May 31–June 4, 2011
Tucson, Arizona, USA

 **Association for
Computing Machinery**

Advancing Computing as a Science & Profession

ICS'11

Proceedings of the 2011 ACM

International Conference on Supercomputing

Sponsored by:

ACM SIGARCH

Supported by:

Intel, AMD, National Science Foundation, Isilon Systems, Nvidia, Microsoft Research, IBM, HP, Rincon Research, Cray, ICT, Reservoir Labs, Chalmers, & Springer

The Association for Computing Machinery
2 Penn Plaza, Suite 701
New York, New York 10121-0701

Notice to Past Authors of ACM-Published Articles
ACM intends to create a complete electronic archive of all articles and/or other material previously published by ACM. If you have written a work that has been previously published by ACM in any journal or conference proceedings prior to 1978, or any SIG Newsletter at any time, and you do NOT want this work to appear in the ACM Digital Library, please inform permissions@acm.org, stating the title of the work, the author(s), and where and when published.

ISBN: 978-1-4503-0102-2

Additional copies may be ordered prepaid from:

ACM Order Department
PO Box 30777
New York, NY 10087-0777, USA

Phone: 1-800-342-6626 (USA and Canada)
+1-212-626-0500 (Global)
Fax: +1-212-944-1318
E-mail: acmhelp@acm.org
Hours of Operation: 8:30 am – 4:30 pm ET

ACM Order Number: 415101

Printed in the USA

Message from the General Chair

It is my pleasure to welcome you to the *25th ACM International Conference on Supercomputing* (*ICS 2011*) in Tucson, Arizona. ICS brings together researchers from several areas to present ground-breaking research related to supercomputing.

In addition to the technical program of papers, workshops, tutorials, posters, and an ACM Student Research Competition, we are pleased to bring you three illustrious keynote speakers addressing important topics in contemporary parallel computing. Sarita Adve of the University of Illinois will talk about which models parallel programming languages should expose and how hardware should support those models. Steve Hammond of the National Renewable Energy Laboratory will talk about renewable energy and energy efficiency. Finally, Bill Gropp of the University of Illinois will talk about developing applications for extreme scale through the use of performance modeling.

Social events include a Tuesday night reception and a conference outing and banquet on Thursday evening at the Pima Air and Space Museum, which, as the largest non-government funded aviation museum, has hundreds of historic aircraft. Tucson also offers a wonderful blend of Southwest culture along with great outdoor adventures.

I particularly thank the companies and universities that made the technical and social programs possible through financial support: Intel, AMD, Microsoft, NVIDIA, Isilon Systems, IBM, HP, Rincon Research, ICT-CAS, Cray, Reservoir Labs, and Chalmers University of Technology. Also, NSF provided funding for student travel support.

In addition, I thank the organizing committee for making this conference possible through all of their hard work. Bronis de Supinski and Sally A. McKee are ideal program co-chairs. They have done an excellent job of creating a top-notch technical program, including recruiting and managing an outstanding program committee to assist them. The rest of the organizing committee was a pleasure to work with. As workshops and tutorials chair, Xipeng Shen helped put together a total of twelve workshops and tutorials; Chris Gniady served as local arrangements chair and expert food consultant. Daniele Scarpazza served as publications chair and ensured that everything flowed smoothly. Daniel Faraj served as registration chair, and Boyana Norris arranged the PC meeting. Shan Lu and Anne Bracy served as poster co-chairs and handled both regular posters and the SRC; they were assisted by several poster PC members. As finance chair, Vince Freeh helped balance the budget, and as web chair Barry Rountree made sure that everything was on-line reliably and promptly. Wu Feng served as industrial chair and was instrumental in bringing in new donors to *ICS* (also, the PC co-chairs both greatly helped in this endeavor). Kirk Cameron and Bernd Mohr served as publicity co-chairs, and Arun Chauhan served as student travel grants chair. Finally, Martin Schulz answered my incessant questions promptly and kept me sane.

David Lowenthal
ICS'11 General Chair

Message from the Program Chairs

It is our pleasure to present the proceedings of the *25th ACM International Conference on Supercomputing (ICS 2011)*. This year's call solicited research on a broad range of topics, including:

- Computationally challenging scientific and commercial applications, particularly studies and experiences on large-scale systems;

- Computer architecture and hardware, including multicore and multiprocessor systems, accelerators, memory, interconnection network and storage and file systems;

- High-performance computational and programming models, including new languages and middleware for high performance computing, autotuning and function-specific code generators;

- High performance system software, including compilers, runtime systems, programming and development tools and operating systems;

- Hardware and software solutions for heterogeneity, reliability and power efficiency;

- Large scale installations, including case studies to guide the design of future systems;

- Novel infrastructures for internet, grid and cloud computing; and

- Performance evaluation studies and theoretical underpinnings of any of the above topics.

We thank all who submitted papers and posters, the program committees for the conference and posters, and the many external reviewers for their hard work. We received 161 submissions by authors from 26 countries. Each submission was assigned to four program committee members for a first round of reviews. For many papers, at least one external review from an outside expert was obtained as well. 70 program committee members and 150 external reviewers produced an average of 4.8 reviews per submission. The review process included an author feedback/rebuttal period in which authors could address questions from reviewers and correct factual errors. In parallel to this rebuttal, papers ranked in the midrange were assigned one or two additional PC members, promoting a more qualified discussion during the program committee meeting.

The program committee did an admirable job of reviewing the papers in a relatively short time frame. On average, each committee member reviewed about 12 papers. The program committee met on Saturday, February 26th, in Chicago. The committee accepted 35 papers, for an acceptance rate of about 22%, demonstrating the continued selectivity and high quality of the ICS conference series.

The technical program includes talks for the 35 papers, three keynotes, and eight poster presentations including an ACM Student Research Competition. The main conference program is augmented with seven tutorials and six workshops.

We hope you find the technical papers included in this volume enlightening.

Bronis R. de Supinski
Lawrence Livermore
National Laboratory

Sally A. McKee
Chalmers University
of Technology

Table of Contents

Session 4a: Novel Hardware/Software Approaches

Session 4b: Power

Keynote Address 2

Session 5: Performance and Resilience for Solver Algorithms

Session 6: Model-Based Techniques

Keynote Address 3

Session 7: Programming Models

Session 8a: Accelerator-Based Mathematics

Session 8b: Caching

Session 9a: Applications

Session 9b: Innovative Architecture Solutions

Session: Student Research Competition Posters & Posters

ACM 25th International Conference on Supercomputing
Conference and Workshop Organization

General Chair: David K. Lowenthal *(University of Arizona)*

Program Co-Chairs: Bronis R. de Supinski *(Lawrence Livermore National Laboratory)*
Sally A. McKee *(Chalmers University of Technology)*

Vice Chair: Martin Schulz *(Lawrence Livermore National Laboratory)*

Local Arrangements Chair: Chris Gniady *(University of Arizona)*

Local Arrangements Chair (PC meeting): Boyana Norris *(Argonne National Laboratory)*

Finance Chair: Vince Freeh *(North Carolina State University)*

Publication Chair: Daniele Paolo Scarpazza *(D. E. Shaw Research)*

Publicity Co-Chairs: Kirk Cameron *(Virginia Tech)*
Bernd Mohr *(Jülich Supercomputing Center)*

Student Travel Grants Chair: Arun Chauhan *(Indiana University)*

Web and Submissions Chair: Barry Rountree *(Lawrence Livermore National Laboratory)*

Posters Co-Chairs: Anne Bracy *(Washington University in St. Louis)*
Shan Lu *(University of Wisconsin)*

Registration Chair: Daniel A. Faraj *(IBM)*

Industry Chair: Wu Feng *(Virginia Tech)*

Workshops/Tutorials Chair: Xipeng Shen *(College of William and Mary)*

Additional reviewers (continued):

Harshvardhan
Yuxiong He
Robert Hesse
Tobias Hilbrich
Lisa Hsu
Hai Huang
Alan Humphrey
Tugrul Ince
Faisal Iqbal
Ciji Isen
Tanzima Islam
Sam Jacobs
Tarun Jain
Djordje Jevdjic
Jungho Jo
Fahed Jubair
Krishnan Kailas
Cansu Kaynak
Mahmut Kandemir
Tejas Karkhanis
Dimitris Kaseridis
Fuat Keceli
Kamil Kedzierski
Youngtaek Kim
Meyrem Kirman
Nevin Kirman
Michael Kluge
Andreas Knuepfer
Onur Kocberber
Christos Kotselidis
Tahsin Kurc
Okwan Kwon
Jean-Yves L'Excellent
Jesus Labarta
Mike Lam
Julien Langou
Sang Ik Lee
Seyong Lee
Chunshu Li
Yue Li
Guangdeng Liao
Matthias Lieber
Charles Lively
Pejman Lotfi-Kamran
Keith Lowery

Mario Donato Marino
Andrea Marongiu
Vernard Martin
Alejandro Martinez
Collin Mccurdy
David Meisner
Jiayuan Meng
Xiaoqiao Meng
Konstantinos Menychtas
Ronald Minnich
Alessandro Morari
Dheya Mustafa
Arun Nair
Sri Hari Krishna Narayanan
David Oehmke
John Owens
Marco Paolieri
Ioannis Papadopoulos
Roger Pearce
Yuval Peress
Josep M. Perez
Howard Pritchard
Tanausu Ramirez
Jonathan Ross
Nick Rutar
Richard Sampson
Prateeksha Satyamoorthy
Lambert Schaelicke
Robert Schoene
Frank Schulze
Sameh Sharkawi
Ashish Sharma
Shishir Sharma
Subodh Sharma
Jeremy Sheaffer
Faissal M. Sleiman
Burton Smith
Huaiming Song
Geoff Stoker
Lukasz Szafaryn
Greg Szubzda
Daisuke Takahashi
Wei Tang
Adrian Tate
Keita Teranishi

Additional reviewers (continued):

Nathan Thomas
Anata Tiwari
Stanimire Tomov
Marc Tremblay
Aniruddha Udipi
Gaurav Uttreja
Sam Vafaee
Nicolas Vasilache
Liang Wang
John-David Wellman
Peng Wu

Weidan Wu
Xingfu Wu
Polychronis Xekalakis
Yuan Xie
Philip Yang
Li Yu
Yongen Yu
Mani Zandifar
Runjie Zhang
Ziming Zheng
Qian Zhu

ICS 2011 Sponsor & Supporters

Sponsor:

Platinum
Supporters:

Gold Supporters:

Silver Supporters:

Keynote Talk

Rethinking Shared-Memory Languages and Hardware

Sarita V. Adve
Department of Computer Science
University of Illinois at Urbana-Champaign
201 N. Goodwin Ave, Urbana, IL 61801, USA
sadve@illinois.edu

Abstract

The era of parallel computing for the masses is here, but writing correct parallel programs remains difficult. For many domains, shared-memory remains an attractive programming model. The memory model, which specifies the meaning of shared variables, is at the heart of this programming model. Unfortunately, it has involved a tradeoff between programmability and performance, and has arguably been one of the most challenging and contentious areas in both hardware architecture and programming language specification. Recent broad community-scale efforts have finally led to a convergence in this debate, with popular languages such as Java and C++ and most hardware vendors publishing compatible memory model specifications. Although this convergence is a dramatic improvement, it has exposed fundamental shortcomings in current popular languages and systems that thwart safe and efficient parallel computing.

I will discuss the path to the above convergence, the hard lessons learned, and their implications. A cornerstone of this convergence has been the view that the memory model should be a contract between the programmer and the system - if the programmer writes disciplined (data-race-free) programs, the system will provide high programmability (sequential consistency) and performance. I will discuss why this view is the best we can do with current popular languages, and why it is inadequate moving forward, requiring rethinking popular parallel languages and hardware. In particular, I will argue that (1) parallel languages should not only promote high-level disciplined models, but they should also enforce the discipline, and (2) for scalable and efficient performance, hardware should be co-designed to take advantage of and support such disciplined models. I will describe the Deterministic Parallel Java (DPJ) language and DeNovo hardware projects at Illinois as examples of such an approach.

This talk draws on collaborations with many colleagues over the last two decades on memory models (in particular, a CACM'10 paper with Hans-J. Boehm) and with faculty, researchers, and students from the DPJ and DeNovo projects.

Categories & Subject Descriptors: B.3.2 Design Styles: Shared memory; D.1.3: [*Software*]: Language Classifications: Concurrent, distributed, and parallel languages

General Terms: Performance, Design, Languages, Verification

Keywords: cache coherence, determinism, memory consistency, memory models

Bio

Sarita Adve is Professor of Computer Science at the University of Illinois at Urbana-Champaign. Her research interests are in computer architecture and systems, parallel computing, and power and reliability-aware systems. Most recently, she co-developed the memory models for the C++ and Java programming languages based on her early work on data-race-free models, and co-invented the concept of lifetime reliability aware processors and dynamic reliability management. She was named an ACM fellow in 2010, received the ACM SIGARCH Maurice Wilkes award in 2008, was named a University Scholar by the University of Illinois in 2004, and received an Alfred P. Sloan Research Fellowship in 1998. She serves on the boards of the Computing Research Association and ACM SIGARCH. She received the Ph.D. in Computer Science from Wisconsin in 1993.

ICS'11, May 31–June 4, 2011, Tucson, Arizona, USA.
ACM 978-1-4503-0102-2/11/05.

An Execution Strategy and Optimized Runtime Support for Parallelizing Irregular Reductions on Modern GPUs

Xin Huo, Vignesh T. Ravi, Wenjing Ma, and Gagan Agrawal
Department of Computer Science and Engineering
The Ohio State University
Columbus, OH 43210
huox@cse.ohio-state.edu, raviv@cse.ohio-state.edu, mawe@cse.ohio-state.edu,
agrawal@cse.ohio-state.edu

ABSTRACT

GPUs have rapidly emerged as a very significant player in high performance computing. However, despite the popularity of CUDA, there are significant challenges in porting different classes of HPC applications on modern GPUs. This paper focuses on the challenges of implementing *irregular applications* arising from *unstructured grids* on modern NVIDIA GPUs. Considering the importance of irregular reductions in scientific and engineering codes, substantial effort was made in developing compiler and runtime support for parallelization or optimization of these codes in the previous two decades, with different efforts targeting distributed memory machines, distributed shared memory machines, shared memory machines, or cache performance improvement on uniprocessor machines. However, there have not been any systematic studies on parallelizing these applications on modern GPUs.

There are at least two significant challenges associated with porting this class of applications on modern GPUs. The first is related to correct and efficient parallelization while using a large number of threads. The second challenge is effective use of *shared memory*. Since data accesses cannot be determined statically, runtime partitioning methods are needed for effectively using the shared memory. This paper describes an execution methodology that can address the above two challenges. We have also developed optimized runtime modules to support our execution methodology. Our approach and runtime methods have been extensively evaluated using two indirection array based applications.

Categories and Subject Descriptors

D.1.3 [**Programming Techniques**]: Concurrent Programming—*Parallel programming*; C.1.2 [**Processor Architectures**]: Multiple Data Stream Architectures (Multiprocessors)—*Single-instruction-stream, multiple-data-stream processors (SIMD)*

General Terms

Performance

Keywords

GPU, CUDA, Irregular Reduction, Partitioning

1. INTRODUCTION

Within the last 2-3 years, *heterogeneous computing* has emerged as the means for achieving *extreme-scale*, *cost-effective*, and *power-efficient* high performance computing. On one hand, some of the fastest machines in the world today are based on NVIDIA GPUs. Specifically, in the top 500 list released in November 2010, three of the top four fastest supercomputers in the world are GPU clusters, including the fastest machine (Tianhe-1A), the third fastest machine (Nebulae) and the fourth fastest machine (Tsubame). At the same time, the very favorable price to performance ratio offered by the GPUs is bringing supercomputing to the masses. It is common for the desktops and laptops today to have a GPU, which can be used for accelerating a compute-intensive application. The peak single-precision performance of a Nvidia Fermi card today is more than 1 Teraflop, giving a price to performance ratio of $2-4 per Giga-flop. Yet another key advantage of GPUs is the very favorable power to performance ratio. Power efficiency is a very important challenge in computing today, as the cost of powering servers is already estimated to be higher than the actual cost of the hardware. In this context, GPUs offer up to a factor of 20 better performance per watt ratio, as compared to the multi-core CPUs.

Despite the above advantages, accelerator and/or heterogeneous systems in general, and GPUs in particular, are not the obvious choice for everyone. There are at least two critical obstacles with the use of these systems, which are *programmability* and *performance efficiency*. Despite the popularity of CUDA, there are significant challenges in porting different classes of HPC applications on modern GPUs. *Performance efficiency*, which can be defined as the ratio between the peak and the sustained performance, is another problem. For example, if we carefully examine the reported data on the top 6 fastest machines from the top 500 list[1], the average ratio between the sustained performance on Linpack and the peak performance is only 0.48 for the three GPU-based machines, whereas it is 0.80 for the other three systems. Moreover, such performance on the GPU-based machines has apparently been obtained with a *"heroic programming"* effort specific to the Linpack modules, and sustained performance on most other applications can be expected to be much lower.

In the last 3-4 years, there have been numerous studies porting a specific application to CUDA. A number of efforts towards code generation, optimization, or providing runtime support have also been undertaken in the last 2-3 years [2, 20, 23, 24, 35, 27, 38].

---

[1]http://www.top500.org/list/2010/11/100

These efforts, however, are in relatively early stages and are in most cases limited to a few application classes.

One feasible approach for improving programmability and performance efficiency for a broad variety of applications could be to focus on particular communication patterns. This approach could be along the lines of using *dwarfs* in the Berkeley view on parallel processing[2]. A dwarf based approach can enable us to identify best application execution strategy and develop corresponding optimized runtime support for each dwarf. The execution strategy identified, in turn, can serve as the basis for automatic code generation in the future, and similarly, the runtime support can be invoked from compilation systems.

Following this approach, this paper focuses on the challenges of porting applications from a particular dwarf, which includes the *irregular applications* arising from *unstructured grids*. Codes from many important scientific and engineering domains contain loops with such indirection arrays. Examples include Computational Fluid Dynamics (CFD) codes that use unstructured meshes [8], and molecular Dynamics applications [17]. In the former case, an unstructured mesh is modeled with nodes and edges, with each edge designating two nodes as end points. While iterating over edges, the node related data can only be accessed through an indirection array. Similarly, in molecular dynamics applications, edges denote interaction between the molecules, and the nodes denote the molecules themselves. Loops iterate over the interactions, and update the values associated with the molecules.

Considering the importance of irregular reductions in scientific and engineering codes, substantial efforts have been made in developing compiler and runtime support for parallelization of these codes in the previous two decades. This included efforts targeting distributed memory machines [1, 7, 14, 16, 21, 22, 33, 37], distributed shared memory machines [32, 12], shared memory machines [4, 13, 25, 39], or those for cache performance improvement on uniprocessors [9, 15, 29, 30]. More recently, this class of computations has been studied for the emerging multi-core and many-core architectures [11]. However, there have not been any systematic studies on porting these applications to modern GPUs.

There are at least two significant challenges associated with porting this class of applications on modern GPUs. The first is related to correct and efficient parallelization while using a large number of threads. Updates to indirection array based computations lead to race conditions while parallelizing the computation. The previous work on shared memory systems assumed a relatively small number of concurrent threads, whereas obtaining efficiency on GPUs requires that the computation be divided among a large number of threads. The second challenge is effective use of *shared memory*, which is a programmable cache on modern GPUs. Judicious use of the shared memory has been shown to be critical in obtaining high performance on GPUs. Since data accesses cannot be determined statically, runtime partitioning methods are needed for effectively using the shared memory.

This paper focuses on the above challenges and makes the following contributions:

A Novel Execution Strategy: We present a novel execution strategy to parallelize this class of applications on GPUs and to effectively use shared memory. Our strategy is referred to as the *partitioning-based locking scheme*, and involves creating disjoint partitions of the reduction space to use shared memory.

Optimized Runtime Support: We have also designed and implemented runtime modules to support our execution strategy. This includes a new partitioning scheme, multi-dimensional partitioning,

which has very low overheads, and efficient modules for reordering the data.

Performance Studies: Using two popular irregular applications, Euler and Molecular Dynamics, we have carried out a detailed experimental study. We show how we clearly outperform other parallelization schemes, and that our proposed multi-dimensional partitioning scheme gives the best trade-offs in terms of partitioning overheads and the resulting application execution time. We also show that our runtime methods are efficient enough to be used for adaptive irregular applications.

2. BACKGROUND

This section provides background on GPU architectures and the nature of computation in irregular reductions.

2.1 Architecture of Modern GPUs

We briefly introduce the architecture of the modern GPUs, with a specific focus on the most recent series of GPUs from NVIDIA, which are the Tesla T20 (Fermi) cards.

A modern Graphical Processing Unit (GPU) architecture consists of two major components, i.e., the processing component and the memory component. The processing component in a typical GPU is composed of a certain number of streaming multiprocessors. Each streaming multiprocessor, in turn, contains a set of simple cores that perform in-order processing of the instructions. To achieve high performance, a large number of threads, typically a few tens of thousands, are launched. These threads execute the same operation on different sets of data. A block of threads are mapped to and executed on a streaming multiprocessor. Furthermore, threads within a block are divided into multiple groups, termed as *warp*. Each warp of threads are co-scheduled on the streaming multiprocessor and execute the same instruction in a given clock cycle (SIMD execution).

The memory component of a modern GPU-based computing system typically contains several layers. One is the *host memory*, which is available on the CPU main memory. This is essential as any general purpose GPU computation can only be launched from the CPU. The second layer is the *device memory*, which resides on the GPU card. This represents the global memory on a GPU and is accessible across all streaming multiprocessors. The device memory is interconnected with the host through a PCI-Express card (version can vary depending upon the card). This interconnectivity enables DMA transfer of data between host and device memory. From the origin of CUDA-based GPUs, a scratch-pad memory, which is programmable and supports high-speed access, has been available private to a streaming multiprocessor. The scratch-pad memory is termed as *shared memory* on NVIDIA cards. Till recently, the size of this shared memory was 16 KB.

Tesla 2050, known as "Fermi", is the latest series of graphic card products by NVIDIA. The architecture of Fermi features 14 or 16 multiprocessors, each of which has 32 cores. The clock rate is 1.215GHz, and memory clock is 3348MT/s. As compared to earlier systems, Fermi has a much larger shared memory/L1 cache, which can be configured as 48KB shared memory and 16KB L1 cache, or 48KB L1 cache and 16KB shared memory. Unlike previous cards, an L2 cache is also available.

Two critical issues in performance on Fermi cards are: 1) partitioning the computation on a sufficient large number of threads, and 2) effectively using its memory hierarchy, particularly, the shared memory. While the same issues have arisen in porting most applications on earlier GPUs, addressing them is particularly challenging for irregular reductions, which are the focus of this paper.

---

[2]Please see http://view.eecs.berkeley.edu/wiki/Dwarf_Mine

```
Real X(numNodes), Y(numEdges);  ! Data arrays
Integer IA(numEdges,2);          ! Indirection array
Real RA(numNodes);               ! Reduction array

for (i=1; i<numEdges; i++) {
    RA(IA(i,1)) = RA(IA(i,1)) op (Y(i) op X(IA(i,1) op X(IA(i,2))))
    RA(IA(i,2)) = RA(IA(i,2)) op (Y(i) op X(IA(i,1) op X(IA(i,2))));
}
```

Figure 1: Typical Structure of *Irregular Reduction*

2.2 Irregular Reductions

A canonical irregular reduction loop is shown in Figure 1. The key characteristics of this loop are as follows. Each element at the *left-hand-side* array might be incremented in multiple iterations of the loop. The set of iterations in which a particular element may be updated depends upon the contents of the *indirection array IA*, but the updates can only be through an associative and commutative operation *op*. We refer to the set of elements for the *left-hand-side* arrays as the *reduction space*. On the other hand, one or more input arrays might be accessed either directly or through an indirection array. A key aspect of the computation loop is that it iterates over the elements of the indirection array. Thus, the set of elements of the indirection array is referred to as the *computation space*.

Overall, the data structures involved in an irregular reduction can be categorized into three different types. The first is the *input* and *read-only* data, i.e, the arrays X and Y in our example. The second is the *reduction* or the *output* array. The third type of data structure include the indirection array(s), which provide the index for accessing some of the data arrays and the reduction array. The indirection shown in Figure 1 includes two portions, which are $IA(i, 1)$ and $IA(i, 2)$. In the ith iteration of the loop, the data array X is accessed by using $IA(i, 1)$ and $IA(i, 2)$. However, some data arrays can also be accessed by loop index, like the data array Y in our example. Reduction array RA is updated using two distinct portions of the indirection array in each iteration of the loop.

The loop with indirection array shown in Figure 1 can be found in a large number of scientific and engineering applications. For example, in a CFD application Euler [8], an unstructured mesh contains nodes and edges. Edges in this application is the indirection array, which provides indices for both end points of the edge. In each iteration, some values (such as face data, velocities, etc.) associated with each of the two end points are updated. Molecular Dynamics applications contain similar loop structure [17]. Here, the nodes represent the molecules, and the edges denote the interaction between a pair of molecules. The loop iterates over set of the interactions, and the corresponding change in forces for the two interacting molecules are updated.

Clearly, applications like Euler and the molecular dynamics involve a large number of loops, not all of which follow the structure shown in Figure 1. However, most of other loops tend to be simple to parallelize, as the data and the iterations can be partitioned in an affine manner. Thus, irregular reduction loops are ones that involve non-trivial challenges in parallelization. These applications, however can involve loops with different indirection arrays. For the rest of the paper, our presentation will focus only on a single indirection array based loop.

A key observation that impacts the parallelization and optimization of the applications is that the size of data structures involved in both the computation space and reduction space are typically extremely large. Thus, they cannot be stored in the shared memory of a GPU.

3. EXECUTION STRATEGY FOR INDIRECTION ARRAY BASED COMPUTATIONS ON GPUS

In the previous section, we had discussed GPU architecture and the nature of irregular reductions. In this section, we first elaborate on the problems associated with the use of two popular methods for parallelizing reductions on shared memory systems, which are *locking* and *replication*. Then, we introduce our proposed *partitioning based locking scheme*, and explain the reason why we choose to partition on the reduction space.

3.1 Overheads with Existing Methods

We now discuss about why the existing methods for parallelizing reductions on any shared memory system are not appropriate for execution of irregular applications on GPUs.

Full Replication: In any shared memory system, one simple method for avoiding race condition is to have a private copy of reduction array for each thread. After each iteration is completed, the results from all threads will be combined by a single thread, or using a *tree structure*. Since each thread has its own replica of the reduction array, no synchronization is needed while updating the array. The combination of results can be performed in two ways. In the first method, we can copy the results from all threads and blocks onto the host and then perform the combination. Alternatively, we perform the combination among the threads within a block on the GPU and then perform the combination across blocks on the host. The second combination method is preferred as the combination among threads within a block can be performed in parallel on GPU.

The main issues with this scheme are the memory and the combination overheads. Particularly, a GPU like Fermi has 14 or 16 multi-processors, and most application studies have shown that 256 or 512 threads per block is desirable for achieving best performance. Such a large number of threads leads to a very high memory overhead. Moreover, this reduces the possibility that any significant portion of the reduction array can be stored in the shared memory. In addition, the cost of combination obviously increases with the number of threads and blocks, and can be quite high when nearly 4,000 to 8,000 copies are involved.

Locking Mechanism: Another approach is to use locking while updating any element of the reduction object. On modern GPUs, this scheme can be implemented using the *atomic operations* provided by CUDA. Particularly, from computation capability 2.0 onwards, NVIDIA GPUs support atomic operations on floating point numbers and on shared memory. In contrast to replication scheme discussed above, all threads within a block will share the same reduction array, and still maintain correctness.

Clearly, an atomic operation is more expensive than a simple update, and similarly, contention among threads trying to update the same element may lead to slowdowns. However, this scheme has the benefits of avoiding memory overheads and the cost of performing the combination. A related benefit is that utilization of shared memory is seemingly possible. But, as we had stated earlier, in most irregular reduction based applications, one copy of reduction array is too large to fit into the shared memory. Thus, additional work is needed to enable effective use of the shared memory. Furthermore, there is still a copy of the reduction array for each thread block or multi-processor. So, a combination among thread blocks is still required.

In summary, while the locking based scheme seems to have cer-

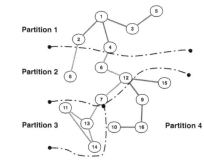

(a) Partitioning on Computation Space

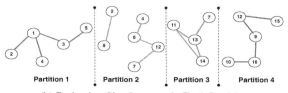

(b) Reduction Size Increase in Each Partition

Figure 2: Computation Space partitioning and reduction size in each partition

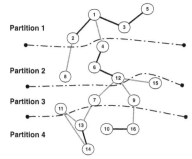

(a) Partitioning on Reduction Space

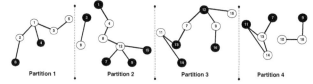

(b) Workload Increase in Each Partition

Figure 3: Reduction Space partitioning and computation size in each partition

tain advantages, both of the above strategies fail to utilize the shared memory effectively. This is the basis for the partitioning-based locking scheme we are proposing.

3.2 Partitioning-Based Locking Scheme

We now discuss our proposed scheme for the execution of irregular reductions. Before getting into the details of this scheme, we summarize the key aspects of this scheme:

- Partition the output or the reduction space, such that the data associated with each resulting partition of the reduction space fits into shared memory.

- Reorder the computation space or the indirection arrays in such a way that iterations updating elements of the same partition are grouped together.

- In the process, completely eliminate the requirement for combination of reduction array across different thread blocks.

We now discuss the strategy in more details, starting with discussion of why partitioning on the reduction space is chosen.

3.2.1 Partitioning Methodologies for Irregular Reductions

As we have discussed earlier, the sizes of arrays involved in any irregular reductions prohibit simple utilization of the shared memory. Thus, clearly, we need to partition the work or data, and execute partitions in a way that a portion of the data can be loaded into shared memory. Now, let us revisit the code example in Figure 1. The indirection array IA and the data array Y have regular memory access patterns. Moreover, there is no reuse of the data within a single loop. Thus, these accesses can be optimized with *coalesced* references to the device memory. On the other hand, accesses through indirection arrays (RA and X) if placed on device memory, have no potential for coalescing. But, there is an opportunity for reuse, and hence placing them on shared memory can be beneficial. Thus, while considering partitioning methods, we focus on the accesses to arrays RA and X.

Now, we can consider two possible partitioning methods:
Computation Space-based Partitioning: One approach is to partition the work or the iterations of the loop into different groups. Subsequently, the reduction array elements that are accessed in the set of iterations from one partition can be stored in the shared memory. To further optimize this, the partitions of iterations can be chosen so that there is a high reuse of the corresponding reduction array elements.

Suppose we have n multi-processors in the GPU. We can create $n \times k$ partitions, such that the size of the set of reduction array elements accessed in each partition fits into the shared memory. Each multi-processor can execute k such partitions, loading the corresponding reduction array elements before execution of each such partition. The partitions can also be chosen in a way that the number of iterations executed by different multi-processors is almost the same.

This simple schemes have several disadvantages, which we illustrate through an example. Figure 2a shows an example of partitioning of the iterations on the computation space. All edges are divided into four partitions, with four edges in each partition. To allocate data in shared memory, we need to determine the set of reduction array elements that will be updated while executing the iterations in each partition. Clearly, an element may be updated by iterations from different partitions. Thus, a reduction element can belong to multiple partitions. Moreover, the number of elements corresponding to one partition may vary significantly, as we show in Figure 2b. There are 6 nodes in the second partition, but only 4 nodes in the third partition. This points to a difficulty in optimally reusing shared memory for each partition. Moreover, as reduction array elements can be updated by multiple partitions, we need to perform the combination operation in the end. This can introduce significant overheads.
Reduction Space-based Partitioning: Based on the discussion above, we can consider another approach. We could start by first partitioning the reduction space, i.e. the set of the elements in the reduction array. The number of partitions can be chosen so that the data corresponding to each partition fits into shared memory.

A simple example of *Reduction Space-based* partitioning is shown

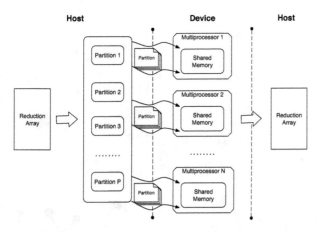

Figure 4: Execution with Partitioning based Locking Scheme

in Figure 3a. Compared to the previous example, partitioning is based on the nodes, instead of edges. Now, we have several edges that are connecting elements from two distinct partitions. In the case of these edges, the corresponding iterations from the loop are updating reduction array elements from two different partitions, i.e. accesses $RA(IA(i,1))$ and $RA(IA(i,2))$ belong to the different partitions. In such a case, we add this iteration i to both the partitions. Most of the computation associated with this iteration is repeated, but only one element is updated during the computing associated with each partition. In Figure 3b, we see that the total number of edges in all the four partitions has been increased to 25, compared to the original number of edges which is 16. This is due to the crossing edges between different partitions. For larger datasets, and with careful partitioning, we can however minimize the number of such crossing edges. Besides redundant computation, this scheme may also lead to computation space imbalance. As an example, the third partition has 7 edges, which is more than the edges in other three partitions.

The single biggest advantage of this scheme is that for the entire GPU, there is only one copy of each reduction array element. Moreover, each thread block performs computation on independent reduction space partitions, thus eliminating the requirement for combination. Thus, while there clearly are tradeoffs between the two schemes, we were driven by the following two observations. First, shared memory is a critical resource on a GPU, and it is important to judiciously utilize it. Second, there is a high degree of parallelism available on a GPU, and thus, redundant computations to an extent are acceptable.

3.2.2 Overall GPU Execution Flow Based on Partitioning

We now summarize the execution of an application with the proposed scheme. Figure 4 outlines the execution of our scheme. Before the computation begins, a partitioning method is used to divide the original reduction space into multiple chunks, such that the reduction data associated with the space should fit in the shared memory. Then, indirection array is also partitioned, with the possibility that some iterations may be inserted in more than one partition. Thus, we have a set of iterations (possibly overlapping) associated with each disjoint partition of the reduction array.

The computation associated with each partition is always performed by a single thread block (executed on one multi-processor), with different threads executing different iterations. Note that different iterations can be simultaneously updating the same reduc-

tion array element. Therefore, the reduction operations are performed using the atomic operations on shared memory, which are supported in modern GPUs. Typically, the number of partitions we create is a multiple of the number of thread blocks, and each thread block executes the same number of partitions. Between the execution of two different partitions, the updated reduction array elements are written back to the device memory, and a new set of reduction array elements are loaded into the shared memory.

Consider again the Figure 1. In our current implementation, only the array RA is stored and updated in shared memory. As we stated previously, there is no reuse on the elements of the arrays IA and Y across iterations of a loop. Therefore, these arrays are kept in device memory, but accesses to their elements are *coalesced*. The array X can be partitioned in the same fashion as the array RA. However, a challenge arises for iterations where $X(IA(i,1))$ and $X(IA(i,2))$ belong to different partitions. In such a case, one of the two accesses will have to be to the device memory. In view of this, we choose not to put X in shared memory at all. Instead, larger (and therefore, fewer) partitions can be created for the array RA, reducing the fraction of iterations that need to be put in more than one partition.

The key observation from the scheme is that the overall reduction space has been divided into disjoint partitions, which can be placed on shared memory. Because the partitions are disjoint, there is no need to perform combination operations at the end of the processing.

However, there are still several challenges, which need to be addressed to maintain efficiency. First, we need methods for partitioning the data over the reduction space, while keeping the overheads low. The existing partitioners tend to be expensive and CPU based, which can introduce unacceptable costs while attempting GPU-based acceleration of the application. Similarly, the computation space needs to be partitioned or reordered. Another challenge is associated with *adaptive* irregular applications, where the indirection array may change between iterations of a *time-step* loop, which is an outer-loop over the loop shown in Figure 1. In the next section, we describe the various partitioning and optimization techniques to address these challenges, and to support the execution efficiently.

4. RUNTIME SUPPORT

To support the execution scheme described in the previous section, we need to develop optimized runtime modules. Though partitioning of unstructured meshes [19, 18] and associated runtime support [33, 34] are very well studied topics, we focus on the specific challenges associated with GPUs. We first discuss the partitioning methods we have implemented, and then discuss efficient reordering of iterations.

4.1 Runtime Partitioning Approaches

We have experimented with three different schemes for partitioning in our system.

METIS Partitioning: METIS is a set of partitioners for graphs and finite element meshes [34], and has been widely disseminated and used in practice. However, METIS based partitioners execute sequentially on CPU, their relative overhead can be very high as compared to the application's execution on a GPU. Particularly, the cost of initialization for METIS is very high. Because it requires analysis on the edges, it needs to reorganize the unstructured mesh. The time complexity for this conversion is $O(numNodes \times numEdges)$.

GPU-based (Trivial) Partitioning: The primary objective of partitioners implemented in METIS (or similar partitioners developed)

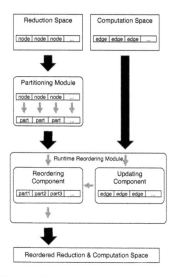

Figure 5: Runtime Iteration Reordering

is to reduce the communication volume while executing the unstructured mesh based computation. In our case, the primary goal is to exploit the shared memory. Thus, we could consider very simple or *trivial* partitioning and implement it on a GPU. The algorithm we have implemented divides the reduction space simply on the order of the input. So, the cost of the partitioning is very low, and the reuse of the shared memory is the same as the other partitioners. However, unlike a smarter algorithm, this method can have a significantly larger number of *cross edges*. Thus, the amount of redundant work can be high, leading to some slow-downs.

Multi-Dimensional Partitioning: We have also developed a more effective yet very efficient partitioning method, which we refer to as *multi-dimensional partitioning*. This method does not utilize the information on the edges, because gathering the adjacencies information is very time consuming. Instead, node coordinates are utilized to partition the space in a fashion that cross edges are significantly reduced. The key step in the algorithm is finding the kth smallest value. Suppose that the total number of partitions desired is 12, and we decide to partition the underlying three-dimensional space into 3 partitions along the x dimension, and 2 partitions along each of the y and z dimensions. In our algorithm, we first find out the coordinate value of the $numNodes/3$th and $numNodes/3 \times 2$th node among a sorted list according to the x dimension. Similarly, we find partitioning points along the y and z dimensions, repeating the process iteratively, and partition the space.

In our algorithm, the dominant cost is for finding the kth smallest value along each dimension, for either the entire dataset or a subset of it. Thus, the time complexity for each such step is $O(n)$. If we create X, Y, and Z partitions along the x, y, and z dimensions, total number of times the above step is invoked is $(X + X \times Y + X \times Y \times Z)$, which is $O(p)$, where p is the number of partitions desired. In practice, the number of partitions is quite small. As we will demonstrate, the execution time of this algorithm is very small, where the number of cross edges is reduced over the GPU-based trivial partitioner. In summary, this method provides a balance between the partitioning time and the efficiency of application execution.

4.2 Iteration Reordering

The goal of the iteration reordering is to ensure that each thread block can process all data from one partition of the reduction space continuously. This not only enables better reuse of shared mem-

ory, but also ensures that the indirection array and other arrays with affine accesses in the original loops are accessed from device memory in a coalesced fashion. The iteration reordering module has two components: *reordering component*, and *updating component*. As shown in Figure 5, after partitioning, all the data associated with nodes will be reordered by reordering component. For example, in the molecular dynamics application, coordinates, velocities, and forces are associated with each molecule. Thus, these structures need to be reordered based on results of the reduction space partitioning. Then, the interactions between every pair of molecules needs to be updated due to the change in the order of molecules. This work is performed by the updating component. The partition an interaction belongs to is determined by its end points. If both the end points of the interaction belong to the partition A, this interaction will be reordered to be in the partition A only. However, if the two nodes on one interaction belong to different partitions, this interaction will be stored into both the partitions. Thus, extra memory is required to store the edges crossing the partitions.

The cost of runtime reordering is as follows. The reordering component involves finding all the elements belonging to the ith partition serially. The complexity of a simple algorithm will be $O(numPartitions \times N)$. When N is large, the overhead can be quite significant. Hence, one optimization is to use $numPartitions$ temporal dynamic vectors to store the elements for each partition. Then, only one iteration of all the nodes is required to group the nodes within the same partition together. Next, we copy all the vectors by increasing partition number to a single data array. The time complexity for this method is only $O(N)$.

5. EXPERIMENTAL RESULTS

5.1 Experimental Platform

Our experiments were conducted using a NVIDIA Tesla C2050 (Fermi) GPU with 448 processor cores (14×32). The GPU has a clock frequency of 1.15 GHz, and a 2.68 GB device memory. This GPU was connected to a machine with Intel 2.27 GHz Quad core Xeon E5520 CPUs, with 48 GB main memory. The sequential CPU execution results we report are also based on this machine.

Our evaluation was based on two representative irregular reduction applications, which have been widely used by studies on this topic [1, 7, 14, 32, 9, 15, 29, 30]. The first application is Euler [8], which is based on Computational Fluid Dynamics (CFD). It takes description of the connectivity of a mesh and calculates quantities like velocities at each mesh point. The second application is Molecular Dynamics (MD) [17], where simulation is used to study the structural, equilibrium, and dynamic properties of molecules. It shows a view of the motion of the molecules and atoms by simulating the interaction of the particles for a period of time.

5.2 Evaluation Goals

Our experiments were conducted with the following goals.

- We evaluate the performance of the two applications with the Partitioning-Based Locking (PBL) scheme introduced in this paper, comparing against simple approaches like full replication and locking, and measuring the speedups against CPU-based sequential versions.

- We further study the performance factors impacting PBL scheme, like the number of partitions used, type of partitioner used, and the choice of configuration of shared memory.

- Last, we focus on the possibility that the irregular application may be adaptive and may require the runtime modules to be reinvoked. We evaluate how we keep the overheads low in such scenarios.

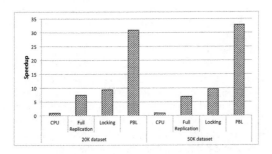

Figure 6: Euler: Comparison of PBL Scheme Over Conventional Strategies and Sequential CPU Execution

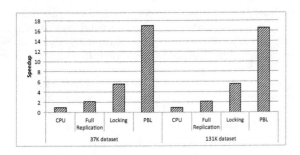

Figure 7: Molecular Dynamics: Comparison of PBL Over Conventional Strategies and Sequential CPU Execution

5.3 Efficiency of Partitioning Based Locking Scheme

Our experiments were conducted using the following datasets. For Euler, the first dataset comprises 20,000 3-dimensional nodes, 120,000 edges, and 12,000 faces. The second dataset involves 50,000 nodes, 300,000 edges, and 29,000 faces. For both of the datasets, the main computation was repeated over 10,000 time-step iterations. For Molecular Dynamics, the first dataset comprises 37,000 molecules and 4,600,000 interactions. The second dataset contains 131,000 nodes and 16,200,000 edges. For both the datasets, we initially consider a non-adaptive version, where the time-step loop involves 100 iterations (with no modifications to the indirection array). Later, in Subsection 5.6, we consider a different version, where the indirection array is modified after every 20 iterations.

For this subsection, the multi-dimensional partitioner is used for the PBL scheme. Also, the results presented for partitioning-based locking scheme, full replication and the locking scheme are all reported with the thread block configuration which gave the best performance.

In Figure 6, for Euler in 20K dataset, the partitioning-based locking scheme outperforms the full replication and locking scheme. The PBL scheme is about a factor of 3.3 times, 4.1 times, and 30.9 times faster over the locking scheme, full replication, and the sequential CPU versions, respectively. The results with the 50K dataset further demonstrate the effectiveness of the PBL scheme.

The results for Molecular Dynamics are similar. Figure 7 summarizes the results for the 37K dataset and 131K dataset, showing the PBL scheme is 3.1 times, 8.2 times, and 17.1 times faster compared to locking, full replication, and the sequential CPU versions,

respectively in 37K dataset. The results from the second dataset again are very similar (Figure 7).

5.4 Impact of Various Partitioning Schemes on Irregular Reductions

In Section 4, we described three kinds of partitioning methods, *Metis Partitioner*, *GPU Partitioner*, and *Multi-Dimensional Partitioner*. Here, we analyze the costs and trade-offs between these three partitioning methods. These three methods are referred to as MP, GP, and MD, respectively.

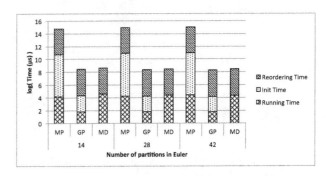

Figure 8: Cost Components of Partitioners (Euler)

Overall Efficiency of Partitioning Methods: In Figure 8, we first compare the running time of the three partitioning methods as we vary the number of partitions desired. For Euler, GP has the shortest running time, across varying number of partitions, as we would expect because of its simplicity. On the other hand, for Euler, MP is around 2.8 times faster than MD when 14 partitions are desired. However, the execution time of MP increases sharply with the increasing number of partitions, whereas MD is not influenced by the number of partitions significantly. Thus, we observe that MD outperforms MP when 42 partitions are desired. For Molecular Dynamics, there is similar trend. GP also gains the best performance. However, the running time of MP is high, because there are more edges (interactions) per node (molecules), and MP performs an analysis of the edge information. In comparison, both MD and GP methods only focus on the node information, and their cost is based on the number of nodes.

Cost Components of Partitioning Methods: The total cost of a partitioning scheme includes not only the *running times* we reported above, but also an initialization cost and the reordering time. Figure 8 considers each of these three costs. The results demonstrate that the most expensive component of MP is its initialization, which takes more than 90% of the total partitioning time. In comparison, the initialization component for GP and MD partitioners is either drastically lower or completely eliminated. The reordering time is similar for all the three methods. The results are very similar for Molecular Dynamics, and are not shown here.

Impact of Partitioners on GPU Computation Time: Different partitioning methods differ not only with respect to the time it takes to partition the data and in reordering iterations, but also in terms of the resulting efficiency during the execution of the application. Particularly, as we partition the reduction space, the workload balance and redundancy in the computation space are critical factors impacting the performance of the application. Figures 9 and 10 show the workload distribution achieved, with different partitioners and number of partitions. *MP-14*, for example, refers to the use of Metis partitioner to obtain 14 partitions.

The work distribution with MP is highly balanced as the algorithm explicitly uses the edge information. The workload distri-

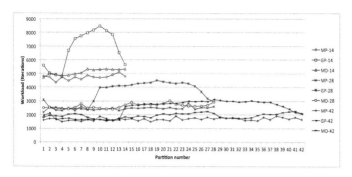

Figure 9: Euler: Workload with Metis, GPU, and Multi-dimensional Partitioners on 14, 28, and 42 Partitions

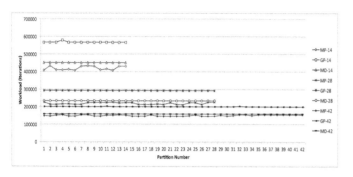

Figure 10: Molecular Dynamics: Workload with Metis, GPU, and Multi-dimensional Partitioners on 14, 28, and 42 Partitions

bution with GP is clearly more imbalanced when compared to the other two partitioners, since it uses neither the spatial locality of nodes, nor the information on the edges. However, we can see that the imbalance per partition reduces as we increase the number of partitions. On the other hand, MD, using only the spatial locality of nodes, achieves a comparable load balance to MP. Similar trends are observed for the redundant workload arising due to cross edges. In view of the earlier observation about the smaller overheads (because the initialization time is eliminated), MD seems to be the best overall option. We further validate this with the next set of results.

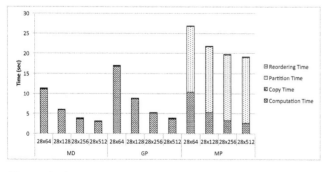

Figure 11: Comparison of Metis, GPU and Multi-dimensional using 28 Partitions for Euler (20K)

End-to-End Execution Time Using Different Partitioning Methods: We now compare the end-to-end execution time using the three partitioning methods. Results with different thread configurations are shown in Figure 11 (Euler - smaller dataset). On one hand, with MP, the partitioning time is even larger than the computation time due to the significant cost of initialization. Whereas, GP has the lowest computation performance because more redundancy

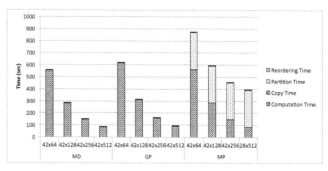

Figure 12: Comparison of Metis, GPU and Multi-dimensional using 42 Partitions for Molecular Dynamics (37K)

and imbalance is introduced. So MD outperforms both of them by achieving a balance between the partitioning time and the execution efficiency. The same comparison for Molecular Dynamics (37K dataset) is shown in Figure 12. The trends are very similar.

Overall, the observation with respect to the choice of partitioners is as follows. Metis package currently does not include any GPU-accelerated implementation of partitioners. As compared to the execution of the application itself on the GPU, the partitioning costs associated with the rigorous algorithms become unreasonably high. Moreover, unlike the use of partitioners for distributed memory machines, the cost of *cross edges* is not as high, since no communication is involved in our proposed scheme for the GPUs. The MD partitioner, which is based on node information only, has a significantly lower overhead, despite being currently implemented on a CPU only. At the same time, it maintains a good load balance, and introduces only a modest amount of redundant computation for the GPU.

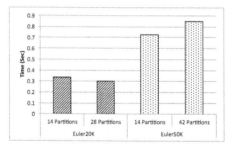

Figure 13: Shared Memory Preferred (14 Partitions) Vs. Cache Preferred (28 Partitions) - (left) Shared Memory Preferred (14 Partitions) Vs. Cache Preferred (42 Partitions) - (right)

5.5 Other Performance Issues

We also evaluated how a very new (and relatively unique) architectural feature of Fermi impacts the performance our PBL scheme. In particular, in the Fermi architecture, application developers can configure a 64 KB fast memory (on each SM) in two ways. It can be configured as a 48 KB programmable shared memory and 16 KB L1 cache or as a 16 KB programmable shared memory and a 48 KB L1 cache. We refer to them as *shared memory preferred* and *L1 preferred* configurations, respectively.

This choice can clearly impact the PBL scheme, as the available shared memory changes the number of partitions we need to create. The number of partitions, in turn, influences performance in the following way. A larger number of partitions can increase the number of cross edges, and increase the amount of computation.

The workload imbalance observed can also vary with number of partitions, though it does not have to be necessarily higher with a higher number of partitions. A larger L1 cache, however, can allow better reuse of data structures not allocated in shared memory.

We conducted an experiment to evaluate this issue using Euler with both 20K and 50K datasets. For the 20K dataset, the L1 preferred strategy (requiring 28 partitions) has better performance over the shared memory preferred strategy (requiring 14 partitions), as we show in Figure 13. The reason seems to be that even with 14 partitions, we use only nearly 20 KB of the 48 KB available (Because there are 14 SMs in the card, fewer partitions will imply that not all SMs can process data). In comparison, with 28 partitions fitting into 16 KB shared memory, we obtain better reuse from L1 cache. The trends change with the larger datasets. Now, while 14 partitions can still fit in 48 KB shared memory, 42 partitions are needed if we have only 16 KB shared memory. This leads to a substantial increase in redundant workload, and worse performance.

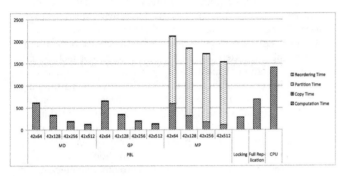

Figure 14: Comparison of MP, GP, and MD for Adaptive Molecular Dynamics (37K dataset, 42 partitions)

5.6 Performance with Adaptive Execution

Our experiments so far with the Molecular Dynamics application executed the main computations for 100 iterations, with no change in interactions between the molecules. In practice, however, this application involves a change in the interactions (set of edges or iterations) over time. Thus, we also experimented with a version that changed the indirection array after every 20 iterations. In comparison to the conventional locking or replication approaches, our PBL scheme needs to perform partitioning and reordering every time the indirection array changes.

Figure 14 shows the comparison among different partitioning methods for Adaptive Molecular Dynamics. For MP a large overhead is introduced. However, for MD, the cost for re-partitioning is only 0.96% of the total running time. Consequently, the PBL scheme still achieves a speedup of 11.6 compared to the sequential CPU version. Figure 14 also shows a comparison of the performance obtained from the PBL scheme against the conventional strategies, in which Locking and Full Replication is shown in their best thread configuration. Again, despite the cost of re-invoking the runtime modules, the PBL scheme achieves a significantly better performance when compared to full replication and locking scheme. Overall, these results show that the PBL scheme with the MD partitioner is effective even for adaptive irregular reductions.

6. RELATED WORK

We now compare our work against similar research efforts.

To the best of our knowledge, there is no existing systematic study considering irregular reductions on modern GPUs, and the use of shared memory for this class of applications. However, there

have been some individual application studies considering Euler, Molecular Dynamics, or very similar applications. Andrew Corrigan et al. [6] have parallelized the Euler computation on a per-element basis on a GPU, with one thread per element. In their approach, a large amount of redundant work arises because of the repeated computation of edges for all the elements they connect to. In comparison, in our approach, through partitioning, redundant work just exists at the boundaries of the partitions. In addition, we are able to use shared memory effectively. Another effort [36] parallelizes Lennard-Jones-based molecular dynamics simulation, in which there is no bond between the molecules. So the computation model in this work is not an irregular reduction. Another study [26] focusing on bond Molecular Dynamics used a parallelization method very similar to full replication. The memory overheads are very significant in this method, and there is a limit on the size of the data that can be processed. The work on Amber 11[3] and Friedrichs' work [10] have both created specific molecular dynamics implementations on GPUs. Details of their implementation schemes are not available and the actual implementations are also not distributed publicly. The limitations on number of molecules that can be simulated using Amber 11 implementation suggests the use of full replication.

The key differences in our work are: 1) our work is general to the irregular reduction class of application, 2) shared memory is utilized by partitioning, 3) a multi-dimensional partitioning method has been introduced, which balances the partitioning time and the execution efficiency, and 4) a detailed comparison of several approaches has been carried out across multiple applications.

A class of applications, which is somewhat similar to irregular reductions involves *sparse matrix computations*, have recently been studied on GPUs as well, including the auto-tuning work at Georgia Tech [5], and earlier studies by Garland [11]. Despite some similarities, there are significant distinct challenges in the parallelization of unstructured mesh computations, which have not been addressed in the efforts on sparse matrix computations.

Several systems have tried automating the use of shared memory on GPUs. Among these, Baskaran et al. have provided an approach for automatically arranging shared memory by using the polyhedral model for affine loops [3]. Moazeni et al. have adapted approaches for register allocation to manage shared memory on GPU [31]. Finally, Ma et al. have considered an integer programming based formulation [28]. None of these efforts have considered irregular applications, where runtime preprocessing needs to be used.

As stated earlier, irregular reductions have been studied widely on different types of architectures. This include efforts targeting distributed memory parallel machines [1, 7, 14, 16, 21, 22, 33, 37], distributed shared memory machines [32, 12], shared memory machines [4, 13, 25, 39] and cache performance improvement on uniprocessor machines [9, 15, 29, 30]. The key distinctive aspect of modern GPUs is the programmable cache or shared memory. Thus, while the use of runtime preprocessing and partitioning is similar to several of the above efforts, the details of our work are clearly distinct.

7. CONCLUSIONS

GPUs have emerged as a major player in high performance computing today. However, programmability and performance efficiency continue to be challenges which can restrict the use of GPUs. Particularly, irregular or unstructured computations can be quite challenging to parallelize and performance-tune on GPUs.

This paper has considered applications that involve unstructured

---

[3]http://ambermd.org/gpus/

meshes. We have developed a general methodology and optimized runtime support for this class of applications. Particularly, we have proposed a novel execution strategy, which we refer to as partitioning-based locking scheme. The main idea is to partition the reduction space, and then reorder the computation. We have developed a new low-cost partitioning scheme, which we refer to as multi-dimensional partitioning. Several optimizations have also been performed to improve the execution time of the runtime modules.

Our detailed evaluation using two popular irregular reductions has demonstrated the following. First, our partitioning-based scheme clearly outperforms the conventional schemes, and results in impressive speedups over sequential CPU versions. Moreover, our multi-dimensional partitioning scheme achieves the best tradeoff between the partitioning time and the application execution time. Our runtime modules are also efficient enough to support adaptive irregular applications.

8. ACKNOWLEDGMENTS

This research was supported by NSF grants IIS-0916196 and CCF-0833101.

9. REFERENCES

[1] G. Agrawal and J. Saltz. Interprocedural data flow based optimizations for distributed memory compilation. *Software Practice and Experience*, 27(5):519 – 546, May 1997.

[2] S. Baghsorkhi, M. Lathara, and W. mei Hwu. CUDA-lite: Reducing GPU Programming Complexity. In *LCPC 2008*, 2008.

[3] M. M. Baskaran, U. Bondhugula, S. Krishnamoorthy, J. Ramanujam, A. Rountev, and P. Sadayappan. Automatic data movement and computation mapping for multi-level parallel architectures with explicitly managed memories. In *PPoPP*, pages 1–10, NY, USA, 2008. ACM.

[4] W. Blume, R. Doallo, R. Eigenman, J. Grout, J. Hoelflinger, T. Lawrence, J. Lee, D. Padua, Y. Paek, B. Pottenger, L. Rauchwerger, and P. Tu. Parallel programming with Polaris. *IEEE Computer*, 29(12):78–82, Dec. 1996.

[5] J. W. Choi, A. Singh, and R. W. Vuduc. Model-driven Autotuning of Sparse Matrix-vector Multiply on GPUs. In *PPoPP*, Feb. 2010.

[6] A. Corrigan, F. Camelli, R. Löhner, and J. Wallin. Running unstructured grid cfd solvers on modern graphics hardware. In *19th AIAA Computational Fluid Dynamics Conference*, number AIAA 2009-4001, June 2009.

[7] R. Das, , P. Havlak, J. Saltz, and K. Kennedy. Index array flattening through program transformation. In *SC95*. IEEE Computer Society Press, Dec. 1995.

[8] R. Das, D. J. Mavriplis, J. Saltz, S. Gupta, and R. Ponnusamy. The design and implementation of a parallel unstructured Euler solver using software primitives. *AIAA Journal*, 32(3):489–496, Mar. 1994.

[9] C. Ding and K. Kennedy. Improving cache performance of dynamic applications with computation and data layout transformations. In *PLDI99*, May 1999.

[10] M. S. Friedrichs, P. Eastman, V. Vaidyanathan, M. Houston, S. Legrand, A. L. Beberg, D. L. Ensign, C. M. Bruns, and V. S. Pande. Accelerating molecular dynamic simulation on graphics processing units. *Journal of Computational Chemistry*, 30(Radeon 4870):864–872, 2009.

[11] M. Garland. Sparse matrix computations on manycore GPUs. In *DAC*, 2008.

[12] E. Gutierrez, O. Plata, and E. L. Zapata. A compiler method for the parallel execution of irregular reductions in scalable shared memory multiprocessors. In *ICS00*, pages 78–87. ACM Press, May 2000.

[13] M. Hall, S. Amarsinghe, B. Murphy, S. Liao, and M. Lam. Maximizing multiprocessor performance with the SUIF compiler. *IEEE Computer*, (12), Dec. 1996.

[14] H. Han and C.-W. Tseng. Improving compiler and runtime support for irregular reductions. In *LCPC98*, Aug. 1998.

[15] H. Han and C.-W. Tseng. A comparison of locality transformations for irregular codes. In *Proceedings of Fifth Workshop on Languages,*

Compilers, and Runtime Systems for Scalable Computers, pages 31 – 36, May 2000.

[16] R. v. Hanxleden. Handling irregular problems with Fortran D - a preliminary report. In *CPC*, Delft, The Netherlands, Dec. 1993. Also available as CRPC Technical Report CRPC-TR93339-S.

[17] Y.-S. Hwang, R. Das, J. H. Saltz, M. Hodoscek, and B. R. Brooks. Parallelizing molecular dynamics programs for distributed memory machines. *IEEE Computational Science & Engineering*, 2(2):18–29, Summer 1995. Also available as University of Maryland Technical Report CS-TR-3374 and UMIACS-TR-94-125.

[18] M. Kaddoura, C.-W. Ou, and S. Ranka. Partitioning unstructured computational graphs for nonuniform and adaptive environments. *IEEE Parallel & Distributed Technology*, 3(3):63–69, Fall 1995.

[19] B. Kernighan and S. Lin. An efficient heuristic procedure for partitioning graphs. *Bell System Technical Journal*, 49(2):291–307, Feb. 1970.

[20] M. Khan, G. Rudy, C. Chen, M. Hall, and J. Chame. Using Compiler-Based Autotuning to Generate High-Performance GPU Libraries. SC 2010 Poster Session, 2010.

[21] C. Koelbel and P. Mehrotra. Compiling global name-space parallel loops for distributed execution. *TPDS*, 2(4):440–451, Oct. 1991.

[22] A. Lain and P. Banerjee. Exploiting spatial regularity in irregular iterative applications. In *IPPS95*, pages 820–826. IEEE Computer Society Press, Apr. 1995.

[23] S. Lee and R. Eigenmann. OpenMPC: Extended OpenMP Programming and Tuning for GPUs. In *SC*, Nov 2010.

[24] S. Lee, S.-J. Min, and R. Eigenmann. OpenMP to GPGPU: A Compiler Framework for Automatic Translation and Optimization. In *PPoPP'09*, 2009.

[25] Y. Lin and D. Padua. On the automatic parallelization of sparse and irregular Fortran programs. In *Proceedings of the Workshop on Languages, Compilers, and Runtime Systems for Scalable Computers (LCR - 98)*, May 1998.

[26] W. Liu, B. Schmidt, G. Voss, and W. Müller-Wittig. Molecular dynamics simulations on commodity gpus with cuda. In *HiPC*, pages 185–196, 2007.

[27] W. Ma and G. Agrawal. A Translation System for Enabling Data Mining Applications on GPUs. In *ICS*, June 2009.

[28] W. Ma and G. Agrawal. An Integer Programming Framework for Optimizing Shared Memory Use on GPUs. In *HiPC*, Dec. 2010.

[29] J. Mellor-Crummey, D. Whalley, and K. Kennedy. Improving memory hierarchy performance of irregular applications. In *ICS*, June 1999.

[30] N. Mitchell, L. Carter, and J. Ferrante. Localizing non-affine array references. In *PACT*, Oct. 1999.

[31] M. Moazeni, A. Bui, and M. Sarrafzadeh. A Memory Optimization Technique for Software-Managed Scratchpad Memory in GPUs. http://www.sasp-conference.org/index.html, Jul 2009.

[32] S. Mukherjee, S. Sharma, M. Hill, J. Larus, A. Rogers, and J. Saltz. Efficient support for irregular applications on distributed-memory machines. In *PPOPP*, pages 68–79. ACM Press, July 1995. ACM SIGPLAN Notices, Vol. 30, No. 8.

[33] R. Ponnusamy, J. Saltz, A. Choudhary, Y.-S. Hwang, and G. Fox. Runtime support and compilation methods for user-specified irregular data distributions. *TPDS*, 6(8):815–831, Aug. 1995.

[34] K. Schloegel, G. Karypis, and V. Kumar. Parallel static and dynamic multi-constraint graph partitioning. *Concurrency and Computation: Practice and Experience*, 14(3):219–240, 2002.

[35] N. Sundaram, A. Raghunathan, and S. Chakradhar. A framework for efficient and scalable execution of domain-specific templates on GPUs. In *IPDPS*, 2009.

[36] J. P. Walters, V. Balu, V. Chaudhary, D. Kofke, and A. Schultz. Accelerating molecular dynamics simulations with gpus. In *ISCA PDCCS*, pages 44–49, 2008.

[37] J. Wu, R. Das, J. Saltz, H. Berryman, and S. Hiranandani. Distributed memory compiler design for sparse problems. *IEEE Transactions on Computers*, 44(6):737–753, June 1995.

[38] Y. Yang, P. Xiang, J. Kong, and H. Zhou. A GPGPU compiler for memory optimization and parallelism management. In *PLDI*, 2010.

[39] H. Yu and L. Rauchwerger. Adaptive reduction parallelization techniques. In *ICS00*, pages 66–75. ACM Press, May 2000.

Automatic Generation of Executable Communication Specifications from Parallel Applications

Xing Wu
North Carolina State
University
xwu3@ncsu.edu

Frank Mueller
North Carolina State
University
mueller@csc.ncsu.edu

Scott Pakin
Los Alamos National
Laboratory
pakin@lanl.gov

ABSTRACT

Portable parallel benchmarks are widely used and highly effective for (a) the evaluation, analysis and procurement of high-performance computing (HPC) systems and (b) quantifying the potential benefits of porting applications for new hardware platforms. Yet, past techniques to synthetically parametrized hand-coded HPC benchmarks prove insufficient for today's rapidly-evolving scientific codes particularly when subject to multi-scale science modeling or when utilizing domain-specific libraries.

To address these problems, this work contributes novel methods to automatically generate highly portable and customizable communication benchmarks from HPC applications. We utilize ScalaTrace, a lossless, yet scalable, parallel application tracing framework to collect selected aspects of the run-time *behavior* of HPC applications, including communication operations and execution time, while abstracting away the *details* of the computation proper. We subsequently generate benchmarks with identical run-time behavior from the collected traces. A unique feature of our approach is that we generate benchmarks in CONCEPTUAL, a domain-specific language that enables the expression of sophisticated communication patterns using a rich and easily understandable grammar yet compiles to ordinary C+MPI. Experimental results demonstrate that the generated benchmarks are able to preserve the run-time behavior—including both the communication pattern and the execution time—of the original applications. Such automated benchmark generation is particularly valuable for proprietary, export-controlled, or classified application codes: when supplied to a third party, our auto-generated benchmarks ensure performance fidelity but without the risks associated with releasing the original code. This ability to automatically generate performance-accurate benchmarks from parallel applications is novel and without any precedence, to our knowledge.

Categories and Subject Descriptors

C.4 [**Performance of Systems**]: Measurement techniques; D.1.3 [**Programming Techniques**]: Concurrent Programming—*Parallel Programming*; D.3.2 [**Programming Languages**]: Language Classifications—*Specialized application languages*

General Terms

Measurement, Performance

Keywords

application-specific benchmark generation, ScalaTrace, CONCEPTUAL, trace compression, communication, performance, domain-specific languages

1. INTRODUCTION

Evaluating and analyzing the performance of high-performance computing (HPC) systems generally involves running complete applications, computational kernels, or microbenchmarks. Complete applications are the truest indicator of how well a system performs. However, they may be time-consuming to port to a target machine's compilers, libraries, and operating system, and their size and intricacy makes them time-consuming to modify, for example, to evaluate the performance of different data decompositions or parallelism strategies. Furthermore, with intense competition to be the first to scientific discovery, computational scientists may be loath to risk granting their rivals access to their application's source code; or, the source code may be more formally protected as a corporate trade secret or as an export-controlled or classified piece of information. Computational kernels address some of these issues by attempting to isolate an application's key algorithms (e.g., a conjugate-gradient solver). Their relative simplicity reduces the porting effort, and they are generally less encumbered than a complete application. While their performance is somewhat indicative of how well an application will perform on a target machine, isolated kernels overlook important performance characteristics that apply when they are combined into a complete application. Finally, microbenchmarks stress individual machine components (e.g., memory, CPU, or network). While they are easy to port, distribute, modify, and run, and they precisely report characteristics of a target machine's performance, they provide little information about how an application might perform when the primitive operations they measure are combined in complex ways in an application.

The research question we propose to answer in this paper is the following: Is it possible to combine the best features of complete applications, computational kernels, and microbenchmarks into a single performance-evaluation methodology? That is, can one evaluate how fast a target HPC system will run a given application without having to migrate it and all of its dependencies to that system, without ignoring the subtleties of how different pieces of an application perform in context, without forsaking the ability to experiment with alternative application structures, and without restricting access to the tools needed to perform the evaluation?

Our approach is based on the insight that application performance is largely a function of the sorts of primitive operations that microbenchmarks measure and that if these operations can be juxtaposed as they appear in an application, the performance ought to be nearly identical. We therefore propose generating *application-specific performance benchmarks*. In fact, by "generating," we imply a fully automatic approach in which a parallel application can be treated as a black box and mechanically converted into an easy-to-build, easy-to-modify, and easy-to-run program with the same performance as the original but absent the original's data structures, numerical methods, and other algorithms.

We take as input an MPI-based [7] message-passing application. To convert this into a benchmark, we utilize the approach illustrated in Figure 1. We begin by tracing the application's communication pattern (including intervening computation time) using ScalaTrace [12]. The resulting trace is fed into the benchmark generator that is the focus of this paper. The benchmark generator outputs a benchmark written in CONCePTuaL, a domain-specific language for specifying communication patterns [15]. The CONCePTuaL code can then be compiled into ordinary C+MPI code for execution on a target machine.

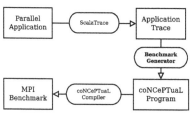

Figure 1: Our benchmark generation system

We utilize ScalaTrace [12] for communication trace collection because ScalaTrace represents the state of the art in parallel application tracing. It benefits benchmark generation in two aspects. First, due to its pattern-based compression techniques, ScalaTrace generates application traces that are lossless in communication semantics yet small and scalable in size. For example, ScalaTrace can represent all processes performing the same operation (e.g., each MPI rank sending a message to rank+4) as a single event, regardless of the number of ranks. Because the application trace is the basis for benchmark generation, this feature helps reduce the size of the generated code, making it more manageable for subsequent hand-modification. In contrast, previous application tracing tools, such as Extrae/Paraver [16], Tau [21], Open|SpeedShop [19], Vampir [11], and Kojak [25], are less suitable for benchmark generation because their traces increase in size with both the number of communication events and the number of MPI ranks traced. Second, ScalaTrace is aware of the structure of the original program. It utilizes the stack signature to distinguish different call sites. Its loop-compression techniques can detect the loop structure of the source code. For example, if an iteration comprises a hundred iterations, and each iteration sends five messages of one size and ten of another, ScalaTrace represents that internally as a set of nested loops rather than as 1500 individual messaging events. These pattern-identification features help benchmark generation maintain the program structure of the original application so that the generated code will be not only be semantically correct but also human comprehensible and editable.

We use the domain-specific CONCePTuaL language [15] instead of a general-purpose language such as C or Fortran as the target language for benchmark generation. (CONCePTuaL does, however, compile to C source code.) Because CONCePTuaL is designed specifically for the expression of communication patterns, benchmarks generated in CONCePTuaL are highly readable. CONCePTuaL code includes almost exclusively communication specifications. Mundane benchmarking details such as error checking, memory allocation, timer calibration, statistics calculation, MPI subcommunicator creation, and so forth are all handled implicitly, which reduces code clutter.

We evaluated our benchmark generation approach with the NAS Parallel Benchmark suite [3] and the Sweep3D code [10]. We per-formed experiments to assess both the correctness and the timing accuracy of the generated parallel benchmarks. Experimental results show that the auto-generated benchmarks preserve the application's semantics, including the communication pattern, the message count and volume, and the temporal ordering of communication events as they appear in the original parallel applications. In addition, the total execution times of the generated codes are very similar to those of the original applications; the mean absolute percentage error across all of our measurements is only 2.9%. Given these experimental results, we conclude that the generated benchmarks are able to reproduce the communication behavior and wall-clock timing characteristics of the source applications.

The contributions of this work are (1) a demonstration and evaluation of the feasibility of automatically converting parallel applications into human-readable benchmark codes, (2) an algorithm for determining precisely when separately appearing collective-communication calls in fact belong to the same logical operation, and (3) an approach and algorithm for ensuring performance repeatability by introducing determinism into benchmarks generated from nondeterministic applications.

We foresee our work benefiting application developers, communication researchers, and HPC system procurers. Application developers can benefit in multiple ways. First, they can quickly gauge what application performance is likely to be on a target machine before exerting the effort to port their applications to that machine. Second, they can use the generated benchmarks for performance debugging, as the benchmarks can separate communication from computation to help isolate observed performance anomalies. Third, application developers can examine the impact of alternative application implementations such as different data decompositions (causing different communication patterns) or the use of computational accelerators (reducing computation time without directly affecting communication time). Communication researchers can benefit by being able to study the impact of novel messaging techniques without incurring the burden of needing to build complex applications with myriad dependencies and without requiring access to codes that are not freely distributable. Finally, people tasked with procuring HPC systems benefit by being able to instruct vendors to deliver specified performance on a given application without having to provide those vendors with the application itself.

This paper is structured as follows. Section 2 contrasts our approach to others' related efforts. Section 3 introduces ScalaTrace and the CONCePTuaL language with respect to their abilities to support benchmark generation. The salient features of our benchmark-generation approach are detailed in Section 4. Section 5 empirically confirms the correctness and accuracy of the benchmarks we generate and presents sample usage of our framework. Finally, Section 7 draws some conclusions from our findings.

2. RELATED WORK

The following characteristics of our benchmark-generation approach make it unique:

- The size of the benchmarks we generate increases sublinearly in the number of processes and in the number of communication operations.
- We exploit run-time information rather than limit ourselves to information available at compile time.
- We preserve all communication performed by the original application.

We utilize ScalaTrace to collect the communication trace of parallel applications. With a set of sophisticated domain-specific trace-compression techniques, ScalaTrace is able to generate traces that preserve the original source-code structure while ensuring scalability in trace size. Other tools for acquiring communication traces such as Vampir [4], Extrae/Paraver [16], and tools based on the Open Trace Format [9] lack structure-aware compression. As a result, the size of a trace file grows linearly with the number of MPI calls and the number of MPI processes, and so too would the size of any benchmark generated from such a trace, making it inconvenient for processing long-running applications executing on large-scale machines. This lack of scalability is addressed in part by call-graph compression techniques [8] but still falls short of our structural compression, which extends to any event parameters. Casas et al. utilize techniques of signal processing to detect internal structures of Paraver traces and extract meaningful parts of the trace files [5]. While this approach could facilitate trace analysis, it is lossy and thus not suitable for benchmark generation.

Xu et al.'s work on constructing coordinated *performance skeletons* to estimate application execution time in new hardware environments [27, 28] exhibits many similarities with our work. However, a key aspect of performance skeletons is that they filter out "local" communication (communication outside the dominant pattern). As a result, the generated code does not fully reproduce the original application, which may cause subtle but important performance characteristics to be overlooked. Because our benchmark generation framework is based on lossless application traces it is able to generate benchmarks with identical communication behavior to the original application. In addition, we generate benchmarks in CONCEPTUAL instead of C so that the generated benchmarks are more human-readable and editable.

Program slicing, statically reducing a program to a minimal form that preserves key properties of the original, offers an alternative approach to generating benchmarks from application traces. Ertvelde et al. utilize program slicing to generate benchmarks that preserve an application's performance characteristics while hiding its functional semantics [6]. This work focuses on resembling the branch and memory access behaviors for sequential applications and may therefore complement our benchmark generator for parallel applications. Shao et al. designed a compiler framework to identify communication patterns for MPI-based parallel applications through static analysis [20], and Zhai et al. built program slices that contain only the variables and code sections related to MPI events and subsequently executed these program slices to acquire communication traces [29]. Program slicing and static benchmark generation in general have a number of shortcomings relative to our run-time, trace-based approach: Their reliance on inter-procedural analysis requires that *all* source code—the application's and all its dependencies—be available; they lack run-time timing information; they cannot accurately handle loops with data-dependent trip counts ("**while not** converged **do**. . ."); and they produce benchmarks that are neither human-readable nor editable.

3. BACKGROUND

Our benchmark generation approach utilizes the ScalaTrace infrastructure [12] to extract the communication behavior of the target application. Based on the application trace, we generate benchmarks in CONCEPTUAL [15], a high-level domain-specific language (with an associated compiler and run-time system) designed for testing the correctness and performance of communication networks. This section introduces the features of ScalaTrace and CONCEPTUAL that enable our benchmark generation methodology.

3.1 ScalaTrace

ScalaTrace is chosen as the trace collection framework because it generates near constant-size communication traces for a parallel applications regardless of the number of nodes while preserving structural information and temporal ordering. This is important because

```
for(i=0; i<1000; i++){
    MPI_Irecv(LEFT, ...);
    MPI_Isend(RIGHT, ...);
    MPI_Waitall(...);
}
```

Figure 2: Sample code for RSD and PRSD generation

it makes the size of the generated benchmarks reasonably small and independent of node count.

ScalaTrace achieves near constant-sized traces through pattern-based compression. It uses extended regular section descriptors (RSDs) to record the participating nodes and parameter values of multiple calls to a single MPI routine in the source code across loop iterations and nodes in a compressed manner. Power-RSDs (PRSDs) recursively specify RSDs nested in loops. For example, the program fragment shown in Figure 2 establishes a ring-style communication across N nodes. The three RSDs,

RSD1: $\{\langle rank \rangle$, MPI_Irecv, LEFT$\}$
RSD2: $\{\langle rank \rangle$, MPI_Isend, RIGHT$\}$
RSD3: $\{\langle rank \rangle$, MPI_Waitall$\}$

denote the MPI_Send, MPI_Receive, and MPI_Waitall operations in a single loop iteration, where $\langle rank \rangle$ takes on each value from 0 to $N - 1$ in turn. ScalaTrace then detects the loop structure and outputs the single PRSD, $\{1000$, RSD1, RSD2, RSD3$\}$, to concisely denote a single, 1000-iteration loop. Note that the intra-node loop compression is done on-the-fly to reduce memory overhead and compression time. Finally, the local traces are combined into a single global trace upon application completion (i.e., within the PMPI interposition wrapper for MPI_Finalize). This inter-node compression detects similarities among the per-node traces and merges the RSDs by combining their lists of participating nodes. For example, in Figure 2, because each MPI routine is called with the same parameters on each node, the RSDs within the PRSD are consequently merged across nodes as

RSD1: $\{0, 1, \ldots, N - 1$, MPI_Irecv, LEFT$\}$
RSD2: $\{0, 1, \ldots, N - 1$, MPI_Isend, RIGHT$\}$
RSD3: $\{0, 1, \ldots, N - 1$, MPI_Waitall$\}$

Besides communication tracing, ScalaTrace also stores application computation times in a scalable way [17]. Computation is defined as the time between consecutive MPI calls. Rather than store individual computation-time measurements, ScalaTrace compresses into a histogram the time taken by all instances of a particular computation (identified by its unique call path) across all loop iterations and all nodes. By grouping computation times in this manner, ScalaTrace achieves good compression while still addressing the time variations that are expected on different call paths. For example, the time spent in computation prior to the first statement of a loop generally differs significantly from the time spent in the first iteration, which generally differs significantly from the times spent in subsequent iterations.

3.2 CONCEPTUAL

CONCEPTUAL is a tool designed to facilitate rapid generation of network benchmarks. CONCEPTUAL includes a compiler for a high-level specification language and an accompanying run-time library. CONCEPTUAL programs are understandable even to non-experts because of its English-like grammar. For example, the following is a *complete* CONCEPTUAL benchmark program corresponding to the code snippet presented in Figure 2:

```
FOR 1000 REPETITIONS {
  ALL TASKS RESET THEIR COUNTERS THEN
  ALL TASKS t ASYNCHRONOUSLY SEND A 1 KILOBYTE
    MESSAGE TO TASK t+1 THEN
  ALL TASKS AWAIT COMPLETION THEN
  ALL TASKS LOG THE MEDIAN OF elapsed_usecs
```

```
      AS "Time (us)".
}
```

Note in the above that no variable or function declarations are required; no buffer allocation is required; no MPI_Request or MPI_Status objects need to be defined; no MPI communicators need to be queried for rank and size; no files need to be opened and written to; no statistics-calculating routines need to be implemented; no error codes need to be checked; no matching receive needs to be posted for each send (but can be if the programmer requires more precise control over posting order); and no special cases for the first and last task (rank) need to be specified. Nevertheless, CONCEPTUAL is able to express sophisticated communication patterns utilizing a variety of collective and point-to-point communication primitives, looping constructs, and conditional operations. When executed, the generated code produces log files that contain a wealth of information about the measured communication performance, code build characteristics, execution environment, and other information needed to yield reproducible performance measurements [14].

The aforementioned features make CONCEPTUAL an ideal language for benchmark generation. In the following section, we present our approach to producing CONCEPTUAL output from ScalaTrace input.

4. BENCHMARK GENERATION

4.1 Overview

The process of automatic code generation from traces is the process of traversing the parallel application trace, interpreting the RSDs and PRSDs, and generating the corresponding CONCEPTUAL program. We designed a trace traversal framework that walks through the trace and invokes a language-dependent code generator for each RSD and PRSD. A code generator is a pluggable function that conforms to a predefined interface. By implementing a generator for a different target language, we can easily generate code for languages other than CONCEPTUAL as well.

Most of the conversion from RSDs and PRSDs to CONCEPTUAL code is straightforward. An RSD representing point-to-point communication (blocking or nonblocking) is converted to a CONCEPTUAL SEND or RECEIVE statement; computation time encoded in an RSD is converted to a CONCEPTUAL COMPUTE statement; and a PRSD is converted to a CONCEPTUAL FOR EACH loop. Behavior that differs across loop iterations (message destinations, compute times, etc.) is implemented with a CONCEPTUAL IF statement conditioned on a loop variable. There are a few subtleties involved in the mapping from ScalaTrace to CONCEPTUAL; Section 4.2 discusses these.

Our view, however, is that a naive conversion from a trace to benchmark code has two important shortcomings. First, one of our goals is for the generated benchmark code to be *readable*, so a human can easily examine, understand, and modify the code. Our second goal is for the performance reported by the benchmark program to be *reproducible*, to make it a more suitable vehicle for experimentation. In short, we want it to be possible to reason about a generated benchmark's behavior and performance. However, achieving the goals of readability and reproducibility is a challenging research problem and is the subject of this section.

One difficulty in improving benchmark readability is the elimination of constructs whose behavior cannot statically be determined. Consider the following snippet of C code:

```
if (rank == 0)
  MPI_Reduce(⟨argument list⟩);
else
  MPI_Reduce(⟨the same argument list⟩);
```

It is not possible to know if those two MPI_Reduce() calls are part of the same collective operation without knowing the complete, run-time control flow of the program—on each rank individually—that led to the execution of the code shown above. The challenge is how to merge per-rank collective operations found in a trace into a single collective operation whose participants can be identified *statically*. An example of such an operation expressed in CONCEPTUAL is "TASKS xyz SUCH THAT 3 DIVIDES xyz REDUCE A DOUBLEWORD TO TASK 0"; no further information is required to know that tasks 0, 3, 6, 9, ... are the participants in that reduction operation. Section 4.3 presents our algorithm for matching collective operations specified separately on each node.

An MPI feature that hinders performance reproducibility is nondeterminism. MPI supports "wildcard receives" (MPI_ANY_SOURCE), which can receive messages from any sender. While this feature *can* lead to correctness issues [23], and we do address this, we are concerned primarily with the different performance that can result from different messages matching a set of wildcard receives. Consider, for example, the following use of the MPI_Recv receive operation:

```
MPI_Recv(..., MPI_ANY_SOURCE, ..., status);
if (status.MPI_SOURCE == 0)
  ⟨Do some long-running computation.⟩
else
  ⟨Do some short-running computation.⟩
MPI_Recv(..., MPI_ANY_SOURCE, ..., status);
```

Depending on the sender's MPI rank (status.MPI_SOURCE), the preceding code can take either a long time or a short time to run. Because the sender whose message matches the MPI_Recv can vary from run to run, the execution time of the preceding code also varies from run to run. While this behavior may be reasonable for an application, we deem it inappropriate for a benchmark program. As benchmarks are commonly used to evaluate system performance, small changes in a target machine's hardware or system software should not result in arbitrarily large changes in a benchmark's execution time. Section 4.4 presents our algorithm for removing performance nondeterminism caused by wildcard receives in the input trace.

4.2 Engineering Details

CONCEPTUAL is not designed to exactly represent MPI features. In fact, the CONCEPTUAL compiler can compile the same source program to C+MPI, C+Unix sockets, or to any other language/ communication library combination for which a compiler backend exists. Consequently, CONCEPTUAL contains collectives that MPI lacks (e.g., arbitrary many-to-many reductions with non-overlapping source and destination task sets), and MPI contains collectives that CONCEPTUAL lacks (e.g., scatters of different-sized messages to different destinations). We therefore had to "impedance match" the benchmark generator's MPI-centric input to CONCEPTUAL output. Our approach is to replace each unsupported MPI collective with one or more CONCEPTUAL collectives that represent a similar communication pattern (i.e., data fan in or fan out) and data volume. Table 1 presents the substitutions we made.

MPI has a notion of a "communicator," which is a subset of the available ranks, renumbered and possibly reordered. Every MPI communication operation takes a communicator as an argument and uses it to specify the participants in the operation. A disturbing consequence of communicators is that a line in the application source code that seems to be sending a message to, say, rank 3 may in fact be sending a message to rank 8 in the primordial MPI_COMM_WORLD communicator. To make the generated benchmarks more readable we keep track of the mapping of every rank within every communicator to an "absolute" rank within MPI_COMM_WORLD and express all

Table 1: Mapping of MPI collectives to CONCEPTUAL

MPI collective	CONCEPTUAL implementation
Allgather	REDUCE + MULTICAST
Allgatherv	REDUCE with averaged message size + MULTICAST
Alltoallv	MULTICAST with averaged message size
Gather	REDUCE
Gatherv	REDUCE with averaged message size
Reduce_scatter	n many-to-one REDUCEs with different message sizes and roots, where n is the communicator size
Scatter	MULTICAST
Scatterv	MULTICAST with averaged message size

generated computation and communication operations in terms of these absolute ranks.

4.3 Combining Per-Node Collectives

As discussed in Section 4.1, MPI allows multiple statements in the source code to represent a single, common collective operation. Because ScalaTrace differentiates call sites by call-stack signatures, this use of collectives generates distinct RSDs in the trace. To improve benchmark readability, before generating CONCEPTUAL code we want to combine these separate RSDs, each representing a subset of the collective's participants, into a single RSD that represents the complete set of participants. Figure 3 illustrates the intention, using C+MPI (with the omission of most MPI arguments) instead of RSDs for clarity. Figure 3(a) presents the initial communication pattern, in which each of ranks 0 and 1 invoke MPI_Barrier from a different source-code line. Assuming these are found to be the same collective, we want to hoist the MPI_Barrier outside of all conditionals on the rank, as shown in Figure 3(b).

```
if(rank == 0) {                 if(rank == 0)
    MPI_Isend(1);                   MPI_Isend(1);
    MPI_Barrier();              MPI_Barrier();
}                               if(rank == 1)
if(rank == 1) {                     MPI_Irecv(0);
    MPI_Barrier(1);             MPI_Wait();
    MPI_Irecv(0);
}
MPI_Wait();
```

(a) C+MPI program	(b) Aligned collectives

Figure 3: Combining collectives across separate source-code statements

To perform this transformation, recall that our benchmark generator operates on communication traces, not on application source code; it therefore does not literally perform the source-code transformation shown in Figure 3. Rather, it follows the sequence of steps presented in Algorithm 1 to align in time the RSDs of the same collective operation across nodes then combine these RSDs into a single RSD specifying the complete set of nodes to which the collective operation applies.

The main idea, illustrated in Figure 4 for RSDs corresponding to the C+MPI code in Figure 3, is to stop the trace traversal for a node at each collective in which it participates until all of the other participating nodes have arrived at the same collective. Algorithm 1 guarantees that (1) a collective operation corresponds to only one RSD in the output trace, (2) the ordering of MPI events for each node is preserved in the trace, and (3) the output trace is still in a compressed format. This algorithm tracks the traversal on different nodes by maintaining a *traversal context* for each node. The traversal context stores the current RSD the node is executing, the loop stack the

execution is in, and the iteration count for each loop in the stack. Upon startup, the algorithm traverses the trace on behalf of node 0, which is called the current *running node*. For each RSD of non-collective MPI routines that the running node is involved in, the algorithm extracts the current MPI event and appends an RSD to the output queue. (Note that an RSD can contain multiple MPI events across loop iterations and across nodes due to compression.) For collectives, however, the traversal stops for the current running node and switches to the next node in the communicator (indicated by the small arrows in Figure 4). When the last node in the communicator arrives at the collective, the algorithm appends the RSD for all the nodes to the output queue and switches the traversal back to the first node that is blocked on the same collective. We treat MPI_Finalize as a collective so that the algorithm cannot finish until the traversal is done for all the nodes. To guarantee that the new trace is scalable in length, we apply ScalaTrace's loop compression algorithm [12] to the output RSD queue each time a new RSD is appended to the queue. The complexity of this algorithm is $O(p \cdot e)$, where p is the number of MPI tasks and e is the number of communication events per task. Nevertheless, we do not blindly run this algorithm for arbitrary input traces. Before applying the algorithm we first check the trace to see if there are unaligned collectives. This check costs only $O(r)$, where r is the number of RSDs in the trace and is typically much smaller than e due to compression.

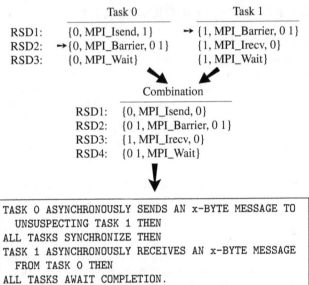

Figure 4: Operation of Algorithm 1

4.4 Eliminating Nondeterminism

MPI supports the use of a wildcard value, MPI_ANY_SOURCE, for the *source* parameter of point-to-point receives. For example, in the NAS Parallel Benchmarks's implementation of LU decomposition [3], nodes use MPI_ANY_SOURCE to receive messages in arbitrary order from their neighbors in a 2-D stencil. The problem with the use of MPI_ANY_SOURCE from a benchmarking perspective is that it has the potential to introduce performance artifacts, as discussed in Section 4.1. That is, each run of LU may stress the communication subsystem slightly differently based on the order in which messages happen to be received. To promote reproducibility of empirical measurements, our benchmark generator removes nondeterminism by replacing wildcard receives with arbitrary but valid non-wildcard receives.

As in Section 4.3's algorithm for combining collectives, Algorithm 2 utilizes a trace-traversal approach to resolve wildcard receives. Let e_{ijk} represent an MPI event k that is issued by node i and has

Algorithm 1 Algorithm to align collectives

Precondition: T_{in}: input trace, N: total number of nodes
Postcondition: T_{out}: the trace for CONCEPTUAL code generation

```
 1: function INITIALIZATION(T_in, N)
 2:     for i ← 1, N do
 3:         Allocate traversal context C[i]
 4:         C[i].RSD ← T_in.head
 5:     end for
 6:     Initialize T_out to am empty trace
 7:     T_out ← ALIGN(0, T_out)            ▷ Start with node 0
 8:     return T_out
 9: end function

10: function ALIGN(n, T_out)
11:     iter ← C[n].RSD
12:     while iter do
13:         if node n is not in iter.rank_list then
14:             iter ← iter.next
15:         else
16:             if iter.op is not a collective then
17:                 Extract current MPI event
18:                 Append a new RSD to T_out
19:                 Compress T_out
20:                 iter ← iter.next
21:                 continue
22:             end if
23:             if iter.op is a collective or MPI_Finalize then
24:                 if some participants have not arrived yet then
25:                     C[n].RSD ← iter
26:                     next ← the next node in the communicator
27:                     ALIGN(next, T_out)
28:                 else
29:                     Append an RSD for all participants to T_out
30:                     Compress T_out
31:                     C[n].RSD ← iter
32:                     for each i ∈ {participants} do
33:                         C[i].RSD ← C[i].RSD.next
34:                     end for
35:                     first ← the first node in the communicator
36:                     ALIGN(first, T_out)
37:                 end if
38:             end if
39:         end if
40:     end while
41:     return T_out
42: end function
```

node j as its peer. We maintain two lists for each node x: a list L_1 of the to-be-matched MPI events $e_{x j_1 1}, e_{x j_2 2}, e_{x j_3 3}, \ldots$ that were issued by node x itself and a list L_2 of the MPI events $e_{i_1 x k_1}, e_{i_2 x k_2}, e_{i_3 x k_3}, \ldots$ specifying the events issued by other nodes that should be matched by node x. Upon startup, this algorithm traverses the input trace on behalf of an arbitrary node x. During the traversal, it adds the unmatched point-to-point operations to list L_1 of node x and to list L_2 of each peer node. The traversal for node x stops when the execution is blocked on (1) a blocking send/receive, (2) a collective, or (3) a wait operation. It then switches the traversal to a node y whose execution will potentially unblock the execution on node x. In order to be selected as the target node to which the traversal switches (i.e., node y), a node must be (1) the destination/source of the blocking send/receive on node x, (2) a node in the same communicator with node x, or (3)

the destination/source of one of the nonblocking sends/receives that node x is waiting on, respectively. During the traversal for node y, we look up every MPI operation we arrived at in list L_2 of node y to detect matches. When a match is found, we delete the event from both lists. If possible, we unblock the execution on node x so that the traversal for it can proceed later on. If the receiver of a match uses MPI_ANY_SOURCE, this value is replaced with the rank of the (first) matching sender so that the wildcard source is resolved. Collectives are handled in a similar way as Algorithm 1 by blocking the traversal until every participating node arrives. We treat MPI_Finalize as a collective that all the nodes participate in, so that every node is traversed before the algorithm finishes. Because Algorithm 2 is again based on traversing a trace and each MPI event is evaluated exactly once, the complexity is also $O(p \cdot e)$, where p is the number of MPI tasks and e is the number of communication events per task. Similarly, the use of wildcard receives is checked at a cost of $O(r)$ before applying this algorithm, where r is the number of RSDs in the trace and, typically, $r \ll e$.

A ScalaTrace trace is obtained from an instance of a correct execution of the original parallel application. However, ScalaTrace does not represent this or any other specific execution because it does not replace the wildcard *source* value with the rank of the actual sender. Consequently, if the original application potentially deadlocks, Algorithm 2 suffers from the same risk. As an example, the code fragment in Figure 5(a) deadlocks if the wildcard receive is matched with node 0 but completes if matched with node 2. One possible execution generates the trace shown in Figure 5(b), which causes Algorithm 2 to hang because node 0 is blocked on MPI_Finalize and node 1 is blocked on MPI_Recv(0) during trace traversal.

```
if(rank == 1){
    MPI_Recv(MPI_ANY_SOURCE);
    MPI_Recv(0);
}
if(rank == 0 || rank == 2){
    MPI_Send(1);
}
```

(a) MPI program with potential deadlock

RSD1:	{1, MPI_Recv, MPI_ANY_SOURCE}
RSD2:	{1, MPI_Recv, 0}
RSD3:	{0, MPI_Send, 1}
RSD4:	{2, MPI_Send, 1}

(b) The trace of (a) that makes Algorithm 2 hang

Figure 5: Potential deadlock

To avoid potential hangs in Algorithm 2 caused by nondeterminism in the original application, our benchmark generator extends Algorithm 2 to detect deadlock conditions during trace traversal. Notice that these deadlocks stem from incorrect MPI semantics of the application, not from our tracing or code-generation framework. We decided to identify such incorrect MPI programs and report the existence of deadlocks to the user. To this end, we track another two types of events during traversal: (1) T_{ijk}, the transfer of traversal from node i to node j due to MPI event e_k, and (2) U, the unblocking event. We append these events to a global list, L_3, in the order they were encountered during the traversal. If the traversal is switched to node n while node n is blocked on an MPI event e_k, the deadlock detection algorithm traverses L_3 to determine if any unblocking event U has taken place since the last time the traversal left node n due to the same MPI event e_k. If there is no unblocking event found, a potential cyclic dependency is detected. If e_k is a blocking send/receive, then a deadlock potential has been uncovered and the algorithm terminates. If e_k is a wait operation blocked on multiple requests, the traversal is

Algorithm 2 Algorithm to resolve wildcard receive (without deadlock detection)

Precondition: T: input trace, N: total number of nodes
Postcondition: T: trace without wildcard receive

```
 1: function INITIALIZATION(T, N)
 2:     for i ← 1, N do
 3:         Allocate list L₁ and list L₂ for node i
 4:         Allocate traversal context C[i]
 5:         C[i].RSD ← T.head
 6:     end for
 7:     T ← Match(0, T)                          ▷ Start with node 0
 8:     return T
 9: end function

10: function MATCH(n, T)
11:     iter ← C[n].RSD
12:     while iter do
13:         if node n is not in iter.rank_list then
14:             iter ← iter.next
15:         else
16:             if iter.op is point-to-point operation then
17:                 if match with an event eₙₖ in L₂ then
18:                     L₂.delete(eₙₖ)
19:                     nodeᵢ.L₁.delete(eₙₖ)
20:                     if nodeᵢ.L₁ is empty then
21:                         C[i].RSD ← C[i].RSD.next   ▷ unblock
22:                     end if
23:                     if iter.peer is MPI_ANY_SOURCE then
24:                         iter.peer = i        ▷ resolve the wildcard
25:                     end if
26:                     iter ← iter.next
27:                     continue
28:                 else
29:                     p ← iter.peer
30:                     L₁.add(eₙₚ₍ₖₙ₊₊₎)
31:                     nodeₚ.L₂.add(eₙₚₖₙ)
32:                     if iter.op is blocking operation then
33:                         C[n].RSD ← iter
34:                         MATCH(p, T)
35:                     else
36:                         iter ← iter.next
37:                         continue
38:                     end if
39:                 end if
40:             end if
41:             if iter.op is collective or MPI_Finalize then
42:                 ...                          ▷ refer to Algorithm 1
43:             end if
44:             if iter.op is wait operation then
45:                 if L₁ is not empty then
46:                     MATCH(L₁.first.getPeer(), T)
47:                 else
48:                     iter ← iter.next
49:                     continue
50:                 end if
51:             end if
52:         end if
53:     end while
54:     return T
55: end function
```

proxied to the peer of another nonblocking communication on which node n is waiting. If the peers of all the pending nonblocking sends/receives have been traversed and the cyclic dependency still exists, a deadlock potential has been detected and the algorithm terminates. This algorithm implements a *sufficient* deadlock detection scheme. As a result, Algorithm 2 is guaranteed to be deadlock-free. However, unlike the DAMPI algorithm [23], Algorithm 2 does not establish or test the permutations of all execution interleavings and thus does not present a *necessary* condition for a deadlock as the approach is based on a single trace sequence of events. It may therefore fail to identify deadlocks in the original application that were not uncovered by the specific trace execution.

4.5 Sources of Performance Inaccuracy

As indicated, there are a number of ways in which our benchmark generator trades off performance fidelity for an improved ability to reason about the generated code and its performance: computation times are summarized across ranks instead of being specified individually (Section 3.1); some complex MPI collectives are implemented in terms of more basic CONCEPTUAL collectives (Section 4.2); and nondeterministic receive ordering is replaced with an arbitrary deterministic ordering (Section 4.4). In Section 5 we examine the impact of these design decisions in the context of a suite of test programs.

5. EVALUATION

5.1 Experimental Framework

To evaluate our benchmark-generation methodology, we generated CONCEPTUAL codes for the NAS Parallel Benchmarks (NPB) suite (version 3.3 for MPI, comprising BT, CG, EP, FT, IS, LU, MG, and SP) using the class C input size [3] and for the Sweep3D neutron-transport kernel [24]. These benchmarks all have either a mesh-neighbor communication pattern or rely heavily on collective communication. Some of them (e.g., Sweep3D) require collective alignment (Section 4.3), and some (e.g., LU) require the resolution of wildcard receives (Section 4.4). Hence, the key features of our code-generation framework are fully tested in this set of experiments. We believe results from the NPB and Sweep3D in this paper, combined with previous ScalaTrace experiments [13, 26], are sufficient to demonstrate the correctness of our approach, and we do not foresee any algorithmic or technical problems with generating code for larger applications. Moreover, these benchmarks are sufficient to demonstrate our ability to retain an application's performance characteristics. In particular, several kernels in the NPB suite, including CG, FT, and MG, are known to be memory-bound [18], which stresses our generated benchmarks' ability to mimic computation with spin loops of the same duration.

Benchmark generation is based on traces obtained on (a) Ocracoke, an IBM Blue Gene/L [1] with 2,048 compute nodes and 1 GB of DRAM per node and (b) ARC, a cluster with 1728 cores on 108 compute nodes, 32 GB memory per node, and an Ethernet interconnect. Due to limited access to these systems our experiments generally run on only a subset of the available nodes. Benchmark generation is performed on a standalone workstation.

5.2 Communication Correctness

Our first set of experiments verifies the correctness of the generated benchmarks, i.e., the benchmark generator's ability to retain the original applications' communication pattern. For these experiments, we acquired traces of our test suite on Blue Gene/L, generated CONCEPTUAL benchmarks, and executed these benchmarks also on Blue Gene/L. To verify the correctness of the generated benchmarks, we linked both them and the original applications with mpiP [22], a lightweight MPI profiling library that gathers run-time statistics of

MPI event counts and the message volumes exchanged. Experimental results (not presented here) showed that, for each type of MPI event, the event count and the message volume measured for each generated benchmarks matched perfectly with those measured for the original application.

We then conducted experiments to verify that the generated benchmarks not only resemble the original applications in overall statistics but also that they preserve the original semantics on a per-event basis. To this end, we instrumented each generated benchmark with ScalaTrace and compared its communication trace with that of its respective original application. Due to differences in the call-site stack signatures between the original application and the generated benchmark, these traces are never bit-for-bit identical. Therefore, we replayed both traces with the ScalaTrace-based ScalaReplay tool [26] to eliminate spurious structural differences and thereby fairly compare the pairs of traces. The results (again, not presented here) show that the original applications and the generated benchmarks generated equivalent traces. That is, the semantics of each of the original applications was precisely reproduced by the corresponding generated benchmark.

5.3 Accuracy of Generated Timings

Having determined that benchmarks produced using our benchmark generator faithfully represent the communication performed by the original applications, we then assessed the generated benchmarks' ability to retain the original applications' performance. To measure the total execution time of the original applications, we extended the PMPI profiling wrappers of MPI_Init and MPI_Finalize to obtain timestamps). The corresponding CONCEPTUAL timing calls were also added to the generated benchmarks. We ran both the original application and the generated benchmark on the Blue Gene/L system and compared the total elapsed times. Figure 6 shows that the timing accuracy is qualitatively extremely good. Quantitatively, the mean absolute percentage error (i.e., $100\% \times |(T_{\text{CONCEPTUAL}} - T_{\text{app}})/T_{\text{app}}|$) across all of Figure 6 is only 2.9%, and only two data points exhibit worse than 10% deviation: LU at 256 nodes observes a deviation of 22% (40 s for the benchmark versus 52 s for the original application), and SP at 16 nodes observes a deviation of 10% (980 s for the benchmark versus 1092 s for the original application).

5.4 Applications of the Benchmark Generator

The experimental results presented in Sections 5.2 and 5.3 indicate that the performance of the generated benchmarks can be trusted. We now present an example of some what-if analysis that is made practical by automatic benchmark generation.

A current trend in high-performance computing is to supplement general-purpose CPUs with more special-purpose computational accelerators (e.g., GPUs).[1] However, by Amdahl's Law [2], accelerating only an application's computational phases does not always lead to proportional overall speedup. Unfortunately, it is nontrivial both to predict how fast a parallel application will run once accelerated and to port a parallel application to an accelerated architecture. Application developers may also optimize performance by overlapping communication and computation. This too takes time to implement and leads to a reduction in execution time that can be difficult to predict.

Because the CONCEPTUAL benchmarks produced by our generator are easy to modify, we can use our framework to estimate how fast an application can be expected to run once accelerated or once communication and computation fully overlap. We generated a benchmark from the NPB BT code on 64 cores using the class C input. We then modified the CONCEPTUAL code to vary the time

[1] In fact, four of the world's ten fastest supercomputers contain accelerators (http://www.top500.org/, November 2010).

spent in all computation phases from 100% down to 0% of their original time to simulate different expected improvements due to acceleration. We ran the resulting benchmark variations on the ARC cluster (cf. Section 5.1) and plotted the results in Figure 7.

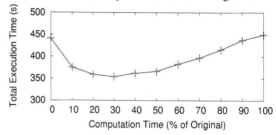

Figure 7: Communication performance of BT

Reading Figure 7 from right to left, the data points ranging from 100% down to 30% of the original application's compute time are essentially what one might expect: a steady but sublinear decrease in total execution time. That is, a fabricated 3.3x speedup of computation leads to only a 21% reduction in total execution time for BT. However, as computation time continues to decrease, rather than reach a plateau, the total execution time *increases*. At the 0% computation mark, which represents infinitely fast processors on a modern Ethernet network, there is essentially *no* speedup over the unmodified BT execution time.

To understand this puzzling behavior, note that BT is a stencil code consisting almost exclusively of asynchronous point-to-point communication operations, with only a few collectives at the beginning and end of the execution. Reducing the time between subsequent communication operations alters the dynamics of the messaging layer and leads to the observed increase in performance. For example, if messages begin arriving faster than they can be processed, they will start being directed to the MPI implementation's unexpected-receive queue, which incurs a performance cost in the form of an extra memory copy to transfer unexpected messages to the target buffer. Once all available space for storing incoming messages on a given node is exhausted, the MPI implementation's flow-control mechanism must stall any senders and later pay a cost in network latency to resume them. It is the nonlinear effects such as those that make it important to quantify potential performance improvements using a framework such as ours before investing the effort to accelerate an application.

We should note that the experimental result presented in Figure 7 is both application-specific and platform-specific. Yet, with our benchmark-generation approach, the experiment can easily be repeated on different platforms without ever needing to port the original application. In addition, our BT experiment can easily be refined to utilize different speedup factors for different computational phases. We foresee this type of performance experimentation, enabled by our benchmark generator, becoming increasingly important as HPC hardware increases in complexity and requires expanded efforts to port large applications (for potentially small performance gains).

6. DISCUSSION AND FUTURE WORK

This work has demonstrated the feasibility of automatically generating performance-accurate and highly readable benchmarks from application traces. The ability to generate benchmarks that can be executed with arbitrary number of MPI processes still remains an open problem. Our prior publication contributed a set of algorithms and techniques to extrapolate a trace of a large-scale execution of an application from traces of several smaller runs [26]. We intend to incorporate that effort into benchmark generation.

Currently, our work focuses on the generation of communication benchmarks. Our approach guarantees that the generated communi-

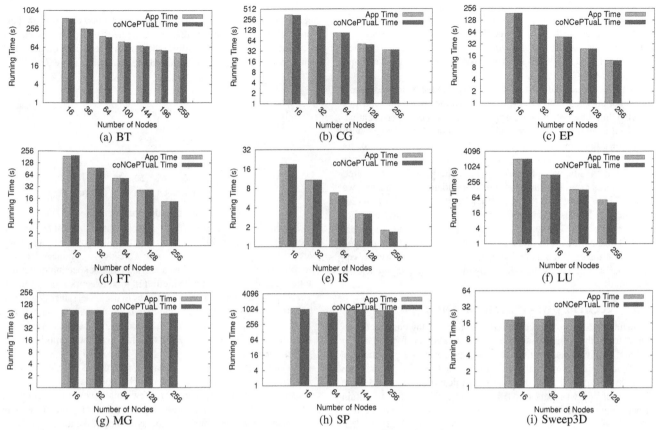

Figure 6: Time accuracy for generated benchmarks

cation is cross-platform performance-portable because we preserve the original communication pattern and can execute it natively on a target machine. However, since computation times are taken from the source machine, the computation performance does not reflect architecture-specific effects of a different platform. One advantage of mimicking computation with spin loops is that this enables studies in which computation time is explicitly varied, as in Section 5.4. Meanwhile, we are also working on scalable memory tracing to complement communication tracing. Automatic generation and replay of memory-access behavior within ScalaTrace is a subject of future work.

7. CONCLUSIONS

To bridge the gap between the performance realism of a complete application and the convenience of porting and modifying a benchmark code, we have designed, implemented, and evaluated a benchmark-generation framework that automatically generates portable, customizable communication benchmarks from parallel applications. Our approach is based on an application's dynamic behavior rather than its statically identifiable characteristics. We use ScalaTrace [12] to recover application structure from a communication trace and CONCEPTUAL [15] to express the resulting benchmarks in a readable, editable, yet executable format.[2] Algorithms we developed to assist in this process merge collective operations described by disparate source-code lines into a single call point and eliminate non-determinism caused by wildcard receives. Empirical measurements indicate that the performance of the generated benchmarks is faithful to that of the original application.

---

[2] ScalaTrace and CONCEPTUAL are freely available from, `http://moss.csc.ncsu.edu/~mueller/ScalaTrace/` and `http://conceptual.sourceforge.net/`.

There are two main conclusions one can draw from this work. First, it is in fact feasible to automatically convert parallel applications into benchmark codes that accurately reproduce the applications' performance yet are easy to port, read, edit, and reason about. Second, as demonstrated in Section 5.4, nonlinear performance effects come into play as applications are modified for nascent architectures, and performance-accurate, application-specific benchmarks are an important new technology for quantifying these effects before exerting the effort involved in application porting.

The benchmarks we generate preserve all communication operations, represent applications' actual run-time behavior, and do not grow proportionally to the process count or message volume. To our knowledge, our work is the first successful attempt at automatically converting parallel applications into performance-accurate benchmarks that exhibit all of those features.

Acknowledgments

This work was supported in part by NSF grants 0937908 and 0958311 and by the U.S. Department of Energy's National Nuclear Security Administration under contract DE-AC52-06NA25396 with Los Alamos National Security, LLC.

8. REFERENCES

[1] N. R. Adiga et al. An overview of the BlueGene/L supercomputer. In *Proceedings of the 2002 ACM/IEEE Conference on Supercomputing*, Baltimore, Maryland, Nov. 16–22, 2002. IEEE Computer Society Press.

[2] G. M. Amdahl. Validity of the single processor approach to achieving large scale computing capabilities. In *Proceedings of the AFIPS Spring Joint Computer Conference*, pages 483–485, Atlantic City, New Jersey, Apr. 18–20, 1967. ACM.

[3] D. H. Bailey, E. Barszcz, J. T. Barton, D. S. Browning, R. L. Carter, D. Dagum, R. A. Fatoohi, P. O. Frederickson, T. A. Lasinski, R. S. Schreiber, H. D. Simon, V. Venkatakrishnan, and S. K. Weeratunga. The NAS Parallel Benchmarks. *The International Journal of Supercomputer Applications*, 5(3):63–73, Fall 1991.

[4] H. Brunst, H.-C. Hoppe, W. E. Nagel, and M. Winkler. Performance optimization for large scale computing: The scalable VAMPIR approach. In *International Conference on Computational Science (2)*, pages 751–760, 2001.

[5] M. Casas, R. Badia, and J. Labarta. Automatic structure extraction from mpi applications tracefiles. In *Euro-Par Conference*, Aug. 2007.

[6] L. V. Ertvelde and L. Eeckhout. Dispersing proprietary applications as benchmarks through code mutation. In *Architectural Support for Programming Languages and Operating Systems*, pages 201–210, 2008.

[7] W. Gropp, E. Lusk, N. Doss, and A. Skjellum. A high-performance, portable implementation of the MPI message passing interface standard. *Parallel Computing*, 22(6):789–828, Sept. 1996.

[8] A. Knupfer. Construction and compression of complete call graphs for post-mortem program trace analysis. In *International Conference on Parallel Processing*, pages 165–172, 2005.

[9] A. Knüpfer, R. Brendel, H. Brunst, H. Mix, and W. E. Nagel. Introducing the Open Trace Format (OTF). In *Int'l Conf. on Computational Science*, pages 526–533, May 2006.

[10] K. R. Koch, R. S. Baker, and R. E. Alcouffe. Solution of the first-order form of the 3-D discrete ordinates equation on a massively parallel processor. *Transactions of the American Nuclear Society*, 65(108):198–199, 1992.

[11] W. E. Nagel, A. Arnold, M. Weber, H. C. Hoppe, and K. Solchenbach. VAMPIR: Visualization and analysis of MPI resources. *Supercomputer*, 12(1):69–80, 1996.

[12] M. Noeth, F. Mueller, M. Schulz, and B. R. de Supinski. Scalable compression and replay of communication traces in massively parallel environments. In *International Parallel and Distributed Processing Symposium*, Apr. 2007.

[13] M. Noeth, F. Mueller, M. Schulz, and B. R. de Supinski. Scalatrace: Scalable compression and replay of communication traces in high performance computing. *Journal of Parallel Distributed Computing*, 69(8):969–710, Aug. 2009.

[14] S. Pakin. Reproducible network benchmarks with CONCEPTUAL. In M. Danelutto, D. Laforenza, and M. Vanneschi, editors, *Proceedings of the 10th International Euro-Par Conference*, volume 3149 of *Lecture Notes in Computer Science*, pages 64–71, Aug. 31–Sept. 3, 2004.

[15] S. Pakin. The design and implementation of a domain-specific language for network performance testing. *IEEE Transactions on Parallel and Distributed Systems*, 18(10):1436–1449, Oct. 2007.

[16] V. Pillet, V. Pillet, J. Labarta, T. Cortes, and S. Girona. PARAVER: A tool to visualize and analyze parallel code. In *Proceedings of the 18th Technical Meeting of WoTUG-18: Transputer and Occam Developments*, pages 17–31, 1995.

[17] P. Ratn, F. Mueller, B. R. de Supinski, and M. Schulz. Preserving time in large-scale communication traces. In *Int'l Conf. on Supercomputing*, pages 46–55, June 2008.

[18] S. Saini, D. Talcott, D. Jespersen, J. Djomehri, H. Jin, and R. Biswas. Scientific application-based performance comparison of sgi altix 4700, ibm power5+, and sgi ice 8200 supercomputers. In *Proceedings of the 2008 ACM/IEEE conference on Supercomputing*, SC '08, pages 7:1–7:12, Piscataway, NJ, USA, 2008. IEEE Press.

[19] M. Schulz, J. Galarowicz, D. Maghrak, W. Hachfeld, D. Montoya, and S. Cranford. Open|SpeedShop: An open source infrastructure for parallel performance analysis. *Scientific Programming*, 16(2–3):105–121, 2008.

[20] S. Shao, A. Jones, and R. Melhem. A compiler-based communication analysis approach for multiprocessor systems. In *In International Parallel and Distributed Processing Symposium*, 2006.

[21] S. S. Shende and A. D. Malony. The Tau parallel performance system. *Int'l Journal of High Performance Computing Applications*, 20(2):287–311, 2006.

[22] J. Vetter and M. McCracken. Statistical scalability analysis of communication operations in distributed applications. In *ACM SIGPLAN Symposium on Principles and Practice of Parallel Programming*, 2001.

[23] A. Vo, S. Aananthakrishnan, G. Gopalakrishnan, B. R. de Supinski, M. Schulz, and G. Bronevetsky. A scalable and distributed dynamic formal verifier for MPI programs. In *Proceedings of the 2010 ACM/IEEE International Conference for High Performance Computing, Networking, Storage and Analysis (SC'10)*, New Orleans, Louisiana, Nov. 13–19, 2010.

[24] H. Wasserman, A. Hoisie, and O. Lubeck. Performance and scalability analysis of teraflop-scale parallel architectures using multidimensional wavefront applications. *The International Journal of High Performance Computing Applications*, 14:330–346, 2000.

[25] F. Wolf and B. Mohr. KOJAK—a tool set for automatic performance analysis of parallel applications. In *Proc. of the European Conference on Parallel Computing (Euro-Par)*, volume 2790 of *Lecture Notes in Computer Science*, pages 1301–1304, Klagenfurt, Austria, August 2003. Springer. Demonstrations of Parallel and Distributed Computing.

[26] X. Wu and F. Mueller. ScalaExtrap: Trace-based communication extrapolation for SPMD programs. In *ACM SIGPLAN Symposium on Principles and Practice of Parallel Programming*, 2011.

[27] Q. Xu, R. Prithivathi, J. Subhlok, and R. Zheng. Logicalization of MPI communication traces. Technical Report UH-CS-08-07, Dept. of Computer Science, University of Houston, 2008.

[28] Q. Xu and J. Subhlok. Construction and evaluation of coordinated performance skeletons. In *International Conference on High Performance Computing*, pages 73–86, 2008.

[29] J. Zhai, T. Sheng, J. He, W. Chen, and W. Zheng. FACT: Fast communication trace collection for parallel applications through program slicing. In *Proceedings of SC'09*, pages 1–12, 2009.

Hystor: Making the Best Use of Solid State Drives in High Performance Storage Systems

Feng Chen   David Koufaty
Circuits and Systems Research
Intel Labs
Hillsboro, OR 97124, USA
{feng.a.chen,david.a.koufaty}@intel.com

Xiaodong Zhang
Dept. of Computer Science & Engineering
The Ohio State University
Columbus, OH 43210, USA
zhang@cse.ohio-state.edu

ABSTRACT

With the fast technical improvement, flash memory based Solid State Drives (SSDs) are becoming an important part of the computer storage hierarchy to significantly improve performance and energy efficiency. However, due to its relatively high price and low capacity, a major system research issue to address is on how to make SSDs play their most effective roles in a high-performance storage system in cost- and performance-effective ways.

In this paper, we will answer several related questions with insights based on the design and implementation of a high performance hybrid storage system, called *Hystor*. We make the best use of SSDs in storage systems by achieving a set of optimization objectives from both system deployment and algorithm design perspectives. Hystor manages both SSDs and hard disk drives (HDDs) as one single block device with minimal changes to existing OS kernels. By monitoring I/O access patterns at runtime, Hystor can effectively identify blocks that (1) can result in long latencies or (2) are semantically critical (e.g. file system metadata), and stores them in SSDs for future accesses to achieve a significant performance improvement. In order to further leverage the exceptionally high performance of writes in the state-of-the-art SSDs, Hystor also serves as a write-back buffer to speed up write requests. Our measurements on Hystor implemented in the Linux kernel 2.6.25.8 show that it can take advantage of the performance merits of SSDs with only a few lines of changes to the stock Linux kernel. Our system study shows that in a highly effective hybrid storage system, SSDs should play a major role as an independent storage where the best suitable data are adaptively and timely migrated in and retained, and it can also be effective to serve as a write-back buffer.

Categories and Subject Descriptors

D.4.2 [**Storage Management**]: Secondary Storage

General Terms

Design, Experimentation, Performance

Keywords

Solid State Drive, Hard Disk Drive, Hybrid Storage System

1. INTRODUCTION

High-performance storage systems are in an unprecedented high demand for data-intensive computing. However, most storage systems, even those specifically designed for high-speed data processing, are still built on conventional hard disk drives (HDDs) with several long-existing technical limitations, such as low random access performance and high power consumption. Unfortunately, these problems essentially stem from the mechanic nature of HDDs and thus are difficult to be addressed via technology evolutions.

Flash memory based Solid State Drive (SSD), an emerging storage technology, plays a critical role in revolutionizing the storage system design. Different from HDDs, SSDs are completely built on semiconductor chips without any moving parts. Such a fundamental difference makes SSD capable of providing one order of magnitude higher performance than rotating media, and makes it an ideal storage medium for building high performance storage systems. For example, San Diego Supercomputer Center (SDSC) has built a large flash-based cluster, called *Gordon*, for high-performance and data-intensive computing [3]. In order to improve storage performance, Gordon adopts 256TB of flash memory as its storage [24]. However, such a design, which is backed by a $20 million funding from the National Science Foundation (NSF), may not be a typical SSD-based storage solution for widespread adoption, because the high cost and relatively small capacity of SSDs will continue to be a concern for a long time [11], and HDDs are still regarded as indispensable in the storage hierarchy due to the merits of low cost, huge capacity, and fast sequential access speed. In fact, building a storage system completely based on SSDs is often above the acceptable threshold in most commercial and daily operated systems, such as data centers. For example, a 32GB Intel® X25-E SSD costs around $12 per GB, which is nearly 100 times more expensive than a typical commodity HDD. To build a server with only 1TB storage, 32 SSDs are needed and as much as $12,000 has to be invested in storage solely. Even considering the price-drop trend, the average cost per GB of SSDs is still unlikely to reach the level of rotating media in the near future [11]. Thus, we believe that in most systems, SSDs should not be simply viewed as a replacement for the existing HDD-based storage, but instead SSDs should be a means to enhance it. Only by finding the fittest position of SSDs in storage systems, we can strike a right balance between performance and cost. Unquestionably, to achieve this goal, it is much more challenging than simply replacing HDDs with fast but expensive SSDs.

1.1 Critical Issues

A straightforward consideration of integrating SSD in the existing memory hierarchy is to treat the state-of-the-art SSDs, whose cost and performance are right in between of DRAM memory and

HDDs, as a *secondary-level cache*, and apply caching policies, such as LRU or its variants, to maintain the most likely-to-be-accessed data for future reuse. However, the SSD performance potential could not be fully exploited unless the following related important issues, from both policy design and system deployment perspectives, be well addressed. In this paper, we present a unique solution that can best fit SSDs in the storage hierarchy and achieve these optimization goals.

1. Effectively identifying the most performance-critical blocks and fully exploiting the unique performance potential of SSDs – Most existing caching policies are temporal locality based and strive to identify the most likely-to-be-reused data. Our experimental studies show that the performance gains of using SSDs over HDDs is highly dependent on workload access patterns. For example, random reads (4KB) on an Intel® X25-E SSD can achieve up to 7.7 times higher bandwidth than that on an HDD, while the speedup for sequential reads (256KB) is only about 2 times. Besides identifying the most likely-to-be-reused blocks as done in most previous studies, we must further identify the blocks that can receive the most significant performance benefits from SSDs. We have systematically analyzed various workloads and identified a simple yet effective metric based on extensive experimental studies. Rather than being randomly selected, this metric considers both *temporal locality* and *data access patterns*, which well meets our goal of distinguishing the most performance-critical blocks.

2. Efficiently maintaining data access history with low overhead for accurately characterizing access patterns – A major weakness of many LRU-based policies is the lack of knowledge about deep data access history (i.e. recency only). As a result, they cannot identify critical blocks for a long-term optimization and thus suffer the well-known cache pollution problem (workloads, such as reading a streaming file, can easily evict all valuable data from the cache [14]). As a key difference from previous studies, we profile and maintain data access history as an important part of our hybrid storage. This avoids the cache pollution problem and facilitates an effective reorganization of data layout across devices. A critical challenge here is how to efficiently maintain such data access history for a large-scale storage system, which is often in Terabytes. In this paper, a special data structure, called *block table*, is used to meet this need efficiently.

3. Avoiding major kernel changes in existing systems while effectively implementing the hybrid storage management policies – Residing at the bottom of the storage hierarchy, a hybrid storage system should improve system performance without intrusively changing upper-level components (e.g. file systems) or radically modifying the common interfaces shared by other components. Some previously proposed solutions attempt to change the existing memory hierarchy design by inserting non-volatile memory as a new layer in the OS kernels (e.g. [18, 19]); some require that the entire file system be redesigned [34], which may not be viable in practice. Our design carefully isolates complex details behind a standard block interface, which minimizes changes to existing systems and guarantees compatibility and portability, which are both critical in practice.

In our solution, compared to prior studies and practices, SSD plays a different role. We treat the high-capacity SSD as a part of storage, instead of a caching place. Correspondingly, different from the conventional caching-based policies, which frequently update the cache content on each data access, we only periodically and asynchronously reorganize the layout of blocks across devices for a long-term optimization. In this paper, we show that this arrangement makes SSDs the best fit in storage hierarchy.

1.2 Hystor: A Hybrid Storage Solution

In this paper, we address the aforesaid four issues by presenting the design and implementation of a practical hybrid storage system, called *Hystor*. Hystor integrates both low-cost HDDs and high-speed SSDs as a *single* block device and isolates complicated details from other system components. This avoids undesirable significant changes to existing OS kernels (e.g. file systems and buffer cache) and applications.

Hystor achieves its optimization objectives of data management through three major components. First, by monitoring I/O traffic on the fly, Hystor automatically learns workload access patterns and identifies performance-critical blocks. Only the blocks that can bring the most performance benefits would be gradually remapped from HDDs to high-speed SSDs. Second, by effectively exploiting high-level information available in existing interfaces, Hystor identifies semantically-critical blocks (e.g. file system metadata) and timely offers them a high priority to stay in the SSD, which further improves system performance. Third, incoming writes are buffered into the low-latency SSD for improving performance of write-intensive workloads. We have prototyped Hystor in the Linux Kernel 2.6.25.8 as a stand-alone kernel module with only a few lines of codes added to the stock OS kernel. Our experimental results show that Hystor can effectively exploit SSD performance potential and improve performance for various workloads

1.3 Our Contributions

The contribution of this work is threefold. (1) We have identified an effective metric to represent the performance-critical blocks by considering both temporal locality and data access patterns. (2) We have designed an efficient mechanism to profile and maintain detailed data access history for a long-term optimization. (3) We present a comprehensive design and implementation of a high performance hybrid storage system, which improves performance for accesses to the high-cost data blocks, semantically-critical (file system metadata) blocks, and write-intensive workloads with minimal changes to existing systems. While we have prototyped Hystor as a kernel module in software, a hardware implementation (e.g. in a RAID controller card) of this scheme is possible, which can further reduce system deployment difficulty as a drop-in solution.

In the rest of this paper, we will first examine the SSD performance advantages in Section 2. We study how to identify the most valuable data blocks and efficiently maintain data access history in Section 3 and 4. Then we present the design and implementation of Hystor in Section 5 and 6. Section 7 presents our experimental results. Related work is presented in Section 8. The last section concludes this paper.

2. SSD PERFORMANCE ADVANTAGES

Understanding the relative performance strengths of SSDs over HDDs is critical to efficiently leverage limited SSD space for the most performance gains. In this section, we evaluate an Intel® X25-E 32GB SSD [13], a representative high-performance SSD, and compare its performance with a 15,000 RPM Seagate® Cheetah® 15.5k SAS hard disk drive, a typical high-end HDD. Details about the two storage devices and experiment system setup are available in Section 7.

In general, a workload can be characterized by its read/write ratio, random/sequential ratio, request size, and think time, etc. We use the Intel® Open Storage Toolkit [21] to generate four typical workloads, namely *random read*, *random write*, *sequential read*, and *sequential write*. For each workload, we set the queue depth of 32 jobs and vary the request size from 1KB to 256KB. All workloads directly access raw block devices to bypass the buffer cache

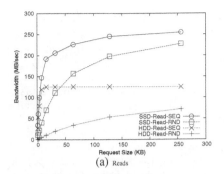 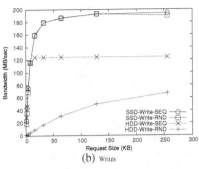 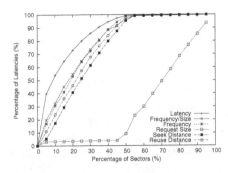

(a) Reads	(b) Writes

Figure 1: I/O Bandwidths for reads and writes on the Intel® X25-E SSD and the Seagate® Cheetah® HDD.

Figure 2: Accumulated HDD latency of sectors sorted using different metrics.

and file system. All reads and writes are synchronous I/O with no think time. Although real-life workloads can be a mix of various access patterns, we use the four synthetic microbenchmarks to qualitatively characterize the SSD. Figure 1 shows the experimental results. We made several findings to guide our system designs.

First, as expected, the most significant performance gain of running workloads on the SSD appears in random data accesses with small request sizes, for both reads and writes. For example, with a request size of 4KB, random reads and random writes on the SSD achieve more than 7.7 times and 28.5 times higher bandwidths than on the HDD, respectively. As request size increases to 256KB, the relative performance gains of sequential reads and writes diminish to 2 times and 1.5 times, respectively. It clearly shows that achievable performance benefits are highly dependent on workload access patterns, and we must identify the blocks that can bring the most performance benefits by migrating them into SSDs.

Second, contrary to the long-existing understanding about low write performance on SSDs, we have observed an exceptionally high write performance on the SSD (up to 194MB/sec). Similar findings have been made in recent performance studies on the state-of-the-art SSDs [5, 6]. As a high-end product, the Intel® X25-E SSD is designed for commercial environments with a sophisticated FTL design [13]. The highly optimized SSD internal designs significantly improve write performance and make it possible to use an SSD as a write-back buffer for speeding up write-intensive workloads, such as email servers.

Third, we can see that write performance on the SSD is largely independent of access patterns, and random writes can achieve almost identical performance as sequential writes. This indicates that it is unnecessary to specially treat random writes for performance purposes like in some prior work. This allows us to remove much unnecessary design complexity. In addition, we also find that writes on the SSD can quickly reach a rather high bandwidth (around 180MB/sec) with a relatively small request size (32KB) for both random and sequential workloads. This means that we can achieve the peak bandwidth on SSDs without need of intentionally organizing large requests as we usually do on HDDs.

Based on these observations, we summarize two key issues that must be considered in the design of Hystor as follows.

1. We need to recognize workload access patterns to identify the most *high-cost* data blocks, especially those blocks being randomly accessed by small requests, which cause the worst performance for HDDs.

2. We can leverage the SSD as a write-back buffer to handle writes, which often raise high latencies in HDDs. Meanwhile, we do not have to treat random writes specifically, since random writes on SSD can perform as fast as sequential writes.

3. HIGH-COST DATA BLOCKS

Many workloads have a *small* data set contributing a *large* percentage of the aggregate latency in data accesses. A critical task for Hystor is to identify the most performance-critical blocks.

3.1 Identifying High-Cost Blocks

A simple way to identify the high-cost blocks is to observe I/O latency of accessing each block and directly use the accumulated latency as an indicator to label the 'cost' of each block. In a hybrid storage, however, once we remap blocks to the SSD, we cannot observe their access latency on HDD any more. Continuing to use the previously observed latency would be misleading, if the access pattern changes after migration. Thus, directly using I/O latency to identify high-cost blocks is infeasible.

Some prior work (e.g. [12, 27]) maintains an on-line hard disk model to predict the latency for each incoming request. Such a solution heavily relies on precise hard disk modeling based on detailed specification data, which is often unavailable in practice. More importantly, as stated in prior work [12], as the HDD internals become increasingly more complicated (e.g. disk cache), it is difficult, if not impossible, to accurately model a modern hard disk and precisely predict the I/O latency for each disk access.

We propose another approach – using a pattern-related metric as an *indicator* to indirectly *infer* access cost without need of knowing the exact latencies. We associate each block with a selected metric and update the metric value by observing accesses to the block. The key issue here is that the selected metric should have a strong correlation to access latency, so that by comparing the metric values, we can effectively estimate the *relative* access latencies associated to blocks and identify the relatively high-cost ones. Since the selected metric is device independent, it also frees us from unnecessary burdens of considering specific hardware details (e.g. disk cache size), which can vary greatly across devices.

3.2 Indicator Metrics

In order to determine an effective indicator metric that is highly correlated to access latencies, we first identify four candidate metrics, namely *request size*, *frequency*, *seek distance*, *reuse distance*, and also consider their combinations. We use the *blktrace* tool [2] to collect I/O traces on an HDD for a variety of workloads. In the off-line analysis, we calculate the accumulated latency for each accessed block, as well as the associated candidate metric values. Then we rank the blocks in the order of their metric values. For example, concerning the metric *frequency*, we sort the blocks from the most frequently accessed one to the least frequently accessed one, and plot the accumulated latency in that order.

Figure 2 shows an example of TPC-H workload (other workloads are not shown due to space constraints). The X axis shows the top percentage of blocks, sorted in a specific metric value, and the Y axis shows the percentage of aggregate latency of these blocks. Directly using latency as the metric represents the ideal case. Thus, the closer a curve is to the *latency* curve, the better the corresponding metric is. Besides the selected four metrics, we have also examined various combinations of them, among which **frequency/request size** is found to be the most effective one. For brevity, we only show the combination of *frequency/request size* in the figure. In our experiments, we found that *frequency/request size* emulates latency consistently better across a variety of workloads, the other metrics and combinations, such as seek distance, work well for some cases but unsatisfactorily for the others.

The metric **frequency/request size** is selected with a strong basis – it essentially describes both **temporal locality** and **access pattern**. In particular, *frequency* describes the temporal locality and *request size* represents the access pattern for a given workload. In contrast to the widely used recency-based policies (e.g. LRU), we use frequency to represent the temporal locality to avoid the well-recognized cache pollution problem for handling weak-locality workloads (e.g. scanning a large file would evict valuable data from the cache) [14]. It is also worth noting here that there is an *intrinsic correlation* between request size and access latency. First of all, the average access latency per block is highly correlated to request size, since a large request can effectively amortize the seek and rotational latency over many blocks. Second, the request size also reflects workload access patterns. As the storage system sits at the bottom of the storage hierarchy, the sequence of data accesses observed at the block device level is an optimized result of multiple upper-level components. For example, the I/O scheduler attempts to merge consecutive small requests into a large one. Thus, a small request observed at the block device often means that either the upper-level components cannot further optimize data accesses, or the application accesses data in such a non-sequential pattern. Finally, small requests also tend to incur high latency, since they are more likely to be intervened by other requests, which would cause high latencies from disk head seeks and rotations. Although this metric cannot perfectly emulate the ideal curve (latency), as we see in the figure, it performs consistently the best in various workloads and works well in our experiments.

4. MAINTAINING DATA ACCESS HISTORY

To use the metric values to profile data access history, we must address two critical challenges – (1) how to represent the metric values in a compact and efficient way, and (2) how to maintain such history information for each block of a large-scale storage space (e.g. Terabytes). In short, we need an efficient mechanism to profile and maintain data access history at a low cost.

4.1 The Block Table

We use the *block table*, which was initially introduced in our previous work [15], to maintain data access history. Akin to the page table used in virtual memory management, the block table has three levels, *Block Global Directory* (BGD), *Block Middle Directory* (BMD), and *Block Table Entry* (BTE), as shown in Figure 3(a). The three levels, namely BGD, BMD, and BTE, of this structure essentially describe the storage space segmented in units of regions, sub-regions, and blocks, accordingly.

In the block table, each level is composed of multiple 4KB pages, each of which consists of multiple entries. A block's logical block number (LBN) is broken into three components, each of which is an index to an entry in the page at the corresponding level. Each BGD or BMD entry has a 32-bit *pointer* field pointing to a (BMD or BTE) page in the next level, a 16-bit *counter* field recording data

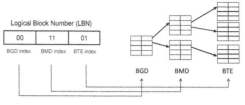

(a) *The block table structure*

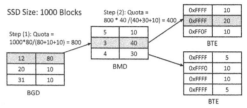

(b) *Traversing the block table*

Figure 3: The Block Table. Each box represents an entry page. In BGD and BMD pages, left and right columns represent *unique* and *counter* fields. In BTE pages, two columns represent *flag* and *counter* fields. The two steps show the order of entries being traversed from BGD to BTE entries.

access information, and a 16-bit *unique* field tracking the number of BTE entries belonging to it. Each BTE entry has a 16-bit *counter* field and a 16-bit *flag* field to record other properties of a block (e.g. whether a block is a metadata block). This three-level tree structure is a very efficient vehicle to maintain storage access information. For a given block, we only need three memory accesses to traverse the block table and locate its corresponding information stored in the BTE entry.

4.2 Representing Indicator Metric

We have developed a technique, called *inverse bitmap*, to encode the *request size* and *frequency* in the block table. When a block is accessed by a request of N sectors, an *inverse bitmap*, b, is calculated using the following equation:

$$b = 2^{max(0, 7 - \lfloor log_2 N \rfloor)} \tag{4.1}$$

As shown above, inverse bitmap encodes request size into a single byte. The smaller a request is, the bigger the inverse bitmap is.

Each entry at each level of the block table maintains a *counter*. The values of the counters in the BGD, BMD, and BTE entries represent the 'hotness' of the regions, sub-regions, and blocks, respectively. Upon an incoming request, we use the block's LBN as an index to traverse the block table through the three levels (BGD→BMD→BTE). At each level, we increment the counter of the corresponding entry by b. So the more frequently a block is accessed, the more often the corresponding counter is incremented. In this way, we use the inverse bitmap to represent the size for a given request, and the counter value, which is updated upon each request, to represent the indicator metric *frequency/request size*. A block with a large counter value is regarded as a high-cost (i.e. hot) block. By comparing the counters associated with blocks, we can identify the blocks that should be relocated to the SSD.

As time elapses, a counter (16 bits) may overflow. In such a case, we right shift all the counters of the entries in the *same* entry page by one bit, so that we can still preserve the information about the relative importance that the counter values represent. Since such a right shift operation is needed for a minimum of 512 updates to a single LBN, this operation would cause little overhead. Also note that we do not need to right shift counters in other pages, because we only need to keep track of the *relative* hotness for entries in a page, and the relative hotness among the pages is represented by the entries in the upper level.

The block table is a very efficient and flexible data structure to maintain the block-level information. For example, the full block table can be maintained in persistent storage (e.g. SSD). During the periodic update of the block table, we can load only the relevant table pages that need to be updated into memory (but at least one page at each level). Also note that the block table is a sparse data structure – we only need to maintain history for *accessed* blocks. This means that the spatial overhead in persistent storage is only proportional to the *working-set size* of workloads. In the worst case, e.g. scanning the whole storage space, the maximum spatial overhead is approximately 0.1% of the storage space (a 32-bit BTE entry per 4KB chunk). In practice, however, since most workloads only access partial storage space, the spatial overhead would be much lower. If needed, we can further release storage space by trimming the rarely updated table pages. This flexibility of the block table provides high scalability when handling a large storage space.

5. THE DESIGN OF HYSTOR

After introducing the indicator metric and the block table, we are now in a position to present the design of Hystor. Our goal is to best fit the SSD in the storage systems and effectively exploit its unique performance potential with minimal system changes.

5.1 Main Architecture

Hystor works as a pseudo block device at the block layer, as shown in Figure 4(a). The upper-level components, such as file systems, view it simply as a *single* block device, despite the complicated internals. Users can create partitions and file systems on it, similar to any directly attached drive. With minimal system changes, Hystor is easy to integrate into existing systems.

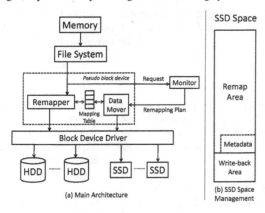

Figure 4: Architecture of Hystor.

Hystor has three major components, namely *remapper*, *monitor*, and *data mover*. The remapper maintains a mapping table to track the original location of blocks on the SSD. When an incoming request arrives at the remapper, the mapping table is first looked up. If the requested block is resident in the SSD, the request is redirected to the SSD, otherwise, it is serviced from the HDD. This remapping process is similar to the software RAID controller. The remapper also intercepts and forwards I/O requests to the monitor, which collects I/O requests and updates the block table to profile workload access patterns. The monitor periodically analyzes the data access history, identifies the blocks that should be remapped to the SSD, and requests the data mover to relocate data blocks across

storage devices. The monitor can run in either kernel mode or user mode. The data mover is responsible for issuing I/O commands to the block devices and updating the mapping table accordingly to reflect the most recent changes.

5.2 Logical Block Mapping

Hystor integrates multiple HDDs and SSDs and exposes a linear array of logical blocks to the upper-level components. Each logical block is directly mapped to a physical block in the HDD and indexed using the logical block number (LBN). A logical block can be selected to remap to the SSD, and its physical location in the SSD is dynamically selected. Hystor maintains a *mapping table* to keep track of the remapped logical blocks. This table is also maintained in a statically specified location in the persistent storage (e.g. the first few MBs of SSD), and it is rebuilt in the volatile memory at startup time. Changes to the mapping table are synchronously written to the storage to survive power failures. In memory, the table is organized as a B-tree to speedup lookups, which only incur minimal overhead with several memory accesses. Since only remapped blocks need to be tracked in the mapping table, the spatial overhead of the mapping table is small and proportional to the SSD size. Techniques, similar to the dynamic mapping table [10], can also be applied to only maintain the most frequently accessed mapping entries to further reduce the in-memory mapping table size.

In essence, Hystor manages remapped blocks in an 'inclusive' manner, which means that, when a block is remapped to the SSD, its original home block in the HDD would not be recycled. We choose such an inclusive design for three reasons. First, the SSD capacity is normally at least one order of magnitude smaller than the HDDs, thus, there is no need to save a small amount of capacity for low-cost HDDs. Also, if we attempt to fully utilize the HDD space, a large mapping table has to be maintained to track every block in the storage space (often in granularity of TBs), which would incur high overhead. Second, when blocks in the SSD need to be moved back to the HDD, extra high-cost I/O operations are required. In contrast, if blocks are duplicated to the SSD, we can simply drop the replicas in the SSD, as long as they are clean. Finally, this design also significantly simplifies the implementation and avoids unnecessary complexity.

5.3 SSD Space Management

In Hystor, the SSD plays *a major role* as a storage to retain the best suitable data, and *a minor role* as a write-back buffer for writes. Accordingly, we logically segment the SSD space into two regions, *remap* area and *write-back* area, as shown in Figure 4(b). The remap area is used to maintain the identified critical blocks, such as the high-cost data blocks and file system metadata blocks. All requests, including both reads and writes, to the blocks in the remap area are directed to the SSD. The write-back area is used as a buffer to temporarily hold dirty data of incoming write requests. All other requests are directed to the HDD. Blocks in the write-back area are periodically synchronized to the HDD and recycled for serving incoming writes. We use a configurable quota to guard the sizes of the two regions, so there is no need to physically segment the two regions on the SSD.

We allocate blocks in the SSD in *chunks*, which is similar in nature to that in RAID [25]. This brings two benefits. First, when moving data into the SSD, each write is organized more efficiently in a reasonably large request. Second, it avoids splitting a request into several excessively small requests. In our prototype, we choose an initial chunk size of 8 sectors (4KB). We will further study the effect of chunk size on performance in Section 7.5. In Hystor, all data allocation and management are performed in chunks.

5.4 Managing the Remap Area

The *remap* area is used to maintain identified critical blocks for a long-term optimization. Two types of blocks can be remapped to the SSD: (1) the high-cost data blocks, which are identified by analyzing data access history using the block table, and (2) file system metadata blocks, which are identified through available semantic information in OS kernels.

5.4.1 Identifying High-Cost Data Blocks

As shown in Section 4, the block table maintains data access history in forms of the *counter* values. By comparing the counter values of entries at the BGD, BMD, or BTE levels, we can easily identify the hot regions, sub-regions, and blocks, accordingly. The rationale guiding our design is that the hottest blocks in the hottest regions should be given the highest priority to stay in the high-speed SSD.

Program 1 Pseudocode of identifying candidate blocks.

```
counter():       the counter value of an entry
total_cnt():     the aggregate value of counters
                 of a block table page
sort_unique_asc(): sort entries by unique values
sort_counter_dsc(): sort entries by counter values
quota:           the num. of available SSD blocks

sort_unique_asc(bgd_page); /*sort bgd entries*/
bgd_count = total_cnt(bgd_page);
for each bgd entry && quota > 0; do
  bmd_quota  = quota*counter(bgd)/bgd_count;
  bgd_count -= counter(bgd);
  quota     -= bmd_quota;

  bmd_page = bgd->bmd;     /*get the bmd page*/
  sort_unique_asc(bmd_page);/*sort bmd entries*/
  bmd_count = total_cnt(bmd_page);
  for each bmd entry && bmd_quota > 0; do
    bte_quota  = bmd_quota*counter(bmd)/bmd_count;
    bmd_count -= counter(bmd);
    bmd_quota -= bte_quota;

    bte_page  = bmd->bte;
    sort_counter_dsc(bte_page);
    for each bte entry && bte_quota > 0; do
      add bte to the update list;
      bte_quota --;
    done
    bmd_quota += bte_quota; /*unused quota*/
  done
  quota += bmd_quota; /*unused quota*/
done
```

Program 1 shows the pseudocode of identifying high-cost blocks. We first proportionally allocate SSD space quota to each BGD entry based on their counter values, since a hot region should be given more chance of being improved. Then we begin from the BGD entry with the least number of BTE entries (with the smallest *unique* value), and repeat this process until reaching the BTE level, where we allocate entries in the descending order of their counter values. The blocks being pointed to by the BTE entries are added into a candidate list until the quota is used up. The unused quota is accumulated to the next step. In this way, we recursively determine the hottest blocks in the region and allocate SSD space to the regions correspondingly. Figure 3(b) illustrates this process, and it is repeated until the available space is allocated.

5.4.2 Reorganizing Data Layout across Devices

Workload access pattern changes over time. In order to adapt to the most recent workload access patterns, Hystor periodically wakes up the monitor, updates the block table, and recommends a list of candidate blocks that should be put in SSD, called *updates*, to update the remap area. Directly replacing all the blocks in the SSD with the updates would be over-sensitive to workload dynamics. Thus we take a 'smooth update' approach as follows.

We manage the blocks in the remap area in a list, called the *resident list*. When a block is added to the resident list or accessed, it is put at the top of the list. Periodically the monitor wakes up and sends a list of updates as described in Section 5.4.1 to the data mover. For each update, the data mover checks whether the block is already in the resident list. If true, it informs the monitor that the block is present. Otherwise, it reclaims the block at the bottom of the resident list and reassign its space for the update. In both cases, the new block (update) is placed at the top of the resident list. The monitor repeats this process until a certain number (e.g. 5-10% of the SSD size) of blocks in the resident list are updated. So we identify the high-cost blocks based on the most recent workloads and place them at the top of the resident list, and meanwhile, we always evict unimportant blocks, which have become rarely accessed and thus reside at the list bottom. In this way, we *gradually* merge the most recently identified high-cost data set into the old one and avoid aggressively shifting the whole set from one to another.

Once the resident list is updated, the data mover is triggered to perform I/O operations to relocate blocks across devices asynchronously in the background. Since the data mover can monitor the I/O traffic online and only reorganize data layout during idle periods (e.g. during low-load hours), the possible interference to foreground jobs can be minimized.

5.4.3 User-level Monitor

As a core engine of Hystor, the monitor receives intercepted requests from the remapper, updates the block table, and generates a list of updates to relocate blocks across devices. The monitor can work in either kernel mode or user mode with the same policy. We implemented both in our prototype.

Our user-level monitor functions similarly to *blktrace* [2]. Requests are temporarily maintained in a small log buffer in the kernel memory and periodically passed over to the monitor, a user-level daemon thread. Our prototype integrates the user-level monitor into *blktrace*, which allows us to efficiently use the existing infrastructure to record I/O trace by periodically passing requests to the monitor. The kernel-level monitor directly conducts the same work in the OS kernel.

Compared to the kernel-level monitor, the user-level monitor incurs lower overhead. Memory allocation in the user-level monitor is only needed when it is woken up, and its memory can even be paged out when not in use. Since each time we only update the data structures partially, this significantly reduces the overhead.

5.4.4 Identifying Metadata Blocks

File system metadata blocks are critical to system performance. Before accessing a file, its metadata blocks must be loaded into memory. With only a small amount of SSD space, relocating file system metadata blocks into SSD can effectively improve I/O performance, especially for metadata-intensive workloads during a cold start. Hystor attempts to identify these *semantically critical* blocks and proactively remap them to the SSD to speed up file accesses at an early stage, which avoids high-cost cold misses at a later time. In order to avoid intrusive system changes, we take a conservative approach to leverage the information that is already available in the existing OS kernels.

In the Linux kernel, metadata blocks are tagged such that an I/O scheduler can improve metadata read performance. So far, this mechanism is used by some file systems (e.g. Ext2/Ext3) for metadata reads. In our prototype, we modified a single line at the block

27

layer to leverage this available information by tagging incoming requests for metadata blocks. No other changes to file systems or applications are needed. Similar tagging technique is also used in Differentiated Storage Services [22]. When the remapper receives a request, we check the incoming request's tags and mark the requested blocks in the block table (using the *flag* field of BTE entries). The identified metadata blocks are remapped to the SSD. Currently, our implementation is effective for Ext2/Ext3, the default file system in Linux. Extending this approach to other file systems needs additional minor changes.

Another optional method, which can identify metadata blocks without any kernel change, is to *statically* infer the property of blocks by examining their logical block numbers (LBN). For example, the Ext2/Ext3 file system segments storage space into 128MB block groups, and the first few blocks of each group are always reserved for storing metadata, such as inode bitmap, etc. Since the location of these blocks is statically determined, we can mark them as metadata blocks. As such a solution assumes certain file systems and default configurations, it has not been adopted in our prototype.

5.5 Managing the Write-back Area

The most recent generation of SSDs has shown an exceptionally good write performance, even for random writes (50-75μs for a 4KB write [5]). This makes the SSD a suitable place for buffering dirty data and reducing latency for write-intensive workloads. As a configurable option, Hystor can leverage the high-speed SSD as a buffer to speed up write-intensive workloads.

The blocks in the write-back area are managed in two lists, a *clean list* and a *dirty list*. When a write request arrives, we first allocate SSD blocks from the *clean list*. The new dirty blocks are written into the SSD and added onto the *dirty list*. We maintain a counter to track the number of dirty blocks in the write-back area. If this number reaches a *high watermark*, a *scrubber* is waken up to write dirty blocks back to the HDD until reaching a *low watermark*. Cleaned blocks are placed onto the clean list for reuse. Since writes can return immediately once the data is written to the SSD, the synchronous write latency observed by foreground jobs is very low. We will examine the scrubbing effect in Section 7.4. Another optional optimization is to only buffer small write requests in the SSD, which further improves the use of the write-back area

As mentioned previously, we do not specifically optimize random writes, since the state-of-the-art SSDs provide high random write performance [5, 6]. One might also be concerned about the potential reliability issues of using SSD as a write-back buffer, since flash memory cells can wear out after a certain number of program/erase cycles. Fortunately, unlike early generations of SSDs, the current high-end SSDs can provide a reasonably high reliability. For example, the Mean Time Before Failure (MTBF) rating of the Intel® X25-E SSDs is as high as 2 million hours [13], which is comparable to that of typical HDDs. In this paper we do not consider the low-end SSDs with poor write performance and low reliability, which are not suitable for our system design goals.

6. IMPLEMENTATION ISSUES

We have prototyped Hystor in the Linux kernel 2.6.25.8 as a stand-alone kernel module with about 2,500 lines of code. The user-level monitor is implemented as a user-level daemon thread with about 2,400 lines of code. Neither one requires any modifications in the Linux kernel. The alternative kernel implementation of the monitor module consists of about 4,800 lines of code and only about 50 lines of code are inserted in the stock Linux kernel.

In our prototype, the remapper is implemented based on the software RAID. When the kernel module is activated, we use `dmsetup`

to create a new block device with appointed HDD and SSD devices. By integrating the Hystor functionality on the block layer, we can avoid dealing with some complex issues, such as splitting and merging requests to different devices, since the block layer already handles these issues. The downside of this design is that requests observed at this layer may be further merged into larger requests later, so we track the LBN of the last request to estimate the mergeable request size. Another merit of this design is that Hystor can work seamlessly with other storage, such as RAID and SAN storage. For example, a RAID device can be built upon Hystor virtual devices, similarly, Hystor can utilize RAID devices too. Such flexibility is highly desirable in commercial systems.

As a core engine of Hystor, the monitor can work in either kernel mode or user mode. In both cases, the monitor is implemented as a daemon thread. Periodically it is triggered to process the collected I/O requests, update the block table, and generate updates to drive the data mover to perform data relocation. In kernel mode, the observed requests are held in two log buffers. If one buffer is full, we swap to the other to accept incoming requests, and the requests in the full buffer are updated to the block table in parallel. In user mode, requests are directly passed to the user-level daemon. The analysis of data access history can also be done offline. In our current prototype, we maintain the block table and the mapping table full in memory, and in our future work we plan to further optimize memory usage by only loading partial tables into memory as discussed previously.

7. EVALUATION

7.1 Experimental System

Our experimental system is an Intel® D975BX system with a 2.66GHz Intel® Core™ 2 Quad CPU and 4GB main memory on board. Our prototype system consists of a Seagate® Cheetah® 15k.5 SAS hard drive and a 32GB Intel® X25-E SSD, both of which are high-end storage devices on the market. Also note that we only use *partial* SSD space in our experiments to avoid overestimating the performance. Table 1 lists the detailed specification of the two devices. The HDDs are connected through an LSI® MegaRaid® 8704 SAS card and the SSD uses a SATA 3.0Gb/s connector.

	X25-E SSD	Cheetah HDD
Capacity	32GB	73GB
Interface	SATA2	SAS
Read Bandwidth	250 MB/Sec	125 MB/Sec
Write Bandwidth	180 MB/Sec	125 MB/Sec

Table 1: Specifications of the SSD and the HDD.

We use Fedora™ Core 8 with the Linux kernel 2.6.25.8 and Ext3 file system with default configurations. In order to minimize the interference, the operating system and home directory are stored in a separate hard disk drive. We use the *noop* (No-op) I/O scheduler, which is suitable for non-HDD devices [5,6], for the SSD. The hard disk drives use the *CFQ* (Completely Fair Queuing) scheduler, the default scheduler in the Linux kernel, to optimize the HDD performance. The on-device caches of all the storage devices are enabled. The other system configurations use the default values.

7.2 Performance of Hystor

In general, the larger the SSD size is, the better the Hystor's performance is. In order to avoid overestimating the performance improvement, we first estimate the working-set size (the number of blocks being accessed during execution) of each workload by

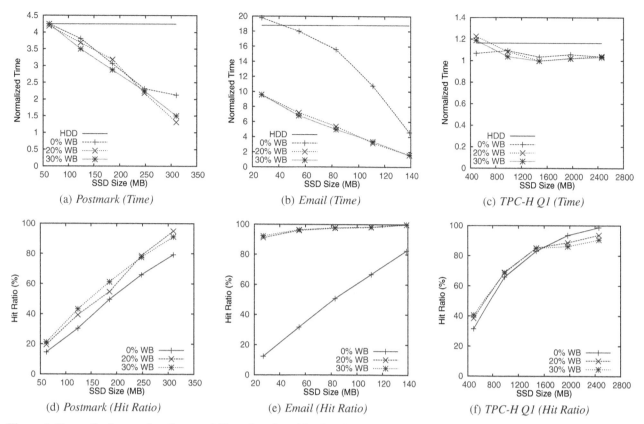

(a) *Postmark (Time)*   (b) *Email (Time)*   (c) *TPC-H Q1 (Time)*

(d) *Postmark (Hit Ratio)*   (e) *Email (Hit Ratio)*   (f) *TPC-H Q1 (Hit Ratio)*

Figure 5: Normalized execution times and hit ratios of workloads. The horizontal line represents the time of running on HDD.

examining the collected I/O traces off line, then we conduct experiments with five configurations of the SSD size, namely 20%, 40%, 60%, 80%, and 100% of the working-set size. Since we only conservatively use *partial* SSD space in our experiments, the performance of Hystor can be even better in practice. To examine the effectiveness of the write-back area, we configure three write-back area sizes, namely 0%, 20%, and 30% of the available SSD space.

For each workload, we perform the baseline experiments on the SSD. We rerun the experiments with various configurations of the SSD space. We show the execution times normalized to that of running on the SSD-only system. Therefore, the normalized execution time '1.0' represents the ideal case. In order to compare with the worst case, running on the HDD-only system, we plot a horizontal line in the figures to denote the case of running on the HDD. Besides the normalized execution times, we also present the hit ratios of I/O requests observed at the remapper. A request to blocks resident in the SSD is considered a *hit*, otherwise, it is a *miss*. The hit ratio describes what percentage of requests are serviced from the SSD. Due to space constraints, we only present results for the user-mode monitor here, and the kernel monitor shows similar results. Figure 5 shows the normalized execution times and hit ratios.

7.2.1 Postmark

Postmark is a widely used file system benchmark [28]. It creates 100 directories and 20,000 files, then performs 100,000 transactions (reads and writes) to stress the file system, and finally deletes files. This workload features intensive small random data accesses.

Figure 5(a) shows that as the worst case, postmark on the HDD-only system runs 4.2 times slower than on the SSD-only system. Hystor effectively improves performance for this workload. With the increase of SSD space, the execution time is reduced till close to an SSD-only system, shown as a linear curve in the figure. In this

case, most data blocks are accessed with similar patterns, which is challenging for Hystor to identify high-cost data blocks based on access patterns. However, Hystor still provides performance gains proportional to available SSD space.

Since this workload features many small writes, allocating a large write-back area helps improve hit ratios as well as execution times. Figure 5(d) shows that with the SSD size of 310MB, allocating 30% of the SSD space for write-back can improve hit ratio from 79% to 91%, compared to without write-back area. Accordingly, the execution time is reduced from 34 seconds to 24 seconds, which is a 29% reduction.

Also note that multiple writes to the same block would cause synchronization issues. With a smaller write-back area, dirty blocks have to be more frequently flushed back to the HDD due to capacity limit. When such an operation is in progress, incoming write requests to the same blocks have to be suspended to maintain consistency, which further artificially increases the request latency. For example, when the cache size grows to 310MB, the amount of hits to the lock-protected blocks decreases by a factor of 4, which translates into a decrease of execution time.

7.2.2 Email

Email was developed by University of Michigan based on Postmark for emulating an email server [31]. It is configured with 500 directories, 500 files, and 5,000 transactions. This workload has intensive synchronous writes with different append sizes and locations based on realistic mail distribution function, and it features a more skewed distribution of latencies. Most data accesses are small random writes, which are significantly faster on the SSD.

Figure 5(b) shows that running *email* exclusively on the SSD is 18.8 times faster than on the HDD. With no write-back area, the performance of Hystor is suboptimal, especially for a small

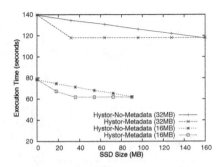 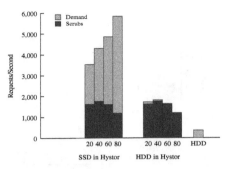 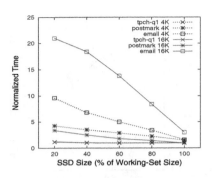

Figure 6: Optimization for metadata blocks. 32MB and 16MB refer to the two workloads. Hystor with and without optimizing metadata are referred to as *Hystor-Metadata* and *Hystor-No-Metadata*.

Figure 7: Request arrival rate in *email*. The numbers on X axis for each bar refer to various configurations of the SSD size (% of the working-set size). HDD refers to the HDD-only system.

Figure 8: Effect of chunk size on performance. 4K and 16K refer to the chunk sizes, respectively. The numbers on X axis refer to various configurations of the SSD size (% of the working-set size).

SSD size. As we see in the figure, with SSD size of 27MB (20% of the working-set size), Hystor may even be slightly worse than the HDD-only system, due to additional I/O operations and increased probability of split requests. Without the write-back area, data blocks remapped in the SSD may not be necessarily to be reaccessed in the next run. This leads to a hit ratio of only 12.4% as shown in Figure 5(e). In contrast, with the write-back area, the hit ratio quickly increases to over 90%. This shows that the write-back area also behaves like a small cache to capture some short-term data reuse. As a result, the execution time is reduced by a half.

7.2.3 TPC-H Query 1

TPC-H Q1 is the query 1 from the TPC-H database benchmark suite [33]. It runs against a database (scale factor 1) managed by PostgreSQL 8.1.4 database server. Different from the other workloads, this workload does not benefit much from running on the SSD, since its data accesses are more sequential and less I/O intensive. As shown in Figure 5(c), running this workload on the HDD-only system is only 16% slower than running on the SSD. However, since the reuse of data blocks is more significant, the hit ratio in this case is higher. Figure 5(f) shows that with SSD size of 492MB, the hit ratio of incoming requests is about 30% to 40%. When the SSD size is small, the write-back area may introduce extra traffic, which leads to a 2-5% slowdown compared to running on HDD. As the write-back area size increases, the number of write-back operations is reduced dramatically, which improves the I/O performance.

7.3 Metadata Blocks

Hystor also identifies metadata blocks of file systems and remaps them to the SSD. We have designed an experiment to show how such an optimization improves performance.

In Ext2/Ext3 file systems, a large file is composed of many data chunks, and *indirect blocks* are used to locate and link these chunks together. As a type of metadata, indirect blocks do not contain file content but are crucial to accessing files. We create a 32GB file and use the Intel® Open Storage Toolkit [21] to generate two workloads, which randomly read 4KB data each time until 16MB and 32MB of data are read. This workload emulates data accesses in files with complex internal structures, such as virtual disk file used by virtual machines. In such random workloads, the accessed file data are unlikely to be reused, while indirect blocks would be reaccessed, thus holding metadata blocks in the SSD would be beneficial. We use this example to compare the performance of Hystor with and without optimization for file system metadata blocks, denoted as *Hystor-Metadata* and *Hystor-No-Metadata* respectively.

Figure 6 shows the experimental results of Hystor-No-Metadata and Hystor-Metadata. Both approaches eventually can speed up the two workloads by about 20 seconds. However, Hystor-Metadata is able to achieve that performance with a much smaller SSD space. For the workload reading 32MB data, Hystor-Metadata identifies and remaps nearly all indirect blocks to the SSD with just 32MB of SSD space. In contrast, Hystor-No-Metadata lacks the capability of identifying metadata blocks. Since only around 20% of the blocks being accessed are metadata blocks, most blocks remapped to the SSD are file content data blocks, which are unfortunately almost never reused. Therefore Hystor-No-Metadata requires about 160MB of SSD space to cover the whole working-set, while Hystor-Metadata needs only 32MB SSD space. A similar pattern can be observed in the case of reading 16MB data.

This experiment shows that optimization for metadata blocks can effectively improve system performance with only a small amount of SSD space, especially for metadata-intensive workloads. More importantly, different from identifying high-cost data blocks by observing workload access patterns, we can proactively identify these *semantically critical* blocks at an early stage, so high-cost cold misses can be avoided. It is also worth noting that the three major components in Hystor are complementary to each other. For example, although the current implementation of Hystor identifies metadata blocks only for read requests, writes to these metadata blocks still can benefit from being buffered in the write-back area.

7.4 Scrubbing

Dirty blocks buffered in the write-back area have to be written back to the HDD in the background, called *scrubbing*. Each scrub operation can cause two additional I/O operations – a read from the SSD and a write to the HDD. Here we use *email*, the worst case for scrubs, to study how scrubbing affects system performance. Figure 7 shows the request arrival rate (number of requests per second) for *email* configured with four SSD sizes (20-80% of the working-set size) and a 20% write-back fraction . The requests are broken down by the source, internal scrubbing daemon or the upper-layer components, denoted as *scrubs* and *demand* in the figure, respectively.

As shown in Figure 7, the request arrival rate in Hystor is much higher than that in the HDD-only system. This is due to two reasons. First, the average request size for HDD-only system is 2.5 times larger than that in Hystor, since a large request in Hystor may split into several small ones to different devices. Second, two additional I/O operations are needed for each scrub. We can see that, as the SSD size increases to 80% of the working-set size, the arrival rate of scrub requests drops by nearly 25% on the SSD, due to less frequent scrubbing. The arrival rate of on-demand requests increases as the SSD size increases, because the execution time is reduced and the number of on-demand requests remains unchanged.

An increase of request arrival rate may not necessarily lead to an increase of latency. In the case with 80% of the working-set size, as many as 5,800 requests arrive on the SSD every second. However, we do not observe a corresponding increase of execution time (see Figure 5(b)) and the SSD I/O queue still remains very short. This is mainly because the high bandwidth of the SSD (up to 250MB/sec) can easily absorb the extra traffic. On the HDD in Hystor, the request arrival rate reaches over 1,800 requests per second. However, since these requests happen in the background, the performance impact on the foreground jobs is minimal.

This case shows that although a considerable increase of request arrival rate is resident on both storage devices, conducting background scrubbing causes minimal performance impact, even for write-intensive workloads.

7.5 Chunk Size

Chunk size is an important parameter in Hystor. A large chunk size is desirable for reducing memory overhead of the mapping table and the block table. On the other hand, a small chunk size can effectively improve utilization of the SSD space, since a large chunk may contain both hot and cold data.

Figure 8 compares performance of using a chunk size of 8 sectors (4 KB) and 32 sectors (16 KB). We only present data for the cache with a 20% write-back fraction here. We can see that with a large chunk size (16KB), the performance of *email* degrades significantly due to the underutilized SSD space. Recall that most of the requests in *email* are small, hot and cold data could co-exist in a large chunk, which causes the miss rate to increase by four-fold. With the increase of SSD size, such a performance gap is reduced, but it is still much worse than using 4KB chunks. The other workloads are less sensitive to chunk size.

This experiment shows that choosing a proper chunk size should consider the SSD size. For a small-capacity SSD, a small chunk size should be used to avoid wasting precious SSD space. A large SSD can use a large chunk size and afford the luxury of increased internal fragmentation in order to reduce overhead. In general, a small chunk size (e.g. 4KB) is normally sufficient for optimizing performance. Our prototype uses a chunk size of 4KB in default.

8. RELATED WORK

Flash memory and SSDs have been actively studied recently. There is a large body of research work on SSDs (e.g. [1, 5–8]). A survey [9] summarizes the key techniques in flash memory based SSDs. Here we present the work most related to this paper.

The first set of work is generally cache-based solutions. An early work [19] uses flash memory as a secondary-level file system buffer cache to reduce power consumption and access latencies for mobile computers. SmartSaver [4] uses a small-factor flash drive to cache and prefetch data for saving disk energy. A hybrid file system, called Conquest [34], merges the persistent RAM storage into the HDD-based storage system. Conquest caches small files, metadata, executables, shared libraries into the RAM storage and it demands a substantial change to file system designs. AutoRAID [35] migrates data inside the HDD-based RAID storage to improve performance and cost-efficiency based on patterns. Sun® Solaris™ [18] can set a high-speed device as a secondary-level buffer cache between main memory and hard disk drives. Microsoft® Windows® ReadyBoost [23] takes a similar approach to use a flash device as an extension of main memory. Intel® TurboMemory [20] uses a small amount of flash memory as a cache to buffer disk data and uses a threshold size to filter large requests. Kgil et al. [16] pro-

pose to use flash memory and DRAM as a disk cache and adopt an LRU-based wear-level aware replacement policy [16]. SieveStore [29] uses a selective caching approach by tracking the access counts and caching the most popular blocks in solid state storage. Hystor views and places SSDs in the storage hierarchy in another way – the high-speed SSD is used as a part of storage rather than an additional caching tier. As such, Hystor only reorganizes data layout across devices periodically and asynchronously, rather than make caching decision on each data access. In addition, recognizing the non-uniform performance gains on SSDs, Hystor not only adopts frequency, rather than recency that has been commonly used in LRU-based caching policies, to better describe the temporal locality, and it also further differentiates various workload access patterns and attempts to make the best use of the SSD space with minimized system changes.

Some other prior work proposes to integrate SSD and HDD together and form a hybrid storage system. Differentiated Storage Services [22] attempts to classify I/O requests and passes information to storage systems for QoS purposes. The upper-level components (e.g. file systems) classify the blocks and the storage system enforces the policy by assigning blocks to different devices. ComboDrive [26] concatenates SSD and HDD into one single address space, and certain selected data and files can be moved into the faster SSD space. As a block-level solution, Hystor hides details from the upper-level components and does not require any modification to applications. Considering the disparity of handling reads and writes in SSDs, Koltsidas and Viglas propose to organize SSD and HDD together and place read-intensive data in SSD and write-intensive data in HDD for performance optimization [17]. Soundararajan et al. propose a solution to utilize HDD as a log buffer to reduce writes and improve the longevity of SSDs [32]. Recently, I-CASH [30] has been proposed to use SSD to store seldom-changed reference data blocks and HDD to store a log of deltas, so that random write traffic to SSD can be reduced. Our experimental studies show that the state-of-the-art SSDs have exceptionally high write performance. Specifically optimizing write performance for SSDs can yield limited benefits on these advanced hardware. In fact, Hystor attempts to leverage the high write performance of SSDs and our experimental results show that such a practice can effectively speed up write-intensive workloads.

9. CONCLUSION

Compared with DRAM and HDD, the cost and performance of SSDs are nicely placed in between. We need to find the fittest position of SSDs in the existing systems to strike a right balance between performance and cost. In this study, through comprehensive experiments and analysis, we show that we can identify the data that are best suitable to be held in SSD by using a simple yet effective metric, and such information can be efficiently maintained in the block table at a low cost. We also show that SSDs should play a major role in the storage hierarchy by adaptively and timely retaining performance- and semantically-critical data, and it can also be effective as a write-back buffer for incoming write requests. By best fitting the SSD into the storage hierarchy and forming a hybrid storage system with HDDs, our hybrid storage prototype, Hystor, can effectively leverage the performance merits of SSDs with minimized system changes. We believe that Hystor lays out a system framework for high-performance storage systems.

10. ACKNOWLEDGMENTS

We are grateful to the anonymous reviewers for their constructive comments. We also thank our colleagues at Intel® Labs, especially Scott Hahn and Michael Mesnier, for their help and support through this work. We also would like to thank Xiaoning Ding at Intel® Labs Pittsburgh, Rubao Lee at the Ohio State University, and Shuang Liang at EMC® DataDomain for our interesting discussions. This work was partially supported by the National Science Foundation (NSF) under grants CCF-0620152, CCF-072380, and CCF-0913150.

11. REFERENCES

[1] N. Agrawal, V. Prabhakaran, T. Wobber, J. D. Davis, M. Manasse, and R. Panigrahy. Design tradeoffs for SSD performance. In *Proceedings of USENIX'08*, Boston, MA, June 2008.

[2] Blktrace. http://linux.die.net/man/8/blktrace.

[3] A. M. Caulfield, L. M. Grupp, and S. Swanson. Gordon: using flash memory to build fast, power-efficient clusters for data-intensive applications. In *Proceedings of ASPLOS'09*, Washington, D.C., March 2009.

[4] F. Chen, S. Jiang, and X. Zhang. SmartSaver: Turning flash drive into a disk energy saver for mobile computers. In *Proceedings of ISLPED'06*, Tegernsee, Germany, Oct. 2006.

[5] F. Chen, D. A. Koufaty, and X. Zhang. Understanding intrinsic characteristics and system implications of flash memory based solid state drives. In *Proceedings of SIGMETRICS/Performance'09*, Seattle, WA, June 2009.

[6] F. Chen, R. Lee, and X. Zhang. Essential roles of exploiting internal parallelism of flash memory based solid state drives in high-speed data processing. In *Proceedings of HPCA'11*, San Antonio, Texas, Feb 12-16 2011.

[7] F. Chen, T. Luo, and X. Zhang. CAFTL: A content-aware flash translation layer enhancing the lifespan of flash memory based solid state drives. In *Proceedings of FAST'11*, San Jose, CA, Feb 15-17 2011.

[8] C. Dirik and B. Jacob. The performance of PC solid-state disks (SSDs) as a function of bandwidth, concurrency, device, architecture, and system organization. In *Proceedings of ISCA'09*, Austin, TX, June 2009.

[9] E. Gal and S. Toledo. Algorithms and data structures for flash memories. In *ACM Computing Survey'05*, volume 37(2), pages 138–163, 2005.

[10] A. Gupta, Y. Kim, and B. Urgaonkar. DFTL: A flash translation layer employing demand-based selective caching of page-level address mappings. In *Proceedings of ASPLOS'09*, Washington, D.C., March 2009.

[11] J. Handy. Flash memory vs. hard disk drives - which will win? http://www.storagesearch.com/semico-art1.html.

[12] L. Huang and T. Chieuh. Experiences in building a software-based SATF scheduler. In *Tech. Rep. ECSL-TR81*, 2001.

[13] Intel. Intel X25-E extreme SATA solid-state drive. http://www.intel.com/design/flash/nand/extreme, 2008.

[14] S. Jiang, F. Chen, and X. Zhang. CLOCK-Pro: An Effective Improvement of the CLOCK Replacement. In *Proceedings of USENIX'05*, Anaheim, CA, April 2005.

[15] S. Jiang, X. Ding, F. Chen, E. Tan, and X. Zhang. DULO: An effective buffer cache management scheme to exploit both temporal and spatial localities. In *Proceedings of FAST'05*, San Francisco, CA, December 2005.

[16] T. Kgil, D. Roberts, and T. Mudge. Improving NAND flash based disk caches. In *Proceedings of ISCA'08*, Beijing, China, June 2008.

[17] I. Koltsidas and S. D. Viglas. Flashing up the storage layer. In *Proceedings of VLDB'08*, Auckland, New Zealand, August 2008.

[18] A. Leventhal. Flash storage memory. In *Communications of the ACM*, volume 51(7), pages 47–51, July 2008.

[19] B. Marsh, F. Douglis, and P. Krishnan. Flash memory file caching for mobile computers. In *Proceedings of the 27th Hawaii Conference on Systems Science*, Wailea, HI, Jan 1994.

[20] J. Matthews, S. Trika, D. Hensgen, R. Coulson, and K. Grimsrud. Intel Turbo Memory: Nonvolatile disk caches in the storage hierarchy of mainstream computer systems. In *ACM Transactions on Storage*, volume 4, May 2008.

[21] M. P. Mesnier. Intel open storage toolkit. http://www.sourceforge.org/projects/intel-iscsi.

[22] M. P. Mesnier and J. B. Akers. Differentiated storage services. *SIGOPS Oper. Syst. Rev.*, 45:45–53, February 2011.

[23] Microsoft. Microsoft Windows Readyboost. http://www.microsoft.com/windows/windows-vista/features/readyboost.aspx, 2008.

[24] A. Patrizio. UCSD plans first flash-based supercomputer. http://www.internetnews.com/hardware/article.php/3847456, November 2009.

[25] D. A. Patterson, G. Gibson, and R. H. Katz. A case for redundant arrays of inexpensive disks (RAID). In *Proceedings of SIGMOD'88*, Chicago, IL, June 1988.

[26] H. Payer, M. A. Sanvido, Z. Z. Bandic, and C. M. Kirsch. Combo Drive: Optimizing cost and performance in a heterogeneous storage device. In *Proceedings of the 1st Workshop on integrating solid-state memory into the storage hierarchy (WISH'09)*, 2009.

[27] F. I. Popovici, A. C. Arpaci-Dusseau, and R. H. Arpaci-Dusseau. Robust, portable I/O scheduling with the disk mimic. In *Proceedings of USENIX'03*, San Antonio, TX, June 2003.

[28] Postmark. A new file system benchmark. http://www.netapp.com/tech_library/3022.html, 1997.

[29] T. Pritchett and M. Thottethodi. SieveStore: A highly-selective, ensemble-level disk cache for cost-performance. In *Proceedings of ISCA'10*, Saint-Malo, France, June 2010.

[30] J. Ren and Q. Yang. I-CASH: Intelligently coupled array of ssd and hdd. In *Proceedings of HPCA'11*, San Antonio, Texas, Feb 2011.

[31] S. Shah and B. D. Noble. A study of e-mail patterns. In *Software Practice and Experience*, volume 37(14), 2007.

[32] G. Soundararajan, V. Prabhakaran, M. Balakrishnan, and T. Wobber. Extending SSD lifetimes with disk-based write caches. In *Proceedings of FAST'10*, San Jose, CA, February 2010.

[33] Transaction Processing Performance Council. TPC Benchmark H. http://www.tpc.org/tpch, 2008.

[34] A. A. Wang, P. Reiher, G. J. Popek, and G. H. Kuenning. Conquest: Better performance through a Disk/Persistent-RAM hybrid file system. In *Proceedings of the USENIX'02*, Monterey, CA, June 2002.

[35] J. Wilkes, R. Golding, C. Staelin, and T. Sullivan. The HP AutoRAID hierarchical storage system. In *ACM Tran. on Computer Systems*, volume 14, pages 108–136, Feb 1996.

Transactional Conflict Decoupling and Value Prediction

Fuad Tabba*
Architecture Technology
Group
Oracle Corporation
fuad.al.tabba@oracle.com

Andrew W. Hay
Computer Science
Department
The University of Auckland
andrewh@cs.auckland.ac.nz

James R. Goodman
Computer Science
Department
The University of Auckland
goodman@cs.auckland.ac.nz

Abstract

This paper explores data speculation for improving the performance of Hardware Transactional Memory (HTM). We attempt to reduce transactional conflicts by decoupling them from cache coherence conflicts; many HTMs do not distinguish between transactional conflicts and coherence conflicts, leading to false transactional conflicts. We also attempt to mitigate the effects of coherence conflicts by using value prediction in transactions. We show that coherence decoupling and value prediction in transactions complement each other, because they both speculate on data in ways that are infeasible in the absence of HTM support.

As a demonstration of how data speculation can improve performance, we introduce DPTM, a best-effort HTM that mitigates the effects of false sharing at the cache line level. DPTM does not alter the underlying cache coherence protocol, and requires only minor, processor-local, modifications.

We evaluate DPTM against a baseline best-effort HTM, and compare it with data restructuring by padding, the most commonly used method to avoid false sharing. Our experiments show that DPTM can dramatically improve performance in the presence of false sharing without degrading performance in its absence, and consistently performs better than restructuring by padding.

Categories and Subject Descriptors: C.1.0 [Computer Systems Organization]: Processor Architectures

General Terms: Design, Performance

Keywords: Transactional Memory, Value Prediction

1. INTRODUCTION

Parallel programming is fast becoming widespread. Most processor manufacturers today are producing chips with an increasing number of cores [16], while software engineering tools have yet to simplify the programming for these cores. Writing correct parallel programs is complicated by deadlock, livelock, starvation, and

---

*This work was done while Fuad Tabba was at the Computer Science Department, the University of Auckland.

data races [21]. Making parallel programs efficient is further complicated by convoying [21] and false sharing [10, 17, 22].

Methods of aggressive speculation in hardware, such as Thread-Level Speculation (TLS) [2, 31, 51], Hardware Transactional Memory (HTM) [24], and Speculative Lock Elision [38, 45], attempt to reduce the challenges of parallel programming. However, processor manufacturers have been slow to adopt such mechanisms, because they may not perceive the cost-benefit tradeoff to be worthwhile.

In this paper, we show that many HTM proposals, and similar methods of aggressive speculation, conservatively infer transactional conflicts from cache coherence conflicts [4, 12, 15, 24, 42, 45–47], which could lead to false transactional conflicts that adversely affect performance. Drawing inspiration from Huh et al. [28], we demonstrate that by decoupling transactional conflicts from coherence conflicts, we can reduce false conflicts between transactions; and that by speculating on data values, we can reduce the delays coherence conflicts incur. Specifically, we explain how decoupling and data speculation can improve performance in the presence of false sharing and silent stores (including temporally silent stores) [32, 33]. We justify the cost of these added mechanisms by showing that, because transactions are already in speculative mode, HTMs can speculate on data in ways that are infeasible in the absence of HTM support.

False sharing can be difficult to mitigate, and its effects are especially pronounced in HTM [25, 42]. Typical methods for mitigating false sharing require data restructuring, which goes against two promises of Transactional Memory (TM): abstraction and composition [21]. Restructuring requires low level knowledge of the system, breaking abstraction; it is also difficult to restructure external code that suffers from false sharing, which hinders composition. In our opinion, for TM to become viable for parallel programming, it should avoid the worst effects of false sharing.

This paper makes the following contributions: (i) we describe how decoupling transactional conflicts from coherence conflicts in HTM reduces apparent transactional conflicts, and how value prediction in HTM complements the decoupling by reducing the delays of coherence conflicts in transactions; (ii) to mitigate the effects of false sharing in transactions, we present DPTM, an enhanced best-effort HTM that relies on a conventional coherence protocol, and adds little processor-local modifications; (iii) we evaluate various design points for DPTM and compare them with data restructuring by padding, the most commonly used method to avoid false sharing.

Our evaluation, using STAMP [40], SPLASH-2 [57], and other benchmarks, shows that DPTM significantly improves performance in benchmarks that exhibit false sharing — more than restructuring by padding — without having adverse effects on benchmarks that do not exhibit false sharing.

Some of the ideas for this work were presented earlier at TRANSACT'09 [53], a workshop with unpublished proceedings. This paper expands on these ideas, proposes additional mechanisms and heuristics for value prediction, and evaluates our proposal using a variety of benchmarks.

2. THE FALSE SHARING PROBLEM

False sharing at the cache line level can have a big impact on the performance of parallel programs [10, 17, 22, 26, 30]. It occurs when different processors access distinct data objects that share the same cache line, and at least one processor is modifying one of the objects. Because the cache line is the unit of granularity for coherence, such *logically* nonconflicting accesses are serialized.

The effects of false sharing are not easy to mitigate. Most methods we have encountered are oriented towards the restructuring and padding of data objects [20, 28, 29, 42, 55], so that logically nonconflicting accesses to different objects are also nonconflicting as far as the coherence protocol is concerned.

Such restructuring of data can be difficult to apply in practice. First, the programmer needs to identify the data objects that cause false sharing. Once the objects are identified, they are aligned to cache line boundaries, which requires knowledge of machine-specific details such as the cache line size.

Then typically, each object is padded so it occupies a whole cache line by itself, which increases memory use and fragmentation, and adversely impacts locality. These changes are often machine-specific, so the benefits of code modified in such ways might not be portable. Moreover, using high-level languages, such as Java, where the underlying virtual machine or interpreter does not lay out the data structure the way it is specified in the program, can make data restructuring impractical.

False sharing may also be introduced to a program by the use of external libraries that suffer from it. Modifying external code is often difficult or infeasible.

False Sharing in Transactions

False sharing is a bigger problem when it occurs in conjunction with HTM, because it leads to the aborting or serialization of whole transactions that could have otherwise executed concurrently [25, 42]. It is a problem that has often been observed by experts on

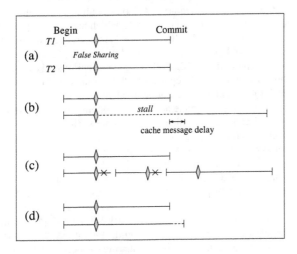

Figure 1: False sharing in HTM

transactional memory and parallel programming [1, 5, 8, 13, 18, 20, 25, 42, 48, 49, 56, 58, 59].

The example in Figure 1 shows the timeline of two concurrent transactions. These transactions access different data on the same cache line at one point during their execution, i.e., they exhibit false sharing. The transactions in this example at no point have any true conflicts, and so any order of their component operations is allowable.

Ideally, these transactions should be able to run completely in parallel, as shown in (a). Because many HTM proposals infer transactional conflicts from coherence conflicts, such implementations do not distinguish between true and false sharing, stalling transactions (b), or aborting them altogether (c).

We expect a solution to the problem of false sharing to result in an execution similar to the one shown in (d). Such a solution would likely not eliminate all the delays caused by false sharing, because some cache data still needs to be communicated. However, it should be able to mitigate these effects by overlapping the delay with other speculative operations.

The typical solution by restructuring and padding, in addition to the difficulties it poses in non-transactional systems, also goes against some of the promises of TM: that of abstraction and composition [21].

Composition in TM is the ability to combine and use different code in transactions. By using external code that is not optimized for false sharing, or that is optimized for a different machine, the usefulness of composition in TM is undermined.

Abstraction aims to hide irrelevant complexity and detail, but restructuring requires exposure to architectural and other low level details, knowledge a typical programmer may not have, and should not need. Therefore, an HTM should also abstract away the adverse effects of false sharing.

3. COHERENCE DECOUPLING AND VALUE PREDICTION IN TRANSACTIONS

From the first HTM proposal [24], the means used by many HTMs to detect cache coherence conflicts has also been employed and extended to assure that transactional conflicts are detected. Coherence conflict detection, however, is implementation dependent, usually classifying certain patterns as a coherence conflict even in some cases where no conflict exists.

One pattern is false sharing. While logically no sharing — and no conflict — occurs, this widely recognized problem is nevertheless treated as a coherence conflict. Likewise with silent stores and temporally silent stores [32, 33], where two or more threads truly share data and at least one of them writes to the data ultimately leaving its value unchanged: no conflict occurs, yet virtually all coherence implementations treat them as a coherence conflict.

None of these constitute a transactional conflict, but are characteristically treated as such because the coherence detection mechanism does not distinguish between them. Yet these patterns may result in significant performance degradation, as their occurrence during transactional speculation can cause a transaction to stall, or even to abort. Aborting may result in much more serious degradation and could, for example, be the cause of livelock.

To mitigate the effects of false conflicts in transactions, we argue that HTMs should decouple transactional conflicts from coherence conflicts. Moreover, because transactions are *already* in speculative execution mode, this makes it easier to use value prediction in transactions.

HTMs that associate transactional conflicts with coherence conflicts also associate cache line states with transactional states, i.e., modified data resides on exclusive cache lines, while read data resides on valid cache lines. These associations enable HTMs to detect potential transactional conflicts using the coherence protocol, but could result in false transactional conflicts.

One alternative is to speculate inside a transaction without this association, then restore it before the transaction tries to commit. This could be done by ensuring that cache lines representing the read and write sets are in their expected state at commit time, and that the read set data matches the current data values.

Therefore, when a cache line containing read data is invalidated, instead of aborting, a transaction continues without triggering a transactional conflict, speculating that the data it has read will still be valid. The transaction tracks which parts of the cache line contains read data; and before it can commit, the transaction must *validate* by re-acquiring the cache line to ensure that the read data is unchanged. If it has changed, only then is a transactional conflict triggered, thereby associating transactional conflicts with *modifications* to the shared data.

This same mechanism can also be used for value prediction in transactions: a transaction could speculate on any value as long as it ensures, that the read cache line is valid and holds the predicted value at the time it commits.

For example, in many HTMs, when a thread attempts to read data that is not in a valid state in its cache, it requests the cache line with the data and stalls waiting for the request. Rather than stall, a transaction could predict the data value because it *already* is in speculative execution and does not have to take an additional checkpoint. When it predicts accurately, the transaction mitigates the effects of the stall.

One method of prediction would use the data value in a *stale* cache line [28], i.e., an invalid cache line still containing the data it held when it was last invalidated. If the cache line is stale, a transaction could predict that the particular part it wants to read has not changed, and speculate using that value. Such predictions would be accurate in the cases of false sharing and silent stores [28].

When a transaction speculates on the value of a cache line, it must verify that the speculation was correct before it is able to commit. A transaction must track the parts of the cache lines on which it is speculating, and validate those cache lines by commit time. It validates the cache line by acquiring the line, and ensuring that the value it predicted matches the current data value in the cache line.

4. DPTM DESCRIPTION

4.1 Overview

This section demonstrates how data speculation could mitigate the effects of false conflicts by example of *Decoupling and Prediction TM* (DPTM), an enhanced *best-effort* HTM [14].

As a baseline, we assume a conventional best-effort HTM that uses eager conflict detection and lazy version management [11, 42], tracks its read and write sets in a transactional cache (such as the L1 cache) [15], and keeps transactional writes in a write buffer until the transaction commits. We also assume a cache coherence protocol that distinguishes stale cache lines from other invalid states. This baseline HTM associates transactional conflicts with coherence conflicts: when a cache line containing transactional data receives an invalidation request (due to a coherence conflict), this triggers a transactional conflict. This baseline is similar to other best-effort HTM proposals [6, 24, 27], and to the one used in Sun's Rock processor [15].

DPTM modifies this baseline HTM as follows.

DPTM decouples transactional conflicts from coherence con-

flicts using value-based conflict detection [43]. The values in a transaction's read set are monitored for change, and a transactional conflict is triggered only if a value changes. This reduces the effects of false sharing, because transactional conflicts are now restricted to changes *only* to the data used inside a transaction, rather than coherence conflicts over whole cache lines.

Moreover, DPTM can speculate when attempting a load from a stale cache line using the value of the stale data and validating it later. When speculating, it assumes that the cache line became stale because of a coherence conflict caused by false sharing. When this prediction is accurate, it could eliminate the stalling due to false sharing.

In addition to mitigating the effects of false sharing, DPTM also mitigates the effects of silent stores. In silent stores, data values do not change; therefore, DPTM's value-based conflict detection does not consider them to be transactional conflicts. Moreover, DPTM's speculation on a stale cache line that became stale because of a silent store would likely be accurate.

4.2 Detailed Description

DPTM does not alter how the baseline HTM begins its transaction. It alters the loading and storing of values inside a transaction, the handling of coherence conflicts and how a transactional conflict is interpreted, and the process of committing a transaction.

4.2.1 Loading a Value

When a transaction in DPTM attempts to load data not present in its transactional cache, it proceeds, as in the baseline, by issuing a request for the cache line and stalling for the request. Otherwise, if the cache line is present and in a valid state, the load is a cache hit.

If the cache line is stale, and DPTM *predicts* that the value has not changed, then it may serve the load using the stale data while simultaneously issuing a cache request for the data. The load proceeds as if it were a cache hit. On the other hand, if it *predicts* that the value has changed, it behaves conventionally, as if the line were not present.

By default, DPTM speculates only on stale data that is already part of a transaction's read set. This is conservative because the transaction has already read that data, and if it has changed, the transactions must abort anyway. Therefore, it has little to lose in the case of a mis-prediction.

Associated with all cache lines in the transactional cache are read mark bits that indicate which parts of each line have been read [39]. Each bit monitors reads from a subset of its cache line, i.e., the bit is set when its associated subset is read inside a transaction. These bits are used for validation, as only the parts of stale cache lines with their associated bits set need to be validated.

The number of read mark bits added per cache line determines the granularity level of DPTM's transactional conflict detection; the greater the number of bits the finer the granularity, and the more cases of false sharing that can be detected.[1] This could conceivably go down to the individual bit level.

When a processor receives a response to a cache request, the data in the cache whose read mark bits are set is validated against the returned data. If the data has not changed, validation succeeds and the transaction proceeds as normal. If the data has changed, validation fails, the transaction aborts, and all read mark bits are cleared. In all cases, the old cache line data is replaced with the returned data.

---

[1]For example, for a 64 byte cache line and a conflict detection granularity level of 4 bytes, DPTM requires an additional 16 bits for each cache line.

4.2.2 Storing a Value

When a transaction performs a store, the baseline HTM requests exclusive permissions for the cache line and stalls while it obtains these permissions, after which it stores the data in the transactional write buffer. Stores in DPTM do not request exclusive permissions at the time of the store; instead, a transaction stores the data in the write buffer immediately and does not stall. However, the transaction must obtain exclusive permissions for all cache lines in the write buffer before it can commit. DPTM, as a starting point in its design, requests exclusive permissions at commit time.

As an extension, DPTM can choose to request exclusive permissions immediately, and does not need to stall for the request. If it postpones the request until commit time, it cannot overlap the stalling for the request with other operations.

Either way, the time taken for the store instruction is equivalent to the time taken for a cache hit.

4.2.3 Conflict Management

When a transaction in the baseline HTM receives an invalidation request for a cache line that is a part of its read or write sets, it invokes a conflict resolution mechanism. If the mechanism decides to acknowledge the request, the receiver's cache line is invalidated, aborting its transaction.

Using DPTM, a transaction that receives an invalidation request acknowledges the request and does *not* abort, anticipating that the invalidation might be due to a coherence conflict caused by false sharing, a silent store, or that the sender of the invalidation is a *doomed transaction* [21], i.e., a transaction that will eventually abort. Therefore, the transaction schedules a request for the now invalidated cache line and continues execution.

When the transaction's request is finally served and it receives the current cache line data, the transaction validates that the read data on that cache line, as specified by the read mark bits, is unchanged. If it has changed, the transaction aborts, and the read mark bits are cleared.

4.2.4 Committing a Transaction

At commit time, the baseline HTM flushes its write buffer by writing all the values in its write buffer to memory. Because this HTM already has all its cache lines in their correct commit states, whereby the coherence states are associated with their transactional states, this is sufficient to complete the transaction.

In DPTM, when a transaction is ready to commit, parts of its read set might not be in a valid state, and parts of its write set might not be in an exclusive state. Therefore, it employs a two stage commit.

In the first stage, DPTM attempts to restore the baseline HTM association of ensuring that all its cache lines are in their correct commit states. It first issues shared cache requests to all stale lines in the cache that are part of the transaction's read set but not its write set. All the while, each incoming cache line is validated, aborting the transaction if data that is part of its read set has changed. DPTM then issues exclusive cache requests to all cache lines that are part of the transaction's write set but are not already in an exclusive state.

Once all the cache lines have been validated and are in their correct commit states, DPTM moves to the second commit phase, which is the same as the baseline HTM's commit. When it finally commits, it clears all the read mark bits.

During the second commit phase, as in the baseline HTM, DPTM must keep all read lines in a valid state, and all written lines in an exclusive state. This results in the serialization of the commit phases in the presence of false conflicts — compared with the serialization of *whole* transactions in the baseline HTM.

The contention management policy during DPTM's commit phases is different from the one during a transaction. Invalidation requests for cache lines that are part of a transaction's read or write sets are denied. To prevent deadlock, the simplest policy is for the committing transaction to abort if a cache request it has sent was denied.

A more elaborate policy, which DPTM uses during its commit phase, is as follows: if a cache line invalidation request comes in during the first commit phase, the transaction acknowledges it only if the requester is also committing and has higher priority, otherwise it denies the request. Therefore, deadlock cannot occur if priority is unique. Invalidation requests during the second commit phase, as in the baseline HTM, are always denied; at that point the transaction is guaranteed to commit and there is no fear of deadlock.

4.3 Additions and Design Alternatives

This section discusses some of the DPTM design alternatives we have investigated.

4.3.1 Eager or Lazy Conflict Detection

DPTM detects transactional conflicts on changed values rather than on coherence conflicts. Because value changes are observable only once a transaction commits, DPTM's conflict detection is *lazy* [21], unlike the baseline HTM which uses eager conflict detection. Because both eager and lazy conflict detection have been shown to be superior under different conditions [9, 11, 40, 50, 54], we introduce *SendSets*, an addition to DPTM which allows eager conflict detection while retaining the benefits of lazy conflict detection.

SendSets leverages the information in a transaction's read and write sets, as represented by the read mark bits and the write buffer. When a transaction in DPTM using *SendSets* issues a cache request, it includes with the request this information as a bit map.

The transaction receiving the request determines whether there could be a transactional conflict by using the read and write set information in the bit map. If it determines that there may be a conflict, it decides, based on priority, whether to deny the request or acknowledge it.

Even if the transaction acknowledges the request it does not abort, anticipating that the request is due to a silent store, or that the sender of the invalidation request might be a doomed transaction. This allows the transaction to eagerly detect conflicts and prioritize requests accordingly, and benefit from the laziness of value-based conflict detection.

4.3.2 Improving Prediction Accuracy by Sending Updates

Because DPTM speculates using stale cache line data, the accuracy of such predictions can increase if the values in the stale cache lines are kept up to date. When a processor requests exclusive permissions to write to a cache line, it could send the value it intends to write along with its request [28]. The receiver, upon receiving this request, would update the value of its now stale cache line.

Other alternatives might go even further; for example, processors could keep track of other processors they have invalidated, and broadcast any subsequent updates of the cache line to those processors [28].

4.4 DPTM Architecture

DPTM is compatible with existing best-effort HTM proposals that associate transactional conflicts with coherence conflicts. DPTM is also compatible with any cache coherence protocol with states denoting cache lines that are not present, present but invalid, valid, and exclusive[2]. It does not matter whether it is a snooping or a directory based protocol.

DPTM does not require modifications of the coherence protocol typically used in HTMs, and adds little, processor-local, hardware. The additional hardware requirements are as follows.

DPTM requires additional bits per transactional cache line for the read mark bits, and assumes the ability of flash-clearing the read mark bits. Flash-clearing is desirable for performance, not required for correctness. If these bits cannot be flash-cleared, they could be cleared sequentially, at the cost of either stalling while the bits are cleared, or potential false conflicts in future transactions for the locations whose bits are still set.

DPTM also requires the ability to validate cache lines that are part of a transaction's read set against incoming data. The incoming data could be buffered in a miss status handling register (MSHR) while the validation takes place. DPTM also requires logic to compare the values being validated, but could be designed to leverage existing logic in a processor.

As for some of the design alternatives, *SendSets* requires the ability to include the read and write sets as a payload with cache requests. Sending updates also requires the ability to add the value being stored as an extra payload to exclusive cache requests and invalidations.

5. EVALUATION

This section reports on our analysis of DPTM. We compare different design alternatives for DPTM and compare them with a best-effort HTM, focusing on false sharing in particular.

5.1 Experiment Environments

The simulation framework we use is based on Virtutech Simics [34], and the University of Wisconsin GEMS 2.1 [36]. The simulator models processors that have best-effort HTM support using Sun's ATMTP [41], itself a component of GEMS. The simulated system is a SPARC/Solaris Sun Fire server; the simulated environment parameters are given in Table 1.

We use ATMTP to simulate the baseline HTM described. To simulate DPTM, we have extended ATMTP without modifying its cache coherence protocol. ATMTP models an eager conflict detection and lazy version management Rock-like best-effort HTM.

---

[2]We note that the extra state introduced for stale data is readily distinguishable in most cache coherence protocols, which conveniently group them together, but in fact can easily distinguish them.

ATMTP uses the L1 cache as its transactional cache, which limits transactional reads and writes by its size and associativity. ATMTP keeps transactional writes in a write buffer until the transaction commits, which also limits transactional writes. Because ATMTP models a best-effort HTM, we use a single global lock as a fallback mechanism when unable to complete a transaction in hardware.

5.2 Benchmarks

For our evaluation, we use STAMP [40], SPLASH-2 [57], micro [23, 35], and our own *SharingPatterns* benchmarks.

We test the STAMP benchmarks (*Table 2–top*), using the parameters suggested by their creators for both *low* and *high* contention tests [40]. We have excluded bayes and yada from our tests, because their transactions are too large to complete successfully in hardware using ATMTP.

STAMP was written by transactional memory experts; its benchmarks exhibit no false sharing inside transactions. However, code not written by experts is unlikely to be optimized for false sharing. We use these benchmarks, anyway, to investigate how DPTM behaves in the absence of false sharing.

The SPLASH-2 suite was not originally meant for evaluating TM. Others have reported that raytrace is particularly susceptible to false sharing in HTM [42]; therefore, we thought it would be interesting to include it in our evaluation (*Table 2–middle*). We use a small image, *teapot*, as an input.

The micro-benchmarks are ones we ported from the Java-based DSTM [23] to C (*Table 2–bottom*). They are concurrent sets implemented with: a chained hash table, a single sorted linked list, and a red-black tree. In these benchmarks, each thread randomly inserts, deletes, or looks up a value in the range of 0–255. The *low* contention distribution of operations is 1:1:1 (insert:delete:lookup), and the *high* one is 1:1:0.

We have also created a group of benchmarks, *SharingPatterns*, to cover a range of sharing patterns. These benchmarks are not meant to represent realistic workloads, but to exaggerate these patterns to better observe the behavior of DPTM in the presence of false and true sharing. The patterns *SharingPatterns* exhibits are the following.

Sharing followed by no sharing: all transactions start by incrementing a value residing on the same cache line, followed by incrementing 19 different lines.

No sharing followed by sharing: all transactions start by incrementing values residing on 19 different cache lines, followed by incrementing the same line.

Item	Model
Processor	in-order, single-issue, single-threaded, CMP
L1 cache	private, transactional, 128 kB, 4-way split, 1 cycle latency
L2 cache	shared, 2 MB, 8-way split, 20 cycle latency
Cache line size	64 bytes
Memory	8 GB, 450 cycle latency
Transactional write buffer	32 entries, 256 for labyrinth
Conflict resolution priority	timestamp [9]
Function calls in transactions	allowed [41]

Table 1: Simulated machine configuration

Benchmark	Tx Length	R/W Set	Contention
genome	medium	medium	low
intruder	short	medium	high
kmeans	short	small	low
labyrinth	long	large	high
ssca2	short	small	low
vacation	medium	medium	low/medium
raytrace	short	small	medium
hash	very short	small	low
list	medium	medium	high
redblack	short	medium	low

Table 2: Qualitative summary, relative to STAMP, of the benchmarks' runtime transactional characteristics: length of transactions (number of instructions), size of the read and write sets, and amount of contention. cf. [40]

Write sharing: all transactions increment values residing on the same 20 cache lines.

The sharing part of each of the three patterns above is tested with false sharing, where processors increment different values on the same cache line; and with true sharing, where processors increment the same value on the same cache line.

5.3 Experiments and Results

The outcome of the experiments, running 16 user threads on 16 processors, is shown in Figures 2, 3, and 4. We measure the time spent in transactional workloads, and present the results of 10 runs with pseudo-random perturbations [3], plotting the standard deviation as error bars.

5.3.1 The effect of different sharing patterns

Because we designed DPTM with the goal of mitigating the effects of false conflicts, we start by looking at different patterns of false and true sharing. We expect DPTM to improve performance over the baseline HTM in the presence of false sharing, and that it would be comparable in the case of true sharing. We also expect that as the amount of false sharing increases, the gap between DPTM's performance and the baseline HTM would also increase.

For these experiments (*Figure 2*), we use the *SharingPatterns* benchmarks, which present an exaggerated form of different sharing patterns. We run the benchmarks using the baseline HTM, and DPTM with conflict detection granularity levels, in bytes, of 4 (one word), 8, 16, 32, and 64 (one cache line); in the presence of false sharing, we expect performance to improve the finer the granularity.

In the presence of false sharing, DPTM with granularity of 4 to 32 bytes always performs significantly better than the baseline HTM (*Figure 2: a, c, e*). DPTM also performs at least as good, if not better, for true sharing (*b, d, f*). The improvement in the case of true sharing is an anomaly due to DPTM's lazy conflict detection, where its transactions are not aborted, as in the baseline HTM, when a cache line is invalidated by a doomed transaction.

We note that DPTM's gains are comparable whether false sharing occurs at the beginning of a transaction (*a*), or at the end (*c*). Because contention in these benchmarks is high, false sharing adversely affects performance in the baseline HTM regardless of where it occurs inside a transaction. This also shows that even one instance of false sharing can be detrimental to performance.

As for the effect of different granularity levels, we find that for the false sharing patterns that do not perform many shared stores (*a*, *c*), the improvement gained by finer granularity is more pronounced than where shared stores dominate (*e*). Moreover, where shared stores — and false conflicts — dominate, DPTM is less effective in mitigating their effects. This is due to DPTM's serialization of commit phases in the presence of false conflicts, which reduces the gains in such workloads.

5.3.2 The effects of restructuring

We have seen that DPTM has potential for improving performance in the presence of false sharing. In the next set of experiments (*Figure 3*), we investigate how DPTM performs using a more diverse set of benchmarks.

We investigate the amount of false sharing present in these benchmarks. Where it is present, we try to mitigate it by padding, and where it is not, we try to instigate it by removing existing padding. This allows us to study the efficacy of using padding, particularly when compared with using DPTM, to mitigate false sharing. We expect DPTM to be at least comparable to, if not better than, padding

Benchmark	False Sharing Aborts	True Conflict Aborts
genome	16%	18%
intruder	7%	104%
labyrinth	16%	300%
ssca2	1%	3%
vacation-high	19%	415%
vacation-low	15%	415%
kmeans-high	5%	18%
kmeans-low	5%	8%
raytrace	67%	28%
hash-high	2%	0%
hash-low	1%	0%
list-high	313%	251%
list-low	269%	156%
redblack-high	17%	9%
redblack-low	12%	6%

Table 3: DPTM–64's abort rates, relative to the number of committed transactions, broken down by cause. The first column presents the percentage of aborting transactions that abort because of false sharing. The second column presents the percentage of transaction that abort because of true conflicts.

in mitigating false sharing, because padding could have adverse effects on locality.

We note that the STAMP suite was developed by TM experts for evaluating TM proposals, so we expect it would be optimized to mitigate false sharing. By analyzing its code, we observed that some of its structures are padded and aligned to cache line boundaries. The only padded data structures used inside transactions, as far as we could tell, are in kmeans. We created a modified version of kmeans with this padding removed. We still use the rest of the STAMP benchmarks in our evaluation, even though we do not expect any performance gains, to study the effect our changes might have in the absence of false conflicts.

Even though the SPLASH-2 suite was written for evaluating multiprocessors, raytrace is known to suffer from false sharing in the context of HTM [42]. To compare against mitigating the effects of false sharing by restructuring, we created a modified version of raytrace in the manner Moore et al. [42] describe.

The micro benchmarks were originally written in Java, and therefore are not padded. In porting them, we created a modified version where each object is padded and aligned to the cache line boundary.

We compare the padded with the unpadded versions (where applicable), running on the baseline HTM, DPTM with conflict detection granularity of 4 bytes (one word — *DPTM*), and 64 bytes (one cache line — *DPTM–64*). We use DPTM–64 to isolate the effects DPTM has on false sharing from other effects, such as DPTM's lazy conflict detection, because DPTM–64 detects conflicts at the granularity level of a whole cache line.

To better understand the impact of false sharing on the benchmarks' transactions, Table 3 presents an analysis of the impact false sharing has on the abort rate of transactions in DPTM–64. We present this analysis for DPTM–64 because it uses the same mechanisms as DPTM–4, yet detects conflict at the granularity level of a whole cache line. Therefore, DPTM–64 isolates the effects of false sharing in transactions from the effects of all the other changes DPTM makes to the baseline.

The results of evaluating DPTM using STAMP show that DPTM is consistently faster than the baseline HTM, with the exception of ssca2, where they are comparable. This improvement is not due

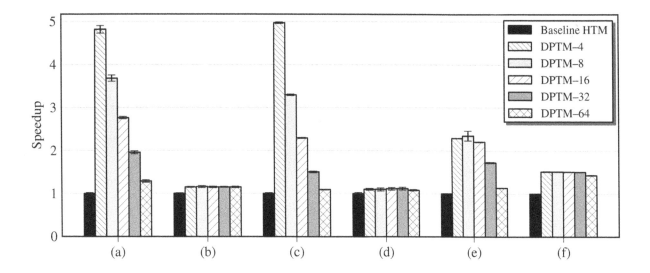

Figure 2: The speedup of the SharingPatterns *benchmarks running at granularities of 4 to 64 bytes, relative to the baseline HTM. (a/b) false/true sharing followed by no sharing (c/d) no sharing followed by false/true sharing (e/f) false/true write sharing*

to the mitigation of false sharing or silent stores, but to DPTM's lazy conflict detection.

For `kmeans`, padding improves performance only slightly. False sharing in `kmeans` does not occur often, because its transactions are small with low contention, and its transactional objects that suffer from false sharing are only slightly bigger than a cache line.

As for the SPLASH-2 benchmark `raytrace`, false sharing has a significant impact. Padding mitigates much of its effects. Furthermore, the cache miss statistics show that padding does not adversely affect locality in this case.

DPTM significantly speeds up `raytrace` compared with the baseline HTM when running either the padded or the unpadded version. Most of this improvement is due to mitigating the effects of false sharing.

DPTM is faster when running the padded version compared with the unpadded version of `raytrace`. This shows that DPTM was able to mitigate most of the effects of false sharing, but not eliminate them. DPTM serializes the commit phases of transactions with false conflicts, whereas the padded version has no false conflicts that cause commit phases to serialize.

For the micro benchmarks running on the baseline HTM, the padded versions of `list` and `redblack` are significantly faster, because padding mitigates false sharing. As for `hash`, there is no significant difference because contention is low and its transactions are very short.

DPTM running the unpadded micro benchmarks is faster than the baseline HTM running either the unpadded or the padded versions. Interestingly in `list`, DPTM performs better using the unpadded version whereas the opposite is true for the baseline HTM; DPTM was able to mitigate the effects of false sharing as well as take advantage of the locality afforded by using the unpadded version.

An observation regarding value prediction, we have until now presented the results using a conservative DPTM, which speculates only on the values already part of a transaction's read set. Most of the gains so far, even in the presence of false sharing, are due to the decoupling of transactional from coherence conflicts; value prediction accounts for less than 5% of the *additional* gains presented.

We also experimented with an aggressive approach, which *always* speculates on the values in a stale cache line, with the results (not shown) consistently slower. This is not surprising, because mis-prediction has the high cost of aborting the whole transaction. Others have also observed that for data speculation to be effective, it should be throttled to avoid the high cost of mis-prediction [52].

5.3.3 The effect of design alternatives

In Section 4, we have discussed some of DPTM's design alternatives. We evaluate the alternatives (*Figure 4*) against the basic DPTM with conflict detection granularity of 4 bytes.

First, we evaluate issuing exclusive requests immediately on stores (*GetX*), rather than waiting until commit time. Issuing the requests immediately can hide the latency for the request. But if contention is high, the transaction may lose exclusive permissions and need to reissue the request later.

We find no significant differences except in `intruder`, `kmeans`, `raytrace`, and `redblack-high`, where *GetX* is noticeably faster. These benchmarks have short transactions, so the window for losing exclusive permissions is small. On the other hand, `hash` is not benefitting much from *GetX*, because its transactions are very short, so there is little time to hide any request latency.

Because *GetX* performs as well as, if not better than, the basic DPTM, the remaining experiments also issue exclusive requests immediately on stores, and are compared against *GetX*.

Next, we evaluate *SendSets*, which makes DPTM more eager by taking advantage of a cache line's read and write set information in detecting transactional conflicts. As mentioned in Section 4.3.1, eager and lazy conflict detection are superior under different conditions; therefore, we expect *SendSets*'s performance to be in line with more eager conflict detection schemes.

For the benchmarks we use, *SendSets* is generally comparable to *GetX*, except for `intruder`, `raytrace`, and `list-high`. There is more improvement in `list-high`, a long benchmark with high contention, because eager conflict detection aids higher priority transactions, i.e., older transactions in this case. On the other hand, `intruder` and `raytrace` are slower, because requests are often denied by doomed transactions, wasting work.

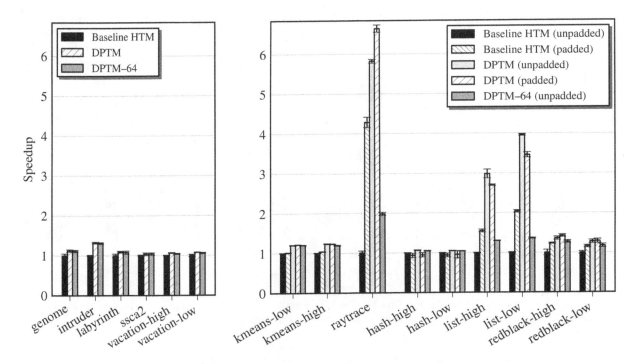

Figure 3: The speedup of running the benchmarks, padded and unpadded where applicable, relative to the baseline HTM. The benchmarks on the left do not exhibit false sharing inside transactions.

Finally, we investigate ways to improve the accuracy of value prediction in DPTM. We first model the instantaneous and free broadcasting of all cache line updates to all processors that have the cache line in a stale state (*Seer*). We use this *unrealistic* approach to evaluate the effects of such a broadcasting mechanism regardless of its cost, in order to give us intuition regarding the benefits of sending updates in general. We then compare *Seer* against the more realistic approach of sending updates only with invalidation requests (*SendUpdates*).

When using either *Seer* or *SendUpdates*, DPTM *always* speculates on stale cache line data, unlike the basic DPTM. Out of all our experiments, *Seer* performs the best.

The gains from value prediction when using *Seer* are substantially higher than in the basic DPTM. For example, in `ssca2`, value prediction now accounts for 50% of the additional gains over the baseline HTM, and 40% in `redblack`, and 30% in `kmeans` and `linklist`. This unrealistic approach demonstrates that broadcasting updates has potential for improving performance gains from value prediction.

On the other hand, *SendUpdates* overall performs poorly; transactions frequently abort because of mis-speculation, especially in `redblack`. This implies that while the sending of updates seems promising, *SendUpdates* is not sufficient to capture this potential.

Finally, to better appreciate the effect the different aspects the design of DPTM has on performance, Figure 5 presents a breakdown of the different speedup components in *Seer*. We present the breakdown for *Seer* because its component parameters perform the best across all workloads in these experiments. Therefore, a breakdown of its components is well suited to examine the relative benefits of the different design options we investigate.

6. RELATED WORK

Other HTMs are also capable of fine-grained conflict detection, e.g., *TCC* [19, 39], *Bulk* [11], and *RETCON* [7]. TCC associates

fine-grained read bits for conflict detection with each cache line; however, TCC proposes an unconventional approach for memory consistency and cache coherence, where transactions are the basic unit of parallel work. Bulk hashes a transaction's access information, and uses this hash for conflict detection. RETCON, which is concurrent with this work, symbolically tracks modifications and constraints that a transaction applies to variables, and uses value-based conflict detection. In contrast to these proposals, we directly address the problem of false sharing using a best-effort HTM with a conventional coherence protocol. We also propose using value prediction to reduce latencies incurred with false sharing, by speculating on the values of stale cache line data.

Concurrently with and independently of our work, Pant and Byrd [44] proposed using value prediction in HTM, in a manner different from ours both in design and in purpose. Their proposal does not address false sharing in transactions, but uses value prediction to reduce load latencies by predicting future updates. It also requires more modifications to the underlying hardware: the value predictor is located at the memory level, near the memory or directory controller; requires the directory to be able to observe all stores, which could be a bottleneck; limits the number of transactions concurrently involved in value prediction; requires additional hardware modifications to the directory to keep prediction history and make further predictions; and requires a *nacking* coherence protocol [42], as well as further changes to that protocol.

Outside the context of HTM, Huh et al. decouple the use of a cache line's data from obtaining permissions for that line to mitigate the effects of false sharing [28]. They propose speculating on the values of stale cache lines, as well as mechanisms of sending write updates and forwarding modified data. In their work, latency tolerance for the coherence permissions was low, effectively limited to the parallelism in the existing reorder buffer. HTM naturally provides a larger scope, and so is better suited for coherence decoupling. Moreover, the additions required for our proposal can be

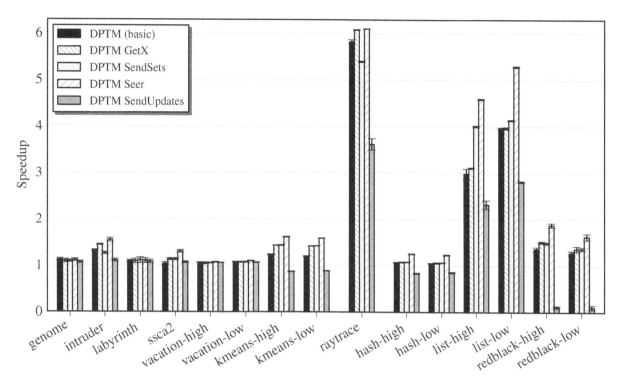

Figure 4: The speedup of design alternatives for DPTM relative to the baseline HTM (not shown)

used to mitigate the effects of false sharing *outside* transactions, in the same manner Huh et al. propose.

Value prediction has also been explored in the context of TLS in works by Knight [31], Akkary and Driscoll [2], Martin et al. [37], Cintra and Torrellas [13], and Steffan et al. [52], among others.

EazyHTM separates conflict detection from conflict resolution in an HTM, allowing it to detect conflicts eagerly, but act on them lazily [54]. Our work on *SendSets* serves a similar purpose using a different technique.

On the software side, Torrellas et al. [55] propose some solutions to the false sharing problem using compiler modifications that optimize the layout of shared data in cache lines to mitigate its effects. Olszewski et al. [43] propose *JudoSTM*, a software TM that uses value-based conflict detection, and is capable of improving performance in the presence of silent stores.

7. CONCLUDING REMARKS

We have demonstrated how data speculation in HTM, by example of DPTM, has the potential for improving performance, particularly in the presence of false conflicts. Benchmarks that exhibit false sharing show dramatic gains, whereas ones that do not exhibit false conflicts are not harmed by the alternative designs — and some even benefit from having lazy conflict detection.

We demonstrated how DPTM could mitigate the effects of false conflicts inside transactions. The modifications DPTM needs could also be applied to mitigate the effects of false sharing *outside* transactions, in the same manner proposed by Huh et al. [28], improving performance over a wider range of workloads.

Although DPTM can significantly mitigate the effects of false sharing, this mitigation is not perfect, because it serializes the commit phases of transactions with false conflicts.

DPTM can also improve performance in the presence of silent stores. Others have noted that silent stores are common in certain workloads [13, 52]; however, they were not common in the bench-

marks we used. We are interested in evaluating DPTM on such workloads in the future.

References

[1] A. Adl-Tabatabai, B. Lewis, V. Menon, B. Murphy, B. Saha, and T. Shpeisman. Compiler and runtime support for efficient software transactional memory. *PLDI*, 2006.

[2] H. Akkary and M. Driscoll. A dynamic multithreading processor. *MICRO*, 1998.

[3] A. Alameldeen and D. Wood. Variability in architectural simulations of multi-threaded workloads. *HPCA*, 2003.

[4] C. Ananian, K. Asanovic, B. Kuszmaul, C. Leiserson, and S. Lie. Unbounded transactional memory. *HPCA*, 2005.

[5] C. Ananian and M. Rinard. Efficient object-based software transactions. *SCOOL*, 2005.

[6] L. Baugh, N. Neelakantam, and C. Zilles. Using hardware memory protection to build a high-performance, strongly-atomic hybrid transactional memory. 2008.

[7] C. Blundell, A. Raghavan, and M. Martin. RETCON: Transactional repair without replay. *ISCA*, 2010.

[8] J. Bobba, N. Goyal, M. Hill, M. Swift, and D. Wood. TokenTM: Efficient execution of large transactions with hardware transactional memory. *ISCA*, 2008.

[9] J. Bobba, K. Moore, H. Volos, L. Yen, M. Hill, M. Swift, and D. Wood. Performance pathologies in hardware transactional memory. *ISCA*, 2007.

[10] W. Bolosky and M. Scott. False sharing and its effect on shared memory. 1993.

[11] L. Ceze, J. Tuck, J. Torrellas, and C. Cascaval. Bulk disambiguation of speculative threads in multiprocessors. *ISCA*, 2006.

[12] W. Chuang, S. Narayanasamy, G. Venkatesh, J. Sampson, M. Biesbrouck, G. Pokam, B. Calder, and O. Colavin. Unbounded page-based transactional memory. *ASPLOS*, 2006.

[13] M. Cintra and J. Torrellas. Eliminating squashes through learning cross-thread violations in speculative parallelization for multiprocessors. *HPCA*, 2002.

[14] P. Damron, A. Fedorova, Y. Lev, V. Luchangco, M. Moir, and D. Nussbaum. Hybrid transactional memory. *ASPLOS*, 2006.

[15] D. Dice, Y. Lev, M. Moir, and D. Nussbaum. Early experience with a commercial hardware transactional memory implementation. *ASPLOS*, 2009.

[16] D. Geer. Chip makers turn to multicore processors. *IEEE Computer*, 2005.

[17] J. Goodman and P. Woest. The Wisconsin Multicube: a new large-scale cache-coherent multiprocessor. *ISCA*, 1988.

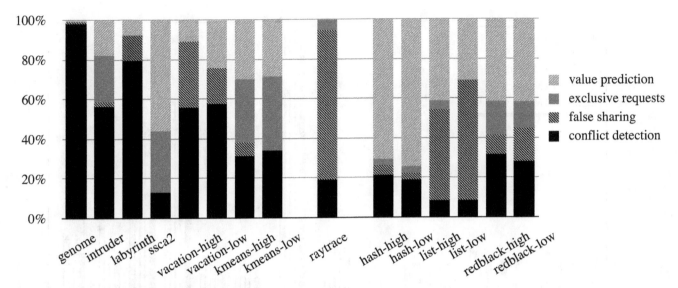

Figure 5: A breakdown of the speedup components of Seer. *The conflict detection component is due to the difference in DPTM's conflict detection from the baseline hardware. The false sharing component is due to the transactions not aborting because of false sharing. The exclusive requests component is due to issuing exclusive requests immediately on stores, rather than waiting until commit time. The value prediction component is due to the reduction in load latency when speculating on data values.*

[18] D. Grossman. The transactional memory / garbage collection analogy. *OOPSLA*, 2007.

[19] L. Hammond, V. Wong, M. Chen, B. Carlstrom, J. Davis, B. Hertzberg, M. Prabhu, H. Wijaya, C. Kozyrakis, and K. Olukotun. Transactional memory coherence and consistency. *ISCA*, 2004.

[20] T. Harris, K. Fraser, and I. Pratt. A practical multi-word compare-and-swap operation. *DISC*, 2002.

[21] T. Harris, J. R. Larus, and R. Rajwar. *Transactional Memory.* Synthesis Lectures on Computer Architecture. Morgan and Claypool Publishers, 2nd edition, 2010.

[22] J. Hennessy and D. Patterson. *Computer Architecture: A Quantitative Approach.* 2006.

[23] M. Herlihy, V. Luchangco, M. Moir, and W. Scherer. Software transactional memory for dynamic-sized data structures. *PODC*, 2003.

[24] M. Herlihy and J. Moss. Transactional memory: Architectural support for lock-free data structures. *ISCA*, 1993.

[25] M. Herlihy and J. Moss. System for achieving atomic non-sequential multi-word operations in shared memory. *US Patent 5,428,761*, 1995.

[26] M. Herlihy and N. Shavit. *The Art of Multiprocessor Programming.* Morgan Kaufmann, 2008.

[27] O. Hofmann, C. Rossbach, and E. Witchel. Maximum benefit from a minimal HTM. 2009.

[28] J. Huh, J. Chang, D. Burger, and G. Sohi. Coherence decoupling: making use of incoherence. *ASPLOS*, 2004.

[29] T. Jeremiassen and S. Eggers. Reducing false sharing on shared memory multiprocessors through compile time data transformations. *PPoPP*, 1995.

[30] M. Kadiyala and L. Bhuyan. A dynamic cache sub-block design to reduce false sharing. *ICCD*, 1995.

[31] T. Knight. An architecture for mostly functional languages. *LFP*, 1986.

[32] K. Lepak and M. Lipasti. Silent stores for free. *MICRO*, 2000.

[33] K. Lepak and M. Lipasti. Temporally silent stores. *ASPLOS*, 2002.

[34] P. Magnusson, M. Christensson, J. Eskilson, D. Forsgren, G. Hallberg, J. Hogberg, F. Larsson, A. Moestedt, and B. Werner. Simics: A full system simulation platform. *Computer*, 2002.

[35] V. Marathe, M. Spear, C. Heriot, and A. Acharya. Lowering the overhead of nonblocking software transactional memory. *TRANSACT*, 2006.

[36] M. Martin, D. Sorin, B. Beckmann, M. Marty, M. Xu, A. Alameldeen, K. Moore, M. Hill, and D. Wood. Multifacet's general execution-driven multiprocessor simulator (GEMS) toolset. 2005.

[37] M. Martin, D. J. Sorin, H. W. Cain, M. D. Hill, and M. H. Lipasti. Correctly implementing value prediction in microprocessors that support multithreading or multiprocessing. *MICRO*, 2001.

[38] J. Martínez and J. Torrellas. Speculative synchronization: applying thread-level speculation to explicitly parallel applications. *ASPLOS*, 2002.

[39] A. McDonald, J. Chung, H. Chafi, C. Minh, B. Carlstrom, L. Hammond, C. Kozyrakis, and K. Olukotun. Characterization of TCC on chip-multiprocessors. *PACT*, 2005

[40] C. Minh, J. Chung, C. Kozyrakis, and K. Olukotun. STAMP: Stanford transactional applications for multi-processing. *IISWC*, 2008.

[41] M. Moir, K. Moore, and D. Nussbaum. The adaptive transactional memory test platform: A tool for experimenting with transactional code for Rock. *TRANSACT*, 2008.

[42] K. Moore, J. Bobba, M. Moravan, M. Hill, and D. Wood. LogTM: Log-based transactional memory. *HPCA*, 2006.

[43] M. Olszewski, J. Cutler, and J. Steffan. JudoSTM: A dynamic binary-rewriting approach to software transactional memory. *PACT*, 2007.

[44] S. Pant and G. Byrd. Extending concurrency of transactional memory programs by using value prediction. *CF*, 2009.

[45] R. Rajwar and J. Goodman. Speculative lock elision: enabling highly concurrent multithreaded execution. *MICRO*, 2001.

[46] R. Rajwar and J. Goodman. Transactional lock-free execution of lock-based programs. *ASPLOS*, 2002.

[47] R. Rajwar, M. Herlihy, and K. Lai. Virtualizing transactional memory. *ISCA*, 2005.

[48] H. Ramadan, C. Rossbach, D. Porter, O. Hofmann, A. Bhandari, and E. Witchel. MetaTM/TxLinux: transactional memory for an operating system. *ISCA*, 2007.

[49] W. Scherer, D. Lea, and M. Scott. A scalable elimination-based exchange channel. *SCOOL*, 2005.

[50] A. Shriraman, S. Dwarkadas, and M. Scott. Flexible decoupled transactional memory support. *ISCA*, 2008.

[51] G. Sohi, S. Breach, and T. Vijaykumar. Multiscalar processors. *ISCA*, 1995.

[52] J. Steffan, C. Colohan, A. Zhai, and T. Mowry. Improving value communication for thread-level speculation. *HPCA*, 2002.

[53] F. Tabba, A. W. Hay, and J. R. Goodman. Transactional value prediction. In *TRANSACT '09: The 4th annual SIGPLAN Workshop on Transactional Memory.* ACM, 2009.

[54] S. Tomić, C. Perfumo, C. Kulkarni, A. Armejach, A. Cristal, O. Unsal, T. Harris, and M. Valero. EazyHTM: eager-lazy hardware transactional memory. *MICRO*, 2009.

[55] J. Torrellas, M. Lam, and J. Hennessy. False sharing and spatial locality in multiprocessor caches. *IEEE Transactions on Computers*, 1994.

[56] E. Vallejo, T. Harris, A. Cristal, O. Unsal, and M. Valero. Hybrid transactional memory to accelerate safe lock-based transactions. *TRANSACT*, 2008.

[57] S. Woo, M. Ohara, E. Torrie, J. Singh, and A. Gupta. The SPLASH-2 programs: characterization and methodological considerations. *ISCA*, 1995.

[58] L. Yen, J. Bobba, M. Marty, K. Moore, H. Volos, M. Hill, M. Swift, and D. Wood. LogTM-SE: Decoupling hardware transactional memory from caches. *HPCA*, 2007.

[59] R. Yoo, Y. Ni, A. Welc, B. Saha, A. Adl-Tabatabai, and H.-H. Lee. Kicking the tires of software transactional memory: why the going gets tough. *SPAA*, 2008.

Multiset Signatures for Transactional Memory

Ricardo Quislant, Eladio Gutierrez, Oscar Plata and Emilio L. Zapata
Dept. of Computer Architecture
University of Malaga, Spain
{quislant, eladio, oplata, zapata}@uma.es

ABSTRACT

Transactional Memory (TM) systems must record the memory locations read and written (read and write sets) by concurrent transactions in order to detect conflicts. Some TM implementations use signatures for this purpose, which summarize read and write sets in bounded hardware at the cost of false positives (detection of non-existing conflicts).

Read/write signatures are usually implemented as two separate Bloom filters with the same size. In contrast, transactions usually exhibit read/write sets of uneven cardinality, where read sets use to be larger than write sets. Thus, the read filter populates earlier than the write one and, consequently the read signature false positive rate may be high while the write filter has still a low occupation.

In this paper, a multiset signature design is proposed which records both the read and write sets in the same Bloom filter without adding significant hardware complexity. Several designs of multiset signatures are analyzed and evaluated. New problems arise related to hardware complexity and the existence of cross false positives, i.e. new false positives coming from the fact that both sets share the same filter. Additionally, multiset signatures are enhanced using locality-sensitive hashing, proposed by the authors in a previous work. Experimental results show that the multiset approach is able to reduce the false positive rate and improve the execution performance in most of the tested codes, without increasing the required hardware area in a noticeable amount.

Categories and Subject Descriptors

B.3 [**Hardware**]: Memory Structures; C.1.4 [**Computer Systems Organization**]: Processor Architectures—*Parallel Architectures*

General Terms

Design, Experimentation, Performance

Keywords

Hardware transactional memory, signatures, Bloom filters, H3 hashing, locality of reference

1. INTRODUCTION

The emerging of the single-chip parallel processors, known as CMPs (Chip Multiprocessors), manycore or multicore processors [9], with an internal architecture similar to a shared-memory multiprocessor, has forced the common programmer to deal with the multithreaded parallel programming model to obtain maximum performance from the processor cores. In general, multithreaded programming introduces complexities which make exploiting multicore processors difficult. Parallelism introduces non-determinism that must be controlled by a careful design of the computational threads and their coordination through explicit synchronization. To avoid race conditions, shared data referenced in critical sections must be accessed in mutual exclusion. Traditionally, locks are used to provide such a mutual exclusion by serializing the execution of concurrent threads. By narrowing these sections (fine granularity locks), the thread serialization may be minimized, but at a cost of increasing the lock overhead and the risk of deadlock. In addition, locks have other disadvantages, like convoying or priority inversion [11], problems difficult to detect and solve. Also, locks lack effective mechanisms for abstraction and composition.

Transactional Memory (TM) [11, 13] represents an alternative to the conventional lock-based multithreaded parallel programming model. TM introduces the concept of transaction that allows semantics to be separated from implementation, with the aim of easing the writing of concurrent programs. A transaction is a block of computations that appears to be executed in an atomic and isolated way. Thus, transactions replace a pessimistic lock-based model by an optimistic one. TM systems execute transactions in parallel committing non-conflicting ones. A conflict occurs when a memory location is accessed by multiple concurrent transactions and at least one access is a write.

In this paper we are mainly interested in hardware implementations of TM (HTM), which include those systems that provide most of the required TM mechanisms implemented in hardware at the core level [10, 2, 6, 22, 19, 8, 28], as well as those systems that provide hardware support to speed up parts of a software TM implementation (STM) [24, 27, 26]. These systems must record all memory reads and writes during the execution of transactions to detect conflicts.

Signatures have been proposed to store the memory addresses read (read set – RS) and written (write set – WS) inside transactions. Some TM proposals include signatures in their systems, like BulkSC [5], LogTM-SE [30], SigTM [18], FlexTM [26], and STMlite [16]. Signatures in these systems are implemented as per-thread Bloom filters [3]. Basically, they use fixed hardware (except for STMlite, that uses a software implementation) to summarize an unbounded amount of read and write memory addresses.

Read/write signatures are usually implemented as two separate Bloom filters with the same size. In contrast, transactions usually exhibit read/write sets of uneven cardinality, where read sets are usually larger than write sets. As a result, the signature for reads populates much more than the one for writes and, consequently, the false positive rate for the read signature may be high while, at the same time, the write filter has still a low occupation, with negligible false positive rate. This situation could be handled by asymmetrically resizing the signatures. However, this solution suffers from a lack of generality because resizing would depend on the specific application, as discussed in [18] where the sensitivity to signature length is analyzed.

In this paper a different approach is followed. We propose a multiset signature design which records both the read and write sets in the same Bloom filter without adding significant hardware complexity. When sharing the filter, both the read and the write false positive rates can be equalized. We analyze and evaluate several designs of multiset signatures. New problems arise related to hardware complexity and the existence of cross false positives, i.e. new false positives coming from the fact that both sets share the same filter. Additionally, as a second contribution, we enhance multiset signatures using locality-sensitive hashing, proposed by the authors in a previous work [21]. Finally, we implement the proposed multiset and locality-sensitive multiset signatures in the Wisconsin GEMS LogTM-SE simulator [15], in order to evaluate their performance, and in CACTI [29] in order to evaluate the hardware area and energy requirements. Experimental results show that the multiset approach is able to reduce the false positive rate and improve the execution performance in most of the tested codes, without increasing the required hardware area in a noticeable amount and slightly increasing the power consumption.

The rest of the paper is organized as follows. In next section we present a background on signatures, describing how they are usually designed and implemented. A brief review of the related work is discussed. In Section 3 we introduce our proposed multiset signature design, discussing its basics, how they are implemented, and a comparison with other signature designs. Section 4 shows an analysis of our proposed signatures and determines false positive rates in different contexts. Next, Section 5 presents the implementation of multiset signatures on the GEMS simulator, and discusses how our novel signature design may improve the execution performance in several cases. In addition, an analysis of area and energy requirements using CACTI is also shown. Finally, Section 6 concludes the paper.

2. BACKGROUND AND RELATED WORK

Ceze et al. [6] first proposed the implementation of signatures by using per-thread Bloom filters. Such filters allow membership queries of elements over a set in a time and space-efficient way. Insertions of an unlimited number of elements can be performed at the cost of false positives (i.e. detection of non-existing conflicts due to address aliasing).

As elements can be added to the set but not removed, the filter is false negative free. A Bloom filter is a data structure which includes a bit array and k independent hash functions mapping the elements into k randomly distributed bits of the array. Initially, the array is zeroed. When an element is to be inserted into the Bloom filter, the k bits indexed by the hash functions are asserted. A positive membership query requires that those k bits are all set to 1.

As a hardware-efficient alternative to regular Bloom filters, Sanchez et al. [25] propose the parallel Bloom filter implementation. Unlike the regular filter, which is implemented as a k-ported SRAM, the parallel one uses k 1-ported SRAMs. The false positive rate is similar or even better. Also [25] concludes that the $H3$ class of hash functions [4] should be used instead of bit-selection ones [23], as $H3$ exhibits better distribution features. Nevertheless, the hardware cost of $H3$ is higher because an XOR tree per hash bit is needed.

Page-Block-XOR hashing (PBX) is a lower hardware cost implementation of $H3$ hash functions proposed by Yen et al. [31]. They use the concept of entropy to find the address bits which exhibit more randomness to use them as the inputs to the hash functions. Notary is also proposed in [31] as a technique to reduce the number of asserted bits in the signature based on privatization strategies. This way, only the shared addresses are recorded in the signature. Notary requires support from the compiler, runtime/library and operating system levels. In addition, the programmer must allocate objects as either private or shared.

Recently, Choi et al. [7] proposed adaptive grain signatures, which keep the history of transaction aborts and dynamically changes the input bit range to the hash functions based on the abort history. The aim of this design is to reduce the number of false positives that harm the execution performance.

First HTM proposals used the cache memory hierarchy to keep the transactional state. However, this approach poses major constraints into TM virtualization. For instance, transactions are limited by the cache size and certain problems can arise with context switching and unbounded transaction nesting. Therefore, signatures have been adopted by several HTM systems. BulkSC [5] uses them to enforce sequential consistency. LogTM-SE [30] ensures paging and context switching with global signatures. SigTM [18] is similar to LogTM-SE. VTM [22] uses a global signature for cache victimization. Finally, signatures have been also used for conflict detection in FPGA-based HTM systems [12].

3. MULTISET SIGNATURE DESIGNS

This section introduces the design and implementation of the different multiset (MS) signature proposals. Regular and parallel separate (SEP) schemes are shown along with its MS versions. Also, a novel and more efficient signature is proposed called parallel multiset shared signature.

3.1 Regular Multiset Signatures

A regular Bloom filter consists of one 2^m bit array and k independent hash functions that index the array. Two operations are provided, insertion and test for membership. Initially, the bit array is set to zero. To insert an address into the filter, first, the address passes through the k hash functions giving k values or indexes. Then those bits in the bit array indexed by the k hash values are set to one. On the

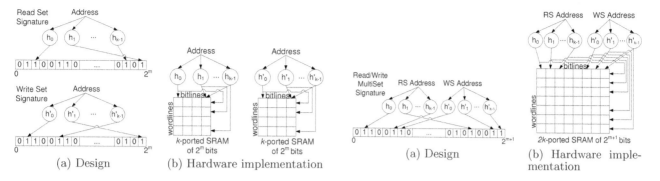

Figure 1: Regular Separate Bloom filters.

Figure 2: Regular MultiSet Bloom filters.

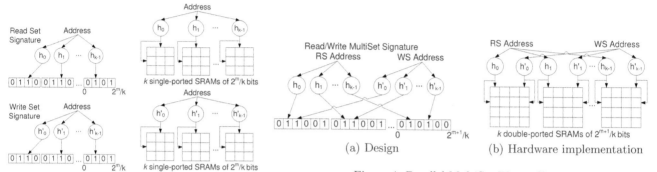

Figure 3: Parallel Separate Bloom filters.

Figure 4: Parallel MultiSet Bloom filters.

other hand, to test for an address the first step is analogous to the insertion operation, that is, compute the hash values for the address. Next, the k bits indexed by such values have to be checked. If they are all set to 1 then the test is positive, otherwise the address is not in the filter.

Figure 1 shows the design and implementation of regular separate signatures. Two Bloom filters are needed, one for the read set and the other one for the write set (see Figure 1a). They are usually of the same length, 2^m bits. Regarding the hardware, a regular Bloom filter can be implemented as an SRAM. The bit array can be divided into words, thus memory cells are placed forming a matrix with wordlines as rows and bitlines as columns, as shown in Figure 1b. This way, the address given by the hash function is divided into word address and bit address. In case of $k > 1$, SRAMs should be multi-ported so that they can perform the operations in parallel in one cycle instead of operating in several cycles. However, multi-ported memories require more hardware than single-ported ones and signatures must keep both concise and fast.

Regular multiset signatures merge the read set and the write set into the same filter of 2^{m+1} bits. Figure 2 shows the design and implementation of this proposal. Now, read set hash functions, $h_0...h_{k-1}$, and write set hash functions, $h'_0...h'_{k-1}$, share the filter. The main drawback of regular MS signatures is that they must be implemented by duplicating the number of ports of the SRAM and it translates into a quadratic growth of the required area. In order to save in area and also to maintain time-efficiency, parallel signatures are used [25] [6] which do not need multi-ported SRAMs.

3.2 Parallel Multiset Signatures

A parallel Bloom filter consists of k arrays of $2^m/k$ bits. Each hash function only indexes its own array, therefore one bit is set into each array on insertion.

Figure 3 shows the design an implementation of parallel separate signatures. They comprise two filters to keep track of read set and write set addresses. Like regular filters, parallel filters can be implemented as SRAMs. However, they use manifold smaller single-ported SRAMs instead of a larger multi-ported one, thus saving in hardware area. Furthermore, parallel Bloom filters have been proven to yield similar or better performance than regular ones [25] [21].

On the other hand, Figure 4 depicts the design and implementation of the multiset counterpart for the parallel signature. In this case, the bit array is also partitioned into k smaller arrays but of $2^{m+1}/k$ bits. Now, each array is indexed by two hash functions, one for the read set, h_i, and the other one for the write set, h'_i. Therefore, parallel multiset filters need 2-ported SRAMs instead of single-ported ones taking about twice the area of parallel separate filters. To alleviate this problem, we propose parallel multiset shared signatures.

3.3 Parallel Multiset Shared Signatures

Several memory locations are read and written inside transactions. Some of them are only read and others are only written but many of them are both read and written (see Section 5.3). In such a case, storing the same address twice may be redundant but the filter must be able to discriminate whether the address was only read or also written. Figure 5 shows the proposed solution. The signature is a parallel mul-

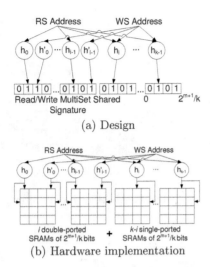

(a) Design

(b) Hardware implementation

Figure 5: Parallel MultiSet Shared Bloom filters.

tiset signature with some arrays indexed by only one hash function. This way, to insert an address into the filter, some arrays do not take into account if the address was either read or written, they simply record one bit representing the address. Therefore, certain read and write hash functions are said to be *shared*. However, the rest of the arrays discriminate between reads and writes since they are addressed by a read hash function h and a write hash function h'. Consequently, in case of an insertion to the write set, h' would set a bit in its array. Then, if the same address is subsequently inserted to the read set, a different bit would be set in the same array.

Figure 5b shows how the parallel multiset shared signature is implemented. Unlike parallel multiset signatures, only i double-ported SRAMs are needed, the rest remains single-ported. Thus, if i is low, parallel MS shared signatures do not require much more area than parallel signatures.

Finally, hash functions are implemented as $H3$ XOR hash functions [4] which only comprise a set of XOR gate trees per function. XOR gate trees do not require significant area and, moreover, they can be replaced by a single line of XOR gates by using PBX hashing [31].

4. MULTISET SIGNATURE ANALYSIS

The following expression is commonly assumed to calculate the false positive probability for a single filter of 2^m bits [25] [21], after inserting a sequence of s elements using k hash functions:

$$p_{\mathrm{FP}}(m, k, s) = \left(1 - \left(1 - \frac{1}{2^m}\right)^{sk}\right)^k . \quad (1)$$

First, consider two different conventional Bloom filters that store the read and write sets separately. A first goal in this section is determining the average false positive rate of the system consisting of these two separate read/write filters. With this purpose, let's suppose an arbitrary address sequence of length s to be inserted in the filters. For such a sequence, let p_R be the probability of an address being exclusively read, p_W the probability of an address being exclusively written and p_{RW} the probability of an address being both read and written ($p_R + p_W + p_{RW} = 1$). Therefore, the

false positive probability in each filter can be expressed as:

$$p_{\mathrm{FP}}^{read}(m, k, s) = \left(1 - \left(1 - \frac{1}{2^m}\right)^{s(p_R + p_{RW})k}\right)^k ,$$
$$p_{\mathrm{FP}}^{write}(m, k, s) = \left(1 - \left(1 - \frac{1}{2^m}\right)^{s(p_W + p_{RW})k}\right)^k . \quad (2)$$

In order to get the mathematical expectation of the false positive rate in this two-filter system, it is necessary to define the probability that both filters (read and write) are checked. By denoting with c_R and c_W such probabilities respectively, we can determine the average false positive rate of the two separate filters as:

$$\overline{p}_{FP}^{\mathrm{SEP}}(m, k, s) = E[p_{\mathrm{FP}}(m, k, s)] = \\ c_R p_{\mathrm{FP}}^{read}(m, k, s) + c_W p_{\mathrm{FP}}^{write}(m, k, s) \quad (3)$$

Note that in real transactions the number of writes is usually lower than the number of reads and consequently it is expected that the false positive rate will be higher for the reads. Additionally, those addresses being read and written will be inserted in both filters, causing for both an increase in occupancy.

In general, the checking pattern will depend on how the threads check each of the filters searching for possible data dependencies. Such a pattern is unknown until run-time and very dependent on the programming strategy used when designing the parallel multithreaded code. Other issues as the coherence protocol and how thread transactions may be aborted or resumed may also have influence. This checking pattern will determine the two weight factors c_R, c_W appearing in the previous expression.

If both filters are joined in a single double-sized one, where both read and write sets are inserted, expression 1 remains valid since reads and writes use a different set of k hashing functions. Thus, the false positive probability for this multiset scheme will be:

$$p_{FP}^{\mathrm{MULTI}}(m, k, s) = p_{\mathrm{FP}}(m + 1, k, s(1 + p_{RW})) \quad (4)$$

Observe that the addresses which are both read and written are inserted using different hash functions, so they are inserted twice in the multiset filter.

Three different scenarios have been analyzed by evaluating equations 3 and 4. In the first case, Figure 6, it is considered that the checking pattern is the same as that of insertion. This corresponds to weight factors $c_R = \frac{p_R + p_{RW}}{p_R + 2*p_{RW} + p_W}$ and $c_W = \frac{p_{RW} + p_W}{p_R + 2*p_{RW} + p_W}$. Figure 7 considers that the probability of checking both read and write filters is the same, that is, $c_R = \frac{1}{2}$ and $c_W = \frac{1}{2}$. On the other hand, Figure 8 assumes that when a read dependence is checked the write filter is probed but when checking a write dependence, both filters, read and write, need to be checked. Under this observation, we can estimate that $c_R = \frac{p_{RW} + p_W}{p_R + 2p_{RW} + 2p_W}$ and $c_W = \frac{p_R + p_{RW} + p_W}{p_R + 2p_{RW} + 2p_W}$. Observe that if the number of addresses both read and written increases, the analyzed configurations (separate filters and multiset) show a trend to be very similar in their expected false positive rate. Actually, for values close to $p_{RW} = 1$ both configurations yield the same rate (not shown). Nevertheless, for low values of p_{RW} the behavior varies greatly with the checking pattern. In such cases, if the number of checks are equalized between the two separated filters (Figure 7) the multiset proposal

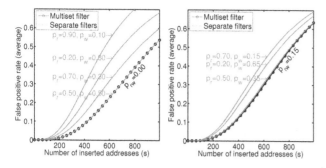

Figure 6: False positive rate average considering that inserting and checking patterns are the same ($k = 4$, $2^m = 1Kbit$).

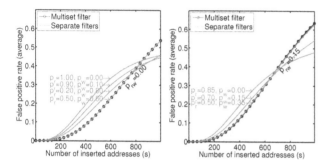

Figure 7: False positive rate average considering that checking patterns for read and write filters are the same ($k = 4$, $2^m = 1Kbit$).

can perform with less false positives when the number of addresses inserted is about $2/3$ of 2^m. In practice, checking patterns are actually closest to Figure 7 because data requested to main memory need to be checked in both filters of every thread to assure strong atomicity [19]. Notice that first level cache hits need no signature checks and the checking pattern of Figure 8 only corresponds to cache misses that can be solved by cache upper levels, which suppose a negligible fraction of total checks.

5. EXPERIMENTAL EVALUATION

In this section, simulation methodology (Section 5.1), experimental results (Sections 5.2, 5.3 and 5.4) and hardware requirements of MS signatures (Section 5.5) are described.

5.1 Simulation Methodology

The full system execution-driven simulator Simics [14] has been used to evaluate MS signatures. Specifically, Simics simulates the Sun Fire server brand and the SPARC architecture and it is able to run an unmodified copy of a Solaris operating system. Solaris 10 has been installed on the simulated machine and all workloads run on top of it.

A 16-core CMP system is considered for simulation. Each in-order single-issue core has a 32KB, 4-way, 64B block private L1 I and D cache. The L2 cache is unified and shared, having a capacity of 8MB organized in 16 banks, 8 ways and 64B blocks. Cache coherence is based on the MESI protocol with an on-chip directory which holds a bit vector of sharers per block. Main memory is 4GB.

Regarding the TM system, the GEMS module [15] has

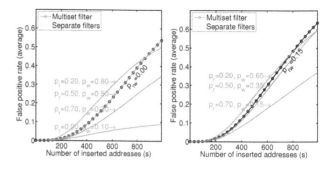

Figure 8: False positive rate average considering that the read filter is checked only for writes, but the write filter is checked both for writes and reads ($k = 4$, $2^m = 1Kbit$).

been used, which is provided by the Wisconsin Multifacet Project as an open-source module for Simics. GEMS's Ruby module implements the LogTM-SE HTM [30] and also includes a detailed timing model for the memory system. Ruby has been modified to include the proposed MS signature designs described in Section 3.

Simulation experiments use perfect signatures (no false positives, hardware unimplementable) as the reference. Filter size ranges from 64 bits, which matches the word length in SPARC architecture, to 8K bits length, which matches the performance of perfect signatures for the simulated benchmarks. All filters use 4 hash functions of the $H3$ family and the same $H3$ matrices of Ruby.

We have tested our MS signatures using all the codes in the STAMP suite [17]. Such a suite is oriented to the evaluation of TM systems. It covers a comprehensive set of codes including long-running transactions and large read and write sets. For signature evaluation, these codes are of special interest as signatures are stressed. STAMP benchmarks have been adapted to GEMS by applying Luke Yen's patches [21]. Table 1 shows the input parameters and main transactional characteristics of the benchmarks. "#xact" is the number of committed transactions. Column "Time in xact" lists the percentage of execution cycles of the benchmarks staying inside transactions. The last columns show the average and the maximum values of RS and WS size distributions in cache blocks.

Finally, Ruby adds pseudorandom delays to the latency of memory accesses to deal with variability in simulation experiments. Therefore, multiple runs of each experiment have been done to obtain confident error bars [1].

5.2 Regular and Parallel Multiset Signature Results

In this section a comparison between regular and parallel separate and multiset signatures is conducted.

Figure 9 shows the results obtained for every benchmark in the suite. The y axis represents the time in cycles which has been normalized to that of the perfect signatures. Light gray lines depict multiset signatures and dark gray lines depict separate ones. Solid line is regular and dashed line is parallel. The x axis represents the size of the filter. For example, the 64bit value means that separate signatures have been configured to use two 64bit filters, one for the RS and the other one for the WS, while multiset signatures use only

Table 1: Workloads: Input parameters and TM characteristics

Bench	Input	#xact	Time in xact	avg $|RS|$	avg $|WS|$	max $|RS|$	max $|WS|$
Bayes	-v32 -r1024 -n2 -p20 -s0 -i2 -e2	523	94%	76.9	40.9	2067	1613
Genome	-g512 -s64 -n8192	30304	86%	12.1	4.2	400	156
Intruder	-a10 -l128 -n128 -s1	12123	96%	19.1	2.5	267	20
Kmeans	-m40 -n40 -t0.05 -i rand-n1024-d1024-c16	1380	6%	99.7	48.5	134	65
Labyrinth	-i rand-x32-y32-z3-n64	158	100%	76.5	62.9	278	257
SSCA2	-s13 -i1.0 -u1.0 -l3 -p3	47295	19%	2.9	1.9	3	2
Vacation	-n4 -q60 -u90 -r16384 -t4096	24722	97%	19.7	3.6	90	30
Yada	-a20 -i 633.2	5384	100%	62.7	38.4	776	510

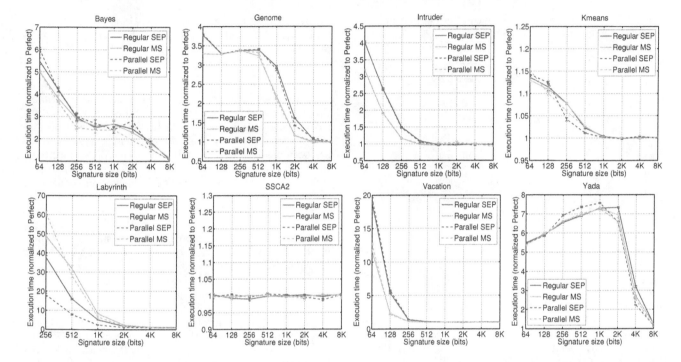

Figure 9: Execution time normalized to perfect signatures (no false positives) comparing regular and parallel separate signatures (SEP) to regular and parallel multiset ones (MS).

one 128bit filter. Let's see that benchmarks can be classified into three behavioral groups:

1. SSCA2: This benchmark is not signature dependent because of its small transactions, the smallest of the whole suite as can be seen in Table 1. In addition, it spends most of the time outside transactions.

2. Bayes, Genome, Intruder, Vacation and Yada: These five workloads behave better when using multiset signatures instead of separate ones.

   Bayes and Yada get a slight improvement of their execution time for certain signature sizes. About 1.2× for Bayes with parallel small signatures and 1.2× for Yada with regular large ones. These benchmarks show large transactions that introduce *cross false positives*. Cross false positives appear in multiset signatures as filter fills. For example, if one transaction reads lots of memory locations the filter will be filled with ones. Then, if no write has been introduced but a test for a write occurs, it could yield a cross false positive, because of filter occupancy, if such a test checks four bits that have been set to 1 by several reads.

On the other hand, Genome, Intruder and Vacation perform better using multiset signatures. Genome is 1.4× faster with filters of 1Kbit and 2Kbit, Intruder also exhibits about 1.4× speedup from 256Kbit filter downwards, and up to 2.5× of speedup is achieved for Vacation. These three benchmarks show relatively small transactions in average (see Table 1) and get not too much affected by cross false positives.

3. Kmeans and Labyrinth: Multiset signatures do not properly work with these workloads. Regular MS signatures perform like regular SEP ones for Kmeans but parallel MS ones perform worse for some filter sizes. In the case of Labyrinth, multiset signatures perform much worse than separate filters specially for parallel ones. Labyrinth's transactions are large in average and many cross false positives come up because of occupancy of the filter. Next sections propose certain configuration enhancements that will ameliorate filter occupancy.

Parallel multiset signatures perform similar than general ones for most cases as shown in Figure 9 and require much

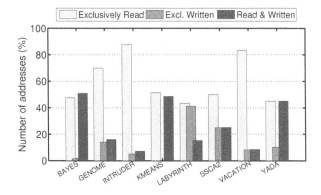

Figure 10: Percentage of addresses that have been both read and written inside transactions.

less area (see Section 5.5). Therefore, subsequent optimizations have been explored using the parallel scheme.

5.3 Parallel Multiset Shared Signature Results

Parallel multiset shared signature design and implementation were described in Section 3.3. The motivation behind such a signature comes from Figure 10 which shows the percentage of addresses that have been both read and written inside transactions for each benchmark. Actually, three bars can be seen per benchmark, from left to right: (i) the number of addresses exclusively read; (ii) the number of addresses exclusively written; and (iii) the number of addresses read and written with respect to the total number of addresses (without repetition). For example, Bayes, Kmeans and Yada exhibit close to 100% of written addresses that have been also read. Overall, about 30% of total locations addressed by each benchmark has been both read and written.

Given that the percentage of addresses both read and written inside transactions is not inconsiderable, next step is to figure out the number of hash functions that can be shared by read set and write set in multiset signatures without losing performance. For that purpose, experiments were conducted where shared functions ranges from 0, which is equivalent to having a parallel multiset signature, to 4 functions, which means that every insertion into the read set is also an insertion into the write set and vice versa.

Figure 11 shows the execution time of parallel multiset shared signatures. As read set and write set hash functions are shared the results get better for all the benchmarks. In fact, MS shared 4 gets the best results for every workload except Bayes and Genome, which execution is slowed down about 1.25× with respect to parallel filters for 8Kbit signatures. Therefore, parallel multiset shared 3 signatures should be used instead of shared 4 since they perform equal or better than parallel separate filters for all signature sizes, while shared 4 signatures perform slightly better than shared 3 for small signature sizes but perform worse than parallel SEP ones for large signatures.

5.4 Parallel Multiset Shared Locality Signature Results

In this section, locality-sensitive hashing [21] is used to enhance parallel multiset shared 3 signatures described in Section 5.3.

Locality-sensitive hashing is able to take advantage of locality of reference, a property which every application exhibits to some extent, to store an address stream more concisely. In a Bloom filter with locality-sensitive hash functions, nearby locations assert non-disjoint bits into the bit array saving in occupancy. Table 2 shows how the locality hash functions operate. Let's see that, for contiguous addresses, the number of hashing outputs with different values is 1. Addresses with distance 2 are different in no more than 2 hashing outputs and, addresses with distance greater than $2^{k-1} - 1$ may have no hashing outputs in common.

Figure 12 shows the results of combining parallel multiset shared 3 signatures with locality-sensitive hashing. Two different combinations are shown:

- Loc1: Shared 3 signatures share hash functions h_1, h_2 and h_3 while h_0 and h'_0 functions remains separate (see Section 3.3) and assert different bits in the same filter, ones for the read set and others for the write set. Locality 1 scheme makes that h_0 and h'_0 behave as h^l_3 in Table 2, h_1 behaves as h^l_2, h_2 behaves as h^l_1 and h_3 behaves as h^l_0. This way, separate functions that discriminate locations from the read set, h_0, from locations from the write set, h'_0, assert less bits in its filter reducing the false positive rate, but the filter fails to discriminate locations read from nearby located writes.

- Loc2: In this case, h_3 behaves as h^l_3, h_2 behaves as h^l_2, h_1 behaves as h^l_1 and h_0 and h'_0 behaves as h^l_0, i.e. the filter which does not share the hash functions stay the same as in shared 3 configuration, thus discriminating between locations read and written, and the other filters get the locality improvement.

As Figure 12 shows, results for Loc1 scheme are practically the same than those for Loc2 for every benchmark but for Labyrinth, Genome and Yada. Labyrinth behaves better with Loc2 for small signatures and, Genome and Yada get slightly worse results for small signatures and Loc2. MS shared locality signatures outperform parallel and locality separate ones in most of cases. Loc2 is 2.4× faster than SEP and 1.5× faster than SEP Loc signatures for Bayes and 2Kbit filters. Genome shows a speedup of 2× using Loc2 compared to SEP and 1.6× compared to SEP Loc and 1Kbit filters. Intruder shows same speedups from 128bit downwards. Kmeans is 1.1× faster than SEP for small signatures. For Labyrinth, Loc2 shows up to 7× speedup over SEP signatures and 4× over SEP Loc for 256bit signatures. Vacation is 3× faster using Loc2 instead of SEP and SEP Loc for 64 and 128bit filters. Finally, Yada is 2× faster than SEP and SEP Loc using Loc2 for 1Kbit to 4Kbit reaching a peak of 5× over SEP for 2Kbit, though it slows down the execution about 1.2× for small filters.

5.5 Hardware Area and Energy Requirements

In this section an analysis of area and energy requirements for the multiset signatures compared to the separate ones is conducted. Area models from CACTI [29] have been used for that purpose.

Table 3 shows area results for different filter sizes. "Filter size" row stands for the size of one set filter, i.e. 4Kbit means two filters of 4Kbit (for RS and WS) for separate signatures and one filter of 8Kbit for multiset ones. CACTI 6.5 [20] was used to model the SRAMs using the 32nm process. Regular

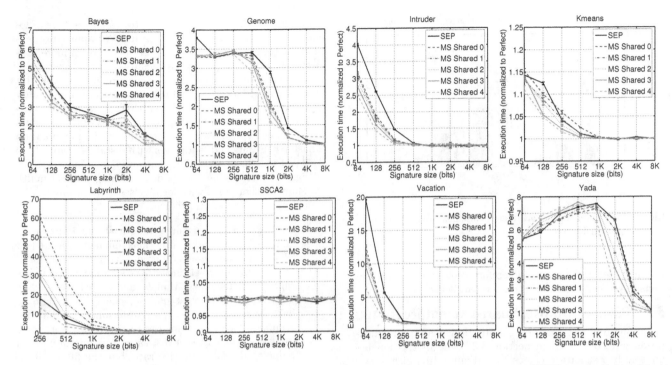

Figure 11: Execution time normalized to perfect signatures comparing parallel separate signatures (SEP) to parallel multiset shared signatures varying the shared functions between 0 (no shared functions) and 4 (all functions shared).

Table 2: Example of locality-sensitive hashing: addresses and its indexes for a Bloom with $k=4$, $2^m=1024$

Address	h_0^l	h_1^l	h_2^l	h_3^l
0xffff0	240	158	889	554
0xffff1	586	158	889	554
0xffff2	90	347	889	554
0xffff3	736	347	889	554
0xffff4	181	906	484	554
0xffff5	527	906	484	554
0xffff6	31	591	484	554
0xffff7	677	591	484	554
0xffff8	718	497	62	163
0xffff9	116	497	62	163
0xffffa	612	52	62	163
0xffffb	222	52	62	163
0xffffc	651	741	675	163
0xffffd	49	741	675	163
0xffffe	545	800	675	163
0xfffff	155	800	675	163

Table 3: Area (mm^2) requirements of separate and multiset signatures. 32nm technology. $k = 4$ hash functions.

Filter size (2^m)	4Kbit	8Kbit	16Kbit
Regular SEP	0.0707	0.1041	0.2540
Regular MS	0.1860	0.4600	0.6776
Parallel SEP	0.0084	0.0135	0.0292
Parallel MS	0.0191	0.0435	0.0640
Parallel MS 3-shared	0.0098	0.0219	0.0331

Table 4: Dynamic energy per access (nJ). 32nm. $k = 4$

Filter size (2^m)	4Kbit	8Kbit	16Kbit
Regular SEP	0.0074	0.0112	0.0219
Regular MS	0.0180	0.0347	0.0623
Parallel SEP	0.0020	0.0025	0.0047
Parallel MS	0.0030	0.0056	0.0081
Parallel MS 3-shared	0.0026	0.0049	0.0068

SEP signatures have two 4-ported SRAMs (one for the RS and one for the WS) since $k = 4$, with separate read/write ports. Regular MS signatures have one 8-ported SRAMs and also separate read/write ports. Parallel SEP signatures comprise eight single-ported SRAMs while parallel MS ones have four double-ported SRAMs. Finally, parallel MS shared 3 signatures have three single-ported SRAMs and only one double-ported SRAM. Ports are dual-ended which means that two lines are required per bitline.

A non-linear behavior can be appreciated in area results for the different array sizes. It is related to CACTI's optimization function which searches for the best partition of the cell array depending on time, power and area efficiency. For example, for 4Kbit regular filters 8 byte words were used re-

sulting a 64×64 bit array. Then CACTI found that the best partition was 4 subarrays by splitting bitlines and wordlines in halves. However, for 8Kbit, 8 byte words were used too, resulting a 128×64 bit array. CACTI also found the best partition to be 4 subarrays but it multiplexed the bitlines to share senses amplifiers, which remained constant, thus providing better area efficiency (memory cell area/total area).

As shown in Table 3, parallel SEP signatures are significantly better than regular SEP configurations. Actually, they get $8\times$ less area. On the other hand, regular MS signatures get the largest area of all. This is because of the multi-ported SRAM which needs 8 ports, four more than the separate one. Regarding the parallel MS signature, it is about twice larger than the parallel signature due to its double-ported SRAMs. The last configuration of MS signa-

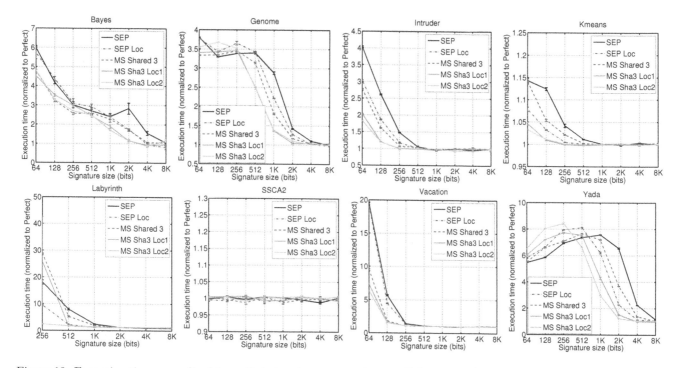

Figure 12: Execution time normalized to perfect signatures comparing parallel separate (SEP), parallel locality separate (SEP Loc) and parallel multiset shared 3 signatures enhanced with locality-sensitive hashing (Loc1 and Loc2).

ture, the 3-shared, is the closest to parallel one in terms of area, it is only a 13% larger because of the double-ported SRAM. However, parallel MS shared 3 signatures outperforms parallel SEP ones as seen in Section 5.4. Therefore, the slight increment in area could be worth.

Regarding energy, Table 4 shows a 30% increment in dynamic read energy consumption per access for parallel MS shared 3 signatures compared to parallel separate ones due to the double-ported SRAM. Regular MS signatures consume more than twice the energy of regular SEP signatures. However, access time is barely affected, e.g. 0.13ns for 4Kbit parallel SEP signatures and 0.14ns for its MS counterpart. Like area, these values concern the SRAMs excluding the hashing logic.

Finally, Sanchez et al. [25] worked out the hashing logic area for 4 XOR hash functions resulting in one-fifth of the SRAM area. Such an area can be halved using PBX hashing [31] without impact in the performance.

6. CONCLUSIONS

In the context of transactional memory, we propose a multiset signature scheme which records both the read and write sets in the same Bloom filter without adding significant hardware complexity. We evaluate and analyze several designs of multiset signatures. New problems arise related to hardware complexity and the existence of cross false positives, i.e. new false positives coming from the fact that both sets share the same filter. Additionally, we enhance multiset signatures using locality-sensitive hashing, proposed by the authors in a previous work.

The proposed multiset and locality-sensitive multiset signatures are implemented in the Wisconsin GEMS simulator, in order to evaluate their performance, and in CACTI in order to evaluate the hardware area and energy requirements.

Experimental results show that the multiset approach reduces the false positive rate and improve the execution performance in most of the tested codes, without increasing the required hardware area in a noticeable amount.

We may conclude that multiset and locality-sensitive multiset signatures are a good alternative to non-multiset ones since they yield similar or better performance without significantly increasing the hardware cost.

7. ACKNOWLEDGMENTS

The authors would like to thank Dr. Luke Yen for providing his patches to adapt STAMP workloads to GEMS simulator. This work has been supported by the Ministry of Education of Spain with project CICYT TIN2006-01078 and by the Junta de Andalucia with project P08-TIC-04341.

8. REFERENCES

[1] A. R. Alameldeen and D. A. Wood. Variability in architectural simulations of multi-threaded workloads. In *9th Int'l Symp. on High-Performance Computer Architecture (HPCA'03)*, pages 7–18, 2003.

[2] C. Ananian, K. Asanovic, B. Kuszmaul, C. Leiserson, and S. Lie. Unbounded transactional memory. In *11th Int'l. Symp. on High-Performance Computer Architecture (HPCA'05)*, pages 316–327, 2005.

[3] B. Bloom. Space/time trade-offs in hash coding with allowable errors. *Communications of the ACM*, 13(7):422–426, 1970.

[4] L. Carter and M. Wegman. Universal classes of hash functions. *J. Computer and System Sciences*, 18(2):143–154, 1979.

[5] L. Ceze, J. Tuck, P. Montesinos, and J. Torrellas. BulkSC: Bulk enforcement of sequential consistency.

In *34th Ann. Int'l. Symp. on Computer Architecture (ISCA'07)*, pages 278–289, 2007.

[6] L. Ceze, J. Tuck, J. Torrellas, and C. Cascaval. Bulk disambiguation of speculative threads in multiprocessors. In *33th Ann. Int'l. Symp. on Computer Architecture (ISCA'06)*, pages 227–238, 2006.

[7] W. Choi and J. Draper. Locality-aware adaptive grain signatures for transactional memories. In *IEEE Int'l. Symp. on Parallel and Distributed Processing (IPDPS'10)*, pages 1–10, 2010.

[8] D. Dice, Y. Lev, M. Moir, and D. Nussbaum. Early experience with a commercial hardware transactional memory implementation. In *14th Int'l. Conf. on Architectural Support for Programming Language and Operating Systems (ASPLOS'09)*, pages 157–168, 2009.

[9] D. Geer. Industry trends: Chip makers turn to multicore processors. *IEEE Computer*, 38(5):11–13, 2005.

[10] L. Hammond, V. Wong, M. Chen, B. Carlstrom, J. Davis, B. Hertzberg, M. Prabhu, H. Wijaya, C. Kozyrakis, and K. Olukotun. Transactional memory coherence and consistency. In *31th Ann. Int'l. Symp. on Computer Architecture (ISCA'04)*, pages 102–113, 2004.

[11] M. Herlihy and J. Moss. Transactional memory: Architectural support for lock-free data structures. In *20th Ann. Int'l. Symp. on Computer Architecture (ISCA'93)*, pages 289–300, 1993.

[12] M. Labrecque, M. Jeffrey, and J. Gregory Steffan. Application-specific signatures for transactional memory in soft processors. In *6th Int'l. Symp. on Applied Reconfigurable Computing (ARC'10)*, 2010.

[13] J. Larus and R. Rajwar. *Transactional Memory*. Morgan & Claypool Pub., 2007.

[14] P. Magnusson, M. Christensson, J. Eskilson, D. Forsgren, G. Hallberg, J. Hogberg, F. Larsson, A. Moestedt, B. Werner, and B. Werner. Simics: A full system simulation platform. *IEEE Computer*, 35(2):50–58, 2002.

[15] M. Martin, D. Sorin, B. Beckmann, M. Marty, M. Xu, A. Alameldeen, K. Moore, M. Hill, and D. Wood. Multifacet's general execution-driven multiprocessor simulator GEMS toolset. *ACM SIGARCH Comput. Archit. News*, 33(4):92–99, 2005.

[16] M. Mehrara, J. Hao, P.-C. Hsu, and S. Mahlke. Parallelizing sequential applications on commodity hardware using a low-cost software transactional memory. In *ACM SIGPLAN Conf. on Programming Language Design and Implementation (PLDI'09)*, pages 166–176, 2009.

[17] C. Minh, J. Chung, C. Kozyrakis, and K. Olukotun. STAMP: Stanford Transactional Applications for Multi-Processing. In *IEEE Int'l Symp. on Workload Characterization (IISWC'08)*, pages 35–46, 2008.

[18] C. Minh, M. Trautmann, J. Chung, A. McDonald, N. Bronson, J. Casper, C. Kozyrakis, and K. Olukotun. An effective hybrid transactional memory system with strong isolation guarantees. In *34th Ann. Int'l. Symp. on Computer Architecture (ISCA'07)*, pages 69–80, 2007.

[19] K. Moore, J. Bobba, M. Moravan, M. Hill, and D. Wood. LogTM: Log-based transactional memory. In *12th Int'l. Symp. on High-Performance Computer Architecture (HPCA'06)*, pages 254–265, 2006.

[20] N. Muralimanohar, R. Balasubramonian, and N. Jouppi. CACTI 6.0: A tool to model large caches. Technical Report HPL-2009-85, HP Laboratories, 2009.

[21] R. Quislant, E. Gutierrez, O. Plata, and E. Zapata. Improving signatures by locality exploitation for transactional memory. In *Int'l Conf. on Parallel Architectures and Compilation Techniques (PACT'09)*, pages 303–312, 2009.

[22] R. Rajwar, M. Herlihy, and K. Lai. Virtualizing transactional memory. In *32th Ann. Int'l. Symp. on Computer Architecture (ISCA'05)*, pages 494–505, 2005.

[23] M. V. Ramakrishna, E. Fu, and E. Bahcekapili. Efficient hardware hashing functions for high performance computers. *IEEE Trans. on Computers*, 46(12):1378–1381, 1997.

[24] B. Saha, A.-R. Adl-Tabatabai, and Q. Jacobson. Architectural support for software transactional memory. In *39st Ann. IEEE/ACM Int'l Symp. on Microarchitecture (MICRO'06)*, pages 185–196, 2006.

[25] D. Sanchez, L. Yen, M. Hill, and K. Sankaralingam. Implementing signatures for transactional memory. In *40th Ann. IEEE/ACM Int'l Symp. on Microarchitecture (MICRO'07)*, pages 123–133, 2007.

[26] A. Shriraman, S. Dwarkadas, and M. Scott. Flexible decoupled transactional memory support. In *35th Ann. Int'l. Symp. on Computer Architecture (ISCA'08)*, pages 139–150, 2008.

[27] A. Shriraman, M. Spear, H. Hossain, V. Marathe, S. Dwarkadas, and M. Scott. An integrated hardware-software approach to flexible transactional memory. In *34th Ann. Int'l. Symp. on Computer Architecture (ISCA'07)*, pages 104–115, 2007.

[28] S. Tomic, C. Perfumo, C. Kulkarni, A. Armejach, A. Cristal, O. Unsal, T. Harris, and M. Valero. EazyHTM: Eager-lazy hardware transactional memory. In *42st Ann. IEEE/ACM Int'l Symp. on Microarchitecture (MICRO'09)*, pages 145–155, 2009.

[29] S. Wilton and N. Jouppi. CACTI: an enhanced cache access and cycle time model. *IEEE Journal of Solid-State Circuits*, 31(5):677–688, 1996.

[30] L. Yen, J. Bobba, M. Marty, K. Moore, H. Volos, M. Hill, M. Swift, and D. Wood. LogTM-SE: Decoupling hardware transactional memory from caches. In *13th Int'l. Symp. on High-Performance Computer Architecture (HPCA'07)*, pages 261–272, 2007.

[31] L. Yen, S. Draper, and M. Hill. Notary: Hardware techniques to enhance signatures. In *41st Ann. IEEE/ACM Int'l Symp. on Microarchitecture (MICRO'08)*, pages 234–245, 2008.

ZEBRA: A Data-Centric, Hybrid-Policy Hardware Transactional Memory Design

Rubén Titos-Gil
Universidad de Murcia, Spain
rtitos@ditec.um.es

Anurag Negi
Chalmers University of
Technology, Sweden
negi@chalmers.se

Manuel E. Acacio
Universidad de Murcia, Spain
meacacio@ditec.um.es

José M. García
Universidad de Murcia, Spain
jmgarcia@ditec.um.es

Per Stenstrom
Chalmers University of
Technology, Sweden
per.stenstrom@chalmers.se

ABSTRACT

Hardware Transactional Memory (HTM) systems, in prior research, have either fixed policies of conflict resolution and data versioning for the entire system or allowed a degree of flexibility at the level of transactions. Unfortunately, this results in susceptibility to pathologies, lower average performance over diverse workload characteristics or high design complexity. In this work we explore a new dimension along which flexibility in policy can be introduced. Recognizing the fact that contention is more a property of data rather than that of an atomic code block, we develop an HTM system that allows selection of versioning and conflict resolution policies at the granularity of cache lines. We discover that this neat match in granularity with that of the cache coherence protocol results in a design that is very simple and yet able to track closely or exceed the performance of the best performing policy for a given workload. It also brings together the benefits of parallel commits (inherent in traditional eager HTMs) and good optimistic concurrency without deadlock avoidance mechanisms (inherent in lazy HTMs), with little increase in complexity.

Categories and Subject Descriptors

D.1.3 [**Programming Techniques**]: Concurrent Programming;
C.1.4 [**Processor architectures**]: Parallel Architectures

General Terms

Performance, Design, Experimentation

Keywords

Hardware Transactional Memory, Contention Management

1. INTRODUCTION

Fast implementations of transactional programming constructs that provide optimistic concurrency control with stringent guar-

antees of atomicity and isolation are necessary for Transactional Memory (TM) to gain widespread usage. Software TM (STM) implementations impose too high an overhead and do not fare well against traditional lock based approaches when performance is important. Hardware TM (HTM) systems show much greater promise. Yet, within the design space of HTM systems, there are tradeoffs to be made among various pertinent metrics like design complexity, speed and scalability. Early work on HTM proposals [6] [19] fixed critical TM policies like versioning (how speculative updates in transactions are dealt with) and conflict resolution (how and when races between concurrent transactions are resolved). These designs choose a point in the HTM design space and analyze utilization of available concurrency in multithreaded applications within that framework.

Results in research so far do not show a clear winner or an optimal design point. Lazy HTMs, that confine speculative updates locally and run past data races until a transaction ends, do seem to be more efficient at extracting concurrency [16] but require elaborate schemes [5][13] to make race free publication of speculative updates (i.e. transaction commit) scalable. Eager HTMs, that version data in place and resolve conflicts as they occur, make such publication rather trivial at the expense of complicating behavior when speculative execution needs to be undone to avoid data races (i.e. transaction abort). Eager HTMs fit very naturally into existing scalable cache coherent architectures and can tolerate spills of speculative data into the shared memory hierarchy, unlike their lazy counterparts. When comparing the performance of the two such designs, a clear winner cannot be established. With workloads that demand high commit throughput eager systems perform substantially better, while with high contention workloads lazy designs come out on top.

This reasoning suggests that a new HTM design that selects the best performing policy (eager or lazy) depending on workload characteristics would be close to the most suitable HTM design for the scalable architectures under consideration. A key factor would then be the complexity involved in realizing such a design in hardware. Some solutions have been proposed that attempt to provide a hybrid-policy HTM design. UTCP [8] is a cache coherence protocol that allows transactions in a multithreaded application run either eagerly or lazily based on some heuristics like prior behavior of transactions. Although it lays down an interesting approach, the authors feel that the protocol is a significant departure from existing cache coherence designs and the additional complexity involved for just supporting TM represents too high a design cost. FlexTM [16] allows flexibility in policy but it does so by implementing critical

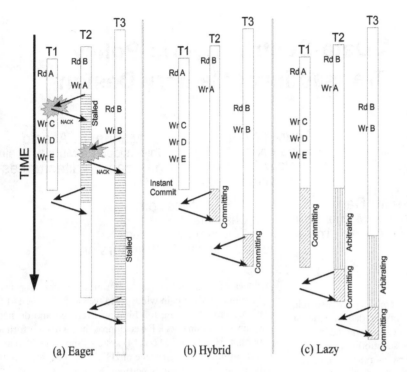

Figure 1: Behavioral differences between different HTM design points.

policy managers in software. It provides a significant improvement in speed over software TM implementations by proposing the use of Alert-On-Update (AOU) hardware, but the considerable cost of software intervention renders a comparison with pure HTMs moot. LV* [12], a proposal that utilizes snoopy coherence, allows programmer control over policy in hardware but with the constraint that all transactions in an application must use the same policy at any given time. A scalable alternative has not yet been proposed. The requirement of programmer-assisted policy change is a drawback too since the same phase of an application can exhibit different behavior with varying datasets.

In this work we propose a solution that is simple and yet powerful and flexible. We recognize the fact that assuming all data accessed in a transaction possesses the same characteristics can lead to sub-optimal solutions. Based on our study of conventional HTM design points we infer that only a relatively small fraction of data accessed inside transactions is actively contended. The rest is either thread-private (stack or thread-local memory) or not actively contended. Treating these two categories of data the same inside transactions leads to inefficiencies – a prolonged publication phase at commit when using a lazy design or increased contention leading to expensive aborts when using an eager approach. This work attempts to break this restriction by choosing a granularity for data at which minimal changes are required in existing scalable architectures – that of the cache line. Efficient scalable cache coherence implementations exist and have been extensively studied for a long time. Our design leverages these by annotating cache lines as being either contended or not. Contended lines are managed lazily thereby permitting greatest concurrency among transactions. It should be noted that eager systems disallow reader-writer concurrency while in lazy systems it can occur quite naturally if the reader commits before the writer. All non-contended lines are versioned eagerly and thus, on transaction commit, only contended lines need to be published. When contention is discovered (e.g. when aborting

or stalling) the offending cache line(s) is (are) marked as contended. Over the course of execution of a workload, versioning of lines that are contended transitions from eager to lazy. In the steady state we can expect only the contended subset of the working dataset to be managed lazily. As we shall show in the analysis presented here, substantial gains over existing fixed policy HTM designs can be seen. The incremental cost of implementing this approach is minimal since only very modest behavioral changes are required in the cache coherence protocol. We call this hybrid-policy HTM protocol *ZEBRA*. An African folktale speaks of how the white zebra fell into a fire and burning sticks scorched black stripes on its flawless coat. Here, transactions manage data purely eagerly (white) to begin with but acquire lazy lines (black stripes) when they conflict (fall into a fire).

Figure 1 depicts an interleaving of three concurrent transactions and highlights some important behavioural aspects of our proposal. In the eager case (Figure 1-a), we see that although transactions *T1* and *T3* are independent, *T3* is stalled because of a chain of dependencies created via transaction *T2*. This does not occur in the hybrid-policy ZEBRA design (Figure 1-b) or the purely lazy case (Figure 1-c) and in the example shown all three transactions commit without conflicts. It should be noted here that in the hybrid case writes to A and B by T2 and T3 are managed lazily, since the lines were annotated as contended at an earlier stage of the execution. On the other hand, in the lazy case *T2*'s commit is delayed because *T1*, having a relatively large write-set, has locked resources that *T2* needs to publish its updates. This in turn delays *T3*'s commit. In the hybrid scenario *T1* is able to perform an instant commit since none of the lines in its write-set are contended and, hence, are managed eagerly, allowing *T2* and *T3* to proceed with their commit operations without any delay on account of *T1*.

There are certain other benefits that stem from using such an approach. Deadlock avoidance mechanisms are not required since contended lines are eventually managed lazily, thereby guarantee-

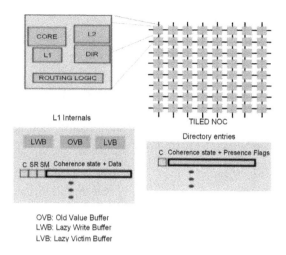

L1 Internals

OVB: Old Value Buffer
LWB: Lazy Write Buffer
LVB: Lazy Victim Buffer

Figure 2: ZEBRA – Salient architectural features

ing forward progress. Significant reductions in transaction commit delays result in a major contraction of the window of contention for concurrent transactions. The burden on lazy versioning mechanisms is considerably reduced enabling much larger transactions to run without resorting to safety nets (like serialization via a single global lock). This effect combines synergistically with a coherence-decoupled lazy version buffer – write-write conflicts, downgrade and abort misses (defined later) can be largely eliminated, amplifying gains achieved from the central idea. Since the design does not lock policy it can adapt to changing workload conditions and is resistant to pathologies that fixed policy HTMs suffer from. The authors feel that this proposal touches upon a sweet spot in the HTM design space that offers both simplicity of design and robust performance.

The rest of this paper is organized as follows. Section 2 describes the salient architectural and behavioral features of the ZEBRA HTM protocol. Section 3 first describes the experimental methodology adopted to evaluate our approach, and then presents our results and analyses. Section 4 puts our work here in perspective of other work in HTM systems on related issues. Section 5 summarizes the paper and looks at future work that can be done to build upon the ideas presented here.

2. DESIGN AND OPERATION

2.1 Conceptual Overview

We choose a tiled CMP (chip multiprocessor) architecture where each tile comprises a processing core, a slice of a shared inclusive L2 cache and corresponding directory entries. The tiles are interconnected by a mesh-based routing network. Figure 2 shows the salient features of the architectural framework. Each processing core has private Level 1 instruction and data caches. The directory keeps private caches coherent using a MESI protocol. Two single-bit speculative access annotations are maintained at the private caches for each cache line - SR (for speculatively read lines) and SM (for speculatively modified lines). Such annotations have been used by several prior HTM proposals [6, 11] to track transactional reads and writes. Read set signatures [4] are employed to permit speculatively read lines to be evicted from private caches.

In order to track contention in the ZEBRA HTM design, we extend per-cache line metadata at the directory and at the private caches with just one additional bit – *"contended bit"* – hereafter referred to as the *C-bit*. The C-bit is transported with all coher-

ence requests and data responses. A C-bit value of "1" indicates that the line has experienced contention in the past. The bit is reset if a line is flushed from the on-chip cache hierarchy or when a non-transactional update is seen by the directory.

The number of contended lines accessed by a transaction is usually quite small in the workloads we have experimented with. Keeping such writes away from the cache improves performance by reducing the number of *contamination misses*[18] – misses due to invalidation of speculatively updated lines on aborts – and redundant permission downgrades from exclusive or dirty state to shared state (which we term *downgrade misses*) that allow detection of conflicts. Moreover, this also mitigates the effect of false writer-writer conflicts. Therefore, we deemed it prudent to introduce a *Lazy Write Buffer (LWB)* to contain speculative updates to contended lines. This buffer is sized to be large enough to accommodate the contended fraction of the write set of a transaction in the common case. We have found that a 32-word buffer is sufficient to handle most commonly occurring cases. This buffer is drained when committing a transaction and discarded when aborting. Writes buffered in this structure do not participate in coherence until the transaction starts commit. Occasional situations when the buffer is completely filled up are handled by buffering subsequent contended-line updates in the cache. Prior to such a cache line update, non-exclusive (shared) access is acquired to the line (line-fill if not present; or downgrade to shared with write-back if dirty) in order to preserve its old value. Figure 4 shows how writes from the processor are dealt with by the private cache controller. To minimize the possibility of spilling lazy speculative state from the L1 cache we prioritize retention of such lines in the private cache and add a small (4 cache lines) *Lazy Victim Buffer (LVB)* to contain rare spills due to limited associativity. This approach works well for the workloads considered here. In the rare case of spills of contended lines, we enforce serialization.

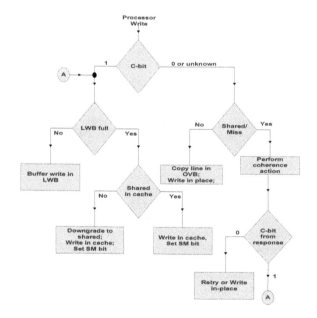

Figure 4: Write handling at the private cache.

Updates to lines that are either non-contended or have unknown C-bit status bypass this buffer (see Figure 4) . This can cause coherence requests to be issued to the directory if L1 line-fill or write permissions are required. If the result of a coherence operation indi-

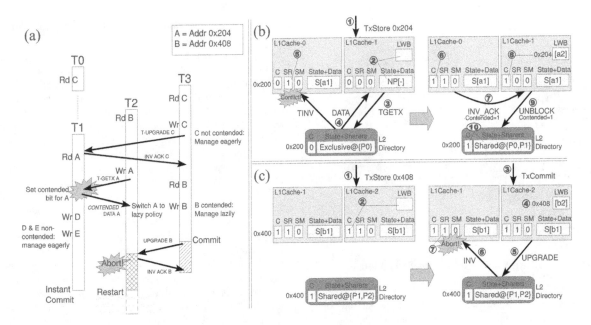

Figure 3: ZEBRA – Key protocol actions.

cates that the line is contended, the write is buffered in the LWB. In either case, the line is allocated in the cache (if not already present) and its C-bit state is updated. If the C-bit is not set, the update happens in place and the old contents of the line are recorded in an *Old Value Buffer (OVB)* or written to a thread-private log in virtual memory in case OVB capacity is exceeded. This aspect of eager behavior is similar to that of LogTM [19].

A transaction with no updates to contended lines can commit without delay, permitting true commit parallelism in such a case. If there are some lazy updates, they must be validated and made globally visible. We adopt the simplest possible approach to do so by having the committer acquire a global commit token. Our results show that in workloads where lazy conflict resolution yields best results we compete very well against or better the performance of the more sophisticated scalable commit approach adopted by STCC [5]. While a more scalable lazy commit scheme would further enhance our proposal, the design choice is orthogonal to the key ideas described in this work. All writes in the LWB are made globally visible at commit. All lines in the shared (S) state in cache with SM indicator set are upgraded to modified (M) state after the directory grants exclusive permissions to the line.

All coherence messages generated in response to speculative accesses by the core are distinguished from ordinary ones by setting a special flag in such messages. An abort occurs when any non-speculative coherence message hits a line speculatively accessed by a transaction. It should be noted that invalidations that result when lazily managed lines are committed are non-transactional. For eagerly managed lines a requester-retry policy similar to the one adopted by LogTM [19] is used. If a cyclic dependency on eager lines is detected (refer usage of possible cycle flag in [19]) at one or more transactions in the dependency chain, they abort to break the deadlock. No software intervention is required. A unique aspect of our design is that offending cache lines will henceforth be treated lazily during re-execution and, thus, will no longer have the potential to cause deadlock. This effect renders LogTM's usage of TLR-like timestamps [14] unnecessary for guaranteeing forward progress.

C-bits at the directory are set when unblock messages sent by

cores to indicate completion of in-flight coherence operations indicate contention. Contention may be reported if a requester discovers a conflict with another transaction or when a committer publishes its contended lines. The directory reports this status in all subsequent coherence messages. The C-bit is cleared when a non-transactional update to the line is completed allowing memory to be recycled without the old C-bit value affecting behavior in the new usage context. In most applications it is highly unusual to find non-transactional updates to a cache line interleaved with transactional accesses. The C-bit is also cleared if a line must be evicted from the directory.

2.2 Protocol behavior

Standard directory-based MESI cache coherence is employed for detecting and managing conflicts. Coherence messages now contain two new flags - *transactional status* and *contended status*. An additional flag, *commit status* is added to UNBLOCK requests indicating whether they correspond to commit-time updates. Figure 3 depicts key protocol actions that occur when contended lines are accessed. All cache lines are managed eagerly by default.

Figure 3-b shows steps taken when a switch to lazy management occurs on encountering contention on a cache line for the first time. The transaction interleaving considered here is the one between transactions *T1* and *T2* shown in Figure 3-a. Core 1 (running *T2*) initiates a write to line A (address *0x204*, step 1). The store misses in the private cache structures (step 2) and results in a *TGETX* (GETX with transactional flag set) request to the directory (step 3). This coherence request results in a *TINV* (transactional invalidation) being sent to the reader, Core 0, and data being sent from the L2 to Core 1 (step 4). Core 0, running transaction *T1*, on receiving *TINV* checks if it is currently managing the line eagerly. It finds that it has only read the line transactionally (SR is set) (step 5). Hence it is in a position to forward data to Core 1 for lazy management (otherwise the requester would be stalled till T1 commits or aborts). It marks the line as contended in its private cache (step 6) causing any future write from Core 0 to be managed lazily. A acknowledgment with *contended status* is sent to Core 1 (step 7). Core 1 on receiving such a response places the line in

56

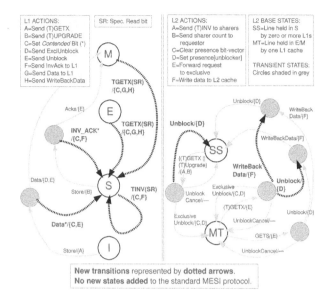

L1 ACTIONS:
A=Send (T)GETX
B=Send (T)UPGRADE
C=Set *Contended* Bit (*)
D=Send ExclUnblock
E=Send Unblock
F=Send InvAck to L1
G=Send Data to L1
H=Send WriteBackData

SR: Spec. Read bit

L2 ACTIONS:
A=Send (T)INV to sharers
B=Send sharer count to requestor
C=Clear presence bit-vector
D=Set presence[unblocker]
E=Forward request to exclusive
F=Write data to L2 cache

L2 BASE STATES:
SS=Line held in S by zero or more L1s
MT=Line held in E/M by one L1 cache

TRANSIENT STATES:
Circles shaded in grey

New transitions represented by **dotted arrows**.
No new states added to the standard MESI protocol.

Figure 5: Support for new transitions at L1 (left) and L2-directory (right) controllers.

shared state in its cache and sets the local C bit. The write, instead of updating the cache line, is now buffered in the LWB (step 8). It then indicates completion of the coherence operation by sending an *UNBLOCK* message with contended status to the directory (step 9). On finding a contended status in the *UNBLOCK* message the corresponding C-bit is set at the directory (step 10). The line will now be managed lazily by all accessors until a non-transactional access causes a C-bit reset.

Figure 3-c shows protocol actions that occur when lazily managed lines are published upon commit. The details correspond to interactions between transactions *T2* and *T3* in Figure 3-a. Core 2 (running *T3*) initiates a write to line B (address 0x408, step 1). The line is found in cache with C-bit set. Hence, the write is buffered in the LWB (step 2). When *T3* commits (step 3), it first acquires a global commit token. It then drains the LWB (step 4) acquiring exclusive ownership over line B by sending a non-transactional *UP-GRADE* request to the directory (step 5).The directory responds by sending a *INV* (non-transactional invalidation) set to Core 1 (step 6). *T2* on Core 1 aborts when a non-transactional invalidation conflicts with a speculatively accessed line (SR is set, step 7). Since *T2* had the lone lazy write to A in its write set, no old value restoration is required. LWB is reset and re-execution of *T2* can start immediately or when deemed right by a back-off algorithm. It should also be noticed that line C, also part of *T3*'s write set, does not need to be published since it was managed eagerly. Core-1 completes its upgrade operation by sending an *UNBLOCK* message to the directory. This message has the *commit flag* set, causing the directory to maintain a value of 1 for the C-bit. Ordinary requests for exclusive ownership generated from non-transactional code result in *UNBLOCK* messages without the *commit-flag* set and cause the directory to reset the bit.

Cache controllers at both L1 and the L2-directory now support a few new transitions summarized in Figure 5. New transitions are represented by black dotted lines in the figure, while transitions that already exist in the baseline MESI protocol are shown in light grey. For clarity, only states and baseline transitions that aid in illustrating the changes are shown. At the directory level, the behavior of *TGETX/TUPGRADE* requests is similar to that of their non-transactional counterparts, but the transactional variants can even-

tually result in the reception of *contended UNBLOCK* messages that cause a transition to shared state (SS). For example, a *TGETX* from Core 3 could cause a directory transition from *SS@{1,2}* (shared by Cores 1 and 2) to *SS@{1,2,3}* if contention is detected. This permits lazy versioning of contended data at the new requester while still allowing conflict detection to happen. Similarly, the transition from *MT@{2}* (exclusive/dirty at Core 2) to *SS@{1,2}* is supported when handling *TGETX* requests. Such a situation might arise if Core 2 forwards a contended line to Core 1, behaving as if the request had been a GETS (the line is also written back to L2). At the L1, we support transitions to shared state on local write misses and upon receiving *TGETX* or *TINV* requests from the directory. This allows coherence mechanisms to be used to detect conflicts on such data after this event has occurred.

The examples above highlight key behavioral aspects of the ZE-BRA protocol. Other cases are handled in a similar fashion. If a transaction is managing a line eagerly, it is given a chance to reach commit by permitting it to stall other requesters. When such events occurred the C-bit for the line is set. This causes the line to be managed lazily once the transaction commits or aborts. The risk of deadlocks is avoided by using a LogTM-like *possible-cycle* bit, but in a different way. The bit is set if the transaction has stalled a requester attempting to access eagerly managed data. When a transaction is stalled by another, it checks if *possible-cycle* flag is set. An abort is triggered if so. The eagerly managed line will henceforth be managed lazily and will no longer be able to cause deadlocks. Transaction timestamps, employed by LogTM for conservative deadlock avoidance, are no longer transported in coherence messages.

Coherence requests generated by non-transactional codes result in an abort if they hit a transactionally accessed line. The flexibility to ask for the requester to retry such requests can be incorporated by transporting the *commit status* flag with invalidation messages. This flag would be set for non-transactional invalidations sent out when the lazy portion of a transaction's write-set is being committed. The receiver, if transactional, would then know that it cannot ask for a retry and must abort if such an invalidation is hits a speculatively accessed line.

3. METHODOLOGY AND EVALUATION

3.1 Experimental Setup

We use a full-system execution-driven simulator based on the Wisconsin GEMS tool-set (v2.1) [10], in conjunction with Wind River Simics [9]. We use the detailed timing model for the memory subsystem provided by GEMS, with the Simics in-order processor model. Simics provides functional simulation of the SPARC-V9 ISA and boots an unmodified Solaris 10 operating system. This simulation infrastructure provides support for LogTM-SE [19], as well as an implementation of a global commit token-based, lazy-lazy (LL) HTM system described by Bobba et al. in [2]. We extend it with detailed implementations of STCC [5] and ZEBRA, our hybrid-policy HTM protocol, allowing fair comparison of several major HTM design points within the same architectural framework. While Bobba's LL system models a private, per processor infinite write buffer, for this study we extended the simulator to precisely model finite buffering for transactional writes. Special status bits are added to coherence messages. Behavior of cache and directory controllers is suitably modified. We use an ideal book-keeping scheme to track read sets (*perfect signatures*) even when some speculatively read lines have been evicted, in an attempt to isolate our study from the effects of false conflicts arising from non-ideal signature schemes like bloom filters.

Table 1: System parameters.

MESI Directory-based CMP	
Core Settings	
Cores	16, single issue
	in-order, non-memory IPC=1
Memory and Directory Settings	
L1 I&D caches	Private, 32KB, split
	4-way, 1-cycle latency
Write Buffer	Non-coherent, private, 128 bytes
L2 cache	Shared, 512KB per tile, unified
	8-way, 12 cycle-latency
L2 Directory	Bit vector, 6-cycle latency
Memory	4GB, 300-cycle latency
Network Settings	
Topology	2D Mesh
Link latency	1 cycle
Link bandwidth	40 bytes/cycle
Flit size	16 bytes

Table 2: STAMP Workload Characteristics.

Workload	Trans Size	Contention	Commit rate
genome	Moderate	Moderate	Moderate
intruder	Small	High	Moderate
kmeans	Small	Low	Low
labyrinth	Large	Moderate	Low
SSCA2	Small	Low	High
vacation	Large	Low	Moderate
yada	Large	High	Moderate

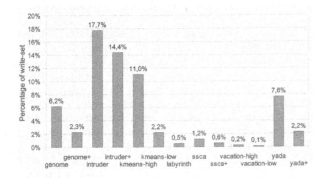

Figure 6: Relative sizes of conflict sets for STAMP applications.

Experiments were performed on a 16-core tiled CMP system, as described in Figure 1. We use a 16-core configuration with private L1I and L1D caches and a shared, multi-banked L2 cache consisting of 16 banks of 512KB each (one L2 slice per tile). For each workload - HTM configuration pair we gathered average statistics over 10 randomized runs designed to produce different interleavings between threads. STAMP workloads were chosen as they are among the most representative TM benchmarks available so far that are suitable for architecture simulation and exhibit a fair diversity in behavior. The parameters for applications have been taken from [3]. We simulate both small and medium datasets for workloads that exhibit differences in transactional behavior across various design points. This not only yields more credible statistics but also allows the hybrid design to achieve steady-state performance.

3.2 Workload Characteristics

STAMP workloads cover a broad spectrum of transactional behavior. Table 2 shows some relevant qualitative characteristics. We have excluded the application, bayes, from our analyses because

it exhibits significant variability in execution times. It should be noted that even labyrinth, which implements Lee's routing algorithm, exhibits divergent executions that depend on thread interleavings but these deviations are not so severe as in the case of bayes and hence, we have retained it in this evaluation.

Conflict set sizes. To measure the proportion of contended data in a typical transaction's write set we define conflict set of a transaction as the set of lines that were written and managed lazily over the duration of execution of a transaction. Figure 6 shows the cardinality of the conflict set as a percentage of the corresponding write set size averaged over an entire run. We see that even in applications with moderate to high contention, like yada and intruder, the conflict set is far smaller than the write set. Workloads like ssca2, that have both high concurrency and a high commit rate, experience contention on less than 1% of the write-set. Moreover, as we move to longer running workloads (small to medium in Figure 6), the ratio of the two set sizes drops even further. The common case size of less than 20% of the write-set bears out our choice to the separately manage the large non-contended fraction of the write set.

3.3 Performance Analysis

Figure 7 shows the relative performance of the four HTM designs evaluated in this study. Results are normalized to the execution time of the LogTM system, represented throughout this evaluation by the *EE* label. The *Hybrid* bar corresponds to the ZEBRA HTM design, while the two right-most bars are the lazy designs, the global commit token scheme (*LL-GCT*) and Scalable TCC (*LL-STCC*), respectively. The average for long running workloads (marked with the suffix +) has been calculated separately (appears as Average+). The ZEBRA HTM shows noticeable improvement in overall performance. It closely tracks the performance of the best policy and excels when applications show mixed transactional behavior – having both contended and non-contended phases of execution. Figure 8 zooms in on TM protocol overheads for different designs, normalized to the LL-GCT design. The hybrid policy shows remarkable overall efficiency here – showing 25-30% improvement over EE or LL-STCC. Figure 9 shows two measures – average deviation from the best observed performance over all workloads and the standard deviation of performance normalized to the best across all workloads. The hybrid approach achieves by far the lowest swings, implying consistent performance and robustness. Figure 10 shows scalability of workloads and design points considered in this study and validates the performance of the parallel architecture modeled in the simulator.

We have further investigated the behavior of the hybrid approach. Figure 11 shows the distribution of purely eager, partly-eager-partly-lazy (hybrid) and purely lazy commits in each application. Table 3 shows utilization of LWB and OVB by each transaction (identified by *TID*) in various STAMP benchmarks. Write-set sizes (WS in the table) and OVB occupancy have been shown in cache lines. LWB occupancy represents the number of bytes that were managed lazily in the structure.

The discussion below highlights important observations and presents insights gained from detailed study of interactions between HTM policies and the behavior of individual workloads.

Genome. This workload exhibits a high contention phase early in its execution where lazy designs outperform the EE system. This phase involves removal of duplicates (hash-table insertions). Reader - writer conflicts dominate at the beginning of the phase and lazy approaches inherently allow greater concurrency in such a situation. The hybrid design quickly switches the management of contended cache lines to lazy and completes the phase faster than EE, but a bit slower than LL-GCT or LL-STCC. The second phase is

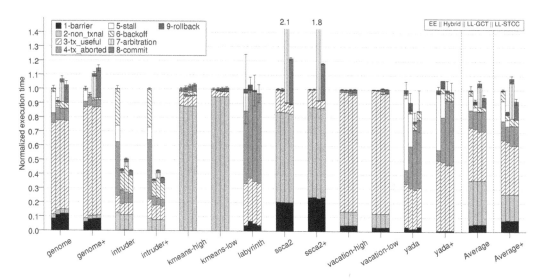

Figure 7: Normalized execution time breakdown.

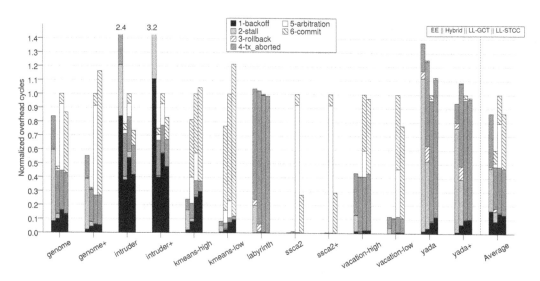

Figure 8: Protocol overheads.

dominated by transactions with moderate write-sets (3.4 cache lines on average) with accesses to predominantly non-contended data and is the determinant of overall performance. The eager approach proves to be the quickest here. The hybrid system run most transactions in a completely eager way and does not suffer from commit overheads seen in the lazy designs. Occupation measurements of the OVB and LWB structures shown in Table 3 confirm how the hybrid system adapts to the transactions of this second phase: TID1 is always eagerly managed (OVB usage equals write-set size), while TID2 and TID3 are purely eager in 70% and 80% of their commits, respectively. No transaction in genome ever commits in a purely lazy fashion (contended lines always comprise only a small fraction of the Wset), demonstrating the benefits of the proposed data-centric approach for policy selection on a per-cache line granularity. The third phase again exhibits low to moderate contention. Since the application shows mixed behavior, the hybrid approach outperforms all others, as depicted in Figure 7. Overall, we find that this result demonstrates the efficacy of quick adaptability to

changing workload conditions in the hybrid approach. Genome+ (genome with a medium sized dataset) shows much less contention, thereby widening the gap between the purely lazy and EE or Hybrid designs. As we show in Figure 11, in the hybrid system almost 90 % of commits happen eagerly for genome+.

Intruder. This workload shows high contention, even with large input sizes. Eager transactions acquire exclusive ownership to data before they are guaranteed to commit. This, in conjunction with a high probability of conflicts, leads to prolonged stalls and pathological cases where transactions form chains of dependencies causing aborts. In this contended scenario, lazy systems are able to exploit concurrency much better resulting in far fewer aborts. This workload has 3 transactions. TID0 extracts elements from a highly contended queue of packets, causing the EE system to experience 15K aborts (out of total of 29K aborts overall). Lazy designs reduce this number to 4K (13K aborts overall). The hybrid system quickly discovers contended lines, and the conflicting location (pointer to the head of the queue) becomes lazy (as indicated by an

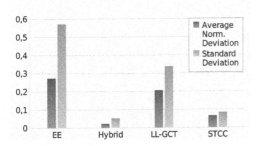

Figure 9: Deviation from best observed performance.

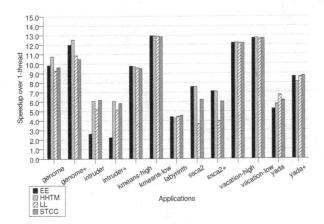

Figure 10: Design scalability.

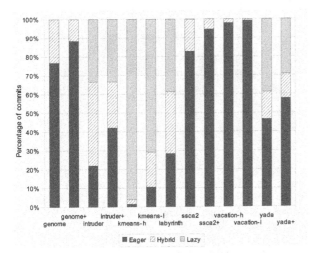

Figure 11: ZEBRA – Policy distribution at commit.

LWB occupancy of 4 bytes in this transaction) decreasing the number of aborts when preforming transactional dequeue operations to 3K (total of 11K). With the hybrid approach, the largest transaction (TID1) can commit eagerly 25% of the time on average, even though it accesses relatively large amounts of contended data (see figure 6). A large fraction of TID1's write set (6.1 lines) is still non-contended and thus an average of 3.8 lines are managed eagerly, as revealed by the OVB occupancy in Table 3. TID2 also exhibits a predominantly eager behavior, committing eagerly about

Table 3: ZEBRA – LWB and OVB utilization.

Workload	TID0			TID1			TID2			TID3			TID4		
	WS	OVB	LWB	WS	OVB	LWB	WS	OVB	LWB	WS	OVB	LWB	WS	OVB	LWB
genome+	1.3	1.2	1.4	1.0	1.0	0.0	**3.4**	**3.3**	**0.7**	3.4	3.4	0.4	2.2	1.8	2.8
genome	1.3	1.1	1.6	1.0	1.0	0.0	**3.5**	**3.1**	**1.9**	3.5	3.3	0.6	2.5	1.4	6.1
intruder+	1.0	0.0	4.0	**5.7**	**4.5**	**7.1**	1.2	1.0	0.9	-	-	-	-	-	-
intruder	1.0	0.0	4.0	**6.1**	**3.8**	**13**	1.5	1.0	2.2	-	-	-	-	-	-
kmeans-h	**2.0**	**0.1**	**65**	1.0	0.0	3.9	1.0	0.0	4.0	-	-	-	-	-	-
kmeans-l	**2.0**	**0.5**	**47**	1.0	0.0	4.0	1.0	0.0	4.0	-	-	-	-	-	-
labyrinth	0.9	0.1	3.1	**217**	**8.0**	**41**	3.8	2.9	4.1	-	-	-	-	-	-
ssca2+	1.0	0.1	3.6	1.0	0.0	4.0	**2.0**	**1.9**	**0.2**	-	-	-	-	-	-
ssca2	1.0	0.1	3.8	1.0	0.0	4.0	**2.0**	**1.8**	**0.7**	-	-	-	-	-	-
vacation-h	**6.8**	**6.8**	**0.2**	5.7	5.7	0.1	4.0	4.0	0.1	-	-	-	-	-	-
vacation-l	**6.1**	**6.1**	**0.1**	5.3	5.3	0.1	2.5	2.5	0.0	-	-	-	-	-	-
yada+	2.5	0.0	11	0.0	0.0	0.0	**70**	**8.0**	**18**	1.0	0.8	0.7	1.3	0.3	5.1
yada	2.0	0.0	8.1	0.0	0.0	0.0	**60**	**8.0**	**40**	1.0	0.5	2.1	1.4	0.2	7.0

50% of the time, with one eagerly managed write on average (out of 1.5 written lines). Hence, it outperforms lazy approaches since commit durations for TID1 and TID2 are significantly shorter as a large number of the transactionally modified lines are not contended and, therefore, committed instantly. We can see in Figure 8 how the overhead due to the arbitration and commit is substantially lower in the hybrid system, in comparison to both LL-GCT and LL-STCC systems.

SSCA2. It has a large number of tiny transactions that demand high commit bandwidth. Inherently parallel commits in eager approaches serve this requirement very well. Lazy approaches suffer, even STCC, which has a degree of scalability. This is clearly evident in 8 where commit delays represent the primary overhead in lazy designs. The hybrid design is able to manage almost the entire write-set eagerly for most transactions. This can be clearly seen in the high proportion of eager commits (see Figure 11) and the low LWB utilization (see Table 3). Hence, the hybrid approach is able to match the performance of the EE design.

Yada. It has a rather large working set and exhibits high contention. The workload traverses the dataset in a manner which makes it longer for the hybrid approach to complete the discovery of contended lines. A longer time to achieve steady state means that in short duration runs we do not perform as well as the lazy systems. TID2, the dominant transaction (see Table 3), exceeds OVB capacity. This coupled with a relatively high fraction of contended data in the write-set (see Figure 6) results in expensive software rollback operations that degrade performance of EE and the hybrid designs. With longer runs we notice that the differences tend to become less marked. The contention in this case is less severe (as is evident the higher proportion of eager commits for yada+ in Figure 11) and the eager approach regains lost performance.

Labyrinth. As noted earlier, the results generated by this workload depend significantly on the interleaving of threads resulting in marked variability in execution times (note the error bars in Figure 7). The data presented thus should be viewed keeping this fact in mind. The dominant transaction is TID1 as can be seen in Table 3. A significant fraction of data is managed eagerly (see Figure 6) but the OVB capacity is exceeded since write-set sizes are large. Thus, relatively high contention results in expensive rollback operations on abort (see Figure 8). Consequently, lazy designs perform slightly better than the EE or the hybrid approach.

Kmeans /Vacation. These applications are highly concurrent and do not show major differences in execution times with changes in policies. Nevertheless, protocol efficiencies at commit in the EE and the hybrid designs result in minor improvements in performance.

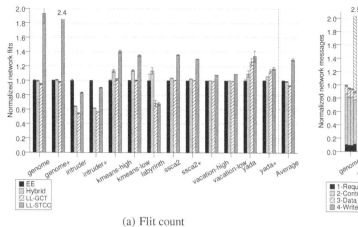

(a) Flit count

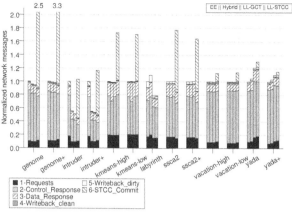

(b) Message Type Distribution

Figure 12: Network Traffic.

3.4 Traffic Considerations

Traffic generated by each HTM design when running STAMP applications is shown in Figure 12. Figure 12-a shows traffic volumes in flits normalized to the EE design. Figure 12-b plots the distribution of various protocol messages types transported through the network. In terms of traffic the hybrid approach performs well across all workloads and puts signficantly lower demands on network bandwidth than LL-STCC. LL-STCC shows remarkably high flit counts for several applications, which, as can be seen in the traffic distribution plot, arises due to messaging for scalable commits. In the experimental setup used for this study, large intra-chip communication bandwidth is available as only 16 in-order cores run. The parallel commit algorithm employed by the design is thus able to hide most of messaging latency. In architectures that have a low peak bandwidth or run workloads that impose high communication demands, this latency may not remain hidden and LL-STCC protocol efficiency could suffer.

4. RELATED WORK

Research in HTM design has been very active since the introduction of multicores in mainstream computing. The early proposal by Herlihy and Moss [7] was revived by new, more elaborate designs like UTM[1], TCC [6] and LogTM [19]. In particular TCC and LogTM explored two opposite corners of the HTM design space. Transactional Coherence and Consistency (TCC) contains speculative updates within private caches and resolves races when a committing transaction broadcasts its write-set. In its basic form it employs a bus to serialize transaction commits. The design was later extended to scalable architectures using directory based coherence. A simple variant employs a global commit token to serialize commits. A more sophisticated approach, Scalable TCC (STCC) [5], employs selective locking of directory banks to avoid arbitration delays and thereby improve commit throughput. LogTM, on the other hand, proposes the use of an undo log to incrementally preserve consistent state and abort handlers that restore it. Directory coherence is used to detect and resolve conflicts eagerly with occasional fallback to handlers in software to break deadlocks.

Parallelism at commit is important when running applications with low contention but a large number of transactions. Transactions that do not conflict should ideally be able to commit simultaneously. The very nature of lazy conflict resolution protocols makes it difficult since only actions taken at commit time permit discovery of data races among transactions. Simple lazy schemes like ones employing a global commit token do not permit such parallelism. Hence most lazy protocols employ more complex approaches like finer-grained locks on shared memory [5], optimizing certain safe interleavings [13] and early discovery of conflicts [17]. Eager schemes do not suffer from this problem and our proposal, under such workload conditions, would allow parallel commits since most transactions would be managed eagerly. Thus, complicated protocol extensions to support higher commit parallelism are not critical to improve common case performance for such workloads.

Sanyal et al. [15] proposed filtering of thread-private data with support from the cores and the operating system. While this reduces pressure on versioning mechanisms in HTMs, it does not separate contended data from non-contended data. This separation is not as distinct as that between thread-private and shared data and can only be known by runtime adaptability, as we propose in this work, or by fine-grained profiling of application behaviour and access patterns. The latter is not always feasible because of large variations due to different datasets and thread interleavings.

Mixed-policy HTM designs like DynTM (UTCP) [8] and LV* [12] have been introduced earlier in this work. DynTM deserves further discussion since it chooses a different dimension and granularity of data to work with when compared to the work presented here. It works at the granularity of a transaction and then develops a cache coherence protocol around it that supports multiple ways to version the same shared memory block. This choice of granularity does not match that of the underlying coherence infrastructure which works at the granularity of cache lines. The result, in the opinion of the authors, is increased complexity of design, which will be a significant criterion in any decision to incorporate TM in silicon.

5. CONCLUSIONS AND FUTURE WORK

In this paper we have outlined a fresh approach to hybrid-policy HTM design. Instead of viewing contention as a characteristic of an atomic section of code, we view it as a characteristic of the data accessed therein. Our observation that contended data forms a relatively small fraction of data written inside transactions reinforces our decision to incorporate mechanisms that support efficient management of such data in the common case. In the process, our proposal – the ZEBRA HTM system – manages to bring together the good aspects of both eager and lazy designs with very modest changes in architecture and protocol. ZEBRA supports parallel commits for transactions that do not access contended data and allows reader-writer concurrency when contention is seen. We have shown, both qualitatively and quantitatively, that it can utilize concurrency better and consistently track or outperform the best performing scalable single-policy design – performing as well as the eager design when high commit rates limit performance of lazy designs and, on average, substantially better than both eager and lazy systems when contention dominates. On average, it places lower demands on intra-chip communication bandwidth. It also achieves the lowest deviation from the best measured performance over a diverse set of workloads corroborating our claim that the design is robust and less susceptible to pathological conditions. We hope this work would spur further efforts in the area of low complexity hybrid-policy HTM systems. More research can be done to develop designs that adapt to workload needs quicker and are still cost-effective enough to attract the attention of computer architects.

Acknowledgments

This collaborative work was supported by the Spanish MEC and MICINN, as well as European Comission FEDER funds, under grants Consolider Ingenio-2010 CSD2006-00046 and TIN2009-14 475-C04. It was also partly supported by the HiPEAC-2 NoE under contract FP7/IST-217068. Anurag's work at Chalmers has been supported by the European Commission FP7 project VELOX (ICT-216852). Rubén Titos has a research grant from the Spanish MEC under the FPU National Plan (AP2006-04152) and was awarded a collaboration grant from HiPEAC to visit Chalmers.

6. REFERENCES

[1] C. Scott Ananian, Krste Asanovic, Bradley C. Kuszmaul, Charles E. Leiserson, and Sean Lie. Unbounded transactional memory. In *Proc. of the 11th Symp. on High-Performance Computer Architecture*, pages 316–327, Feb 2005.

[2] Jayaram Bobba, Kevin E. Moore, Luke Yen, Haris Volos, Mark D. Hill, Michael M. Swift, and David A. Wood. Performance pathologies in hardware transactional memory. In *Proc. of the 34th Int'l Symp. on Computer Architecture*, pages 81–91, Jun 2007.

[3] Chi Cao Minh, JaeWoong Chung, Christos Kozyrakis, and Kunle Olukotun. STAMP: Stanford transactional applications for multi-processing. In *Proc. of the IEEE Intl. Symposium on Workload Characterization*, pages 35–46. Sept 2008.

[4] Luis Ceze, James Tuck, Calin Cascaval, and Josep Torrellas. Bulk disambiguation of speculative threads in multiprocessors. In *Proc. of the 33rd Int'l Symp. on Computer Architecture*, pages 227–238, Jun 2006.

[5] Hassan Chafi, Jared Casper, Brian D. Carlstrom, Austen McDonald, Chi Cao Minh, Woongki Baek, Christos Kozyrakis, and Kunle Olukotun. A scalable, non-blocking approach to transactional memory. In *Proc. of the 13th Symp. on High-Performance Computer Architecture*, pages 97–108, 2007.

[6] Lance Hammond, Vicky Wong, Mike Chen, Brian D. Carlstrom, John D. Davis, Ben Hertzberg, Manohar K. Prabhu, Honggo Wijaya, Christos Kozyrakis, and Kunle Olukotun. Transactional memory coherence and consistency. In *Proc. of the 31st Int'l Symp. on Computer Architecture*, pages 102–113, Jun 2004.

[7] Maurice Herlihy and J. Eliot B. Moss. Transactional memory: Architectural support for lock-free data structures. In *Proc. of the 20th Int'l Symp. on Computer Architecture*, pages 289–300. May 1993.

[8] Marc Lupon, Grigorios Magklis, and Antonio González. A dynamically adaptable hardware transactional memory. In *Proc. of the 43rd Int'l Symp. on Microarchitecture*, Dec 2010.

[9] Peter S. Magnusson, Magnus Christensson, Jesper Eskilson, Daniel Forsgren, Gustav Hallberg, Johan Hogberg, Fredrik Larsson, Andreas Moestedt, and Bengt Werner. Simics: A full system simulation platform. *IEEE Computer*, 35(2):50–58, Feb 2002.

[10] Milo M.K. Martin, Daniel J. Sorin, Bradford M. Beckmann, Michael R. Marty, Min Xu, Alaa R. Alameldeen, Kevin E. Moore, Mark D. Hill, and David A. Wood. Multifacet's general execution-driven multiprocessor simulator (GEMS) toolset. *Computer Architecture News*, pages 92–99, Sept 2005.

[11] Kevin E. Moore, Jayaram Bobba, Michelle J. Moravan, Mark D. Hill, and David A. Wood. LogTM: Log-based transactional memory. In *Proc. of the 12th Symp. on High-Performance Computer Architecture*, pages 254–265, Feb 2006.

[12] Anurag Negi, M.M. Waliullah, and Per Stenstrom. LV*: A low complexity lazy versioning HTM infrastructure. In *Proc. of the Intl. Conference on Embedded Computer Systems: Architectures, Modeling, and Simulation (IC-SAMOS 2010)*, pages 231–240, July 2010.

[13] Seth H. Pugsley, Manu Awasthi, Niti Madan, Naveen Muralimanohar, and Rajeev Balasubramonian. Scalable and reliable communication for hardware transactional memory. In *Proc. of the 17th Int'l Conf. on Parallel Architectures and Compilation Techniques*, pages 144–154, Oct 2008.

[14] Ravi Rajwar and James R. Goodman. Transactional lock-free execution of lock-based programs. In *Proc. of the 10th Int'l Symposium on Architectural Support for Programming Language and Operating Systems*, pages 5–17, Oct 2002.

[15] Sutirtha Sanyal, Adrián Cristal, Osman S. Unsal, Mateo Valero, and Sourav Roy. Dynamically filtering thread-local variables in lazy-lazy hardware transactional memory. In *HPCC '09: Proc. 11th Conference on High Performance Computing and Communications*, jun 2009.

[16] Arrvindh Shriraman, Sandhya Dwarkadas, and Michael L. Scott. Flexible decoupled transactional memory support. In *Proc. of the 35th Int'l Symp. on Computer Architecture*. Jun 2008.

[17] Sasa Tomic, Cristian Perfumo, Chinmay Kulkarni, Adria Armejach, Adrián Cristal, Osman Unsal, Tim Harris, and Mateo Valero. EazyHTM: Eager-lazy hardware transactional memory. In *Proc. of the 42nd Int'l Symp. on Microarchitecture*, 2009.

[18] M.M. Waliullah and P. Stenstrom, Classification and Elimination of Conflicts in Transactional Memory Systems. Tech. Report 2010:09, Dept. of Computer Engineering, Chalmers University of Technology, Sweden, 2010.

[19] Luke Yen, Jayaram Bobba, Michael R. Marty, Kevin E. Moore, Haris Volos, Mark D. Hill, Michael M. Swift, and David A. Wood. LogTM-SE: Decoupling hardware transactional memory from caches. In *Proc. of the 13th Symp. on High-Performance Computer Architecture*, pages 261–272, Feb 2007.

Scalable Fine-grained Call Path Tracing

Nathan R. Tallent
Rice University
tallent@rice.edu

John Mellor-Crummey
Rice University
johnmc@rice.edu

Michael Franco
Rice University
mrf1@rice.edu

Reed Landrum
Stanford University
rlandrum@stanford.edu

Laksono Adhianto
Rice University
laksono@rice.edu

ABSTRACT

Applications must scale well to make efficient use of even medium-scale parallel systems. Because scaling problems are often difficult to diagnose, there is a critical need for scalable tools that guide scientists to the root causes of performance bottlenecks.

Although tracing is a powerful performance-analysis technique, tools that employ it can quickly become bottlenecks themselves. Moreover, to obtain actionable performance feedback for modular parallel software systems, it is often necessary to collect and present fine-grained context-sensitive data — the very thing scalable tools avoid. While existing tracing tools can collect calling contexts, they do so only in a coarse-grained fashion; and no prior tool scalably presents both context- and time-sensitive data.

This paper describes how to collect, analyze and present fine-grained call path traces for parallel programs. To scale our measurements, we use asynchronous sampling, whose granularity is controlled by a sampling frequency, and a compact representation. To present traces at multiple levels of abstraction and at arbitrary resolutions, we use sampling to render complementary slices of calling-context-sensitive trace data. Because our techniques are general, they can be used on applications that use different parallel programming models (MPI, OpenMP, PGAS). This work is implemented in HPCTOOLKIT.

Categories and Subject Descriptors

C.4 [**Performance of systems**]: Measurement techniques, Performance attributes

General Terms

Algorithms, Measurement, Performance

Keywords

tracing, calling context, statistical sampling, performance tools, HPCTOOLKIT

1. INTRODUCTION

As hardware-thread counts increase in supercomputers, applications must scale to make effective use of computing resources. However, inefficiencies that do not even appear at smaller scales can become major bottlenecks at larger scales. Because scaling problems are often difficult to diagnose, there is a critical need for tools that guide scientists to the root causes of performance bottlenecks.

Tracing has long been a method of choice for many performance tools [6,8,9,12,15,17,19,22,24,30,31,33,35,43,44]. Because performance traces show how a program's behavior changes over time — or, more generally, with respect to a progress metric — tracing is an especially powerful technique for identifying critical scalability bottlenecks such as load imbalance, excessive synchronization, or inefficiencies that develop over time. For example, consider a trace that distinguishes between, on one hand, periods of useful work and, on the other, communication within the processes of a parallel execution. Presenting this trace as a Gantt chart, or process/time diagram, can easily show that load imbalance causes many processes to (unproductively) wait at a collective operation. In contrast, such a conclusion is often difficult to draw from a performance *profile* in which an execution's time dimension has been collapsed.

Although trace-based performance tools can yield powerful insight, they can quickly become a performance bottleneck themselves. With most tracing techniques, the size of *each* thread's trace is proportional to the length of its execution. Consequently, for even medium-scale executions, extensive tracing can easily generate gigabytes or terabytes of data, causing significant perturbations in an execution when this data is flushed to a shared file system [5,8,14,15,23,25]. Moreover, massive trace databases create additional scaling challenges for analyzing and presenting the corresponding performance measurements.

Because traces are so useful but so difficult to scale, much recent work has focused on ways to reduce the volume of trace data. Methods for reducing trace-data volume include lossless online compression [20,30]; 'lossy' online compression [12]; online clustering for monitoring only a portion of an execution [13,14,25]; post-mortem clustering [5,16,24]; online filtering [16]; selective tracing (static filtering) [8,15,35]; and throttling [19,35].

However, prior work on enhancing the scalability of tracing does not address three concerns that we believe are critical for achieving effective performance analysis that leads to actionable performance feedback.

First, prior work largely emphasizes *flat* trace data, i.e., traces that exclude additional execution context such as calling context. Because new applications employ modular design principles, it is often important to know not simply what an application is doing at a particular point, but also that point's calling context. For instance, consider a case where one process in an execution causes all others to wait by performing additional work in a memory copy. The memory copy routine is likely called from many different contexts. To begin resolving the performance problem, it is necessary to know the calling contexts of the problematic memory copies. While some tracing tools have recently added support for collecting calling contexts, they do so in a relatively coarse-grained fashion, usually with respect to a limited set of function calls [12, 19, 21, 33]. Moreover, while these tools can show calling context for an individual trace record, no tool presents context- and time-sensitive data, across multiple threads, for arbitrary portions of an execution. In this paper, we show how to use sampling to present arbitrary and complementary slices of calling-context-sensitive trace data.

Second, to reduce trace-data volume, prior tracing tools use, among other things, coarse-grained instrumentation to produce coarse-grained trace data. Examples of coarse-grained instrumentation include only monitoring high-level 'effort loops' [12] or MPI communication routines [44]. One problem with coarse-grained instrumentation is that, except where there is a pre-defined (coarse) monitoring interface (as with MPI [28]), manual effort or a training session is required to select instrumentation points. Another problem is that coarse-grained instrumentation may be insufficient to provide actionable insight into a program's performance. For example, although a tool that only traces MPI communication can easily confirm the presence of load imbalance in SPMD (Single Program Multiple Data) programs, that tool may not be able to pinpoint the source of that imbalance in a complex modular application. Therefore, it is often desirable to scalably generate relatively fine-grained traces across all of an application's procedures.

However, using fine-grained instrumentation to generate a fine-grained trace has not been shown to be scalable. Indeed, instrumentation-based measurement faces an inelastic tension between accuracy and precision. For instance, instrumentation of small frequently executing procedures — which are common in modular applications — introduces overhead and generates as many trace records as procedure invocations. To avoid measurement overhead, we use asynchronous sampling to collect call path traces.[1] Both coarse-grained instrumentation and sampling reduce the volume of trace data by selectively tracing. However, coarse-grained instrumentation often ignores that which is important for performance (such as small math or communication routines), whereas asynchronous sampling tends to ignore that which is least relevant to performance (such as routines that, over all instances, consume little execution time). Thus, because we use *asynchronous* sampling, our tracer monitors an execution through *any procedure* and at *any point* within a procedure, irrespective of a procedure's execution frequency or length and irrespective of application and library boundaries. Because asynchronous *sampling* uses a controllable

sampling frequency, our tracer has controllable measurement granularity and overhead. By combining sampling with a compact call path representation, our tracer can collect comparatively fine-grained call path traces (hundreds of samples/second) of large-scale executions and present them on a laptop.

Third, while tools like ScalaTrace [30] exploit model-specific knowledge to great effect, recent interest in hybrid models (e.g., OpenMP + MPI) and PGAS languages suggests that a more general approach can be valuable. Our sampling-based measurement approach is programming-model independent and can be used on standard operating systems (OS), as well as the microkernels used on the IBM Blue Gene/P and Cray XT supercomputers [39]. While we affirm the utility of exploiting model-specific properties, having the ability to place such insight in the context of an application's OS-level execution is also valuable.

In this paper, we describe measurement, analysis and presentation techniques for scalable fine-grained call path tracing. We make the following contributions:

- We use asynchronous sampling to collect informative call path traces with modest cost in space and time. By combining sampling with a compact representation, we can generate detailed traces of large-scale executions with controllable granularity and overhead. Our method is general in that, instead of tracing certain aspects of a thread's execution (such as MPI calls), we sample all activity that occurs in user mode.

- We describe scalable techniques for analyzing a trace. In particular, we combine in parallel every thread-level call path trace so that all thread-level call paths are compactly represented in a data structure called a calling context tree.

- We show how to use sampling to present (out-of-core) call path traces using two complementary views: (1) a process/time view that shows how different slices of an execution's call path change over time; and (2) a call-path/time view that shows how a single process's (or thread's) call path changes over time. These techniques enable us to use a laptop to rapidly present trace files of arbitrary length for executions with an arbitrary number of threads. In particular, given a display window of height h and width w (in pixels), our presentation tool can render both views in time $O(hw \log t)$, where t is the number of trace records in the largest trace file.

Our work is implemented within HPCTOOLKIT [1, 32], an integrated suite of tools for measurement and analysis of program performance on computers ranging from multicore desktop systems to supercomputers.

The rest of this paper is organized as follows. First, Section 2 presents a taxonomy of existing techniques for collecting and presenting traces of large-scale applications. Then, Sections 3, 4 and 5 respectively describe how we (a) collect call path traces of large-scale executions; (b) prepare those measurements for presentation using post-mortem analysis; and (c) present those measurements both in a scalable fashion and in a way that exposes an execution's dynamic hierarchy. To demonstrate the utility of our approach, Section 6 presents several case studies. Finally, Section 7 summarizes our contributions and ongoing work.

---

[1]Sampling can be synchronous or asynchronous with respect to program execution. Although we focus on the latter, there are important cases where the former is useful [40].

2. RELATED WORK

There has been much prior work on tracing. This section analyzes the most relevant work on call path tracing from the perspectives of measurement, presentation and scalability.

2.1 Collecting Call Path Traces

Because it is important to associate performance problems with source code, recently several tracing tools have added support for collecting the calling context of trace events [3, 12, 19, 21, 33]. However, instead of collecting detailed call path traces, these tools, with perhaps two exceptions, trace in a relatively coarse-grained manner. The reason is that most of these tools measure using forms of static or dynamic instrumentation. Because instrumentation is inherently synchronous with respect to a program's execution, fine-grained instrumentation — such as instrumenting every primitive in a math library — causes both high measurement overhead and an unmanageable volume of trace data. Consequently, to scale well, instrumentation-based tools rely on coarse-grained instrumentation, which results in coarse-grained traces. For instance, a common tracing technique is to trace MPI calls and collect the calling context of either (a) each MPI call [19, 21, 33] or (b) the computation between certain MPI calls [12]. Moreover, some of these tools encourage truncated calling contexts. With the CEPBA Tools, one can specify a 'routine of interest' to stop unwinds [21]; with VampirTrace, one specifies a call stack depth [41].

Two existing tools — the exceptions mentioned above — can collect fine-grained traces. The CEPBA Tools combine coarse-grained instrumentation and asynchronous sampling to generate flat fine-grained traces supplemented with coarse-grained calling contexts [21, 34]. Apple Shark uses asynchronous sampling and stack unwinding to collect fine-grained call path traces [3]. Both of these tools collect fine-grained data because they employ asynchronous sampling.

Apple Shark [3] is perhaps the closest to our work, at least with respect to measurement. However, there are three critical differences. First, as a single-node system-level tracer, Shark is designed to collect data, not at the application level, but at the level of a hardware thread. As a result, it cannot per se trace a parallel application with multiple processes. Second, to our knowledge, Shark does not use a compact structure (like a calling context tree [2]) to store call paths. Third, Shark is not always able to unwind a thread's call stack. It turns out that unwinding a call stack from an arbitrary asynchronous sample is quite challenging when executing optimized application binaries. Because we base our work on dynamic binary analysis for unwinding call stacks [38], HPCTOOLKIT can accurately collect full call path traces, even when using asynchronous sampling of optimized code.

Besides affecting trace granularity, a tool's measurement technique also affects the class of applications the tool supports. Because MPI is dominant in large-scale computing, a number of tools primarily monitor MPI communication [12, 30, 31, 34, 44]; some also include support for certain OpenMP events. However, both technology pressure and programming-productivity concerns have generated much interest in alternative models such as PGAS languages. Our approach, which measures arbitrary computation within all threads of an execution, easily maps to all of these models. Additionally, an approach that monitors at the system level can take advantage of a specific model's semantics to provide trace information both at the run-time level (for run-time tuning) and at the application level [37].

2.2 Presenting Call Path Traces

Although a few tools collect coarse call path traces, no tool presents context-sensitive data for arbitrary portions of the process and time dimensions. For instance, one especially important feature for supporting top-down contextual analysis is the ability to arbitrarily zoom. To do this, a tool must be able to (a) appropriately summarize a large trace within a relatively small amount of display real estate; (b) render high-resolution views of interesting portions of the execution; and (c) expose context. While presentation tools such as Paraver [22], Vampir [19] and Libra [12] display flat trace data across arbitrary portions of the process and time dimensions, they do not analogously present call path data.

Instead, current presentation techniques for call path traces are limited to displaying different forms of one thread's call path. For instance, Apple Shark [3] presents call path depth with respect to one hardware thread. Thus, it shows stylized call paths (i.e., the depth component) for all application threads that execute on a particular hardware thread. While this is interesting from a system perspective, it is not helpful from the perspective of a parallel application. Open|SpeedShop displays call paths of individual trace events [33]. While this is very useful for finding where in source code a trace event originates, it does not provide a high-level view of the dynamic structure of an execution. Vampir can display a 'Process Timeline' that shows how caller-callee relationships unfold over time for a single process [19]. While the ability to see call paths unfolding over time is helpful, only focusing on one process can be limiting.

2.3 Scaling Trace Collection and Presentation

Because traces are so useful but so difficult to scale, much recent work has focused on ways to reduce the volume of trace measurement data. Broadly speaking, there are two basic techniques for reducing the amount of trace information: coarse measurement granularity and data compression. Since as discussed above (Subsection 2.1), nearly all tools measure in a coarse-grained fashion, here we focus primarily on compression techniques, which can be lossless or 'lossy.'

As an example of lossless compression, ScalaTrace relies on program analysis to compress traces by compactly representing certain commonly occurring trace patterns [30]. For applications that have analyzable patterns, ScalaTrace's approach is extremely effective for generating compressed communication traces. VampirTrace uses a data structure called a Compressed Complete Call Graph to represent commonality among several trace records [20]. Similarly, we use a calling context tree [2] to compactly represent trace samples.

There are several forms of 'lossy' compression. Gamblin et al. have explored techniques for dynamically reducing the volume of trace information such as (a) 'lossy' online compression [12]; and (b) online clustering for monitoring only a subset of the processes in an execution [13, 14]. They report impressively low overheads, but they also, in part, use selective instrumentation that results in coarse measurements.

A popular form of 'lossy' compression is clustering. Lee et al. reduce trace file size by using k-Means clustering to select representative data [23, 24]. However, because their data-reduction technique is post-mortem rather than online, it assumes all trace data is stored in memory. This is feasible only with coarse-grained tracing.

The CEPBA Tools can use both offline and online clustering techniques for reducing data [5,16,22,25]. To make trace analysis and presentation more manageable, Casas et al. developed a post-mortem technique to compress a trace by identifying and retaining representative trace structure [5]. Going one step further, to reduce the amount of generated trace data, Gonzalez et al. [16] and Llort et al. [25] developed online clustering algorithms to retain only a representative portion of the trace. It is not clear how well these techniques would work for fine-grained call path tracing.

Yet another way to 'lossily' compress trace data is to filter it. As already mentioned, to manage overhead, all instrumentation-based tools statically filter data by selectively instrumenting. Scalasca and TAU support feedback-directed selective tracing, which uses the results of a prior performance profile to avoid instrumenting frequently executing procedures [15, 35]. Others tools support forms of manual selective tracing [8]. Since feedback-directed trace reduction requires an additional execution, it is likely impractical in some situations; and manual instrumentation is usually undesirable.

In contrast to static filtering, it is also possible to dynamically filter trace information. For example, the CEPBA Tools dynamically filter trace records by discarding periods of computation that consume less than a certain time threshold [16]. While dynamic filtering can effectively reduce trace data volume, it must be applied carefully to avoid systematic error by discarding frequent computation periods just under the filtering threshold. As another example of dynamic filtering, TAU and VAMPIR can optionally throttle a procedure by disabling its instrumentation after that procedure has been executed a certain number of times [19,35].

In contrast to all of these techniques, by using asynchronous sampling, we have taken a fundamentally different approach to scale the process of collecting a call path trace. Although, we do use a form of lossless compression (a calling context tree), that compression would be ineffective without sampling. With a reasonable sampling period and the absence of a correlation between the execution and sampling period, asynchronous sampling can collect representative and fine-grained call path traces for little overhead. Sampling naturally focuses attention on important execution contexts without relying on possibly premature local filtering tests. Additionally, because asynchronous sampling provides controllable measurement granularity, it naturally scales to very large-scale and long-running executions.

Sampling can also be employed to present call path traces at multiple levels of abstraction and at arbitrary resolutions. Here the basic problem is that a display window typically has many fewer pixels than available trace records. Given one pixel and the trace data that could map to it, sophisticated presentation tools like Paraver attempt to select the most interesting datum to define that pixel's color [22]. However, such techniques require examination of all trace data to render one display. Because this is impractical for fine-grained traces of large-scale executions, we use various forms of sampling to rapidly render complementary slices of calling-context-sensitive data. In particular, by sampling trace data for presentation, we can accurately render views by consulting only a fraction of the available data.

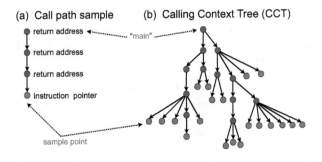

Figure 1: (a) The call path for a sample point; (b) several call path samples form a calling context tree.

Other work on scalably presenting traces at multiple levels of resolution has focused on flat traces; and none, to our knowledge, has used sampling. To scale in the time dimension, Jumpshot's SLOG2 format organizes trace events with a binary tree to quickly select trace events for rendering [7]. To scale in the time and process dimensions, Gamblin et al. use multi-level wavelet compression [12]. Lee et al. precompute certain summary views [23].

2.4 Summary

By using sampling both for measurement and presentation, we can collect and present fine-grained large-scale traces for applications written in several programming models. In prior work [1], we presented a terse overview of an early prototype of our tool. This paper, besides describing the key ideas behind our work, additionally presents new techniques for (a) scalable post-mortem trace analyses and (b) scalable presentation, including a combined process/time and call-path/time display.

3. COLLECTING CALL PATH TRACES

To collect call path traces with controllable granularity and measurement overhead, we use asynchronous sampling. Sampling-based measurement uses a recurring event trigger, with a configurable period, to raise signals within the program being monitored. When an event trigger occurs, raising a signal, we collect the calling context of that sample — the set of procedure frames active on the call stack — by unwinding the call stack. Because unwinding call stacks from an arbitrary execution point can be quite challenging, we base our work on HPCTOOLKIT's call path profiler [38, 39].

To make a call path tracer scalable, we need a way to compactly represent a series of timestamped call paths. Rather than storing a call path independently for each sample event, we represent all of the call paths for all samples (in a thread) as a calling context tree (CCT) [2], which is shown in Figure 1. A CCT is a weighted tree whose root is the program entry point and whose leaves represent sample points. Given a sample point (leaf), the path from the tree's root to the leaf's parent represents a sample's calling context. Although not strictly necessary for a trace, leaves of the tree can be weighted with metric values such as sample counts that represent program performance in context (a call path profile). The critical thing for tracing is that with a CCT, the calling context for a sample may be completely represented by a leaf node. Thus, to form a trace, we simply generate a sequence of tuples (or trace records), each consisting of a 4-byte CCT node id and an 8-byte timestamp (in microseconds).

With this approach, it is possible to obtain a very detailed call path trace for very modest costs. Assuming both a reasonable sampling rate — we frequently use rates of hundreds to thousands of samples per second — and a time-related sampling trigger, we can make several observations. First, assuming no correlation between an application's behavior and the sampling frequency, our traces should be quite representative. Second, in contrast to instrumentation-based methods where trace-record generation is related to a procedure's execution frequency, our rate of trace-record generation is constant. For instance, using a sampling rate of 1024 samples per second, our tracer generates 12 KB/s per thread of trace records (which are written to disk using buffered I/O); it writes the corresponding calling context tree at the end of the execution. Such modest I/O bandwidth demands are easily met. For instance, consider tracing an execution using all cores ($\approx 160,000$) of Argonne National Laboratory's Blue Gene/P system, Intrepid. At 12 KB/s per core, our bandwidth needs would be 0.0028% of Intrepid's disk bandwidth per core [42]. Third, the total volume of trace records is proportional to the product of the sampling frequency and the length of an execution. (The size of the CCT is proportional to the number of distinct calling contexts exposed by sampling.) This means that an analyst has significant control over the total amount of trace data generated for an execution. Fourth, because our tracer uses a technique to memoize call stack unwinds [11], the overhead of collecting call paths is proportional only to the call stack's *new* procedure frames with respect to the prior sample.

Of course, there are conditions under which sampling will not produce accurate data. If the sampling frequency is too high, measurement overhead can significantly perturb the application. Another more subtle problem is when the sampling frequency is below the natural frequency of the data. Although typically not a problem with profiling (which conceptually generates a histogram of contexts and therefore aggregates small contexts), under-sampling is a real concern for tracing since traces approximate instantaneous behavior over time. It turns out, however, that under-sampling is not a significant problem for our tracer because of two reasons. First, most of the interesting time-based patterns occur not at call-path leaves, but within call-path interiors, which have lower natural frequencies. This might seem to defeat the purpose of fine-grained sampling. However, it is helpful to observe that our tracer's call paths expose all implementation layers of math and communication libraries. Thus, frequently it is the case that moving out a few levels from a singly-sampled leaf brings an analyst to a multiply-sampled interior frame that is *still* in a library external to the application's source code (cf. Section 6). Second, for typical applications, selecting reasonable sampling frequencies that highlight an application's representative behavior is not difficult. In particular, we typically use frequencies in the hundreds and thousands of samples per second which yields several samples for instances of interior procedure frames. Of course, any one sample may correspond to noise and one cannot assume that any particular call path leaf executed for the duration of the virtual time represented by a pixel. But our experience is that trace patterns at interior call-path frames are representative of an application's execution.

4. ANALYZING CALL PATH TRACES

To present the large-scale trace measurements of Section 3, it is helpful to perform several post-mortem analyses. These analyses are designed to (a) compress the measurement data; (b) enable its rapid presentation; and (c) associate measurements with static source code structure. Our work extends HPCTOOLKIT's analysis tool [36, 38]. This section focuses on the most important of these analyses.

Recall that a thread's trace is represented as a sequence of trace records and a calling context tree (CCT). Although generating distinct CCTs avoids communication and synchronization during measurement, it generates more total data than is necessary. For instance, in SPMD scientific applications, many thread-level CCTs have common structure. To significantly compress the total trace data, we create a canonical CCT that represents all thread-level CCTs. In many situations, we expect the canonical CCT to be no more than a small constant factor larger than a typical thread-level CCT.

To form the canonical CCT, we union each thread-level CCT so that a call path appears in the canonical CCT if and only if it appears in some thread-level CCT. We do this in parallel using a (tree-based) CCT reduction.

An important detail is that the CCT reduction must ensure trace-file consistency, because each trace file must now refer to call paths in the canonical CCT instead of that thread's CCT. Consider the case of merging a path from a thread-level CCT into the canonical CCT. Either the path (1) already or (2) does not yet exist in the canonical CCT. For case (1), let the path in the CCT be x and the other path be y. Even though x and y have exactly the same structure (call chain), in general, they have different path identifiers (IDs). When these paths are merged to form one path, we only want to retain one ID. Assuming that we keep x's ID, it is then necessary to update trace records that refer to y. For case (2), when adding a path to the canonical CCT, it is necessary to ensure that that a path's ID does not conflict with any other ID currently in the canonical CCT. If there is a conflict, we generate a new ID and update the corresponding trace records. For efficiency, we batch all updates to a particular trace file.

5. PRESENTING CALL PATH TRACES

The result of Section 4's analysis is a trace database. To interactively present these trace measurements, an analyst uses HPCTOOLKIT's `hpctraceviewer` presentation tool, which can present a large-scale trace without concern for the scale of parallelism it represents. To make this scalability possible, and to show call path hierarchy, we designed several novel presentation techniques for `hpctraceviewer`. This section discusses those techniques.

5.1 Presenting Call Path Hierarchy

To analyze performance effectively, it is necessary to rapidly identify inefficient execution within vast quantities of performance data. This means that, among other things, it is necessary to present data at several levels of detail, beginning with high-level data from which one can descend to lower-level data to understand program inefficiencies in more detail. Additionally, to understand multi-dimensional data, it is often necessary to view it from several different angles. Consequently, we have designed `hpctraceviewer`'s interface to facilitate rapid top-down performance analysis

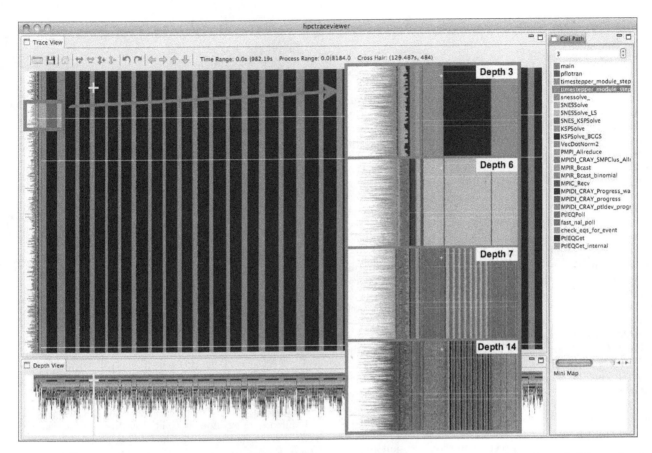

Figure 2: An 8184-core execution of PFLOTRAN on a Cray XT5. The inset exposes call path hierarchy by showing the selected region (top left) at different call path depths.

by displaying trace measurements in different views and at arbitrary levels of detail. In discussing the interface, we first describe `hpctraceviewer`'s views and then how those views can be manipulated; we defer case studies to Section 6.

Figure 2 shows `hpctraceviewer`'s main display. It represents an execution of PFLOTRAN (see Section 6.1) that took 982 seconds on 8184 cores of a Cray XT5. The figure is divided into three panes. The two stacked horizontal panes on the left consume most of the figure and display the Trace View and Depth View. The third slender vertical pane on the right shows the Call Path View and, on the very bottom, the Mini Map. These four coordinated views are designed to show complementary aspects of the call path trace data:

- *Trace View* (left, top): This is `hpctraceviewer`'s primary view. This view, which is similar to a conventional process/time (or space/time) view, shows time on the horizontal axis and process (or thread) rank on the vertical axis; time moves from left to right. Compared to typical process/time views, there is one key difference. To show call path hierarchy, the view is actually a user-controllable slice of the process/time/callpath space. Given a call path depth, the view shows the color of the currently active procedure at a given time and process rank. (If the requested depth is deeper than a particular call path, then `hpctraceviewer` simply displays the deepest procedure frame and, space permitting, overlays an annotation indicating the fact that this frame represents a shallower

depth.) Figure 2 shows that at depth 3, PFLOTRAN's execution alternates between two phases (purple and black). The figure contains an inset that shows the boxed area (top left) in greater detail at call path depths of 3, 6, 7 and 14. At depth 6, it is apparent that the two phases use the *same* solver (tan), though depths 7 and 14 show that they do so in different ways.

`hpctraceviewer` assigns colors to procedures based on (static) source code procedures. Although the color assignment is currently random, it is consistent across the different views. Thus, the same color within the Trace and Depth Views refers to the same procedure.

The Trace View has a white crosshair that represents a selected point in time and process space. For this selected point, the Call Path View shows the corresponding call path. The Depth View shows the selected process.

- *Depth View* (left, bottom): This is a call-path/time view for the process rank selected by the Trace View's crosshair. Given a process rank, the view shows for each virtual time along the horizontal axis a stylized call path along the vertical axis, where 'main' is at the top and leaves (samples) are at the bottom. In other words, this view shows for the whole time range, in qualitative fashion, what the Call Path View shows for a selected point. The horizontal time axis is exactly aligned with the Trace View's time axis; and the colors are consistent across both views. This view has its own crosshair that corresponds to the currently selected time and call path depth.

- *Call Path View* (right, top): This view shows two things: (1) the current call path depth that defines the hierarchical slice shown in the Trace View; and (2) the actual call path for the point selected by the Trace View's crosshair. (To easily coordinate the call path depth value with the call path, the Call Path View currently suppresses details such as loop structure and call sites; we may use indentation or other techniques to display this in the future.)

- *Mini Map* (right, bottom): The Mini Map shows, relative to the process/time dimensions, the portion of the execution shown by the Trace View. The Mini Map enables one to zoom and to move from one close-up to another quickly.

To further support top-down analysis, `hpctraceviewer` includes several controls for changing a view's aspect and navigating through various levels of data:

- The Trace View can be zoomed arbitrarily in both of its process and time dimensions. To zoom in both dimensions at once, one may (a) select a sub-region of the current view; or (b) select an arbitrary region of the Mini Map. To zoom in only one of the above dimensions, one may use the appropriate control buttons at the top of the Trace View. At any time, one may return to the entire execution's view by using the 'Home' button.

- To expose call path hierarchy, the call-path-depth slice shown in the Trace View can be changed by using the Call Path View's depth text box or by selecting a procedure frame within the Call Path View.

- To pan the Trace and Depth Views horizontally or vertically, one may (a) use buttons at the top of the Trace View pane; or (b) adjust the Mini Map's current focus.

Even though `hpctraceviewer` supports panning, it is worth noting that zooming is much more important because it permits viewing the execution at different levels of abstraction. In contrast, a tool that requires scrolling through vast quantities of data is difficult to use because, at any one time, the tool can only present a fraction of the execution.

5.2   Using Sampling for Scalable Presentation

To implement the arbitrary zooming that is required to support top-down analysis, it is clearly not feasible either (a) to examine all trace data repeatedly and exhaustively or (b) to precompute all possible (or likely) views. One possible solution for displaying data at multiple resolutions is to precompute select summary views [23]. We prefer a method that dynamically and rapidly renders views at arbitrary resolutions.

Consider a large-scale execution that has tens of thousands of processor ranks and that runs for thousands of seconds, where time granularity is a microsecond. A trace of this scale dwarfs any typical computer display; today, a high-end 30-inch display we use has a width and height of 2560×1600 pixels. Thus, the basic problem that a trace presentation tool faces is the following: Given a display window of a certain size, how should that window be rendered in time that is proportional not to the total amount of trace data, but to the window size? Alternatively, we can ask: given that one pixel maps to many trace records from many process ranks, how should we color that pixel without consulting all of the associated trace records?

In this connection, it is helpful to briefly consider the presentation technique of conveying the maximum possible information about an application's behavior [22]; cf. [23]. For example, to color one pixel, one could use either the minimum or maximum of the metric values associated with the trace records mapped to the pixel. While this can be a very effective way of rendering performance, it limits the scalability of a presentation tool because it requires examining every trace record mapped to the pixel.

In contrast, to render the views described in Section 5.1 without concern for the scale of parallelism they represent, we use various forms of sampling. For example, consider the Trace View, which displays procedures at a given call path depth along the process and time axes. To render this view in a display window of height h and width w, `hpctraceviewer` does two things. First, it systematically samples the execution's process ranks to select h ranks and their corresponding trace files. (For the trivial case where the number of process ranks is less than or equal to h, all ranks are represented.) Second, `hpctraceviewer` uses a form of systematic sampling to select the call path frames displayed along the process rank's time lines. It subdivides the time interval represented by the entire execution into a series of consecutive and equal intervals using w virtual timestamps. Then, for each virtual timestamp, it binary searches the corresponding trace file — our trace file format is effectively a vector of trace records — to locate the record with the closest actual timestamp; this record's call path is used to define the pixel's color.

We can make several observations about this scheme. Because we consult at most h trace files and perform at most w binary searches in each trace file, the time it takes to render the Trace View is $O(hw \log t)$, where t is the number of trace records in the largest trace file. In practice, the $\log t$ factor is often negligible because we use linear extrapolation to predict the locations of the w trace records. Next, as with the Trace View, the Depth View can also be rendered in time $O(hw \log t)$ by considering at most h frames of each call path. For some zooms and scrolling it is possible to reuse previously computed information to further reduce rendering costs. Finally, by generating virtual timestamps and using binary search, we effectively overlay a binary tree on the trace data, which is the basic idea behind Jumpshot's SLOG2 trace format [7].

One problem with sampling-based methods is that while they tend to show representative behavior, they might miss interesting extreme behavior. While this will always be a problem with statistical methods, two things attenuate these concerns. First, we (scalably) precompute special constant-sized values (instead of views) for `hpctraceviewer`. For example, we compute, for all trace files, the minimum beginning timestamp and the maximum ending timestamp, which takes work proportional to the number of processor ranks. Though a minor contribution, these timestamps enable `hpctraceviewer`'s Trace View to expose, e.g., extreme variation in an application's launch or teardown. Second, and more to the point, assuming an appropriately sized and uncorrelated sample, we expect sampling-based methods to expose anomalies that generally affect an execution. In other words, although using sampling-based methods for rendering a high-level view can easily miss a specific anomaly, those same methods will expose the anomaly's general effects. If the anomaly does not interfere with the application's execution, then a high-level view will show no effects. But if process synchronization transfers the anomaly's effects to other process ranks, we expect sampling-based methods to expose that fact. It is worth noting that Figure 2 actually exposes an interesting anomaly. The thin horizontal white lines in the Trace View represent a few processes for which sampling simply stopped, most likely (we suspect) because of a kernel bug.[2] One possible avenue of future work is for an analyst to identify a region and request a more exhaustive root-cause analysis.

We are currently working on a Summary View that shows for each virtual timestamp a stacked histogram that qualitatively represents the number of process ranks executing a given procedure at a given call path depth. This view would be similar to Vampir's 'Summary Timeline' [19]. However, in contrast to Vampir, which, to our knowledge, computes its view based on examining the activity of each thread at each time interval, we will use a sampling-based method to scalably render the view. To render this view for a window of height h and width w, we will first generate a series of w virtual timestamps as with the Trace View. Then, to create a stacked histogram for a given virtual timestamp, we will take a random sample of the process ranks and from there determine the set of currently executing procedures. The time complexity of rendering this view is the same as for the Trace View.

Unlike many other tools, hpctraceviewer does not render inter-process communication arcs. We are uncertain how to do this effectively and scalably. Instead, we are exploring ways of using a special color, say red, to indicate, at all levels of a call path, when a sample corresponds to communication.

6. CASE STUDIES

To demonstrate the ability of our tracing techniques to yield insight into the performance of parallel executions, we apply them to study the performance of the PFLO-TRAN ground water flow simulation application [26, 29]; the FLASH [10] astrophysical thermonuclear flash code; and two HPC Challenge benchmark codes [18] written in Coarray Fortran 2.0, one implementing a parallel one-dimensional Fast Fourier Transform (FFT), and the second implementing High Performance Linpack, (HPL) which solves a dense linear system on distributed memory computers. We describe our experiences with each of these applications in turn.

6.1 PFLOTRAN

PFLOTRAN models multi-phase, multi-component subsurface flow and reactive transport on massively parallel computers [26, 29]. It uses the PETSc [4] library's Newton-Krylov solver framework.

We collected call path traces of PFLOTRAN running on 8184 cores of a Cray XT5 system known as JaguarPF, which

is installed at Oak Ridge National Laboratory. The input for the PFLOTRAN run was a steady-state groundwater flow problem. To collect traces, we configured HPCTOOLKIT's hpcrun to sample wallclock time at a frequency of 200 samples/second. Tracing dilated the application's execution by 5% and the total job (including the time for hpcrun to flush measurements to disk) by 10%. hpcrun generated 13 GB of data (1.6 MB/process); a parallel version of HPCTOOLKIT's hpcprof analyzed the measurements in 13.5 minutes using 48 cores and generated a 7.5 GB trace database.

Figure 2 shows hpctraceviewer displaying a high level overview of a complete call path trace of a 16 minute execution of PFLOTRAN on 8184 cores. Recall from Section 5.1 that (a) the Trace View (top) shows a process/time view; (b) the Depth View shows a time-line view of the call path for the selected process; and (c) the Call Path View (right) shows a call path for the selected time and process. A process's activity over time unfolds from left to right.

Unlike other trace visualizers, hpctraceviewer's visualizations are hierarchical. Since each sample in each process's timeline represents a call path, we can view the process timelines at different call path depths to show more or less detailed views of the execution. The figure shows the execution at a call path depth of 3. Each distinct color on the timelines represents a different procedure executing at this depth. The figure clearly shows the alternation between PFLOTRAN's flow (purple) and transport (black) phases. The beginning of the execution shows different behavior as the application reads its input using the HDF5 library. The figure contains an inset that shows the boxed area (top left) in greater detail at call path depths of 3, 6, 7 and 14. At depth 6, it is apparent that the flow and transport phases use the *same* solver (tan), though depths 7 and 14 show that they do so in different ways. The point selected by the crosshair shows the flow phase performing an MPI_Allreduce on behalf of a vector dot product (VecDotNorm2) deep within the PETSc library. The call path also descends into Cray's MPI implementation. Given that the routine MPIDI_CRAY_Progress_wait (eighth from the bottom) is associated with exposed waiting, we can infer that the flow phase is currently busy-waiting for collective communication to complete.

6.2 FLASH

Next we consider FLASH [10], a code for modeling astrophysical thermonuclear flashes. Figure 3 shows hpctraceviewer displaying an 8184-core JaguarPF-execution of FLASH. We used an input for simulating a white dwarf detonation. It is immediately apparent that the first 60% of execution is quite different than the regular patterns that appear thereafter. The Trace View's crosshair marks the approximate transition point. At this point, the Call Path View makes clear that the execution is still in its initialization phase (cf. driver_initflash at depth 2). Note the large light purple region on the left that consumes about one-third of the execution. A small amount of additional inspection reveals that this corresponds to a routine which simply calls MPI_Init. Note also that there are a few white lines that span the length of this light purple segment. These lines correspond to straggler MPI ranks which took about 190 seconds to launch — no samples can be collected until a process starts — and arrive at MPI_Init, which is acting like a collective operation. In other words, recalling the discussion in Section 5.2, a few anomalous processors had

---

[2]This process could not have stopped because the execution's many successful collective-communication operations would not have completed.

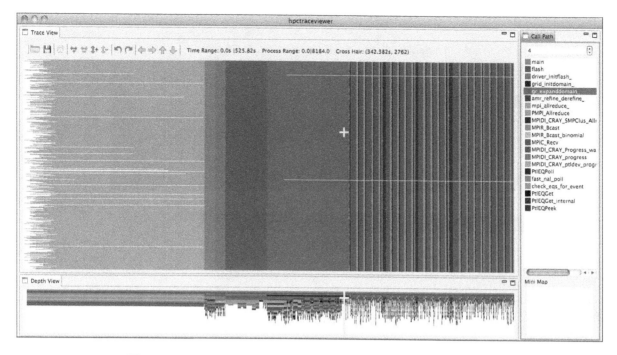

Figure 3: An 8184-core execution of FLASH on a Cray XT5.

enormous effects on the execution and sampling-based presentation techniques immediately exposed them.

6.3 High Performance Linpack (HPL)

Figure 4 shows our tool displaying a 5000 second execution of an implementation of High Performance Linpack written in Rice University's Coarray Fortran 2.0 [27] running on 256 cores of a Cray XT4. The blue triangular sections show serialization present in initialization and finalization code. The center section of the figure shows the heart of the LU decomposition. The irregular moire patterns arise because of the use of asynchronous broadcast communication, which allows the execution to proceed without tight synchronization between the processes.

6.4 Fast Fourier Transform (FFT)

Figure 5 shows our tool displaying a 76 second execution of an implementation of a one-dimensional implementation of Fast Fourier Transform (FFT) written in Rice University's Coarray Fortran 2.0 [27] running on 256 cores. The figure displayed here shows the first execution we traced to begin to understand (a) the overall performance of the code, (b) the impact of different regions of the code on its execution time, and (c) the transient behavior of the code. We were surprised by what we found in the trace. The FFT computation has several distinct phases: an all-to-all permutation, a local computation phase that is proportional to $N \log N$ (where N is the size of the local data), and finally a global computation phase that requires $N \log P$ time and $\log P$ rounds of pairwise asynchronous communication. In the Trace View, the green samples represent execution of calls to barrier synchronization. The application has only two barriers: one at the beginning of the global communication phase and one end. While the first (leftmost) barrier is short — indicated by the narrow green band, the barrier at the end consumes 30% of the total execution time! This

diagram revealed that even though the global communication phase should be evenly balanced across the processors, in practice some processors were finishing much later than others. Processors that finish in a timely fashion wait at the barrier until the stragglers arrive.

The inset figure shows detail from the interior of the execution. The blue areas show processors waiting for asynchronous get operations to complete. We have concluded that this is an effect rather than a cause of the imbalance. The cursor selection in the inset shows an unexpected stall inside our asynchronous progress engine. The stall occurred within a call to the GASNet communication library that checks for the completion of a non-blocking get. In our use of GASNet, we had not anticipated that calls to non-blocking primitives would ever block. Clearly, our expectations were wrong.

Based on the feedback from hpctraceviewer, we implemented an alternate version of FFT that used all-to-all communication rather than the problematic asynchronous pairwise communication. The changes resulted in a 50% speedup when executed on 4096 cores of a Cray XT4 known as Franklin.

6.5 Summary

We have demonstrated our tools on applications with several different behaviors and over two very different programming models (MPI and Coarry Fortran 2.0). Our sampling-based trace presentation quickly exposed several things: extremely late launching for a few processes (FLASH), serialization during HPL's initialization and finalization; and delays caused by asynchronous communication in what should have been a balanced phase (FFT). We show call paths that begin at 'main,' descend into libraries (e.g., PETSc), and continue into libraries used by those libraries (e.g., MPI). By exposing this detail, an informed analyst can form very precise hypotheses about what is happening, such as our

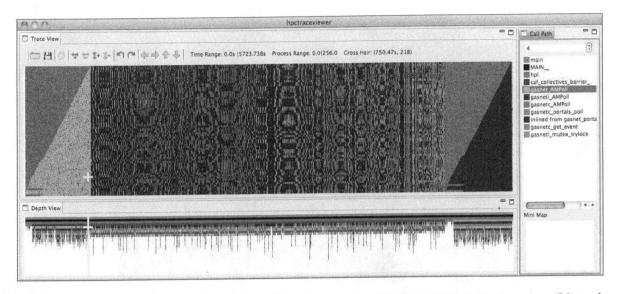

Figure 4: A 256-core execution of a Coarray Fortran 2.0 implementation of High Performance Linpack on a Cray XT4.

hypothesis that FFT is using GASNet in such a way as to exhaust its asynchronous `get` resource tickets. We believe this provides strong evidence that our sampling-based trace presentation is not only scalable, but is also highly effective in exposing performance problems and even some anomalies.

7. CONCLUSIONS

The fundamental theme of this paper is how to use various forms of sampling to collect and present fine-grained call path traces. To collect call path traces of large-scale executions with controllable measurement granularity and overhead, we use asynchronous sampling. By combining sampling with a compact representation of call path trace data, we generate trace data at a very moderate, constant and controllable rate. (Additionally, by using a technique to memoize call stack unwinds, it is only necessary to unwind procedure frames that are new with respect to the prior sample.) To rapidly present trace data at multiple levels of abstraction and in complementary views, `hpctraceviewer`, again, uses various sampling techniques. We showed that sampling-based presentation is not only rapid, but can also be effective. Given all this, we would argue that HPC-TOOLKIT's call path tracer manages measurement overhead and data size better than a typical flat tracer — while providing more detail.

Our sampling-based measurement approach naturally applies to many programming models because it measures all aspects of a thread's user-level execution. While there are cases, such as over-threading, where measuring system-level threads does not well match the application-level programming model, our approach does not preclude exploiting model-specific knowledge as well.

There are a number of directions that we are actively exploring. First, we want to use our sampling-based call path trace information to identify root causes of performance bottlenecks; related work would be pattern analyzers for instrumentation based-tracing. A starting point is to use a special color, say red, to indicate, at all levels of a call path, when a sample corresponds to communication. Second, with an eye

toward exascale computers, we are exploring measurement techniques that involve sampling at multiple levels, such as randomly sampling processes that are then monitored for a period using asynchronous sampling. Third, we want to add several modest but very useful features. As one example, we would like to expose structure within a procedure frame (including sample points) and link it to source code, just as we do with HPCTOOLKIT's `hpcviewer` tool for presenting call path profiles. As another example, we plan to track a sampled procedure's return to distinguish, in the Depth View, between several samples (a) within the same procedure instance and (b) spread over different procedure instances. Finally, we are considering techniques for addressing clock skew, a classic problem with tracing.

Acknowledgments

Guohua Jin wrote the Coarry Fortran (CAF) 2.0 version of HPL; Bill Scherer wrote the CAF 2.0 version of FFT.

Development of HPCTOOLKIT is supported by the Department of Energy's Office of Science under cooperative agreements DE-FC02-07ER25800 and DE-FC02-06ER25762. This research used resources of (a) the National Center for Computational Sciences at Oak Ridge National Laboratory, which is supported by the Office of Science of the U.S. Department of Energy under contract DE-AC05-00OR22725; (b) the National Energy Research Scientific Computing Center, which is supported by the Office of Science of the U.S. Department of Energy under contract DE-AC02-05CH11231; and (c) the Argonne Leadership Computing Facility at Argonne National Laboratory, which is supported by the Office of Science of the U.S. Department of Energy under contract DE-AC02-06CH11357.

8. REFERENCES

[1] L. Adhianto, S. Banerjee, M. Fagan, M. Krentel, G. Marin, J. Mellor-Crummey, and N. R. Tallent. HPCToolkit: Tools for performance analysis of optimized parallel programs. *Concurrency and*

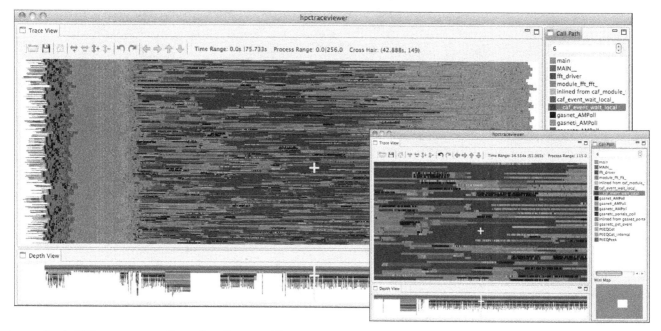

Figure 5: A 256-core execution of a Coarray Fortran 2.0 FFT benchmark on a Cray XT4. The inset shows detail around the main crosshair.

Computation: Practice and Experience, 22(6):685–701, 2010.

[2] G. Ammons, T. Ball, and J. R. Larus. Exploiting hardware performance counters with flow and context sensitive profiling. In *Proc. of the 1997 ACM SIGPLAN Conf. on Programming Language Design and Implementation*, pages 85–96, New York, NY, USA, 1997. ACM.

[3] Apple Computer. *Shark User Guide*, April 2008.

[4] S. Balay, K. Buschelman, V. Eijkhout, W. D. Gropp, D. Kaushik, M. G. Knepley, L. C. McInnes, B. F. Smith, and H. Zhang. PETSc users manual. Technical Report ANL-95/11 - Revision 3.0.0, Argonne National Laboratory, 2008.

[5] M. Casas, R. Badia, and J. Labarta. Automatic structure extraction from MPI applications tracefiles. In A.-M. Kermarrec, L. Bougé, and T. Priol, editors, *Proc. of the 13th Intl. Euro-Par Conference*, volume 4641 of *Lecture Notes in Computer Science*, pages 3–12. Springer, 2007.

[6] J. Caubet, J. Gimenez, J. Labarta, L. De Rose, and J. S. Vetter. A dynamic tracing mechanism for performance analysis of OpenMP applications. In *Proc. of the Intl. Workshop on OpenMP Appl. and Tools*, pages 53–67, London, UK, 2001. Springer-Verlag.

[7] A. Chan, W. Gropp, and E. Lusk. An efficient format for nearly constant-time access to arbitrary time intervals in large trace files. *Scientific Programming*, 16(2-3):155–165, 2008.

[8] I.-H. Chung, R. E. Walkup, H.-F. Wen, and H. Yu. MPI performance analysis tools on Blue Gene/L. In *Proc. of the 2006 ACM/IEEE Conf. on Supercomputing*, page 123, New York, NY, USA, 2006. ACM.

[9] L. De Rose, B. Homer, D. Johnson, S. Kaufmann, and H. Poxon. Cray performance analysis tools. In *Tools for High Performance Computing*, pages 191–199. Springer, 2008.

[10] A. Dubey, L. B. Reid, and R. Fisher. Introduction to FLASH 3.0, with application to supersonic turbulence. *Physica Scripta*, 132:014046, 2008.

[11] N. Froyd, J. Mellor-Crummey, and R. Fowler. Low-overhead call path profiling of unmodified, optimized code. In *Proc. of the 19th Intl. Conf. on Supercomputing*, pages 81–90, New York, NY, USA, 2005. ACM.

[12] T. Gamblin, B. R. de Supinski, M. Schulz, R. Fowler, and D. A. Reed. Scalable load-balance measurement for SPMD codes. In *Proc. of the 2008 ACM/IEEE Conf. on Supercomputing*, pages 1–12, Piscataway, NJ, USA, 2008. IEEE Press.

[13] T. Gamblin, B. R. de Supinski, M. Schulz, R. Fowler, and D. A. Reed. Clustering performance data efficiently at massive scales. In *Proc. of the 24th ACM Intl. Conf. on Supercomputing*, pages 243–252, New York, NY, USA, 2010. ACM.

[14] T. Gamblin, R. Fowler, and D. A. Reed. Scalable methods for monitoring and detecting behavioral equivalence classes in scientific codes. In *Proc. of the 22nd IEEE Intl. Parallel and Distributed Processing Symp.*, pages 1–12, 2008.

[15] M. Geimer, F. Wolf, B. J. N. Wylie, E. Ábrahám, D. Becker, and B. Mohr. The Scalasca performance toolset architecture. *Concurrency and Computation: Practice and Experience*, 22(6):702–719, 2010.

[16] J. Gonzalez, J. Gimenez, and J. Labarta. Automatic detection of parallel applications computation phases. In *Proc. of the 23rd IEEE Intl. Parallel and Distributed Processing Symp.*, pages 1–11, 2009.

[17] W. Gu, G. Eisenhauer, K. Schwan, and J. Vetter. Falcon: On-line monitoring for steering parallel

programs. *Concurrency: Practice and Experience*, 10(9):699–736, 1998.

[18] Innovative Computing Laboratory, University of Tennessee. HPC Challenge benchmarks. `http://icl.cs.utk.edu/hpcc`.

[19] A. Knüpfer, H. Brunst, J. Doleschal, M. Jurenz, M. Lieber, H. Mickler, M. S. Müller, and W. E. Nagel. The Vampir performance analysis tool-set. In M. Resch, R. Keller, V. Himmler, B. Krammer, and A. Schulz, editors, *Tools for High Performance Computing*, pages 139–155. Springer, 2008.

[20] A. Knüpfer and W. Nagel. Construction and compression of complete call graphs for post-mortem program trace analysis. In *Proc. of the 2005 Intl. Conf. on Parallel Processing*, pages 165–172, 2005.

[21] J. Labarta. Obtaining extremely detailed information at scale. 2009 Workshop on Performance Tools for Petascale Computing (Center for Scalable Application Development Software), July 2009.

[22] J. Labarta, J. Gimenez, E. Martínez, P. González, H. Servat, G. Llort, and X. Aguilar. Scalability of visualization and tracing tools. In G. Joubert, W. Nagel, F. Peters, O. Plata, P. Tirado, and E. Zapata, editors, *Parallel Computing: Current & Future Issues of High-End Computing: Proc. of the Intl. Conf. ParCo 2005*, volume 33 of *NIC Series*, pages 869–876, Jülich, September 2006. John von Neumann Institute for Computing.

[23] C. W. Lee and L. V. Kalé. Scalable techniques for performance analysis. Technical Report 07-06, Dept. of Computer Science, University of Illinois, Urbana-Champaign, May 2007.

[24] C. W. Lee, C. Mendes, and L. V. Kalé. Towards scalable performance analysis and visualization through data reduction. In *Proc. of the 22nd IEEE Intl. Parallel and Distributed Processing Symp.*, pages 1–8, 2008.

[25] G. Llort, J. Gonzalez, H. Servat, J. Gimenez, and J. Labarta. On-line detection of large-scale parallel application's structure. In *Proc. of the 24th IEEE Intl. Parallel and Distributed Processing Symp.*, pages 1–10, 2010.

[26] Los Alamos National Laboratory. PFLOTRAN project. `https://software.lanl.gov/pflotran`, 2010.

[27] J. Mellor-Crummey, L. Adhianto, G. Jin, and W. N. Scherer III. A new vision for Coarray Fortran. In *Proc. of the Third Conf. on Partitioned Global Address Space Programming Models*, 2009.

[28] Message Passing Interface Forum. *MPI: A Message Passing Interface Standard*, June 1999. `http://www.mpi-forum.org/docs/mpi-11.ps`.

[29] R. T. Mills, G. E. Hammond, P. C. Lichtner, V. Sripathi, G. K. Mahinthakumar, and B. F. Smith. Modeling subsurface reactive flows using leadership-class computing. *Journal of Physics: Conference Series*, 180(1):012062, 2009.

[30] M. Noeth, P. Ratn, F. Mueller, M. Schulz, and B. R. de Supinski. ScalaTrace: Scalable compression and replay of communication traces for high-performance computing. *J. Parallel Distrib. Comput.*, 69(8):696–710, 2009.

[31] Oracle. Oracle Solaris Studio 12.2: Performance Analyzer. `http://download.oracle.com/docs/cd/E18659_01/pdf/821-1379.pdf`, September 2010.

[32] Rice University. HPCToolkit performance tools. `http://hpctoolkit.org`.

[33] M. Schulz, J. Galarowicz, D. Maghrak, W. Hachfeld, D. Montoya, and S. Cranford. Open|SpeedShop: An open source infrastructure for parallel performance analysis. *Sci. Program.*, 16(2-3):105–121, 2008.

[34] H. Servat, G. Llort, J. Giménez, and J. Labarta. Detailed performance analysis using coarse grain sampling. In H.-X. Lin, M. Alexander, M. Forsell, A. Knüpfer, R. Prodan, L. Sousa, and A. Streit, editors, *Euro-Par 2009 Workshops*, volume 6043 of *Lecture Notes in Computer Science*, pages 185–198. Springer-Verlag, 2010.

[35] S. S. Shende and A. D. Malony. The TAU parallel performance system. *Int. J. High Perform. Comput. Appl.*, 20(2):287–311, 2006.

[36] N. R. Tallent, L. Adhianto, and J. M. Mellor-Crummey. Scalable identification of load imbalance in parallel executions using call path profiles. In *Proc. of the 2010 ACM/IEEE Conf. on Supercomputing*, 2010.

[37] N. R. Tallent and J. Mellor-Crummey. Effective performance measurement and analysis of multithreaded applications. In *Proc. of the 14th ACM SIGPLAN Symp. on Principles and Practice of Parallel Programming*, pages 229–240, New York, NY, USA, 2009. ACM.

[38] N. R. Tallent, J. Mellor-Crummey, and M. W. Fagan. Binary analysis for measurement and attribution of program performance. In *Proc. of the 2009 ACM SIGPLAN Conf. on Programming Language Design and Implementation*, pages 441–452, New York, NY, USA, 2009. ACM.

[39] N. R. Tallent, J. M. Mellor-Crummey, L. Adhianto, M. W. Fagan, and M. Krentel. Diagnosing performance bottlenecks in emerging petascale applications. In *Proc. of the 2009 ACM/IEEE Conf. on Supercomputing*, pages 1–11, New York, NY, USA, 2009. ACM.

[40] N. R. Tallent, J. M. Mellor-Crummey, and A. Porterfield. Analyzing lock contention in multithreaded applications. In *Proc. of the 15th ACM SIGPLAN Symp. on Principles and Practice of Parallel Programming*, pages 269–280, New York, NY, USA, 2010. ACM.

[41] TU Dresden Center for Information Services and High Performance Computing (ZIH). VampirTrace 5.10.1 user manual. `http://www.tu-dresden.de/zih/vampirtrace`, March 2011.

[42] V. Vishwanath, M. Hereld, K. Iskra, D. Kimpe, V. Morozov, M. E. Paper, R. Ross, and K. Yoshii. Accelerating I/O forwarding in IBM Blue Gene/P systems. Technical Report ANL/MCS-P1745-0410, Argonne National Laboratory, April 2010.

[43] P. H. Worley. MPICL: A port of the PICL tracing logic to MPI. `http://www.epm.ornl.gov/picl`.

[44] O. Zaki, E. Lusk, W. Gropp, and D. Swider. Toward scalable performance visualization with Jumpshot. *High Performance Computing Applications*, 13(2):277–288, Fall 1999.

Generic Topology Mapping Strategies for Large-scale Parallel Architectures

Torsten Hoefler
University of Illinois at Urbana-Champaign
Urbana, IL, USA
htor@illinois.edu

Marc Snir
University of Illinois at Urbana-Champaign
Urbana, IL, USA
snir@illinois.edu

ABSTRACT

The steadily increasing number of nodes in high-performance computing systems and the technology and power constraints lead to sparse network topologies. Efficient mapping of application communication patterns to the network topology gains importance as systems grow to petascale and beyond. Such mapping is supported in parallel programming frameworks such as MPI, but is often not well implemented. We show that the topology mapping problem is NP-complete and analyze and compare different practical topology mapping heuristics. We demonstrate an efficient and fast new heuristic which is based on graph similarity and show its utility with application communication patterns on real topologies. Our mapping strategies support heterogeneous networks and show significant reduction of congestion on torus, fat-tree, and the PERCS network topologies, for irregular communication patterns. We also demonstrate that the benefit of topology mapping grows with the network size and show how our algorithms can be used in a practical setting to optimize communication performance. Our efficient topology mapping strategies are shown to reduce network congestion by up to 80%, reduce average dilation by up to 50%, and improve benchmarked communication performance by 18%.

Categories and Subject Descriptors

D.1.3 [**Concurrent Programming**]: Parallel Programming—*Topology Mapping*

General Terms

Performance

Keywords

Topology Mapping, MPI Graph Topologies

1. MOTIVATION

The number of nodes in the largest computing systems, and, hence, the size of their interconnection networks, is increasing rapidly: The Jaguar system at ORNL has over

18,000 nodes and larger systems are expected in the near future. These networks are built by interconnecting *nodes* (*switches* and *processors*) with *links*. Pin count, power and gate count constraints restrict the number of links per switch; typical sizes are: 24 (InfiniBand), 36 (Myrinet, InfiniBand), or 6 (Sea Star or BlueGene/P). Different topologies are used to construct large-scale networks from crossbars; e.g., k-ary n-cubes (hypercube, torus), k-ary n-trees (fat-trees), or folded Clos networks. Networks also differ in their routing protocols.

As the number of nodes grows larger, the *diameter* of the network (i.e., the maximum distance between two processors) increases; for many topologies, the *bisection bandwidth* (i.e., the minimum total bandwidth of links that need to be cut in order to divide the processors into two equal sets) decreases relative to the number of nodes.

This effect is well understood and it is generally accepted that dense communication patterns (such as an all-to-all communication where each node communicates to each other) are hard to scale beyond petascale systems. Luckily, the communication patterns of many applications are relatively sparse (each node communicate with a few others), and dense communications can be replaced by repeated sparse communications (e.g., the all-to-all communication used for the transpose in a parallel Fast Fourier Transform can be replaced by two phases of group transposes, each involving only $\Theta(\sqrt{P})$ processors [17]). Furthermore, the communication pattern often has significant *locality*, e.g., when most communication occurs between adjacent cells in a 3D domain. However, an inappropriate mapping of processes to the nodes of the interconnection network can map a logical communication pattern that is sparse and local into traffic that has no locality.

Finding an allocation of processes to nodes such that the sparse application communication topology efficiently utilizes the physical links in the network is called *topology mapping*. The problem has been much studied for regular communication graph and regular interconnection network topologies. In practice, both graphs are likely to be irregular: The communication pattern may be data-dependent (e.g., for finite-element on irregular meshes); it may consist of a superposition of multiple regular graphs (e.g., for computations that combine nearest-neighbor communications with global communication). The interconnection network may have a complex topology, with different links having different bandwidths (e.g., copper vs. optics), and with some links being disabled. The general problem has been much less studied.

Our previous argument suggests that mapping regular and irregular applications to the network topology is becoming more and more important at large scale. MPI offers support for topology mapping. A user can specify the (regular or irregular) communication topology of the application and request the library to provide a good mapping to the physical topology [16, 7]. An MPI implementation then re-numbers the processes in the communicator so as to improve the mapping.The scalability and usability of the topology interface was recently improved in MPI-2.2 [12] to allow a scalable specification and edge weights that represent communication characteristics. Finding a good mapping is non trivial and MPI implementations tend to use the trivial identify mapping.

Our work supports the optimization of arbitrary process topologies for arbitrary network topologies and thus an efficient implementation of the MPI process topology interface. This enables transparent and portable topology mapping for all network topologies. Our work also addresses heterogeneous networks such as PERCS, where different physical links may have different bandwidths.

Our implementation is intended for renumbering processes as suggested by MPI, however, the developed techniques and our open-source library can also be applied to other parallel programming frameworks such as UPC or CAF.

1.1 Related Work

The mapping of regular Cartesian structures to different target architectures is well understood. Yu, Chung, and Moreira present different topology mapping strategies of torus process topologies into the torus network of BlueGene/L [23]. Bhatelé, Kalé and Kumar discuss topology-aware load-balancing strategies for molecular dynamic CHARM++ applications [2]. Their analysis enables mapping from mesh and torus process topologies to other mesh and torus network topologies and provides performance gains of up to 10%.

Several researchers investigated techniques to optimize process mappings with arbitrary topologies on parallel computers. Bokhari [3] reduces the mapping problem to graph isomorphism. However, his strategy ignores edges that are not mapped. It was shown later that such edges can have a detrimental effect on the congestion and dilation of the mapping. Lee and Aggarwal [15] improve those results and define a more accurate model which includes all edges of the communication graph and propose a two-stage optimization function consisting of initial greedy assignment and later pairwise swaps. Bollinger and Midkiff [4] use a similar model and simulated annealing to optimize process mappings.

Träff proposes an implementation strategy for strictly hierarchical networks such as clusters of SMPs [22]. He defines different optimization criteria and shows the potential of MPI topology mapping for several artificial graphs.

2. TOPOLOGY MAPPING

2.1 Terms and Conventions

We use a notation that extends that used for graph embeddings [19]. The formulation is similar to the fluid flow approximation used to study Internet traffic [13]. We represent the (logical) communication pattern using a weighted, directed graph $\mathcal{G} = (V_\mathcal{G}, \omega_\mathcal{G})$ $V_\mathcal{G}$ is the set of processes; the weight $\omega(uv)$ of the edge connecting $u \in V_\mathcal{G}$ to $v \in V_\mathcal{G}$ rep-

resents the volume of communication from process u to process v; the weight is zero if no such communication occurs. The graph $\mathcal{G}$ might be disconnected and isolated vertices can exist – representing the concurrent execution of multiple unrelated jobs.

Likewise, the (physical) interconnection network is represented by a weighted, directed graph $\mathcal{H} = (V_\mathcal{H}, C_\mathcal{H}, c_\mathcal{H}, \mathcal{R}_\mathcal{H})$. $V_\mathcal{H}$ is the set of physical nodes (processors and switches). If $u \in V_\mathcal{H}$ then $C_\mathcal{H}(u)$ is the number of processes that can be hosted at u (this represents multicore processors); $C_\mathcal{H}(u) = 0$ if u contains no processors (e.g., is a switch). $c_\mathcal{H}(uv)$ is the *capacity* (bandwidth) of the link connecting u to v (zero if there is no such link).

The function $\mathcal{R}_\mathcal{H}$ represents the routing algorithm. Let $\mathcal{P}(uv)$ be the set of simple paths (paths where each edge occurs at most once) connecting node $u \in V_\mathcal{H}$ to node $v \in V_\mathcal{H}$ For each pair of nodes uv, $\mathcal{R}_\mathcal{H}(uv)$ is a probability distribution on $\mathcal{P}(uv)$. Thus, if $p \in \mathcal{P}(uv)$ then $\mathcal{R}_\mathcal{H}(uv)(p)$ is the fraction of traffic from u to v that is routed through path p. In practice, routing algorithms tend to use a small fraction of the possible paths (e.g., only shortest paths), and the traffic is often distributed evenly across all used paths.

The topology mapping is specified by a function $\Gamma: V_\mathcal{G} \to V_\mathcal{H}$ which maps the vertices of $\mathcal{G}$ (processes) to vertices in $V_\mathcal{H}$ (nodes) such that no more than $C(v)$ vertices in $\mathcal{G}$ are mapped to each vertex $v \in V_\mathcal{H}$. We use the terms mapping and embedding interchangeably.

We now define two quality measures for a mapping: *Worst Case Congestion* (for short, *congestion*) and *Average Dilation* (for short, *dilation*). Let $|p|$ denote the length of path p. Then, the expected dilation of an edge uv of the communication graph is defined as

$$Dilation(uv) = \sum_{p \in \mathcal{P}(\Gamma(u)\Gamma(v))} \mathcal{R}_\mathcal{H}(\Gamma(u)\Gamma(v))(p) \cdot |p| \quad (1)$$

$Dilation(uv)$ is the average length of the path taken by a message sent from process u to process v. The average dilation is computed by weighting each inter-process communication by its frequency:

$$Dilation(\Gamma) = \sum_{u,v \in V_\mathcal{G}} \omega_\mathcal{G}(uv) \cdot Dilation(uv) \quad (2)$$

Dilation is the average number of edges traversed by packets – hence is a measure of the total "communication work" performed by the interconnection network; it is indicative of the total energy consumption of the interconnection network.

The congestion of a link uv of the interconnection network is the ratio between the amount of traffic on that link and the capacity of the link. The total traffic crossing an edge $e \in E_\mathcal{H}$ is

$$Traffic(e) =$$

$$\sum_{u,v \in V_\mathcal{G}} \omega_\mathcal{G}(uv) \left(\sum_{p \in \mathcal{P}(\Gamma(u)\Gamma(v)), e \in p} \mathcal{R}_\mathcal{H}(\Gamma(u)\Gamma(v))(p) \right) \quad (3)$$

The congestion of edge e is defined as

$$Congestion(e) = \frac{Traffic(e)}{c_\mathcal{H}(e)}, \quad (4)$$

and the worst-case congestion is

$$Congestion(\Gamma) = \max_e Congestion(e) \quad (5)$$

$Congestion(\Gamma)$ is a lower bound on the time needed for communication. Both congestion and dilation can be computed in polynomial time.

The chosen representation embodies certain assumptions that are satisfied in many cases:

We assume that bandwidth between processes hosted at the same processor node is practically unbounded. To do so formally, we add to each processor node a self-loop with infinite capacity.

We assume that switches are not a performance bottleneck: the traffic flowing through a switch is constrained by the bandwidth of the incoming and outgoing links, but not by the internal switch structure. If this is not the case, the internal switch structure needs to be represented, too.

We assume oblivious routing: the distribution of traffic between two nodes does not depend on other ongoing traffic.

We assume that the routing algorithm is fixed, and does not depend on the embedded communication graph: The knowledge of the application communication pattern is used to map processes to processors, but is not used to change the routing algorithm. The formalism can be adjusted to handle routing protocols that are application dependent, in which case, the routing function becomes part of the mapping.

The mapping problem is often expressed as a permutation of processes, following an initial assignment of processes to processors. The remapping is defined by a permutation π on the set $0 \ldots P-1$ of processes. For example, in MPI, the user can specify a logical communication graph for a communicator, and request that the processes in the communicator be physically mapped so as to improve the performance of this communication pattern; the permutation π is returned as a new rank order for the processes in the communicator if the `reorder` argument is set to true.

2.2 Practical Issues

The mapping framework presented in this paper assumes that a communication pattern is defined once for all processes running on the system, and the processes are mapped to processors once. In practice, it may be advantageous to periodically readjust the mapping; and remapping of the processes of a job may be restricted to the set of nodes allocated to the job. We discuss below how our framework can be extended to handle these concerns; a detailed performance analysis of these enhancements is beyond the scope of this paper.

The jobs running on the system can be periodically reconfigured, based on the observed communication pattern and the overall network topology. A remapping might be beneficial whenever the communication pattern of a job changes, or when jobs start or terminate. When we do so, we need to balance the overhead of remapping against the benefit of improved communication performance. We do not consider in this paper the problem of selecting an optimal remapping schedule, and focus only on the choice of an optimal mapping when (re)mapping is performed.

If each job is mapped independently, then the host graph for a job is taken to be the partition used for this job (we assume space partitioning): the processors allocated to the job and the switches that can be used to route between these nodes. If there is little interference between the traffic of different parallel jobs, then the capacity of each link in this host graph equals its physical capacity; if the interference is significant, then the traffic of other jobs can be represented

as a reduction in the capacity of edges in the host graph seen by the job being mapped. A significant change in the background traffic may necessitate a remapping of processes to nodes.

2.3 An Example Mapping

Figure 1 shows a simple example. The host network topology $\mathcal{H}$ is a 2-ary 3-cube (3D cube) with $V_{\mathcal{H}} = \{0,1\}^3$ and $E_{\mathcal{H}} = \{(u,v) \in V_{\mathcal{H}} \times V_{\mathcal{H}} \mid u \text{ and } v \text{ differ in one bit}\}$; we assume dimension order routing in x,y,z-order. We use a four process job with the communication topology shown in Figure 1(b) as example. A possible initial mapping that maps $(0,1,2,3)$ to $(000,111,101,100)$, in this order, is shown in Figure 1(c); the edges in $\mathcal{H}$ are annotated with the number of connections that are routed through the edge. The maximum congestion and dilation for this initial mapping are 2 and 3, respectively. A better mapping, shown in Figure 1(d), maps $(0,1,2,3)$ to $(101,111,000,100)$, with both maximum congestion and dilation of 1.

2.4 The Mapping Problem

The mapping problem can be defined as finding a mapping Γ that minimizes some measure of the congestion or dilation. In this work, we focus on minimizing the maximum congestion (the algorithm runtime) and average dilation (the needed power to move the data). Our work is equally applicable to other optimization metrics.

We define the Topology Mapping Problem TMP as the problem of deciding if there exists a mapping Γ (or permutation π) that has congestion less or equal to x.

THEOREM 1. *TMP is NP-complete.*

PROOF. The congestion of a mapping can be computed in polynomial time, using Equations (3), (4) and (5). It follows that TMP is in NP: The NP algorithm guesses a mapping Γ, computes its congestion and returns TRUE is the congestion is less than x.

We now show a reduction to the "MINIMUM CUT INTO BOUNDED SETS" NP-complete problem' [10, ND17] to conclude our proof. The (reduced) min cut problem takes as input an undirected graph $G = <V, E>$, two specified vertices $s, t \in V$ and an integer L; it decides whether there exist a partition of the vertices into two disjoint sets V_1, V_2 such that $s \in V_1$, $t \in V_2$, $|V_1| = |V_2|$ and the number of edges between V_1 and V_2 is no more than L. an

Let $G = <V, E>, s, t, L$ be an instance of the min-cut problem. Let $P = |V|$. We construct a "dumbbell" host graph $\mathcal{H} = (V_{\mathcal{H}}, E_{\mathcal{H}}, C, c)$ that consists of two fully connected graphs $L_1 = L_2 = K_{P/2}$ and a single bidirectional edge $\bar{e}$ between arbitrary vertices $u_1 \in L_1$ and $u_2 \in L_2$. We set $C(v) = 1$ and $c(e) = 1$ for all edges, except edge $u_1 u_2$; $c(u_1 u_2) = c(u_2 u_1) = P$. The construction is shown, for $P = 8$ in Figure 2. The routing function $\mathcal{R}_{\mathcal{H}}$ is defined to

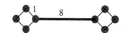

Figure 2: Dumbbell graph

route all traffic between two nodes in $\mathcal{H}$ through the unique shortest path connecting them.

We define the communication graph $\mathcal{G}$ to be the graph G with weight $\omega(e) = 1$ for each edge $e \in E$; the edge st is given weight P^4 if $st \notin E$, and weight $P^4 + 1$ if $st \in E$.

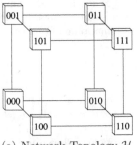
(a) Network Topology $\mathcal{H}$.

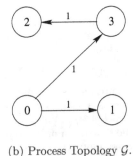
(b) Process Topology $\mathcal{G}$.

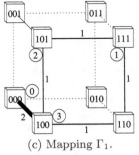
(c) Mapping Γ_1.

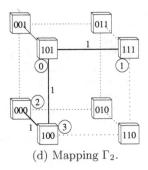
(d) Mapping Γ_2.

Figure 1: A simple example for topology-aware mappings.

Any mapping of $\mathcal{G}$ to $\mathcal{H}$ defines a partition of $V_{\mathcal{G}}$ into two equal size sets $V_1 = \Gamma^{-1}(L_1)$ and $V_2 = \Gamma^{-1}(L_2)$. A mapping that minimizes congestion must map $\{s, t\}$ to $\{u_1, u_2\}$: This results in a congestion of $\leq P^3 + P$ whereas any other mapping will result in a congestion of $\geq P^4$ (since traffic from s to t will flow through an edge of capacity 1). In such a mapping, the most congested edge will be the edge $u_1 u_2$; its congestion will be

$$P^3 + \frac{1}{P} \cdot |\{(v_1 v_2) \in E \text{ s.t. } v_1 \in V_1 \text{ and } v_2 \in V_2\}|$$

Thus, any solution to the TMP instance, with $x = P^3 + L/P$, can be used to build a solution to the partition problem in polynomial time. It is easy to see that the converse is also true. $\square$

2.5 Restricted Mapping Problem

We shall focus, from now on, on the simpler problem where routing only uses shortest paths and all shortest paths are used with equal probability.

The dumbbell graph $\mathcal{H}$ used in the proof of Theorem 1 has a unique shortest path between any two nodes; the routing function routes all traffic between two nodes on that shortest paths. Thus, the problem of finding an optimal mapping is still NP-hard if routing is restricted as above.

For the restricted routing problem, we do not need to specify explicitly the routing function; the host graph is defined as $(V_{\mathcal{H}}, C_{\mathcal{H}}, c_{\mathcal{H}})$, and the routing function is determined implicitly. The number of shortest paths between two nodes can be exponential in the number of vertices, so that the concise representation of the host graph can be exponentially smaller than an explicit one. Therefore, it is not obvious that computing the congestion or dilation of a mapping takes polynomial time, with this input representation. We show this is the case, below.

Determining the dilation of an edge $(u, v) \in \mathcal{G}$ is straightforward by computing the length of the shortest path from $\Gamma(u)$ to $\Gamma(v)$ in $\mathcal{H}$. This can be implemented with single-source-shortest-path (SSSP) from each vertex in time $\mathcal{O}(|V_{\mathcal{G}}| \cdot (|E_{\mathcal{H}}| + |V_{\mathcal{H}}| \cdot \log |V_{\mathcal{H}}|))$.

The congestion of an edge can be computed in polynomial time using an algorithm similar to the one used for computing betweenness centrality [5]. We present below a simple (nonoptimal) polynomial time algorithm.

Let $\sigma_i(s, t)$ be the number of paths of length i from s to t. Then

$$\sigma_0(s, t) = \begin{cases} 1 & \text{if } s = t \\ 0 & \text{otherwise} \end{cases}$$

and

$$\sigma_i(s, t) = \sum_{u \text{ adjacent to } t} \sigma_{i-1}(s, u)$$

We compute $\sigma_i(s, t))$ for all pairs of nodes s, t and all $i \leq P$ in time $O(|V_{\mathcal{H}}|^2 |E_{\mathcal{H}}|)$. The distance (the shortest path length) between any two nodes is equal to

$$d(s, t) = \min\{i : \sigma_i(s, t) > 0\}$$

and the number of shortest paths from s to t is equal to

$$\tau(s, t) = \sigma_{d(s,t)}(s, t)$$

Let $\tau(s, t, e)$ be the number of shortest paths from s to t going through edge e, Then, if $e = uv$, then

$$\tau(s, t, e) = \sum_{j+k=d(s,t)-1} \sigma_j(s, u) \cdot \sigma_k(v, t)$$

The traffic through edge e can now be computed as

$$Traffic(e) = \sum_{s,t} \omega(s, t) \frac{\tau(s, t, e)}{\tau(s, t)}$$

and the congestion equals to

$$\max_e \frac{Traffic(e)}{c(e)}$$

3. TOPOLOGY MAPPING ALGORITHMS

Previous work discussed different options for topology mapping. We start with an extension to a simple greedy algorithm which supports heterogeneous networks, discuss recursive bisection mapping and then discuss a new mapping strategy based on graph similarity. We also show how to support multicore nodes with established graph partitioning techniques.

3.1 Greedy Heuristic

Similar greedy algorithms have been proposed in previous work. Our greedy strategy, however, considers edge weights and thus enables mapping to heterogeneous network architectures.

Let the weight of a vertex $v \in V_{\mathcal{G}}$ be the sum of the weights of all edges $e = (v, u)$. The greedy mapping strategy starts at some vertex in $\mathcal{H}$, chooses the *heaviest* vertex in $\mathcal{G}$ and greedily maps its heaviest neighboring vertices in $\mathcal{G}$ to the neighboring vertices in $\mathcal{H}$ with the heaviest connections. The process is continued recursively. The detailed algorithm is presented in Algorithm 1. The greedy heuristic would find an optimal solution for the example in Figure 1 if it is started at vertex 100. This greedy approach is the most generic

Algorithm 1: Greedy Graph Embedding.

Input: Graphs $\mathcal{H}$ and $\mathcal{G}$, $C(v)$ for all $v \in V_{\mathcal{H}}$.
Output: Mapping $\Gamma : V_{\mathcal{G}} \to V_{\mathcal{H}}$, congestion $\rho(e)$ for all $e \in E_{\mathcal{H}}$.

1 $S \leftarrow V_{\mathcal{G}}$;
2 $Q \leftarrow$ empty priority queue;
3 $\hat{\omega} = \max_{e \in E_{\mathcal{G}}} \{\omega(e)\} \cdot |V_{\mathcal{H}}|^2$
4 initialize all $\rho(e)$ with $\hat{\omega}$; // forces minimal edge count
5 pick start vertex $s \in V_{\mathcal{H}}$;
6 **while** $S \neq \emptyset$ **do**
7   find vertex m with heaviest out-edges in S;
8   **if** $C(s) = 0$ **then**
9   pick new $s \in V_{\mathcal{H}}$ such that $C(s) \geq 1$;
10    $\Gamma(m) = s$; // map m to s
11    $S = S \backslash m$; // remove m from S
12    $C(s) = C(s) - 1$;
13   **foreach** $u|(m,u) \in E_{\mathcal{G}}$ and $u \in S$ **do**
14       $Q \leftarrow (m,u)|u \in S$; // add all neighbors
15   // ... of m that are still in S to Q
16   **while** $Q \neq \emptyset$ **do**
17       $(u,m) \leftarrow Q$; // heaviest edge in Q
18   **if** $C(s) = 0$ **then**
19   // find closest vertex $t \in V_{\mathcal{H}}$ to s with
20   // ... $C(t) \geq 1$ using a SSSP
21   // ... (e.g., Dijkstra's) algorithm
22          $s = t$;
23       $\Gamma(m) = s$; // map m to s
24       $S = S \backslash m$; // remove m from S
25       $C(s) = C(s) - 1$;
26   add $\omega((m,u))/c(f)$ to each $\rho(f)$ for all edges f on the shortest path $\Gamma(u) \rightsquigarrow \Gamma(m)$
27   **foreach** $u|(m,u) \in E_{\mathcal{G}}$ and $u \in S$ **do**
28          $Q \leftarrow (m,u)|u \in S$; // add all neighbors
29   // ... of m that are still in S to Q
30 subtract $\hat{\omega}$ from all $\rho(e)$; // correction from line 4

Algorithm 2: Function $map\_recursive()$.

Input: Graphs $\mathcal{H}$ and $\mathcal{G}$, $C(v)$ for all $v \in V_{\mathcal{H}}$.
Output: Mapping $\Gamma : V_{\mathcal{G}} \to V_{\mathcal{H}}$.

1 // pre-condition: $\sum_{v \in V_{\mathcal{H}}} C(v) == |V_{\mathcal{G}}|$
2 **if** *more than one vertex* $v \in V_{\mathcal{H}}$ *with* $C(v) \neq 0$ **then**
3     $(C_1, C_2) = \text{bisect}(\mathcal{H}, C)$;
4     $(\mathcal{G}_1, \mathcal{G}_2) = \text{bisect}(\mathcal{G})$;
5   **if** $\sum_{c \in C_1} c == |V_{\mathcal{G}_1}|$ **then**
6   map_recursive$(\mathcal{H}, \mathcal{G}_1, C_1)$;
7   map_recursive$(\mathcal{H}, \mathcal{G}_2, C_2)$;
8   **else**
9   map_recursive$(\mathcal{H}, \mathcal{G}_1, C_2)$;
10   map_recursive$(\mathcal{H}, \mathcal{G}_2, C_1)$;
11 **else**
12   // map all n vertices in $\mathcal{G}$ to vertex with load n in $\mathcal{H}$

---

is expected to compute relatively good mappings. However, Simon and Teng show that in some cases, the recursive bisection approach might result in bad p-way partitions [21].

THEOREM 3. *The runtime of the recursive mapping algorithm is* $\mathcal{O}(|E_{\mathcal{G}}| \log(|V_{\mathcal{G}}|) + |E_{\mathcal{H}}| \cdot |V_{\mathcal{G}}|)$.

PROOF. The runtime of the multilevel k-way partitioning approach to bisect a graph $G = (V, E)$ is $\mathcal{O}(|E|)$ [20]. The depth of recursive calls to bisect $\mathcal{G}$ is $\lceil \log_2(|V_{\mathcal{G}}|) \rceil$ and the size of the graph G is halved in each step. Thus, the total runtime is $\sum_{k=0}^{\lceil \log_2(|V_{\mathcal{G}}|) \rceil - 1} 2^k \mathcal{O}(|E_{\mathcal{G}}|)/2^k = \log_2(|V_{\mathcal{G}}|)|E_{\mathcal{G}}| = \mathcal{O}(|E_{\mathcal{G}}| \log(|V_{\mathcal{G}}|))$. The depth of recursive calls to bisect $\mathcal{H}$ is the same as for $\mathcal{G}$ because the number of processors in $\mathcal{H}$ ($\sum_{v \in V_{\mathcal{H}}} C(v) == |V_{\mathcal{G}}|$) is equal to the $|V_{\mathcal{G}}|$. However, in $\mathcal{H}$, all vertices are considered at each recursion level of the bisection (only edges cut in previous recursions are removed). If we assume that no edges are cut (removed), then the runtime is $\sum_{k=0}^{\lceil \log_2(|V_{\mathcal{G}}|) \rceil - 1} 2^k \cdot \mathcal{O}(|E_{\mathcal{H}}|) = \mathcal{O}(|E_{\mathcal{H}}|) \cdot (|V_{\mathcal{G}}| - 1) = \mathcal{O}(|E_{\mathcal{H}}| \cdot |V_{\mathcal{G}}|)$. $\square$

We used the METIS library [20] to compute a $(2, 1+\epsilon)$-balanced bisection. The bisection had to be balanced in some rare cases. Our library does this by moving the vertex with the lowest cumulative edge weight from the bigger to the smaller partition.

In the following, we discuss a new algorithm based on graph similarity. This algorithm has significantly lower time complexity and improves dilation and congestion.

3.3 Mapping based on Graph Similarity

It is well known that there is a duality between graphs and sparse matrices and techniques from sparse linear algebra have been applied to solve graph problems [11]. The basic idea is that a graph's adjacency matrix can be modeled as a sparse matrix which enables the application of established techniques from sparse linear algebra.

A well-studied NP-hard problem is the reduction of the bandwidth of a sparse matrix which tries to eliminate non-zero elements that are far from the diagonal elements by re-numbering columns of the matrix. This can be used to bring the adjacency matrices two graphs $\mathcal{G}$ and $\mathcal{H}$ in a similar shape. This technique effectively transforms both graphs into a shape where edges are localized. The Reverse Cuthill

---

approach and works with all graphs and arbitrary values for $C(v)$.

THEOREM 2. *The runtime of the greedy mapping algorithm is* $\mathcal{O}(|V_{\mathcal{G}}| \cdot (|E_{\mathcal{H}}| + |V_{\mathcal{H}}| \log |V_{\mathcal{H}}| + |V_{\mathcal{G}}| \log |V_{\mathcal{G}}|))$.

PROOF. Each vertex in $\mathcal{G}$ will be removed exactly once from S. Picking a new vertex (lines 7/8) takes $\mathcal{O}(|V_{\mathcal{G}}|)$ with a linear scan. Checking if each of the neighbors of m should be added to Q (lines 13,24) can be done in $\mathcal{O}(|V_{\mathcal{G}}| \log |V_{\mathcal{G}}|)$. Line 16-19 issues an SSSP-run in $\mathcal{H}$ (e.g., Dijkstra's algorithm using a Fibonacci heap) for $\forall v \in V_{\mathcal{G}}$. Thus, the asymptotic run-time is $\mathcal{O}(|V_{\mathcal{G}}| \cdot (|E_{\mathcal{H}}| + |V_{\mathcal{H}}| \log |V_{\mathcal{H}}| + |V_{\mathcal{G}}| \log |V_{\mathcal{G}}|))$ $\square$

3.2 Recursive Bisection Mapping

A second method to find a good topology mapping is recursive bisection. In this method, the weighted graphs $\mathcal{H}$ and $\mathcal{G}$ are recursively split with minimum weighted edge-cut into equal halves to determine the mapping. This technique proved successful to determine "static mappings" in the software package SCOTCH [18].

The minimal edge cut in the bisections maps "heavy" clusters in $\mathcal{G}$ to "strong" clusters in $\mathcal{H}$. Thus, this mechanism

McKee (RCM) algorithm [6] is a successful heuristic for the bandwidth reduction problem.

RCM mapping applies the RCM algorithm to $\mathcal{G}$ and $\mathcal{H}$ to compute $\pi_{\mathcal{G}}$ and $\pi_{\mathcal{H}}$ and then computes the final process permutation $\pi(\pi_{\mathcal{G}}) = \pi_{\mathcal{H}}$, that is, $\pi = \pi_{\mathcal{H}} \circ \pi_{\mathcal{G}}^{-1}$. To handle mappings with $|\mathcal{G}| < |\mathcal{H}|$ correctly, all vertices v with $C(v) = 0$ are removed from $\mathcal{H}$. Despite potential disconnectivity on the sub-graph, RCM handles the proximity condition well and produces mappings with low dilation and congestion.

Figures 3(a) and 3(b) show the adjacency matrices for the problem graph $\mathcal{G}$ and the network graph $\mathcal{H}$, respectively.

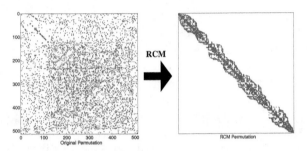

(a) $\mathcal{G}$ adjacency map of the F1 matrix on 512 processes.

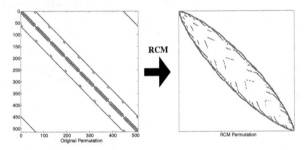

(b) $\mathcal{H}$ adjacency map for an 8x8x8 torus.

Figure 3: Example for RCM topology mapping of the F1 matrix to a torus network.

Figure 3(a) shows the adjacency matrix of the communication topology for a sparse matrix-vector product of the F1 matrix on 512 processes. This represents one of our application-use-cases and described in detail in Section 5.2. Figure 3(b) shows the physical topology of an 8x8x8 3-d torus network with 512 processes.

Both figures show the original permutation on the left and the RCM permutation on the right. RCM mapping is now based on the similarity between both RCM graphs. This effectively minimizes dilation and congestion.

THEOREM 4. *Let $m = \max\{degree(v)|v$ in $V\}$. RCM topology mapping computes a mapping in time $\mathcal{O}(m_{\mathcal{H}} \log(m_{\mathcal{H}})|V_{\mathcal{H}}| + m_{\mathcal{G}} \log(m_{\mathcal{G}})|V_{\mathcal{G}}|)$.*

PROOF. The complexity of RCM is $\mathcal{O}(m \log(m)|V|)$ [6] where $m = \max\{degree(v)|v$ in $V\}$. The algorithm applies RCM to $\mathcal{H}$ and $\mathcal{G}$ and the mapping can be computed from the results in $\mathcal{O}(|V_{\mathcal{G}}|)$. □

The discussions in the introduction suggests that $m_{\mathcal{H}} = \mathcal{O}(1)$ and scalable parallel algorithms often have $m_{\mathcal{G}} = \mathcal{O}(\log(|V_{\mathcal{G}}|))$. RCM is thus significantly faster than the greedy and the recursive mapping approaches and is a good candidate for large-scale systems.

3.4 Supporting Multicore Nodes

If compute nodes (vertices $v \in V_{\mathcal{H}}$) execute more than one process, then a graph partitioner can be used to divide $\mathcal{G}$ before other mapping strategies are applied. The common case where each allocated node executes the same number of processes $C(v) = p \; \forall v \in \Gamma(V_{\mathcal{G}})$ and the topology graph $\mathcal{G}$ needs to be partitioned into P/p equal pieces is supported by graph partitioners.

This technique benefits from the long experience in serial and parallel graph partitioning. Multiple heuristics for $(k,1+\epsilon)$-balanced partitioning using geometric, combinatorial, spectral and multilevel schemes exist [8, §18].

Libraries, such as METIS [20] or SCOTCH [18] and their parallel versions offer optimized partitioning heuristics. However, most graph partitioners cannot guarantee perfectly $(k,1)$-balanced but $(k,1+\epsilon)$-balanced partitions (for small ϵ). Thus, the partition might need to be corrected to be $(k,1)$-balanced. We use the ParMeTiS partitioner (Multilevel k-way Partitioning in $\mathcal{O}(|E_{\mathcal{G}}|)$ [20]) to compute $(k,1+\epsilon)$-balanced partitions and balance the partitions if necessary.

3.5 Improving the Initial Solution

We now describe a heuristic that might further improve the found solution as was used in several previous works. Several heuristics exist for such problems. Threshold Accepting [9] is an improved algorithm for simulated annealing or hill climbing which takes an initial solution and tries to optimize it further by searching a local minimum. We use 20 iterations in the inner optimization loop and a time limit to determine the number of outer optimization iterations. Candidate solutions are modified by swapping two random positions in the mapping π. We will introduce a fast algorithm to estimate the congestion in Section 5.1 which is also used as weight function to minimize the optimization in our TA implementation. The asymptotic running time of each iteration of TA is equal to the running time of Algorithm 3 (cf. Theorem 5).

In the next section we describe how to effectively compose all strategies into a topology mapping framework and apply them to real-world network architectures.

4. A TOPOLOGY MAPPING LIBRARY

Several problems need to be solved in addition to the mapping problem in order to use topology mapping in practice. We show a mechanism that supports most interconnection networks and implement it in a portable library to perform automated topology mapping for parallel applications.

4.1 Determining the Network Topology

The first practical problem is to determine the network topology graph $\mathcal{H}$. This task can be handled manually based on the physical connections between compute nodes. However, many interconnection networks offer automated tools to query the topology and connectivity. Table 1 lists the tools that can be used to query the topology of different networks. All listed networks are supported by our implementation. The result of running those tools, the graph $\mathcal{H}$, is stored as an adjacency list in a configuration file on disk. When a parallel job starts up, each process loads $\mathcal{H}$ and identifies the vertex that it runs on. The identification is done with the hostname of the machine, that is, each vertex in the $\mathcal{H}$ file (representing a compute node) has its hostname

Figure 4: Optimization process flow. The mapping with the lowest congestion is chosen at the end.

Input: Graphs $\mathcal{H}$ and $\mathcal{G}$, mapping $\Gamma : V_{\mathcal{G}} \to V_{\mathcal{H}}$.
Output: congestion $\rho(e)$ for all $e \in E_{\mathcal{H}}$.

1   $\hat{\omega} = \max_{e \in E_{\mathcal{G}}}\{\omega(e)\} \cdot |V_{\mathcal{H}}|^2$
2   initialize all $\rho(e)$ with $\hat{\omega}$; // enforce paths with minimal number of edges in SSSP
3   **foreach** $e = (u, v) \in E_{\mathcal{G}}$ **do**
4   find shortest path $\Gamma(u) \rightsquigarrow \Gamma(v)$ in $\mathcal{H}$;
5   // implicitly minimizing congestion
6   increase edge weight $\rho(f)$ of each edge $f \in E_{\mathcal{H}}$ along path $\Gamma(u) \rightsquigarrow \Gamma(v)$ by $\omega(e)/c(f)$;
7   subtract $\hat{\omega}$ from all $\rho(e)$; // correct edge weights

Algorithm 3: Determine Congestion.

Interconnection Network (API)	Topology Query Tool(s)
Myrinet (MX)	`fm_db2wirelist`
InfiniBand (OFED)	`ibdiagnet` & `ibnet-discover`
SeaStar (Cray XT)	`xtprocadmin` & `xtdb2proc`
BlueGene/P (DCMF)	`DCMF API`

Table 1: Supported Topology Query Tools.

as attribute attached. Each process p has now access to the initial mapping $\Gamma(p)$ which is often not under the user's control (e.g., determined by the batch system). BlueGene/P is an exception where $\mathcal{H}$ is created on the fly after querying the Deep Computing Messaging Framework (DCMF) for all topology information.

4.2 Composing a Mapping Strategy

We now seek to permute processes so as to reduce congestion and dilation. We assume that interference with other jobs is negligible, so that congestion can be computed from the network topology, the location of the allocated processes and the communication graph.

If all $C(v) = p$ are all equal, then an optional graph partitioning phase as described in Section 3.4 is used to divide $\mathcal{G}$ into P/p partitions. The *topomapper* library uses ParMETIS [20] to perform partitioning and corrects the resulting (k,1+ϵ)-balanced partitioning by moving vertices from partitions with more then p vertices to partitions with less than p vertices. The correction step moves vertices with the least cumulative edge weight. After this optional partitioning step, a new graph $\mathcal{G}'$ that contains the partitions as vertices with $|V_{\mathcal{G}}'| = P/p$ is created. Only inter-partition edges from $\mathcal{G}$ remain in $\mathcal{G}'$ and vertices are numbered from 0 to $\frac{P}{p} - 1$.

A second step applies Greedy, Recursive, or RCM mapping as described in Sections 3.1, 3.2, and 3.3 respectively. The mappings can be optimized additionally by applying the threshold accepting algorithm discussed in Section 3.5.

The complete control flow of the optimization process is shown in Figure 4. All processes apply the optimization process, subsets of processes can perform different optimizations, for example, each process chooses a different starting vertex for the Greedy mapping. The permutation with the

lowest congestion is chosen at the end of the optimization process and returned.

5. EXPERIMENTAL ANALYSIS

We analyze the efficiency and performance of mappings of irregular process topologies onto different multicore network topologies.

5.1 A Fast Algorithm to Assess Congestion

Assessing the congestion with the technique described in Section 2.5 is, due to the high time complexity $(\mathcal{O}(|V_{\mathcal{H}}|^2|E_{\mathcal{H}}|) = \mathcal{O}(|V_{\mathcal{H}}|^4))$, impractical at large scale. Thus, we propose a portable and fast heuristic for determining the approximate congestion of all edges in $\mathcal{H}$ in Algorithm 3. The congestion is computed by repeated shortest path calculations. To find the minimal congestion, the edge weights along used (shortest) paths are updated after each search to reflect the current load. This leads to an automatic balancing of edges along all paths. However, with this scheme, paths with more edges and less congestion on those edges might have shorter weighted distances. This is avoided by initializing the edges to a high weight $\hat{\omega} = \max_{e \in E_{\mathcal{G}}}\{\omega(e)\} \cdot |V_{\mathcal{H}}|^2$ so that a path with less edges always has a shorter weighted distance regardless of the congestion. Among all paths with the minimal number of edges, those with minimal congestion are then preferred.

THEOREM 5. *The runtime of Algorithm 3 is* $\mathcal{O}(|E_{\mathcal{G}}| \cdot (|E_{\mathcal{H}}| + |V_{\mathcal{H}}| \cdot \log|V_{\mathcal{H}}|))$.

PROOF. Exactly one SSSP-run on $\mathcal{H}$ (e.g., Dijkstra'a algorithm using a Fibonacci heap) is started for each edge in $\mathcal{G}$ (line 3–4). Thus, the asymptotic runtime of Algorithm 3 is $\mathcal{O}(|E_{\mathcal{G}}| \cdot (|E_{\mathcal{H}}| + |V_{\mathcal{H}}| \cdot \log|V_{\mathcal{H}}|))$. □

5.2 Real-world Irregular Process Topologies

Sparse matrix-vector multiplication is one of the most important kernels in large-scale scientific applications and can be used to solve a large class of scientific computing problems [8]. In order to capture the characteristics of real irregular applications, we use parallel sparse matrix-vector products with real-world input matrices from the University of Florida Sparse Matrix Collection [7]: F1, nlp-kkt240, and audikw_1. All three matrices represent un-

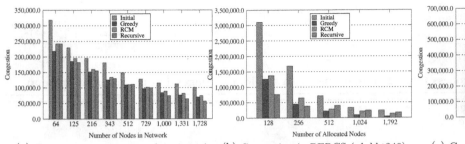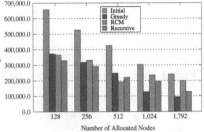

(a) Congestion on 3d Torus (nlpkkt240).   (b) Congestion in PERCS (nlpkkt240)   (c) Congestion for Juropa (audikw_1)

Figure 5: Topology mapping results for different topologies.

structured matrices/grids. F1 and audikw_1 are symmetric stiffness matrices—approximating elasticities in structural mechanics—modeling automotive crankshafts. The nlpkkt240 matrix is the largest matrix in the collection and represents a nonlinear programming problem for a 3d PDE-constrained optimization. Table 2 lists the dimensions and number of non-zero (nnz) entries for each matrix.

Matrix Name	Rows and Columns	NNZ (sparsity)
F1	343,791	$26,837,113$ $(2.27 \cdot 10^{-4}\%)$
audikw_1	943,695	$39,297,771$ $(4.4 \cdot 10^{-5}\%)$
nlpkkt240	27,993,600	$401,232,976$ $(5 \cdot 10^{-7}\%)$

Table 2: Properties of the test matrices.

The vector of a sparse matrix-vector product is initially distributed block-wise. Each element i of the vector requires all elements j where the matrix element $A_{i,j}$ is nonzero. Most matrix elements are zero and the pattern of nonzero elements depends on the structure of the input system. Thus, in order to minimize the communication, scientific codes usually partition the matrix with a graph partitioner and redistribute matrix and vector elements accordingly. We use ParMeTiS to find a decomposition of the matrix in order to minimize communication.[1] The domain-optimized decomposition is then used to derive the number of vector elements that need to be communicated from and to each process. We build a weighted MPI-2.2 process topology that reflects the communication requirements of the decomposition. The resulting distributed topology communicator [12] is used by our topology mapping library to optimize the process-to-node mapping.

All experiments presented below use the same input matrices which means that they simulate a strong scaling problem. We ran all experiments with up to 1,792 processes (or the maximum supported by the physical topology). All presented results used TA to refine the mapping until otherwise noted. Results without TA are omitted for brevity. TA improved the congestion between 2% and 9%.

5.3 Petascale Network Topologies

We investigate topologies that are used to build current and future petascale-class systems: A three-dimensional torus is used in the Cray XT-5 and IBM Blue Gene architectures. The IBM PERCS network [1] uses a heterogeneous hierarchical fully-connected topology to construct a 10 petaflop computer.

---

[1] This step should not be confused with graph partitioning for multicore topology mapping even though it uses the same tools!

We present only one representative matrix for each network topology due to space limitations. We also analyze only one process per node in Sections 5.3 and 5.4 because we assume that hybrid programming schemes will be used to exploit the full potential of those machines.

5.3.1 Three-Dimensional Torus

A k-dimensional torus of size $x_1 \times \cdots \times x_k$ has vertices $< m_1 \ldots m_k >$, where $0 \leq m_i < x_i$ and edges connecting $< m_1 \ldots m_k >$ to $< m_1 \ldots m_i \pm 1 (\mod x_i) \ldots m_k >$, for $i = 1, \ldots, k$.

We investigate 3-dimensional toruses with cube topologies ($x_1 = x_2 = x_3$) which maximize bisection bandwidth. Processes are mapped in lexicographical order, i.e., $< 0, 0, 0 >, < 0, 0, 1 >, \ldots, < x_1 - 1, x_2 - 1, x_3 - 2 >, < x_1 - 1, x_2 - 1, x_3 - 1 >$ in the initial allocation.

Figure 5(a) shows the maximum congestion of mapping the communication topology that results from a domain-decomposition of the nlpkkt240 matrix to different 3d-Torus networks. The relative gain over the initial consecutive mapping increases with the network size. Greedy mapping reduces the maximum congestion by 27% for a 3^3 and up to 32% for a 12^3 torus network. RCM is slightly worse than greedy in all configurations, however, it reduces the dilation significantly. The recursive mapping algorithm delivers the best results at large scale where it outperforms greedy with a relative gain of 44% for a 12^3 network. The average dilation a 12^3 torus was 9.00, 9.03, 7.02, 4.50 for the initial, Greedy, RCM, and Recursive mappings, respectively. Recursive reduces the average dilation by 50% and might thus result in lowest power consumption.

The memory overhead to start the physical topology was between 0.63 kiB for 3^3 and 31.20 kiB for 12^3 respectively. It shows that RCM takes basically constant time (never more than 0.01 s) and Greedy and Recursive take up to 1s while TA can be infeasibly expensive with nearly 10 minutes.

5.3.2 PERCS Network

The PERCS topology [1] was designed by IBM to construct a multi-petaflop machine. The network consists of three different link types: LL, LR, and D with different speeds. Each endpoint connects to 7 neighbors via LL links with a rate of 24 GiB/s, 24 neighbors via LR links at a rate of 5 GiB/s, and up to 16 neighbors via D links with 10 GiB/s. Each stage (link-type) forms a fully-connected network. A set of nodes that is fully connected with LL links is called drawer and a set of nodes fully-connected with LL+LR links is called supernode; supernodes are fully connected by D links. Each drawer consists of 8 nodes and each supernode consists of 4 drawers. The size of the network is determined by the number of D links. The maximum distance between any two nodes is three. A detailed description of the network and the topology can be found in [1]. We assume 9 D links per node which results in 9248 nodes total and we connect all D links randomly. The total topology occupies 1,445 kiB in main memory.

For the first simple example, we assume that processes are allocated and mapped consecutively to nodes in drawers and then drawers in supernodes. Figure 5(b) shows the result of topology mapping for this heterogeneous network architecture. Topology mapping can reduce the maximum congestion by up to 80% (P=1,792). The huge improvement comes from the effective exploitation of the different link speeds in the greedy strategy. RCM performs consistently slightly worse than greedy because it does not take the link capacities into account. Recursive achieves with 1.82 a lower average congestion than Greedy with 2.89 with 1,728 nodes. The benefits grow with the size of the allocation.

Again, RCM mapping consistently takes less than 0.01s while Greedy grows from 0.8s to 22s and Recursive from 4.51s to 7.51s. TA took 41 minutes at P=512 and was thus disabled for $P > 512$.

5.4 InfiniBand Network Topologies

We now investigate our topology mapping strategies on large-scale InfiniBand installations. We used the tools described in Section 4 to query the network topology of two large-scale systems, Juropa at the Jülich Supercomputing Center and Ranger at the Texas Advanced Computing Center. Both systems use InfiniBand topologies that are similar to fat-trees. The number of nodes in the systems were 3,292 for Juropa and 4,081 for Ranger. For our initial allocations, we use the order of hostnames like a batch-system does by default. As before, we assume one process per core in our analyses to investigate the quality of topology mapping separately from multicore mapping.

5.4.1 Juropa

Figure 5(c) shows the results for topology mapping of the communication patterns for the audikw_1 matrix on the Juropa cluster. The improvements are between 40% and 61% and grow with the number of mapped tasks. Greedy shows significantly better congestion results than RCM mapping. RCM provides a lower average dilation of 4.45 in comparison to Greedy with 5.8 and Recursive with 5.13 at P=1,792.

RCM is again fastest with less than 0.01s. Greedy takes between 0.16 s and 2.6s and Recursive between 0.63s and 1.21s, while TA is with up to 9 minutes only feasible at small scales. Juropa's complete topology occupied 87 kiB memory.

5.4.2 Ranger

Figure 6(a) shows the results of topology mapping on the Ranger cluster. The maximum congestion was improved by up to 50%, depending on the allocation size. Figure 6(b) shows the mapping times for the Ranger system. Again, Greedy performs significantly better than RCM at a much higher cost. RCM finished all mapping problems in less than 0.01s while Greedy used between 0.26s and 3.85s and Recursive between 0.76s and 1.5s. TA took up to 14 minutes for the largest problem and only improved it modestly. Ranger's complete topology occupied 134 kiB memory.

5.5 Benchmark Results

In our theoretical analysis and simulations, we made several assumptions on the (ideal) routing scheme and network behavior. The improvements reported by our mapping strategies are thus lower bounds and are hard to achieve in practice.

We now show benchmark results on Surveyor, an IBM BlueGene/P system at the Argonne National Lab, to demonstrate the utility of our topology mapping library and algorithms in practice.

As for the simulation, each process loads a part of the matrix, decomposes it with a graph partitioner, constructs an MPI-2.2 graph topology, and calls the topomapper library to optimize the mapping. The library exercises all options as described in Section 4 and returns an optimized mapping.

We measured the time to perform 100 communication phases in isolation and report the maximum time across all ranks before and after applying the mapping. We also compute a predicted time from the improvement in maximum congestion which is a lower bound to the actual improvement.

Figure 6(c) shows the time to perform the communication on the initial (consecutive) mapping, the time to perform the communication on an optimized (renumbered) mapping and the prediction of a run with 512 nodes. The mapping took 0.34s in all cases and the physical topology graph occupied 12 kiB memory. The measured performance gains lie between 10% and 18% depending on the matrix while the predictions were between 18% and 32%.

These experiments show that topology mapping leads to significant improvements in practical settings.

6. CONCLUSIONS AND FUTURE WORK

In this work, we defined the topology mapping problem and presented a proof that an finding an optimal solution to the problem is NP-hard. This opens the door to investigate the efficiency of different heuristics for topology mapping.

We propose different topology mapping algorithms that support arbitrary heterogeneous network and application topologies and showed their effective use in the context of sparse linear algebra computation. The proposed topology mapping algorithms have been implemented to support reordering in the intuitive distributed graph topology interface in MPI-2.2.

We showed improvements of the maximum congestion of up to 80% and our results indicate that the benefits of topology mapping grow with the system size. We analyzed the scalability of the different mapping approaches. Our theoretical and practical analysis shows that Greedy and Recursive are slower than RCM and that additional optimization with threshold accepting (TA) might be prohibitively expensive. Greedy scales approximately linearly with the system size for all our investigated application and network topologies which means that it might not be suitable for large mappings. Recursive mapping is faster but might result in worse congestion. However, RCM is fastest in theory and never took longer than 0.01s in our experiments. We also found that the Greedy performs well for minimizing congestion and Recursive and RCM for minimizing dilation. This creates interesting opportunities for further investigation. We conclude that TA can improve most mappings further but it is not scalable to large systems.

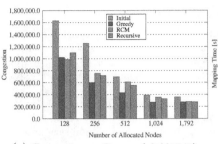 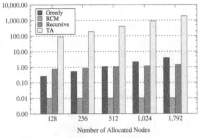 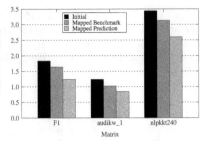

(a) Congestion on Ranger (nlpkkt240)   (b) Times for Ranger (nlpkkt240)   (c) Benchmark Results on BlueGene/P.

Figure 6: Topology mapping results for different networks.

Our proposed optimization framework utilizes the available parallelism in the system. It starts the Greedy algorithm at different source vertices on each node and simultaneously applies RCM and Recursive on one node each and selects the best solution found. We demonstrated speedups of up to 18% of the communication phase of a sparse matrix-vector multiplication on 512 BlueGene/P nodes.

We plan to investigate optimized strategies for initial process-to-node mappings on different architectures. The PERCS network topology presents multiple interesting challenges in this area.

Our implementation can immediately be used to optimize communication on petascale systems. However, the proposed mapping algorithms can scale to the size of exascale systems. The two metrics, maximum congestion and average dilation can be used to optimize and trade application runtime and power consumption on such systems. Exascale systems will need to exhibit substantially improved communication locality in order to achieve acceptable energy consumption [14]. The use of high quality mapping procedures will be essential to achieving this goal.

The topology mapper library is available at http://www.unixer.de/research/libtopomap.

Acknowledgments. We thank Peter Gottschling and Andrew Lumsdaine for many helpful discussions and comments. Thanks to Bernd Mohr for providing the Juropa topology and Len Wisniewski and the TACC for providing the Ranger topology. This work is supported by the Blue Waters sustained-petascale computing project, which is supported by the National Science Foundation (award number OCI 07-25070) and the state of Illinois.

7. REFERENCES

[1] B. Arimilli, R. Arimilli, V. Chung, S. Clark, W. Denzel, B. Drerup, T. Hoefler, J. Joyner, J. Lewis, J. Li, N. Ni, and R. Rajamony. The PERCS High-Performance Interconnect. In *Proc. of 18th Symposium on High-Performance Interconnects (HotI'10)*, Aug. 2010.

[2] A. Bhatelé, L. V. Kalé, and S. Kumar. Dynamic topology aware load balancing algorithms for molecular dynamics applications. In *ICS '09*, pages 110–116, New York, NY, USA, 2009. ACM.

[3] S. H. Bokhari. On the mapping problem. *IEEE Trans. Comput.*, 30(3):207–214, 1981.

[4] S. W. Bollinger and S. F. Midkiff. Heuristic technique for processor and link assignment in multicomputers. *IEEE Trans. Comput.*, 40(3):325–333, 1991.

[5] U. Brandes. A faster algorithm for betweenness centrality. *The Journal of Math. Sociology*, 25(2):163–177, 2001.

[6] E. Cuthill and J. McKee. Reducing the bandwidth of sparse symmetric matrices. In *Proceedings of the 1969 24th national conference*, ACM '69, pages 157–172, New York, NY, USA, 1969. ACM.

[7] T. A. Davis. University of Florida Sparse Matrix Collection. *NA Digest*, 92, 1994.

[8] J. Dongarra, I. Foster, G. Fox, W. Gropp, K. Kennedy, L. Torczon, and A. White, editors. *Sourcebook of parallel computing*. Morgan Kaufmann Publishers Inc., San Francisco, CA, USA, 2003.

[9] G. Dueck and T. Scheuer. Threshold accepting: a general purpose optimization algorithm appearing superior to simulated annealing. *J. Comput. Phys.*, 90(1):161–175, 1990.

[10] M. Gary and D. Johnson. *Computers and Intractability: A Guide to NP-Completeness*. New York: W H. Freeman and Company, 1979.

[11] J. R. Gilbert, S. Reinhardt, and V. B. Shah. High-performance graph algorithms from parallel sparse matrices. In *PARA'06: Proceedings of the 8th international conference on Applied parallel computing*, pages 260–269, 2007.

[12] T. Hoefler, R. Rabenseifner, H. Ritzdorf, B. R. de Supinski, R. Thakur, and J. L. Traeff. The Scalable Process Topology Interface of MPI 2.2. *Concurrency and Computation: Practice and Experience*, 23(4):293–310, Aug. 2010.

[13] R. Johari and D. Tan. End-to-end congestion control for the internet: delays and stability. *Networking, IEEE/ACM Transactions on*, 9(6):818–832, Dec. 2001.

[14] P. Kogge et al. Exascale computing study: Technology challenges in achieving exascale systems. *DARPA Information Processing Techniques Office, Washington, DC*, 2008.

[15] S.-Y. Lee and J. K. Aggarwal. A mapping strategy for parallel processing. *IEEE Trans. Comput.*, 36(4):433–442, 1987.

[16] MPI Forum. *MPI: A Message-Passing Interface Standard. Version 2.2*, June 23rd 2009. www.mpi-forum.org.

[17] D. Pekurovsky. P3DFFT - Highly scalable parallel 3D Fast Fourier Transforms library. Technical report, 2010.

[18] F. Pellegrini and J. Roman. Scotch: A software package for static mapping by dual recursive bipartitioning of process and architecture graphs. In *HPCN Europe'96*, pages 493–498, 1996.

[19] A. L. Rosenberg. Issues in the study of graph embeddings. In *WG'80*, pages 150–176, London, UK, 1981.

[20] K. Schloegel, G. Karypis, and V. Kumar. Parallel static and dynamic multi-constraint graph partitioning. *Concurrency and Computation: Practice and Experience*, 14(3):219–240, 2002.

[21] H. D. Simon and S.-H. Teng. How good is recursive bisection? *SIAM J. Sci. Comput.*, 18:1436–1445, September 1997.

[22] J. L. Träff. Implementing the MPI process topology mechanism. In *Supercomputing '02: Proceedings of the 2002 ACM/IEEE conference on Supercomputing*, pages 1–14, 2002.

[23] H. Yu, I.-H. Chung, and J. Moreira. Topology mapping for Blue Gene/L supercomputer. In *SC'06*, page 116, New York, NY, USA, 2006. ACM.

Page Placement in Hybrid Memory Systems

Luiz Ramos
Rutgers University
Piscataway, NJ, USA
luramos@cs.rutgers.edu

Eugene Gorbatov
Intel Corporation
Hillsboro, OR, USA
eugene.gorbatov@intel.com

Ricardo Bianchini
Rutgers University
Piscataway, NJ, USA
ricardob@cs.rutgers.edu

ABSTRACT

Phase-Change Memory (PCM) technology has received substantial attention recently. Because PCM is byte-addressable and exhibits access times in the nanosecond range, it can be used in main memory designs. In fact, PCM has higher density and lower idle power consumption than DRAM. Unfortunately, PCM is also slower than DRAM and has limited endurance. For these reasons, researchers have proposed memory systems that combine a small amount of DRAM and a large amount of PCM. In this paper, we propose a new hybrid design that features a hardware-driven page placement policy. The policy relies on the memory controller (MC) to monitor access patterns, migrate pages between DRAM and PCM, and translate the memory addresses coming from the cores. Periodically, the operating system updates its page mappings based on the translation information used by the MC. Detailed simulations of 27 workloads show that our system is more robust and exhibits lower energy-delay^2 than state-of-the-art hybrid systems.

Categories and Subject Descriptors

C.5.5 [**Computer system implementation**]: Servers

General Terms

Design, Performance

1. INTRODUCTION

Main memory capacity is becoming a critical issue for many systems. As the number of processor cores in each CPU chip increases, so do the number of concurrent threads, applications, and/or virtual machines that must have their working sets simultaneously in main memory. Unfortunately, current trends suggest that meeting these capacity requirements using DRAM will not be ideal. DRAM exhibits low access times, but consumes significant amounts of energy (idle, refresh, and precharge energies). As a result, the amount of energy consumed by the memory is

approaching (and sometimes surpassing) that consumed by the processors in many servers [2, 21].

For these reasons, architects have started to consider Phase-Change Memory (PCM) as a potential replacement for DRAM [20, 28, 37, 38]. PCM is byte-addressable, consumes little idle energy, does not require refreshing or precharging (its contents are persistent), and exhibits access times in the nanosecond range. Furthermore, PCM cells have feature size comparable to DRAM cells, but can store more information in the same physical area. However, PCM's read/write times, read/write energies, and write endurance are worse than those of DRAM. To take advantage of the low latencies of DRAM and the high capacity of PCM, researchers have proposed hybrid memory systems that combine a small amount of DRAM and a large amount of PCM [28, 37, 38]. Unfortunately, those systems exhibit poor behavior for certain workloads, as we shall demonstrate. For example, the system proposed in [28] degrades performance significantly for workloads with poor locality, whereas that from [37] suffers when cache write-backs represent a small fraction of the memory traffic.

In this paper, we propose a new DRAM+PCM memory system design that is robust across a wide range of workloads. The design comprises a sophisticated memory controller (MC) that implements a page placement policy called "Rank-based Page Placement" (RaPP). The policy efficiently ranks pages according to popularity (access frequency) and write intensity, migrating top-ranked pages to DRAM. While monitoring popularity, RaPP penalizes pages that are unlikely to produce benefits if migrated. To improve PCM's endurance, each migration involves two PCM memory frames and one DRAM frame. The MC monitors access patterns and, when necessary, migrates pages. The migrations are not immediately visible by the operating system (OS), as the MC uses its own address translation table. Periodically (or when the table fills up), the OS updates its mapping of virtual pages to physical frames based on the translation table and clears it.

We evaluate our memory system design and RaPP using a detailed simulator that computes the energy, performance, and endurance of workloads running on an 8-core CPU. For comparison with our system, we simulate two state-of-the-art hybrid memory designs [28, 37], as well as a baseline hybrid system without page management (called "unmanaged") and a PCM-only system.

Our results for 27 workloads show that our system consumes roughly the same amount of power on average as its competitors and the baselines, but with significantly better performance. In terms of energy-delay^2, our system is on average 36% better than the PCM-only baseline and 24% better than the unmanaged hybrid system. Compared to the state-of-the-art hybrid systems, our system exhibits at least 13% better energy-delay^2 on average, especially for workloads with large memory footprints. Our system also improves lifetime, as compared to the baselines, but not enough to enable system operation for 5 years assuming current PCM endurance. Nevertheless, PCM endurance is expected to increase by orders of magnitude in the next few years [1, 9]. Until then, our system can be easily combined with previously proposed endurance-improvement techniques [8, 18, 20, 38].

We conclude that existing hybrid memory systems are useful, but they need to be more robust and efficient. Our system is a demonstration that these characteristics can be achieved through a sophisticated MC, and careful page ranking and migration.

2. BACKGROUND

A server's memory system typically comprises a few key elements, namely a memory controller (MC), a few memory channels, and a number of dual-inline memory module (DIMMs). Each DIMM includes memory devices (chips) that contain a memory cell array and peripheral circuitry.

The MC is responsible for handling memory access requests from the CPU, resulting from last-level cache (LLC) misses or write-backs. The MC operates the memory chips to fetch and store data, as well as refresh their memory arrays (in the case of DRAM). Operating the memory chips entails forwarding physical addresses to the peripheral circuitry, and issuing commands to drive the chips while respecting certain timing constraints. Due to its central role, an MC can be designed with varying complexity to optimize the memory system for different purposes. For example, to improve access throughput, the MC may choose to buffer particular requests (e.g., LLC write-backs) and/or reorder requests according to the system's current state [3, 17, 30].

At a high level, a memory chip can be logically viewed as an array of bit cells with some interface circuitry. Memory chips are read and written in groups called ranks. A rank can transfer a number of bits equal to the memory channel's width (e.g., 64 bits) in one memory cycle, so it takes several memory cycles to transfer an entire LLC line. At a low level, the memory chips are subdivided into banks that can be accessed concurrently, and further into bitcell arrays. On a read to a bank, part of the target address (provided by the MC) is used to activate a row of bitcells, and amplify and latch their contents into a row buffer. Then, a column (subset of a row) can be selected, causing its data to be transferred from the row buffer to the MC. The MC then delivers the data to the CPU. An access to a column of another row causes the activation of the new row. On a LLC write-back, the data flows in the opposite direction, is stored in the row buffer, and eventually written to the memory array.

2.1 Synchronous Dynamic RAM (DRAM)

A DRAM cell is a transistor-capacitor pair (1T/1C) where each transistor allows reading and writing, and the capacitor stores a bit as an electrical charge (Figure 1). Since DRAM's capacitors discharge over time, they need to be refreshed at regular intervals to prevent data loss. In addition, reading a DRAM cell destroys its original content; the "precharge" operation restores the data from the row buffer into the array. Under a close-page management scheme, the MC precharges (closes) a row after every column access, unless there is another pending access for the same row. If there is a pending access, the row buffer remains open and the access can be serviced from there. Under open-page management, the row buffer remains open until another row needs to be loaded into it; only at that point is the precharge operation performed.

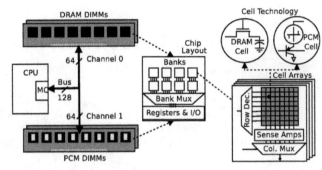

Figure 1: Memory system using DRAM and PCM DIMMs. DRAM and PCM arrays are slightly different (cells and sense amplifiers).

Close-page management typically works better than open-page management for multi-core systems [31].

Double Data Rate 3 (DDR3) is the current standard for Synchronous DRAM interfaces. DDR3 channels are 64-bit wide (72-bit wide with ECC), so it takes four memory cycles (8 transfers) to access a 64-byte LCC line. In server systems, typically one, two, or four ranks of 8 (x8) or 16 (x4) chips (plus additional chips when using ECC) are laid out on each DIMM. When designed to operate at high frequencies, only one or two DDR3 DIMMs can lie on a single memory channel due to electrical limitations.

DRAM energy can be broken down into background, activation/precharge, read/write, and termination energies. Background energy is independent of activity and is due to the peripheral circuitry (e.g., row decoder, column muxes, sense amplifiers, and bus drivers), transistor leakage, and refresh operations. The activation/precharge energy is due to these two operations on the memory arrays. The read/write energy is due to column accesses to row buffers. The termination energy is due to terminating data and strobe signals at each chip, as well as signals of other ranks on the same channel. The three latter classes are often referred to as "dynamic DRAM energy". Most of the energy consumed by DRAM is background and activation/precharge energy.

2.2 Phase-Change Memory (PCM)

A PCM cell comprises an NMOS access transistor and a storage resistor (1T/1R) made of a chalcogenide alloy. With the application of heat, the alloy can be transitioned between physical states with particular resistances, used to represent binary values. When the alloy is heated to a very high temperature ($> 600^{\circ}C$) and quickly cooled down, it turns into an amorphous glass with high electrical resistance, representing 0. When the alloy is heated to a temperature between the crystalization ($300^{\circ}C$) and melting ($600^{\circ}C$) points and cools down slowly, it crystalizes to a state with lower resistance, representing 1. This programming process can be carried out by peripheral write drivers.

A cell's content can be read using current sense amplifiers to measure its electrical resistance, as opposed to DRAM's slower but smaller voltage sense amplifiers. PCM can thus interface with most CMOS peripheral circuitry used in DRAM [37]. Unlike in DRAM, PCM's reads are non-destructive and cells can retain data for several years. On the downside, PCM cells exhibit worse access performance than DRAM.

Regarding density, PCM has similar cell size ($4F^2$ to $12F^2$) compared to DRAM ($6F^2$ to $8F^2$). However, PCM enables manufacturing of multi-level cells (MLC), which produce intermediate resistances (the alloy is partially crystalline and partially amorphous) and therefore can store multiple bits. Current MLC prototypes have two- or four-bit cells, capable of storing four and sixteen binary values, respectively [24]. Assuming the same cell size for both technologies, these MLCs hold twice and eight times more data than DRAM cells in the same area.

Our assumptions for PCM. To evaluate MLCs in the middle of this range of storage densities, we assume three-bit MLCs for the PCM array. This assumption makes PCM four times more storage-dense than DRAM, as in [28]. For easier adoption, we expect that the peripheral circuitry for PCM (e.g., row buffers, row and column decoders, DIMM interface) will be equivalent to that for DRAM, except for sense amplifiers. Thus, we assume this circuitry to have the same performance and power characteristics for both PCM and DRAM. Previous papers have made the same assumption [20, 37]. Only the written cache lines in a row buffer are written back to the PCM cell array (DRAM needs the entire buffer to be written back to precharge its cells). Similar optimizations have been used before as well [20, 38]. To expose the entire overhead of PCM accesses to the cores, we study a CPU with in-order cores and a single outstanding miss per core.

PCM does not require cell refreshing or precharging, thereby lowering background energy relative to DRAM and eliminating precharge energy. However, PCM increases activation and termination energies, since its activations (actual accesses to memory cells) are slower than with DRAM. Our assumptions for peripheral circuitry imply that row buffer read/write energy is the same for DRAM and PCM.

3. HYBRID MAIN MEMORY DESIGN

Given the speed of DRAM and the high density of PCM, there is a clear incentive for combining these two technologies into a single, hybrid memory system. However, PCM has undesirable characteristics (poor performance, dynamic energy, and endurance) that must be properly managed. Similarly, DRAM has a relatively high idle energy consumption compared to that of PCM.

A few previous works have realized the benefits of combining DRAM and PCM [28, 37] and the associated tradeoffs. Unfortunately, the previous approaches have serious limitations. Qureshi et al. [28] proposed to use DRAM as a buffer in front of PCM. Since the buffer is managed as an inclusive hardware cache, the DRAM space does not add to the overall memory capacity. More importantly, for workloads with poor locality, the cache actually lowers performance and increases energy consumption. Zhang et al. [37] combine the DRAM and PCM areas in a large flat memory and migrate pages between the areas. However, the migrations are performed by the OS and target the frequently written pages, leaving read-intensive pages in the slower PCM area.

Next, we describe our hardware-software page placement policy, called RaPP (Rank-based Page Placement), which manages pages without the limitations of previous works. After that, we detail our implementation of the two prior hybrid systems. Throughout our descriptions, we differentiate between *virtual memory* pages (or simply pages) and *physical memory* frames (or simply frames).

3.1 Rank-based Page Placement

Given the characteristics of DRAM and PCM, RaPP seeks to (1) place performance-critical pages and frequently written pages in DRAM, (2) place non-critical pages and rarely written pages in PCM, and (3) spread writes to PCM across many physical frames.

The justification for these goals is that previous works have shown that typically only a relatively small subset of pages is performance-critical during the execution of a workload [15]. This

observation suggests that (a) this subset may fit entirely in the DRAM part of the hybrid memory, and (b) the majority of lightly accessed pages should consume little energy, if stored in the PCM part. Moreover, previous work has found that the subset of critical pages may change over time, along with the criticality of individual pages [15]. This second observation suggests that the system must dynamically identify the critical pages and adjust their placements accordingly.

Since the OS is not on the path of most memory accesses, RaPP must be collaboratively executed by the OS and the MC. An interesting challenge is that neither the MC nor the OS has complete information about the performance criticality of the pages in a workload. For example, the latency of the cache misses associated with a page may be hidden behind out-of-order execution or multithreading by the processor cores. Interestingly, previous work [4] has shown that the frequency of cache misses is a very good proxy for a thread's performance criticality, regardless of the details of the microarchitecture (in-order vs out-of-order execution). Thus, pages that experience more misses also tend to be more performance critical.

RaPP relies on the MC to monitor the misses in the LLC to each physical memory frame. In addition, the MC monitors the LLC write-backs directed to each frame. Using this information, RaPP dynamically ranks frames based on frequency and recency of accesses, as detailed below. Frames that rank high are called "popular", and frames that rank low are called "unpopular". Whenever the most popular PCM frame reaches a threshold number of accesses (called the "migration threshold"), the MC considers migrating its content into DRAM transparently to the OS. If the DRAM area is full, the MC selects the page stored in an unpopular DRAM frame to migrate to PCM.

Ranking frames. RaPP simultaneously considers frame access frequency and recency in its dynamic ranking of pages (i.e., the pages stored in the frames), using a modified version of the Multi-Queue (MQ) [39] algorithm for second-level buffer cache replacements. As originally designed, MQ defines M LRU queues of block descriptors, numbered from 0 to $M - 1$. Each descriptor includes the block number, a reference counter, and a logical expiration time. The descriptors in queue $M - 1$ represent the blocks that are most frequently used. On the first access to a block, its descriptor is placed in the tail of queue 0. In addition, the block's expiration time $ExpirationTime$ is set to $CurrentTime + LifeTime$, where both times are measured in number of accesses and $LifeTime$ specifies the number of consecutive accesses that must directed to other blocks before we expire the block. Every time the block is accessed, its reference counter is incremented, its expiration time is reset to $CurrentTime + LifeTime$, and its descriptor is moved to the tail of its current queue. The descriptor of a frequently used block is promoted to a higher queue (saturating at queue $M - 1$, of course) after a certain number of accesses to the block. Specifically, if the descriptor is currently in queue i, it will be upgraded to queue $i + 1$ when its reference counter reaches 2^{i+1}. Conversely, MQ demotes blocks that have not been accessed recently. On each access, the descriptors at the heads of all M queues (representing the LRU block of each queue) are checked for expiration ($CurrentTime > ExpirationTime$). If a block descriptor expires, it is placed at the tail of the immediately inferior queue, and has its expiration time again set to $CurrentTime + LifeTime$.

We use the modified MQ to rank memory frames (it was originally designed to rank disk blocks). We do so for two main rea-

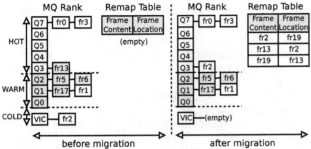

Figure 2: RaPP example. Before and after we migrate a PCM page (stored in frame 13) that crossed over to the DRAM side of the ranking to a frame from the victim list (frame 2). Dark shading represents PCM frames and no shading represents DRAM frames.

sons: (1) as page migrations are expensive operations, it is important to select the pages to migrate as intelligently and accurately as possible. MQ has been proven superior to other algorithms in selecting the blocks to replace [39]; (2) modern memory controllers are becoming increasingly complex and sophisticated (as discussed below), as a result of the increasing importance of the memory system (in terms of performance and energy) and relentless technology scaling. To avoid performance degradation, *the updates to the MQ queues are performed by the MC off the critical path of memory accesses,* using a separate queue of updates and a small on-chip SRAM cache. To find the MQ entry of a frame, the MC hashes the corresponding frame number.

We create 15 queues (numbered 0–14) plus a 16th victim list (described below). Pages stored in PCM frames that become popular (i.e., get to higher queues) are scheduled for migration to DRAM. However, we modified MQ in two important ways. First, instead of counting all accesses, we only count an access if it occurs more than a threshold time (measured in memory cycles) after the last access to the same frame. This latter threshold is called the "filter threshold". The MC stores the time of the last access in the descriptor for the frame. The reason for filtering rapid-fire accesses out is that there is no point in trying to migrate a page that is accessed in such a way; before we get to migrate the page, the needed data has already been loaded to the LLC (or evicted from it). In fact, it is possible that the page will not even be accessed again in memory. Using a 2-competitive approach, we set the filter threshold to be $MigrationCost/MigrationThreshold$, where $MigrationCost$ is the uncontended number of memory cycles needed to migrate a page. ($MigrationCost$ is roughly $1.6\mu s$ in our experiments.)

Second, we modified the demotion policy in the following ways: (a) we use time, not number of accesses, as the metric for demotion to reduce space requirements (in our experiments, we set $LifeTime$ to $100\mu s$, which works well for our workloads); (b) we only demote from one queue at a time (in round-robin fashion) to reduce runtime overhead; and (c) a DRAM frame that is demoted twice without any intervening accesses leaves the MQ queues and becomes a candidate to receive a popular PCM page. The reason for the latter modification is that frames that undergo multiple demotions tend to have already been cached in the LCC and will not be accessed in a while. We store the MQ queues and the victim list in the lowest DRAM addresses.

Migrating pages. As mentioned above, RaPP schedules the page stored in a PCM frame for migration to DRAM after its reference counter reaches the migration threshold. In particular, the page stored at any PCM frame that reaches queue 5 (i.e., the reference

counter for the frame has reached $2^5 = 32$) is scheduled for migration to DRAM. (Thus, the maximum number of frames that can be in queues 5–14 is the size of DRAM. For symmetry, the maximum size of queues 0–4 is also set to the size of DRAM.)

We find these values for M and the migration threshold to work well for our extensive set of workloads. The rationale is that in many workloads, a large number of pages would end up in queue $M - 1$ if M is small, compromising the accuracy of the hot page identification. On the other hand, if M is high, RaPP can correctly identify hot pages, but the MQ overhead increases. As for the migration threshold, we must select a value that enables early migrations but without migrating pages unnecessarily.

To select a destination DRAM frame for a page, the MC maintains an LRU list of victim DRAM frames. The victim frames are not in any of the LRU queues (the list is initialized with all DRAM frames). Whenever a frame on the victim list is accessed, it is removed from the list and added to queue 0. A frame demoted from queue 0 or demoted twice without intervening accesses is moved to the tail of the list. The destination DRAM frame is the first frame on the list. If the list is empty, no destination is selected and the migration is delayed until a frame is added to the list.

To effect a page migration to DRAM, the MC (1) migrates the page stored in the selected DRAM frame to one of the unranked PCM frames, (2) migrates the content of this latter frame to the most popular PCM frame, and finally (3) migrates the content of the most popular PCM frame to the selected DRAM frame. Figure 2 shows an example, where shaded frames are PCM frames and non-shaded frames are DRAM frames. In the example, the MC migrates the content of frame 13 to frame 2, the content of frame 2 to frame 19, and the content of frame 19 to frame 13.

To allow the three migrations to proceed concurrently, the MC uses three intermediate frame-size buffers located in the MC itself. The contents of the frames are first copied to the buffers, and only later copied to the destination frames. In addition, to avoid excessively delaying LLC misses due to row conflicts while migrating, the PCM DIMMs are equipped with an extra pair of row-buffers per rank, used exclusively for migrations. Operated by the MC, these buffers communicate with the internal prefetching circuitry of the PCM DIMM [11, 12], bypassing the original bank's row buffer. Since our migrations occur in sequence, two of these buffers are necessary only when the migration involves two banks of the same rank, and one buffer would suffice otherwise. This modification is not applied to DRAM DIMMs to avoid their redesign. (The energy and delay costs of these extra PCM DIMM buffers are taken into account in our simulations.)

RaPP uses a different destination unranked (and thus unpopular) PCM frame every time it needs to migrate a page out of DRAM. The reason is that migrations involve writes to the PCM cells. Using different unpopular pages guarantees that these writes are evenly spread across the PCM area for wear leveling. We start picking unranked frames from the bottom of the physical address space (which maps to the end of the PCM area), and move upward from there whenever a new PCM frame is needed.

The set of scheduled migrations is maintained in a list. We deschedule migrations whenever the corresponding PCM pages cross back down to queue 4 before the migrations start. The MC performs migrations from the list whenever there are no LLC misses or write-backs to perform. Any misses that arrive for a page undergoing a migration are directed to the original address or to one of the intermediate buffers. Write-backs are buffered until the migration is concluded.

For best performance, our goal is to execute the migrations completely in the background and without OS involvement. Thus, the MC maintains the $RemapTable$, a hash table for translating frame addresses coming from the LLC to actual remapped frame addresses. Figure 2 shows an example $RemapTable$. The $RemapTable$ is accessible by the OS as well. Periodically or when the $RemapTable$ fills up (at which point the MC interrupts the CPU), the OS commits the new translations to its page table and invalidates the corresponding TLB entries. (When non-virtually addressed hardware caches are used, some lines may have to be invalidated as well.) We assume that the OS uses a hashed inverted page table, as in the UltraSparc and PowerPC architectures, which considerably simplifies the commit operation. Since a commit clears the $RemapTable$, the OS sets a flag in a memory-mapped register in the MC to make sure that the MC refrains from migrating pages during the commit process.

The $RemapTable$ also includes two bits for communication between the MC and the OS. One bit is called $MigratingNow$, which when set means that the corresponding frame is currently scheduled for a migration. The other bit is called $ReplacingNow$, which when set means that the OS is replacing the page currently stored in that frame. The MC is responsible for $MigratingNow$, whereas the OS is responsible for $ReplacingNow$. Before the OS tries to replace a page, it must check the $RemapTable$ first. There are three possible scenarios here. Scenario 1: If there is no entry for the physical frame in which the page lies, the OS creates one, sets $ReplacingNow$, and programs the DMA engine to use the frame. The MC does not migrate any page to that same frame while $ReplacingNow$ is set. When the replacement is done, the OS resets $ReplacingNow$. Scenario 2: If there is an entry for the corresponding frame and $MigratingNow$ is set, the OS should select another page for replacement. Scenario 3: If the frame has already changed addresses (i.e., the entry for the frame exists and $MigratingNow$ is not set), the OS can set $ReplacingNow$ and proceed using the new frame address.

Finally, for robustness, RaPP uses a self-disabling mechanism that disables access monitoring, queue maintenance, and migrations whenever too many "bad migrations" occur. A bad migration occurs in one of two cases: (1) when a page originally in PCM is migrated to DRAM and then back to PCM without being referenced enough times while in DRAM; or (2) when a page originally in DRAM is evicted to PCM and then back to DRAM with too many accesses while in PCM. To implement this mechanism, we use a single counter of bad migrations (CBM) and a 2-bit saturating counter per MQ entry. Whenever a ranked page is touched, the saturating counter is incremented. Whenever a migration is completed, using the $RemapTable$, RaPP can identify where the page was since the last commit to the OS page table. If the migration falls into case (1) and the counter is not saturated, or it falls into case (2) and the counter is saturated, CBM is incremented. The saturating counter for a page is reset whenever the page migrates. At the end of each 1ms epoch, if the number of bad migrations reached 5% (the "disable threshold") or more of the maximum number of migrations possible within the epoch, RaPP is disabled.

Controller structure. Our MC adds a few components to a vanilla MC. Our MC (Figure 3) extends a programmable MC from [34] by adding RaPP's own modules (shaded in the figure). The MC receives read/write requests from the LLC controller via the CMD queue. The Arbiter iteratively dequeues requests, which the Controller converts into commands to be sent to the memory devices.

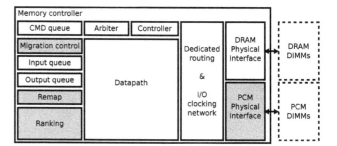

Figure 3: Memory controller with RaPP's new modules highlighted.

The Controller routes those commands by frame address to the appropriate Physical Interface (DRAM or PCM), which converts commands into timing relationships and signals for operating memory devices and coordinating data transfers. The Interfaces also control the power states of their respective memory ranks. The Datapath handles the data flow from the memory devices to the LLC controller and vice-versa. The module places data read from memory into the Output queue, where the LLC controller can read it. On write-back requests, the Datapath reads data (provided by the LLC controller) from the Input queue. For consistency, the CMD queue logic checks if the target address of a read or write-back collides with older write-backs in the Input queue. A colliding read is serviced from the queue without actually reaching the memory devices, thus finishing faster. A colliding write-back invalidates the older write-back command and data.

RaPP's Ranking module (RKMOD) contains the small on-chip cache of MQ and victim entries (entry cache) and the queue for updates to the MQ queues and the victim list (update queue). Misses in the entry cache produce requests to DRAM. RKMOD's logic snoops the CMD queue, creating one update per new request. To reduce the lag between an access and its corresponding MQ entry update, the update queue is implemented as a small circular buffer (32 entries), where an entering update precludes any currently queued update to the same entry.

The Migration Control module (MIGMOD) contains the queue of scheduled migrations (migration queue) and three page-sized buffers for the migrations (transfer buffers). MIGMOD processes migrations sequentially, each one occurring in two stages: (1) read and buffer frames; and (2) write frames to their new locations. Stage (2) does not start until stage (1) is completed. MIGMOD latches the base addresses of the frames undergoing a migration, as well as an offset address within each frame. The Controller module detects memory accesses that target one of the frames undergoing migrations by checking the base addresses. The Controller serves an access that targets a migrating frame by accessing the appropriate structure (main memory or a transfer buffer).

The Remap module (REMOD) contains the $RemapTable$ and the logic to remap target addresses. At the end of a migration, MIGMOD submits the three latched frame numbers to REMOD, which creates new mappings in the $RemapTable$. REMOD snoops the CMD queue to check if it is necessary to remap its entries. Each $RemapTable$ lookup and each remapping take 1 memory cycle. However, these operations only delay a request if it finds the CMQ queue empty.

Note that many previous works have proposed MCs with similar levels of sophistication and complexity, e.g. [10, 17, 18, 25, 36, 37, 13]. For example, [17] implements a learning algorithm in the memory controller itself.

Storage overhead. The bulk of our MC design is in the storage structures that it contains. The total on-chip storage in our design is 126 KBytes. By design, the page buffers require 24 KBytes (3 pages). The other structures have empirically selected sizes: 28 KBytes for the $RemapTable$ (4K entries), 64 KBytes for the cache of MQ and victim entries (4K entries), and 10 KBytes for the update and migration queues. This amount of on-chip storage is small compared to the multi-MByte shared LLC.

Our design also has limited DRAM space requirements. Taking a system with 1GB of DRAM + 32GB of PCM as a base for calculation, the total DRAM space consumed by descriptors is 6 MBytes (0.59% of the DRAM space). Each frame descriptor in the MQ queues or in the victim list takes 124 bits, which we round to 128 bits. Each descriptor contains the corresponding frame number (22 bits), the reference counter (14 bits), the queue number, including victim list (4 bits), the last-access time (27 bits), three pointers to other descriptors (54 bits), a flag indicating that the frame has been demoted (1 bit) and the counter for bad migrations (2 bits). For the configurations with which we experiment, the space taken by the descriptors is 0.63 MBytes.

3.2 Comparable Hybrid Memory Systems

We compare our design to the two most closely related hybrid memory systems: DBUFF [28] and WP [37].

DRAM Buffer (DBUFF) relies on a DRAM buffer logically placed between the CPU and a main memory composed solely of PCM [28]. The DRAM buffer is implemented as a set-associative cache managed entirely by the MC and invisible to the OS. Cache blocks (corresponding to virtual memory pages) coming from secondary storage are initially installed in the DRAM buffer, but also take space in PCM. From then on, the memory accesses are directed to the DRAM buffer. On a buffer miss, the page containing the desired cache line is brought into the buffer from PCM. When a block is replaced from the buffer (using the clock algorithm), it is written to its PCM frame if this is the first eviction of the block or the block was written in the buffer. Block writes to PCM are enqueued in an write buffer and done lazily in background. Like in our design, only the cache lines that were actually written are written to PCM.

When workloads exhibit good locality, most accesses hit the DRAM buffer, which leads to good performance and dynamic energy. Endurance is also good since the lazy block writes and cache-line-level writes substantially reduce the write traffic to the PCM array. (In fact, our implementation of DBUFF does not include the Fine-Grained Wear Leveling and Page-Level Bypass techniques proposed in [28]. The reason is that the endurance produced by the other techniques is sufficient in our experiments; adding extra complexity does not seem justified for our workloads and endurance assumptions.) However, workloads with poor locality may lead to poor performance and energy consumption. In addition, the inclusive DRAM caching in DBUFF reduces the amount of available memory space, potentially leading to a larger number of page faults than our design.

Our simulations of DBUFF are optimistic in many ways. First, we consider a DRAM buffer of size approximately 8% of the total memory size (rather than the original 3%). Second, we assume no DRAM buffer lookup overhead in performance or energy. Third, we implement the DRAM buffer as a fully associative structure (rather than set associative) with LRU replacement (rather than clock). Fourth, on a DRAM buffer miss requiring a page write-back, the dirty blocks (only) are written back at the same time as the missing page's content is fetched from PCM or disk.

Despite these optimistic assumptions, RaPP improves on DBUFF

in two fundamental ways: (1) it uses the entire memory as a flat space, relying on page migration rather than replication; and (2) it detects when most migrations are useless and turns itself off.

Hot-modified Pages in Write Partition (WP) places DRAM and PCM in a flat address space and treats DRAM as an OS-managed write partition [37]. All pages are initially stored in PCM. The idea is to keep the cold-modified (infrequently written) pages in PCM, trying to take advantage of its low idle power consumption, and the hot-modified (frequently written) pages in DRAM to avoid PCM's high write latency and poor endurance. The MC implements a variation of the MQ algorithm with 16 LRU queues, but only counts write accesses to the physical frames. Frames that reach queue 8 (receive 2^8 writes) are considered to store hot-modified pages. On a page fault, the OS brings the page from secondary storage to the PCM area. Over time, the pages that become hot-modified are migrated to DRAM by the OS. At the same time, a page currently in DRAM but with fewer writes may have to be migrated back to PCM.

Our simulations of WP are also optimistic, as we do not charge any performance or energy overheads for the data structures and hardware modifications necessary to implement WP.

Despite these optimistic assumptions, there are three main problems with WP. First, it can hurt the performance of read-dominated workloads under less optimistic assumptions about PCM read performance. Second, migrating pages using a core at the OS quantum boundary wastes opportunities to improve performance and energy-delay within that timespan. Third, endurance also suffers because it takes a large number of writes until the OS will consider migrating a heavily written page to DRAM. Our evaluation studies mainly how WP compares to other approaches. However, in our longer technical report [29], we also isolate the impact of migrating frequently-read pages and enabling migrations within the OS quantum via hardware.

RaPP improves on WP by: (1) migrating pages that are read-intensive as well; (2) migrating pages in the background, without OS involvement; (3) including mechanisms for identifying pages worthy of migration and self-disabling for when migrations are mostly useless; and (4) spreading migrations across many physical frames. Moreover, this paper improves on [37] by: (5) assuming more realistic PCM characteristics; and (6) presenting a comparison of RaPP and WP to DBUFF, across a large set of workloads and parameters. We study variations of WP in [29].

4. EVALUATION

In this section, we evaluate hybrid memory systems using energy and performance as first-order metrics. Although we also report endurance results, we give them lower emphasis because our system can be easily combined with many previously proposed techniques to mitigate the PCM endurance problem (Section 5).

4.1 Methodology

Our evaluation is based on simulation, since PCM hardware is not yet available. We simulate combinations of benchmarks from the SPEC 2000, SPEC 2006, and Stream suites forming a total of 27 workloads (Table 1). Because our workloads have widely different memory footprints, we group them with respect to footprint size into Large (LG), Medium (MD), and Small (SM) classes.

To reduce simulation times, our simulations are done in two steps. In the first step, we use M5 [5] to collect memory access (LLC misses and write-backs) traces from our workloads running on an 8-core server. Each benchmark in a workload is represented

Table 1: Workload described by tag, memory footprint in MB (Foot), LLC misses per 1000 instructions (MKPI), and percentage of LLC write-backs as a fraction of all memory accesses (WB%). *Spec 2006.

Tag	Foot	MKPI	WB%	Applications (x2 each)
LG1	993	12	33	milc*, gobmk*, sjeng*, libquantum*
LG2	992	29	32	S.add, S.copy, apsi, milc*
LG3	746	24	27	mcf*, S.triad, sjeng*, facerec
LG4	743	4	25	vortex, milc*, sixtrack, mesa
LG5	702	24	26	sjeng*, S.triad, S.add, swim
LG6	683	4	28	perlbmk, crafty, gzip, milc*
LG7	645	25	32	lucas, gcc, mcf*, sphinx3*
LG8	594	18	32	wupwise, vpr, mcf*, parser
LG9	557	17	32	swim, eon, art, lucas
MD1	486	13	49	applu, lucas, gap, apsi
MD2	467	23	32	S.scale, S.triad, swim, eon
MD3	414	20	30	mcf*, parser, twolf, facerec
MD4	407	8	24	namd*, S.triad, sjeng*, wupwise
MD5	394	13	32	art, lucas, mgrid, fma3d
MD6	385	24	28	art, mcf*, gzip, vpr
MD7	381	14	23	S.add, h264ref*, equake, hmmer*
MD8	367	46	33	S.triad, S.add, S.copy, S.scale
MD9	356	30	27	equake, S.scale, S.triad, mgrid
SM1	295	2	21	wupwise, gobmk*, vortex, h264ref*
SM2	285	5	33	swim, perlbmk, namd*, eon
SM3	283	6	33	swim, crafty, twolf, gcc
SM4	276	16	33	lucas, h264ref*, libquantum*, sphinx3*
SM5	271	15	27	wupwise, equake, ammp, libquantum*
SM6	260	11	24	fma3d, mgrid, galgel, equake
SM7	247	12	32	fma3d, sphinx3*, galgel, lucas
SM8	243	15	21	S.triad, h264ref*, fma3d, equake
SM9	243	2	29	ammp, gap, wupwise, vpr

Table 2: System settings.

Feature		Value	
CPU cores (2.668GHz, Alpha ISA)		8 in-order, one thread/core	
TLB per-core size, hit/miss time		128 entries, 8/120 CPU cycles	
L1 I/D cache (per core)		64KB, 2-way, 1 CPU cycle hit	
L2 cache (shared)		8MB, 8-way, 10 CPU cycle hit	
Cache block size / OS page size		64 bytes / 8KB	
Memory (667MHz/DDR3-1333)		8KB rows, close-page	
Memory devices (x8 width, 1.5V)		DRAM	PCM
Delay	tRCD	15ns	56ns
	tRP	15ns	150ns
	tRRDact	6ns	5ns
	tRRDpre	6ns	27ns
	Refresh time	64ms	n/a
	tRFC / tREFI	110ns / 7.8μs	n/a
Current	Row Buffer Read	200mA	200mA
	Row Buffer Write	220mA	220mA
	Avg Array R/W	110mA	242mA
	Active Standby	62mA	62mA
	Precharge Powerdown	40mA	40mA
	Refresh	240mA	n/a
Normalized Density		1	4
Data Retention		64 ms	> 10 years
Cell endurance (writes)		$> 10^{16}$	$10^8 - 10^9$

by its best 100M-instruction simulation point (selected using Simpoints 3.0 [26]). A workload terminates when the slowest application has executed 100M instructions.

In the second step, we replay the traces using our own detailed memory system simulator. This simulator models all the relevant aspects of the OS, memory controller, and memory devices, including inverted page tables and TLB management, page replacements, memory channel and bank contention, memory device power and timing, and row buffer management.

The main architectural characteristics of the simulated server are listed in Table 2. We simulate in-order cores to expose the overheads associated with PCM accesses to workloads. The cores have private 64-Kbyte 2-way instruction and data L1 caches, as well as an 8-MByte 8-way combined shared cache. For this cache architecture, Table 1 reports the LLC misses per kilo instruction (MPKI) and the percentage of LLC write-backs (WB%) for each workload. The memory system has 4 DDR3 channels, each one occupied by a single-rank DIMM with 8 devices (x8 width) and 8 banks per device. In all simulations, we assume an initially warm memory (no cold page faults). The MC implements cache-block-level bank interleaving and page-level channel interleaving. Memory accesses are served on a FCFS basis. The MC uses close-page row buffer management. (More sophisticated access scheduling is not necessary for our simulated system and workloads, as opportunities to increase their bank hit rate via scheduling are rare, and such improvements are orthogonal to our study.)

A memory rank can be in (1) Active Standby state, when at least one of its banks is serving requests; or (2) Precharge Power Down, when all banks are idle and the clock enable line is turned off to save energy. Additionally, PCM is enhanced to avoid writing unmodified cache lines back to the cell array. The table shows power parameters [20] of DRAM and PCM chips, and the timing parameters that change across memory technologies [20, 28, 37] (although we simulate all relevant parameters [22, 32]).

Besides RaPP, we simulate the two hybrid approaches mentioned in Section 3 (DBUFF and WP) and an additional "Unman-

aged" system, in which pages remain in the frames originally assigned to them by the OS. We use Unmanaged as the baseline for comparison. *Only RaPP is assumed to have energy and performance overheads stemming from its data structures. Our assumptions for RaPP are consistent with those of other authors [14].* For example, the RaPP SRAM consumes 0.13W of background power and 0.017nJ per 16-byte operation; the transfer buffers consume 0.06W of background power and 0.06nJ per 64-byte operation; and each DIMM-level row buffer increases the rank background power by 12.5% when active (and as much dynamic power as a regular row buffer). The four hybrid systems have 1 channel equipped with 1 DRAM DIMM (128MB) and the remaining 3 channels with 1 PCM DIMM each (3x128x4MB=1536MB), totaling 1.664 GBytes of memory. We picked these small memory sizes to match the footprint of the workloads' simulation points.

As another basis for comparison, we use a PCM-only system with 2 GBytes of memory (4x128x4MB). Previous works have shown that the DRAM-only system exhibits much worse performance than PCM-only and hybrid systems [28], due to its lower storage capacity, so we do not consider it in this paper.

4.2 Results

4.2.1 Performance and energy

We now compare the behavior of RaPP, DBUFF, WP, and the two baseline systems. Due to space limitations, we do not present separate performance and energy results for all workloads; instead, we plot these results for the MD workloads and discuss the results for other workloads in the absence of figures. Later, we plot energy-delay^2 (ED2) results for all workloads.

Figure 4 presents the running time (top graph, including the geometric mean of the MD results), average memory power consumption (middle graph, including the power consumed by the SRAM cache used in RaPP), and number of page migrations in RaPP and WP and page fetches from PCM in DBUFF (bottom graph, again including the geometric mean). We refer to page migrations and fetches collectively as page transfers. The performance and power results are normalized to Unmanaged. Note that we plot average power, rather than energy, to remove the impact of different running times (which are plotted in the top graph).

Running time. The top graph shows that RaPP exhibits the low-

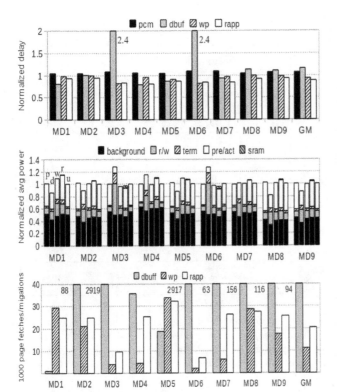

Figure 4: Comparing performance, average power, and page transfers for the MD workloads. In the middle figure, p = PCM-only, d = DBUFF, w = WP, r = RaPP and u = Unmanaged.

est average running times, followed by WP, Unmanaged, PCM-only, and then DBUFF. In fact, RaPP performs better than PCM-only and Unmanaged for all workloads (including the LG and SM workloads). RaPP achieves these results by migrating popular pages to the DRAM area, which has substantially better performance in the presence of row buffer misses than PCM. WP and DBUFF do not always outperform PCM-only and Unmanaged. RaPP is more robust than WP and DBUFF, achieving good performance in most cases and preventing degradation in others by disabling itself.

WP attempts to migrate pages to DRAM as well, but focuses solely on those pages that experience a large number of write-backs (or writes of disk data read into memory). In addition, the fact that WP migrates pages at the end of the OS quantum has two sides. On the negative side, WP misses opportunities to migrate popular pages as their popularity shifts within the OS quantum. MD2 and MD8, for example, suffer from this problem. On the positive side, migrating infrequently reduces the number of migrations in workloads where most migrations will turn out useless. However, RaPP is more effective than WP at preventing unnecessary migrations, as it includes mechanisms designed explicitly for this purpose. For example, in SM2, a large fraction of pages is hot-modified, but performance-irrelevant. In that case, RaPP disables itself at about a quarter of the execution. A similar phenomenon occurs in 6 other workloads in our experiments. In essence, RaPP is more effective at migrating the actual performance-critical pages to DRAM, improving performance by 6% for MD workloads and 7% overall with respect to WP.

The most extreme results happen for DBUFF. It achieves the lowest running time for MD1, but dismal running times for MD3 and MD6. The reason for DBUFF's poor performance is that

MD3 and MD6 exhibit poor locality (their working sets are substantially larger than the size of the DRAM buffer). The same effect occurs for several LG workloads. Poor locality forces frequent page fetching from PCM into DRAM, with the eviction of dirty blocks (if any) within victim pages done in the background. Without the problematic workloads, RaPP still performs 14% and 8% better than DBUFF for the LG and MD workloads, respectively. On the other hand, the SM workloads have working sets that easily fit in the DRAM buffer, so DBUFF performs best for 6 of them. However, RaPP's overall average performance is still slightly better than DBUFF's for the SM workloads.

Finally, note that Unmanaged consistently outperforms PCM-only. The reason is that Unmanaged benefits from accessing data in its DRAM section, which is substantially faster than accessing data in PCM when row buffer misses occur. (Excluding the effect of page transfers, the row buffer miss ratio we observe is always higher than 80%. This effect has been observed in previous studies of multi-core servers as well, e.g. [31].)

Average memory power. Considering the middle graph of Figure 4, we see that all systems exhibit similar average power consumption for the MD workloads (the same happens for the LG and SM workloads). The average power correlates well with the total number of accesses in each approach. As expected, page transfers increase read/write and activation/precharge (activation/write to array for PCM) power somewhat. We also see that DBUFF produces lower background power. The reason is that the PCM area can be in precharge powerdown state more often in DBUFF.

Interestingly, although RaPP uses an SRAM cache for its ranking of pages, the power consumed by this cache is negligible. Most rank accesses become cache hits (at least 90% in our experiments). The SRAM results in the figure account for the static and hit energies. The energy consumed by the misses is reported in the other categories.

Page transfers. The bottom graph shows that RaPP migrates more pages than WP for most (all but 3) MD workloads. The same happens for most SM (all but 1) and LG (all but 2) workloads. The reason is that each migration operation in RaPP actually transfers 3 pages, instead of 1 or 2 pages in WP. Interestingly, DBUFF fetches many more pages from PCM than RaPP and WP migrate in the MD workloads. Again, the reason is that these (and the LG) workloads have working sets that do not fit in the DRAM buffer. For the SM workloads, DBUFF fetches pages much less frequently than for the MD and LG workloads. In fact, DBUFF transfers fewer pages than WP in 4 SM workloads and fewer than RaPP in 6 of them.

Putting performance and energy together: ED2. Figure 5 plots the ED2 of each workload and system normalized to Unmanaged. The rightmost set of bars in each graph shows the geometric mean of the results presented in the same graph. The graphs show that RaPP is the only system to achieve ED2 no higher than Unmanaged and PCM-only for all workloads. (In the few instances where RaPP achieves roughly the same ED2 as Unmanaged, it disabled itself due to a large percentage of bad migrations.) Considering the workload classes independently, we find that RaPP achieves the lowest average ED2 for the LG and MD workloads. For the SM workloads, the combination of low run time, very few migrations, and idle PCM ranks (as discussed before) leads DBUFF to the lowest average ED2 (14% lower than RaPP). Over-

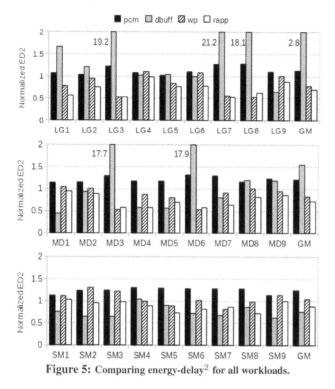

Figure 5: Comparing energy-delay^2 for all workloads.

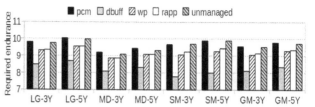

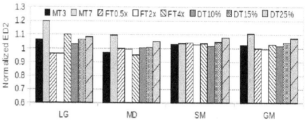

Figure 6: Required Endurance projected over 3 and 5 years.

Figure 7: RaPP's sensitivity to migration threshold (MT), filter threshold (FT), disable threshold (DT).

all, RaPP achieves 13%, 24%, 36%, and 49% lower ED2 than WP, Unmanaged, PCM-only, and DBUFF, respectively.

As mentioned above, RaPP improves ED2 over PCM-only and Unmanaged by migrating popular pages from PCM to DRAM. The comparison to WP is more interesting. RaPP and WP achieve comparable ED2 for some workloads. However, WP achieves worse ED2 than Unmanaged for 2 LG, 1 MD, and 4 SM workloads. In many of these cases, RaPP did very well but in others it simply disabled itself. Compared to DBUFF, RaPP wins for workloads with working sets larger than the DRAM buffer (i.e., 9 of our workloads).

4.2.2 Endurance

To evaluate the system lifetimes (limited by PCM's endurance), we resort to the Required Endurance metric [6]: $T_{life} \times \frac{B}{\alpha\,C}$, where B is the memory bandwidth in bytes per second, T_{life} is the desired system lifetime in seconds, α is the wear-leveling efficiency of the system, and C is the memory capacity in bytes. For each workload, we consider T_{life} the typical 3- to 5-year server lifespan. α is A/M, where A is the average number of writes per PCM cache block and M is the number of writes to the most written cache block in the PCM area of the system. A low value of α suggests poor wear-leveling. Required Endurance determines the number of writes that a PCM cache block must be able to withstand during the server's lifespan.

Figure 6 compares the base-10 logarithm of the Required Endurance of the systems we consider, using the 3- and the 5-year projections. For comparison, PCM's endurance today is $10^8 - 10^9$. The figure shows that RaPP requires roughly 10% more endurance than DBUFF, but only 1% more than WP on average. In contrast, it requires 5% and 4% less endurance than PCM-only and Unmanaged, respectively. DBUFF provides the best Required Endurance.

In RaPP's 5-year projection, most MD and SM workloads require endurance only slightly higher than 10^9, whereas a few LG

workloads require closer to 10^{10} endurance. The reason for these results is that in RaPP the frequently read and frequently written pages compete for space in the DRAM area, trying to strike a balance between performance and endurance. In addition, in some cases, RaPP's self-disabling mechanism is triggered, making it behave as Unmanaged from that point on.

However, we argue that RaPP's endurance results are not a cause of concern for two reasons. First, as we mention in Section 5, many proposals already extend the lifetime of PCM greatly. Several of them are orthogonal to RaPP [8, 18, 20, 38] and can enhance PCM independently from our approach. Second, the predictions for future PCM cells suggest significant endurance improvement compared to DRAM (10^{12} writes by 2012 [9] and 10^{15} writes by 2022 [1]), but performance and energy will still lag. Better PCM endurance justifies a shift towards reducing energy and delay, as we do in this paper.

4.3 Sensitivity analysis

RaPP parameters. We now study the impact of the migration threshold (MT), which defines the number of accesses to a PCM page before deciding to migrate it to DRAM; the filter threshold (FT), which defines the window of time for filtering consecutive page references; and the disable threshold (DT), which defines the percentage of bad migrations before RaPP disables itself.

Figure 7 depicts the ED2 results for the three workload classes and the overall geometric mean. Each bar is normalized to the ED2 resulting from the default value of the corresponding parameter. Specifically, the default value for MT is 2^5 and we compare it to 2^3 (labeled MT3) and 2^7 (MT7); the default value for FT is $MigrationTime/32$ and we compare it to 0.5x default FT (FT0.5x), 2x default FT (FT2x), and 4x default FT (FT4x); and the default value for DT is 5% and we compare it to 10% (DT10%), 15% (DT15%), and 25% (DT25%). We always vary one parameter at a time, keeping others at their default values.

The figure shows that RaPP is most sensitive to MT, especially for the LG workloads. In particular, MT7 degrades ED2 by 20% on average for the LG workloads, compared to the default. It also degrades ED2 for the MD and SM workloads. In contrast, MT3 degrades ED2 for the LG and SM workloads, but not by as much and not for the MD workloads. RaPP exhibits relatively low sensitivity to FT, except for FT4x for LG workloads. Finally, RaPP consistently showed more ED2 degradation as DT increases.

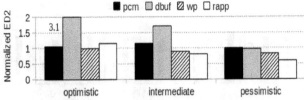

Figure 8: Sensitivity to PCM's characteristics.

These results suggest that (1) overshooting the ideal MT is more harmful on average than undershooting it; and (2) lower values for FT and DT provide better behavior. In contrast, varying these settings has a negligible impact on Required Endurance; it varies only within 1% compared to our default RaPP results.

PCM's characteristics. We now evaluate the impact of the performance and energy characteristics of PCM devices. We consider three additional settings for PCM performance: optimistic, intermediate, and pessimistic; the PCM energy varies along with its performance settings. Specifically, the optimistic setting assumes that row activations are 40% faster than our default value, bringing them close to DRAM's activations; the array writes stay with their default values. [37] assumed similarly high-performing PCM activations. The pessimistic setting assumes that activations and array writes are 25% and 2.5x slower than our defaults, respectively. [12] assumed similarly pessimistic parameters. Finally, the intermediate setting assumes that activations are 25% faster and array writes are 50% slower than our defaults.

Figure 8 shows the average ED2 results (across all workloads) normalized to Unmanaged. We can see that RaPP achieves the best average ED2 for the pessimistic and intermediate cases. The advantage of RaPP is particularly significant in the pessimistic scenario. For the optimistic setting, PCM-only and WP achieve roughly the same ED2 as Unmanaged. This is not surprising since the optimistic performance and energy of PCM become comparable to those of DRAM. Because RaPP attempts to migrate pages to DRAM despite the optimistic assumptions for PCM, it achieves slightly higher ED2. In contrast, DBUFF achieves worse ED2 because of the workloads with poor locality.

These results suggest that RaPP behaves better than the other systems for different sets of expected PCM characteristics (default and intermediate). RaPP's benefits will be even more pronounced, if commercial PCM devices turn out to be worse than our expectations. Again, the Required Endurance varies negligibly (less than 2%) across these parameter settings.

5. RELATED WORK

Using technologies other than DRAM for main memory. Despite the problems with Flash technology (page-level interface of NAND Flash, very high write and block-erase times, low cell endurance), two studies have considered combining Flash and DRAM in main memory. ENVy [33] focused on sidestepping the write-related problems of Flash using battery-backed SRAM and virtual memory techniques. A more recent position paper [23] considered a flat DRAM+Flash (or PCM) address space with the OS responsible for predicting page access patterns and migrating read-only pages from DRAM to (write-protected) Flash. Although the paper did not include an evaluation of their system, we expect that an OS-only approach to page management would cause unacceptable overhead for most types of pages.

With better characteristics than Flash, PCM is a more promising technology for use in main memory. In fact, several recent works [7, 8, 20, 27, 28, 35, 37, 38] have proposed systems that use PCM as a partial or complete replacement for DRAM. We compared our design to two of these works.

Tackling PCM's endurance problem. Many previous works focused extensively on the work-arounds needed to mitigate this problem. Lee *et al.* [20] proposed tracking data modifications at the cache block and data word levels to avoid unnecessary traffic to the MC and writes to the PCM array. The technique was combined with narrow row buffer sets organized to exploit locality.

Yang *et al.* [35] proposed the Data-Comparison Write (DCW) approach, which only allows a write to a PCM cell if the new value differs from the previously stored one. Flip-and-Write [8] improves DCW by storing extra "flip bits" that denote the encoding of each PCM word and performing hamming distance calculations to verify if reversing the encoding (by inverting flip bits) will reduce the number of writes. Alternatively, Zhou *et al.* [38] improved DCW using periodic byte rotation at the cache block level and segment swaps across memory areas.

A complementary technique named Fine-Grained Wear-Leveling (FGWL) seeks to balance the wear-out across cache blocks within a physical PCM frame by rotating blocks within the frame [28]. FGWL inspired Start-Gap [27], a technique that applies a simple algebraic function to transform a logical memory address into a physical one. [27] also combined Start-Gap with simple address-space randomization techniques.

Another approach [18] improves endurance by reusing a pair of physical frames with complementary faulty cells as a single logical frame. The system creates the pairs periodically, as new faults may alter previous pairings.

Differently than these previous systems, our work takes a higher level, page-based approach to wear leveling. First, we migrate write-intensive pages to DRAM. Second, we migrate pages coming from DRAM to unpopular PCM frames. Importantly, their low-level techniques are orthogonal and can be nicely combined with our page-based techniques to extend endurance further.

Page migration in main memory. A few works have considered page migration for memory energy conservation. Lebeck *et al.* [19] conducted a preliminary investigation of popularity-based page allocations to enable sending (unpopular) memory devices to low-power state. In [16], the OS migrates pages periodically based on their reference bits, without any support from the MC. In contrast, Pandey *et al.* [25] proposed to implement popularity-based page ranking and migration using the MC to reduce the energy consumed by DMA transfers. Dong *et al.* [13] migrate hot pages from the off-chip memory to a chip-integrated memory. In a position paper [3], Bellosa proposed "memory management controllers" (MMCs) that would take away the responsibility for memory management (e.g., page migration) from the OS.

Although an OS-only approach to page migration [16] may work for energy conservation, it does not react quickly and efficiently enough to mitigate the problems with PCM. Thus, it is critical to involve the MC (or an MMC) as well. In this context, the closest prior work to this paper is [25]. However, as our environment (a DRAM+PCM hybrid in a multiprocessing system) and goal (improve performance at the same energy consumption) are quite different than theirs (DRAM-only memory and DMA-related energy conservation in a uniprocessor system), there are many differences between the two approaches. First, we had to adapt a sophisticated ranking algorithm to address the poor performance and endurance of PCM. Pandey *et al.* used a much simpler histogram-based ranking. Second, our migration approach is also more complex, as it needs to consider the limitations of PCM and involve an additional, properly selected PCM frame. Third, we considered many multiprocessing workloads and the increased pressure they put on the memory system. Because of this pressure, migrations need to be done very selectively, so we had to devise heuristics to avoid certain migrations.

6. CONCLUSIONS

In this work, we introduced a novel hybrid memory system design combining DRAM and phase-change memory. Our design features a sophisticated memory controller, and a page ranking and migration policy called RaPP. The memory controller monitors the memory accesses and implements RaPP. RaPP seeks to benefit from the best characteristics of DRAM and PCM, while avoiding their limitations. The policy takes into account the recency and frequency of page accesses, as well as the write traffic to each page, to rank pages and lay them out in physical memory. Our results demonstrate that our design behaves significantly better than two state-of-the-art hybrid designs, despite our optimistic assumptions for the latter systems.

We conclude that, although useful, existing designs are not robust to certain workloads. This robustness can be achieved by relying on page migration (rather than caching-style replication) in the background, optimizing read traffic as well as write traffic, and self-monitoring and disabling. Our controller and policy are good examples of how to achieve these characteristics.

Acknowledgments

We thank Rekha Bachwani, Kien Le, and Wei Zheng for their help in the early stages of this work. We are also grateful to Qingyuan Deng, Stijn Eyerman, Daniel Jimenez, Yoshio Turner, and Hongzhong Zheng for their help with our simulation infrastructure. We thank Abhishek Bhattacharjee for comments that helped us improve this paper. Finally, we thank our sponsors: NSF grant #CCF-0916539, Intel, and CAPES (Brazil).

7. REFERENCES

[1] Emerging Research Devices. International Technology Roadmap for Semiconductors (ITRS), 2007.

[2] L. Barroso and U. Holzle. *The Datacenter as a Computer: An Introduction to the Design of Warehouse-Scale Machines*. Morgan and Claypool Publishers, 2009.

[3] F. Bellosa. When Physical Is Not Real Enough. In *ACM SIGOPS European Workshop*, 2004.

[4] A. Bhattacharjee and M. Martonosi. Thread Criticality Predictors for Dynamic Performance, Power, and Resource Management in Chip Multiprocessors. In *ISCA*, 2009.

[5] N. Binkert et al. The M5 Simulator: Modeling Networked Systems. *IEEE Micro*, 26(4), 2006.

[6] G. W. Burr et al. Phase change memory technology. 2010. Journal of Vacuum Science & Technology B.

[7] A. Caulfield et al. Understanding the Impact of Emerging Non-Volatile Memories on High-Performance, IO-Intensive Computing. In *SC*, 2010.

[8] S. Cho and H. Lee. Flip-N-Write: A Simple Deterministic Technique to Improve PRAM Write Performance, Energy and Endurance. In *MICRO*, 2009.

[9] J. Condit et al. Better I/O Through Byte-Addressable, Persistent Memory. In *SOSP*, 2009.

[10] B. Diniz et al. Limiting the Power Consumption of Main Memory. In *ISCA*, 2007.

[11] X. Dong et al. Leveraging 3D PCRAM Technologies to Reduce Checkpoint Overhead for Future Exascale Systems. In *SC*, 2009.

[12] X. Dong, N. Jouppi, and Y. Xie. PCRAMsim: System-Level Performance, Energy, and Area Modeling for Phase-Change RAM. In *ICCAD*, 2009.

[13] X. Dong, Y. Xie, N. Muralimanohar, and N. P. Jouppi. Simple but Effective Heterogeneous Main Memory with On-Chip Memory Controller Support. In *SC*, 2010.

[14] X. Guo, E. Ipek, and T. Soyata. Resistive Computation: Avoiding the Power Wall with Low-Leakage, STT-MRAM Based Computing. In *ISCA*, 2010.

[15] H. Huang et al. Improving Energy Efficiency by Making DRAM Less Randomly Accessed. In *ISLPED*, 2005.

[16] H. Huang, P. Pillai, and K. G. Shin. Design and implementation of power-aware virtual memory. In *USENIX*, 2003.

[17] E. Ipek et al. Self-Optimizing Memory Controllers: A Reinforcement Learning Approach. In *ISCA*, 2008.

[18] E. Ipek et al. Dynamically Replicated Memory: Building Reliable Systems From Nanoscale Resistive Memories. In *ASPLOS*, 2010.

[19] A. Lebeck et al. Power Aware Page Allocation. In *ASPLOS*, 2000.

[20] B. Lee et al. Architecting Phase Change Memory as a Scalable DRAM Architecture. In *ISCA*, 2009.

[21] C. Lefurgy et al. Energy Management for Commercial Servers. *IEEE Computer*, 36(12), December 2003.

[22] Micron. 1Gb: x4, x8, x16 DDR3 SDRAM Features. http://download.micron.com/pdf/datasheets/dram/ddr3/1Gb_DDR3_SDRAM.pdf, 2006.

[23] J. C. Mogul et al. Operating System Support for NVM+DRAM Hybrid Main Memory. In *HotOS*, 2009.

[24] T. Nirschl et al. Write Strategies for 2 and 4-bit Multi-Level Phase-Change Memory. In *IEDM*, 2007.

[25] V. Pandey et al. DMA-Aware Memory Energy Management. In *HPCA*, 2006.

[26] E. Perelman et al. Using Simpoint for Accurate and Efficient Simulation. In *SIGMETRICS*, 2003.

[27] M. K. Qureshi et al. Enhancing Lifetime and Security of PCM-Based Main Memory with Start-Gap Wear Leveling. In *MICRO*, 2009.

[28] M. K. Qureshi, V. Srinivasan, and J. A. Rivers. Scalable High Performance Main Memory System Using Phase-Change Memory Technology. In *ISCA*, 2009.

[29] L. Ramos, E. Gorbatov, and R. Bianchini. Page Placement in Hybrid Memory Systems. Technical Report DCS–TR–675, Dept. of Comp. Science, Rutgers Univ., Sept. 2010, Revised Mar. 2011.

[30] S. Rixner et al. Memory Access Scheduling. In *ISCA*, 2000.

[31] K. Sudan et al. Micro-Pages: Increasing DRAM Efficiency with Locality-Aware Data Placement. In *ASPLOS*, 2010.

[32] D. Wang et al. DRAMsim: A Memory System Simulator. *SIGARCH Computer Architecture News*, 33(4), 2005.

[33] M. Wu and W. Zwaenepoel. eNVy: a Non-Volatile, Main Memory Storage System. In *ASPLOS*, 1994.

[34] Xilinx. Spartan-6 FPGA Memory Controller User Guide. 2010. http://www.xilinx.com/support/documentation/user_guides/ug388.pdf.

[35] B.-D. Yang et al. A Low Power Phase-Change Random Access Memory using a Data-Comparison Write Scheme. In *ISCAS*, 2007.

[36] L. Zhang et al. The Impulse Memory Controller. *IEEE Transactions on Computers, Special Issue on Advances in High-Performance Memory Systems*, November 2001.

[37] W. Zhang and T. Li. Exploring Phase Change Memory and 3D Die-Stacking for Power/Thermal Friendly, Fast and Durable Memory Architectures. In *PACT*, 2009.

[38] P. Zhou et al. A Durable and Energy Efficient Main Memory Using Phase Change Memory Technology. In *ISCA*, 2009.

[39] Y. Zhou, P. Chen, and K. Li. The Multi-Queue Replacement Algorithm for Second-Level Buffer Caches. In *USENIX*, 2001.

Performance Impact and Interplay of SSD Parallelism through Advanced Commands, Allocation Strategy and Data Granularity

Yang Hu[†‡], Hong Jiang[§], Dan Feng[‡ ✉],

Lei Tian[‡§], Hao Luo[†], Shuping Zhang[✗]

[†]School of Computer, Huazhong University of Science and Technology, Wuhan, China, 430074
[‡]Wuhan National Laboratory for Optoelectronics, Wuhan, China, 430074
[§]University of Nebraska-Lincoln, Lincoln, United States, 68588
[✗]Beijing Institute of Computer Technology and Application, Beijing, China, 100039
✉Corresponding author: dfeng@hust.edu.cn
{yanghu, hluo}@foxmail.com, jiang@cse.unl.edu, ltian@hust.edu.cn, zsp7098@sina.com

ABSTRACT

With the development of the NAND-Flash technology, NAND-Flash based Solid-State Disk (SSD) has been attracting a great deal of attention from both industry and academia. While a range of SSD research topics, from interface techniques to buffer management and Flash Translation Layer (FTL), from performance to endurance and energy efficiency, have been extensively studied in the literature, the SSD being studied was by and large treated as a grey or black box in that many of the internal features such as advanced commands, physical-page allocation schemes and data granularity are hidden or assumed away. We argue that, based on our experimental study, it is these internal features and their interplay that will help provide the missing but significant insights to designing high-performance and high-endurance SSDs.

In this paper, we use our highly accurate and multi-tiered SSD simulator, called SSDsim, to analyze several key internal SSD factors to characterize their performance impacts, interplay and parallelisms for the purpose of performance and endurance enhancement of SSDs. From the results of our experiments, we found that: (1) larger pages tend to have significantly negative impact on SSD performance under many workloads; (2) different physical-page allocation schemes have different deployment environments, where an optimal allocation scheme can be found for each workload; (3) although advanced commands provided by flash manufacturers can improve performance in some cases, they may jeopardize the SSD performance and endurance when used inappropriately; (4) since the parallelisms of SSD can be classified into four levels, namely, channel-level, chip-level, die-level and plane-level, the priority order of SSD parallelism, resulting from the strong interplay among physical-page allocation schemes and advanced commands, can have a very significant impact on SSD performance and endurance.

Categories and Subject Descriptors

B.1.4 [**Hardware**]: Microprogram Design Aids– *Firmware engineering*. B.3.3 [**Memory Structure**]: Performance Analysis and Design Aids– *Simulation*. D.4.2 [**Operating Systems**]: Storage Management– *Secondary storage*.

General Terms

Measurement and Performance

Keywords

NAND-Flash, SSD, simulator, advanced commands, parallelism

1. INTRODUCTION

NAND-Flash based Solid State Drive (SSD) has experienced tremendous development and growth during the last two decades. The enterprise-quality Flash memory storage has dropped in price, increased in per-unit capacity, improved in reliability, and addressed the random write performance penalty, which is traditionally associated with the technology, by various ingenious methods [1-6]. These advantages enable SSDs to be widely used in almost every aspect of modern computing systems, from low-end PCs to high-end servers in supercomputing, thus making the performance and endurance issues of solid-state storage system increasingly attractive to both academia and industry [7-11].

Several topics related to the performance and endurance of SSD, including FTL designs [12-15] and buffer schemes [16-19], have been extensively discussed in the literatures. Other studies in the literature deduce or infer the characteristics of flash or SSD by extended measurement [20-23]. However, some SSD internal behaviors with potentially important impacts on the system performance and endurance have been largely ignored. While very little has been studied and reported in the literature about the performance and endurance impacts and interplay of data granularity of SSD, allocation strategy and advanced commands, our experiences with SSD design and evaluation indicate that judicious use of these features can have significant performance and endurance impacts. For example, we found that diverse allocation schemes can result in different performance level and the way in which parallelism in SSD is exploited can be a key performance-impact factor. Moreover, when these internal SSD behaviors did get discussed in the literature they were studied in isolation without considering their interplay and interaction [14][17][24-27]. In fact, we found that it is this interplay and interaction among them that tend to have the most profound impact on system performance and endurance of SSD.

To thoroughly investigate the aforementioned performance impact and interplay of SSD advanced commands, allocation strategy, and data granularity, in this paper, we carefully examine several internal behaviors rarely discussed in the literature, which may have potentially important impact on the performance and endurance of SSD. Specifically, we carry out in-depth evaluations of these features and their interplay, obtaining the following main insights.

1. *Flash page size*

   With the capacity growth of NAND flash chips, the size of an SSD page has increased significantly over the past few years, for example, from 512B in the 1990s to 16KB in 2010 [28-34]. However, when a page is updated partially (e.g., with small and random I/O requests in such workloads as MSN [35]), bigger pages are more prone to the problem in which some data must be read from the old page and written to a new page after being merged with the new data. This problem leads to degraded performance. In fact, enlarging the flash page size leads to that the average response time is increased to 1.8 times, compared to that of the best performing flash page-size, under the MSN workload. Considering the different access patterns of various workloads, there is no one-size-fits-all page size and an optimal page size must be and can be dynamically determined to optimize performance, adapting to different workloads.

2. *Allocation schemes*

   Static allocation is based on fixed striping while dynamic allocation assigns pages dynamically. Although dynamic allocation is more flexible and adaptive in exploiting parallelisms, thus resulting in better performance in most cases, static allocation is simple in implementation and can be very effective in some workloads. Static allocation is found to perform the best in read operations under all workloads. Dynamic allocation performs the best overall performance and endurance under the most of workloads in aged SSDs.

3. *Advanced commands*

   The SSD manufacturers have provided advanced commands, such as copy-back, multi-plane and interleave operations, with an intention to improve the performance of SSD by handling read, write and erase operations more efficiently. However, we find that some strict restrictions must be adhered to when using these commands, making their appropriate use extremely important. For example, using copy-back blindly leads to that the average response time and erasure count are increase to 7.7 and 17.8 times respectively, compared to that of only using basic commands, under the MSN workload.

4. *Priority order of SSD parallelism*

   Parallelism has been regarded as a key to achieving the peak performance. There are four levels of parallelism in SSD: (1) among channels (channel-level), (2) among chips in a channel (chip-level), (3) among dies in a chip (die-level) and (4) among planes in a die (plane-level). Allocation schemes can effectively utilize the first two levels of parallelisms, while the last two levels of parallelisms can be exploited by advanced commands. We found that the four levels of parallelisms tend to have an optimal priority order. An incorrectly placed order of priority can result in a performance degradation of up to 60%.

The rest of the paper is organized as follows. Section 2 introduces the necessary background and related work to motivate our research. Section 3 presents and validates the evaluation platform – SSDsim, a highly accurate and multi-tiered simulator for the evaluation of various SSD internal behaviors. Then we present our extensive trace-driven evaluations of the internal behaviors of SSD on SSDsim in Section 4. Section 5 summarizes the key observations and insights obtained from our evaluations.

2. BACKGROUND AND MOTIVATION

2.1 Flash Memory Basics

In general, Flash memory can be classified into two categories: NOR and NAND [3]. NOR-Flash memory supports byte-level random accesses and is typically used in read-only applications such as storing firmware codes. NAND-Flash memory, in contrast, has higher density, larger capacity and lower cost than NOR-Flash, but only supports block-level random accesses. It is thus typically used for more general-purpose applications.

There are two NAND-Flash technologies, Single-Level Cell (SLC) and Multi-Level Cell (MLC) [4][5]. While the former stores only one bit per cell, the latter stores two or even more bits per cell. Throughout this paper, we will use the term Flash to refer specifically to NAND-Flash memory.

To increase storage density, flash manufactories package several flash chips together, a model called package [28-34]. All chips in a package share the same 8/16-bit I/O bus of the package but have separate chip enable and ready/busy control signals. Each chip is composed of two or more dies. Each die has one internal ready/busy signal that is different from the external ready/busy signal of a chip. The internal ready/busy signal is invisible to user. It will only be used in *advanced commands*. Each die is composed of multiple planes. Each plane contains thousands of flash blocks and one or two data/cache registers used as an I/O buffer. A flash block typically consists of 64 or 128 pages, where a page is further divided into many 512B sub-pages. Each sub-page has a 16B spare space used to store a variety of information, such as error correction code (ECC), logical page number and sub-page state. The size of a page has been steadily increasing due to the technology development as well as the growing size of a single chip. While chip and die are not clearly distinguished and often confused with each other in many previous studies in the literature, chip enable and read/busy signals make them clearly distinct from each other.   A chip is the basic functional unit that has its independent chip enable and read/busy signals. A die is a component of a chip, which only has an internal read/busy signal.

There are two key and unique flash characteristics, namely, *write-after-erase* and *erase cycle*. A write operation can only change the value of each target bit from `1` to `0`. Once a page is written, it must be erased, where all bits are reset to `1`, before the next write operation can be performed on the same page. Each flash block has a limited number of erase cycles before it is worn out. After wearing out, a block can no longer store any data. A typical MLC Flash has an erase-cycle limit of about 10K, while a typical SLC Flash has an erase-cycle limit of about 100K with a 1bit/512byte ECC [4].

The page size of early NAND-Flash products is typically 512 bytes, consistent with a hard disk drive (HDD) sector [36]. With the development of fabrication technology, the storage density has been steadily increasing, resulting in a diverse set of page sizes among NAND-Flash products, including 2KB, 4KB, 8KB and 16KB [28-34]. In the pursuit of higher capacity, SSD products are employing increasingly large page size.

2.2 Flash Commands: Basic Commands and Advanced Commands

There are three basic operations in Flash: read, program (write) and erase. A read operation fetches data from a target page. A write operation writes data to a target page. An erase operation resets all bits of a target block to `1`. All operations are initiated by writing the command code to the command register and the address of the request to the address register. The address points to the target data of the request inside the package. An address is separated into six segments: chip address, die address, plane address, block address, page address and in-page address, as illustrated in Figure 1. Within a block, the pages must be programmed consecutively in the increasing order of page address. Random-page-address programming is prohibited. We call this Restriction (a).

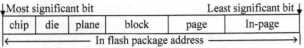

Most significant bit					Least significant bit
chip	die	plane	block	page	In-page

In flash package address

Figure 1. Flash package address format.

Most flash manufacturers provide advanced commands, such as *copy-back*, *multi-plane* and *interleave*, to further improve the performance of SSD. Advanced commands are extensions of the basic read, program and erase commands but with some usage restrictions [28-34][37].

Copy-back (internal data move) command moves one page of data from one page to another in the same plane, without occupying the I/O bus. Some manufacturers also call this command internal data move [38-39]. We will call it copy-back in the remainder of the paper. The source page and the target page must have the same chip, die and plane addresses. The addresses of the source page and destination page must be both odd or both even. As shown in Figure 4, a copy-back operation can only move data from page 0 to page 2, or from page 1 to page 3, etc. Moving data from page 0 to page 1 or page 3 is prohibited. We call this Restriction (b).

Multi-plane command activates multiple read, program or erase operations in all planes of the same die. It only costs the time of one read, write or erase operation, while executing multiple such operations, as illustrated in Figure 2 (a). The pages executing a multi-plane read/write operation must have the same chip, die, block and page addresses. And the blocks executing a multi-plane erase operation must have the same chip, die and block addresses. As shown in Figure 4, only page 1 from plane 0 and page 1 from plane 1 of the same die can be read/written simultaneously by using a multi-plane read/write operation. Reading/writing page 1 from plane 0 and page 3 from plane 1 using a multi-plane read/write operation is prohibited. We call this Restriction (c).

Interleave command executes several page read, page write, block erase and multi-plane read/write/erase operations in different dies of the same chip simultaneously. The interleave command is different from the interleave operation mentioned in [17][25-27]. The former is a flash command that is executed among different dies in the same chip, while the latter is executed among different chips in the same channel. An interleave write command is illustrated in Figure 2 (b). Other than the restriction that pages operated simultaneously must belong to different dies on the same chip, there are no other restrictions when using the interleave command.

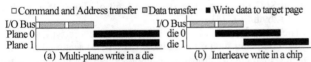

Figure 2. The multi-plane write and interleave write command process

2.3 Allocation Schemes

An allocation scheme determines how to choose free physical page(s) to accommodate logical page(s) being written to the SSD. To locate a particular physical page, one must know the channel address and package address, in addition to the chip address, die address, plane address, block address and page address, as shown in Figure 1. The format of a full address of SSD is shown in Figure 3.

Allocation schemes are classified into two categories: dynamic and static.

Static allocation first assigns a logical page to a *pre-determined* channel, package, chip, die and plane, before allocating it to any free physical page of the plane. The channel, package, chip, die and plane addresses assigned to each logical page are typically calculated by some formulas that define a special allocation scheme.

Dynamic allocation assigns a logical page to any free physical page of the entire SSD. When a write request arrives, a dynamic allocation scheme chooses a free physical page by considering several factors, such as the idle/busy state of channels, the idle/busy state of chips, the erasure count of blocks, the priority order of parallelism and so on. The scheme that assigns a logical page to any free physical page of the pre-determined channel is also classified in the dynamic allocation category.

There are many existing static allocation schemes, of which the scheme shown in Figure 11(b) has been shown to perform the best by an extensive comparative study in [14].

There has not been any direct comparison between the static and dynamic allocation schemes in the literature, to the best of our knowledge. In this paper, we will evaluate and directly compare the static and dynamic allocation schemes in terms of performance and wear-leveling.

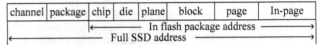

channel	package	chip	die	plane	block	page	In-page

In flash package address

Full SSD address

Figure 3. The format of a full SSD address.

2.4 Parallelism inside SSDs

There are four levels of parallelism in SSD: (1) among channels (*channel-level*), (2) among chips in a channel (*chip-level*), (3) among dies in a chip (*die-level*), and (4) among planes in a die (*plane-level*). For example, in Figure 4, if a request is served by channel 0 and channel 1 simultaneously, it exploits the channel-level parallelism; if it is served by chip 0 of package 0, chip 1 of package 0 and chip 0 of package 1 in channel 0 simultaneously, it leverages the chip-level parallelism; if it is served by plane 0 of die 0 and plane 1 of die 1 on the same chip, it utilizes the die-level parallelism; if it is served by plane 0 and plane 1 of the same die, it makes use of the plane-level parallelism.

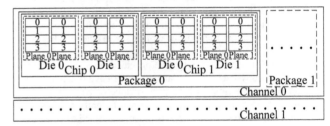

Figure 4. An SSD internals.

[25] and [27] exploit the channel-level parallelism; [17] makes use of the chip-level parallelism; and [26] employs the plane-level parallelism. Previous studies in the literature mainly focus on the first two levels of parallelism. In this paper, we will evaluate the performance impact of exploiting all four levels of SSD parallelisms through the interplay of the aforementioned internal behaviors of SSD.

2.5 SSD Simulator

At present, there are only two open-source SSD simulators [40-41] available in the public domain. They provide basic research platforms for researchers to evaluate their designs of FTL. They provide the first two levels of parallelism, including channel-level and chip-level. They only support one of the three advanced commands, copy-back. However, they both fail to adhere to Restriction (b) (Section 2.2) when using the copy-back command. Furthermore, they did not validate their measurement accuracy against a real SSD system by directly comparing the simulation measurements with the real SSD system measurements.

To address the drawbacks of the existing SSD simulators, we designed and implemented a new SSD simulator, called SSDsim, which provides the detailed and accurate simulation of each level of SSD, including hardware, FTL and buffer layer. It provides four levels of parallelism, supports all the advanced commands that adhere to all the aforementioned restrictions. It is directly validated against a real SSD prototype. The aim of design and implementation of SSDsim is to provide an open-source and high-accuracy SSD research tool for all researchers.

2.6 Research Motivation

To design a high-performance and high-endurance SSD, we must comprehensively consider many factors that have been discussed so far. More specifically, we must answer the following research questions that have not been fully addressed, if at all, in the literature, to the best of our knowledge.

Question 1: Is the flash page size a factor impacting the SSD performance? And if so, to what extent? Enlarging the flash page size can increase the capacity of SSD. But does it also help performance?

Question 2: How to choose allocation schemes?

The question has been partially answered by previous studies in the literature. However, a comprehensive answer is still elusive. Since different workloads have diverse characteristics, no one allocation scheme can possibly fit all workloads. On the other hand, are there certain workloads that will be best suitable for a particular type of scheme? For example, we found that in all cases, the read performance of the static allocation scheme is consistently superior to that of the dynamic allocation scheme. Conversely, in an aged SSD, the dynamic allocation scheme significantly outperforms the static allocation scheme.

Question 3: Do advanced commands always improve performance? If not, how should they be appropriately used to promote performance?

Question 4: Given the four levels of parallelism in SSD, what is their priority order that optimizes the performance and endurance of SSD?

To comprehensively answer these questions, we conduct a series of trace-driven experiments and evaluations detailed in Section 4, on the SSDsim simulator to be described next.

3. EVALUATION PLATFORM

In this section we present the evaluation platform on which the in-depth investigation into the internal SSD behaviors and their interplay (to be detailed in Section 4) are conducted by first introducing and validating the core of this platform, the SSDsim simulator. This is followed by a description of the real-world workloads chosen for this investigation and the configuration of the evaluation platform.

3.1 SSDsim Simulator and Its Validation against a Hardware SSD Prototype

We design and implement an SSD simulator, called SSDsim, which is event-driven, modularly structured, and multi-tiered. SSDsim is a single-threaded program written in C, which has about 15 thousand lines of C code. SSDsim is capable of simulating most SSD hardware platforms, mainstream FTL schemes, allocation schemes, buffer management algorithms and request scheduling algorithms. The three-tiered SSDsim design consists of the buffer and request-scheduling module at the top, the FTL and allocation module in the middle, and the low-level hardware platform module at the bottom. The top module is responsible for buffer organization and scheduling requests; In the middle module, the FTL sub-module simulates many state-of-the-art FTL schemes including pure page-FTL [43][44], pure block-FTL [43][44], DFTL [12] and FAST [15], and the allocation sub-module provides the choice of allocation schemes including the dynamic allocation and the static allocation. The bottom module simulates the behaviors of all the Flash operations based on the Open NAND Flash Interface Specification (ONFI) 2.2 [37]. This module supports four levels of parallelism and all advanced

commands that are adhered to all aforementioned restrictions. By feeding block-level trace files and configuring with the parameter files, we can obtain the waiting time, processing time, response time of each request, total erasure count, buffer hit count and other detailed information.

In the design of SSDsim, we take into explicit account the time consumed by the necessary internal SSD software cost so as to achieve a high fidelity of the simulator. This, we argue, is one of the key features distinguishing SSDsim from the existing open-source SSD simulators. As a known fact in HDD, a typical request's response time is in the millisecond-scale, with negligible amount of program code being executed while processing the request. In SSD, on the other hand, a request's response time is in the microsecond-scale and there is significantly more program code being executed to service the request than in HDD, including address mapping, data merge and migration, among other things. Assuming a frequency of 100MHz for the SSD controller, one instruction executed by the controller will cost 10 nanoseconds. The time cost of 100 lines of assembly code will be about 1 microsecond, which is no longer negligible as part of SSD's response time. In fact, we found that the software processing cost as part of the response time of SSD is not only non-negligible, but actually a significant part of the response time. For example, in the response time of one read request, the software processing cost accounted for up to 18.9%.

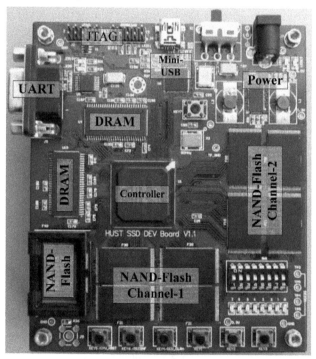

Figure 5. Real SSD hardware prototype.

To validate the accuracy of SSDsim, we have implemented a real SSD hardware prototype, as shown in Figure 5. In this prototype, an FPGA chip acts as the controller; eight SUMSANG flash chips [28] are organized into two independent channels, and four 16MB DRAM chips are used to store the mapping table and data buffer. For validation purposes, the same buffer management schemes, FTL and allocation schemes are implemented in the hardware prototype and SSDsim, the configuration parameter file based on the hardware prototype is fed to SSDsim, and the same request streams are fed to both the hardware prototype and SSDsim. Four workloads, which are detailed in Section 3.2 and reflect the high-performance computing environment with diverse write/read request ratios, request sizes, request characteristics, are used in our SSDsim validation.

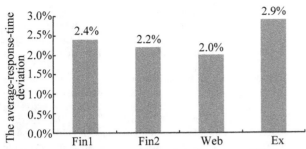

Figure 6. The average-response-time deviation of SSDsim from the prototype.

The main evaluation results from SSDsim and the hardware prototype are presented in Figures 6 and 7. In Figure 6, the average-response-time deviation of SSDsim from the prototype is plotted as a function of the four workloads. With a deviation of only 2%~2.9% shown in this figure, it is clear that the average response time obtained from SSDsim is very close to that obtained from the prototype, indicating the high accuracy of SSDsim.

Figure 7 plots the simulation accuracy as a Cumulative Distribution Function (CDF) of the response time. The sub-figure in each of the four parts of Figure 7 is a microscopic illustration of inflexion of each part. In Figure 7, the blue lines represent the prototype and the red lines represent SSDsim. It is evident that the two curves in each part almost completely overlap, suggesting that SSDsim matches extremely well with the prototype in the response-time measurement.

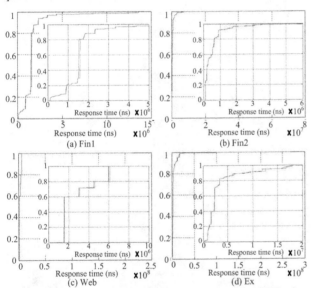

Figure 7. The Cumulative Distribution Function (CDF) of the response time.

3.2 Workloads

We use a set of real-world workloads, shown in Table 1 and reflecting the high-performance computing environments, to study the performance and endurance impacts of the internal behaviors/features of SSD, including the flash page size, allocation schemes, advanced commands, and their interplay. Financial1, Financial2 and Websearch were collected at a large financial institution and a popular Internet web search machine respectively [45]. Exchange [35] was collected at the Microsoft Exchange 2007 SP1 server, which is a mail server for 5000 corporate users. MSN [35] was collected at the Microsoft's several Live file servers. Develop [35] was obtained from a file server accessed by more than 3000 users to download various daily builds of Microsoft Visual Studio. Radius [35] was obtained from a RADIUS authentication server that

is responsible for worldwide corporate remote access and wireless authentication. Table 1 summarizes the basic characteristics of these traces, including the average request size for reads and writes percentage of read requests, and request inter-arrival time.

Table 1. Workload characteristics of the traces

Workloads	Abb.	Avg. req. size read/write(KB)	Read(%)	Int. arrv. Time(ms)
Financial1	Fin1	2.25/3.75	23.2	8.19
Financial2	Fin2	2.3/2.9	82.3	11.08
Websearch	Web	15.15/8.6	99.9	2.99
Exchange	Ex	15.15/14.5	30.8	1179
MSN	MSN	9.6/11.1	67.2	513
Develop	Dev	18.45/10.95	88.6	1985
Radius	Rad	124.25/12.45	17.1	9475

3.3 Configuration of the Evaluation Platform

In our evaluation experiments, we assume a multiple-channel, multiple-package, multiple-chip, multiple-die and multiple-plane SSD organization. There are many ways to organize channels and packages based on the sharing methods of I/O bus, chip enable signal and ready/busy signal. Since our focus is on the use of SSD in the high-performance computing environment, we will concentrate on an organization that offers potentially the best performance. As shown in Figure 8, each channel has its independent I/O bus, and each chip has its independent chip enable signal and ready/busy signal. Both of them constitute the independent service units in the SSD. Since a package simply overlaps several chips, we only give sketches of chips without packages. The timing and organization characteristics of the configuration are based on a real NAND-Flash product [28], as summarized in Table 2. In the evaluations we also assume two types of SSD, the aged and the non-aged. While the former is used to show the case where a great number of physical pages have been previously written and thus garbage collection and erase operations are far more likely to be triggered by new requests, the latter is used to show the opposite situation. In particular, the former will allow us to examine the performance and endurance impact of garbage collection and erase operations that cause channels and chips to be in the busy state.

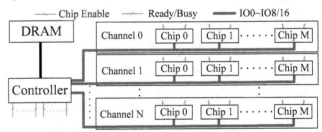

Figure 8. The evaluation platform of high-performance SSD.

Table 2. Configuration parameters used in SSDsim (Channel-Chip-Die-Plane-Block-Page indicates the number of channels in the SSD, chips in a channel, dies in a chip, planes in a die, blocks in a plane and pages in a block, respectively. Unless otherwise noted, they are default experiment parameters)

Parameters	Values
Page read to register	20us
Page write from register	200us
Block erase	1.5ms
Read one byte data from register	25ns
Write one byte data to register	25ns
Channel-Chip-Die-Plane-Block-Page	4-4-2-2-2048-64
Page size	2KB

4. EXPERIMENTAL EVALUATIONS

In this section we evaluate three SSD internal behaviors, or characteristics, which have notable impact on SSD performance and endurance, namely, (1) flash page size, (2) allocation schemes and (3) advanced commands. This is followed by a study on the interplay of these characteristics and the priority order of parallelism in SSD, presented in Section 4.4. We obtain our experimental results from SSDsim rather than the hardware SSD prototype. Since it is not easy to reconfigure some parameters of the hardware SSD prototype, such as the flash page size and the numbers of channels and chips, conducting experiments on the hardware SSD prototype is both costly and time consuming.

4.1 Flash Page Size

There are two scenarios in which a logical page is written to the flash memory, the logical page is written for the very first time and the logical page is rewritten or *updated* in the flash memory. The update operation can lead to two types of SSD internal data movement depending on whether the new data of the page fully overlaps, called "covered", or partially overlaps, called "un-covered", the old data of the page. Figure 9 shows the covered (Figure 9(a)) and un-covered (Figure 9(b)) cases of a page update assuming a page size of 2KB (i.e., the equivalent of 4 sectors), where the shaded sectors of the page represent valid data while the un-shaded sectors represent invalid data. In the case of a covered update, shown in Figure 9(a) the new data (sectors 0-2) is written to a new physical page, invalidating the old physical page containing the old data (sectors 1-2) of the logical page and modifying the mapping information of the logical page. In the case of an un-covered update, shown in Figure 9(b), the old data (sector 3) is read out to be combined with the new data (sectors 0-2) of the logical page before the combined data (sectors 0-3) is written to a new physical page, invaliding the old physical page containing the old data and modifying the mapping information of this logical page.

Figure 9. The covered and un-covered update operations.

In other words, an un-covered operation requires one more flash read operation than a covered update operation, which can have a negative impact on the request's response time. Given the same average request size, the larger the page size is, the more likely it is for un-covered update operations to be induced. This is because, in a large-size page, a small write request will more likely find itself updating a subset of the sectors in a page with at least one valid sector to be combined, resulting in an un-covered update operation. On the other hand, a large page size also has its advantages, since a read/write operation in an SSD with a large page-size can fetch/send more data to/from the register, which allows a large read/write request to be more efficiently executed.

In Figure 10, we plot the percentage of un-covered update operations among all write operations, shown as the line plots and labeled on the Y-axis on the right side of the figure, as a function of the flash page-size under five different workloads. The performance impact of these un-covered update operations, measured in the average response time normalized to that of the best performing flash page-size, shown as the bars and labeled on the Y-axis on the left side of the figure, is plotted as a function of the flash page sizes under five different workloads.

From Figure 10, it is clear that, under the Dev, MSN, Ex and Rad workloads, the page size of 4KB results in the best average response time. This is because 78.6%, 74.3%, 99.2% and 33.4% of write requests in MSN, Ex, Dev and Rad, respectively, are of size 4KB or the multiples of 4KB, which induce fewer un-covered update operations than the 8KB-page and 16KB-page SSDs. The

4KB page-size also results in the least average response time under these four workloads. Although the un-covered update operation count in the 2KB-page SSD is smaller than that in the 4KB-page SSD, a 4KB write request in the 2KB-page SSD requires two or three write operations, in contrast to the one or two write operations required in the 4KB-page SSD, giving rise to a higher average response time in the former. Under the Fin1 workload, the average response time is the best in the 16KB-page SSD, because the un-covered update-operation count changes very little with an increase in the page size while the larger page size favors the large requests in this workload.

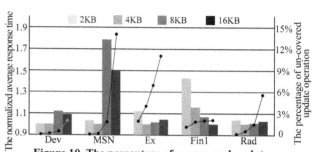

Figure 10. The percentage of un-covered update operations and normalized average response time as functions of flash page-size under different workloads.

Insight 1: Enlarging the storage capacity of SSD by means of increasing the page size may not be a wise choice under some workloads. Instead, we argue that a better choice for large capacity and stable performance is to use more packages with an appropriate page size in the same channel, or overlap more chips of an appropriate page size in a flash package. Since the controller provides a chip enable signal and a busy/ready signal to each chip, the storage capacity of SSD can be enlarged without decreasing the I/O performance by increasing some control signals of the controller in this way. Further, to design high-performance and large-capacity SSDs, the request size and the percentage of the un-covered update operations of the workload must be taken into account to choose flash chip with an appropriate page size.

4.2 Allocation Schemes

In this subsection, we compare the performances of the static allocation and dynamic allocation schemes, and evaluate the related wear-leveling issues.

Figure 11 illustrates six different static allocation schemes (including static allocation 2 proposed by J. Shin et al. [14]), which are referred to as s1, s2, s3, s4, s5 and s6.

As mentioned in Section 2.3, dynamic allocation schemes assign a logical page to any free physical page of the entire SSD or the pre-determined channel, according to the idle/busy state of channels, the idle/busy state of chips, the erasure count of blocks, and the priority order of parallelism. Different combinations of these factors will derive many different dynamic allocation schemes. For example, when a 4KB write request arrives in an SSD of 2KB-page-size Flash, assuming that 2 channels as well as 2 chips in each channel are idle, the request can be served by 2 channels or 2 chips in a channel, when applying different priority order of parallelism. The former is channel-level parallelism first, and the latter is chip-level parallelism first. Since we discuss advanced commands and priority order of parallelism in SSD in Sections 4.3 and 4.4, respectively, die-level parallelism and plane-level parallelism will not be explored in this section. In other words, the multi-plane and the interleave advanced commands will not be used, and the priority order of parallelisms will be channel-level parallelism first, followed by the chip-level parallelism.

We compare the average response time of the dynamic allocation scheme with that of s2, because s2 is shown to achieve the best performance when advanced commands are not employed [14].

The read/write/overall performance impact of different allocation schemes, measured in the average response time normalized to that of the s2 is plotted in Figure 12, under six different workloads.

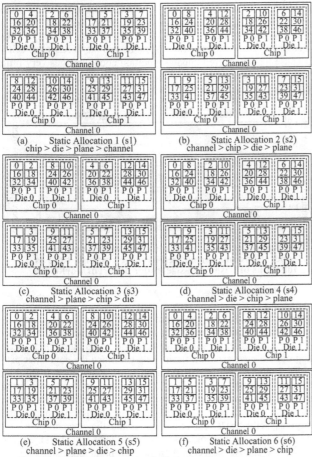

Figure 11. Six kinds of typical static allocation schemes.
(A > B > C > D means the priority order of allocating logical page. In other word, it is striping address to A first, then to B, then to C, and finally to D.)

From Figure 12, it is clear that the static allocation scheme performs the best for read requests in both the non-aged SSD and the aged SSD, under all workloads. For a given read request whose size is a multiple of a logical page size, the striping nature of the static allocation is likely to distribute the sequential logical pages of the request to different channels and chips, which tends to exploit more parallelisms of the multi-channel and multi-chip structured SSD, thus decreasing the response time of this request. In the dynamic allocation, on the other hand, it is entirely possible that the sequential logical pages are stored in the same channel, or even the same chip, so that these sequential logical pages will be operated in the same channel or chip one by one, failing to exploit the parallelism of SSD. Since 99.99% of the requests are read requests in the Web workload, the overall performance of the static allocation is better than dynamic allocation, in both the non-aged SSD and the aged SSD.

Insight 2: The static allocation scheme consistently outperforms the dynamic allocation scheme in serving read requests. Thus, in the application environments that demand fast reads, or are read-dominant in their workloads, the static allocation scheme should be employed.

For the non-aged SSD, Figure 12 (a) shows that the dynamic allocation scheme outperforms the static allocation scheme under all workloads for write requests and overall under the Fin2, MSN, Ex, and Fin1 workloads. This is because the sequential logical pages of a multi-page write request are likely to be serviced by multiple chips

in several channels in the static allocation, while the response time of the request is determined by the logical page completing the last. If any one of the logical pages happens to be on a busy chip, which is very likely, the response time of the request will be severely delayed. This, however, does not happen in the dynamic allocation, since write requests can be adaptively distributed to idle chips.

In the aged SSD, the write-performance advantage of the dynamic allocation scheme becomes more pronounced, as shown in Figure 12 (b). This is because there are more garbage collection and erase operations in an aged SSD than in a non-aged SSD, which can cause more chips to be in the busy state and further decrease the write performance of the static allocation scheme.

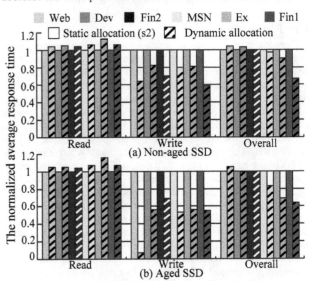

Figure 12. The normalized average response time when using static allocation and dynamic allocation schemes, in non-aged and aged SSDs, under the six workloads.

Insight 3: In a non-aged SSD, the static allocation scheme is preferable when the workload is read-dominant. Otherwise, the dynamic allocation scheme should be employed. In an aged SSD, the dynamic allocation scheme consistently outperforms of the static allocation scheme, with the only exception being the read-only workloads.

Wear-leveling algorithms are used to distribute the erase operations evenly to the entire SSD for the purpose of enhancing flash endurance. To balance erasure count, wear-leveling usually writes hot data to the least frequently erased blocks and migrates cool data to blocks with higher erasure counts [46]. Obviously, such data migrations will lead to extra read write and erase operations that have negative impact on performance and endurance. In Table 3, we list the standard deviation of the total erasure counts of blocks in each plane for the static and dynamic allocation schemes under the five workloads, where a low standard deviation indicates a more evenly distributed erase operations. It is clear from the table that the dynamic scheme has a much better wear-leveling performance than the static scheme.

Insight 4: The dynamic allocation scheme consistently outperforms the static scheme on the wear-leveling performance.

Table 3. The standard deviations of total erasure count of blocks in each plane when employing either static allocation scheme or dynamic allocation scheme.

Workloads	Static allocation	Dynamic allocation
Dev	284.9	2.5
Ex	409.1	39.5
Fin1	207.3	3.9
MSN	3534.4	112.6
Rad	7.5	2.6

4.3 Advanced Commands

In this subsection, we evaluate the impact of the advanced commands provided by Flash manufacturers, and how Restrictions (a)-(c) make these advanced commands a double-edged sword.

To better examine the performance impact of the multi-plane read/write/erase commands that exploit the plane-level parallelism and the interleave read/write/erase commands that exploit the die-level parallelism, we exclude the interference of the channel-level parallelism by employing a single-channel SSD in the experiments of this section.

4.3.1 Copy-back

When using the copy-back command, Restriction (a) and Restriction (b) must be adhered to. Figure 13 illustrates the process of executing a copy-back command, where the data stored in PPN =82 needs to be migrated to a free physical page. Since the pages in a block must be programmed sequentially, the next available page is PPN =641. However, Restriction (b) forbids us to write the data to PPN =641, forcing the invalidation of PPN =641 and migration of the data into PPN =642. It is obvious that using the copy-back command blindly will lead to a waste of flash pages. In fact, our experiments reveal that using the copy-back command blindly can cause almost half of the copy-back operations to each invalidate one extra page under all workloads.

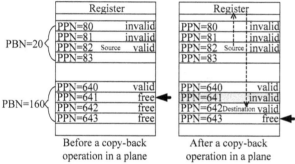

Figure 13. The exemplar process of executing a copy-back command.

To use the copy-back command wisely to minimize the number of invalidated pages, we recommend its use only when the addresses of the source page and the destination page have the same parity.

The performance impact of the way in which the copy-back command is used, measured in the average response time normalized to that of only using the basic commands, is plotted as a function of the workloads and labeled on the Y-axis on the left side of Figure 14. The erasure count of using the copy-back command blindly, normalized to that of only using basic commands, is shown by small triangles and labeled on the Y-axis on the right side of the figure. In the experiments presented in this subsection, the dynamic allocation scheme employs the same priority order of parallelisms as that used in Section 4.2.

In Figure 14, it is clear that using the copy-back command blindly has a notable negative impact on the average response time and the erasure count measures under the Dev, MSN and Ex workloads. This is because a large number of the copy-back commands lead to many pages being invalidated under these workloads, which in turn trigger frequent garbage collections. During a garbage collection, more copy-back operations and erase operations will be performed, which further decreases the overall performance and increases erasure count. On the other hand, using the copy-back command wisely does improve performance without increasing the erasure count. This is because there are no extra pages invalidated and no extra erasure operation induced.

In Figure 14, we only present the results of an aged SSD, since garbage collections are rarely triggered in a non-aged SSD.

Insight 5: The copy-back command should only be used wisely when the addresses of the source page and the destination page have the same parity, otherwise the I/O performance and endurance of SSD can be significantly reduced.

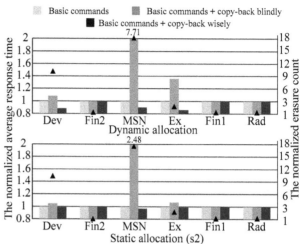

Figure 14. The performance comparison of different the methods of using copy-back command.

4.3.2 Multi-Plane

In this section, we analyze the multi-plane command for reads and writes, which we call MPW (Multi-Plane Write) and MPR (Multi-Plane Read) for short in the remainder of the paper.

As mentioned in Section 2.2, a multi-plane command can execute the same basic command in all planes on the same die. Therefore, it exploits the parallelism among the planes of the same die. When using multi-plane write command, Restriction (a) and Restriction (c) must be adhered to.

Figure 15 illustrates an MPW operation. Two different planes of the same die, plane 0 and plane 1, are shown in the figure. The page address of the next available page in plane 0 is 26 while that in plane 1 is 24. When using the MPW command in these two planes, PPN =24 and PPN =25 in plane 1 will be invalidated. Therefore, in this case, executing the MPW command invalidates (and wastes) two free pages.

Similar to the copy-back command, the MPW command can be used blindly or wisely. In Figure 16, we plot the average response times and erasure count of the MPW command in the same way as in Figure 14. In the experiments of this sub-section, the dynamic allocation scheme exploits MPW/MPR and adheres to the parallelism priority order of channel-level first, plane-level second and chip-level last. The static scheme s3 performs the best I/O performance when employing MPW/MPR among all the static allocation schemes.

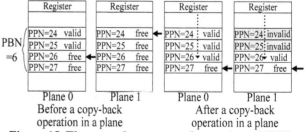

Figure 15. The exemplar process of executing a MPW.

As shown in the upper sub-figure of Figure 16, when employing the dynamic allocation, using MPW blindly improves average response time over basic commands. However, a large number of free pages are invalidated, which leads to more extra erase operations. Note that the benefit of plane-level parallelism outweighs the loss caused by the extra erase operations. Therefore using MPW blindly can improve response time under all workloads. On the other hand, since the condition required for the wise MPW, i.e., the target pages executing an MPW must have the same chip, die, block and page addresses, can rarely be met, the improvement by the wise MPW is insignificant.

As shown in the bottom sub-figure of Figure 16, when employing the static allocation, MPW has a similar performance to that in the dynamic allocation.

We only show the experiment results in an aged SSD because using MPW blindly will not likely trigger garbage collection and resulting erase operations.

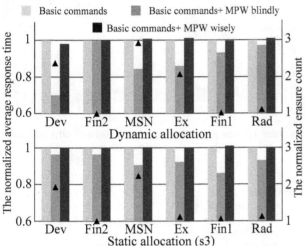

Figure 16. Performance comparison of different the methods of using MPW.

Insight 6: Using MPW blindly improves the I/O performance but reduces the endurance under most workloads. The impact of the wise MPW is negligible because the condition required for its application can rarely be met.

MPR performs multiple-page read operations in different planes of the same die simultaneously. When using MPR, Restriction (c) must be adhered to. In Table 4, we list the performance gains due to MPR under the dynamic and static allocation schemes, respectively. We found that the performance gains are negligible under a majority of the workloads. A speedup of only 1.16 is observed for a two-page MPR command. Moreover, since Ex and Fin1 are write-dominant workloads, the performance gain due to MPR is negligible. Since the request size of Fin2 is too small to be striped onto multiple pages, MPR is not applicable there. Under Web, Dev and MSN, the performance gains will be higher compared to other workloads, since these three workloads are read-dominant, whose request sizes are multiples of a flash page size.

Table 4. The performance gain due to MPR (RS is short for response time speedup. Baseline is based on basic command alone.)

	Web	Dev	Fin2	MSN	Ex	Fin1
Dynamic RS	1.15	1.11	1.02	1.04	1.00	1.00
Static RS	1.09	1.01	1.00	1.01	1.00	1.00

Insight 7 : MPR cannot provide significant performance improvement, under most workloads. But in the application environments whose workloads are read-dominant and comprise of large reads (i.e., Web, Dev and MSN), using MPR can help improve I/O performance.

In addition to MPW and MPR, the multi-plane command can also activate multiple erase operations in all planes of the same die. However, since the extent to which the erase operations are triggered in all planes of the same die at the same time is heavily

dependent on the specific garbage collection algorithm and weal-leveling algorithm used, which are beyond the scope of this paper, we will not evaluate the impact due to the multi-plane erase command independently.

4.3.3 Interleave

The interleave command exploits the parallelism among dies on the same chip. Pages and blocks from different dies on a chip can be read/written and erased simultaneously by executing an interleave command. The command is different from other advanced commands in that only Restriction (a) must be adhered to. Therefore, there is no endurance loss when using the interleave command, unlike using other advanced commands.

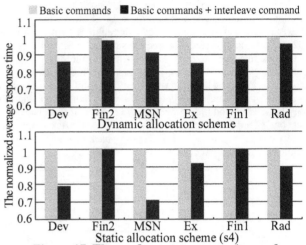

Figure 17. The performance comparisons of employing interleave command or not.

We plot the performance gain due to the interleave read/write/erase command as a function of the workloads in Figure 17, measured in the average response time normalized to that based on basic commands. In the experiments of this sub-section, the dynamic allocation scheme exploits the interleave command and adheres to the parallelism priority order of channel-level first, die-level second and chip-level last. The static scheme s4 performs the best when employing the interleave command among all the static allocation schemes.

The results from the figure show that, while the I/O performance is improved, SSD endurance is not notably impacted. The only exceptions are Fin1 and Fin2, where no significant performance gains are observed when using the static allocation, since the request sizes of these two workloads are small, thus depriving the interleave command the opportunity to be applicable.

Insight 8: The interleave command can help improve the I/O performance without any endurance degradation. Therefore the interleave command should be applied under all circumstances.

For the same reason given to the case of the multi-plane erase command at the end of Section 4.3.2, we will not evaluate the impact of using the interleave erase command independently. The interleave command can be combined with MPW and MPR, which we will discuss next.

4.3.4 The combinations of the three advanced commands

In this sub-section, we employ the three advanced commands simultaneously, and evaluate their combined impacts on the performance and endurance of SSDs. Based on Insights 5-8, there are two recommended approaches to using the advanced commands, namely, (1) use the copy-back command, the MPW command, and the interleave command wisely (i.e., with matching parity in addresses) under all circumstances; and (2) use the copy-back command wisely, the MPW command blindly, and the interleave command ubiquitously.

In Figure 18, we plot the average response time and erasure count of using advanced commands in the two recommended ways as a function of workloads, in the same way in which Figures 14, 16 are plotted. We only display the results of the static scheme s6 that is shown to achieve the best performance when the advanced commands are employed. We also only list the experimental results in an aged SSD for the reason discussed earlier.

From the figure, we found that the combined use of advanced commands based on Approach (2) achieves the best performance but leads to SSD endurance degradation, while Approach (1) achieves the less performance gain but without any endurance loss.

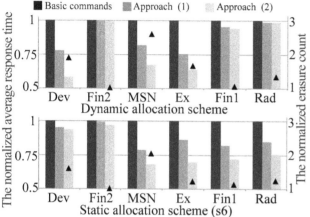

Figure 18. The performance comparison of two approaches to using the advanced commands.

4.4 Priority Order of Parallelism in SSD

As discussed in Section 2.4, there are four levels of parallelism in SSD, namely, channel-level, chip-level, die-level and plane-level. To determine the priority order of these levels that optimizes the performance and endurance of SSD, we first infer the optimal priority order qualitatively, and then confirm the optimality quantitatively by a series of experiments with different allocation schemes.

Strictly speaking, each read/write operation consists of two steps, (1) data transfer and (2) reading/writing data from/to the target page to/from the data register of the plane. The aim of parallelism is to overlap or pipeline these two steps. Chip-level parallelism, die-level parallelism and plane-level parallelism are executed on the same channel, which share the same channel bus. As a result, these three levels of parallelism can only overlap or pipeline step (2) of an operation. On the other hand, the channel-level parallelism overlaps not only step (2), but also step (1) of an operation. Therefore channel-level parallelism should be given the highest priority among the four levels of parallelism.

Chip-level parallelism renders multiple chips busy. When the chips on the channel are servicing requests, the subsequent requests cannot be serviced until these chips return to the idle state. On the other hand, die-level parallelism and plane-level parallelism only involve a single chip, thus making them a higher priority than the chip-level parallelism.

As shown in Figure 19, to serve a four-page-write request, two MPW operations are executed when exploiting the plane-level parallelism. To exploit the die-level parallelism, however, two interleave write commands are executed. From the figure, we find that the latter to be superior to the former. Moreover, exploiting the plane-level parallelism requires the execution of the MPW/MPR command, which often invalidates free pages. On the contrary, the interleave command required for exploiting the

die-level parallelism has no such disadvantages. Therefore, die-level parallelism should be given a higher priority than plane-level parallelism.

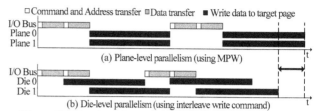
(a) Plane-level parallelism (using MPW)

(b) Die-level parallelism (using interleave write command)

Figure 19. The plane-level parallelism compares to die-level parallelism

4.4.1 Evaluation of priority order of SSD parallelism under the dynamic allocation

In this sub-section, we use six different SSDs to conduct a set of experiments to evaluate the priority order of SSD parallelism. The configuration parameters of the six SSDs are shown in Table 5.

Table 5. Six kinds of configured SSDs. (A>B in the "Priority" field signifies that choosing a free page from A is preferred to choosing one from B. Cl.-Cp.-D.-P. indicates the numbers of channels in the SSD, chips in a channel, dies in a chip, and planes in a die, respectively. The "AC" row indicates whether advanced commands are used (Yes) or not (No))

SSD	Cl.-Cp.-D.-P.	AC	Page	Priority
SSD1	8-4-2-2	Yes	2KB	chip >die>plane>channel
SSD2	8-4-2-2	Yes	2KB	channel> chip>die>plane
SSD3	1-4-2-2	Yes	2KB	channel>chip>die>plane
SSD4	1-4-2-2	Yes	2KB	channel>die>chip>plane
SSD5	1-4-2-2	Yes	2KB	channel>die>plane>chip
SSD6	1-4-2-2	Yes	2KB	channel>plane>die>chip

The hardware organizations of SSD1 and SSD2 (see Table 5) are different to those of SSD3, SSD4, SSD5 and SSD6, thus we compare their performance in two separated sub-figures (Figure 20 (a) and Figure 20 (b)). Figure 20 (a) shows that SSD2 outperforms SSD1 consistently. In SSD2, we distribute the requests to different channels. When 8 channels are deployed, steps (1) and (2) of an operation can be perfectly overlapped under all workloads. In SSD1, several pages of a request are distributed to some chips of the same channel, which results in multiple data transfers (i.e., step (1)) and one reading/writing flash media (i.e., step (2)). This explains SSD2's superiority to SSD1 and confirms quantitatively that channel-level parallelism should be given the first priority.

Figure 20 (b) shows that SSD4 consistently outperforms SSD3. While SSD3 prefers the chip-level parallelism to the die-level parallelism, the reverse is true for SSD4. Thus, when a request involving two pages is served by SSD3, two chips become busy. On the contrary, only one chip becomes busy in SSD4, allowing SSD4 to serve more subsequent requests than SSD3. This confirms that the die-level parallelism should be given a higher priority than the chip-level parallelism.

SSD5 outperforms SSD6 because the former uses an interleave write operation while the latter employs an MPW operation when a request that needs to write two pages arrives. Since using MPW blindly leads to render free pages invalidated, as discussed in Section 4.3.2, more erase operations will be triggered in SSD6 than in SSD5. Therefore, the die-level parallelism must be given a higher priority than the plane-level parallelism.

SSD5 is superior to SSD4, because a request that needs to read/write four pages can render two chips busy in SSD4 by executing two consecutive interleave read/write operations. On the other hand, for the same request only one chip is rendered busy in

SSD5 with the execution of a single interleave multi-plane read/write operation. Therefore, the priority of the chip-level parallelism should be the lowest.

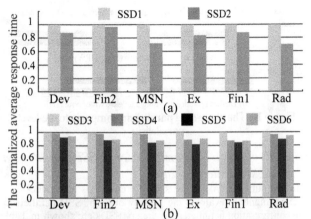

Figure 20. The normalized average response time of SSD1, SSD2, SSD3, SSD4, SSD5 and SSD6.

4.4.2 *Evaluation of priority order under the static allocation*

In the experiments of this subsection, we use six SSDs, SSD-s1, SSD-s2, SSD-s3, SSD-s4, SSD-s5 and SSD-s6, that employ six different static allocation schemes, s1, s2, s3, s4, s5, s6, as shown in Figure 11. These six SSDs share the following common configuration parameters: 8 channels in the SSDs, 4 chips in each channel, 2 dies on each chip, 2 plane on each die, 2048-block planes on each die, and each block contains 64 2KB pages. All advanced commands are used. In addition to the six real-world workloads listed in Table 1, we use a set of synthetic workloads in our experiments, whose key characteristics are shown in Table 6.

Table 6. The characteristics of synthetic workloads

Workload	Write ratio	Req. size	Interval time
Syn1	100%	16KB	30us (75%)
Syn2	25%	16KB	30us (75%)
Syn3	100%	20KB	200us (75%)
Syn4	25%	20KB	200us(75%)

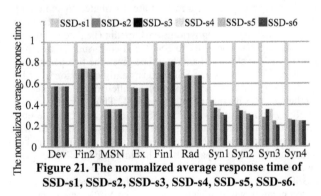

Figure 21. The normalized average response time of SSD-s1, SSD-s2, SSD-s3, SSD-s4, SSD-s5, SSD-s6.

The performance comparisons of SSD-s1, SSD-s2, SSD-s3, SSD-s4, SSD-s5 and SSD-s6 are shown in Figure 21. We found that SSD-s1 performs the worst among all the SSDs. It further confirms that the channel-level parallelism should be given the highest priority. With the exception of SSD-s1, all SSDs perform almost the equal under the real-world workloads. This is because the request intensities of these workloads are relatively low, which can be fully served by the channel-level parallelism. Therefore we use a set of higher-intensity synthetic workloads in our experi-

ments. Under these synthetic workloads, SSD-s6 performs the best, since the allocation scheme of SSD-s6 is adhered to the priority order of parallelism inferred at the beginning of Section 4.4.

Insight 9: The optimal priority order of parallelisms in SSD should be (1) the channel-level parallelism, (2) the die-level parallelism, (3) the plane-level parallelism, and (4) the chip-level parallelism.

5. CONCLUSION

We presented and validated an event-driven, modularly structured, multi-tiered and high accuracy SSD simulator, called SSDsim. Through extensive performance analysis conducted on SSDsim, we obtained important insights into the design and use of SSDs. Based on these insights, we argue that Flash page sizes, allocation schemes, advanced commands and the priority order of SSD parallelisms have significantly important impacts on the performance and endurance of SSD. More specifically, from the in-depth evaluations of these features and their interplay, our work provides the following important insights: (1) to design high-performance and large-capacity SSDs, the request size and the percentage of the un-covered update operations of the workload must be taken into considerations to choose an appropriate page size; (2) the static allocation is found to perform the best on read performance under all workloads. The dynamic allocation performs the best on overall performance and endurance under the most of workloads in aged SSDs; (3) there are two recommended approaches to using the advanced commands, namely, use the copy-back command, the MPW command, and the interleave command wisely as well as use the copy-back command wisely, the MPW command blindly, and the interleave command ubiquitously; (4) the optimal priority order of parallelisms in SSD should be the channel-level parallelism first, the die-level parallelism second, the plane-level parallelism third, and the chip-level parallelism last.

6. AVAILABILITY

We intend to release SSDsim source code for public use in the near future. Please check http://storage.hust.edu.cn/SSDsim to obtain a copy.

7. ACKNOWLEDGMENTS

We are grateful to the anonymous reviewers for their constructive comments. This research was partially supported by the National Basic Research 973 Program of China under Grant N o. 2011CB302301, 863 project 2009AA01A402, NSFC No.61025 008, 60933002,60873028,60703046, Changjiang innovative group of Education of China No. IRT0725, US NSF under Grants IIS-0916859, CCF-0937993, and CNS-1016609.

8. REFERENCES

[1] A. R. Olson and D. J. Langlois. 2008. Solid State Drives Data Reliability and Lifetime. White Paper. Imation Corp. http://www. imation.com/PageFiles/1189/SSD_Gov_DataReliability_WP.pdf

[2] W. Hutsell, J. Bowen and N. Ekker. 2008. Flash Solid State Disk Reliability. White Paper. Texas Memory Systems. http://www.ramsan.com/files/f000252.pdf

[3] M-System. Two Technologies Compared: NOR vs NAND. In white paper, 2003. http://maltiel-consulting.com/Nonvolatile_ Memory_NOR_vs_NAND.pdf

[4] SLV vs. MLC: An Analysis of Flash Memory. In white paper. Super Talent Technology, Inc. http://www.supertalent.com/ datasheets/SLC_vs_MLC%20whitepaper.pdf

[5] J. Cooke. Introduction to Flash Memory (T1A). Slides. 2008. http://www.slideshare.net/Flashdomain/introduction-to-flash-m emory-t1a

[6] K. M. Greenan, D. D. E. Long, E. L. Miller, T. Schwarz and A. Wildani. Building Flexible, Fault-Tolerant Flash-based Storage Systems. In *Proc. of* HotDep'09, June 2009.

[7] M. Moshayedi and P Wilkison. Enterprise SSDs. ACM QUEUE. July/August 2008

[8] C. Dirik and B. Jacob. The Performance of PC Solid-State Disks (SSDs) as a Function of Bandwidth, Concurrency, Device Architecture, and System Organization. In *Proc. of* ISCA'09, June 2009.

[9] A. M. Caulfield, J. Coburn, T. I. Mollov, A. De, A. Akel, J. He, A. Jagatheesan, R. K. Gupta, A. Snavely and S. Swanson. Understanding the Impact of Emerging Non-Volatile Memories on High-Performance, IO-Intensive Computing. In *Proc. of* SC'10, November 2010.

[10] A. Leventhal. Flash Storage Today. ACM QUEUE. July/August 2008.

[11] G. Graefe. The Five-minute Rule Twenty Years Later, and How Flash Memory Changes the Rules. In *Proc. of* DaMoN'07. June 15, 2007

[12] A. Gupta, Y. Kim and B. Urgaonkar. DFTL: A Flash Translation Layer Employing Demand-based Selective of Page-level Address Mapping. In *Proc. of* ASPLOS'09. March 7-11, 2009.

[13] Y. Hu, H. Jiang, D. Feng, L. Tian, S. Zhang, J. Liu, W. Tong, Y. Qin and L. Wang. Achieving Page-Mapping FTL Performance at Block-Mapping FTL Cost by Hiding Address Translation. In *Proc. of* MSST'10. May 3-7, 2010.

[14] J. Shin, Z. Xia, N. Xu, R. Gao, X. Cai, S. Maeng and E. Hsu. FTL Design Exploration in Reconfigurable High-Performance SSD for Server Applications. In *Proc. of* ICS'09, June 2009.

[15] S. Lee, D. Park, T. Chung, D. Lee, S. Park and H. Song. A Log Buffer-Based Flash Translation Layer Using Fully-Associative Sector Translation. ACM Transactions on Embedded Computing Systems, Vol.6, No.3, Article 18, July 2007.

[16] H. Kim and S. Ahn. BPLRU: A Buffer Management Scheme for Improving Random Writes in Flash Storage. In *Proc. of* FAST'08. February 26-29, 2008.

[17] J. Seol, H. Shim, J. Kim and S. Maeng. A buffer replacement algorithm exploiting multi-chip parallelism in solid state disks. In *Proc. of* CASES'09, October 2009.

[18] S. Park, D. Jung, J. Kang, J. Kim and J. Lee. CFLRU: A Replacement Algorithm for Flash Memory. In *Proc. of* CASES'06, October 2006.

[19] H. Jo, J. Kang, S Park, J. Kim and J. Lee. FAB: Flash-Aware Buffer Management Policy for Portable Media Players. IEEE Transaction on Consumer Electronics, Vol.52, No.2, M ay 2006.

[20] F. Chen, D. A. Koufaty and X. Zhang. Understanding Intrinsic Characteristics and System Implications of Flash Memory based Solid State Drives. In *Proc. of* SIGMETRICS /performance'09. June 15-19, 2009

[21] L. M. Grupp, A. M. Caulfield, J. Coburn, S. Swanson, E. Yaakobi, P. H. Siegel and J. K. Wolf. Characterizing Flash Memory: Anomalies, Observations, and Applications. In *Proc. of* MICRO'09. December 12-16, 2009.

[22] S. Boboila and P. Desnoyers. Write Endurance in Flash Drives: Measurements and Analysis. In *Proc. of* FAST'10. February 23-26, 2010.

[23] P. Desnoyers. Empirical Evaluation of NAND Flash Memory Performance. In *Proc. of* HotStorage'09, October 2009.

[24] N. Agrawal, V. Prabhakaran, T. Wobber, J. D. Davis, M. Manasse and R. Panigrahy. Design Tradeoffs for SSD Performance. In *Proc. of* USENIX'08, June 2008

[25] J. Kang, J. Kim, C. Park, H. Park and J. Lee. A multi-channel architecture for high-performance and flash-based storage system. Jounal of Systems Architecture. 53: 644-658, 2007.

[26] S. Park, E. Seo, J. Shin, S. Maeng and J. Lee. Exploiting internal parallelism of flash-based SSDs. IEEE Computer Architecture Letters. 03-Feb-2010.

[27] S. Park, S. Ha, K. Bang and E. Chuang. Design and analysis of flash translation layers for multi-channel NAND flash based storage devices. IEEE Transaction on Consumer Electronics, Vol.55, No.3, August 2009.

[28] K9XXG08UXA datasheet. http://www.samsung.com/products /semiconductor/flash/technicalinfo/datasheets.htm.

[29] K9NCG08U5M datasheet. http://www.samsung.com/products /semiconductor/flash/technicalinfo/datasheets.htm.

[30] Micro MT29F16G08FAA NAND Flash Memory datasheet. http://www.micron.com//document_download/?documentId=4308

[31] Micro MT29F256G08CUCBB NAND Flash Memory datasheet. http://www.micron.com//document_download/?documentId=4368

[32] Intel JS29F64G08CAMD1 MD332 NAND Flash Memory datasheet. http://www.intel.com/design

[33] Toshiba TH58TVG7S2F NAND Flash Memory datasheet. http://www.toshiba.com/

[34] Hynix H27UCG8U5(D)A Series 64Gb NAND Flash datasheet. http://www.hynix.com/datasheet/

[35] Microsoft Enterprise Traces. http://iotta.snia.org/traces/list/BlockIO

[36] Application note for nand flash memory (revision 2.0) http://www.samsung.com/global/business/semiconductor/produ cts/flash/downloads/applicationnote/app_nand.pdf

[37] Open NAND Flash Interface SpecificaRion. revision2.2.http://onfi. org/wp-content/uploads/2009/02/ ONFI%202_2%20 Gold.pdf

[38] NAND Flash Performance Improvement Using Internal Data Move. Technical Note TN-29-15. http://download.micron.com/ pdf/technotes/nand/tn2915.pdf

[39] Using COPYBACK Operations to Maintain Data Integrity in NAND Devices. Technical Note TN-29-41. http://www.eeta-sia.com/STATIC/PDF/200903/EEOL_2009MAR02_STOR_A N_01.pdf?SOURCES=DOWNLOAD

[40] SSD Extension for DiskSim Simulation Environment. http://research.microsoft.com/en-us/downloads/b41019e2-1d2b -44d8-b512-ba35ab814cd4/

[41] Y. Kim, B.Tauras, A. Gupta, D. M. Nistor and B. Urgaonkar. FlashSim: A Simulator for NAND Flash-based Solid-State Drives. Technical Report CSE-09-008

[42] J. Bucy, J. Schindler, S. W. Schlosser and G. R. Ganger. The DiskSim Simulation Environment Version 4.0 Reference Manual. May 2008.

[43] E. Fal and S. Toledo. Algorithms and Data Structures for Flash Memories. ACM Computing Surveys, Vol.37, No.2, June 2005, pp.138-163.

[44] T. Chung, D. Park, S. Park, D. Lee, S. Lee and H. Song. System Software for Flash Memory: A Survey. International Federation for Information Processing 2006. EUC 2006, LNCS 4096, pp. 394-404. 2006.

[45] UMass Trace Repository. http://traces.cs.umass.edu

[46] Weal-Leveling Techniques in NAND Flash Devices. Technical Note TN-29-42. http://download.micron.com/pdf/technotes/ nand/tn2942_nand_wear_leveling.pdf

SecureME: A Hardware-Software Approach to Full System Security[*]

Siddhartha Chhabra[1][†], Brian Rogers[1][‡], Yan Solihin[1], and Milos Prvulovic[2]

[1]Dept. of Electrical and Computer Engineering
North Carolina State University
{schhabr,bmrogers,solihin}@ncsu.edu

[2]College of Computing
Georgia Institute of Technology
milos@cc.gatech.edu

ABSTRACT

With computing increasingly becoming more dispersed, relying on mobile devices, distributed computing, cloud computing, etc. there is an increasing threat from adversaries obtaining physical access to some of the computer systems through theft or security breaches. With such an untrusted computing node, a key challenge is how to provide secure computing environment where we provide privacy and integrity for data and code of the application. We propose SecureME, a hardware-software mechanism that provides such a secure computing environment. SecureME protects an application from hardware attacks by using a secure processor substrate, and also from the Operating System (OS) through memory cloaking, permission paging, and system call protection. Memory cloaking hides data from the OS but allows the OS to perform regular virtual memory management functions, such as page initialization, copying, and swapping. Permission paging extends the OS paging mechanism to provide a secure way for two applications to establish shared pages for inter-process communication. Finally, system call protection applies spatio-temporal protection for arguments that are passed between the application and the OS. Based on our performance evaluation using microbenchmarks, single-program workloads, and multi-programmed workloads, we found that SecureME only adds a small execution time overhead compared to a fully unprotected system. Roughly half of the overheads are contributed by the secure processor substrate. SecureME also incurs a negligible additional storage overhead over the secure processor substrate.

Categories and Subject Descriptors

D.4.6 [**Operating Systems**]: Security and Protection; C.1.0 [**Processor Architectures**]: General

---

[*]This work was supported in part by NSF Award CCF-0915501 and CCF-0916464.

[†]Now works at Intel Labs (siddhartha.chhabra@intel.com)

[‡]Now works at IBM (bmrogers@us.ibm.com)

General Terms

Security

Keywords

Operating Systems, Security, Hardware attacks, Cloaking

1. INTRODUCTION

Computing is increasingly becoming more dispersed, relying on various computer systems that are distributed physically, yet working together to solve a common problem. Examples include mobile devices (laptops, PDAs, cellphones), distributed computing, cloud computing, remote data center, etc. The increasing reliance on physically remote computer systems for solving a computing problem carries some security risks in that adversaries may obtain physical access to some of the computer systems through theft or security breaches. Example scenarios include an adversary stealing a company laptop in order to obtain secret company information, combat robotic vehicles confiscated by enemies who try to reverse engineer code or steal data stored in the vehicles, or even owners of gaming consoles who try to bypass security protection of the consoles. In such environments, a key question is how to provide a secure computing environment on untrusted computing nodes.

If we assume that attackers can gain physical access to computer systems for which we want to provide secure computing environment, we must assume that all off-chip hardware components and all software components are vulnerable to both passive (eavesdropping) attacks as well as active attacks. Therefore, the goal of a secure computing environment on untrusted computing node is to provide *privacy* (a guarantee that plaintext of code or data will not be leaked to the adversary) and *integrity* (a guarantee that program behavior or data cannot be modified by the adversary). Vulnerable components include many hardware components (all components outside of the processor die including the main memory, the system bus, I/O, etc.) as well as software components especially the Operating System (OS). Hence, a complete security solution *must* protect applications against vulnerabilities in *both the hardware and the OS*.

Providing complete security to untrusted computing nodes is a very challenging problem. At the heart of the problem is that in traditional systems, the OS is *implicitly entrusted* to manage the memory resources of the application. OS performs context switching, memory protection, memory allocation, initialization, sharing, etc. on behalf of applications. This automatically exposes an application to security vulnerabilities of the OS. One can envision an approach where core OS functionality like virtual memory management, context switching etc. is delegated to a *security kernel*. However, a security kernel can be quite large (e.g. 74K lines of code just for virtual management alone in AEGIS[29]) but simultaneously must be free from bugs and security vulnerabilities. As another option, one can envisage to restructure the OS such that key memory management functions are either disallowed, or relegated to special secure processor mechanisms, hence removing the implicit trust assumption completely. Such approach has been pursued in XOM OS [18] and AEGIS [29]. For example, regular OS mechanisms to allow sharing between processes (e.g. inter-process communication), copy on write, and dynamic linked library are not allowed under AEGIS, or special mechanisms are in place to bypass regular OS mechanisms in XOM OS. Such an approach requires significant modifications or restrictions to the OS, making it impractical to use in general purpose systems.

A promising alternative is to adapt the hypervisor based approach in the untrusted-OS but trusted-hardware studies, such as Overshadow [5] and SP^3 [34]. The approach is to avoid OS modifications, but before the OS performs any vital management functions, a hypervisor intercepts such events and hides the application data plaintext from the OS, using a technique called *cloaking* [5]. In this approach, the OS is allowed to do its vital management functions, but on data that is already encrypted and hashed. Upon the completion of such functions, the hypervisor decrypts the data and verifies its integrity, before returning control to the application.

Unfortunately, existing cloaking mechanisms do not provide protection against untrusted hardware and are incompatible with *secure processor technology* [9, 16, 17, 22, 23, 25, 26, 27, 30, 33, 35, 36] that protects against hardware attacks, for several reasons. First, they keep each application data page in both encrypted and non-encrypted forms in the main memory, making the non-encrypted pages vulnerable to hardware eavesdropping. Secondly, they require direct encryption, where the encryption function is address-independent. That is, two ciphertext pages corresponding to the same plaintext data must be identical, regardless of where the pages are located in the main memory. This allows OS to operate solely on a ciphertext basis, for example it can create a perfect copy of data by copying the ciphertext of a page from one location to another. However, as pointed out in prior studies [26, 33, 35], address-dependent counter mode encryption has been shown to be superior to address-independent direct encryption in terms of security protection and performance. Direct encryption provides weaker security protection than counter mode encryption because the statistical distribution of the ciphertext and plaintext are identical. In addition, direct encryption has been shown to impose significant performance overheads of up to 35% [35] even when the decryption is implemented in hardware, due to the inability of the processor to overlap the decryption delay with cache miss delay. These security and performance drawbacks are eliminated when we use counter mode encryption [30, 35], which is unfortunately incompatible with current cloaking mechanisms.

The goal of this study is to investigate how to provide privacy and integrity to applications that run on untrusted computing nodes, where both hardware and the OS are vulnerable to security attacks. To achieve that, we propose an integrated security protection framework which we refer to as Secure My Execution (SecureME). SecureME consists of a secure processor substrate controlled by small trusted software which can be cleanly implemented as a thin hypervisor layer. In SecureME, an application can explicitly request the processor to protect its address space by invok-

ing a special instruction that traps to the hardware. Unlike SP^3 and Overshadow, the entire address space of the application is cloaked (encrypted and hashed) at all time, avoiding hardware eavesdropping from discovering plaintext data. Only when the application accesses its own data, data is decrypted and its integrity checked on chip. SecureME is compatible with the state-of-the-art secure processor technology, which employs counter-mode encryption and Merkle Tree for integrity protection. We show mechanisms to ensure this compatibility. SecureME allows a commodity OS to be employed nearly unmodified, requiring only the addition of two virtual instructions to indicate the intent of the OS for page copying and initialization. The addition of these virtual instructions can be automated, for example, through a compiler pass, and does not in any way change the OS functionality. Hence the OS is free to implement vital management functions on application's data using whatever policies it wants. SecureME leverages the secure processor to perform validation of the OS virtual memory management functions. Despite this flexibility, SecureME ensures the privacy and integrity of the application, from both hardware and OS vulnerabilities.

SecureME also provides an additional protection mechanism for system calls. By making system calls, an application explicitly trusts the OS to perform service with data it supplies or will receive. Thus, system call parameters must be uncloaked, and there is no guarantee that a compromised OS will perform the service correctly. However, SecureME ensures that the OS only accesses data it is supposed to (spatial protection), and only within the window of time of the system call invocation (temporal protection). Again, we demonstrate that such spatio-temporal protection can be achieved by leveraging secure processor mechanisms, without much additional complexities.

To evaluate the performance overheads of SecureME, we implement SecureME's software component through dynamic instrumentation of Linux OS, and SecureME's architecture component on detailed processor simulator based on Simics [19]. Our results show that SecureME adds only a small runtime overhead, averaging 5.2% for SPEC2006 applications over an unprotected system; of that, 2.2% is caused by the use of secure processor itself, while only the remaining (3%) is caused by SecureME mechanisms. Even on a multicore system consisting of two cores and two applications running on different cores concurrently, SecureME runtime overheads remain negligible. Furthermore, SecureME incurs trivial storage overheads of 0.58% apart from the meta-data needed by the secure processors (counters and Merkle Tree nodes), in contrast to cloaking in software, which can incur storage overheads of up to 100%. Finally, SecureME mechanisms require only approximately 700 lines of code (vs >74,000 lines of code in secure kernel approach), making it much easier to guarantee a secure bug-free implementation.

The rest of the paper is organized as follows. Section 2 presents related work. Section 3 discusses our attack model and assumptions. Section 4 presents SecureME design. Section 5 describes the implementation details for SecureME. Section 6 describes our experimental setup, and Section 7 discusses our evaluation results and findings. Finally, we conclude in Section 8.

2. RELATED WORK

Figure 1 shows a classification of related security works and forms the basis of our discussion in this section.

Secure Processor Technology (Cluster A). Research on secure processor architectures [9, 12, 16, 17, 22, 23, 25, 26, 27, 29, 30, 33, 35, 36] assumes that the processor die boundary provides a natural secure boundary, and off-chip

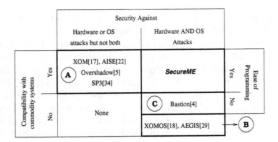

Figure 1: Classification of related work.

components are vulnerable. Secure processors use memory encryption for ensuring data *privacy* and memory integrity verification for ensuring data *integrity*. While secure processor architectures provide defense against hardware attacks, they implicitly assume a trusted OS.

Dealing with an Untrusted OS but Trusted Hardware (also Cluster A) Hypervisors or Virtual Machine Monitors (VMMs) running directly on bare hardware (e.g. VMWare ESX Server [32] and Xen [3]) have become popular. Several hypervisor-based security protection schemes have been proposed, assuming software-based attacks but not hardware attacks. SecVisor [24] is a tiny hypervisor designed to ensure kernel code integrity against software attacks. Proxos [31] is a hypervisor-based trust partitioning system. It partitions the system into multiple Virtual Machines (VMs), one running an untrusted full-blown OS and the others running trusted, application-specific OSes. Chen et al. [5] and Yang et al. [34] propose *multi-shadowing*, that presents different cryptographic views of the physical memory (ciphertext or plaintext) depending on whether the data is accessed by the application or by the OS. McCune et al. propose Flicker [20] which relies on a secure co-processor like TPM [10] to provide a secure execution environment. Flicker provides protection from other software and OS, however, it requires the applications to be re-written to identify the code segments requiring security and linked against the Flicker library.

Dealing with an Untrusted OS on Secure Processor (Cluster B). Lie et al. proposed XOM OS [18], an OS for XOM secure processor. To deal with the untrusted OS assumption, XOM provides compartments to fully isolate one process from others. Suh et al. proposed AEGIS [29], and presented two alternative implementations. One implementation requires a secure implementation of OS called secure kernels, and another assumes untrusted OS and enforces isolation between processes similar to compartments in XOM OS. A protected application has a compartment ID that is stored as tags for processor registers and all cache blocks. The processor prevents a process to access registers or cache blocks with a different compartment ID. Hence, even if the OS is compromised and allows a malicious application to map its address space to a good application, the malicious application still cannot read the data of the good application due to the compartment ID mismatch. However, compartments are incompatible with how a modern OS manages protection and sharing between processes, through virtual memory management features such as inter-process communication, copy on write, and dynamic linked library. AEGIS prohibits such OS features, while XOM OS uses special hardware and OS mechanisms to provide the features. Significant modifications to the OS make the system incompatible and less applicable for general purpose systems, and may present backdoors to new security vulnerabilities.

Dealing with Untrusted OS and Untrusted Hardware (Cluster C). The closest related work to ours is Bastion [4], a hypervisor based solution that assumes untrusted OS and hardware. Bastion security protection revolves around a *security module*, an encapsulation of code section, data it uses, access permission for data, that forms the basic unit of security protection. To enjoy the processor and hypervisor protection from hardware/OS vulnerabilities, an application programmer must identify statically a module and the permission (read/write/execute) for all pages that the module uses. Module information is given to the compiler which generates a security compartment for that module, which is enforced by the hypervisor and secure processor at run time.

3. ATTACK MODEL, SECURITY MODEL, AND ASSUMPTIONS

3.1 Attack Model

The attack model that we are interested in is a case in which attackers gain full physical access to the computer systems. The main goal of attackers will be to steal secret data that is processed by the applications. In order to do that, the attackers may mount physical attacks on the hardware (such as by inserting a bus snooper or memory scanner to read the plaintext data stored in off-chip memory, or communicated between the processor and off-chip memory), or mount software attacks on the OS in order to leak secret data that belongs to an application process. Alternatively, the attackers may attempt to change the code or data of the application in order to modify its behavior so that it leaks out its secret data. Therefore, the goal of a secure computing environment on untrusted computing node is to provide *privacy* (a guarantee that plaintext of code or data will not be leaked to the adversary) and *integrity* (a guarantee that program behavior or data cannot be modified by the adversary). We do not consider denial of service attacks or side channel attacks in this paper.

3.2 Security Model

Our goal is to provide privacy and integrity protection for an application from hardware and OS vulnerabilities. There are at least two possible security models to achieve this. One possible security model is one proposed by Bastion [4] where users define a *security module*, a basic unit of security protection that encapsulates code section, data it uses, and access permission for data. With Bastion, the critical question is who should determine modules and what should be the optimum module granularity. If a program is broken into many small modules, figuring out which modules should be allowed to share data or not is tricky. On the other hand, encapsulating the entire program as a single security module presents intractable operational challenges such as (1) Data Sharing: the application must conform to share-everything or share-nothing semantics for a module. (2) System calls: to avoid the OS from having access to the entire application's data, code implementing system calls must be broken into modules with different security permissions, which complicates OS design. (3) Copy-on-write: The application will need to provide access to its entire address space to the OS to allow this optimization on forking a process. (4) Dynamic memory allocation: Since the location of dynamically allocated memory is not known at compile time, it is infeasible to define permissions for data residing on the heap using Bastion, hence critical data cannot be placed in the heap or else its security is compromised. Therefore, we view Bastion's module-based security model to be more suitable for well-defined functions such as subroutines or functions that perform cryptographic algorithms, but is too restrictive for protecting user data or an entire application.

Thus, SecureME uses a security model in which it automatically protects the entire address space of an application from the OS through cloaking. An application must explicitly ask for hardware protection at the start of program by requesting a hardware ID. If two applications want to establish inter-process communication, they have to explicitly request for shared memory to be established.

3.3 Assumptions

We assume that a proper infrastructure is in place for a hypervisor and applications to be distributed to the end users securely, for use on secure processors. In general, we assume that a feature similar to IBM Cell *runtime secure boot* [13] is present on the system which verifies an application each time it is launched. Hence, an attempt to modify the application before launch will be caught as an integrity failure and the application will not be launched. We also assume a secure booting infrastructure utilizing establishing a chain of trust and verification to be used [2, 6], to prevent against any attacks that may happen during or before the booting of a system, and launching of the hypervisor and applications. These features ensure that an application/system has not been compromised before launch/bootup and before SecureME runtime mechanisms can take effect to protect the system.

4. SecureME DESIGN

4.1 Secure Processor Substrate

In this section, we provide an overview of the secure processor used by SecureME. The secure processor architecture itself is not a contribution of this paper.

The secure processor substrate we assume uses Address-Independent Seed Encryption (AISE) [22] for counter-mode encryption, and Merkle Tree for integrity verification [9]. In counter mode encryption, data block is not directly encrypted or decrypted. Instead, a *seed* is encrypted to generate a pseudo random pad that is then XORed with data block in order to encrypt (or decrypt) the data block. Since a data block is not needed for generating the pad (which is the time consuming step), decryption delay can be overlapped with cache miss delay, which is a unique feature of counter-mode encryption.

Figure 2 illustrates the components of a secure processor, shown in gray boxes. Suppose a data block is evicted from the last level cache, the physical address of the block is sent to the *counter cache* (Step 1). A counter cache stores a collection of blocks, each block containing a logical per-page identifier (LPID), and multiple per-block counter values. LPID is unique for a page, assigned at the first allocation of the page, and its value is unaffected by where the page may be located (in physical memory or swap space in disk), and is unrelated to the address of the application. The encryption seed for the block is a concatenation of the page's LPID, the block's counter, page offset, and some initial vector (Step 2). The LPID and page offset give the seed spatial uniqueness (each block has a unique LPID and page offset combination), while the per-block counter gives the seed temporal uniqueness (each time a block is written back to the main memory, the block's counter is incremented to ensure no seed reuse is possible). The encryption seed of a block is input to the encryption engine in order to obtain a pseudo-random *pad* (Step 3). The pad is XORed with the data block in order to encrypt it. The ciphertext itself is fed into the message authentication code (MAC) generator

to produce a hash code (Step 4). Finally, the hash code updates the Merkle Tree, to provide a full integrity protection (Step 5).

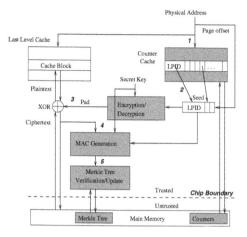

Figure 2: Secure processor substrate used by SecureME.

SecureME uses Merkle Tree for memory integrity verification. A Merkle Tree is a tree of hash codes where a parent node contains a hash of all its children nodes. A Merkle Tree has been shown to offer the strongest protection for data as it protects against splicing, spoofing, as well as replay attacks [9]. Since a hash code is smaller than the data it protects (e.g. 128 bits of hash code for a 64-byte block), ultimately at some level there is only one root node. This root node covers the entire tree, and is always stored on-chip in order to avoid hardware attacks from tampering it. The intermediate nodes can be stored on the L2 cache on-chip as needed. By allowing intermediate nodes to be cached, when a data block is modified (read) and is evicted from the cache, the Merkle Tree is updated (verified) until the first parent node that resides on chip, not all the way to the root. Merkle trees with better performance characteristics have been proposed [9, 22]. However, since Merkle Tree is not a focus of this paper, we use a standard Merkle Tree with 128 bits of hash code covering each 64-byte cache block.

4.2 Overview of SecureME

SecureME architecture is illustrated in Figure 3. Figure 3(a) shows hardware components added to the processor. Figure 3(b) shows the five new instructions introduced for SecureME mechanisms and Figure 3(c) shows how the application, the OS, hypervisor, and the secure processor interact, through the execution of various instructions and the occurrence of various processor events. The purpose of each of the new components and the interactions will become clear in the following sections when we discuss SecureME mechanisms.

4.3 Protecting an Application from OS Vulnerabilities

To ensure the privacy and integrity of an application's data from a compromised OS, SecureME relies on *hardware-based memory cloaking*. Memory cloaking is a concept introduced in Overshadow [5] and SP[3] [34], where the OS is given access only to application data's ciphertext. Cloaking is enabled based on the observation that for most memory management functions (such as page allocation, copying, and swapping), the OS does not need to have access to the plaintext data of the application. Hence, the OS can carry

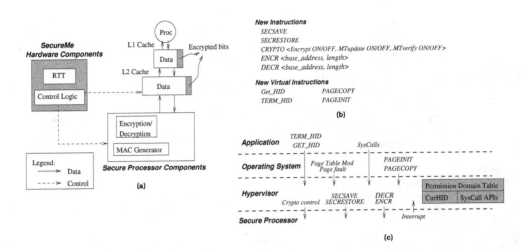

Figure 3: SecureME Architecture: hardware components (a), new instructions (b), and the interaction of applications, the OS, hypervisor, and secure processor (c).

out most of its functions on cloaked (i.e. encrypted and hashed) data. It may seem straightforward to implement software-based cloaking of Overshadow or SP^3 on the secure processor substrate to achieve the same security goal of SecureME. However, the fundamental incompatibility in their attack models makes it hard or even impractical to combine them directly. For example, imagine an access to an application page which is stored in ciphertext in the main memory by the Overshadow mechanisms, because it was previously accessed by the OS. This access will first be decrypted in software by Overshadow mechanisms and the processor will decrypt it again using its own key before supplying to the processor, resulting in unnecessary power and performance overheads. In addition, software-based cloaking can result in storage overheads of up to 100%, because an application page is kept in both encrypted and non-encrypted forms to minimize performance overheads. Finally, software-based cloaking intrinsically requires direct encryption, which is address independent, to allow OS to operate on pages solely on ciphertext basis. However, the secure processor substrate uses counter-mode encryption due to its performance and security advantages and hence is fundamentally incompatible with current software-based cloaking mechanisms in Overshadow or SP^3. XOMOS [18] provides an example where an attempt to add protection against OS attacks to XOM resulted in requiring significant OS redesign.

In contrast, SecureME is designed from bottom-up to make the interaction between the secure processor substrate and hypervisor synergistic, in order to provide the desired protection while meeting the other goals of low performance overheads, compatibility and ease of programming. Unlike Overshadow and SP^3, SecureME's cloaking leverages hardware mechanisms already present in the secure processor substrate, by selectively turning on or off various components of the secure processor's cryptographic engine.

A pre-requirement for providing memory cloaking is that we must distinguish between when an application needing protection is running and when the OS is running. To achieve that, an application requesting protection by SecureME is required to obtain a unique identifier to be associated with it. We refer to this unique identifier as a *hardware identifier (HID)*. A HID must be immutable by the OS, hence it must be assigned and managed by the hypervisor and the processor. The OS itself is given its own unique HID to distinguish it from applications being protected. To obtain a HID, a secure application executes a

special instruction *GET_HID*, which, because it is a virtual instruction, generates an *Invalid Opcode fault*. This fault traps to the hypervisor which then assigns a new HID to the application and initializes its *permission domain table*. HIDs do not need to be unique across system reboots and can be reused by the hypervisor. Hence, the hypervisor can maintain a software counter to assign HIDs to requesting applications. In addition, the hypervisor also keeps track of the HID of the currently running context.

A HID is saved and restored by the hypervisor across interrupts or context switching. An application can give up its HID upon exit by calling another virtual instruction which we refer to as *TERM_HID*. It should be noted that we do not rely on an applications terminating reliably for the security of the system. If an application exits without calling *TERM_HID*, resources allocated for its security in the hypervisor will not be released but in no event will the security of the system be compromised. The addition of GET_HID and TERM_HID to the beginning and the end of the application is the only change required by SecureME for an application which requests for security protection. Unlike modules in Bastion [4] which require programmers to identify static code, data, and security permission to encapsulate as a security module, in SecureME programmers (or compilers) can obtain protection for the program's entire data, oblivious of various types of code and data structures used in the program.

Note that the notion of cloaked access includes not just privacy protection, but also integrity protection. In SecureME, the on-chip cryptographic engine alternates between two modes: *cloaked mode* and *uncloaked mode*. In an uncloaked mode, all parts of the cryptographic engine are turned on: encryption/decryption, integrity verification, and Merkle Tree update. Data that is brought on chip is decrypted, and its integrity is verified against the Merkle Tree. If data is modified, the Merkle Tree is updated to reflect the new data. In a cloaked mode, all parts of the cryptographic engine are turned off. Ciphertext data fetched from off-chip memory is not decrypted, hence the OS only views the ciphertext of data. Integrity verification is not performed. And finally, if the OS modifies some of the application's ciphertext data, the modification does not result in the Merkle Tree being updated. Hence, if a compromised OS modifies cloaked data, the illegitimate modification is detected later when the application accesses the data, and the integrity verification of the data against the Merkle Tree fails. Therefore, it is as if cloaked access only grants read permission on the ciphertext form of data.

The hypervisor controls the transition from cloaked to uncloaked mode and vice versa, using the cryptographic control instruction, i.e. CRYPTO<>, which enables the hypervisor to independently turn on or off various parts of the cryptographic engine: the encryption/decryption engine, Merkle Tree update, Merkle Tree integrity checking. When the processor switches mode from user to kernel, for example, the mode switch traps to the hypervisor, which then remembers the new HID as the currently running HID (CurHID).

Note, however, that data that is already cached (i.e. not fetched from off-chip memory), already resides in a certain form, either in plaintext form (if brought in by the application to whom the data belongs), or in ciphertext form (if brought in by the OS). The mix of data forms in the same cache introduces a vulnerability as the OS may directly access an application's plaintext data that was brought into the cache in the past by the application. To remove this vulnerability, there are several possible solutions. One possible solution is to flush the caches across mode switches. However, flushing the entire on-chip caches is too costly to be practical. Another possible solution that is actually used by Overshadow [5] and SP^3 [34] is to unmap (invalidate) the page of the application that the OS accesses, and remap it to the kernel address space. Unmapping a page removes the corresponding page translation entry (PTE) from the TLB, and causes all data of that page to be flushed from the cache. The flush forces the OS to refetch it into the cache in a ciphertext form. While this solution works, its performance overheads are not trivial since it involves cache and TLB invalidations, and a page table modification. It also incurs subsequent page faults, cache and TLB refills when the application resumes execution.

In order to avoid such costly overheads, in SecureME we exploit the capability of the secure processor. First, in order to distinguish the current form of a particular cache block, we tag each cache block with an "encrypted" bit. The encrypted bit is set to 1 when a block is stored in the cache in its ciphertext form, otherwise it is set to 0. Under an uncloaked mode, data blocks brought from off-chip memory are decrypted before they are stored in the cache, hence their encrypted bits are set to 0. Under cloaked mode, data blocks brought from off-chip memory are stored in the cache without being decrypted, hence their encrypted bits are set to 1. Since the OS should only be given access to cloaked data, when it accesses a block whose encrypted bit is not set to 1, the block is passed to the cryptographic engine in order to be encrypted and stored back into the cache.

In the previous discussion, we have assumed that in order to perform memory management functions (page allocation, copying, swapping), it is sufficient for the OS to have access to cloaked data. This in turn implicitly assumes that direct encryption scheme is used, in that the encryption function is position-independent, that is, two ciphertext pages corresponding to the same plaintext data are identical, regardless of where the pages are located in the main memory. This allows OS to operate solely on a ciphertext basis, for example it can create a perfect copy of data by copying the ciphertext of a page from one location to another. The same assumption is used by Overshadow [5] and SP^3 [34].

However, counter mode encryption has been shown to be superior to direct encryption in terms of security protection and performance [26, 33, 35]. Direct encryption provides weaker security protection than counter mode encryption because the statistical distribution of the ciphertext and plaintext are identical. In addition, direct encryption has been shown to impose a significant performance overheads

of up to 35% [35] even when the decryption is implemented in hardware, due to the inability of the processor to overlap the decryption delay with cache miss delay. These security and performance drawbacks are eliminated when we use counter mode encryption [30, 35]. However, with counter mode encryption, the same plaintext page will have different ciphertext values depending on where they are located in the memory. Thus, it is incorrect for an OS to copy a ciphertext application page verbatim to a different location.

Therefore, a novel mechanism is needed to achieve seemingly conflicting goals of *allowing the OS to work on cloaked data while at the same time allowing the use of counter-mode encryption in the secure processor substrate*. As a part of virtual memory management, the OS is frequently required to copy a page that belongs to an application to another location. Page copying is often employed during forking of a child process. When a parent process forks a child process, the two are made to share the memory pages of the parent, in order to return from the fork quickly, and to reduce the memory requirement of the child process. However, the memory pages of the parent are set to read-only. When either of the process tries to write to the shared pages, a write protection fault occurs and at that time, the OS copies the content of the source page to a new destination page, so that now the parent and child have their own page. After the page copying due to "copy-on-write" completes, the write is allowed to resume.

In order to satisfy the contradictory goals of allowing the OS to perform page copying as it pleases, while at the same time allow us to use counter-mode encryption in the secure processor substrate, the only solution is to allow the OS to perform the page copying oblivious of the use of counter-mode encryption (i.e. verbatim), and then fix the destination page afterwards. To support this, there are important questions that need to be addressed: how to ensure that integrity verification failure does not occur under correct OS operation, who should fix the destination page and how, and how to validate that the OS has indeed performed page copying correctly.

Recall that when the OS runs, the cryptographic engine is in the cloaked mode, where decryption, Merkle tree verification and update are turned off for data that the OS operates on. This means that a data block from the source page is not decrypted as it is read by the processor, and is also written verbatim to the destination as it is written by the processor. Integrity verification cannot fail at this time as it is turned off. However, once the application resumes execution and accesses data in the destination page, it will suffer from integrity verification failure as the Merkle Tree has not reflected the new data. To avoid integrity verification failure, prior to the copying by the OS, the LPID, counters used for encrypting the page, and hash codes that cover the page, are copied over to the destination page. When the application resumes, if the OS indeed has copied the page verbatim, the seed components (LPID and counters) are available for the page to be decrypted to the correct plaintext. In addition, integrity verification will succeed using the copied-over hash codes. Failures in integrity signify that the OS has not performed the copying correctly, which implies a compromised OS.

Another issue to deal with is regarding fixing the destination page. The destination and source page currently share the same content, LPID, and page root. This is not a security vulnerability because currently the destination page is the direct outcome of OS page copying, which is not a secret operation. However, once the source or destination page is written to, they can no longer share the same LPID because then they may use the same encryption seed and knowledge of the plaintext of data in one of the page can reveal the plaintext of the corresponding data in the other page. Hence, on completion of copying, the hypervisor write protects the page and on the first write protection fault to the newly copied page, the hypervisor triggers re-encryption of the page.

Page re-encryption can be designed to incur very little overheads. In order to re-encrypt a page, all that is needed is to bring each block in the page into the on-chip cache (in plaintext), and as the page is naturally evicted from the cache, each evicted block is encrypted with a new LPID. Hence, re-encryption occurs over a stretched period of time, and it is off the critical path as the processor is never stalled during the process. Furthermore, during OS page copying, blocks of the destination page were already being brought into the on-chip cache, hence few or no extra cache misses occur due to page re-encryption. The only actual overhead comes from the fact that blocks of the destination page that were brought on-chip by the OS are stored in ciphertext form. Thus, they need to be converted into plaintext form once the application resumes. Hence, the cryptographic engine will have additional work to decrypt the blocks. However, this can be done at the background without hogging the cryptographic engine. To achieve that, for a page that needs to be re-encrypted after page copying, we keep a *re-encryption tracking table* (RTT), where each entry contains a page address and a bitmap of re-encryption progress. The RTT does not need to have many entries, since only a few pages are being re-encrypted at any given time, and in the case where the RTT runs out of entries, the re-encryption is performed synchronously where the page is re-encrypted completely before allowing the application to continue. Each bit in the bitmap corresponds to a cache block. For example, for a 4KB page, we will have 64 bits to track 64 blocks of the page. As each block is re-encrypted (i.e. decrypted using the old LPID), the corresponding bit is set to 1. Whenever the cryptographic engine is idle, we schedule another block to be decrypted, until all blocks of a page are decrypted. Once that is completed, re-encryption process for the page is completed, and its entry from the RTT is removed.

Page initialization is handled in a similar manner to page copying. We provide a reference zero-page having all zero values. When the OS initializes a page to zeros, SecureME treats it as if it copies the zero-page to a destination page. The rest of the mechanism is then identical to page copying.

One final issue is how the hypervisor knows when the OS performs page initialization or copying. While analyzing the change in the page table may allow us to do that, it is relatively tricky to do so. Hence, we require the OS to be annotated with PAGEINIT and PAGECOPY virtual instructions prior to initializing or copying a page. These instructions can be added to the kernel code base after kernel development, for example, by dynamic instrumentation. Let us examine the security implications of this new requirement. If the OS adds these instructions, while maliciously doing other operations, it will result in integrity verification failures as the data in the destination page mismatches the hash codes that are copied over from the source page. Another possible attack is the removal of the virtual instructions. In this case, as the kernel runs in the cloaked mode (cryptographic engine turned OFF), the ciphertext of the source page will be copied to the destination page without its accompanying LPID, counters, and hash codes. Once again, when the application resumes execution, this will be caught as an integrity verification failure by the secure processor. Hence, in SecureME, the secure processor mechanisms are used to verify the outcome of these operations reliably.

4.4 Inter-Application Protection

Different applications must be protected from one another, and at the same time they must also be allowed to establish data sharing for *inter-process communication* (IPC). Different applications can be distinguished from their HIDs. One way to enforce protection between applications is by tagging data with the owning application's HID, and only allow access when the currently running application's HID matches with the HID tag value of the data. Such an approach is employed in XOM [18] and AEGIS [29]. Overshadow [5] and SP[3] [34] also use a context-based approach, hence it allows applications to either share nothing, or share everything in their address space.

Context-based protection is incompatible with the way contemporary OSes allow protection and sharing between different applications. Contemporary OSes allow shared memory based IPC to be established between two processes by mapping two virtual pages from the two processes to map to a single physical page. One of the goals of SecureME is to be compatible with current OS mechanisms, including allowing different applications to establish a common shared memory for IPC. To achieve that, we extend regular demand paging mechanism by keeping track of an application's *permission domain*, which essentially specifies what pages an application should be allowed to have access to. If a page resides in the permission domain of an application, the application is allowed to map the page into its address space. Otherwise, it is not allowed to do so. To establish a shared page, the page identity is added to the sharing applications' permission domains. Permission domain may be updated or checked when a page fault occurs.

When a page fault occurs, the OS constructs the new virtual to physical page translation information, and attempts to record that information in the page table of the application. This attempt will trap to the hypervisor. The hypervisor then checks to see if the page already has an LPID associated with it. If it does not, indicating an allocation of a new page, the hypervisor assigns a new LPID by inquiring the secure processor (e.g. by executing a special instruction called RDAGPC [22]), which in turn gives a globally-unique number for the page's LPID. The hypervisor then adds the LPID of the new page to the permission domain of the faulting process. If a page already has an LPID, indicating that it is an already-allocated page that needs to be brought back in to the physical memory, the permission domain of the currently executing process is checked for a match. A match indicates that the application should be allowed to map the page to its address space. A mismatch indicates that the application should not be allowed to map the page to its address space, effectively denying the access.

If an application with a different HID, or an unprotected application having no HID, attempts to map a page that belongs to a protected application, a mismatch will occur since the page does not belong to them. Therefore, they would not be able to map the page to their address space. For example, consider an attack where the OS changes the virtual-to-physical mapping to allow a rogue application (R) to access the data of a secure application (S). It will construct this new translation and write to R's page table to allow the access. This will trap to the hypervisor. The hypervisor's permission paging semantics will now verify if the access is allowed or not. Since the page belonged to S, it already has an LPID associated with it. This will result in the hypervisor to lookup R's permission domain, thereby raising a security exception, because the LPID is not in the permission domain of R. If on the other hand, an application wants to establish a page for IPC with another application having a different HID, it can do so by explicitly giving the

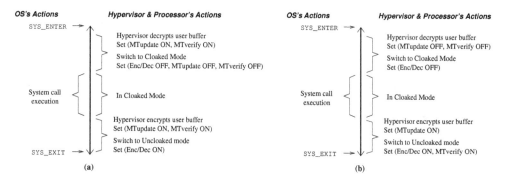

Figure 4: Temporary access mechanism for System Calls with read-only arguments (a), and read-write arguments (b).

hypervisor permission to add the page's LPID to the other application's permission domain. This gives applications an ability to share only a part of their address space without revealing the entire address space to one another.

When an application sets up shared memory segment using a system call, it is required to specify the permissions on that page. The hypervisor examines the arguments of the system call and when a different application tries to map the shared page to its address space, the hypervisor can lookup the permissions set up on that page to allow/disallow this mapping. The first application does not need to be aware of the existence of the sharing application. By ensuring that no application other than the ones indicated by the owner of shared memory segment can read/modify the page, shared memory communication is secured.

4.5 Additional Protection for System Calls

Unlike virtual memory management functions where it is sufficient to provide cloaked data access to the OS, system calls imply that an application *explicitly* entrusts the OS to carry out a service on its behalf. Therefore, short of validating each of OS service's functionality [1], SecureME cannot guarantee that the service will be performed correctly, or data that is passed to the OS will not be leaked to attackers. Hence, it is the responsibility of the application to encrypt system call parameters before making a system call if they need privacy protection.

However, a limited *spatio-temporal* protection is possible in SecureME. The protection ensures that the OS can only access the data that the system call is authorized to access (spatial protection), and only within the window of time of the system call invocation (temporal protection). We will demonstrate that such spatio-temporal protection can be achieved mostly without explicit validation, relying on the hardware's cryptographic engine to provide much of the protection.

The requirement for this system call protection is that the hypervisor must know the input and output of each system call in terms of all register arguments, memory buffers, and whether they will be read or written by the system call. While some system calls do not take any arguments, many others require arguments.

To restrict the OS access to just the arguments of the system call and nothing else, Overshadow [5] uses argument marshalling (system call arguments are copied from user space to the kernel space) and demarshalling (output of system calls is copied from the kernel space to user space). We view such copying to be too expensive, especially for applications that invoke system calls frequently, such as web servers, network applications, and disk utilities. Hence, in SecureME, we allow the OS to directly access the part of the

application's address space that stores the argument. However, the hypervisor controls the cryptographic engine such that spatio-temporal protection is still provided.

To provide temporary read access to user arguments, Figure 4(a) illustrates the steps taken in SecureME. When the system call is encountered, it traps to the hypervisor. The hypervisor reads a register that identifies which system call has been invoked. It checks a table that records the specifications of the system calls: what arguments are read and their addresses and lengths. It then instructs the the application's buffer containing the arguments to be decrypted (using the *DECR* instruction). In addition, since only read access is required, the OS should not be allowed to make any modifications to the user buffer. This is achieved by updating the Merkle tree as the buffer is decrypted which brings the decrypted buffer under Merkle tree protection. Then, the cryptographic engine is completely turned off (encryption/decryption, Merkle Tree update, and Merkle Tree integrity verification), before the system call is allowed to proceed. During system call execution, the OS can only view user arguments in plaintext while the rest of the user address space is cloaked. Upon the completion of the system call, the OS tries to return control to the application, which traps to the hypervisor. The hypervisor instructs the user buffer to be re-encrypted (using the *ENCR* instruction) with the Merkle tree verification mechanism turned on so that any illegal modifications by the OS to user buffer results in integrity verification failure. In parallel, the Merkle tree is updated to reflect the ciphertext of the user buffer. Finally, encryption/decryption is turned on and control is returned to the application.

Figure 4(b) illustrates the steps to provide spatio-temporal write protection to application's arguments in user buffer. As the system call is invoked, the hypervisor decrypts the user buffer, this time with Merkle Tree not being updated or verified. System call is executed under the cloaked mode. At the completion of the system call, the hypervisor re-encrypts the user buffer, with the Merkle Tree updated (but not verified) to reflect the new values. Modifications by the OS to user buffer will not trigger integrity verification failure in this case because integrity verification is turned on at the completion of the system call.

4.6 Other Design Issues

On an interrupt, the processor saves the register state of the interrupted process in an exception frame on the kernel stack. This leaves a possibility for the OS to read the register state of the interrupted process. Since hypervisors are designed to naturally intercept all interrupts, SecureME lets the hypervisor to use the intercept to securely store the state of the application that is interrupted (by executing

SECSAVE). The hypervisor or the processor can encrypt the register state along with the HID of the application, before storing the exception frame on the kernel stack. In addition, a hash code is computed over the encrypted exception frame to prevent the kernel from modifying the register contents. The hash may also include a unique counter value that is incremented across interrupts to provide protection against replay on register state saved across interrupts (similar to XOM [18]). Once the interrupt is serviced, SecureME can decrypt the exception frame and restore the register state and HID of the application (by executing SECRESTORE), after verifying the hash code associated with it to ensure its integrity and defense against replay attacks.

5. SecureME IMPLEMENTATION

SecureME consists of two components: a hardware component implementing the secure processor mechanisms and a software component implementing the mechanisms described for application-to-OS and application-to-application protection.

Hardware Components: We simulate the secure processors mechanisms and the other processor changes for SecureME using Simics [19], a full-system simulator, as the hardware proposed for SecureME does not exist in any contemporary processor.

Software Components: In a virtualized environment, the hypervisor virtualizes the hardware resources by causing a trap when the guest OS attempts to modify the privileged state. These include events for virtual memory management such as page initialization and copying, context switches, interrupts, and system calls. Hence, SecureME thin software layer can be captured cleanly as a hypervisor. However, our full-system simulator simulating the hardware components is not capable of supporting an Operating system running in a virtualized environment. Hence, in order to model the overheads for the software components of SecureME, in our current implementation, we use an approach where the OS is dynamically instrumented by inserting probes into the Linux OS kernel. The probes are inserted at the kernel functions to match the traps that will happen in a virtualized environment. Probing the kernel closely models the performance of a virtualized environment as probes also result in a trap when execution reaches the probe, emulating the behavior of a virtualized environment. In particular, we use `jprobes` and `kretprobes` [21], which allows us to get a handle to the probed kernel function arguments and return values respectively. We implement the code that manages permission paging, HIDs, and LPIDs, as trap handlers. Table 1 provides details of our modifications to the Linux kernel to simulate SecureME.

6. EXPERIMENTAL SETUP

Simulated machine configuration. For our benchmark-driven performance evaluation study, we implement our secure processor substrate on a full-system simulator, Simics [19]. We model a 2GHz, in-order processor with split L1 data and instruction caches. Both caches are 32KB in size, 2-way set associative and have a 2-cycle round-trip hit latency. The L2 cache is unified and is 1MB in size, 8-way set-associative, and has a 10-cycle round-trip hit latency. L1 and L2 cache lines are tagged with the "encryption bit" to simulate our cache protection mechanism. For counter mode encryption, the processor includes a 16-way set-associative 32KB counter cache at the L2 cache level. All caches have 64B blocks and use LRU replacement. We assume a 1GB main memory with an access latency of 350 cycles. The encryption/decryption engine models a 128-bit, 16-stage pipelined, AES engine with a total latency of 80-cycles. The MAC computation assumes HMAC [11], based on SHA-1 [8], with an 80-cycle latency [14]. The seed used for encryption is the concatenation of a 64-bit per-page LPID and a 7-bit per-block counter. On a counter cache block, a 64-bit LPID is co-located with 64 7-bit counters, occupying exactly a 64-byte block, and corresponding exactly to a 4KB memory page [33]. The default authentication code size is 128-bits.

The simulated machine runs Linux kernel that is dynamically instrumented with traps to implement SecureME. We add to the cost of an interrupt (e.g. a context switch) an extra 100 cycles needed to encrypt or decrypt the architecture register file.

Real machine configuration: To evaluate just the software components of SecureME, we run SPEC 2006 [28] benchmarks on a real machine (not a secure processor). We use the modified Linux kernel version 2.6.24 as our OS, running on a 2GHz Intel Pentium 4 processor. The processor has 32KB split L1 data and instruction caches, and a 1MB L2 cache.

Benchmarks. To evaluate SecureME, we use all (but one) C/C++ benchmarks from SPEC 2006 benchmark suite: *astar, bzip2, gcc, gobmk, h264ref, hmmer, lbm, libquantum, mcf, milc, namd, omnetpp, perlbench, povray, sjeng, soplex, sphinx,* and *xalancbmk*. Only one benchmark, *dealII*, is excluded, due to compilation error. The benchmarks are run on the simulated machine with reference input set. We intentionally avoid skipping any instructions since the initialization phase of the benchmark is where most page faults will occur. This stresses the performance of SecureME. Each benchmark is simulated for 2-billion *user-mode* instructions. The SPEC benchmarks do not involve many system calls or fork a process, hence to test these specific aspects, we wrote three microbenchmarks: *ReadBench* to test read system call performance, *WriteBench* to test write system call performance, and *COWBench* to test copy-on-write performance. We further present results for several real, system call intensive benchmarks. We use Linux *find* utility, disk usage utility, *du*, and I/O performance tool *iozone3*, with tests performed on a 4MB file.

For multiprogrammed evaluation on a CMP, we have constructed nine benchmark pairs from SPEC 2006, by pairing two benchmarks. We divide the benchmarks into two groups: those that are cache miss-intensive, measured as having an L2 miss rate of more than 20% when they run alone, and those that are not cache miss-intensive, measured as having an L2 miss rate of 20% or less when they run alone. We pair two cache miss-intensive benchmarks (*gcc_libquantum, gcc_mcf, mcf_libquantum*), one cache miss intensive benchmark with one non cache miss intensive benchmark (*gcc_hmmer, perl_gcc, perl_mcf*), and two non cache miss-intensive benchmarks (*perl_hmmer, soplex_perl, soplex _hmmer*). For each simulation, we use the reference input set and simulate for a combined number of 2 billion user-mode instructions.

7. EVALUATION

7.1 Microbenchmark Results

In order to evaluate the overhead of SecureME on system calls and copy-on-write events, we have constructed three microbenchmarks: ReadBench, WriteBench, and CopyBench. ReadBench (WriteBench) reads (writes) 1MB of data from (to) a file, at varying granularity at each call. Hence, a smaller granularity increases the system call frequencies. In CopyBench, we allocate an array of varying size, and fork a child process that writes to the entire array to force the

Table 1: Kernel instrumentation to implement SecureME code

SecureME Feature	Kernel Function Probed	Probe Type and Entity Probed	Description
Assigning HIDs	None	None	Process ID assigned by the OS used as HID
Maintaining CurHID	_switch_to	jprobe, function argument for next task	Kernel function called by scheduler to do a context switch with the task structure of the next task passed as an argument
Maintaining LPIDs	None		Kernel page structure changed to include a field for LPID
	_alloc_pages	kretprobe, structure representing the allocated page	Kernel function called to allocate a new page, if LPID is 0, new LPID assigned and added to permission domain, else permission domain checked to determine if access is allowed
	_free_pages	jprobe, function argument for structure of page to be freed	Kernel function called to free pages, resets the LPID to 0
Page Initialization	_alloc_pages	jprobe, function argument for flags for allocation	Flag value of _GFP_ZERO used by the kernel to initialize a page
Page COW	cow_user_page	jprobe, function argument for destination page	Kernel symbol was exported to allow probing
Page Re-encryption on Initialization and COW	None	None	Kernel function page_address was used to obtain the virtual address and initiate a read to the page requiring re-encryption. Closely models the re-encryption latency, as in AISE, a re-encryption requires a read of the page and changing the LPID associated with the page. The blocks will be naturally re-encrypted as and when they are evicted off the processor chip, using the new LPID for the page.
System Calls	System call code in kernel	jprobe, function arguments based on the system call	Encryption/decryption required is simulated by reading the buffer passed to the call, similar to Page Initialization and copy-on-write

OS's copy-on-write mechanism to cause page copying. The microbenchmarks only have system calls or page copying and have no computation at all, hence at small granularities, they represent the worst-case execution time overheads on SecureME. Figure 5 shows the execution time overheads for these microbenchmarks on SecureME (which includes secure processor substrate) over a system with no protection.

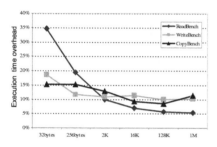

Figure 5: Execution time overhead breakdown for SecureME.

The figure shows that in the worst case (at the smallest granularity), ReadBench, WriteBench, and CopyBench incur execution time overheads of 35%, 19%, and 15%, which are significant but relatively low considering that there is no computation performed other than those of the system calls and page copying. The overheads decline steeply as the number of traps is reduced with the increase in granularities, reaching 5.3%, 10%, and 11% on 1MB case, respectively. We believe such overheads are manageable, and real-benchmarks suffering less than 1% overhead (0.98% for *find*, 0.6% for *du* and 0.28% for *iozone*) corroborate that.

7.2 Real Benchmark Evaluation Results

Figure 6(a) shows the execution time overheads of secure processor alone, and SecureME (including secure processor substrate) for SPEC 2006 applications. The overheads are over a system with no security protection at all. On average, SecureME adds an execution time overhead of 5.2%. Roughly 42% of those overheads come from the use of secure processor, with an average of 2.2%. Hence, on top of secure processor, SecureME adds only a small performance overhead of about 3%.

To analyze the source of these overheads, we profile the number of user-mode and kernel-mode instructions before and after SecureME is added, in Figure 6(b). The figure shows that while the number of user-mode instructions are largely unaffected, the number of kernel-mode instructions (due to the thin software layer of SecureME) may increase significantly. This is especially true for the two benchmarks that suffer from a large execution time overhead with SecureME (astar and bzip), and we observe a strong correlation between the increase in kernel mode instructions and SecureME execution time overheads for other benchmarks as well.

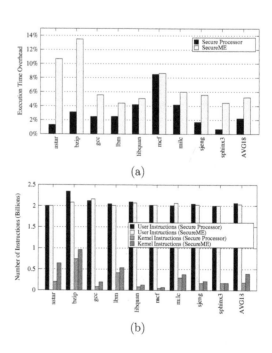

(a)

(b)

Figure 6: Execution time overheads of secure processor and SecureME (a), and the breakdown of kernel and user-mode instructions (b).

Figure 7(a) presents the L2 cache miss rate and Figure 7(b) presents the number of misses per thousand instruction or MPKI for SecureME compared to a system with only secure processor substrate. The figure shows that the L2 miss rates are either unchanged or slightly reduced in SecureME. The reason for this reduction in L2 miss rates can be seen in Figure 7(b), which shows that the new kernel instructions introduced by SecureME have much lower MPKIs compared to regular kernel instructions. This is because the kernel code and data in SecureME code exhibits better temporal locality than regular kernel code. This better temporal locality and the resulting lower MPKIs help mask the performance overheads that would result from higher number of kernel instructions. Note, however, that the significant increase in the number of kernel instructions can be attributed to the unusually high page fault rate of the benchmarks at the initialization phase of their execution (the first 2 billion instructions are simulated). Steady-state execution page fault rate would be significantly lower than this, and the overheads from SecureME will be significantly lower as well.

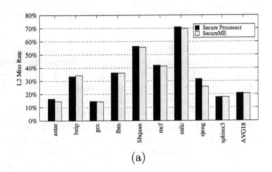

(a)

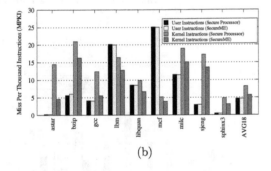

(b)

Figure 7: L2 cache miss rate (a), and L2 misses per thousand instructions (b), for secure processor vs. SecureME.

To understand the source of SecureME overheads better, Figure 8 breaks down the overheads into their components: permission table lookup, page initialization, page copying that results from copy-on-write, and secure interrupt handling. The figure shows that the permission table lookup is the dominant component of overheads (44.7% on average), with page initialization at second place (34.1% on average), followed by secure interrupt handling (20.44% on average), and copy on write that is incurred by the OS and not by the application (0.76% on average). The relatively-high overhead contribution due to permission table lookup is due to our current permission table implementation that must be linearly searched on a page fault. We believe a better implementation, such as a hash table, can improve performance significantly by eliminating linear searches.

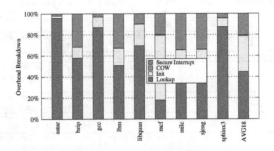

Figure 8: Execution time overhead breakdown for SecureME.

Figure 9 shows execution time overheads for multiprogrammed workload running on a dual core CMP. The figure shows an average overhead of 1.5% for secure processor alone and 3.4% for SecureME. The total overheads from SecureME for all nine workloads are below 5%.

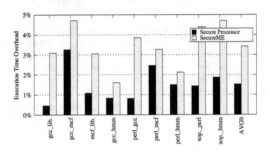

Figure 9: Evaluation results for multiprogrammed workload on a two-core CMP.

7.3 Sensitivity Studies

Figure 10(left) shows the average execution time overhead for single-benchmark workloads as well as multiprogrammed workloads on CMP when the L2 cache sizes vary from 512KB, 1MB to 2MB, over secure processor only. The figure shows that the overheads for SecureME are relatively unaffected by the cache size, and stay below 3.5% for all cases. Figure 10(right) shows the average execution time overheads when the latency of the AES engine is varied from 80 cycles (base case), to 160 cycles (2X) or 320 cycles (4X), which is almost equivalent to the memory latency. The overheads are not much affected.

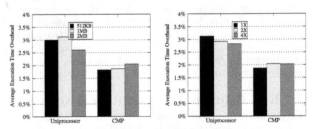

Figure 10: Sensitivity to Cache size (left), and Sensitivity to AES latency (right).

7.4 Other Evaluation Results

Real Machine Evaluation. We also measure SecureME dynamically instrumented Linux kernel on a real machine.

The processor (2GHz Intel Pentium 4) has no cryptographic engine, hence the overheads mainly come from the extra traps, code to lookup and update permission domain tables. All benchmarks are run five times using reference input set from the beginning to completion, and the average of five runs is taken. The execution time overheads we observe approximately match the simulation results, averaging 2.3% across the SPEC benchmarks, with individual benchmark overheads showing similar trends to those of simulation runs.

Memory Overheads. The permission table requires a storage of 286KB in the main memory on an average across all SPEC benchmarks, which is less than 0.03% of size of the 1GB physical memory. The theoretical maximum overhead for a 1GB physical memory and 2GB swap space on disk assuming 64bit LPID is 6MB ($\frac{3GB}{4KB} * 64bits = 6MB$), equivalent to 0.58% storage overhead.

Memory Allocation-Intensive Benchmarks. To stress SecureME, we also run eight memory allocation-intensive benchmarks that are often used in memory allocation studies [7, 15] (*boxed, cfrac, deltaBlue, espresso, lindsay, LRUsim, richards, and roboop*). Even for these benchmarks, the performance overheads of SecureME remains low, at 4% on average with a worst case overhead of 9.08% for deltaBlue.

8. CONCLUSIONS

We have proposed and presented SecureME, a new mechanism consisting of architecture support and a hypervisor, built on top of secure processor substrate, that provides secure computing environment on untrusted computing nodes. SecureME shows how an application can be protected from vulnerabilities of the hardware and the OS, through memory cloaking built on top of secure processor mechanisms. We show how memory cloaking can be integrated with counter-mode encryption and Merkle Tree integrity verification. SecureME also allows traditional inter-process communication to be supported. SecureME requires minimum changes to the OS (dynamically inserted annotation is sufficient) and to the application (only one instruction to get hardware identifier is needed). We show how spatio-temporal protection can be provided to guard against some attacks utilizing system calls, relying on just selective activation or deactivation of various components of the cryptographic engine of a secure processor. Finally, our evaluation results with single-benchmark and multiprogrammed workloads show that the execution time overheads of SecureME, inclusive of overheads from the secure processor substrate, is low on average (5.2%), and still acceptable even in the worst case (13.5%).

9. REFERENCES

[1] N. Q. Anh and Y. Takefuji. Towards a tamper-resistant kernel rootkit detector. In *SAC*, New York, NY, USA, 2007.
[2] W. Arbaugh, D. Farber, and J. Smith. A Secure and Reliable Bootstrap Architecture. In *ISSP*, 1997.
[3] P. Barham, B. Dragovic, K. Fraser, S. Hand, T. Harris, A. Ho, R. Neugebar, I. Pratt, and A. Warfield. Xen and the art of virtualization. In *SOSP*, New York, NY, 2003.
[4] D. Champagne and R. Lee. Scalable Architectural Support for Trusted Software. In *HPCA*, 2010.
[5] X. Chen, T. Garfinkel, E. C. Lewis, P. Subrahmanyam, C. A. Waldspurger, D. Boneh, J. Dwoskin, and D. R. K. Ports. Overshadow: A virtualization-based approach to retrofitting protection in commodity operating systems. In *ASPLOS*, Seattle, WA, USA, 2008.
[6] S. Chhabra, B. Rogers, and Y. Solihin. SHIELDSTRAP: Making Secure Processors Truly Secure. In *ICCD*, 2009.
[7] Emery D. Berger and Kathryn S. Mckinley and Robert D. Blumofe and Paul R. Wilson. Hoard: A scalable memory allocator for multithreaded applications. In *ASPLOS*, 2000.
[8] FIPS Publication 180-1. Secure Hash Standard. NIST, Federal Information Processing Standards, 1995.
[9] B. Gassend, G. Suh, D. Clarke, M. Dijk, and S. Devadas. Caches and Hash Trees for Efficient Memory Integrity Verification. In *HPCA*, 2003.
[10] T. C. Group. Trusted platform module (TPM) Main - Part 1 Design Principles.
[11] H. Krawczyk and M. Bellare and R. Caneti. HMAC: Keyed-hashing for message authentication. http://www.ietf.org/, 1997.
[12] IBM. IBM Extends Enhanced Data Security to Consumer Electronics Products. *http://domino.research.ibm.com/comm/pr.nsf/pages/ news.20060410_security.html*, April 2006.
[13] IBM Corporation. The Cell Broadband Engine processor security architecture. http://www-128.ibm.com/developerworks/power/library/pa-cellsecurity/, 2006.
[14] T. Kgil, L. Falk, and T. Mudge. ChipLock: Support for Secure Microarchitectures. In *Proc. of the Workshop on Architectural Support for Security and Anti-Virus*, Oct. 2004.
[15] M. Kharbutli, X. Jiang, Y. Solihin, G. Venkataramani, and M. Prvulovic. Comprehensively and efficiently protecting the heap. *SIGOPS Oper. Syst. Rev.*, 40(5):207–218, 2006.
[16] D. Lie, J. Mitchell, C. Thekkath, and M. Horowitz. Specifying and Verifying Hardware for Tamper-Resistant Software. In *ISSP*, 2003.
[17] D. Lie, C. Thekkath, M. Mitchell, P. Lincoln, D. Boneh, J. MItchell, and M. Horowitz. Architectural Support for Copy and Tamper Resistant Software. In *ASPLOS*, 2000.
[18] D. Lie, C. A. Thekkath, and M. Horowitz. Implementing an untrusted operating system on trusted hardware. In *SOSP*, 2003.
[19] P. S. Magnusson, M. Christensson, J. Eskilson, D. Forsgren, G. Hallberg, J. Hogberg, F. Larsson, A. Moestedt, and B. Werner. Simics: A Full System Simulation Platform. *IEEE Computer Society*, 35(2):50–58, 2002.
[20] J. M. McCune, B. J. Parno, A. Perrig, M. K. Reiter, and H. Isozaki. Flicker: an execution infrastructure for tcb minimization. In *Eurosys*, Glasgow, Scotland UK, 2008.
[21] Redhat. Gaining insight into the Linux kernel with kprobes. *http://www.redhat.com/magazine/005mar05/features/kprobes/*, 2005.
[22] B. Rogers, S. Chhabra, Y. Solihin, and M. Prvulovic. Using Address Independent Seed Encryption and Bonsai Merkle Trees to Make Secure Processors OS- and Performance-Friendly. In *MICRO*, 2007.
[23] B. Rogers, Y. Solihin, and M. Prvulovic. Efficient Data Protection for Distributed Shared Memory Multiprocessors. In *PACT*, 2006.
[24] A. Seshadri, M. Luk, N. Qu, and A. Perrig. Secvisor: a tiny hypervisor to provide lifetime kernel code integrity for commodity oses. In *SOSP*, 2007.
[25] W. Shi and H.-H. Lee. Authentication Control Point and Its Implications for Secure Processor Design. In *MICRO*, 2006.
[26] W. Shi, H.-H. Lee, M. Ghosh, and C. Lu. Architectural Support for High Speed Protection of Memory Integrity and Confidentiality in Multiprocessor Systems. In *PACT*, 2004.
[27] W. Shi, H.-H. Lee, M. Ghosh, C. Lu, and A. Boldyreva. High Efficiency Counter Mode Security Architecture via Prediction and Precomputation. In *ISCA*, 2005.
[28] Standard Performance Evaluation Corporation. http://www. spec.org, 2006.
[29] G. Suh, D. Clarke, B. Gassend, M. van Dijk, and S. Devadas. AEGIS: Architecture for Tamper-Evident and Tamper-Resistant Processing. In *ICS*, 2003.
[30] G. Suh, D. Clarke, B. Gassend, M. van Dijk, and S. Devadas. Efficient Memory Integrity Verification and Encryption for Secure Processor. In *MICRO*, 2003.
[31] R. Ta-min, L. Litty, and D. Lie. Splitting interfaces: Making trust between applications and operating systems configurable. In *OSDI*, 2006.
[32] C. A. Waldspurger. Memory resource management in vmware esx server. *SIGOPS Operating Systems Review*, 36(SI):181–194, 2002.
[33] C. Yan, B. Rogers, D. Englender, Y. Solihin, and M. Prvulovic. Improving Cost, Performance, and Security of Memory Encryption and Authentication. In *ISCA*, 2006.
[34] J. Yang and K. G. Shin. Using hypervisor to provide data secrecy for user applications on a per-page basis. In *VEE*, 2008.
[35] J. Yang, Y. Zhang, and L. Gao. Fast Secure Processor for Inhibiting Software Piracy and Tampering. In *MICRO*, 2003.
[36] Y. Zhang, L. Gao, J. Yang, X. Zhang, and R. Gupta. SENSS: Security Enhancement to Symmetric Shared Memory Multiprocessors. In *HPCA*, 2005.

Processing Data Streams with Hard Real-time Constraints on Heterogeneous Systems

Uri Verner
uriv@cs.technion.ac.il

Assaf Schuster
assaf@cs.technion.ac.il

Mark Silberstein
marks@cs.technion.ac.il

Computer Science Department, Technion, Israel

ABSTRACT

Data stream processing applications such as stock exchange data analysis, VoIP streaming, and sensor data processing pose two conflicting challenges: short per-stream latency – to satisfy the milliseconds-long, hard real-time constraints of each stream, and high throughput – to enable efficient processing of as many streams as possible. High-throughput programmable accelerators such as modern GPUs hold high potential to speed up the computations. However, their use for hard real-time stream processing is complicated by slow communications with CPUs, variable throughput changing non-linearly with the input size, and weak consistency of their local memory with respect to CPU accesses. Furthermore, their coarse grain hardware scheduler renders them unsuitable for unbalanced multi-stream workloads.

We present a general, efficient and practical algorithm for hard real-time stream scheduling in heterogeneous systems. The algorithm assigns incoming streams of different rates and deadlines to CPUs and accelerators. By employing novel stream schedulability criteria for accelerators, the algorithm finds the assignment which simultaneously satisfies the aggregate throughput requirements of all the streams and the deadline constraint of each stream alone.

Using the AES-CBC encryption kernel, we experimented extensively on thousands of streams with realistic rate and deadline distributions. Our framework outperformed the alternative methods by allowing 50% more streams to be processed with provably deadline-compliant execution even for deadlines as short as tens milliseconds. Overall, the combined GPU-CPU execution allows for up to 4-fold throughput increase over highly-optimized multi-threaded CPU-only implementations.

Categories and Subject Descriptors

C.1.3 [**Other Architecture Styles**]: Heterogeneous (hybrid) systems

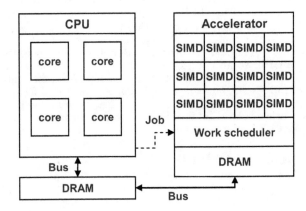

Figure 1: A model of a heterogeneous system composed of a CPU and an accelerator

General Terms

Management, Performance

Keywords

Accelerator, data streams, hard real-time, scheduling

1. INTRODUCTION

Stream processing is one of the most difficult problems from the algorithmic and system design perspectives. This is because the data processing rate should not fall behind the aggregate throughput of arriving data streams, otherwise leading to buffer explosion or packet loss. *Stateful* processing, which is the focus of this work, also requires the previous processing results to be available for computations on newly arrived data.

Even more challenging is the problem of *hard real-time stream processing*. Many life-critical and latency-sensitive applications such as medical data processing, traffic control, and stock exchange monitoring require strict performance guarantees to be satisfied along with the common requirement of sufficient overall system throughput. In such applications, each stream specifies its *deadline*, which restricts the maximum time arrived data may stay in the system.

The deadline requirement fundamentally changes the system design space, rendering throughput-optimized stream processing techniques inappropriate for several reasons. First, tight deadlines may prevent computations from being distributed across multiple computers because of unpredictable network delay. Furthermore, *schedulability criteria* must be devised in order to predetermine whether a given set of streams can be processed without violating their deadline requirements and exceeding the aggregate system throughput. Runtime predictions must thus take into account every aspect of the processing pipeline. A precise and detailed performance model is therefore crucial. The runtime prediction problem, hard in the general case, is even more challenging here: to allow deadline-compliant processing, the predictions must be conservative, in conflict with the goal of higher aggregate throughput.

High performance, massively parallel accelerators such as GPUs are natural candidates for speeding up multiple data stream processing. However, because of their unique architectural characteristics their use in this context is not straightforward, and becomes complicated for hard real-time workloads.

- **Low per-thread performance.** Accelerators are optimized for throughput. They multiplex thousands of lightweight threads on a few SIMD cores, thereby trading single-thread performance for higher throughput. Furthermore, they are connected to a CPU via a bus with limited throughput and high latency. Data-parallel processing is inapplicable to single streams because of the stateful processing requirement. Thus, per-stream accelerator performance may be much lower than that of a CPU, which essentially precludes streams with tight deadlines from being processed on an accelerator.
- **Weak inter-device memory model.** Accelerators cannot access the main CPU memory. They have their own separate memory, where the input and output data are staged by a CPU prior to and after execution respectively. No consistency is guaranteed if that memory is accessed by a CPU while the accelerator is performing computations. Consequently, streaming the input dynamically from a CPU is not possible; rather, a bulk of data from multiple streams must be *batched* together for non-preemptive, finite-time processing[1].
- **Non-linear throughput scaling.** For better hardware utilization, accelerators require many concurrently active threads. Thus, effective throughput depends non-linearly on the number of concurrently processed streams, making run-time prediction difficult.

Previous works on hard real-time processing [3, 7, 20, 21, 2] dealt with homogeneous, multiprocessor, CPU-only systems and cannot be directly applied here. They schedule the input streams assuming only one stream being processed by each processor at any instant, whereas the accelerator's advantage is in the concurrent processing of multiple streams.

Contribution. We designed a framework for hard real-time stateful processing of multiple streams on heterogeneous platforms with multiple CPUs and a single accelerator. The framework employs the CPUs together with the accelerator, thus reaping the benefits of fast single-stream processing of a CPU and high-throughput multi-stream performance of an accelerator. To the best of our knowledge, this is the first time accelerators are used in hard real-time computations.

The core of the framework is an algorithm for scheduling of input streams to processors that is deadline-compliant

and allows sufficient aggregate throughput. The algorithm partitions the streams into two subsets, one for processing by the accelerator, and the other for all the available CPUs. A user-supplied schedulability criterion validates that each subset is schedulable. Non-linear throughput scaling in accelerators makes this partitioning problem computationally hard in general, as it requires every two subsets of streams to be tested for schedulability. The exact solution requires exhaustive search in an exponential space of subsets and does not scale beyond a few input streams.

We develop a fast polynomial-time heuristic for scheduling thousands of streams. Each stream is represented using its deadline and rate properties as a point in the two-dimensional (rate-deadline) space. The heuristic finds a rectangle in this space, so that all the streams with their respective points in the rectangle are schedulable on the accelerator, and the rest are schedulable on the CPUs. We show that this simple heuristic does, in fact, optimize many of the considerations above.

We implement and evaluate our stream processing framework by using it to accelerate AES-CBC encryption of multiple streams on NVIDIA GPUs. AES is widely used in the hard real time context. As it is integral to encrypted data processing, AES must meet hard real time constraints in systems where hard deadlines are part of Service Level Agreements (SLAs). For instance, it is a part of the SSL and IPSEC used in Web and VPN gateways. Other examples include encrypted VoIP, IPTV, and media streaming services.

AES framework is universally applicable to a large family of streaming workloads fully characterized by the rate and deadline parameters, and whose data processing time is determined by size (rather than content). Besides AES-CBC, additional applications in this family include SVD, digital noise filters, convolutions, FFT, and threshold-crossing detection.

Unlike the previous works on AES encryption on GPUs [17, 9, 10], AES-CBC encryption is stateful and does not permit independent processing of different data blocks of the same stream. This constraint necessitates multiple streams with different rates to be scheduled concurrently on a GPU, thereby creating a highly unbalanced workload that leads to much lower throughput. We describe a method for the static balancing of multiple streams that achieves high GPU throughput even for harshly unbalanced workloads, and then develop the schedulability criterion for AES-CBC processing on a GPU, used in conjunction with the scheduling algorithm described above.

We perform extensive experiments on a variety of inputs with thousands of streams, using exponential and normal distributions of rates and deadlines. The framework achieves a maximum throughput of 13 Gbit/sec even with deadlines as short as 50ms while processing 12,000 streams. We show that our algorithm achieves up to 50% higher throughput than alternatives that partition the streams according to rate or deadline alone. Overall, adding a single GPU to a quadcore machine allows 4-fold throughput improvement over highly optimized CPU-only execution.

---

[1] NVIDIA GPUs enable dedicated write-shared memory regions in the CPU memory, but it has low bandwidth and high access latency.

2. MODEL

2.1 Application model

A real-time data stream s is described by a tuple $O\langle r,d\rangle$, where r denotes the stream rate, and d denotes the processing deadline. Each data item that arrives at time t must be processed to completion by time $t+d$. The stream rates and deadlines may differ for different streams, and are constant.

We transform a data stream $s:\langle r,d\rangle$ into a stream of *jobs*, where each job is created by collecting data items from the stream s during an interval of time I. The interval I is determined as a part of the algorithm, as discussed later. After transformation, every stream is represented as an infinite sequence of jobs $J = \{J^0, J^1, J^2...\}$ arriving at times $I, 2I, 3I, ...$. Job J^k is described by a tuple $\langle w_k, d_k\rangle$, where $w_k = r \cdot I$ is the amount of work – or, the number of data items – to be processed by that job, and $d_k = kI + d$ is the deadline of the job.

Job J^{i+1} cannot be processed until the processing of J^i is complete; stateful execution implies that parallel processing of different jobs of the same stream is impossible. Such data dependency between subsequent jobs of the same stream forces pipelined processing of that stream. Namely, at every given moment, one job of a stream is being processed while the data for the next one is being collected.

The system receives a set S containing multiple independent streams, where each stream $s_i : \langle r_i, d_i\rangle \in S$ has its own rate and deadline. Jobs of different streams can be processed concurrently. For simplicity we assume a constant number of streams $|S|$.

Dynamic inputs can in fact be treated by activating our methods periodically or in response to changes in the system status. Consequently, when arrival rates change steadily over time, the methods developed in this paper provide an adequate solution. However, when arrival rates change drastically and unpredictably, light-weight load balancing techniques must be invoked on-the-fly in order to utilize the accelerator; these are beyond the scope of this work.

2.2 Hardware model

We focus on heterogeneous systems composed of different types of *computing units (CU)*: general-purpose processors (CPUs) and accelerators with multiple SIMD cores, as presented in Figure 1. A CPU initiates the execution of the accelerator by invoking a subroutine, called *kernel*, comprising a batch of jobs. The accelerator processes one batch at a time in a non-preemptive manner. Jobs in the batch are scheduled on the SIMD cores by the hardware scheduler. We have very limited information and no control over how these jobs are actually scheduled. We assume that the scheduler strives to maximize accelerator throughput.

An accelerator has a separate memory, to which all the data must be copied by a CPU prior to kernel execution. Data transfers are carried out via an external bus. A CPU and an accelerator implement the release consistency memory model, whereby the data transferred to and from an accelerator during kernel execution may be inconsistent with that observed by the running kernel. Consistency is enforced only at the kernel boundaries. We develop an algorithm for a system with multiple CPUs and a single accelerator. Extending to multiple accelerators is a subject of the future work.

3. SCHEDULING OF MULTIPLE STREAMS

We define the scheduling problem as follows: Given a set of input streams $\{s_i : \langle r_i, d_i\rangle\}$, each with its own rate r_i and deadline d_i, find the assignment of streams to CUs, s.t. the obtained total processing throughput $T \geq \sum_i r_i$, and no stream misses its deadline. This problem has an optimal algorithm for a uniprocessor CPU [16]; that is, it produces a valid schedule for every feasible system. However, scheduling jobs with arbitrary deadlines on multiprocessor systems is a hard, exponential problem [20]. The existing CPU-only scheduling approaches [20, 16, 3] cannot be applied in our setup because they schedule jobs one- or a-few-at-a-time. In contrast, accelerators require batches of thousands jobs to be packed together, raising the question of how to select those to be executed together so that all of them comply with their respective deadlines.

Two main approaches are known for scheduling real-time streams on multiple CUs: dynamic global scheduling and static partitioning [21]. In global scheduling, idle processors are dynamically assigned the highest priority job available for execution. This approach is not practical in our system for two reasons:

1. The accelerator's weak memory consistency makes it impossible to push new input data from a CPU to a running kernel. Thus, the batch of jobs being executed by an accelerator must be completed before a new batch can be started. Hence, the new batch for the accelerator should be statically created in advance on a CPU, under the constraint of timely completion of all jobs in the batch. In fact, proper batch creation is the main focus of this work.
2. The stream state is carried from one job in a stream to the next job of the same stream. Slow communication between the CPU and the accelerator makes the overhead of moving jobs of the same stream between CUs too high. Furthermore, since a steady state is assumed, migration can be avoided with proper batch creation.

These considerations led us to choose the static partitioning method where multiple streams are batched together and statically assigned to a particular CU. The main challenge is to select the streams for the batch to achieve the required throughput under the deadline constraints.

3.1 Batch execution

Accelerator execution is performed in batches of jobs. Batch execution time depends on parameters such as the number of jobs, distribution of job sizes, and the total amount of work to be processed. Our design for efficient job batching was guided by the following principles.

1. Batch as many jobs as are ready to be executed. Batches with many independent jobs have higher parallelism and provide more opportunities for throughput optimization by the hardware scheduler.
2. For every job, aggregate as much data as possible (this means aggregate as long as possible). This is because batch invocation on an accelerator incurs some overhead which is better amortized when the job is large. Moreover, transferring larger bulks of data between an accelerator and a CPU improves the transfer throughput. Aggregation time is limited by the deadlines of the jobs in the batch. More precisely, the deadline for a batch execution is the earliest deadline of any of the jobs in it.

Distribution of job sizes in a batch affects the load balancing on the accelerator. The longest job puts a lower bound on the execution time of the whole batch. Suppose w_i is the amount of work in job i. Then, if $\sum_i w_i < \max_i w_i \cdot C$ for a batch $\{\langle w_i, d_i \rangle\}$ and an accelerator with C cores, accelerator utilization is at most $\frac{\sum_i w_i}{\max_i w_i \cdot C}$. The equation shows that for a given batch size $\sum_i w_i$, the load cannot be efficiently balanced if the amount of work in one job greatly exceeds that of other jobs. We use this observation and the previous principles to batch jobs in a way that minimizes their overall execution time, while all batches complete on time.

3.2 Rectangle method

A set of jobs is called *schedulable* on a CU if there exists a schedule where no stream misses its deadline and job dependencies are enforced (see Section 2.1). We aim to find an assignment of streams to CUs such that the set of jobs assigned to each device is schedulable on it. We call this a *schedulable assignment*. Schedulability testing in our setup is equivalent to schedulability testing of synchronous periodic jobs, which is coNP-Hard even on a uniprocessor [8].

Due to the different constraints imposed by the different components, it makes sense to partition the streams into two sets: one for the homogeneous collection of CPUs and another for the accelerator. Each partition is then tested for schedulability on the target devices: if both tests return positive then the assignment is accepted as a *schedulable partition*. The streams assigned to the CPUs are scheduled using known algorithms for homogeneous multiprocessor systems. In turn, those assigned to the accelerator are batched, tested for schedulability using the schedulability criterion (see Section 3.3), and then scheduled using the accelerator's hardware scheduler. Unfortunately, even with two partitions, the search space is exponential in the number of streams, which makes exhaustive search impractical. We thus develop a heuristic that reduces the number of tested partitions to polynomial in the number of streams.

An accelerator poses several harsh constraints on its workload if the jobs are to be schedulable. It is thus more efficient to prune first the jobs which are not schedulable on the accelerator. Most importantly, invoking the accelerator incurs overhead, which, coupled with the latency of data transfers to and from the accelerator's memory, determine a lower bound on job processing time. Thus, any job whose deadline is below this lower bound cannot be processed on the accelerator and should be removed from its partition.

We next consider the job with the shortest deadline in the batch of jobs in the accelerator's partition. Because the batch completes as a whole, this job effectively determines the deadline for all the jobs in the batch. We will denote by d_{low} the threshold for the shortest deadline of jobs assigned to the accelerator's partition. By lowering d_{low} we restrict the maximum execution time of a batch, thus effectively decreasing the number of jobs that can be assigned to the accelerator. By increasing d_{low} we increase this number, with the penalty of having more short deadline jobs assigned to the CPUs.

A simple heuristic is thus to test all partitions induced by d_{low}, where all jobs with the deadlines above d_{low} are assigned to the accelerator's partition, and all the rest allocated to the CPUs. This heuristic exhaustively tests all the created partitions for different values of d_{low}. It may fail, however, to find a schedulable partition for inputs with

too many short-deadline jobs, even if one exists. For such a workload, decreasing d_{low} would result in too tight a deadline for the accelerator, while increasing d_{low} would overwhelm the CPUs with too many short-deadline jobs. A possible solution is to move a few longer-deadline jobs to the CPUs' partition, thereby decreasing the load on the accelerator and allowing it to assist the CPUs in handling shorter-deadline jobs. The longer-deadline jobs impose no extra burden on CPU scheduling, as short-deadline jobs would do. Thus, a natural extension to a single threshold heuristic is to add an upper bound d_{high} to limit the deadlines for jobs assigned to the accelerator's partition.

Both heuristics, however, ignore the amount of work per job. Consequently, the accelerator may be assigned a highly unbalanced workload, which would seriously decrease its throughput (as explained in section 3.1), thus rendering the partition not schedulable. A reasonable approach to better load balancing is to remove work-intensive jobs (data aggregated from streams of high rate) from the accelerator's partition. The increased load on the CPUs can be compensated by moving jobs with shorter deadlines and lower rates to the accelerator, whose overall throughput would thus increase. Two other thresholds are thus introduced: r_{high} and r_{low}, which set an upper (lower) bound on the amount of work for jobs assigned to the accelerator's partition.

We end up with a heuristic for partitioning streams to CUs, which we call the *Rectangle method*. It considers partitions in which streams within a certain range of rates and deadlines are assigned to the accelerator, and the rest to the CPUs. Visually, the selected streams can be represented as a rectangle in the rate-deadline space. For example, Figure 2 shows a partition of 10,000 streams with normally distributed rates and deadlines. Each dot represents a stream. All streams inside the black rectangle are assigned to the accelerator, while the others are assigned to the CPUs. We see that a stream is assigned to the accelerator if its rate is in the range [0bps,1.8Mbps] and its deadline is in the range [27ms,81ms].

The Rectangle method tests the schedulability of all rectangles. The number of rectangles in an $n \times n$ space is $\left(\frac{n(n-1)}{2}\right)^2 = O\left(n^4\right)$. We reduce the number of tested partitions to $O\left(n^2 \lg n\right)$, first, by setting the lower rate bound r_{low} to 0 (since slower streams improve accelerator utilization), and second, by testing $O(\lg n)$ upper rate bounds r_{high} for each pair of deadline bounds. Correctness is implied by the following property of schedulability: If a set of streams is schedulable on the accelerator, its sub-sets are schedulable as well. Similarly, if it is not schedulable, then no containing set is schedulable. Using binary search, it is enough to test $O(\lg n)$ upper bounds on rate in order to find a schedulable assignment, if one exists for the given pair of deadline bounds. A more advanced algorithm allows for $O(n^2)$ complexity but for simplicity we describe the slower one. Further details are omitted for lack of space.

This algorithm produces deadline-compliant schedules, otherwise marking the input as unschedulable. Following existing methods for real-time scheduling, it assumes perfect runtime prediction by the performance model [21, 8, 2]. However, to compensate for imprecision, a safety margin is taken, which ensures 100% precision at the expense of slight degradation in schedulable throughput. Furthermore, out of all the schedulable partitions (rectangles), we choose the one

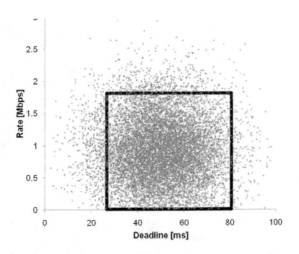

Figure 2: A partition of N=10K data streams (represented by dots) with generation parameters: normally distributed rate, $\mu_R = 1\,Mbps$, $\sigma_R = 0.5\,Mbps$; normally distributed deadline, $\mu_D = 50\,ms$, $\sigma_D = 15\,ms$. Streams within the rectangle are assigned to the accelerator.

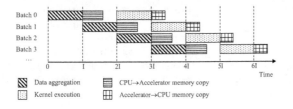

Figure 3: Batches are processed in a four-stage pipeline

for which the performance model predicts the largest safety (error) margin.

3.3 Batch scheduling and schedulability

Job are scheduled on the accelerator in batches. Every batch goes through a four stage pipeline: data aggregation, data transfer to local memory on accelerator, kernel execution, transfer of results to main memory. These stages are illustrated in Figure 3. Processing must be complete before any job deadline is missed, i.e., before the earliest deadline of any job in the batch. One batching guideline(see subsection 3.1) is to aggregate data for the jobs as long as possible, to reduce batching overhead. Therefore, the best aggregation time is $\frac{d_{min}}{4}$, where $d_{min} = \min_i d_i$ for a set of streams $\{\langle r_i, d_i \rangle\}$ assigned to the accelerator. The system produces a new batch to the pipeline every $\frac{d_{min}}{4}$ time with all data accumulated since the previous batch. A batch of jobs will be schedulable if no stage of the pipeline exceeds $\frac{d_{min}}{4}$ time during its processing. Given a batch of jobs, we rely on an accelerator performance model to calculate the length of each pipeline stage. Efficient methods for schedulability of the CPUs are presented in [6, 7, 2].

4. CASE STUDY: CPU/GPU SYSTEM

A GPU is a processor with multiple processing elements adjusted for graphics acceleration. Each processing element,

or *streaming multiprocessor* (SM), is a SIMD processor with several arithmetic units, capable of simultaneous execution of an instruction on a vector of operands. Modern GPUs are fully programmable many-core devices, supported by programming models, such as CUDA and OpenCL, and compatible with general-purpose programming. In this work, we use a system with a multi-core CPU and a CUDA-enabled GPU accelerator. The application running on the CPU (*host*) invokes the GPU (*device*) by calling GPU methods (*kernels*). Kernel calls are asynchronous; they return immediately.

A GPU has its own local memory accessible to a CPU via explicit data transfer operations. The kernel input and output are transferred from CPU memory over a PCI-E bus prior to the kernel execution, possibly overlapped with the kernel processing another data set. The GPU memory consistency model does not guarantee that the CPU updates of GPU memory will be visible to the running GPU kernel. This restriction prevents continuous data streaming from a CPU to a running GPU kernel. Kernel execution must terminate and be invoked again in order to read new data.

4.1 GPU execution model

When a kernel is called, multiple threads are invoked on the GPU. A hardware scheduler schedules the threads to the SMs during kernel execution.

Scheduling is hierarchical. The minimum schedulable unit is a *warp*, a group of 32 threads in CUDA. Each warp is assigned to an SM and executed on it in SIMD fashion. When a warp executes a high-latency command, such as accessing the off-chip memory, the scheduler attempts to hide this latency by executing other warps that are scheduled to this SM and are ready to be executed.

Warps are grouped into *thread-blocks*. Upon kernel invocation, a queue of thread blocks is created. A global GPU scheduler then distributes full thread-blocks between SMs, and each SM then internally schedules its warps. Multiple thread blocks can be concurrently assigned to the same SM, thereby providing more opportunities for latency hiding. When all threads of the thread block are complete, the global scheduler assigns an unscheduled thread block from the queue. The execution parameters – the number of thread-blocks and the number of threads in a thread-block – are specified at runtime for every kernel invocation. In our scenario, jobs are executed on the GPU in batches and equally partitioned between thread-blocks. Each job is processed by one or more CUDA threads in the same thread block.

4.2 Batch execution on a GPU

4.2.1 GPU load balancing

A GPU attains the best performance for massively parallel SPMD programs, with all the threads having the same execution path and runtime. Multi-stream processing, however, may deviate from this pattern. The difference in the rates of different streams results in greatly varying job sizes in the same thread block and degraded performance. Figure 4 shows that kernels that processed jobs with a wide spectrum of sizes took 48% more time to process than kernels that processed equal-size jobs with the same total amount of work.

Threads that execute different jobs may follow different

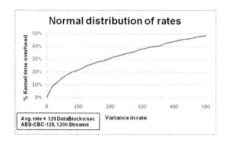

Figure 4: Rate variance overhead

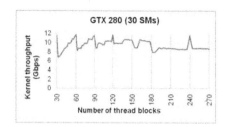

Figure 5: Choosing the number of thread-blocks. Workload: AES-CBC encryption of 3840 data streams with equal rates.

$$U(x) = \min\left(\frac{x}{0.004898[x]^2 + 0.005148[x] + 49.62}, 1\right)$$

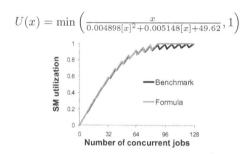

Figure 6: Non-linear SM utilization

execution paths (*diverge*), resulting in serialized execution. Thus, limited fine-grain parallelism per job may require assigning several jobs to the same warp, where thread divergence and load imbalance might affect performance. We found, however, very little divergence for data stream processing, due to the periodicity of data stream functions. But load imbalance between the threads of a warp is detrimental to performance since the warp execution time is dominated by the longest job.

The distribution of jobs among warps and thread blocks is crucial to kernel performance. We use the following simple algorithm to increase GPU utilization.

1. Create warps with jobs of similar size;
2. Partition warps to M bins such that total job size in each bin is about the same[2], where M is the number of SMs;
3. Assign the warps in each of the M bins to thread-blocks, such that warps with similar size are assigned to the same block.

Since the thread-blocks are scheduled by the hardware, not all thread-blocks created from a single bin can be guaranteed to execute on the same SM. Our approach attempts to combine good latency hiding, by creating thread-blocks that process jobs of similar size, with balanced overall load on the SMs, by creating equally-sized bins. Our experience shows that the hardware scheduler can leverage these benefits to find an optimal schedule for the thread-blocks. Experimentally, this approach provides better throughput than creating thread-blocks with equal total job size and with maximally-similar job size.

Existing dynamic job scheduling methods for GPU, e.g. [4, 5], use software load balancing mechanisms, such as job queues. The required synchronization incurs large overhead, especially for short jobs. These methods can be used in addition to ours since our method is offline.

4.2.2 Selecting kernel execution parameters

The total number of thread blocks plays an important role in GPU performance. Figure 5 shows the throughput of an AES-CBC encryption kernel as a function of the number of thread-blocks on a GPU with 30 SMs. We see that choosing the number of thread-blocks as a multiple of the number of SMs maximizes utilization of the cores, whereas other choices cause up to 42% performance loss. Our threads-per-block choice satisfies two conditions: (1) the number of threads per block is maximized to allow better SM utiliza-

tion; (2) the total number of thread blocks is a multiple of the number of SMs to balance the load between them.

4.3 GPU empirical performance model

The GPU performance model, or more precisely, its schedulability function (Section 3.3), is used by our partitioning algorithm to estimate the kernel time for processing a batch of jobs. In the model we assume that the jobs in a given batch are distributed among the SMs so that each SM is assigned the same number of jobs, regardless of job size. Such distribution is equivalent to a random one which ignores load balancing considerations. Hence the runtime estimate for this distribution gives us an upper bound on the expected runtime for a distribution which is optimized for load balancing. The problem is thus reduced to estimating the runtime of the jobs on a single SM, and taking the longest one among the SMs as the estimate of the runtime of the whole batch on a GPU.

We now consider execution of jobs on an SM. For convenience, we express the performance of an SM as utilization: the fraction of the maximum throughput achievable by a single SM. The maximum throughput for a given GPU stream processing kernel can be easily obtained by measuring the throughput of that kernel on tens of thousands of identical jobs.

We call *a utilization function* the relation describing the SM utilization as a function of the number of jobs invoked on that SM. The utilization function can be calculated by means of a lookup table generated by benchmarking a GPU kernel for different numbers of jobs. Figure 6 demonstrates the utilization function for the AES-CBC kernel with 4 threads per data stream (we also show a best-fitting quadratic curve for that function). The saw-like form of this function is due to the execution of multiple jobs in a single warp. Thus, in Figure 6, $[x]$ is the rounding of the number of jobs (x) to the closest multiple of the number of jobs per warp that is higher than or equal to x.

---

[2]This is a version of the PARTITION problem which is NP-Complete. We use a popular greedy algorithm which provides $4/3 - approximation$ to the optimal solution.

5. EVALUATION

In this section we evaluate our framework using state-of-the-art hardware on thousands of streams.

5.1 Experimental platform

Our platform was an Intel Core2 Quad 2.33Ghz CPU and a NVIDIA GeForce GTX 285 GPU card. The GPU has thirty 8-way SIMD cores and is connected to the main board by a 3GB/s PCI-E bus.

The workload is based on the AES-CBC data stream, stateful encryption application. The AES 128 bit symmetric block cipher is a standard algorithm for encryption, considered safe, and widely used for secure connections and classified information transfers (e.g., SSL). Several modes of operation exist for block ciphers. CBC is the most common – it enforces sequential encryption of data blocks by passing the encryption result of one block as the input for the encryption of the following block.

The CPU implementation is Crypto++ 5.6.0 open-source cryptographic library with machine-dependent assembly-level optimizations and support for SSE2 instructions. For the GPU we developed a CUDA-based multiple stream execution of AES. The implementation uses a parallel version of AES, in which every block is processed by four threads concurrently. Streaming data is simulated by an Input Generator that periodically generates random input for each data stream according to its preset rate. During the simulation we dedicate one CPU to the input generator and another to control the GPU execution. Data is processed on two CPU cores and the GPU as an accelerator.

We compare the Rectangle method with two baseline techniques: *MinRate,* which attempts to optimize the scheduling of streams with respect to their rates, and *MaxDeadline,* which does the same with respect to the deadlines. In MinRate streams are sorted by rate in non-increasing order $\{s_i : \langle r_i, d_i \rangle\}$. The first k streams (those with the highest rates) are assigned to the CPU and all others to the GPU, where k satisfies $\sum_{i=1}^{k} r_i \leq \tau_{CPU} \leq \sum_{i=1}^{k+1} r_i$, and τ_{CPU} is CPU throughput. In MaxDeadline streams are sorted by deadline in non-decreasing order, so that the CPU is assigned the streams with the shortest deadlines up to its capacity τ_{CPU}, and the GPU processes the rest.

5.2 Setting parameters

System throughput was measured as the highest total processing rate with all the data processed on time. We use the following notations:

N	Number of streams
R_{tot}	Total stream rate (Gbps)
μ_R, μ_D	Average stream rate (Mbps), deadline (ms)
σ_R, σ_D	Standard deviation of rate (Mbps), deadline (ms)
Δ_R, Δ_D	Rate and deadline distribution functions

In the experiments we used Exponential (Exp) and Normal (Norm) distribution functions for rate and deadline. Such workloads are common in data streaming applications. To avoid generating extremely high or low values, we limited generated figures to $[0.1\mu, 30\mu]$ for the exponential distribution, and to $[0.002\mu, 100\mu]$ for the normal distribution, where μ denotes the average distribution value. Figure 2 displays an example of a randomly generated workload with the following parameters: $N = 10K$, $\Delta_R = \Delta_D = Norm$, $\mu_R = 1\,Mbps$, $\sigma_R = 0.5\,Mbps$, $\mu_D = 50\,ms$, $\sigma_D = 15\,ms$.

5.3 Results

We tested the efficiency of the Rectangle method on workloads with different distributions of stream rates and deadlines in three experiments. Each workload consisted of $N = 12,000$ streams. Figure 7 shows results of experiments where the average deadline is long ($\mu_D = 500\,ms$), the standard deviation of the rate is high, and the distribution is exponential. In this experiment, the throughput of the Rectangle method was 30% higher than that of MaxDeadline and similar to that of MinRate. MaxDeadline suffered from insufficient load balancing on the GPU, caused by simultaneous processing of streams with a wide range of rates. MinRate was effective because all deadlines were long, resulting in GPU processing of big batches.

Figure 8 presents the performance of processing input with shorter average deadlines ($\mu_D = 50\,ms$). The workloads in this experiment are more time constrained, causing lower throughput in all three scheduling methods. MaxDeadline failed to produce a valid schedule for any value of the total rate larger than $2\,Gbps$, because CPU was assigned more short-deadline streams it could handle. For both MaxDeadline and MinRate, GPU throughput was limited by $r_{tot} \leq 5\,Gbps$. For MaxDeadline, the reason is inefficient load balancing due to high-rate streams, whereas for MinRate, the limiting factor is the batch scheduling overhead created by short-deadline streams. In comparison, the Rectangle method provides up to $7\,Gbps$ throughput by finding the correct balance between rate and deadline.

Figure 9 presents results of experiments using normal distribution for rates and deadlines. Here we allow generation of values within a higher range, as described in section 5.2. However, values are closer to μ on average due to lower variance. The shorter deadlines greatly reduce the throughput of MinRate, which makes no effort to avoid assigning short-deadline streams to the GPU. In contrast, MaxDeadline assigns these streams to the CPU, and benefits from a lower variance of stream rate than in the previous experiments. However, for low values of total rate, MaxDeadline puts more short-deadline streams than it can handle.

The number of processed data streams defines the amount of parallelism in the workload. We tested the efficiency of our method for $4K$ streams, where the GPU is underutilized because there are not enough jobs that can execute in parallel. Figure 10 shows that the Rectangle method outperformed the baseline methods by finding a balance between the rates and deadlines. Assignment of high-rate streams to the CPU increases the number of parallel jobs on the accelerator. Controlling the deadline increases batch size and reduces batch scheduling overhead.

In the last experiment we created workloads with exponentially distributed rates and deadlines while increasing the number of streams. Figure 11 shows that the high overhead of batch scheduling – a result of processing short-deadline streams on the accelerator – reduced the throughput of MinRate to below the measured range.

5.4 Performance model

The estimation error of our GPU performance model is shown in Table 1. Jobs of different sizes were randomly generated according to exponential and constant distributions. For each batch we calculated the estimated kernel time and data copying time, and measured its running time on the GPU. Then, we calculated the average and maximum preci-

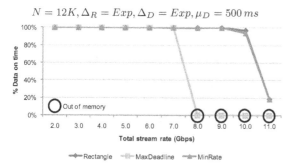

Figure 7: MaxDeadline fails on exponential rate distribution due to inefficient GPU utilization

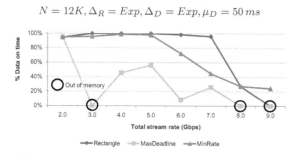

Figure 8: MaxDeadline overloads the CPU with low-deadline streams. MinRate suffers from high batch scheduling overhead because low-deadline streams are processed on the GPU.

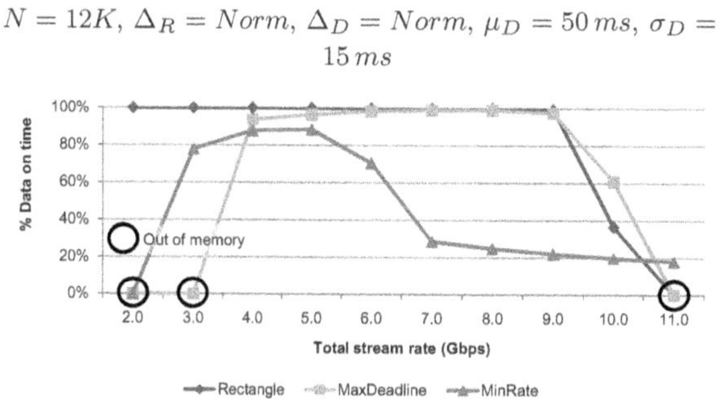

$N = 12K$, $\Delta_R = Norm$, $\Delta_D = Norm$, $\mu_D = 50\,ms$, $\sigma_D = 15\,ms$

Figure 9: Both baseline methods overload the CPU on low rates. MinRate fails for all rates.

	COPY		KERNEL	
	AVG	MAX	AVG	MAX
CONST	3.3%	4.8%	3.7%	7.0%
EXP	3.0%	4.7%	5.8%	11.3%

Table 1: Performance model estimation error

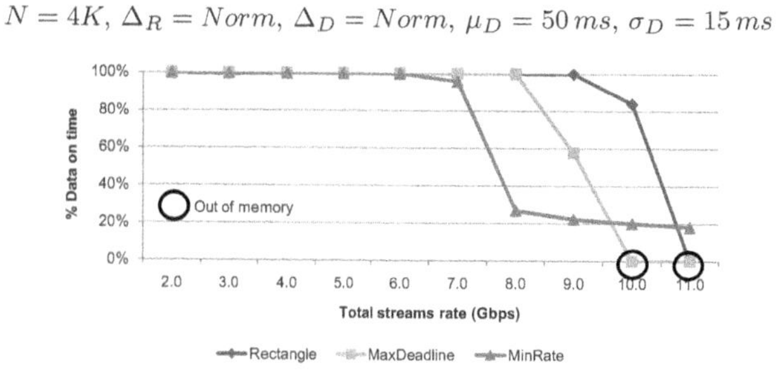

Figure 10: Low level of parallelism (4000 streams). The average rate of each stream is higher than in previous experiments. The highest throughput is achieved by the Rectangle method, which balances rate (increases the number of parallel jobs on the accelerator) and deadline (reduces batch scheduling overhead).

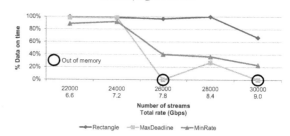

Figure 11: Increasing the number of streams. The Rectangle method finds a schedulable solution for 17% more streams than MaxDeadline. MinRate chokes on the overhead of batch scheduling.

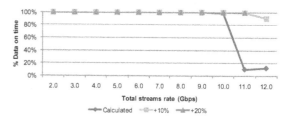

Figure 12: Safety margin for kernel time estimation. No misses with 20% margin. Same input as in Figure 9.

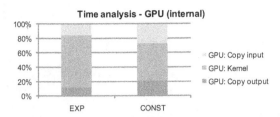

Figure 13: GPU breakdown of pipeline stages for exponential and normal rate distributions

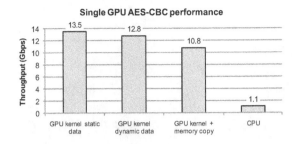

Figure 14: Optimal results for single GPU

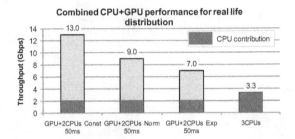

Figure 15: Throughput of GPU+2CPUs is 4 times higher than that of 3CPUs

sion errors. Figure 12 shows that with a 20% safety margin no deadlines are missed.

5.5 Time breakdown

We analyzed the CPU and GPU states during processing. The results show that CPU scheduling overhead is less than 3% on all tested workloads. On average, this overhead is 1.4% for streams with constant rate distribution and 2.8% for streams with exponential rate distribution. The CPUs reach full occupancy with constant rates; idling is <1%. With exponential distribution, the assignment puts more load on the GPU and does not fully occupy the CPUs. Therefore, the CPUs have idle periods for low values of total rate. In the GPU, we see that processing time is not linear in the load. This is most apparent for the constant rate, where execution time grows more slowly than load.

Figure 13 shows a breakdown of GPU relative execution time for three pipeline stages: copy input to accelerator, kernel execution, and copy output to main memory. We see that in the case of constant rate distribution the running time of the kernel is similar to the total copying time, about 50% of the total time. For exponentially distributed streams, the share of kernel execution time is significantly larger (72%), because batches of higher variance of job size do not fully utilize the GPU.

5.6 How far are we from optimum?

Figure 14 presents AES-CBC performance results on a single GPU for workloads consisting of batches with equal-size jobs. Since scheduling is trivial in this case, the results can be considered optimal for the given total aggregated rate. The columns show the throughput results for the following execution modes: (1) a GPU kernel executes a single, large, batch of jobs; (2) a kernel executes a stream of relatively large batches; (3) a GPU executes a stream of relatively large batches, including memory copies from/to the CPU memory; (4) a CPU executes a stream of jobs.

According to these results, the performance of dynamic data processing on the GPU is 5% lower than for static processing. This is a result of additional accesses to the off-chip memory required for streaming data. Dynamic data is stored in memory as a chain of data blocks, and threads must perform memory accesses to follow the pointers between these blocks. This overhead does not exist for static data, as jobs are simply stored sequentially (further implementation details are omitted for lack of space). Interestingly, there is an order of magnitude GPU to CPU maximum throughput ratio for this algorithm.

The throughput of a system with a GPU and two CPUs for real-life workloads is compared to a system with three CPUs in Figure 15. In the experiments, both rates and deadlines of $12K$ streams were generated using the constant, normal and exponential distributions, with $50ms$ average deadline. The chart shows that our system achieves up to 4-fold speedup over a CPU-only system even for streams with $50ms$ deadlines.

6. RELATED WORK

The problem of hard real-time stream processing can be mapped to the domain of real-time periodic task scheduling. A series of studies dealt with different aspects of task scheduling and load balancing in GPU-CPU systems. Joselli et al. [11, 12] proposed automatic task scheduling for CPU and GPU, based on sampling of their load. These methods are not suitable for hard real-time tasks, as there is no guarantee of task completion times. In specialized applications, such as FFT [18] or the matrix multiplication library [19], application-specific mechanisms for task scheduling and load balancing were developed.

Dynamic load balancing methods for single and multi GPU systems using task queues and work-stealing techniques were developed[5, 4, 27, 1]. In [1], a set of *workers* on the accelerator execute tasks taken from local EDF (earliest deadline first) queues. These approaches cannot be used in our case as it is very hard to guarantee hard real-time schedulability in such a dynamic environment. An important work of Kerr et al. [13] describes *Ocelot*, an infrastructure for modeling the GPU. Modeling can be used in our work to create a precise performance model without benchmarking.

Kuo and Hai [14] presented an EDF-based algorithm to schedule real-time tasks in a heterogeneous system. Their work is based on a system with a CPU and an on-chip DSP. This algorithm is not compatible with our system model because of the high latency of CPU to GPU communication. The problem of optimal scheduling of hard real-time tasks on a multiprocessor is computationally-hard [20]. Our work borrows some partitioning ideas from [21].

The term *stream processing* is often used in the context of GPUs, and refers to a programming paradigm for parallel computations. As such it is irrelevant to our work. To prevent confusion, we use the term *data stream processing*.

7. CONCLUSIONS AND FUTURE WORK

We have shown the first hard-deadline data stream processing framework on a heterogeneous system with CPU cores and a GPU accelerator. We have developed the Rectangle method, an efficient polynomial-time scheduling approach that uses simple geometric principles to find schedulable stream assignments. Rectangle method throughput was shown to be stable for different workloads and is higher than that of the compared baseline methods in all of the experiments. It is especially preferable for workloads with shorter deadlines and more streams.

Our future work will study ways to overcome some limitations of the proposed method. A formal treatment of the Rectangle method is required to prove its completeness (correctness is true by construction). Generalization of the Rectangle for multiple accelerators would make it applicable to a wider range of systems.

8. REFERENCES

[1] C. Augonnet, S. Thibault, R. Namyst, and P. A. Wacrenier. StarPU: a unified platform for task scheduling on heterogeneous multicore architectures. *Euro-Par 2009 Parallel Processing*, pages 863–874, 2009.

[2] S. K. Baruah. The non-preemptive scheduling of periodic tasks upon multiprocessors. *Real-Time Syst.*, 32:9–20, 2006.

[3] S. K. Baruah, N. K. Cohen, C. G. Plaxton, and D. A. Varvel. Proportionate progress: A notion of fairness in resource allocation. *Algorithmica*, 15(6):600–625, 1996.

[4] D. Cederman and P. Tsigas. On sorting and load balancing on GPUs. *SIGARCH Comput. Archit. News*, 36:11–18, 2009.

[5] L. Chen, O. Villa, S. Krishnamoorthy, and G. Gao. Dynamic load balancing on single- and multi-GPU systems. In *IEEE Intl. Symp. on Parallel and Distributed Processing (IPDPS)*, pages 1 –12, 2010.

[6] S. Davari and S. K. Dhall. An on line algorithm for real-time tasks allocation. In *IEEE Real-Time Systems Symp.*, pages 194–200, 1986.

[7] U. C. Devi. An improved schedulability test for uniprocessor periodic task systems. *Euromicro Conf. on Real-Time Systems*, 0:23, 2003.

[8] F. Eisenbrand and T. Rothvoß. EDF-schedulability of synchronous periodic task systems is coNP-hard. In *SODA*, pages 1029–1034, 2010.

[9] O. Harrison and J. Waldron. AES encryption implementation and analysis on commodity graphics processing units. In *CHES*, pages 209–226, 2007.

[10] D. A. O. Joppe W. Bos and D. Stefan. Fast implementations of aes on various platforms. Cryptology ePrint Archive, Report 2009/501, 2009. http://eprint.iacr.org/.

[11] M. Joselli, M. Zamith, E. Clua, A. Montenegro, A. Conci, R. Leal-Toledo, L. Valente, B. Feijo,

M. d' Ornellas, and C. Pozzer. Automatic dynamic task distribution between CPU and GPU for real-time systems. *11th IEEE Intl. Conf. on Comp. Science and Engineering (CSE 08)*., 0:48–55, 2008.

[12] M. Joselli, M. Zamith, E. Clua, A. Montenegro, R. Leal-Toledo, A. Conci, P. Pagliosa, L. Valente, and B. Feijó. An adaptive game loop architecture with automatic distribution of tasks between CPU and GPU. *Comput. Entertain.*, 7, 2009.

[13] A. Kerr, G. Diamos, and S. Yalamanchili. Modeling GPU-CPU workloads and systems. In *GPGPU*, pages 31–42, 2010.

[14] C.-F. Kuo and Y.-C. Hai. Real-time task scheduling on heterogeneous two-processor systems. In C.-H. Hsu, L. Yang, J. Park, and S.-S. Yeo, editors, *Algorithms and Architectures for Parallel Processing*. 2010.

[15] S. Lee, S. Min, and R. Eigenmann. OpenMP to GPGPU: a compiler framework for automatic translation and optimization. In *PPOPP*, pages 101–110, 2009.

[16] C. L. Liu and J. W. Layland. Scheduling algorithms for multiprogramming in a hard-real-time environment. *J. ACM*, 20:46–61, 1973.

[17] S. Manavski. CUDA compatible GPU as an efficient hardware accelerator for AES cryptography. In *Signal Processing and Communications, 2007.*, 2007.

[18] Y. Ogata, T. Endo, N. Maruyama, and S. Matsuoka. An efficient, model-based CPU-GPU heterogeneous FFT library. In *IPDPS*, pages 1–10, 2008.

[19] S. Ohshima, K. Kise, T. Katagiri, and T. Yuba. Parallel processing of matrix multiplication in a CPU and GPU heterogeneous environment. In *Proc. of the 7th intl. conf. on High performance computing for comp. science*, VECPAR'06, pages 305–318, 2007.

[20] S. Ramamurthy. Scheduling periodic hard real-time tasks with arbitrary deadlines on multiprocessors. In *Proc. of the 23rd IEEE Real-Time Systems Symp.*, RTSS '02. IEEE Computer Society, 2002.

[21] S. Rarnarnurthy and M. Moir. Static-priority periodic scheduling on multiprocessors. *Proc. of the IEEE Real-Time Systems Symp.*, 0:69, 2000.

[22] L. D. Rose, B. Homer, and D. Johnson. Detecting application load imbalance on high end massively parallel systems. In *Euro-Par*, pages 150–159, 2007.

[23] S. Schneider, H. Andrade, B. Gedik, K.-L. Wu, and D. S. Nikolopoulos. Evaluation of streaming aggregation on parallel hardware architectures. In *DEBS*, pages 248–257, 2010.

[24] M. Själander, A. Terechko, and M. Duranton. A look-ahead task management unit for embedded multi-core architectures. In *DSD*, pages 149–157, 2008.

[25] N. R. Tallent and J. M. Mellor-Crummey. Identifying performance bottlenecks in work-stealing computations. *IEEE Computer*, 42(11):44–50, 2009.

[26] W. Tang, Z. Lan, N. Desai, and D. Buettner. Fault-aware, utility-based job scheduling on Blue Gene/P systems. In *CLUSTER*, pages 1–10, 2009.

[27] S. Tzeng, A. Patney, and J. D. Owens. Task management for irregular-parallel workloads on the GPU. In *High Performance Graphics*, pages 29–37, 2010.

Coordinating Processor and Main Memory for Efficient Server Power Control

Ming Chen, Xiaorui Wang, and Xue Li
Department of Electrical Engineering and Computer Science
University of Tennessee, Knoxville, TN 37996
{mchen11, xwang, xli44}@utk.edu

ABSTRACT

With the number of high-density servers in data centers rapidly increasing, power control with performance optimization has become a key challenge to gain a high return on investment, by safely accommodating the maximized number of servers allowed by the limited power supply and cooling facilities in a data center. Various power control solutions have been recently proposed for high-density servers and different components in a server to avoid system failures due to power overload or overheating. Existing solutions, unfortunately, either rely only on the processor for server power control, with the assumption that it is the only major power consumer, or limit power only for a single component, such as main memory. As a result, the synergy between the processor and main memory is impaired by uncoordinated power adaptations, resulting in degraded overall system performance. In this paper, we propose a novel power control solution that can precisely limit the peak power consumption of a server below a desired budget. Our solution adapts the power states of both the processor and memory in a coordinated manner, based on their power demands, to achieve optimized system performance. Our solution also features a control algorithm that is designed rigorously based on advanced feedback control theory for guaranteed control accuracy and system stability. Compared with two state-of-the-art server power control solutions, experimental results show that our solution, on average, achieves up to 23% better performance than one baseline for CPU-intensive benchmarks and doubles the performance of the other baseline when the power budget is tight.

Categories and Subject Descriptors

C.4 [**Performance of Systems**]: Design studies; C.5.5 [**Computer System Implementation**]: Servers

General Terms

Design, Management, Performance

Keywords

Power control, server, power capping, memory, data center

ICS'11, May 31–June 4, 2011, Tucson, Arizona, USA.
Copyright 2011 ACM 978-1-4503-0102-2/11/05...$10.00.

1. INTRODUCTION

Power management has become one of the first-order considerations in modern enterprise data centers in recent years. The constant quest for high performance leads to high peak power consumption when the system is fully utilized. The power problem is further exacerbated by the wide adoption of high-density servers and the increasing demand for high-capacity, high-bandwidth main memory subsystems. This is especially true for supercomputers, which are usually equipped with very large memory size. As a result, the power supply and cooling facilities become expensive and bulky, which may hinder the deployment of new servers in the data centers in turn. More importantly, high peak power may cause system failures due to power capacity overload and thermal violations. In response, power control techniques have been proposed at different levels in data centers [25][31]. For example, a data center may allocate its power budget to different Power Distribution Units (PDU) and then, a group of racks. Further, the power budget of a single server may be allocated by the rack in which the server resides. Likewise, the server-level budget may be further divided among multiple components in a server. Hence, it is important that power is controlled at all the levels.

Power control at the server level faces several major challenges. *First*, multiple components need to be manipulated simultaneously to control the power consumption of a server. The widespread adoption of multi-core processors and the rapid increase of applications' memory footprints have dramatically increased the demand on memory bandwidth and capacity. As a result, it is no longer valid to assume that the processor is the only major power consumer in a server. For example, Lin et al. [19] reported that the main memory systems in a multi-core server box, which has $32GB$ of Fully-Buffered DIMMs, might have power consumption in the same range as the processor. Hence, we need Multi-Input-Multi-Output (MIMO) strategies to coordinate both processor and memory for server power control. *Second*, the components in a server are usually heterogeneous. Thus, we cannot simply allocate power proportional to the activities of each individual component since the power consumption of a single activity varies for different components. For example, an instruction dispatched in a processor may contribute a different amount of power from a memory request. Therefore, we need to optimize power allocation based on performance indicators that can characterize the real power demands of the components. *Third*, workloads in different components in a server are usually synergetic. For example, processor frequency downscaling may decrease the number of memory requests so that the memory power consumption decreases accordingly. Therefore, the synergy among components should be carefully addressed during power allocation at the server level. *Fourth and most importantly*, the workloads of different components are unpredictable at design time and may vary significantly at runtime. As a result, power control algorithms cannot rely on static power models or open-loop estimations. They must be self-adaptive to workload variations for improved server performance.

In recent years, various power control solutions have been proposed for high-density servers. A recent solution [15] relies only on the processor for server power control, with the assumption that it is the only major power consumer in the server. As a result, that solution is limited to those small form-factor servers with small-size memory systems. Another recent paper [5] proposes to shift power between the processor and main memory proportionally to the number of activities. However, their solution relies on power estimation based on measured activities and off-line profiled power models, which may result in either power violations or performance degradation when the workload varies. In addition, their power actuation method relies only on throttling the number of activities and does not exploit low-power states in the processor and main memory to minimize idle power. As a result, it has unnecessarily high idle power and a limited capacity of power adaptation.

In this paper, we propose a novel server power control solution that can precisely control the server power consumption to a desired budget. We periodically coordinate the processor and main memory to achieve improved performance, based on the memory queue level, by dynamically adjusting the voltage/frequency of the processor and placing memory ranks into different power states. Our coordinated solution is systematically designed based on Model Predicative Control (MPC) theory, which is an advanced optimal MIMO control theory. Compared with two state-of-the-art server power control solutions, our solution has the following improvements. First, our solution, on average, achieves up to 23% better performance than one baseline for CPU-intensive benchmarks and doubles the performance of the other baseline when the power budget is tight. Second, our solution significantly improves the power adaptation capacity, which is the range between the maximum and minimum power consumption that the server can have, due to coordinating the power states of both processor and main memory. As a result, our solution can still manage to conduct power control even when the power budget becomes very tight (e.g., due to thermal emergency without having to shutdown the server). Third, our solution has better power control accuracy so that it is more robust and less vulnerable to workload variations. Specifically, the contributions of this paper are three-fold:

- We mathematically model the power dynamics of the memory system by varying the number of memory ranks in low power states based on a recently proposed memory power actuation method.

- We design and analyze a MIMO power control algorithm to control the total power of a high-density server to a budget, while coordinating the processor and main memory for improved server performance.

- We propose a new technique that uses the memory queue level as the power demand indicator to optimally allocate power between the processor and main memory.

The reminder of this paper is organized as follows. Section 2 introduces the power adaptation methods and provides a high-level description of the coordinated power control architecture. Section 3 presents the system modeling, design, and analysis of our power controller. Section 4 introduces the simulation environment and discusses the impact of DDR3 technology on our solution. Section 5 presents the results of our experiments. Section 6 discusses related work and Section 7 concludes the paper.

Table 1: DRAM power states

Power state/Transition	Power/Delay
Active standby (ACT)	104.5 mW
Precharged (PRE)	76 mW
Active powerdown (APD)	19 mW
Precharged powerdown (PPD)	13.3 mW
Self refreshing (SR)	5 mW
$PRE \rightleftharpoons PPD$	6 ns
$APD \rightleftharpoons ACT$	6 ns
$SR \rightarrow PRE$	≥ 137.5 ns

2. SYSTEM DESIGN

In this section, we first introduce the power adaptation methods used in this paper. We next provide a high-level description of the coordinated power control architecture.

2.1 Power Adaptation for the Main Memory

To effectively enforce the power budget of a server, it is important to find efficient power actuators for the processor and main memory. In this paper, we adapt the processor power consumption by conducting the widely used *DVFS* technique. Our power adaptation method for the main memory leverages the fact that modern memory devices have multiple power states that retain stored data. Each power state consumes a different amount of power, whereas the transitions between states involve different performance overheads. As an example, Table 1 lists the power states, power consumption, and transition overheads of DDR2 SDRAM chips with 1Gb capacity [24]. Diniz et al. [3] have shown that dynamically adjusting the power states of different memory devices can efficiently limit memory power consumption. By making a compromise between power saving and transition overhead based on Table 1, we utilize two power states: the precharged (PRE) state and precharged powerdown (PPD) state. The PRE state is an idle mode in which all banks are precharged and awaiting row activation commands to service a request, while the PPD state is the lowest power mode, other than the self-refreshing mode, in which all banks are precharged [11]. Hereinafter, we refer to the PRE state as *active state* and the PPD state as *sleep state*, for simplicity. We use the number of ranks in the active state as the actuator to dynamically change the memory power consumption. We place each memory rank either in the active state or in the sleep state. A rank in the sleep state needs to be activated first to service any arriving memory requests, which involves some overhead. We define the *active ratio* as the number of memory ranks in the active state normalized to the total number of ranks in the memory system. For example, if we keep 4 out of 16 ranks in the active state, the active ratio is 0.25.

The active ratio is kept constant within each control period while it is re-calculated at the end of each control period. The memory scheduler, shown in Figure 1, maintains a Most Recently Used (MRU) queue which records the most recently accessed rank at the head of the queue, and a status array which records the power state of each rank (i.e., active state or sleep state). Its working process is based, generally, on an approach proposed by a recent paper [3]. We briefly introduce it as follows.

- At the end of each control period, based on the difference between the ratios in the current and previous control periods, some sleeping ranks at the head of the MRU queue are transitioned to the active state, or some active ranks from the tail of the MRU queue are transitioned to the sleep state.

- Within a control period, when a memory request arrives, if the accessed rank is in the sleep state, the active ratio is kept unchanged by firstly switching an active rank to the sleep state and then activating the accessed rank. Before the accessed rank becomes active, the memory access is held in the memory queue. To avoid frequent transitioning, a rank is chosen to be switched only if the time it has been in the active state is longer than the *break-even time* [3].

Please note that the active ratio mechanism does not conflict with existing memory power management solutions implemented in nowadays' commercial servers (*e.g.*, transition memory ranks into the sleep state when they are idle for a certain period of time.). Our solution only throttles the maximum number of active ranks. If the number of ranks in the active state is smaller than our decision, nothing needs to be done. If it is greater, some extra ranks have to be put into the sleep state to make sure the power budget is not violated.

2.2 Coordinated Power Control Architecture

Figure 1 is a simplified illustration of a memory controller with multiple memory channels that can sustain multiple memory requests at a given time. The memory requests generated by the processor are sent to a memory queue in the memory controller after a certain bus delay. The memory scheduler converts the physical address of the requests into the memory address via an address mapping scheme. It then forwards them to the corresponding channels if the transaction queue in the channel has space. The channel scheduler reorders and schedules the requests in the transaction queue based on a scheduling algorithm (*e.g.*, Read or Instruction Fetch First). Finally, the scheduled requests are converted into a sequence of DRAM commands and serviced by the DRAM system.

As shown in Figure 1, the key components in the server power control loop include a power controller and a power monitor at the server level, a queue monitor and an active ratio modulator in the memory controller, and a DVFS modulator in the processor. The control loop is invoked periodically. At the end of each control period: 1) The power monitor (*e.g.*, a power meter) measures the average server power consumption and sends the value to the power controller. The total server power consumption is the *controlled variable*. 2) The queue monitor samples the memory queue level (*i.e.*, the number of memory requests waiting in the queue) multiple times in each control period. The average queue level is calculated at the end of each control period and used as a power demand indicator for the power controller to coordinate the processor and main memory for improved server performance. 3) The power controller collects the power value and queue level, calculates the new frequency level for the processor and the new active ratio for the main memory, respectively. The processor frequency level and active ratio are the *manipulated variables*. 4) The DVFS modulator changes the processor frequency level, and the active ratio modulator notifies the memory scheduler to power up/down memory ranks as introduced in Section 2.1, accordingly.

3. COORDINATED POWER CONTROLLER

In this section, we present the system modeling, design, and analysis of the coordinated power controller.

3.1 System Models

In order to have an effective controller design, it is important to model the dynamics of the controlled system, namely the relation between the controlled variable (*i.e.*, server power consumption) and the manipulated variables (*i.e.*, processor frequency level and memory active ratio). Since the total power is the sum of the processor power and the main memory power[1], we have two power models: the processor power model and the memory power model. We first introduce some notation. T_s is the control period. $f(k)$ is the average processor frequency in the kth control period. $r(k)$ is the active ratio of the main memory. $\Delta f(k)$ is the difference between $f(k+1)$ and $f(k)$, *i.e.*, $\Delta f(k) = f(k+1) - f(k)$. $\Delta r(k)$ is the difference between $r(k+1)$ and $r(k)$, *i.e.*, $\Delta r(k) = r(k+1) - r(k)$. $F_{max} = 1$ and F_{min} are the maximum and minimum processor frequency (normalized to the maximum) while $R_{max} = 1$ and $R_{min} = 0$ are the maximum and minimum active ratio, respectively. $p_p(k)$, $p_m(k)$, and $p(k)$ are the power consumption of the processor, the main memory, and the whole server, respectively.

Memory Power Modeling. Based on the power adaptation method of the main memory introduced in Section 2.1, we need to model the dynamics of the relationship between the memory power consumption (*i.e.*, $p_m(k)$) and active ratio (*i.e.*, $r(k)$). However, a well-established physical equation is unavailable between $p_m(k)$ and $r(k)$. Therefore, we use a standard approach to this problem called *system identification* [6]. Instead of trying to build an analytical equation between $p_m(k)$ and $r(k)$, we infer their relationship by collecting data in the simulation environment introduced in Section 4 and establish a statistical model based on the measured data.

First, we examine the relationship between $p_m(k)$ and $r(k)$ based on experiments with 12 randomly selected workloads from SPEC CPU2000. Figure 2 plots the memory power consumption with the standard deviation under different active ratios for 5 workloads. Each data point in the curve is the average of 10 values which are sampled every 64 million CPU cycles (*i.e.*, the control period introduced in Section 4). The data points in the same curve are produced by forwarding the same number of instructions of the workload. As shown in Figure 2, the memory power consumption decreases when the active ratio decreases. The reduction of the memory power has two parts: the reduction of idle power due to the decreased number of ranks in the active state and the reduction of activity power due to the reduced available memory bandwidth. As shown in the figure, the curves of CPU-intensive workloads (*e.g.*, *gzip* and *mesa*) are closer to a linear model than those of memory-intensive workloads (*e.g.*, *mcf*, *swim*, and *art*). This is because the decrease of the active ratio for CPU-intensive workloads has a smaller impact on the bandwidth, compared with the memory-intensive workloads. Based on these experiments, we make three important observations:

1. There exhibits an approximately linear relationship between the memory power consumption and active ratio for each workload, except some offset.

2. The slope of all curves varies within a limited range, which is [34.42, 53.68], based on our analysis.

3. The memory power consumption is stable with a fixed active ratio within a certain phase. The maximum standard deviation of all the data points in Figure 2 is only 6.63 W, compared with the average power of $95.63W$.

Using the system identification approach for each randomly selected workload, we find that a linear model fits very well for all of them (smallest $R^2 > 94\%$). Therefore, it is valid to assume that there exists a model between the memory power consumption and active ratio as follows:

---

[1]In this paper, since we do not change the power states of other components in a server, we assume that their power consumption can be approximated as a constant and is thus eliminated in the difference power model (5) introduced later.

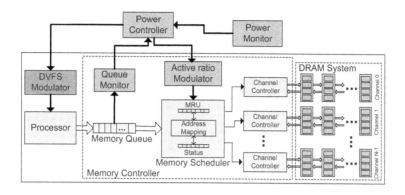

Figure 1: Coordinated Power Control Architecture

$$p_m(k) = k_r r(k) + C_i, \qquad (1)$$

where k_r is a generalized parameter that may vary for different workloads and C_i is a constant representing the offset. The dynamic model as a difference equation is

$$p_m(k+1) = p_m(k) + k_r \Delta r(k). \qquad (2)$$

To validate our system model, we first stimulate the main memory system with pseudo-random white-noise input to change the active ratio in a random manner. We then compare the actual power consumption with the value predicted by our model. Figure 3 plots the predicted power and measured power by running *swim* which has the largest standard deviation. We can see that the predicted power is adequately close to the actual power of the memory system, even for the workload with a significant power variation.

Please note that we are not trying to find a fixed k_r for all workloads, but to validate the linearity observed in our experiments by using 12 randomly selected workloads from SPEC CPU2000 (5 of them shown in Figure 2). As we prove in Section 3.4, only if the workload exhibits an approximately linear memory power model and the slope k_r (together with the slope for the processor power model as we discuss later) varies within a certain range, the stability of our coordinated power control algorithm can be guaranteed. A key advantage of the control-theoretic design approach is that it can tolerate a certain degree of modeling errors and can adapt to online model variations based on dynamic feedback [6]. As a result, our solution does not need to rely on power models that are 100% accurate, which is in sharp contrast to open-loop solutions that would fail without an accurate model.

Processor Power Modeling. Raghavendra et al. [25] and Lefurgy et al. [15] have shown that the processor power is approximately linear to the DVFS level. In this paper, we model the processor power in the same way as the memory power by using system identification. The power consumption of a processor is modeled as:

$$p_p(k) = p_p(k-1) + k_f \Delta f(k), \qquad (3)$$

where k_f is a generalized parameter that may vary for different workloads running in the processor. The detailed analysis of the processor power model can be found in [15].

Server Power Modeling. The server power consumption is the sum of power of all components in the server:

$$p(k) = p_p(k) + p_m(k) + p_o, \qquad (4)$$

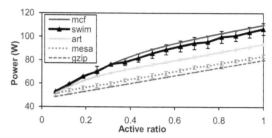

Figure 2: Relationship between memory power and active ratio

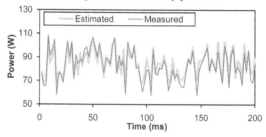

Figure 3: Memory Power Model Validation

where p_o is the power consumption of other components, which can be eliminated in a difference power model. Based on (2) and (3), we can get the difference power model as follows:

$$p(k+1) = p(k) + \mathbf{K}\Delta\mathbf{v}(k), \qquad (5)$$

where $\mathbf{K} = \begin{bmatrix} k_f & k_r \end{bmatrix}$ and $\Delta\mathbf{v}(k) = \begin{bmatrix} \Delta f(k) & \Delta r(k) \end{bmatrix}^T$. The actual values of k_f and k_r at runtime may change for different workloads and are unknown at design time. In Section 3.4, we prove that a system, controlled by the controller designed with the estimated parameters, can remain stable as long as the variations of k_f and k_r are within allowed ranges.

3.2 Controller Design

We apply *Model Predictive Control* (MPC) theory [21] to design the controller based on the system model (5). MPC is an advanced control technique that can deal with coupled MIMO control problems with constraints on the plant and the actuators. MPC enables us to combine power prediction, optimization, constraint satisfaction, and feedback control into a single algorithm. This property makes MPC well suited for coordinating the processor and main memory for server power control.

A model predictive controller optimizes a *cost function* defined over a time interval in the future. The controller uses the system model to predict the control behavior over P control periods, which is referred to as the *prediction horizon*, based on the feedback $p(k)$

from the power monitor. The control objective is to select an input trajectory that minimizes the cost function while satisfying the constraints. An input trajectory includes the control inputs in the M control periods, which is referred to as *control horizon*. The controller includes a least squares solver, a cost function, a reference trajectory, and a system model. At the end of every control period, the controller computes the control input $\Delta \mathbf{v}(\mathbf{k})$ that minimizes the following cost function under constraints.

$$V(k) = \sum_{i=1}^{P} \|p(k+i|k) - ref(k+i|k)\|_{Q(i)}^2 +$$

$$\sum_{i=0}^{M-1} \|\Delta \mathbf{v}(\mathbf{k+i}|\mathbf{k}) + \mathbf{v}(\mathbf{k+i}|\mathbf{k}) - \mathbf{V_{max}}\|_{\mathbf{R(i)}}^2 \quad (6)$$

where $\mathbf{V_{max}} = \begin{bmatrix} F_{max} & R_{max} \end{bmatrix}^T$, $Q(i)$ is the *tracking error weight*, and $\mathbf{R(i)}$ is the *control penalty weight vector*. The notation $x(k+i|k)$ means that the value of variable x at time $(k+i)T$ depends on the conditions at time kT. The first term in the cost function represents the *tracking error*, *i.e.*, the difference between the total power $p(k+i|k)$ and a reference trajectory $ref(k+i|k)$. The reference trajectory defines an ideal trajectory along which the total power $p(k+i|k)$ should change from the current value $p(k)$ to the set point P_s (*i.e.*, power budget of the server)[21]. The second term in the cost function (6) represents the *control penalty*. The control penalty term causes the controller to optimize system performance by minimizing the difference between the highest power states of the processor and the main memory, $\mathbf{V_{max}}$, and the new power states, $\mathbf{v(k+i+1|k)} = \Delta \mathbf{v(k+i|k)} + \mathbf{v(k+i|k)}$, along the control horizon. The control weight vector, $\mathbf{R(i)} = \begin{bmatrix} R_c & R_m \end{bmatrix}_{1 \times M}$, is tuned, based on the memory queue level, to shift power to either the processor (*i.e.*, R_c) or the main memory (*i.e.*, R_m), which will be discussed in Section 3.3. This control problem is subject to two sets of constraints. First, both the DVFS level of the processor and the active ratio of the main memory should be within allowed physical ranges. Second, the total power consumption should not be higher than the desired power constraint.

Based on the above analysis, the problem of server power control has been modeled as a constrained MIMO optimal control problem, which can be easily transformed to a standard constrained least-squares problem [21]. Please note that the computational complexity and runtime overhead of an MPC controller can be significantly reduced by optimizing the original MPC algorithm. For example, a hardware implementation of an improved MPC algorithm with 4 inputs (we have 2 inputs in the paper) and 1 output (e.g., the server power) only takes $4.7\mu s$ at a clock frequency of $20MHz$ [12]. Compared with the power control period (*i.e.*, $20ms$) as discussed in Section 4.1, the computation overhead can be considered small ($< 0.02\%$). Therefore, it is feasible to use MPC in practice for server power control.

3.3 Weight Allocation in Coordinated Controller

The power controller discussed above can precisely control the total server power consumption to the desired budget by solving an optimization problem. However, it cannot guarantee that the power states of the processor and main memory are coordinated to achieve further improved performance. The experiments in Section 5.4 demonstrate that the system performance, in terms of Instructions Per Cycle (IPC), differs significantly by giving different preferences to the processor and main memory. In this subsection, we introduce a simple, but efficient, coordination scheme that allocates the control penalty weights for the processor and main memory based on the memory queue level, so that improved performance

can be achieved. The reason why we use the memory queue level as the indicator is as follows: (1) the memory queue physically exists in many memory controllers [9], so it does not incur any other implementation overhead. (2) More importantly, when compared with other related metrics such as CPU stall time or L2 cache miss ratio, the queue level is a fair indicator for all workloads and can quantitatively reflect the power demand of the memory system. For example, if the queue level increases, it means that the memory requires more power to increase its capability so that the waiting time of the memory requests in the queue can be decreased.

In this paper, we propose an algorithm called *Moving Average* (MA) to assign weights in the coordinated controller as follows. We keep the weight of the processor (*i.e.*, R_c) constant at 1 and adjust the weight of the memory (*i.e.*, R_m) at runtime. At the end of each control period, the controller calculates the moving average of the queue level $q_a(k)$ in a window with a size of L, after receiving the queue level $q(k)$ from the queue level monitor. Specifically, $q_a(k) = \sum_{i=0}^{L-1} q(k-i)$. Clearly, the selection of the window size is a trade-off between a smooth weight allocation for the main memory and the response speed to memory workload variations. Based on our experiments, we found that the window size of 4 works well for most workloads. If the moving average of queue level $q_a(k)$ is higher than the reference level Q_{ref}, we set the weight of the memory as $(q_a(k) - Q_{ref})\alpha + 1$ to indicate that the memory needs more power. If $q_a(k)$ is smaller than Q_{ref}, the weight of the memory is set as $(q_a(k)/Q_{ref})^\beta$, which is lower than 1, to indicate that the processor needs more power. Both α and β are experiential parameters that map the queue level to the weight. Based on our profiling experiments with SPEC CPU 2000, we find that $\alpha = 10$ and $\beta = 2$ have approximately the best results.

The selection of the reference level Q_{ref} also plays an important role in the allocation scheme. Due to the dependencies among instructions, the length of the memory queue usually stops increasing when the processor stalls, instead of increasing infinitely. We define the *saturation level* as the maximum queue level that can be accumulated before the processor stalls. Clearly, the saturation level relies highly on the degree of dependency among the instructions. The stronger the dependency, the smaller the saturation level. If Q_{ref} is too high (*e.g.*, higher than the saturation level), the processor may stall before the queue level can be accumulated to the reference level. Likewise, if Q_{ref} is too low, the preference is more likely to be always given to the processor. Both of these may lead to degraded performance. Based on our profiling experiments, most workloads have a saturation level from 6 to 50. Without loss of generality, we set the reference level Q_{ref} as 4. Note that no reference level can be guaranteed to be always optimal in terms of performance for all workloads, since the interaction between the processor and memory is interleaved among instructions at runtime.

3.4 Control Analysis for Model Variations

A fundamental benefit of the control-theoretic approach is that it gives us confidence for system stability, even when the system power model (5) may change at runtime due to workload variations. We say that a system is *stable* if the total power $p(k)$ converges to the desired set point P_s, that is, $\lim_{k \to \infty} p(k) = P_s$.

We now outline the general steps to analyze the stability of the system controlled by the coordinated power controller, when the actual system model is different from the *estimated* model used to design the coordinated controller. First, given a specific system, we derive the control inputs $\Delta \mathbf{v}(\mathbf{k})$ that minimize the cost function based on the estimated system model (5) with estimated parameters $\mathbf{K}$. Second, we construct the *actual* system model by assuming the actual parameter $k_f' = g_f k_f$ and $k_r' = g_r k_r$ for the processor and memory, respectively, where g_f and g_r represent the unknown system gain. Third, we derive the closed-loop system model by substituting the control inputs derived in the first step into the actual system model. Finally, we analyze the stability of the closed-loop system by computing the poles of the closed-loop system. According to control theory, if all the poles locate inside the unit circle in the complex space, the controlled system is stable.

Following the steps above, we have proven that the closed-loop system is guaranteed to be stable when $0 < g_f, g_r < 5.3$. This means that a system, controlled by the coordinated controller designed based on the estimated model (5), can remain stable as long as the real system parameters k'_f and k'_r are smaller than 5.3 times of the values used to design the controller. This stability analysis gives us confidence in the performance of our controller since we use the average k_f and k_r of all workloads from SPEC CPU2000 at the controller design time. It is reasonable to consider that our closed-loop system is stable for all workloads.

4. SYSTEM IMPLEMENTATION

In this section, we introduce our simulation environment and discuss the impact of DDR3 technology on our solution.

4.1 Simulation Environment

It would be ideal to test the proposed coordinated solution on a hardware testbed. However, to our best knowledge, currently there are few DRAM devices that are commercially available and provide external interfaces for power state adaptation, though DVFS is widely available in many processors. Therefore, as in other memory power management projects [3][5], we can only use simulations to evaluate the proposed coordinated solution. We integrate two cycle-accurate simulators: SimpleScalar [2] and DRAMsim [29], to simulate both the processor and main memory. SimpleScalar is heavily modified to simulate a quad-core CMP with one thread per core. To accurately simulate memory dependency, we modify the static main memory latency in SimpleScalar and hold all instructions which require main memory accesses from dispatching until the main memory accesses they depend on are returned by DRAMsim. Since the proposed solution is designed for high-end servers with large memory capacity, DRAMsim is configured to simulate a FB-DIMM DDR2 SDRAM system for its high bandwidth. The memory system has a capacity of 32 GB with four channels and specifications are based on the Micron data sheet [22]. The major parameters of the processor and main memory are shown in Table 2. We integrate Wattch [1] with SimpleScalar to estimate the power consumption of the processor. The power calculation in DRAMsim is based on the power model proposed by Micron [23]. We assume that the simulated quad-core CMP has an idle power of 50 W when running at the lowest frequency, based on a recent quad-core Xeon processor from Intel. Hence, the peak power of the simulated system can be as high as 270 W. In this paper, we assume that the processor and memory contribute the majority of the total power consumption in a server. However, our framework described above can be extended to include other components, such as network or disks.

Since the new frequency level periodically received from the controller could be any value that is not exactly one of the four supported DVFS levels shown in Table 2, we implement the first-order delta-sigma modulator proposed by Lefurgy et al. [15]. The modulator approximates the desired value via a series of supported DVFS levels. For example, to approximate $3GHz$ during a control period, the modulator would output the sequence, 2.8, 3.2, 2.8, and 3.2, on a smaller timescale. Apparently, the more subintervals the modulator is invoked within one control period, the better

the approximation is, but with a higher overhead. In this paper, we choose to use 20 subintervals to approximate the desired DVFS level. Based on Skadron et al. [27], the DVFS overhead is approximately $10\mu s$. As a result, we choose a subinterval of $1ms$ so that the overhead is up to 1% in the worst case when the DVFS level is changed every subinterval. Therefore, the coordinated control period is $20ms$, which is 64 million CPU cycles in our simulation environment. To simulate the overhead of DVFS, we assume there is no instruction executed during transitions [10].

The server power is calculated every control period (i.e., 64 million CPU cycles) in our simulation environment. Many of today's high-density servers are equipped with built-in power measurement circuit, such as IBM system x and p servers [14]. Those circuits can accurately measure the server power with a sampling period as short as $1ms$, which is much shorter than the sampling period of $20ms$ used in this paper. Therefore, it is realistic to precisely measure server power at runtime at a low cost.

In real systems, the controller can be implemented in the service processor firmware. In our simulation environment, the coordinated controller is implemented as a separate process and communicates with the processor-memory simulator via a pipe. The controller executes the control algorithm presented in Section 3 by calling a Matlab library which implements a standard constrained least-square solver. Our experiments are driven by pre-compiled alpha binaries of SEPC CPU2000. Since our goal is to validate the idea of shifting power between processors and memory for improved performance within a certain power constraint, we generate 4 identical threads of the same workload and run each thread on each core. To test our solution by running other coupled multi-threaded workloads, we need to incorporate advanced workload scheduling algorithms that can guarantee performance fairness by allocating power among different cores, which will be our future work. The performance is accumulated across all the cores in term of IPC. Please note that the length of cycle is normalized to the reciprocal of the highest frequency (i.e., $3.2GHz$). Therefore, the performance metric of IPC is equivalent to instructions per second.

4.2 Impact of DDR3 Technology

In this paper, we aim for high-end servers with high memory bandwidth. We chose FB-DIMM memory architecture for it high bandwidth [7]. However, our solution is not limited to a certain DRAM technology, and can also be applied on other memory systems such as DDR3. In this section, we discuss the impact of DDR3 technology on our solution, which will be part of our future work.

Memory power model. The coordinated power control solution is designed based on the processor and memory power models presented in Section 3.1. A similar memory power model can be derived as long as the system consists of multiple memory ranks whose power states can be transitioned independently, as in a DDR3 memory system. Therefore, it is reasonable to infer that a similar memory power model can be derived for DDR3, but with a different parameter k_m.

High power of FB-DIMM. FB-DIMM memory modules have relatively higher power consumption compared with conventional memory modules, mainly due to the Advanced Memory Buffer (AMB). For each AMB, the idle power (4-5 Watts) takes a major part of the total power (4-8 Watts) [18][19]. However, we do not take advantage of the high idle power of AMB. In our memory power model (1), the high idle AMB power is part of the offset C_i, which is eliminated in the difference model (2). As a result, the power dynamics of the memory system mainly come from the power difference between the different power modes of memory ranks, instead of the high idle power of FB-DIMM. If the coordi-

Table 2: Simulator parameters

Parameters	Values
Processor Frequency scaling Functional unit	4 cores, 8 issues per core 3.2GHz at 1.3V, 2.8GHz at 1.15V, 1.6GHz at 0.95V, 0.8GHz at 0.8V 4 IntALU, 2 IntMult, 2 FPALU, 1 FPMult
L1 caches (per core) L2 cache (shared)	64KB Inst/64KB Data, 2-way, 64B line size, 3-cycle hit latency 8MB, 8-way, 64B line size, 12-cycle hit latency
Memory Channel bandwidth	4 channels, 4 DIMMs/channel, 8 banks/DIMM, 1 rank/DIMM 667MT/s, FB-DIMM DDR2

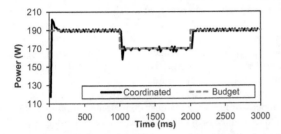

Figure 4: A typical run of the coordinated solution

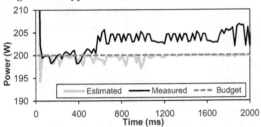

Figure 5: Estimation error of PLI

nated solution is applied to DDR3 memory systems, similar power dynamics can be achieved as long as DDR3 memory chips have a similar power reduction from the PRE state to the PPD state and the available memory bandwidth decreases similarly. Therefore, it is reasonable to believe that DDR3 memory systems may have power dynamics similar to FB-DIMM configured in our testbed. As a result, the coordinated solution can achieve similar performance improvement in DDR3 memory systems.

5. EVALUATION

In this section, we first introduce two state-of-the-art baselines. We then compare the coordinated solution with the two baselines, in terms of power control performance and application performance. Finally, we investigate the impact of weight allocation on server performance.

5.1 Baselines

Our first baseline, referred to as *ProcOnly*, is a server power control solution based on feedback control theory, proposed by Lefurgy et al. [15]. ProcOnly represents a typical server power control solution that assumes the processor is the only major power consumer in a server. ProcOnly leverages frequency scaling in the processor to control the power consumption of the whole server to be within a certain power budget. We compare the proposed coordinated solution against ProcOnly to highlight that coordinating the processor and main memory, when power budget is limited, is important to achieve better performance than only considering the processor. A fundamental difference between the coordinated solution and ProcOnly is that ProcOnly only manipulates the CPU frequency while disregarding the synergy between the processor and main memory.

In contrast, the coordinated solution manipulates the power states of both the processor and memory, and adaptively adjusts the power states of the two components in a coordinated way.

The second baseline, referred to as *Proportional-by-Last-Interval* (PLI), is a server power control scheme that shifts power between the processor and main memory based on the number of activities, proposed by Felter et al. [5]. PLI profiles the processor power model as a function of the number of dispatched instruction per cycle (DPC), while the memory power is modeled as a function of memory bandwidth. It periodically estimates the server power consumption based on the two off-line power models. Given a power budget, in every period, PLI calculates the maximum number of activities in the processor (*i.e.*, dispatched instructions) and memory (*i.e.*, memory requests) that can occur in the next period without violating the power budget, as the thresholds, proportionally to the measured number of activities in the last period. The power budget is enforced by only running the calculated numbers of activities in the processor and main memory. There are three fundamental differences between PLI and the coordinated solution. *First of all*, PLI is based on an estimation strategy that does not explicitly measure the power but relies on estimation, and thus cannot guarantee budget enforcement when the runtime power model becomes different from the profiled power model. Although the coordinated solution also predicts the power consumption based on profiled power models, the fundamental advantage of the coordination solution is that the prediction is continuously corrected based on feedback information, as discussed in Section 3.2. *Second*, the power allocation of PLI is proportional to the number of activities. In contrast, in the coordinated solution, the power allocation is driven by a performance indicator, the memory queue level. *Finally*, PLI enforces the power budget by directly throttling the number of activities. In contrast, the coordinated solution exploits different power states to effectively reduce idle power for both the processor and memory. When the budget is tight, our solution can allow more system activities by utilizing the reduced idle power. As a result, our solution has a higher capacity of power adaptation and can achieve better application performance.

5.2 Power Control Performance

In this experiment, we compare the power control performance of the coordinated solution with the two baselines, in terms of power control accuracy and power adaptation capacity.

Power Control Accuracy. To test the power control accuracy of the coordinated solution in a scenario where the power budget of the system needs to be changed at runtime due to various reasons (*e.g.*, thermal emergencies), we select a workload from SPEC benchmarks that is not used in the profiling of the memory power model in Section 3.1, *twolf*. As shown in Figure 4, the power budget is reduced from $190W$ to $170W$ at time $1,000ms$, and then restored to $190W$ at time $2,000ms$. We can see that the coordinated solution quickly responds to the power budget reduction and

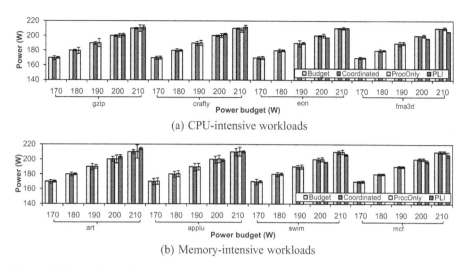

(a) CPU-intensive workloads

(b) Memory-intensive workloads

Figure 6: Comparison of power control among the coordinated solution, ProcOnly, and PLI

Table 3: Power adaptation capacity of the proposed coordinated solution and two baselines.

	Coordinated	ProcOnly	PLI
Lowest budget (W)	105	132	191

precisely control the total power consumption of the server to the budget by adjusting the CPU frequency of the processor and the active ratio of the memory.

Figures 6(a) and (b) show the average power consumption under the proposed coordinated solution, ProcOnly, and PLI with standard deviations for CPU-intensive and memory-intensive workloads, respectively. Each bar in the figures is the average of 110 data points after the controllers enter the steady state. The reason why there are no results for PLI at the budgets of $190W$, $180W$, and $170W$ is because PLI is incapable of lowering the power below its idle power (*i.e.*, $191W$). The smaller the standard deviation is, the smaller power variation will be, that is, the less dangerous to have a power violation. We can see that the average power consumption under both the coordinated solution and ProcOnly precisely converges to the budgets. However, the standard deviation of ProcOnly tends to be greater than the coordinated solution. For example, the maximum standard deviation of ProcOnly in all runs is 8.94W compared to 5.1W for the coordinated solution. This is because the coordinated solution has two manipulated variables (*i.e.*, CPU frequency and active ratio) which can handle larger workload variations than ProcOnly, which has only one manipulated variable (*i.e.*, processor frequency). The result is consistent with the stability analysis of the coordinated solution presented in Section 3.4, and the analysis of ProcOnly presented in [15]. The analyses show that the stability range of the coordinated solution (*i.e.*, $(0, 5.3]$) is larger than that of ProcOnly (*i.e.*, $(0, 2)$). Therefore, the coordinated solution is less vulnerable to workload variations and more robust.

As for PLI, the average power consumption fails to converge to the power budget due to estimation errors in most runs. For example, the average power consumption under PLI is either smaller (*e.g.*, *fma3a* and *mcf*) or larger (*e.g.*, *art*) than the power budget. As a result, PLI either violates the power budget or leads to degraded performance. This is because PLI features a strategy that does not explicitly measure power but estimates power based on measured activities. As a result, it relies heavily on the accuracy of the offline profiling of power models so that it has the risk of violating the power budget. To further verify our analysis of estimation inac-

curacy about PLI, Figure 5 plots both the measured and estimated power consumption in a typical run of PLI by using *lucas* ($0.8B$ instructions are forwarded) under a power budget of $200W$. We can see that the actual power consumption (*i.e.*, measured) is successfully enforced to the power budget at the beginning because the power characteristic of activities in the processor and main memory are accurately captured by the power models used by PLI for estimation. After the time around 580ms, the power characteristic varies. However, PLI neglects the variation due to the lack of feedback information and still allocates power between the processor and memory based on the measured number of activities. This results in a constant power violation of approximately $4.5W$, which is highly undesirable and may cause system failures in real systems.

Power Adaptation Capacity. Power adaptation capacity is defined as the power budget range that a control solution can achieve. A higher power adaptation capacity means that a control solution can still manage to conduct power control even when the power budget becomes very tight (*e.g.*, due to thermal emergency). PLI caps power by throttling the number of dispatched instructions in the processor and the number of memory requests in the main memory, instead of exploiting the low-power states. As a result, it has the smallest power adaptation capacity among the three solutions. As introduced in Section 5.1, a fundamental difference between the coordinated solution and ProcOnly is that the coordinated solution utilizes the low-power states of both the processor and main memory while ProcOnly only manipulates the DVFS level of the processor. Therefore, the coordinated solution has the largest power adaptation capacity. Table 3 shows the average minimum power budget that can be achieved by the three power control algorithms using 8 workloads randomly selected from SPEC CPU2000. If the maximum power budget can be achieved is 270 W, we can see that the coordinated solution improves the power adaptation capacity up to 20% and 120%, compared with ProcOnly and PLI, respectively.

5.3 Application Performance

Now we compare the coordinated solution with the two baselines in terms of application performance.

ProcOnly. In this experiment, we run ProcOnly and the coordinated solution by using *gzip* under a power budget of 200 W. Figure 7(a) shows the memory bandwidth of running *gzip* in our simulation environment by forwarding $0.4B$ instructions. Figures 7(b) and (c) show the power consumption of the whole server, the processor, and the main memory in a typical run of ProcOnly and the

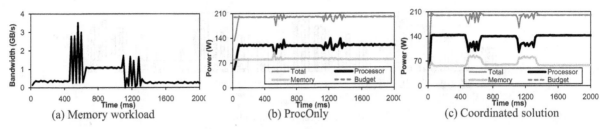

(a) Memory workload   (b) ProcOnly   (c) Coordinated solution

Figure 7: Comparison with ProcOnly during a typical run of gzip

coordinated solution, respectively. We can see tha *gzip* experiences time-varying memory workload from a bandwidth of $0.3GB/s$ to more than $3GB/s$ at runtime. However, ProcOnly only adjusts the power states of the processor, disregarding the variations of memory workload. Consequently, the power consumption of the memory system is unnecessarily high even at the time when the memory system experiences a low workload. In contrast, the proposed coordinated solution adapts to the low memory workload by putting the main memory in low-power states and putting the processor in relatively high-power states. When the memory workload increases significantly, the coordinated solution shifts power from the processor to the main memory. As a result, performance increases by approximately 11% when compared with ProcOnly, due to the coordination between the processor and main memory. Please note that, though the power temporarily violates the budget due to severe workload variations in Figures 7(b) and (c), these overshoots are instantaneous (*i.e.*, in tens of milliseconds) and the system is safe as long as the server power can be controlled back to the desired budget within the designed time interval that the power supply can sustain a power overload.

To more thoroughly investigate the performance comparison between the coordinated solution and ProcOnly, we run experiments by using a variety of workloads under different power budgets. Figures 8(a) and (b) show the performance comparison for CPU-intensive and memory-intensive workloads, respectively. Performance is measured as the average IPC of 120 data points from the beginning of each run. As we can see, the coordinated solution has better performance for all CPU-intensive workloads. The average improvement of the coordinated solution over ProcOnly at each power budget is shown in Figures 8(a) (*i.e.*, up to 23% on average at the budget of $170W$). This is because the coordinated solution can coordinate the power states of the processor and main memory by dynamically shifting power between them. We can also see that the lower the budget, the better improvement that the coordinated solution can achieve over ProcOnly (*i.e.*, the improvement increases from 6% to 23% as the budget decreases from $210W$ to $170W$). This is because when the power resource becomes more constrained, it is more important to efficiently allocate it between the processor and main memory for improved performance. As for the memory-intensive workloads shown in Figure 8(b), the coordinated solution has similar performance to ProcOnly. This is because those memory-intensive workloads have high memory traffic at the majority of time. As a result, the coordinated solution places the memory in high-power states almost all the time which is similar to what ProcOnly does. The reason why the coordinated solution has a very slightly lower performance (around 1%) than ProcOnly for *applu* and *art* is because *applu* and *art*'s memory workload oscillates more than other memory-intensive workloads so that the queue level varies significantly at runtime. As a result, the coordinated solution has a higher overhead by frequently adjusting the power states of the processor and main memory. This set of experiments demonstrates that the coordinated solution achieves considerably better application performance than ProcOnly for CPU-

intensive workloads and similar performance for memory-intensive workloads.

It is important to note that the *runtime* complexity of the proposed coordinated solution is comparable to that of ProcOnly, as discussed in Section 3.2. Please also note that the performance improvement is highly dependent on the percentage of memory power in the total power consumption of the system. The higher the percentage is, the higher the improvement will be. As presented in [14], memory power may have a much higher percentage in many high-end servers than our configuration (*i.e.*, around 50%). Therefore, the performance improvement of the coordinated solution can be even more significant.

PLI. The high idle power places PLI in a disadvantageous situation when the power budget is tight (*e.g.*, lower than the average power consumption). As shown in Figures 8(a) and (b), PLI has much lower performance than both the coordinated solution and ProcOnly. On average across all the budgets, the coordinated solution improves PLI by 110% and 120% for CPU-intensive and memory-intensive workloads, respectively. However, as the power budget increases, differences between PLI and the other two solutions becomes smaller.

5.4 Weight Allocation Schemes

Now we investigate the control penalty weight $\mathbf{R}(i)$ in the cost function (6) and the impacts of different allocation schemes on the coordination between the processor and main memory. To highlight the importance of the dynamic weight allocation based on the memory queue level, we compare the proposed moving average scheme (MA) with three static allocation schemes. The first one, referred to as *Equal*, gives the same preference to the processor and main memory by assigning an equal weight to them. The other two, referred to as *Proc-preferred* and *Mem-preferred*, always give preference to the processor and main memory, respectively.

To stress test the allocation schemes, we select 8 workloads and run all of them under a tight budget, $150W$, which is only approximately 56% of the system's peak power. We plot the average IPC of 200 control periods from the beginning in Figure 9. We can observe that: 1) For CPU-intensive workloads, MA has better performance than both Equal and Mem-preferred. The reason is that using lower processor power states unnecessarily for CPU-intensive workloads may hurt performance significantly. At the same time, MA has similar performance to Proc-preferred. Note that Proc-preferred has slightly better performance than MA (around 2%) for *gcc*. This is because MA has some overhead to find the best allocation weight based on the memory queue level, which results in slightly worse performance. 2) For memory-intensive workloads, MA has significantly better performance than Proc-preferred. In addition, MA has slightly better performance than both Equal and Mem-preferred (with the average 2% and 6%, respectively). This is because shifting power to the main memory for memory-intensive workloads has less impact on performance than shifting power to the processor for CPU-intensive workloads, since the memory latency dominates the performance bottleneck.

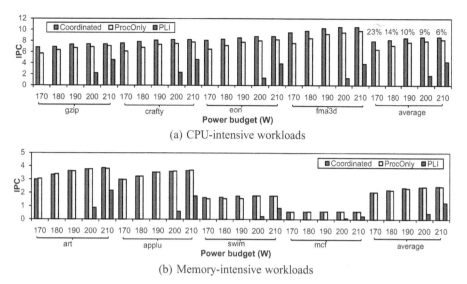

(a) CPU-intensive workloads

(b) Memory-intensive workloads

Figure 8: Comparison of performance among the coordinated solution, ProcOnly, and PLI

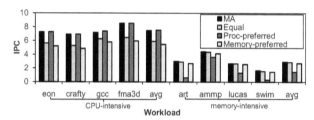

Figure 9: Comparison of weight allocation schemes

In general, MA, which dynamically allocates control penalty weights to the processor and main memory based on the memory queue level, is superior to other static allocation schemes.

6. RELATED WORK

Power consumption has become one of the most important design concerns for computing systems. Much prior work has focused on minimizing the power consumption within a specified performance guarantee. At the cluster level, Verma et al. [28] and Horvath et al. [8] propose different power management schemes to minimize power consumption while guaranteeing the application performance. At the server level, Li et al. develop algorithms for power adaptation between processor and memory so that energy can be minimized [16]. At the component level, energy conserving algorithms have been presented for processors [33], DRAM systems [34], disks [17], and caches [13]. However, all of the solutions cannot provide any explicit guarantees for the power consumption to stay below the desired budget though the performance is guaranteed. Our work is different in that we focus on a different but equally important problem, *i.e.*, power control to avoid power overload or thermal violations.

Several power provisioning strategies have been proposed by [4] to host the maximized number of servers allowed by the limited power supply in data centers. Different power control solutions have been proposed at different levels in data centers [25][31] to maximize application performance. Shang et al. present Power-Herd to control the peak power of interconnection networks [26]. At the server level, Lefurgy et al. propose a server power control solution based on basic feedback control theory by assuming that CPU is the major power contributor in servers [15]. Felter et al. propose to cap server peak power by shifting power between the processor and memory proportionally to the number of activities

[5]. At the cluster level, Wang et al. propose a MIMO controller to cap the cluster power consumption [30]. Raghavendr et al. also propose a hierarchical power control solution for server clusters [25]. However, those solutions conduct power control by adjusting only the DVFS levels of the server processors. In contrast, our work coordinates the processor and main memory for efficient server power capping based on an advanced optimal MIMO control theory. Our server-level power control solution can be used in a cluster setting with a cluster-level power control loop, such as the ones in [25] [31]. The cluster-level loop allocates power budget to each server, where our loop precisely controls the server power to the desired budget. As shown in Figure 4, our controller can react quickly to a sudden budget change. The settling time is just several control periods. Since our control period can be as short as $20ms$, the settling time is acceptably short compared with the time interval for a PDU-level circuit breaker to trip, which is about $2s$ for a power overload of 20% over the rated capacity [31].

Power control solutions have also been applied on different server components to address cooling and thermal problems. For example, Diniz et al. propose several policies to limit power consumption for DRAM systems [3]. Lin et al. develop dynamic thermal management (DTM) techniques for FB-DIMM memory systems by DVFS [18]. Various power control solutions have also been proposed to cap the power consumption of a chip multiprocessor with per-core DVFS [10][20][32]. However, all of them focus on a single component in servers and cannot be directly applied to server power control.

7. CONCLUSIONS

Existing power control solutions either rely solely on processor frequency scaling or shift power simply based on estimated system activities. In this paper, we propose a novel server power control solution that can precisely control the power consumption of a server to the desired budget. Our solution shifts power between processor and main memory in a coordinated manner by dynamically adjusting the voltage/frequency of the processor and placing memory ranks into different power states, based on their power demands indicated by the memory queue level, to achieve improved server performance. We compare with two state-of-the-art server power control solutions. One baseline relies only on processor frequency scaling while the other one uses estimated system activities for power shifting. Our experimental results demonstrate that our solution, on average, achieves up to 23% better performance than the first baseline for CPU-intensive benchmarks and doubles the performance of the second baseline when the power budget is tight. In addition, our solution significantly improves the power adaptation range and has better power control accuracy.

8. ACKNOWLEDGEMENTS

This work was supported, in part, by NSF under CAREER Award CNS-0845390 and Grants CCF-1017336, CNS-0915959, and CNS-0720663, and by ONR under Grant N00014-09-1-0750.

9. REFERENCES

[1] D. Brooks, V. Tiwari, and M. Martonosi. Wattch: a Framework for Architectural-level Power Analysis and Optimizations. In *ISCA*, 2000.

[2] D. Burger and T. M. Austin. The SimpleScalar Tool Set, Version 2.0. In *Technical Report CS-TR-1997-1342, University of Wisconsin, Madison*, 1997.

[3] B. Diniz, D. Guedes, W. Meira, and R. Bianchini. Limiting the Power Consumption of Main Memory. In *ISCA*, 2007.

[4] X. Fan, W.-D. Weber, and L. A. Barroso. Power Provisioning for a Warehouse-sized Computer. In *ISCA*, 2007.

[5] W. Felter, K. Rajamani, and T. W. Keller. A Performance-Conserving Approach for Reducing Peak Power Consumption in Server Systems. In *ICS*, 2005.

[6] G. F. Franklin, J. D. Powell, and M. Workman. *Digital Control of Dynamic Systems, 3rd edition*. Addition-Wesley, 1997.

[7] B. Ganesh, A. Jaleel, D. Wang, and B. Jacob. Fully-Buffered DIMM Memory Architectures: Understanding Mechanisms, Overheads and Scaling. In *HPCA*, 2007.

[8] T. Horvath, T. Abdelzaher, K. Skadron, and X. Liu. Dynamic Voltage Scaling in Multi-tier Web Servers with End-to-end Delay Control. *IEEE Transactions on Computers*, 56(4), 2007.

[9] Intel. Intel 845 Chipset: 82845 Memory Controller Hub (MCH) Datasheet. http://developer.intel.com/Assets/PDF/datasheet/290725.pdf, 2002.

[10] C. Isci, A. Buyuktosunoglu, C.-Y. Cher, P. Bose, and M. Martonosi. An Analysis of Efficient Multi-Core Global Power Management Policies: Maximizing Performance for a Given Power Budget. In *MICRO*, 2006.

[11] B. Jacob, Spencer, and D. Wang. *Memory Systems: Cache, DRAM, Disk*. Morgan Kaufmann, 2007.

[12] T. A. Johansen, W. Jackson, R. Schreiber, and P. Tøndel. Hardware Synthesis of Explicit Model Predictive Controllers. *IEEE Control Systems Technology*, 15(1), Jan. 2007.

[13] S. Kaxiras, Z. Hu, and M. Martonosi. Cache Decay: Exploiting Generational Behavior to Reduce Cache Leakage Power. In *ISCA*, July 2001.

[14] C. Lefurgy, K. Rajamani, F. Rawson, W. Felter, M. Kistler, and T. W. Keller. Energy Management for Commercial Servers. *IEEE Computer*, 36(12), Dec. 2003.

[15] C. Lefurgy, X. Wang, and M. Ware. Power capping: a prelude to power shifting. *Cluster Computing*, 11, 2008.

[16] X. Li, R. Gupta, S. V. Adve, and Y. Zhou. Cross-Component Energy Management: Joint Adaptation of Processor and Memory. *ACM Transactions on Architecture and Code Optimization*, 4, 2007.

[17] X. Li, Z. Li, F. David, P. Zhou, Y. Zhou, S. Adve, and S. Kumar. Performance Directed Energy Management for Main Memory and Disks. In *ASPLOS*, 2004.

[18] J. Lin, H. Zheng, Z. Zhu, H. David, and Z. Zhang. Thermal Modeling and Management of DRAM Memory Systems. In *ISCA*, July 2007.

[19] J. Lin, H. Zheng, Z. Zhu, E. Gorbatov, H. David, and Z. Zhang. Software Thermal Management of DRAM Memory for Multicore Systems. In *SIGMETRICS*, 2008.

[20] K. Ma, X. Li, M. Chen, and X. Wang. Scalable Power Control for Many-Core Architectures Running Multi-threaded Applications. In *ISCA*, 2011.

[21] J. M. Maciejowski. *Predictive Control with Constraints*. Prentice Hall, 2002.

[22] Micron. Data Sheet. http://download.micron.com/pdf/datasheets/modules/ddr2/HTF9C64_128x72F.pdf, 2007.

[23] Micron. Micron System Power Calculator. http://download.micron.com/downloads/misc/ddr2_power_calc_web.xls, 2007.

[24] Micron. Data Sheet. http://download.micron.com/pdf/datasheets/dram/ddr2/1GbDDR2.pdf, 2009.

[25] R. Raghavendra, P. Ranganathan, V. Talwar, Z. Wang, and X. Zhu. No Power Struggle: Coordinated Multi-level Power Management for the Data Center. In *ASPLOS*, 2008.

[26] L. Shang, L.-S. Peh, and N. K. Jha. PowerHerd: A Distributed Scheme for Dynamically Satisfying Peak-Power Constraints in Interconnection Networks. *IEEE Transactions on Computer-Aided Design of Circuits and Systems*, 25(1), 2006.

[27] K. Skadron, M. R. Stan, W. Huang, S. Velusamy, K. Sankaranarayanan, and D. Tarjan. Temperature-aware Microarchitecture: Modeling and Implementation. *ACM Transactions on Architecture and Code Optimization*, 1, Mar. 2004.

[28] A. Verma, G. Dasgupta, T. K. Nayak, P. De, and R. Kothari. Server Workload Analysis for Power Minimization using Consolidation. In *USENIX*, 2009.

[29] D. Wang, B. Ganesh, N. Tuaycharoen, K. Baynes, A. Jaleel, , and B. Jacob. DRAMsim: A Memory System Simulator. *SIGARCH Computer Architecture News*, 33, Nov. 2005.

[30] X. Wang, M. Chen, and X. Fu. MIMO Power Control for High-Density Servers in an Enclosure. *IEEE Transactions on Parallel and Distributed Systems*, 21(10), Oct. 2010.

[31] X. Wang, M. Chen, C. Lefurgy, and T. W. Keller. SHIP: Scalable Hierarchical Power Control for Large-Scale Data Centers. In *PACT*, 2009.

[32] Y. Wang, K. Ma, and X. Wang. Temperature-Constrained Power Control for Chip Multiprocessors with Online Model Estimation. In *ISCA*, 2009.

[33] Q. Wu, P. Juang, M. Martonosi, and D. W. Clark. Formal Online Methods for Voltage/Frequency Control in Multiple Clock Domain Microprocessors. In *ASPLOS*, 2004.

[34] H. Zheng, J. Lin, Z. Zhang, E. Gorbatov, H. David, and Z. Zhu. Mini-Rank: Adaptive DRAM Architecture for Improving Memory Power Efficiency. In *MICRO*, 2008.

Optimizing Throughput/Power Trade-offs in Hardware Transactional Memory Using DVFS and Intelligent Scheduling

Clay Hughes
ECE Department
Florida State University
Panama City, FL 32405
chughes@pc.fsu.edu

Tao Li
ECE Department
University of Florida
Gainesville, FL 32611
taoli@ece.ufl.edu

ABSTRACT

Power has emerged as a first-order design constraint in modern processors and has energized microarchitecture researchers to produce a growing number of power optimization proposals. Almost in tandem with the move toward more energy-efficient designs, architects have been increasing the number of processing elements (PEs) on a single chip and promoting the concept of running multithreaded workloads. Nevertheless, software is still lagging behind and is often unable to exploit these additional resources – giving rise to transactional memory. Transactional memory is a promising programming abstraction that makes it easier for programmers to exploit the resources available in many-core processor systems by removing some of the complexity associated with traditional lock-based programming. This paper proposes new techniques to merge the power and transactional memory domains.

An analysis of the per-core and chip-wide power consumption of hardware transactional memory systems (HTMs) pinpoints two areas ripe for power management policies: transactional stalls and aborts. The first proposed policy uses dynamic voltage and frequency scaling (DVFS) during transactional stall periods. By frequency scaling PEs based on their transactional state, DVFS can increase the throughput and energy efficiency of HTMs. The second method uses a transaction's conflict probability to reschedule transactions and clock gate aborted PEs to reduce overall contention and power consumption within the system. The proposed techniques are evaluated using three HTM configurations and are shown to reduce the energy delay squared product (ED2P) of the STAMP and SPLASH-2 benchmarks by an average of 18% when combined. Synthetic workloads are used to explore a wider range of program behaviors and the optimizations are shown to reduce the ED2P by an average of 29%. For a comparison, this work is shown reduce the ED2P by up to 30% relative to previous proposals for energy reduction in HTMs (e.g. transaction serialization).

Categories and Subject Descriptors

C.5.0 [**Computer System Implementation**]: General

General Terms

Performance, Design.

Keywords

Transactional memory, power.

1. INTRODUCTION

Power dissipation continues to be a first-order design constraint for modern computer designs from the chip level to data centers. At the chip level, power consumption can affect its reliability and performance and can increase packaging and manufacturing costs. And while chip multi-processors (CMPs) offer better energy efficiency than previous uniprocessors [14], they still suffer from the same heat removal problems as previous generations. However, unlike previous generations, CMPs provide more opportunities for balancing energy use. CMPs are designed for running multiple threads of execution, which often vary in performance and resource requirements, making them ideal candidates for runtime optimizations that can maximize program performance while minimizing chip power consumption.

Many of the threads executing in modern machines are actually disparate processes each running with a single thread. In order to exploit the types of resources offered by CMPs, programmers need to begin changing the way they write code, writing programs that consist of multiple threads that are able to take advantage of the ever-increasing number of processing elements (PEs). However, exploiting the available data and task parallelism in a program is often a challenging and time-consuming process, requiring significant time investments to extract performance and guarantee correctness. Transactional memory (TM) [7] has been proposed as a programming technique to replace locks, shifting some of the burden of synchronization from the programmer to the system architecture – in effect providing an abstraction of the implementation. While transactional memory was conceived of as a means to shift the programming burden, hardware implementations have ancillary benefits such as increased performance over locks and potential energy savings [21].

This work focuses on how transactional memory can be leveraged for energy and performance optimizations, making the following contributions:

- Dynamic frequency and scaling (DVFS) is introduced to reduce the power consumption of stalled processing elements and increase overall throughput by setting the clock frequency and supply voltage for each PE based on its current execution state and those of the collocated PEs. The optimization decreases the amount of **time** that a processor holds its read and write sets by increasing the clock frequency of NACKing PEs and decreases the **power consumption** of NACK'd PEs by throttling the clock frequency. Using this DVFS policy improves the energy

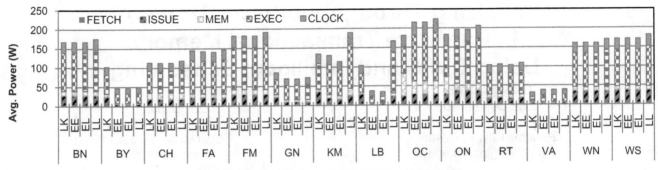

Figure 1. Benchmark Power (SPLASH-2 and STAMP)

delay product (ED2P), which is a joint measurement of the system power and performance, by up to 43%.

- A new preemptive transaction scheduler is introduced based on the system's conflict density. This scheduling policy prevents potentially contentious transactions from issuing and clock gates the resident PE, reducing the system power. Furthermore, because there are fewer executing transactions those that remain running have a lower probability of experiencing an abort, which increases total throughput and reduces the system ED2P by as much as 76%.

- The new policies are then combined and compared against previously proposed power management techniques for transactional memory that use clock gating and transactional serialization. The new policies show improvements between 12% and 30% relative to the previous work.

The next section describes the motivation behind the proposed schemes. Section 3 contains the evaluation methodology and implementation details. The proposed power management policies and results are described in Section 4. The paper concludes with a discussion of related work in Section 5 and concludes in Section 6.

2. MOTIVATION

This section provides an overview of the power of the different hardware transactional memory systems using the SPLASH-2 [31] and STAMP [19] benchmarks. Benchmarks are referenced by the abbreviations in Table 3 and the transactional memory systems are described using their primary design points: conflict detection and version management. Conflict detection defines when conflicts are detected and version management defines where new and old values within a transaction are stored. Both use the same basic nomenclature and can be either eager or lazy. With eager conflict detection, addresses are checked for conflicts on each read and write within the transaction whereas lazy checks addresses when a transaction attempts to commit. Eager version management writes new values in place and copies old values elsewhere; lazy does the opposite, leaving old values in place and writing new values elsewhere. The system designs are referenced as LK – lock, EE – eager conflict/eager versioning, EL – eager conflict/lazy versioning, and LL – lazy conflict/lazy versioning.

Consider Figure 1, which shows a breakdown of the power consumption from 14 benchmarks using locks, eager-eager, eager-lazy, and lazy-lazy. There is no measurable difference in the average power consumption of the SPLASH-2 benchmarks for the lock and eager conflict detection schemes but the average power for lazy conflict detection is slightly higher due to increased log utilization. For the STAMP benchmarks, the average power varies from 32W to 192W. While any model would suffice for the

SPLASH-2 benchmarks, eager-lazy minimizes the average power for the STAMP benchmarks. However, the ED2P for these benchmarks suggests that because their behavior is so diverse, there is no clear design choice that minimizes the power-performance. These experimental results show that when there is little or no contention, hardware transactional memory consumes approximately the same amount of power as a lock-based system. Under moderate or heavy contention, some of the transactional memory designs have much lower average power than their lock counterparts. What is important is that the slack power available in these benchmarks can be exploited to improve the performance while limiting the maximum chip power and temperature.

3. METHODOLOGY

This section describes the specific implementation details of the hardware transactional memory systems as well as the simulation environment, methodology, and benchmarks used to evaluate the power and energy characteristics of transactional memory workloads.

3.1 CMP DESIGN

Figure 2 shows the basic system architecture and Table 1 summarizes the design parameters. The CMP system consists of 4 processing elements based on 65nm technology; the base number of processors was chosen to reflect currently available configurations. The processors are 4-issue out-of-order with a split 64kB 4-way set associative write-back L1 cache. There is a 4MB 8-way set associative shared L2 cache split into 8 banks. The off chip memory is modeled as 4GB of DDR3. Cache coherence is maintained using a snoop-based MESI protocol. The power management structures are discussed in Section 3.2.

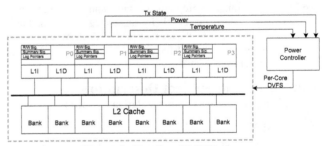

Figure 2. Baseline CMP Design

3.2 SIMULATOR DESIGN

The transactional memory simulator is a modified version of SuperTrans [22], a cycle-accurate detailed hardware transactional memory model that includes support for eager and lazy versioning and conflict detection modes. The conflict detection and version management schemes in SuperTrans are abstract, meaning while they were guided by previously proposed implementations [6]

Table 1. Baseline Configuration

		Parameters
Core Model	Processing Elements	2.4GHz, out-of-order, 4-issue, 65nm
	L1D Cache	64kB, 4-way, 32B blks, 2-cycle latency
	L2 Cache	4MB, 8-way, 32B blks, 9-cycle latency
	Off-chip memory	240 cycle latency
	V_{DD}	0.6-1V (default of 1V)
Transactional Model	Conflict Detection	Eager and lazy
	Version Management	Eager and lazy
	Conflict Resolution	Requester/Committer wins with exponential backoff
	Conflict Granularity	32B
	Primary Baseline	50
	Primary Variable	9
	Secondary Baseline	12

[20], they do not strictly follow any specific transactional memory design; they are idealized representations. SuperTrans was modified to mimic a generic signature-based transactional memory system similar to LogTM-SE [32] and BulkSC [4] and tracks read- and write-sets using per-processor Bloom filters [2]. Both versioning schemes implement a cacheable logging structure, which holds the virtual addresses and old (eager) or new (lazy) values of memory blocks modified during a transaction.

Table 1 lists both the core and transactional model parameters. Conflict detection is carried out per-cache line. The primary/secondary baseline latencies and primary variable latency quantify the latencies associated with a commit or an abort. The primary latency is associated with the long operation for the selected versioning scheme – abort for eager and commit for lazy. The secondary latency is the opposite; it sets the delays for a fast operation – commit for eager and abort for lazy. The baseline latency is the static overhead associated with a transaction (*e.g.* the sum of the bus arbitration and log overhead) and the variable latency is the additional time required for a transaction based on the transaction size.

The signature implementation uses the results from Sanchez *et al.* [25] and Yen *et al.* [33] for modeling the hardware implementation of signatures. Each 1024b signature is represented as 2 64B SRAMs along with the logic gates necessary to implement the H_3 hashing functions. Each hash function consists of $\frac{n}{2}$ 2-input XORs for each bit of the hash and each XOR is assumed to consist of 6 transistors [30]. The dynamic power for each XOR was estimated using the following formula: $\sum_{i=1}^{N} \frac{1}{2} C_i V_{dd}^2 f_i$ where C_i is the output capacitance of the ith gate, V_{dd} is the supply voltage, f_i is the switching frequency, and N is the total number of gates. The values were estimated using CACTI [28] and the switching frequency was assumed to be the clock frequency, which gives a worst-case estimation.

The power management system was modeled after Intel's Foxton Technology (FT) [18] and includes on-chip power and temperature sensors and a small microcontroller. Internally, the microcontroller was modeled as a single structure that consumes 0.5% of the total chip power. DVFS was added to SESC with the levels shown in Table 2. Wattch [3] was integrated into the simulator to estimate the energy consumption for 64 individual structures per processor plus an additional 18 global structures based on values obtained from CACTI [28]. HotSpot [27] was used to estimate on-chip temperature, which is based on the current chip power and feeds into HotLeakage [35] to estimate the leakage power. Although recent work has explored the feasibility of on-chip regulators [12], this work assumes that voltage transitions require approximately 50k cycles at the base frequency or 20µs. When down-scaling the DVFS level, the frequency drop occurs over a two cycle period with the voltage lagging behind over the transition period. Up-scaling the DVFS level increases the frequency and voltage simultaneously over the transition period.

3.3 WORKLOADS

For the evaluation, 14 benchmarks from two different benchmarking suites (SPLASH-2 and STAMP) along with 15 synthetic benchmarks were used. While SPLASH-2 provides a good comparison of design points for fine-grained transactions and highly optimized lock-behavior, it is believed that future transactional workloads will also be comprised of coarse granularity transactions that may not be well tuned. To capture this trend, workloads from the STAMP suite (ver. 0.9.6) of transactional benchmarks are used in the evaluation. Since the STAMP suite does not provide lock-based equivalents of the transactional benchmarks, lock versions were generated using the same level of granularity as the transactions. Table 3 gives the input set used for each benchmark. All benchmarks were run to completion.

TransPlant [23], a parameterized transactional memory benchmark creation tool, was used to generate the synthetic benchmarks. TransPlant takes a statistical descriptor file as an input and produces C-code that can be compiled and run on a simulator. Table 4 describes the first order design parameters that the user can specify. One of the goals of this work is to isolate those program characteristics that have the largest impact on the power. To accomplish this, the workloads are constructed so that the transactional work, in terms of instruction count and composition, is held constant. While task decomposition in real applications is not straight forward, keeping the total work

Table 3. Benchmark Parameters

Benchmark	Abbreviation	Input	Benchmark	Abbreviation	Input
barnes	BN	16K particles	*labyrinth*	LB	x32-y32-z3-n96
bayes	BY	1024 records	*ocean-con*	OC	258x258
cholesky	CH	tk15.O	*ocean-non*	ON	66x66
fluidanimate	FA	35kMips	*raytrace*	RT	Teapot
fmm	FM	16K particles	*vacation*	VA	4096 tasks
genome	GN	g256 s16 n16384	*water-nsq*	WN	512 molecules
kmeans	KM	Random1000_12	*water-sp*	WS	512 molecules

Table 2. Frequency and Supply Voltage

Freq (GHz)	2.93	2.67	2.40	2.27	2.20	2.13	2.00	1.87	1.73	1.60	1.47	1.33	1.20	1.07
V_{dd} (V)	1.00	1.00	1.00	0.97	0.95	0.93	0.90	0.87	0.84	0.80	0.77	0.72	0.67	0.60

Table 4. Transactional- and Microarchitecture-Independent Characteristics From TransPlant

Characteristic	Description
Threads	Total number of threads in the program
Homogeneity	All threads have the same characteristics
Tx Granularity	Number of instructions in a transaction
Tx Stride	Number of instructions between transactions
Read Set	Number of unique reads in a transaction
Write Set	Number of unique writes in a transaction
Shared Memory	Number of global memory accesses
Conflict Dist.	Distribution of global memory accesses
Tx Inst. Mix	Instruction mix of transactional section(s)
Sq Inst. Mix	Instruction mix of sequential section(s)

constant allows variables to be isolated. For example, if work was not held constant, transaction granularity could not be used as an independent variable in these workloads. Unless otherwise noted, transactions are evenly spaced throughout the program, allowing for a direct comparison across dimensions. Each transaction is responsible for at least one unique load and one unique store so that all transactions have at least some chance of conflicting; the probability of a conflict is random for each benchmark. In the granularity experiments, the work is broken down into successively smaller granularities so that as the granularity of the transactions becomes finer, transactions contain fewer instructions but the total number of transactions required to complete the work increases proportionately. While TransPlant provides two modes of conflict modeling, a high mode in which the distance between pairs of load/store operations to the same cache line is maximized and a random mode where this distance is randomized, only the random mode is used for the granularity experiments. Finally, it should be noted that since transactional work is calculated on a per-thread basis, trends can be compared across a varying number of processing elements, however the raw total cycle counts will differ based upon the number of threads. As such, all of the results for the synthetic benchmarks are reported as the mean of 50 trials.

4. SCHEDULING AND DVFS FOR IMPROVED POWER-PERFORMANCE

The discussion in Section 2 suggests that aborts and stalls have a large impact on the power and performance of many of the benchmarks. If true then there should be a net power-performance gain by avoiding time-intensive aborts and stalls. The first proposed policy leverages dynamic voltage and frequency scaling (DVFS) to decrease the amount of time processing elements are stalled during a NACK. A second policy, based on transaction scheduling, is proposed that utilizes a transaction's current conflict density [9] and its past performance to determine whether a transaction should be preemptively stalled, reducing a program's contention. A further extension, clock gating, is used to reduce the dynamic power of the stalled transaction.

4.1 DVFS FOR IMPROVED THROUGHPUT

Dynamic voltage and frequency scaling (DVFS) was introduced [16] as a means to reduce system power by dynamically controlling the voltage and frequency of PEs based on the system load. DVFS can be implemented at many levels within a system – in the microarchitecture [17], the operating system [11], or at the compiler level [8]. In this work, the power controller is modeled as Intel's FT controller and embedded in the microarchitecture.

On each 2μs probe interval, the conflict manager is queried. If a stall is detected, the DVFS manager is invoked and the stalled

core's frequency is decreased by 266MHz while the stalling core frequency is increased by 133MHz until the upper and lower bounds are reached, at 2.93GHz and 1.07GHz, respectively. If there are multiple stalled transactions residing on multiple processing elements, then the processor frequency is increased an additional step for each stalled processing element. On a successful commit, the power manager is preempted and all processing elements are returned to their default operating frequency. In the event of an abort, the process is repeated. However, if the abort count exceeds some allowable threshold, the aborted processing element is put into an idle state. While in this state, the core's clocks are gated (phase locked loops are disabled) and its caches flushed. The aborting processing element is then assigned to the highest performance state. The processing element remains at this frequency unless the chip-wide power approaches its threshold or unless there is a thermal emergency. On a successful commit, it returns to its default operating frequency and sends a signal to wake the idle processing element. By relaxing the contention between the transactions and exploiting the newly available slack power, total throughput is increased while maintaining or reducing average chip-wide and per-processing element power beneath the package's allowed electrical and thermal limits.

4.2 DVFS RESULTS

Figure 3 shows the ED2P (Et^2) of the transactional execution normalized to the baseline of each implementation when using the dynamic voltage and frequency scaling scheme described in Section 4.1. As can be seen from the figure, the proposed scheme improves the ED2P by 8% for eager-eager, 7% for eager-lazy, and 7% for lazy-lazy. Because only one processor is allowed to have an up-scaled frequency and multiple processors can be down-scaled, much of the improvement comes from a reduction in energy consumption. There is a greater improvement in the ED2P for benchmarks that spend long periods of time with multiple processors in a NACK'd state such as *bayes*, *kmeans*, and *labyrinth*, but the reasons for the improvements can be applied to the remaining benchmarks.

Bayes: This is the longest running benchmark and is comprised of very large critical sections, averaging 87k instructions. However, the parent thread has a long setup time and skews cycle calculations, making it appear that there is very little contention. Once the program reaches the parallel regions, *bayes* is highly contentious. The read and write sets, while large, are small relative to the transaction size with very few circular conflicts. This composition allows the eager conflict detection scheme to resolve most conflicts through NACKs, which benefits from the DVFS policy. While the eager schemes can NACK while waiting for a potentially conflicting address, lazy schemes only check for conflicts when a transaction commits. The DVFS policy considers contention for the commit bus as a NACK, which along with the abort policy is why there is moderate improvement for the lazy conflict detection scheme but less so, for all benchmarks, than the eager conflict detection schemes.

Kmeans: This benchmark has the highest ratio of stall cycles to total cycles of all of the benchmarks. The DVFS policy reduces the average power of eager-eager by 13%, eager-lazy by 14%, and lazy-lazy by 16% while reducing the execution time by 2% in all cases. For *kmeans*, lazy-lazy obtains more benefit because, for the baseline case, the transactions suffer from contention for the commit bus as well as aborts, extending the execution time and increasing the energy consumption due to rollbacks. The DVFS

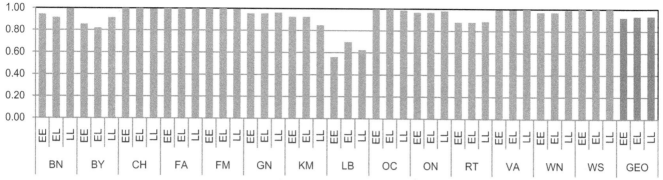

Figure 3. ED2P (Et²) Using DVFS Normalized to Base Case

policy helps by reducing the number of aborts from 412 to 278, decreasing the total energy and the execution time.

Labyrinth: This benchmark consists of very coarse-grain critical regions, averaging almost 400k instructions each, making it the coarsest of the benchmarks and giving it the highest ratio of contentious work – both in terms of aborts and stalls. All of the transactional implementations suffer from multiple rollbacks and stalls. This is the only benchmark where the average power increases with the proposed DVFS. From Figure 1, the average power for the eager conflict detection schemes is 30W. The power is low because rollbacks are expensive in terms of cycles but only require the L1D, L2, and data buses, resulting in lower power density. By scaling the frequency and allowing one thread to complete faster than others many of the aborts are avoided (36%), which has a twofold effect. First, the power density is higher because the pipeline is active more often. Second, because there is not as much time spent performing bookkeeping and rollbacks, the execution time is shortened, which increases the power density but decreases total execution time. However, despite the fact that the average power increases to 62.2W for both eager schemes, it remains low enough that there is never a thermal emergency. The average power for the lazy-lazy platform decreases by 26%. The reduction is primarily due to the decrease in aborts with a small decrease in the average power consumption.

While these three benchmarks show the most improvement, the causes of the reduction in ED2P can be extended to all of the benchmarks, to some degree. The average power of *cholesky*, *fmm*, *ocean-contiguous*, *vacation*, and *water-spatial* remains roughly the same for all of the transactional models when using DVFS but the execution time is reduced. For the remaining benchmarks, the average power is reduced along with the execution time (with the exception of *labyrinth* when using eager conflict detection).

4.3 CONFLICT PROBABILITY

While the DVFS policy discussed in Section 4.1 primarily targeted NACKing transactions, the preemptive stalling policy is targeted at aborting transactions and perceived contention within the transactional system. When a transaction aborts, the contention manager resolves the conflict using the prescribed resolution policy. In the systems discussed in Section 2, the contention manager invokes an exponential backoff policy that prevents a transaction from reissuing using an exponentially increasing interval, up to some maximum. The proposed addition to the contention manager is called when a transaction begins its execution and works in conjunction with the contention manager. A software manager is invoked within the power controller to compute the transaction's conflict potential for the current iteration, $C[n]$, given by $C[n] = \alpha C[n-1] + (1-\alpha)(C_p)$. Where the conflict probability, C_p, is:

$$C_p = \left(\frac{CurrentAborts}{CurrentAborts + \beta} * \frac{ActiveTransactions}{TotalAvailableProcessors}\right)$$

α and β are scaling factors used to weight the effect of the previous conflict potential and to determine how responsive the system is to the number of aborts, respectively. If the conflict potential exceeds some threshold, ρ, then the transaction is preempted and stalled for a brief interval before it attempts to reissue. If the potential is below the threshold, the transaction is allowed to issue normally. When a transaction begins, a software manager is invoked on the on-chip microcontroller to calculate the new conflict probability. In the simulator, this is modeled as seven floating-point instructions that must be completed before the transaction begins. The result is stored in a special register in the calling PE. Clock gating is instant while wake-up from clock gating takes two cycles.

Initial tests showed a minor improvement in the ED2P for lazy conflict detection but almost no change for eager. This was because eager is already adept at avoiding many of the aborts that affect the lazy implementation and, although there was measurably reduced energy for some of the more contentious benchmarks, much of the improvement in lazy came from reduced runtime. To improve the results, clock gating was introduced to work in tandem with the contention manager and the new scheduling policy. The new scheme works the same as above with two modifications. First, when a transaction is stalled, the processor's clocks are halted, effectively setting the dynamic power to zero for the processor on which the transaction is executing. Second, the processor does not wakeup after a given interval, instead it waits for another transaction to commit before un-gating occurs.

4.4 CONFLICT PROBABILITY RESULTS

This evaluation is based on the same configurations from Section 4.2 with the addition of the conflict probability scheme. Figure 4 shows the new ED2P using the scheduling enhancement normalized to the base case for each design point. Improvement in the ED2P is seen for all but two benchmarks, *genome* and *raytrace* on the lazy-lazy platform. For most of the benchmarks, the reduction in ED2P is the same across all of the transactional implementations, which is due to the lack of contention in the benchmarks. However, the scheduling scheme does reduce both the static and dynamic power of the benchmarks. On average, the proposed scheduling policy produces in a 6% decrease in the static power due to the reduction in execution time and a 9% decrease in dynamic power because of the clock gating scheme. The reduction in energy use and execution times leads to an ED2P

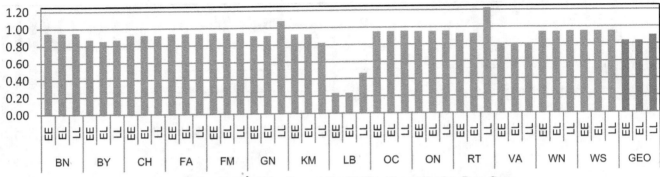

Figure 4. ED2P (Et²) Using Preemptive Stalling Normalized to Base Case

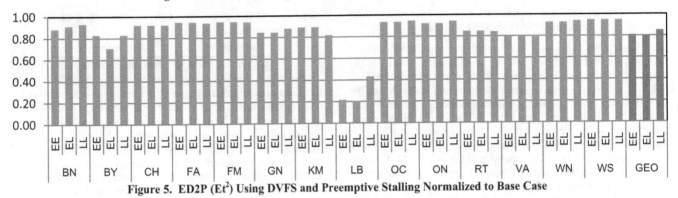

Figure 5. ED2P (Et²) Using DVFS and Preemptive Stalling Normalized to Base Case

reduction of 17% for eager-eager, 17% for eager-lazy, and 10% for lazy-lazy.

Of the benchmarks, *labyrinth* shows the largest improvement across all three implementations while the remainder of the applications show modest improvements. The reason is that *labyrinth* spends more than 98% of its cycles in a NACK or abort state while the other benchmarks typically spend less than 1% of their time in these states. This benchmark consists of very coarse-grain critical regions, averaging almost 400k instructions each, making it the coarsest of the benchmarks and giving it the highest ratio of contentious work. The transactional implementations suffer from multiple rollbacks and stalls and the lazy-lazy scheme suffers from twice as many aborts. All three schemes obtain more than a 2x ED2P improvement for *labyrinth* with the eager conflict detection schemes reaching a 5x improvement. For lazy-lazy, the total runtime remains roughly the same but there are 78% fewer aborts, which means that the dynamic power used for speculative execution of these transactions has been saved through preemption and clock gating. For the eager conflict detection schemes, preemptive stalling provides more than 50% reduction in runtime, which directly reduces ED2P.

The outliers on the lazy conflict detection scheme, *genome* and *raytrace*, are due to the restrictive scheduling algorithm. Although their total energy is lower than in the base cases, the execution time for these benchmarks is increased by several million cycles, which leads to the increased ED2P. For example, *genome* contains nearly 6k critical sections but less than 1% of them result in aborts for the transactional models. The critical sections in *genome* average 2.4k instructions over 4.9k cycles and comprise 70% of the dynamic execution. When the algorithm is applied to *genome*, the number of aborts is reduced from 106 to 87 and the number of NACKs is reduced from 3794 to 2988 but the average number of cycles consumed by each transaction increases to 5.7k. The algorithm does not consider individual transactions, meaning that

it only knows that there are *t* active transactions and not the program counter of each transaction. If each available processor has an active transaction and if the abort count increases too quickly, the result is an overly pessimistic representation of the contention, stalling transactions longer than may be necessary. The end result of which is akin to the serialization scheme discussed in Section 4.6. The scaling factors, α and β, are fixed; a feedback mechanism that can shift these for each active process may provide a better prediction mechanism but the philosophy behind both of the proposed designs was to provide a simple implementation with very little runtime overhead.

4.5 COMBINING THE SCHEMES

Although both of the policies described in Sections 4.1 and 4.3 are linked with aborts, the DVFS policy relies on NACKs as the primary motivator while the preemptive scheduler relies on perceived contention, allowing the schemes to be use together. Figure 5 shows the ED2P when both DVFS and the probabilistic conflict scheduler are used together. The proposed policies effectively work together, providing a reduction in the ED2P of 19% for eager-eager, 20% for eager-lazy, and 15% for lazy-lazy. The trend is similar to that of Figure 4 because the contention management policy provides the majority of the energy reduction for most of the benchmarks. The exceptions are *barnes*, *bayes*, and *raytrace* (and *genome* for lazy-lazy), which benefit more from the DVFS policy.

4.6 MEASURING UP

In this section, the proposed DVFS and scheduling policies are compared with two previous studies. The first comparison is based on work done by Sanyal *et al.* [26]. When a transaction is aborted by a committing transaction, the clocks of the aborted processor are halted and remain so until a local timer expires. The timer value is derived from an equation that takes into account the abort count and how long the blocked processor has been gated.

146

Table 5. Performance Comparison (nJ·s²)

	EE			EL			LL		
	DVFS+CS	Gating	Serial	DVFS+CS	Gating	Serial	DVFS+CS	Gating	Serial
BN	4.10E+10	4.65E+10	4.65E+10	4.24E+10	4.64E+10	4.65E+10	4.34E+10	4.65E+10	4.66E+10
BY	2.98E+11	3.58E+11	3.63E+11	2.53E+11	3.57E+11	3.62E+11	2.92E+11	3.50E+11	3.37E+11
CH	1.92E+08	2.09E+08	2.09E+08	1.92E+08	2.09E+08	2.09E+08	1.93E+08	2.09E+08	2.10E+08
FA	1.86E+10	1.98E+10	1.98E+10	1.86E+10	1.98E+10	1.98E+10	1.86E+10	1.99E+10	1.99E+10
FM	6.76E+10	7.15E+10	7.15E+10	6.76E+10	7.15E+10	7.15E+10	6.73E+10	7.15E+10	7.15E+10
GN	5.13E+04	5.63E+04	5.77E+04	5.13E+04	5.63E+04	5.77E+04	5.65E+04	5.72E+04	5.85E+04
KM	8.38E+08	9.22E+08	9.41E+08	8.38E+08	9.22E+08	9.41E+08	1.47E+09	9.03E+08	
LB	3.47E+07	2.85E+08	1.03E+09	3.29E+07	2.85E+08	1.03E+09	2.85E+07	1.12E+08	
OC	5.83E+09	6.23E+09	6.24E+09	5.83E+09	6.23E+09	6.24E+09	5.90E+09	6.23E+09	6.24E+09
ON	9.51E+06	9.76E+06	1.03E+07	9.51E+06	9.76E+06	1.03E+07	9.74E+06	9.94E+06	1.03E+07
RT	9.33E+07	9.95E+07	1.16E+08	9.33E+07	9.95E+07	1.16E+08	1.02E+08	1.15E+08	1.40E+08
VA	3.21E+07	4.03E+07	4.03E+07	3.21E+07	4.03E+07	4.03E+07	3.23E+07	4.03E+07	4.03E+07
WN	2.88E+08	3.10E+08	3.11E+08	2.88E+08	3.10E+08	3.11E+08	2.93E+08	3.11E+08	3.11E+08
WS	1.92E+08	2.03E+08	2.03E+08	1.92E+08	2.03E+08	2.03E+08	1.93E+08	2.03E+08	2.03E+08
GEO	4.86E+08	6.15E+08	6.88E+08	4.79E+08	6.15E+08	6.88E+08	5.08E+08	5.82E+08	6.56E+08

For the experiments presented here, the model is ideal – meaning that the structures proposed in their work are not modeled at the microarchitecture level and the delay algorithm is able to complete instantly. It should be noted that the original paper used an analytical model to derive results based on memory traces, not integrated functional and timing models. The second comparison is from Moreshet *et al.* [21] who proposed a serialization algorithm for power-savings in hardware transactional memory. When a conflict is detected and a transaction is forced to abort, instead of reissuing the transaction it is placed in a queue until a successful commit is detected at which point it is reissued. When the queue is empty, the system returns to its default state. For their work, the authors only reported the power of the memory subsystem; the results reported here are for the entire processor and main memory.

Table 5 provides the results for both the gating (**gating**) and serialization (**serial**) schemes along with the proposed DVFS and scheduling (**DVFS+CS**) policies proposed in this paper. Clock gating alone does not noticeably reduce the ED2P for most of the benchmarks. Although the average power of the benchmarks is reduced by an average of 0.9% for eager-eager, 0.7% for eager-lazy, and 1.1% for lazy-lazy, the execution time is increased as well, offsetting any benefit. The exceptions are *kmeans* and *labyrinth*. The ED2P for *kmeans* is an improvement over DVFS+CS using clock gating and is explained in the discussion in Section 4.4 For *labyrinth*, the average power increases by 118% for eager-eager and eager-lazy but whose execution time is decreased by 37%, resulting in a net loss in the power-performance domain. While the gating algorithm can save some energy in a hardware transactional memory system, it has the drawback of limiting the performance. For the serialization algorithm, the results are much the same (note that *kmeans* and *labyrinth* on the lazy-lazy system would not complete). Although there is a slight reduction (less than 1% on average) in the average power for most of the benchmarks, as with the clock gating method most of the reduction is offset by increased execution time.

The combined policies proposed in this paper provide between 21-30% improvement in ED2P reduction relative to clock gating and serialization for eager conflict detection and 12-22% for lazy conflict detection. It is clear that for transactional programs with an abundance of contention, serialization and clock gating cannot improve the power and performance jointly and both the DVFS

method and the contention prediction algorithm proposed in Sections 4.1 and 4.3 provide superior results. If the future of transactional memory is to increase the efficiency of parallel programming, then it can be expected that highly optimized programs like *cholesky* and *ocean* will not be the norm and programs are more likely to resemble some of the STAMP benchmarks. Regardless, to highlight the effect that the proposed methods have on a range of transactional memory program behavior, synthetic benchmarks are needed.

4.7 SYNTHETIC WORKLOADS

This section provides an analysis of the power and performance of the different hardware transactional memory systems using synthetic benchmarks. Synthetic benchmarks [1] are miniature programs for use in early design evaluations. The advantage of synthetic benchmarks is that they can be used when the simulation time of real benchmarks is prohibitively long or for design space evaluation where no suitable benchmark exists, as is the case for this research. The benchmarks for this analysis are derived by employing a parameterized form of workload synthesis using the TransPlant [23] tool.

For these experiments, the transactional granularity is scaled by powers of 2 beginning with 8 instructions and continuing to 128k instructions; the transaction stride, the distance between transactions, is equal to the transaction size so that the static number of transactional and sequential instructions remains equal. Memory accesses are modeled as circular arrays. On a per-thread basis, there is no reuse outside of the transaction that first references a specific location, ensuring that a single transaction in each thread can only interfere with a single transaction in another thread. For example in a program with n threads, TX_1-A can interfere with TX_2-A, TX_3-A, ..., and TX_{n-1}-A but never with TX_n-B, where n is the thread ID.

4.8 SYNTHETIC WORKLOAD RESULTS

Figure 6 shows the ED2P of the synthetic benchmarks normalized to the base case for each example as transaction granularity increases. Immediately apparent is the abrupt shift in the trend at the 4k granularity. The reason for this relates to the average power of the transactional models. On the base system, the eager-lazy model has the highest average power out of the three designs – peaking at 70W. At 4k, there is an abrupt drop in the average power for the two eager conflict detection schemes; eager-eager drops by 54% to 32W and eager-lazy drops by 60% to 41W while

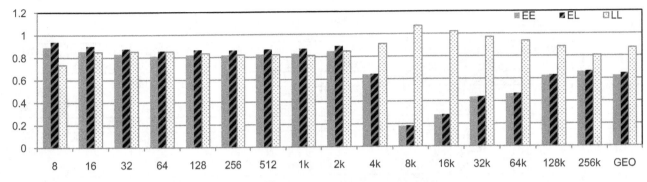

Figure 6. ED2P (Et²) Normalized to Base Case

the average power for the lazy versioning scheme increases by an average of 6% until the granularity reaches 32k at which point it begins slowly decreasing. A breakdown of the transactional cycles, shown in Figure 7, is needed to further explain these phenomena.

The top graph in Figure 7 shows the relative execution time for the eager-eager system. Referring back to Figure 6, the reduction in ED2P remains roughly flat until the transaction size reaches 4k and is a result of reduced power consumption from the conflict-aware scheduling policy; execution time remains mostly unchanged. At 4k, the benchmarks begin to spend more and more time in a NACKd state and the system is able to avoid aborting by stalling the processor, which itself reduces the average by 54% to 32W as pipelines become idle. DVFS and the conflict-aware scheduling policy are able to further reduce the power for all three schemes by an additional 60% and decrease the execution time by of the eager-conflict detection schemes by as much as 7%.

The eager-lazy behavior is shown in the middle graph of Figure 7. Again, until the transaction size reaches 4k, the average power remains roughly constant and is reflected by the almost constant ED2P reduction. This is because the processors are able to spend almost 100% of the time performing useful work; there are no aborts and fewer stalls than the eager-eager model. The runtime is slightly increased by the proposed policies but is offset by moderate power reductions from the new scheduling policy. At 4k, aborts and stalls completely overtake successful execution causing a 40% drop in the average power of the base system, from 67W to 41W. The proposed DVFS and conflict-aware scheduling policies are able to further reduce the power as well as the runtime, providing an additional 66% drop in power consumption and a 45% reduction in runtime.

The lazy-lazy cycle breakdown is shown in the bottom graph of Figure 7. There is more contention for lazy conflict detection than eager. For the 8- and 16-instruction transactions, the average power in the base system is lower than the other two by more than 30%. This is because the execution becomes serialized as transactions are waiting to commit, resulting in idle time for the processors. The DVFS scheme proposed in Section 4.1 is able to take full advantage of this fact, which is why there is a greater improvement in the power-performance domain for lazy-lazy. However, the potential for power and performance gains quickly diminishes as the transactions begin overlapping and aborts begin occurring. Beginning at 8k, the aborts become so persistent that the power manager essentially halts all but one processing element. Note that this is a different situation from the one in Section 4.4 where the scheduler was unnecessarily penalizing *raytrace* and *genome* but the result is the same – reduced power

consumption relative to the baseline system but increased runtime, which increases the ED2P.

5. RELATED WORK

The new work discussed in this paper is related to prior work on power management techniques. In [15], the authors show how processes can be mapped onto a variable number of processing elements while sleeping unused ones and guaranteeing some minimum performance threshold. Isci *et al.* [10] proposed managing per-core voltage and frequency levels based on application behavior to manage total chip power. [29] proposed using linear programming to identify the optimal voltage and frequency levels for each core in a CMP to increase throughput and reduce ED2P. Rangan *et al.* [24] show how threads can migrate between different PEs to achieve nearly the same power reduction as per-core DVFS while [13] propose an algorithm to improve fairness between co-executing threads. The drawback with all of these approaches is that they require online profiling of the runtime environment and computationally-intensive algorithms to meet their desired goals. The proposals outlined in this paper are less intrusive and achieve excellent results with minimal overhead.

There has been some recent research into the energy use of transactional memory for embedded and multiprocessor systems. Ferri recently proposed unifying the L1 and transactional cache in an embedded system and showed that using a small victim cache to reduce the pressure from sharing improved the energy-delay product [5]. Moreshet *et al.* [21] showed that hardware transactional memory systems can be more energy efficient than locks in the absence of contention. They then proposed a serialization mechanism for HTMs and showed that it lowered energy consumption for their microbenchmarks. However, their work relied on four non-contentious SPLASH-2 benchmarks and one in-house microbenchmark, making it difficult to draw any meaningful conclusions. Using an analytical model to estimate the additional power for an Alpha 21264, Sanyal *et al.* [26] proposed a technique for clock gating on an abort using TCC. Neither of these proposals exploit the feedback inherently available in transactional memory like the scheduler proposed by Yoo and Lee [34] who proposed an adaptive scheduler using parallelism feedback and showed speedups of almost 2x for his selected benchmarks. While the energy reduction scheme proposed here has some similarities to previous work, it differs in two main regards. First, it abstracts the differences in the hardware, allowing for an almost direct comparison of power for different conflict detection and version management schemes. Secondly, the proposed method does not assume that contentious transactions should be serialized like [21] and is much less complicated than [26].

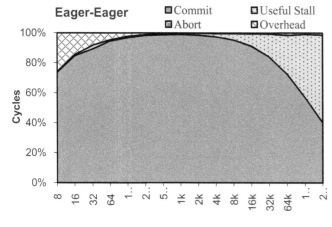

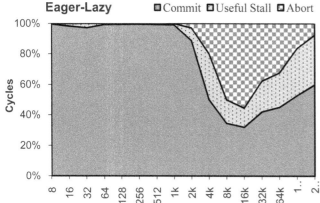

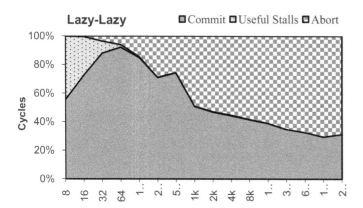

Figure 7. Relative Execution Time

6. CONCLUSIONS

Although there have been many proposed transactional memory designs, few have focused on the power-performances aspects of transactional memory. This research uses the SPLASH-2 and STAMP benchmark suites as well as synthetic workloads to analyze the power and energy for three different transactional systems: eager conflict/eager versioning, eager conflict/lazy versioning, and lazy conflict/lazy versioning and proposes two enhancements to HTM systems. The designs are kept simple by relying on power features available in modern processors and in proposed HTM designs. By targeting the idle periods in HTMs, the proposed optimizations reduce the average power and increase total throughput with minimal overhead.

To reduce system power and increase throughput when transactions are in a NACK state, a dynamic frequency and scaling system is proposed. By increasing the clock frequency of NACKing PEs and throttling the clock frequency of NACK'd PEs, the number of stall and abort cycles is reduced, increasing throughput. The PEs in low-power states serve to reduce or maintain the average system power. Together these effects serve to reduce the system ED2P, or improve the power-performance of the system by 8% for eager-eager, 7% for eager-lazy, and 7% for lazy-lazy. To limit the number of aborts a program experiences and control power usage during these periods, a new transaction scheduling policy is proposed that utilizes a transaction's current and past conflict density to determine whether a transaction should be preemptively stalled and its clock disabled. This technique provides an average reduction in the ED2P of 17% for eager-eager, 17% for eager-lazy, and 10% for lazy-lazy. When applied together, the DVFS and scheduling policies provide a reduction in the ED2P of 19% for eager-eager, 20% for eager-lazy, and 15% for lazy-lazy. More importantly, the benchmarks with greater contention (*labyrinth*) obtained even greater reductions – up to 76%. These results show the potential for manipulating clock frequencies for transactional memory for improved throughput while maintaining or reducing local and chip-wide power budgets and lay the foundation for future work in aggressive power management strategies for multithreaded workloads in the many-core era.

7. ACKNOWLEDGEMENTS

This work was supported by NSF grants CNS-0834288 and CCF-0845721 (CAREER) and SRC grant 2008-HJ-1798 and by three IBM Faculty Awards. The authors would also like to thank the UF HPC Center for providing computational resources and the anonymous reviewers for their valuable suggestions.

8. REFERENCES

[1] Bell, R. H. and John, L. K. Improved Automatic Testcase Synthesis for Performance Model Validation. In *International Conference on Supercomputing* (2005).

[2] Bloom, B. H. Space/Time Trade-offs in Hash Coding with Allowable Errors. *Communications of the ACM* (July 1970), 422-426.

[3] Brooks, D., Tiwari, V., and Martonosi, M. Wattch: A Framework for Architectural-level Power Analysis and Optimization. In *International Symposium on Computer Architecture* (2007).

[4] Ceze, L., Tuck, J., Montesinos, P., and Torrellas, J. BulkSC: Bulk Enforcement of sequential Consistency. In *International Symposium on Computer Architecture* (2007).

[5] Ferri, C., Wood, S., Moreshet, T., Bahar, I., and Herlihy, M. Energy and Throughput Efficient Transactional Memory for Embedded Multicore Systems. In *International Conference on High-Performance Embedded Architectures and Compilers* (2010).

[6] Hammond, L., Wong, V., Chen, M. et al. Transactional Memory Coherence and Consistency. In *International Symposium on Computer Architecture* (2005).

[7] Herlihy, M. P. and Moss, J. E. B. Transactional Memory: Architectural Support for Lock-Free Data STructures. In *International Symposium on Computer Architecture* (1993).

[8] Hsu, C. and Kremer, U. The Design, Implementation, and Evaluation of a Compiler Algorithm for CPU Energy Reduction. In *Conference on Programming Language Design and Implementation* (2003).

[9] Hughes, C., Poe, J., Qouneh, A., and Li, T. On The (Dis)similarity of Transactional Memory Workloads. In *IEEE International Symposium on Workload Characterization* (2009).

[10] Isci, C., Buyuktosunoglu, A., Cher, C., Bose, P., and Martonosi, M. An Analysis of Efficient Multi-Core Global Power Management Policies: Maximizing Performance for a Given Power Budget. In *International Symposium on Microarchitecture* (2006).

[11] Ishihara, T. and Yasuura, H. Voltage Scheduling Problem for Dynamically Variable Voltage Processors. In *International Symposium on Low Power Electronics and Design* (1998).

[12] Kim, W., Gupta, M., Wei, G. -Y., and Brooks, D. System Level Analysis of Fast, Per-Core DVFS Using On-Chip Switching Regulators. In *International Symposium on High-Performance Computer Architecture* (2008).

[13] Kondo, M., Sasaki, H., and Nakamura, H. Improving Fairness, Throughput, and Energy-Efficiency on a Chip Multiprocessor Through DVFS. *SIGARCH Computer ARchitecture News*, 35 (2007).

[14] Li, Y., Brooks, D., Hu, Z., and Skadron, K. Performance, Energy, and Thermal Considerations For SMT and CMP Architectures. In *International Symposium on High-Performance Computer Architecture* (2005).

[15] Li, J. and Martinez, J. F. Dynamic Power-Performance Adaptation of Parallel Computation on Chip Multiprocessors. In *International Symposium on High-Performance Computer Architecture* (2006).

[16] Macken, P., Degrauwe, M., Paemel, M. V., and Oguey, H. A Voltage Reduction Technique For Digital Systems. In *IIEEE International Solid State Circuits Conference* (1990), 238-239.

[17] Marcalescu, D. On the Use of Microarchitecure-Driven Dynamic Voltage Scaling. In *Workshop on Complexity-Effective Design* (2000).

[18] McGowen, R., Poirier, C. A., Bostak, C., Ignowski, J., Millican, M., Parks, W. H., and Naffziger, S. Power and Temperature Control on a 90nm Itanium Family Processor. *Journal of Solid-State Circuits* (2006).

[19] Minh, C. C., Olukotun, K., Kozyrakis, C., and Chung, J. STAMP: Stanford Transactional Applications for Multi-Processing. In *IEEE International Symposium on Workload Characterization* (2008).

[20] Moore, K. E., Bobba, J., Moravan, M. J., Hill, M. D., and Wood, D. A. LogTM: Log-based Transactional Memory. In *International Symposium on High-Performance Computer Architecture* (2006).

[21] Moreshet, T., Bahar, R. I., and Herlihy, M. Energy-Aware Microprocessor Synchronization: Transactional Memory vs. Locks. In *Workshop on Memory Performance Issues* (2006).

[22] Poe, J., Cho, C., and Li, T. Using Analytical Models to Efficiently Explore Hardware Transactional Memory and Multicore Co-Design. In *Computer Architecture and High Performance Computing* (2008).

[23] Poe, J., Hughes, C., and Li, T. TransPlant: A Parameterized Methodology For Generating Transactional Memory Workloads. In *International Symposium on Modeling, Analysis, and Simulation of Computer and Telecommunication Systems* (2009).

[24] Rangan, K. K., Wei, G., and Brooks, D. Thread Motion: Fine-Grained Power Management for Multi-Core Systems. In *International Symposium on Computer Architecture* (2009).

[25] Sanchez, D., Yen, L., Hill, M. D., and Sankaralingam, K. Implemetning Signatures for Transactional Memory. In *International Symposium on Microarchitecture* (2009).

[26] Sanyal, S., Roy, S., Cristal, A., Unsal, O. S., and Valero, M. Clock Gate on Abort: Towards Energy-efficient Hardware Transactional Memory. In *IEEE International Symposium on Parallel & Distributed Processing* (2009).

[27] Skadron, K., Stan, M. R., Huang, W., Velusamy, S., Sankaranarayanan, K., and Tarjan, D. Temperature-Aware Microarchitecure. In *International Symposium on Computer Architecture* (2003).

[28] Tarjan, D., Thoziyoor, S., and Jouppi, N. P. *CACTI 4.0.* HP Labs, 2006.

[29] Teodorescu, R. and Torrellas, J. Variation-Aware Application Scheduling and power Management for Chip Multiprocessors. In *International Symposium on Computer Architecture* (2008).

[30] Wang, J., Fang, S., and Fen, W. New Efficient Designs for XOR and XNOR Functions on the Transistor Level. *IEEE Journal of Solid-State Circuits*, 29, 7 (1994).

[31] Woo, S. C., Ohara, M., Torrie, E., Singh, J. P., and Gupta, A. The SPLASH-2 Programs: Characterization and Methodological Considerations. In *International Symposium on Computer Architecture* (1995).

[32] Yen, L., Bobba, J., Marty, M. R. et al. LogTM-SE: Decoupling Hardware Transactional Memory From Caches. In *International Symposium on High-Performance Computer Architecture* (2007).

[33] Yen, L., Draper, S. C., and Hill, M. D. Notary: Hardware Techniques to Enhance Signatures. In *International Symposium on Microarchitecture* (2008).

[34] Yoo, R. and Lee, H. S. Adaptive Transaction Scheduling for Transactional Memory Systems. In *Symposium on Parallelism in Algorithms and Architecture* (2008).

[35] Zhang, Y., Parikh, D., Sankaranarayanan, K., Skadron, K., and Stan, M. *HotLeakage: A Temperature-Aware Model of Subthreshold and Gate Leakage for Architects.* CS-2003-05, University of Virginia, 2003.

Keynote Talk

Challenges and Opportunities in Renewable Energy and Energy Efficiency

Steven Hammond
National Renewable Energy Laboratory
Golden, CO, USA
steven.hammond@nrel.gov

Abstract

The National Renewable Energy Laboratory (NREL) in Golden, Colorado is the nation's premier laboratory for renewable energy and energy efficiency research. In this talk we will give a brief overview of NREL and then focus on some of the challenges and opportunities in meeting future global energy challenges. Computational modeling, high performance computing, data management and visual informatics is playing a key role in advancing our fundamental understanding of processes and systems at temporal and spatial scales that evade direct observation and helping meet U.S. goals for energy efficiency and clean energy production. This discussion will include details of new, highly energy efficient buildings and social behaviors impacting energy use, fundamental understanding of plants and proteins leading to lower cost renewable fuels, novel computational chemistry approaches for low cost photovoltaic materials, and computational fluid dynamics challenges in simulating complex behaviors within and between large-scale deployment of wind farms and understanding their potential impacts to local and regional climate.

Categories & Subject Descriptors: Computer Applications; Physical Sciences and Engineering; Chemistry; Physics; Earth and atmospheric sciences

General Terms: Performance, Design, Economics, Reliability, Experimentation, Security, Human Factors, Standardization, Languages, Theory, Legal Aspects, Verification.

Keywords: renewable, energy, efficiency, climate

Bio

Steve is the director of Computational Science at the National Renewable Energy Laboratory (NREL) located in Golden, CO where he leads the laboratory efforts in high performance computing and energy efficient data centers. Prior to joining NREL in 2002, Steve spent ten years at the National Center for Atmospheric Research in Boulder, CO leading efforts to develop efficient massively parallel climate models.

Before NCAR, Steve did Post Doctoral work at the European Center for Advanced Scientific Computing in Toulouse, France; was a Research Associate at the Research Institute for Advanced Computer Science, NASA Ames Research Center, Moffett Field, CA; and a Computer Scientist at GE's Corporate Research and Development Center, in Schenectady, New York.

Education:

BA Mathematics, University of Rochester, Rochester, New York
MS Computer Science, University of Rochester, Rochester, New York
PhD Computer Science, Rensselaer Polytechnic Institute, Troy, New York

Characterizing the Impact of Soft Errors on Iterative Methods in Scientific Computing [*]

Manu Shantharam
The Pennsylvania State
University
(shanthar@cse.psu.edu)

Sowmyalatha
Srinivasmurthy
The Pennsylvania State
University
(sowmya@cse.psu.edu)

Padma Raghavan
The Pennsylvania State
University
(raghavan@cse.psu.edu)

ABSTRACT

The increase in on-chip transistor count facilitates achieving higher performance, but at the expense of higher susceptibility to soft errors. In this paper, we characterize the challenges posed by soft errors for large scale applications representative of workloads on supercomputing systems. Such applications are typically based on the computational solution of partial differential equation models using either explicit or implicit methods. In both cases, the execution time of such applications is typically dominated by the time spent in their underlying sparse matrix vector multiplication kernel (SpMV, $t \leftarrow A \cdot y$). We provide a theoretical analysis of the impact of a single soft error through its propagation by a sequence of sparse matrix vector multiplication operations. Our analysis indicates that a single soft error in some i^{th} component of the vector y can corrupt the entire resultant vector in a relatively short sequence of SpMV operations. Additionally, the propagation pattern corresponds to the sparsity structure of the coefficient matrix A and the magnitude of the error grows non-linearly as $(||A_{i*}||_2)^k$, after k SpMV operations, where, $||A_{i*}||_2$ is the 2-norm of the ith row of A. We corroborate this analysis with empirical observations on a model heat equation using explicit method and well known sparse matrix systems (matrices from a test suite) for the implicit method using iterative solvers such as CG, PCG and SOR. Our results indicate that explicit schemes will suffer from soft error induced numerical instabilities, thus exacerbating intrinsic stability issues for such methods, that impose constraints on relative time and space step sizes. For implicit schemes, linear solver performance through widely used CG and PCG schemes, degrades by a factor as high as 200x, whereas, a stationary scheme such as SOR is inherently soft error resilient. Our results thus indicate the need for new approaches to achieve soft error resiliency in such methods and a critical evaluation of the

tradeoffs among multiple metrics, including, performance, reliability and energy.

Categories and Subject Descriptors

G.4 [**Mathematical Software**]: Algorithm design and analysis, Efficiency, Reliability and robustness; G.1.3 [**Numerical Linear Algebra**]: Sparse, structured, and very large systems (direct and iterative methods)

General Terms

Theoretical underpinning, Algorithms, Reliability

Keywords

Scientific computing, Iterative methods, Soft errors, Efficiency

1. INTRODUCTION

A current trend among chip manufacturers is to increase transistor densities on the chip using small feature sizes. This facilitates achieving higher performance, at the expense of greater soft error susceptibility [1–3]. Increasing soft errors will increase intermittent error rate by almost two orders of magnitude [4]. Consequently, the scientific simulation applications that comprise the majority of long running workloads on large scale high performance computing installations [5] are at a greater risk of being hit by a soft error. In this paper, we seek to assess the vulnerability of such scientific applications that are often based on the solution of partial differential equation (PDE) models [6] through explicit and implicit schemes [7].

Soft errors can be seen as transient errors that result in bit flips in memory and errors in logic circuit output, leaving the computing system state corrupt. The errors can be caused by cosmic radiations [8], radiation from packaging materials [9], as well as voltage fluctuation [10]. Although the increase in transistor density facilitates higher performance, it also leads to a higher soft error susceptibility. In fact, with increases in the transistor densities the soft error rates have been growing exponentially, with typical values ranging between 1k and 10k FIT/Mb [9] (FIT is failure per billion hours of operation). The 106,496 dual-processor compute node BlueGene/L, for example [11], experiences one soft error in its L1 cache every 4-6 hours induced by the radioactive decay in lead solders. Michalak et al. [12] report that the ASCI Q experienced 27.7 CPU failures per week due to radiation. These high soft error rates are a cause of concern for long running scientific applications as it could

[*]This research is supported in part by grants CSR-SMA 0720749, CCF 0830679 and OCI 0821527 from the National Science Foundation.

potentially degrade the performance or produce erroneous solutions.

A majority of large-scale scientific applications including those that run on multicores and their multiprocessor clusters (supercomputers) involve solving PDE based systems, such as those found in heat diffusion, computational fluid dynamics (CFD) and structural mechanics [5]. Such applications typically use software tool kits such as PETSc [6], for solutions using explicit and implicit schemes; with the latter requiring the use of solvers packages such as hypre [13] and Trinilos [14, 15]. At the lower levels, the basic underlying computation in such methods is a sequence of SpMV operations of the form $t \leftarrow A \cdot y$ that are performed iteratively. The explicit schemes may directly use SpMV operations to find the solution across different time steps, while in the implicit methods, SpMV operation is often within an iterative sparse linear solver such as conjugate gradient (CG) and its preconditioned forms. Across all cases, reliable and accurate fast simulations can be viewed as depending on the performance of the SpMV kernel and the propagation of numerical attributes through relevant sequence of SpMV operations [7]. In this paper, we seek to characterize the impact of soft errors on such PDE-based applications by an in-depth analysis of soft error propagation through series of underlying SpMV operations.

The earlier studies related to soft errors in scientific applications focus on error detection and mitigation of their effect using algorithmic techniques [11], and, compiler and hardware based soft error prevention techniques [16]. Unlike these studies, we focus on theoretical analysis and characterization of the impact of soft errors on scientific simulations. We show that a single soft error is capable of causing multiple errors, and this propagation has a pattern corresponding to the sparsity structure of the coefficient matrix. In the case of an explicit method, we show that the growing magnitude of the error makes the final solution inviable. For the implicit methods, we show that, although, it may converge to a viable solution, the total iterations required for the convergence may increase significantly leading to performance degradation. Additionally, we prove that the magnitude of the error grows non-linearly with the 2-norm of the matrix rows. Further, we provide empirical evaluation of performance degradation in terms of the relative increase in iteration count due to the presence of a soft error. Our results indicate that for practical problems, a single soft error could potentially degrade the preconditioned conjugate gradient (PCG) performance by as much as 200x compared to soft error free PCG performance.

The paper is organized as follows. In Section 2, we discuss our work in the context of recent results related to the detection and mitigation of soft errors in sparse linear solvers, [11, 16]. In Section 3, we use the heat equation as an example to indicate the pivotal role of SpMV operations in the explicit and implicit solution of PDE-based models. In Section 4, we provide an analysis on the propagation and growth of a single soft error through a sequence of SpMV operations. In Section 5, we present our experimental methodology and the results of empirical tests in support our theoretical analysis. Additionally, we provide an in-depth evaluation of the practical impact of soft errors on implicit schemes using popular solvers such as PCG and successive over relaxation (SOR). In Section 6, we provide

brief concluding remarks and motivate potential directions for future work.

2. RELATED WORK

Prior work considers dealing with soft errors in silicon as well as at the application level. We can categorize the earlier results into three directions: soft error detection [2,3,17,18], soft error protection [19–22], and soft error characterization in microarchitecture [23], [24], [25]. Smolens et al. [3] propose an error detection technique, called fingerprinting, which detects differences in execution across a dual modular redundant processor pair. This technique requires special hardware modifications to the processor pipeline. On the other hand, to avoid any hardware overhead, software based techniques have been developed to detect soft errors [17], [18]. For example, Rebaudengo et al. [17] propose a technique to automatically transform programs written in a high-level language so that they can detect most of the errors affecting data and code. The scheme proposed by Hu et al. [18] enlists the compiler's help in duplicating instructions for error detection in VLIW datapaths. It is further supported by a hardware enhancement for efficient result verification, which also avoids the need of additional comparison instructions. In their proposed approach, the trade-off between performance, reliability and energy consumption is achieved using the compiler by determining degree of instruction duplication.

Recently there has been interest in understanding the effect of soft errors on sparse linear solvers. Bronevetsky et al. [11] report observations on the effect of soft errors on iterative solvers like, CG, preconditioned Richardson, and Chebyshev methods in SparseLib [26]. Based on the experimental observations, the paper groups the impact of soft errors as (i) no effect, (ii) silent error, (iii) application hangs, and (iv) application crashes. The paper also proposes and evaluates several soft error detection and tolerance schemes, like, residual tracking, checkpointing and data structure encoding that could potentially lead to significant improvements in the reliability of these libraries. Malkowski et al. [16] consider PCG and GMRES and they focus on utilizing the manner in which the coefficient matrix A is resident in L1 and L2 caches in these methods. They use the concept of vulnerable time to propose and evaluate energy and reliability tradeoffs for two schemes, for adaptively turn-off the Error Correction Code (ECC) for L1 cache and L2 caches. They assume little or no cache reuse for the vector v and therefore is not protected. The data structures having higher resident time in the caches than their corresponding vulnerable time, are protected.

Our proposed work differs from the earlier work as follows: first, we focus on a sequence of SpMV operations as the common core of PDE-based simulations using explicit or implicit schemes. Second, we provide an in-depth analysis of the propagation of a single soft error through a sequence of SpMV operations in terms of the sparsity structure of the coefficient matrix A and growth of this error in terms of the numerical properties of A. Third, we relate this analysis to the stability of explicit schemes and the convergence of iterative solvers in an implicit scheme. We thus characterize algorithmic aspects of computational schemes for such large scale applications, to motivate the need for soft error resilient approaches in software libraries, such as, PETSc [6], Trinilos [14, 15], hypre [13], SparseLib [26].

3. BACKGROUND AND THE ROLE OF SPMV

In this section, we use the heat equation [27] to provide a brief overview of explicit and implicit methods with a focus on the central role of a sequence of SpMV operations. PDE-based simulations play a vital role in many problems, ranging from astrophysics to material science and there are many complex underlying issues related to the type of the PDE (like elliptic, parabolic), discretization methods, the choice of explicit or implicit schemes, the non-linearity of the underlying operator among other factors. The material in the section is highly simplified for illustrative purposes and the reader is referred to the book by Heath [27] for an accessible overview including references to classical text on this very broad topic.

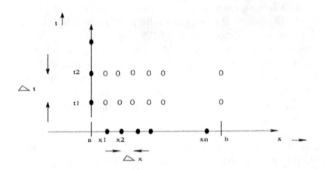

Figure 1: One dimensional heat flow problem.

Figure 1 shows an example of one dimensional heat flow problem. The x-axis represents discretization of space (a physical object) and the y-axis represents time steps over which the PDE solution evolves. In general, a PDE can be solved using either an explicit or implicit method as reviewed below.

Explicit Methods. An explicit method calculates the state of a system (u), as a function of time (t) and space (x), at a later time from the state of the system at the current time. For example, a one dimensional heat equation for an explicit method can be written as

$$u_i^{m+1} = u_i^m + \mu\{u_{i+1}^m - 2u_i^m + u_{i-1}^m\} \tag{1}$$

where the temperature at point x_i at time t_m is denoted by u_i^m and μ is a constant related to the discretization sizes and the material property. Equation 1 can be rewritten as:

$$\mathbf{u}^{m+1} = \mathbf{u}^m + \mu\mathbf{A}\mathbf{u}^m \tag{2}$$

where $\mathbf{A}$ is a sparse coefficient matrix. Note that solution to every time step involves a SpMV operation of the form $\mathbf{A}\mathbf{u}^m$.

Implicit Methods. Unlike an explicit method, an implicit method finds the solution of a PDE by solving the system of equations involving both the current state of the system and the state at a later time. The following equation shows a one dimensional heat equation obtained using an implicit method.

$$u_i^m = (1+2\mu)u_i^{m+1} - \mu\{u_{i+1}^{m+1} + u_{i-1}^{m+1}\} \tag{3}$$

where the temperature at point x_i at time t_m is denoted by u_i^m and μ is a constant related to the discretization sizes and the material property. Equation 3 can be reformulated as:

$$\mathbf{A}\mathbf{u}^{m+1} = \mathbf{u}^m \tag{4}$$

where $\mathbf{A}$ is a tridiagonal coefficient matrix.

The above methods can be similarly extended to 2D and 3D heat flow problems [7]. The method selection to solve a given PDE depends on the computational overheads and numerical stability tradeoffs. The explicit methods are simple to use and computationally less expensive per time step compared to implicit methods. However, the explicit methods are prone to numerical instabilities if the discretization intervals are not chosen accurately.

Role of SpMV. For easy of analysis, we henceforth focus on systems where the matrix $\mathbf{A}$ is sparse, symmetric and positive definite. Such systems represent a large class of widely used PDE-based simulations on large scale high performance computers [5]. Additionally, methods developed for such systems often form the basis for extensions relating to non-symmetric $\mathbf{A}$ [5, 7, 27].

Explicit Method: Observe from Equation 2 for the explicit method that SpMV propagates $\mathbf{u}^m$ into $\mathbf{u}^{m+1}$ by the factor of $\mu\mathbf{A}$. Consequently, $\mathbf{u}^{m+1}$ directly holds the effects of a sequence of m SpMV operations.

Implicit Method: Equation 4 for the implicit method indicates that $\mathbf{u}^{m+1}$ is obtained by a linear system solution involving A and $\mathbf{u}^m$. Now, a sequence of SpMV operations occur in each linear system solution using popular iterative methods such as Conjugate Gradient (CG) and its preconditioned forms (PCG) or stationary iterative methods such as successive over relaxation (SOR). To illustrate the role of SpMV in such sparse linear solutions consider Algorithm 1. Line 9 in the algorithm represents the SpMV kernel which is executed in every iteration until termination. Observe that an occurrence of soft error in $\mathbf{v}$ leads to an error in the other vectors like $\mathbf{t}$ and $\mathbf{r}$. Since these vectors govern the convergence time of CG, the number of iterations executed by CG may change due to soft errors in $\mathbf{v}$. In most practical settings, the convergence of CG is accelerated through preconditioning; such preconditioned CG methods involve the use of SpMV as in Algorithm 1.

Algorithm 1 Conjugate Gradient

procedure CG(A, b, MAXIT, TOL)
 1: $x = 0$
 2: $iters = 0$
 3: $nb = norm(b)$
 4: $r = b$
 5: $rsq = r' * r$
 6: $v = r$
 7: **while** iters < MAXIT && sqrt(rsq)/nb > TOL **do**
 8:     $iters = iters + 1$
 9:     $t = SpMV(A, v)$
10:     $alpha = rsq/(v' * t)$
11:     $x = x + alpha * v$
12:     $r = r - alpha * t$
13:     $rsqprev = rsq$
14:     $rsq = r' * r$
15:     $beta = rsq/rsqprev$
16:     $v = r + beta * v$
17: **end while**

To illustrate the role of SpMV in the SOR method, consider a linear system $\mathbf{Ax} = \mathbf{b}$, where, $\mathbf{A}$ is an $N \times N$ coefficient matrix, $\mathbf{b}$ is a known vector and $\mathbf{x}$ is an unknown vector. To solve this system, $\mathbf{A}$ is decomposed into a diagonal ($\mathbf{D}$), strict lower and upper triangular ($\mathbf{U}$, $\mathbf{L}$) matrices such that $\mathbf{A} = \mathbf{L} + \mathbf{D} + \mathbf{U}$. The linear system is reformulated as Equation 5, that represents SOR iteration.

$$\mathbf{Mx}^{k+1} = \mathbf{Nx}^k + \omega\mathbf{b} \qquad (5)$$

where, $\mathbf{M} = \mathbf{D} + \omega\mathbf{L}$, $\mathbf{N} = (1-\omega)\mathbf{D} - \omega\mathbf{U}$, $\mathbf{x}^k$ and $\mathbf{x}^{k+1}$ are vectors that represent the solution of the system at time t_k and t_{k+1}, and ω is a fixed search parameter. As indicated in the equation, the SpMV kernel is executed to solve for $\mathbf{x}^{k+1}$.

4. ANALYSIS OF SOFT ERROR PROPAGATION

In this section, we focus on analytically characterizing the propagation and growth of a single soft error in the vector $\mathbf{y}^0$ for a sequence of SpMV operations given by $\{\mathbf{y}^0, \mathbf{y}^1 \leftarrow \mathbf{Ay}^0..., \mathbf{y}^k \leftarrow \mathbf{Ay}^{k-1}\}$. Observe that this sequence is equivalent to $\{\mathbf{y}^0, \mathbf{Ay}^0..., \mathbf{A}^k\mathbf{y}^0\}$. We use a graph formulation that corresponds to the SpMV sequence to capture effects related to sparsity structure of A (zero-nonzero pattern) and its numeric attributes.

Notation. In the rest of this paper, matrices are represented by bold uppercase letters such as $\mathbf{A}$, and vectors are represented by bold lowercase letters such as $\mathbf{y}$. The matrices are assumed to be of size $N \times N$ and vectors are correspondingly $N \times 1$. Additionally, superscripts, such as $\mathbf{y}^j$ are used to represent a vector within the sequence $\{\mathbf{y}^0, \mathbf{y}^1, .., \mathbf{y}^p\}$ and $\mathbf{y}^k_i$ represent the ith component in the vector $\mathbf{y}^k$. $\mathbf{A}_{i*}$ represents the elements in the ith row of $\mathbf{A}$. $NNZIndex(\mathbf{x})$ represents the set of indices that correspond to the non-zeroes in the vector $\mathbf{x}$. E.g., if $\mathbf{x} = [0,0,-,-,0,-]$ where '$-$' indicates non-zeroes and $NNZIndex(\mathbf{x}) = [3,4,6]$.

Graph Representation. For our analysis, we assume that the coefficient matrix $\mathbf{A}$ has a single connected component. In general, it is observed that many matrices arising from practical problems have a single connected component.

We consider the traditional graph representation $\mathbf{G(A)} = (V, E)$ for an $N \times N$ sparse symmetric coefficient matrix $\mathbf{A}$. Now the vertex set $V = \{v_1..v_N\}$, where v_i represents i^{th} row or column of $\mathbf{A}$; the edge set $E = \{(v_i v_j) : i \neq j, 1 \leq i, j \leq N, A_{ij} \neq 0\}$, where A_{ij} is an element of $\mathbf{A}$. Define a level set partitioning of the vertex set $V = \{\bigcup_{i=0}^p S_i, \; S_r \bigcap S_q = \phi, r \neq q, 0 \leq r, q \leq p\}$, where S_i is the set of vertices in the ith partition. Let $Reach[S_i]$ represent the set of all the immediate neighbors of the vertices in the set S_i. It can be defined as, $Reach[S_i] = \bar{S}_i = \{v_j | v_j \in V, (v_i v_j) \in E \; \& \; v_i \in S_i\}$. Additionally, define $NewReach(S_{j-1}) = S_j = \bar{S}_{j-1} \backslash S_{j-1}$.

For a given $\mathbf{G(A)}$ and $S_0 = \{v_i\}$, define $Depth(\mathbf{G(A)}, v_i) = p$, such that $NewReach(S_p) = S_{p+1} = \phi$. Observe that such a level set partitioning can be obtained starting with $S_0 = v_i$ and a breadth first search (BFS) in $\mathbf{G(A)}$ from v_i, where S_1 represents vertices in the next level of the search tree and so on.

Analysis. Using the notation and definitions above, we now state and prove theorems related to soft error propagation in a sequence of SpMV operations with respect to the sparsity structure and numerical properties of matrix $\mathbf{A}$.

THEOREM 1. *Consider an $N \times N$ sparse symmetric coefficient matrix $\mathbf{A}$, an initial $N \times 1$ vector $\mathbf{y}^0$, and a sequence of SpMV operations that generate the vector set $\{\mathbf{y}^0, \mathbf{y}^1, .., \mathbf{y}^p\}$ where $\mathbf{y}^i = \mathbf{A}^i\mathbf{y}^0$. Consider a single soft error inserted in $\mathbf{y}^0$ in the ith position (y_i^0). At the end of the pth SpMV operation, the vector $\bar{\mathbf{y}}^p$ will have errors in all its components, where $p = Depth(\mathbf{G(A)}, v_i)$, i.e., the maximum depth of the tree starting at vertex v_i in $\mathbf{G(A)}$.*

PROOF. Let us assume without loss of generality that a soft occurs in $\mathbf{y}_1^0$, i.e., $i = 1$. For example, we can use symmetric reordering of $\mathbf{A}$ and induced reordering of $\mathbf{y}^0$ that permutes the ith position to the 1st position. Let the vector with the change due to error be $\bar{\mathbf{y}}^0 = \mathbf{y}^0 + \mathbf{e}^0$, where, $\mathbf{e}^0 = [\delta, 0, 0, ..., 0]^T$. Observe that $NNZIndex(\mathbf{e}^0) = [1]$.

At the end of the 1st SpMV operation we have $\bar{\mathbf{y}}^1 = \mathbf{A}\bar{\mathbf{y}}^0 = \mathbf{y}^1 + \mathbf{e}^1$, where $\mathbf{y}^1 = \mathbf{Ay}^0$ and $\mathbf{e}^1 = \mathbf{Ae}^0$. Here $\mathbf{e}_j^1 \neq 0$ iff $\mathbf{A}_{1j} \neq 0$ (or equivalently, from symmetry $\mathbf{A}_{j1} \neq 0$). Next, consider in $\mathbf{G(A)}$, $S_0 = \{v_1\}$ and $\bar{S}_0 = Reach\{S_0\}$. Observe that $NNZIndex(\mathbf{e}^1)$ corresponds to $\{j : v_j \in \bar{S}_0\}$. Additionally, indices in $\mathbf{e}^1$ that now have error propagated from $\mathbf{e}^0$ are given by $NNZIndex(\mathbf{e}^1) - NNZIndex(\mathbf{e}^0) = \{j : v_j \in NewReach(S_0)\}$.

By applying this inductively, we can show that $NNZIndex(\mathbf{e}^p) = \{1..n\}$, where $p = Depth(\mathbf{G(A)}, v_1)$.

The output vector $\bar{\mathbf{y}}^p$ can be defined as $\bar{\mathbf{y}}^p = \mathbf{y}^p + \mathbf{e}^p$, where $\mathbf{e}^p = \mathbf{A}^p\mathbf{e}_0$. Thus, the output vector $\bar{\mathbf{y}}^p$ will have errors in all its components at the end of the pth SpMV operation, where p is the depth of the BFS tree starting at vertex v_1 in $\mathbf{G(A)}$. $\square$

We illustrate Theorem 1 with a small example matrix and its graph counterpart shown in Figures 2-4. Figure 2 shows a sparse symmetric coefficient matrix $\mathbf{A}$, where 'X' represents a non-zero value; an initial vector $\mathbf{y}^0$, where 'x' represents a non-erroneous value and 'δ' represents erroneous value; and the resultant vectors of a sequence of SpMV operations ($\bar{\mathbf{y}}^1, \bar{\mathbf{y}}^2, \bar{\mathbf{y}}^3, \bar{\mathbf{y}}^4$). Figure 3 and Figure 4 show the growth of the BFS tree in which elements of $\mathbf{y}^i$ are corrupted. In this figure, we assume that the 1st element of $\mathbf{y}^0$ is affected by a soft error initially. Figure 4 shows the order and positions (1, 6, 7, 2, 5, 3, 4) in which the elements of $\mathbf{y}^i$ are affected. We observe that the resultant vector at the end of the 4th iteration has an error in all of its components and the depth of the BFS tree is 4.

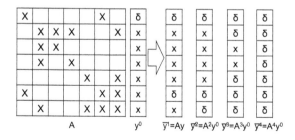

Figure 2: Sparse matrix A, vector y, and the sequence of SpMV operations on A and y.

THEOREM 2. *Consider an $N \times N$ sparse symmetric coefficient matrix $\mathbf{A}$, an initial $N \times 1$ vector $\mathbf{y}^0$, and a sequence of SpMV operations that generate the vector set $\{\mathbf{y}^0, \mathbf{y}^1, .., \mathbf{y}^p\}$*

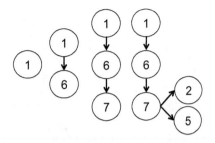

Figure 3: Intermediate tree representations (0-3 iterations) .

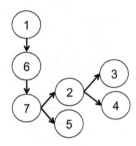

Figure 4: Final BFS tree representation

where $\mathbf{y}^i = \mathbf{A}^i\mathbf{y}^0$. Consider a single soft error inserted in $\mathbf{y}^0$ in the ith position ($\mathbf{y}^0_i$). The magnitude of error in the element $\mathbf{y}^k_i$ (at the end of the kth iteration) grows non-linearly as $(||\mathbf{A}_{i*}||_2)^k$, i.e., the kth power of the 2-norm of ith row of $\mathbf{A}$.

PROOF. Assume that a soft error occurs in $\mathbf{y}^0_1$, i.e., $i = 1$. Let the vector with the change due to error be $\bar{\mathbf{y}}^0 = \mathbf{y}^0 + \mathbf{e}^0$. Consider the set of vectors $\{\bar{\mathbf{y}}^0, \bar{\mathbf{y}}^1, ..., \bar{\mathbf{y}}^k\}$ corresponding to a sequence of SpMV operations $\bar{\mathbf{y}}^i = \mathbf{A}\bar{\mathbf{y}}^{i-1}$ or equivalently, $\bar{\mathbf{y}}^i = \mathbf{A}^i\bar{\mathbf{y}}^0$; now, $\bar{y}^i = \mathbf{y}^i + \mathbf{e}^i$, where, $\mathbf{y}^i = \mathbf{A}\mathbf{y}^{i-1}$ and $\mathbf{e}^i = \mathbf{A}\mathbf{e}^{i-1}$.

By Theorem 1, $NNZIndex(\mathbf{e}^1) = \{j : v_j \in \bar{S}_0\}$, where $\bar{S}_0 = Reach(S_0) = \{v_1\}$.

At the end of the 1st iteration we have
$\bar{\mathbf{y}}^1 = \mathbf{A}\bar{\mathbf{y}}^0$
$\quad = \mathbf{A}\mathbf{y}^0 + \mathbf{A}\mathbf{e}^0$
$\quad = \mathbf{y}^1 + \mathbf{e}^1$
Additionally, for each $j \in NNZIndex(\mathbf{e}^1)$, $\mathbf{e}^1_j = \mathbf{A}_{j1}\delta$
Next consider $\bar{\mathbf{y}}^2 = \mathbf{y} + \mathbf{e}^2$. Here
$\mathbf{e}^2_1 = \sum \mathbf{A}_{1j}\mathbf{e}^1_j$, where $j \in NNZIndex(\mathbf{e}^1)$
$\quad = \sum \mathbf{A}_{1j}\mathbf{A}_{j1}\delta$, where $j \in NNZIndex(\mathbf{e}^1)$
$\quad = \delta \sum \mathbf{A}^2_{1j}$, by the symmetric property of the matrix $\mathbf{A}$
$\quad = (||\mathbf{A}_{1*}||_2)^2\delta$
By repeating this analysis for $\bar{\mathbf{y}}^3$ and $\bar{\mathbf{y}}^4$ consequently we see that

$$\mathbf{e}^4_1 = (||\mathbf{A}_{1*}||_2)^4\delta + \beta \qquad (6)$$

where β represents additional error from non-zero components in $\mathbf{e}^1$, $\mathbf{e}^2$ and $\mathbf{e}^3$ and their propagation.

Now writing the resultant vector $\bar{\mathbf{y}}^4$ we have

$$\bar{\mathbf{y}}^4 = \mathbf{y}^4 + \mathbf{e}^4 \qquad (7)$$

Using Equation 6 in Equation 7 we see that the error is the resultant vector $\bar{\mathbf{y}}^4$ grows non-linearly as $(||\mathbf{A}_{1*}||_2)^4$

By applying this inductively, we can show that
$\mathbf{e}^k_i = (||\mathbf{A}_{i*}||_2)^k\delta + \beta \ (for \ k \ mod \ 2 = 0)$
Therefore we prove that the magnitude of error in the element $\mathbf{y}^k_i$ (at the end of the kth iteration) grows non-linearly as $(||\mathbf{A}_{i*}||_2)^k$, i.e., the kth power of the 2-norm of ith row of $\mathbf{A}$. □

Theorems 1 and 2 indicate that absolute errors in $\bar{\mathbf{y}}^k$ can be much higher if the initial soft error occurred in a component $\bar{\mathbf{y}}^0_i$ corresponding to a row i of $\mathbf{A}$ with the highest 2-norm. Additionally, a single error would propagate the fastest to all components if it were to initially occur in a component i such that $Depth(\mathbf{G}(\mathbf{A}), v_i) = min\{\forall j, Depth(\mathbf{G}(\mathbf{A}), v_i), v_j \in V\}$. Sparse matrices from many PDE applications tend to have graphs where the depth measure starting from any vertex does not vary dramatically. Consequently, for such systems, we expect the highest norm position to be more critical in error growth.

5. EXPERIMENTAL METHODOLOGY AND RESULTS

We present our experimental setup and methodology in Section 5.1. Subsequently, in Section 5.2, we report empirical observations in support of the theoretical analysis in Section 4 and the impacts for both explicit and implicit methods. In Section 5.3, we assess in-depth how soft errors can dramatically change the space of tradeoffs in the relative performance of PCG vs SOR for the sparse linear system solution within implicit methods. We thus highlight how soft errors add to the complexity of managing performance and reliability tradeoffs of sparse solvers, a key challenge in enabling fast simulations of large scale PDE-based models.

5.1 Experimental Methodology

We use the model heat equation (Equation 2) using a 5-point finite stencil to analyze the effects of soft errors on the explicit method. For the implicit methods, we use PCG with incomplete Cholesky preconditioner [28] with threshold as a representative iterative linear solver. We evaluate PCG with two different threshold values, 0.01 (PCG1) and 0.001 (PCG2). We use 28 symmetric positive definite matrices[1] from The University of Florida Sparse Matrix Collection [29]. Table 1 gives the properties of the these matrices. The first column represents matrix ids and the second column gives matrix names. The third and fourth columns represent, respectively, the matrix dimension and number of non-zero elements in the matrix.

Soft error insertion: As we intend to study the impact of soft errors with respect to the SpMV kernel, we insert an error within the SpMV kernel. For the explicit method, we insert a soft error in an element of $\mathbf{u}^m$ that is involved in the SpMV operation (see Equation 2). For the CG and PCG methods, we insert a soft error in the vector $\mathbf{v}$ within the SpMV kernel of Algorithm 1. For SOR, we insert a soft error in the vector $\mathbf{x}$, that is involved in the SpMV operation (see Equation 5). We use small and large perturbations to simulate bit flips near the least significant bit and most significant bit of the exponent, respectively. To study the in-depth behavior of the performance impact of a soft error, we insert soft errors in each component of the vector iteratively

---
[1]A symmetric matrix $\mathbf{A}$ is positive definite if $\mathbf{x}^T\mathbf{A}\mathbf{x} > 0$ for all non-zero vectors $\mathbf{x}$, where $\mathbf{x}^T$ denotes the transpose of $\mathbf{x}$.

and record the required data. The fault injection schemes proposed in [11] and [16] insert an error at a random location of a random data structure. However, to analyze the varying performance impacts due to a soft error, we take a more systematic error insertion scheme as described above.

Matrix ID	Matrix	N	NNZ
1	bcsstk01	48	400
2	mesh1e1	48	306
3	lund_b	147	2,441
4	mesh2e1	306	2,018
5	mesh2em5	306	2,018
6	mhdb416	416	2,312
7	bcsstk07	420	7,860
8	nos5	468	5,172
9	nos6	675	3,255
10	msc00726	726	34,518
11	bcsstk09	1,083	18,437
12	plbuckle	1,282	30,644
13	bcsstk15	3,948	117,816
14	mhd4800b	4,800	27,520
15	crystm01	4,875	105,339
16	bcsstk16	4,884	290,378
17	Kuu	7,102	340,200
18	Muu	7,102	170,134
19	fv1	9,604	85,264
20	fv2	9,801	87,025
21	fv3	9,801	87,025
22	tedB	10,605	144,579
23	t2dahe	11,445	176,117
24	bcsstk18	11,948	149,090
25	cbuckle	13,681	676,515
26	crystm02	13,965	322,905
27	gyrom	17,361	340,431
28	bodyy4	17,546	121,550

Table 1: The UFL benchmark matrices with their dimension (N) and number of nonzeroes (NNZ).

5.2 Empirical Corroboration of Analysis

We support our theoretical analysis (in Section 4) with experimental observations in this section. Consider the explicit method to find the solution of the heat equation in Equation 2. We insert an error in $\mathbf{u}^0$ to give $\bar{\mathbf{u}}^0$ (here, $\mathbf{u}^0$ represents the solution in the first time step of the explicit method). We track $\mathbf{u}^m$ (original solution without soft error) and $\bar{\mathbf{u}}^m$ (solution with a soft error). Figure 5 shows the relative norm of the solutions, $\mathbf{u}^m$ and $\bar{\mathbf{u}}^m$, for 100 iterations for a relatively small 40x40 grid based PDE using an explicit method. The y-axis represents the relative norm of the solutions, defined as, $\frac{norm(\mathbf{norm}(\bar{\mathbf{u}}^m - \mathbf{u}^m))}{norm(\mathbf{u}^m)}$. It illustrates relative norms for three different error insertion positions corresponding to the highest (red), median (black), and , lowest (blue) row norms of $\mathbf{A}$. For the problem in this figure, the depth measure (see Theorem 1) is nearly the same for all positions of $\mathbf{u}^m$, implying that similar iterations are required to corrupt all the elements in $\mathbf{u}^m$. Hence, row norm of $\mathbf{A}$ plays a major role in the growth of a soft error (see Theorem 2). The plots in Figure 5 support this theorem. A key point to observe is that the magnitude of relative error growth easily surpass 200, making the solutions physically

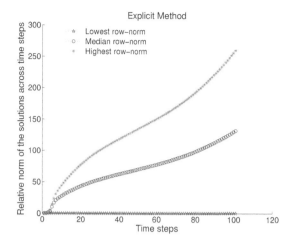

Figure 5: Relative errors in the solution of a model heat flow problem using an explicit method.

meaningless. Further, propagation of a soft error could potentially manifest as a change in the value of μ in Equation 2 leading to numerical instabilities.

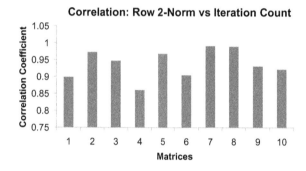

Figure 6: Correlation between row 2-norm values of a matrix and iteration count when a soft error is inserted in the corresponding position of the vector.

Now, consider solving an implicit scheme. It typically uses an iterative linear solver such as, CG, to find the solution. CG works on the vectors represented by a SpMV sequence, $span\{\mathbf{r}, \mathbf{A}\mathbf{r}, ... \mathbf{A}^n\mathbf{r}\}$ to find a solution for the linear system, where, $\mathbf{A}$ is the coefficient matrix and $\mathbf{r}$ is the initial residual vector. This span of vectors is known as Krylov subspace [7]. Let us assume that $span\{\bar{\mathbf{r}}, \mathbf{A}\bar{\mathbf{r}}, ... \mathbf{A}^n\bar{\mathbf{r}}\}$ and $span\{\mathbf{r}, \mathbf{A}\mathbf{r}, ... \mathbf{A}^n\mathbf{r}\}$ represent Krylov subspaces of CG with and without soft error inserted in the residual vector. Figure 7(a) tracks the relative norm of the Krylov vectors for three sample matrices. Observe that an error in the highest row norm position (red) of the vector propagates faster in terms of relative norm compared to an error in either the median (black) or the lowest (blue) row norm positions. Unlike the explicit method, the SpMV sequence of CG (Krylov subspace) alone, does not provide enough insights about the solution, but manifests on the measure, A-norm of errors. We define A-norm of errors, as $\sqrt{(\mathbf{x} - \hat{\mathbf{x}})' * \mathbf{A} * (\mathbf{x} - \hat{\mathbf{x}})}$, where, $\mathbf{x}$ is the true solution and $\hat{\mathbf{x}}$ is an intermediate solution during a CG iteration. It plays an important role in the conver-

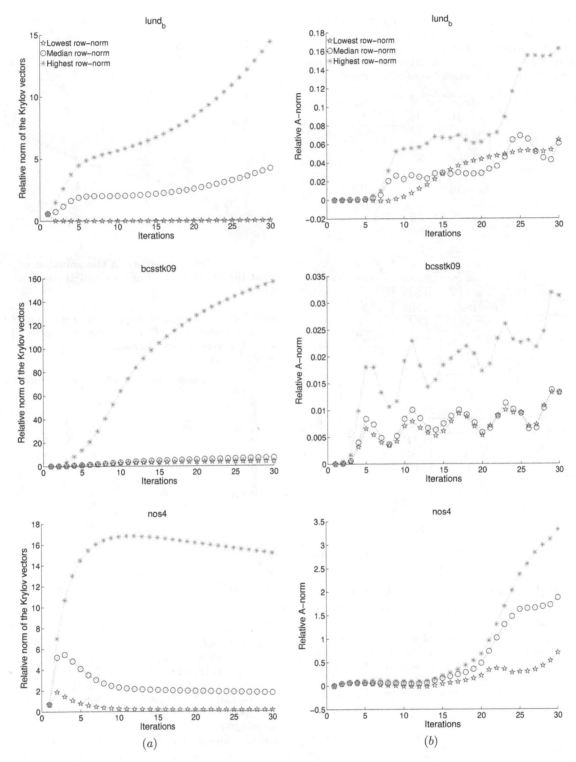

Figure 7: Relative errors in (a) Krylov subspace, (b) A-norm error during CG iterations. Note that red, black and blue colors indicate that a soft error was inserted in a vector position corresponding to the highest, median and lowest row norm positions, respectively.

gence of CG [30]. Figure 7(b) tracks relative A-norm errors, defined as, $\frac{ANormErr - \overline{ANormErr}}{\overline{ANormErr}}$, where, $ANormErr$ and $\overline{ANormErr}$ are the A-norm errors for CG with and without soft errors, respectively. The behavior of relative A-

norm error is similar to that of the relative norm of Krylov vectors with respect to the position of a soft error. Observe that unlike plots in Figure 7(a), the plots in Figure 7(b) are not smooth but oscillating, but both follow similar trends.

As A-norm of errors plays an important role in the convergence of CG, we conjecture that a soft error in an element of the vector corresponding to the highest 2-norm row of the matrix could potentially lead to significant performance degradation in terms of iteration count. Figure 6 shows the correlation between the row 2-norm values of the matrix and the iteration count of CG. Observe that these two are highly correlated, with correlation coefficient greater than 0.8. Hence, our conjecture about the performance degradation is correct.

5.3 Discussion

The correlation between a soft error (propagation and magnitude), numerical property (row-norm) and sparsity structure of a sparse matrix is evident from the previous section. We have shown that explicit methods are highly vulnerable to soft errors and could potentially produce erroneous results, and the convergence of implicit methods are affected (as indicated by the relative A-norm in Figure 7(b)). Now, we discuss the impact of soft errors on two of the implicit methods. For ease of analysis, we provided a theoretical study of the error propagation pattern and the growth of error with respect to the Krylov subspace and A-norm of errors for CG. However, for most practical purposes, CG has slow convergence rate, making it prohibitively expensive in terms of computational time. Hence, a majority of implicit schemes usually employ faster solvers like PCG. However, the choice of an effective solver that accounts for both performance and reliability is not clear [31]. We use PCG and SOR as representative fast solvers, to analyze the impact of soft errors on practical problem.

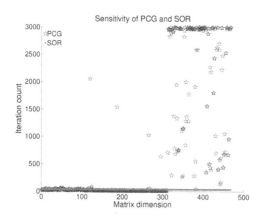

Figure 8: Sensitivity to error insertion position in SOR and PCG.

Figure 8 shows the sensitivity of SOR (red) and PCG (black) to error insertion position. We observe an increase in the number of iterations in the case of PCG for certain error insertions positions, while, SOR is not affected. Here, it is important to note that we obtain all the relevant data by exhaustive experimentation, which involves inserting a soft error in each position of the vector and recording the corresponding iteration count. Figure 9 shows the impact of a soft error on the convergence of PCG and SOR. Figure 9(a) illustrates the maximum observed performance degradation due to an error. Observe that performance of PCG

on matrices like, Matrices 4, 5, and, 10, could potentially degrade by more than 150 times. However, observe that SOR has no degradation due to a soft error. We conjecture that these results for SOR robustness is due to the inherent solution correction property of the SOR algorithm. Figure 9(b) shows the potential average performance degradation is much less when compared to maximum performance degradation for PCG. This implies that a small fraction of the vector elements are more impacted by a soft error than the remaining elements.

Figure 10 illustrates the tradeoffs of using PCG and SOR in the presence of soft errors for a sample set of matrices. A soft error was inserted in the same vector position for both PCG and SOR for both *Average Error* and *Maximum Error* cases. The y-axis represents relative performance, defined as, the ratio of execution times of SOR and PCG, in *log2* scale. A positive value indicates that PCG performs better than SOR and a negative value indicates SOR is better. A key observation from this figure is the variable behavior of PCG in the presence of a soft error. We observe that, in the absence of a soft error, PCG performs significantly better than SOR. However, in the presence of an error, SOR tends to perform substantially better than PCG.

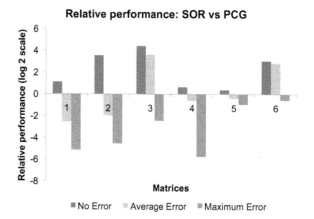

Figure 10: Performance tradeoffs of PCG and SOR in the presence of soft errors. Average and maximum error corresponds to the average increase and highest iteration count observed in PCG and SOR on soft error insertion.

6. CONCLUSION AND FUTURE WORK

The efficient and reliable simulation of PDE-based models using explicit and implicit methods on high performance multicore multiprocessors is an area of active research. Such simulations are needed for enabling advances in multiple areas of science, ranging from biology, materials, energy and environmental sciences. Many recent results concern new formulations reflecting effective tradeoffs between multiple metric including the scalability, performance, reliability and accuracy of solution methods. In this context, our results indicate that the stability of explicit methods can be greatly degraded by the occurrence of a single soft error. Additionally, for the inherently numerically stable implicit methods, a single soft error can have a serious impact on performance, with potential degradation by factors of 200x when using

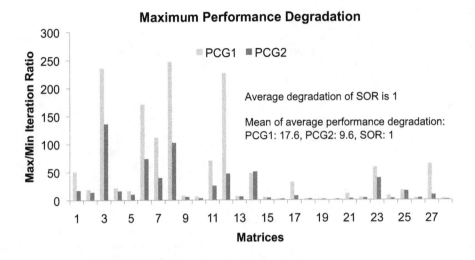

(a)

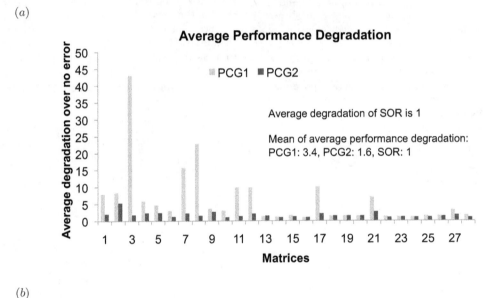

(b)

Figure 9: Performance impact of soft errors on PCG: (a) maximum performance degradation, and (b) average performance degradation.

PCG for linear system solution. On the other hand we observed that there are essentially no performance degradation for the stationary SOR scheme. Consequently, there are interesting crossover instances, i.e., systems where PCG has vastly superior performance relative to SOR by a factor of 21x when there are no soft errors while SOR outperforms PCG by a factor of 12x given a single soft error. We expect to see an interesting spectrum of vastly different impacts of soft errors if we consider a broader array of linear solvers including methods from direct [32], domain decomposition [33] and multigrid approaches [34]. These results motivate and indicate the need for developing cost effective soft error detection and mitigation strategies. Additionally, they also motivate the development of new techniques for the selection of sparse linear solution methods that take into account distortions in the tradeoffs between performance and reliability due to the differential impacts of soft errors.

7. REFERENCES

[1] M. Rebaudengo, M. Sonza Reorda, and M. Violante, "An accurate analysis of the effects of soft errors in the instruction and data caches of a pipelined microprocessor," in *DATE '03: Proceedings of the conference on Design, Automation and Test in Europe*. Washington, DC, USA: IEEE Computer Society, 2003, p. 10602.

[2] B. T. Gold, J. C. Smolens, B. Falsafi, and J. C. Hoe, "The Granularity of Soft-Error Containment in Shared-Memory Multiprocessors," 2006.

[3] J. C. Smolens, B. T. Gold, J. Kim, B. Falsafi, J. C. Hoe, and A. G. Nowatzyk, "Fingerprinting: Bounding soft-error detection latency and bandwidth," in *In Proc. of the Symposium on Architectural Support for Programming Languages and Operating Systems (ASPLOS*, 2004, pp. 224–234.

[4] S. Borkar, *Probabilistic and Statistical Design: The Wave of the Future*. Springer Boston, 2008.

[5] M. A. Heroux, P. Raghavan, and H. D. Simon, *Parallel Processing for Scientific Computing (Software, Environments and Tools)*. Philadelphia, PA, USA: Society for Industrial and Applied Mathematics, 2006.

[6] L. C. McInnes, Mcinnes, and B. F. Smith, "Petsc 2.0: A case study of using mpi to develop numerical software libraries."

[7] G. Golub and J. M. Ortega, *Scientific Computing: An Introduction with Parallel Computing*. Academic Press, 1993.

[8] J. F. Ziegler, "Terrestrial cosmic rays," *IBM J. Res. Dev.*, vol. 40, no. 1, pp. 19–39, 1996.

[9] R. Baumann, "Radiation-induced soft errors in advanced semiconductor technologies," vol. 5, no. 3, sept. 2005, pp. 305 – 316.

[10] S. Krishnamohan and N. R. Mahapatra, "A highly-efficient technique for reducing soft errors in static cmos circuits," in *ICCD '04: Proceedings of the IEEE International Conference on Computer Design*. Washington, DC, USA: IEEE Computer Society, 2004, pp. 126–131.

[11] G. Bronevetsky and B. de Supinski, "Soft error vulnerability of iterative linear algebra methods," in *ICS '08: Proceedings of the 22nd Annual International Conference on Supercomputing*. New York, NY, USA: ACM, 2008, pp. 155–164.

[12] S. Michalak, K. Harris, N. Hengartner, B. Takala, and S. Wender, "Predicting the number of fatal soft errors in los alamos national laboratory's asc q supercomputer," vol. 5, no. 3, sept. 2005, pp. 329 – 335.

[13] R. D. Falgout and U. M. Yang, "hypre: a library of high performance preconditioners," in *Preconditioners,Ó Lecture Notes in Computer Science*, 2002, pp. 632–641.

[14] M. Heroux, R. Bartlett, V. H. R. Hoekstra, J. Hu, T. Kolda, R. Lehoucq, K. Long, R. Pawlowski, E. Phipps, A. Salinger, H. Thornquist, R. Tuminaro, J. Willenbring, and A. Williams, "An Overview of Trilinos," Sandia National Laboratories, Tech. Rep. SAND2003-2927, 2003.

[15] M. A. Heroux, J. M. Willenbring, and R. Heaphy, "Trilinos Developers Guide," Sandia National Laboratories, Tech. Rep. SAND2003-1898, 2003.

[16] K. Malkowski, "Analyzing the soft-error resilience of linear solvers on multicore multiprocessors," in *IPDPS '10: 24th IEEE International Parallel and Distributed Processing Symposium*, 2010.

[17] M. Rebaudengo, M. S. Reorda, M. Torchiano, and M. Violante, "Soft-error detection through software fault-tolerance techniques," in *DFT '99: Proceedings of the 14th International Symposium on Defect and Fault-Tolerance in VLSI Systems*. Washington, DC, USA: IEEE Computer Society, 1999, pp. 210–218.

[18] J. Hu, F. Li, V. Degalahal, M. Kandemir, N. Vijaykrishnan, and M. J. Irwin, "Compiler-assisted soft error detection under performance and energy constraints in embedded systems," *ACM Trans. Embed. Comput. Syst.*, vol. 8, no. 4, pp. 1–30, 2009.

[19] J. Blome, S. Mahlke, D. Bradley, and K. Flautner, "A microarchitectural analysis of soft error propagation in a production-level embedded microprocessor," in *Proceedings of the 1st Workshop on Architectural Reliability, 38th International Symposium on Microarchitecture, Barcelona, Spain*, 2005.

[20] P. Montesinos, W. Liu, and J. Torrellas, "Shield: Cost-effective soft-error protection for register files," in *Third IBM TJ Watson Conference on Interaction between Architecture, Circuits and Compilers (PAC2)*, 2006.

[21] M. Latif, M, R. Ramaseshan, and F. Meuller, "Soft error protection via fault-resilient data representations," *Workshop on Silicon Errors in Logic - System Effects*, 2007.

[22] M. Sadi, D. Myers, and C. Sanchez, "A design approach for soft error protection in real-time embedded systems," in *ASWEC 2008: 19th Australian Conference on Software Engineering*, March 2008, pp. 639–643.

[23] W. Zhang and T. Li, "Microarchitecture soft error vulnerability characterization and mitigation under 3d integration technology," in *MICRO '08: Proceedings of the 2008 41st IEEE/ACM International Symposium on Microarchitecture*. Washington, DC, USA: IEEE Computer Society, 2008, pp. 435–446.

[24] R. Naseer, Y. Boulghassoul, M. Bajura, A, J. Sondeen, S. Stansberry, and J. Draper, "Single-event effects characterization and soft error mitigation in 90nm commercial-density srams," in *Proceedings of IASTED International Conference*, 2008.

[25] X. Fu, J. Poe, T. Li, and J. Fortes, "Characterizing microarchitecture soft error vulnerability phase behavior," in *Modeling, Analysis, and Simulation of Computer and Telecommunication Systems, 2006. MASCOTS 2006. 14th IEEE International Symposium on*, Sept. 2006, pp. 147–155.

[26] J. Dongarra, A. Lumsdaine, X. Niu, R. Pozo, and K. Remington, "A sparse matrix library in c++ for high performance architectures," 1994.

[27] M. T. Heath, *Scientific Computing, An Introductory Survey*. New York, NY, USA: McGraw-Hill, 2002.

[28] D. S. Kershaw, "The incomplete cholesky–conjugate gradient method for the iterative solution of systems of linear equations," *Journal of Computational Physics*, vol. 26, no. 1, pp. 43 – 65, 1978. [Online]. Available: http://www.sciencedirect.com/science/article/B6WHY-4DD1NST-H9/2/2eec10d2aeb383a70b831c65d01844cf

[29] T. Davis, "The University of Florida Sparse Matrix Collection," *NA Digest*, vol. 97, 1997.

[30] G. Meurant, *The Lanczos and Conjugate Gradient Algorithms*. Philadelphia, PA, USA: Society for Industrial and Applied Mathematics, 2006.

[31] A. Ern, V. Giovangigli, D. Keyes, and M. D. Snooke, "Towards polyalgorithmic linear system solvers for nonlinear," *sjsc*, vol. 15, pp. 681–703, 1994.

[32] M. T. Heath, E. Ng, and B. W. Peyton, "Parallel algorithms for sparse linear systems," *sirev*, vol. 33, pp. 420–460, 1991.

[33] B. Smith, P. Bjorstad, and W. Gropp, *Domain Decomposition: Parallel Multilevel Methods for Elliptic PDES*. Cambridge University Press, 1996.

[34] V. Henson and U. Yang, "BoomerAMG: a parallel algebraic multigrid solver and preconditioner," *Appl. Numer. Math.*, vol. 41, pp. 151–177, 2002.

High Performance Linpack Benchmark: A Fault Tolerant Implementation without Checkpointing

Teresa Davies, Christer Karlsson, Hui Liu, Chong Ding, and Zizhong Chen
Colorado School of Mines
Golden, CO, USA
{tdavies, ckarlsso, huliu, cding, zchen}@mines.edu

ABSTRACT

The probability that a failure will occur before the end of the computation increases as the number of processors used in a high performance computing application increases. For long running applications using a large number of processors, it is essential that fault tolerance be used to prevent a total loss of all finished computations after a failure. While checkpointing has been very useful to tolerate failures for a long time, it often introduces a considerable overhead especially when applications modify a large amount of memory between checkpoints and the number of processors is large. In this paper, we propose an algorithm-based recovery scheme for the High Performance Linpack benchmark (which modifies a large amount of memory in each iteration) to tolerate fail-stop failures without checkpointing. It was proved by Huang and Abraham that a checksum added to a matrix will be maintained after the matrix is factored. We demonstrate that, for the right-looking LU factorization algorithm, the checksum is maintained at each step of the computation. Based on this checksum relationship maintained at each step in the middle of the computation, we demonstrate that fail-stop process failures in High Performance Linpack can be tolerated without checkpointing. Because no periodical checkpoint is necessary during computation and no roll-back is necessary during recovery, the proposed recovery scheme is highly scalable and has a good potential to scale to extreme scale computing and beyond. Experimental results on the supercomputer Jaguar demonstrate that the fault tolerance overhead introduced by the proposed recovery scheme is negligible.

Categories and Subject Descriptors

C.4 [**Performance of Systems**]: Fault tolerance

General Terms

Performance, Reliability

Keywords

High Performance Linpack benchmark, LU factorization, fault tolerance, algorithm-based recovery

1. INTRODUCTION

Fault tolerance is becoming more important as the number of processors used for a single calculation increases [26]. When more processors are used, the probability that one will fail increases [14]. Therefore, it is necessary, especially for long-running calculations, that they be able to survive the failure of one or more processors. One critical part of recovery from failure is recovering the lost data. General methods for recovery exist, but for some applications specialized optimizations are possible. There is usually overhead associated with preparing for a failure, even during the runs when no failure occurs, so it is important to choose the method with the lowest possible overhead so as not to hurt the performance more than necessary.

There are various approaches to the problem of recovering lost data involving saving the processor state periodically in different ways, either by saving the data directly [9,20,25,28] or by maintaining some sort of checksum of the data [6,8,17,21] from which it can be recovered. A method that can be used for any application is Plank's diskless checkpointing [4,11,12,15,22,25,27], where a copy of the data is saved in memory, and when a node is lost the data can be recovered from the other nodes. However, its performance degrades when there is a large amount of data changed between checkpoints [20], as in for instance matrix operations. Since matrix operations are an important part of most large calculations, it is desirable to make them fault tolerant in a way that has lower overhead than diskless checkpointing.

Chen and Dongarra discovered that, for some algorithms that perform matrix multiplication, it is possible to add a checksum to the matrix and have it maintained at every step of the algorithm [5,7]. If this is the case, then a checksum in the matrix can be used in place of a checkpoint to recover data that is lost in the event of a processor failure. In addition to matrix multiplication, this technique has been applied to the Cholesky factorization [17]. In this paper, we extend the checksum technique to the LU decomposition used by High Performance Linpack (HPL) [23].

LU is different from other matrix operations because of pivoting, which makes it more costly to maintain a column checksum. Maintaining a column checksum with pivoting would require additional communication. However, we show in this paper that HPL has a feature that makes the column checksum unnecessary. We prove that the row checksum is maintained at each step of the algorithm used by HPL, and that it can be used to recover the required part of the matrix. Therefore, in this method we use only a row checksum, and it is enough to recover in the event of a failure. Additionally, we show that two other algorithms for calculating the LU factorization do not maintain a checksum.

The checksum-based approach that we have used to provide fault tolerance for the dense matrix operation LU factorization has a number of advantages over checkpointing. The operation to perform a checksum or a checkpoint is the same or similar, but the checksum is only done once and then maintained by the algorithm, while the checkpoint has to be redone periodically. The checkpoint approach requires that a copy of the data be kept for rolling back, whereas no copy is required in the checksum method, nor is rolling back required. The operation of recovery is the same for each method, but since the checksum method does not roll back its overhead is less. Because of all of these reasons, the overhead of fault tolerance using a checksum is significantly less than with checkpointing.

The rest of this paper will explain related work that leads to this result in section 2; the features of HPL that are important to our application of the checksum technique in section 3; the type of failure that this work is able to handle in section 4; the details of adding a checksum to the matrix in sections 5; proof that the checksum is maintained in section 6; and analysis of the performance with experimental results in sections 7 and 8.

2. RELATED WORK

2.1 Diskless Checkpoint

In order to do a checkpoint, it is necessary to save the data so that it can be recovered in the event of a failure. One approach is to save the data to disk periodically [28]. In the event of a failure, all processes are rolled back to the point of the previous checkpoint, and their data is restored from the data saved on the disk. Unfortunately, this method does not scale well. For most scientific computations, all processes make a checkpoint at the same time, so that all of the processes will simultaneously attempt to write their data to the disk. Most systems are not optimized for a large amount of data to go to the disk at once, so this is a serious bottleneck, made worse by the fact that disk accesses are typically extremely slow.

In response to this issue diskless checkpointing [25] was introduced. Each processor saves its own checkpoint state in memory, thereby eliminating the need for a slow write to disk. Additionally, an extra processor is used just for redundancy, which would be parity, checksum, or some other appropriate reduction. Typically there would be a number of such processors, each one for a different group of the worker processors. This way, upon the failure of a processor in one group, all of the other processors can revert to their stored checkpoint, and the redundant data along with the data of all the other processors in the group is used to recover the data of the failed processor.

Diskless checkpointing has several similarities to the checksum-based approach. When a checksum row is added to a processor grid, each checksum processor plays the role of the redundancy processor in a diskless checkpoint. The difference is that the redundancy of the checksum data is maintained naturally by the algorithm. Therefore there are two main

benefits: the working processors do not have to use extra memory keeping their checkpoint data, and less overhead is introduced in the form of communication to the checkpoint processors when a checkpoint is made. A key factor in the performance of diskless checkpointing is the size of the checkpoint. The overhead is reduced when only data that has been changed since the last checkpoint is saved [10]. However, matrix operations are not susceptible to this optimization [20], since many elements, up to the entire matrix, could be changed at each step of the algorithm. When the checkpoint is large, the overhead is large [24].

2.2 Algorithm-Based Fault Tolerance

Algorithm-based fault tolerance [1–3, 16, 18, 19, 21] is a technique that has been used to detect miscalculations in matrix operations. This technique consists of adding a checksum row or column to the matrices being operated on. For many matrix operations, some sort of checksum can be shown to be correct at the end of the calculation, and can be used to find errors after the fact. A checksum of a matrix can be used to locate and correct entries in the solution matrix that are incorrect, although we are most interested in recovery. Failure location is determined by the message passing library in the case of the failure of a processor.

The existence of a checksum that is correct at the end raises the question: is the checksum correct also in the middle? It turns out that it is not maintained for all algorithms [8], but there do exist some for which it is maintained. In other cases, it is possible to maintain a checksum with only minor modifications to the algorithm, while still keeping an advantage in overhead over a diskless checkpoint. It may also be possible to use a checksum to maintain redundancy of part of the data, while checkpointing the rest. Even a reduction in the amount of data needing to be checkpointed should give a gain in performance. The checksum approach has been used for many matrix operations to detect errors and correct them at the end of the calculation, which indicates that it may be possible to use it for recovery in the middle of the calculation as well.

2.3 Applications of Checksum-Based Recovery

It has been shown in [8] how a checksum is maintained in the outer product matrix-matrix multiply. It is also made clear that not all algorithms will maintain the checksum in the middle of the calculation, even if the checksum can be shown to be correct at the end. So it is important to ensure that the algorithm being used is one for which a checksum is maintained before using a checksum for recovery. Another application of a checksum is described in [17]. Here a checksum is used to recover from a failure during the ScaLAPACK Cholesky decomposition.

3. HIGH PERFORMANCE LINPACK

HPL performs a dense LU decomposition using a right-looking partial pivoting algorithm. The matrix is stored in two-dimensional block-cyclic data distribution. These are the most important features of HPL to our technique.

3.1 2D Block-Cyclic Data Distribution

For many parallel matrix operations, the matrix involved is very large. The number of processors needed for the operation may be selected based on how many it takes to have

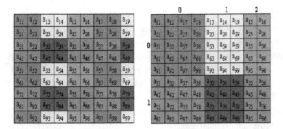

Figure 1: Global and local matrices under the 2D block cyclic distribution [8].

enough memory to fit the entire matrix. It is common to divide the matrix up among the processors in some way, so that the section of the matrix on a particular processor is not duplicated anywhere else. Therefore an important fact about recovering from the failure of a processor is that a part of the partially finished matrix is lost, and it is necessary to recover the lost part in order to continue from the middle of the calculation rather than going back to the beginning.

Matrices are often stored in 2D block cyclic fashion [8, 17, 20]. Block cyclic distribution is used in HPL. This storage pattern creates a good load balance for many operations, since it is typical to go through the matrix row by row or column by column (or in blocks of rows or columns). With a block cyclic arrangement, matrix elements on a particular processor are accessed periodically throughout the calculation, instead of all at once. An example of 2D block cyclic distribution is shown in figure 1. As this figure indicates, the global matrix will not necessarily divide evenly among the processors. However, we currently are assuming matrices that divide evenly along both rows and columns of the processor grid to simplify the problem. The block size is how many contiguous elements of the matrix are put in a processor together. Blocks are mapped to processors cyclically along both rows and columns.

3.2 Right-looking Algorithm

In Gaussian elimination, the elements of L are found by dividing some elements of the original matrix by the element on the diagonal. If this element is zero the division is clearly not possible, but with floating point numbers a number that is very close to zero could be on the diagonal and not be obvious as a problem. In order to ensure that this does not happen, algorithms for LU factorization use pivoting, where the row with the largest element in a the current column is swapped with the current row. The swaps are not done in the L matrix, which enforces our idea that it is not necessary to be able to recover it. The equation $Ax = b$ can be rewritten as $LUx = b$ using the LU decomposition, where $Ux = y$, so that $Ly = b$. The algorithm transforms b to y, so that L is not needed to find x at the end. The factorization is performed in place, which means that the original matrix is replaced by L and U.

The right-looking variation is the version of LU that updates the trailing matrix. When one row and column are factored in basic Gaussian elimination, the remaining piece of the original matrix is updated by subtracting the product of the row and column. It is possible to put off the update of a particular section of the matrix until that section is

Figure 2: Three different algorithms for LU decomposition [20]. The part of the matrix that changes color is the part that is modified by one iteration. Unlike right-looking, left- and top-looking variants change only a small part of the matrix in one iteration.

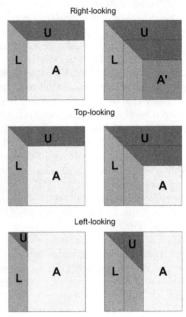

going to be factored. However, this approach means that large sections of the matrix are unchanged after each iteration. Figure 2 shows how the matrix is changed in each of the three variations. Because of the data distribution, the load balance is best when each processor does some work on its section of the matrix during each iteration. When the trailing matrix is not updated at each step, the work of updating it has to be done consecutively by a small set of processors when the factorization reaches each new part. When the update is done at every step, the work is done at the same time that other processors are doing factorization work, taking less total time.

4. FAILURE MODEL

The type of failure that we focus on in this work is a fail-stop failure, which means that a process stops and loses all of its data. The main task that we are able to perform is to recover the lost data. Another type of failure that this technique could handle is a soft failure, where one or more numbers become incorrect without any outwardly detectable signs. A checksum can be used to detect and correct these types of errors as well. However, it has higher overhead than handling only fail-stop failures. Detecting a soft failure requires that all elements of the matrix be made redundant by two different checksums, where different elements of the matrix go into each checksum. The other way in which the overhead of detecting and recovering from soft failures is greater than recovering from fail-stop failures is that detecting soft failures requires periodically checking to see if a failure has occurred. This does not have to be done every step, but it should be done often enough that a second failure is not likely to occur and make it impossible to recover.

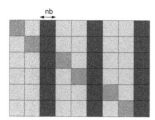

Figure 3: Global view of a matrix with checksum blocks and diagonal blocks marked. Because of the checksum blocks, the diagonal of the original matrix is displaced in the global matrix.

Soft failures are a task for later research, although the idea behind having multiple sums for the same set of elements is similar. Instead, we are focused on recovering from one hard failure, where the fact of the failure and the processor that failed are provided by some other source, presumably the MPI library. The ability to continue after a process failure is not something that is currently provided by most MPI implementations. However, for testing purposes it is possible to simulate a failure in a reasonable manner. When one process fails, no communication is possible, but the surviving processes can still do work. Therefore, the general approach to recovery is to have the surviving processes write a copy of their state to the disk. This information can then be used to restart the computation. The state of the surviving processes is used to recover the failed process.

5. CHECKSUM

Adding checksums to a matrix stored in block cyclic fashion is most easily done by adding an extra row, column, or both of processors to the processor grid. The extra processors hold an element by element sum of the local matrices on the processors in the same row for a row checksum or the same column for a column checksum. This way processors hold either entirely checksum elements or entirely normal matrix elements. If this were not the case it might make recovery impossible.

The block cyclic distribution makes it so that the checksum elements are interpreted as being spread throughout the global matrix, rather than all in the last rows or columns as they would be in a sequential matrix operation. Figure 3 shows the global view of a matrix with a row checksum. The width of each checksum block in the global matrix is the block size nb. The block size is also used as the width of a column block that is factored in one iteration. Periodically during the calculation checksum elements may need to be treated differently from normal elements. In the LU factorization, when a checksum block on the main diagonal is come to, that iteration can be skipped because the work done in it is not necessary to maintaining the checksum. When there is only a row checksum, as in this case, the elements on the diagonal of the original matrix are not all on the diagonal of the checksum matrix. Instead of considering every element $a_{i,i}$ of the matrix during Gaussian elimination, the element is $a_{i,i+c\cdot nb}$, where c is the number of checksum blocks to the left of the element under consideration.

Another feature of the matrix storage for LU that is worth noting is that the factorization is done in place, so that L and U replace the original matrix one panel at a time. An implication of this fact is that the local matrix in a particular processor may have sections of all three matrices. However, both U and the original matrix A are recovered using row checksums, so the elements of L in the row are simply set to zero so that they do not affect the outcome. The recovery is done by a reduce across the row containing the failed process.

The checksum is most useful when it is maintained at every step of the calculation. The shorter the period of time when the checksum is not correct or all processors do not have the information necessary to update the checksum, the less vulnerable the method is. This period of time is equivalent to the time it takes to perform a checkpoint when the checkpointing method is used. If a failure occurs during the checkpoint, it is likely that the data cannot be recovered. The same might be true for the checksum method.

Specifically for HPL, it is necessary to take some extra steps to reduce this vulnerability. One iteration of the factorization is broken down into two parts: the panel factorization and the trailing matrix update. During the panel factorization, only the panel is changed, and the rest of the matrix is not affected. This operation makes the checksum incorrect. Fortunately, simply keeping a copy of the panel before factorization starts is enough to eliminate this problem. The size of the panel is small compared to the total matrix. HPL already keeps copies of panels for some of the variations available for optimization.

Once the panel factorization is completed, the factored panel is broadcast to the other processors, and the panel is used to update the trailing matrix. If a failure occurs while the panel is being factored, recovery consists of replacing the partially factored panel with its stored earlier version, then using the checksums to recover the part of the matrix that was kept on the failed processor.

It is not guaranteed that the checksum can be maintained for any algorithm for calculating the LU decomposition. The method relies on whole rows of the matrix being operated on in the same iteration.

The right-looking LU factorization can be used with our technique, but the left-looking LU factorization cannot. In the left-looking variation, columns to the left of the currently factored column are not updated. So the row checksum will not be maintained, and it will not be possible to recover U.

6. ALGORITHMS FOR LU DECOMPOSITION

Like all matrix operations, there are different algorithms for the LU decomposition, not all of which will necessarily maintain a checksum at each step. However, there is at least one algorithm for LU that maintains the checksum in a way that is useful for recovery. This is the right-looking algorithm with partial pivoting. If pivoting is not used at all, the right-looking algorithm also maintains a checksum, but without pivoting the outcome of the algorithm is not as numerically stable.

The right-looking algorithm for LU maintains a checksum at each step as is required because each iteration operates on entire rows and columns. If an entire row is multiplied by a constant, or rows are added together, the checksum will still be correct. The same is true of columns. When an operation finishes factoring a part of the matrix into part of L or U, the checksums in that part will be sums on L or U only. Elements belonging to L will go into column checksums only, and elements belonging to U will go into row checksums only. The elements of L and U that are not stored in the matrix-ones on the diagonal of L and zeros above or below the diagonal-also go into the checksums.

Left-looking and top-looking LU decomposition do not maintain a checksum because various parts of the matrix are not updated in a given step, shown in figure 2 by the sections that do not change color. When some sections of the matrix are changed and others are not, a sum that includes elements from both sections will not be maintained. Only the right-looking variant updates the entire matrix at every step, maintaining the checksum. Interestingly, this characteristic makes the right-looking variant the least favorable for diskless checkpointing.

6.1 Proof

Right-looking LU factorization maintains a checksum at each step, as shown below. This version is also faster than the others, left-looking and top-looking.

The right-looking algorithm is:

```
for i = 1 to n-1
    A(i+1:n,1) = A(i+1:n,1)/A(i,i)
    A(i+1:n,i+1:n) = A(i+1:n,i+1:n)
                   - A(i+1:n,i)*A(i,i+1:n)
```

In an iteration of the loop, the original matrix is:

$$
\begin{pmatrix}
a_{11} & a_{12} & \cdots & a_{1n} & \sum_{j=1}^{n} a_{1j} \\
a_{21} & a_{22} & \cdots & a_{2n} & \sum_{j=1}^{n} a_{2j} \\
\vdots & \vdots & & \vdots & \vdots \\
a_{n1} & a_{n2} & \cdots & a_{nn} & \sum_{j=1}^{n} a_{nj}
\end{pmatrix}
$$

Dividing it up by the sections that are relevant to the step, this matrix is

$$
\begin{pmatrix}
a_{11} & A_{12} & \sum A_{12} \\
A_{21} & A_{22} & \sum A_{22}
\end{pmatrix}
$$

where

$$ A_{12} = \begin{pmatrix} a_{12} & \cdots & a_{1n} \end{pmatrix} $$

$$ \sum A_{12} = \begin{pmatrix} \sum_{j=1}^{n} a_{1j} \end{pmatrix} $$

$$ A_{21} = \begin{pmatrix} a_{21} \\ \vdots \\ a_{n1} \end{pmatrix} $$

$$ A_{22} = \begin{pmatrix} a_{22} & \cdots & a_{2n} \\ \vdots & & \vdots \\ a_{n2} & \cdots & a_{nn} \end{pmatrix} $$

$$ \sum A_{22} = \begin{pmatrix} \sum_{j=1}^{n} a_{2j} \\ \vdots \\ \sum_{j=1}^{n} a_{nj} \end{pmatrix} $$

The first part of the iteration makes the matrix into

$$
\begin{pmatrix}
a_{11} & A_{12} & \sum A_{12} \\
A_{21}/a_{11} & A_{22} & \sum A_{22}
\end{pmatrix}
$$

The second step modifies the trailing matrix as follows:

$$
\begin{aligned}
& \begin{pmatrix} A_{22} & \sum A_{22} \end{pmatrix} - \begin{pmatrix} A_{21}/a_{11} \end{pmatrix} \begin{pmatrix} A_{12} & \sum A_{12} \end{pmatrix} \\
=~ & \begin{pmatrix} A_{22} & \sum A_{22} \end{pmatrix} - \begin{pmatrix} A_{21}A_{12}/a_{11} & A_{21}/a_{11}\sum A_{12} \end{pmatrix} \\
=~ & \begin{pmatrix} A_{22} - A_{21}A_{12}/a_{11} & \sum A_{22} - A_{21}/a_{11}\sum A_{12} \end{pmatrix}
\end{aligned}
$$

Note that $A_{22} - A_{21}A_{12}/a_{11} = a_{ij} - a_{i1}a_{1j}/a_{11}$ for $i = 2, \ldots n$ and $j = 2, \ldots n$.

The term representing the sums is

$$
\begin{aligned}
& \sum A_{22} - A_{21}/a_{11} \sum A_{12} \\
=~ & \begin{pmatrix} \sum_{j=1}^{n} a_{2j} \\ \vdots \\ \sum_{j=1}^{n} a_{nj} \end{pmatrix} - \begin{pmatrix} a_{21}/a_{11} \\ \vdots \\ a_{n1}/a_{11} \end{pmatrix} \begin{pmatrix} \sum_{j=1}^{n} a_{1j} \end{pmatrix} \\
=~ & \begin{pmatrix} \sum_{j=1}^{n} a_{2j} - a_{21}a_{1j}/a_{11} \\ \vdots \\ \sum_{j=1}^{n} a_{nj} - a_{n1}a_{1j}/a_{11} \end{pmatrix} \\
=~ & \begin{pmatrix} \sum_{j=2}^{n} a_{2j} - a_{21}a_{1j}/a_{11} \\ \vdots \\ \sum_{j=2}^{n} a_{nj} - a_{n1}a_{1j}/a_{11} \end{pmatrix}
\end{aligned}
$$

The first term of each sum is zero. Therefore they become sums of the elements in the trailing matrix only. The trailing matrix contains correct checksums at the end of the iteration. The row that became part of U has a checksum for itself. The column that is part of L no longer has a checksum that it is part of, but with the HPL algorithm it is no longer needed for the final result.

7. PERFORMANCE

One way to evaluate the relative merit of the checkpointing and checksum techniques is to compare their overhead. The most straightforward way of measuring overhead is to find how much longer a run on the same matrix size takes with fault tolerance than without. This way all of the effects of the additional work will be included.

A problem with this comparison is that the optimal rate of checkpointing depends on the expected rate of failure, among other factors. The time between checkpoints that gives the best performance is given in [13]. This means that it is impossible to absolutely state that checkpointing has higher overhead. However, it is possible to show that the interval would have to be extremely long, which is only possible when the failure rate is extremely low, for checkpointing to achieve overhead as low as that of the checksum method.

Making a checkpoint is the same operation as making the checksum, the difference being that a checksum is only done once while the checkpoint is done many times. Aside from that fact, the difference lies in the fact that the checksum needs to have some work done to keep it correct, while the checkpoint ends with doing the sum periodically. The extra work comes from the fact that the blocks with the sums in them are treated as part of the matrix. However, no extra iterations are added because it is possible to skip over the sum blocks and keep the sums correct. So the number of steps is the same; the only difference is how much longer each step takes when there are more processors in the grid.

The only parts of an iteration that are affected by there being more processors are the parts with communication. There are broadcasts in both rows and columns, but only broadcasting in rows is affected because there are no column checksums. If the original matrix dimension is P, then with a checksum added it is $P+1$. So the overhead of each iteration is the difference between a broadcast among P+1 processors and a broadcast among P processors. Depending on the implementation, the value varies. With a binomial tree, the overhead would be $\log(P+1) - \log P$. Using pipelining, where the time for the broadcast is nearly proportional to the size of the message, the overhead is even smaller.

The total overhead of the checksum technique is

$$T_{P+1} + (T_{P+1} - T_P) \cdot \frac{N}{nb}$$

where T_P is the time for either a broadcast or a reduce on P processors, N is the matrix dimension, and nb is the block size. N/nb is the number of iterations. It seems reasonable to assume that $T_{P+1} - T_P$ is a very small quantity. Whether this term is significant depends on the exact value and the number of iterations, but for certain ranges of matrix size the overhead is essentially the time to do one reduce across rows. The total overhead of checkpointing is

$$T_{P+1} \cdot \frac{N}{nb}/I$$

where I is the number of iterations in the checkpointing interval. There is an interval for which these overheads are the same:

$$T_{P+1} + (T_{P+1} - T_P) \cdot \frac{N}{nb} = T_{P+1} \cdot \frac{N}{nb}/I$$
$$I = \frac{T_{P+1} \cdot \frac{N}{nb}}{T_{P+1} + (T_{P+1} - T_P) \cdot \frac{N}{nb}}$$

If $\frac{N}{nb}$ is large, the number of iterations required in the interval would be approximately $\frac{T_{P+1}}{T_{P+1} - T_P}$, which could be a very large number, depending on the implementation of broadcast and reduce.

Another consideration is how the overhead scales. If the checkpoint is done at the same interval regardless of the matrix size, then the overhead would remain nearly constant. However, when more processors are added, the expected rate of failure increases, so that in practice the checkpoint interval would likely have to be shorter when a larger matrix is used. In contrast, the fraction of total time that is overhead in the checksum technique should decrease as the size of the matrix increases. Since much of the overhead comes from making the sum at the beginning of the calculation, the overhead as a fraction of the total time will decrease as the length of the calculation increases.

Even when there is no failure, the process of preparing for one has a cost. For this method, the cost is performing the checksum at the beginning, as well as the extra processors required to hold the checksums. The checksum is done by a reduce. The number of extra processors required is the number of rows in the processor grid, since an extra processor is added to each row. The number of iterations is not

increased because the checksum rows are skipped. Performing the factorization on checksum blocks is not necessary for maintaining a correct checksum, so the work done in that step would be pointless.

This method competes with diskless checkpointing for overhead. Because the extra processors do the same sort of tasks as the normal processors in the same row, the time to do an iteration is not significantly increased by adding the checksums. In contrast, in order to do a checkpoint it is necessary to do extra work periodically to update the checkpoint. If the checkpoint is done every iteration, then the cost of recovery is the same as with a checksum, but the cost during the calculation is clearly higher.

When no error occurs, the overhead of performing a checkpoint is the time it takes to do one checkpoint multiplied by the number of checkpoints done. For checkpointing, the optimum interval depends on the failure rate and the time it takes to do a checkpoint. The more frequently failures are likely to occur, the smaller the interval must be. The longer the checkpoint itself takes, the fewer checkpoints there should be in the total running time, so the interval is longer for a larger checkpoint. Whatever the optimum interval is, the additional overhead from the checkpoint when no failure occurs is Nt_c, where N is the total number of checkpoints and t_c is the time to perform one checkpoint.

The checksum technique, in contrast, does not take any extra time to keep the sum up to date. The only overhead when no failure occurs is the time to calculate the sum at the beginning. Since both the sum and the checkpoint operation will use some sort of reduce, the time to calculate the checksum is comparable to the time to perform one checkpoint.

In addition to the time overhead, both techniques have the overhead of additional processors that are required to hold either the checksum or checkpoint. However, with the trend of using more and more processors, processors can be considered cheap. Additionally, the overhead in number of processors for the checksum is approximately $\sqrt{P}$, where P is the number of processors, so the relative increase in processors is smaller the more processors there are.

Whether fault tolerance is used or not, a failure means that some amount of calculation time is lost and has to be repeated. When no fault tolerance is used, the time that has to be repeated is everything that has been done up to the point of the failure. The higher the probability of failure, the less likely it is that the computation will ever be able to finish.

Both checkpoint and checksum methods make it so that at any particular time, only a small part of the total execution is vulnerable to a failure. With either method, only the time spent in the most recent interval can be lost. With a checkpoint this interval depends on the failure rate of the system, but with a checksum the interval is always one iteration. For the checksum method, the checksums are consistent at the beginning of each iteration. To recover from a failure, it is necessary to go back to the beginning of the current iteration and restart from there.

Both checkpoint and checksum recoveries use a reduce of some sort to calculate the lost values, so that the recovery time t_r is comparable for the two methods.

The other aspect of the overhead of recovery, beside t_r, is the amount of calculation that has to be redone. Since the checkpoint interval can be varied while the checksum interval

Table 1: Jaguar: local matrix size 2000×2000**, block size 64**

N	P	Total time (s)	Checksum time (s)	Overhead (%)	Performance (Gflops)
192000	9312	161.83	1.22	0.759	29160
216000	11772	186.24	1.24	0.670	36070
240000	14520	206.08	1.26	0.615	44720
264000	17556	238.56	1.29	0.541	51420

Table 3: Jaguar: local matrix size 2000×2000**, block size 128**

N	P	Total time (s)	Checksum time (s)	Overhead (%)	Performance (Gflops)
192000	9312	162.52	1.29	0.800	29030
216000	11772	184.92	1.28	0.697	36330
240000	14520	210.50	1.29	0.617	43780
264000	17556	244.63	1.33	0.547	50140

Table 2: Jaguar: local matrix size 4000×4000**, block size 64**

N	P	Total time (s)	Checksum time (s)	Overhead (%)	Performance (Gflops)
384000	9312	913.16	5.72	0.630	41340
432000	11772	995.98	5.70	0.576	53960
480000	14520	1137.26	5.69	0.503	64830
528000	17556	1254.81	5.91	0.473	78200

cannot, it seems that this overhead could favor one method or the other depending on the circumstances. However, the optimum checkpointing interval is determined partly by the time it takes to perform a checkpoint, and one of the main points emphasized in this paper is that the time to perform a checkpoint is very long for matrix operations because of the large amount of data that changes between checkpoints. Therefore it is reasonable to assume that the interval required by the checkpoint will be larger than that of the checksum method, and the overhead introduced by the repeated work will be less with the checksum method.

There are two ways in which the overhead of the checksum method is less than that of checkpointing: the time added even when there is no failure, and the time lost when a failure occurs.

8. EXPERIMENTS

8.1 Platforms

We evaluate the proposed fault tolerance scheme on the following platforms:

Jaguar at Oak Ridge National Laboratory (ranks No. 2 in the current TOP500 Supercomputer List): 224,256 cores in 18,688 nodes. Each node has two Opteron 2435 "Istanbul" processors linked with dual HyperTransport connections. Each processor has six cores with a clock rate of 2600 MHz supporting 4 floating-point operations per clock period per core. Each node is a dual-socket, twelve-core node with 16 gigabytes of shared memory. Each processor has directly attached 8 gigabytes of DDR2-800 memory. Each node has a peak processing performance of 124.8 gigaflops. Each core has a peak processing performance of 10.4 gigaflops. The network is a 3D torus interconnection network. We used Cray MPI implementation MPT 3.1.02.

Kraken at the University of Tennessee (ranks No. 8 in the current TOP500 Supercomputer List): 99,072 cores in 8,256

nodes. Each node has two Opteron 2435 "Istanbul" processors linked with dual HyperTransport connections. Each processor has six cores with a clock rate of 2600 MHz supporting 4 floating-point operations per clock period per core. Each node is a dual-socket, twelve-core node with 16 gigabytes of shared memory. Each processor has directly attached 8 gigabytes of DDR2-800 memory. Each node has a peak processing performance of 124.8 gigaflops. Each core has a peak processing performance of 10.4 gigaflops. The network is a 3D torus interconnection network. We used Cray MPI implementation MPT 3.1.02.

Ra at Colorado School of Mines: 2,144 cores in 268 nodes. Each node has two 512 Clovertown E5355 quad-core processor at a clock rate of 2670 MHz supporting 4 floating-point operations per clock period per core. Each node has 16 GB memory. Each node has a peak processing performance of 85.44 gigaflops. The network uses a Cisco SFS 7024 IB Server Switch. We used Open MPI 1.4.

8.2 Overhead without recovery

We ran our code on both a larger scale (Jaguar and Kraken) and on a smaller scale (Ra). Since the time required to perform the checksum can be kept almost constant when the matrix size is increased, the larger scale shows lower overhead as a fraction of the total time.

Tables 1, 2, and 3 show the overhead of making a checksum at the beginning of the calculation for a matrix of size $N \times N$ on P processes. The processes are arranged in a a grid of size $p \times (p + 1) = P$. The sum is kept on the extra processes in the last column of the processor grid. When the local matrix on each process is the same size, the time to perform the checksum is nearly the same for different total matrix sizes. The overhead of the checksum method consists almost entirely of the time taken to perform the checksum at the beginning, so it decreases as a fraction of the total time. Changing the block size has very little effect on the overhead. However, when the local matrix on each process is increased from 2000×2000 to 4000×4000, the overhead is less for the same number of processes, while the performance is greater.

Table 4 shows the results on a different large system. Here also the overhead is typically less than 1%. Table 5 shows the results for small matrices. Even with few processes the overhead is low, and it decreases as the size increases.

Figure 4 shows runtimes with and without fault tolerance. The difference in times between the two cases is smaller than the variation that can arise from other causes, as in the case of sizes 264000 and 288000, where the untouched code took longer for some reason.

Table 4: Kraken: local matrix size 2000×2000**, block size 64**

N	P	Total time (s)	Checksum time (s)	Overhead (%)	Performance (Gflops)
144000	5256	214.71	1.16	0.543	9272
168000	7140	195.06	1.18	0.609	16210
192000	9312	256.91	1.17	0.457	18370
216000	11772	307.34	1.18	0.385	21860
240000	14520	342.28	1.18	0.346	26930

Table 5: Ra: local matrix size 4000×4000**, block size 64**

N	P	Total time (s)	Checksum time (s)	Overhead (%)	Performance (Gflops)
16000	20	36.51	2.16	6.29	74.81
20000	30	44.44	1.84	4.32	120.0
24000	42	54.98	1.97	3.72	167.7
28000	56	65.82	2.23	3.51	222.4
32000	72	77.20	2.43	3.25	283.0
36000	90	89.95	2.46	2.81	345.8
40000	110	81.44	2.27	2.87	523.9

Figure 4: On Jaguar, when run with and without checksum fault tolerance, the times are very similar. In fact, variations in the runtime from other causes are greater than the time added by the fault tolerance, with all effects included.

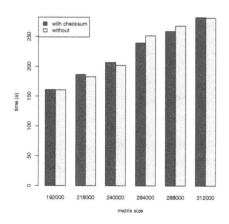

Table 6: Jaguar: local matrix size 2000×2000**, block size 64**

N	P	Total time (s)	Recovery time (s)
192000	9312	161.83	1.19
216000	11772	186.24	1.24
240000	14520	206.08	1.24
264000	17556	238.56	1.25

Table 7: Ra: local matrix size 4000×4000**, block size 64**

N	P	Total time (s)	Recovery time (s)
16000	20	36.51	1.52
20000	30	44.44	1.94
24000	42	54.98	2.60
28000	56	65.82	3.03
32000	72	77.20	3.41
36000	90	89.95	4.25

8.3 Overhead with recovery

Tables 6 and 7 show simple recovery times for a single failure. Here the recovery is done at the end of an iteration, and requires only a reduce. Consequently, the time needed to recover is very similar to the time needed to perform the checksum in the beginning. In order to find the recovery time, we did the recovery operation to a copy of the local matrix of an arbitrary process, using this to both time the recovery operation and to check its correctness by comparing to the original local matrix.

By this measure, the recovery time is only the time needed for a reduce. In the case of a real failure it may be necessary to repeat at most one iteration. As an example of the amount of work that is repeated, the first entry in table 6 did 3000 iterations, which means that each iteration took less than 0.05 seconds, which is not very significant compared to the other cost of recovery.

8.4 Algorithm-based recovery versus diskless checkpointing

According to [29], an approximation for the optimum checkpoint interval is

$$I = \sqrt{\frac{2t_c(P)M}{P}}$$

where $t_c(P)$ is the time to perform one checkpoint when there are P processes and M is the mean time to failure of one process, assuming that the process failures are independent so that, if the failure rate of one is $\frac{1}{M}$, then the failure rate for the entire system is $\frac{P}{M}$. This formula illustrates the balance between the two main factors that determine the optimum interval. The longer it takes to perform a checkpoint, the less often it should be done for the sake of overhead. The term M/P is the mean time to failure for the entire system. When the expected time until a failure is less, checkpoints need to be done more often for the optimum expected runtime. Since the time to perform a checkpoint only increases slightly as the number of processes increases, the significant

Figure 5: Fault tolerance overhead without recovery: Algorithm-based recovery versus diskless checkpointing

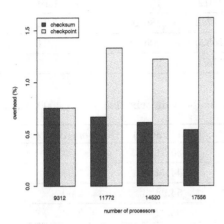

Figure 7: Fault tolerance overhead with recovery: Algorithm-based recovery versus diskless checkpointing

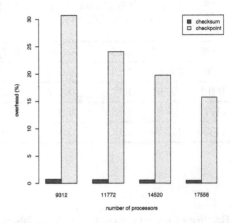

Figure 6: On smaller runs on Ra, the difference between checksum and checkpoint can be easily seen.

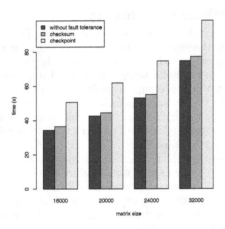

factor is the number of processes, which makes failures more likely and decreases the length of the checkpoint interval.

As an example of possible checkpoint overhead, figure 5 shows the overhead when the mean time to failure is 10000 hours for one process. Because both the operation to create the backup (checksum or checkpoint) and the operation to recover from a failure are essentially the same between the two different approaches, using the same values for both the checksum and the checkpoint approach gives an approximation for how the overheads compare that is fair to the checkpointing approach.

The checkpoint interval decreases as more processes are added because the probability of a failure increases. This means that the amount of work repeated because of one failure is less, but the expected number of failures during the run increases. On average, half of the checkpoint interval will have to be repeated. The running time increases as the problem size is larger, while the checkpoint interval decreases. So there will be an increasing number of checkpoints, and therefore the overhead increases as the number of processes increases. With the checksum method, on

the other hand, the overhead decreases as the number of processes increases. Figure 6 shows the results of smaller runs, comparing checksum and checkpoint overhead without a failure. Figure 7 shows the cost of one recovery with the algorithm-based recovery scheme. Here the overhead is less than one percent for each case, compared to at least 15 percent with a checkpoint.

9. CONCLUSION

By adding a row checksum to the matrix, we are able to make the right-looking LU decomposition with partial pivoting fault tolerant. We can recover lost data from the original matrix and from U resulting from one process failure. The overhead of the method consists mostly of the time to calculate the checksum at the beginning, using a reduce. The time to perform the checksum is approximately proportional to the size of the local matrix stored on one process, so that the overhead time can be kept almost constant when the matrix size is increased, decreasing the overhead as a fraction of the total time. This method can perform with much lower overhead than diskless checkpointing, which is a very good option in general. Although this method is specific to matrix operations, it can offer much better performance than diskless checkpointing for those operations.

In this work we have used only one checksum to handle one failure. However, with weighted checksums it is possible to recover from multiple failures, or to use the additional checksums to detect as well as recover from errors. These possibilities will be explored in future work.

Acknowledgments

This research is partly supported by National Science Foundation under grant #OCI-0905019 and Department of Energy under grant DE FE#0000988.

We would like thank the following institutions for the use of their computing resources:

- The National Center for Computational Sciences: Jaguar
- The National Institute for Computational Sciences: Kraken
- The Golden Energy Computing Organization: Ra

10. REFERENCES

[1] C. J. Anfinson and F. T. Luk. A linear algebraic model of algorithm-based fault tolerance. *IEEE Transactions on Computers*, 37(12), December 1988.

[2] P. Banerjee and J. Abraham. Bounds on algorithm-based fault tolerance in multiple processor systems. *IEEE Transactions on Computers*, 2006.

[3] P. Banerjee, J. T. Rahmeh, C. B. Stunkel, V. S. S. Nair, K. Roy, V. Balasubramanian, and J. A. Abraham. Algorithm-based fault tolerance on a hypercube multiprocessor. *IEEE Transactions on Computers*, C-39:1132–1145, 1990.

[4] F. Cappello. Fault tolerance in petascale/ exascale systems: Current knowledge, challenges and research opportunities. *International Journal of High Performance Computing Applications*, 23(3), August 2009.

[5] Z. Chen. Extending algorithm-based fault tolerance to tolerate fail-stop failures in high performance distributed environments. In *Proceedings of the 22nd IEEE International Parallel and Distributed Processing Symposium*, Miami, FL, USA, April 2008.

[6] Z. Chen. Optimal real number codes for fault tolerant matrix operations. In *Proceedings of the ACM/IEEE SC2009 Conference on High Performance Networking, Computing, Storage, and Analysis*, Portland, OR, USA, November 2009.

[7] Z. Chen and J. Dongarra. Algorithm-based checkpoint-free fault tolerance for parallel matrix computations on volatile resources. In *Proceedings of the 20th IEEE International Parallel and Distributed Processing Symposium*, Rhodes Island, Greece, April 2006.

[8] Z. Chen and J. Dongarra. Algorithm-based fault tolerance for fail-stop failures. *IEEE Transactions on Parallel and Distributed Systems*, 19(12), 2008.

[9] Z. Chen and J. Dongarra. Highly scalable self-healing algorithms for high performance scientific computing. *IEEE Transactions on Computers*, July 2009.

[10] Z. Chen, G. E. Fagg, E. Gabriel, J. Langou, T. Angskun, G. Bosilca, and J. Dongarra. Fault tolerant high performance computing by a coding approach. In *Proceedings of the ACM SIG-PLAN Symposium on Principles and Practice of Parallel Programming*, Chicago, IL, USA, June 2005.

[11] T. Chiueh and P. Deng. Evaluation of checkpoint mechanisms for massively parallel machines. In *The Twenty-Sixth Annual International Symposium on Fault-Tolerant Computing*, 1996.

[12] C. da Lu. *Scalable diskless checkpointing for large parallel systems*. PhD thesis, Univ. of Illinois Computer Science in the Graduate College of the University of Illinois at Urbana-Champaign, 2005.

[13] J. Daly. A higher order estimate of the optimum checkpoint interval for restart dumps. *Future Generation Computer Systems*, 22(3):303–312, 2006.

[14] G. A. Gibson, B. Schroeder, and J. Digney. Failure tolerance in petascale computers. *CTWatchQuarterly*, 3(4), November 2007.

[15] L. A. B. Gomez, N. Maruyama, F. Cappello, and S. Matsuoka. Distributed diskless checkpoint for large scale systems. In *2010 10th IEEE/ACM International Conference on Cluster, Cloud and Grid Computing*, 2010.

[16] J. A. Gunnels, R. A. van de Geijn, D. S. Katz, and E. S. Quintana-Orti. Fault-tolerant high-performance matrix multiplication: Theory and practice. In *The International Conference on Dependable Systems and Networks*, 2001.

[17] D. Hakkarinen and Z. Chen. Algorithmic cholesky factorization fault recovery. In *Proceedings of the 24th IEEE International Parallel and Distributed Processing Symposium*, Atlanta, GA, USA, April 2010.

[18] K.-H. Huang and J. A. Abraham. Algorithm-based fault tolerance for matrix operations. *IEEE Transactions on Computers*, C-33:518–528, 1984.

[19] J. Jou and J. Abraham. Fault-tolerant matrix arithmetic and signal processing on highly concurrent computing structures. In *Proceedings of the IEEE*, volume 74, May 1986.

[20] Y. Kim. *Fault Tolerant Matrix Operations for Parallel and Distributed Systems*. PhD thesis, University of Tennessee, Knoxville, June 1996.

[21] F. T. Luk and H. Park. An analysis of algorithm-based fault tolerance techniques. *Journal of Parallel and Distributed Computing*, 5(2):172–184, 1988.

[22] A. Moody, G. Bronevetsky, K. Mohror, and B. R. de Supinski. Design, modeling, and evaluation of a scalable multi-level checkpointing system. In *IEEE/ACM Supercomputing Conference*, November 2010.

[23] A. Petitet, R. C. Whaley, J. Dongarra, and A. Cleary. HPL - a portable implementation of the high-performance linpack benchmark for distributed-memory computers. http://www.netlib.org/benchmark/hpl, September 2008.

[24] J. S. Plank, Y. Kim, and J. Dongarra. Fault tolerant matrix operations for networks of workstations using diskless checkpointing. *IEEE Journal of Parallel and Distributed Computing*, 43:125–138, 1997.

[25] J. S. Plank, K. Li, and M. A. Puening. Diskless checkpointing. *IEEE Transactions on Parallel and Distributed Systems*, 9(10):972–986, 1998.

[26] B. Schroeder and G. A. Gibson. A large-scale study of failures in high-performance computing systems. In *Proceedings of the International Conference on Dependable Systems and Networks*, Philadelphia, PA, USA, June 2006.

[27] L. M. Silva and J. G. Silva. An experimental study about diskless checkpointing. In *24th EUROMICRO Conference*, 1998.

[28] C. Wang, F. Mueller, C. Engelmann, and S. Scot. Job pause service under lam/mpi+blcr for transparent fault tolerance. In *Proceedings of the 21st IEEE International Parallel and Distributed Processing Symposium*, Long Beach, CA, USA, March 2007.

[29] J. W. Young. A first order approximation to the optimum checkpoint interval. *Commun. ACM*, 17:530–531, September 1974.

Modeling the Performance of an Algebraic Multigrid Cycle on HPC Platforms

Hormozd Gahvari[1], Allison H. Baker[2], Martin Schulz[2]
Ulrike Meier Yang[2], Kirk E. Jordan[3], William Gropp[1]

[1]Computer Science Department, University of Illinois at Urbana-Champaign, Urbana, IL 61801
[2]Center for Applied Scientific Computing, Lawrence Livermore National Laboratory, Livermore, CA 94551
[3]IBM TJ Watson Research Center, Cambridge, MA 02142

gahvari@illinois.edu, abaker@llnl.gov, schulzm@llnl.gov
umyang@llnl.gov, kjordan@us.ibm.com, wgropp@illinois.edu

ABSTRACT

Now that the performance of individual cores has plateaued, future supercomputers will depend upon increasing parallelism for performance. Processor counts are now in the hundreds of thousands for the largest machines and will soon be in the millions. There is an urgent need to model application performance at these scales and to understand what changes need to be made to ensure continued scalability. This paper considers algebraic multigrid (AMG), a popular and highly efficient iterative solver for large sparse linear systems that is used in many applications. We discuss the challenges for AMG on current parallel computers and future exascale architectures, and we present a performance model for an AMG solve cycle as well as performance measurements on several massively-parallel platforms.

Categories and Subject Descriptors

G.4 [**Mathematical Software**]: Algorithm design and analysis, Parallel and vector implementations; G.1.3 [**Numerical Analysis**]: Numerical Linear Algebra—*Linear systems (direct and iterative methods)*

General Terms

Algorithms, Performance

Keywords

Algebraic Multigrid, Scaling, Performance Modeling, Massively Parallel Architectures

1. INTRODUCTION

Multigrid methods are popular for the solution of large sparse linear systems, which is a necessary and often time-consuming element of many large-scale scientific simulation codes. The parallel AMG solver BoomerAMG [11] in the

hypre software library [12], for example, is an integral component in simulations in diverse areas such as groundwater flow, explosive materials modeling, electromagnetic applications, fusion energy simulations, and image-guided facial surgery. Multigrid methods have the "optimal" property that, when they work well, the amount of work per unknown stays constant. This property is especially attractive for parallel computing: as the size of supercomputers increases, we can solve increasingly larger problems in a roughly fixed amount of time.

Since the performance of AMG has a profound impact on a wide variety of applications across a wide range of disciplines, it is crucial to understand the challenges for future architectures with increased parallelism as well as to predict and locate performance bottlenecks that hinder performance. Therefore, given that currently no computers exist with several millions or billions of cores available, the development of performance models to evaluate algorithm performance has become very important to prepare application codes for exascale computing and beyond.

In this paper, we develop a novel performance model for the solve phase of the AMG algorithm. To our knowledge this is the first formal characterization of this important application. We start with the basic α-β model for communication combined with an analytical model of the computation. We then add penalties based on machine constraints, including distance effects, reduced per core bandwidth, and the number of cores per node. We validate the model on several parallel platforms and illustrate various challenges to the scalability of AMG, including the increasing communication complexity on coarser grids and the effects of increasing numbers of cores per node on the performance.

We make the following contributions:

- We present a performance model for the AMG solve cycle and validate it across various multicore architectures.

- We expose several bottlenecks on the various architectures using the AMG model.

- We discuss model-based predictions for the scalability of AMG on future machines.

This paper proceeds as follows. Section 2 discusses related work. Section 3 summarizes AMG and the performance challenges it faces on parallel machines. Section 4 describes our performance model, and Section 5 presents experiments done to validate it. Section 6 discusses lessons from the model results, followed by concluding remarks in Section 7.

2. RELATED WORK

A wide range of related projects target the modeling of numerical codes on large scale parallel systems. For example, [13] provides an analytical model for the application SAGE, [15] describes an approach to combine computation and communication profiles into a general performance model, and [3] targets the prediction of large scale performance behavior based on the extrapolation of small scale performance results.

While the issue of scaling AMG to higher and higher process counts has been a subject of much study recently, no performance models for AMG have been developed yet. In [2] and [1], changing the programming model is investigated as a means of better matching emerging multicore clusters and improving AMG performance. Performance models and their implications for geometric multigrid on exascale systems were considered in [8], but geometric multigrid is a less complex algorithm than AMG and does not suffer from the same performance degradation on the coarser grid levels. Also of interest is a brief analysis of when it would be preferable to use redundant computation to replace communication in [10], but again this analysis is for geometric multigrid, not AMG. Finally, the moving of data between main memory and cache can be a significant factor in the application performance, and this is examined for multigrid in [5]. We have not considered this at this time, but the underlying message of reducing data movement also motivates our work.

3. ALGEBRAIC MULTIGRID

Multigrid methods are well-suited for large-scale scientific applications because they are algorithmically scalable, i.e. they solve a sparse linear system $A^{(0)}u = f^0$ with n unknowns with $O(n)$ computations. They obtain this optimality by eliminating "smooth error", e, that is not removed by relaxation (or smoothing) by coarse-grid correction using successively smaller grids. Algebraic multigrid (AMG) does not require an explicit grid. Instead coarse grid selection and the generation of interpolation and restriction operators depend entirely on the matrix coefficients. For a detailed description of AMG, see [18], for example.

AMG consists of a setup phase and a solve phase, as illustrated in Figure 1. We describe and analyze the simplest multigrid cycle, the V-cycle, but our approach can be straightforwardly extended to analyze the more complicated W-cycle and full multigrid cycle. In the setup phase, the coarse grid variables, interpolation operators $P^{(m)}$, restriction operators $R^{(m)}$ and the coarse grid matrices $A^{(m+1)}$, are determined for $m = 0, ..., k - 1$. The coarsest level $k - 1$ is reached when $A^{(k)}$ is sufficiently small. In our experiments, $A^{(k)}$ has at most nine unknowns. Note from Figure 1 that the coarse grid matrices are determined via a triple matrix product, and, as a result, the "stencil size" on each grid level tends to increase as we coarsen. In other words, the coarse grid matrices are less sparse and require communication with more neighbor processes (to perform a matrix-vector multiplication, for example) than the fine grid matrices.

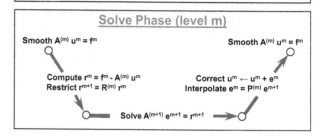

Figure 1: AMG building blocks.

In the solve phase, a smoother is applied on each level $m = 0, ..., k - 1$, and then the residual r^m is transferred to the next coarser grid, where the process continues. On the coarsest level, the linear system $A^{(k)}e^k = r^k$ is solved by Gaussian elimination. The error e^k is then interpolated back up to the next finer grid, followed by relaxation. This is continued all the way up to the finest grid. The m-th level of the solve phase is described in Figure 1. The primary components of the solve phase are the matrix-vector multiplication (MatVec) and the smoother. The classical smoother used for algebraic multigrid is Gauss-Seidel, which is highly sequential. Therefore, we use a parallel variant, called hybrid Gauss-Seidel, which can be viewed as an inexact block-diagonal (Jacobi) smoother with Gauss-Seidel sweeps inside each process. In other words, we use a sequential Gauss-Seidel algorithm locally on each process, with delayed updates across processes. One sweep of hybrid Gauss-Seidel is very similar to a MatVec.

For our experiments, we use BoomerAMG, the parallel AMG code in the hypre software library. We use HMIS coarsening [17] with extended+i interpolation [16] truncated to at most 4 coefficients per row and aggressive coarsening with multipass interpolation [19] on the finest level.

3.1 Parallel Implementation

BoomerAMG uses the ParCSR matrix data structure, which is based on the sequential compressed sparse row (CSR) storage format. The ParCSR matrix A consists of p parts $A_k, k = 1, ..., p$, where A_k is stored locally on process k. Each A_k is split into two matrices D_k and O_k. D_k contains all coefficients of A_k, whose column indices point to rows that are stored locally on process k. O_k contains the remaining coefficients of A_k. Both matrices are stored in CSR format. Whereas D_k is a CSR matrix in the usual sense, for O_k, which in general is extremely sparse with many zero columns and rows, all non-zero columns are renumbered for greater efficiency, requiring an additional array that defines the mapping of local to global column indices.

In order to perform a parallel MatVec or smoothing step, process k needs to evaluate $A_k x = D_k x^D + O_k x^O$, where x^D is the local part of vector x and x^O the portion that needs to be received from other processes (receive processes). In order to receive the required information as well as to send information needed by other processes (send processes), each process has a communication package that contains the fol-

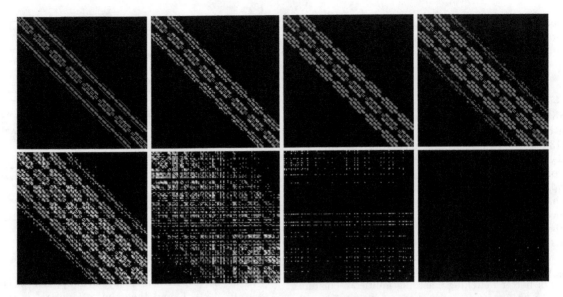

Figure 2: Level-by-level communication patterns for an AMG solve on a 7-point $200 \times 200 \times 200$ Laplace problem using 128 processes. Levels 0 (finest grid) through 3 (left to right) are on the top row, and levels 4 through 7 (left to right) are on the bottom row. Areas of black indicate zero messages between processes.

lowing information: the IDs of the receive processes, the size of the data to be received by each receive process, the IDs of the send processes, and the indices of the elements that need to be sent to each send process. The actual communication is then performed by posting non-blocking receives (MPI_Irecv) to each receive process followed by non-blocking sends (MPI_Isend) and finalized by an MPI_Waitall to all posted operations. See [6] for more discussion on the implementation details.

Regarding the distribution of data on the coarser levels, coarse points are kept on the same processes that they were located on at the finer levels. Because the number of coarse points will eventually be smaller than the total number of processes, on the coarser levels processes will start "dropping out" when they no longer own any rows in the matrix. Therefore, while a process's neighbors will be "close" in terms of process ranks at the fine levels, on the coarser levels neighbors will be farther away and messages will be smaller in size. On the coarsest level, where at most nine processes are still active, the remaining data (matrix and vectors) is distributed to all active processes, each of which then solves the coarsest system using Gaussian elimination.

3.2 Performance Challenges

The challenges to achieving good parallel AMG performance mainly center around performance degradation on coarse grids. As mentioned before, each process's communication partners will be farther away on the coarser grids than on the fine grids. There is also little computation on the coarser levels due to the smaller matrix sizes, so communication dominates the time spent here. Delays in sending messages to distant processes can cause scalability concerns, as an analysis in [8] found. This analysis, however, targeted only geometric multigrid for five-point and seven-point Laplace problems, where the communication pattern remains a simple, fixed stencil on all grids. When AMG is employed to solve the same problems, the communication pattern starts off as a simple stencil, but eventually becomes

more irregular and involves far more communication partners, or in other words, increases the communication neighborhood for each process.

An initial performance experiment confirms this behavior: Figure 2 (obtained using the performance analysis tool TAU [14]) shows the communication between pairs of processes on each level of an AMG solve using 128 processes. Initially, on level 0, communication is regular and mostly focused on nearest neighbors. In subsequent levels, the communication neighborhood grows until, in level 5, it covers almost the complete process space. At the same time, we see several processes leave the communication pattern (black horizontal and vertical lines). In level 6, these dropped processes start to dominate, and in level 7, only a few processes remain. The communication and computation statistics from our subsequent experiments to validate our performance model, which are in Table 1, also highlight this trend. On the finer grids, computation time dominates the execution time, but then on the coarser grids, the amount of data per process gets small and communication time dominates instead.

Further challenges arise due to the trend of increasing numbers of cores on each node of a massively-parallel machine. The numerous cores on a single node contend for access to the interconnect, which slows down coarse grid performance even further because of the large number of messages that need to be sent on those coarse levels. Despite the fine grid matrix being many orders of magnitude larger than those matrices on the coarsest levels, the solve on the coarse grid can take as long as the solve on the fine grid. For example, this performance problem occurs when using 1024 processes on the Hera machine (machine specifications are given in Section 5). The computation on the fine grid problem, which has 64 million unknowns, took 25.9 ms, but the computation on a much coarser grid level with only 1224 unknowns took 42.3 ms. More generally, further examples of this unexpected and troubling phenomenon are seen in the results in Section 5. Note that two prior studies [2, 1] have examined this issue to a limited extent and found that using OpenMP on the individual nodes and pinning threads to cores and processes to sockets can alleviate these problems to some degree, but not completely. We discuss multicore issues when presenting our performance models, but the use of OpenMP and pinning of threads and processes is beyond the scope of this paper.

4. MODELING PERFORMANCE

To understand the performance of AMG and predict its performance on future machines, we develop a performance model for the solve cycle that requires minimal machine-specific information. We first start with models for local computation and communication. Combined, these two models form our baseline model, which we consequently refine to reach a complete model that is able to cover the relevant system architecture properties.

For this we define the following terms:

- P – total number of processes

- C_i – number of unknowns on grid level i

- s_i, $\hat{s}_i$ – average number of nonzeros per row in the level i solve and interpolation operators, respectively

- p_i, $\hat{p}_i$ – maximum number of sends over all processes in the level i solve and interpolation operators, respectively

- n_i, $\hat{n}_i$ – maximum number of elements sent over all processes in the level i solve and interpolation operators, respectively

- t_i – time per flop on level i

We do not consider the overlap of communication and computation here, as on coarse grids there is hardly any computation available for this purpose. The use of maximum numbers of sends accounts for the use of nonblocking communication and MPI_Waitall, as the processes that are waiting are waiting for the one that is doing the most communication to finish. For all AMG solves, we assume one smoothing step before restricting and one smoothing step after interpolation (the default in BoomerAMG).

4.1 Modeling the AMG Steps

The computation time is modeled by multiplying the number of floating-point operations by the time per flop t_c. The flops in the AMG solve cycle are incurred as a result of a sparse matrix-vector multiplication (MatVec) for the interpolation and restriction steps and the similar operation of applying the smoother. Note that an in-depth study [7] found the floating-point rate for the MatVec operation to vary widely depending on the size of the matrix and vector. For this reason, we allow t_c to vary depending on the level, and denote the time per flop on level i with t_i.

We model the AMG solve cycle by modeling each level individually and write the total time of one AMG solve cycle as

$$T_{\text{solve}}^{\text{AMG}} = \sum_{i=0}^{G} T_{\text{solve}}^i,$$

where G is the number of grid levels and T_{solve}^i is the time spent in the solve cycle at level i. We then split the time at each level, T_{solve}^i, into the time spent smoothing, restricting, and interpolating on that level:

$$T_{\text{solve}}^i = T_{\text{smooth}}^i + T_{\text{restrict}}^i + T_{\text{interp}}^i.$$

Here, T_{smooth}^i is the time spent smoothing on level i, T_{restrict}^i is the time spent restricting from level i to level $i+1$, and T_{interp}^i is the time spent interpolating from level i to level $i-1$.

4.2 Modeling Communication

For communication, we start with the basic α-β model for interprocess communication, which breaks down the cost of communication into the start-up time α (latency) and the per-element send time β (inverse bandwidth). If a message has n elements in it, then the send cost is

$$T_{\text{send}} = \alpha + n\beta.$$

Note that α covers both the software overhead and the latency involved in message passing, and β is tied to the achievable bandwidth.

To improve upon the basic model, we then add penalties to the parameters to take into account machine-specific performance issues. In particular, we add a γ term to take into account communication distance and switching delays on the interconnect. We penalize β to account for limited bandwidth, and we penalize α and γ to account for performance degradation arising from multiple cores on a single node contending for available resources.

4.3 Baseline Model (α-β Model)

To reach our baseline model, we apply the communication model in the description of the three main steps and deduce formulas for each step based on the algorithmic requirements of the AMG implementation.

The complete time for the smoother at level i is given by

$$T_{\text{smooth}}^i(\alpha, \beta) = 6\frac{C_i}{P}s_i t_i + 3(p_i \alpha + n_i \beta).$$

This reflects one smoother application before restricting, one MatVec to form the residual, and one smoother application after interpolation, with two flops (one multiplication and one addition) per matrix entry.

The time for restricting on level i is given by

$$T_{\text{restrict}}^i(\alpha, \beta) = \begin{cases} 2\frac{C_{i+1}}{P}\hat{s}_i t_i + \hat{p}_i \alpha + \hat{n}_i \beta & \text{if } i < G \\ 0 & \text{if } i = G. \end{cases}$$

This reflects the cost of one MatVec that represents restriction from level i to level $i+1$.

The time for interpolation on level i given by

$$T_{\text{interp}}^i(\alpha, \beta) = \begin{cases} 0 & \text{if } i = 0 \\ 2\frac{C_{i-1}}{P}\hat{s}_{i-1} t_i + \hat{p}_{i-1} \alpha + \hat{n}_{i-1} \beta & \text{if } i > 0. \end{cases}$$

This reflects the cost of one MatVec that represents interpolation from level i to level $i-1$.

Therefore the complete baseline model is given by

$$T_{\text{solve}}^{\text{AMG}}(\alpha, \beta) = \sum_{i=0}^{G} T_{\text{solve}}^i(\alpha, \beta),$$

where

$$T_{\text{solve}}^i(\alpha, \beta) = T_{\text{smooth}}^i(\alpha, \beta) + T_{\text{restrict}}^i(\alpha, \beta) + T_{\text{interp}}^i(\alpha, \beta).$$

4.4 Distance Penalty (α-β-γ Model)

In modern interconnection networks it is assumed that distance does not have much effect on communication time. However, with many messages being sent at once, as is the case for coarse grids in AMG, this is no longer a safe assumption. On larger machines distance will be an even bigger factor. To take this into account, we replace the α in the baseline model by $\alpha(h) = \alpha(h_m) + (h - h_m)\gamma$, where h is the number of hops a message travels, h_m is the smallest possible number of hops a message can travel in the network, and γ is the delay per extra hop. This covers issues of switching delays and, to some extent, network contention. For machines with a mesh or torus interconnect, $h_m = 1$, and h is assumed to be the diameter of the network formed by the number of nodes being used, to take into account routing delays and possible "long hops" across a large machine room. For machines with a fat-tree interconnect, the shortest message travels one switch, or two links, so $h_m = 2$. The fat-tree machines we consider here have two-level trees, so h is 4, as each message passes through at most four links.

In terms of the baseline model, which was expressed as $T_{\text{solve}}^{\text{AMG}}(\alpha, \beta)$, a function of α and β, we get

$$\tilde{T}_{\text{solve}}^{\text{AMG}}(\alpha, \beta, \gamma) = T_{\text{solve}}^{\text{AMG}}(\alpha(h_m) + (h - h_m)\gamma, \beta).$$

4.5 Bandwidth Penalty (on β)

The peak hardware bandwidth is rarely achieved in message passing under ideal conditions using typical message sizes. This achievable bandwidth is in turn rarely achieved under non-ideal conditions. We take this into account by multiplying β by $\frac{B_{\max}}{B}$, where $B_{\max}$ is the peak hardware per-node bandwidth, and B is the bandwidth corresponding to β (if B is in bytes per second, and β is the time to send one double-precision floating point value, we would have $B = \frac{8}{\beta}$). The fraction $\frac{B_{\max}}{B}$ provides a measure of how much worse than ideal the available bandwidth actually is. The formula for the resulting model becomes

$$T_{\text{penalty}}^{\beta} = \tilde{T}_{\text{solve}}^{\text{AMG}}\left(\alpha, \frac{B_{\max}}{B}\beta, \gamma\right).$$

4.6 Multicore Penalty (on α and/or γ)

As mentioned previously, the increasing number of cores per node on parallel machines brings an additional set of challenges. Among other issues, there is increased contention between cores on a node to get onto the interconnect as well as additional noise caused by accesses to resources shared by multiple cores. While a precise accounting of all of these problems is essentially impossible, we model these effects with a focus on worst-case behavior, in particular on machines in which the aggregate bandwidth that could be generated by all cores communicating exceeds the per node bandwidth. We address this by multiplying one or both of the terms $\alpha(h_m)$ and γ by $\left\lceil c\frac{P_i}{P} \right\rceil$. Parameter c is the number of cores per node, and P_i is the number of active processes on level i, meaning those processes that have not "dropped out" and have work to do on that level. The resulting models become

$$T_{\text{penalty}}^{\alpha} = \tilde{T}_{\text{solve}}^{\text{AMG}}\left(\left\lceil c\frac{P_i}{P} \right\rceil \alpha, \beta, \gamma\right)$$

and

$$T_{\text{penalty}}^{\gamma} = \tilde{T}_{\text{solve}}^{\text{AMG}}\left(\alpha, \beta, \left\lceil c\frac{P_i}{P} \right\rceil \gamma\right).$$

5. MODEL VALIDATION

In this section, we first describe the considered architectures and the experimental setup, including the test problem, and then present experimental results to validate the model.

5.1 Machine Descriptions

To test our performance models, we run a series of experiments on the five architectures described in this section.

Intrepid is a large IBM BlueGene/P system at Argonne National Laboratory, consisting of 40 racks with 1024 compute nodes per rack. On each node is a quad-core 850 MHz PowerPC 450 processor. The nodes are connected by a proprietary 3D torus interconnect. The hardware bandwidth between nodes is 5.1 GB/s. On the software side, the compute nodes run a specialized small footprint compute node kernel. Further, for all experiments we use IBM's compiler and the BG/P derivative MPICH-2 version.

Jaguar is a hybrid Cray system at Oak Ridge National Laboratory consisting of both XT5 and XT4 nodes. These are organized into two partitions, one that is XT5 and one that is XT4. We run on the XT5 partition, which has 18,688 compute nodes in all. On each node are two hex-core 2.6 GHz AMD Opteron processors. However, we only use eight cores per node, as our test problem was created with power-of-two core counts in mind. The nodes are connected by a 3D torus interconnect. The hardware bandwidth between nodes is 6.4 GB/s. On the software side, the compute nodes run Compute Node Linux. Further, for all experiments we used PGI's compiler suite and Cray's native MPI implementation.

Hera is a Linux cluster at Lawrence Livermore National Laboratory consisting of 800 compute nodes, with four quad-core 2.3 GHz AMD Opteron processors per node. The nodes are connected by Infiniband, and organized as a two-level fat-tree topology. The first-stage switches have 24 ports, and the second-stage switches have 288 ports. The hardware bandwidth between nodes is 2.5 GB/s. On the software side, Hera runs CHAOS, a specialized version of RHEL5 adapted for HPC. Further, for all experiments we use gcc 4.1.2 and the MPI implementation is MVAPICH v0.99.

Zeus is a Linux cluster at Lawrence Livermore National Laboratory consisting of 260 compute nodes, with two four-core 2.5 GHz Intel Xeon processors per node. The nodes are connected by an Infiniband interconnect similar to Hera's. The software setup is identical to Hera.

Atlas is a Linux cluster at Lawrence Livermore National Laboratory consisting of 1,072 compute nodes, with four dual-core 2.4 GHz AMD Opteron processors per node. The nodes are connected by an Infiniband interconnect similar to Hera's. The software setup is identical to Hera.

5.2 Experimental Setup

On each of the architectures described above, we ran 10 AMG solve cycles and measured the amount of time spent in each level. We then divided the results by 10 to get a measurement of the time spent in each level for an average solve cycle. While each process takes its own time measurements, because some processes have no work on the coarser grid levels, we report times from the process that takes the most time on the coarsest grid. This strategy ensures that all measurements of time spent in each level are fair. We note that the maximum time spent in each level over all processes, which is the intuitive quantity to measure, is not

Level	No. Sends	Elems. Sent	Unknowns	NNZ/row	Active Procs.	No. Sends	Elems. Sent	NNZ/row
		Solve, 1024 Processes				Interpolation, 1024 Processes		
0	6	10000	64000000	7.0	1024	19	1290	2.1
1	25	3101	4865878	19.2	1024	21	493	3.4
2	26	1808	945465	53.5	1024	23	152	3.7
3	37	812	103412	81.5	1024	25	73	3.7
4	72	401	10442	86.8	1024	36	50	3.6
5	148	318	1201	69.8	709	97	113	3.3
6	93	159	140	45.7	131	48	48	2.2
7	18	18	19	17.7	19	2	2	0.16
8	0	0	1	1.0	1	–	–	–
		Solve, 65536 Processes				Interpolation, 65536 Processes		
0	6	10000	4096000000	7.0	65536	21	1357	2.1
1	26	3122	309040872	19.4	65536	24	536	3.4
2	26	1887	59587160	54.6	65536	25	178	3.7
3	40	826	6337442	85.5	65536	26	89	3.7
4	87	495	583594	99.6	65534	42	73	3.7
5	187	463	57923	97.0	39692	96	140	3.6
6	203	445	6746	86.0	6365	138	153	3.3
7	245	248	842	79.3	832	100	100	2.8
8	125	125	135	59.4	135	64	64	2.6
9	20	20	21	19.5	21	13	13	1.3
10	1	1	2	2.0	2	–	–	–

Table 1: AMG solve and interpolation operator statistics for Intrepid with 1024 and 65536 processes.

appropriate for a multigrid solve cycle. The reason is that once a process does not own any rows on a level (drops out), it quickly moves between levels, going down the grid hierarchy and then back up until the point when the interpolation results in rows on that process. Then, it sits idle until the the other processes catch up to it. This idle time, which is essentially the sum of the time spent on the level where the process drops out and all levels below it, is reported as being spent in just the level where the process drops out, and so the maximum time spent in each level gives times that are far too large on coarse grids.

Our test problem is a 3D 7-point Laplace problem on a cube, which was also considered in [2]. On Intrepid, Jaguar and Hera, the problem size per core is $50 \times 50 \times 25$. The problem is solved using 128, 1024, 8192 and 65,536 cores on Intrepid and Jaguar, and 128, 1024 and 3456 cores on Hera. On Zeus and Atlas, fewer cores were available to us, so we solve the same problem on 512 cores using $50 \times 50 \times 50$ variables per core. We additionally run the problem on 1728 cores on Atlas. Table 1 shows problem sizes and communication information for the runs on Intrepid. Statistics for the other architectures are similar and hence omitted. When viewing the data in Table 1, there are several things to note. First, one can observe that as the level number increases, the grid becomes coarser as indicated by the column labeled 'Unknowns'. At some coarser level, processes begin to drop out, as indicated by a decreasing number in the 'Active Procs.' column. After processes begin to drop, we also see a increase in the number of sends, though at this point the number of elements sent in each message is getting smaller ('Elems. Sent' column). In the middle levels we also see the increase in stencil size as indicated by 'NNZ/row', meaning the number of nonzero elements in each row on average. The restriction operator is not shown because, for all

our experiments, the restriction operator is the transpose of the interpolation operator.

The mappings of MPI processes to nodes used were the defaults on each machine. On Intrepid, this is a block mapping, where each node is filled with successive MPI ranks before assigning processes to the next one. Each job is also guaranteed a contiguous piece of the interconnect. On Hera, Zeus, and Atlas, the positions of the nodes on the interconnect varies from job to job, and the mapping is either block or cyclic, with the choice left to the scheduler. In a cyclic mapping, successive MPI ranks are assigned to different nodes, until each node has one. Then the next task is assigned to the first node, and the process repeated until all the processes are assigned. On Jaguar, information about which nodes the scheduler allocates and how MPI processes are mapped to them is proprietary and thus unavailable to us.

5.3 Machine Parameters

We use benchmark measurements to obtain values for machine parameters. Parameters α and β are determined from best-case latency and bandwidth measurements taken by the latency-bandwidth benchmark in the HPC Challenge suite [4]. Parameter γ is determined as follows. We start with the formulation of α in the distance penalty model, written as a function of the number of hops h:

$$\alpha(h) = \alpha(h_m) + \gamma(h - h_m).$$

Here, $\alpha(h_m)$ is the latency for the shortest possible message distance, corresponding with the minimum latency number reported in the benchmark results. The maximum latency possible is

$$\alpha(D) = \alpha(h_m) + \gamma(D - h_m),$$

where D is the diameter of the network. Taking the

	Intrepid	Jaguar	Hera	Zeus	Atlas
α	3.42 μs	6.05 μs	1.31 μs	0.583 μs	4.62 μs
β	19.3 ns	4.47 ns	6.08 ns	5.80 ns	7.29 ns
γ	28.5 ns	39.9 ns	2.68 μs	3.04 μs	0.88 μs
t_0	27.4 ns	3.27 ns	5.12 ns	4.67 ns	6.22 ns
t_1	12.8 ns	1.18 ns	1.39 ns	1.45 ns	3.22 ns
t_2	7.66 ns	0.935 ns	1.09 ns	1.45 ns	2.23 ns

Table 2: Machine parameters for the architectures evaluated.

maximum latency reported in the benchmark results to be $\alpha(D)$, we have

$$\gamma = \frac{\alpha(D) - \alpha(h_m)}{D - h_m}.$$

The computation rates t_i are measured using a serial sparse MatVec benchmark [9] run on one node, simultaneously on the number of cores per node used in our experiments to properly stress the memory system. Specific values are obtained for the first three levels (t_0, t_1, and t_2), and the value obtained for t_2 is used to approximate the computation rate on all coarser levels. The values are determined from the observed computation rate for sparse MatVec problems matching the dimension and number of nonzero entries per row of the solve operators for the respective levels. Values for all parameters appear in Table 2.

5.4 Validations Results

We apply the possible penalties outlined in the previous section to the basic performance model and show results for the following six combinations. Recall that the penalties in options 2 through 6 are all applied to the baseline model and note that in parentheses are the corresponding legend entries for the plots that follow.

1. Baseline model *(α-β Model)*

2. Baseline plus distance penalty *(α-β-γ Model)*

3. Baseline plus distance penalty and bandwidth penalty on β *(β Penalty)*

4. Baseline plus distance penalty, bandwidth penalty on β, and multicore penalty on α *(α, β Penalties)*

5. Baseline plus distance penalty, bandwidth penalty on β, and multicore penalty on γ *(β, γ Penalties)*

6. Baseline plus distance penalty, bandwidth penalty on β, and multicore penalty on α and γ *(α, β, γ Penalties)*

We model AMG using the models above and contrast their performance. In the following graphs, the best fit option is shown as a solid line in the plots, while the others are shown as lighter weight dotted lines. The actual measured performance is shown as a black line. The coarsest grid, which is solved using Gaussian Elimination instead of smoothing, is not shown. The results are shown in Figure 3 (Intrepid), Figure 4 (Jaguar), Figure 5 (Hera, Zeus), and Figure 6 (Atlas).

On Intrepid, once there is little computation, the performance generally tracks the communication counts, with little overall degradation. The best fit is obtained by the β penalty model, so distance effects and the bandwidth

penalty play a role as well. The total cycle time is on average predicted with 71% accuracy. Most of this error is due to the MatVec benchmark mispredicting the computation rate on the finest level. The predicted cycle time without this level has an average accuracy of 94%.

On Jaguar, the other machine with a torus topology, our results are different; the models with penalties to α do the best job of tracking the actual performance, with the α, β, γ penalty model doing the best job overall, though there is some deviation. This deviation can be partially attributed to the MatVec benchmark underestimating the time per flop on the machine. However, the fit that the models provide, with an average cycle time prediction accuracy of 80%, is still sufficient to suggest that endpoint contention is primarily responsible for the performance problems here.

The performance on Hera and Zeus is best tracked by models with a γ penalty, all of which are very close to each other. The best fit comes from the α, β, γ penalty model, with average cycle time prediction accuracies of 82% and 98% for Hera and Zeus, respectively. On Atlas, the best fit is the β, γ penalty model, with an average cycle time prediction accuracy of 87%, though the model does not do an ideal job of tracking the level-by-level performance. Note that Atlas has a much higher latency than Hera and Zeus, and the models with an α penalty substantially underpredict performance on Atlas. The common theme for these three machines, though, is that the best-fit models all have penalties to γ. As these machines have fat-tree interconnects with large switching costs, this indicates that the problem lies with messages contending for the switches.

6. LESSONS ON SCALABILITY

Our performance model has significantly contributed to our understanding of the scalability of AMG for large parallel machines. In particular, both distance of communication and contention among multicore nodes are major factors in observed performance and including their effects into our AMG model was essential to achieve a good fit. In this section, we discuss the important lessons learned for ensuring the scalability of AMG (and other HPC applications), both for the design of HPC architectures and for AMG algorithms themselves.

On the architectural side, interconnects must be able to handle both distance and contention effectively. This problem was most noticeable on fat-tree machines where communication distance was a big factor in performance, with γ larger than α or not far from it in magnitude on each platform. Most of this cost came from the top-level switch, as the value of α reflected the cost of communication through one of the lower-level switches. In addition, there was contention in the switches, reflected by the models with penalties to γ giving the best approximation to the performance on these machines. Future machines with the fat-tree topology will need switches that can handle growing amounts of traffic with smaller and smaller delays. Furthermore, machines with a torus interconnect are not immune from penalties to distance or contention either, as the results on Jaguar showed. The main factor was contention among the cores, as shown in the effectiveness of the penalty to α. As is the case with the fat-tree machines, future machines with a mesh or torus topology will also need to be able to handle increasing communication distances and contention among the cores on each node.

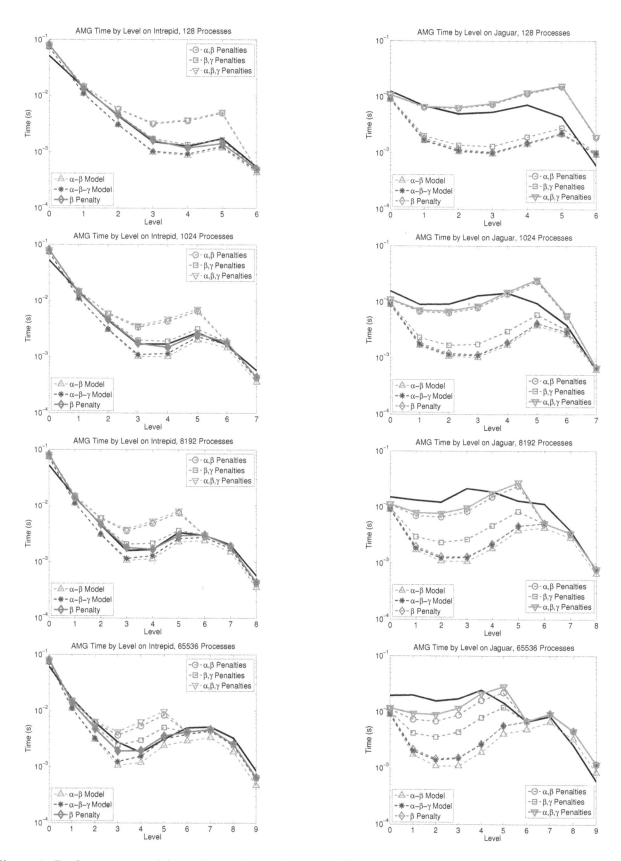

Figure 3: Performance model results on Intrepid.

Figure 4: Performance model results on Jaguar.

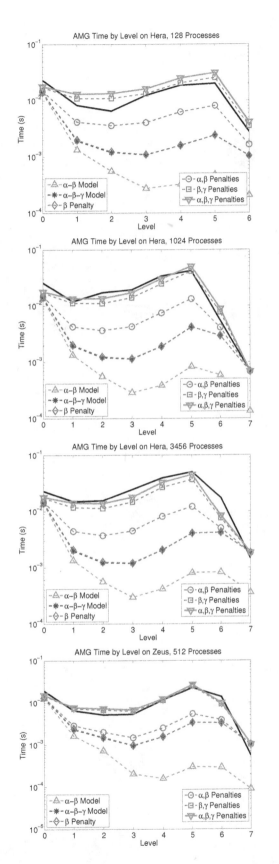

Figure 5: Performance model results on Hera and Zeus.

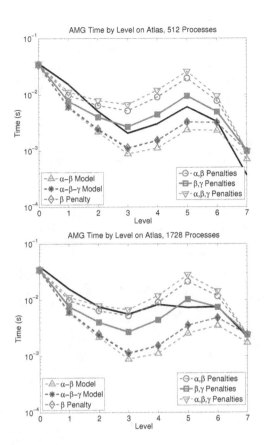

Figure 6: Performance model results on Atlas.

It is likely, though, that improvements in interconnection networks will not be enough to ensure the scalability of AMG in the future. Increasing numbers of cores and cores per node in future parallel machines will make the problems of distance and contention even greater. AMG itself will have to adapt to the changing landscape through algorithmic changes to better handle its performance problems on coarse grids. These changes will have to reduce the amount of communication, whether by trading it for redundant computation, or by using new coarsening and interpolation schemes to create operators that involve less communication.

7. CONCLUSIONS

Motivated by a desire to understand the issues impeding the scalability of AMG on HPC platforms, we developed a performance model for the AMG solve cycle, with penalties to account for various performance problems: distance of communication, low effective bandwidth, and contention among the multiple cores on each node. Our results found that distance and contention were both substantial performance bottlenecks for AMG. With core counts soon to reach the millions, and eventually the billions in future exascale machines, we expect these bottlenecks to become more severe unless changes are made to AMG to alleviate the extensive communication requirements on the coarser grid levels.

In the future, we will use the models developed in this work to guide changes to the AMG solve cycle. In particular, we will reduce AMG's communication burden and explore possibilities that include the use of redundant computation in place of communication and algorithmic changes that reduce the amount of required data movements. We will also investigate and model the setup phase on AMG, looking for ways to reduce its communication burden as well. Other issues of interest are the impact of data movement through the memory hierarchy, using threads, different sparse storage formats, and the influence of the mapping of tasks to nodes in the machine. Our ultimate goal is to ensure the scalability of AMG for the exascale machines of tomorrow.

Acknowledgments

We thank the reviewers for their constructive and very helpful comments. This work was supported in part by the Office of Advanced Scientific Computing Research, Office of Science, U.S. Department of Energy, under award DE-FG02-08ER25835, and in part by the National Science Foundation award 0837719. Part of this work was performed under the auspices of the U.S. Department of Energy by Lawrence Livermore National Laboratory under contract DE-AC52-07NA27344 (LLNL-CONF-473462). It also used resources of the Argonne Leadership Computing Facility at Argonne National Laboratory, which is supported by the Office of Science of the U.S. Department of Energy under contract DE-AC02-06CH11357, as well as resources of the National Center for Computational Sciences at Oak Ridge National Laboratory, which is supported by the Office of Science of the U.S. Department of Energy under Contract No. DE-AC05-00OR22725. These resources were made available via the Performance Evaluation and Analysis Consortium End Station, a Department of Energy INCITE project. Neither Contractor, DOE, or the U.S. Government, nor any person acting on their behalf: (a) makes any warranty or representation, express or implied, with respect to the information contained in this document; or (b) assumes any liabilities with respect to the use of, or damages resulting from the use of any information contained in the document.

8. REFERENCES

[1] A. H. Baker, T. Gamblin, M. Schulz, and U. M. Yang. Challenges of Scaling Algebraic Multigrid across Modern Multicore Architectures. In *25th IEEE Parallel and Distributed Processing Symposium*, Anchorage, AK, May 2011.

[2] A. H. Baker, M. Schulz, and U. M. Yang. On the Performance of an Algebraic Multigrid Solver on Multicore Clusters. In *VECPAR'10: 9th International Meeting on High Performance Computing for Computational Science*, Berkeley, CA, June 2010.

[3] B. Barnes, B. Rountree, D. Lowenthal, J. Reeves, B. R. de Supinski, and M. Schulz. A Regression-Based Approach to Scalability Prediction. June 2008.

[4] J. Dongarra and P. Luszczek. Introduction to the HPCChallenge Benchmark Suite. Technical Report ICL-UT-05-01, University of Tennessee, Knoxville, March 2005.

[5] C. C. Douglas, J. Hu, M. Kowarschik, U. Rüde, and C. Weiss. Cache Optimization for Structured and Unstructured Grid Multigrid. *Electronic Transactions on Numerical Analysis*, 10:21–40, 2000.

[6] R. D. Falgout, J. E. Jones, and U. M. Yang. Pursuing Scalability for *hypre*'s Conceptual Interfaces. *ACM Transactions on Mathematical Software*, 31:326–350, September 2005.

[7] H. Gahvari. Benchmarking Sparse Matrix-Vector Multiply. Master's thesis, University of California, Berkeley, December 2006.

[8] H. Gahvari and W. Gropp. An Introductory Exascale Feasibility Study for FFTs and Multigrid. In *24th IEEE International Parallel and Distributed Processing Symposium*, Atlanta, GA, April 2010.

[9] H. Gahvari, M. Hoemmen, J. Demmel, and K. Yelick. Benchmarking Sparse Matrix-Vector Multiply in Five Minutes. In *SPEC Benchmark Workshop 2007*, Austin, TX, January 2007.

[10] W. Gropp. Parallel Computing and Domain Decomposition. In T. Chan, D. Keyes, G. Meurant, J. Scroggs, and R. Voigt, editors, *Fifth Conference on Domain Decomposition Methods for Partial Differential Equations*, pages 349–361. SIAM, 1992.

[11] V. E. Henson and U. M. Yang. BoomerAMG: A parallel algebraic multigrid solver and preconditioner. *Applied Numerical Mathematics*, 41:155–177, April 2002.

[12] *hypre*: High performance preconditioners. http://www.llnl.gov/CASC/hypre/.

[13] D. Kerbyson, H. Alme, A. Hoisie, F. Petrini, A. Wasserman, and M. Gittings. Predictive performance and scalability modeling of a large-scale application. Nov. 2001.

[14] S. S. Shende and A. D. Malony. The TAU Parallel Performance System. *International Journal of High Performance Computing Applications*, 20:287–311, May 2006.

[15] A. Snavely, N. Wolter, and L. Carrington. Modeling application performance by convolving machine signatures with application profiles. In *IEEE Workshop on Workload Characterization, 2001.*, December 2001.

[16] H. D. Sterck, R. D. Falgout, J. W. Nolting, and U. M. Yang. Distance-two interpolation for parallel algebraic multigrid. *Numerical Linear Algebra With Applications*, 15:115–139, April 2008.

[17] H. D. Sterck, U. M. Yang, and J. J. Heys. Reducing complexity in parallel algebraic multigrid preconditioners. *SIAM Journal on Matrix Analysis and Applications*, 27:1019–1039, 2006.

[18] K. Stüben. An introduction to algebraic multigrid. In U. Trottenberg, C. Oosterlee, and A. Schüller, editors, *Multigrid*, pages 413–528. Academic Press, San Diego, CA, 2001.

[19] U. M. Yang. On long-range interpolation operators for aggressive coarsening. *Numerical Linear Algebra With Applications*, 17:453–472, April 2010.

Optimizing the Datacenter for Data-Centric Workloads

Stijn Polfliet   Frederick Ryckbosch   Lieven Eeckhout

ELIS Department, Ghent University
Sint-Pietersnieuwstraat 41, B-9000 Gent, Belgium
{stijn.polfliet, frederick.ryckbosch, lieven.eeckhout}@elis.UGent.be

ABSTRACT

The amount of data produced on the internet is growing rapidly. Along with data explosion comes the trend towards more and more diverse data, including rich media such as audio and video. Data explosion and diversity leads to the emergence of data-centric workloads to manipulate, manage and analyze the vast amounts of data. These data-centric workloads are likely to run in the background and include application domains such as data mining, indexing, compression, encryption, audio/video manipulation, data warehousing, etc.

Given that datacenters are very much cost sensitive, reducing the cost of a single component by a small fraction immediately translates into huge cost savings because of the large scale. Hence, when designing a datacenter, it is important to understand data-centric workloads and optimize the ensemble for these workloads so that the best possible performance per dollar is achieved.

This paper studies how the emerging class of data-centric workloads affects design decisions in the datacenter. Through the architectural simulation of minutes of run time on a validated full-system x86 simulator, we derive the insight that for some data-centric workloads, a high-end server optimizes performance per total cost of ownership (TCO), whereas for other workloads, a low-end server is the winner. This observation suggests heterogeneity in the datacenter, in which a job is run on the most cost-efficient server. Our experimental results report that a heterogeneous datacenter achieves an up to 88%, 24% and 17% improvement in cost-efficiency over a homogeneous high-end, commodity and low-end server datacenter, respectively.

Categories and Subject Descriptors

C.0 [**Computer Systems Organization**]: Modeling of computer architecture; C.4 [**Computer Systems Organization**]: Performance of Systems—*Modeling Techniques*

General Terms

Design, Performance, Measurement, Experimentation

Keywords

Datacenter, data-centric workloads, workload characterization, heterogeneity

1. INTRODUCTION

The internet-sector server market is growing at a fast pace, by 40 to 65% per year according to various market trend studies (including by IDC). This fast increase is due to various novel internet services that are being offered, along with ubiquitous internet access possibilities through various devices including mobile devices such as smartphones and netbooks. In particular, smartphones enable their users to be permanently in touch with email, the internet, social networking sites such as Facebook and Twitter, e-commerce, etc. There are around 400 million smartphones worldwide today, and trend analysis estimates the number of smartphones to exceed 1.1 billion by 2013[1]. Hence, the number of people using internet services of various kinds is increasing rapidly and demonstrates the large scale of the applications and systems behind these services. For example, there are more than 500 million active Facebook users of which 50% log in on a daily basis; 200 million Facebook users use mobile devices and these users are twice as active as non-mobile users — according to Facebook's statistics as of Jan 2011[2]. As another example, there are 175M registered Twitter users generating more than 95M Twitter messages a day, as of Sept 2010[3].

Designing the servers to support these services is challenging, for a number of reasons. Online services have hundreds of millions of users, which requires distributed applications to run on tens to hundreds of thousands of servers [4], e.g., Facebook has 60,000 servers as of June 2010[4]. The ensemble of servers is often referred to as a warehouse-scale computer [5] and scaling out to this large a scale clearly is a key design challenge. Because of its scale, warehouse-scale computers are very much cost driven — optimizing the cost per server even by only a couple tens of dollars results in millions of dollars of cost savings and thus an increase in

---

[1] http://www.i4u.com/29160/11-billion-smartphones-2013
[2] http://www.facebook.com/press/info.php?statistics
[3] http://twitter.com/about
[4] http://www.datacenterknowledge.com/archives/2010/06/28/facebook-server-count-60000-or-more/

millions of dollars in revenue. There are various factors affecting the cost of a datacenter, such as the hardware infrastructure (the servers as well as the rack and switch infrastructure), power and cooling infrastructure as well as operating expenditure, and real estate. Hence, warehouse-sized computers are very cost-sensitive, need to be optimized for the ensemble, and operators drive their datacenter design decisions towards a sweet spot that optimizes performance per dollar. For example, commercial offerings by companies such as SeaMicro[5] as well as ongoing research and advanced development projects such as the EuroCloud project[6], target low-end servers to optimize datacenter cost-efficiency.

The emergence of warehouse-scale computers also leads to a dramatic shift in the workloads run on today's datacenters. Whereas traditional datacenter workloads include commercial workloads such as database management systems (DBMS) and enterprise resource planning (ERP), the datacenters in the cloud now run a new set of emerging workloads for online web services, e.g., e-commerce, webmail, video hosting, social networks. Users accessing these online web services generate huge amounts of data, both text and rich media (i.e., images, audio and video). The workloads running on a warehouse-scale computer not only include the interactive interface with the end user but also distributed data processing and storage infrastructure. In addition, data analytics workloads need to run in the datacenter 'behind the scenes' to manage, manipulate, and extract trends from the vast amounts of online data. For example, an e-commerce application will feature a data mining workload running in the background to collect user profiles and make suggestions to its end users for future purchases. Similarly, web search engines feature indexing workloads running in the background to build up indices. Whereas traditional datacenter workloads are well studied historically, see for example [9, 13, 19], and online interactive workloads have emerged as a workload of interest in recent research efforts [1, 12, 20], data-centric workloads have received limited attention so far.

1.1 Data-centric workloads

In this paper we focus on the data-centric workloads that are likely to run as background processes in datacenters in the cloud, i.e., workloads such as data mining, indexing, compression, encryption, rich media applications and data warehousing. And we study how these data-centric workloads affect some of the design decisions in the datacenter. Through full-system simulations using a validated x86 simulator while simulating minutes of run time, we explore which server type optimizes the performance per dollar target metric. We conclude that there is no clear winner: for some workloads, a high-end server yields the best performance per cost ratio, whereas for others, a middle-of-the-road server is a winner, and for yet other workloads, a low-end server yields the best performance-cost efficiency.

This result suggests the case for heterogeneous datacenters in which a workload is run on its most performance-cost efficient server. For our set of workloads and experimental setup (which assumes equal weight for all workloads), a homogeneous low-end server datacenter improves performance-cost efficiency by 14% compared to a homogeneous high-end server datacenter; we report an

18% better performance-cost efficiency for a heterogeneous datacenter relative to a homogeneous datacenter with high-end servers only. We also observe that a heterogeneous datacenter with a collection of high-end servers and low-end servers achieves most of the benefits that can be achieved through heterogeneity; adding middle-of-the-road servers does not contribute much.

Obviously, the improvement achieved through heterogeneity very much depends on the workloads that co-execute in the datacenter. Considering a wide range of workload mixes, we report performance-cost efficiency improvements for a heterogeneous datacenter up to 88%, 24% and 17% compared to homogeneous high-end, commodity and low-end server datacenters, respectively. Because estimating a datacenter's total cost of ownership is non-trivial, we also report results quantifying the performance-cost efficiency as a function of the cost ratio between the various server types, and by doing so, we determine the sweet spot for heterogeneous datacenters. Finally, we present a comprehensive analysis on where the benefit comes from. In the cases where the high-end server achieves a better performance-cost efficiency, the higher cost is offset by the higher throughput achieved through higher clock frequency, lower execution cycle counts and larger core counts. For the benchmarks for which the low-end processor is more performance-cost beneficial, the higher throughput achieved on the server is not offset by its higher cost.

We believe this is an interesting result given the current debate in the community on high-end versus commodity (middle-of-the-road) versus low-end servers for the datacenter [14, 17]. In particular, Lim et al. [12] conclude that lower-end consumer platforms and low-cost, low-power components from the high-volume embedded/mobile space may lead to a $2\times$ improvement in performance per dollar. Reddi et al. [20] similarly conclude that a low-end Atom processor is more favorable than a high-end Intel Xeon for an industry-strength online web search engine, although these processor would benefit from better performance to achieve better quality-of-service and service-level agreements. In spite of these recent studies pointing towards low-end embedded servers for performance-cost efficient datacenters, there is no consensus as to whether contemporary datacenters should consider high-end versus low-end versus middle-of-the-road server nodes [14, 17]. Some argue for low-end 'wimpy' servers (see T. Mudge's statement in [14]) whereas others argue for high-end servers, and yet others argue for middle-of-the-road 'brawny' servers (see U. Hölzle's statement in [14]). This paper concludes there is no single answer. For some workloads, high-end servers are most performance-cost efficient, whereas for other workloads, low-end embedded processors are most efficient.

1.2 Paper contributions and outline

This paper makes the following contributions.

- We collect a set of data-centric workloads and we study how these workloads affect design decisions in the datacenter. Recent work in architectural studies for the datacenter considered online interactive workloads for the most part, and did not consider data-centric workloads. Running data-centric workloads requires minutes of run time on large data sets. We employ full-system simulation for doing so using a validated architectural simulator.

---

[5]http://www.seamicro.com/

[6]http://www.eurocloudserver.com/

- We obtain the result that high-end and middle-of-the-road servers can be more cost-efficient than low-end servers for running data-centric workloads. This is in contrast to recent work, see for example [1, 12, 20], which argues for lower-end servers to optimize cost-efficiency and/or energy-efficiency in the datacenter. The reason for this outcome is that data-centric workloads are computation-intensive and frequency-sensitive, hence, high-end and middle-of-the-road servers yield a substantially better performance per cost ratio.

- We demonstrate that for some sets of data-centric workloads, a heterogeneous datacenter in which each workload runs on its most cost-efficient server, can yield significant cost savings.

- We provide detailed sensitivity analyses to gain insight in the benefits of heterogeneity and how it varies with workload mixes, server infrastructure cost and energy cost. In particular, we demonstrate that heterogeneity is beneficial for a range of cost ratios between a high-end versus a low-end server. Further, we demonstrate that the benefit from heterogeneity is higher at lower energy costs.

The remainder of this paper is organized as follows. We first describe the data-centric workloads that we consider in this study (Section 2). We subsequently detail on the datacenter modeling aspects and our experimental setup (Section 3). We then describe our results (Section 4) and provide sensitivity analyses (Section 5). Finally, we discuss related work (Section 6) and conclude (Section 7).

2. DATA-CENTRIC WORKLOADS

2.1 Data explosion and diversity in the cloud

A prominent trend that we observe in the cloud is data explosion. The amount of online data has grown by a factor of $56\times$ over 7 years, from 5 exabytes of online data in 2002 to 281 exabytes in 2009 — a substantially larger increase compared to Moore's law ($16\times$ over 7 years) [18]. The reason comes from the emergence of interactive internet services (e.g., e-commerce, web mail) and Web 2.0 applications such as social networking (e.g., Facebook, Twitter), blogs, wikis, etc., as well as ubiquitous access to online data through various mobile devices such as netbooks and smartphones.

Along with data explosion comes the trend of increasingly diverse data, including structured data, unstructured data and semi-structured data. In addition, the data stored in Web 2.0 applications is increasingly rich media, including images, audio and video.

Data explosion and diversity preludes a novel area of data-centric workloads in the cloud to manipulate the data, manage this huge data volume, extract useful information from it, derive insight from it, and eventually act on it. Hence, it is important to study these workloads and understand how this emerging class of workloads may change how datacenters are optimized for performance-cost efficiency.

2.2 A data-centric benchmark suite

Motivated by this observation, we collected a number of benchmarks to represent the emerging application domain of data-centric workloads. We identify a number of categories such as data mining, indexing, security, rich media, compression, and data warehousing. Each of these categories prelude important emerging applications in data-centric workloads. We select benchmarks for each of these categories, see also Table 1.

Data mining.

Analyzing the data is absolutely crucial to gain insight from it and eventually act on it. This requires data mining, statistical analysis and machine learning to extract and understand the underlying phenomena. We include three data mining benchmarks, namely kmeans, eclat and hmmer. The kmeans benchmark is a clustering workload that discovers groups of similar objects in a database to characterize the underlying data distribution. Clustering algorithms are often used in customer segmentation, pattern recognition, spatial data analysis, etc. Our dataset includes 100K data points in an 18-dimensional space and groups these points in 50 clusters. The eclat benchmark is a typical Association Rule Mining (ARM) workload to find interesting relationships in large data sets (466MB in our case). The benchmark tries to find all subsets of items that occur frequently in a database. The hmmer benchmark involves the pfam collection of multiple sequence alignments and hidden Markov models (HMM) covering many common protein domains and families. It is used for running the hmmpfam executable, part of the HMMER package. Its input is a sequence of 9,000 residues that is being compared against 2,000 HMMs.

Indexing.

Analyzing the data often requires indexing the data to enable efficient searching. We include the Apache lucene text search engine. In our case, lucene builds an index for 50K Wikipedia pages (647MB in total). The lucene benchmark is a Java workload and runs on the Open JDK JVM v6.

Data compression.

Storing huge volumes of data requires compression and decompression in order to be able to store the data on disk in an efficient way. Our benchmark suite includes the tarz application which consists of the standard GNU Tar utility to create an archive from, in our case, a set of PDF and text files. The archive is compressed using gzip (GNU zip). Gzip reduces the size of the archive using Lempel-Ziv (LZ77) encoding. The uncompressed input equals 1.2GB in size and is compressed to 273MB.

Data security.

Data stored in the cloud may be proprietary or personal, and third parties should not access this data. Data encryption is thus required to secure the data. We consider gpg (GNU Privacy Guard) as part of our benchmark suite. We sign and encrypt the same 1.2GB archive as for the compression benchmark.

Rich media applications.

As mentioned before, the data stored online is becoming more and more rich media, including audio (e.g., iTunes, MySpace), images (e.g., flickr), video (e.g., YouTube), as well as virtual reality (e.g., online games). We include three benchmarks to cover rich media applications, namely blender, bodytrack and x264. The

category	benchmark	source	description	run time
data compression	tarz	GNU	Create an archive and compress the files	1m10s
data mining	kmeans	MineBench	Mean-based data clustering	1m50s
	eclat	MineBench	Association rule mining to find interesting relationships in large data sets	1m56s
	hmmer	BioPerf	Compares sequence alignments against hidden Markov models	3m30s
data indexing	lucene	Apache	Apache text search indexer library written in Java	1m59s
data security	gpg	GNU	Sign and encrypt files	1m30s
rich media	blender	Blender Foundation	3D graphics rendering for creating 3D games, animated film or visual effects	2m15s
	bodytrack	PARSEC	Body tracking using multiple cameras	1m38s
	x264	PARSEC	Encoding video streams in H.264 format	1m15s
business	SPECjbb2005	SPEC	Middle-tier of server-side Java performance	2m09s

Table 1: Our set of data-centric benchmarks: their category, source, description and run time on a dual-socket dual-core AMD Opteron 2212 machine.

blender benchmark is a 3D graphics rendering application for creating 3D games, animated film and visual effects. We render 40 frames from a 3D scene including objects, and shadow, lightning and mirroring effects. The bodytrack benchmark is a computer vision application that tracks a human body with multiple cameras through an image sequence. As input data we consider 200 frames from 4 cameras with 4,000 particles in 5 annealing layers (input data set of 477MB). The x264 benchmark is an application for encoding videostreams in H.264 format. Its input is a 1.5GB video file.

Classical business logic.

Next to these emerging workloads, classical business logic will remain to be an important workload. We include PseudoSPECjbb2005, a modified version of SPECjbb2005 that executes a fixed amount of work rather than for a fixed amount of time. SPECjbb models the middle tier (the business logic) of a three-tier business system containing a number of warehouses that serve a number of districts. There are a set of operations that customers can initiate, such as placing orders or requesting the status of an existing order. PseudoSPECjbb, in our setup, processes 4M operations in total.

Both multi-threaded as single-threaded workloads.

As mentioned in Table 1, we gathered these benchmarks from various sources. Some benchmarks come from existing benchmark suites (PARSEC [7], MineBench [15], BioPerf [3]), while others were derived from real-life applications (Apache lucene, blender, GNU gpg, GNU tarz). Half the benchmarks are multi-threaded workloads (blender, bodytrack, kmeans, specjbb, x264); the others are single-threaded (hmmer, eclat, gpg, lucene, tarz). The inputs for these workloads were chosen such that the run time on a dual-processor dual-core AMD Opteron 2212 machine is on order of minutes, see also Table 1. We simulate these workloads to completion.

Workload data set sizes.

All the workloads run on data sets with hundreds of MBs or on the order of GBs of data. Although the data sets may be even bigger in real setups, we believe this is a reasonable assumption for our purpose, because these data sets do not fit in the processor's caches anyway. Hence, simulating even larger data sets is unlikely to change the overall conclusions. We simulate these workloads

for minutes of real time, see also Table 1, or hundreds of billions of instructions, which is unusual for architecture simulation studies.

3. DATACENTER MODELING

Datacenter design is very much cost driven, and design decisions are driven by two key metrics, namely performance and cost [5]. Cost is not limited to hardware cost, but also includes power and cooling as well as datacenter infrastructure cost. A recently proposed metric for internet-sector environments is performance divided by total cost of ownership (TCO) and quantifies the performance achieved per dollar [12]. We now describe how we quantify cost and performance in the following two subsections, respectively.

3.1 TCO modeling

We build on the work by Lim et al. [12] to quantify datacenter cost. A three-year depreciation cycle is assumed and cost models are provided for hardware cost, as well as power and cooling costs. Hardware cost includes the individual components (CPU, memory, disk, board, power and cooling supplies, etc.) per server. Power and cooling cost includes the power consumption of the various server and rack components. The cooling cost includes infrastructure cost for power delivery, infrastructure cost for cooling, and the electricity cost for cooling.

We consider three server types: a high-end server, a low-end embedded processor and a middle-of-the-road (commodity) server. Table 2 describes their configurations and their cost models. The high-end server that we simulate is modeled after the Intel Xeon X5570; we assume an eight-core machine[7] running at 3GHz with a fairly aggressive out-of-order processor core along with an aggressive memory hierarchy. The low-end processor is a dual-core embedded processor running at 1.2GHz with a modest core and memory hierarchy, and is modeled after the Intel Atom Z515 processor. The commodity system is somewhat in the middle of the road between the high-end and low-end systems. We assume 4 cores at 2GHz and we model it after the Intel Core 2 Quad. The cost for each of the components is derived from a variety of sources[8].

---

[7] The Intel Xeon X5570 implements 4 cores and 2 hardware threads per core.

[8] http://ark.intel.com/Product.aspx?id=40740;
http://www.newegg.com/Product/Product.aspx?Item=N82E16813131358;
http://ark.intel.com/Product.aspx?id=40816&processor=Q8200S&spec-codes=SLG9T

Processor configuration			
	high-end	middle	low-end
frequency	3GHz	2GHz	1.2GHz
#cores	8	4	2
OOO core	4-wide	3-wide	2-wide
ROB size (#insns)	160	90	40
mem latency (cycles)	120	80	40
private L1 caches	64KB	32KB	32KB
L1 prefetching	yes	yes	no
private L2 caches	256KB	NA	NA
shared LLC cache	8MB	2MB	1MB
LLC prefetching	yes	no	no
branch predictor	4KB, 14b hist	2KB, 10b hist	1KB, 8b hist
Cost model			
	high-end	middle	low-end
CPU	1,386	213	45
board and mngmnt	330	145	50
memory	265	113	98
total hardware cost	1,981	471	193
CPU power (TDP)	95	65	1.4
server & rack power	300	100	22
cooling	300	100	22
total power (Watt)	600	200	44
power cost 3-year	2,680	894	197
total cost 3-year	4,662	1,365	390

Table 2: Processor configurations and their cost models (in Euro).

We use these default costs for reporting a reasonable design point given today's technology. Note that we do account for the server NIC cost as part of the 'board and management' cost. We do not account for the network itself; we basically assume that network cost is constant across different datacenter configurations. We believe this is a reasonable first-order approximation, given that networking accounts for 8% of the total datacenter cost only [8]. Further, because cost depends on many sources and varies over time, we vary the relative cost ratios across platforms in order to understand cost sensitivity in Section 5. In other words, if server cost and/or network cost were to differ across datacenter configurations, this can be accounted for through these cost ratios.

We consider a default energy cost of 17 Eurocent per kWh, unless mentioned otherwise. This is a typical private tariff rate; industry tariff rate may be as low as 10 Eurocent per kWh and below, hence, we explore a range of electricity costs in the evaluation section of this paper.

3.2 Performance modeling

We use HP Labs' COTSon simulation infrastructure [2] which uses AMD's SimNow [6] as its functional simulator to feed a trace of instructions into a timing model. COTSon can simulate full-system workloads, including the operating system, middleware (e.g., Java virtual machine) and the application stack. In this study, we use the COTSon-based simulator by Ryckbosch et al. [21], which has been validated against real hardware and which runs at a simulation speed of 37 MIPS with sampling enabled. This high simulation speed enables us to run the data-centric workloads on sufficiently large datasets for minutes of real time. The sampling strategy assumed is periodic sampling: we consider 100K instruction

sampling units every 100M instructions and 1M instructions prior to each sampling unit for warming the caches and predictors.

We quantify performance as throughput or the number of jobs that can be completed per unit of time. Because the workloads that we consider are supposed to run as background processes in the cloud — these workloads are non-interactive with the end users — we believe throughput is the right performance metric. For each platform we compute the best possible throughput that can be achieved. For the single-threaded benchmarks this means we run multiple copies of the same benchmark concurrently on the multicore processor and we vary the number of copies (e.g., for the high-end server, from one copy up to eight copies), and we then report the best possible throughput that was achieved. For the multi-threaded benchmarks, we vary both the number of copies and the number of threads (e.g., on an 8-core system we consider 1 copy with 8 threads, 2 copies with 4 threads, etc.), and we report the best possible throughput.

4. OPTIMIZING THE DATACENTER

4.1 Which server type is optimal?

Figure 1 quantifies performance per TCO efficiency for the high-end, middle-of-the-road and low-end servers, normalized to the high-end server. Performance per TCO efficiency is defined as TCO divided by performance, or the reciprocal of performance per TCO. Hence, performance per TCO efficiency is a lower-is-better metric. The interesting observation from Figure 1 is that there is no single winner: there is no single server that yields the best performance per TCO across all the workloads. For most workloads, the low-end server results in the lowest performance per TCO efficiency, however, for a couple workloads, the high-end server is the most performance per TCO efficient system, see for example kmeans and x264. It is also interesting to note that for a couple workloads, namely gpg, hmmer and tarz, the middle-of-the-road server yields the best performance per TCO efficiency, albeit the difference with the low-end server is very small. The result that high-end and middle-of-the-road servers are more cost-efficient than low-end servers for some data-centric workloads is surprising and is in contrast to common wisdom and recently reported studies [1, 12, 20] which argued for lower-end servers to optimize cost-efficiency in the datacenter. The reason is that these workloads are computation-intensive which makes the high-end and commodity servers yield a better performance per cost ratio, as we explain next. It must be noted that these conclusions hold true for our workloads, but more study is needed before we can generalize these results to a much broader range of data-centric workloads, and internet-sector workloads in general.

4.2 Where does the benefit come from?

In order to get some insight as to why a particular server type is a winner for a particular workload, we break up the performance per TCO metric into its contributing components, using the following formula:

$$performance\ per\ TCO = \frac{no.\ parallel\ jobs \cdot \frac{freq}{\#cycles}}{TCO}. \quad (1)$$

The denominator quantifies cost for which we assume a 3-year de-

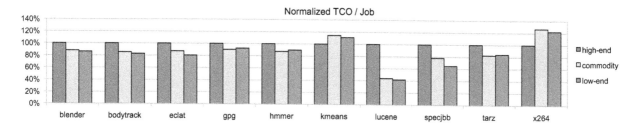

Figure 1: Normalized performance per TCO efficiency (lower is better) for the high-end, the middle-of-the-road and the low-end servers.

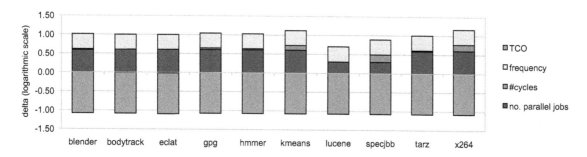

Figure 2: Performance per TCO stacks for quantifying the different factors; high-end versus low-end processors.

preciation cost cycle. The nominator quantifies throughput as the number of parallel jobs multiplied by the performance per job, or the reciprocal of the job's execution time; we measure throughput as the number of jobs that can be completed over a three-year time period. Figure 2 quantifies the contributing components when comparing the high-end versus the low-end server. The vertical axis is on a logarithmic scale. The contributing components are additive on a logarithmic scale, or multiplicative on a nominal scale. A negative component means that the component is a contributor in favor of the low-end server. In particular, TCO is always in favor of the low-end server because the TCO for the low-end server is about 12 times as low as for the high-end server. A positive component implies that the component is a contributor in favor of the high-end server. For example, frequency is a significant positive contributor for the high-end server: 3GHz versus 1.2 GHz, a 2.5× improvement. Also, the number of parallel jobs is a significant contributor for the high-end server for most workloads. This means that the high-end server benefits from its ability to run multiple jobs in parallel, and hence achieve a higher throughput than the low-end server. Note that for some benchmarks, e.g., lucene and specjbb, this component is only half as large as for the other benchmarks. This is due to the fact that 4 copies is the optimum for these benchmarks on the high-end servers versus 2 copies on the embedded server, whereas for the other benchmarks 8 copies is the optimum on the high-end server. Finally, the third positive contributor is the number of execution cycles; this means that the execution time in number of cycles is smaller on the high-end server compared to the low-end server. For most benchmarks, the number of execution cycles is roughly the same for the high-end and low-end servers, which implies that on the low-end server, the reduction in memory access time (in cycles) is compensated for by the increase in the number of cycles to do useful work (smaller processor width

on the low-end server) and the increase in the number of branch mispredictions and cache misses (due to a smaller branch predictor and smaller caches on the low-end server). The number of execution cycles is a positive contributor for the high-end server for three benchmarks though, namely kmeans, specjbb and x264. In other words, the high-end server benefits significantly from the larger caches and branch predictor as well as the larger width compared to the low-end server for these workloads.

4.3 Does multi-threading help?

As mentioned before, half the workloads are multi-threaded and we optimize the datacenter for optimum throughput at the lowest possible cost. An interesting question is whether multi-threading helps if one aims for maximizing throughput. In other words, for a given workload for which there exists both a sequential and a parallel version, should we run multiple copies of the sequential version simultaneously, or are we better off running a single copy of the multi-threaded version? This is a non-trivial question for which an answer cannot be provided without detailed experimentation. On the one hand, parallel execution of sequential versions does not incur the overhead that is likely to be observed for the parallel version because of inter-thread communication and synchronization. On the other hand, multiple copies of sequential versions may incur conflict behavior in shared resources, e.g., the various sequential copies may incur conflict misses in the shared cache.

Table 3 summarizes the optimum workload configuration on each of the servers in terms of the number of instances of each workload and the number of threads per workload. For all of the multi-threaded workloads, except for specjbb, running multiple copies of the single-threaded workload version optimizes throughput. It is remarkable to see that multi-threading does not help in maximizing throughput for the data-centric workloads. Running multiple se-

	high-end	middle	low-end
blender	c8t1	c4t1	
bodytrack	c8t1	c4t1	
eclat	c8t1	c4t1	
gpg	c8t1	c4t1	
hmmer	c8t1	c4t1	c2t1
kmeans	c8t1	c4t1	
lucene	c4t1	c4t1	
specjbb	c4t2	c2t2	
tarz	c8t1	c4t1	
x264	c8t1	c4t1	

Table 3: Workload configurations that maximize throughput on the high-end, commodity and low-end servers; 'cxty' means 'x' copies of the same workload with 'y' threads.

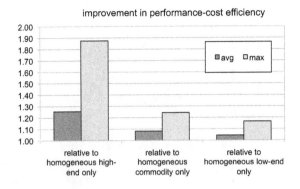

Figure 4: Cost reduction for a heterogeneous datacenter relative to homogeneous datacenter configurations across all possible two-benchmark workloads.

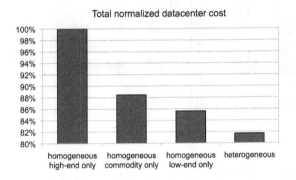

Figure 3: Normalized cost for iso-throughput homogeneous datacenters with high-end, middle-of-the-road and low-end servers only, versus a heterogeneous datacenter.

quential versions yields higher throughput compared to running a single parallel version; co-running sequential versions do not incur significant conflict behavior in shared resources.

4.4 The case for a heterogeneous datacenter

The results shown above suggest that a heterogeneous datacenter in which a job is executed on the most cost-efficient server, may be beneficial. In order to quantify the potential of a heterogeneous datacenter for data-centric workloads, we consider four iso-throughput datacenter configurations. We consider three homogeneous datacenters (with high-end servers only, middle-of-the-road servers only, and low-end servers only) as well as a heterogeneous datacenter. We assume the same workloads as before and we assume that all of these workloads are equally important — they all get the same weight. All of the datacenter configurations achieve the same throughput (for all of the workloads), hence, a datacenter with low-end servers needs to deploy more servers to achieve the same throughput as the homogeneous high-end server datacenter. The heterogeneous datacenter is configured such that it minimizes cost while achieving the same throughput as the homogeneous datacenters.

Figure 3 quantifies datacenter cost normalized to the homogeneous high-end server datacenter. A homogeneous datacenter with commodity servers reduces cost by almost 12% and low-end servers reduce datacenter cost by 14%. A heterogeneous datacenter reduces cost by 18%. Clearly, optimizing the datacenter's architec-

ture has a significant impact on cost. Even homogeneous datacenters with commodity and low-end servers can reduce cost significantly. Heterogeneity reduces cost even further, although not by a large margin. However, this is very much tied to the workloads considered in this study. As shown in Figure 1, only two out of the ten workloads are run most efficiently on the high-end server. Hence, depending on the workloads, cost reduction may be larger or smaller.

In order to get a better view on the potential of heterogeneity as a function of its workload, we now consider a large variety of different workload mixes. The previous experiment assumed that all the workloads are equally important, simply because we do not have a way for determining the relative importance of these workloads in real datacenters. We now consider a more diverse range of workload types: we consider all possible two-benchmark workload mixes and determine the potential benefit from heterogeneity; this is to study how sensitive a heterogeneous datacenter is with respect to its workload. In other words, for each possible two-benchmark workload mix, we determine the cost reduction through heterogeneity relative to homogeneous datacenters, see Figure 4. On average, a heterogeneous datacenter improves cost by 25%, 8% and 4%, and up to 88%, 24% and 17% relative to a homogeneous high-end, commodity and low-end server datacenter, respectively. (We consider the two-benchmark workload mixes for the remainder of the paper.)

We now zoom in on the architecture of a heterogeneous datacenter. We therefore consider the workload mixes for which we observe a throughput benefit of at least 30% for heterogeneity compared to a homogeneous datacenter consisting of high-end servers only. Figure 5 plots the fraction of low-end and commodity servers in a heterogeneous datacenter; one minus these two fractions is the fraction of high-end servers. The size of the disks relate to the number of cases (workload mixes) for which we observe a particular configuration. We observe that the optimum heterogeneous datacenter typically consists of a relatively large fraction low-end servers and smaller fractions of commodity and high-end servers.

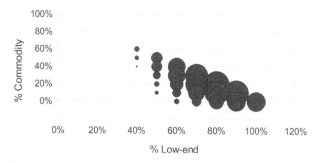

Figure 5: Configuration of the optimum heterogeneous data-center: the fraction of low-end and commodity servers; the fraction of high-end servers equals one minus the fraction of low-end and commodity servers.

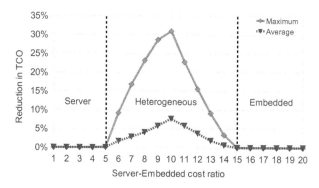

Figure 6: Cost reduction through heterogeneity as a function of the cost ratio between the high-end vs low-end servers.

5. SENSITIVITY ANALYSES

The results presented so far assumed the default parameters relating to datacenter cost mentioned in Section 3. Meaningful cost parameters are not easy to obtain because they are subject to a particular context, e.g., energy cost relates to where the datacenter is located, hardware purchase cost depends on the number of hardware items purchased, etc. In order to deal with the cost uncertainties, we therefore perform a sensitivity analysis with respect to the two main cost factors, hardware purchase cost and energy cost.

5.1 Varying the cost ratio

So far, we considered fixed costs for the various server types, as shown in Table 2. However, cost may vary depending on the number of servers that are bought — we assumed a fixed price per server. In addition, prices fluctuate over time. Hence, making a quantitative statement about which system is most performance-cost efficient at a given point in time, is subject to the cost ratios and thus it is not very informative. Instead, we also report the cost reduction through heterogeneity as a function of the cost ratio between the high-end and the low-end server, see Figure 6. The cost reduction reported here is the cost reduction over the best possible homogeneous datacenter. In case a high-end server is less than 5 times more expensive than a low-end server, then a high-end server is the clear winner, and there is no need for heterogeneity: a homogeneous high-end server datacenter optimizes the performance per dollar metric. In case a high-end server is more than 15 times more expensive that a low-end server, then a homogeneous data-

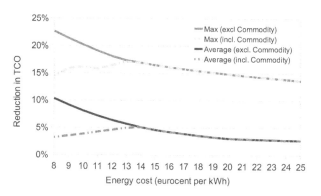

Figure 7: Cost reduction for a heterogeneous datacenter relative to the best possible homogeneous datacenter as a function of energy cost.

center with low-end servers is the optimal datacenter configuration. For cost ratios between 5× and 15×, performance per cost is optimized through heterogeneity. A 10× cost ratio yields the best possible benefit through heterogeneity, with an average reduction in cost of 8% and up to 31% for some workload mixes. As a point of reference, the cost ratio between the high-end and low-end server assumed in the rest of the paper equals 12, see Table 2.

5.2 Varying energy cost

Along the same line, energy cost is variable as well: it varies from one location to another, and it varies over time. Figure 7 quantifies the cost reduction of a heterogeneous datacenter relative to the best possible homogeneous datacenter as a function of energy cost. We report the average and maximum cost reduction through heterogeneity, and we consider two heterogeneous datacenter setups: one setup includes high-end, commodity and low-end servers, while the other includes high-end and low-end servers only (no commodity servers). The reason for considering both configurations is that the performance-cost efficiency is comparable for the commodity and low-end servers, as seen in Figure 1, which implies that heterogeneous datacenters with high-end and low-end servers only would achieve most of the benefits from heterogeneity — including commodity servers does not add much benefit. This is indeed the case for the 17 Eurocent per kWh assumed so far.

The interesting observation from Figure 7 is that there is a cost benefit from heterogeneity across a broad range of energy prices. Second, when considering high-end and low-end servers only (i.e., 'excluding commodity' servers in Figure 7) for both the homogeneous and heterogeneous design points, the benefit from heterogeneity tends to be higher at lower energy costs. At lower energy costs, the performance argument outweighs the cost argument, shifting the optimum towards high-end servers for a larger fraction of the workloads. At higher energy costs, the performance per cost metric drives the optimum design point towards low-end servers for most of the workloads, hence, the benefit from heterogeneity is decreasing. Finally, commodity servers fit a sweet spot at lower energy costs (see the 'including commodity' curves in Figure 7). Commodity servers have interesting performance-cost properties at low electricity costs — they yield good throughput at relatively low cost. Nevertheless, heterogeneity is still beneficial and can reduce the datacenter's TCO by up to 15%.

5.3 Discussion

The results discussed so far made the case for heterogeneous datacenters. Significant cost reductions can be obtained compared to homogeneous datacenters while achieving the same overall system throughput. The results also revealed that the extent to which cost is reduced is subject to various factors including the workloads, server cost ratio for different server types, energy cost, etc. Hence, in some cases, depending on the constraints, the benefit from heterogeneity may be limited. However, in a number of cases (for specific sets of workloads, server cost ratios and energy cost), heterogeneity may yield substantial cost benefits, which may translate into millions of dollars of cost savings.

6. RELATED WORK

Prior work in architectural studies for warehouse-sized computers considered online interactive workloads for the most part. In particular, Lim et al. [12] consider four internet-sector benchmarks, namely websearch (search a very large dataset within sub-seconds), webmail (interactive sessions of reading, composing and sending emails), YouTube (media servers servicing requests for video files), and mapreduce (series of map and reduce functions performed on key/value pairs in a distributed file system). These benchmarks are network-intensive (webmail), I/O-bound (YouTube) or exhibit mixed CPU and I/O activity (websearch and mapreduce). The data-centric benchmarks considered in this paper are data-intensive and are primarily compute- as well as memory-intensive, and barely involve network and I/O activity. It is to be expected that cloud datacenters will feature both types of workloads, interactive internet-sector workloads as well as data-intensive background workloads. Lim et al. reach the conclusion that lower-end consumer platforms are more performance-cost efficient — leading to a $2\times$ improvement relative to high-end servers. Low-end embedded servers have the potential to offer even more cost savings at the same performance, but the choice of embedded platform is important. We conclude that heterogeneity with both high-end and low-end servers can yield substantial cost savings.

Andersen et al. [1] propose the Fast Array of Wimpy Nodes (FAWN) datacenter architecture with low-power embedded servers coupled with flash memory for random read I/O-intensive workloads. Vasudevan et al. [22] evaluate under what workloads the FAWN architecture performs well while considering a broad set of microbenchmarks ranging from I/O-bound workloads to CPU- and memory-intensive benchmarks. They conclude that low-end nodes are more energy-efficient than high-end CPUs, except for problems that cannot be parallelized or whose working set cannot be split to fit in the cache or memory available to the smaller nodes — wimpy cores are too low-end for these workloads. Whereas the FAWN project focuses on energy-efficiency, we focus on cost-efficiency, i.e., performance per TCO. While focusing on data-centric workloads, we reach the conclusion that both high-end and low-end CPUs can be cost-efficient, depending on the workload.

Reddi et al. [20] evaluate the Microsoft Bing web search engine on Intel Xeon and Atom processors. They conclude that this web search engine is more computationally demanding than traditional enterprise workloads such as file servers, mail servers, web servers, etc. Hence, they conclude that embedded mobile-space processors are beneficial in terms of their power efficiency, however, these processors would benefit from better performance to achieve better service-level agreements and quality-of-service.

Keys et al. [10] consider a broad set of workloads as well as different processor types, ranging from embedded, mobile, desktop to server, and they aim for determining energy-efficient building blocks for the datacenter. They conclude that high-end mobile processors have the right mix of power and performance. We, in contrast, aim for identifying the most cost-efficient processor type taking into account total cost of ownership (TCO), not energy-efficiency only. We conclude that a mix of high-end servers and low-end servers optimizes performance per TCO.

Nathuji et al. [16] study job scheduling mechanisms for optimizing power efficiency in heterogeneous datacenters. The heterogeneous datacenters considered by Nathuji et al. stem from upgrade cycles, in contrast to the heterogeneity 'by design' in this paper. Also, Nathuji et al. consider high-end servers only and they do not include commodity and low-end servers as part of their design space.

Kumar et al. [11] propose heterogeneity to optimize power efficiency in multicore processors. Whereas Kumar et al. focus on a single chip and power efficiency, our work considers a datacenter, considers total cost (including hardware, power and cooling cost) and data-centric workloads.

7. CONCLUSION

Data explosion and diversity in the internet drives the emergence of a new set of data-centric workloads to manage, manipulate, mine, index, compress, encrypt, etc. huge amounts of data. In addition, the data is increasingly rich media, and includes images, audio and video, in addition to text. Given that the datacenters hosting the online data and running these data-centric workloads are very much cost driven, it is important to understand how this emerging class of applications affects some of the design decisions in the datacenter.

Through the architectural simulation of minutes of run time of a set of data-centric workloads on a validated full-system x86 simulator, we derived the insight that high-end servers are more performance-cost efficient compared to commodity and low-end embedded servers for some workloads; for others, the low-end server or the commodity server is more performance-cost efficient. This suggests heterogeneous datacenters as the optimum datacenter configuration. We conclude that the benefit from heterogeneity is very much workload and server-cost and electricity-cost dependent, and, for a specific setup, we report improvements up to 88%, 24% and 17% over a homogeneous high-end, commodity and low-end server datacenter, respectively. We also identify the sweet spot for heterogeneity as a function of high-end versus low-end server cost, and we provide the insight that the benefit from heterogeneity increases at lower energy costs.

Acknowledgements

We thank the anonymous reviewers for their constructive and insightful feedback. Stijn Polfliet is supported through a doctoral fellowship by the Agency for Innovation by Science and Technology (IWT). Frederick Ryckbosch is supported through a doctoral fellowship by the Research Foundation–Flanders (FWO). Additional support is provided by the FWO projects G.0232.06, G.0255.08, and G.0179.10, the UGent-BOF projects 01J14407 and 01Z04109, and the European Research Council under the European Community's Seventh Framework Programme (FP7/2007-2013) / ERC Grant agreement no. 259295.

8. REFERENCES

[1] D. G. Andersen, J. Franklin, M. Kaminsky, A. Phanishayee, L. Tan, and V. Vasudevan. FAWN: A fast array of wimpy nodes. In *Proceedings of the International ACM Symposium on Operating Systems Principles (SOSP)*, pages 1–14, Oct. 2009.

[2] E. Argollo, A. Falcón, P. Faraboschi, M. Monchiero, and D. Ortega. COTSon: Infrastructure for full system simulation. *SIGOPS Operating System Review*, 43(1):52–61, Jan. 2009.

[3] D. A. Bader, Y. Li, T. Li, and V. Sachdeva. BioPerf: A benchmark suite to evaluate high-performance computer architecture on bioinformatics applications. In *Proceedings of the 2005 IEEE International Symposium on Workload Characterization (IISWC)*, pages 163–173, Oct. 2005.

[4] L. A. Barroso, J. Dean, and U. Hölzle. Web search for a planet: The google cluster architecture. *IEEE Micro*, 23(2):22–28, Mar. 2003.

[5] L. A. Barroso and U. Hölzle. *The Datacenter as a Computer: An Introduction to the Design of Warehouse-Scale Machines*. Synthesis Lectures on Computer Architecture. Morgan and Claypool Publishers, 2009.

[6] R. Bedichek. SimNow: Fast platform simulation purely in software. In *Proceedings of the Symposium on High Performance Chips (HOT CHIPS)*, Aug. 2004.

[7] C. Bienia, S. Kumar, J. P. Singh, and K. Li. The PARSEC benchmark suite: Characterization and architectural implications. In *Proceedings of the International Conference on Parallel Architectures and Compilation Techniques (PACT)*, pages 72–81, Oct. 2008.

[8] J. Hamilton. Datacenter networks are in my way. Principals of Amazon, Oct. 2010.

[9] K. Keeton, D. A. Patterson, Y. Q. He, R. C. Raphael, and W. E. Baker. Performance characterization of a quad Pentium Pro SMP using OLTP workloads. In *Proceedings of the International Symposium on Computer Architecture (ISCA)*, pages 15–26, June 1998.

[10] L. Keys, S. Rivoire, and J. D. Davis. The search for energy-efficient building blocks for the data center. In *The Second Workshop on Energy-Efficient Design (WEED), held in conjunction with the International Symposium on Computer Architecture (ISCA)*, June 2010.

[11] R. Kumar, K. I. Farkas, N. P. Jouppi, P. Ranganathan, and D. M. Tullsen. Single-ISA heterogeneous multi-core architectures: The potential for processor power reduction. In *Proceedings of the ACM/IEEE Annual International Symposium on Microarchitecture (MICRO)*, pages 81–92, Dec. 2003.

[12] K. Lim, P. Ranganathan, J. Chang, C. Patel, T. Mudge, and S. Reinhardt. Understanding and designing new server architectures for emerging warehouse-computing environments. In *Proceedings of the International Symposium on Computer Architecture (ISCA)*, pages 315–326, June 2008.

[13] Y. Luo, J. Rubio, L. K. John, P. Seshadri, and A. Mericas. Benchmarking internet servers on superscalar machines. *IEEE Computer*, 36(2):34–40, Feb. 2003.

[14] T. Mudge and U. Hölzle. Challenges and opportunities for extremely energy-efficient processors. *IEEE Micro*, 30(4):20–24, July 2010.

[15] R. Narayanan, B. Ozisikyilmaz, J. Zambreno, G. Memik, A. Choudhary, and J. Pisharath. MineBench: A benchmark suite for data mining workloads. In *Proceedings of the International Symposium on Computer Architecture (IISWC)*, pages 182–188, Oct. 2006.

[16] R. Nathuji, C. Isci, and E. Gorbatov. Exploiting platform heterogeneity for power efficient data centers. In *Proceedings of the International Conference on Autonomic Computing (ICAC)*, Oct. 2007.

[17] K. Olukotun, J. Laudon, and B. Lee. Mega-servers versus micro-blades for datacenter workloads. Panel debate at the Workshop on Architectural Concerns in Large Datacenters (ACLD), held with ISCA, June 2010.

[18] P. Ranganathan. Green clouds and black swans in the exascale era. Keynote at the IEEE International Symposium on Workload Characterization (IISWC), Oct. 2009.

[19] P. Ranganathan, K. Gharachorloo, S. V. Adve, and L. A. Barroso. Performance of database workloads on shared-memory systems with out-of-order processors. In *Proceedings of the Eighth International Conference on Architectural Support for Programming Languages and Operating Systems (ASPLOS)*, Oct. 1998.

[20] V. J. Reddi, B. C. Lee, T. Chilimbi, and K. Vaid. Web search using mobile cores: Quantifying and mitigating the price of efficiency. In *Proceedings of the International Symposium on Computer Architecture (ISCA)*, pages 26–36, June 2010.

[21] F. Ryckbosch, S. Polfliet, and L. Eeckhout. Fast, accurate and validated full-system software simulation of x86 hardware. *IEEE Micro*, 30(6):46–56, Nov/Dec 2010.

[22] V. Vasudevan, D. Andersen, M. Kaminsky, L. Tan, J. Franklin, and I. Moraru. Energy-efficient cluster computing with FAWN: Workloads and implications. In *Proceedings of the 1st International Conference on Energy-Efficient Computing and Networking (e-Energy)*, pages 195–204, Apr. 2010.

Predictive Coordination of Multiple On-Chip Resources for Chip Multiprocessors

Jian Chen and Lizy K. John
Department of Electrical and Computer Engineering
The University of Texas at Austin, Austin, Texas, USA
chenjian@mail.utexas.edu, ljohn@ece.utexas.edu

ABSTRACT

Efficient on-chip resource management is crucial for Chip Multi-processors (CMP) to achieve high resource utilization and enforce system-level performance objectives. Existing multiple resource management schemes either focus on intra-core resources or inter-core resources, missing the opportunity for exploiting the interaction between these two level resources. Moreover, these resource management schemes either rely on trial runs or complex on-line machine learning model to search for the appropriate resource allocation, which makes resource management inefficient and expensive. To address these limitations, this paper presents a predictive yet cost effective mechanism for multiple resource management in CMP. It uses a set of hardware-efficient online profilers and an analytical performance model to predict the application's performance with different intra-core and/or inter-core resource allocations. Based on the predicted performance, the resource allocator identifies and enforces near optimum resource partitions for each epoch without any trial runs. The experimental results show that the proposed predictive resource management framework could improve the weighted speedup of the CMP system by an average of 11.6% compared with the equal partition scheme, and 9.3% compared with existing reactive resource management scheme.

Categories and Subject Descriptors

C.4 [**Performance of Systems**]: Modeling techniques

General Terms

Performance

Keywords

Microprocessor, Resource management, Program characteristics, Performance modeling

1. INTRODUCTION

Chip Multiprocessors (CMP) have become mainstream platforms to improve the system throughput for multi-threaded and multi-programmed workloads in high-performance computing. However, their energy efficiency and end-performance is strongly dependent on management of the ever-increasing on-chip resources. It is well

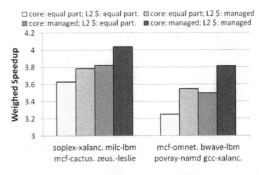

Figure 1: **Performance comparison for different resource management policies. Results are based on a quad-core CMP with per-core 2-way SMT (Detailed configurations in table 3).**

known that unrestricted sharing of inter-core resources such as L2 cache and memory bandwidth, can lead to destructive interference between the running threads [20], resulting in large performance variation and throughput degradation. Yet, managing inter-core resources alone is not sufficient as modern CMPs, such as Intel Nehalem processor [6], support per-core Simultaneous Multi-threading (SMT). Under such circumstance, the resource sharing in a CMP is compounded with both inter-core and intra-core resources, and any resource management scheme without coordinating between these two types of resources could lead to suboptimal system performance and inability to enforce system performance objectives.

As an example, Figure 1 shows the comparison of the weighted speedups for different combination of inter-core and intra-core resource management schemes in a quad-core 2-way SMT CMP system. Inter-core resource here is represented by L2 cache, and intra-core resources include issue queue (IQ), reorder buffer (ROB), and physical registers, all partitioned in proportion to each other [9]. As we can see, although separate management of L2 cache or intra-core resources improves the performance over the scheme of equal partition, it still misses a large amount of potential for improving system performance compared with the one that coordinates the allocation of L2 cache and intra-core resources. This is because the application's demands on different resources are correlated, and the change of the application's intra-core resource allocation could affect the its demands on inter-core resources. For example, the increase of ROB size may expose more memory level parallelism (MLP), and consequently increase the number of outstanding load misses. Since multiple outstanding load misses could hide the latency with each other, the average cache miss penalty is reduced, hence the requirement of L2 cache size is smaller in order to maintain the same performance. Therefore, coordinating between intra-core and inter-core resources is necessary to achieve high utilization and system performance in the CMP+SMT environment.

However, existing management schemes for multiple interacting resources focus on either intra-core resource partitioning for a single-core SMT processor or inter-core resource allocation for a chip multiprocessor. Cazorla et al. [8] proposed a resource sharing model to estimate the anticipated resource needs of a thread, and dynamically allocate shared resources to the thread that utilizes the resource most efficiently. Yet, this method only *indirectly* improves the performance and is unable to control the end performance. Choi and Yeung [9] improve the SMT resource partition by using the *direct* performance feedback to learn the desired resource allocation via *hill-climbing*. However, this method requires tentative runs to explore a large amount of trial resource partitions, fundamentally limiting its potential for performance improvement. Moreover, these methods only address intra-core resource allocation, and are not suitable for CMP inter-core resource management. To manage multiple inter-core resources, Bitirgen et al. [3] proposed an on-line machine learning model to capture the performance impact of multiple interacting resources. However, their model requires extensive training/re-training before it can accurately predict the application's performance, and incurs significant cost in hardware implementation and validation. Moreover, the original proposal of their model only addresses inter-core resource management, hence yields only suboptimal performance in the CMP+SMT scenario. Finally, while these existing policies recognize the importance of providing Quality-of-Service (QoS) on performance [13] for the co-executing applications, none of them provide a comprehensive solution to enforce performance objectives on a CMP platform where both inter-core and intra-core resources can vary simultaneously.

To address these limitations, this paper presents a comprehensive yet cost-effective resource management framework that can coordinate both intra-core and inter-core shared resources meanwhile simultaneously enforce QoS performance objectives. Unlike the existing resource management schemes, the proposed framework leverages an analytical performance model to predict the performance, and enforces resource allocations without any trial resource partitioning or training. By using the application characteristics dynamically collected during the application's execution, the performance model can update the performance prediction at each resource adaptation epoch, allowing the resource allocation to dynamically adapt to program phase changes. In particular, the contributions of this paper are as follows:

- We build a comprehensive yet cost-effective dynamic on-line profiler, and a performance model that utilizes the online profile to accurately predict the performance of the applications under different allocations of both inter-core and intra-core resources. We show that with about 22kilobytes of hardware, the performance model could predict the performance with an average relative error of 8.1%.

- We propose a framework for multiple resource management based on this performance model. This framework eliminates the need of trial-runs or training for dynamic resource allocation, and allows the enforcement of QoS performance objectives. We compare our approach with a set of resource management schemes from prior work, and show that on average, our approach improves the weighted speedup by 11.6% over the equal partition management scheme, and 9.3% over the reactive *hill-climbing* method [9].

The organization of this paper is as follows. Section 2 gives the overview of the proposed resource management framework. Section 3 describes the performance model. Section 4 shows the

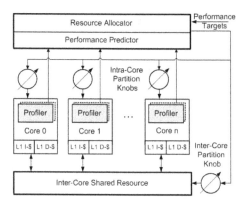

Figure 2: The overview of the predictive resource management framework.

structures of the online profilers. Section 5 presents the resource partitioning algorithm. Section 6 analyzes the hardware cost of the implementation. Section 7 describes the experiment methodology. Section 8 discusses the results. Section 9 describes the related works, and section 10 concludes of this paper.

2. OVERVIEW OF THE FRAMEWORK

The proposed framework for multiple resource management consists of three major components: the on-line profilers, the performance predictor, and the resource allocator, as shown in Figure 2. The on-line profiler non-invasively profiles each thread running on each core, and extracts the inherent characteristics of the thread for performance prediction. The performance predictor collects the profiled characteristics of the thread at the end of each resource allocation epoch, and estimates the thread's performance for different resource allocations. The resource allocator uses a built-in search engine to identify the appropriate resource allocations under the constraint of the given performance targets, and enforces the resource partition for each thread through a set of partition knobs.

The intra-core partition knobs regulate the allocation of the intra-core resources, which include IQ, ROB, and physical registers. These resources are interdependent, and are allocated *in proportion to* each other, similar with the way employed in the work by Choi et al. [9]. On the other hand, the inter-core partition knobs control the distribution of Last Level Cache (LLC) size and the power consumption of each core. In this paper, we assume that the CMP uses L2 cache as LLC and supports per-core Dynamic Voltage and Frequency Scaling (DVFS). In DVFS, the voltage and frequency are correlated, hence the power management can be achieved by controlling the operating frequency of each core meanwhile keeping the total power within the budget. This framework does not explicitly manage the memory bandwidth. Instead, it uses PAR-BS memory scheduling policy [19] to ensure the fairness and QoS of bandwidth usage.

While this framework addresses the resource allocation issues in the CMP+SMT scenario, it could also be applied in the cases where each core only supports single thread but can be dynamically reconfigured. Nevertheless, this paper focuses on the CMP platform with each core supporting 2-way SMT to demonstrate the effectiveness of the framework. In the following sections, we explain each component of the proposed framework in detail.

3. PERFORMANCE PREDICTOR

Predicting the performance impact of different resource allocations is the key step to avoid expensive trial runs and enable fast identification of appropriate resource distributions. Unlike the machine learning model proposed by Bitirgen et al. [3], our performance predictor is based on an analytical model, which does not require training/retraining and is easy to implement and validate.

3.1 Basic Performance Model

The performance model is based on the previously proposed interval analysis [15][11], which treats the exhibited Instruction-Per-Cycle (IPC) rate as a sustained ideal execution rate intermittently disrupted by long time miss events, such as, L2 cache misses and branch misprediction, etc. With the interval analysis, the total Cycle-Per-Instruction (CPI) of an application can be treated as the sum of three CPI components:

$$CPI_{total} = CPI_{exe} + CPI_{mem} + CPI_{other} \qquad (1)$$

CPI_{exe} represents the steady-state execution rate when the execution is free from any miss events. It is fundamentally constrained by the inherent Instruction Level Parallelism (ILP) of the application and the issue width of the processor. The ILP of the application is typically characterized by the critical dependency chain of the instructions in the instruction window. Assume an instruction window size w, and average critical dependency chain length l_w. On an idealized machine with unit execution latency, l_w indicates the average number of cycles required to execute the instructions in the instruction window, hence the average throughput is w/l_w. For a more realistic machine with non-unit execution latency, this number should be further divided by the average execution latency lat_{avg} according to Little's law [15]. Therefore, the average ILP, α_{avg}, can be obtained by $w/(lat_{avg} \cdot l_w)$, which also represents the steady-state execution rate if the instruction issue width is unlimited. However, for a realistic processor with limited issue width β, the ideal execution rate would be saturated at either the average ILP or the issue width, whichever is smaller. As a result, CPI_{exe} can be obtained by $1/min(\alpha_{avg}, \beta)$.

CPI_{mem} represents the penalty caused by the load misses in the last level cache (L2 cache in this paper). It can be calculated by the multiplication between the number of L2 load misses N_{L2}, and the average memory access latency lat_{mem}, assuming there are no multiple L2 cache misses outstanding. In practice, in order to hide the load miss latency, L2 caches are usually non-blocking and multiple L2 cache load misses could be outstanding. Under this circumstance, it has been proven that the average load miss latency is reduced to lat_{mem}/m_{ovp} [15], where m_{ovp} is the average number of outstanding load misses. Therefore, CPI_{mem} can be calculated by $lat_{mem} \cdot N_{L2}/(m_{ovp} \cdot N_{inst})$, where N_{inst} is the total number of retired instructions. Note that the term N_{L2}/m_{ovp} could also be treated as the number of L2 load misses that are not overlapping with each other, and hence is referred to as the *non-overlapped L2 load misses* N_{novp}.

CPI_{other} is the CPI component caused by other miss events, such as instruction cache misses, branch mispredictions, etc. In this paper, we do not change the resources related with these miss events. Therefore, this CPI component is approximately constant for an application with different resource allocations, as long as the application is in a stable execution phase. This CPI component can be obtained by transforming equation (1) to $CPI_{other} = CPI_{total} - CPI_{exe} - CPI_{mem}$, where CPI_{total} can be obtained from the performance counter, CPI_{ideal} and CPI_{mem} can be derived from the observed program characteristics. Once CPI_{other} has been deduced, it can be plugged into the performance model to estimate the performance of other cores. As a result, we have our basic performance model as follows:

$$CPI_{total} = \frac{1}{min(\alpha_{avg}, \beta)} + \frac{lat_{mem} \cdot N_{novp}}{N_{inst}} + CPI_{other}$$

With the basic performance model, the performance impact of different clock frequencies can be captured by converting the CPI to the delay in terms of absolute execution time. Hence, we have:

$$Delay = \frac{N_{inst}}{min(\alpha_{avg}, \beta) \cdot f} + t_{mem} \cdot N_{novp} + C_{other}/f \qquad (2)$$

where f is the operating frequency, t_{mem} represents the absolute memory access latency, and C_{other} refers to $CPI_{other} \cdot N_{inst}$, representing the cycles spent on other miss events.

3.2 Interaction of Co-executing Threads

The basic performance model only captures the performance of a thread when it is executed alone on a core and is free to access all available intra-core resources. However, when multiple threads simultaneously execute on a core, these threads will compete each other for the shared intra-core resources, causing interference on the performance of each co-executing thread. In practice, to achieve controllable performance for each thread, the shared intra-core resources are dynamically partitioned among the threads [9] except for the issue/dispatch width, which often remains as shared such that one thread can exploit the full execution bandwidth when the other thread is waiting for its miss events to be served [10]. In such case, the effective issue width of each thread may be significantly different from the physical issue width, and the basic performance model needs to be augmented accordingly.

Assuming a processor with 2-way SMT and per-thread retirement capability, the effective execution rate of the thread can be estimated by analyzing the ILP of the co-executing threads. For example, if the ILP of thread T_0 (referred to as α_{T0}) and the ILP of thread T_1 (referred to as α_{T1}) are both larger than the issue width β of the processor core, on average each thread can execute at a rate equal to half of the issue width. If we could further obtain the fraction of the time that T_0 is in long latency miss event, the effective execution rate of T_1 can be derived by considering the additional execution bandwidth T_1 has during that fraction of time. Similarly, if α_{T0} and α_{T1} are both smaller than β but the sum of these two is larger than β, on average the effective issue width of a thread is determined by the occupancy of its ready instructions: $\alpha_{T0} \cdot \beta/(\alpha_{T0} + \alpha_{T1})$ for T_0 and $\alpha_{T1} \cdot \beta/(\alpha_{T0} + \alpha_{T1})$ for T_1. By considering the fraction of the time in serving the long latency miss event, the effective execution rate can be also derived. Table 1 summarizes the calculation of the effective execution rate under different scenarios. These values are used as the background steady-state execution rates of the performance model in the presence of SMT. Note that these estimations are based on the assumption that IQ uses the oldest-first policy to dispatch ready instructions.

3.3 Non-overlapped L2 Load Misses

For a given application, the number of non-overlapped L2 Load Misses (LLM) is affected by two factors: the L2 cache size, which determines the total number of L2 load misses, and the ROB size, which controls the amount of exposed MLP. Therefore, when both ROB size and L2 cache size can be reconfigured, their compounded effect has to be modeled in order to estimate the number of non-overlapped LLM.

To do so, we introduce the *load histogram* to hold the statistics of the number of loads occurred within a certain ROB size. Specifically, each time when the number of retired instructions equals the given ROB size, the number of loads observed in those retired instructions is used as an index to the load histogram, and corresponding entry in the load histogram is incremented by one. With the load histogram, we are able to model the "*window*" effect the ROB has on the non-overlapped LLM. As illustrated in Pseudocode 1, if the calculated number of LLM in an instruction window is less

Table 1: Estimation of Average Execution Rate for 2-Way SMT

Cases:	Effective Average Execution Rate		Notes
	Thread 0 (T_0)	Thread 1 (T_1)	
$\alpha_{T0} < \beta, \alpha_{T1} < \beta,$ $\alpha_{T0} + \alpha_{T1} < \beta$	α_{T0}	α_{T1}	
$\alpha_{T0} < \beta, \alpha_{T1} < \beta,$ $\alpha_{T0} + \alpha_{T1} > \beta$	$\frac{\alpha_{T0}*\beta}{\alpha_{T0}+\alpha_{T1}} * (1 - f_{T1}) + \alpha_{T0} * f_{T1}$	$\frac{\alpha_{T1}*\beta}{\alpha_{T0}+\alpha_{T1}} * (1 - f_{T0}) + \alpha_{T1} * f_{T0}$	α_{T0}: average ILP of thread 0 α_{T1}: average ILP of thread 1 β: issue width of the core f_{T0}: the fraction of time that thread 0 is in long latency events f_{T1}: the fraction of time that thread 1 is in long latency events
$\alpha_{T0} > \beta, \alpha_{T1} < \beta,$ $\alpha_{T0} + \alpha_{T1} < 2\beta$	$\frac{\alpha_{T0}*\beta}{\alpha_{T0}+\alpha_{T1}} * (1 - f_{T1}) + \beta * f_{T1}$	$\frac{\alpha_{T1}*\beta}{\alpha_{T0}+\alpha_{T1}} * (1 - f_{T0}) + \alpha_{T1} * f_{T0}$	
$\alpha_{T0} > \beta, \alpha_{T1} < \beta,$ $\alpha_{T0} + \alpha_{T1} > 2\beta$	$\frac{2*\beta-\alpha_{T1}}{2.0} * (1 - f_{T1}) + \beta * f_{T1}$	$\frac{\alpha_{T1}}{2.0} * (1 - f_{T0}) + \alpha_{T1} * f_{T0}$	
$\alpha_{T0} < \beta, \alpha_{T1} > \beta,$ $\alpha_{T0} + \alpha_{T1} < 2\beta$	$\frac{\alpha_{T0}*\beta}{\alpha_{T0}+\alpha_{T1}} * (1 - f_{T1}) + \alpha_{T0} * f_{T1}$	$\frac{\alpha_{T1}*\beta}{\alpha_{T0}+\alpha_{T1}} * (1 - f_{T0}) + \beta * f_{T0}$	
$\alpha_{T0} < \beta, \alpha_{T1} > \beta,$ $\alpha_{T0} + \alpha_{T1} > 2\beta$	$\frac{\alpha_{T0}}{2.0} * (1 - f_{T1}) + \beta * f_{T1}$	$\frac{2*\beta-\alpha_{T0}}{2.0} * (1 - f_{T0}) + \beta * f_{T0}$	
$\alpha_{T0} > \beta, \alpha_{T1} > \beta$	$\frac{\beta}{2.0} * (1 - f_{T1}) + \beta * f_{T1}$	$\frac{\beta}{2.0} * (1 - f_{T0}) + \beta * f_{T0}$	

Pseudocode 1 Non-overlapped L2 Load Miss Estimation

```
#def N_l //maximum number of loads in the ROB size i
#def N_novp //number of non-overlapped L2 load misses
#def MLP_i //average load MLP rate in ROB size i
#def ld_miss_rate //L2 load miss rate
#def ld_hist_i[N_l] //load histogram for ROB size i

1   for ( j=0; j < N_l; j++ )
2     if (j * ld_miss_rate < 1)
3         temp = ld_hist_i[j] * j * ld_miss_rate;
4     else
5         if (j * ld_miss_rate/MLP_i < 1)
6           temp = ld_hist_i[j];
7         else
8           temp = ld_hist_i[j] * j * ld_miss_rate/MLP_i;
9         end if
10    end if
11    temp_novp = temp_novp + temp;
12  end for
13  N_novp = ceiling(temp_novp);
```

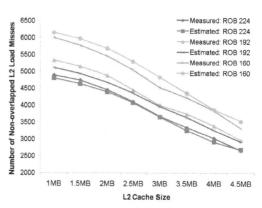

Figure 3: Comparison of the estimated and measured non-overlapped L2 load misses for SPECCPU2006 program *libquantum*. Data are collected at a 2M instructions interval.

than 1 (line 2), there is no overlapped LLM and MLP is not considered. Otherwise, this number is divided by MLP. A result less than 1 (line 5) means all L2 load misses are overlapped and the number of non-overlapped LLM is 1. The total number of non-overlapped LLM can be obtained by accumulating these values in all cases. By using a set of load histograms with each dedicated to a certain ROB size, we are able to estimate the non-overlapped LLM for different ROB sizes. On the other hand, the L2 load miss rates for different L2 cache sizes can be estimated with the stack distance model, which is explained in section 4.3.

Figure 3 shows the accuracy of the estimation technique for program *libquantum* under different ROB and L2 cache sizes. We observe a close match between the measured and the estimated non-overlapped L2 load misses when both ROB size and L2 cache size vary. We also validate this technique using other SPEC CPU2006 programs, and we observe the average error rate of the estimation is 12.2%. Most of the errors are caused by the artifact that a small number of L2 load misses leads to a large relative error even though the absolute difference between the measured and the estimated is small. However, since a small number of L2 load misses means a small impact on the overall CPI, the influence of the estimation error passed down to the estimated CPI is also insignificant.

4. ONLINE PROFILER

The proposed performance model requires a set of program characteristics from which the key parameters for the model can be derived. These characteristics include: a). the critical dependency chain, for deriving the average ILP; b). the dependent load miss statistics, for estimating the memory level parallelism under differ-

ent ROB sizes; c). the stack distance statistics [18], for estimating the number of L2 load misses with different L2 cache sizes. In this section, we present a set of non-invasive and cost-effective online profilers to dynamically extract these characteristics during the application's execution.

4.1 Critical Dependency Chain Profiler

The critical dependency chain in this paper refers to the longest instruction dependency chain in the instruction window. To capture the length of the critical dependency chain, we propose a token-passing technique inspired by Fields et al's work [12]. A token is a field in each issue queue entry that keeps track of the dependency chain length, as shown in Figure 4(a). When an instruction enters the issue queue, its token field is set to zero; when an instruction leaves the issue queue for execution, its token field is incremented by one. The incremented token is propagated along with the result tag of the instruction. When the instruction finishes execution and its result tag matches the source tag of the waiting instruction in the issue queue, the propagated token also compares the token of the waiting instruction. The larger one between these two is stored in the token field of the waiting instruction. Hence, by the time an instruction is ready for execution, its token holds the length of the longest dependency chain for this instruction.

For each thread, the critical dependency chain profiler compares the token of every issued instruction of that thread, and keeps track of the maximum observed token, which is further used as an index to the critical dependency chain histogram. The histogram is controlled by an instruction counter that monitors the number of issued instructions. When this number reaches the interested ROB size, the histogram entry indexed with the maximum observed token is

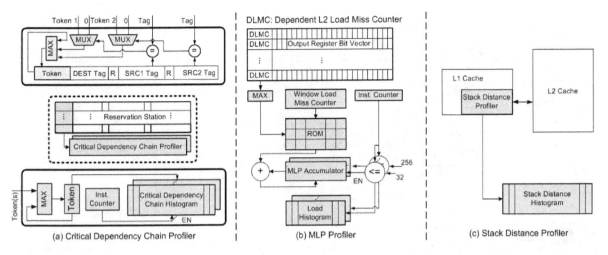

Figure 4: The structure of the online profilers.

incremented by 1. Meanwhile the register that holds the maximum token is reset to zero. Consequently, the critical dependency chain histogram holds the information of the longest dependency chain length for each instruction window. At the end of each epoch, this histogram is used to calculated the average length of the critical dependency chains, and then reset to zeros for the next epoch.

In order to obtain the dependency chain length for different ROB sizes, we need a set of critical dependency chain histograms, with one histogram dedicated to one specific ROB size. All histograms share one instruction counter to count the number of issued instructions. When the number equals one of the interested ROB sizes, the corresponding histogram is updated, and the counter continues counting until it equals the largest ROB size. Then, the counter is reset and starts counting from zero again. In this way, the token fields designed to profile for the largest ROB size can be reused by multiple histograms for different ROB sizes.

4.2 MLP Profiler

The MLP profiler is to capture the L2 load miss parallelism for different ROB sizes. As shown Figure 4(b), this profiler contains a L2 *Load Miss Event Table* (LMET), which has a *Dependent Load Miss Counter* (DLMC) and a *Output Register Bit Vector* (ORBV) in each table entry, similar with the one proposed by Eyerman and Eeckhout [10]. Each time a load that missed L2 cache is retired, a new entry in the table is created and the corresponding DLMC is updated with the number of L2 load misses that this load is dependent on in the current window. Meanwhile, the ORBV is initialized by setting '1' to the bit indexed by the output register ID of this load, and setting '0' to the remaining bits. Each retired instruction thereafter needs to check its dependency on this long-latency load by looking up the ORBV bit at the position corresponding to the input register ID of the retired instruction. A '1' in this bit position indicates this instruction depends on the previous long-latency load, and hence the bit indexed by the output register ID of the retired instruction is also set to '1'; whereas a '0' means this instruction is independent with the previous long-latency loads, and no further actions is needed. This process continues until the number of analyzed instructions reaches the largest ROB size of interest, in this paper, 256, and then the table is reset.

Besides the load miss event table, the profiler also has a MLP lookup table, which is a Read-Only-Memory (ROM) structure populated with pre-computed MLP values. The MLP value is obtained by dividing the its column index with the row index, and is represented in a 8-bit fixed-point format with 4 bits for integer and 4

bits for fraction. Each time when the analyzed instruction number equals an interested ROB size R, the MLP table is looked up by the largest DLMC in LMET and the Window Load Miss Counter (WLMC) that holds the number of L2 load misses occurred in the ROB window. The corresponding MLP value is then added to the MLP accumulator associated with the interested ROB size R. At the end of each epoch, the average load MLP rate of ROB size R can be obtained by dividing the values in the MLP accumulator with the number of accumulations occurred on this accumulator in the epoch.

The profiler also has a load histogram for each possible ROB size. The histogram collects the number of loads occurred in each ROB window, and is used to estimate the non-overlapped L2 load misses.

4.3 Stack Distance Profiler

To estimate the number of L2 load misses for different cache sizes, we employ the previously proposed Mattson's stack distance histogram at the granularity of cache ways [18][20]. This stack distance model exploits the inclusion property of Least Recently Used (LRU) replacement policy, i.e., the content of an N-way cache line is a subset of the content of any cache line with associativity larger than N. As an example, figure 5 shows the MSA histogram of program *xalancbmk* on an 8-way associative cache, organized from MRU position to LRU position. For caches with its associativity reduced to 6-ways (dash line in the figure), the data with stack distance larger than 6 could not be hold in the cache, generating cache misses. Therefore, with the stack distance histogram, we are able to estimate the cache miss rate for any cache ways less than the profiled ways and consequently derive the number of L2 misses.

Profiling the stack distance requires an Auxiliary Tag Directory (ATD) and hit counters for each cache set [20]. The ATD has the same associativity with L2 cache in the chip and uses LRU replacement; whereas the hit counter counts the number of hits on each cache way. To reduce the hardware overhead caused by ATD, we employ the Dynamic Set Sampling (DSS) technique, which essentially uses a few sets (in our case 32 sets) to approximate the entire cache behavior [20].

4.4 Profiling for Other Parameters

Other parameters in the performance model can be obtained from the standard performance counters. For example, the performance counters in Intel® Core™ architecture [1] are able to provide the instruction mix and cache hit/miss statistics. With these statistics,

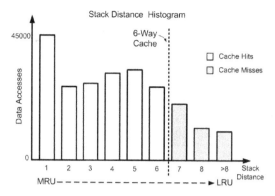

Figure 5: Stack Distance Histogram of SPEC CPU2006 program *xalancbmk*.

the average latency lat_{avg} can be derived by weight-averaging the percentage of each instruction type with the corresponding execution latency. Note that the load that misses L1 cache but hits in L2 cache is treated as an instruction with long execution latency.

5. ALLOCATION ALGORITHMS

With the online profilers and the performance predictor, the performance of the application under different resource allocations can be estimated by simply evaluating an equation, which fundamentally eliminates the need of trial runs and significantly improves the quality and efficiency of multiple resource management.

Pseudocode 2 Coordinated Predictive Hill-Climbing

```
   #def N_tt //total number of threads
   #def N_res //the number of resources independently partitioned
   #def delta //resource partition granularity
   #def P_th //convergence threshold
   #def part[0 : N_tt][0 : N_res] //the resource partition array
   #def max_id(A, n) //get the index of the largest value in A[0:n]
   #def max(A, n) //get the largest value in A[0:n]
   #def perf_eval(part)
   //estimate the overall performance for resource array part
   #def perf(part, i)
   //estimate the performance of thread i for resource array part

1  old_part_perf = perf_eval(part);
2  copy part[0 : N_tt][0 : [N_res] to temp_part[0 : N_tt][0 : N_res];
3  while(TRUE)
4    for( i = 0; i < N_res; i++)
5      for( j = 0; j < N_tt; j++ )
6        temp_part[i][j] = part[i][j] + delta;
7        pos_perf[j] = perf(temp_part, j);
8        temp_part[i][j] = part[i][j] − delta;
9        neg_perf[j] = perf(temp_part, j);
10     end for
11     pos_tid[i] = max_id(pos_perf, N_tt);
12     neg_tid[i] = max_id(neg_perf, N_tt);
13     if(max(pos_perf, N_tt) > max(neg_perf, N_tt))
14       part[pos_tid[i]][i] = part[pos_tid[i]][i] + delta;
15       part[neg_tid[i]][i] = part[neg_tid[i]][i] − delta;
16     end if
17   end for
18   new_part_perf = perf_eval(part);
19   if ( abs(new_part_perf − old_part_perf) < P_th) break;
20   else old_part_perf = new_part_perf;
21 end while
```

To efficiently manage multiple resources, this paper presents a predictive and coordinated resource management algorithm that leverages the performance predictor to identify the optimum resource distribution for the workload. As shown in Pseudocode 2, the proposed algorithm uses *hill-climbing* to search for the appropriate re-

source distribution, hence the name *Coordinated Predictive Hill-Climbing* (CPHC). Specifically, it first uses the performance model to evaluate the performance of each thread as one of the resources is incremented or decremented by a certain amount *delta* (line 5 to line 10). It then moves *delta* amount of the resource from the thread that has the lowest performance degradation to the thread that benefits most from the additional resource, provided that the overall performance gain is positive (line 13 to line 16). This process iterates through different resources, and repeats itself until the estimated performance reaches the given target or no noticeable performance gain is attainable (line 19). In this way, this algorithm explores the resource allocation in the positive-gradient direction, and hence achieves fast convergence.

In this algorithm, power as a resource is *indirectly* managed by controlling the operating frequency of each core in a CMP. Specifically, for a quad-core CMP, the total power consumption can be written as $a_1 v_1^2 f_1 + a_2 v_2^2 f_2 + a_3 v_3^2 f_3 + a_4 v_4^2 f_4$, where v_i and $f_i (i = 1..4)$ are the voltage and frequency of core i respectively, and $a_i (i = 1..4)$ is the product of the activity factor and the effective capacitance for core i. In a fully-loaded CMP system, the power is usually consumed as close to the given power budget as possible to maximize performance, and $a_1, .., a_4$ are generally very close to each other. Therefore, the problem of power management can be transformed to the problem of allocating frequencies such that $v_1^2 f_1 + v_2^2 f_2 + v_3^2 f_3 + v_4^2 f_4$ remains constant. Note that the frequency and voltage are correlated with each other under DVFS, and for a given frequency, the corresponding voltage can be found by looking up a table. Therefore, by controlling the frequencies, the power can be allocated the same way as other resources.

Besides this proposed algorithm, we also evaluate a set of other resource allocation algorithms for comparison, which include:

Equal Partition: This algorithm distributes all shared resources equally among the threads. Specifically, the inter-core resources are equally partitioned for all active threads in the CMP, and the intra-core resources are equally partitioned for the threads that are simultaneously executed in the core. This algorithm is used as the baseline management scheme in this paper.

Coordinated Reactive Hill-Climbing (CRHC): Like the proposed predictive scheme, this algorithm also attempts to manage both intra-core and inter-core resources, but without a performance prediction model. Therefore, it has to rely on trial runs to explore the gradient direction for resource allocation. Specifically, the algorithm randomly selects two threads (for inter-core resource) or a pair of co-executing threads (for intra-core resource), tentatively moves *delta* amount of resource from one thread to the other, and runs the workload for one epoch. It then moves the resource in opposite direction for these two threads, and runs the workload for another epoch. The resource allocation that gives the higher performance during these two trial runs is enforced in the next epoch. The process keeps on repeating itself for different resources and different threads.

Intra-core Reactive Hill-Climbing (Intra-RHC): This algorithm is similar with the one proposed by Choi et al. [9], and it uses trial runs to search for the appropriate resource allocations. The resource adaptation only happens on the intra-core level, and the inter-core resources are equally partition for all threads.

Inter-core Reactive Hill-Climbing (Inter-RHC): This algorithm is similar with CRHC except that the resource adaptation only happens on the inter-core level, and the intra-core resources are equally partition for the co-executing threads in the core.

Oracle: This algorithm assumes the application's performance under different resource allocation in the next epoch is known *a priori*. It uses these *future* performance data to enforce the resource allocation that gives highest performance in the next epoch. While it is unrealistic in practice, it sets an upper bound of the potential performance improvement.

6. IMPLEMENTATION COST ANALYSIS

Both the on-line profilers and the resource allocator are implemented in hardware, and they are the major sources of the implementation cost in the proposed framework. The cost of the profilers depends on the ROB size, the L2 cache size, the number of SMT threads, as well as the partition granularity. Assuming a 256-entry ROB with 32-entry partition granularity, 160 issue queue size, 32-bit physical address space, 16MB 32-way shared L2 cache, and 2-way SMT, the total hardware cost amounts to approximately 22KB, as shown in Table 2. Under this circumstance, the dimension of MLP lookup table is set to 16-by-16, and the profilers need 8 critical dependency chain histograms and 8 load histograms since there are 8 possible ROB sizes. Note that the hardware cost may be further reduced by using a smaller number of histogram counters based on the observation that the critical dependency chain length is far smaller than the ROB size. However, even without such optimization, the hardware overhead incurred by the online profilers only amounts to 0.14% of the 16MB L2 cache size. Note also that these profilers are not in the critical path, and does not affect the application's execution.

Table 2: Hardware Cost of the Online Profilers

Profiler	Components	Costs
Critical Dependency Chain Profiler	token fields	8*256 bits
	multiplexors, comparator	(8*2+8)*160bits
	histogram counters	16*256*8*2bits
MLP Profiler	LMET	(4+32)*16*2bits
	MLP accumulator	16*8*2 bits
	WLMC	5*8*2 bits
	MLP lookup table	16*16*8 bits
	comparators	8*8*2 bits
	load histogram	16*256*8*2 bits
Stack Distance Profiler	valid bits per ATD entry	1 bits
	addr. bits per ATD entry	12 bits
	total ATD cost (32 sampled sets, 2 threads)	(3+1+12)* 32*32*2 bits
	Hit Counters	16*32*2 bits
Total Cost of Profilers per core		21812 Bytes

On the other hand, the cost of the resource allocator is mainly caused by converting the profiled histograms to the parameters for the performance model and searching for the appropriate resource allocation with the performance model. For example, to obtain the average critical dependency chain length from the dependency chain histogram, approximately 300 multiply-add operations are required. To further quantify the hardware cost, we implemented the resource allocator in Verilog HDL, and synthesized it into a netlist. The design employs pipelining so that arithmetic units can be reused. Overall, it has two adders, two multipliers and one divider, all in 32-bit fixed-point. The total area of the resource allocator is estimated to be $0.632\ mm^2$ under 65nm technology. Each performance estimation requires 20 cycles to complete, and the search process takes less than 30000 cycles before it converges (we enforce convergence if the iterations is larger than 20). Since the resource allocation is made only once every epoch, the latency can be completely hidden by starting resource exploration procedure several thousands of instructions before the end of the epoch.

7. EXPERIMENT METHODOLOGY

7.1 Simulation Platform

We use Simics [16], extended with the Gems toolset [17], to simulate a quad-core SPARCv9 CMP system running under OpenSo-

laris operating system. Each core in the CMP is a 4-issue out-of-order processor and supports 2-way SMT with ICOUNT [23] instruction fetch policy. The simulated CMP system also contains a detailed memory subsystem model, which includes an inter-core last-level cache network and a detailed memory controller. Table 3 lists the configurations of the CMP system in detail. We use Wattch [4] to estimate the dynamic power of the processor as well as the resource allocator, and use Cacti 5 [22] to estimate the leakage power on caches and other SRAM structures in the core. We use Orion [24] to estimate the power on the interconnection network of last level caches. These estimated power data are used in evaluating the efficiency of the system.

Table 3: Configurations of the CMP system

	Parameter	Configurations
Core	Max. Clock Frequency	4GHz
	Fetch/Issue/Commit	4/4/4
	Ld/St Units	2/2
	I-ALU	4(fused multiply/add for I-ALU)
	FP Units/FP Multipliers	4/2
	ROB size/Issue Queue	256/160
	Load/Store Queue Size	64/64
	Branch Predictor	YAGS, 16 PHT bits, 10 Tag bits
	Physical Register Number	380
Cache	L1 I-Cache/D-Cache	32KB, 2-way, 64B, LRU, 1 cycle
	L2 Cache size	16MB shared
	L2 Cache parameter	32-way, 64B, LRU, 12 cycle
	L2 MSHR Entry	32
	Coherence Protocol	Directory-based MOESI
Memory	Size/Model	4GB/DDR2-800
	Controller	PAR-BS policy [19]
	Organization	8 banks per rank, 2 ranks per DIMM

The ROB in the core is partitioned at the granularity of 32 entries. Other intra-core resources such as issue queue size and physical register number are partitioned in proportion to the ROB size. Each thread is guaranteed to have at least 32 entries of ROB size. The L2 cache size is partitioned at the granularity of cache ways, with each thread allocated with at least one cache way. The CMP system supports per-core DVFS, with the frequency of each core ranging from 2GHz to 4GHz at the step of 0.1GHz. We assume that the CMP system reaches the power budget when it is fully loaded and each core is running at 3GHz.

Table 4: Workloads and Their Characteristics

Workload Mix	Symbol	Category
povray, calculix, sjeng, hmmer perlbench, wrf, dealII, tonto	pcshpwdt	ILP
gcc, povray, astar, calculix gobmk, hmmer, bzip2, dealII	gpacghbd	
astar, bzip2, gobmk, povray sjeng, perlbench, dealII, gamess	abgpspdg	
namd, gcc, gromacs, perlbench h264ref, tonto, sphinx3, sjeng	nggphtss	
mcf,omnetpp,bwaves,lbm povray, namd, gcc, xalancbmk	moblpngx	MIX
dealII, sjeng, libquantum, omnetpp povray, soplex, perlbench, milc	dslopspm	
libquantum, cactusADM, xalancbmk calculix,wrf,mcf, soplex, omnetpp	lcxcwmso	
leslie3d,tonto,sphinx3, omnetpp hmmer, libquanutm, astar, zeusmp	ltsohlaz	
soplex, xalancbmk, milc, lbm mcf, cactusADM, zeusmp, leslie3d	sxmlmczl	MEM
leslie3d,soplex, zeusmp, bwaves wrf, cactusADM, xalancbmk, lbm	lszbwcxl	
lbm, milc, xalancbmk, leslie3d zeusmp, wrf, mcf, soplex	lmxlzwms	
milc, xalancbmk, mcf, cactusADM soplex, leslie3d, bwaves, wrf	mxmcslbw	

7.2 Workloads

The workload of the experiment is composed of the programs from SPEC CPU2006 benchmark suite [2], with each compiled

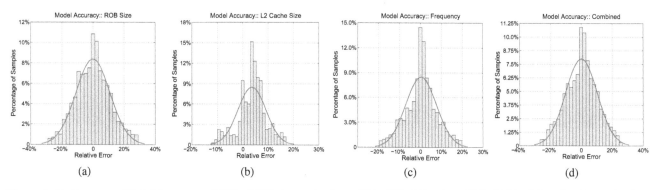

(a)   (b)   (c)   (d)

Figure 6: Performance Model Accuracy. (a)The ROB size varies from 32 to 256 at the step of 32. (b)The L2 cache size varies from 512KB to 4MB at the step of 512KB. (c) Frequency varies from 2GHz to 4GHz at the step of 0.1GHz. (d) 500 random configurations when all three resources vary simultaneously.

to SPARC ISA. We construct 12 heterogeneous multiprogrammed workloads, each containing 8 programs, as shown in Table 4. These workloads are grouped into three categories: CPU-intensive (high-ILP), memory-intensive, and the mixture of both. Each workload will be running on the aforementioned CMP systems. For each run, we fast-forward the workload for 4 billion instructions to reach its steady state execution, and then use the next 100 million instructions to warmup the cache subsystem. We then simulate the full system for 200M instructions to evaluate the performance of various resource allocation policies.

7.3 Metrics

The metric we use to evaluate the system performance is the weighted speedup, which is defined as $\sum_i IPC_i^{shared}/IPC_i^{alone}$ [21]. To measure the efficiency of the system, we use the metric $mips^3/W$, which is inverse to energy-delay-square (ED^2) and has been accepted as the efficiency metric for high-performance systems [5].

8. EVALUATION

8.1 Model Accuracy

The accuracy of the performance model could largely impact the effectiveness of the proposed resource management framework. To evaluate the model accuracy, we run every SPEC CPU2006 program on a simulated processor for an interval of 2 million instructions, and use the performance model to estimate the program's CPI on processors with different resource configurations. Meanwhile, we also simulate the program on those processors for the same interval and compare the observed CPI values with the estimated ones. Figure 6(a)-(c) show the accuracy when only one resource changes. As we can see, the relative error between the estimated CPI and the observed one follows normal distribution. The average errors (using absolute values) are 8.7% for different ROB sizes, 5.3% for different L2 cache sizes, and 6.7% for different frequencies, indicating the performance model tracks well with the observed performance when only one resource varies its configuration. Figure 6(d) further shows the relative estimation error for 500 random configurations when all three resources vary simultaneously. The average CPI estimation error in this scenario is 8.1%, and the largest one is 26.7%. We also observe that this relative error follows normal distribution.

8.2 Epoch Size Sensitivity

The epoch size determines the frequency of resource adaptation during the execution of the workload, and can indirectly influence

the overall performance of our resource management framework. Figure 7 shows the performance trend of three workloads as the epoch size increases from 0.5 million to 5 million instructions. We observe that as the epoch size increases, the weighted speedup first increases, then reaches a plateau, and then gradually decreases. This is because with a relatively small epoch size, the on-line profilers may not be fully warmed up to capture the corresponding program characteristics, which could affect the accuracy of the performance predictor, and in turn pulls down the performance of the resource management. This is particularly true for the stack distance profiler since this profiler employs set sampling technique, which provides a good accuracy only when it has been exercised with sufficient amount of L2 accesses. On the other hand, a large epoch size would miss the opportunity for adapting resource distribution to some finer grain program phases, which also degrades the end performance. In this work, we find that 2 million instruction is a reasonable epoch size that balances the accuracy of the performance predictor and the responsiveness of the resource allocation.

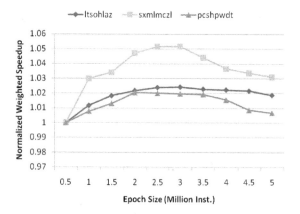

Figure 7: Performance impact of epoch size.

Note that such choice of epoch size is based on the assumption that different voltage and frequency pairs can be enforced instantaneously. In practice, this is not true because it may take the voltage regulator hundreds of micro-seconds to stabilize voltage. Under such circumstance, the epoch size need to incorporate this additional time for voltage regulation.

8.3 Performance & Efficiency

Figure 8(a) shows the comparison of the weighted speedups between different resource allocation policies. As expected, equal partition policy usually yields lowest weighted speedup among all

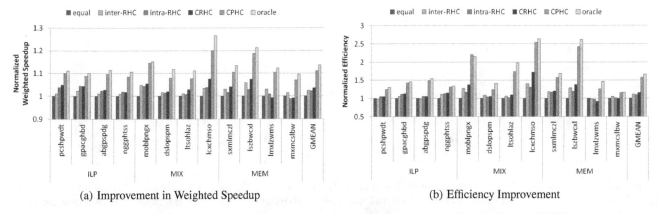

(a) Improvement in Weighted Speedup   (b) Efficiency Improvement

Figure 8: Performance and efficiency comparison for different resource management policies.

the policies investigated in this paper. Inter-RHC and Intra-RHC improves the performance over equal partition policy as it dynamically adapts allocations for either inter-core or intra-core resources. CRHC further improves the weighted speedup, as it attempts to adjust the resource allocation on both inter-core and intra-core level. However, for some workloads, these reactive allocation policies may leads to inferior performance compared with equal partition. This is because they rely on the trial runs to search for the appropriate resource allocation, which means workloads may spend some trial runs in an inappropriate resource allocation. That also explains why these dynamic policies only have a small improvement over the equal partition policy. Our proposed predictive hill-climbing scheme avoids trial runs, and achieves an average of 11.6% over the baseline scheme and 9.3% over the CRHC scheme. In general, CPHC yields higher speedup in the workloads that belong to the MIX category because in such workloads, the resource requirements of the programs are more diversified, resulting in higher potential for resource management. Compared with the oracle scheme, the CPHC has approximately 3% less speedup. This is attributed to: (a) the imperfection of the performance model;(b) the lack of future knowledge of program phase behavior; (c) hill-climbing being trapped in local optima.

Figure 8(b) further shows the efficiency improvements for different resource allocation policies. We observe that CPHC has an average efficiency improvement of 57.4% over the baseline, and 36.5% over CRHC.

8.4 QoS Enforcement

The QoS target is defined as the target IPC relative to the alone-execution IPC, expressed in the form of percentages [13][7]. The proposed resource management framework can convert this QoS target into resource usage requirements [13], thereby enforce QoS for an application by regulating the amount of allocated resources. The quality of such QoS enforcement is demonstrated in Figure 9, where for each workload, only one program is enforced with the QoS targets and the remaining programs do not have QoS objectives. The resource allocator attempts to satisfy the QoS target for that program and maximize the overall performance for the remaining programs. As we can see, the relative IPCs of the programs keep a good track of the QoS targets. For some programs, such as *povray*, *gcc*, and *astar*, the relative IPC at the 20% QoS target is significantly off the target. This is because even with the minimum allocation on each resource, the relative performance of these programs are still much larger than 20%. Hence, such QoS target is *ill-suited* for these programs. Overall, we observe that the proposed framework could enforce QoS within 6.1% for 80% target, 6.7%

for 60% target, and 5.9% for 40% target. Hence, this framework is suitable for the enforcement of elastic QoS objectives [13].

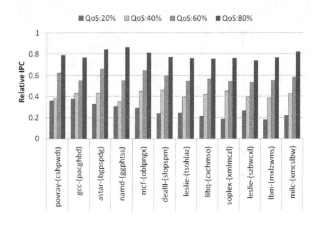

Figure 9: QoS targets enforcement.

9. RELATED WORK

Dynamic Resource Partition for SMT Threads: Cazorla et al. [8] proposed a DCRA mechanism to dynamically allocate shared resources to each thread in an SMT processor. Their method uses a resource sharing model to estimate the thread's anticipated resource needs, and allocate resources to the thread that utilizes the resource most efficiently. Like other SMT resource sharing policies [23], this method improves the SMT performance only *indirectly*, not only potentially missing opportunities for further performance improvement but also unable to control the end performance. Choi and Yeung [9] improves the SMT resource distribution by *directly* using the performance feedback to partition the resources for a specific performance goal. Their method requires a number of trial resource partitions before it learns the appropriate resource distribution, fundamentally limiting its potential for performance improvement. In contrast, our work uses an analytical model to predict the performance, hence eliminating the need of trial partitions. In addition, our work coordinates both intra-core and inter-core resources, whereas previous SMT resource partition techniques only consider the intra-core resources.

CMP Shared Resource Partition: Qureshi and Patt [20] propose to partition the last level cache to prevent negative interference between threads and maximize the utilization of the cache capacity. However, this utility based cache partitioning scheme is only applicable to cache, and can not manage the partition of multiple resources. Isci et al. [14] propose to manage global power by estimating the performance impact of per-core DVFS with an analytical model. Again, their proposal is only applicable to managing power alone. Bitirgen et al. [3] proposed a technique based on online machine learning to manage multiple CMP resources. However, the on-line machine learning model requires extensive training and retraining before it can accurately predict the application's performance. Moreover, it incurs significant hardware cost and is hard to implement and validate. On the contrary, our scheme uses cost-effective online profilers and an analytical model to predict the performance. It does not require any training and could manage the partition of multiple inter-core and intra-core resources.

Resource Partition for QoS: Guo et al. [13] propose a mechanism to support QoS in CMP by controlling the L2 cache allocation. Cazorla et al. [7] leverages OS-processor interaction to achieve QoS in SMT processors. These works address QoS problem separately at either inter-core or intra-core level. In contrast, our framework provides QoS support by coordinating both inter-core and intra-core resources.

10. CONCLUSIONS

This paper presents a showcase study of using an on-line analytical model to manage multiple interacting resources for throughput and QoS. In this paper, we find that for a Chip Multiprocessors (CMP) supporting per-core Simultaneous Multithreading (SMT), both intra-core and inter-core resources need to be managed simultaneously in order to achieve high resource utilization and deliver controllable performance. We thereby present a predictive resource management framework that coordinates both inter-core and intra-core resources. This framework uses a set of hardware-efficient online profilers and an analytical performance model to predict the application's performance with different intra-core and/or inter-core resource allocations. Based on the predicted performance, the resource allocator identifies and enforces near optimum resource partitions for each epoch without any trial runs. Our study shows that the proposed framework improves weighted speedup by an average of 11.6% compared with equal partition scheme, and 9.3% compared with the learning-based resource manager. We also show this framework enforces QoS targets within 6.7%. We believe that this predictive resource management framework offers a promising way to coordinate both inter-core and intra-core resources in CMPs.

11. ACKNOWLEDGMENT

The authors would like to thank anonymous reviewers for their valuable feedback. This work is supported in part through the NSF Award number 0702694. Any opinions, findings, and conclusions or recommendations expressed herein are those of the authors and do not necessarily reflect the views of NSF.

12. REFERENCES

[1] Intel® 64 and IA-32 Architectures Software Developer's Manual, Volume 3B: System Programming Guide.

[2] Spec cpu2006 benchmark suit. In http://www.spec.org.

[3] R. Bitirgen, E. Ipek, and J. F. Martinez. Coordinated management of multiple interacting resources in chip multiprocessors: A machine learning approach. In Proceedings of the 41st Int'l Symposium on Microarchitecture, pages 318–329, 2008.

[4] D. Brooks, V. Tiwari, and M. Martonosi. Wattch: a framework for architectural-level power analysis and optimizations. In Proceedings of the 27th Int'l symposium on Computer architecture, pages 83–94, 2000.

[5] D. M. Brooks, et al. Power-aware microarchitecture: Design and modeling challenges for next-generation microprocessors. IEEE Micro, 20(6):26–44, 2000.

[6] J. Casazza. White paper first tick, now tock: Intel microarchitecture (nehalem). 2009.

[7] F. J. Cazorla, et al. Predictable performance in smt processors. In Proceedings of the 1st conference on Computing frontiers, pages 433–443, 2004.

[8] F. J. Cazorla, et al. Dynamically controlled resource allocation in smt processors. In Proceedings of the 37th Int'l Symposium on Microarchitecture, pages 171–182, 2004.

[9] S. Choi and D. Yeung. Learning-based smt processor resource distribution via hill-climbing. In Proceedings of the 33rd int'l symposium on Computer Architecture, pages 239–251, 2006.

[10] S. Eyerman and L. Eeckhout. Per-thread cycle accounting in smt processors. In Proceeding of the 14th ASPLOS, pages 133–144, 2009.

[11] S. Eyerman, et al. A performance counter architecture for computing accurate cpi components. In Proceeddings of the 11th ASPLOS, pages 175–184, 2006.

[12] B. Fields, et al. Focusing processor policies via critical-path prediction. In Proceedings of the 28th Int'l symposium on Computer architecture, pages 74–85, 2001.

[13] F. Guo, et al. A framework for providing quality of service in chip multi-processors. In Proceedings of the 40th Int'l Symposium on Microarchitecture, pages 343–355, 2007.

[14] C. Isci, et al. An analysis of efficient multi-core global power management policies: Maximizing performance for a given power budget. In Proceedings of the 39th Int'l Symposium on Microarchitecture, pages 347–358, 2006.

[15] T. S. Karkhanis and J. E. Smith. A first-order superscalar processor model. In Proceedings of the 31st Int'l symposium on Computer architecture, pages 338–349, 2004.

[16] P. Magnusson, et al. Simics: A full system simulation platform. IEEE Computer, 35(2):50–58, 2 2002.

[17] M. M. K. Martin, et al. Multifacet's general execution-driven multiprocessor simulator (gems) toolset. SIGARCH Comput. Archit. News, 33(4):92–99, 2005.

[18] R. L. Mattson, et al. Evaluation techniques for storage hierarchies. IBM Syst. J., 9(2):78–117, 1970.

[19] O. Mutlu and T. Moscibroda. Parallelism-aware batch scheduling: Enhancing both performance and fairness of shared dram systems. In Proceedings of the 35th Int'l Symposium on Computer Architecture, pages 63–74, 2008.

[20] M. K. Qureshi and Y. N. Patt. Utility-based cache partitioning: A low-overhead, high-performance, runtime mechanism to partition shared caches. In Proceedings of the 39th Int'l Symposium on Microarch., pages 423–432, 2006.

[21] A. Snavely and D. M. Tullsen. Symbiotic jobscheduling for a simultaneous multithreaded processor. In Proceedings of ASPLOS-IX, pages 234–244, 2000.

[22] S. Thoziyoor, et al. Cacti 5.1. HP Technical Reports, 2008.

[23] D. M. Tullsen, et al. Exploiting choice: instruction fetch and issue on an implementable simultaneous multithreading processor. In Proceedings of the 23rd Int'l symposium on Computer architecture, pages 191–202, 1996.

[24] H.-S. Wang, et al. Orion: a power-performance simulator for interconnection networks. In Proceedings. 35th Int'l Symposium on Microarchitecture, pages 294 – 305, 2002.

An Idiom-finding Tool for Increasing Productivity of Accelerators

Laura Carrington
UCSD/SDSC
9500 Gilman Dr. MC0505
La Jolla, CA 92093-0505
1-858-534-5063
lcarring@sdsc.edu

Mustafa M. Tikir[1]
Google Inc.
1600 Amphitheatre Parkway
Mountain View, CA 94043
1-858-357-1681
mustafa.m.tikir@gmail.com

Catherine Olschanowsky
UCSD/SDSC
9500 Gilman Dr. MC0505
La Jolla, CA 92093-0505
1-858-246-0744
cmills@sdsc.edu

Michael Laurenzano
UCSD/SDSC
9500 Gilman Dr. MC0505
La Jolla, CA 92093-0505
1-858-822-2798
michaell@sdsc.edu

Joshua Peraza
UCSD/SDSC
9500 Gilman Dr. MC0505
La Jolla, CA 92093-0505
1-909-292-6970
jperaza@ucsd.edu

Allan Snavely
UCSD/SDSC
9500 Gilman Dr. MC0505
La Jolla, CA 92093-0505
1-858-534-5158
allans@sdsc.edu

Stephen Poole
ORNL
PO BOX 2008 MS6173
Oak Ridge, TN 37831-6173
1-865-574-9008
spoole@ornl.gov

ABSTRACT

Suppose one is considering purchase of a computer equipped with accelerators. Or suppose one has access to such a computer and is considering porting code to take advantage of the accelerators. Is there a reason to suppose the purchase cost or programmer effort will be worth it? It would be nice to able to estimate the expected improvements in advance of paying money or time. We exhibit an analytical framework and tool-set for providing such estimates: the tools first look for user-defined idioms that are patterns of computation and data access identified in advance as possibly being able to benefit from accelerator hardware. A performance model is then applied to estimate how much faster these idioms would be if they were ported and run on the accelerators, and a recommendation is made as to whether or not each idiom is worth the porting effort to put them on the accelerator and an estimate is provided of what the *overall application speedup* would be if this were done.

As a proof-of-concept we focus our investigations on Gather/Scatter (G/S) operations and means to accelerate these available on the Convey HC-1 which has a special-purpose "personality" for accelerating G/S. We test the methodology on two large-scale HPC applications. The idiom recognizer tool saves weeks of programmer effort compared to having the programmer examine the code visually looking for idioms; performance models save yet more time by rank-ordering the best candidates for porting; and the performance models are accurate, predicting G/S runtime speedup resulting from porting to within 10% of speedup actually achieved. The G/S hardware on the Convey sped up these operations 20x, and the overall impact on total application runtime was to improve it by as much as 21%.

---

[1] This work is completed while Dr. Tikir was an active member of PMaC

General Terms
B8.2 Performance Analysis and Design Aids

Descriptors
Performance

Keywords
Benchmarking, performance prediction, performance modeling, FPGAs, accelerators, HPC.

1 INTRODUCTION

Tools to help programmers identify optimization opportunities are useful for improving application scalability [1-4], improving throughput of applications [5], and improving programmer productivity[6, 7]. Lately Scalable hybrid-multi-core computing systems are becoming ubiquitous in the HPC environment. These systems typically have host cores and accelerator hardware thus offering the promise of enhanced compute power. For example the recently announced #1 on the Top500 list augments 14,336 Intel Westmere-EP processors with 7,168 NVIDIA M2050 general purpose GPUs and is capable of 2.57 petaflops on LINPACK. Because some real-world applications are more memory bound than compute bound, other accelerator-based systems such as Convey-HC-1 focus on speeding up memory accesses rather than flops. Yet common wisdom is that all these systems are difficult to program. They require writing code in new language extensions such as CUDA of even (in the case of Convey) coming up with VHDL-level descriptions of the problem to be solved. So at issue is to determine to what extent real-world applications would benefit from the accelerators on such systems? And assuming they would benefit, what portions of the applications would benefit most and how much work would it be to port the application, or portions of it, to these accelerators? PIR (PMaC's Idiom Recognizer) [8] is a static analysis tool that automates the process of identifying sections of code that are candidates for acceleration. PIR automatically recognizes and identifies user-specified compute and memory access patterns, called idioms [41] within application source code. This greatly reduces the amount of code that an expert must analyze "by hand" (visually). Once a section of code is identified that *could* be run on an accelerator, there still remains the question *should* it be? Often the startup overhead of moving the data to/from the accelerator outweighs the performance benefits. Also this question may depend on input. In this work we develop a general performance model for accelerators that can estimate whether the identified idiom would be worth computing on an accelerator depending on input. The combined tool-stream (PIR + model) helps programmers to be productive in two ways 1) it saves them the labor of analyzing thousands lines of legacy code "by hand" to identify idioms that are candidates for acceleration and 2) it saves the time of porting candidate idioms by identifying sections of code/idioms to be ported only when the forecasted performance improvement will benefit overall performance 3) it triages the idioms that should be ported in order best-candidate-for-porting-first.

In this paper we focus our investigations on local Gather/Scatter (G/S) operations and means to accelerate these available on the Convey HC-1 which has a vendor supplied function (i.e. Convey personality) for accelerating local G/S. A local G/S is one where the data is gathered or scattered from memory local to the core and doesn't require communication among cores. G/S is a very difficult memory access pattern for most commodity systems to do well [9-11] and therefore some real applications may benefit more from this kind of acceleration than the more common "flops" accelerators. We test the methodology on two large-scale HPC applications. The idiom recognizer tool saves weeks of programmer effort compared to having the programmer examine the code "by hand" looking for idioms; performance models save yet more time by rank-ordering the idioms, best-candidate-for-porting-first; the models themselves are highly accurate and predict the G/S runtime speedup resulting from going ahead and porting to within 10% of what was actually achieved. The G/S hardware on the Convey sped up these operations 20x, the overall impact on total application runtime was to improve it by as much as 21%. In what follows we describe first in Section II our tool for recognizing idioms, section III describes our performance modeling methodology applied to G/S, section IV provides experimental results, section V concludes, and section VI gives background and related work.

2 IDIOMS

PIR (PMaC Idiom Recognizer)[8] is a tool for searching source code for idioms. An idiom [41] is a local pattern of computation that a user may expect to occur frequently in certain applications. For example, a stream idiom is a pattern where memory is read from an array, some computation may be done on this data, and then the data is written to another array. A stream reads sequentially from the source array and writes sequentially to the destination array. A stream may arise from the presence of the statement A[i] = B[i] within a loop over i.

Idioms are useful for describing patterns of computation that have the potential to be optimized, for example, by loading the piece of code to a coprocessor or accelerator.

The PIR tool allows us to automate searching for idioms in a powerful way by using data-flow analysis to augment the identification process. It would be very difficult to use a simpler searching tool, such as regular expressions, because a regular expression does not naturally discern the meaning of the text it

identifies. For example, in the code shown in Figure 1, a simple regular expression based on (for example) "grep" that searches for stream idioms of the form "A[i]= B[i]" would incorrectly identify line 1 as a stream and it would miss the stream at lines 3-4 because the assignment is broken into multiple statements.

```
1. values[c] = constants[c];
2. for( i = 0; i < 10; ++i ) {
3.     item = source_array[i];
4.     dest_array[i] = item;
5. }
```

Figure 1. Sample stream idiom code.

PIR, however, is able to determine that line 1 is not in a loop and that c is a constant. This indicates that the meaning of this statement is simply a variable assignment, rather than a stream. In lines 3-4, PIR uses data-flow analysis to determine that item in line 4 holds a value from the source array making this a stream.

PIR's design provides the flexibility to identify optimization opportunities for many different hardware configurations. The user provides descriptions of the idioms to be identified. As a starting point, PIR provides a set of commonly useful idioms and access to an Idiom definition syntax that allows for user customization of the idioms.

PIR includes seven idiom definitions we have found to be common in HPC applications. The user is free to define more via a simple pattern describing API. The pre-defined idioms are described in the following. All of the code samples are assumed to be part of a loop, i (and j) are loop induction variables.

- Stream: A[i] = A[i] + B[i]

The stream idiom includes accesses that step through arrays. In the above example two arrays are being stepped through simultaneously, but the stream idiom is not limited to this case. Stepping through any array in a loop where the index is determined by a loop induction variable is considered a stream.

- Transpose: A[i][j] = B[j][i]

The transpose idiom involves a matrix transpose, essentially reordering an array using the loop induction variable.

- Gather: A[i] = B[C[i]]

The gather idiom includes gathering data from a potentially random access area in memory to a sequential array. In this example the random accesses are created using an index array, C.

- Scatter: A[B[i]] = C[i]

The scatter idiom is essentially the opposite of gather. Values are read from a sequential area of memory and saved to an area accessed in a potentially random manner.

- Reduction: s = s + A[i]

A reduction can be formed from a stream, as in the working example, or a gather. It implies that the value returned from the read portion of the idiom is assigned to a temporary variable.

- Stencil: A[i] = A[i-1] + A[i+1]

A stencil idiom involves accessing an array in a sequential manner, including a dependency between iterations of the loop.

Table 1 presents just a sample of the report for an application. The sample shows how PIR is able to classify the idiom, capture the source file, source line, function name and even the line number of source code used for the identification(additional information about loop depth, start, and end are captured but not shown).

Table 1. Sample output from PIR analysis on HYCOM.

File Name	Line #	Function	Idiom	Code
mod_tides.F	623	tides_set	gather	pf(i)=f(index(i))
mxkrt.f	992	mxkrtbaj	reduction	sdp=sdp+ssal(k)*q

The PIR user manual and programmers guide can be found online at www.sdsc.edu/pmac.

3 MODELING GATHER-SCATTER OPERATIONS

Once the idioms are identified having an accurate estimate of which ones will perform well on the new accelerator could save a lot of human hours in porting efforts. Some idioms that can be executed on an accelerator should not be because the overhead of moving the data to the accelerator is greater than the performance gains of executing them there. It is not uncommon anecdotally for users to invest a fair amount of time in porting to accelerators only to discover the whole code as a whole runs slower[1]. Having an accurate performance model avoids these situations.

In this work we develop a general methodology to model idiom operations on accelerators. The focus of this paper is on the G/S idiom due to its ability to exacerbate a systems memory performance. The Von Neumann Bottleneck is particularly aggravated by memory access patterns that have a substantial amount of randomness or indirection in the address stream such as Gather/Scatter idioms. In a Gather, non-contiguous memory locations are collected up into a contiguous array; in a Scatter, contiguous array elements are distributed to non-contiguous memory locations; because these species of operations are 1) prevalent in many scientific applications 2) performance-limited on many architecture by the latency of main memory, various architectural features have been proposed to try to accelerate them. An access to main-memory on today's deep-memory-hierarchy machines commonly takes two orders-of-magnitude longer than either floating-point or integer operations, thus these operations will be performance bottlenecks unless some means can be found to accelerate them.

Our motive was to develop models and methodology to be able to assist in the prediction of the benefit of having G/S accelerators directly in future HPC architectures without just building the

[1] Negative results are rarely published in computer science: at a recent DoD GP GPU workshop most application developers reported spending considerable time porting codes to accelerators without getting any speedup.

hardware first and finding out if it is useful afterwards. Building a model of the interaction of the hardware and the application requires three main components: the machine component, the application component, and the model component. The machine component involves measuring the performance benefits of using the acceleration hardware for Gather/Scatter operations and identifying the parameters that affect that performance (i.e. locality, vector length, etc.). The application component entails automating the detection of Gather/Scatter operations in a large scale HPC application and measuring the parameters of these operations that affect performance on the acceleration hardware. The final piece, the model component, combines the machine component and application component to complete the model and detail the performance of the application on the hardware.

3.1 Machine Component- Measuring Gather/Scatter Operations

The Machine Component of the G/S model consists of a way to measure the typical performance of running Gather/Scatter operations on acceleration hardware and determine what parameters affect their performance. A simple benchmark was developed, SGBench[12]. SGBench has two main loop bodies; one for a local scatter operations and one for a local gather operations.

Figure 2 and Figure 3 represents the code snippets from SGBench for the scatter and gather operations respectively. The code represents local operations that do not require communication among cores. Figure 2 illustrates a scatter operation. In this loop the array A is filled by the contents of array B at non-contiguous locations in local memory, determined by the index array. In Figure 3 the gather operation is shown. Here a contiguous piece of array B is filled by the contents of a non-contiguous piece of array A in local memory. In both loops the index array is filled with integers representing elements of an array.

```
for(i=0;i<n;i++){
    A[index[i]] = B[i];
}
```

Figure 2. Loop for Scatter operation.

```
for(i=0;i<n;i++){
    B[i] = A[index[i]];
}
```

Figure 3. Loop for Gather operation.

In considering Gather/Scatter operation and ways to accelerate them, it is important to understand if there is locality in the index set. If there is locality the accelerator hardware may be able exploit it; also accelerator hardware may exist at different levels of the memory hierarchy (cache, local main memory, global memory, etc.). The size of the array accessed then matters but also any clustering or patterns of the index set matters. G/S accelerator hardware basically works by packing and reordering memory requests and pulling in chunks of random locations at a time. So even though the index set is by definition random, if reordered it may have some locality properties that G/S hardware can take advantage of. To study different modes of Gather/Scatter operations, the addresses in the index array in SGBench was varied. This work focused on three specific modes.

Figure 4 depicts the three kinds of locality modes we consider in the index set. Figure 4a *random indices* has no locality, that is to say the index set is a set of entirely random indices that span the entire array from 0 to size of A. The second mode, *clustered indices,* shown in Figure 4b, has locality clusters within the random index set. In this case the indices in the index array span certain sections of the A array and within those sections the indices of the index array are random. In the third mode, *spread indices*, illustrated in Figure 4c, the indices have, if reordered, some spatial locality (predictable or constant strides) spanning the entire array from 0 to size of A.

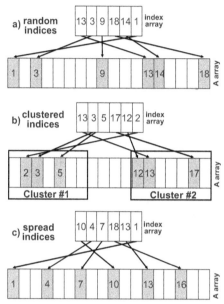

Figure 4. Type of index arrays for gather-scatter operations, a) random index, b) clustered index, c) spread index.

Random indices (Figure 3a) might be typical of a graph problem or similar to the RandomAccess (GUPs) kernel [13, 14], Clustered (Figure 3b) is typical of sorting partially-sorted input, Spread (Figure 3c) typical of a sparse matrix problem which can arise in Finite Element or Finite Difference codes. Along with enabling the index array to be filled in the three different modes, SGBench also allows the user to vary the padding or offset between the A, B and index arrays as these parameters may interact with memory banking.

3.1.1 Machine Component – measuring the FPGAs

To study the performance effects of Gather/Scatter operations on acceleration hardware, SGBench was ported to the Convey HC-1[15]. The Convey HC-1, shown in Figure 5, uses a tightly integrated Intel 5138 processor (Xeon Woodcrest) with a FPGA-based, reconfigurable coprocessor. The coprocessor can be targeted at specific workloads by reloading it with different instruction sets, called personalities. By enabling the implementation of a new instruction set, the coprocessor can be tailored to specific applications and algorithms. In addition the coprocessor shares memory with the Intel processor, which

reduces the data transfer time between the computing elements and eliminates much implementation complexity.

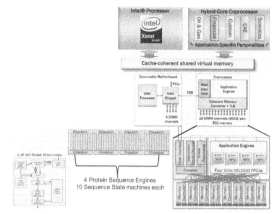

Figure 5. Convey HC-1.

For this work, a Convey supplied personality was used to accelerate local Gather/Scatter operations illustrated in Figure 2 and Figure 3. This personality was used both to gather performance data used as input for the model and to port sections of the application for model verification.

The SGBench benchmark was used to measure both the performance of Scatter operation and Gather operation. SGBench was run on two ways; first the entire SGBench execution was run on the host processors of the HC-1. Second the majority of the SGBench execution was run on the host processor with just the loops containing Gather or Scatter operations running on the FPGAs. The measurements were taken to determine the performance effects of running G/S operations at increasing data set sizes (i.e. total address range of the arrays). The measurements were made using an index array of stride-1 and an index array of random-stride, this was intended to cover the range of performance for the operations shown in Figure 4a through Figure 4c. The measurements were taken both on the host Xeon processor and the FPGA coprocessor. Figure 6 and Figure 7 illustrate the results of these measurements as a function of the size of the address range of the test loop and compare performance of operations on the host Xeon processor with those on the FPGAs.

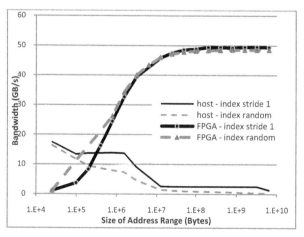

Figure 6. Performance of Scatter loop as a function of |Address Range| on Convey HC-1 using host and FPGA.

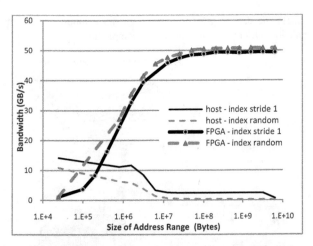

Figure 7. Performance of Gather loop as a function of |Address Range| on Convey HC-1 using host and FPGA.

Figure 6 shows Scatter operations run at different data set sizes. The first curve is for SGBench run at increasing sizes on the host processor (Xeon) of the Convey HC-1 with an index array of stride-1, while the second curve is for an index of random-stride. These curves illustrate that as the size is increased the performance decreases in a stepwise fashion on the host processor an exemplar of today's deep-memory-hierarchy machines comprised of levels of cache. The next two curves, in Figure 6, are Scatter operations run on the FPGA with stride-1 and random-stride index arrays. This illustrates that at a few small data set sizes, it is more beneficial to run Scatter operations on the host but that performance on the FPGA *increases* with size asymptotically and for large sizes ~200x performance improvement over the host can be gained. More importantly, the performance does not change much when using random-stride vs. stride-1 index array on the FPGA for larger data sizes.

Figure 7 represents similar measurements for Gather operations. Both figures illustrate that there are only small changes in performance when running Gather vs. Scatter operations on the FPGAs and the FPGA's performance is not significantly affected by the randomness of the index array. The figures illustrate that the data footprint of these operations can dramatically affect performance; in other words there is no such thing as "the performance of a machine on Gather/Scatter" rather one needs more information such as the size of the range of array address arguments to accurately estimate performance.

3.2 Application Component

In order to have a general scheme for modeling and predicting Gather/Scatter operation performance, we first need to identify instances of Gather/Scatter operations within the source code. Secondly, we need to capture the parameters of each individual G/S instance that will affect their performance (locate them on the benchmark graph) if they were to be ported to the accelerated hardware. As identified above, size or range of addresses in the G/S loop, are important in determining performance on the Convey HC-1 and thus were identified as the main modeling parameter. Figure 6 and Figure 7 illustrates how the Gather/Scatter operations benefit for large address ranges more when using the FPGAs, which would also likely be true of commodity (HPC) processors with built-in G/S capabilities. In fact in retrospect we can look back at the vector systems of the

80' and 90's and see how this was also true back then. Back then G/S was inherent in the hardware and on the Crays it was in the ISA as an assembler vector instruction.

3.2.1 Identifying Gather/Scatter operations

Once the basic Gather/Scatter operation is defined the next step is to automate the detection of these operations in large scientific application because without automated detection the task of identifying candidates for G/S acceleration by hand would be extremely time consuming. The PIR tool, described in section 2, was used to automate the search for G/S instances in large scale scientific application.

Identification of the idioms in an application in an automated way allows for the easy detection of Gather/Scatter instances. Once the G/S instances are detected the second step is capturing the address ranges for each instance. This needs to be done dynamically by instrumentation.

3.2.2 Measuring range Gather/Scatter operations

Once operations in an application are identified as Gather/Scatter, the next step, as suggested by the benchmark results, is to measure the address range of each instance as they occur within the application. It should be clear that the range may depend on input, thus a static analysis tools such as PIR, while sufficient to *identify* instances of Gather/Scatter in applications, provides insufficient information to accurately model them since performance may vary more than an order-of-magnitude just depending on range of addresses (see Figure 6 and Figure 7). Therefore we used the binary instrumentation tool PmacInst[16] to instrument the instances of Gather/Scatter identified by PIR.

PmacInst is used to gather the memory traces of an application for the general PMaC performance model. It is designed to instrument an identified set of basic-blocks in an application and capture the memory addresses of those blocks during the execution of the application. To conserve time and space the address stream is simulated against architectural features of interest (caches, Gather/Scatter hardware) on-the-fly while the application is running.

In order to capture the range of the Gather/Scatter operations identified by PIR two steps were required. First the information gathered from PIR needed to be translated and conveyed between the two tools because PIR works on source code while PmacInst works on the binary—we need to identify the binary code corresponding to the source code. This translation allows PmacInst to add additional instrumentation to those basic-blocks identified by PIR. Secondly, an address range function was developed to process the address streams from Gather/Scatter operations and calculate the range and distribution of those operations.

In order to translate identified PIR operations to basic-blocks by PmacInst a special feature of PmacInst was utilized. This feature allowed the source file and line number to be collected along with the basic-block number. This same information is collected by PIR, so by using additional parsing scripts, the PIR output was connected to and combined with the static analysis from PmacInst to automate the identification and additional instrumentation of all Gather/Scatter instances. This extra instrumentation allowed for the addresses of these operations to be processed by the function to calculate address range for each G/S instance.

To calculate the range of addresses in a Gather/Scatter operation the function was designed to minimize overhead while maintaining sufficient accuracy by determining the memory regions touched by each basic-block. One way to gather information on memory regions for an address stream is to use binary search tree that holds the boundary addresses for memory regions and at every memory access searches for the region the memory access fits in [17]. This requires additional split and merge operations of memory regions according to some heuristics for accurate region identification. Even though such an approach would potentially identify the memory regions very accurately, it would also introduce a significant overhead since a search in the binary tree would be required for every memory access and would rely on accurate split and merge heuristics.

To avoid this large overhead, the function tracks the addresses accessed by each memory operation (instruction) in the basic-block separately. Since the instrumentation code already passes information about the memory operation for each access, we identify the region accessed by the memory operation by keeping track of the minimum and maximum addresses touched.

This method is faster at instrumentation time but requires additional post processing to be accurate enough. The overall overhead required for this additional instrumentation is less than 10%. The additional post-processing is needed due to the fact that even though the list of memory regions accessed by all memory operations can be used as the memory regions accessed by the block, some of these memory regions may overlap. This is can be a result of multiple memory operations accessing the same data structures and arrays, which can be an outcome of heavy code optimizations such as loop unrolling. To correct for such overlap, we post process the trace data to find the minimal number of memory regions accessed by a basic block. We accomplish this by first sorting the list of memory regions accessed by all memory operations in ascending order of their minimum addresses and then merging the overlapping regions.

Table 2 shows the results of using this range calculation on an instrumented run of the SGBench benchmark. The table presents the measured and actual ranges for a given array in the scatter loop shown in Figure 2. The instrumented SGBench was run at 8 different size scatter loops and the results for 4 of those are shown in Table 2 below. The relative absolute error for all the runs was less than 1% for all sizes.

Table 2. Actual and measured ranges in SGBench.

Array name	Actual size (bytes)	Measured size (bytes)	% Error[2]
A	20,480	20,400	0.4
B	5,120	5,080	0.8
Index	2,560	2,540	0.8
A	65,536	65,520	0.0
B	16,384	16,344	0.3
Index	8,192	8,192	0.3
A	16,777,216	16,777,128	0.0
B	4,194,304	4,194,264	0.0
Index	2,097,152	2,097,132	0.0
A	33,554,432	33,554,352	0.0
B	8,388,608	8,388,568	0.0
Index	4,194,304	4,194,284	0.0

$$1\quad \% \, Error = abs\left(\frac{actual\, size \, - \, measured\, size}{actual\, size}\right) \times 100$$

The automated process of using PIR to identify Gather/Scatter operations and PmacInst to measure ranges was further tested using spot checking of two large scale applications (HYCOM and Flash) and showed similar absolute relative error with all loops measured with less than 1% error.

Thus by combining the PIR and PmacInst tools we have a tool to automate the process of first identifying Gather/Scatter operations and second measuring the range of each of those operations in a tractable fashion, which is an important step in modeling their performance on acceleration hardware.

3.3 Modeling Gather/Scatter operations

We extended our existing performance modeling framework to account for the performance effects of acceleration hardware on Gather/Scatter operations. Here we briefly describe the PMaC framework designed to model large scale parallel applications and then present how the Gather/Scatter model is incorporated into the framework.

3.3.1 PMaC Performance prediction framework

The PMaC prediction framework is designed to accurately model parallel applications on HPC systems. In order to model a parallel application, the framework is composed of two models, a computational model and a communication model. The computational model models work done on the processor in between communication event, while the communication model deals with modeling communication events. Below a brief description is provided but for a detailed description of the framework, please see Snavely et al.[18], Carrington et al.[19] and Tikir et al. [20].

For each model, the computational and communication is comprised of three primary components: an application signature, a machine profile, and a convolution method. The machine profile captures that rates that a machine can perform fundamental operations through simple benchmarks. These simple benchmarks includes tests for performance of different kinds of memory access patterns, arithmetic operations, and communications events, at various working set sizes and message sizes. The application signature includes detailed information about the required operations the applications needs as well as the locality of its data and its message sizes, and is collected via trace tools. The machine profile and application signature are combined by mapping the required operation of the application to their expected rate on the target machine. This mapping takes place in the PSiNS simulator that re-plays the entire execution of the HPC application on the target/predicted system to calculate the runtime of the target system. The models generated by the framework have shown good accuracy (i.e. <15% absolute relative error) predicting full-scale application running production datasets on existing systems [21].

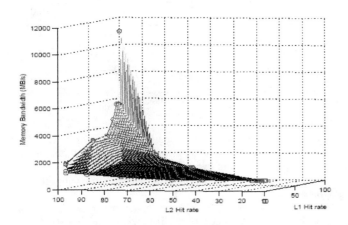

Figure 8. . Measured bandwidth as function of cache hit rates for Opteron.

For this work we focused on extending the computational or core model, which is comprised of the work done on the processor or core in between communication events or computational work. We extended the model to account for the effect of having accelerators in each node; and modeling the work that is off-loaded to the accelerator.

For the computational model there are two main operations that normally comprise a majority of the run time: arithmetic time and memory time. Arithmetic time is the time required to perform floating-point and other math operations. Memory time is the time required to load and store memory references and it is this time that usually dominates the computational model's run time. To accurately model memory time we need to determine the number of bytes that need to be loaded or stored but also the location and access pattern of those references. This is because references from different locations and access patterns can perform orders of magnitude better or worse. For example, a stride-one load from L1 cache can perform significantly faster than a random stride load from main memory. Figure 8 is an example of the MultiMAPS benchmark[20] used to capture the complex interaction of spatial and temporal locality and performance on memory reference on a two level Opteron processor. The MultiMAPS surface allows the model to determine the performance of memory references with different spatial and temporal locality.

To capture this temporal and spatial locality information in an application for each reference that occurs in the execution an augmented memory trace of the application is used. The memory trace is captured using the pmacInst[16] tool which has the ability to instrument each memory reference in order to capture the memory address stream from each core of the running application. This address stream is then processed on-the-fly through a cache simulator for the target system or system to predict. The result of this trace is for each basic block of the application information is provided on: 1) the location of the block in the source code, 2) number of floating-point operations and type, 3) number of memory references and type (e.g. load and/or store), 4) size of references in bytes, and 5) the expected cache hit rates for those references on the target system. It is the hit rates that provide information about the spatial and temporal locality of the reference and enable accurate predictions of their performance via the corresponding data on the MultiMAPS surface. The

framework enables the application to be traced on a one system (i.e. the base system) but by simulating a difference cache structure (i.e. the target system) the model can predict the performance of a completely different system. For this work the applications were trace on an IBM Power 6 system but simulated the cache structures for AMD and Intel based systems, these are referred to cross-architectural predictions.

In the computational model the majority of the time comes from the memory time or time to move data through the memory hierarchy (arithmetic time is also modeled but memory time tends to dominate in the cases we studied). A detailed description of the memory time calculation can be found at Tikir et al.[20]. The general memory time equation is:

1) $\quad$ memory $\quad$ time $= \sum_{i}^{all\ BB} \dfrac{(memory\ ref._{i,j} \times size\ of\ reference)}{memory\ BW_{j}}$

Where:

Memory bandwidth$_j$ = $\quad$ memory bandwidth of the jth type of memory reference on a target system.

Size of reference = $\quad$ size in bytes of the reference

memory ref.$_{i,j}$ = $\quad$ number of memory references for basic-block i of the jth type (locality information encompassed in type)

Equation 1 represents the memory time of an application as being the sum of all basic-block's memory time for the application.

To model Gather/Scatter operations, an additional equation needed to be developed to compute the time for operations off-loaded to the accelerator or Convey HC-1 FPGAs and additions to the simulator on which equation is used for which basic-block.

3.3.2 Gather/Scatter memory model

In order to add the modeling of Gather/Scatter operations the simulator requires two additional pieces of data. First, how the performance of Gather/Scatter operations vary with size of operation and second which basic-blocks in the application contains these operations and what is their size.

In developing a model of the performance of Gather/Scatter operation based on size, we first investigated the trends displayed in Figure 6. The concept in designing the model is to start as simple as possible and only add complexity when needed. Therefore we started with a piece-wise fit to the data in Figure 6. The equation for modeling Gather/Scatter operations on the FPGAs is as follows:

2) $\quad$ memory $\quad$ time $= \sum_{i}^{all\ BB} \dfrac{(\#\ memory\ ref._{i,j} \times size\ of\ reference)}{memory\ BW_{gs}}$

Where:

3) $\quad$ memory $BW_{gs} = 1E - 5 \times size + 12.6$ for $192KB < size < 3MB$

4) $\quad$ memory $BW_{gs} = 48 \geq 3MB$

Where:

Memory BW$_j$ = $\quad$ memory bandwidth of the jth type of memory reference on the target system.

Size = $\quad$ size in bytes of the reference

Equation 2 represents the memory bandwidth as a function of size in bytes detailed in Equations 3 and 4. The framework was modified so that the simulator incorporated the trace data of the PIR recognized Gather/Scatter operations, its measured size, and Equations 2, 3, and 4 to model the performance impact the Convey would have on applications. Note that the simulator includes a conditional that would only run those Gather/Scatter operations that are predicted to see a performance improvement on the FPGA (from Figure 6 and Figure 7 only those with array address ranges larger than 192 KB).

4 EXPERIMENTAL MODEL AND RESULTS

In the experiment we used two full-scale scientific applications to test the model, HYCOM and FLASH. FLASH is an astrophysics application developed at the "FLASH Center" funded by DOE ASC/Alliance Program. It is a state-of-the-art simulator code for solving nuclear astrophysical problems related to exploding stars. It is 126,478 lines of code. HYCOM is an ocean modeling application developed by The Naval Research Laboratory (NRL), Los Alamos National Laboratory (LANL), and the University of Miami as an upgrade to MICOM (well-known ocean modeling code) by enhancing the vertical layer definitions within the model to better capture the underlying science. It is 54,085 lines of code.

The main goal of the research was to design a modeling framework to explore the question "Would a given HPC application benefit from accelerators?". We designed a general modeling methodology around this but to verify the methodology we chose a specific set of operations (e.g. G/S) and a specific accelerator (e.g. the FPGA). In order to verify the models two main experiments were conducted. The first experiment was to simply verify the model for the two large scale applications running on a large scale HPC system. In addition verify the model at a finer-grain level for only Gather/Scatter operations still running on the same system, see section 4.1. The second experiment dealt with a smaller data set for the FLASH application. In this experiment we wanted to verify the FPGA Gather/Scatter model by running the application on the Convey HC-1 and porting a single loop of the application to the FPGA for the verification of the FPGA model. The smaller data set was used because the HC-1 only had 4 host cores and we were unable to run a bigger data set. Figure 2 and Figure 3 had already verified the accuracy of the FPGA Gather/Scatter model on benchmarks on the HC-1 but this experiment verified the model working within a full-scale application on that system.

4.1 Models and fine grain verification experiment

In this experiment we needed to first verify the full application model for the two applications running on a large scale HPC system. In addition verify the accuracy of the full application model at a finer-grain level by capturing the model time for only Gather/Scatter operations of the application. To accomplish this a large data set was used as input to the application. For this experiment we identified all of the Gather/Scatter instances within both applications, modeled the entire computational time of the applications (using the full framework), then inside the simulator captured the modeled time for just the Gather/Scatter idioms within the applications, and verified those modeled times on a large scale HPC system by measuring those times with a light weight profiling tool and individual timers.

For this experiment, models were developed for HYCOM and FLASH for Oakridge National Laboratory's (ORNL) Jaguar XT4 to verify the accuracy and the granularity of the models. Jaguar is an XT4 with seastar2 interconnect [22]. FLASH was run on Jaguar with 128 processors using the white dwarf input and HYCOM was run with 59 processors using the 26-layer 1/4 degree fully global HYCOM benchmark input deck. While the framework is designed and is used at much larger processor counts, both applications were run at small core counts to minimize the contribution of runtime from communication, thus focusing the modeling on computational aspects of the application such as their ability to benefit from Gather/Scatter accelerators.

PIR was used to capture the number and location of Gather/Scatter operations in FLASH and HYCOM source codes. An additional feature was added so that PIR automatically inserted tags at the identified Gather/Scatter operations to enable timer insertion to aid in model accuracy verification. This feature could further be enhanced to automate the process of modifying the identified Gather/Scatter loops to call the FPGA personality, a valuable aid in the porting process (future work).

After the PIR analysis, 140 Gather/Scatter idioms were identified for FLASH and 64 in HYCOM. PIR only captures the number of G/S idioms but gives no indication on their contribution to the overall runtime; for that, the performance model is required. A performance model for FLASH and HYCOM executing on Jaguar was developed to investigate the performance benefit these applications would see from FPGA accelerators.

Table 3 shows the results for both predicted/modeled and measured computational time of FLASH and further breaking down the time spent in Gather/Scatter operations for both predicted/model and measured time. It also has the predicted/modeled computational time on Jaguar for HYCOM compared to the measured computational time.

Table 3. Prediction of FLASH on ORNL Jaguar.

Code segment	Predicted time (sec)	Measured time (sec)	% error[1]
FLASH – full	262	250	4.6%
FLASH G/S ops	69	68	1.4%
HYCOM – full	5956	5781	2.9%

[1] $\% \text{ Error} = abs\left(\frac{\text{measured - predicted}}{\text{measured}}\right) \times 100$

Table 3 shows that the accuracy of modeling FLASH and HYCOM on existing hardware is accurate to within 5% (e.g. rows 2 and 4). Additionally at finer granularity models of the Gather/Scatter operations of FLASH with the same level of accuracy (e.g. <2% error, row 3). Due to the nature of the HYCOM G/S operations (e.g. inner loops with other operations) we were unable to capture the fine grain G/S operation time alone without disturbing the overall runtime significantly due to number of calls to the timer routines (the measurement was affecting the execution significantly). Therefore we were only able to compare the overall runtime and not the G/S operations on HYCOM.

4.2 Convey HC-1 models and verification

Once the accuracy of the applications' models on an existing system was confirmed then the exploration of the Gather/Scatter operations on the Convey system was investigated. It is one thing to verify the accuracy of a kernel extracted from an application (e.g. SGBench) but this experiment was designed to verify the accuracy of the model during execution of the entire application.

To verify the accuracy of the FPGA Gather/Scatter model and simulation for large scale applications, one of the identified Gather/Scatter operations (i.e. loop) of FLASH was ported to the Convey system and timed to compare the simulated FPGA model time with the measured time. So a majority of the FLASH application could then be executed on the HC-1 host processors with one loop being executed on the FPGA. Porting loops to the Convey requires some additional work; the whole point of our technique is to focus programmer efforts on the parts of the code where the effort will result in the most reward. From FLASH we chose porting a loop that ranked the highest among the Gather/Scatter operations for overall runtime contribution.

Due to the size of the Convey HC-1 we were accessing (only 4 host processors) we had to choose a smaller FLASH input, sedov-2d problem rather than the white dwarf input, in order to run FLASH at full-scale with the single ported loop executing on the FPGAs. Alternately we could have extracted the loop into a small kernel but that might not fully capture the data transfer penalties associated with the many visits to the loop throughout the execution. A full application model was developed for the sedov-2d input similar to the white dwarf input verified in Table 3. This time the model was developed for not only Jaguar but the host processors of the HC-1. In addition for both models the simulation time for the identified loop was captured in order to verify the model accuracy at the loop level. Then a model was generated for the HC-1 with that loop executing on the FPGA, this allowed verification of the FPGA G/S model. The sedov-2d input computational time was predicted/modeled and measured on Jaguar and the Convey host; the results are shown in Table 4 below. This illustrates the accuracy of the Gather/Scatter model on the Convey HC-1 system for the sedov-2d input with a relative absolute error less than 10%.

Table 4. Simulated and measured Gather/Scatter times for FLASH on the Convey HC-1.

Code/section (system)	Measured time (s)	Predicted time (s)	% Error[1]
FLASH-full (Jaguar)	518.6	487.7	6.0%
#1 FLASH-G/S loop (Jaguar)	3.4	3.7	9.3%
FLASH-full (Convey Host)	491.9	489.7	5.0%
#1 FLASH-G/S loop (Convey FPGAs)	2.8	3.0	8.6%

[1]
$$\% \, Error = abs \left(\frac{measured - predicted}{measured} \right) \times 100$$

Table 4 verifies the accuracy of the FPGA G/S model when implemented in a full-scale application even at a fine grain loop level with only 8.6% abs. relative error. Table 3 and Table 4 confirms the accuracy of the full application models for FLASH and HYCOM, the accuracy of the models on a finer-grain level (i.e. gather/scatter operations in FLASH), and the accuracy of the FPGA Gather/Scatter model on the Convey HC-1 FPGAs.

4.3 Exploring the benefits of G/S on FPGAs

In section 4.1 we verified the Jaguar models accuracy for full scale applications and sub-sections (e.g. G/S loops) of the application. In section 4.2 we verified the FPGA G/S model executing in the context of a full scale application. After verifying these components of the modeling framework we then began to investigate the original question the methodology was designed to explore, "Do applications benefit from running G/S operations on FPGAs?" Since we have verified large scale runs of HYCOM and FLASH on Jaguar nodes we will start our exploration there.

To explore this space we need to create a hypothetical system consisting of 32 Jaguar nodes (e.g. 128 cores) with FPGAs attached to the cores, essentially a hypothetical Convey system where the host processors are Barcelona (i.e. XT4- Jaguar) processors rather than Xeon's. We then use the models to predict the performance of FLASH and HYCOM on this system to answers the question "What if all Gather/Scatter operation that would perform faster on the FPGAs were ported and run on them how that would affect overall application runtime?"

These new simulations give insight into not only whether an application might benefit from accelerated G/S operations but how much and which ones. The G/S operations in FLASH took 68 seconds on Jaguar and were predicted to take 3.5 seconds if run on the FPGAs an almost 20X speedup. HYCOM showed slightly different behavior since a significant number of the HYCOM G/S operations did not benefit from the FPGAs (were too small). HYCOM showed G/S operations predicted to run on the FPGAs at a 7X speed up compared to Jaguar. The overall runtime speed up of FLASH and HYCOM resulting from the FPGAs on the new hypothetical system was 21% and 3.2% respectively.

The model showed that while there are over 140 Gather/Scatter operations in FLASH that contributes to 27% of the runtime, the FPGAs can potentially speedup these by close to 20X. The model allows users to focus porting efforts by identifying only those applications and idioms that would benefit most. While the speedup of the G/S operations was significant, due to the nature of the applications this speedup had only a modest contribution to the speedup of the overall runtime. This speedup could potentially be significantly improved if other idioms were ported to the FPGAs (future work).

If we look at Figure 6 we see that G/S operating on arrays smaller than 16K would be faster on the host. The performance models predict that the 33 largest instances of G/S (out of 140) correspond to 95% of predicted total G/S execution time. Quantitatively, the predicted time with FPGA G/S model is 197.2 seconds if all G/S in FLASH larger than 16K are ported while porting the top 33 results in execution time of 198.7 seconds for accelerator system. That is, even though we eliminated 107 blocks from porting to G/S hardware, we did not lose anything from the benefits of the accelerators. We only lost 1.42 seconds of optimized time but we were able to reduce the port time by a significant factor.

5 CONCLUSIONS

This work showed a general modeling methodology to automate the prediction of HPC applications on acceleration hardware. The models were confirmed using two large scale applications with an average absolute relative error of 5% and fine-grain accuracy of the model was confirmed with similar results. The fine-grain model for FPGA G/S operations was proven to have less than 8.6% absolute relative error using a loop from FLASH running on the FPGAs for verification. The performance modeling methodology estimated that >100 instances of the G/S idiom were not worth porting thus saving additional programmer's time and improving performance and avoiding illogical results such as incorrectly assuming Convey can't accelerate G/S because blind porting all G/S would make the code run slower. While speedup of 21% and 3.2% may not seem significant for some developers this amount may be worth the effort. The tools and models make the porting effort less challenging by identifying which sections of the application would benefit from porting and indicating their contribution to the overall runtime, leaving the final decision up to the developer. In addition, this work focused only on Gather/Scatter operations but the tools and methodology can be applied to other operations (i.e. stream, reduction, etc.). And with additional work on PIR and its source code tagging feature, porting could become quite effortless for the user/developer. In future work we also intend to extend this to model other idioms and also in using these potential calculations to predict how much energy we could save (FPGA's consume less energy than their host processors). Also, the methodology described in this work could easily be extended to other accelerators such as GPUs. Such an extension would involve similar steps as using PIR to identify code blocks which might perform efficiently on GPUs, developing a model for those blocks on the GPU, develop trace tools to capture relevant model inputs, and modify the simulator to incorporate new trace data and models. Such work is saved for future work.

6 BACKGROUND

The prevalence of Gather/Scatter operation in application can be seen in sorting algorithms, hash searches, and sparse-matrix vector multiplication[23] to name a few. For many parallel algorithms scatter and gather are two fundamental operations[24] for instance radix sort is a parallel sorting algorithm[25], hash used in databases, and any linear solvers use sparse-matrix vector multiplication[26]. The use of acceleration hardware to speed-up Gather/Scatter operations has mainly focused on GPU-based acceleration hardware. In He et al[23] they used gather scatter operations optimize using GPUs to implement three memory intensive algorithms radix sort, the hash search, and the sparse-matrix vector multiplication with models for just the GPU.

On traditional architectures there are varying techniques for modeling the performance of HPC applications [18, 27-46], spanning derived analytical models, trace-based models, to a combination of the two. Analytical based models require a detailed understanding of the application and/or its algorithm and the method doesn't lend itself to automated model generation, unlike trace-based methods.

Understanding the performance of acceleration hardware through modeling is a task that many researchers have focused on. Alam et al[47] investigate using their Modeling Assertions to model the multi-streaming, vector processing capabilities of the X1E on the NAS SP kernel[48]. Hong and Kim[49] developed an analytical model for GPU performance and applied it to micro-kernel and benchmarks, but not full scale HPC applications. Govindaraju et al [50] developed a memory model for GPUs for a set of algorithms used in scientific applications. They tested the model on benchmark kernels but not full-scale HPC applications.

This work offers a unique contribution in that it develops a general framework to model acceleration hardware on full-scale HPC applications and validates the model using full-scale applications and the acceleration hardware offered by the Convey FPGA system.

ACKNOWLEDGMENT

This work was supported by the DoD and used elements at the Extreme Scale Systems Center, located at ORNL and funded by the DoD. The software used in this work was in part developed by the DOE-supported ASC / Alliance Center for Astrophysical Thermonuclear Flashes at the University of Chicago. This research used resources of the National Center for Computational Sciences at Oak Ridge National Laboratory, which is supported by the Office of Science of the U.S. Department of Energy under Contract No. DE-AC05-00OR22725. Special thanks to Mark Kelly and Glen Edwards for all their help.

REFERENCES

[1] B. Miller, et al., "The Paradyn Parallel Performance Measurement Tool," Computer, vol. 28, pp. 37-46, 2002.

[2] S. Shende and A. Maloney, "The TAU Parallel Performance System," International Journal of High Performance Computing Applications, vol. 20, 2006.

[3] V. Adve, et al., "An Integrated Compilation and Performance Analysis Environment for Data Parallel Programs," Proceedings of the IEEE/ACM SC95 Conference, 1995.

[4] V. Freeh, et al., "Analyzing the Energy-time Trade-off in High-Performance Computing Applications," IEEE Transactions on Parallel and Distributed Systems, vol. 18, pp. 835-848, 2007.

[5] J. Shin, et al., "Autotuning and Specialization: Speeding up Nek5000 with Compiler Technology," presented at the International Conference on Supercomputing, 2010.

[6] J. Kepner, "HPC Productivity: An Overarching View," International Journal of High Performance Computing Applications, vol. 18, 2004.

[7] L. Hochstein, et al., "Parallel Programmer Productivity: A Case Study of Novice Parallel Programmers," Proceedings of the 2005 ACM/IEEE conference on Supercomputing, 2005.

[8] C. Olschanowsky, et al., "PIR: A Static Idiom Recognizer," in First International Workshop on Parallel Software Tools and Tool Infrastructures (PSTI 2010), San Diego, CA, 2010.

[9] J. Nieplocha, et al., "Global Arrays: A Non-uniform Memory Access Programming Model for High-Performance Computers," Journal of Supercomputing, vol. 10, pp. 169-189, 1996.

[10] J. Lewis and H. Simon, "The Impact of Hardware Gather/Scatter On Sparse Gaussian Elimination," SIAM J. Sci. Stat. Comput., vol. 9, pp. 304-311, 1988.

[11] S. Mukherjee, et al., "Efficient Support for Irregular Applications on Distributed-memory Machines," ACM SIGPLAN Notices, vol. 30, pp. 68-79, 1995.

[12] SGBench see, http://www.sdsc.edu/pmac/SGBench.

[13] J. Dongarra and P. Luszczek, "Introduction to the HPC Challenge Benchmark Suite," ICL-UT-05-01, 2005.

[14] G. Fox, et al., "Solving Problems on Concurrent Processors: Volume 1, Chapter 22," P. Hall, Ed., ed Englewood Cluffs, NJ, 1988.

[15] C. HC-1, "http://www.conveycomputer.com/ConveyArchitectureWhiteP.pdf," ed.

[16] M. Tikir, *et al.*, "The PMaC Binary Instrumentation Library for PowerPC," *Workshop on Binary Instrumentation and Applications, San Jose,* 2006.

[17] C. Olschanowsky, *et al.*, "PSnAP: Accurate Synthetic Address Streams Through Memory Profiles," *The 22nd International Workshop on Languages and Compilers for Parallel Computing,* Oct. 8-10 2009.

[18] A. Snavely, *et al.*, "A Framework for Application Performance Modeling and Prediction," *ACM/IEEE Conference on High Performance Networking and Computing,* 2002.

[19] L. Carrington, *et al.*, "How well can simple metrics represent the performance of HPC applications?," *Proceedings of the ACM/IEEE SC2005 Conference on High Performance Networking and Computing,* 2005.

[20] M. Tikir, *et al.*, "Genetic Algorithm Approach to Modeling the Performance of Memory-bound Codes," *The Proceeding of the ACM/IEEE Conference on High Performance Networking and Computing,* 2007.

[21] M. Tikir, *et al.*, "PSINS: An Open Source Event Tracer and Execution Simulator for model prediction," presented at the HPCMP User Group Conference, San Diego, CA, 2009.

[22] "ORNL Jaguar see http://www.nccs.gov/computing-resources/jaguar/."

[23] B. He, *et al.*, "Efficient Gather and Scatter Operations on Graphics Processors," *SC07,* 2007.

[24] J. D. Owens, *et al.*, "A Survey of general purpose compuation on graphics hardware," *Computer Graphics Forum,* vol. 26, 2007.

[25] M. Zagha and G. E. Blelloch, "Radix sort for vector multiprocessors.," in *Supercomputing 1991,* 1991.

[26] J. Bolz, *et al.*, "Sparse matrix solvers on the GPU: conjugate gradients and multigrid," *ACM Transactions on Graphics,* pp. 917-924, 2003.

[27] V. Adve and R. Sakellariou, "Application representations for multiparadigm performance modeling of large-scale parallel scientific codes," *The International Journal of High Performance Computing Applications,* vol. 14, 2000.

[28] S. Alam and J. Vetter, "A Framework to Develop Symbolic Performance Models of Parallel Applications," presented at the 5th International Workshop on Performance Modeling, Evaluation, and Optimization of Parallel and Distributed Systems, 2006.

[29] G. Almasi, *et al.*, "Demonstrating the scalability of a molecular dynamics application on a Petaflop computer," presented at the Proceedings of the 15th international conference on Supercomputing, Sorrento, Italy, 2001.

[30] B. Armstrong and R. Eigenmann, "Performance forecasting: Towards a methodology for characterizing large computationals applications," in *Internationals Conference on Parallel Processing,* 1998.

[31] D. Bailey and A. Snavely, "Performance Modeling: Understanding the Present and Predicting the Future," *EuroPar,* 2005.

[32] J. Bourgeois and F. Spies, "Performance prediction of an NAS benchmark program with chronosmix enviroment," presented at the 6th International Euro-Par Conference, 2000.

[33] M. Clement and M. Quinn, "Automated performance prediction for scalable parallel computing," *Parallel Computing,* vol. 23, 1997.

[34] M. J. Clement and M. J. Quinn, "Analytical performance prediction on multicomputers," *Supercomputing,* pp. 886-894, 1993.

[35] D. Culler, *et al.*, "LogP: Towards a realistic modle of parallel computation," in *4th ACM SIGPLAN Symposium on Principles and Practice of Parallel Programming,* 1993.

[36] M. Faerman, *et al.*, "Adaptive performance prediction for distributed data-intensive applications," presented at the Supercomputing, 1999.

[37] T. Fahringer and M. Zima, "A static parameter based performance prediction tool for parallel programs," presented at the The International Conference on Supercomputing, 1993.

[38] D. J. Kerbyson, *et al.*, "Predictive Performance and Scalability Modeling of Large-Scale Application," *Supercomputing,* 2001.

[39] C. Lim, *et al.*, "Implementation lessons of performance prediction tool for parallel conservative simulation," presented at the 6th International Euro-Par Conference, 2000.

[40] G. Marin and J. Mellor-Crummey, "Cross Architecture Performance Predictions for Scientific Applications Using Parameterized Models," *In Proceedings of the Joint International Conference on Measurement and Modeling of Computer Systems,* June 2004.

[41] B. Mohr and F. Wolf, "KOJAK - A Tool Set for Automatic Performance Analysis of Parallel Applications," presented at the European Converence on Parallel Computing (EuroPar), 2003.

[42] J. Simon and J.-M. Wierum, "Accurate Performance Prediction for Massively Parallel Systems and its Applications," *Euro-Par'96 Parallel Processing,* vol. 1124, pp. 675-688, 1996.

[43] A. van Gemund, "Symbolic performance modeling of parallel systems," *IEEE Transactions on Parallel and Distributed Systems,* vol. 14, 2003.

[44] A. Wagner, *et al.*, "Performance models for the processor farm paradigm," *IEEE Transactions on Parallel and Distributed Systems,* vol. 8, 1997.

[45] L. Yang, *et al.*, "Cross-Platform Performance Prediction of Parallel Applications Using Partial Execution," presented at the Proceedings of the 2005 ACM/IEEE conference on Supercomputing, 2005.

[46] X. Zhang and Z. Xu, "Multiprocessor Scalability Predictions Through Detailed Program Execution Analysis," *International Conference on Supercomputing,* pp. 97-106, 1995.

[47] S. Alam, *et al.*, "An Exploration of Performance Attributes for Symbolic Modeling of Emerging Processing Devices," presented at the HPCC, 2007.

[48] *NAS Parallel Benchmarks (NPB) see, http://www.nas.nasa.gov/Resources/Software/npb.html.*

[49] S. Hong and H. Kim, "An Analytical Model for a GPU Architecture with Memory-level and Thread-level Parallelism Awareness," presented at the ISCA'09, Austin, Texas, USA, 2009.

[50] N. Govindaraju, *et al.*, "A Memory Model for Scientific Algorithms on Graphics Processors," presented at the Supercomputing, Tampa, Florida USA, 2006.

Keynote Talk

Performance Modeling as the Key to Extreme Scale Computing

William D. Gropp
University of Illinois at Urbana-Champaign
wgropp@illinois.edu

Abstract

Parallel computing is primarily about achieving greater performance than is possible without using parallelism. Especially for the high-end, where systems cost tens to hundreds of millions of dollars, making the best use of these valuable and scarce systems is important. Yet few applications really understand how well they are performing with respect to the achievable performance on the system. The Blue Waters system, currently being installed at the University of Illinois, will offer sustained performance in excess of 1 PetaFLOPS for many applications. However, achieving this level of performance requires careful attention to many details, as this system has many features that must be used to get the best performance. To address this problem, the Blue Waters project is exploring the use of performance models that provide enough information to guide the development and tuning of applications, ranging from improving the performance of small loops to identifying the need for new algorithms. Using Blue Waters as an example of an extreme scale system, this talk will describe some of the challenges faced by applications at this scale, the role that performance modeling can play in preparing applications for extreme scale, and some ways in which performance modeling has guided performance enhancements for those applications.

Categories & Subject Descriptors: D.2.8 Software Engineering, Metrics, Performance measures; D.1.3 Programming Techniques, Concurrent Programming, Parallel programming

General Terms: Performance.

Mint: Realizing CUDA Performance in 3D Stencil Methods with Annotated C

Didem Unat
Dept. of Computer Science
and Engineering
Univ. of California, San Diego
La Jolla, CA, USA
dunat@cs.ucsd.edu

Xing Cai
Simula Research Laboratory,
Department of Informatics
University of Oslo
Norway
xingca@simula.no

Scott B. Baden
Dept. of Computer Science
and Engineering
Univ. of California, San Diego
La Jolla, CA, USA
baden@cs.ucsd.edu

ABSTRACT

We present Mint, a programming model that enables the non-expert to enjoy the performance benefits of hand coded CUDA without becoming entangled in the details. Mint targets stencil methods, which are an important class of scientific applications. We have implemented the Mint programming model with a source-to-source translator that generates optimized CUDA C from traditional C source. The translator relies on annotations to guide translation at a high level. The set of pragmas is small, and the model is compact and simple. Yet, Mint is able to deliver performance competitive with painstakingly hand-optimized CUDA. We show that, for a set of widely used stencil kernels, Mint realized 80% of the performance obtained from aggressively optimized CUDA on the 200 series NVIDIA GPUs. Our optimizations target three dimensional kernels, which present a daunting array of optimizations.

Categories and Subject Descriptors

D.3.4 [**Programming Languages**]: Processors—*Optimization, Compilers, Code generation*

General Terms

Algorithms, Design, Languages, Performance

Keywords

Automatic Translation and Optimization, CUDA, Parallel Programming Model, Stencil Computation

1. INTRODUCTION

GPUs are an effective means of accelerating certain types of applications, but an outstanding problem is how to manage the expansion of detail entailed in a highly tuned implementation. The details are well known; managing on-chip locality is perhaps the most challenging, and when managed

effectively it offers considerable rewards. Finding a way around this stumbling block is crucial, not only at the desktop but also on high-end mainframes. Many top-500 systems [1] are populated with GPUs and their number is growing.

In order to make GPU technology more accessible to the user, we have developed Mint: a programming model based on programmer annotations (pragmas) and a source-to-source translator that implements the model. The Mint translator takes annotated C source code, and produces legal CUDA code that is subsequently compiled by nvcc, the CUDA C compiler [2]. Mint targets stencil methods, an important problem domain with a wide range of applications, with an emphasis on optimizations for 3-dimensional stencils.

A general-purpose translator is the philosopher's stone of high performance computing. One of the most successful compilers was CFT, the Cray vectorizing compiler that came into its own in the early to mid 1980s. This success story was a consequence of the fact that the Cray architecture possessed a reasonable "cartoon" for how to obtain high performance, a simple set of guidelines the programmer could grasp intuitively[1]. We contend that no such cartoon (yet) exists for GPUs; a general-purpose compiler would have to wade through a sea of possible optimizations, specific to each problem class [3, 4, 5, 6, 7].

We advocate a "middle ground" approach. We restrict the application space so that we can incorporate semantic content into the translation process, but choose an application space that is important enough to make the restriction reasonable. Mint, a domain-specific approach for stencil methods, embodies this approach. Like OpenMP [8], Mint employs pragmas to guide translation. Some Mint pragmas are inherited from OpenMP, but interpreted differently in order to address the requirements of GPU hardware.

The benefit of our approach is improved productivity. The Mint pragmas enable the programmer to control the hardware at a much higher level than that of CUDA C. In exchange for a restricted application space, we reap the benefits of specialization–namely a reduced optimization space– leading to improved performance compared to a general-purpose compiler. As a result, application developers use their valuable time to focus on the application, rather than on the idiosyncratic features of the hardware.

The contribution of this paper is as follows. We introduce a CUDA-free interface to implement stencil methods on GPU hardware, which is based on modest amounts of program annotation. We identify a set of pragmas with an

---

[1]Phil Colella, private communications

OpenMP-like syntax that address system requirements not met by OpenMP, for example, in managing locality on the device, with an emphasis on supporting three-dimensional problems. We provide a source-to-source translator that incorporates domain specific knowledge to generate highly efficient CUDA C code, delivering performance that is competitive with hand-optimized CUDA. For a set of widely used stencil kernels, the Mint translator realized 80% of the performance of highly optimized hand-written CUDA on the Tesla C1060. The corresponding result on Fermi is 76%.

The paper is organized as follows. §2 provides background on the characteristics of stencil methods, and explains the motivation behind our work. §3 introduces the Mint programming model, §4 describes the translator and optimizer. We present performance results and evaluation in §5. §6 discusses related work. We conclude by evaluating the limitations of the model and translator.

2. STENCIL COMPUTATIONS

Stencil computations arise in some important classes of applications, notably finite difference discretization of partial differential equations [9] and in image processing [10]. They are good candidates for acceleration because they are highly data parallel and are typically implemented as nested for-loops. Many stencil methods are iterative; they sweep the mesh repeatedly, updating the mesh (or meshes) over a series of iterations. Each sweep will update each point of the mesh as a function of a surrounding neighborhood of points in space and time. We refer to a *stencil* as the neighborhood in the spatial domain. The most well known examples are the 5-point stencil approximation of the 2D Laplacian operator and the corresponding 7-point stencil in 3D, both shown in Fig. 1.

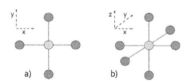

Figure 1: a) 5-point Stencil b) 7-point Stencil

As a motivating example, we consider the 3D heat equation $\partial u/\partial t = \kappa \nabla^2 u$, where ∇^2 is the Laplacian operator, and we assume a constant heat conduction coefficient κ and no heat sources. We use the following explicit finite difference scheme to solve the problem on a uniform mesh of points.

$$\frac{u_{i,j,k}^{n+1} - u_{i,j,k}^n}{\Delta t} = \frac{\kappa}{\Delta x^2} \big(u_{i,j,k-1}^n + u_{i,j-1,k}^n + u_{i-1,j,k}^n - 6u_{i,j,k}^n$$
$$+ u_{i+1,j,k}^n + u_{i,j+1,k}^n + u_{i,j,k+1}^n \big).$$

The superscript n denotes the discrete time step number (an iteration), the triple-subscript i, j, k denotes the spatial index. The quantity Δt is the temporal discretization (the timestep) and the mesh spacing Δx is equal in all directions. Note that the above formula is a 7-point computational stencil applicable only to inner grid points, and for simplicity we have omitted the treatment of boundary points.

The Mint program for solving this equation appears in Listing 1. (This program is also legal C, since a standard compiler will simply ignore the pragmas). Fig. 2 compares the double precision performance of three implementations

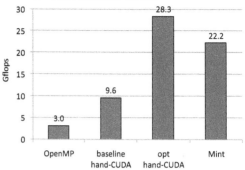

Figure 2: Comparing performance of OpenMP with 4 threads, hand-written unoptimized CUDA (unopt hand-CUDA), manually optimized CUDA (opt hand-CUDA), and Mint.

of the 3D heat equation solver running on an NVIDIA Tesla C1060 GPU. Our performance basis is an OpenMP implementation running on 4 cores of an Intel Nehalem processor. (§5 describes the testbeds used to obtain these results). The three CUDA versions are: baseline CUDA, aggressively hand-optimized CUDA, and Mint-generated CUDA. The baseline CUDA variant resolves all references to solution arrays through global (device) memory. It does not take advantage of fast on-chip shared memory. The heroically hand-optimized CUDA version improves performance by a factor of 3 over the baseline version. Running at 28.3 Gflops on the Tesla C1060 performance is comparable to previously published results [6] for this kernel[2], and is 9.4 times faster than the OpenMP variant. The programming effort required to realize this performance milestone is substantial; not only it manages threads and host-device transfers as in the baseline version, but also it tiles the iteration space to utilize fast on-chip device memory.

```
1  #pragma mint copy(U,toDevice,(n+2),(m+2),(k+2))
2  #pragma mint copy(Unew,toDevice,(n+2),(m+2),(k+2))
3
4  #pragma mint parallel default(shared)
5  {
6    int t=0;
7    while( t++ < T ){
8
9  #pragma mint for nest(all) tile(16,16,1)
10     for (int z=1; z<= k; z++)
11       for (int y=1; y<= m; y++)
12         for (int x=1; x<= n; x++)
13           Unew[z][y][x] = c0 * U[z][y][x] +
14             c1 * (U[z][y][x-1] + U[z][y][x+1] +
15                   U[z][y-1][x] + U[z][y+1][x] +
16                   U[z-1][y][x] + U[z+1][y][x]);
17  #pragma mint single{
18     double*** tmp;
19     tmp = U; U = Unew; Unew = tmp;
20     }//end of single
21   }//end of while
22  }//end of parallel region
23
24  #pragma mint copy(U,fromDevice,(n+2),(m+2),(k+2))
```

Listing 1: Mint program for the 3D heat equation. (Unew corresponds to u^{n+1} and U to u^n and $c_0 = 1 - 6\kappa\Delta t/\Delta x^2$ and $c_1 = \kappa\Delta t/\Delta x^2$.)

---

[2]Vasily Volkov kindly provided the 7-point stencil used in [6] which is equivalent to our 7-pt 3D heat equation kernel.

By comparison, the Mint-annotated version shown in Listing 1 came within 78% of the performance achieved by the heroically optimized CUDA, and required a much more modest programming effort. Only 6 pragmas were introduced and no existing source code was modified. The Mint `for` directive appearing at line 9 enables the translator to parallelize the `for` loop nest on lines (10-16). The `nest(all)` clause specifies that all loops should be parallelized. It is important to clarify that the Mint keyword `nest` specifies that a loop nest is to be parallelized using multi-dimensional thread structures. This is different from the nested parallelism in OpenMP, which specifies trees of threads. We need to specify higher dimensional threading structures in order to effectively utilize the GPU hardware, especially for three dimensional kernels.

3. MINT PROGRAMMING MODEL

3.1 System Assumptions

The Mint programming model assumes a system design depicted in Fig. 3, comprising a host processor and an accelerator[3]. Since accelerator technology is in a state of flux, our model abstracts away some aspects of how the system functions. For example, in an NVIDIA-based system, the host and device have physically distinct memories and the host controls all data motion between the two. However, Mint is neutral about how the data motion is brought about. Future systems may treat data motion differently, for example, the device may be able to initiate data transfers.

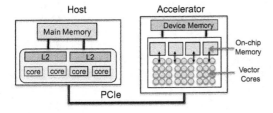

Figure 3: System Design

The accelerator contains several vector units that see a global device memory address space. The host invokes multithreaded kernels on the accelerator, which execute as a sequence of long vector operations that are partitioned into pieces by the accelerator and assigned to vector units. The vector elements are computed independently in an undefined order.

Each vector unit has a small local storage hierarchy that delivers much higher bandwidth (and a lower access time) than device memory. In NVIDIA 200 series devices, each vector processor has a private, software-managed on-chip memory. Fermi's on-chip memory is partitioned into a first level of cache and shared memory, and there is a second level of cache to back up L1. Mint does not assume a specific memory hierarchy, other than that there is fast and slow memory. We believe that Mint will not require special clauses to handle the Fermi architecture, except perhaps a flag to set the relative amounts of shared memory and L1 cache. Currently, Mint uses default configurations for Fermi: 48KB shared memory and 16KB L1.

---

[3]Extensions are required to handle multi-GPU platforms in Mint.

3.2 The Model

With the non-expert GPU user in mind, simplicity is our principal design goal for the Mint programming model. The principal effort should be to (1) identify and effectively parallelize time consuming-loop nests that can benefit from acceleration and (2) move data between host and accelerator.

A pragma-based programmer interface is a natural way of meeting our requirements. It allows us to optimize code for GPU execution incrementally, while maintaining a code base that can always run on a conventional CPU. Mint parallelizes a loop nest by associating one logical thread with some number of points in the iteration space of the nest. It then partitions and maps the logical threads onto physical ones, guided by any clauses that the programmer employs to tune the pragmas. The details come at a high level. For example, the programmers need not concern themselves with "flattening" a multidimensional array, which is common in GPU implementations. The translator takes care of the details.

Mint employs just five different directives, four of which appear in Listing 1. The `for` directive is the most important, as it identifies a parallel `for` loop nest and helps guide optimization. This construct resembles the familiar OpenMP directive, but is interpreted differently to meet the device capabilities. Mint creates a multi-dimensional array of threads to parallelize the specified loop nest. This capability of Mint is crucial; it enables the user to employ higher dimensional CUDA thread blocks, which are required to use the device effectively. Lastly, Mint helps the user manage the separate host and device memory spaces. The Mint programmer specifies transfers at a high level through the Mint `copy` directive, avoiding storage management and setup.

3.3 The Mint Pragmas

We next describe the 5 pragmas of Mint.

- **mint parallel [clauses]** indicates the start of a parallel region containing parallel work. These regions will be accelerated. Before control enters the parallel region, any data used in the region must have previously been transferred using the `copy` directive. Mint provides the `shared` clause as in OpenMP to indicate the data sharing rule between threads. Mint maps a shared array onto device memory and it is visible to all threads employed by the launched kernel. Variables not declared as shared are thread-private, and typically reside in registers.

- **mint for [clauses]** marks the succeeding `for` loop (or nested loops) for GPU acceleration and manages data decomposition and work assignment. Each such parallel `for` loop becomes a CUDA kernel. Mint may merge kernels if there is `no-wait` clause attached to a for loop directive. Other optional `for` clauses are followings:

  nest(# | all) indicates the depth of `for`-loop parallelization within a loop nest, which can be an integer, or the keyword `all` to indicate that all the loops are independent, and hence parallelizable. This clause supports multi-dimensional thread geometries. If the `nest` clause is not specified, Mint assumes that only the outermost `for` loop is parallelizable.

tile(t_x, t_y, t_z) specifies how the iteration space of a loop nest is to be subdivided into *tiles*. A data tile is assigned to a group of threads and the sizes are passed as parameters to the clause. In the CUDA context, a tile corresponds to the number of data points computed by a thread block.

chunksize(c_x, c_y, c_z) aggregates logical threads into a single CUDA thread. Each CUDA thread serially executes these logical threads via a C `for` loop. This clause is similar to the OpenMP *schedule* clause, though OpenMP confines chunking to a single dimension. Together with the `tile` clause, the `chunksize` clause establishes the number of CUDA threads that execute a tile. Specifically, the size of a CUDA thread block is $threads(t_x/c_x, t_y/c_y, t_z/c_z)$, as depicted in Fig. 4. In the absence of `tile` and `chunksize` clauses, the compiler will choose default values[4].

- **mint barrier** synchronizes all the threads.
- **mint single** indicates serial regions. Depending on the requirements, either a host or a single device thread executes the region.
- **mint copy(src | dst, toDevice | fromDevice, [N_x, N_y, N_z, ...])** expresses data transfers between the host and device. Mint binds a host array to the corresponding device array using this directive. Mint handles the declaration, allocation/deallocation, and data transfers (with padding for alignment) on the device. The parameters *toDevice* and *fromDevice* indicate the direction of the copy. The remaining parameters are optional, and specify the array dimensions. This directive in fact is the only hint to a reader of Mint code about the use of an accelerator. We choose to get help from the programmer for the sake of better performance in terms of *when* the copy should occur, and between *which* arrays.

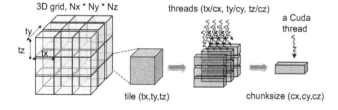

Figure 4: A 3D grid is broken into 3D tiles based on the tile clause. Elements in a tile are divided among a thread block based on chunksize clause.

To summarize, Mint will attempt to migrate a parallel region that contains at least one for-loop to the accelerator. The `barrier` directive will be translated into costly global synchronization among CUDA threads. The `single` directive will cause the indicated code segment to run on the host or as a single device thread.

Those familiar with OpenMP will recognize the `parallel`, `for`, `single` and `barrier` pragmas. A legal Mint program can be converted to a legal OpenMP program using string substitution, or, it could be compiled as it is by a standard C compiler, which would ignore the Mint pragmas. Thus, the code can always be run on conventional hardware.

---

[4]Mint currently chooses 16x16x1 tiles with a chunksize of 1 in all dimensions, but the default is configurable.

4. C TO CUDA TRANSLATION

We have developed a fully automated translation and optimization system for the Mint programming model. To construct our source-to-source translation and analysis tools, we used the ROSE compiler framework[11, 12], open source software developed and maintained at Lawrence Livermore National Laboratory. ROSE is a convenient tool for developing our infrastructure, because it provides an API for generating and manipulating in memory representations of Abstract Syntax Trees (ASTs).

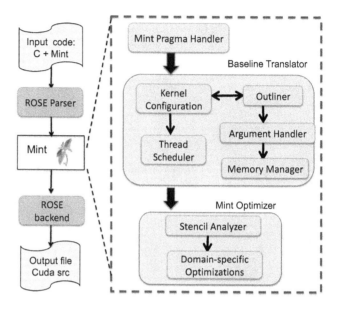

Figure 5: Modular design of Mint Translator and translation flow.

4.1 Mint Translator

Fig. 5 shows the modular design of the Mint translator and the translation work flow. The input to the compiler is C source code annotated with Mint pragmas. The *Pragma Handler* parses the Mint directives and clauses. Once the translator has constructed the AST, it queries the parallel regions containing data parallel for-loops. Directives in a candidate parallel region go through several transformation steps inside the Baseline Translator: *Outliner, Kernel Configuration, Argument Handler, Memory Manager*, and *Thread Scheduler*.

The *Baseline Translator* generates both device kernel code and host code. With the help of the `mint for` directive and attendant clauses, the transformer determines the kernel configuration parameters, i.e. CUDA thread block and grid sizes. *Outliner* outlines the candidate parallel for-loop into a function: a CUDA kernel. It moves the body of the loop into a newly-created `__global__` function and replaces the statement it vacates (including the original `for` directive) with a launch of the newly-created kernel. *Argument handler* works with *Outliner* and determines which variables are local to the function and which need to be passed as arguments. Naturally, all the parameters in the function argument become kernel call parameters. Depending on whether these parameters are vectors or scalars, they may require data transfers.

Unless already residing on the device (say from a previous loop body), any vector arguments need to be transferred to device memory. The *Memory Manager* checks whether or not the programmer requested the transfer of vector variables via the Mint `copy` pragma. If not, then the compiler tries to infer the information necessary to generate the code for the transfer. In the case of statically declared arrays, it will carry out the translation, but it cannot determine this information for dynamically allocated arrays. In such cases it will issue a message and abort.

The *Thread Scheduler* inserts code into the generated kernel body to compute global thread IDs. It also rewrites references (i.e array subscripts) to original `for` loop indices to use these global thread IDs instead. When `chunksize` is set to 1, the loop iteration space is mapped one-to-one onto physical threads. Otherwise, the compiler inserts a serial loop into the kernel so that the thread can compute the multiple points assigned to it.

The output of the *Baseline Translator* makes all memory references through device memory. If the optimization flag is turned on, the *Mint optimizer* performs both general and stencil method-specific optimizations on the generated code. We will discuss these optimizations in depth shortly.

```
1  /* Mint: Replaced Pragma: #pragma mint copy */
2  cudaExtent ext_dU = make_cudaExtent(...);
3
4  /* Mint: Malloc on the device */
5  cudaPitchedPtr ptr_dU;
6  cudaMalloc3D(&ptr_dU,ext_dU);
7  ...
8  /* Mint: Copy host to device */
9  cudaMemcpy3DParms param_dU = {0};
10 param_dU.srcPtr = make_cudaPitchedPtr(...);
11 param_dU.dstPtr = ptr_dU;
12 param_dU.extent = ext_dU;
13 param_dU.kind = cudaMemcpyHostToDevice;
14 stat_dU = cudaMemcpy3D(&param_dU);
15 ...
16 while(t++ < T){
17
18     //Kernel configuration parameters
19     int num3block = (k-1+1)%1 == 0?(k-1+1)/1:(k-1+1)/1+1;
20     int num2block = (m-1+1)%16 == 0?(m-1+1)/16:(m-1+1)/16+1;
21     int num1block = (n-1+1)%16 == 0?(n-1+1)/16:(n-1+1)/16+1;
22
23     dim3 blockDim(16,16,1);
24     dim3 gridDim(num1block, num2block * num3block);
25
26     float invYnumblock = 1.0/num2block;
27     //kernel launch
28     mint_1_1527<<<gridDim,blockDim>>>(...);
29
30     cudaThreadSynchronize();
31     ...
32     double* tmp = (double*)ptr_dU.ptr;
33     ptr_dU.ptr = ptr_dUnew.ptr;
34     ptr_dUnew.ptr = (void*)tmp;
35
36 }//end of while
37 /* Mint: Replaced Pragma: #pragma mint copy */
38 /* Mint: Copy device to host */
```

Listing 2: Host code generated by the Mint translator for the 7-point 3D stencil input.

Listing 2 shows the host code generated by the Mint translator for the 7-point 3D stencil example provided in Listing 1. For the sake of clarity, we have omitted some of the details. Lines (1-14) perform memory allocation and data transfer for the variable *U*, corresponding to line 1 in Listing 1. Mint uses CUDA *pitched* pointer type and *cudaMalloc3D* to pad storage allocation on the device to ensure

hardware alignment requirements are met [13]. Lines (18-24) compute the kernel configuration parameters based on values provided by the user (i.e. via pragma clauses), if there are any, else it chooses default values. Under CUDA, a grid of thread blocks can not have more than 2 dimensions. A common trick in CUDA is to emulate 3D grids (lines (24-26)) by mapping two dimensions of the original iteration space onto one dimension of the kernel. Line (28) launches the kernel and line (30) is a global barrier across all threads employed in the kernel launch. Lines (32-34) perform the pointer swap on the device pointers.

```
1  __global__ void mint_1_1527(cudaPitchedPtr ptr_dU,
2    cudaPitchedPtr ptr_dUnew,int n,int m, int k,
3    double c0,double c1,int blocksInY,float invBlocksInY)
4  {
5    double* U = (double *)(ptr_dU.ptr);
6    int widthU = ptr_dU.pitch / sizeof(double );
7    int sliceU = ptr_dU.ysize * widthU;
8    ...
9    int _idx = threadIdx.x + 1;
10   int _gidx = _idx + blockDim.x * blockIdx.x;
11   int _idy = threadIdx.y + 1;
12   int _idz = 1;
13   int blockIdxz = blockIdx.y * invBlocksInY;
14   int blockIdxy = blockIdx.y - blockIdxz * blocksInY;
15   int _gidy = _idy + blockIdxy * blockDim.y;
16   int _gidz = _idz + blockIdxz;
17   int indU = _gidx +_gidy*widthU +_gidz*sliceU;
18   int indUnew = _gidx +_gidy*widthUnew +_gidz*sliceUnew;
19
20   if (_gidz >= 1 && _gidz <= k)
21    if (_gidy >= 1 && _gidy <= m)
22     if (_gidx >= 1 && _gidx <= n)
23       Unew[indUnew] = c0 * U[indU]
24        + c1 * (U[indU - 1] + U[indU + 1]
25           + U[indU - widthU] + U[indU + widthU]
26           + U[indU - sliceU] + U[indU + sliceU]);
27 }//end of function
```

Listing 3: Unoptimized kernel generated by Mint for the 7-point 3D stencil input.

Listing 3 shows the unoptimized kernel generated by Mint. All the memory accesses pass through global memory. Lines (5-7) unpack the CUDA pitched pointer *U*, while lines (9-18) compute local and global indices using thread and block IDs. Lines (20-22) are `if` statements derived from the `for` statements in the original annotated source. Finally, the lines (23-26) perform the stencil mesh sweep on the flattened arrays. In CUDA, multi-dimensional indexing works correctly only if the `nvcc` compiler knows the pitch of the array at compile time. Therefore, Mint converts such indices appearing in the annotated code into their 1D equivalents.

In the generated kernel code shown in Listing 3, each CUDA thread updates a single element of `Unew`. However, there is a performance benefit to aggregating array elements so that each CUDA thread computes more than one point. Mint allows the programmer to easily manage the mapping of work to threads using the `chunksize` clause. The following code fragment shows part of the generated kernel when the programmer sets a chunking factor in the z dimension, the 3rd argument of the `chunksize` clause. As an optimization, the translator moves `if` statements outside the `for` statement. It also computes the bounds of the `for`-loop.

```
1  if (_gidy >= 1 && _gidy <= m)
2   if (_gidx >= 1 && _gidx <= n)
3    for (_gidz = _gidz; _gidz <= _upper_gidz; _gidz++)
4      Unew[indUnew] = c0 * U[indU] + ...
```

Chunking affects the kernel configuration (i.e. size of the thread blocks) by rendering a smaller number of thread blocks with "fatter" threads. This clause is particularly helpful when combined with on-chip memory optimizations because it enables re-use of data. The reason will be explained in more detail in §4.2.3.

4.2 Mint Optimizer

The Mint optimizer incorporates a number of optimizations that we have found to be useful in optimizing stencil methods written in CUDA. Our insight is that occupancy should not be maximized to the exclusion of properly managed on-chip locality. Although we need a sufficient number of threads to overlap data transfers with computation, if global memory accesses are too frequent, we may not be able to hide their latency.

4.2.1 Stencil Analyzer

To optimize for on-chip memory re-use, the optimizer must analyze the structure of the stencil(s) appearing in the application. Based on this analysis, it then chooses an optimization strategy appropriate for the determined stencil pattern. The analyzer first determines if the kernel is eligible for optimization by checking to see if the pattern of array subscripts involves a central point and nearest neighbors only, that is, index expressions of the form $i \pm k$, where i is an index variable and k is a small constant.

Next, the analyzer determines the shape of the stencil. The shape affects not only the number of ghost cell loads, but also the amount of shared memory needed to optimize the kernel. Consider two 3D stencils as shown in Fig. 6. A common case is the 7-point stencil that couples the 6 nearest neighbor points (in the Manhattan directions) to the central point. The 7-point stencil requires that only one xy-plane of data be kept in shared memory at a time. By comparison, the 19-point stencil shares data in all three xy-planes because of the diagonal points, and thus has a different shared memory requirement.

Stencils may also differ in the required number of ghost cell loads depending on whether they are symmetric or cover a large neighborhood. For instance, a thread block processing a 3D tile (t_x, t_y, t_z) for a non-compact, 4th order, 13-point stencil would load a tile with size $(t_x + 2k, t_y + 2k, t_z + 2k)$ including ghost cells, where k is 2. The analyzer passes this information to the optimizer.

4.2.2 On-chip Memory Optimizer

When Mint optimizations are not enabled, the translated code does not utilize on-chip memory to handle array references. All array references go through global memory, and frequently referenced data is not re-used. For example, in the 7-point stencil kernel, each thread independently loads all six nearest neighbors even though each nearest neighbor is used by 6 nearby points. Owing to this high volume of potential re-use, the key optimization for stencil kernels is to buffer global memory accesses on chip, i.e. in shared memory and registers.

Shared Memory. The optimizer lets a thread block load a block of data –with respective ghost cells–into shared memory. One of the issues of using shared memory effectively is that ghost cells require special handling. We have two choices. In the first case we adjust the thread block size so

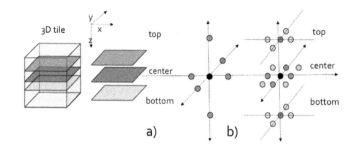

Figure 6: The black point is the central point of the stencil. a) 7-point stencil, b) 19-point stencil.

that each thread is assigned a single interior point[5]. Some threads are then responsible for loading ghost cells as well as performing computation. In the second case, the thread block is large enough to cover ghost cells as well as interior points. The drawback of this approach is that we leave some border threads idle during computation. Mint implements the former approach.

There may be various choices regarding which array(s) to place in shared memory. The optimizer chooses the most frequently referenced array(s). In case of a tie involving more than one array, the array(s) accessed along the fastest varying dimension are given priority since they require that fewer planes be kept in shared memory. However, because shared memory is a scarce resource (16KB per vector unit in the 200 series GPUs) there are obvious limitations to how many arrays we can buffer in shared memory, especially for stencils with many points. For example, owing to diagonal points, a 19-point stencil would require 3 times the space needed for a 7-point stencil. If we needed an extra mesh, say, for a variable coefficient problem, and we choose to keep it in shared memory as well, then we further increase the shared memory requirement: we double it.

Registers. We use registers to alleviate pressure on shared memory, enabling us to increase device occupancy by increasing the number of thread blocks. We improve performance still further, since an instruction with operands in shared memory runs at a lower rate (about 66% of the peak) compared to when its operands are in registers [3]. The optimizer stores, in registers, stencils that use a center point. As a result, a thread will read values from registers if available instead of reading from shared memory.

The optimizer conducts a def-use analysis to retrieve information about when to transfer data between on-chip and device memory. For example, read-only arrays are not written back to device memory and write-only arrays are not read from memory.

4.2.3 Loop Aggregation

As described previously, we can improve re-use still further by employing the `chunksize` clause in tandem with on-chip memory optimizations. The effect is to assign each CUDA thread more than one point in the iteration space of the loop nest, enabling values stored in shared memory to be shared in updating adjacent points. This optimization is particularly helpful for 3D stencils as it allows the reuse of data already in shared memory, by chunking along

---

[5]Without any loss of generality, we assume a chunk size of one.

Stencil kernel	Mathematical description	In,Out arrays	Read,Write per point	Operations per point
2D Heat 5-point	$u_{i,j}^{n+1} = c_0 u_{i,j}^n + c_1 \left(u_{i\pm1,j}^n + u_{i,j\pm1}^n \right)$	1,1	5,1	2(*),4(+)
3D Heat 7-point	$u_{i,j,k}^{n+1} = c_0 u_{i,j,k}^n + c_1 \left(u_{i\pm1,j,k}^n + u_{i,j\pm1,k}^n + u_{i,j,k\pm1}^n \right)$	1,1	7,1	2(*),6(+)
3D Poisson 7-point	$u_{i,j,k}^{n+1} = c_0 b_{i,j,k} + c_1 \left(u_{i\pm1,j,k}^n + u_{i,j\pm1,k}^n + u_{i,j,k\pm1}^n \right)$	2,1	7,1	2(*),6(+)
3D Heat 7-point variable coefficient	$u_{i,j,k}^{n+1} = u_{i,j,k}^n + b_{i,j,k}$ $+ c \left[\kappa_{i+\frac{1}{2},j,k} \left(u_{i+1,j,k}^n - u_{i,j,k}^n \right) - \kappa_{i-\frac{1}{2},j,k} \left(u_{i,j,k}^n - u_{i-1,j,k}^n \right) \right.$ $+ \kappa_{i,j+\frac{1}{2},k} \left(u_{i,j+1,k}^n - u_{i,j,k}^n \right) - \kappa_{i,j-\frac{1}{2},k} \left(u_{i,j,k}^n - u_{i,j-1,k}^n \right)$ $\left. + \kappa_{i,j,k+\frac{1}{2}} \left(u_{i,j,k+1}^n - u_{i,j,k}^n \right) - \kappa_{i,j,k-\frac{1}{2}} \left(u_{i,j,k}^n - u_{i,j,k-1}^n \right) \right]$	3,1	15,1	7(*),13(+),6(−)
3D Poisson 19-point	$u_{i,j,k}^{n+1} = c_0 \left[b_{i,j,k} + c_1 \left(u_{i\pm1,j,k}^n + u_{i,j\pm1,k}^n + u_{i,j,k\pm1}^n \right) \right.$ $\left. + u_{i\pm1,j\pm1,k}^n + u_{i\pm1,j,k\pm1}^n + u_{i,j\pm1,k\pm1}^n \right]$	2,1	19,1	2(*),18(+)

Table 1: A summary of stencil kernels used in this paper. The $\pm$ notation is short hand to save space, $u_{i\pm1,j}^n = u_{i-1,j}^n + u_{i+1,j}^n$. 19-pt stencil Gflop/s rate is calculated based on the reduced flop counts which is 14.

the z-dimension. The programmer can explicitly trigger this optimization by setting a chunking factor in the z-dimension (the 3rd argument of `chunksize` clause). Mint implements the optimization with the help of registers and shared memory. As shown in Fig. 4, a 3D input grid is subdivided into 3D tiles and then each 3D tile is further divided into a series of 2D planes. In this scheme, we use a buffer with three rotating planes. A plane that has been read from global memory starts as the bottom plane, continues as the center plane and then migrates to the top.

This optimization is referred to as partial 3D blocking in the literature. Rivera and Tseng [14] proposed the method for stencil-based computation on traditional processors. The technique is shown to be highly effective [15] on software-managed memory architectures such as the STI Cell Broadband Engine [16]. We incorporated this optimization into our compiler through a simple clause, `chunksize`, saving a good deal of programming overhead in managing data decomposition and index computation.

Since we let a thread compute multiple elements in the slowest varying dimension, we can reduce some of the index calculations by assigning a thread more than one row in the y-dimension. We do this by setting the y-dimension of the `chunksize` clause to a value greater than one. However, there is a potential drawback. If we allow a thread to compute multiple elements we increase the number of registers used by the thread, constraining the range of usable chunk sizes in the y-dimension. It is disadvantageous to apply loop aggregation to the x-dimension because it disrupts the temporal locality across threads, assigning successive elements to a thread in the fastest varying dimension. Such locality is needed to ensure coalesced accesses to global memory in the NVIDIA GPU [13].

4.3 Limitations

An obvious limitation of our translator is that it is domain-specific. Mint targets stencil computations and our optimizations are specific to this problem domain. We believe that the benefit of this approach outweighs the disadvantages of the limitations. We can incorporate domain-specific optimizations into our compiler, resulting in improved performance.

Our translator can perform subscript analysis on multi-dimensional array references only. It cannot analyze "flattened" array references, for example, when determining stencil structures, and may incorrectly disqualify a computation as not expressing a stencil pattern. In addition, the compiler cannot determine the shapes of dynamically allocated arrays. In this case we require that the programmer use the `copy` pragma to express data transfers, though many of the details are hidden from view.

Our translator is currently capable of generating code that utilizes only a single CUDA device. Generating code for multi-GPU execution would require more complex analysis to manage the ghost cell communication. This remains as future work.

5. PERFORMANCE RESULTS

We next demonstrate the effectiveness of the Mint translator, using a set of widely used stencil kernels in two and three dimensions. The kernels were chosen because of their different patterns of memory access and computational intensity. Tab. 1 summarizes the characteristics of each kernel.

We compare the performance of Mint-generated CUDA with hand-written (and optimized) CUDA and with OpenMP. All GPU results were obtained from an NVIDIA Tesla C1060 with 4GB device memory. The device is 1.3 capable. It has 30 streaming multiprocessors (each with 8 cores), which we will refer to as vector units [6], each running at 1.3 GHz. Each vector unit has substantial fast on-chip memory in the form of a 16KB scratch-pad memory and 64KB of registers. Both hand-coded and translated CUDA codes were compiled with `nvcc 3.2` and `-O3` optimization. The host CPU is a server based on a 2.0 GHz quad-core Intel Nehalem-EP processor (E5504, or "Gainstown") with 4MB of L3 cache and 16GB of main memory. OpenMP programs were compiled using `gcc 4.4.3` and command line options `-O3 -fopenmp`. All computations were run in double precision.

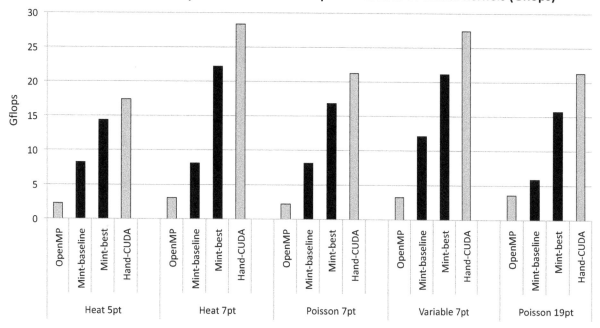

Performance Comparison of Different Implementations of Stencil Kernels (Gflops)

Figure 7: Performance comparison of the kernels. OpenMP ran with 4 threads on conventional hardware. Mint-baseline corresponds to the Mint baseline translation without using the Mint optimizer, Mint-best with optimizations turned on, and Hand-CUDA is hand-optimized CUDA. The Y-axis shows the measured Gflop rate. Heat 5-pt is a 2D kernel, the rest are 3D.

5.1 Performance Comparison

Fig. 7 compares the performance of the stencil kernels and their 4 different implementations. *OpenMP* results were obtained by running 4 OpenMP threads on the host. The remaining versions ran on the device. *Mint-baseline* is the result of compiling Mint-annotated C source without enabling any Mint optimizations, and *Mint-best* turns on all Mint optimizations. (Mint-generated CUDA was compiled with nvcc without any modification.) Lastly, *Hand-CUDA* refers to manually implemented and optimized CUDA C. Mint was **not** used to produce this code. The figure shows that even our baseline Mint code outperforms the OpenMP code running on 4 CPU cores and provides on average a 3x speedup. The Mint optimizer improves performance still further, achieving between 78% and 83% of the performance of the aggressively hand-optimized CUDA versions. The optimizer delivers 4.5 to 8 times the performance of OpenMP running with 4 threads.

We have also run the Mint-generated code on Fermi (Tesla C2050). On average, Mint achieved 76% of the performance of hand-written CUDA. Fermi results were obtained without modifying either the translator or the hand-written CUDA kernels, thus neither Mint nor our hand-coded implementations have been tuned for Fermi. Our preliminary results are therefore subject to change though they are quite promising.

5.2 Optimization Levels

The Mint optimizer provides three levels of optimization: *opt-1, opt-2 and opt-3*. The optimizations are cumulative, thus opt-3 includes all three optimizations.

- *Opt-1* turns on shared memory optimization (§4.2.2).
- *Opt-2* adds loop aggregation, which benefits shared memory (§4.2.3).
- *Opt-3* adds register optimizations (§4.2.2).

As mentioned previously, *baseline* refers to the performance of the Mint baseline translator. This variant resolves all array references through device memory. It does not buffer these references in on-chip memory and makes many redundant global memory accesses. On the other hand, it does create multi-dimensional thread blocks, if the nest clause is used in the mint-for directive.

Fig. 8 compares the performance of 4 kernels at different levels of optimization. We report performance as a speedup over Mint-generated code without any compiler optimization turned on, though we do allow source code optimization via pragmas. In all Mint code, loops are annotated with nest(all). In 3D we chose tile sizes as follows, all resulting in 16 × 16 thread blocks, except for the 2D Heat kernel, which uses a (16,16) tile size.

- *baseline* and *opt-1* use 2D tiles: tile(16,16,1). Each thread computes just one element.
- *opt-2* and *opt-3* use 3D tiles: tile(16,16,64). Each thread computes 64 elements in the z-dimension.

Fig. 8 shows the performance impacts of the different optimizations. Generally, performance improves with the level of optimization, though not in all cases. Not all optimizations are relevant in two dimensions, for example, loop aggregation (*opt-2*). Shared memory optimization (*opt-1*) is always

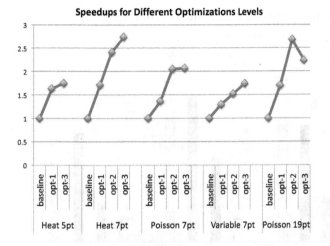

Figure 8: Effect of the Mint optimizer on the performance. The baseline resolves all the array references through device memory.

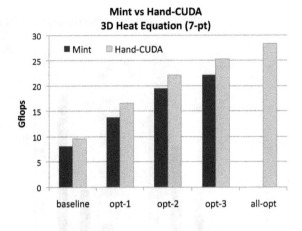

Figure 9: Comparing the performance of Mint-generated code and hand-coded CUDA. *All-opt* indicates additional optimizations on top of *opt-3*.

helpful. It takes advantage of significant opportunities for re-use in stencil kernels, reducing global memory traffic significantly. We observed performance improvements in the range of 30-70%.

The speedups attributed to tiling for shared memory differ according to the number of data streams that exhibit reuse. The Poisson 7-pt and Heat 7-pt stencils have the same flop counts but Poisson 7-pt requires an additional input grid, increasing the number of data streams from 2 to 3. As a result, its performance lags behind the Heat 7-pt because one of the input arrays (the right hand side) does not exhibit data reuse and cannot benefit from shared memory. On the other hand, the 7-pt variable coefficient kernel (Variable 7-pt) has 4 data streams, and 2 of the streams exhibit reuse. The Mint optimizer places the corresponding two meshes in shared memory, trading off occupancy for reduced global memory traffic. Since Variable 7-pt uses twice the shared memory as Heat 7-pt, occupancy is cut in half, and performance suffers. Nevertheless, shared memory still improves performance of Variable 7-pt. To see why, we experimented with hand-coded CUDA implementations. We found that if we allowed only one of the two data streams in question to reside in shared memory, then overall performance increased by 45% compared to when we used no shared memory. When we put both data streams in shared memory, the overall improvement increased to 85%.

The *opt-2* flag applies loop aggregation on top of shared memory optimization. In *opt-1*, threads can share data (reads) within the xy-plane only, whereas loop aggregation assigns each thread a column of values, allowing reuse in z-dimension as well. Thus, the thread block is responsible for 3D tile of data and can share the work across xy-planes. The generated kernels perform only the necessary loads and stores to device memory for the inner points. Once an element is read, no other thread will load the value, except for the ghost cells. This optimization has a significant impact on performance. The effect is particularly pronounced for the Poisson 19-pt stencil, owing to the high degree of sharing between threads.

The *opt-3* flag implements register optimizations on top of *opt-2*. This optimization helps in two ways: (1) an instruction executes more quickly if its operands are in registers [3] and (2) registers augment shared memory with plentiful on-chip storage (64KB compared with 16KB of shared memory). We can store more information on-chip and reduce pressure on shared memory. By reducing pressure on shared memory, the device can execute more thread blocks concurrently, i.e. with higher occupancy. Indeed, the register optimization improves performance in nearly all the kernels. The one exception is the 19-point stencil. This is an artifact of the current state of our optimizer. The hand-CUDA version of the 19-point kernel uses registers more effectively. It eliminates common expressions appearing in multiple slices of the input grid. It also uses registers to store intermediate sums along edges, and reuses the computed sums in multiple slices[6]. The effect is to reduce the number of flops performed per data point. The opportunity does not arise in the 7-pt stencils owing to limited sharing: only one value is used from the top and bottom slices. We are currently working on this optimization in Mint and expect to increase the performance of the 19-pt stencil further and hence close the performance gap with hand-coded CUDA.

5.3 Mint vs Hand-CUDA

To better understand the source of performance gap between the Mint-generated and hand-optimized CUDA code, we analyze the Heat 7-pt kernel in greater depth. Fig. 9 compares the performance of Mint-generated code for the available optimizations and compares with hand-coded CUDA (*Hand-CUDA*) that implements the same strategies. While the two variants implement the same optimization *strategies*, they may *implement* the strategies differently.

One way in which the implementations differ is in how they treat padding, which helps ensure that shared memory accesses coalesce. Mint relies on *cudaMalloc3D* to pad the storage allocation. This function aligns memory to the start of the mesh array, which includes the ghost cells. On the

---

[6]More information about this optimization on traditional multi-core architecture can be found in [17].

other hand, the *Hand-CUDA* implementation pre-processes the input arrays and pads them to ensure that all the global memory accesses are perfectly aligned. Memory is aligned to the inner region of the input arrays, where the solution is updated. Ghost cells are far less numerous so it pays to align to the inner region, which accounts for the lion's share of the global memory accesses.

We can achieve this effect in the Mint implementation if we pad the arrays manually prior to translation. In so doing, we observed a 10% performance improvement, on average, in the Mint-generated code at all optimization levels. Mint *opt-3* closes the gap from 86% to 90% of Hand-CUDA *opt-3* with padding.

Mint generates code that uses more registers than the hand-optimized code. This mainly stems from the fact that it maintains separate index variables to address different arrays even when the subscript expressions are shared among references to the different arrays. For example, in Listing 3, the compiler uses separate *width, surface,* and *index* variables for *U* and *Unew*. By comparison, Hand-CUDA shares the common index expressions. Combined with manual padding, reduction in index variables improved the performance by 10% and provided us with the same performance for Mint *opt-3* and the Hand-CUDA *opt-3*.

There is also an additional hand coded variant in Fig. 9, called *all-opt*, that do not appear in the compiler. This variant supports an optimization we haven't yet included in Mint, and we built the optimization on top of the *opt-3 HandCuda* variant. Currently, Mint supports `chunksize` for the z-dimension only. The *all-opt* variant implements chunking in y-dimension as well, providing a 12% improvement over Hand-CUDA *opt-3*.

6. RELATED WORK

By and large, source-to-source translation for GPU programming has taken two approaches according to the form of the user input. In the first approach the user input is a domain specific language. Liu et al. [18] implemented a source-to-source translator to automatically optimize a kernel against program inputs, and uses statistical learning techniques to search the optimization space. Lionetti et al. [19] implemented a domain-specific translator for a cardiac simulation framework, which solved a reaction diffusion system. Included was an off-line software managed cache. The translator encapsulates expert knowledge about CUDA optimization, enabling the non-expert to remain aloof of the hardware. Another domain-specific approach is taken by Kamil et al. [20]. The authors developed a translator that takes ordinary Fortran 95 as input, and can produce CUDA source code. The code generator utilizes device memory only and does not take advantage of shared memory. As previously mentioned, shared memory plays an important role in the performance of stencil methods. Indeed, our 3D Heat 7-pt kernel performs at nearly twice the performance presented by the authors.

The second approach takes input in the form of a traditional programming language, e.g., annotated with pragmas such as OpenMP. Eichenberger et al. [21] describe a source-to-source translator for the Cell Broadband Engine [16] that takes OpenMP source code as input and distributes computation across the 9 cores of the processor. The translator implements function partitioning and an on-line software managed cache.

The PGI Accelerator model [22] and OpenMPC [23, 24] take a directive-based approach, and are closest to our work. The PGI Accelerator model is a commercial compiler and is intended to be general purpose. OpenMPC supports an extended OpenMP syntax for GPUs. The compiler generates many optimization variants, and the user guides optimization through a performing tuning system.

We compared the performance of code generated by OpenMPC and the PGI compiler with code generated by Mint. For the Heat 7-pt kernel, Mint realized 22.2 Gflops while performance dropped to 1.06 Gflops for OpenMPC. The PGI compiler delivered about half the performance of Mint: 9.0 Gflops.

OpenMPC has fundamental limitations. Notably, OpenMPC only parallelizes the outermost loop of a loop nest whereas Mint parallelizes an entire loop nest. As a result, Mint can generate multi-dimensional CUDA thread blocks. The results show the significant benefit of parallelizing all levels of a loop nest in three dimensions. Moreover, because shared memory plays an important role in performance, Mint heavily invests in shared memory optimizations. By comparison, OpenMPC uses shared memory for scalar variables only and cannot buffer arrays in shared memory.

The PGI compiler uses shared memory and multi dimensional thread blocks but not as effectively as Mint. Mint uses registers in lieu of shared memory, reducing pressure on shared memory and thereby increasing device occupancy. In addition, Mint implements loop aggregation through the `chunksize` clause, improving reuse. Mint uses domain-specific knowledge to realize this optimization and the benefit of the approach is to greatly reduce the optimization search space. The payoff is improved performance for the selected application domain.

7. CONCLUSIONS

We have introduced the Mint programming model for accelerating stencil computations on the NVIDIA GPU. The user needs only annotate a traditional C source with a few intuitive Mint directives. The accompanying source-to-source translator of Mint generates highly optimized CUDA C that is competitive with heroic hand coding. The benefit of our approach is to simplify the view of the hardware while incurring a reasonable abstraction overhead.

On-chip memory and thread aggregation optimizations are crucial to delivering high performance. For a set of widely used stencil kernels, Mint realized 78% to 83% of the performance obtained by aggressively hand-optimized CUDA. Most of the kernels were 3-dimensional, where the payoff for successful optimization is high, but so are the difficulties in optimizing CUDA code by hand. We are currently applying Mint to more complex stencil applications involving many input grids and several parallel regions. As a result, our extensions to the translator in the future will focus on more inter-kernel optimizations and data movement. Moreover, we are re-targeting to the Fermi architecture, and shall report on this work in the future. We expect that many of the same optimization strategies will apply to Fermi. More up-to-date information about the Mint source to source translator can be found on our project website: https://sites.google.com/site/mintmodel.

Acknowledgments

The authors would like to thank Vasily Volkov for stimulating conversations about the 7-point stencil kernel, Everett Phillips from NVIDIA for his insightful comments on CUDA-related issues, and Seyong Lee for the private communication over the OpenMPC framework. Didem Unat was supported by a Center of Excellence grant from the Norwegian Research Council to the Center for Biomedical Computing at the Simula Research Laboratory. Scott Baden dedicates his portion of this research to the memory of *Shirley D. Wallach*. He was supported by the Simula Research Laboratory and the University of California, San Diego. The work of Xing Cai was partly supported by the Research Council of Norway through Grant 200879/V11. Computations on the NVIDIA Tesla system located at UCSD were supported by NSF DMS/MRI Award 0821816.

8. REFERENCES

[1] "http://www.top500.org/."

[2] J. Nickolls, I. Buck, M. Garland, and K. Skadron, "Scalable parallel programming with CUDA," in *SIGGRAPH '08: ACM SIGGRAPH 2008 classes*, pp. 1–14, ACM, 2008.

[3] V. Volkov and J. W. Demmel, "Benchmarking GPUs to tune dense linear algebra," in *Proceedings of the 2008 ACM/IEEE conference on Supercomputing*, SC '08, pp. 31:1–31:11, IEEE Press, 2008.

[4] N. Bell and M. Garland, "Implementing sparse matrix-vector multiplication on throughput-oriented processors," in *Proceedings of the Conference on High Performance Computing Networking, Storage and Analysis*, SC '09, pp. 18:1–18:11, ACM, 2009.

[5] P. Micikevicius, "3D finite difference computation on GPUs using CUDA," in *GPGPU-2: Proceedings of 2nd Workshop on General Purpose Processing on Graphics Processing Units*, pp. 79–84, ACM, 2009.

[6] K. Datta, M. Murphy, V. Volkov, S. Williams, J. Carter, L. Oliker, D. Patterson, J. Shalf, and K. Yelick, "Stencil computation optimization and auto-tuning on state-of-the-art multicore architectures," in *Proceedings of the 2008 ACM/IEEE conference on Supercomputing*, SC '08, pp. 4:1–4:12, IEEE Press, 2008.

[7] K. Moreland and E. Angel, "The FFT on a GPU," in *Proceedings of the ACM SIGGRAPH/EUROGRAPHICS conference on Graphics hardware*, HWWS '03, pp. 112–119, Eurographics Association, 2003.

[8] B. Chapman, G. Jost, and R. van der Pas, *Using OpenMP: Portable Shared Memory Parallel Programming (Scientific and Engineering Computation)*. The MIT Press, 2007.

[9] J. C. Strikwerda, *Finite Difference Schemes and Partial Differential Equations, 2nd Edition*. SIAM, 2004.

[10] R. C. Gonzalez and R. E. Woods, *Digital Image Processing, 3rd Edition*. Prentice Hall, 2008.

[11] D. J. Quinlan, B. Miller, B. Philip, and M. Schordan, "Treating a user-defined parallel library as a domain-specific language," in *Proceedings of the 16th International Parallel and Distributed Processing Symposium*, IPDPS '02, pp. 324–, IEEE Computer Society, 2002.

[12] "Rose." http://www.rosecompiler.org.

[13] NVIDIA, *CUDA programming guide 3.2*. 2010.

[14] G. Rivera and C.-W. Tseng, "Tiling optimizations for 3D scientific computations," in *Proceedings of the 2000 ACM/IEEE conference on Supercomputing (CDROM)*, SC '00, IEEE Computer Society, 2000.

[15] S. Williams, J. Shalf, L. Oliker, S. Kamil, P. Husbands, and K. Yelick, "Scientific computing kernels on the Cell processor," *Int. J. Parallel Program.*, vol. 35, pp. 263–298, June 2007.

[16] J. A. Kahle, M. N. Day, H. P. Hofstee, C. R. Johns, T. R. Maeurer, and D. Shippy, "Introduction to the Cell multiprocessor," *IBM J. Res. Dev.*, vol. 49, pp. 589–604, July 2005.

[17] K. Datta, S. Williams, V. Volkov, J. Carter, L. Oliker, J. Shalf, and K. Yelick, "Auto-tuning the 27-point stencil for multicore," in *iWAPT, 4th International Workshop on Automatic Performance Tuning*, 2009.

[18] Y. Liu, E. Z. Zhang, and X. Shen, "A cross-input adaptive framework for GPU program optimizations," in *Int. Parallel and Distributed Processing Symp.*, pp. 1–10, 2009.

[19] F. V. Lionetti, A. D. McCulloch, and S. B. Baden, "Source-to-source optimization of CUDA C for GPU accelerated cardiac cell modeling," in *Proceedings of the 16th international Euro-Par conference on Parallel processing: Part I*, EuroPar'10, pp. 38–49, Springer-Verlag, 2010.

[20] S. Kamil, C. Chan, L. Oliker, J. Shalf, and S. Williams, "An auto-tuning framework for parallel multicore stencil computations," in *Interational Conference on Parallel and Distributed Computing Systems (IPDPS)*, 2010.

[21] A. E. Eichenberger, J. K. O'Brien, K. M. O'Brien, P. Wu, T. Chen, P. H. Oden, D. A. Prener, J. C. Shepherd, B. So, Z. Sura, A. Wang, T. Zhang, P. Zhao, M. K. Gschwind, R. Archambault, Y. Gao, and R. Koo, "Using advanced compiler technology to exploit the performance of the Cell Broadband Engine architecture," *IBM Syst. J.*, vol. 45, pp. 59–84, January 2006.

[22] M. Wolfe, "Implementing the PGI Accelerator model," in *Proceedings of the 3rd Workshop on General-Purpose Computation on Graphics Processing Units*, GPGPU '10, pp. 43–50, 2010.

[23] S. Lee, S.-J. Min, and R. Eigenmann, "OpenMP to GPGPU: a compiler framework for automatic translation and optimization," *SIGPLAN Not.*, vol. 44, pp. 101–110, February 2009.

[24] S. Lee and R. Eigenmann, "OpenMPC: Extended OpenMP Programming and Tuning for GPUs," in *Proceedings of the 2010 ACM/IEEE International Conference for High Performance Computing, Networking, Storage and Analysis*, SC '10, pp. 1–11, IEEE Computer Society, 2010.

MDR: Performance Model Driven Runtime for Heterogeneous Parallel Platforms

Jacques A. Pienaar
Purdue University
West Lafayette, IN
jpienaar@purdue.edu

Anand Raghunathan
Purdue University
West Lafayette, IN
raghunathan@purdue.edu

Srimat Chakradhar
NEC Laboratories America
Princeton, NJ
chak@nec-labs.com

ABSTRACT

We present a runtime framework for the execution of workloads represented as parallel-operator directed acyclic graphs (PO-DAGs) on heterogeneous multi-core platforms. PO-DAGs combine coarse-grained parallelism at the graph level with fine-grained parallelism within each node, lending naturally to exploiting the intra- and inter-processing element parallelism present in heterogeneous platforms. We identify four important criteria — Suitability, Locality, Availability and Criticality (SLAC) — and show that all these criteria must be considered by a heterogeneous runtime framework in order to achieve good performance under varying application and platform characteristics.

The proposed model driven runtime (MDR) considers all the aforementioned factors, and tradeoffs among them, by utilizing performance models. These performance models are used to drive key run-time decisions such as mapping of tasks to PEs, scheduling of tasks on each PE, and copying data between memory spaces.

We discuss the software architecture and implementation of MDR, and evaluate it using several benchmark programs on three different heterogeneous platforms that contain multi-core CPUs and GPUs. The hardware platforms represent server, laptop, and netbook class systems. MDR achieves up to 4.2X speedup (1.5X on average) over the best of CPU-only, GPU-only, round-robin, GPU-first, and utilization-driven schedulers. We also perform a sensitivity analysis that establishes the importance of considering all four SLAC criteria in order to achieve high performance execution in a heterogeneous runtime framework.

Categories and Subject Descriptors

D.1.3 [**Concurrent Programming**]: Parallel Programming;
D.4.1 [**Process Management**]: Scheduling

General Terms

Measurement, Performance

Keywords

Parallel computing, Heterogeneous platforms, Multi-core, Many-core, GPUs, Runtime system, Performance model

1. INTRODUCTION

Heterogeneous parallel computing platforms, which contain multiple processing elements (PEs) with distinct architectures, offer a potential for significant improvements in performance and power efficiency [10]. Applications from numerous domains have demonstrated large speedups on heterogeneous platforms consisting of multi-core CPUs and GPUs [20]. While these results make a compelling case for heterogeneous parallel computing, exploiting such platforms at a larger scale requires suitable programming frameworks.

Frameworks such as CUDA [19] and OpenCL [22] have substantially raised the level of abstraction of GPU programming. However, programming heterogeneous platforms is still quite challenging. Programmers must manually partition workload between the PEs (CPUs and GPUs), schedule calls to PE-specific implementations of kernels, and manage coherence between distinct memory spaces. In addition, the lack of performance portability across hardware platforms necessitates repeated programmer effort.

We have developed a heterogeneous runtime framework for executing computations that are specified as parallel-operator directed acyclic graphs (PO-DAGs). PO-DAGs naturally capture computations that manifest in a wide range of applications. Previous efforts have used graph-based programming models for programming parallel computing platforms ranging from GPUs [24] to clusters [13, 25].

We use the PO-DAG model to specify and exploit parallelism at two levels: coarse-grained graph-level parallelism is exploited across PEs, and fine-grained intra-node parallelism is exploited within a PE.

While high-level programming abstractions facilitate programmability, the design of the runtime system is key to achieving high performance. We identify four important factors that need to be considered in order to achieve high performance in a heterogeneous parallel runtime.

- *Suitability:* which processing element is inherently better suited (faster) to execute a given task.

- *Locality:* whether the data required for a task is present in the local memory of the processing element.

- *Availability:* when next a processing element will become available to execute a given task.

- *Criticality:* how a given task's execution is likely to affect the overall program execution time.

Previous work on heterogeneous runtimes has considered some but not all of these factors [16, 6, 17, 1].

Paper Contributions

In this paper, we propose a performance model driven runtime system that addresses the above challenges. The key contributions of our work are as follows:

- We identify four factors that need to be considered in heterogeneous runtime frameworks, namely *S*uitability of computations to PEs, *L*ocality of data, *A*vailability of PEs, and *C*riticality of computations (SLAC).

- We propose a Model Driven Runtime (MDR) that considers the SLAC factors by using performance models to drive key runtime decisions. MDR utilizes graph-based application-level performance models, online history-based models for kernel-level execution time, and analytical models for communication time.

- We have implemented MDR on top of Intel's TBB [12] and NVIDIA's CUDA [19] and evaluate the proposed framework on several benchmarks, demonstrating the benefits with respect to a range of baselines. We illustrate the adaptivity of MDR by evaluating it on three different heterogeneous multi-core platforms with widely varying characteristics. We also performs a sensitivity analysis to demonstrate the importance of the SLAC factors in achieving good performance.

The rest of the paper is organized as follows. Section 2 presents a motivation for considering SLAC in a heterogeneous runtime system. Section 3 presents an overview of MDR and the performance modeling techniques that drive runtime decisions. Section 4 presents an empirical evaluation of MDR on three different heterogeneous platforms. Section 5 places our work in the context of previous work on the topic, and Section 6 concludes with a summary.

2. MOTIVATION

In this section we describe the intuition behind the SLAC criteria using an simple example (Figure 1), indicate the attributes extracted that correspond to each criterion, and discuss what a programmer would need to do to obtain the same benefits without MDR.

2.1 Example

Let us consider the PO-DAG in Figure 1(a). For this discussion, we assume that the computation times of each node and communication times associated with each edge are known (annotated as node and edge labels in the figure). Suppose that we wish to schedule the PO-DAG for execution on a two-PE system consisting of a CPU and a GPU. The baseline scheduling policies we will consider in this example are PE$_2$-only (GPU-only) and utilization-based. The utilization-based scheduler tries to keep both PEs utilized (*i.e.,* busy) by assigning a task to an idle PE. If all PEs are idle, it assigns tasks to different PEs in an alternating fashion.

Execution times for PE$_2$-only and utilization-based schedules (shown in Figures 1(b) and 1(c)) are 37 untis and 28 units, respectively. Note that PE$_2$-only is better than utilization-based even though in PE$_2$-only we are "wasting" computing resources.

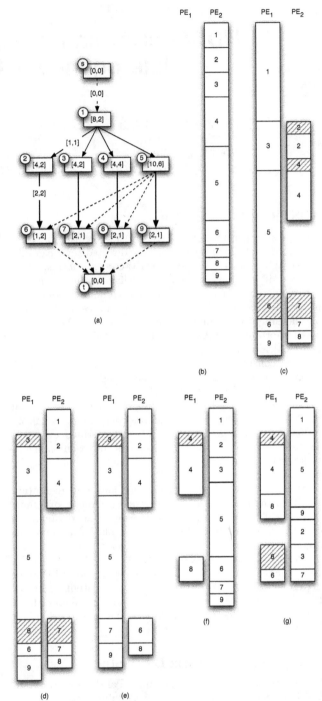

Figure 1: (a) Example PO-DAG. Node labels correspond to execution time, edge labels to communication cost, edges with equal weights are assigned same line type. In the next graphs schedules are given where labels corresponds to task numbers, shaded regions to communication required for computation, circle's in these graph denote why a task was allocated to that PE: R for Round Robin, U for Utilization, and F for any SLAC factor. (b) PE$_2$ only schedule. (c) Utilization-based schedule. Schedules (d)—(e) incrementally adds on the utilization-based schedule first consideration of suitability (d), then locality (e), availability (f) and finally criticality (g).

226

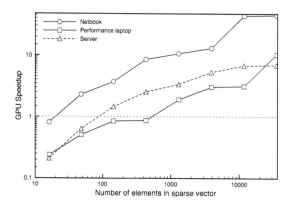

Figure 2: GPU speedup for the sparse-vector dense matrix multiplication kernel.

2.2 Suitability

How well does a task perform on a processing element? A good indicator for suitability is the execution time of a kernel on the different PEs. A kernel is better suited to PE_i than PE_j if the expected runtime on PE_i is less than the expected runtime on PE_j. Suitability is a first-order effect and can completely determine the scheduling decisions made.

In the example, when suitability is considered along with utilization, the executing time reduces to 22 time units (Figure 1(d)). This is due to scheduling tasks on the better suited PE when both PEs are idle. Task 5 is still scheduled on PE_1 (its least desired PE) due to utilization.

The suitability of a kernel to a PE often depends on the inputs to the kernel. For example, consider the speedup of the sparse-vector dense-matrix multiplication (SVDM) kernel shown in Figure 2. In this case, suitability depends on the size of the vector. MDR uses the concept of a signature to capture such dependencies. A *signature* is a per-kernel programmer specified n-tuple of ordinal characteristics that separates kernel instances from a performance modeling point of view.

While our framework is general enough to consider arbitrary signatures, in almost all kernels that we have encountered, the sizes of data structures used are adequate to model performance for the purpose of guiding runtime decisions.

From Figure 2 one can additionally see that suitability differs across different hardware platforms (details of the platforms are given in Section 4). Therefore, one needs a per-platform model of suitability and a programmer who wants to capture suitability would thus have to create a parameterized model of the kernel per platform. MDR alleviates the programmer of this cumbersome task.

2.3 Locality

Where is the kernel's dependent data located? Using data locality as factor in the scheduling process is based on the realization that the time a kernel requires to complete is not determined purely by its execution time. Rather, the time required to move the associated data between different memory spaces has to be taken into account as well.

In the example, task 6 is better suited to PE_1 and considering only suitability it was assigned to PE_1 (Figures 1(c) and 1(d)). However, if one considers the communication cost

of its input/output data, then assigning task 6 to PE_2 results in quicker completion (Figure 1(d) to 1(e)). Communication cost can significantly impact performance [23] and therefore great care should be taken to minimize communication as well as remove redundant communication.

To take locality into account a programmer would have to keep track of the location of the most recent copy of a data item and have some means of computing the transfer time for a data item. The transfer time is dependent on the platform as well as the direction of transfer (*i.e.*, from CPU to GPU, or from GPU to CPU). Again, MDR automates these steps, alleviating the programmer from the need to perform them.

2.4 Availability

When will a processing element be available next? Incorporating availability into the runtime framework addresses the following scenarios:

1. Sometimes it is much better to wait a little bit for a more desirable PE to become available, rather than focussing purely on utilization.

2. At other times, even though a computation might be better suited for PE_i than PE_j, it would be best to schedule it on PE_j if PE_i is executing a long running task.

Task 5, in the example, is 1.67x faster on PE_2 than on PE_1, but due to utilization it gets assigned to PE_1. In taking PE_2's availability into account it is clear that it is worthwhile to wait for PE_2 and keep PE_1 idle. Considering availability reduces the execution time from 21 units to 16 units (Figure 1(f)).

In contention-aware scheduling [9] Gregg *et al.* considered the binary version of availability (*i.e.*, "Is PE_i available **now**?") and showed the benefits of considering availability as part of scheduling. A contention-factor was used to scale the runtime of a task being scheduled if a desired PE is not available. This approach ignores contention with the tasks already enqueued for execution on a PE and only considers the task that is currently scheduled. MDR keeps track of all tasks scheduled, executing and completed and uses performance models to estimate their execution times. Therefore, it is able to model when a PE will next become available with reasonable accuracy.

2.5 Criticality

What effect does this kernel have on the total execution time? Critical path scheduling algorithms [15] are among the most successful class of heuristic scheduling algorithms. Kernels that are on the critical path need to be given priority as scheduling them on their least desirable PE *will* result in a larger execution time. Furthermore the amount of inter-task parallelism available can also be affected by criticality.

The critical path in the example is $1 \rightarrow 5 \rightarrow 9$ and by scheduling these tasks on their best PE (considering suitability, locality and availability) reduces overall execution time.

Criticality adds a more global consideration to the scheduling process and it depends on the graph structure, in addition to computation and communication costs. For some applications, the critical nodes can be determined statically, while, in general, the criticality of a node is dependent on input data and therefore requires runtime analysis, making it very difficult for a programmer.

In the example in Figure 1 we we find that the schedule that considers all the SLAC criteria (Figure 1(g)) has 1.5X speedup over the best of PE_1-, PE_2-only and utilization-based schedules. This clearly motivates the need to consider these factors in a heterogeneous runtime framework.

3. MDR SYSTEM

MDR is a heterogeneous runtime framework that models task execution, orchestrates data movement and intelligently schedules tasks using online performance models, thereby considering suitability, locality, availability, and criticality. MDR consists of a programming abstraction, which eases program specification and analysis, a coarse-grained data coherence layer, which reduces programmer burden in managing memory and communication, and a runtime that intelligently schedules computations, and constructs/refines the performance models that drive the scheduler. MDR does not attempt to manage parallelism within each PE — this is left to PE-specific runtimes such as TBB and CUDA. Therefore, the MDR scheduler can be viewed as a meta-scheduler on top of PE-specific schedulers.

We provide an overview of the key aspects of MDR in the following sub-sections.

3.1 Programming abstraction

The programming abstraction provided to the programmer by MDR is PO-DAGs. PO-DAGs can be nested within regular code sections such as functions and loops. This abstraction allows for easy assembly of parallel operators while presenting parallelism at two levels: different vertices without any dependencies may execute in parallel, and each vertex itself may represent a parallel computation. PO-DAGs can also combine architecture-agnostic expression of parallelism at the graph level with encapsulation of architecture-specific implementations at the node level.

PO-DAGs are not a new programming model and have also been utilized in a wide range of parallel frameworks [24, 13, 25]. We also do not claim that PO-DAGs are an appropriate representation for all problems or require that the entire program be constructed using them. Programs that fit the MapReduce paradigm, for example, can be expressed as PO-DAGs but the dynamic communication pattern is poorly captured and adaptability is lost in doing so.

The abstraction and framework provided by MDR divides heterogeneous programming into four parts:

- *Application.* End-user applications are developed using the PO-DAG abstraction, as illustrated in Figure 3. The code preceding `schedule` in Figure 3 symbolically executes to construct the PO-DAG. During this phase no memory allocation or actual computation is performed. Symbolic data structures allow MDR to track data across function boundaries and drives the data coherency layer, relieving the programmer from the burden of manually allocating, copying and freeing data.

- *Computational kernel.* Graph nodes in the MDR programming model correspond to computational kernels, which the developer may specify by encapsulating functions that correspond to PE-specific implementations (for example, MKL and CUBLAS routines for the same function). MDR allows for specification of new kernels

```
// Data element defined
class matrix : public MDR::data {
 public:
    blas_matrix(int m, int n) { ... }
    float *dataOnPE(PE nextPE) { ... }
    int m, n;
 private:
    bool copyFromToPE(PE oldPE, PE newPE) { ... }
    bool freeOnPE(PE curPE) {  ...  }
    bool allocateOnPE(PE newPE) { ...  }
    float intCopyTime(PE fromPE, PE toPE) {
       return MDR::transferTime(sizeof(float)*n*m,    ↩
         fromPE, toPE);
    }
};
// Computational kernel defined
class MatrixMult : MDR::task<MatrixMult> {
  matrix *A, *B, out;
  ...
  MatrixMult(MatrixMult *inA, MatrixMult *inB) :    ↩
    A(inA->out), B(inB->out), out(A->out->m,B->out->n) {
     dependsOnData(A); dependsOnData(B);
     producesData(out);
     dependsOn(inA); dependsOn(inB);
  }
  ...
  void operator()() {
     switch (scheduledOn) {
     case CPU: cblas(...)
     case GPU: cublas_sgemm(...)   }
  }
  MDR_SIGNATURE(3,{A->n, A->m, B->n})
  // Possible to define complex signature
  // MDR_SIGNATURE(3,{A->n * A->m * B->n})
}
...
// Application code
MDR_INIT_SCHEDULER
MDR::graph g;
matrix A(128,128), B(128,128), C(128,128);

≪ Matrix initialization here ≫

MatrixMult *t1, *t2, *t3;
t1 = MDR_ADD(g, MatrixMult(A, A));
t2 = MDR_ADD(g, MatrixMult(B, C));
t3 = MDR_ADD(g, MatrixMult(t1, t2));
   g.source->referencedBy(t1);
   g.sink->dependsOn(t3);

schedule<util_functor>();

MDR_FINI_SCHEDULER
```

Figure 3: Snippets of usage of MDR's programming interface to define custom data components, kernels, scheduler functors and application code sections.

via inheritance and templating from a set of provided base classes. The programmer should specify the signature (Section 2.2) for custom kernels. These signatures can be arbitrary functions but the expectation is that they are computationally inexpensive.

- *Data.* MDR provides templated array data types, *e.g.*, `MDR::data_type::array<T>`, and a framework for developers who want to define custom types such as linked lists and trees, which require specific functions for allocation, serialization and copying.

MDR's MSI-based data coherence layer is similar to

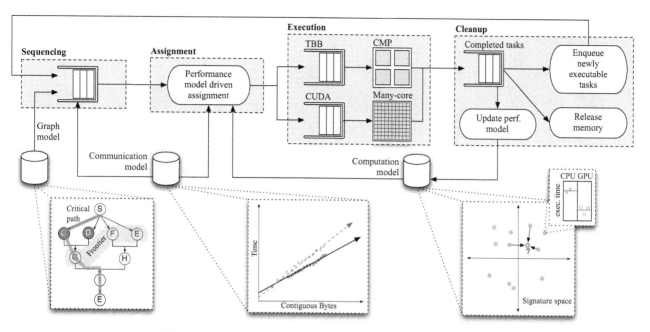

Figure 4: Schematic representation of MDR pipeline.

ADSM [8] except that the PO-DAG structure is exploited by MDR to lazily allocate and eagerly reclaim memory. Using the PO-DAG structure allows MDR, in contrast to [8], to avoid unnecessary allocations (*i.e.*, if a PE never uses an array then space for that array is never allocated in said PE's memory), redundant copying (the PO-DAG model specifies which memory objects a kernel will read/write), and determine when memory can be reclaimed. Lazy allocation also allows the programmer to specify a program consuming (in total) more memory than is available on the platform.

The coherence layer also breaks the so-called cyclic communication pattern present in some (simple) heterogeneous approaches, by copying data only if the values of a data object on which a computation is dependent have changed.

- *Scheduler.* The default SLAC-based scheduler in MDR performs well across a wide range of workload characteristics and hardware platforms. However, scheduling is an NP-Hard problem and therefore different scheduling heuristics may be superior for different applications. A programmer who wishes to extend MDR to include a new scheduler just has to define an appropriate functor. Within this functor, one could access utility functions provided by MDR, such as the performance models, graph-level analysis info, location of dependent data, predecessor scheduling information and so forth.

3.2 Runtime

The MDR runtime constructs the graph-level model, schedules tasks, updates performance models of the tasks, and orchestrates data movement. MDR is built using TBB and assigns tasks to the TBB and CUDA runtime queues. The scheduling problem faced is a dynamic scheduling problem as the runtimes of tasks are not known a priori.

MDR uses the performance models (kernel, communica-

tion and graph-level) to incorporate the SLAC criteria into runtime decisions. These models are built during actual runs, *i.e.*, there is no offline training, rather performance models are continuously adapted based on observed execution history.

The software architecture of MDR resembles a non-blocking pipeline with four stages (see Figure 4):

1. *Sequencing.* During the sequencing phase the frontier of tasks that are ready to execute are ordered according to their criticality (Section 3.3.3). The task among these with the highest criticality is selected and passed to the assignment stage.

2. *Assignment.* The task selected is assigned to an underlying PE's runtime queue based on the computation cost of the task, the communication cost of the dependent data, and PE availability.

3. *Execution.* Once the assignment step has assigned a computation to a specific PE, the task gets passed on to the execution phase. The required memory allocation and data coherence actions are performed prior to executing the task using TBB and CUDA runtimes.

4. *Clean-up.* The clean-up phase is responsible for (aggressively) reclaiming memory, determining which tasks are ready to execute and updating the kernel models.

MDR does not update the graph-level model during execution as this would add significant run-time overhead.

3.3 Performance Models

Intelligent scheduling and assignment of tasks onto different processing elements is at the core of MDR and communication, kernel and graph-level performance models provide the inputs to drive these decisions.

3.3.1 Communication model

The communication model consists of two parts: a data object model and a byte-level communication model. The

$$\text{EST}[s; p_i] := \min \left\{ \max\{\text{EST}[r; p_j] + c'(r, p_j) : r \in \text{pred}(s)\} : p_j \in \text{PE}[s] \right\} \tag{1}$$

$$\text{LTE}[s; p_i] := \min \left\{ c'(s, p_j) + \max\{\text{LTE}[t; p_i] : t \in \text{succ}(s)\} + \sum_{d \in \text{prod}(s)} c(d, p_j \rightarrow p_i) : p_j \in \text{PE}[s] \right\} \tag{2}$$

$$c'(t, p_i) = \begin{cases} c(t, p_i) & \text{if } p_i \in \text{PE}[t] \\ \min\{c(t, p_j) + \sum_{d \in \text{prod}(t)} c(d, p_j \rightarrow p_i) : p_j \in \text{PE}[t]\} & \text{otherwise} \end{cases} \tag{3}$$

$$\rho(t) = \min\{\text{EST}[t, p] + \text{LTE}[t, p] : p \in \text{PE}[t]\} + \min\{\text{LTE}[t, p] : p \in \text{PE}[t]\} \tag{4}$$

$$\text{assignment}(s) := \arg\min \left\{ \sum_{d \in \text{dep}[s]} c(d, \cdot \rightarrow p) + \text{delay}(p) + c'(s, p) : p \in \text{PE}[s] \right\} \tag{5}$$

Figure 5: Equations used by MDR for determining EST, LTE, criticality, and the PE assignment.

byte-level model is constructed by MDR using linear regression and estimates the time required to move x contiguous bytes from one memory space to another. The coefficients determined by linear regression are stored as system parameters for use across runs. In our experiments we found that, if one takes the direction of data movement into account, a simple linear model suffices ($R^2 \approx 0.94$).

MDR uses the data object model during execution, and programmers creating custom data types are expected to define the data object model in terms of this byte-level model.

3.3.2 Kernel model

The kernel model is used to predict a task's execution time. These models, parametrized by the computational kernel and signature, are built online using performance history from actual kernel executions. Recall from Section 2.2 that each computation has a signature which is an ordinal n-tuple specified by the programmer that, from a performance point of view, aims to uniquely characterize a kernel instance. The signature is used to identify the most similar previous executions of a kernel, this recorded execution times is used to predict current instance's execution time.

For a given kernel and signature, if the kernel has been previously executed with exactly the same signature, the median of the previous (at most) three executions of a kernel is used as a prediction of the runtime on that PE. For a task with an unseen signature, MDR uses the k-Nearest Neighbor instance-based learning method [18] to predict the performance by performing linear interpolation of its three nearest neighbors in the signature space. In practice, we observed that this approach provides estimates that are tolerant to outliers and sufficiently accurate for the purpose driving of runtime decisions.

We note that the specification of appropriate signatures is an overhead for the programmer. MDR allows arbitrarily complex signatures that the programmer can use to return more accurate approximations. The decision of what would be a suitable signature is left to the progammer. A poorly chosen signature (either overly simplistic or overly complex) can harm performance.

3.3.3 Graph-level model

The order in which tasks that are ready to execute are processed, is an important runtime decision. A graph-level model of the program, constructed using the communication and kernel models, is used to determine a suitable ordering by identifying which tasks are critical [15] to execution.

To identify tasks that are on the critical path, we use standard metrics such as earliest starting time (EST) and length to end (LTE) [15]. We compute the EST and LTE using Equations 1 and 2 respectively. In these formulae, the predecessors of a task t are indicated by $\text{pred}(t)$, the successors by $\text{succ}(t)$, the set of dependent data by $\text{dep}(t)$, the set of data produced by $\text{prod}(t)$, and the set of PEs which t can execute upon by $\text{PE}[t]$. $c(t, p)$, where t is a task and p a PE, would correspond to the expected runtime of t on p, while $c(d, i \rightarrow j)$ would correspond to the expected cost of copying data object d from PE_i to PE_j.

Note that the equations in Figure 5 attempt to model the execution of the un-executed part of the program, which is not known a priori. For computational efficiency, these formulae make simplifying assumptions, such as there are an infinite number of PEs, no communication contention, *etc*. The rationale is that tasks identified as critical using these optimistic assumptions, will likely also be bottlenecks during actual execution.

3.4 Work-list based scheduler

MDR is prototypically a work-list based scheduler and its scheduling algorithm was inspired, in part, by the theoretical analysis in [15]. Tasks that are ready to execute are ordered in decreasing order of ρ (Equation 4). ρ consists of two terms, the first is large for computations on the critical path and the second tries to maintain parallelism (balance execution) by giving higher value to nodes that are predicted to be on a longer path to end. Combined, these factors steer MDR to consider tasks on the critical path with longest path to end. Initially, when no kernel model exists, the ordering reduces to prioritizing tasks with the most tasks on its shortest path to the end.

The function used by the assignment phase of MDR is shown in Equation 5. It performs a direct comparison between the PEs on which the task may be scheduled and selects the PE for which the sum of the wait time due to already enqueued kernels, communication time, and kernel execution time is minimized.

The formulae shown in Figure 5 encapsulate the factors MDR considers: suitability of tasks to PEs, locality of data,

Table 1: Platforms used for experimentation.

		Netbook	Laptop	Server
CPU	Cores	2	2	8
	Processor	1.6 GHz Intel Atom 330	2.26 GHz Intel Core 2 Duo	2.26 GHz Dual Intel Xeon 5500
	Memory	2 GB	8 GB	16 GB
	L2/3 cache	1 MB	3 MB	1/8 MB
	System bus	533 MHz	1066 MHz	1066 MHz
GPU	SM	16	48	240
	Processor	Nvidia ION	Nvidia 320M	Tesla C1060
	Memory	256 MB (shared)	256 MB (shared)	4 GB

availability of PEs and criticality of tasks to total execution time. Separately, the importance of some these factors have been demonstrated [15, 7, 2, 23]. MDR is the first heterogeneous runtime system to automatically consider all of the SLAC factors and use performance models to consider their effect and drive runtime decisions.

4. RESULTS

4.1 Methodology

We evaluate MDR on three different platforms (described in Table 1), which span a large segment the GPGPU programming spectrum starting from the low-power commodity Atom-ION combination to the server-class Xeon-Tesla pairing. These diverse platforms allow us to test MDR's performance across greatly varying performance characteristics and investigate the portability, scalability and performance robustness of the runtime. We use benchmarks drawn from the domains of computational fluid dynamics, semantic indexing, linear algebra, and bioinformatics. We compare MDR against multiple baselines described in Section 4.3. Each trial was run multiple times and the average execution times for all runs excluding the first run are reported. In addition, we also report the runtime of the last execution of MDR. As MDR is adaptive the last execution gives an indicator of MDR's performance after refining its performance models. We believe the last execution is a good indicator as we did not observe any oscillating behaviour in the performance of MDR. All numbers are reported as speedups normalized to the CPU-only execution time on the same platform.

4.2 Benchmarks

We use selected benchmarks from the Rodinia benchmark suite [5], StarPU [1] that demonstrate potential for utilizing both PEs (i.e., we did not consider benchmarks where executing on only the CPU or only the GPU was the best across all three platforms). In addition, we use a semantic indexing application SSI [4].

- **CFD** CFD solver [5] is an unstructured grid CFD solver using three-dimensional Euler equations for inviscid, compressible flow.

- **NW** Needleman-Wunsch [5] is an algorithm commonly used in bioinformatics for global alignment of two sequences. At a coarse granularity, the Needleman-Wunsch algorithm consists of three tasks and we considered aligning multiple pairs of sequences.

- **LU** and **CHO** LU- and Cholesky-decomposition are procedures for decomposing a matrix into a product of upper and lower triangular matrices. We used the algorithms described in [1].

- **SSI** Semantic indexing is a popular technique used to access and organize large amounts of unstructured data. We specifically considered the problem of assigning documents to semantic classes [4].

We note that, when expressing the benchmarks as PO-DAGs, we did not attempt to optimize the application in any manner. For example, we did not consider different block sizes and blocking strategies for LU.

4.3 Baseline Schedulers

We compare MDR against the following schedulers.

- *CPU-only (GPU-only)* These baselines simply assign any available task to the CPU (GPU).

- *Random* Tasks are arbitrarily assigned to either PE.

- *Round-robin* Tasks are alternately assigned to either CPU or GPU. Tasks that are constrained to execute on a specific PE do not effect the alternating assignment.

- *Utilization* This scheduler tries to keep both PEs utilized by assigning a task to the least utilized PE, as determined by the performance model.

- GPU-FIRST Try to keep both PEs utilized but if faced with a choice (i.e., both CPU and GPU are idle) always assign on the GPU first.

Execution restrictions of tasks are respected by all the above schedulers and in all of the schedulers, except MDR, no ordering is imposed on the order in which executable tasks are considered.

4.4 Results

Our results are summarized in Table 2. The results suggest that:

- The performance of MDR is at worst 3% worse than the best baseline and at best 4.24x faster than the best baseline. MDR is consistently one of the best performers across the different platforms and benchmarks.

- CFD is a worst-case application for MDR as it is highly GPU-friendly and has no inter-node parallelism, obviating the need for an intelligent scheduler (which will only add overhead).

- The difference between intelligent and naïve scheduling approaches is more pronounced when the performance difference between PEs is large.

- Aiming to keep both PEs utilized can in fact significantly increase the runtime over even the slowest PE.

- On the netbook-class platform the communication cost affects performance significantly, while on the performance laptop the communication cost is a lot less, although on both these platforms GPUs share memory

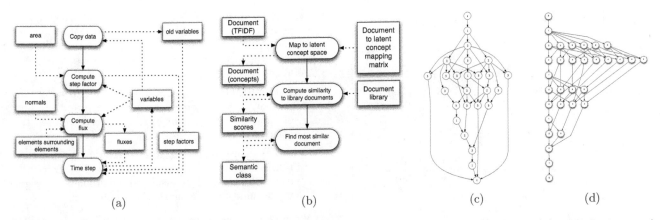

Figure 6: Graphical representations of the PO-DAGs used (a) per iteration in CFD, (b) per document in SSI, (c) in Cholesky- and (d) in LU-decomposition. For Cholesky- and LU-decomposition the graph shown is, due to space and readability, the 16 block case and not the 169 block version used.

Table 2: Speedup relative to CPU-only of the benchmarks on the different systems.

Platforms	Netbook					Performance Laptop					Server				
Benchmarks	CFD	SSI	NW	LU	CHO	CFD	SSI	NW	LU	CHO	CFD	SSI	NW	LU	CHO
CPU-only	1.0	1.0	1.0	1.0	1.0	1.0	1.0	1.0	1.0	1.0	1.0	1.0	1.0	1.0	1.0
GPU-only	25.04	8.08	3.46	5.41	1.34	3.62	2.36	1.68	2.95	1.89	7.88	1.55	1.93	3.18	1.39
Random	0.19	2.65	1.65	1.34	1.18	1.14	1.55	1.05	2.17	1.59	1.00	1.18	1.34	1.76	1.22
R-robin	0.10	1.81	1.58	1.81	1.18	1.23	1.25	1.11	2.12	1.64	0.89	1.09	1.25	1.82	1.23
Utilization	0.12	4.10	1.89	3.12	1.37	1.07	2.24	1.18	2.76	1.85	0.83	1.38	1.66	2.87	1.40
GPU-first	24.66	4.86	2.92	3.57	1.33	3.60	2.24	1.50	2.98	2.20	7.73	1.23	1.74	2.89	1.37
MDR$_{avg}$	24.80	9.22	3.03	8.28	1.52	3.62	3.45	1.71	12.64	2.91	7.65	1.75	1.97	7.04	2.11
MDR$_{last}$	24.86	9.39	4.05	8.37	1.52	3.63	3.86	2.36	12.56	2.87	7.68	1.91	2.01	7.08	2.06
MDR/best	0.99	1.16	1.17	1.55	1.11	1.00	1.63	1.41	4.24	1.32	0.97	1.23	1.04	2.23	1.50

with the CPU. In both cases, we considered the memory spaces as distinct, *i.e.*, we didn't use the *mapped* functionality these platforms provide.

- One cannot just scale by the number of CPU and GPU cores to obtain performance figures: the netbook CPU to GPU performance ratio is much greater than the core & frequency ratio compared to the server-class platform would suggest. This underscores the need for per-platform models.

- The performance benefit of the intelligent decisions made by MDR offsets the overhead incurred by the more complex scheduling function.

We performed a sensitivity analysis to compare the effects of each of the SLAC factors on the final execution time. In each case, we compared the execution time of full MDR versus a modified version of MDR excluding this factor from Equation 5. For example, when determining sensitivity to locality the communication cost was omitted from Equation 5, but the data state was still accurately tracked and unnecessary communication avoided. The results are shown in Figures 7, 8 and 9.

The sensitivity analysis shows the importance and impact of each of the factors considered. Suitability proved to have the greatest effect across workloads and platforms.

In SSI, the relative importance of each factor differed across platforms. Criticality plays an important role in SSI as the document to the latent concept mapping matrix has a large communication cost which some of the smaller tasks cannot offset. However, if this matrix were already resident on the GPU then these tasks would have likely been scheduled there. This results in different factors being more or less important as the different PEs have, in addition, different communication and computation cost models: copying this matrix to the GPU on the netbook costs 1.95x more than on the server, and the server is additionally about 6.39x faster than the netbook on this benchmark.

The importance of suitability is clearest on the netbook class platform and CFD benchmark (where the performance difference between CPU-only and GPU-only is greatest), while the importance of availability is clearest on the performance laptop platform for LU (where the performance difference between CPU-only and GPU-only is small). This shows that for workloads with more heterogeneity between tasks, and for workloads where the performance difference between the PEs are not exorbitant, the impact of these factors are more marked.

The importance of locality is also shown clearly by CFD on the netbook with the round-robin scheduler: the GPU is 25x faster than the CPU but if one mindlessly assigns

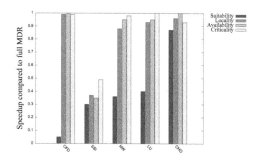

Figure 7: Sensitivity analysis of runtime on the different factors considered on the netbook class platform.

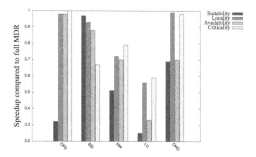

Figure 8: Sensitivity analysis of runtime on the different factors considered on the performance laptop class platform.

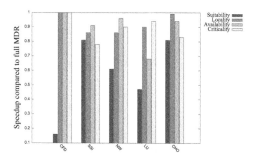

Figure 9: Sensitivity analysis of runtime on the different factors considered on the server class platform.

tasks to different PEs then the communication cost will result in the heterogeneous schedule being ten times slower than CPU-only.

The relative impact of the different factors vary noticeably across platforms for the same workload, and the relative impact of a factor across workloads on the same platform also differs greatly. This emphasizes the need to consider all these factors and also highlights the importance of an adaptive runtime: No static rule can capture these effects across such diverse platforms and workloads.

4.5 Overheads

Any runtime will introduce overheads when compared to an identically scheduled static execution. This is normally offset by the difficulty/impossibility of producing such a static schedule, and the adaptability, robustness and performance portability provided by a runtime framework. The overhead is further amortized for longer running programs and for programs where the tasks are sufficiently large.

For MDR we measured the overhead added by the runtime framework and found that it varied between 1% to 7%. In cases where GPU-only was the best scheduling decision we found the MDR scheduler to add, at worst, a 3% runtime overhead compared to using the GPU-only scheduler and the MDR runtime. In other words, using the performance models to come to the foregone conclusion that the GPU is better cost 3%. Finally, we used Intel VTune to profile the execution of applications under MDR on the server class platform, and found that 97.2% of the execution time was spent in application code. These results suggest that the runtime overheads incurred by MDR are low and are easily offset by the performance gains produced as a result of better runtime decisions, as well as the improved programmability provided by MDR.

5. RELATED WORK

We describe other efforts towards frameworks for heterogeneous multi-core platforms.

MapCG [11] and Merge [16], among others, use the MapReduce formalism to specify tasks that can be offloaded to CPUs and GPUs. Merge allows the specification of processor and function variants but does not automatically map tasks to PEs. Merge allows the programmer to specify predicates, which are used to select the most appropriate function variant and PE. MapCG allows one to concurrently use both the CPU and GPU to perform MapReduce tasks, but they found no performance improvement in using both over the best of CPU- and GPU-only for their benchmarks.

The problem of scheduling computations on multi-core machines with accelerators was considered in [14], [17], [6] and [3]. The granularity of computations considered in [14] and [17] differ from MDR. Jiménez *et al.* [14] consider programs as a scheduling unit and schedule computations without regard to input data. In Qilin [17], an application corresponds to a node in MDR and is split between PEs using a linear model while ignoring communication. Diamos et al. [6] presented some preliminary results for a runtime supported programming and execution model called Harmony. Harmony did not consider criticality of computations or data locality. CellSs/StarSs [3] uses compiler annotations to define PE variants for functions. StarSs uses various schedulers but none of them consider suitability.

Maestro [21] proposes a runtime on top of OpenCL. They consider automating transfers, task decomposition across multiple devices, and autotuning of dynamic execution parameters for some types of problems.

Becchi *et al.* [2] considered the problem of scheduling, in a data-aware manner, legacy kernels on heterogeneous platforms with distributed memory. They showed the importance of locality for legacy kernels. Using library variants and page protection mechanisms, they were able to provide a unified memory view and execute on a heterogeneous platform without rewriting the application.

StarPU [1] uses a library-based approach to allow applications to explicitly enqueue tasks in the underlying runtime while MDR uses the PO-DAG programming abstraction. The lower level of abstraction of the StarPU API is broader and gives application developers greater control on the one hand, while making it difficult to analyze global application structure on the other. Using the PO-DAG abstraction provides a structured model that allows MDR to predict program performance. In addition, decisions are made in MDR with global (graph-level) visibility, enabling us to consider factors such as criticality which cannot be computed with a purely local view. StarPU considers each core of a multi-core CPU as a PE, while MDR considers each PE as an atomic unit that is managed by a lower-level runtime.

In summary, the key distinguinshing attributes of MDR are the consideration of all four (SLAC) criteria, and the use of performance models to drive key runtime decisions.

6. CONCLUSION

We presented a programming model and runtime framework for executing computations that can be represented as PO-DAGs on heterogeneous parallel platforms. We showed that suitability, locality, availability, and criticality (SLAC) have a significant impact on key runtime decisions such as how to assign tasks to processing elements, when to schedule tasks, and when to copy data between memory spaces. Considering them is especially important in order to sustain good performance under diverse workload and hardware platform characteristics. We described a runtime framework where performance models are used to drive key runtime decisions, consider the impact of the SLAC factors. We believe that the proposed heterogeneous runtime framework will be especially useful as larger applications that have a complex mixture of computations are developed on heterogeneous parallel platforms.

Acknowledgments

This work was supported in part by the National Science Foundation under Grant No. 0916817, and in part by NEC Laboratories America.

7. REFERENCES

[1] C. Augonnet, S. Thibault, R. Namyst, and P.-A. Wacrenier. StarPU: A Unified Platform for Task Scheduling on Heterogeneous Multicore Architectures. In *Euro-Par '09*, volume 5704 of *Lecture Notes in Computer Science*, pages 863–874, Delft, The Netherlands, Aug. 2009. Springer.

[2] M. Becchi, S. Byna, S. Cadambi, and S. Chakradhar. Data-aware scheduling of legacy kernels on heterogeneous platforms with distributed memory. In *SPAA '10*, pages 82–91, New York, NY, USA, 2010.

[3] P. Bellens, J. M. Perez, F. Cabarcas, A. Ramirez, R. M. Badia, and J. Labarta. CellSs: Scheduling techniques to better exploit memory hierarchy. *Sci. Program.*, 17:77–95, January 2009.

[4] S. Byna, J. Meng, A. Raghunathan, S. Chakradhar, and S. Cadambi. Best-effort semantic document search on GPUs. In *GPGPU '10*, pages 86–93, New York, NY, USA, 2010. ACM.

[5] S. Che, M. Boyer, J. Meng, D. Tarjan, J. W. Sheaffer, S.-H. Lee, and K. Skadron. Rodinia: A benchmark suite for heterogeneous computing. In *IISWC '09*, pages 44–54, Washington, DC, USA, 2009.

[6] G. F. Diamos and S. Yalamanchili. Harmony: an execution model and runtime for heterogeneous many core systems. In *HPDC '08*, pages 197–200, New York, NY, USA, 2008. ACM.

[7] M. Frigo, C. E. Leiserson, and K. H. Randall. The implementation of the Cilk-5 multithreaded language. *SIGPLAN Not.*, 33:212–223, May 1998.

[8] I. Gelado et al. An asymmetric distributed shared memory model for heterogeneous parallel systems. *SIGPLAN Not.*, 45(3):347–358, 2010.

[9] C. Gregg, J. Brantley, and K. Hazelwood. Contention-aware scheduling of parallel code for heterogeneous systems. In *HotPar 10*, 2010.

[10] M. Hill and M. Marty. Amdahl's law in the multicore era. *Computer*, 41(7):33–38, July 2008.

[11] C. Hong, D. Chen, W. Chen, W. Zheng, and H. Lin. MapCG: writing parallel program portable between CPU and GPU. In *PACT '10*, pages 217–226, New York, NY, USA, 2010. ACM.

[12] Intel. Intel threading building blocks (TBB), 2010.

[13] M. Isard, M. Budiu, Y. Yu, A. Birrell, and D. Fetterly. Dryad: distributed data-parallel programs from sequential building blocks. In *EuroSys '07*, pages 59–72, New York, NY, USA, 2007. ACM.

[14] V. J. Jiménez, L. Vilanova, I. Gelado, M. Gil, G. Fursin, and N. Navarro. Predictive runtime code scheduling for heterogeneous architectures. In *HiPEAC '09*, pages 19–33, Berlin, Heidelberg, 2009.

[15] Y.-K. Kwok and I. Ahmad. Dynamic critical-path scheduling: an effective technique for allocating task graphs to multiprocessors. *IEEE Trans. on Parallel and Distributed Systems*, 7(5):506–521, May 1996.

[16] M. D. Linderman, J. D. Collins, H. Wang, and T. H. Meng. Merge: a programming model for heterogeneous multi-core systems. In *ASPLOS XIII*, pages 287–296, New York, NY, USA, 2008. ACM.

[17] C.-K. Luk, S. Hong, and H. Kim. Qilin: exploiting parallelism on heterogeneous multiprocessors with adaptive mapping. In *MICRO 42*, pages 45–55, New York, NY, USA, 2009. ACM.

[18] T. M. Mitchell. *Machine Learning*. McGraw-Hill, New York, 1997.

[19] J. Nickolls, I. Buck, M. Garland, and K. Skadron. Scalable parallel programming with CUDA. *Queue*, 6(2):40–53, 2008.

[20] NVIDIA. CUDA Zone, 2010.

[21] K. Spafford, J. Meredith, and J. Vetter. Maestro: data orchestration and tuning for OpenCL devices. In *Euro-Par'10*, pages 275–286, Berlin, Heidelberg, 2010. Springer-Verlag.

[22] J. E. Stone, D. Gohara, and G. Shi. OpenCL: A parallel programming standard for heterogeneous computing systems. *Computing in Science and Engineering*, 12:66–73, 2010.

[23] N. Sundaram, A. Raghunathan, and S. T. Chakradhar. A framework for efficient and scalable execution of domain-specific templates on GPUs. In *IPDPS '09*, pages 1–12, Washington, DC, USA, 2009.

[24] D. Tarditi, S. Puri, and J. Oglesby. Accelerator: using data parallelism to program GPUs for general-purpose uses. In *ASPLOS-XII*, pages 325–335, New York, NY, USA, 2006. ACM.

[25] J. Yu and R. Buyya. A taxonomy of scientific workflow systems for grid computing. *SIGMOD Rec.*, 34:44–49, September 2005.

Active Pebbles: Parallel Programming for Data-Driven Applications

Jeremiah J. Willcock
Open Systems Lab
Indiana University
jewillco@cs.indiana.edu

Torsten Hoefler
University of Illinois at
Urbana-Champaign
htor@illinois.edu

Nicholas Edmonds,
Andrew Lumsdaine
Open Systems Lab
Indiana University
$\left\{ \begin{array}{c} \text{ngedmond} \\ \text{lums} \end{array} \right\}$ @cs.indiana.edu

ABSTRACT

The scope of scientific computing continues to grow and now includes diverse application areas such as network analysis, combinatorial computing, and knowledge discovery, to name just a few. Large problems in these application areas require HPC resources, but they exhibit computation and communication patterns that are irregular, fine-grained, and non-local, making it difficult to apply traditional HPC approaches to achieve scalable solutions. In this paper we present Active Pebbles, a programming and execution model developed explicitly to enable the development of scalable software for these emerging application areas. Our approach relies on five main techniques—scalable addressing, active routing, message coalescing, message reduction, and termination detection—to separate algorithm expression from communication optimization. Using this approach, algorithms can be expressed in their natural forms, with their natural levels of granularity, while optimizations necessary for scalability can be applied automatically to match the characteristics of particular machines. We implement several example kernels using both Active Pebbles and existing programming models, evaluating both programmability and performance. Our experimental results demonstrate that the Active Pebbles model can succinctly and directly express irregular application kernels, while still achieving performance comparable to MPI-based implementations that are significantly more complex.

Categories and Subject Descriptors

D.1.3 [**Programming Techniques**]: Concurrent Programming—*Parallel Programming*

General Terms

Performance, Design

Keywords

Irregular applications, programming models, active messages

1. INTRODUCTION

Computation is now well-accepted as a "third pillar" of science (complementary to theory and experimentation). High-performance computing (HPC) in particular has enabled computational scientists to expand the frontiers of their disciplines. More recently, a "fourth pillar" of science has been proposed, namely, data-intensive science [14]. The computational resource requirements for data-intensive science are just as vast as for traditional compute-intensive science (consider Google or the Human Genome Project as exemplars). Thus, there is a pressing need to expand the scope of HPC to include data-intensive applications. An important sub-class of data-intensive applications is data-driven applications. In this class of problems, the computational dependencies are embedded in the data and discovered dynamically at run-time.

Traditional compute-intensive applications, such as those based on discretized systems of PDEs, have natural locality (from the local nature of the underlying operators). Scalable applications can therefore be written to solve such problems using a relatively coarse-grained approach, such as the BSP "compute-communicate" model [28]; the communication operations themselves can also be coarse, involving only a few (local) peers per process.

In contrast, data-driven problems tend to be **fine-grained**, i.e., a large number of small objects; **irregular**, i.e., connections between objects cannot be expressed analytically; and **non-local**, i.e., the dependency graph does not have good separators [24]. As a result, these problems are not well suited to the parallel programming approaches that have proven to be so effective for compute-intensive applications. Additionally, most HPC hardware has been developed for problems with compute-intensive characteristics. This hardware has also become increasingly complex, including clusters of multi-core systems that have widely varying communication characteristics within the same machine. These developments further hinder programming with standard models.

Many data-driven problems can scale on traditional HPC hardware. The difficulty is in expressing fine-grained, irregular, non-local computations in such a way as to be able to fully exploit hardware that was designed for coarse-grained, regular, local computations. This can be done (and has been done), with great difficulty, by hand. However, with home-grown solutions like this, the application developer is responsible for developing all layers of the solution stack, not just the application. Furthermore, the application developer is responsible for re-implementing this entire stack when target platforms change, or when new applications must be developed. In many ways, this is similar to the state of affairs that faced the compute-intensive community prior to the standardization of MPI.

Accordingly, an approach is needed that separates data-driven applications from the underlying hardware so that they can be expressed at their natural levels of granularity, while still being able to (portably) achieve high performance.

To address this need, we have developed Active Pebbles[1] (AP), a new programming model accompanied by an execution model specialized for data-driven computations. AP defines control and data flow constructs for fine-grained data-driven computations that enable low implementation complexity and high execution performance. That is, with the Active Pebbles programming model, applications can be expressed at their "natural" granularities and with their natural structures. The Active Pebbles execution environment in turn coalesces fine-grained data accesses and maps the resulting collective operations to optimized communication patterns in order to achieve performance and scalability.

At the core of the Active Pebbles model are *pebbles*, light-weight active messages that are managed and scheduled in a scalable way, and which generally have no order enforced between them. In addition to pebbles, the AP model includes *handlers* and *distribution objects*. Handlers are functions that are executed in response to pebbles (or ensembles of pebbles) and are bound to data objects with distribution objects to create *targets*. To provide the simultaneous benefits of fine-grained programmability with scalable performance, our model relies on the following five integrated techniques:

1. **Fine-grained Pebble Addressing** — light-weight global addressing to route pebbles to targets.
2. **Message Coalescing** — combining messages to trade message rate for latency and bandwidth.
3. **Active Routing** — restricting the network topology to trade message throughput for latency for large numbers of processes.
4. **Message Reductions** — pebble processing at sources and intermediate routing hops (where possible).
5. **Termination Detection** — customizable detection of system quiescence.

The Active Pebbles model has two distinct aspects: a programming model plus an execution model. Pebbles and targets, in combination with Pebble Addressing (1), define an abstract programming model. The techniques in 2–5 describe an execution model which translates programs expressed using the programming model into high-performance implementations. Accordingly, techniques used in the execution model are not simply implementation details: e.g., message reductions in combination with routing cause a decrease in the asymptotic message complexity of some algorithms and are thus essential to our model.

2. RELATED WORK

Solutions to data-driven problems on shared memory machines has been studied by several groups [2, 4, 18]. A fundamental result from these efforts is that locking can limit performance due to lock contention and additional memory traffic, decrease programmer productivity, and stop progress in faulty environments [12]. Predefined atomic memory operations such as *compare and swap* or *fetch and add* allow the design of non-blocking and wait-free algorithms but their expressiveness is limited [13] (e.g., to integer addition). Transactional Memory provides an extension to the shared memory programming model by allowing user-defined operations (*transactions*) which succeed or fail atomically, thus reducing programming complexity while still enabling non-blocking and wait-free algorithms [12, 25].

[1]The term Active Pebbles expresses the idea that messages are active and independent, but without individual identity (transported and processed in bulk).

Scalable computing systems are by necessity distributed memory machines with multiple coherence domains, and are thus more complex to program. Message passing, an effective programming model for regular HPC applications, provides a clear separation of address spaces and makes all communication explicit. The Message Passing Interface (MPI) is the de facto standard for programming such systems [21]. However, irregular and dynamic applications often need shared access to data structures which naturally cross address spaces. MPI-2 One Sided [21, §11] and Partitioned Global Address Space (PGAS) [22, 27] models strive to fill this gap by allowing transparent access to remote memory in an emulated global address space. However, mechanisms for concurrency control are limited to locks and critical sections; some models support weak predefined atomic operations (e.g., *MPI_Accumulate()*). Stronger atomic operations (e.g., compare and swap, fetch and add) and user-defined atomic operations are either not supported or do not perform well. Thus, we claim that these approaches do not provide the appropriate primitives for fine-grained data-driven applications. Just as Transactional Memory generalizes processor atomic operations to arbitrary transactions, Active Pebbles generalizes one-sided operations to user-defined pebble handlers.

Active Pebbles are similar to active messages [29]. However, active messages are mostly used for low-level communication layers that are not exposed to the users. Other advanced object communication models like Charm++ [17], X10 [7], and ParalleX [10] are also based on active messages behind the scenes. Our approach differs from these approaches in that AP has a much finer natural granularity (i.e., AP naturally expresses fine-grained problems while also obtaining high performance). Moreover, our approach allows direct expression of operations on fine-grained distributed items. The figure below compares the natural granularities of AP with other programming models.

Our execution model could be a compilation target for an active PGAS language such as X10 or Chapel [6]; however, we claim that the techniques described in our execution model are required to allow those languages to efficiently target fine-grained applications—and are thus a substantial part of our contribution.

2.1 Comparative Example

We compare and contrast related approaches with a simple example problem. Assume that each of P processes wants to insert n items into a hash table which is statically distributed across the P processes and uses chaining to resolve collisions. The keys for the hash table are uniformly distributed in $[0, N)$, $N \gg P$. We now compare possible implementations in different programming models.

MPI. In one possible MPI implementation, each process would collect distinct sets of items, each destined for one remote process. After each process inserted all n requests, all processes would participate in a complete exchange. This communication can either be done with direct sends or with a single *MPI_Alltoallv()* operation (plus an *MPI_Alltoall()* stage to determine the pairwise message sizes). Each process would receive and add items to its local portion of the hash table. On average, each would receive and process $\Omega(n)$ items from $\Omega(P)$ peers, incurring a cost of $\Omega(n + P)$.

PGAS. A possible PGAS implementation would create the hash table in the global address space and each process would add items directly ensuring mutual exclusion by locking. This would need $\Omega(n)$ lock/unlock messages in addition to the $\Omega(n)$ data transfers per process. Resolving collisions is likely to require further messages and locks (e.g., to allocate additional space).

Object-Oriented. In object-oriented parallel languages, such as Charm++ [17] or X10 [7], the hash table would be a global object (e.g., a *Chare*). Each item would trigger a member function (e.g., insert) of the hash table object. For large n and P the vast number of remote invocations and their associated management overhead, as well as the small amount of computation per object, would impact performance significantly.

Active Pebbles. Figure 1 shows a schematic view of the Active Pebbles execution model. In an Active Pebbles implementation the user would specify a handler function which adds data items to the local hash table. The user would then send all data elements successively to the handler for each individual key (which is globally addressable). The Active Pebbles framework takes these pebbles and coalesces them into groups bound for the same remote process (two items with keys 6 and 7 sent from process P2 to P3 in Figure 1). It can also perform reductions on these coalesced groups of messages to eliminate duplicates and combine messages to the same target key (shown at P3 "single-source reduction" in Figure 1). Active routing sends all (coalesced) messages along a virtual topology and applies additional coalescing and reductions at intermediate hops (Figure 1 shows routing along a hypercube, i.e., P0 sends messages to P3 through P1 where they are coalesced and reduced, "multi-source reduction," with other messages).

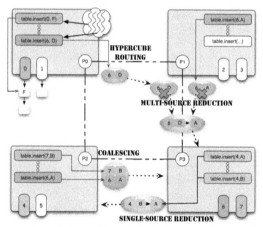

Figure 1: Overview of the Active Pebbles model.

This example shows the advantages of the Active Pebbles model, and how PGAS and object oriented models are inherently limited by the per-process message rate. Although MPI's flexibility allows the use of collective communication, high programming effort would be required to implement coalescing and multi-stage communication manually. The Active Pebbles model performs such optimizations transparently and eliminates redundant communication.

3. THE ACTIVE PEBBLES MODEL

In this section we analyze each of the Active Pebbles mechanisms in detail. Sections 3.1 and 3.2 describe the programming model while Sections 3.3–3.6 describe the execution model. We utilize the well-known LogGP model [1] as a framework for formal analysis. The LogGP model incorporates four network parameters: L, the maximum latency between any two processes; o, the CPU

injection overhead of a single message; g, the "gap" between two messages, i.e., the inverse of the injection rate; G, the "gap" per byte, i.e., the inverse bandwidth; and P, the number of processes. We make two modifications to the original model: small, individual messages (pebbles) are considered to be of one-byte size, and we assume that the coefficient of G for an n-byte message is n rather than $n-1$ as in the original LogGP model. LogGP parameters written with a subscript p refer to pebble-specific parameters imposed by our *synthetic network*. For example, L_p is the per-pebble latency, which might be higher than the network latency L due to active routing or coalescing; analogously, o_p, g_p, and G_p are the overhead, gap, and gap per byte for a pebble.

3.1 Active Pebbles Abstractions

The primary abstractions in the Active Pebbles model are pebbles and targets. Pebbles are light-weight active messages that operate on targets (which can, transparently, be local or remote). Targets are created by binding together a data object with a message handler, through the use of a distribution object. In Figure 1, targets are the destination buckets and their keys are used directly as destination addresses. The distribution object in this example maps each key i to process $\lfloor i/2 \rfloor$. Pebbles flow through the network from their source ranks to their destination ranks (determined by the distribution object). Pebbles are unordered (other than by termination detection), allowing flexibility in processing (such as threading, when the underlying handler function is thread-safe, or other forms of acceleration).

3.2 Fine-Grained Pebble Addressing

In the Active Pebbles model, messages are sent to individual targets, not process ranks. Target identifiers (which are typically domain-specific) are converted to ranks using a user-defined distribution object. Target identifiers form a global address space, as in other GAS models. Active Pebbles supports both static and dynamic distributions. When a static distribution is used, the distribution will often require only constant space and constant time for location computations. A dynamic distribution is likely to require larger amounts of storage; however, applications need not use dynamic distributions if static ones will suffice. Note that, unlike some other object-based messaging systems, Active Pebbles does not require any particular information to be kept to communicate with a target; i.e., there is no setup required to communicate, and a sending thread does not require any local information about the destination target (other than the distribution, which can be shared by many targets). A target identifier can be as simple as a global index into a distributed array; such identifiers can be created and destroyed at will, and are thus very lightweight. This mechanism is similar to *places* in X10 or *Chare arrays* in Charm++ but those mechanisms enable migration and other other advanced management and thus require $\mathcal{O}(n)$ time and space overhead to manage n elements; a statically-distributed array in Active Pebbles would only require $\mathcal{O}(1)$ space overhead to manage n elements, on the other hand. To simplify applications, the fine-grained addressing layer traps pebbles destined for the sending node and calls the corresponding handler directly, avoiding overheads from message coalescing, serialization, etc. In LogGP terms, addressing moves some time from the application to the model's o_p term without an overall change to performance.

3.3 Message Coalescing

A standard technique for increasing bandwidth utilization is message coalescing. Message coalescing combines multiple pebbles to the same destination into a single, larger message. This

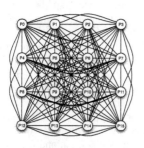 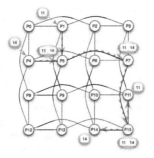 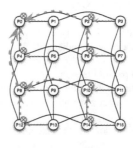 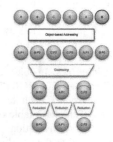

(a) Full system (as exposed by MPI). (b) Pebble routing in a synthetic hypercube network.

(c) Pebble reduction in a synthetic hypercube network.

(d) Coalescing and reductions on idempotent objects bound for processes $P0$, $P1$, and $P2$.

Figure 2: The Different Active Pebbles Features.

technique is well-known in the MPI arena and often performed manually. In LogGP terms, the packing of n 1-byte messages into one, n-byte message changes the overall message latency from $(n+1)o + L + G + (n-1)g$ to $2o + L + nG$. Thus, coalescing improves performance if $G < o + g$, which is true for all practical networks. However, coalescing works against pipelining. While without coalescing, the first pebble can be processed at the sender after $2o + L + G$, coalescing delays this to $2o + L + nG$. Thus, coalescing improves bandwidth utilization and reduces the use of g and o at cost of per-pebble latency L_p. Finding the optimal coalescing factor is system-dependent and subject to active research. Our LogGP discussion can be used as a good starting point and, in Active Pebbles, a user can specify the coalescing factor at run-time. Also, it may not be known exactly when the stream of pebbles will end, and so a timeout or similar scheme can be used to know when to stop accumulating pebbles. Active Pebbles includes a *flush()* call to send pebbles immediately.

One disadvantage of message coalescing is its use of memory. For fast access to buffers, one buffer must typically be kept for each possible message destination. Some implementations also use an individual, preallocated message buffer to receive messages from each possible sender. Those buffers can be established lazily, i.e., allocated at first use, however, reserving space for P buffers per process is impractical for large P if the communication is dense. The next feature, active routing, is an efficient technique to reduce the number of such buffers and increase performance.

3.4 Active Routing

Highly irregular applications often send messages from each process to almost every other process. Thus, the packet injection rate on each process's outgoing network links and the number of coalescing buffers become performance bottlenecks. To work around these limitations, our implementation of the Active Pebbles model can route messages through one or more intermediate hops on their ways to their destinations. For example, a hypercube topology can be embedded, with messages routed in such a way that they are only sent along the edges of the hypercube. Thus, each node only sends directly to a small number of other nodes, allowing fewer, but larger, coalesced messages to be sent. Users can also define their own routing schemes, including dynamic routing for fault tolerance.

Several researchers have found (e.g., Bruck et al [5]) that software-based routing improves performance on personalized (all-to-all) communications. For example, Bader, Helman, and JáJá show that adding one intermediate node into each message's path leads to a substantial performance improvement [3]; Plimpton et al show a performance benefit, both in theory and in practice, of simulating a hypercube topology for the HPCC RandomAccess benchmark [23].

Garg and Sabharwal discuss the benefits of manual software routing along a virtual torus on Blue Gene/L [11] and Yoo et al. [32] use manual routing and message reductions to optimize breadth-first search at large-scale. The original paper that introduced the LogGP model shows a personalized broadcast (*MPI_Scatter()*) operation that uses tree-based routing [1], reducing the number of messages sent from $\mathcal{O}(P^2)$ to $\mathcal{O}(P \log P)$, although the total number of message bytes is increased by a factor of $\log P$. In LogGP terms, the assumption made is that $o + g$ is large enough compared to G that it is acceptable to use extra bandwidth to reduce the number of messages sent.

In many networks, routing increases the number of links used by any given pebble, leading to greater bandwidth utilization. However, routing allows pebbles from multiple sources and/or to multiple destinations to be packed together into a single, larger message, increasing the effectiveness of coalescing compared to a non-routed network. A similar argument applies to reductions across pebbles from multiple source nodes to the same destination target; see Section 3.5 for an analysis. Thus, active routing can reduce the number of packets sent across the network, potentially leading to less congestion and a performance improvement.

Active routing also reduces the amount of memory needed for message coalescing because it limits k, the number of other processes that each process communicates with. Without routing, $k = P - 1$, and thus each node requires a large number of communication buffers. Hypercube routing, with $k = \log_2 P$, reduces the number of buffers needed from $\Theta(P)$ to $\Theta(\log P)$.

Active routing, in combination with other AP features, effectively converts fine-grained point-to-point messaging operations into coarse-grained optimized "collective" operations. For example, one source sending separate pebbles to different destinations will, by combining routing and message coalescing, actually use a tree-based scatter operation that takes advantage of large message support in the network (as in [1]). Similarly, a number of sources sending pebbles to the same target will combine them into a tree-based, optimized gather operation (similar to [5]).

Figure 2(b) shows routing along a hypercube (two messages are coalesced at $P5$ and split up at $P15$; routing reduces the message volume significantly). Messages flow only along the edges of the hypercube compared with (logically) direct all-to-all routing in Figure 2(a). Active Pebbles' synthetic topologies can be optimized for the topology of the physical communication network, as with MPI collective operations (e.g., [5]).

3.5 Message Reductions

In many applications, multiple pebbles of the same type to the same object are redundant: duplicate messages can be removed or combined in some way. We call this optimization message reduction; it can occur either at a message's sender or—with active routing—at an intermediate node. Reduction is implemented using a cache. For duplicate removal, previous messages are stored in a cache at each process; messages found in the cache are ignored. As analyzed below, lookup cost is important for the benefit of message reductions, requiring a fast, constant-time cache lookup at the expense of hit rate. In our experiments, we use a direct-mapped cache with runtime-configurable size; a miss replaces the contents of a cache slot with the new pebble.

For messages with data payloads, two cases are possible: the reduction operation is max (in some ordering; min is dual), in which case the cache simply removes messages with suboptimal values; or the reduction operation is something else that requires messages to be combined. In the latter case, message data payloads can be concatenated or combined (e.g., additively) as shown in Figure 1. In LogGP terms, reductions replace n messages by $n(1-h)$ messages (where h is the cache hit rate), but they also increase the value of o_p for each pebble to $o_p + c$, where c is the average cost of searching and maintaining the cache. The decrease in messages from n to $n(1-h)$ is equivalent to sending n messages but replacing G by $c+(1-h)G$. With message coalescing, G, c, and the message count are the only important factors in messaging performance; other factors are constant overheads. Without reductions, the time to send one pebble is G; reductions reduce the (expected) time to $c+(1-h)G$, leading to a benefit when $hG > c$.

This analysis only considers the effect of reductions on message latencies and bandwidth consumption; however, the reduction in computation at the target is likely to be even more important. Reductions reduce the expected processing cost p for each pebble to $p(1-h)$. Messages requiring expensive computation thus benefit from reductions by reducing the number of those computations that occur. In particular, if a message can trigger a tree of other messages, one reduction at the source of that message can prevent many others from being sent at all.

Active routing can increase the benefit of reductions by allowing reductions across messages from multiple sources to the same target. With routing, a message is tested against the cache of every node along its path, increasing the chance of a match being found. For example, in a hypercube, each message is tested against up to $\log_2 P$ caches. Assuming the probabilities of hitting in each cache are independent, the overall hit rate becomes $1-(1-h)^{\log_2 P}$ (approximately $h\log_2 P$) rather than the rate h for a single cache. These multiple checks thus may lead to a greater reduction in message volume than would occur without routing.

When messages are sent from different sources to one target, routing and local message reductions at intermediate nodes combine to synthesize a reduction tree as would be used by an optimized implementation of *MPI_Reduce()*. This emergent property creates an efficient collective operation from point-to-point messages, with the routing algorithm defining the structure of the generated tree. Hypercube routing, for example, would generate binary reduction trees (Figure 2(c) shows an all-to-P0 reduction) with a logarithmic number of stages.

3.6 Termination Detection

The Active Pebbles model allows the handler for each pebble to trigger new communications. Thus, in a message-driven computation, it is non-trivial to detect the global termination (quiescence) of the algorithm. In the standard model for termination detection [8], each process can either be active or passive. Active processes perform computation and can send messages, as well as become passive. Passive processes can only be activated by incoming messages. A computation starts with one or more active processes and

is terminated when all processes are passive and no messages are in flight. Many algorithms are available to detect termination [20], both for specialized networks and general, asynchronous message passing environments.

The optimal termination detection algorithm for an algorithm can depend on the features of the communication subsystem and on the structure of the communication (dense or sparse). Our framework enables easy implementation of different algorithms by providing several hooks into the messaging layer. We implement one fully general termination detection scheme (SKR [26]), using a nonblocking *allreduce()* operation [15], similar to the four-counter algorithm in [20].

3.6.1 Depth-Limited Termination Detection

Some applications can provide an upper bound for the longest chain of messages that is triggered from handlers. For example, a simple application where each message only accumulates or deposits data into its target's memory does not require a generic termination detection scheme. Another example would be an application that performs atomic updates on target locations that return results (e.g., read-modify-write). These examples would require termination detection of depths one and two, respectively. Graph traversals can generate chains of handler-triggered messages of unbounded depth (up to the diameter of the graph), however. Several message-counting algorithms meet the lower bound discussed in [16] and detect termination in $\log P$ steps for depth one, while unlimited-depth termination detection algorithms usually need multiple iterations to converge. In the SKR algorithm, termination detection takes at least $2\log P$ steps (two *allreduce()* operations). Our framework offers hooks to specify the desired termination detection depth to exploit this application-specific knowledge. We implement two depth-one termination detection schemes: a message-counting algorithm based on nonblocking *reduce_scatter()* [15], and an algorithm that uses nonblocking barrier semantics and is able to leverage high-speed synchronization primitives [16]. Both algorithms are invoked n times to handle depth-n termination detection.

3.6.2 Termination Detection and Active Routing

In active routing, each message travels over multiple hops which increases the depth of termination detection. For example in hypercube routing, an additional $\log_2 P$ hops are added to the termination detection. This is not an issue for detectors that can handle unlimited depths, but it affects limited-depth detection. With s-stage active routing and a depth-n termination requested by the application, limited-depth termination detection would take $n \cdot s$ steps. However, termination detection could take advantage of the smaller set of possible neighbors from active routing, such as the $\log_2 P$ neighbors of each node in a hypercube. This would reduce the per-round time to $\mathcal{O}(\log\log P)$, for a total time of $\mathcal{O}(\log P \log\log P)$ as compared to $\mathcal{O}(\log P)$ without routing. Routing may benefit the rest of the application enough to justify that increase in termination detection time, however.

3.7 Synthetic Network Tradeoffs

The Active Pebbles model uses coalescing, reductions, active routing, and termination detection to present an easy-to-use programming model to the user while still being able to exploit the capabilities of large-scale computing systems. Active Pebbles transforms fine-grained object access and the resulting all-to-all messaging into coarse-grained messages in a synthetic, or overlay, network. The synthetic network transparently transforms message streams into optimized communication schedules similar to those used by MPI collective operations. Various aspects of the Active

Pebbles execution model can be adjusted to match the synthetic network to a particular application, such as the coalescing factor, the synthetic topology, and termination detection. The programming interface remains identical for all of those options. Active Pebbles can thus be optimized for specific machines without changes to application source code, allowing performance-portability.

4. APPLICATION EXAMPLES

We examine four example applications using the Active Pebbles model in order to explore the expressiveness and performance of applications written using it. Implementations of these applications in three models are evaluated: Active Pebbles; MPI; and Unified Parallel C (UPC), which we use to illustrate the programming techniques used in PGAS languages.[2] We first present a simple summary of these applications with more detailed explanations to follow:

RandomAccess randomly updates a global table in the style of the HPCC RandomAccess benchmark [19]. We use optimized reference implementations where appropriate, as well as simplified implementations.

PointerChase creates a random ring of processes and sends messages around the ring.

Permutation permutes a data array distributed across P processes according to another distributed array, as might be used to redistribute unordered data after loading it.

Breadth First Search (BFS) is a graph kernel that explores a random Erdős-Rényi [9] graph breadth-first.

4.1 RandomAccess

The parallel RandomAccess benchmark measures the performance of updating random locations in a globally distributed table [19]. The benchmark resembles access patterns from distributed databases and distributed hash tables. It uses a global *table* of N elements distributed across P processes. The timed kernel consists of $4N$ updates to the table of the form $table[ran \% N] \mathbin{\char`\^}= ran$ where *ran* is the output of a random number generator. Processes may not buffer more than 1024 updates locally.

PGAS. In UPC the *table* can be allocated in the shared space and accessed just as in the sequential version of the algorithm:

```
uint64_t ran;                                              UPC
shared uint64_t* table = upc_all_alloc(N ,sizeof(uint64_t));
for (int i = 0 ; i < 1024 ; ++i) {
    ran = (ran << 1) ^ (((int64_t)ran < 0) ? 7 : 0); // compute index
    table[ran % N] ^= ran; // perform update
}
```

The UPC compiler/runtime then performs the necessary communication to perform the update to *table*.

MPI. MPI has no notion of shared data structures, so the updates to non-local portions of the table must be explicitly communicated to the remote process which then applies them. Rather than sending individual updates we buffer 1024 updates sorted by destination then communicate them collectively. The MPI implementation of the RandomAccess application first buffers local updates, then communicates the number of updates followed by the updates themselves:

---

[2]"PGAS" here refers to fine-grained remote memory accesses (the basic PGAS model), without active message extensions.

```
for (int i = 0 ; i < 1024 ; ++i) {                         MPI
    ran = (ran << 1) ^ (((int64_t)ran < 0) ? 7 : 0); // compute index
    long index = ran % N;
    int owner = index / (N/P);

    // perform local update
    if (rank == owner)
        table[index % (N/P)] ^= ran;
    else // remote
        out_bufs[owner].buf[out_bufs[owner].count++] = ran;
}
// ... allocate and prepare all-to-all communication buffers
MPI_Alltoall(out_bufs.count,. . . ,in_bufs.count,. . . );
// ... allocate and prepare all-to-allv communication buffers
MPI_Alltoallv(out_bufs.buf,out_bufs.count,. . . ,
              in_bufs.buf,in_bufs.count,. . . );
```

AP. In Active Pebbles we invoke remote handlers using pebbles. To implement RandomAccess we first encapsulate the update operation inside a handler:

```
struct update_handler {                                    AP
    bool operator()(uint64_t ran) const
    { table[ran % (N/P)] ^= ran; } // update to table
};
```

This handler is then invoked from a remote process by creating a pebble type and assigning the handler to it. The pebble type encapsulates pebble addressing (through the *block_owner_map* type) and routing (through the *hypercube_routing* object passed to the type's constructor). A separate operation attaches a particular handler object to the pebble type:

```
pebble_addressing_dest_hbr<. . . >                         AP
update_msg(transport, . . . , block_owner_map(N/P),
              hypercube_routing(rank, size));
update_msg.set_handler(update_handler(table));
```

Active Pebbles detects messages which would be sent to the current rank using pebble addressing and simply calls the appropriate handler directly. This eliminates the need for applications to treat local and remote data differently:

```
for (int i = 0 ; i < 1024 ; ++i) {                         AP
    ran = (ran << 1) ^ (((int64_t)ran < 0) ? 7 : 0);
    update_msg.send(ran);
}
```

4.2 PointerChase

The PointerChase application creates a random permutation of $[0, P)$; each processor i then relays a single, small message to element $(i+1) \bmod P$ of the permutation. This benchmark is intended to model the performance of chains of dependent operations in an irregular application. It primarily tests message latency, and thus is expected to favor PGAS models.

PGAS. In UPC, notifying the next process to relay the message can be implemented by polling on a counter allocated in the shared space and waiting for its value to be updated:

```
shared int* flags = upc_all_alloc(THREADS, sizeof(int));   | UPC |
for (int i = 0; i < rounds; ++i) {
   while (flags[MYTHREAD] != i) {}
   flags[next_rank] = i;
}
```

MPI. The implementation of the PointerChase application is similar in MPI, except that messages replace the memory operations and *MPI_Wait()* is used instead of polling (example simplified):

```
for (int i = 0; i < rounds; ++i) {                         | MPI |
   MPI_Recv(&data, 1, MPI_ANY_SOURCE, . . . );
   MPI_Send(&next_rank, 1, next_rank, . . . );
}
```

AP. In Active Pebbles there is no main loop at all; the control flow is entirely represented in the message handler:

```
struct msg_handler {                                        | AP |
   bool operator()(int source, const int* data, int count) {
      if (rank != start) msg->send(round, next);
      else if (--round > 0) msg->send(round, next);
} };
```

The message handler is initialized with the rank which sends the first message (*start*), the number of loops around the ring to perform (*round*), and the next rank in the ring (*next*). After the handlers are initialized all that is required to start the application is for the *start* rank to send the first message:

```
typed_message<. . .>::type                                  | AP |
   msg(typed_message<. . .>
         ::make(transport, 1, msg_handler(0, rounds, next, msg)));
if (rank == start) msg.send(0, next);
```

4.3   Permutation

The Permutation application is designed to be representative of a common task in scientific computing: distributing and permuting unsorted data (e.g., after it has been read from a file). The data distribution may exist to optimize locality, provide load-balancing, or for domain-specific reasons. Permutation uses three arrays representing input data (*data*), a permutation (*perm*), and the re-ordered data (*data_perm*). These arrays each contain N elements, and each is distributed across P processors. The *data* array contains an index into the *perm* array which functions as a unique identifier for the data element, as well as some associated data. The *perm* array contains the destination for each input element; the inverse of the permutation *perm* is applied. The result satisfies $\{\forall i \in [0, N) : data_{perm}[perm[data[i]]] = i\}$.

PGAS. In UPC we allocate the arrays in the shared space and use *upc_forall()* to distribute the work:

```
upc_forall (uint64_t i = 0; i < N; ++i; &data[i])           | UPC |
   data_perm[perm[data[i]]] = i;
```

In the preceding example we simply store the indices i into $data_{perm}$; a real application using this technique would assign the application data associated with index i.

MPI. In the MPI implementation of Permutation a similar communication pattern to that described in Section 4.1 is used. Rather than a single *Alltoall()/Alltoallv()* round, two rounds are required for Permutation. In the first round, elements of *data* are sent to the process that stores *perm[data[i]]*. In the second round *perm* is applied and the data sent to the process which owns $data_{perm}[perm[data[i]]]$. We have omitted the lengthy code for the MPI implementation of Permutation in the interest of brevity.

AP. The Active Pebbles implementation combines the movement of *data* and the application of *perm* into a single phase using dependent messages and depth-two termination detection to detect completion. The MPI implementation must address the situations where some dependent elements of *data*, *perm*, and *data_perm* may be local and others remote. Active Pebbles handles these locality concerns automatically because pebbles sent to local targets will simply call the correct underlying handler with no performance penalty. The Active Pebbles implementation uses two handlers, the first receives elements of *data*, applies *perm*, and sends a pebble to the owner of the appropriate target in *data_perm*:

```
struct permute_handler {                                    | AP |
   bool operator()(const pair<uint64_t, uint64_t>& x) const {
      uint64_t target_idx = perm[get(local_map, x.first)];
      put->send(make_pair(target_idx, x.second));
} };
```

The second handler is the *put* handler used by the *permute_handler*. This handler writes values to the specified target in *data_perm*:

```
struct put_handler {                                        | AP |
   bool operator()(const put_data& x) const
   { data_perm[get(local_map, x.first)] = x.second; }
};
```

After the message handlers are initialized, each process simply sends pebbles for all of its local data:

```
make_coalesced_mt<. . .>::type data_permute(transport, . . . );   | AP |
for (int i = 0; i < N/P; ++i)
   data_permute.send(make_pair(data[i], N/P * rank + i));
```

Once termination detection completes, all pebbles sent (both originally and from handlers) will have been processed, and so all elements of *data_perm* will have been updated.

4.4   BFS

The final application we consider is breadth-first search on a directed graph. Graph algorithms are an excellent application of the Active Pebbles model because they often create many fine-grained asynchronous tasks. All of the implementations use an Erdős-Rényi random graph with a one-dimensional vertex distribution across the P processors.

In a bulk-synchronous implementation BFS is implemented with a single logical distributed queue, composed of logical queues on each process. A *push()* operation on any process results in a vertex being placed on the local queue of the vertex's owning process. Neither MPI nor UPC support dynamic shared data structures such as queues directly. Buffering queue operations at the source and applying them collectively addresses this limitation in both cases. In the case of MPI, this is necessary because *MPI_Accumulate()* is not expressive enough to implement queue update operations; e.g., it cannot atomically fetch and increment a counter. In UPC, vertices could be pushed directly onto the targets' local queues, but the queues would then need to be locked remotely, limiting concurrency.

PGAS + MPI. The MPI and UPC implementations use similar algorithms:

```
                                          MPI/UPC Pseudocode
if (source is local) Q.push(source);
while (!Q.empty()) {
  for (v : Q)
    if (visited[v] == 0) {
      visited[v] = 1;
      for (w : neighbors[v]) {Q2.push(w);}
    }
  Q.clear(); swap(Q, Q2);
}
```

AP. In Active Pebbles we can choose a formulation of the BFS algorithm that expresses a better mapping to the programming model. Level-wise traversals of the BFS tree are possible using a queue to buffer pebbles, as are versions which compute a BFS numbering using a single-source shortest path algorithm. The latter approach is asymptotically more expensive, but significantly reduces the synchronization required and thus may be desirable in practice. An implementation in Active Pebbles would define a handler which utilized a *distance* property for each vertex:

```
                                                      AP
struct bfs_handler {
  // x is a ⟨vertex, distance⟩ pair
  bool operator ()(const pair<Vertex, int>& x) const {
    if (x.second < distance[x.first]) {
      distance[x.first] = x.second;
      explore->send(x.first, x.second + 1);
} } }; // explore is an instance of a message type
```

In this formulation there is no need for any queues: all the message buffering and work coalescing performed by the queue in the other implementations is performed by Active Pebbles. Running the algorithm simply requires exploring the source vertex by sending a message to a *bfs_handler()*.

5. EXPERIMENTAL EVALUATION

We used Odin, a 128-node InfiniBand cluster (Single Data Rate), for our performance experiments. Each node has two 2 GHz dual-core Opteron 270 CPUs and 4 GiB of RAM. Our experiments used Open MPI 1.4.1, OFED 1.3.1, and Berkeley UPC 2.10.2 (compiled with `--disable-multirail --enable-pshm`). We used g++ 4.4.0 as the compiler in our experiments (including the back-end compiler for MPI and UPC). Except for single-node runs, all tests used four MPI processes per node. Our Active Pebbles implementation, written in standard C++ using the AM++ active message library [31], uses MPI as its underlying communication mechanism. All scaling experiments test weak scaling, so data sizes are reported per processor rather than globally.

5.1 Implementation Details

The coalescing buffer size (Section 3.3) was 4096 elements for BFS and Permutation, 1024 for RandomAccess (due to the lookahead limit in that benchmark), and no coalescing was used for PointerChase. Our implementation uses advanced C++ features to allow all pebble handlers for a coalesced message buffer to run in a single, statically analyzable loop, avoiding dynamic dispatch at the level of a single pebble. Routing experiments use a hypercube

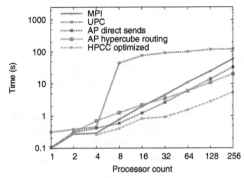

(a) RandomAccess (2^{19} elements per processor).

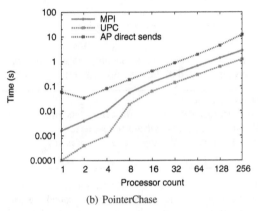

(b) PointerChase

Figure 3: Benchmark Results (part 1).

topology (as in [23]), the best-performing of the four topologies implemented; termination detection used the PCX (reduce-scatter) algorithm from [16], generalized to support multiple termination detection levels but unaware of message routing.

5.2 Results

RandomAccess. In Figure 3(a), we see the performance of the RandomAccess benchmark implementations. Because of the availability of official, highly optimized, MPI-based implementations of the benchmark, we also compared to those (HPCC version 1.4.1 using Sandia Opt 2, the fastest version on Odin). The graph shows that our current Active Pebbles implementation performs worse than the optimized, specialized, and more complex HPCC implementation [23]. However, Active Pebbles performs better than the reference UPC implementation and our MPI implementation of similar implementation complexity (see Section 4). Active routing is slower than a non-routed implementation on small node counts; routing has a cost in latency and its advantages (such as reduced buffer memory usage) do not appear at small scales. Once beyond 128 processors (32 nodes), however, hypercube routing provides a performance benefit. Similarly, our MPI implementation is fast on small process counts, but it too suffers from the use of many sends (through the *MPI_Alltoallv()* collective) at large scales.

PointerChase. Figure 3(b) shows Odin's performance on the PointerChase latency benchmark. This benchmark shows a clear performance benefit for UPC over both MPI and Active Pebbles, which is expected because PGAS models are designed for sending fine-grained, asynchronous messages with very low latencies and the network supports remote direct memory access (RDMA). Active Pebbles, unlike UPC, is designed to support a large *volume*

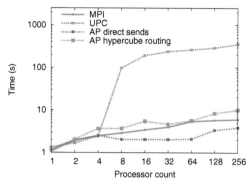

(a) Permutation (2^{22} elements per processor).

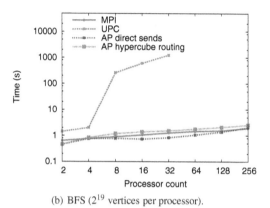

(b) BFS (2^{19} vertices per processor).

Figure 4: Benchmark Results (part 2).

of small messages, emphasizing throughput for millions or billions of messages over individual message latency. Even with message coalescing disabled, overheads from dynamic memory allocation and other features to support asynchronous messages still hindered Active Pebbles's performance.

Permutation. The results for the Permutation benchmark are shown in Figure 4(a). For this experiment, 2^{22} eight-byte elements were permuted on each processor. As can be seen from the graph, once multiple nodes (rather than processors on the same node) are in use, UPC's performance degrades substantially. On the other hand, the Active Pebbles and MPI versions exhibit almost linear weak scaling. In this benchmark, active routing was not useful—sending messages directly between processes performed better. Unlike RandomAccess's 1024-element lookahead limit, elements in Permutation can be streamed at any rate and elements never need to wait for previous elements to complete. Thus, termination detection is done only at the end of the overall benchmark, rather than periodically within it. Additionally, without routing, message handlers only send messages to a limited, fixed depth, enabling use of a specialized termination detection algorithm. When routing is used, on the other hand, messages can be nested to depth $2 \log_2 P$, and so the generalized PCX termination detection algorithm must perform that many global communications. An optimized implementation could replace those by localized operations with each node's neighbors in the hypercube.

BFS. Figure 4(b) shows the performance of the BFS benchmark on Odin. Note that the BFS implementation for AP tested here is level-synchronized; i.e., the message handler inserts each incoming vertex into a queue to be processed in the next level, but does

not itself directly trigger the exploration of other vertices. As in the other benchmarks (except PointerChase), the MPI and AP implementations show minimal increase in runtime as problem size is increased (because the experiment uses weak scaling), while the UPC version's time grows quickly as more nodes are added. UPC results beyond 32 processors were not shown because the version failed to finish in an acceptable time. The BFS benchmark is level-synchronized [32], so termination detection is performed for every vertex level.

6. CONCLUSION

We have presented a programming model, Active Pebbles, designed for the direct expression of highly irregular applications at their "natural" granularities. The key elements of the model are pebbles sent between very fine-grained objects: targets. These pebbles trigger actions on the receiving targets, as in a model such as Charm++, but allow for finer object granularities. For example, sending messages to a target does not require any explicit bookkeeping. Our model allows high-performance, performance-portable, and intuitive high-level expression of fine-grained algorithms such as graph traversals. We implement a corresponding execution model that effectively converts fine-grained, point-to-point communications into optimized collective operations using five main techniques: fine-grained target addressing, message coalescing, active routing, message reductions, and configurable termination detection. These techniques combine to allow fine-grained algorithms, expressed at their natural granularities, to perform as well as more complicated, MPI-based implementations.

7. ACKNOWLEDGMENTS

We thank the anonymous reviewers for their helpful comments. This work was supported by a grants from the Lilly Foundation and Intel Corporation, NSF grant CNS-0834722, and DOE FASTOS II (LAB 07-23). The Odin system was funded by NSF grant EIA-0202048. Portions of this work were presented as a research poster in [30].

8. REFERENCES

[1] A. Alexandrov, M. F. Ionescu, K. E. Schauser, and C. Scheiman. LogGP: Incorporating long messages into the LogP model. *J. of Par. and Dist. Comp.*, 44(1):71–79, 1995.

[2] D. Bader and K. Madduri. Designing multithreaded algorithms for breadth-first search and st-connectivity on the Cray MTA-2. In *Intl. Conference on Parallel Processing*, pages 523–530, August 2006.

[3] D. A. Bader, D. R. Helman, and J. JáJá. Practical parallel algorithms for personalized communication and integer sorting. *Journal of Experimental Algorithmics*, 1, 1996.

[4] J. W. Berry, B. Hendrickson, S. Kahan, and P. Konecny. Software and algorithms for graph queries on multithreaded architectures. In *Intl. Parallel and Distributed Processing Symposium*, Mar. 2007.

[5] J. Bruck, C.-T. Ho, S. Kipnis, and D. Weathersby. Efficient algorithms for all-to-all communications in multi-port message-passing systems. In *Symposium on Parallel Algorithms and Architectures*, pages 298–309, 1994.

[6] D. Callahan, B. L. Chamberlain, and H. P. Zima. The Cascade High Productivity Language. In *Intl. Workshop on High-Level Parallel Programming Models and Supportive Environments*, pages 52–60, April 2004.

[7] P. Charles, C. Grothoff, V. A. Saraswat, et al. X10: An object-oriented approach to non-uniform cluster computing. In *Obj. Oriented Prog., Sys., Lang., and Apps.*, 2005.

[8] E. W. Dijkstra and C. S. Scholten. Termination detection for diffusing computations. *Information Processing Letters*, 11(1):1–4, 1980.

[9] P. Erdős and A. Rényi. On random graphs. *Publ. Math. Debrecen*, 6:290–297, 1959.

[10] G. Gao, T. Sterling, R. Stevens, M. Hereld, and W. Zhu. ParalleX: A study of a new parallel computation model. In *IPDPS*, pages 1–6, 2007.

[11] R. Garg and Y. Sabharwal. Software routing and aggregation of messages to optimize the performance of HPCC RandomAccess benchmark. In *Supercomputing*, pages 109–, 2006.

[12] M. Herlihy and J. E. B. Moss. Transactional memory: Architectural support for lock-free data structures. *SIGARCH Comput. Archit. News*, 21(2):289–300, 1993.

[13] M. P. Herlihy. Impossibility and universality results for wait-free synchronization. In *Principles of Distributed Computing*, pages 276–290, 1988.

[14] T. Hey, S. Tansley, and K. Tolle, editors. *The Fourth Paradigm: Data-Intensive Scientific Discovery*. Microsoft Research, 2009.

[15] T. Hoefler, A. Lumsdaine, and W. Rehm. Implementation and performance analysis of non-blocking collective operations for MPI. In *Supercomputing*, Nov. 2007.

[16] T. Hoefler, C. Siebert, and A. Lumsdaine. Scalable communication protocols for dynamic sparse data exchange. In *Principles and Practice of Parallel Programming*, pages 159–168, Jan. 2010.

[17] L. V. Kalé and S. Krishnan. CHARM++: A portable concurrent object oriented system based on C++. *SIGPLAN Notices*, 28(10):91–108, 1993.

[18] A. Lumsdaine, D. Gregor, B. Hendrickson, and J. Berry. Challenges in parallel graph processing. *Parallel Processing Letters*, 17(1):5–20, 2007.

[19] P. R. Luszczek, D. H. Bailey, J. J. Dongarra, et al. The HPC Challenge (HPCC) benchmark suite. In *Supercomputing*, pages 213–, 2006.

[20] F. Mattern. Algorithms for distributed termination detection. *Distributed Computing*, 2(3):161–175, 1987.

[21] MPI Forum. MPI: A Message-Passing Interface Standard. Version 2.2, Sept. 2009.

[22] R. W. Numrich and J. Reid. Co-array Fortran for parallel programming. *SIGPLAN Fortran Forum*, 17(2):1–31, 1998.

[23] S. Plimpton, R. Brightwell, C. Vaughan, and K. Underwood. A simple synchronous distributed-memory algorithm for the HPCC RandomAccess benchmark. In *Intl. Conf. on Cluster Comp.*, pages 1–7, 2006.

[24] A. L. Rosenberg and L. S. Heath. *Graph Separators, with Applications*. Kluwer Academic Publishers, Norwell, MA, USA, 2001.

[25] N. Shavit and D. Touitou. Software transactional memory. In *Principles of Dist. Computing*, pages 204–213, 1995.

[26] A. B. Sinha, L. V. Kalé, and B. Ramkumar. A dynamic and adaptive quiescence detection algorithm. Technical Report 93-11, Parallel Programming Laboratory, UIUC, 1993.

[27] UPC Consortium. UPC Language Specifications, v1.2. Technical report, Lawrence Berkeley National Laboratory, 2005. LBNL-59208.

[28] L. G. Valiant. A bridging model for parallel computation. *Communications of the ACM*, 33(8):103–111, 1990.

[29] T. von Eicken, D. E. Culler, S. C. Goldstein, and K. E. Schauser. Active Messages: A mechanism for integrated communication and computation. In *Intl. Symposium on Computer Architecture*, pages 256–266, 1992.

[30] J. Willcock, T. Hoefler, N. Edmonds, and A. Lumsdaine. Active Pebbles: A programming model for highly parallel fine-grained data-driven computations. In *Principles and Practice of Parallel Programming*, Feb. 2011. Poster.

[31] J. J. Willcock, T. Hoefler, N. G. Edmonds, and A. Lumsdaine. AM++: A generalized active message framework. In *Par. Arch. and Comp. Tech.*, 2010.

[32] A. Yoo, E. Chow, K. Henderson, et al. A scalable distributed parallel breadth-first search algorithm on BlueGene/L. In *Supercomputing*, pages 25–. IEEE, 2005.

Automating GPU Computing in MATLAB

Chun-Yu Shei
cshei@cs.indiana.edu

Pushkar Ratnalikar
pratnali@cs.indiana.edu

Arun Chauhan
achauhan@cs.indiana.edu

School of Informatics and Computing
Indiana University
Bloomington, IN

ABSTRACT

MATLAB is a popular software platform for scientific and engineering software writers. It offers a high level of abstraction for fundamental mathematical operations and extensive highly optimized domain-specific libraries for several scientific and engineering disciplines. With the recent availability of GPU libraries for MATLAB, it has become possible to easily exploit GPGPUs as coprocessors. However, this requires changing the code by carefully declaring variables that would live on the GPU, breaking the simplicity of the MATLAB programming model.

We present a fully automatic source-level compilation technique to exploit a given GPU library for MATLAB, enabling coarse-grained heterogeneous parallelism across CPU and GPU. Our approach is based on empirically characterizing the library's functions, in order to build a comparative model of their performance on the CPU and GPU, which is then used along with a data communication cost model to maximize parallelism by selectively offloading some computation on the GPU. We achieve this by phrasing the problem as a binary integer linear programming problem aimed at minimizing CPU-GPU data movement, and using a hierarchical approach to keep the computational complexity in check. We have implemented our approach in a source-level MATLAB compiler, and present experimental results on a set of MATLAB kernels and applications using the GPUmat library. We show speedups of up to 7 times when the GPU is harnessed, compared to a standalone 8-core CPU.

Categories and Subject Descriptors

D [**3**]: 4—*compilers*

General Terms

Experimentation, Languages, Performance

Keywords

GPGPU, MATLAB, source-level, heterogeneous parallelism

1. INTRODUCTION

With a greater reliance on computing in diverse areas than in the past, many domain experts find themselves writing programs, even though they may not be expert programmers. This has resulted in a growing popularity of many high level dynamically typed languages, sometime called *scripting* languages, that are more expressive, and easy to use and debug. One such highly popular language for scientific and engineering computing is MATLAB. Even though it leverages libraries that have been painstakingly optimized, and often parallelized, there can still be significant differences in performance between a program written in MATLAB and one written in a lower-level language, say C. It is important to note that the dramatically higher productivity afforded by MATLAB often more than compensates for the performance difference. However, for certain classes of applications that difference can be sufficiently high to trigger costly redevelopment effort in another language.

Recent general-purpose programmability of GPUs[1] has opened an avenue for improving the performance of MATLAB, by offloading part of the computation onto a GPU. However, even with simplified programming models such as CUDA or OpenCL [8, 14], programming GPUs effectively remains a challenge that typical MATLAB programmers might be unwilling to take on directly. Fortunately, several library developers have used this opportunity to develop MATLAB libraries that hide the complexities of programming GPUs while providing most of their benefits to users [1, 22, 15, 16]. Recent versions of MATLAB also include GPU versions of some of the functions in the Parallel Computing Toolbox [13]. In order to utilize such a library, a MATLAB program usually needs to be modified with declarations registering the variables that would participate in GPU operations. Subsequent operations on those variables are then automatically scheduled on the GPU. Invariably, not all MATLAB operations are supported, or can be supported, by GPU libraries, forcing the users to go through the arduous task of identifying supported operations and carefully inserting declarations, for the relevant variables. This manual process is tedious, and also makes it difficult to port code to target a different library at a later date.

In this paper we describe an automatic source-level method to transform MATLAB programs to utilize a given GPU li-

---

[1]We will consistently used the term "GPU" when we mean both Graphics Processing Unit (GPU) that can be used for general purpose computing and also General Purpose GPU (GPGPU) that is specifically designed for general purpose computing.

brary. We present an algorithm that uses type inference to guide the partitioning of a data dependence graph of the MATLAB program into statements that run on CPU and GPU, while attempting to minimize load imbalance and data transfer between CPU and GPU. The algorithm uses an analytical model to predict CPU and GPU performance, based on empirical measurements on sample data sets.

Information about the target GPU library is abstracted out so that the algorithm can be easily retargeted to a new library, and our approach does not require any user input beyond the source code[2]. We implement our approach in a source-level MATLAB compiler and experimentally evaluate it on programs and kernels drawn from a variety of domains. We make the following contributions:

- We present an algorithm to leverage type inference to automatically offload portions of a MATLAB program onto a GPU. Hierarchical handling of control flow statements keeps the computational complexity low in practice. We believe that the findings of our work are applicable to other similar array-based languages, such as Fortran.

- The partitioning strategy may be staged, performing as much of the partitioning as possible statically and deferring the rest until run time. This becomes possible since the partitioning algorithm leverages MATLAB libraries.

- We evaluate our strategy on a wide variety of applications and kernels, using the GPUmat library [22]. We measure the performance of these benchmarks when a GPU is used as a cooperating processor, and demonstrate speedups of up to 7.0x over the original code running on an 8-core CPU.

- The coarse-grained parallelism exposed by our approach opens an avenue to perform further automatic fine-tuning to better exploit hardware features.

2. MATLAB ON GPU

MATLAB is a dynamically typed high-level language targeted towards numerical computation, with an emphasis on ease of use. MATLAB supports structured control flow and heavily overloaded operators to present math-like abstraction. For example, to solve the linear system $Ax = B$ in MATLAB, the user simply needs to write x = A \ B, with the matrix A and vector B defined, and the overloaded \ operator checks the types of A and B and performs matrix left-division automatically. Through the range syntax, with optional stride, MATLAB syntax allows rectangular array sections.

Through the use of highly optimized libraries such as BLAS [4], MATLAB achieves high performance on common operations such as matrix multiplication. Additionally, a large collection of domain-specific libraries (toolboxes) is also available. Data-parallelism and coarse-grained parallelism are supported though an MPI interface and **parfor** loops. However, despite the existence of a proprietary just-in-time compiler, code which contains a significant amount of control-flow and scalar operations does not perform well, compared to equivalent C implementations.

MATLAB supports a limited form of object-oriented programming. This is most commonly used to overload operators for user-defined types. Even though veriables are not declared, there is an implicit type associated with each variable. Libraries like Star-P [18], GPUmat [22] and other parallel libraries employ user-defined operator overloading to automatically direct computations to a cluster or a GPU. For example, the following GPUmat code declares A and B as GPU variables, so that the subsequent * operation is performed on the GPU:

```
A = GPUdouble(a); B = GPUdouble(b); C = A*B
```

A and B are initialized using standard MATLAB variables a and b. The result, C, is also of GPUdouble type. One way to think about the declarations of A and B is as type casting CPU types to GPU types. This type casting involves copying the data from CPU main memory to GPU memory (*global* memory in the case of CUDA [14]). MATLAB is oblivious to the fact that A and B live on the GPU. The variables are represented on the CPU by proxies of the same names, which may be freely copied or passed as arguments to functions. Type casting in the reverse direction can be accomplished using the **double** function, which is overloaded by the GPUmat library when the argument is of **GPUdouble** type, and involves copying data from the GPU to main memory. The GPUmat library also supports single precision floating point and complex numbers.

3. APPROACH

Our strategy for automatic partitioning of a MATLAB program into CPU and GPU computations relies on type inference for MATLAB by Shei et al. [19]. The type inference algorithm works by making all type disambiguation explicit by inserting valid MATLAB code that infers types into specially named variables derived from user variable names. An aggressive partial evaluation phase then statically evaluates as much of the type inference code as possible. In most cases, the partial evaluator statically evaluates almost all the explicit type inference code that is inserted by the compiler. The advantage of this approach is that type inference can be expressed using MATLAB code, and it can leverage the MATLAB interpreter as well as MATLAB's features for reflection. Any code that cannot be statically evaluated gets left behind to be evaluated at run time to be used for run time optimization. A subsequent dead code elimination pass eliminates all run time type inference code that would not be used for any run time optimization. Once types have been statically inferred, or appropriate code inserted for inference at run time, type information can be used to determine which variables are arrays and to estimate their sizes.

As an optimization, it is possible to reduce dynamic type inference by supplying optional annotations in the form of hints to the compiler about types of specific variables. Annotating input arguments turns out to be particularly useful since many local variables, and hence their types, may depend on input arguments to a function.

A given MATLAB program is processed one function at a time, which involves three steps:

1. Identifying statements that could potentially be executed on the GPU. We call these *schedulable* statements.
2. Estimating computation costs of performing each schedulable statement on the CPU and the GPU, and estimating data communication costs of moving operands and results between the CPU and GPU based on data dependencies.
3. Partitioning schedulable statements between the CPU and GPU while minimizing data communication overhead and load imbalance.

---

[2]Except, optional annotations for aiding type inference, as explained later in Section 3.

The rest of this section describes each of these steps and code generation. Throughout our discussion we use the terms *operations* and *functions* interchangeably. This is literally true in MATLAB since almost all operations have equivalent function names and can be performed using explicit function names.

3.1 Identifying Schedulable Statements

We use the GPUmat library [22] for our implementation, although our approach would work with any similar library. GPUmat implements about 50 common MATLAB functions, which is a small, but important, subset of all MATLAB functions. The library includes most dense matrix operations, FFT, trigonometric functions, relational operations, and several other miscellaneous functions. Unsupported functions include various factorization algorithms and sparse matrix operations. Only vector forms of these functions are supported.

For a function to be eligible to run on the GPU, that function must be in the list of the supported functions. Additionally, not all arguments can be scalar. In the use case anticipated by GPUmat, GPU variables are declared manually and the user must make sure that only variables that are input arguments to supported functions are declared as GPU variables. Similarly, the user must ensure that only vector functions are farmed out to the GPU.

In automating this process, our compiler makes use of a library-specific list to identify supported functions. It uses inferred variable types to determine when a specific function call is a vector operation. The accuracy of this process depends directly on the accuracy of type inference. If part of type inference must happen at run time, then the process of identifying schedulable statements and deciding whether to run those on the GPU can also easily be done at run time, due to our use of MATLAB for computing statement schedules.

3.2 Estimating Costs

To decide whether or not to run a function on the GPU, we need a way to estimate the computation cost of each operation. It is much trickier to estimate the cost of scalar operations than array operations due to MATLAB's large function call overheads that may be hard to model accurately. Fortunately, we need only estimate the costs of array statements, since those are the only types that can be offloaded onto the GPU.

Almost all the GPU supported functions are either unary (e.g., trigonometric functions) or binary (e.g., matrix functions). All binary operations, except matrix multiplication, expect their input arguments to either both be arrays of matching size, or the scalar argument is logically expanded to an array of the same size as the other argument. Recall that both arguments cannot be scalar for a function to be executable on the GPU. The only exceptions are functions that generate matrices, i.e., `rand`, `zeros`, and `ones`.

For all the unary and binary functions (except matrix multiplication), we empirically collect running time data on the CPU as well as GPU for varying input sizes. A small degree polynomial (up to degree 3) in one variable is fitted on the empirically collected data and the polynomial is used to interpolate or extrapolate the running time of the function using the inferred sizes of the actual parameters. This works because all the functions have polynomial time complexity.

The curve fitting simply extracts the exact coefficients of the polynomial from the empirical data. For all operations except matrix multiplication, it took us about nine hours to collect all the empirical data for an 8-core 3 GHz Intel Core2-duo machine and an NVIDIA Tesla GPGPU card, when each test was run five times.

Matrix multiplication expects the arguments to be arrays of compatible sizes. If the first argument is of size $p \times q$, then the second argument must be of size $q \times r$. Thus, a univariate polynomial is insufficient to model the cost of matrix multiplication. Instead, we need a trivariate polynomial. Due to a large number of sample points, matrix multiplication took much longer—about 10 days—to collect all the CPU and GPU data. However, we took overly refined samples for matrix multiplication (a total of 10^9 samples) for this study, while a much more sparse set of samples would have likely sufficed. In order to compute the cost of matrix multiplication for a given input size, we use 3-D interpolation on the sampled data.

Of all the functions supported by the library, `fft` has the unique characteristic that its running time does not vary smoothly with the input size. The reason is that the FFT algorithm works differently when the input size has large prime factors. As a result, it is practically impossible to fit a low degree polynomial curve on the running time data of FFT. One possible solution is to approximate the running time with a least square fit of a low degree polynomial.

3.3 Partitioning Computation

The general problem of scheduling a directed acyclic task graph on a heterogenous set of processors is known to be NP-complete [9]. The scheduling problem is hard even in several restricted cases, including scheduling on two processors. In order to minimize the average time complexity, we adopt a hierarchical technique by choosing to schedule statements at one level in the abstract syntax tree (AST) independently of the other levels. In other words, we schedule a list of statements that might include compound statements, treating the compound statements as atomic statements that are not schedulable. The bodies of the compound statements are then scheduled recursively. This is an approximation, since the schedule of the statements surrounding the compound statements might influence the optimal schedule of the statements within the compound statement due to data dependencies. The hierarchical approach forgoes this opportunity and trades off solving a single large problem for solving several smaller problems.

In order to estimate if such a strategy would work in practice, we analyzed 756 MATLAB functions (.m files) from a variety of application domains to collect statistics about basic blocks and GPU schedulable statements. Figure 1 shows three histograms, summarizing the number of basic blocks in each function, the sizes of all the basic blocks across all analyzed functions, and the number of schedulable statements per basic block. Each histogram has a bin size of

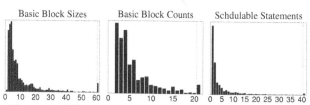

Figure 1: Histograms for 756 MATLAB functions.

```
if (~a_on_cpu)                 x_on_cpu = true;
  a = double(gpu_a);
end                            if (~x_on_gpu)
a_on_cpu = true;                 gpu_x = GPUdouble(x);
if (~b_on_cpu)                 end
  b = double(gpu_b);           x_on_gpu = true;
end                            gpu_y = gpu_x * gpu_x;
b_on_cpu = true;               y_on_gpu = true;
x = a + b;
```

Figure 2: Runtime code inserted by the compiler to ensure input arguments are located correctly.

one, and each histogram has been truncated at an upper limit with the rightmost bar showing the sum of all the remaining counts. The exact counts are unimportant, so we have omitted labeling the vertical axis. We note that a vast majority of MATLAB code has very small basic blocks, even though the number of basic blocks can sometimes be large. The number of schedulable statements per basic block is predominantly in the single digits or low double digits. This indicates that a recursive strategy that handles basic blocks individually—even if it has to solve a hard problem for each—can be practically feasible.

We divide the scheduling process into two steps, partitioning the statements into CPU and GPU computations, and ordering the statements to achieve maximal concurrency across the CPU and GPU. Partitioning the statements, described in greater detail in Section 4, is the more expensive step while reordering statements, described next, is relatively straightforward.

3.4 Reordering Statements

Once the set of statements to run on the GPU have been identified, we next try to maximize the overlap of CPU and GPU operations. This is possible since GPUmat function calls are asynchronous, which results in a simple strategy to maximize overlap. The GPU function calls are hoisted as high as the dependencies allow within each basic block.

As the partitioning step, the reordering step also works recursively through the statements, working at one level of statements at a time to reorder the statements. Unlike partitioning, this process is, in fact, optimal as long as the code has already gone through other optimizations such as loop-invariant code motion and unreachable code elimination.

3.5 Code Generation

After code has been scheduled to run on either the CPU or GPU, additional MATLAB code is inserted to ensure that all input arguments are present at the appropriate location for each statement. We use the convention of appending a `gpu_` prefix to variable names corresponding to GPU variables introduced by our compiler, and leaving CPU variables as-is. We also introduce two "flag" variables by appending a `_on_cpu` and `_on_gpu` suffix to each base variable name, that indicate whether a variable is available on the CPU or GPU respectively. Thus, for a base variable `foo`, if it is involved in any GPU computations, a `gpu_foo` variable will be introduced to hold the GPU copy, and the variables `foo_on_cpu` and `foo_on_gpu` will be set to `true`.

The flag variables are used in the code inserted to ensure that all input arguments are present in the appropriate location. For every statement that is to be run on the GPU, each input argument's `_on_gpu` flag is tested in an `if`, and if it is unset, the necessary GPU variable is created from the CPU variable using `GPUdouble()`. The `_on_gpu` flag of every GPU variable created is then set to `true`, as well as the output variable's. Statements to be run on the CPU are handled similarly, with the exception that the `_on_cpu` flag is checked instead, and conversions are performed using `double()`. For example, Figure 2 shows the compiler generated output for the input `x = a + b; y = x * x;` when the first statement is scheduled on the CPU and the second on the GPU. This strategy facilitates dynamic scheduling of statements.

Although this strategy seems to introduce a large amount of code as an intermediate step, it is still linear in the size of the input program. Subsequent partial evaluation and dead-code elimination passes get rid of all extra code except that needed for run time correctness or optimization.

3.6 Assumptions

We make a core assumption that the amount of computation involved in a MATLAB operation (or function) is proportional to the size of the inputs and outputs for that operation (or function). This assumption is obviously incorrect for certain functions, such as the MATLAB `size` function, for which the compiler maintains a table of known exceptions. We assume that most computationally intensive portions of the MATLAB program are statements that are schedulable on the GPU. This is not a drastic assumption, since GPU libraries try to support most computationally intensive functions. For the purpose of this work, we also assume that array sizes can be estimated at compile time. Although this sounds overly constraining, the staged design of our algorithm allows us to perform the scheduling just-in-time when array sizes and loop bounds can be resolved. In those cases where just-in-time resolution is impossible, compiler annotations let the compiler proceed assuming "typical" array sizes. Given that even manual parallelization efforts need to make an assumption about array sizes, it is reasonable for a compiler to expect this information. If widely different array sizes are expected then, in principle, it is possible to generate multiple schedules by appropriately partitioning the set of possible sizes [2]. However, that is outside the scope of this paper.

4. STATEMENT PARTITIONING

Let $S = \{s_1, s_2, \ldots, s_n\}$ be a sequence of n schedulable statements. A dependence graph D for the sequence S is a directed graph consisting of n nodes, one for each statement, and edges $s_i \rightarrow s_j$ if, and only if, there is a data dependence from statement s_i to s_j. The dependence graph can be equivalently represented as an adjacency matrix, $\mathbf{A}_d$, of size $n \times n$. We assume that edges in the dependence graph are weighted with the amount of data that flows along that dependence edge. Thus, the matrix $\mathbf{A}_d$ contains the edge weights instead of binary values. The weighted dependence graph for straight line code, as in our case, is easily constructed efficiently using type information that provides us array sizes.

We solve the partitioning problem by reducing it to a binary integer linear programming (BILP) problem:

$$
\begin{aligned}
\text{Minimize} \quad & \vec{f}'\vec{x} \\
\text{such that} \quad & \mathbf{A}\vec{x} \leq \vec{b} \\
\text{and} \quad & \mathbf{A}_{\text{eq}}\vec{x} = \vec{b}_{\text{eq}}
\end{aligned}
$$

Here, $\vec{x}$ is a vector of n binary variables that is to be determined, $\mathbf{A}$ and $\mathbf{A}_{eq}$ are matrices of size $n \times n$ each, and $\vec{b}$ and $\vec{b}_{eq}$ are vectors of size n each.

We phrase the partitioning problem as a BILP problem with the goal of minimizing data transfer costs between main memory and GPU. We express this by creating suitable inequality constraints, while trying to minimize the objective function of total running time on CPU plus GPU.

We define $\vec{x}$ to be of size $2n$, where the first n variables determine whether a statement will be computed on the CPU and the last n variables determine whether a statement will be computed on the GPU. In other words, $\vec{x} = [x_1\ x_2\ \ldots\ x_{2n}]'$, and exactly one of x_i and x_{i+n} is 1, where $1 \leq i \leq n$. We will find it convenient to write $\vec{x}$ as $\begin{bmatrix} \vec{x}_c \\ \vec{x}_g \end{bmatrix}$, where $\vec{x}_c$ and $\vec{x}_g$ are vectors of size n each.

Suppose that c_i is the cost of computing statement s_i on the CPU and g_i is the cost on GPU. We define $\vec{f}$ as $[c_1\ c_2\ \ldots\ c_n\ g_1\ g_2\ \ldots\ g_n]'$. Thus, minimizing $\vec{f}'\vec{x}$ minimizes the total cost of CPU and GPU computations. Similarly to $\vec{x}$, we may write $\vec{f}$ as $\begin{bmatrix} \vec{c} \\ \vec{g} \end{bmatrix}$.

In order to constrain $\vec{x}$ such that exactly one corresponding entry in either $\vec{x}_c$ or $\vec{x}_g$ is 1, we define $\mathbf{A}_{eq}$ as $[\mathbf{I}\ \mathbf{I}]$, where $\mathbf{I}$ is an $n \times n$ identity matrix, and $\vec{b}_{eq}$ as $[1\ 1\ \ldots\ 1]'$ of size n.

Using the weighted adjacency matrix $\mathbf{A}_d$ and the strategy outlined in Section 3.2 we can estimate the costs of data transfer between any two statements that have a data dependence between them. Suppose that the cost of moving the data related to statement i is cg_{ij} when statement i is computed on the CPU and j is computed on GPU. Similarly, gc_{ij} is the data movement cost when statement i executes on GPU and j executes on CPU. We assume that the cost of moving data within a single device is zero. Suppose the per-unit cost of moving data are given by functions C_{c2g} and C_{g2c} for CPU-GPU and GPU-CPU, respectively. Thus:

$$cg_{ij} = \begin{cases} 0 & \text{if } i = j \\ C_{c2g}(\mathbf{A}_d(i,j)) & \text{if } i \neq j \end{cases}$$

We define the matrix $\mathbf{CG}$ by combining all cg_{ij} in the obvious manner. The matrix $\mathbf{GC}$ is similarly defined for data transfer costs from GPU to CPU, using C_{g2c}. Notice that CG and GC are both symmetric with zero diagonal. We follow the convention of reading off the costs for statement i from the row i of a cost matrix. Since rows are arranged in the statement order, on any given row costs to the left of the diagonal correspond to incoming dependencies and those to the right correspond to the outgoing dependencies.

In order to arrive at appropriate constraints, we observe that we would like i to be scheduled on the CPU if the cost of transferring all the incoming and outgoing data from/to the GPU is smaller that the corresponding cost of data transfer if i was to run on the GPU. Thus, statement i should be scheduled on the CPU if the expression

$$-\sum_{j=1}^{i-1} cg_{ij}\, x_j - \sum_{j=i+1}^{n} gc_{ij}\, x_j + \sum_{j=1}^{i-1} gc_{ij}\, x_{j+n} + \sum_{j=i+1}^{n} cg_{ij}\, x_{j+n}$$

is ≤ 0. Given that the diagonals of $\mathbf{CG}$ and $\mathbf{GC}$ are zero, we can combine the above constraint for all statements into

a matrix form:

$$-(\mathbf{CG}_L + \mathbf{GC}_U)\,\vec{x}_c + (\mathbf{GC}_L + \mathbf{CG}_U)\,\vec{x}_g\ \leq\ \vec{0} \quad (1)$$

where the subscripts U and L denote, respectively, the upper and lower triangle of a matrix, and $\vec{0}$ denotes a zero vector of size n. Combining $\vec{x}_c$ and $\vec{x}_g$ into $\vec{x}$, we get:

$$[-\mathbf{CG}_L - \mathbf{GC}_U\quad \mathbf{GC}_L + \mathbf{CG}_U]\,\vec{x}\ \leq\ \vec{0} \quad (2)$$

We can similarly derive the constraints that we would like to satisfy if statement i is scheduled on the GPU:

$$[\mathbf{CG}_L + \mathbf{GC}_U\quad -\mathbf{GC}_L - \mathbf{CG}_U]\,\vec{x}\ \leq\ \vec{0} \quad (3)$$

Since each statement is scheduled either on the GPU or the CPU, but not both, Equations 2 and 3 cannot be satisfied at the same time. In order to activate only the relevant constraints, we introduce two relaxation matrices to "nullify" the constraints that are not applicable. Thus, if statement i is scheduled on the GPU then we nullify the constraint for statement i in Equation 2. The $n \times n$ relaxation matrix $\mathbf{R}_c$ is defined as follows by defining its (i,j) element:

$$\mathbf{R}_c(i,j)\ =\ \begin{cases} 0 & \text{if } i \neq j \\ -\sum_{k=1}^{i-1} gc_{ik} - \sum_{k=i+1}^{n} cg_{ik} & \text{if } i = j \end{cases}$$

We can now modify Equation 2:

$$([\mathbf{0}\quad \mathbf{R}_c] + [-\mathbf{CG}_L - \mathbf{GC}_U\quad \mathbf{GC}_L + \mathbf{CG}_U])\,\vec{x}\ \leq\ \vec{0} \quad (4)$$

where $\mathbf{0}$ is an $n \times n$ zero matrix. Equation 4 ensures that when a statement i is scheduled on the GPU (i.e., $x_i = 0$ and $x_{i+n} = 1$), the constraint for statement i (i.e., row i) is trivially satisfied since the left hand side is guaranteed to be smaller than the right hand side.

Analogously, we construct the relaxation matrix $\mathbf{R}_g$ to "nullify" the constraints for GPU scheduling when a statement actually gets scheduled on the CPU. From Equation 4 and an analogous equation that uses $\mathbf{R}_g$, we derive the final set of constraints, defining the matrix $\mathbf{A}$ and vector $\vec{b}$ as follows:

$$\mathbf{A} = \begin{bmatrix} -\mathbf{CG}_L - \mathbf{GC}_U & \mathbf{R}_c + \mathbf{GC}_L + \mathbf{CG}_U \\ \mathbf{R}_g + \mathbf{CG}_L + \mathbf{GC}_U & -\mathbf{GC}_L - \mathbf{CG}_U \end{bmatrix}, \quad \vec{b} = \begin{bmatrix} \vec{0} \\ \vec{0} \end{bmatrix}$$

$\mathbf{A}$ is of size $2n \times 2n$ and $\vec{b}$ is of size $2n$. The first n rows of $\mathbf{A}$ impose the constraint that if a statement executes on CPU, then the cost of moving the data related to that statement to/from the CPU must not exceed the similar cost if the statement were to be executed on the GPU. The next n rows impose similar constraints when statements are scheduled to execute on the GPU.

4.1 Load Balancing

The BILP approach described above can be extended to include a constraint on load balance between CPU and GPU. This would be particularly useful if there is sufficient parallelism to completely overlap GPU and CPU computations. In that case, the additional constraint on load balance may result in better schedules. We add the load balance constraint by extending $\mathbf{A}$ and $\vec{b}$ each by two rows:

$$\mathbf{A} = \begin{bmatrix} \cdots & \cdots \\ \vec{c}' & -\vec{g}' \\ -\vec{c}' & \vec{g}' \end{bmatrix} \quad \vec{b} = \begin{bmatrix} \cdots \\ \epsilon \\ \epsilon \end{bmatrix}$$

The last two rows bound the load imbalance between the CPU and GPU from above as well as below by ϵ. The value of ϵ could be as low as 0, however, the BILP solver is unlikely to succeed with such a tight constraint. In practice, we would set ϵ to a value that is comparable to at least the difference between the most expensive and the least expensive operations.

4.2 Pinning Statements

While considering load balancing, it is often helpful to pin certain statements to either the CPU or GPU. For example, we may wish to include CPU-only statements in determining a load-balanced schedule. In the future, certain operations or functions might be available only on the GPUs through a GPU library. We modify the model described before by extending $\vec{x}$ to also include all the pinned statements. The matrix $\mathbf{A}$ is constructed as before using extended versions of $\mathbf{A}_d$, $\vec{c}$, and $\vec{g}$. For statement i pinned to CPU, $\vec{g}_i$ is set to ∞. Similarly, appropriate elements of $\vec{c}$ are set to ∞ for those statements that are pinned to the GPU. Finally, to enforce pinning we modify $\mathbf{A}_{eq}$ to $[\mathbf{I}_c \ \mathbf{I}_g]$, where $\mathbf{I}_c$ and $\mathbf{I}_g$ are both diagonal matrices such that $\mathbf{I}_c(i,i)$ is 0 if statement i is pinned to GPU, and 1 for all others. $\mathbf{I}_g$ is analogously defined. In practice, instead of ∞ in $\vec{c}$ and $\vec{g}$, it is adequate to use a sufficiently large value. In all our benchmarks, there were no substantial computational statements that needed to be pinned to the CPU.

4.3 Practical Considerations

Quick Selection of Special Cases We can identify some special cases that can be partitioned with simple checks. The two most common cases are when we would like to assign all schedulable statements to the GPU or all to the CPU. These cases are relatively easy to identify. We define a threshold factor, $\gamma < 1$. If the ratio of the time it takes to run all the schedulable statements on GPU to the time it takes to run all of them on the CPU is less than γ, then we assign all the schedulable statements to GPU. γ serves as an elastic factor for the partitioning heuristic so that it resists switching to another device immediately. It helps robustness in the face of small errors in estimating compute times.

Tweaking the solver parameters MATLAB allows its binary integer linear program solver to be fine-tuned with parameters such as permitted running time in CPU seconds, the strategy to traverse the solution space, initial feasible solution, and tolerances on fractional parts of the integer variables and objective functions. These did not have a large impact on the solver's ability to finish successfully.

5. IMPLEMENTATION

We have implemented our scheduling algorithm in a source-to-source MATLAB compiler. The compiler uses GNU Octave for parsing and MATLAB[3] for partial evaluation that is used in type inference and GPU scheduling algorithm. The compiler is written in Ruby, using an embedded domain-specific language (DSL), called RUBYWRITE, for tree rewriting.

The use of MATLAB for aiding type inference and computation partitioning lets the compiler stage these two steps. It performs all it can statically, and generates code to perform the rest at run time. The compiler leverages the built-in ca-

---

[3]The compiler can optionally use GNU Octave for partial evaluation, restricted to the subset of MATLAB libraries that Octave implements.

pability of MATLAB's BILP solver to terminate the computation after a predetermined amount of time, by restricting the time it may consume at run time to solve the integer linear programming problem. In practice, we have not encountered a case where the time ran out. If the BILP solver does not terminate within the time limit, the compiler reverts to a simple greedy strategy for scheduling computations on the GPU. The implementation supports running the MATLAB or Octave instance used for partial evaluation on a remote machine, allowing the compiler to be used on a machine different from where MATLAB may be available.

Our current implementation does not make use of profile data, although it is a straightforward extension of the current compiler. In computing the amount of data that flows along dependence edges, the current implementation ignores array sections, treating them as full arrays. This does not significantly affect the benchmarks that we studied. However, improving the accuracy of flow estimation is part of the future planned work.

We make several **key observations** about our implementation strategy.

1. The partition solver uses MATLAB for solving the integer linear programming problem, which means that it can be easily used at run time to stage the partitioning process. This works in conjunction with our staged type inference algorithm.

2. The solver can be interrupted at any time with appropriate timeout options, which acts as a safety valve if the compiler encounters a particularly difficult problem instance.

3. The greedy strategy can be used as a fall-back mechanism if the integer linear programming problem proves too difficult to solve.

4. The implementation is not limited to using a single library. Multiple libraries complementing each other may be used as a single library.

6. EXPERIMENTAL EVALUATION

To evaluate our approach, we ran our compiler on several benchmarks. Experiments were run in MATLAB version 2010b on an 8-core Intel Xeon X5365 (3 GHz, 8 GB DDR2 memory, 8 MB L2 cache) running 64-bit Gentoo Linux 2.6.32, and GPUmat version 0.25 on an NVIDIA Tesla C1060 card (4 GB memory). Each test was run five times, distributed over a wide range of time, on an unloaded machine and the median time selected. The results presented here are for those benchmarks that contained array statements that could run on the GPU. We explored over 50 applications and kernels collected from a variety of sources, including code used in research work in engineering and science departments, standard benchmarks ported to MATLAB, and contributed code available freely at the MATLAB Central on MathWorks web-site [13]. Out of these, about a dozen benefited from coarse-grained heterogeneous parallelism involving cooperating CPU and GPU, while others had no significant portions of code that could take advantage of a GPU library.

Whenever a piece of code benefited from this type of parallelism, it showed significant improvement in a large majority of cases. This indicates that leveraging a GPU as a coprocessor can be very useful when key functions are available as library functions on the GPU. On the other hand, this also shows that a library-based approach has its limitations. In

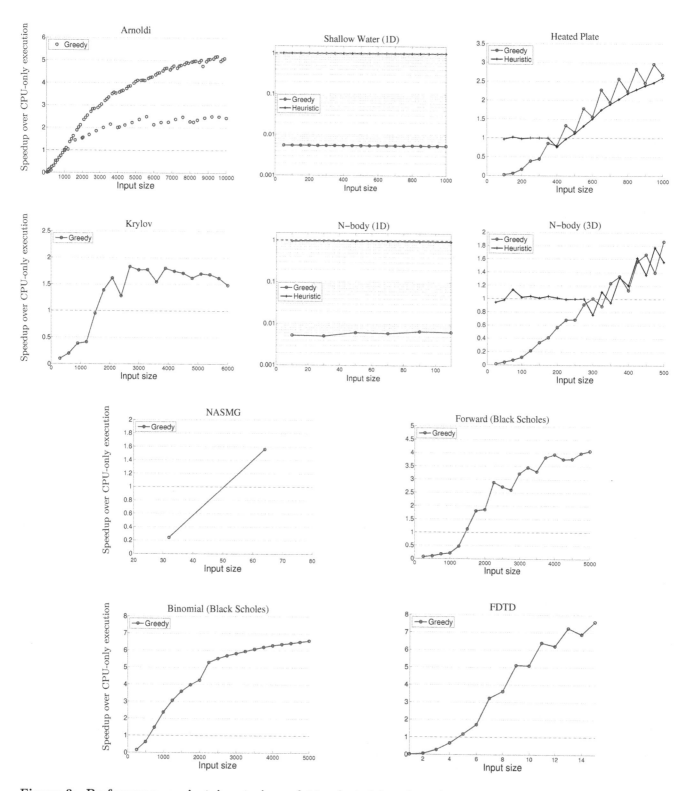

Figure 3: Performance against input sizes of 10 selected benchmarks on a heterogeneous coarse-grained CPU+GPU parallel environment.

those applications that did not significantly use GPU-ported operations, it might be possible to directly compile computationally intensive loops into GPU kernels. We did not investigate this option thoroughly, although it appears that the current restricted support for writing GPU kernels in MATLAB may be inadequate in handling many of these applications. Finally, the fact that there is a significant fraction of applications that are not at all amenable to GPU execution suggests that there are real-life limitations to leveraging the current generation of GPUs, and until those are addressed, CPUs will continue to play an important role in scientific applications.

We ran performance tests on all array operations used in our benchmarks, over a uniform sample of input sizes that would fit in memory. The results from these performance tests constituted one of the inputs to our model, as described in Section 3. Somewhat surprisingly, we discovered that the GPU does not perform uniformly better than the CPU, even for dense matrix operations, contradicting the commonly held belief that GPUs are orders of magnitude faster on dense matrix operations. We attribute this to the more realistic scenario that we use for performance comparison by using multi-threaded optimized versions of operations on the multi-core CPU. Some recent studies also seem to point in this direction [10]. This observation is clearly a function of the hardware as well as the quality of the libraries, and these conclusions are likely to need adjusting in future generations of hardware and software. Our strategy for partitioning tasks between the CPU and GPU makes no assumption about the relative performance of the two.

In the remainder of this section we describe performance results on some selected benchmarks. The statement partitioning was performed completely statically in each case and input size was increased until the code could no longer fit in CPU or GPU memory.

Arnoldi is an algorithm to find the eigenvalues of general matrices. **Krylov** is a code to construct a Krylov matrix with columns normalized to have length one. **Heated plate** is a thermal simulation code. **NBody 3D** performs a three-dimensional N-body simulation. **NASMG** is the multigrid benchmark from the NAS benchmark suite, ported to MATLAB. **Black Scholes** is a finance application for analyzing stock-market data and **Forward** and **Binomial** are two computationally intensive kernels employed within the code. **FDTD** applies the Finite Difference Time Domain technique on a hexahedral cavity with conducting walls. **Shallow water 1D** is a solver for shallow water equations in 1D. **NBody 1D** performs a one-dimensional N-body simulation.

We ran the programs within MATLAB in fully-threaded mode on the 8-core machine in order to compute the base running times for various input sizes. In order to evaluate the effectiveness of our approach, we compared the performance of code resulting from our strategy with a simple method of selecting every schedulable statement in the program to run on the GPU. We call this simple method the *greedy* strategy of scheduling code on GPU. We could not compare our results to the best possible schedule since the benchmarks all contained too many schedulable statements to be searched exhaustively for the optimal partitioning. Figure 3 plots speedup results for 10 benchmarks with increasing input sizes. In each case, we plot speedups obtained with the greedy strategy and those obtained with the strategy described in Section 3, which is labeled as "heuris-

tic" in the figure. In order to isolate the impact of reordering statements to achieve potentially better overlap between CPU and GPU operations, we also ran the tests with reordering disabled. However, for these set of benchmarks, we observed no significant difference, indicating that there were not enough opportunities to reorder statements to improve GPU-CPU computation overlap.

Arnoldi and Krylov have a unique characteristic among all the benchmarks that their main computational loops contain statements that operate on arrays that grow in size with each iteration. As a result, our heuristic strategy would need to be invoked dynamically at the beginning of each iteration. Since we restricted ourselves to studying static scheduling, we did not use Arnoldi and Krylov to evaluate the heuristic approach. However, even a simple greedy strategy in these cases can result in significant speedup for larger input sizes. The speedup for Arnoldi dips significantly for specific matrix sizes (these are *not* powers of two) because the GPU performance for these sizes is substantially lower than for other sizes. Similar, but less pronounced, dips occur in some other benchmarks as well.

In 8 out of the 10 cases there is a significant performance improvement when GPU is leveraged. However, the performance advantage exists only for larger input sizes. This is because for smaller input sizes, the GPU has low occupancy, and data transfer overheads more than compensate for any performance improvements on the GPU. The speedup improves with larger inputs.

In 2 of the 10 cases, i.e., N-body 1D and Shallow Water 1D, the performance degrades dramatically when the GPU is involved. In these cases, the CPU performance on operations that are candidates for GPU execution is sufficiently good that it is not worthwhile paying the price of transferring data to and from GPU. Clearly, the greedy strategy does not take this into account. However, the heuristic approach picks the CPU schedules in these cases, showing the value of being selective about using GPUs. In two benchmarks, Heated Plate and N-Body 3D, the heuristic strategy completely eliminates the cases that would slow down the applications if statements were scheduled greedily on the GPU. Finally, in four of the benchmarks, the heuristic strategy did not improve on the greedy strategy (therefore, we do not show separate plots for the heuristic schedules). This is likely related to the tuning of the γ parameter. Unfortunately, we do not yet have a systematic method to estimate or tweak γ.

Overall, the results demonstrate that a fully automatic strategy to expose and exploit heterogeneous coarse-grained parallelism in MATLAB (and similar array-based languages) is feasible and can result in improved performance for large problem sizes, if deployed carefully.

6.1 Accuracy of the Model

Our empirical model can predict the computation time very accurately (to within about 95% accuracy) on both CPU and GPU for all but the smallest input sizes. However, the model accuracy drops in predicting the GPU run times for very small sizes and also in estimating the total time spent on communication. The inaccuracy in GPU run times comes due to the jitter in kernel set up time, which becomes significant at very small sizes. The inaccuracy in communication arises due to latency hiding techniques employed by the library and the hardware, as well as variations

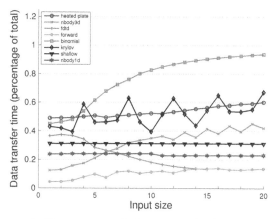

Figure 4: Percentage of time spent in data transfers.

in the GPU card's memory access speeds based on memory access patterns, which are not modeled in our simple scheme. However, the γ factor described in Section 4.3, helps in hiding some of these inaccuracies.

6.2 Communication Overheads

Figure 4 shows the fraction of time spent by the benchmarks (we have omitted Arnoldi to avoid clutter) on data transfers back and forth between CPU and GPU. In all cases, this is a significant fraction, going up to almost 90% for large sizes for `binomial`. Even with such high communication overheads, involving the GPU can improve performance. However, this also points to the existence of further opportunities in leveraging data locality.

7. RELATED WORK

There have been earlier attempts at parallelizing MATLAB, but almost all of them require human intervention in one form or another and are mostly library based implementations. The few that do detect parallelism automatically require source-level changes in MATLAB programs.

Threaded or cluster-level parallelism in MATLAB: MATLAB operations are threaded internally to utilize multicore CPUs, which occurs transparently to users, providing a fork-join style of parallelism.

Star-P enables leveraging a remote cluster from a MATLAB program running on a client machine [7]. It works by overloading MATLAB operations to replace standard operations by their parallelized variant. The user must declare variables that would be manipulated on the remote cluster. Star-P is relatively easy to use for embarrassingly parallel applications, but the programmer must perform data distribution and manage communication manually.

Several other library-based solutions have also been developed that work similarly with overloaded operators or minor syntactic extensions. MATLAB*G is parallel MATLAB for the grid [21]. It provides distributed matrices and also a `parallel-for` construct, but relies on the user to specify parallelism. pMATLAB offers a set of MATLAB data structures and functions that implement distributed MATLAB arrays [5]. It assumes that parallel array programming is an effective programming style for a variety of applications. MatPAR allows MATLAB users to replace calls to certain built-in MATLAB functions with calls to MatPAR functions which are implemented as standard MATLAB external calls to C libraries [20].

An earlier effort attempts to analyze MATLAB source to identify avenues for task and data parallelism [17]. It then converts intrinsic MATLAB functions and operators to ScaLA-PACK or other routines. This approach is not completely automatic, and depends on the user supplying directives about the size and types of input variables. This implies change to MATLAB syntax, which is not desirable. To the best of our knowledge the implementation of this compiler is somewhat incomplete.

The Parallel Computing Toolbox from MathWorks [13] makes several parallel programming constructs, such as **parallel for**, available to users. However, it depends on the users to have expertise in using these constructs and very little is done to automatically detect parallelism and produce code for the underlying architecture. When combined with the MathWorks Distributed Computing Server, it also enables users to deploy applications on a cluster.

Parallelization for GPUs: With the advent of GPUs and GPGPUs, there have been attempts to accelerate MATLAB by moving computation to the GPU. CUDA has been the preferred way of programming NVIDIA GPUs [18, 14]. However, the CUDA APIs are only available for C and there is no MATLAB equivalent. Several third party GPU libraries have been developed to interface directly from MATLAB [1, 22]. These libraries hide all the low-level implementation details behind a user-level MATLAB data-type. This approach depends on the users to identify tasks that are best run on the GPU and to schedule computations manually if they desire concurrency across the CPU and GPU.

The most recent version of MathWorks Parallel Computing Toolbox also lets users offload parts of their computation on GPUs in a way similar to the GPUmat library used in our study [22]. Additionally, this version lets users write simple CUDA-compatible GPU kernels in MATLAB syntax. However, the kernel may only contain scalar operations and may not contain any control-flow statements.

The Cetus framework translates OpenMP programs to CUDA code [11]. In an extension of their earlier work, the authors have developed an annotation language, called OpenMPC, based on OpenMP [10], which allows finer control over thread scheduling and memory allocation. The compiler performs data flow analysis to determine if values need to be moved between CPU and GPU. However, a more direct approach appears feasible in the context of MATLAB, since it is an array-based language and computationally intensive array statements and loops are easily vectorized.

The Pluto compiler uses the polyhedral model for optimizing loop nests and converting them to CUDA kernels [3]. This approach is most useful for detecting and exploiting fine-grained parallelism, which can potentially complement the approach described in this paper.

Scheduling: Scheduling of tasks on heterogeneous systems has been studied for a long time [12]. Traditionally, the problem of scheduling of tasks is abstracted into the problem of scheduling vertices of a directed acyclic graph (DAG), where vertices represent tasks and edges represent dependencies among them. Optimal DAG scheduling is a known NP-complete problem [9]. Therefore, it is not surprising that the problem of scheduling statements on CPU and GPU can be reduced to binary integer linear programming, which is itself an NP-complete problem. Our heuristic to schedule statements hierarchically based on control flow constructs is aimed at reducing the average case time complexity.

8. FURTHER RESEARCH

Enabling users to write GPU kernels within MATLAB is a powerful notion. An alternative would be to compile the kernels down to code in a lower-level language, such as CUDA C, which could in turn be compiled with a back-end compiler. This route could make the optimizations performed by the back-end compiler available to MATLAB programs. Such an approach is not entirely unknown in the MATLAB world, where it is common to compile pieces into so-called MEX libraries that get dynamically loaded at run-time.

A deeper question in exploiting parallelism at the multiple levels of granularity that becomes available with GPUs is how to best express the parallelism. Array statements naturally express Single Instruction Multiple Data (SIMD)-style parallelism, which maps well to CUDA blocks. However, expressing coarser parallelism is still an open problem. While our work is able to expose an intermediate level of parallelism, still coarser levels of parallelism are possible, indeed desirable, if we want to operate on a cluster.

Working recursively through control-flow structures controls the time complexity of the scheduling process but prevents the algorithm from taking advantage of loop-level parallelism. The algorithm presented here could be extended to work with parallelizable loops, if the loop body could be abstracted out in a kernel. This would build on techniques involved in C to CUDA translation or optimizing CUDA programs that have been used in published work [3, 6]. However, vector statements inside parallelizable loops can potentially produce higher levels of parallelism in array-based languages such as MATLAB.

While we attempt to minimize data movement between CPU and GPU, this could be extended to minimize data movements between CUDA blocks, if an automatic translation of MATLAB to CUDA kernels is undertaken.

Our strategy of empirically measuring the running times on a sample of inputs will need to be refined to apply to sparse data sets. On the other hand, the performance benefits of GPUs when working with sparse data sets are not always clear.

9. CONCLUSION

In this paper we have shown that a fully automatic method of partitioning computation across the CPU and GPU is possible for MATLAB programs, given a library that implements computationally intensive MATLAB functions on the GPU. The approach can achieve optimal results at the basic-block level. The optimality of the solution is guaranteed by mapping it to a binary integer linear programming problem. We implemented our approach in a source-level MATLAB compiler and demonstrated its effectiveness using a set of benchmarks from a variety of problem domains. A statistical analysis of a large number of real-life MATLAB examples indicates that a globally optimal approach would be infeasible in practice. Our approach is not only practically feasible, but is also able to achieve significant performance improvements in a large number of benchmarks.

10. REFERENCES

[1] Accelreyes. GPU Computing with MATLAB. On the web. http://www.accelereyes.com/.

[2] Amina Aslam and Laurie Hendren. McFLAT: A profile-based framework for MATLAB loop analysis and transformations. In *Proceedings of the 23rd International Workshop on Languages and Compilers for Parallel Computing (LCPC)*, 2010.

[3] Muthu Manikandan Baskaran, J. Ramanujam, and P. Sadayappan. Automatic C-to-CUDA Code Generation for Affine Programs. In *In Proceedings of the 19th International Conference on Compiler Construction (CC)*, pages 244–263, 2010.

[4] L. Susan Blackford, James Demmel, Jack Dongarra, Iain Duff, Sven Hamarling, Greg Henry, Michael Heroux, Linda Kaufman, Andrew Lumsdaine, Antoine Petitet, Roldan Pozo, Karin Remington, and R. Clint Whaley. An Updated Set of Basic Linear Algebra Subprograms (BLAS). *ACM Transactions on Mathematical Software (TOMS)*, 28(2):135–151, June 2002.

[5] N. Travinin Bliss and J. Kepner. pMATLAB Parallel MATLAB Library. *International Journal of High Performance Computing Applications*, 21(3):336–359, 2007.

[6] Snaider Carrillo, Jakob Siegel, and Xiaoming Li. A Control-structure Splitting Optimization for GPGPU. In *Proceedings of the 6th ACM Symposium on Computing Frontiers*, pages 147–150, 2009.

[7] Ron Choy, Alan Edelman, John R. Gilbert, Viral Shah, and David Cheng. Star-P: High productivity parallel computing. In *In 8th Annual Workshop on High-Performance Embedded Computing (HPEC 04)*, 2004.

[8] Khronos Group. OpenCL: The open standard for parallel programming of heterogeneous systems. On the web. http://www.khronos.org/opencl/.

[9] Yu-Kwong Kwok and Ishfaq Ahmad. Static Scheduling Algorithms for Allocating Directed Task Graphs to Multiprocessors. *ACM Computing Surveys*, 31(4):406–471, 1999.

[10] Seyong Lee and Rudolf Eigenmann. OpenMPC: Extended OpenMP Programming and Tuning for GPUs. In *Proceedings of the International Conference for High Performance Computing, Networking, Storage and Analysis (SC 2010)*, 2010.

[11] Seyong Lee, Seung-Jai Min, and Rudolf Eigenmann. OpenMP to GPGPU: A Compiler Framework for Automatic Translation and Optimization. In *Proceedings of the 14th ACM SIGPLAN Symposium on Principles and Practice of Parallel Programming (PPoPP)*, 2009.

[12] Jane W S Liu and Ai-Tsung Yang. Optimal Scheduling of Independent Tasks on Heterogeneous Computing Systems. In *Proceedings of the 1974 Annual Conference*, volume 1, pages 38–45, 1974.

[13] Mathworks inc. On the web. http://www.mathworks.com/.

[14] NVIDIA. *NVIDIA CUDA Compute Unified Device Architecture: Programming Guide*, version 1.1 edition, November 2007.

[15] NVIDIA Corporation, 2701 San Tomas Expressway, Santa Clara, CA 95050. *CUDA CUBLAS Library: Version 2.0*.

[16] EM Photonics. CULA: GPU accelerated linear algebra. On the web. http://www.culatools.com/.

[17] Shankar Ramaswamy, Eugene W. Hodges IV, and Prithviraj Banerjee. Compiling MATLAB Programs to ScaLAPACK: Exploiting Task and Data Parallelism. In *Proceedings of the 10th International Parallel Processing Symposium (IPPS)*, pages 613–619, 1996.

[18] Shane Ryoo, Christopher I. Rodrigues, Sara S. Baghsorkhi, Sam S. Stone, David B. Kirk, and Wen mei W Hwu. Optimization Principles and Application Performance Evaluation of a Multithreaded GPU using CUDA. In *Proceedings of the 13th ACM SIGPLAN Symposium on Principles and Practice of Parallel Programming (PPoPP)*, pages 73–82, 2008.

[19] Chun-Yu Shei, Arun Chauhan, and Sidney Shaw. Compile-time Disambiguation of MATLAB Types through Concrete Interpretation with Automatic Run-time Fallback. In *Proceedings of the 16th annual IEEE International Conference on High Performance Computing (HiPC)*, 2009.

[20] Paul L Springer. Matpar: Parallel Extensions for MATLAB. Technical report, Jet Propulsion Laboratory, July 1998.

[21] Yong-Meng Teo, Ying Chen, and Xianbing Wang. On Grid Programming and MATLAB*G. In *Proceedings of Third International Conference on Grid and Cooperative Computing*, pages 761–768, 2004.

[22] The GP-you Group. GPUmat: GPU toolbox for MATLAB. On the web. http://gp-you.org/.

Using GPUs to Compute Large Out-of-card FFTs

Liang Gu
Department of ECE
University of Delaware
Newark, DE, USA
lianggu@udel.edu

Jakob Siegel
Department of ECE
University of Delaware
Newark, DE, USA
jakob@udel.edu

Xiaoming Li
Department of ECE
University of Delaware
Newark, DE, USA
xli@ece.udel.edu

ABSTRACT

The optimization of Fast Fourier Transfer (FFT) problems that can fit into GPU memory has been studied extensively. Such on-card FFT libraries like CUFFT can generally achieve much better performance than their counterparts on a CPU, as the data transfer between CPU and GPU is usually not counted in their performance. This high performance, however, is limited by the GPU memory size. When the FFT problem size increases, the data transfer between system and GPU memory can comprise a substantial part of the overall execution time. Therefore, optimizations for FFT problems that outgrow the GPU memory can not bypass the tuning of data transfer between CPU and GPU. However, no prior study has attacked this problem. This paper is the first effort of using GPUs to efficiently compute large FFTs in the CPU memory of a single compute node.

In this paper, the performance of the PCI bus during the transfer of a batch of FFT subarrays is studied and a blocked buffer algorithm is proposed to improve the effective bandwidth. More importantly, several FFT decomposition algorithms are proposed so as to increase the data locality, further improve the PCI bus efficiency and balance computation between kernels. By integrating the above two methods, we demonstrate an out-of-card FFT optimization strategy and develop an FFT library that efficiently computes large 1D, 2D and 3D FFTs that can not fit into the GPU's memory. On three of the latest GPUs, our large FFT library achieves much better double precision performance than two of the most efficient CPU based libraries, FFTW and Intel MKL. On average, our large FFTs on a single GeForce GTX480 are 46% faster than FFTW and 57% faster than MKL with multiple threads running on a four-core Intel i7 CPU. The speedup on a Tesla C2070 is $1.93\times$ and $2.11\times$ over FFTW and MKL. A peak performance of 21GFLOPS is achieved for a 2D FFT of size 2048×65536 on C2070 with double precision.

Categories and Subject Descriptors

G.4 [**Mathematical Software**]: Parallel and Vector Implementation

General Terms

Algorithms, Design, Performance

Keywords

FFT, DFT, Library, GPU, CUDA

1. INTRODUCTION

FFT is the fast algorithms to compute Discrete Fourier Transform (DFT), which transfers an input series from time or space domain to frequency domain (Inverse DFT does the opposite). FFT reduces the complexity of a DFT from $O(N^2)$, N being the size of input series, to O(Nlog(N)) by recursively adopting a divide-and-conquer approach. FFT is an important tool in spectral analysis, signal processing, data compression and many other fields. Meanwhile, it is frequently the most time-consuming part of a program. This is particularly true for a large sized FFT due to its heavy demand in memory bandwidth and computational resources.

In order to compute an FFT more efficiently, many FFT libraries have been built on both, general purpose CPUs and computation accelerators such as GPUs. Examples of FFT libraries on CPUs include FFTW [1], SPIRAL [2, 3] and Intel's MKL [4], etc. In our tests, FFTW and MKL typically achieve about 10GFLOPS in double precision on an Intel i7 CPU with multi-threading and vectorization enabled. On the GPU side, best-performing FFT libraries include CUFFT [5], a vendor-provided implementation, and several other research FFT libraries, [6, 7, 8]. Benefiting from GPU's high bandwidth of their off-chip memory and abundant ALUs, these FFT libraries usually out-perform their counterparts on CPUs by a large margin. For example, CUFFT can achieve more than 50GFLOPS in double precision on a high end GPU, Tesla C2070.

The impressive performance of the current GPU-based FFT libraries has a prerequisite, however, that is *all* the input and output data of the computation must reside in the GPU's off-chip memory. Before those libraries are called, all the input data of an FFT has to be transferred from the system memory to the GPU by the user. After the library is called, the output data of the FFT needs to be transferred back as well. This prerequisite leads to two implications. First of all, those libraries cannot handle very large FFT problems, which happen to be required in many applications such as large-scale physics simulations. The maximum problem size for those libraries is limited by the size of the GPU memory. The latest NVIDIA's GeForce GPU, GTX480, has 1.5GB global memory which can only hold a 3D out-of-place FFT of size 256^3 with double precision. Second, the performance advantage of those GPU FFT libraries over their CPU counterparts will be discounted when the data transfer is counted in. The CPU-GPU data channel, in most cases the PCI bus, has larger latency and smaller bandwidth than the GPU memory. For example, PCIe 2.0 with 16 lanes has only a theoretical peak bandwidth of 8GB/s, only 10% of the 80GB/s bandwidth of the GPU off-chip memory.

Computing large FFTs that cannot fit into the GPU memory needs to transfer the FFT data back and forth over PCI bus at least $\frac{2 \times problem\_size}{GPU\_memory\_size}$ times. This is because each data point of an FFT's output mathematically depends on *all* the input data. Therefore, when part of the input is copied to the GPU memory, only intermediate results can be calculated. All the intermediate results on the CPU need at least another round of GPU computations to get the final FFT output. In particular, the same argument applies to not only 1D but 2D and 3D FFTs as well. Another challenge of the problem is that the effective bandwidth of the CPU-GPU data channel is sensitive to the layouts of the data array. Without optimization, a naive implementation of data transfer needs to transfer the FFT data in many non-contiguous chunks in the CPU memory and each PCI transfer can be small. A large number of small transfers is particularly inefficient for the CPU-GPU data channel.

Previous works have studied FFTs on external or hierarchical memory. Bailey [9] proposed a two-round algorithm to compute 1D FFT on a hierarchical memory system including a solid state disk and main memory. However, streaming technique that could overlap the memory communication with FFT computation was not introduced in that work. Moreover, the data transfer between the disk and the main memory is unoptimized in the previous work, while it could be further optimized by a blocked buffer on the disk as suggested later in this paper.

There are cluster based works that can compute large sized FFTs [10, 11]. Particularly, Chen et.al reported the implementation of a large 3D FFT on a 16-node GPU cluster [12]. That work used CUFFT as their solution of in-node FFT and optimized the 3D FFT on a particular cluster architecture. Most cluster based FFT implementations are limited to 3D FFTs, which have abundant natural parallelism. Hence, high performance can be easily achieved with more compute nodes. Most important, the effective PCI bus bandwidth during the transfer of FFTs, a challenge that cannot be bypassed for in-node FFT implementation, is not well studied nor optimized.

This paper is the first effort to address these unique challenges in the implementation of large out-of-card FFTs on a single GPU. The paper makes two main contributions: (1) We propose a Cooley-Tukey algorithm based decomposition framework that co-optimizes both CPU-GPU data transfer and balance of on-GPU computation for 1D, 2D, and 3D FFTs. (2) We develop a blocked buffer technique for 1D FFTs to achieve a high effective bandwidth on the CPU-GPU data channel. Moreover, this technique may be applied to more general data transfer problems as well.

2. OVERVIEW AND BACKGROUND

This work targets FFT problems whose input and output data is larger than the GPU memory and therefore is allocated in system memory. A key difference between our work and other on-card GPU libraries is that these libraries only need to optimize the computation on GPU but our library needs to optimize the data transfer over the PCI bus as well. The data transfer for an on-card GPU FFT library is quite straightforward and is done by the library users. the whole input data allocated on the CPU memory is copied into the GPU in one pass. After the library finishes the FFT computation, the output is transferred back to the host, again, in one pass. However, in this work, the data transfer itself needs to be optimized along with the on-card FFT computation. The interface of our library is on the CPU side just like FFTW or MKL. Specifically, this work deals with double precision complex 1D, 2D and 3D FFTs

with power-of-two sizes, which are the most commonly used FFT problems. The input and output arrays of an FFT are allocated as unpagable CPU memory, also called pinned memory, to maximize PCI bus transfer bandwidth.

In this paper, FFT problems and the algorithm we use are denoted in an extended I/O tensor format [8, 13]. We use this concise representation to specify an FFT of any dimension. Optimization algorithms are described as transformations in this representation space as well. In short, an I/O dimension d_1 is defined as $d_1 = d(n, i, o, I, O)$, where n is the FFT size, i and o are the input and output strides and I and O are the addresses of the input and output arrays. One I/O dimension represents the FFT problem on one dimension, and a sequence of I/O dimensions compose an I/O tensor $t = \{d_1, d_2, ..., d_p\}$ which can neatly represent a multi-dimensional FFT. The two pointers, I and O, specify where to store the data (on CPU memory, GPU's global or shared memory) and whether the computation is in-place or out-of-place. However, in this work they are not shown because it is evident that during a PCI transfer one of the pointers is on CPU memory and the other is on GPU memory. Moreover, we can tell that an I/O dimension needs to be out-of-place if the input stride is not equal to the output stride, which suggests there is a transposition. Otherwise, it does not matter whether the I/O dimension is in-place or out-of-place. Without showing the I/O pointers, a 2D FFT of size Y × X can be represented as $t = \{d(Y, X, X), d(X, 1, 1)\}$ in tensor format.

FFT transforms used in our method are based on the Cooley-Tukey algorithm [14] which decomposes a single $r \times m$ sized FFT into three steps. First, compute r number of FFTs of size m. Second, transpose r with m and multiply a constant matrix called twiddle factors on the intermediate results. Finally, compute m number of FFTs of size r. The Cooley-Tukey algorithm can be precisely represented in tensor form in equation (1), called Decimation In Time(DIT), or equation (2), called Decimation In Frequency(DIF), depending on where the transposition is performed.

$$\{d(rm, i, o)\} = \{d(m, ir, o)t_r^m d(r, mo, mo)\} \quad (1)$$
$$\{d(rm, i, o)\} = \{d(r, im, im)t_m^r d(m, i, ro)\} \quad (2)$$

Here t_r^m represents multiplication of twiddle factors with size $m \times r$. In the real computation, this part will be combined with the adjacent computation steps. These two tensor representations are the basic components of the Cooley-Tukey algorithm and they can be recursively applied in all four direct FFT parts in equation (1) and (2). Different combinations of how to apply the decomposition will derive a DIT, a DIF or hybrid algorithm.

After decomposing a large sized FFT using the Cooley-Tukey algorithm, the smaller sub-FFTs can usually fit into the GPU memory. A batch of such FFTs, possibly with a stride, is transferred to the GPU and is computed using our own FFT kernels, sometimes along with the twiddle factor multiplication. In some cases, NVIDIA's CUFFT is used to solve small 1D and 2D FFTs with a stride equal to one, i.e., the data is contiguous in memory, when CUFFT is faster than our own kernel. Our FFT kernels are optimized using the tensor representation and the Cooley-Tukey algorithm. Specifically, a FFT is recursively decomposed until it is small enough to be directly solved efficiently. Typically, the sizes are 4 to 16 on our tested GPUs.

We have therefore two levels of decomposition: the decomposition of large FFT problems into subproblems that can fit into a GPU and the further decomposition of those on-card FFTs to optimize the kernel computation. A particular way of performing these two levels of decomposition will deliver a different implementation of the target FFT problem. The result of the decomposition will be denoted as a sequence of FFTs in tensor format, which represents all necessary FFT computation, transposition and twiddle factor multiplication. Please note that a sequence of I/O dimensions implicitly determines the number of FFTs for each I/O dimension. For example, there are $\frac{n_1 \cdot n_2 \cdot \ldots \cdot n_j}{n_i}$ number of FFTs of size n_i for the I/O dimension $d(n_i, i, o)$ in a sequence of j I/O dimensions.

We follow the same approach as is shown in paper [8] for on-GPU optimization. To summarize, specially revised codelets [15], [16], which are compiler generated C programs to solve small FFTs in FFTW, are used to compute FFTs on a GPU. High dimensional FFTs are computed on that dimension without being transposed to a lower dimension first. Codelets within one FFT dimension or across multiple dimensions are grouped into the fewest number of kernels. Each kernel has one pass of global and multiple passes of shared memory accesses. Therefore, the overall global memory accesses are minimized. Moreover, 16 or 32 threads are coalesced into a single memory transfer when accessing adjacent data so that a higher global memory bandwidth is achieved.

The new architectural features in the latest Fermi GPUs [17] also affect optimization decisions. Compared with older GPUs, Fermi introduces a larger shared memory size(48KB vs 16KB), more banks in shared memory(32 banks vs 16 banks) and more coalescing threads(32 threads vs 16 threads). Those new features are incorporated into the optimization through the parametrization of the algorithm. Fermi's newly added L1 and L2 cache, is not really helpful to FFT because of its highly regular and non-repeating data access pattern. Concurrent kernel execution is not applicable either because the kernels corresponding to a sequence of I/O dimensions (or codelets) have data dependency among each other, and therefore can not be executed concurrently.

Overall, we use FFT decomposition algorithms based on the I/O tensor framework to maximize the data transfer PCI bandwidth and balance computation kernels to have better overlap with communication. As we will show later, the transfer of subarrays over the PCI bus can have an order of magnitude difference in effective bandwidth depending on the width of the subarray. With our proposed FFT algorithms, a close to optimum PCI bus bandwidth is achieved and computation kernels between rounds are of comparable size. The last key component in the optimization of large FFTs is a blocked buffer algorithm which is applicable to a wide class of data transfer problems. Particularly, this algorithm is used to increase the effective PCI bus bandwidth of 1D FFTs when other FFT related optimizations are not applicable.

3. PCI TRANSFER OF SUBARRAYS

In this section, we illustrate the general scheme of how to move partial data of a large FFT between CPU and GPU memory. Several methods are proposed to improve the performance of such data movement over a communication channel such as the PCI bus.

When the FFT is larger than the GPU memory size, only a portion of the whole data can be transferred each time. If we have a large high dimensional FFT or a 1D FFT divided by the Cooley-Tukey algorithm, a batch of the smaller FFTs will take a block of subarrays within the original large array as input. Since these subarrays have the same length and a constant stride between each other, we call them *regular subarrays*. Figure 1 shows C regular subarrays of length W and stride X between each other in a large array of size $C \times X$. Note that the large array is contiguous on the X dimension, and the regular subarrays as a whole are not contiguous in system memory. But they need to be copied to a single contiguous array in GPU memory, as is shown on the right side of Figure 1.

This large array in CPU memory can actually be a 1D, 2D or 3D array but is just shown in a 2D point of view. Assume the total size

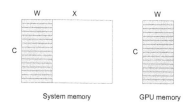

Figure 1: regular subarrays within a large array

of the large FFT is $C \times X$. For a large 1D FFT, the regular subarrays contain a part of the small FFTs in one computation step of the Cooley-Tukey algorithm, i.e. W FFTs of length C. If the large FFT is a 2D problem of size $Y \times X$, then the regular subarrays comprise part of the Y dimensional FFTs, where $Y = C$. In order to copy the whole chunk of subarrays to or back from GPU memory, there need to be C number of *cudaMemcpyAsync()* function calls and each call copies a subarray of width W. As we want to use as much GPU memory as possible to reduce passes of subarray transfers, $C \times W$ is usually chosen to be the largest value allowed on the GPU memory. For example, if the FFT problem has an input and an output arrays with complex double precision data type, the maximum power-of-two size of $C \times W$ is 32M on a NVIDIA's GTX480 with 1.5GB global memory,

The choice of how a large FFT problem is divided has a great impact on the data transfer performance. In other words, even if we know the maximal value of $C \times W$, the different choices of C or W can lead to almost one magnitude difference in transfer time. As we fix the $C \times W = 32M$, for example, and change W from 8 to 32M (C changes accordingly), the effective PCI bandwidth is illustrated in Figure 2. The curves 'H2D' (host to device, i.e., CPU

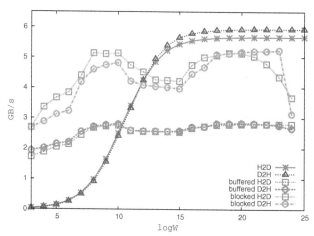

Figure 2: PCI bandwidth test of subarray transfer

memory to GPU memory) and 'D2H' (device to host) in figure 2 show the overall effective bandwidth of the transfer with different W. The value of W is shown in log_2 scale and $16 \times W$ is the actual width in Bytes. These two curves show that PCI bus keeps a fairly high bandwidth (about 6GB/s out of 8GB/s theoretical peak) with large W and a small numbers of *cudaMemcpyAsync()* calls. The PCI bandwidth, however, quickly decreases by an order of magnitude when W decreases to be smaller than 2^{13} to 2^{14}. We also consider whether the stride between two adjacent subarrays, i.e. X value, will affect the transfer performance or not. However, test results show that it does not have much influence on the effective bandwidth of the PCI bus.

In order to increase the effective PCI bandwidth of the subarray transfer for small W values, we introduce a buffer on CPU memory. The buffer has the same total size of the regular subarrays. All the data on the subarrays is transferred to this buffer first and then the whole buffer is copied to GPU using a single PCI transfer. Device to host transfer is exactly the opposite process. The benefit of this approach is that the rearrangement of the subarrays to a continuous chunk of memory using *memcpy()* can lead to lower total overhead than transferring subarrays directly using additional *cudaMemcpyAsync()* calls. The host to device and device to host bandwidth with a buffer on system memory is shown as the curves 'buffered H2D' and 'buffered D2H' in figure 2. This method generally achieves a bandwidth of 2GB/s to 3GB/s and can improve the performance of the direct transfer method when W is smaller than 2^{11}.

To further increase the bandwidth, the preparation of the buffer can be done concurrently with the the transfer of the buffer over the PCI bus. The key issue is the synchronization between the two steps. A further optimization we propose is that the buffer on system memory can be divided into blocks as is shown in figure 3 and we can overlap the preparing time of a block with the PCI transfer time of another block. More specifically, when *memcpy()* is

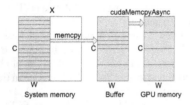

Figure 3: PCI transfer of subarrays with blocked buffer

used to transfer a block of data from the large array to the buffer, *cudaMemcpyAsync()* can be used to transfer the previous block to GPU at the same time. Additional threads are needed for the device to host subarray transfer. First, *cudaMemcpyAsync()* is called to move a block of data from the GPU memory to the buffer. Then after calling the cudaStreamSynchronize() function, a signal is sent by the first thread and the second thread will handle the data movement of the block from the buffer to the large global array. The curves 'blocked H2D' and 'blocked D2H' in figure 2 show the effective bandwidth of transferring subarrays using a blocked buffer. The optimum number of blocks for each (C,W) pair is found by an empirical search. As a result of the overlap between the two steps of data movement, this method can greatly increase the PCI bandwidth to about 5GB/s when W is smaller than 2^{12}.

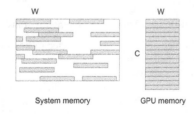

Figure 4: More general case of subarray transfer

So far, we have presented multiple methods to increase the effective PCI bus bandwidth of transferring regular subarrays. The proposed blocked buffer algorithm can be applied to communication channels other than PCI bus and much more general random-stride subarray transfer problems as is shown in figure 4. For reg-

ular subarrays with W larger than 2^{12}, we can improve the PCI bus bandwidth to more than $3GB/s$ without using any FFT related optimization. We will shown in the following sections that we can further improve the PCI bandwidth of FFT problems to almost optimum by co-optimizing the Cooley-Tukey algorithm based decomposition and the parameter tuning of the PCI transfer step.

4. LARGE 1D FFT

First, we will discuss the computation of 1D FFTs with size larger than GPU memory. 1D FFT has no natural parallelism that can be extracted from simple problem division. However, the Cooley-Tukey decomposition algorithm can be applied on a large 1D FFT to get smaller sized 1D sub-problems that can fit into GPU memory and be computed on card. As is discussed before, at least two rounds of partial computation is needed for a large sized FFT. The simplest way to compute a large sized 1D FFT is to decompose the original problem once and compute the sub-problems with a two-round algorithm.

4.1 Two-Round 1D FFT algorithm

A 1D FFT of size $X = X_1 \times X_2$, represented as $d(X,1,1)$ in the I/O tensor format, is divided with the DIT Cooley-Tukey algorithm represented in equation (1) by choosing $m = X_1$ and $r = X_2$. Then, we have the following decomposition equation, $d(X_1, X_2, 1) t_{X_2}^{X_1} d(X_2, X_1, X_1)$. Figure 5 shows the overview of our two-round large 1D FFT algorithm. The computation of a

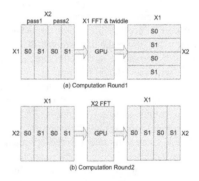

(a) Computation Round1

(b) Computation Round2

Figure 5: Two-round computation for large 1D FFT

large 1D FFT is divided into two rounds. Each round includes several passes of GPU computation and the number of passes is $\frac{X \times data\_size}{GPU\_memory\_size}$.

Each pass of GPU computation can use multiple streams to overlap the computation with communication. For example, figure 5 shows the case of using two streams, S0 and S1, in each round. The relation between the stream size, the number of streams and the number of passes is shown in equation (3).

$$stream\_size \times (\#streams) \times (\#passes)$$
$$\leq GPU\_memory\_size \quad (3)$$

We use empirical search to find the optimum number of streams and the stream size.

For the host to device data transfer, round one needs $C = X_1$ number of PCI transfers and a width of $W = \frac{X_2}{(\#passes) \times (\#streams)}$ for each transfer. For example, if $X_1 = X_2 = 2^{13}$, W will be smaller than 2^{11}. The blocked buffer method can be used to perform the host to device subarray transfer and about $5GB/s$ PCI bus bandwidth is achieved according to the results in figure 2.

On the GPU, FFTs of size X_1 are further decomposed by the Cooley-Tukey and are computed using a sequence of codelets. The last codelet is rewritten to include twiddle factors of size $X_1 \times X_2$. The transposition of X_1 to the low dimension is performed on GPU instead of on CPU because of GPU's higher bandwidth. Moreover, this transposition is incorporated in the computation of the codelets with the help of shared memory, so no explicit transposition is needed. Finally, the output of round one is copied back to the CPU in a single PCI transfer. Close to 6GB/s PCI bus bandwidth is achieved in this step.

In round two of the computation, a host to device and a device to host PCI subarray transfer with $C = X_2$ and $W = \frac{X_1}{(\#passes) \times (\#streams)}$ is performed. Similar to the host to device transfer in round one, about 5GB/s PCI bandwidth can be achieved. The number of passes and streams in round two need not to be the same as for round one. No transposition is needed on the GPU in this round.

In order to keep a high PCI bandwidth of all three transfers, we want to keep both the W value large and the C value small. Therefore, X_2 is chosen to be equal or slightly larger than X_1. Another reason to choose equal or close X_1 and X_2 values is that the two computation kernels in the two rounds will be balanced. This helps to overlap the computation time with the PCI transfer time.

4.2 Three-Round 1D FFT algorithm

When the problem size X increases, X_1 and X_2 in the above two-round algorithm will increase, and more subarrays with smaller size need to be transferred in one pass. The decrease of width of subarray will hurt bandwidth significantly in both rounds. In this case, we propose another alternative algorithm using three rounds of PCI bus transfer with higher bandwidth for each round. If $X = X_1 \times X_2 \times X_3$, applying the DIT Cooley-Tukey algorithm (1) twice gives equation (4), which suggests a three-round 1D FFT algorithm.

$$\{d(X_1, X_2X_3, 1)t_{X_2}^{X_1}d(X_2, X_1, X_1)$$
$$t_{X_3}^{X_1X_2}d(X_3, X_1X_2, X_1X_2)\} \quad (4)$$

There are other valid decomposition schemes that can be derived from recursively applying DIT or DIF algorithm on different parts of the previous equation.

The three-round computation of equation (4) is illustrated in figure 6. Different data transfer strategies are needed for the

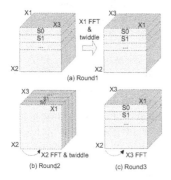

Figure 6: Three-round computation for large 1D FFT

three rounds of computation. In round one, reading from system memory needs $C = X_1$ PCI transfers, each with a width of $W = \frac{X_3X_2}{(\#passes) \times (\#streams)}$. Writing backs in round one and both accesses in round three have $C = X_3$ and $W = $

$\frac{X_1X_2}{(\#passes) \times (\#streams)}$. To keep W large and C small, X_2 is chosen to be larger than both X_1 and X_3. Arrays that need to be transferred in round two occupy a contiguous chunk of system memory. Only one PCI transfer is needed for round two, so it already has the best bandwidth over the PCI bus.

By adding one more round of GPU computation, the bandwidth of each round is improved. However, this three-round 1D FFT algorithm is only beneficial for very large 1D FFTs where a two-round algorithm has low PCI bandwidth. Thus the overhead of adding one round of PCI communication is justified. In our case, due to the limitation of our system memory, the largest 1D FFT we can test is 256M and a two-round algorithm still has a good PCI transfer bandwidth for this size. So this three-round 1D FFT algorithm should be used for even larger 1D FFTs.

5. LARGE 2D FFT

5.1 Naive 2D FFT algorithm

For a large 2D FFT of total size $N = Y \times X$ where $16N$ is larger than the GPU's global memory size, there are naturally 2 rounds of computation by definition, i.e. Y dimensional FFTs and X dimensional FFTs. One can easily takes advantage of this natural parallelism and compute a batch of these smaller sub-FFTs on the GPU if these Y dimension sub-problems or X dimensional sub-problems can fit into the GPU memory. The data layout in system memory of this straightforward algorithm is shown in figure 7. Y dimensional

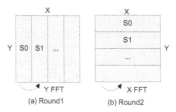

Figure 7: Naive algorithm for large 2D FFT

FFTs are computed in round one and X dimensional FFTs in round two. Similarly, each round is divided into several passes and each pass has a couple of streams. Round two has no PCI bandwidth issue because each stream needs only one PCI transfer between host and device. In round one, there are $C = Y$ number of reads from and writes to subarrays on system memory. Each access over PCI has a width of $W = \frac{X}{(\#passes) \times (\#streams)}$. According to the PCI performance curves in figure 2, when X is large and Y is small, the data transfer pattern has a good PCI bandwidth. However, this naive algorithm may lose up to 50% of the peak PCI performance when Y is large. Moreover, the amount of GPU computation between two rounds is also unbalanced when Y is much larger than X. Therefore, this naive algorithm is only used when Y is small.

5.2 Y decomposition 2D FFT algorithm

In order to increase the effective PCI bus bandwidth of round one in the naive 2D FFT algorithm, we apply the Cooley-Tukey algorithm once on the Y dimensional FFTs. The original 2D FFT in tensor form, $\{d(Y, X, X), d(X, 1, 1)\}$, becomes equation (5) for $Y = Y_1 \times Y_2$.

$$\{d(Y_1, Y_2X, X)t_{Y_2}^{Y_1}d(Y_2, Y_1X, YX)d(X, 1, 1)\} \quad (5)$$

FFTs of size Y_1 and Y_2 are further decomposed on the GPU using the Cooley-Tukey and are eventually computed by codelets. In particular, we rewrite the last codelet of the Y_1 codelet sequence so that the twiddle factor computation between Y_1 and Y_2 can be computed within that codelet. X dimensional FFTs are computed using the CUFFT library due to its good on-GPU performance for 1D FFTs.

Figure 8 visualizes this decomposition in equation (5). FFTs of

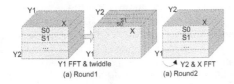

Figure 8: Y decomposition algorithm for large 2D FFT

size Y_1 is computed and a transposition between Y_1 and Y_2 is performed on GPU in round one of the algorithm. The device to host copy of round one needs a single PCI transfer (C=1) and thus has the best PCI bandwidth. The host to device copy in round one and the two-way communications in round two need $C=Y_1$ and $C=Y_2$ number of PCI transfers. All of them have smaller C and better bandwidth than the naive algorithm. To achieve high bandwidth for both rounds, both Y_1 and Y_2 need to be small. Round one computes Y_1 sized FFTs and round two computes Y_2 and X sized FFTs. We want the amount of computation in two rounds to be similar so that they can be better hidden by the PCI communication. The best choice depends on the size of the 2D FFT and is found empirically.

Suppose there is a 2D FFT of size $Y = X = 8192$ with $\#passes = \#streams = 2$, $Y_1 = 128$ and $Y_2 = 64$. Round one in the naive algorithm has a copy width of $W = 2^{11}$ for each PCI transfer, and roughly 4.7GB/s host to device and 4.2GB/s device to host PCI bus bandwidth can be achieved if the blocked buffer algorithm is used. Without a blocked buffer, only 3.4GB/s and 3.3GB/s are available for direct PCI transfers. The Y decomposition 2D FFT algorithm, however, has a copy width of $W = 2^{17}$ for the host to device transfers in round one and a bandwidth of 5.6GB/s is achieved by a direct PCI transfer. Round two of the algorithm has a copy width of $W = 2^{18}$ for each PCI transfer and can achieve 5.6GB/s and 5.9GB/s for each direction. In other words, close to theoretical peak bandwidth is achieved in all two rounds of PCI transfers by using this Y decomposition 2D FFT algorithm.

A special case where the above 2D FFT algorithms will not work is when the X dimension of a 2D FFT is larger than the GPU memory size. In this case, a naive algorithm needs two rounds PCI transfer and GPU computation just for the X dimensional FFTs and another round for the Y dimensional FFTs. The solution we propose is to decompose the X dimensional FFT using our large 1D FFT algorithm and combine the Y dimensional FFT into one of the two rounds of X dimensional computation. Therefore, still only two rounds of PCI transfer are needed.

6. LARGE 3D FFT

6.1 Naive 3D FFT algorithm

Similar to the 2D FFT case, the natural parallelism in 3D FFTs of size $X \times Y \times Z$ can be translated into a straightforward way to compute large sized 3D FFTs on a GPU if $X \times Z$ and $X \times Y$ can fit into the GPU memory. The data layout in system memory of the naive two round algorithm is shown in figure 9. Z dimensional FFTs are computed in the first round and Y dimensional FFTs in the second round. X dimensional FFTs can be combined into either round depending on which one has less computation. Again the on-GPU Z and Y dimensional FFTs are further decomposed

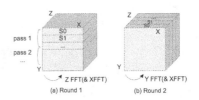

Figure 9: Naive algorithm for large 3D FFT

using the Cooley-Tukey algorithm and are computed by our own kernels. X dimensional FFTs are computed by calling CUFFT for better performance. Each stream in round two accesses a continuous chunk of data on the host memory and therefore has optimum PCI bandwidth during data transfer. However, round one has $C = Z$ number of PCI transfers and each transfer has a data width $W = \frac{XY}{(\#passes) \times (\#streams)}$. For large Z and small $X \times Y$, this round of PCI transfer will have a low effective PCI bus bandwidth according to figure 2. We need to further decompose the Z dimension to avoid this scenario.

6.2 Z decomposition 3D FFT algorithm

Similar to the Y decomposition 2D FFT algorithm, we apply the Cooley-Tukey algorithm once on Z dimensional FFTs of a 3D FFT when Z is large. For $Z = Z_1 \times Z_2$, a direct 3D FFT represented as $\{d(Z, XY, XY)d(Y, X, X)d(x, 1, 1)\}$ is transformed into the tensor format as is shown in equation (6) after applying a DIT algorithm on Z.

$$\{d(Z_1, XYZ_2, XY)t_{Z_2}^{Z_1}d(Z_2, XYZ_1, XYZ_1)$$
$$d(Y, X, X)d(X, 1, 1)\} \quad (6)$$

The system memory layout of this Z decomposition algorithm for 3D FFT with large Z is illustrated in figure 10. The PCI bandwidth

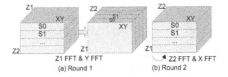

Figure 10: Z decomposition algorithm for large 3D FFT

analysis of this algorithm is similar to that of the Y decomposition 2D FFT algorithm except that Y becomes Z and X becomes $X \times Y$ in this case. A close to optimum PCI bandwidth is achieved for all four transfers between the host and device if Z_1 and Z_2 are chosen to be close.

Strictly following equation (6), only FFTs of size Z_1 will be computed in round one and all Z_2, Y and X kernels will be in round two. The computation will be extremely unbalanced between the two rounds. Particularly, the computation time in round two will be difficult to be hidden in the communication time. Instead, we apply an optimization proposed in paper [8] to rearrange the computation order. The general reorder rule is that the order of these I/O dimensions can be adjusted as long as FFTs of size Z_1 appears before FFTs of size Z_2. Therefore, we can exchange the I/O dimension $d(Z_2, XYZ_1, XYZ_1)$ and $d(Y, X, X)$ and still have the correct output. The result of this reordered 3D FFT is shown in formula (7).

$$\{d(Z_1, XYZ_2, XY)t_{Z_2}^{Z_1}d(Y, X, X)$$
$$d(Z_2, XYZ_1, XYZ_1)d(X, 1, 1)\} \quad (7)$$

260

Now, Y dimensional FFT is computed in the first round of computation and X dimensional in the second round as is shown in figure 10. Moreover, size Y FFTs and size X FFTs can be exchanged as well in order to best balance the computation between two rounds.

There are two corner cases of large 3D FFTs that can not be handled by the above two algorithms. One is that $X \times Y$ is larger than the GPU's memory size (but X is still smaller). The other one is that X alone is larger than the GPU memory size. In the first case, the Y dimensional FFT can be decomposed and, in the second case, X can be decomposed using the Cooley-Tukey. A two-round decomposition algorithm can be derived using the I/O tensor representation to achieve a good bandwidth over PCI. These two-round decomposition schemes are similar to our large 1D FFT and the large 2D FFT algorithms and therefore are not further discussed here.

7. EVALUATION

In this section, we present the performance of our large 1D, 2D and 3D FFT implementations on three NVIDIA GPUs, i.e. GeForce GTX480, Tesla C1060 and Tesla C2070. Of the three GPUs, the GTX480 and the C2070 are based on the latest GF400/Fermi architecture while the C1060 is based on the slightly older GT200 architecture. Details of the three NVIDIA GPUs and the related configurations of their host systems are listed in table 1.

The host machine of the GTX480 and C2070 has a high-end Intel i7 920 CPU. The performance of FFTW and MKL on this CPU is compared with that of our FFT library on the two Fermi-based GPUs. The host CPU for the C1060 is an Intel server CPU Xeon E5405. The configuration of the CPUs and the CPU based FFT libraries are listed in table 2. In FFTW, the support of the Single Instruction Multiple Data (SIMD) extension is enabled to take advantage of the vector instructions (SSE2) on the Intel CPUs. FFTW's *patient level*, choices of search method and search space size, is set as 'MEASURE'. This method takes around 30 minutes on searching for large sized FFTs in our test but it provides much better performance than a lower patient level, 'ESTIMATE'. Since all host CPUs are multi-core processors, multithreading is enabled and the performance with different number of threads is shown for both FFTW and MKL. In short, the performance of FFTW and MKL is configured to be their best on our test systems.

Currently this work handles 1D, 2D and 3D FFTs with power-of-two sizes, and other sizes can be easily included by adding codelets of different sizes. The FFT computation is performed out-of-place, which preserves the input array. The input and output are complex number and can be in either double precision or single precision. Only double precision results are shown due to its higher accuracy, which is valuable particularly for large FFT sizes. The correctness of our FFT's output is checked by a comparison with FFTW and MKL on the same input.

The range of the FFT size in our test is determined by both the size of the system memory and the size of the GPU memory. The smallest test case is the smallest FFT problem that cannot fit into GPU memory or computed by CUFFT, and the largest test case is the largest power-of-two FFT that can fit into pinned system memory. For a D dimensional out-of-place complex FFT with double precision, the total number of elements $M = N_1 \cdot N_2 \cdot ... \cdot N_D$ should be equal or larger than 32M for GTX480, 64M for C1060 and 128M for C2070 and should be equal or smaller than 256M due to the available CPU memory on our system. In fact, our algorithm is able to handle much larger FFTs if given more system memory. Finally, as a convention, the performance of FFT is reported in GFLOPS defined in equation (8) where t is the execution time in seconds.

$$GFlops = \frac{5M \sum_{d=1}^{D} log_2 N_d}{t} * 10^{-9} \qquad (8)$$

7.1 Performance of Large 1D FFTs

Figure 11 shows the performance of 1D FFTs of size 32M to 256M in log_2 scale on GTX480 and C2070. FFTW and Intel MKL's performance on the host system with an Intel i7 920 CPU is listed as a comparison. FFTW shows good scalability when the number of threads is within 4. FFTW with 8 threads has similar performance to 4 threads on this 4-core CPU, and both achieve around 6 to 7.5GFLOPS. MKL has similar scalability but performs significantly worse than FFTW on sizes of 128M and 256M. Our large 1D FFT on the GTX480 achieves 11GFLOPS, on average, and is 62% faster than FFTW and $2.4\times$ faster than MKL with 4 threads. Compared with a single thread on a CPU, our GPU FFT is $4.5\times$ faster than FFTW and $3.3\times$ faster than MKL. Our peak performance of 15.5GFLOPS is achieved on the size of 32M. This problem size can actually fit into the GPU but CUFFT is somehow unable to compute it. In this particular case, our approach needs only one round of PCI transfer although a global synchronization in between two rounds of computation remains necessary.

A Tesla C2070, on the other hand, supports duplex communication on the PCIe bus, which theoretically has bi-directional bandwidth of 16GB/s. However, its 1D FFT performance is only 10% to 15% faster than that of GTX480. A possible reason is that duplex PCI transfers cannot properly overlap with a memory-bound kernel like FFT, because host to device transfer, device to host transfer and kernel accesses on global memory may result in a bottleneck in global memory bandwidth or its memory control unit. For the two largest 1D FFTs, the C2070 achieves 11GFLOPs and is $1.7\times$ times faster than FFTW and $3.55\times$ faster than MKL with 4 threads. Compared with a single CPU thread, the C2070 is $4.5-4.8\times$ faster.

Figure 12 shows the performance of 1D FFTs of size 64M to 256M on a Tesla C1060. Intel MKL crashes when performing a 1D FFT of size 256M and therefore this point is not shown. On the Intel Xeon E5405, FFTW with 4 threads achieves 3.6GFLOPS and MKL achieves 3.0GFLOPS for large 1D FFTs on average. Our library on the C1060 achieves 4.2GFLOPS, which is 16.7% faster than the 4-thread FFTW but is much worse than our library on Fermi GPUs. This is because the C1060 has much fewer double precision ALUs compared with the Fermi cards. The double-precision performance of pre-Fermi GPUs is about only 10% of the single-precision performance.

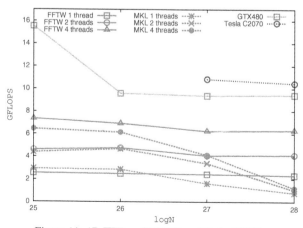

Figure 11: 1D FFT on GTX480 and Tesla C2070

GPU	Global Memory	CUDA Driver	Nvcc & Cufft	PCI	System Memory
GeForce GTX480	1.5GB	260.19.21	3.2	PCIe2.0 x16	12GB
Tesla C2070	6GB	260.19.21	3.2	PCIe2.0 x16	12GB
Tesla C1060	4GB	256.53	3.1	PCIe2.0 x16	9GB

Table 1: Configuration of GPUs

CPU	Frequency	Cores	GCC	FFTW	MKL	System Memory
i7 920	2.66GHz	4	4.4.3	3.2.2	10.2.6	12GB
Xeon E5405	2.00GHz	4	4.1.2	3.2.2	10.2.6	9GB

Table 2: Configuration CPUs and FFT libraries

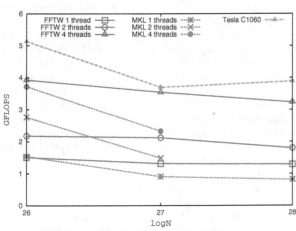

Figure 12: 1D FFT on Tesla C1060

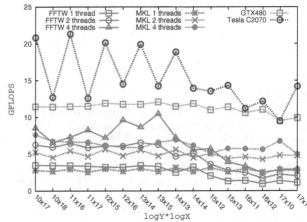

Figure 14: 2D FFT $Y \times X \geq 128M$ on GTX480 and Tesla C2070

Moreover, C1060's best PCI bandwidth of a single array transfer (when C=1 and W=64M) is only 5.6GB/s for host to device and 4.3GB/s for device to host transfers, which is much worse than that of Fermi GPUs. As a result, our blocked buffer algorithm achieves lower PCI bus bandwidth on the C1060 as well.

7.2 Performance of Large 2D FFTs

This section shows the performance of 2D FFTs with size $Y \times X$, where $32M \leq Y \times X \leq 256M$. Due to a large number of test points, the results on GTX480 are divided into two figures. Figure 13 shows the 2D FFTs where $Y \times X \leq 64M$ and figure 14 shows those $Y \times X \geq 128M$. Different $Y \times X$ sizes are indexed in an increasing order of Y. Similar to 1D, FFTW shows a good scalability up to 4 threads in

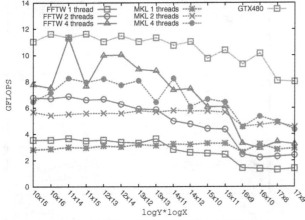

Figure 13: 2D FFT $Y \times X \leq 64M$ on GTX480

both figures. FFTW with 8 threads has almost the same performance as 4 threads, and therefore is not shown. As we can see, FFTW's performance decreases dramatically from 10GFLOPS to less than 3GFLOPS with the increase of Y due to the loss of data locality in the Y dimensional computation. However, MKL with 2 threads and 4 threads suffers less from the loss of Y dimensional locality on this Intel CPU and performs better than FFTW.

Because we divide the Y computation into two rounds, our 2D FFTs on a GTX480 has a much smaller performance decrease with the increase of Y than FFTW. We achieve an average of 10.9GFLOPS, which is 64% and 69% faster than FFTW and MKL with 4 threads. Since CUFFT on the C2070 can compute 2D FFTs with size $Y \times X \leq 64M$, our FFT results on C2070 are only shown in figure 14. The fluctuation in figure 14 is because 2D FFTs of size $Y \times X = 128M$ can fit into the 6GB global memory on the C2070 but somehow cannot be handled by CUFFT. For these sizes, we only need the host to device transfer of round one and the device to host transfer of round two in our algorithm, and can eliminate the PCI transfer of intermediate results. The best 2D FFT performance on the C2070 is 21GFLOPS for a size of 1024×65536. On average, the C2070 achieves 15.2GFLOPS and is 2.3× faster than FFTW and 2.4× faster than MKL with 4 threads on an Intel i7. C2070 has four times more double precision ALU than GTX480, however its speedup over GTX480 is not big for a communication bound problem like FFT.

Figure 15 shows our large 2D FFT test results on the Tesla C1060 and the performance of FFTW and MKL on the Intel Xeon machine. FFTW's performance decreases with the increase of the Y dimension but MKL is much better for these sizes. Our 2D FFT achieves 7.88GFLOPS and is 2.66× faster than FFTW and 2.13× faster than MKL with 4 threads.

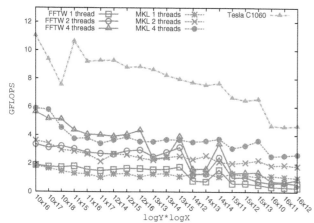

Figure 15: 2D FFT $Y \times X$ on C1060

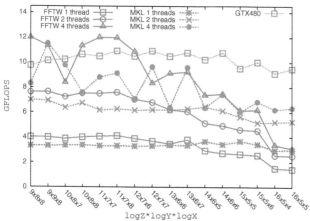

Figure 16: 3D FFT $Z \times Y \times X \leq 64M$ on GTX480

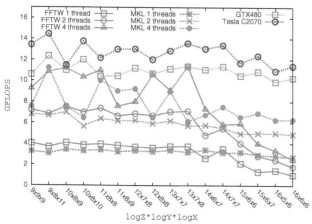

Figure 17: 3D FFT $Z \times Y \times X \leq 128M$ on GTX480 and Tesla C2070

7.3 Performance of Large 3D FFTs

Figures16 and 17 illustrate the performance comparison of our large FFT library with FFTW and MKL for 3D FFTs of size $N = Z \times Y \times X$, where $32M \leq N \leq 256M$. FFTW with 4 threads performs slightly better than our GPU library for small Z values, but its performance decreases quickly as Z increases. MKL's 3D FFTs with 4 threads have similar performance with FFTW and is better than FFTW for large Z. Our high dimensional decomposition algorithm shows a big advantage when the highest dimension of the FFT is larger than 2048. FFTW and MKL quickly lose data

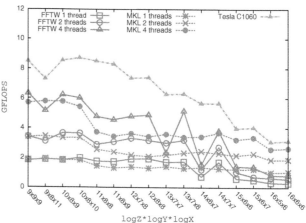

Figure 18: 3D FFT $Z \times Y \times X \leq 64M$ on C1060

locality for these sizes and therefore perform much worse than our GPU library. Overall, our library has an average of 10.6GFLOPS on the GTX480 and is 27% faster than FFTW and 52% faster than MKL. The C2070, on the other hand, achieves 12.7GFLOPS for large 3D FFTs which can be attributed to its duplex PCI communication ability.

The performance of FFTW and MKL on the Xeon E5405 and our 3D FFTs on the Tesla C1060 is shown in figure 18. Compared with the Fermi GPU cards, 3D FFTs on the C1060 have an obvious performance decrease with the increase of the Z dimension. Our Z decomposition algorithm decreases the number of PCI transfers from Z to Z_1 and Z_2. However, with the increase of Z, the number of PCI transfers still increases slowly. The effective PCI bus bandwidth for the C1060 card decreases faster than for Fermi based GPUs. This leads to an obvious decrease in performance for 3D FFTs on the C1060 when Z is large. Overall, the C1060 still achieves 6.4GFLOPS, on average, and is 72% faster than FFTW with 4 threads and and 64% faster than MKL' best performance.

Overall, our GPU based large FFT library is faster than multithreaded FFTW and MKL on almost all 1D, 2D and 3D FFT sizes. The performance of the Tesla C2070 is slightly better than the GeForce GTX480 and both Fermi cards are much faster than the GT200 based Tesla C1060. Across 1D, 2D and 3D sizes, the C1060 has an average performance of 7GFLOPS, a GTX480 achieves 11GFLOPS and the C2070 achieves 14GFLOPS. As a comparison, both FFTW and MKL achieve only 3.5GFLOPS on the Xeon and about 7GFLOPS on i7. We also tested our library with single precision data. Because FFT is a communication bounded problem, both the performance of our large FFT library and CPU based libraries have 50% to 100% speedup over their double precision results. The speedup of our GPU FFT library over the CPU libraries is similar to the double precision case. We do not show these single precision results here simply due to limited space.

7.4 Precision of Our Large FFTs

The correctness of our large GPU FFT library is verified by a comparison with FFTW and MKL. All three libraries are tested with the same double precision pseudo-random input data in the range of $[-0.5, 0.5)$ and the difference in output is quantized as root mean square error (RMSE) over the whole data set. Let us assume there are two complex FFT output arrays of length N, (x_i, y_i) and (X_i, Y_i). The RMSE between these two output arrays is calculated as shown in equation (9)

$$RMSE = \sqrt{\frac{\sum_{i=1}^{N} \left((x_i - X_i)^2 + (y_i - Y_i)^2 \right)}{N}} \qquad (9)$$

The RMSE is a widely used metric to measure the relative accuracy of two computations. Lower RMSE value means the two computation routines produce more similar result. The RMSE results of the 1D, 2D and 3D FFTs between our GPU FFT and FFTW are shown as the solid bars in figure 19. Overall, the RMSE is extremely small and is in the range of $(1.4 \times 10^{-12}, 3.6 \times 10^{-12})$. With the increase of FFT size, the RMSE increase almost linearly. The RMSE between MKL and our GPU FFT library, shown as the shadowed bars in figure19, is of the same order of magnitude as the FFTW results.

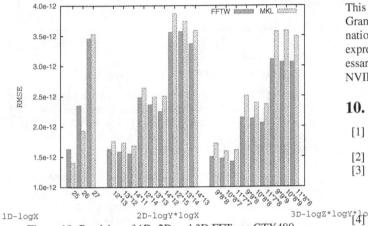

Figure 19: Precision of 1D, 2D and 3D FFTs on GTX480

8. CONCLUSION AND FUTURE WORKS

This is the first work that enables GPUs to efficiently compute FFTs of such large sizes on a single compute node. So far, CUFFT and many other CUDA based FFT libraries have mostly been focusing on FFT's on-card performance. There are at least two limitations of the FFT performance they have achieved. First, their FFT size is limited by the GPU on-card memory. Second, a user has to transfer the FFT's input and output data between CPU and GPU memory via PCI bus. When the data transfer over PCI bus is counted in, this transfer time can easily eliminate the majority of the GPU's on-card performance advantage. This work is the first step in attacking the above two realistic problems in the case of FFT and has achieved success in the comparison with CPU based FFT libraries.

In this paper, we propose a computation framework for GPUs to efficiently compute large 1D, 2D and 3D FFTs that do not fit into GPU memory. Unlike on-card FFT problems, whose performance depends on the speed of the GPU memory and the number of ALUs, the dominant performance factor for such large FFTs is the PCI bus bandwidth and the balance of computation. Specifically, we propose a couple of FFT related decomposition algorithms and a general blocked buffer algorithm to maximize the effective PCI bus bandwidth and best hide the computation time. The FFT computation kernels on GPUs are generated following an on-card FFT computation work proposed in paper [8]. For a high-end GPU, NVIDIA's GTX480, our algorithms achieve a speedup of 1.62× for 1D, 1.65× for 2D and 1.28× for 3D over FFTW with multithreading enabled on an Intel i7 CPU. Even higher speedup is achieved on a Tesla C2070, i.e. 1.5×, 2.3× and 1.53×, over FFTW.

This work can be easily extended to higher dimensional FFTs, FFTs with non power-of-two sizes and multi-GPU architectures. The idea behind our decomposition algorithm is to maximize the data locality of arrays to be transferred over the PCI bus, through

both algorithmic manipulation and implementation optimization, so that a better bandwidth can be achieved. This FFT decomposition framework and the algorithms proposed in this paper may also be applied to FFTs in other hierarchical memory or communication bound problems other than FFT, where high performance can also be achieved by maximizing the memory or network bandwidth.

9. ACKNOWLEDGMENTS

We thank the anonymous reviewers for their helpful suggestions. This work is supported by the National Science Foundation under Grant No. 0746034 and 0904534 and NVIDIA's equipment donation. Any opinions, findings, conclusions or recommendations expressed in this material are those of the authors and do not necessarily reflect the views of the National Science Foundation or NVIDIA.

10. REFERENCES

[1] M. Frigo and SG Johnson. "The FFTW web page" http://www.fftw.org, 2010.

[2] "The SPIRAL Project" http://www.spiral.net, 2010.

[3] F. Franchetti and Y. etc. Voronenko. FFT program generation for shared memory: SMP and multicore. In *SC 2006 Conference, Proceedings of the ACM/IEEE*, pages 51–51. IEEE, 2006.

[4] "Intel Math Kernel Library" http://software.intel.com/en-us/articles/intel-mkl/, 2010.

[5] "NVIDIA CUFFT Library" http://developer.nvidia.com/object/cuda_3_2_downloads.html, 2010.

[6] N.K. Govindaraju and B. etc. Lloyd. High performance discrete Fourier transforms on graphics processors. In *Proceedings of the 2008 ACM/IEEE conference on Supercomputing*, pages 1–12. IEEE Press, 2008.

[7] A. Nukada and S. Matsuoka. Auto-tuning 3-D FFT library for CUDA GPUs. In *Proceedings of the Conference on High Performance Computing Networking, Storage and Analysis*, pages 1–10. ACM, 2009.

[8] L. Gu, X. Li, and J. Siegel. An empirically tuned 2D and 3D FFT library on CUDA GPU. In *Proceedings of the 24th ACM International Conference on Supercomputing*, pages 305–314. ACM, 2010.

[9] D.H. Bailey. FFTs in external of hierarchical memory. In *Proceedings of the 1989 ACM/IEEE conference on Supercomputing*, pages 234–242. ACM, 1989.

[10] A. Gupta and V. Kumar. The scalability of FFT on parallel computers. *IEEE Transactions on Parallel and Distributed Systems*, pages 922–932, 1993.

[11] D. Takahashi and Y. Kanada. High-performance radix-2, 3 and 5 parallel 1-D complex FFT algorithms for distributed-memory parallel computers. *The Journal of Supercomputing*, 15(2):207–228, 2000.

[12] Y. Chen and X. etc. Cui. Large-scale FFT on GPU clusters. In *Proceedings of the 24th ACM International Conference on Supercomputing*, pages 315–324. ACM, 2010.

[13] Matteo Frigo and Steven G. Johnson. The design and implementation of fftw3. *Proceeding of the IEEE*, 93(2):216–231, February 2005.

[14] J.W. Cooley and J.W. Tukey. An algorithm for the machine computation of complex Fourier series. *Mathematics of Computation*, 19(90):297–301, 1965.

[15] M. Frigo and SG Johnson. The Fastest Fourier Transform in the West. 1997.

[16] M. Frigo. A fast Fourier transform compiler. *ACM SIGPLAN Notices*, 34(5):169–180, 1999.

[17] Whitepaper NVIDIA's next generation cuda compute architecture: Fermi, 2009.

Automatic SIMD Vectorization of Fast Fourier Transforms for the Larrabee and AVX Instruction Sets

Daniel S. McFarlin
Department of Electrical and
Computer Engineering
Carnegie Mellon University
Pittsburgh, PA USA 15213
dmcfarli@ece.cmu.edu

Volodymyr Arbatov
Department of Electrical and
Computer Engineering
Carnegie Mellon University
Pittsburgh, PA USA 15213
arbatov@ece.cmu.edu

Franz Franchetti
Department of Electrical and
Computer Engineering
Carnegie Mellon University
Pittsburgh, PA USA 15213
franzf@ece.cmu.edu

Markus Püschel
Department of Computer
Science
ETH Zurich
8092 Zurich, Switzerland
pueschel@inf.ethz.ch

ABSTRACT

The well-known shift to parallelism in CPUs is often associated with multicores. However another trend is equally salient: the increasing parallelism in per-core single-instruction multiple-date (SIMD) vector units. Intel's SSE and IBM's VMX (compatible to AltiVec) both offer 4-way (single precision) floating point, but the recent Intel instruction sets AVX and Larrabee (LRB) offer 8-way and 16-way, respectively. Compilation and optimization for vector extensions is hard, and often the achievable speed-up by using vectorizing compilers is small compared to hand-optimization using intrinsic function interfaces. Unfortunately, the complexity of these intrinsics interfaces increases considerably with the vector length, making hand-optimization a nightmare. In this paper, we present a peephole-based vectorization system that takes as input the vector instruction semantics and outputs a library of basic data reorganization blocks such as small transpositions and perfect shuffles that are needed in a variety of high performance computing applications. We evaluate the system by generating the blocks needed by the program generator Spiral for vectorized fast Fourier transforms (FFTs). With the generated FFTs we achieve a vectorization speed-up of 5.5–6.5 for 8-way AVX and 10–12.5 for 16-way LRB. For the latter instruction counts are used since no timing information is available. The combination of the proposed system and Spiral thus automates the production of high performance FFTs for current and future vector architectures.

Categories and Subject Descriptors

D.3.4 [**Software**]: Programming Languages—*Code generation, Optimization*

General Terms

Performance

Keywords

Autovectorization, super-optimization, SIMD, program generation, Fourier transform

1. Introduction

Power and area constraints are increasingly dictating microarchitectural developments in the commodity and high-performance (HPC) CPU space. Consequently, the once dominant approach of dynamically extracting instruction-level parallelism (ILP) through monolithic out-of-order microarchitectures is being supplanted by designs with simpler, replicable architectural features. This trend is most evident in the proliferation of architectures containing many symmetrical processing cores. Such designs provide for flexible power management and reduced area by trading dynamic ILP for static, software-defined thread-level parallelism. A similar trade-off is occurring with the steadily increasing vector-width and complexity of single-instruction-multiple-data (SIMD) vector instruction sets.

AVX and Larrabee. Intel's recent AVX and Larrabee (LRB) architectures feature 256-bit and 512-bit vector-lengths respectively; architectures with 1024-bit long vectors are already planned [2, 24]. Vector functional units and vector registers are regular structures which are fairly easy to replicate and expand. Like multiple cores, vector units provide for flexible power management in that individual vector functional units can be selectively idled. SIMD instructions also represent a form of scalar instruction compression thereby reducing the power and area consumed by instruction decoding. Collectively, this architectural trend towards multiple cores and wide vectors has fundamentally shifted the burden of achieving performance from hardware to software.

Programming SIMD extensions. In contrast to multiple cores, SIMD architectures require software to explicitly encode fine-grain data-level parallelism using the SIMD instruction set. These SIMD instruction sets are quickly evolving as vendors add new instructions with every CPU generation, and SIMD extensions are incompatible across CPU vendors. Consequently, explicitly vectorized code is hard to write and inherently non-portable. The complexity of SIMD instruction sets complicates hand-vectorization while auto-vectorization just like auto-parallelization poses a continuing challenge for compilers.

The latest version of production compilers (Intel C++, IBM XL C, and Gnu C) all contain autovectorization technology [17, 36, 15] that provides speed-up across a large class of computation kernels. However, for many kernels like the fast Fourier transform (FFT) and matrix multiplication, the results are usually suboptimal [8] since optimal vectorization requires algorithm knowledge or there are simply too many choices that the compiler cannot evaluate.

Much of the difficulty in vectorization lies in the instructions required to transform and keep data in vector form. These shuffle or permutation instructions are generally the most complex and expensive operations in the SIMD instruction set. They tend to scale poorly, may not support arbitrary permutations and their parameters become increasingly non-obvious to use, especially with wider vector units. From a performance point of view, shuffle instructions are the overhead imposed by vectorization, which prevents the perfect speedup linear in the vector length. Consequently, minimizing the number and cost of shuffles is crucial.

Contribution. This paper makes two key contributions. First, we present a super-optimization infrastructure that takes as input the instruction set specification and automates the discovery of efficient SIMD instruction sequences for basic data reorganization operations such as small matrix transpositions and stride permutations. These are required, for example, by many high performance computing kernels including the FFT and linear algebra kernels.

Second, we incorporate this infrastructure into the library generator Spiral to generate the reordering blocks needed for FFT vectorization [8]. This approach effectively automates the porting of FFTs to new vector architectures. We then evaluate efficacy by automatically generating vectorized FFTs for AVX and LRB. We demonstrate speed-ups (measured using runtime or instruction counts) of 5.5–6.5 for 8-way AVX and 10–12.5 for 16-way LRB. We also compare the AVX code against Intel's IPP. For LRB, no benchmarks are available at the time of writing.

Besides this main contribution, with AVX and Larrabee it now becomes possible to study efficiency and overhead of vectorization methods across a range of vector lengths: 2, 4, 8, and 16 for single-precision floating-point. We include such a study for Spiral's FFT vectorization.

2. Related Work

The work in this paper extends the SIMD support in the Spiral system. It is related to vectorization techniques developed for traditional vector computers, SIMDization techniques developed for short length SIMD vector instruction sets, superoptimization, and SIMD support by program generators like FFTW.

SIMD instructions in Spiral. The inspiration for this work comes from earlier work extending Spiral [29, 7, 9] to SIMD vector architectures. Spiral is a domain-specific library generator that automates the production of high performance code for linear transforms, notably the discrete Fourier Transform [35]. Previous efforts to extend Spiral to SIMD vector architectures are described in [6, 8, 10]. Spiral's approach breaks the vectorization problem into two stages. First, rewriting produces SIMD FFTs [6, 8, 10] that reduce the problem to a small set of basic reordering operations (matrix transpositions of small matrices held in SIMD registers). Second, a small code generator is used to produce short instruction sequences for these operations [11] given only the instruction set specification as input. Unfortunately, experiments showed that the method in [11] does not scale (i.e., is too expensive) to AVX and LRB. Hence the motivation for this paper, which offers a replacement for [11]

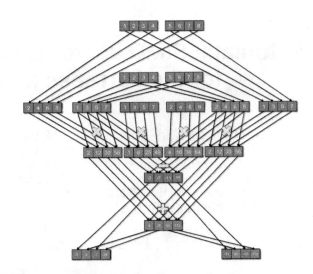

Figure 1: The dataflow of an SSE-vectorized kernel. The computation is an element-wise multiplication of two complex input arrays (blue and red) of length four in interleaved format.

that is designed for both longer vector lengths and more complex instruction sets.

Vectorization. Automatic vectorization has been the subject of extensive study in the literature. Two excellent references are [21, 37]. Vectorization becomes (again) increasingly important for SIMD extensions like Larrabee and the latest versions of SSE (SSE 4.1) that allow for efficient implementation of gather/scatter operations and large data caches, since the conditions on such architectures are similar to traditional vector computers.

SIMDization. Originating from SIMD within a register (SWAR) [5, 34], SIMDization was recognized as a hybrid between vectorization and instruction level parallelism extraction [1]. Recent advances in compilation techniques for SIMD vector instruction sets in the presence of alignment and stride constraints are described in [4, 28]. SIMD instruction extraction for two-way architectures aimed at basic blocks is presented in [22]. This technique is included in FFTW 2.1.5 [13, 12] and has shown good performance improvements across multiple two-way SIMD extensions. FFTW3 [14] contains SIMD codelets for SSE and AltiVec, supporting vector lengths of 2 and 4.

Superoptimization. The classic paper on super-optimization is [26] while [3] presents a modern approach that is close in spirit to our own. A dataflow-graph and integer-linear programming based approach to finding SIMD permutations was described by [23] and is similar to our approach though it is unclear what sort of vectorization efficiencies are attained. The approach explored in [30] also focuses on SIMD permutations with an emphasis on linear transforms including the FFT. However, only small kernels (max size: 64-point FFT) are investigated and the overall scalability of their solution to larger vector widths and larger kernels is not addressed. The difficulties of optimizing for a wide range of SIMD vector architectures are well explored in [27, 16].

3. Vectorization Efficiency and Motivation

Vectorization overhead impacts even simple kernels. Consider the case of the element-wise product of two arrays each containing four complex element in interleaved form (alternating real and imaginary parts). On a traditional scalar processor, this kernel requires 24 floating point operations: 4 multiplications, 1 addition and 1 subtraction per complex product. Figure 1 shows the dataflow

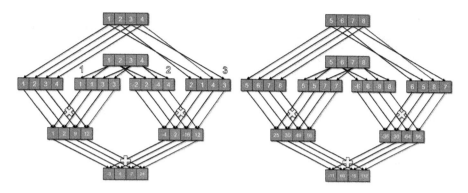

Figure 2: The same computation as in Fig. 1 performed on LRB using again a vector width of size four.

of a vectorized version of this kernel on Intel's SSE SIMD architecture with a vector width of four (4-way). The six vectorized arithmetic instructions (yellow symbols) in this figure are straightforward but the de- and re-interleaving of real and imaginary elements is less obvious and requires six shuffle instructions as overhead.

We quantify the vectorization efficiency by calculating the ratio of total floating point operations in the scalar kernel to the total number of vector instructions in the vectorized kernel. In Fig. 1 the efficiency is $24/(6+6) = 2$. An ideal vectorization (not possible in this case) would yield $24/6 = 4 =$ vector length as efficiency.

Vectorization efficiency is a good first-order indicator of performance and enables the study of different vector architectures even if the architecture is not yet available.

Figure 2 gives a first idea of the difficulties in vectorization. It shows the same kernel as in Fig. 1 this time 4-way vectorized for LRB (only 4 out of the 16 slots in the vector register are shown for simplicity; the labels 1–3 are explained later). The data flow is non-intuitive but now has an overhead of only 4 shuffles and thus an improved efficiency of $24/(6+4) = 2.4$.

4. AVX and Larrabee

We give a brief overview of Intel's AVX instruction set and a more in-depth view of LRB, with focus on the Larrabee new instructions (LRBni).

4.1 Advanced Vector Extension

Intel's latest extension to the SSE family is the Advanced Vector Extension (AVX) [2]. It extends the 128-bit SSE register into 256-bit AVX registers, that consist of two 128-bit lanes. An AVX lane is an extension of SSE4.2 functionality, including fused multiply-add instructions and three-operand instructions. AVX operates most efficiently when the same operations are performed on both lanes. Cross-lane operations are limited and expensive. AVX defines 4-way 64-bit double precision, 8-way 32-bit single precision, and integer operations.

AVX shuffle instructions. AVX essentially implements SSE's 128-bit shuffle operation for both lanes, with some extensions to support parameter vectors. In addition it defines one cross-lane shuffle operation. This leads to higher shuffle-overhead since many operations now require both cross-lane and intra-lane shuffling. In Listing 4.1 we show the intrinsic function prototypes of 4-way double and 8-way single AVX shuffle instructions. The parameter space of AVX shuffle instructions is much larger compared to 2-way and 4-way SSE instructions.

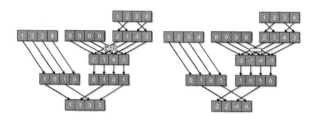

Figure 3: An expanded view of the LRB swizzle and writemask features used to sign-change and reorder vectors for complex multiplication. The left and right image corresponds to labels 1 and 2 in Figure 2, respectively. Each is a single LRB instruction.

Listing 1: AVX shuffle instructions.

```
__m256d _mm256_unpacklo_pd(__m256d a, __m256d b);
__m256d _mm256_unpackhi_pd(__m256d a, __m256d b);
__m256d _mm256_shuffle_pd(__m256d a, __m256d b, const int select);
__m256d _mm256_permute2_pd(__m256d a, __m256d b, __m256i control, int imm);
__m256d _mm256_permute2f128_pd(__m256d a, __m256d b, int control);
__m256d _mm256_permute_pd(__m256d a, int control);

__m256 _mm256_unpacklo_ps(__m256 a, __m256 b);
__m256 _mm256_unpackhi_ps(__m256 a, __m256 b);
__m256 _mm256_permute2f128_ps(__m256 a, __m256 b, int control);
__m256 _mm256_permute2_ps(__m256 a, __m256 b, __m256i control, int imm);
__m256 _mm256_shuffle_ps(__m256 a, __m256 b, const int select);
__m256 _mm256_permute_ps(__m256 a, int control);
__m256 _mm256_permutevar_ps(__m256 a, __m256i control);
```

4.2 Larrabee

Intel's LRB architecture can be described as a chip-level multiprocessor containing a large number of cache-coherent, in-order x86 cores. LRB leverages legacy code through compatibility with the standard Intel x86 32/64 scalar instruction set but features a novel and powerful SIMD vector instruction set known as LRBni (Larrabee New Instructions). We restrict our discussion of LRB to the architectural features most relevant to vectorization and refer the reader to [31, 24] for a more comprehensive discussion.

The LRB core is a dual-pipeline architecture that shares many similarities with the well known P5 Pentium architecture. LRB's vector unit and LRBni, however represent a significant departure from previous commodity vector architectures. To elaborate, we return to Figure 2. Label 1 shows data reordering on the second vector input. Label 2 shows data reordering and a sign-change of the same input vector. Label 3 shows data reordering being performed on the remaining input vector. This reordering operation is folded into the subsequent computation while Labels 1 and 2 require one instruction each. All told, there are 4 reordering instructions in this kernel compared to 6 reordering instructions in the SSE kernel shown in Figure 1.

LRBni ISA. We now briefly discuss the LRBni vector exten-

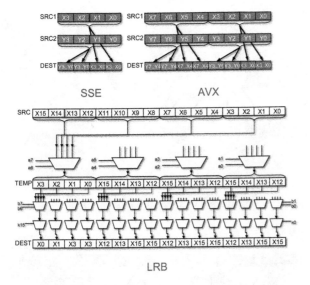

Figure 4: The LRBni vector extension.

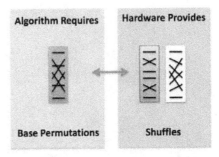

Figure 5: The problem of mapping basic permutations to vector shuffle instructions

sion. The 512-bit registers are grouped into 4 128-bit lanes. The 512-bit registers can hold either 8 double-precision numbers or 16 single-precision numbers. The 16-way vector can be interpreted as 4-by-4 matrix. Instructions (see Figure 3) contain multiple parts: 1) Source operands can be reordered (within lanes) before being used. 2) All standard arithmetic operations are supported (including addition, subtraction, multiplication, fused multiply-add and add-sub) and performed in parallel on all vector slots. 3) A selector describes which of the result vector slots are actually written into the destination, and which results are discarded. In addition, step 1 is exposed as instructions as well. LRBni instructions are complicated with may parameters, and the intrinsic interface decouples LRBni instructions into multiple intrinsics to make programming manageable. We show examples of LRBni instructions in Listing 4.2 Below we discuss some of the LRBni instructions important for this paper in more detail.

Swizzles. Returning to Figure 3 we note that the reduction in reordering instructions is achievable due to the dedicated reorder HW in LRB's vector unit. This HW provides for a limited set of nondestructive shuffles, known as swizzles, which can be performed on one in-register vector operand per vector instruction. The swizzles used to implement Labels 1 and 2 in Figure 2 are shown in Figure 3. Label 1's implementation is shown on the left and uses a binary-OR taking three vector inputs; vector instructions in LRB are ternary. The first and third operands are sourced from the same register. We binary-OR the swizzled third operand with the zero vector and merge the result with the first vector operand in accordance with a writemask. This writemask is stored in one of the mask registers and is an optional argument to most vector instructions. It dictates which elements in the third vector operand are overwritten.

Listing 2: Implementation of complex multiplication using LRB intrinsics

```
// v0, v1: input vectors of interleaved complex floats
__m512 zero  = _mm512_setzero();
__m512 s0    = _mm512_swizzle_r32(v0, _MM_SWIZ_REG_CDAB);
__m512 reals = _mm512_mask_or_pi(v0, 0xAAAA, zero, s0);
__m512 imags = _mm512_mask_sub_ps(v0, 0x5555, zero, s0);
__m512 t0    = _mm512_mul_ps(reals, v1);
__m512 s1    = _mm512_swizzle_r32(v1, _MM_SWIZ_REG_CDAB);
__m512 res   = _mm512_madd231_ps(t0, imags, s1);
```

The computation required for Label 2 is similar with the use

of a subtraction instruction to affect a sign-change and a different writemask. For completeness, we show the C code with LRB intrinsics that implements the entire kernel in Listing 4.2. This code listing also shows the use of one of LRB's many fused multiply-add (FMA) instructions. The combination of FMAs and swizzles enables LRB's complex multiplication kernel to attain a vectorization efficiency of 3 for the simplified 4-way case; the 16-way case has the same relative efficiency at 12 floating-point operations/vector instruction.

Broadcasts, gathers, and memory operations. LRB's vector unit also features extensive support for L1-cache-to-register operations. Of particular interest is the replicate hardware which enables efficient scalar broadcasts from memory and can be used with virtually all vector instructions. Scatter/gather functionality exists in the form of two instructions which take a base address and a vector of offsets. Another useful pair of instructions are those which can pack/unpack data and handle unaligned memory accesses. For LRB's remaining non-reordering vector instructions we refer the reader to [25].

LRBni shuffle operations. Finally, there is the unary LRB shuffle, depicted at the bottom of Figure 4. Because the reorder hardware only supports a limited set of shuffles we must rely on the dedicated shuffle instruction for more general, arbitrary reorderings. As stated before, shuffle instructions are generally the most expensive vector instructions and do not particularly scale well; encoding a fully general unary shuffle for a 16-way architecture requires 64 bits. If this 64 bit value is stored directly in the shuffle instruction it complicates the instruction decoders. Conversely, storing this value in a separate, scalar register complicates the datapath.

5. Superoptimizer for Data Permutations

In this section we explain how we automatically derive short (efficient) instruction sequences to implement important basic data reorganizations (permutations). The data to be permuted fits into a few vector registers and the data permutations we consider have a regular structure. Two important examples are 1) the interleaving/deinterleaving of two vectors of complex numbers into/from one vector of real parts and one vector of imaginary parts, and 2) the in-register transposition of a square matrix whose number of rows is the vector length. Both can be viewed as transpositions of a small matrix. The motivation for considering these permutations is from [6], which shows that these are the only in-register shuffles needed to implement FFTs. The same permutations are also important in numerical linear algebra kernels and many other functions.

Fundamentally, we are faced with the challenge of mapping the basic permutations needed to a class of hardware reordering instructions that we refer to collectively as shuffles (see Figure 5).

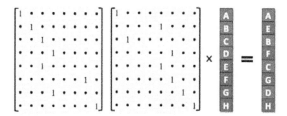

Figure 6: The basic permutation (perfect shuffle) that interleaves two 4-way vectors represented as a product of two binary matrices and two input vectors

Our goal is to generate efficient sequences of these reordering instructions in order to minimize the vectorization overhead. Efficient sequences are difficult to generate due to the complexity of shuffles and other reordering instructions in wide-vector architectures. To overcome these challenges, we developed an infrastructure to automate the generation of efficient reordering sequences.

Problem statement. Given a vector ISA and its shuffle operations and a transposition of a small matrix that is held in a few vector registers. We aim to generate a short instruction sequence that implements this matrix transposition with the minimal number of in-register shuffles.

Approach. We find the shortest instruction sequence that implements the required matrix transposition by 1) modeling instructions as binary matrices, 2) instruction sequences as products of binary matrices, 3) and transpositions as *stride permutation* matrices [20, 11]. Checking that an instruction sequence implements a certain transposition then is equivalent of checking that a product of matrices evaluates to the required stride permutation matrix. Based on this observation we build a superoptimizer based on matrix factorization to find the shortest instruction sequence that implements the required permutation.

5.1 Implementing the Superoptimizer

Formalization. The key insight to our approach is that we can represent permutations and the shuffle instructions that implement them as binary matrices [11]. This can be seen in Figure 6, which shows the permutation that reinterleaves a real vector and an imaginary vector into a vector of complex numbers as a product of two binary matrices operating on two concatenated input vectors of size 4.

This particular factorization of the permutation maps to two different sets of instructions on Intel SSE each with different performance characteristics. With the binary matrix representation in hand, we can formalize the generation of shuffle sequences as equivalent to finding a binary matrix factorization (BMF) of a given permutation matrix, P_m where each factor, F_i is a valid shuffle instruction in the vector instruction set architecture (ISA). For efficient shuffle sequences we generally want the least expensive sequence for some per-instruction cost function cost:

$$\text{minimize} \sum_{i=0}^{n} \text{cost}(F_i)$$

subject to $P_m = F_0 F_1 \cdots F_{n-1} \wedge F_0, \ldots, F_{n-1} \in \text{ISA}$

Binary matrix factorization (BMF). While BMF is a convenient formalization it is known to be NP-hard [33]. The problem is further complicated by our need for exact factorizations and factors with specific matrix dimensions (2ν x 2ν for a vector width ν); existing solvers generally find approximate factorizations with factors of arbitrary dimension [32]. We therefore elected to go in the other

direction by generating sequences of binary matrices where each binary matrix corresponds to a particular configuration of a particular shuffle instruction. The code implementing this description is shown in Listing 3. We then evaluate the sequence by matrix multiplying the sequence elements and comparing the Hamming distance to the desired base permutation matrix.

Super-optimization. In a sense, we are performing a kind of super-optimization on a limited number of complex shuffle instructions [26]. While conceptually straightforward, this approach, like general super-optimization, has limitations. One basic problem is that we have no indication of the minimal sequence size required to implement a particular base permutation. Furthermore, even though the matrices in the candidate sequences are all derived from a small set of shuffle instructions, we are still left with a very large search space; there are four billion variants of the unary LRB shuffle alone. More concretely, the code shown in Listing 3 produces k^n different sequences of shuffle instructions for a sequence length of n and vector ISA with k shuffle instructions. Considering the number of variants per shuffle instruction (or the number of different matrices each shuffle instruction represents) gives us a total number of different instruction sequences of:

$$\sum_{i=0}^{k^n-1} \left(\prod_{j=0}^{n} |S_{i,j}| \right)$$

where $S_{i,j}$ is the jth shuffle instruction in the ith instruction sequence and $|S_{i,j}|$ is the number of shuffle variants.

Guided search. Our solution for searching this space efficiently is a vector-instruction aware, heuristic-guided search system that can be integrated with the program generator Spiral, which is itself already a form of expert system.

Sequence length estimation. An example heuristic uses the vector width of the architecture, combined with a representation of the intrinsic interface of the most general shuffle instruction in the vector ISA to help determine a likely lower bound on the minimum number of shuffle instructions required to implement a particular base permutation. For example, a fully general unary shuffle can be used to implement the reinterleaving of an vector of real and imaginary parts to a complex vector in about four instructions.

Sequence culling. Other heuristics allow us to cull individual shuffle configurations from consideration (e.g. the identity shuffle) as well as instruction sequences (e.g. interleaving followed by immediate de-interleaving). The system also requires a generator program for each prospective shuffle instruction. The generator produces a binary matrix for a given configuration of the shuffle.

Listing 3: Building Sequences (Schedules) of Shuffle Instructions

```
// idx: index in the current schedule, numInstrs: # of shuf instrs in ISA
// schedLen: size of an instruction sequence, sched: the existing schedule
// instrs: array of shuffle instructions
void build_schedules(int idx,int numInstrs,int schedLen,schedule_t* sched){
    for(int i=0;i<numInstrs;++i){
        schedule_t nSched = new schedule_t(schedLen);
        // append the existing schedule
        nSched.add(sched);
        // add the ith instruction to the schedule
        nSched.add(idx,instrs[i]);
        if(idx+1 == schedLen){
            // finished creating the schedule
            // enqueue the schedule for processing
            threadQueue.enqueue(nSched);
        }else{
            // recursively build the remaining schedules
            build_schedules(idx+1,numInstrs,schedLen,nSched);
        }
    }
}
```

μ-op decomposition. We also decompose complex instructions into multiple stages; encoding each stage as a separate shuffle instruction to provide much finer grain resolution for the pattern

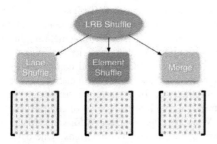

Figure 7: A decomposition of the LRB shuffle instruction into μ-ops

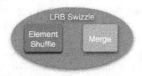

Figure 8: μ-op fusion: this particular element shuffle and merge can be implemented by one swizzle instruction

matching and rewriting that we employ to cull candidates and perform other optimizations. We show an example of this decomposition for the LRB shuffle in Figure 7 where we refer to individual stages as μ-ops. The μ-ops depicted in the figure are generally sufficient to describe most reordering operations. Ideally, we hope to subsume a sequence of these μ-ops with a less expensive instruction, performing in effect a type of strength reduction by "μ-op fusion." Figure 8 shows two μ-ops originating from a LRB shuffle which can be performed by a less expensive swizzle.

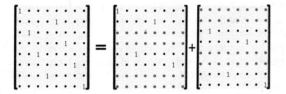

Figure 9: Partitioning of a stride permutation matrix (reinterleaving a real and an imaginary vector into a complex vector) for a 4-way vector architecture

Base permutation partitioning. Another technique used to accelerate search involves partitioning a base permutation matrix into a sequence of "hollow" matrices. These matrices have the same dimensions and initial contents as the source base permutation matrix. However, certain rows are converted into "don't care" rows; an example is shown in Figure 9.

Searches are then performed on a set of these "hollow" matrices in parallel using reduced length instruction sequences. The hope is that the shorter instruction sequences found for each "hollow" matrix can be inexpensively combined in a later pass to produce the full base permutation matrix. Because these shorter instruction sequences potentially contain many redundancies we employ a prefix tree to filter out common sub-sequences. The search mechanism is fully parallelized and can run on shared-memory and cluster machines and relies on a hand-tuned binary multiplication kernel shown in Listing 4. We describe its performance and efficacy in generating vectorized code presently.

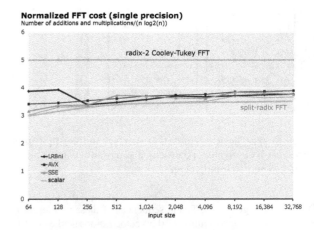

Figure 10: Number of additions and multiplications for Spiral-generated FFTs

Listing 4: Binary matrix multiplication kernel optimized for permutation matrices

```
// c: output binary matrices, a,b: input binary matrices, all matrices
// are represented as an  array of bit-vectors with n as the vector width
void binmat_mult(unsigned int* a, unsigned int* b, unsigned int* c){
  unsigned int mask = exp2(n-1);
  for(int j=0;j<n;++j){
    unsigned int bb = b[j];
    unsigned int w = 0;
    unsigned int m = mask;
    #pragma unroll(n)
    for(int i=0;i<n;++i) {
      unsigned int v = a[i] & bb; bool f = !(v & (v - 1)) && v;
      w = (w & ~m) | (-f & m); m >>= 1;
    }
    c[j] = w;
  }
}
```

6. Experimental Results

In this section we evaluate both the performance of the superoptimizer and the quality of the generated code. The latter is assessed by using the generated permutations inside Spiral-generated FFT code, whose efficiency and performance is then evaluated. For LRB we use instruction counts since no hardware is available. For compilation, we used Intel icc version 12.0.2 on Linux with the -O3 optimization flag as well as unrolling and alignment pragmas.

Generated FFTs. We experimentally evaluate our generator with 1D complex FFTs, both with 2-power sizes $n = 64, \ldots, 32768$ as well as for kernel sizes $n = 2, 3, \ldots, 32$. To do this we connected our generator with the program generation system Spiral effectively inserting the generated permutations into the generated FFT code. On LRB, Spiral's feedback-driven search uses the number of vector instructions instead of runtime as cost function. All FFTs used are $O(n \log(n))$ algorithms. For small sizes we also perform an experiment with direct $O(n^2)$ implementation.

First, we evaluate the impact of vectorization on the mathematical operations count (counting additions and multiplication) of the generated FFTs. Vectorization introduces overhead in the form of superfluous multiplications by 1 and superfluous additions with 0 due to data packing in registers. A degenerate strategy for minimizing this overhead could generate kernels with higher operations count and simpler structure. Figure 10 shows that this is not the approach with Spiral-generated FFTs. The y-axis shows the number of mathematical additions and multiplications of Spiral-generated vectorized code divided by $n \log_2 n$ where n is the input size shown on the x-axis. As upper bound we show the radix-2

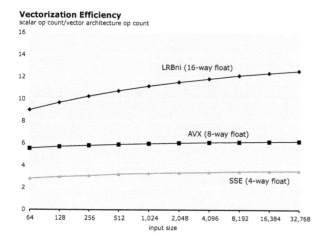

Figure 11: Spiral's vectorization efficiency across three Intel SIMD architectures

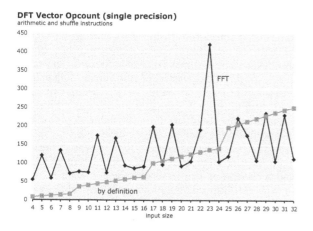

Figure 12: Comparison of vector operation counts for FFTs and "DFTs by definition" on LRB

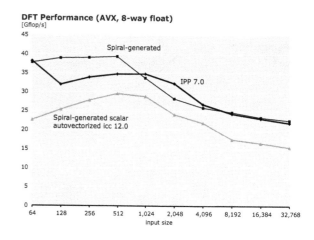

Figure 13: Comparison of 8-way AVX vectorized DFT implementations

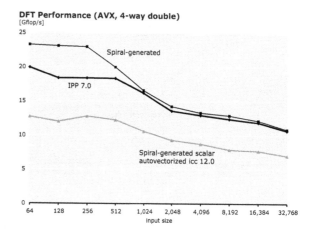

Figure 14: Comparison of 4-way AVX vectorized DFT implementations

Cooley-Tukey FFT, which requires $5n \log_2(n)$ operations. This number is usually (and also in this paper) used for FFT performance comparisons in Gflop/s, thus slightly overestimating the performance. As lower bound we show the split-radix FFT which requires $4n \log_2(n) - 6n + 8$ many operations. The plot shows that Spiral-generated vector code on all architectures is close to the latter.

Vectorization efficiency. We now examine the vectorization efficiency, defined in Section 3, of the Spiral-generated vectorized FFT. Ideally, the vectorization efficiency should approach the architecture's vector width. However, due to the required shuffles, this is not achievable. Figure 11 shows that across vector architectures and lengths, we achieve an efficiency of up to about 80% of the vector length. For AVX and LRB, this is mainly due to the superoptimizer presented in this paper.

We also note that AVX ramps up faster due to its more general, binary shuffle but LRB eventually achieves the same relative efficiency.

Next we investigate the trade-off between fast $O(n \log_2 n)$ algorithms and direct $O(n^2)$ computations for small kernel sizes. For these sizes the shuffles required by the fast algorithms can become prohibitive while the regular, FMA-friendly structure of the matrix-vector product allows for high efficiency. Figure 12 shows that

indeed up to a size of about $n = 20$, the direct computation is preferable, even though the mathematical operations count (counting only additions and multiplications) is inferior. The reason is in LRB's dedicated replicate HW, which enables efficient scalar broadcasts and FMA instructions which are well-suited for a direct computation.

Evaluation against FFT libraries. We cannot evaluate our FFT implementations against state-of-the-art third-party FFT implementations using the vectorization efficiency metric. The Intel Integrated Performance Primitives (IPP) [18] and Math Kernel Library (MKL) [19] would be the ideal base line for comparisons, but are only distributed as binaries; thus, instruction counts are not available. The recent (Jan 2011) release of hardware implementing the AVX ISA allows for a runtime comparison. Figures 13 and 14 show a runtime performance comparison of 4-way (double precision) and 8-way (single precision) AVX vectorized FFTs from Intel IPP 7.0 with those generated by Spiral on a 3.3 GHz Intel Core i5-2500. Spiral's AVX performance compares well with IPP 7.0 on the full range of DFT sizes. Note, that this early platform implementing the AVX ISA does not feature support for FMAs. FFTW [14] is available in source code and thus amenable to instruction statistics, but at this point only supports 2-way double precision 4-way

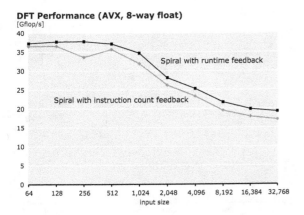

DFT Performance (AVX, 8-way float)
[Gflop/s]

Spiral with runtime feedback

Spiral with instruction count feedback

input size

Figure 15: Comparison of 8-way AVX vectorized DFT implementations generated using different search metrics

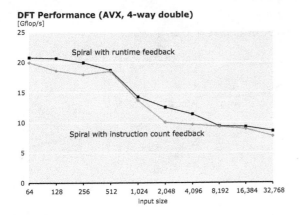

DFT Performance (AVX, 4-way double)
[Gflop/s]

Spiral with runtime feedback

Spiral with instruction count feedback

input size

Figure 16: Comparison of 4-way AVX vectorized DFT implementations generated using different search metrics

single-precision SSE on Intel architectures. At the time of this writing there is no AVX or LRBni support.

Comparison to Intel's compiler vectorization. Intel's C/C++ compiler (icc) 12.0.1 supports AVX as a vectorization target. However, the auto-vectorizer does not utilize the AVX fused multiply-add instructions. We instruct the Intel C compiler to generate AVX assembly code from scalar (ANSI C with the necessary pragmas) and count the AVX arithmetic and reorder instructions, taking loop trips into account. No comparison for LRBni is possible. The Intel compiler performs well and achieves a vectorization efficiency of about 5.6 on 8-way single-precision AVX, thus achieving about 72% of our vectorization efficiency. Note that this high efficiency is in large parts due to Spiral's search, which in effect finds the code with the best structure for the compiler to succeed. Also the use of vectorization pragmas and buffer alignment declarations contributes.

Figures 13 and 14 include the performance of Spiral-generated scalar code, autovectorized by the compiler as described. For the 8-way and 4-way cases, Spiral vectorized DFTs were 30% and 40% faster, respectively, than icc compiled DFTs.

Vectorization efficiency as a performance guide. Spiral's conventional search for the best performing DFTs relies heavily on runtime performance feedback as a guiding metric. We have argued that in the absence of runtime performance feedback, vectorization efficiency can serve as substitute metric for guiding search. Figures

System	Million instruction sequences/sec
2.6 GHz Core i7	2.1
3.0 GHz Core 2 Quad	1.3
2.8 GHz Opteron 2200	0.8

Table 1: Search throughput on three x86-based CPUs

15 and 16 compare the performance of Spiral generated, AVX vectorized DFTs produced using two different metrics to guide search: runtime performance feedback and vectorization efficiency. In the 8-way case, the vectorization efficiency guided code approaches to within 7.4% on average of the performance of the code generated using runtime feedback. Similarly, in the 4-way case, the performance difference between the two generation methods is 8% on average. The relatively small performance disparity for smaller sizes is attributable to the delicate balance of arithmetic instructions and permutations required to handle functional unit latencies and port conflicts. For larger sizes, vectorization efficiency has difficulty achieving the right balance between loading precomputed constants and calculating the constants on the fly.

Permutation search results. Table 1 summarizes the throughput of our search mechanism on three different architectures. On average, finding a base permutation matrix for LRB required about two hours, roughly the equivalent of evaluating 14 billion instruction sequences of length six on the Core i7, which took about 2 hours. To put this figure in perspective, when expanded to μ-ops an instruction sequence of length six is roughly 16 μ-ops. An exhaustive search would need to evaluate more than 512^{16} different instruction sequences requiring about 10^{29} years on a Core i7. The shortest LRB instruction sequences discovered were for interleaving and deinterleaving two vectors of complex numbers, both of which require six instructions each: four shuffles and two swizzles. In contrast, both of these operations can be done in two instructions each on SSE. These sequence lengths compare favorably with the heuristic described above which estimated four shuffle instructions based on a fully general unary shuffle.

7. Conclusion

Near-term designs in the commodity architecture space show a clear trend towards more sophisticated SIMD vector instruction sets featuring ever wider vectors. Effectively vectorizing code for such architectures is a major challenge due to highly complex, nonintuitive and expensive vector reordering instructions. In this paper we presented a superoptimizer for data reorganization (permutations) that are important building blocks in many computations in linear algebra and signal processing. We show that—using enough resources—highly efficient automatic vectorization is possible for the the rather complex recently announced SIMD vector extensions: Our superoptimizer evaluated 14 billion instruction sequences in about 2 hours to find an efficient 6-instruction implementation of the core data reorganization. Using our optimizer we generated a library of building blocks required for implementing FFTs on AVX and Larrabee. We connected our optimizer to the program generation system Spiral and used it to generate efficient FFT implementations for AVX and Larrabee's LRBni vector instructions achieving a vectorization efficiency of up to 80% of the vector length across vector architectures.

8. Acknowledgments

This work was supported by a gift from Intel Corporation and by NSF through award 0702386. Daniel S. McFarlin was supported by an NPSC and NDSEG graduate fellowship. We are indebted to Scott Buck, Randy Roost, Joshua Fryman and Mitchell Lum of Intel Corporation for granting early access to Larrabee and AVX and their technical advice and guidance.

9. References

[1] Saman Amarasinghe, Samuel Larsen, and Samuel Larsen. Exploiting superword level parallelism with multimedia instruction sets, 2000.

[2] Intel Advanced Vector Extensions programming reference, 2008. http://software.intel.com/en-us/avx/.

[3] Sorav Bansal and Alex Aiken. Automatic generation of peephole superoptimizers. *SIGPLAN Not.*, 41(11):394–403, 2006.

[4] Alexandre E. Eichenberger, Peng Wu, and Kevin O'Brien. Vectorization for SIMD architectures with alignment constraints. *SIGPLAN Not.*, 39(6):82–93, 2004.

[5] Randall J. Fisher, All J. Fisher, and Henry G. Dietz. Compiling for simd within a register. In *11th Annual Workshop on Languages and Compilers for Parallel Computing (LCPC98*, pages 290–304. Springer Verlag, Chapel Hill, 1998.

[6] F. Franchetti and M Püschel. Short vector code generation for the discrete Fourier transform. In *Proc. IEEE Int'l Parallel and Distributed Processing Symposium (IPDPS)*, pages 58–67, 2003.

[7] F. Franchetti, Y. Voronenko, and M. Püschel. Loop merging for signal transforms. In *Proc. Programming Language Design and Implementation (PLDI)*, pages 315–326, 2005.

[8] F. Franchetti, Y. Voronenko, and M. Püschel. A rewriting system for the vectorization of signal transforms. In *Proc. High Performance Computing for Computational Science (VECPAR)*, 2006.

[9] Franz Franchetti, Frédéric de Mesmay, Daniel McFarlin, and Markus Püschel. Operator language: A program generation framework for fast kernels. In *IFIP Working Conference on Domain Specific Languages (DSL WC)*, 2009.

[10] Franz Franchetti and Markus Püschel. SIMD vectorization of non-two-power sized FFTs. In *International Conference on Acoustics, Speech, and Signal Processing (ICASSP)*, volume 2, pages II–17, 2007.

[11] Franz Franchetti and Markus Püschel. Generating SIMD vectorized permutations. In *International Conference on Compiler Construction (CC)*, volume 4959 of *Lecture Notes in Computer Science*, pages 116–131. Springer, 2008.

[12] M. Frigo. A fast Fourier transform compiler. In *Proc. ACM PLDI*, pages 169–180, 1999.

[13] M. Frigo and S. G. Johnson. FFTW: An adaptive software architecture for the FFT. In *Proc. IEEE Int'l Conf. Acoustics, Speech, and Signal Processing (ICASSP)*, volume 3, pages 1381–1384, 1998.

[14] Matteo Frigo and Steven G. Johnson. The design and implementation of FFTW3. *Proceedings of the IEEE*, 93(2):216–231, 2005. Special issue on "Program Generation, Optimization, and Adaptation".

[15] The Gnu C compiler web site. gcc.gnu.org.

[16] Manuel Hohenauer, Felix Engel, Rainer Leupers, Gerd Ascheid, and Heinrich Meyr. A simd optimization framework for retargetable compilers. *ACM Trans. Archit. Code Optim.*, 6(1):1–27, 2009.

[17] The Intel C compiler web site. software.intel.com/en-us/intel-compilers.

[18] Intel. Integrated performance primitives 5.3, User Guide.

[19] Intel. Math kernel library 10.0, Reference Manual.

[20] J. R. Johnson, R. W. Johnson, D. Rodriguez, and R. Tolimieri. A methodology for designing, modifying, and implementing FFT algorithms on various architectures. *Circuits Systems Signal Processing*, 9:449–500, 1990.

[21] Ken Kennedy and John R. Allen. *Optimizing compilers for modern architectures: a dependence-based approach*. Morgan Kaufmann Publishers Inc., San Francisco, CA, USA, 2002.

[22] Stefan Kral, Franz Franchetti, Juergen Lorenz, Christoph W. Ueberhuber, and Peter Wurzinger. Fft compiler techniques. In *In Compiler Construction: 13th International Conference, CC 2004, Held as Part of the Joint European Conferences on Theory and Practice of Software, ETAPS 2004*, pages 217–231, 2004.

[23] Alexei Kudriavtsev and Peter Kogge. Generation of permutations for simd processors. In *LCTES '05: Proceedings of the 2005 ACM SIGPLAN/SIGBED conference on Languages, compilers, and tools for embedded systems*, pages 147–156, New York, NY, USA, 2005. ACM.

[24] C++ Larrabee Prototype Library, 2009. http://software.intel.com/en-us/articles/prototype-primitives-guide.

[25] A first look at the Larrabee New Instructions (LRBni), 2009. http://www.ddj.com/hpc-high-performance-computing/216402188.

[26] Henry Massalin. Superoptimizer: a look at the smallest program. *SIGPLAN Not.*, 22(10):122–126, 1987.

[27] Dorit Nuzman and Richard Henderson. Multi-platform auto-vectorization. In *CGO '06: Proceedings of the International Symposium on Code Generation and Optimization*, pages 281–294, Washington, DC, USA, 2006. IEEE Computer Society.

[28] Dorit Nuzman, Ira Rosen, and Ayal Zaks. Auto-vectorization of interleaved data for simd. *SIGPLAN Not.*, 41(6):132–143, 2006.

[29] Markus Püschel, José M. F. Moura, Jeremy Johnson, David Padua, Manuela Veloso, Bryan W. Singer, Jianxin Xiong, Franz Franchetti, Aca Gačić, Yevgen Voronenko, Kang Chen, Robert W. Johnson, and Nick Rizzolo. SPIRAL: Code generation for DSP transforms. *Proc. of the IEEE*, 93(2):232–275, 2005. Special issue on *Program Generation, Optimization, and Adaptation*.

[30] Gang Ren, Peng Wu, and David Padua. Optimizing data permutations for simd devices. In *PLDI '06: Proceedings of the 2006 ACM SIGPLAN conference on Programming language design and implementation*, pages 118–131, New York, NY, USA, 2006. ACM.

[31] Larry Seiler, Doug Carmean, Eric Sprangle, Tom Forsyth, Michael Abrash, Pradeep Dubey, Stephen Junkins, Adam Lake, Jeremy Sugerman, Robert Cavin, Roger Espasa, Ed Grochowski, Toni Juan, and Pat Hanrahan. Larrabee: a many-core x86 architecture for visual computing. *ACM Trans. Graph.*, 27(3):1–15, August 2008.

[32] Bao-Hong Shen, Shuiwang Ji, and Jieping Ye. Mining discrete patterns via binary matrix factorization. In *KDD '09: Proceedings of the 15th ACM SIGKDD international conference on Knowledge discovery and data mining*, pages 757–766, New York, NY, USA, 2009. ACM.

[33] V. Snasel, J. Platos, and P. Kromer. On genetic algorithms for

boolean matrix factorization. *Intelligent Systems Design and Applications, International Conference on*, 2:170–175, 2008.

[34] N. Sreraman and R. Govindarajan. A vectorizing compiler for multimedia extensions. *International Journal of Parallel Programming*, 28:363–400, 2000.

[35] C. Van Loan. *Computational Framework of the Fast Fourier Transform*. SIAM, 1992.

[36] The IBM XL C compiler web site. www-01.ibm.com/software/awdtools/xlcpp.

[37] Hans Zima and Barbara Chapman. *Supercompilers for parallel and vector computers*. ACM, New York, NY, USA, 1991.

Cost-Effectively Offering Private Buffers in SoCs and CMPs

Zhen Fang[1], Li Zhao[1], Ravi Iyer[1], Carlos Flores Fajardo[2],
German Fabila Garcia[2], Seung Eun Lee[3], Bin Li[1], Steve King[1],
Xiaowei Jiang[1], Srihari Makineni[1]

[1]Intel Labs, Intel Corp, Hillsboro, OR, U.S.A.
[2]Intel Labs, Intel Corp, Guadalajara, Jalisco, Mexico
[3]Seoul National University of Science and Technology, Seoul, Korea
{zhen.fang | li.zhao | ravishankar.iyer | carlos.a.flores.fajardo |
german.fabila.garcia @ intel.com }

ABSTRACT

High performance SoCs and CMPs integrate multiple cores and hardware accelerators such as network interface devices and speech recognition engines. Cores make use of SRAM organized as a cache. Accelerators make use of SRAM as special-purpose storage such as FIFOs, scratchpad memory, or other forms of private buffers. Dedicated private buffers provide benefits such as deterministic access, but are highly area inefficient due to the lower average utilization of the total available storage.

We propose Buffer-integrated-Caching (BiC), which integrates private buffers and traditional caches into a single shared SRAM block. Much like shared caches improve SRAM utilization on CMPs, the BiC architecture generalizes this advantage for a heterogeneous mix of cores and accelerators in future SoCs and CMPs.

We demonstrate cost-effectiveness of the BiC using SoC-based low-power servers and CMP-based servers with on-chip NIC. We show that with a small extra area added to the baseline cache, BiC removes the need for large, dedicated SRAMs, with minimal performance impact.

Categories and Subject Descriptors

C.0 [Computer Systems Organization]: System architectures

General Terms

Design, Performance

Keywords

Cache, SRAM, Accelerators

1. INTRODUCTION

An increasing number of applications are available on smartphones, but the computational power of such devices is still too limited for many 'killer' applications. There are three schemes that can help to solve the performance issues. The first is to build application- or domain-specific hardware accelerators, shown in Figure 1(a). This model allows the smartphone to reach Quality-of-Service targets, but increases the cost of the phone and is unappealing to customers who do not use those particular applications. In the second scheme, shown in Figure 1(b), user data are sent over a wireless network to a data center, where compute- and data-intensive functions are executed on high-performance servers. Heat density challenges of the data centers [24, 38] have led academia and industry to low-power, low-cost servers built with mobile cores to enhance performance-per-watt and performance-per-dollar [6, 39, 53]. However, the low single-thread performance of the mobile cores can lead to unacceptable response time for interactive applications [32, 36]. To improve power efficiency and reduce response time on the low-cost processors, researchers have recently proposed server SoCs (system-on-chips) with hardware accelerators [18]. Figure 1(c) represents such a model, which we assume in this study.

To illustrate the types of applications that will benefit from this architecture, Figure 1(d) describes the general flow of an emerging application, Mobile Augmented Reality (MAR) [10, 42, 44]. MAR is becoming available as a commercial service on several platforms, including Google Android and Apple iPhone.

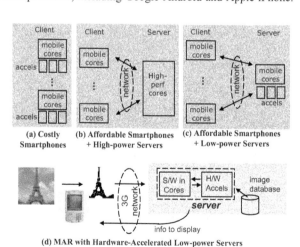

(a) Costly Smartphones
(b) Affordable Smartphones + High-power Servers
(c) Affordable Smartphones + Low-power Servers

(d) MAR with Hardware-Accelerated Low-power Servers

Figure 1. Low-Power Servers with Accelerators: a Mobile Augmented Reality Example

In MAR, the user takes a picture with a smartphone and sends the minimally pre-processed query image to the server. The shaded block in Figure 1(d) denotes a MAR server with software functions running in the core and accelerated functions running in hardware. Software and hardware work together to extract interest points in the query image, and match them against those of database images. Information associated with the closest matching database image is sent back to the smartphone.

SoCs typically employ a few power-efficient cores along with a number of hardware accelerators [46, 34]. The small cores use SRAM as caches, and accelerators use SRAM for local storage such as message FIFOs, scratchpad memory, etc. Figure 2(a) illustrates such an SoC. We use the term *buffer* to refer to these explicitly addressed, explicitly managed SRAM stores. Since these buffer structures have different organizations from caches, they are conventionally implemented as distinct physical resources.

The trend of migrating discrete devices and accelerators onto the processor chip has also started in CMPs (Chip-Multiprocessors) [4, 5, 13, 21, 41]. Intel's Sandy Bridge includes MPEG4 encoder and decoder, 3D graphics and display controller onto the processor die [5]. Sun Niagara2 [13] and IBM PowerEN [21] respectively integrate two and four 10Gbps network interface controllers (NICs) . Based on an estimate given by Binkert et. al [8], each 10Gbps integrated NIC requires adding about 400KB of dedicated SRAM used as packet FIFOs, a significant cost factor in wider adoption of NIC integration.

With each new accelerator integrated, the area devoted to dedicated buffers increases. *Chip-level inefficiency* arises due to the fact that all accelerators on one chip are not simultaneously active. Within each individual accelerator, buffer size requirements can vary drastically depending on the actual parameters. At design time, however, a private SRAM has to accommodate the worst-case requirements of the accelerator (i.e., largest size), leading to *block-level inefficiency*. The multiplicative effect of both types of inefficiency inevitably results in severely over-provisioned SRAM real estate.

Inefficiency in SRAM utilization motivates sharing across various forms of buffers and caches: it could be highly beneficial to allow SRAM to be dynamically shared between cores and accelerators, repurposed as cache space or private buffers. Our goal is to reduce total silicon cost via SRAM sharing. At the same time, performance of non-accelerated software running on the cores should not be significantly penalized, and QoS requirements of accelerated functions must not be violated.

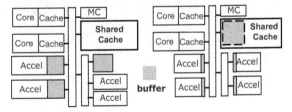

(a) Today's Platforms   (b) A Shared Buffer-Integrated-Cache

Figure 2. A Case for Sharing SRAM in SoC/CMP Platforms

The key challenges in consolidating the cache and buffers into a same piece of SRAM lie in three aspects: (a) addressing the heterogeneity in organization of buffer structures and caches, (b) reconciling the determinism of a private buffer versus the best-effort policy of the cache, and (c) minimizing SRAM waste

by allowing unused buffer portions to be used as cache space at a fine granularity.

In this paper, we address these challenges by proposing a Buffer-Integrated-Cache (BiC) architecture. The BiC architecture allows buffers and a cache to reside in the same SRAM block, shown in Figure 2(b). Cores can view and access the SRAM as a cache, whereas accelerators can view and access other portions of the SRAM as local storage. Much like shared caches improve SRAM utilization on CMPs [3, 35], the BiC architecture generalizes this advantage for a heterogeneous mix of cores and accelerators in future SoCs and CMPs. We present the design and implementation of the BiC architecture, and evaluate it using two usage models: 1) core/accelerator sharing in low-power SoCs, and 2) core/device sharing in CMPs.

When private buffers are provided by a shared structure, one downside is that local SRAM accesses now must traverse the system interconnect. To accommodate the extra latency, the accelerators need to keep some private buffers. But since the shared SRAM covers the bulk of memory access bandwidth and latency jitters caused by DRAM and I/O peripherals like NAND devices, the local buffers physically residing in each accelerator can be negligible in number, e.g., under 1KB compared to 64KB. System interconnect and cache port contention could also become performance bottlenecks when buffers are heavily accessed. We examine these concerns along with the cost of increasing interconnect bandwidth and adding cache ports, if necessary. The contributions of this paper are as follows:

(a) We present the efficiency-driven need to dynamically share SRAM between on-die cores and accelerators in a heterogeneous CMP and SoC architecture.

(b) We introduce a novel architecture (BiC) for fine-grain SRAM sharing in a cost-effective manner.

(c) We present two CMP/SoC usage models that highlight the BiC efficacy in achieving the goals set out.

2. BiC ARCHITECTURE AND IMPLEMENTATION

2.1 Overview of the BiC Architecture

The BiC includes three components (Figure 3): a traditional cache controller, a buffer controller, and the shared substrate. We first describe the buffer controller and the BiC substrate, followed by more details in subsequent sections.

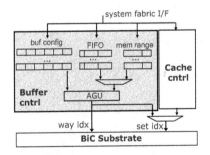

Figure 3. BiC Block Diagram

The buffer controller, alongside the cache controller, enables a cache view and multiple buffer views to the cores and accelerators on top of a single SRAM substrate. At buffer allocation time, the buffer controller manages buffer location in SRAM and provides buffer ids to the cores or accelerators for use in identifying particular buffers. At buffer access time, it converts incoming buffer requests to signals appropriate for the BiC substrate to perform lookup and data access.

The BiC substrate is based on a conventional cache organization, with extensions to integrate multiple buffers in a fine-grain, deterministic and flexible manner. The BiC substrate is fine-grain because it allows allocation of buffers in the cache, as well as alignment of the allocation, at cache line granularity, not at way granularity as proposed earlier. The BiC substrate is flexible by allowing SRAM to be dynamically repurposed as buffer or cache. The BiC substrate is deterministic by ensuring that data in the buffer is always resident in SRAM and cannot be evicted.

In addition to the existing read/write/snoop transactions for a typical cache, the BiC introduces new buffer access transactions:

```
Bread       BufferId [Offset]
Breadinv    BufferId [Offset]
Bwrite      BufferId [Offset] Data
DMA_MtoB    BufferId Offset Size memaddress
DMA_BtoM    BufferId Offset Size memaddress
```

Breadinv is similar to Bread, but also marks the entry as invalid after providing the data. If the buffer type was a FIFO, Breadinv is the transaction that should be used for read accesses since the read is destructive. Of the above transactions, only the DMAs touch system memory. Coherency with cached copies of the DMA data is automatically maintained by the baseline architecture.

Compared with existing software-controlled cache design, our implementation 1) does not expose cache organizational details (associativity, total number of sets, cacheline size) to software. 2) In addition to a generic view of local memory, we provide support for commonly used higher-level abstracts that can simplify agents' buffer management tasks.

2.2 Design of the Buffer Controller

The buffer controller provides the following hardware support for access to buffers: buffer setup, scratchpad access, memory-mapped buffer access, FIFO buffer access.

2.2.1 Support for Buffer Setup

The buffer controller maintains a set of buffer descriptors, one descriptor for each buffer. The buffer controller stores the buffer descriptors in a master buffer. The master buffer is otherwise a normal BiC buffer, except that the buffer controller stores the descriptor for the master buffer in a dedicated hardware register. System software initializes the size and contents of the master buffer to manage the runtime BiC buffers needed in the system. Although allocation of cache space to buffers is at cacheline granularity, the size of each buffer entry can be larger or smaller.

The buffer descriptor consists of the following fields:

Agent ID(s)	Stride Size	Entry Size	Buffer Size	Base Way	Base Set

Base Set and *Base Way* indicate the set and way indices of the first entry of the buffer location. Both are determined by the buffer controller hardware instead of given by software. *Agent ID(s)* is a bit vector indicating the cores and accelerators that will initiate a request for this buffer. The rest of the fields are self-evident.

2.2.2 Handling Buffer Accesses

Depending on whether the transaction type is scratchpad, FIFO, or memory-mapped, a buffer request goes through one of three

sets of descriptors (`buf config`, `FIFO`, and `mem range` in Figure 3). Based on the buffer id, the offset to the location inside the buffer, and an optional size, an address generation unit (AGU) computes way and set indices using the buffer descriptor. In addition, the buffer controller checks whether the request is the last use of the buffer entry, indicated via an encoded bit. If so, a mask, located in the unused tag of the buffer cache line, is updated to indicate that the entry is free. If all bits in the mask are marked free, the cacheline is returned to being allocated to the cache. Releasing a cacheline from a buffer is achieved by clearing its sticky bit, to be explained in Section 2.3.

To support access to a FIFO buffer type, the buffer controller maintains a set of head and tail pointers, and full/empty bits. The buffer controller compares the head and tail at every FIFO update to appropriately mark the F/E bits for this buffer.

Memory-mapped buffers are convenient for fast communication between accelerators and processor cores. Memory range registers contain the physical base address and size for each memory-mapped buffer. As a memory request comes to the BiC, the memory range registers are searched in parallel with the cache access. A match to one of them nullifies the cache access, and the request is converted to a buffer id and offset.

2.2.3 Support for Buffer Access QoS

The buffer controller can prioritize requests to enable bandwidth and latency guarantees for accelerators that need them. For the case studies that we presented in this paper, prioritizing buffer accesses over cache accesses while giving equal priorities to buffer accesses serves the workloads well. More complex QoS mechanisms [20, 33] for bandwidth sharing could be necessary for future applications.

2.3 Design of the BiC Substrate

The BiC substrate design requires two cache extensions. One is direct addressability, in addition to caches' associative tag comparisons. The other extension is deterministic access.

2.3.1 Buffer Location in BiC

System agents identify buffers using buffer id's and offsets. Internally, the BiC substrate allows each buffer to start at any location in the cache, identified by a set index and a way index. Given the starting location of the buffer, the buffer controller calculates each subsequent cache line belonging to the buffer based on the stride chosen in the cache.

All ways of a given set of cache lines should not be used up by the buffers because it would starve any cache allocation into this set. Hence we allocate contiguous buffer entries within the same way across sets as opposed to within the same set across ways.

2.3.2 Buffer Determinism in BiC

To ensure that a buffer entry is always found in the cache, we add an additional B/C sticky bit to each cache line to indicate whether it is currently in buffer mode (B/C = 1) or cache mode (B/C = 0). We modify the cache replacement policy such that the cache controller never evicts cache lines marked with a B/C=1. The baseline cache performs serialized tag check and data array access, which is typical for L2 and L3 caches. In a cache read, the extra logic adds only one gate delay to the data array access. In general, this will not change the

Table 1. Buffer Size Requirement in the MAR Accelerator

IPD Accelerator of MAR				Match Accelerator of MAR			
Parameter	SRAM Buffer Size			Parameter	SRAM Buffer Size		
Filter size, sampling interval	Theoretical requirement	**Dedicated Buffer**	**BiC**	DRAM b/w target	Theoretical requirement	**Dedicated Buffer**	**BiC**
124, 2	127KB	**127KB**	**127KB**	840 MB/s	32KB	**32KB**	**32KB**
64, 4	51KB	**127KB**	**51KB**	690 MB/s	16KB	**32KB**	**16KB**
34, 2	14KB	**127KB**	**14KB**	530 MB/s	8KB	**32KB**	**8KB**

cache hit cycle. In a buffer read, the sticky bit value of '1' disables the tag actions which are performed only for cache accesses. At the same time, (set index, way index) generated by the buffer controller causes the wordlines and bitlines to be charged/discharged in the data array, and thus the right data line fetched. Detailed design can be found in [14].

In addition to space determinism, it is also important to address the bandwidth requirement for the accelerators. In theory, bandwidth could be problematic at two locations: cache port and system interconnect. In this paper, we study the potential for optionally adding an additional read/write port in the cache and/or doubling the width of the system fabric.

3 EVALUATION OF BiC

In this section, we first describe the workloads to be used in the study, with an emphasis on their buffer requirements. Then we explain the evaluation methodology, and quantify the benefits and cost of using BiC.

3.1 Workload Description

3.1.1 Mobile Augmented Reality (MAR)

Using the system architecture that we described in Section 1, the MAR server goes through three serialized phases. (1) Interest Point Detection (IPD) on the query image, (2) Descriptor Generation for the identified interest points, and (3) Match compares descriptor of the query image against those of the reference images in the database. To meet a performance target of sub-second response time and achieve power efficiency, hardware accelerators for IPD and Match are needed [26]. Descriptor Generation is rich in floating-point operations, and would not be cost-effective to accelerate.

The SRAM capacity requirement in the IPD accelerator is a function of two orthogonal parameters: block filter size and sampling interval. Intuitively, they determine how thoroughly we sample the image pixels, which translates to the accuracy and total number of identified interest points. Different filter sizes are often chosen for different objects. For example, recognizing a historic building aided by GPS information is much easier than recognizing a particular type of flower in an arboretum. The SRAM capacity requirement for the Match accelerator starts at 8KB. However, larger sizes are helpful to reduce DRAM read bandwidth and IO power. The SRAM sizes for the two accelerator components are shown in Table 1.

Using the conventional solution of dedicated SRAM blocks, both IPD and Match would have to build the largest SRAM sizes at design time even though they are only relevant in some rare usage cases. BiC allows us to tailor buffer allocation optimally for IPD and Match at runtime.

3.1.2 Speech Recognition (SR)

Cloud service providers such as Google have initiated SR features such as voiced-based search. In this paper, we address the more difficult SR applications such as meeting transcription and in-vehicle email. Speech recognition engines like Sphinx3 [11] usually consist of three steps: acoustic processing, Gaussian Mixture Model (GMM) scoring, and LM/AM (language model/acoustic model) search. Acoustic processing is a light-weight task that is well within the computation power of a medium- to high-end mobile processor. GMM scoring and LM/AM search are heavy-weight functions that are best executed on the server side. In Sphinx3, GMM scoring takes about 75% of total decoding time if executed in software. To enable real-time decoding of continuous speech with power efficiency, we implemented a GMM scoring accelerator [2].

The GMM accelerator has different capacity requirements for SRAM buffers depending on different parameters, shown in Table 2. The three parameters (feature vector dimension, grouping factor, and number of Gaussian mixtures) are orthogonal. Also note that the buffer size numbers are just minimum requirements for the algorithm to work; larger total buffer capacity would be needed, for example, if ping-pong buffering is to be used to improve DMA efficiency. Obviously, there are many possible combinations. A conventional design using double buffering would need dedicated SRAM of size (12KB + 29 KB) x 2 = 82KB. BiC only needs to allocate enough buffer space from shared cache.

Table 2. (Minimum) Buffer Sizes in the GMM Accelerator

For Audio Feature Vectors		For Gaussian Table	
Feat vector dimension, Grouping factor	Buffer size	Number of Gaussian mixtures	Buffer size
60, 50	12 KB	37	29 KB
39, 20	3.2 KB	16	5 KB
39, 10	1.6 KB	10	2 KB

3.1.3 Packet Processing with Integrated NIC

Memory operations and I/O adaptor register accesses constitute two of the major bottlenecks in 10Gb/s and higher speed Ethernet [27, 29], especially receive-side processing. On-chip integrated network interface controller (INIC) naturally reduces I/O register access latency from 200+ ns to the PCIe to under 100ns. But memory operations do not necessarily benefit from NIC integration.

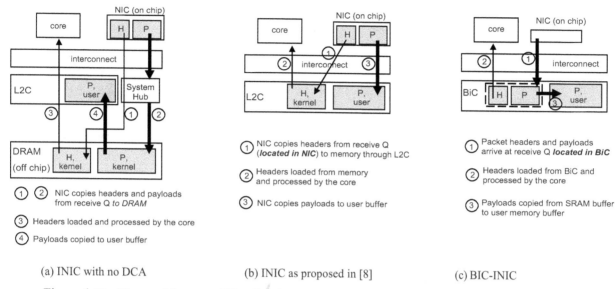

Figure 4. Key Memory Movement When Receiving a Packet with On-chip NICs (Blocks Not Drawn to Scale)

In this paper we use Niagara2's INIC[13, 28] as our baseline, which performs same memory copy operations as with a discrete NIC. In Figure 4(a), packet headers and payloads in the NIC's receive queue first get DMA-ed to a kernel buffer in system memory. In Niagara2, this DMA does not use the Direct Cache Access (DCA) technique [19]. In other words, the processor caches are snooped but the data do not get cached; they get written directly to DRAM (steps 1 and 2). The device driver loads the headers from DRAM and processes them, before it can copy the payloads from kernel buffer to a user buffer – this time the data get cached, as is denoted with the "P, user" box in L2C in Figure 4(a). There are other memory access overheads, like those to retrieve and update DMA descriptors. But to focus on differences between INIC implementations, we omit these other memory operations in Figure 4.

In the INIC architecture proposed by Binkert et. al [8], the kernel payload buffer is eliminated, so is the associated data copying overhead. The device driver inspects the headers from kernel memory and decides where the incoming payloads should go. When the receiving application's buffer address is known, the driver copies the payloads from the NIC buffer directly to the user buffer. The user buffer content gets cached in the L2C. Subsequent reads by the receiving application often hit the L2C lines in M state. The process is shown in Figure 4(b). The so-called zero-copy (which is indeed one-copy) is achieved by delaying the copying out of the NIC FIFO until the user buffer is available to use.

The ability to defer NIC-to-user copying relies critically on buffer capacity in the INIC. With more processor cores to perform protocol stack processing, the NIC buffer size will likely pose an upper bound on maximum packet throughput. Binkert [8] finds that one 10Gbps Ethernet requires a 384 KB NIC buffer. Since the amount of buffering required is proportional to the network bandwidth, only about 40KB is necessary in the INIC if the MAC works at 1Gbps. Similarly, a 40Gbps MAC would require about 1.5MB of buffering in the INIC. At design time, the maximum capacity must be built to cater for the peak speed, even though the server may work in a low network bandwidth mode

most of the time. Due to the wide variation of network traffic dynamics [38, 43], building dedicated buffers in the NIC for peak traffic apparently results in low SRAM utilization.

BiC offers a flexible way to provide the NIC buffer. We call this INIC design BiC-INIC. Two buffers are created in BiC-INIC, one to receive packet headers, and the other to receive payloads. These are represented by the H and P blocks in the dashed box in Figure 4(c). When a packet arrives, the header and payload are split and put into the two buffers. The H buffer is shared between the NIC and core via memory mapping. The core processes packet headers from the BiC's H buffer. A copy engine in the shared L2 cache copies payloads from the P buffer to user space. Comparing Figure 4(b) against 4(c), BiC-INIC saves packet header copying, but requires copying packet data from P to P-user. Page flipping [37] can avoid payload copying by remapping the P buffer to user memory. Investigating this optimization is beyond the scope of this paper.

With BIC-NIC, the OS can dynamically adjust the H and P buffer sizes in response to the actually packet arrival rate, as opposed to building mega bytes of dedicated local SRAM in the NIC to accommodate for the theoretical maximum bandwidth. Table 3 compares the NIC buffer requirement of a chip that has a peak network bandwidth of 40Gbps.

Table 3. Buffer Requirements in the Integrated NIC

Network Mode	Theoretical	Dedicated NIC Buffer	BiC
40Gbps	1536KB	1536KB	1536KB
10Gbps	384KB	1536KB	384KB
1Gbps	38KB	1536KB	38KB

3.2 Evaluation Methodology

3.2.1 Evaluation Metrics

We use two metrics to quantitatively evaluate the BiC architecture:

279

1) performance degradation when buffers are allocated out of the L2C capacity. In theory, both the hardware accelerated functions and CPU software functions could be negatively impacted. The source of performance degradation can be three-fold: interconnect bandwidth, cache port contention, and cache capacity loss. The baseline is an otherwise same processor, except that it uses dedicated private SRAM buffers.

2) hardware cost of total SRAM plus the system interconnect. Net savings in silicon will be reduced on-die SRAM minus the extra logic for buffer management, and cost for increasing the system interconnect width and cache port should they become necessary.

Two important aspects that we leave for future work are security [17, 49] and power implications of BiC

3.2.2 Evaluated Platforms

We evaluate the BiC design based on two platforms.

The first platform, illustrated in Figures 5 and 6, is a recognition processor that we are implementing for a research test-chip. The SoC serves the two recognition tasks we described, MAR and SR. The SoC integrates Intel® Pentium cores, a BiC, interconnect, a DDR2 controller, and two fixed-function accelerators.

To evaluate BiC, at any given time we run two applications, one from SPEC CPU2000 and the other either MAR (Figure 5a)or SR (Figure 5b). When we activate both recognition tasks as well as one SPEC application, all three processor cores and both accelerators are active, shown in Figure 6.

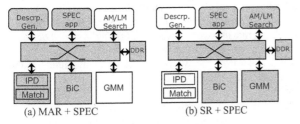

(a) MAR + SPEC   (b) SR + SPEC

Figure 5. Recognition SoC with 2 Cores Active

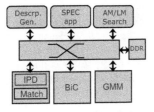

Figure 6. Recognition SoC with 3 Cores Active

The other platform, illustrated in Figure 7, is a hypothetical high-end CMP processor with two on-chip network interface devices.

3.3 Hardware Cost

We implemented BiC in RTL on a 512KB, 8-way set-associative cache with 64-byte cachelines and LRU replacement policy. Based on synthesized results using 32nm process, Figure 8 compares area of the baseline cache and that of the BiC. BiC area is 1.3% larger than the traditional cache. Detailed hardware implementation information can be found in [14].

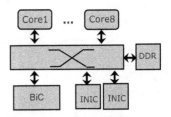

Figure 7. CMP with an Integrated NIC

In stark contrast to general-purpose processor cores which usually benefit from any reduction in individual load/store latencies, fixed-function accelerators have strict bandwidth requirements but are usually relaxed with respect to latency. With pipelined cache and buffer controllers, BiC maintains sustained bandwidth, although it introduces a few clock cycles of initial delay. A few local staging registers, approximately 400 bytes in each accelerator, absorb much of the traffic. The residual buffer accesses issued by each of the MAR and GMM accelerators are about 32 bytes for every six core clock cycles. Both workloads on our recognition processor were able to sustain the same throughput as when dedicated local buffers are used. In other words, the performance of neither accelerator in our recognition processor has been impacted by the BiC design.

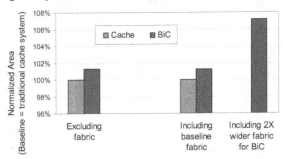

Figure 8. Hardware Cost of BiC

To address potential bandwidth issues, in some SoC designs we may need to increase the system fabric bandwidth. We will give such an example in Section 3.4. Figure 8 shows that area of BiC + baseline interconnect is about 1.2% higher than that of cache + baseline interconnect, while BiC + 2X wider interconnect consumes 7.2% larger area than cache + baseline interconnect. The numbers in the figure include all components of the coherent interconnect: wires, cache miss transaction tables, arbitration logic, etc. The wider interconnect transfers twice as many data as the baseline at the same clock frequency.

For the usage cases that we evaluated (details in Section 3.4), we did not find compelling needs to add an extra port in the BiC. If future applications prefer more cache bandwidth, e.g., by adding a dedicated port for buffer accesses, the additional cost is rather small.

A conventional architecture needs to build buffers whose sizes meet the need of the worst cases (i.e., largest setups) that the applications use, even though they may only be required in some rare usage cases. Based on the minimum buffer requirements for worst-case scenarios in Tables 1 and 2, we estimate the dedicated SRAM buffers for this recognition processor to be about 205KB, assuming ping-pong buffering. Using BiC, we allocate just the necessary amount of buffer space at run time from the shared L2 cache, obviating the need to build the 205KB dedicated SRAM. If we take the system interconnect into account, the BiC design reduces SRAM+fabric area by 36.5%. If a 2X wider interconnect is used with BiC, the area reduction is 28.9% compared with a L2C+dedicated buffer design with the baseline interconnect. This is shown in Table 4.

Table 4. Silicon Cost Savings in the Recognition Processor

	SRAM Size	Area(μm^2)	Savings
L2C + buf + baseline fabric	717 KB	10,501,273	baseline
BiC + baseline fabric	512 KB	7,694,331	36.5%
BiC + 2X wider fabric	512 KB	8,144,331	28.9%

3.4 Simulation Results

We use a performance simulator, ManySim [52], to estimate performance of software threads running in the processor cores.

Table 5 shows simulation parameters. The cache and buffer controllers share an SRAM port with different priorities; a cache access is serviced only when there is no pending buffer request. One key set of parameters in the table are buffer space used by the accelerators. In the recognition SoC, we use two numbers, 70KB and 32KB, based on common-case usage scenarios. For the INIC packet buffers in the CMP, we allocate 768KB out of the L2C based on [8], for a dual-NIC setup that Niagara2 [13] uses.

3.4.1 Recognition Server Simulation Results

Both recognition applications have clearly pre-defined performance targets. For MAR, it is one second response time. For SR, it is real time decoding. The performance targets translate to specific bandwidth requirements, achieved by time stamps that we inserted in the traces. More available bandwidth is not necessary and will not be utilized by the accelerators. The SPEC applications, quite differently, will benefit from any reduction in memory latency and consume memory bandwidth on a best-effort basis.

To understand the degree of performance degradation for application processing on the core caused by L2 cache sharing, we run the accelerators at full speed and simulate cycles-per-instruction (CPI) of the SPEC benchmarks. Figure 9 shows performance of SPEC CPU benchmarks when they compete for L2 cache capacity and bandwidth with accelerated MAR or SR applications. The normalization baseline is the same workload mix running with dedicated private SRAM buffers in the accelerator.

We observe occasional major performance impact to the SPEC applications. For example, *parser* performance is down by over 5.6% when taking 70KB of L2C away, primarily because of the consequent conflict and capacity misses. The average performance degradation of SPEC processes when using BiC buffers is just ~2% and ~1% respectively than using dedicated SRAM buffers. For the low-power recognition servers, we consider this good cost-performance tradeoff.

We also find that neither an extra cache port nor higher interconnect bandwidth yield noticeably different SPEC performance (data not shown here) for this scenario since the default interconnect and single-ported cache supply ample bandwidth when MAR and SR do not run simultaneously.

When we add one more core in the SoC and run both workloads simultaneously on the SoC, the performance targets of both recognition workloads are still well met. In this setup, the three cores are used for descriptor generation of MAR, Viterbi search of SR, and one SPEC benchmark, respectively. Thanks to priority given to the buffer accesses over cache accesses, the accelerators are able to sustain their normal throughput. We observe performance impact, about 0.5% and 5.4% respectively, in the software portions of MAR and SR. But neither thread violates its deadline. However, the best-effort SPEC applications are more noticeably impacted due to loss of cache capacity and increased contentions, shown as the *Default* bars in Figure 10.

We added one extra cache port to allow a buffer access and a cache access to be served in a same clock cycle. We also made the system interconnect twice as wide. As is shown in Figure 10, the cache port enhancement only improves the SPEC applications' performance by an average of 0.8%. System interconnect bandwidth turned out to be a more severe bottleneck; the 2X wider fabric completely solves the contention issue. In fact, with the faster interconnect, the benchmarks

Table 5. Simulation Parameters for the SoC and CMP

Parameter	Recognition on low-power MPSoC server	INIC in a high-performance CMP
Core and L1C	1.6Ghz, in-order; IL1=DL1=32KB, 4-way	4Ghz, out-of-order; IL1=DL1=32KB, 4-way
Active Cores	2 if either MAR or SR runs; 3 if both run	8
Shared BiC (L2C)	512KB total capacity , 8-way SA, 1.6Ghz	8MB total capacity , 8-way SA, 2Ghz
Buffer out of L2C	**70KB for MAR and 32KB for SR**	**768KB for INIC buffer**
Memory latency	L1 hit = 3 cyc, L2 hit = 9 cyc, DRAM = 110ns.	
MAR information	1M pixel images, 500 interest points. Running in software on the core: Descriptor generation. Accelerated: IPD and Matching. 400Mhz.	
SR information	65000-word vocabulary. Wall Street Journal article in clean audio Running in software on the core: Viterbi search. Accelerated: GMM scoring. 400Mhz	
Workload mix	Core1: One SPEC00 benchmark Core2/3: Software portion of MAR and/or SR; Accelerator: MAR (IPD+Match) or GMM.	Cores 1-8: Eight SPEC00 benchmarks, plus receive-side TCP/IP packet processing Accelerator: Two on-die NIC for MAC functions, each 10Gb/s network rate

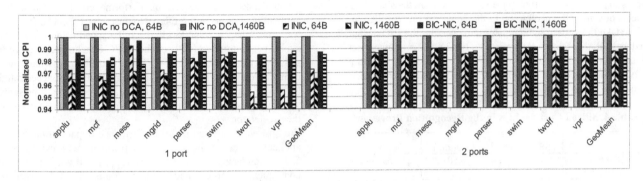

Figure 9. Performance Impact to the SPEC00 Applications When Using BiC on a 2-Core SoC (MAR and SR Run in Isolation)

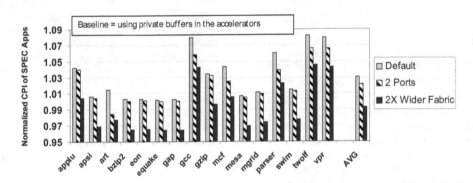

Figure 10. Performance Impact to the SPEC00 Applications When Using BiC on a 3-Core SoC (MAR and SR Run Simultaneously)

performed higher than the baseline because L1 misses are filled 2 core clocks earlier.

3.4.2 On-Chip NIC Simulations Results

To study the benefits of the proposed BiC-NiC, we simulate receive-side packet processing for an on-chip NIC shown in Figure 7. All eight cores run SPEC CPU2000 applications, and the device driver for the NICs is invoked randomly from these cores. All cores share an 8M cache.

In Figure 11, we present the simulated SPEC benchmark performance when they compete for processor and memory system resources with receive-side packet processing. We evaluate three models, INIC with no DCA, INIC, and BIC-NIC, corresponding respectively to the three on-chip NIC architectures described in Section 3.1.3. In each model, two packet sizes are used, 64B and 1460B, representing control messages and bulk data transfers, respectively. We also vary the number of cache/BiC ports. The CPIs are normalized to those of INIC with no DCA.

As the packets arrive at each of the BIC-NICs at a rate of 10Gb/s, we found that overall, the utilization of the stack processing core and memory bandwidth is lower with DCA than the baseline, reconfirming the observations in [19]. Both INIC and BIC-NIC yield better performance relative to the INIC with no DCA when the packet size is 1460 bytes compared to 64B, because more DRAM accesses are converted to L2 cache hits.

Between INIC and BIC-INIC, the average performance difference is 1.1% and 2.5% for 1 cache port for the two packet sizes. BIC-NIC affects the core threads more because of two reasons: higher cache port contention due to payload copying and smaller cache capacity due to buffer use, with port contention being the major factor. Referring to Figure 4 (c), copying payloads from P (in BiC) to P-user (in cacheable memory space) causes extra cache port contention. As a result, BIC-NIC performance is slightly worse than INIC by up to 4.5% for larger packets on a 1-port cache. With two ports, the performance advantage of INIC over BIC-INIC drops to 0.2% (shown in the right half of Figure 11) as more cache bandwidth become available to the SPEC processes. The loss of 768 KB cache capacity to NIC buffer in an 8MB shared L2C with aggressive processor cores causes the small performance difference between INIC and BIC-INIC.

We thus conclude that BIC-INIC saves 768KB of dedicated SRAM in the two integrated NICs, at the cost of no more than 2.5% performance degradation on SPEC workloads with 1-port BiC when compared with INIC with DCA. With an additional port, the performance impact of the BiC architecture is negligible.

4 RELATED WORK

While general-purpose processors rely on caches to bridge the speed gap between computation logic and main memory [35, 50], embedded systems widely use addressable on-chip memory [51]. As transistor cost drops, it becomes natural for embedded processors to include caches [7]. But adoption of software-visible memory buffers in general-purpose processors is much more challenging due to its many ramifications in context switch, virtual memory management, and programming interface. Nevertheless, researchers start to investigate potential benefits and associated complexities of using memory buffers in the cache hierarchy [12, 23, 48]. The BiC architecture complements these studies by providing a cost-effective way of *providing* the on-chip SRAM buffers.

A closely related work is Column Caching [9]. Column Caching exposes part of the cache as software-visible memory. Some DSP processors [1, 45] have similar designs. To the best of our knowledge, our paper is the first to systematically evaluate performance impact using realistic workloads. It is also the first and only paper to present the tradeoff between performance degradation and hardware cost. Earlier publications on the subject [3, 9] only present qualitative descriptions of the architecture, and evaluate it with simplistic computation kernels. Another major drawback of these as compared to BiC is that the coarse granularity of SRAM allocation is one way (or larger) of the whole set-associative cache. This causes fragmentation of the precious on-die SRAM resources. BiC allows accelerators to allocate/release buffers at cacheline granularity. For some workloads, the difference can be big. For example, in our image recognition accelerator, one of the buffer setups is 70 KB. If implemented by allocating capacity from the cache on a way granularity, the over-provisioning is significant due to round to the nearest way-size. On an Intel Atom processor which contains a 512KB 8-way cache, accommodating a 70KB private buffer with column caching consumes two 64KB cache-ways, wasting 58KB of SRAM.

SAM (Syncretic Adaptive Memory) in the FT64 scientific stream accelerator [47] can be accessed both as a stream register file and as a direct-mapped cache. SAM is inherently tied to stream semantics and not used for general data structures.

Way Stealing [25] uses the cache space to implement local memory for accelerators. Software accesses data in the stolen ways by explicitly specifying way numbers in instructions and through special per-way AGUs, which requires that layout of the cache be exposed to software. In BiC, we purposefully hide from software implementational details of the baseline cache structure. Another difference is that their study focuses on L1 cache sharing to enhance instruction set extensions, while our work is on L2/L3 cache sharing for coarse grained accelerators. Compiler-controlled way-placement [22] write/read data to/from specified ways of the cache to achieve guaranteed cache hits. Gummaraju et al. [16] take a software-only approach to provide deterministic accesses on a hardware-managed cache. In their implementation, the software carefully manages sequences of data accesses and makes sure that references to cacheable data do not trigger replacement of a memory-mapped cacheline.

Recognizing the difficulty of application software managing SRAM memory, researchers use software instructions to implement a cache on top of an SRAM memory [31, 40]. Compared with hardware-managed caches, software-managed caches can be tailored to cater for different applications' behavior by using the best parameters such as associativity, line size and replacement logic.

5 SUMMARY

In this paper, we show that the trend of accelerator integration into SoC and CMP platforms introduces a plethora of buffers and caches that occupy SRAM. To address the SRAM area inefficiency, we propose a Buffer-Integrated-Caching architecture that extends a conventional cache organization to integrate multiple buffers. We show that the BiC architecture enables best-effort cache views and deterministic buffers to cores and accelerators accessing the BiC. Using detailed case studies, we show that the BiC architecture provides significant area savings by eliminating most of the private dedicated SRAM blocks and introduces very minor performance degradation for memory-intensive CPU threads. As more hardware accelerators are integrated on to the CPU die, and hence the need for more buffer space, we believe that BiC offers a cost-effective solution to the SRAM challenge.

6 ACKNOWLEDGEMENTS

We thank Sally McKee for her help to improve the quality of this paper. Many of our colleagues contributed to the recognition SoC, including May Wu, Steve Zhang, Jenny Chang, Anthony Chun, David Bormann, Mike Deisher, Sadagopan Srinivasan, et al.

7 REFERENCES

[1] S. Agarwala, et. al, "A Multi-level Memory System for High Performance DSP Applications,", ICCD 2000

[2] J. Chang, et al., "ISIS: An Accelerator for Sphinx Speech Recognition", SASP 2011

[3] F. Liu, et al., "Understanding How Off-chip Memory Bandwidth Partitioning in Chip-Multiprocessors Affects System Performance", HPCA 2010

[4] AMD Fusion, http://fusion.amd.com

[5] Anandtech, "Intel's Sandy Bridge Architecture Exposed", http://www.anandtech.com

[6] D. Andersen et al., "FAWN: a Fast Array of Wimpy Nodes", SOSP 2009

[7] ARM, "Accelerator Coherency Port", http://www.arm.com

[8] N. Binkert, A. Saidi, S. Reinhardt, "Integrated network interfaces for high-bandwidth TCP/IP", ASPLOS 2006

[9] D. Chiou, et al. "Application-Specific Memory Management for Embedded Systems Using Software-Controlled Caches", DAC 2000

[10] M. Choubassi and Y. Wu, "Augmented Reality on Mobile Internet Devices", Intel Technology Journal, 14(1), 2010

[11] CMU Sphinx Project, http://www.cmusphinx.org

[12] H. Cook, et al, "Virtual Local Stores", Technical Report UCB/EECS-2009-131, 2009

[13] G. Grohoski and R.Golla, "Niagara2: a Highly Threaded Server-on-a-Chip", HOTCHIPS 2006

[14] C. Fajardo, et al., "Buffer-Integrated Cache: A cost Effective SRAM Architecture for Handheld and Embedded Platforms", DAC 2011

[15] M. Gschwind, et al, "Synergistic Processing in Cell's Multicore Architecture", IEEE Micro, 26(1), 2006

[16] J. Gummaraju, et. al, "Architectural Support for the Stream Execution Model", PACT 2007

[17] M. Kharbutli, et al., "Comprehensively and Efficiently Protecting the Heap", ASPLOS, 2006

[18] R. Iyer, et.al, "CogniServe: Heterogeneous Server Architecture for Large-Scale Recognition", IEEE Micro, May/June, 2011

[19] R. Huggahalli, R.Iyer and S. Tetrick, "Direct Cache Access for High Bandwidth Network I/O", ISCA 2005

[20] R. Iyer, et al., "QoS Policies and Architecture for Cache/Memory in CMP Platforms", SIGMETRICS 2007

[21] C. Johnson, et al, "A Wire-Speed Power Processor: 2.3Ghz, 45nm, SOI with 16 Cores and 64 Threads", ISSCC 2010

[22] T. Jones, et. al, "Instruction Cache Energy Saving through Compiler Way-Placement", DATE 2008

[23] M. Katevenis, et. al, "Explicit Communication and Synchronization in SARC", IEEE Micro, 30(5), 2010

[24] R. H. Katz, "Tech Titans Building Boom", IEEE Spectrum, Feburary 2009, pp.40-54

[25] T. Kluter, P. Brisk, P. Ienne and E. Charbon, "Way Stealing: Cache-assisted Automatic Instruction Set Extensions", DAC, 2009

[26] S. Lee, et al, "Accelerating Mobile Augmented Reality on a Handheld Platform", ICCD 2009

[27] G. Liao, et.al, "A New TCP Cache to Efficiently Manage TCP Sessions for Web Servers", ANCS 2010

[28] G. Liao and L. Bhuyan, "Performance Measurement of an Integrated NIC Architecture with 10GbE", Hot Interconnect, 2009

[29] S. Makineni and R. Iyer, "Architectural Characterization of TCP/IP Packet Processing on the Pentium M Processor", HPCA 2004

[30] B. Mathew, et al., "A Low-Power Accelerator for the SPHINX3 Speech Recognition System", CASES 2003

[31] J. Miller and A. Agarwal, "Software-based Instruction Caching for Embedded Processors", ASPLOS-XII, 2006

[32] T. Mudge and U. Holzle, "Challenges and Opportunities for Extremely Energy-Efficient Processors", Micro, 30(4), 2010

[33] K. J. Nesbit, et al, "Virtual Private Caches", ISCA, 2007.

[34] R. Patel, "Moorestown Platform: Based on Lincroft SoC Designed for Next-Generation Smartphones", HOTCHIPS 2009

[35] B. Rogers, et al., "Scaling the Bandwidth Wall: Challenges in and Avenues for CMP Scaling", ISCA 2009

[36] V. Reddi, et al, "Web Search Using Mobile Cores: Quantifying and Mitigating the Price of Efficiency", ISCA 2010

[37] J. Ronciak, et al., "Page-Flip Technology for use within the Linux Networking Stack", the Linux Sym., 2004

[38] A. Qureshi, et. al, "Cutting the Electric Bill for Internet-Scale Systems", SIGCOMM 2009

[39] SeeMicro, Atom-based Servers, http://www.seemicro.com

[40] S. Seo, et al, "Design and Implementation of Software-managed Caches for Multicores with Local Memory", HPCA 2009

[41] L. Spracklen, "Sun's Third-Generation On-chip UltraSPARC Security Accelerator", HOTCHIPS, 2009

[42] S. Srinivasan, et. al., "Performance Characterization and Optimization of Mobile Augmented Reality on Handheld Platforms", IISWC 2009

[43] N. Taft, et al, "Understanding Traffic Dynamics at a Backbone POP", SPIE ITCOM Workshop on Scalability and Traffic Control on IP Networks, 2001

[44] G. Takacs, et al, "Outdoors Augmented Reality on Mobile Phone Using Loxel-Based Visual Feature Organization", ICMIR 2008

[45] Texas Instruments, "TMS320C Flexible Cache", http://focus.ti.com.cn/cn/lit/ug/sprug82a/sprug82a.pdf

[46] Texas Instruments, "OMAP4 Mobile Applications Platform", http://focus.ti.com/lit/ml/swpt034/swpt034.pdf

[47] M. Wen, et al, "On-chip Memory System Optimization Design for the FT64 Scientific Stream Accelerator", IEEE Micro, 28(4), 2008, pp.51-70

[48] T. Wenisch, et al, "Store-Ordered Streaming of Shared Memory", PACT 2005

[49] X.Jiang and Y. Solihin, "Architectural Framework for Supporting Operating System Survivability", HPCA 2011

[50] X.Jiang, et al., "CHOP: Adaptive Filter-based DRAM Caching for CMP Server Platforms", HPCA 2010

[51] R.Banakar, et al., "Scratchpad Memory: a Design Alternative for Cache On-chip Memory in Embedded Systems", CODES 2002

[52] L.Zhao, et. al, "Exploring Large-Scale CMP Architectures Using ManySim", IEEE Micro, 27(4)

[53] ZTsystems, "R1801e Data Center Servers based on ARM A9 cores", http://www.ztsystems.com

A Composite and Scalable Cache Coherence Protocol for Large Scale CMPs

Yi Xu[†], Yu Du[‡], Youtao Zhang[‡], Jun Yang[†]
[†] Department of Electrical and Computer Engineering
[‡] Department of Computer Science
University of Pittsburgh, Pittsburgh, Pennsylvania, USA
[†]{yix13, juy9}@pitt.edu, [‡]{fisherdu, zhangyt}@cs.pitt.edu

ABSTRACT

The number of on-chip cores of modern chip multiprocessors (CMPs) is growing fast with technology scaling. However, it remains a big challenge to efficiently support cache coherence for large scale CMPs. The conventional snoopy and directory coherence protocols cannot be smoothly scaled to many-core or thousand-core processors. Snoopy protocols introduce large power overhead due to enormous amount of cache tag probing triggered by broadcast. Directory protocols introduce performance penalty due to indirection, and large storage overhead due to storing directories.

This paper addresses the efficiency problem when supporting cache coherency for large-scale CMPs. By leveraging emerging optical on-chip interconnect (OP-I) technology to provide high bandwidth density, low propagation delay and natural support for multicast/broadcast in a hierarchical network organization, we propose a composite cache coherence (C^3) protocol that benefits from direct cache-to-cache accesses as in snoopy protocol and small amount of cache probing as in directory protocol. Targeting at quickly completing coherence transactions, C^3 organizes accesses in a three-tier hierarchy by combining a mix of designs including local broadcast prediction, filtering, and a coarse-grained directory. Compared to directory-based protocol [18], our evaluations on a thousand-core CMP show that C^3 improves performance by 21%, reduces network latency of coherence messages by 41% and saves network energy consumption by 5.5% on average for PARSEC applications.

Categories and Subject Descriptors

C.1.2 [**Computer Systems Organization**]: Processor Architectures—*Multiple Data Stream Architectures (Multiprocessors)*; B.3.2 [**Memory Structures**]: Design Styles—*Cache memories, shared memories*; B.4.3 [**Hardware**]: Input/Output and Data Communications—*Interconnections (subsystems)*

General Terms

Performance

Keywords

Cache Coherence Protocol, Thousand-Core, CMP, Optical Network, Nanophotonics

1. INTRODUCTION

Chip multiprocessors (CMP) have emerged as a promising microarchitecture for keeping up performance with integration density [20, 41]. Today, the number of on-chip cores has reached low hundreds, e.g. Intel's 80-core Terascale chip [48] and nVidia's 128-core Quadro GPU [40]. In near future, the on-chip core count will likely to reach upper hundreds or even a thousand [11].

Designing hardware cache coherence protocols for future many-core CMPs is challenging. There are mainly two classes of protocols to enforce cache coherence: snooping-based and directory-based protocols [3]. There have been many proposals for small- and mid- scale CMPs [4, 5, 17, 23, 24, 34, 35, 46]. However, supporting coherence for large scale CMPs remains difficult. Snoopy protocols introduce large power overhead due to enormous amount of cache tag probing triggered by broadcast. Directory protocols introduce large storage and performance overhead due to directory store and lookup. In addition, the efficiency of coherence protocols depends on the network topology. Traditional topologies, such as Mesh, face challenge in performance scalability. For example, core-to-core communications require up to 64 hops for a 1024-core mesh network, making it prohibitively expensive to support indirection in directory protocols. Mesh-based snoopy protocols [5, 4, 23], on the other hand, require additional hardware to support broadcast and message ordering, making it difficult to scale with increased core count and cache sizes.

Recent efforts have embraced the emerging nanophotonic technologies for networks-on-chip. Optical interconnects (OP-I) naturally supports broadcast, provides high bandwidth density, low propagation delay, and low power consumption for remote communications [8, 36, 37]. However, few optical designs address the intrinsic scalability issues of coherence protocols in large-scale CMPs. For example, optical crossbars [29, 42, 49] did not reduce the cache tag probing overhead in snoopy protocols. Hence, new designs are necessary for large-scale cache coherence protocols to be efficient and scalable.

In this paper, we address the cache coherence problem for thousand-core CMPs leveraging benefits of OP-I. We first alleviate the scalability pressure by shrinking the network size with cache clustering and network concentration. We then utilize optical crossbars to provide inter-cluster communications for high bandwidth and low network diameter. We greatly reduce snooping messages through local broadcast with prediction, and message filtering. Finally, we use extremely small directories to avoid unnecessary global broadcast. Comparing to various directory and snoopy protocols in a thousand-core architecture, our composite protocol achieves 21% performance improvement and 5.5% energy savings with modest storage. The last-level cache probing is only 5.8% of a snoopy protocol. In summary, we make these contributions:

- We introduce a composite cache coherence (C^3) protocol that strives to achieve both direct cache-to-cache accesses as in snoopy protocol, and small amount of cache probing as in directory protocol.

- We integrate recent research and technology advances including OP-I, 3D die-stacking and network concentration to design a viable NoC architecture for thousand-core CMPs.

- We design a new mechanism to order coherence messages in global network to remove racing situations and ensure correctness.

The remainder of this paper is organized as follows. Section 2 presents the background of nanophotonics. Section 3 discusses the details of the proposed C^3 protocol as well as architecture design of thousand-core CMP. The implementation details are described in Section 4. The experimental results are analyzed in Section 5. Section 6 summarizes the related work. Finally, Section 7 concludes this paper.

2. NANOPHOTONICS BACKGROUND

Recent ITRS report [21] identified limitations in using metal wires for global links: (i) the wire performance does not scale well; (ii) long RC wires require large number of repeaters that consume significant portion of total power; and (iii) the slow increase of pin count restricts the bandwidth between core and memory. In contrast, nanophotonic links can provide high bandwidth density, low propagation delay, communication-target-independent power consumption, and natural support for multicast/broadcast. Recent advances in photonic devices and integration technology have made it a promising candidate for future global interconnects.

A typical optical network includes off-chip laser source that provides on-chip light, waveguides that route optical signal, ring modulators that convert electrical signals to optical ones, and ring filters to detect lights and translate it into electrical signals. Fig. 1 illustrates a typical dense wavelength division multiplexing (DWDM) nanophotonic link. Light of multiple wavelengths is generated by the off-chip laser source and then coupled into the on-chip waveguide. Though on-chip light source exists [51], it consumes significant precious on-chip power and area [37]. Waveguide, which uses high refraction index material as the core part and low index material on the outside, confines and guides the light around the chip with losses on the order of 0.1dB/mm [30]. Since light of different wavelengths can be transmitted and modulated in the single waveguide, DWDM technology enables multiple data channels per waveguide, providing high network bandwidth density. At the sender side, electrical signals are imprinted to laser light by wavelength-selective silicon modulators that absorb and pass the light for signal '0' and '1' respectively. The modulators are built based on

ring resonators of less than $50\mu m^2$/ring [37] performing at 20Gbps. At the receiver side, the optical filter extracts the light of specific wavelength from the waveguide and transfers it to the photo detector which can be built with CMOS-compatible germanium to convert optical signals to electrical ones which are then passed to amplifiers. In global broadcast, optical signal is able to reach the furthest receiver in the network because of the low-loss property of those optical filters in the intermediate nodes. The power and energy loss of different optical modules are listed in Section 4.2.

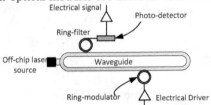

Figure 1: Photonic components.

3. COMPOSITE CACHE COHERENCE (C^3) PROTOCOL DESIGN

In this section, we present the composite cache coherence protocol to address the efficiency problem in large-scale CMPs. We first discuss the chip architecture and cache organization that our protocol is based upon, and then elaborate the protocol details.

3.1 Thousand-Core Chip Architecture

Fig. 2 illustrates an overview of our 1000-core chip architecture. It adopts emerging 3D die-stacking technology [10, 27] to integrate CMOS logic and memories into different layers. All cores are in one layer and caches are in other layers. In our design, there are three levels of cache in the hierarchy: L1 and L2 are private; they are relatively small and fast. L3 (LLC) is shared; it is relatively large and slow. L1 is placed in the core layer for fast access. L2 and L3 are stacked atop.

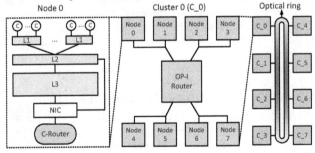

Figure 2: A thousand-core cache and NoC architecture.

3.1.1 Cache Clustering

In typical small-scale CMPs, the private cache tile of each core is directly connected to an NoC node. However, this would be inappropriate for thousand-core processors because the NoC size would be too large and average latency would too high. Also, each node's traffic injection rate is not very high because they are from a single core's private cache misses, indicating that such NoC is not very efficient. Therefore, a better way is to employ the concentration technique to share the network channel among core-cache tiles [6, 28]. We choose to cluster several cores and their L1 and L2 cache slices. Sharing caches results in less global coherence traffic, better utilization of the limited cache capacity and network resources. However, too much sharing may create contention in cache, especially in L1 which is performance critical. Hence, we let four cores share one L1, and four L1s share one L2, similar to the design of the Rock processor [15]. Each L2 is connected to one concentrated router (C-Router) via network interface module (NIC), resulting in only 64 nodes in the NoC, as shown in left part of Fig. 2.

3.1.2 Optical Interconnection Topology

To support high traffic volume generated from up to thousand on-chip cores, we employ the single-write-multiple-read (SWMR) optical buses [29, 37, 42] because it provides contention free connections between senders and receivers. Each node in the network has a dedicated channel to send requests and all remaining nodes listen to the channel to receive requests. We choose this topology due to its contention-free communication, high performance and low design complexity. However, the power consumption of this design increases quadratically with the network size. This is because all microrings need to consume the "listening" power and there are N^2 microrings (N is the network size) in the crossbar. We have already reduced the network size from 1000 to 64 through cache clustering. But a 64×64 optical crossbar is still quite large. Hence, a hierarchical network architecture [29, 37] is necessary to keep the crossbar small. Adopting such a hierarchy divides the network into C clusters. Each cluster has $64/C$ nodes that share one OP-I router. The SWMR crossbar then connects all OP-I routers to form a network of C nodes.

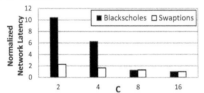

Figure 3: Network latency with different Cs.

Determining an appropriate C represents the design trade-off between bandwidth and power in 1) the aggregated traffic load per cluster. If cluster size is large, then the bandwidth requirement within a cluster may be high for the OP-I router, resulting in contention delay and performance degradation; 2) the power consumed by microrings. If the cluster size is small, then C is large, which results in quadratic increase in power consumption as discussed earlier; 3) the power consumed by laser source. More ring resonators on a waveguide will cause more energy loss during light propagation, which leads to higher laser power at the source. Fig. 3 compares the network latency of two applications with different Cs. The 8- and 16-cluster networks obtain better performance over others. We choose C=8 in this paper. Electrical network is used to connect 8 L2 banks within each OP-I router (Fig. 2). These links are bidirectional. A coherence message generated by a node (L2 bank) is first sent to either local L3 if it is the home node, or the NIC that packs it as a network message and then sends to the corresponding C-router which routes the message through local electrical network to the OP-I router and then onto the global OP-I network (Fig. 2).

Data messages are much larger than coherence messages. The latter often requires broadcast or multicast while the former is always unicast. Since the laser power for broadcast or multicast is higher than unicast [8, 29], it is inefficient to use the same network for both coherence and data messages. In our scheme, we use a separate network that employs a reservation-assisted SWMR crossbar for data messages [42], which saves filter power and laser source power. Lastly, we use multiple network layers to supply necessary bandwidth required by both networks. This is more effective than increasing the network bandwidth directly [16]. DWDM technology is adopted to implement multiple network layers through partitioning the wavelengths according to address space. The details of the network layers used are discussed in section 4.2.

3.2 The C^3 Protocol

The goal of the C^3 protocol is to provide as much as possible direct cache-to-cache communication between requester and destination as in a snoopy protocol, while minimizing the amount of cache tag probing, and storage space as required in a directory protocol.

3.2.1 Local Broadcast for Reads

Let us first perform a simple traffic analysis on a set of PARSEC workloads [9] to motivate our design.

The left bar in Fig. 4 shows the probability of a read request finding a sharer ("shared data"), or the owner ("dirty data") in its local cluster, i.e., if the requested data present in a local L2 cache bank. On average, there is a 50% chance that a read can find the desired data locally, without having to use the global optical crossbar. For some benchmarks such as blackscholes and swaptions, the probability can be as high as 85%. This simple observation suggests that for read requests, it is beneficial to perform a local broadcast. When it is likely to obtain the target data directly from a local L2 cache, this design choice is not only fast but also energy efficient.

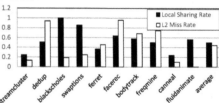

Figure 4: The probability of a read request finding a sharer/owner in the local cluster upon L2 hit and L2 miss rate of read requests.

However, blindly broadcasting read requests is not always beneficial because 1) some benchmarks such as canneal have low local sharing rate; 2) some benchmarks do not even have many reads that can find owner or sharers in global L2 due to L2 miss, as is also plotted in Fig. 4. Some of workloads cannot fit in private L2 cache and miss rate is over 90%. Hence, performing a local broadcast for every read in those benchmarks indeed introduces extra cycles and energy. To prevent unnecessary broadcast in those cases, we implement a simple 1-bit predictor for every core in each OP-I router to determine if a broadcast should be performed. If a local owner or sharer is found in the previous broadcast, then the bit is set, and the next read request will also be broadcast. Otherwise, the bit is reset, preventing the next local broadcast. If the later activity, e.g. from directory, indicates there is a local owner or sharer, the bit is set again. In Section 5, we will show that the simple 1-bit predictor can remove above 60% blind local broadcast.

Although a large portion of read requests benefit from local broadcast, write requests cannot because local forwarding is only allowed when the the owner is in the local cluster and dirty. Otherwise the write requests have to be broadcast to other clusters to invalidate all the sharers. Fig. 5 shows the possibility of the write request finishing transactions locally. The benchmarks not shown here hardly have any owner status during our experimental phase. As we can see the success rate is much lower than that of a read request in Fig. 4.

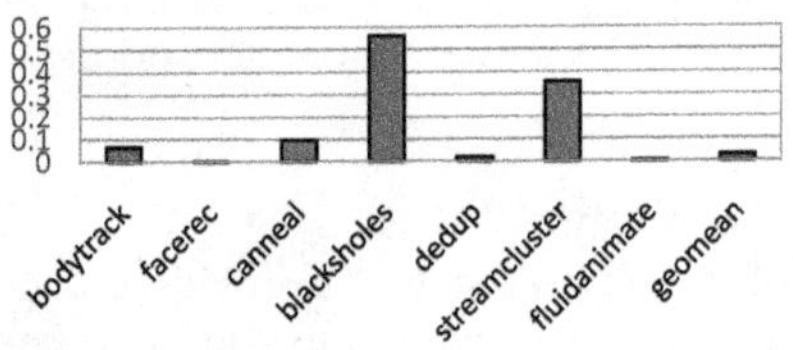

Figure 5: The probability of a write request finding a owner in the local cluster.

3.2.2 Filtering Requests for Global Broadcasts

In this section, we discuss how to handle requests that either skip local broadcast (writes) or fail to find a local sharer/owner (reads). We take advantage of direct cache-to-cache transfer using snooping, which can quickly locate the owner of the requested data. But broadcasting such requests to all nodes still incurs enormous probing energy costs and long queuing delay at L2 cache side. In our design, we use carefully designed filters to remove unnecessary broadcast overhead in snooping. That is, requests that hit in filters are turned into direct message or multicast messages. Requests that missed filters are sent directly to the home node. Most of them are also global L2 misses and should be sent to L3 anyway.

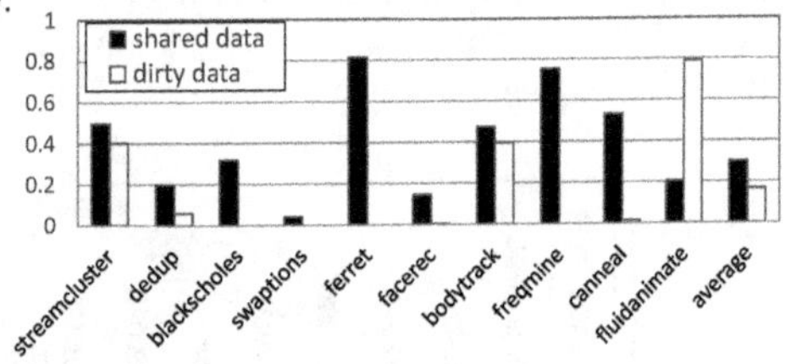

Figure 6: Categorizing read requests. There are more shared data than dirty data.

We put filters in OP-I routers to capture broadcast messages upon first sight. To determine what information is kept in filters, we analyzed read requests that are satisfied by read sharers and dirty owner in Fig. 6. We can see that for most benchmarks such as `ferret` and `freqmine`, shared-data reads predominate the total reads. For others such as `fluidanimate`, `streamcluster` and `bodytrack`, dirty-data reads occupy significant portion of the total reads. For the rest, i.e., `swaptions` and `facerec`, most read requests are simply L2 misses. Thus, if we store sharers in the filter, we can filter out more global broadcast messages. In addition, we can further reduce invalidation messages inside the cluster by utilizing the information of the sharer list in the filter.

Based on above observations, each entry of the filter stores an 8-bit *cluster* sharer vector and an 8-bit *local* sharer ID, as shown in Fig. 7. Each bit of the cluster sharer vector indicates if there is at least one sharer in the cluster. The local sharer records sharers within the local cluster. We use an example to illustrate how filter reduces snoopy messages upon write and read requests in Fig. 7. The request is first broadcast to all the OP-I routers through the optical waveguide. Once an OP-I router receives a remote write/read request, it queries both the cluster and local filter. If there are more than one cluster sharers, the filters spontaneously

pick one cluster closest to the requester, such as C_3 in the figure, to forward data. Other cluster sharers will invalidate their local sharers if it is a write request. Note that if there is a dirty owner, both the cluster and the local sharer vector should contain a single "1". Hence, we also implicitly store the dirty owner for requests, covering larger percent of broadcast. We also want to make a note that all filters are always synchronized, which we will discuss with details in Section 3.2.3. Later in Section 5, we will show that our filter together with the predicted local broadcast result in extremely small amount of cache probing while providing direct cache-to-cache transfer for majority of read and write requests. The former is almost comparable to that in a directory based coherence protocol while the latter is similar to that in a snooping protocol.

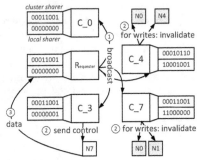

Figure 7: An example of filter access upon a request. A write request has extra local invalidation messages.

We implement the simple MSI coherence states in our protocol to remove remaining snoopy messages. "M" stands for "modify" (dirty data); "S" stands for "share" (clean data) and "I" indicates that no data copy in L2 cache. Keeping directory helps to handle messages such as L2 misses — they cannot benefit from further snooping. Using a coarse-grained vector directory helps to control the storage overhead, making it scalable to large scale CMPs. We use only an 8-bit vector to record either cluster sharers or the precise owner ID of the data.

Putting everything together, upon a local L2 *read* miss, the C-router first sends the request to its OP-I router and consults the predictor to determine if the request should be broadcast locally. If yes, the router sends message to all the local nodes and waits for their responses. Upon a hit, the requester receives data from a local sharer. Comparing to traditional directory protocols, a request with successful local prediction does not use the global network, which saves hop count and is more energy efficient. However, the write requests omit this step due to its low success rate.

For writes and those reads that failed to find sharer/owner in local broadcast, a global broadcast is then necessary. Upon seeing such messages, every OP-I router looks up in the filters trying to locate the corresponding owner/sharer ID. If a sharer/owner is found in the requester's cluster, the router simply forwards the data inside this cluster locally. Otherwise, the cluster (with a sharer) closest to the requester will forward the data. Finally, the OP-I router of the home node's cluster will forward the message to the home node to update the directory.

3.2.3 Message Ordering and Synchronization

The correctness of cache coherence protocols depends on the ordering in handling request racing. For example, two writes requesting the same data should be ordered such that only one owner exists at any time. In this section we discuss this ordering problem and present our mechanism to guarantee the correctness.

Ordering in global network. If a single transmission channel is used for broadcast, it is essentially a global ordered bus which needs arbitration for multiple requests. To improve the throughput of this network, we used as many channels as the number of nodes: 8. The problem arising from such a multi-bus broadcast network is how to order the broadcast messages sent by different nodes. In a conventional snoopy protocol implemented on a shared bus, the arbitration procedure of the bus will naturally grant permissions in a specific order for the receivers. In a conventional directory-based protocol, the directory in the home node orders the requests. In this paper, we use the filters in OP-I routers as the natural ordering points. Since the requests in the optical network can be received in one cycle (details in section 4), broadcast messages sent at the same cycle will be received by every optical router simultaneously. Next, messages arriving at the same cycle are processed in the same order in all the filters as arbitration algorithms are the same. Thus in the ordered global network, every filter observes the same sequence of broadcast messages.

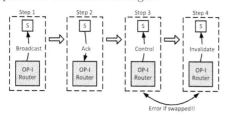

Figure 8: An example of ordering scheme in local network. The in-flight broadcast transaction is preferred over the global write/invalidation requests.

Ordering in local network. When arbitrating among local broadcast request and remote write/invalidation messages, we always check whether there is an in-flight local broadcast request before forwarding global ones to the local nodes. A write request will change cache status, so incorrect order of message handling would result in errors of an ongoing snoopy message. For example in Fig 8, a read request is first broadcast locally by the OP-I router. A local sharer S responds with a positive Ack to the router. Next the router should send a control message to S to require data forwarding. If, however, the router grants a remote invalidation message to the same address over the control message, the data in S would be invalidated before being forwarded to the requester, which is an error. Hence, only after the transaction of local broadcast is finished (the control message is sent or no positive Ack is received), can an invalidation/write message use the local link between the OP-I router and destination nodes. Note that it does not create starvation of remote write requests because the buffer size for the local broadcasts in the router is limited, so is the number of in-flight messages. Besides new broadcast is not issued until current invalidation message is sent. Second, messages sent by directory have fixed index of Virtual Channel (VC) and network layer via address mapping. The directory serves as ordering point if filters miss. The acknowledgments of invalidation and owners are not necessarily in the ordered network. Thus the ordered messages leaving from directory should stay in order until they arrive at the corresponding nodes. The same network layer and virtual channel can en-

sure that local arbitration in router will not reorder them to maintain the correctness.

Filter synchronization. The main reason of using same filters for every cluster is to let home node be aware if other node (the owner/sharer) is in charge of data forwarding. When the request is broadcast in the global network, filter in the home cluster can tell if the request hits in any other filter and if home node should send control message to the owner node without receiving the responds from other clusters, introducing additional network latency and messages. So in our protocol, filters in different clusters should be synchronized. Otherwise, it may introduce error: different filters indicate different owner/sharer. Filter is updated immediately after it is queried by current request sent via global network. However not all the local broadcast request is used to modify filter in case that they introduces differences. Only successful broadcast request meaning that predicted local broadcast helps find a local sharer and related reply messages could update the filter if the entry already exists and the status of the entry remains the same to avoid changes on replacement. Most of the actions of update are finished with the implication of the read/write requests. The network bandwidth overhead for filter updating is small as only write back message and eviction of sharers in whole cluster result broadcast in optical network. The filters in all the clusters are cache structures which have the same settings, initialization, and replacement policy. Besides, the accessing requests which update the filters are broadcast to all the clusters, arriving at the same cycle and arranged in the same order. Hence, the synchronization of filter is achieved via these organizations. Because filter space is not statically allocated for each cluster. The actual occupancy for the entries belonging to one of the clusters can vary vastly during this period of time. It helps improve the usage efficiency of the filter space.

4. IMPLEMENTATION

4.1 Router Microarchitecture

The OP-I router connects each local cluster to the global optical network. Since our optical network employs SWMR crossbar, each router includes eight input/output local ports, one output port that transfers flit in optical network (through Electric/Optical conversion), and seven input ports from optical detectors. Messages from local nodes are stored in virtual-channel (VC) buffer. If it is sent by the home node, the VC is assigned based on two address bits, as mentioned in section 3.2.3. Otherwise, there is no need for static mapping. After buffering message, the broadcast predictor and route unit are acquired. Based on the prediction result, message is either routed to local nodes or global network and forwarded to the switch allocation (SW) stage. If the message is to be broadcast in global network, the SW is similar to conventional two-stage design. Otherwise, it competes the local output ports with messages from remote clusters.

The messages from optical network go through a crossbar, which is designed for load balance and message ordering, before being stored into a shared buffer [43]. The buffer index of each message is exactly the same in all routers. And the filters process messages in the buffers in the same order, which depends on the arriving time of the message and a priority order based on sender's ID for the simultaneous requests. To reduce the unfairness, all routers periodically rotate the priority of the clusters.

To obtain the usage of electrical links to the local nodes, the winners from both local and global networks send requests to the round-robin based arbiter. When current local broadcasts do not finish, meaning that the OP-I router does not receive or respond to corresponding reply messages, the arbiter will not grant write and invalidation messages from remote clusters or following local broadcast requests to guarantee the order. However other type requests are processed normally and does not require waiting for on-fighting local broadcasts. Upon passing the arbitration, the messages stored in the buffer go through the second switch to be forwarded to the local ejected ports. And one credit per message is sent back to increment the buffer count in upstream node or router.

To ensure that message arrives at different clusters in the same cycle, the cycle time should accommodate the propagation delay in the worst case. We assume a 400 mm^2 die size. And the light speed is 10.45 ps/mm, the latency of E/O and O/E conversion is 75ps [29]. Therefore the network can support 1GHz adequately. The OP-I router requires 4 pipeline stages: buffering, (prediction and routing)/filter accessing, switch allocation and transferring to downstream router/local node. For the router implemented in directory protocol, it also has 4 stages except that the second stage is replaced by VC allocation. VC help improve the throughput of the un-ordered network, which is feasible for directory-based coherence protocol.

4.2 Power Model

To estimate the power consumption of on-chip network, including electrical and optical components, we adopted the nanophotonics power model in [7]. The total dynamic energy consumption of the optical link is 158 fJ/bit. This includes energy consumption from modulators, detectors, amplifiers, driver and clock circuits. In addition, to maintain corresponding wavelength, micro-rings require consistent heating power as they are sensitive to temperature. This introduces 16-32fJ/bit/heater [25] thermal tuning energy cost.

Our on-chip optical network adopts dense wavelength division multiplexing (DWDM) support such that 64 wavelengths can be transmitted in single waveguide. Each modulator can run at 20 Gb/s bit rate [49]. There are five-layer coherence network of 64-bit width and single data layer of 512-bit width. There are in total 2.6 k micro-rings for both modulators and filters. The same network design is used to evaluate our proposed C^3 protocol and traditional snoopy and directory protocols. The only difference is that traditional full-vector directory protocol has wider invalidation message size and requires an extra of 0.2k rings. To summarize, the thermal power required to tune the rings over a temperature range of 20K is 104 mW and 112 mW [25] for C^3 and directory protocols, respectively.

The power of off-chip laser is large enough to sustain all types of light loss such that the detector can receive sufficient optical power. In table 1, we listed the losses from different optical components [25, 30]. We performed detailed power calculation of our optical network that consists of 4 broadcast network layers for read/write requests, one unicast network for control messages, and one unicast data network. The estimated laser power is 582 mW. The di-

rectory requires a multi-cast network with twice bandwidth of ours for invalidation, the laser power is 326 mW as the aggregate broadcast bandwidth is less than ours. In this study, the electrical power estimations of buffers, crossbars and electrical links are modeled at 32nm technology, which is scaled from 45nm PTM HSPICE device models [45] at 1.1V and temperature 90°C.

Photonic device	Loss (dB)	Photonic device	Loss (dB)
Waveguide loss	0.5/cm	Waveguide bend	0.005
Splitter	0.2	Coupler	1
Modulator insertion	0.1	Detector insertion	0.1
Filter drop	1.5	Ring through	0.01
Laser efficiency	30%	detector sensitivity (μw)	10

Table 1: Optical losses of different optical components [25, 30].

5. EVALUATION

We evaluated and compared the performance and energy-efficiency of proposed C^3 protocol with directory-based, snoopy-based coherence and DASH [31] protocols. In the evaluation, we used the same hierarchical network (see section 3.1.1).

5.1 Simulation Methodology

We extended Noxim [39], a cycle-accurate NoC SystemC-based simulator, to model our proposed hierarchical network (Fig. 2) that uses electrical concentration organization and optical crossbar respectively for intra- and inter- cluster communications. The routing for our topology is deterministic routing within each cluster. We modeled all major components of the network and additional components in C^3: predictors, filters and other control logics. The energy models for both electrical and optical modules are augmented. Table 2 lists other essential parameters.

Execution Pipeline	2GHz, in-order, 2-issue
Core Organization	8 clusters, 8 nodes per cluster, 4 groups per node, 4 cores per group. Total 64 nodes, 256 groups and 1K cores
Private L1I/D	32KB per cluster, 8-way, 64B line, 2-cycle hit time, write-through, shared by 4 cores in the same group
Local Shared L2	2MB per node, 16-way, 64B line, 10-cycle hit time, write-back, shared by 4 clusters in the same node
Global Shared LLC	Distributed 3D stacking, 4 layers, 64 tiles per layer. 2GB, 16-way, 512B line, 30-cycle hit time, write-back
Memory Controller	Four, located in the edges of the chip
Interconnect	Hierarchical optical-electrical network, 8 clusters with 8 nodes per cluster, 1GHz frequency, 4-stage router.

Table 2: Chip configuration.

Since existing OS may not be scalable to thousand-core architecture, we choose a user level simulator to collect cache transaction traces. We extended PTLsim [44] to simulate parallel kernels with up to thousands of threads. The detailed processor parameters are listed in Table 2. We used workloads from PARSEC [9] to evaluate different protocols, similar to the approach in the thousand-core simulation in ATAC [37]. For each PARSEC workload, we used *sim-large* input set and collected all L2 cache transactions into trace files. Four memory controllers are placed along the edges of the chip. Since a large LLC is integrated in our architecture, the memory bandwidth in our system is not a bottleneck.

We compared C^3 to three widely adopted cache coherence protocol designs:

Snoop-based protocol — snoopy. Every request is broadcast to all the nodes through the ordered network. To enable simulation with high core count, we alleviate the bandwidth overhead by removing the respond messages of the snoopy request, and implemented a simple 1-bit directory in LLC to indicate if the line is clean. If the line is dirty, the owner forwards the data copy to the requester, otherwise, the home node is in charge of data forwarding.

Directory protocol — directory. We evaluated a full-vector MSI directory protocol. Although a full directory keeps all sharers of the shared cache line and helps to remove unnecessary probings, it brings significant storage and power overheads and needs large invalidation messages. In this protocol, the directory serves as the order point to ensure correctness.

ACKwise protocol — ATAC [37]. ATAC is a directory based protocol that only stores limited number (5 in this paper) of sharers, in a 1024-core CMP. Broadcast is still required if sharers are more than 5. The number of sharers is tracked to reduce the acknowledgment messages.

DASH protocol — DASH [31]. DASH protocol is a hybrid design of directory and snoopy protocols. Each request is broadcast inside the cluster firstly. If it can not be served locally, it will be sent to global network to access directory. The sharing information in the directory is the bit vector of pointers to clusters. Thus additional local broadcast is necessary to look for the owner node or to invalidate the sharers inside the cluster.

5.2 Filter Configuration

Filter efficiency is the key point of C^3 performance since higher hit rate indicates more direct cache-to-cache accesses and less directory queries. In addition, filter hits reduce the number of write-initiated local broadcasts. The filter efficiency depends on its capacity, set-associativity, replacement policy and throughput. We adopted a recently proposed replacement policy — dynamic re-reference interval prediction (DRRIP) [22], in the filter to achieve better hit rate. Each filter has 2 read/write ports to achieve improved throughput without incurring significant area and power overheads.

We performed a study of hit rates with different configurations of capacity and set-associativity. The estimations of delay, energy and area under different settings are based on CACTI [12]. Both energy consumption and area overhead increase almost linearly with the capacity of filter but much slower with the set-associativity. In our assumption, filter access completes within one cycle. This timing constraint (1ns) limit the number of entries to be less than 16K. Besides, the hit rate shows visible increase when the set count goes up from 1K to 8K. Therefore C^3 employs the 8K-set 16-way filter design which incurs 0.28% of total area overhead.

5.3 Performance Evaluation

In this section, we evaluated the efficiency of filters and broadcast predictors and overall performance of four different cache coherence protocols.

Filter efficiency. We compared the effectiveness of our proposed cache-based filter, to an owner predictor that predicts the locations of dirty lines [1]. The latter is a two-level

prediction design. The first-level predictor predicts whether a cache miss can be served by a cache-to-cache forwarding based on the PC of the instruction that generates the miss. The second-level predictor further improves the prediction accuracy with the combination of the PC and the load/store addresses. We chose its default implementation parameters, which has 2K L1 entries and 16K L2 entries. Each L2 entry includes 4 prediction nodes. The first-level table is indexed by the lowest 11-bit of PC. The second-level table is indexed by the XOR result of the tag address of the missing cache line and bits from 2 to 15 of the PC.

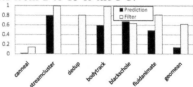

Figure 9: Comparisons of efficiency in locating owner between owner prediction and filter.

Fig. 9 depicts the percentage of owners caught by either predictor or filter. The benchmarks not shown here hardly have any owner status during our experimental phase. The geometric means of success rate are 13.4% and 62.2% respectively. In particular, workloads facerec and freqmine have above 98% success rates. To summarize, the filter is effective in finding the owners for majority requests.

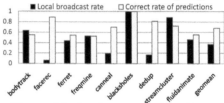

Figure 10: Performance of predictor.

Predictor efficiency. Although C^3 uses 1-bit predictor with trivial overhead, it helps to remove a large number of snoopy and reply messages, as shown in Fig. 10. The geometric mean of broadcast rate from our predictor is 36.7% while DASH requires 100% local broadcasts. And the broadcast rate of workload is compatible with local sharing rate. For example, as we can see in Fig. 4, the local sharing rate of blackscholes is above 90%, meaning that most local broadcasts are necessary for fast data forwarding. Fig. 10 shows that the broadcast rate of blackscholes reaches 99%. The figure also presents the the correct prediction rate of our proposed predictor which is over 50% on average and up to 98% for blackscholes case.

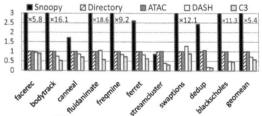

Figure 11: Network latency.

Network latency. We then integrated filters and predictors with our coarse-vector directory, and compared C^3 protocol with three baseline designs. The network latency is the total delay of round-trip for the request and its reply, including the queuing delay at network and cache, the time spent on the optical and electrical network, and the access latency of filters and directory/cache.

Fig. 11 compared the network latency of C^3, snoopy, ATAC, DASH (all are normalized to directory). From the figure, C^3 protocol outperforms directory and ATAC by 41% on average and a maximum of 84% (in streamcluster). It is mainly due to the high hit rates of the filter, which removes remote accesses to the directory. The access latency of L2 cache is lower than that of L3 due to its smaller sizes. Although ATAC requires broadcast when sharers are more than 5, it does not inccur significant network latency compared to full-vector directory since cases with more than five sharers are rare and both the global optical network and local concentration topology support broadcast for invalidation messages.

On average, C^3 outperforms DASH protocol by 18.7%. This is because the failed local broadcast could still gain benefits from filters to visit the owner directly, and successful prediction could reduce redundant local broadcasts.

Snoopy protocol does not perform well almost in every protocol due to the bottleneck of the bandwidth through most of the benchmarks. And the contention in the network results in long queuing delay since the buffers of the router are full and the packet cannot be injected into the network.

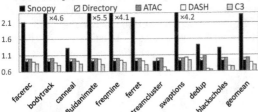

Figure 12: Normalized execution time.

Execution time. Fig. 12 summarizes the normalized execution time of all the protocols (normalized to directory). C^3 protocol consistently outperforms other protocols with a maximum reduction of 35% over tt directory or ATAC and 17% over DASH. This is due to shorter network latency in C^3 protocol (Fig. 11). Snoopy only performs better than directory in streamcluster when the traffic is low. In other cases, snoopy is not a scalable option for a many-core CMP.

5.4 Broadcast Overhead

One major drawback of snoopy is the amount of activities triggered by a broadcast message: all local cache tags are probed for the coherence status of the requested data. This not only generates significant energy overhead but also harms performance. We measured the amount of redundant snooping messages, i.e., those that do not have a copy of requested data and so the lookup is redundant. Over 90% of total broadcast traffic is unnecessary for PARSEC benchmarks [9].

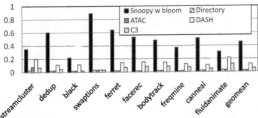

Figure 13: Cache probing for directory, snoopy protocol with bloom filter [47], DASH and C^3, normalized to snoopy protocol without filter.

C^3 adopted a mix of three-level blocking scheme to effectively remove most of the redundancy: (1) local broadcast

predictor is able to reduce the unnecessary local broadcasts. Successful local broadcasts also prevent global broadcasts; (2) The filters in OP-I routers also reduces the global snoopy; (3) coarse-grained vector directory indicates the location of the owner or cluster index of shares to avoid snooping every cache. The comparisons with other protocol designs are shown in Fig. 13. One can see that the predictor removes about half number of messages and is able to reduce the number of snoopy messages to only 5.8% and 12% on average of snoopy, with and without bloom filter, respectively. In ATAC, if the number of sharers is over five, broadcasting invalidation messages could generate more traffic than in full-map directory (e.g. streamcluster), though overall, ATAC is low on cache probing. Redundancy only exists in two cases of C^3 compared to precise full-map directory protocol: (1) local broadcast to look for sharer/owner and (2) invalidation. So the snoopy traffic is still higher than directory protocol, however the storage overhead is only 16.4% of a baseline directory.

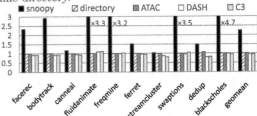

Figure 14: Energy consumption of directory, snoopy protocol with bloom filter [47], DASH and C^3, normalized to snoopy protocol without filter.

5.5 Energy Comparison

We also estimated the energy consumption of on-chip optical and electrical networks in different protocols. Fig. 14 demonstrates that both C^3 and DASH save about 5% energy over directory. This is because: (1) they shorten the execution time, which results in the overall reduced leakage energy consumption. (2) the average path of coherence messages in C^3 and DASH is shorter as most requests can be served either by a local broadcast or by the filter. This helps to reduce the communication energy further. (3) coarse-grain directory requires small message size (8-bit vs 64-bit in the baseline directory) and less number of micro-rings to transfer the message, thus C^3 saves both communication and heating power. On average C^3 has slightly larger energy consumption than DASH.

6. PRIOR ART

There are a myriad of prior research works on coherence protocol optimization, network optimizations for better cache coherence management and nanophotonic based interconnection designs. In this section, we categorize and discuss those works.

Optical interconnect. Optical interconnect (OP-I) often adopts crossbar topology to achieve fast all-to-all connection [29, 49]. The overhead of micro-rings becomes a serious issue for high node count, requiring high optical and thermal tuning power. Different topologies such as Clos [25] or mesh [14] were proposed to reduce the number of optical devices although with an increase of dynamic energy consumption in intermediate routers. Adopting hybrid networks of both metal and OP-I connections, utilizing OP-I in global communication [37, 42], and/or clustering [29] were proposed to shrink the crossbar size. A reservation mechanism [42] was proposed to tune off the idle rings to avoid optical energy loss of broadcast on the data channels. FlexiShare [43] and wavelength-based routing [30] presented the topologies that allow channel or wavelength sharing among the network nodes to improve the power-efficiency. However, they both have to deal with contention introduced by multiple senders, which results in additional network latency due to waiting for the dedicated token or acknowledgment.

For snoopy-based coherence traffic, Corona [49] and optical bus [29] leveraged single broadcast bus and arbitration scheme while spectrum [32] employed antennas to form multiple broadcast channels. In this paper, we adopted contention-free SWMR [42] crossbar topology and the reservation scheme for the wide data channel to save optical power, considering its broadcast support and low design and fabrication complexity. But we also leverage the benefit of the topology and optical technology to introduce a new cache coherence policy.

Cache coherence protocol. A major obstacle that restricts the adoption of directory-based protocol in large-scale CMPs is its prohibitive storage overhead as the size of full-map directory scheme [13] increases linearly with the core count. Optimizations have been proposed to deal with this problem, e.g., the schemes that save limited pointers with broadcast backup [3, 37], WayPoint that uses sparse directory [26] to allow evicting entries to memory, and tagless directory (TL) [52] that builds sharing information based on a set of bloom filters. Coarse vector scheme has been proven to have similar or even better performance than limited pointer scheme and generate less traffic than sparse directory [18]. Thus we employ the coarse vector as one of building blocks in this paper, which enables us to achieve comparable performance as snoopy protocol but with small storage overhead.

The major challenge to scale snoopy protocol is that enormous cache tag look-ups consume significant network bandwidth and power. Several schemes have been proposed [4, 38, 47] to address this problem through filtering redundant messages. However, when scaling this approach to a thousand cores, challenges remain such as the dilemma between filter storage space and its efficiency, and network overhead of updating traffics for previous filter designs. In this paper, we analyze the traffic of thousand-core CMPs using real traces and propose a mix of three building components, (1) local broadcast predictor, (2) filters in the router, and (3) coarse-vector directory, to eliminate the majority of unnecessary broadcast messages.

Another difficulty to implement snoopy protocol is to maintain ordering in the network. Uncorq [46] presented an approach to ensure the correctness for ring-based network, which does not scale well when the number of cores grows to one thousand. Token coherence protocol [34, 35] can achieve direct cache-to-cache transfer in un-ordered network by decoupling the performance from correct substrate. The order is guaranteed by requesting and forwarding tokens. However tokenB protocol requires additional storage for tokens and broadcasting requests. Atomic coherence [50] serializes the transactions with mutexes to reduce additional racing transitions in directory protocol but brings performance penalty due to atomic coherence and large number of mutexes occupy non-trivial bandwidth. In our case, we implemented an ordered network to ensure the correctness.

Several hybrid cache coherence protocols have been previously proposed. DASH [31] uses bus-based snoopy to maintain consistency for intra-cluster cache coherence and full-vector directory for inter-cluster coherence. However, every coherence request demands at least one local broadcast which brings unnecessary snoopy messages and extra network latency. If local broadcast fails, additional access to directory is always required. In our scheme, broadcast predictor and filters introduce much less overhead and harvests more direct cache-to-cache accesses. The hybrid coherence protocol proposed in [19] decouples the read and write traffic to reduce contentions on the broadcast network. The directory scheme is used exclusively for read over optical fully-connected network while the remaining messages are handled by snoopy-based protocol. This results in worse write latency than that through a shared bus. Our work differs from this design as follows: (1) The C^3 protocol is not designed to speedup any specific request type. Both read and write requests can benefit from snoopy as it eliminates the extra indirection. (2) Write requests in C^3 do not always require global broadcasting as both the filter and the directory help to remove unnecessary broadcast messages.

Bandwidth adaptive snooping hybrid (BASH) [33] is a protocol that employs snoopy protocol when network bandwidth is plentiful and switches to directory protocol when bandwidth becomes limitation. It neither addresses the probing overhead problem in snoopy protocol nor optimizes the performance under heavy traffic loads. In contrast, our scheme let one request achieve direct access without looking up all the cache-tags. Owner prediction [1] and sharer prediction [2] introduced an approach to improve the performance of directory protocol by predicting the owner or sharers. Their works were motivated by some observations, such as the total number of sharers is small, 1 in some cases, are based on a small-scale CMP. It may not stand in a large-scale CMP or use a different application. Besides, the accesses extend to the 4-step when the prediction fails. Moreover, the prediction is not always allowed [1]. The filter in our scheme shows better performance than the predication in section 5.

7. CONCLUSION

The conventional snoopy and directory coherence protocols face several challenges when scaling to many-core or thousand-core CMPs. Snoopy protocol incurs enormous amount of cache tag probing. Directory protocol requires an indirection through directory in all coherence requests, and potentially large storage overhead from the directory itself. We observed that while the emerging OP-I network provides high bandwidth density, low propagation delay and natural support for multicast, it cannot satisfy the overwhelming broadcast requests in snoopy protocols.

In this paper, we addressed the efficiency problem by proposing C^3, a composite cache coherence (C^3) protocol that integrates a set of of effective building blocks including local broadcast predictor, filtering, and a coarse-grained directory, to improve the performance of the coherence transactions on large-scale CMPs. C^3 helps to achieve direct cache-to-cache accesses as in snoopy protocol and small amount of cache probing as in directory protocol. Our experimental results showed that on average, it reduces the snoopy messages to only 5.8% of that in snoopy protocol, improves performance by 21%, reduces network latency of coherence messages by 41% and saves network energy consumption by 5.5%. Thus the proposed C^3 protocol with hierarchical optical interconnect support is a promising candidate for implementing cache coherence scheme in large-scale CMPs.

8. ACKNOWLEDGMENT

This work is supported in part by NSF grants CAREER CNS-0747242 and CNS-1012070.

9. REFERENCES

[1] M. E. Acacio, et. al., "Owner Prediction for Accelerating Cache-to-Cache Transfer Misses in a cc-NUMA Architecture," In *SC*, 2002.

[2] M. E. Acacio, et. al., "The use of Prediction for Accelerating Upgrade Misses in a cc-NUMA Multiprocessors," In *PACT*, pp. 155-164, 2002.

[3] A. Agarwal, et. al., "An Evaluation of Directory Schemes for Cache Coherence," In *ISCA*, pp.353-362, 1988.

[4] N. Agarwal, et. al., "In-Network Coherence Filtering: Snoopy Coherence without Broadcasts," In *MICRO*, 2009.

[5] N. Agarwal, et. al., "In-Network Snoop Ordering: Snoopy Coherence on Unordered Interconnects," In *HPCA*, 2009.

[6] J. Balfour and W. J. Dally, "Design tradeoffs for tiled cmp onchip networks," In *ICS*, pp.187-198, 2006.

[7] C. Batten and et. al., "Building Manycore Processor-to-DRAM Networks with Monolithic Silicon Photonics," In *High Performance Interconnects*, pp.21-30, 2008.

[8] S. Beamer, et. al., "Re-Architecting DRAM Memory Systems with Monolithically Integrated Silicon Photonics," In *ISCA*, pp.117-128, 2010.

[9] C. Bienia, et. al., "The parsec benchmark suite: Characterization and architectural implications," In *PACT*, pp.72-81,2008.

[10] B. Black, et. al., "Die stacking (3d) microarchitecture," In *MICRO* pp. 469-479, 2006.

[11] S. Borkar, "Thousand core chips - a technology perspective," In *DAC*, pp.746-749, 2007.

[12] CACTI, http://www.hpl.hp.com/research/cacti/

[13] L. M. Censier and P. Feautrier, " A New Solution to Coherence Problems in Multicache Systems," In *IEEE Trans. on Computers*, pp. 1112-1118, 1978.

[14] M. J. Cianchetti, et. al., "Phastlane: A Rapid Transit Optical Routing Network," In *ISCA*, pp.441-450, 2009.

[15] S. Chaudhry, et. al., "Rock: A High-Performance Sparc CMT Processor," In *IEEE Micro*, 29(2):6-16, 2009.

[16] W. J. Dally and B. Towles, "Principles and practices of Interconnection Networks," Morgan Kaufmann, 2004.

[17] N. Eisley, et. al., "In-network cache coherence," In *MICRO*, pp. 321-332, 2006.

[18] A. Gupta, et. al., "Reducing Memory and Traffic Requirements for Scalable Directory-Based Cache Coherence Schemes," In *ICPP*, pp. 312-321, 1990.

[19] J.-H. Ha and T. M. Pinkston, " A Hybrid Cache Coherence Protocol for a Decoupled Multi-Channel Optical Network: SPEED DMON, " In *ICPP*, pp.164-171, 1996.

[20] L. Hammond, et. al., "A single-chip multiprocessor," In *IEEE Computer*, 30(9):79-85, 1997.

[21] Semiconductor Industry Association, "International Technology Roadmap for Semiconductors," http://www.itrs.net/Links/2009ITRS/Home2009.htm, 2009.

[22] A. Jaleel, et. al., "High performance cache replacement using re-reference interval prediction (RRIP)," In *ISCA*, pp.60-71, 2010.

[23] N. Enright-Jerger, et. al., " Virtual Circuit Tree Multicasting: A Case for On-Chip Hardware Multicast Support," In *ISCA*, 2008.

[24] N. Enright-Jerger, et. al., "Virtual Tree Coherence: Leveraging Regions and In-Network Multicast Trees for Scalable Cache Coherence," In *MICRO*, 2008.

[25] A. Joshi, et. al., "Silicon-Photonic Clos Networks for Global On-Chip Communication," In *NOCS*, 2009.

[26] J. H. Kelm, et. al., "WAYPOINT: scaling coherence to 1000-core architectures," In *PACT*, pp. 99-109, 2010.

[27] T. Kgil, et. al., "Picoserver:Using 3d stacking technology to enable a compact energy efficient chip multiprocessor," In *ASPLOS*, pp. 117-128, 2006.

[28] J. Kim, et. al., "Flattened butterfly topology for on-chip networks," In *MICRO*, 2007.

[29] N. Kirman, et. al., " Leveraging optical technology in future bus-based chip multiprocessors," In *MICRO*, pp. 492-503, 2006.

[30] N. Kirman and J. Martinez, "An efficient all-optical on-chip interconnect based on oblivious routing," In *ASPLOS*, 2010.

[31] D. Lenoski, et. al., " Design and Scalble Shared-Memory Multiprocessors: The DASH Approach," In *COMPCON*, pp. 62-67, 1990.

[32] Z. Li, et. al., "Spectrum: A Hybrid Nanophotonic-Electric On-Chip Network," In *DAC*, pp. 575-580, 2009.

[33] M. M. K. Martin, et. al., "Bandwidth Adaptive Routing," In *HPCA*, 2002.

[34] M. M. K. Martin, et. al., "Token Coherence: Decoupling Performance and Correctness," In *ISCA*, 2003.

[35] M. Marty, et. al., "Improving multiple-cmp systems using token coherence," In *HPCA*, 2005.

[36] D. Miller, "Rationale and Challenges for Optical Interconnects to Electronic Chips," In *Proceedings of the IEEE*, 88(6):728-749, 2000.

[37] G. Kurian, et. al., "ATAC: A 1000-core cache-coherent processor with on-chip optical network," In *PACT*, pp.447-488, 2010.

[38] A. Moshovos, et. al., "JETTY: Filtering snoops for reduced energy consumption in SMP servers," In *HPCA*, pp.85-96, 2001.

[39] "Noxim, An Open Network-on-Chip Simulator," http://noxim.sourceforge.net

[40] nVidia, "Quadro fx 3700m, " http://www.nvidia.com/object/product_quadro_fx_3700_m_us.html.

[41] K. Olukotun, et. al., "The case for a single-chip multiprocessor," In *ASPLOS*, pp. 2-11, 1996.

[42] Y. Pan, et. al., " Firefly: Illuminating Future Network-on-Chip with Nanophotonics," *Int. Symp. on Computer Architecture, ISCA'09*, pp. 429-440, 2009.

[43] Y. Pan, et. al., "FlexiShare: Channel Sharing for an Energy-Efficient Nanophotonic Crossbar," *In Int. Symp. on High-Performance Computer Architecture (HPCA)*, 2010.

[44] PTLsim. http://www.ptlsim.org/

[45] PTM interconnect model. http://www.eas.asu.edu/ ptm/interconnect.html

[46] K. Strauss, et. al., "Uncorq: Unconstrained snoop request delivery in embedded-ring multiprocessors," *In Int. Symp. on Micorarchitecture*, pp. 327-342, 2007.

[47] A. N. Udipi, et. al., "Towards Scalable, Energy-Efficient Bus-Based On-Chip Networks," *In Int. Symp. on High-Performance Computer Architecture (HPCA)*, pp. 1 - 12, 2010.

[48] S. Vangal, et. al., "An 80-tile 1.28tflops network-on-chip in 65nm cmos," *In IEEE Int. Solid-State Circuits Conf.*, pp. 98-590, 2007.

[49] D. Vantrease, et. al., "Corona: System implications of emerging nanophotonic technology," *In Int. Symp. on Computer Architecture*, pp.153-164, 2008.

[50] D. Vantrease, et. al., "Atomic Coherence: Leveraging Nanophotonics to Build Race-Free Cachec Coherence Protocols," *In Int. Symp. on High-Performance Computer Architecture (HPCA)*, 2011.

[51] J. Xue, et. al., "An Intra-Chip Free-Space Opitcal Interconnect," *Int. Symp. on Computer Architecture, ISCA* 2010.

[52] J. Zebchuk, et. al., "A Tagless Coherence Directory," *In Int. Symp. on Microarchitecture, MICRO*, pp. 423-434, 2009.

Controlling Cache Utilization of HPC Applications

Swann Perarnau   Marc Tchiboukdjian   Guillaume Huard

INRIA MOAIS Team, CNRS LIG Lab, Grenoble University, France
{swann.perarnau,marc.tchiboukdjian,guillaume.huard}@imag.fr

ABSTRACT

This paper discusses the use of software cache partitioning techniques to study and improve cache behavior of HPC applications. Most existing studies use this partitioning to solve quality of service issues, like fair distribution of a shared cache among running processes. We believe that, in the HPC context of a single application being studied/optimized on the system, with a single thread per core, cache partitioning can be used in new and interesting ways.

First, we propose an implementation of software cache partitioning using the well known page coloring technique. This implementation differs from existing ones by giving control of the partitioning to the application programmer. Developed on the most popular OS in HPC (Linux), this cache control scheme has low overhead both in memory and CPU while being simple to use.

Second, we illustrate how this user-controlled cache partitioning can lead to efficient measurements of cache behavior of a parallel scientific visualization application. While current tools require expensive binary instrumentation of an application to obtain its working sets, our method only needs a few unmodified runs on the target platform.

Finally, we discuss the use of our scheme to optimize memory intensive applications by isolating each of their critical data structures into dedicated cache partitions. This isolation allows the analysis of each structure cache requirements and leads to new and significant optimization strategies. To the best of our knowledge, no other existing tool enables such tuning of HPC applications.

Categories and Subject Descriptors

C.4 [**Performance of Systems**]: Measurement Techniques

General Terms

Experimentation, Performance

Keywords

page coloring, cache partitioning, working set

1. INTRODUCTION

The memory cache behavior of high performance computing (HPC) applications is a topic that has been the focus of numerous studies. Most of those studies analyze the cache usage ratio of a target application: how much cache is efficiently used. This usage ratio is closely related to *working sets* [2,10].

From a general point of view, the working sets model the performance of a process relative to its resource utilization during a time interval. In particular, these working sets highlight specific ranges of values of the quantity of resources assigned to the process for which the process performance does not vary. Applied to the full execution period, it outlines the resources an application requires to reach a given performance level. In [2,10], this model has been applied successively to cache performance analysis.

Closely related to working sets, the reuse distance of an application, introduced by Beyls and D'Hollander in 2001 [1], plays a major role in its cache performance. The reuse distance is defined, for each memory access performed by the application, as the number of different memory accesses realized before the next access to the same location, if any. Under the assumption that the application runs on a machine equipped with a fully associative cache using the least recently used (LRU) policy, this metric expresses exactly the efficiency in cache of the application: measuring the reuse distance of each memory access will determine if a cache miss will be triggered by this access. Regarding set associative caches, where line eviction depends on memory accesses in the same set and where the LRU implementation usually presents slight modifications, several papers studied and confirmed the accuracy of the reuse distance [1,24].

Formally, if the number of accesses having a reuse distance of d is $H(d)$, then the number of cache misses $Q(C)$ occurring on a cache of size C is: $Q(C) = \sum_{d=C+1}^{\infty} H(d)$ where a reuse distance of ∞ is associated to the initial access to each element. Thus, the working sets of an application are directly related to its reuse distance: if there exists a range $[i,j]$ for which H is null (*i.e.* $\forall d \in [i,j]\ H(d) = 0$), then $Q(C)$ will stay the same for values of C in this range $[i,j]$. This is obvious: if giving slightly more cache to an application does not change any cache miss into a hit, then its performance will stay constant. More precisely, working sets can be deduced from reuse distances as the integral function of their distribution.

Unfortunately, despite its obvious usefulness, the evaluation of the reuse distances of a given application is tremendously difficult. Static analysis of the source code is quickly limited by its complexity and by missing runtime data. As an alternative, reuse distance are often determined by gathering the application's memory accesses using tools like Pin [20] or Valgrind [22]. They can also be used to measure working sets by feeding the memory access trace to a cache simulator (Valgrind even include a virtually indexed one). Nevertheless, the simulation of all the memory accesses of an application requires huge computational resources, limiting those experiments to short runs.

Our first contribution is a tool and a method for measuring working sets of an application. Our method does not suffer from the huge computational overhead induced by simulation methods. Indeed, the determination of one point of the working sets function just requires one regular run of the application. To achieve this result, we make use of well known page coloring techniques [16] to implement a cache control mechanism. Then, we use this cache control mechanism to assign to a given application a chosen fraction of the hardware cache. The resulting performance is a point of the working set function Q.

Our second contribution aims at improving the cache performance of a single HPC application. In particular, we show that our cache control method can be used to evaluate how memory accesses to each distinct data structure contribute to the working set function of an application. We deduce from this information an estimation of the cache requirements of each of these data structures. Combining this information with our cache control tool, we allocate to each data structure a well chosen fraction of the cache: memory accesses to this structure are then cached only to this fraction of the hardware cache. Finally we demonstrate that carefully choosing the partition size of each data structure can result in significant performance improvements.

The remainder of this paper is organized as follows. The next section presents a simple software cache partitioning mechanism based on page coloring. It differs from previously presented works as it gives control of partitions to users (application programmers) instead of the OS. Section 3 describes the implementation of our proposal on the Linux Operating System as well as its interfaces. We validate this implementation both as a page coloring facility and a cache controller in Section 4. This validation is based on working sets detection of a perfectly understood application, it makes sure that the working set changes accordingly to the cache partition in use.

This working set analysis is then applied in Section 5 to a parallel visualization application having more complex memory access patterns. This application can be configured to use different parallelization schemes. Thus, using our tool, we determined its working sets to select the most cache efficient parallelization scheme. To the best of our knowledge this paper is the first to focus on such working set analysis on actual application executions in the HPC context.

Section 6 presents various possible uses of our cache partitioning scheme to improve the cache performance of several parallel applications. First, we show how the noise of a data structure with close-to-none reuse distance can be suppressed, giving more cache to the remaining data structures of a visualization application. Then, we analyze in detail an application (a multigrid stencil) to determine the work-

ing set of each of its data structures. Those working sets are evaluated by isolating each data structure inside its own partition and making the partition size vary. This analysis leads to a global partitioning of the application, dramatically improving its performance.

Finally we compare our tool to related works in Section 7 and summarize our results in Section 8.

2. CACHE CONTROL BY PAGE COLORING

Our cache control tool is based on a straightforward and lightweight method: page coloring. It has been designed for way-associative, physically indexed caches, but can also be applied to direct mapped ones. As most cache architectures are nowadays way-associative or direct mapped caches, our control scheme can be applied on almost all recent systems. For clarity we define C as the cache size, A as its associativity (i.e. its number of ways), L as the cache line size and P as the page size. All sizes are in bytes.

As page coloring is critical to understand both our cache control mechanism and the experiments in the remainder of the paper, we recall its principle in the following subsection.

2.1 Page Coloring

Most modern architectures use physically indexed caches. In such systems, if the mapping of virtual pages to physical ones performed by the virtual memory (VM) subsystem is not properly chosen, unnecessary cache conflicts can be triggered during processes execution. Kessler et al. [16] showed that a VM subsystem choosing page mappings arbitrarily contributed up to 30% of total cache conflicts in an application execution. They proposed several *careful-mapping* algorithms to solve this problem, of which page coloring is the most popular in Operating System research. Several major OS implement it in their virtual memory subsystems (FreeBSD and Windows NT among others) and it has been praised as a key component of cache optimization of applications as well as a good performance stabilizer [8, 17].

Page coloring identifies with a color the group of physical pages that conflict (or overlap) in a cache. This definition arises from the inner working of physically indexed caches. It can be summarized as follows. Physical memory is cached line by line and each page is several lines long. As lines are mapped to associative sets in a round-robin fashion, consecutive lines of the same physical page are mapped to several, consecutive associative sets. The number of lines (and sets) in a cache being limited, many pages map to the same associative sets. A color identifies indiscriminately the group of pages overlapping in cache or the group of associative sets they map to. As a cache possesses C/AL associative sets and a page occupies P/L cache lines, the number of colors in a cache is C/AP. Figure 1 illustrates this page mapping and the corresponding colors on an hypothetical cache with 8 associative sets of 8 ways and physical pages being two lines long.

An OS virtual memory subsystem implementing page coloring tries to optimize cache utilization by giving different colors to consecutive virtual pages. As a page color never changes, page coloring is easily implemented in an efficient way. Of course, as the number of colors in a system is limited, it might still be necessary to give some pages of the same colors to a memory demanding process.

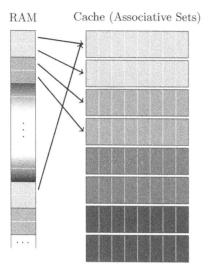

RAM   Cache (Associative Sets)

Figure 1: Page coloring in an hypothetical system with 2 lines per page and a 4 colored cache with 8 ways. Pages are placed in the cache in round robin, each line in a different associative set. Pages of the same color are placed in the same associative sets.

In a multiprogrammed environment this definition of page coloring does not suffice. To ensure fair resource sharing, page coloring is also tuned to give different colors to distinct processes. This way, applications competing for the same core will not trash each other's cache. This well studied issue [14, 18] is close to our work although we focus on cache sharing inside a single application. Indeed, our goal is to provide a cache partitioning interface based on page coloring directly to applications. Furthermore, in most HPC context, applications only have one thread per core. Thus, the precise issues we study relate to cache sharing (which is discussed later in this article), rather than resources contention.

2.2 Cache Control

In a sense, page coloring was one of the first cache partitioning algorithms. In this special case, each color represents a partition and giving processes different colors ensures they use different portions of the cache. Our cache control mechanism is a direct extension of this partitioning scheme, allowing a partition to span several colors. It works in two phases: first, the user sets a portion of physical memory aside for the page coloring scheme. Then he is provided with a specific memory allocation *device* which returns pages of a configurable set of colors in response to allocation requests. This control scheme allows an application programmer to select the colors allocated to some dynamic memory allocations (*i.e.* data structures), creating custom cache partitions, usable concurrently. As further sections of this paper will show, letting applications control their cache partitioning can greatly improve their performance. Because the memory accesses of most HPC applications are well understood, our scheme should be easy to apply.

Our mechanism does not provide automatic page recoloring, a classical feature of cache partitioning schemes. This is a design choice: we consider the whole automatic recoloring mechanism as too intrusive in the context of HPC applications. Furthermore, a programmer knows better the key

phases of its application and when to trigger recoloring. Indeed he can implement it by creating two different devices (with different colors) and copy data from one to the other.

We should also mention that partitioning cache induces a partition of the memory. This means that, as with any other cache partitioning scheme, the memory available for one partition is limited to the pages that can fall into it (in our case, the ones with the good color). In other words, a small cache partition will contain few colors, thus few pages to use. Since we provide those partitions to applications as memory mappable devices, a small partition will limit the size of the virtual memory mapped to it. This sounds like a constraining limitation, but our cache control scheme is only remapping available memory to specific parts of a process address space. Applications having enough memory without cache control should have enough while it is enabled. However, it might be necessary to use larger partitions than needed (regarding reuse distance) for data structures that occupy a large space in memory.

Most modern processors are composed of several cores and a cache hierarchy. Caches far from cores are shared by all while closer ones are private to a single core. In the remaining of this article we do not address the complex problem of cache partitioning across the whole hierarchy. We have chosen to enforce the partitioning according to the last level cache only, to benefit from the greater flexibility it provides and to avoid noise during experimental measurements. This choice already gives promising results and does not change our analysis of presented applications. Nevertheless, we plan to inspect the additional improvements that could result from a multilevel partitioning scheme in our future works.

3. IMPLEMENTATION

We implemented our cache control mechanism on Linux. We chose this OS for several reasons. First, Linux does not implement page coloring. This makes our implementation easier as no existing mechanism needs to be bypassed. Second, according to the latest TOP500 [21], Linux (or its variants) is the most popular OS in HPC.

3.1 Linux Memory Subsystem

Before explaining how our cache control scheme has been implemented, some information on virtual memory management in Linux is necessary. Using the standard GNU C library, a process calling the memory allocation functions can trigger two events. If the requested allocation size is large (more than a page) the library will call the system function *mmap*. In the other case, the library will return a memory location coming from a pool of pages. In the latter case, the pools are managed dynamically, thus, along with new allocation requests, new pages will be asked eventually. Consequently any memory allocation will eventually ask the OS for more virtual pages.

This request is always handled in the same way: Linux creates or expands an *area*. Such an area represents a region of the address space of a process that is managed by the same memory handler. Once new pages are made available to the process, the Linux kernel returns without having touched any of the pages (no page faults are triggered). For each area, a particular memory handler inside Linux is in charge of page faults handling. Thus, when a process accesses a virtual page for the first time, the kernel dispatches the page fault to the fault handler of the corresponding area.

Classically this means a physical page will be allocated to the process, but it could also trigger a DMA to fetch a file region on disk or instruct a particular device to send data on a network for example. Thus, in the Linux kernel, virtual memory management works in two steps: virtual pages are made available inside the virtual address space and physical pages are allocated when page faults occur.

Linux is a modular kernel: modules (code) can be loaded at runtime to enable additional functionalities. Such modularity also extends to virtual memory management: the new code can add to the system special (virtual) files having their dedicated page fault handler. Once a process will have those files mapped to its virtual memory, the first access to this *area* will trigger the dedicated page fault handler. Thus, kernel modules can add functionalities to the memory subsystem.

3.2 Cache Control as a Kernel Module

Cache control is implemented as a very simple module and a set of special devices. The kernel module is responsible for the management of a configurable number of contiguous physical page blocks (obtained from the kernel memory allocator). Once the color of each allocated page has been identified, users can ask for the creation of memory mappable virtual devices to the module by issuing the `ioctl` system call on a special control file. Such commands contain the size and the authorized colors of the new device.

When an application maps one of the devices into its address space, every page fault in the corresponding area will trigger our module page fault handler, which will provide a page with an allowed color. Thus, the user can create cache partitions dynamically during the execution of its application.

When allocating memory, the module tries to reserve the same number of pages for each color. This design is motivated by the Linux physical memory allocator behavior: to obtain several pages of the same color, it is necessary to allocate all the memory between them. Such behavior makes allocating the same number of pages to each color much simpler than any other possibility (like asking the desired number of pages for each partition). As a result, the module allocates physical memory by contiguous blocks as large as the requested memory and partitions it according to colors.

Once the module is loaded, two interfaces to the control mechanism are available to users. The first one is a library providing simple functions to define a set of colors and a *zone*: a memory allocator working inside a specific device. This interface is close in design to systems like the Linux `hugepages`: a function creates a zone using a size (maximum number of bytes that can be allocated) and a color set, and memory allocations can then be made inside the zone. The zone corresponds exactly to a colored device. To ease development and to enable the use of our control scheme by existing applications, we provide a second interface which is a memory allocation hijack. Such interface enables any user to install a custom library intercepting any standard POSIX memory allocation call (`malloc,realloc,calloc,free`) on any C application. Upon loading, this custom library will create various partitions and map them to the process address space, creating various memory allocation pools inside the application. Upon an allocation request, the library will determine the pool to use and return a part of this memory

```
#include<ccontrol.h>

void do_stuff(char *t, size_t s);

int main(void) {
    char *t;
    struct ccontrol_zone *z;
    color_set c;

    /* use first 32 colors */
    COLOR_ZERO(&c);
    for(int i = 0; i < 32; i++)
        COLOR_SET(i,&c);

    z = ccontrol_new(); // bookkeeping struct
    ccontrol_create_zone(z,&c,400); // create colored device

    /* alloc our char array in colored memory */
    t = (char *) ccontrol_malloc(z,100*sizeof(char));

    do_stuff(t,100);

    ccontrol_free(z,t); // free char array
    ccontrol_destroy_zone(z); // destroy device
    ccontrol_delete(z); // delete bookkeeping struct
    return 0;
}
```

Figure 2: Code snippet using our cache control library to create a cache partition of 32 colors and to allocate a character array into it.

pool to the user process. It is, of course, possible to tune this library by changing the function determining for each allocation the pool to use.

Figure 2 gives a code snippet describing the few functions calls needed to create a cache partition of 32 colors and allocate some character array into it.

The kernel module is a lightweight process (both in CPU and memory). During the execution of the target application it is only triggered by page faults in the virtually mapped partitions. The Linux kernel calls our page fault handler with the page number (as an offset to the first virtual page of the area) to allocate. Thus our fault handler only retrieves one page pointer from its color arrays and returns it. The setup phase of the module, during which physical memory is requested from the kernel might seems more costly. It is not the case, even if a huge number of physical page allocations is made, the kernel is still able to respond quickly. For example, in the experimentation system used in the following sections, allocating 24 GB of physical memory to our module takes approximately 1 second. Our module also has low memory requirements as it only saves one pointer per physical page managed.

4. VALIDATION

We validated our cache control mechanism on two aspects: its capability to provide memory allocations with a good page coloring and its capability to partition the hardware cache.

4.1 Experimental Setup

All experiments were conducted on a Quad Intel Xeon E5530 System. Each CPU possesses 4 cores, with a L_1 Data cache size of 32 KB, a L_2 Unified cache, 8 ways associative of 256 KB and a L_3 Shared Unified cache, 16 ways associative of 8 MB. All caches have 64 B lines.

All our validation experiments use the same memory in-

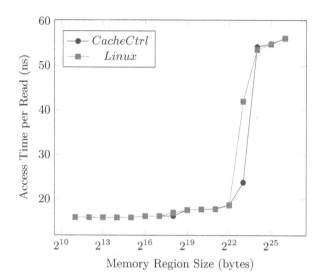

Figure 3: Random reads: access time per element on a memory region of varying size. Performance comparison between Linux page allocation and cache controlled one.

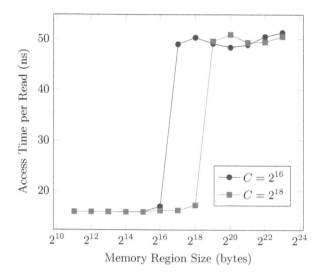

Figure 4: Random reads: access time per element on a memory region of varying size. Performance comparison between two cache partition sizes.

tensive application. This program consists only of a huge number of random accesses (reads) to a single memory region dynamically allocated. The size of this memory region can be configured. Given the fact that the number of accesses performed on the memory region outnumbers the number of elements in it, this application will have performance depending on its ability to cache said memory region. If the region fit in L_1 cache then the first access to each element will cache it and further accesses will all be hits. As the region size grows, other levels of the cache hierarchy will be required until the last level cache does not suffice (then the application will touch frequently the physical memory).

Thus, if we measure the average access time per read on our setup, the application will exhibits 3 working sets: a first one when the region is smaller than L_2 cache, a second one when the region fits in L_3 and the third one when the region is bigger than L_3. A fourth working set could have appeared when the region fits the L_1 cache, but practically the performance drop is too small to be noticed on our system. Notice that a similar program was used dy Ulrich Drepper [10] to demonstrate this working set effect with Valgrind as a cache simulator.

Each data point in the following experiments is the result of 100 executions of 5 000 000 reads on a memory region. The program was fixed on a single core, running on real-time scheduling policy (SCHED_FIFO) with max priority (ensuring no other program disturbs the measurements). Confidence intervals were too small to be included.

For the remainder of this paper, we refer to partition size as the number of colors used by a partition: it directly maps to the amount of cache made available.

4.2 Results

In the first experiment (Figure 3) we compare working sets of our application when the region is managed by the Linux kernel to a cache controlled region allocated by our tool and having access to the whole cache. In such a setup, because of our pages allocation method, our cache control

is only performing a classical page coloring on the memory region. Thus, as the Linux kernel does not implement page coloring the performance of the measured application should drop faster when the memory region size is close to the L_3 size. This experiment also validates our page fault handler: if it performs poorly the whole application performance will suffer from it.

As both physical memory allocators give the whole cache to the application, we can observe what we expected: 3 working sets corresponding to the size of each cache in the hierarchy. A small performance drop appears at region size 2^{17} which is the size of the L_2 and a big performance drop around 2^{23} (the size of the L_3 cache). Notice that under cache control the program still achieves good performance for a region of the same size as the L_3, whereas the imperfect page allocation of Linux make performance drop faster. This validates that our cache controller performs a proper page coloring. Those results were confirmed by measuring cache misses during the same experiment with hardware performance counters [3].

Next we validate the cache partitioning in itself: by making the available cache size vary, the application should exhibit working sets at different sizes. We compare several partition sizes given to the whole random access application. Each cache size should make the last working set of this program appear when the memory region get close to it. Figure 4 reports our measurements. The performance drop in access time follows closely the cache partition size. This assesses that our program behaves as if its cache was only the size of the partition it uses.

5. WORKING SETS ANALYSIS FOR ALGO-RITHMIC CHOICES

This section presents an analysis of the cache performance of a parallel application from the scientific visualization domain. In particular it shows how the analysis of its working sets can lead to appropriate algorithmic choices for its parallelization.

5.1 Isosurface Extraction with Marching Tetrahedron (MT)

Isosurface extraction is one on the most classical filters of scientific visualization. It provides a way to understand the structure of a scalar field in a three dimensional mesh by visualizing surfaces having the same scalar value.

Our application is based on the marching tetrahedrons (MT) algorithm, known for its good performance [15]. For each cell of a mesh, the MT algorithm reads the point coordinates and scalar values and computes a triangulation of the isosurface going through this cell. The triangulation consists of 0, 1 or 2 triangles according to how the isosurface intersects the tetrahedron.

The cache misses induced by MT can be analyzed as follows. The mesh data structure consists of two multidimensional arrays: an array storing, for each point, the coordinates and a scalar value and an array storing, for each cell, the indexes of its points (*cf.* Figure 5). Due to the mesh construction process, the order of points and cells has some locality: points and cells close to each other in the mesh space often have close indexes.

Thus, processing cells in the order of their indexes induces fewer cache misses when accessing the point array due to an improved locality: successive cells often share common points or points located in the same cache line. This locality can even be optimized by reordering points and cells to obtain better cache performance [27].

5.2 Parallel MT for Shared Cache

As each cell can be processed independently, it is relatively easy to parallelize the MT algorithm. One can logically divide the cell sequence into contiguous chunks and assign one chunk to each processor core. Since cell processing time differs according to the number of triangles generated, we used a work stealing scheduler to dynamically balance the load. When a core becomes idle, it selects another core at random and steals half of its remaining cells. This scheme efficiently uses the private caches of a multicore processor: each core processes contiguous cells and maximizes the reuse of points loaded in its private cache. However, cores operate on parts located far from each other in the cell sequence (and thus in the mesh space), reducing the chance that two cores use common points. Therefore, this parallel algorithm, denoted NoWINDOW, does not efficiently use the last level of cache of multicore processors which is shared amongst all cores.

To improve the reuse of data stored in the shared cache, a new parallel algorithm denoted SLIDINGWINDOW has been introduced in a previous work [26]. A fixed size window sliding on the cell sequence constrains cores to operate on cells close in mesh space. Threads still process chunks of contiguous cells for efficient private cache usage but these chunks are now smaller and closer to each other in the cell sequence thus improving shared cache usage. The SLIDINGWINDOW algorithm can be efficiently implemented using work stealing. The core operating at the beginning of the window has a specific status and is called the master. Steal operations to other cores are treated in the same way as the previous algorithm. However, when another core steals the master, it can only steal cells inside the window. The master is responsible for sliding the window on the sequence to enable new cells to be processed. This stealing mechanism guarantees that cores are operating inside the window at all time.

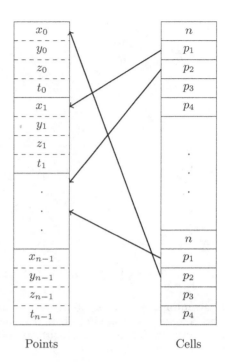

Figure 5: Mesh Data Structure. The point array stores coordinates and scalar values (t) and the cells array contains indexes to points defining each cell.

5.3 Shared Cache Misses Analysis with Reuse Distances

The SLIDINGWINDOW algorithm improves shared cache usage but increases synchronization overheads compared to the NoWINDOW algorithm: cores steal smaller amounts of work. We would like to use the SLIDINGWINDOW algorithm only when it significantly reduces the number of shared cache misses. We show in this section how we can predict the gain in shared cache misses of the SLIDINGWINDOW algorithm over the NoWINDOW algorithm using the working sets function Q of the sequential algorithm which processes the cell sequence in order.

Let $H(d)$ denote the number of memory references with a reuse distance d in the sequential algorithm. The number of cache misses on a fully associative cache of size C is given by $Q(C) = \sum_{d=C+1}^{\infty} H(d)$. We assume that the sequential algorithm has good temporal locality, *i.e.* cells far away from each other in the sequence use distinct points while cells having close indexes use common points. We first consider the NoWINDOW parallel algorithm on p cores sharing a cache of size C. In this case, as distinct cores do not operate on common points, the reuse distance is equal to the reuse distance of the sequential algorithm multiplied by p: each access performed by a core is followed by $p-1$ unrelated accesses performed by the other cores in parallel. Thus, $H_{\text{no-win}}(d) = H(\frac{d}{p})$ and the number of cache misses of the NoWINDOWalgorithm is

$$Q_{\text{no-win}}(C) = \sum_{d=C+1}^{\infty} H\left(\frac{d}{p}\right) = \sum_{d=\frac{C}{p}+1}^{\infty} H(d) = Q\left(\frac{C}{p}\right).$$

The NoWINDOWalgorithm induces as many cache misses as the sequential algorithm with a cache p times smaller.

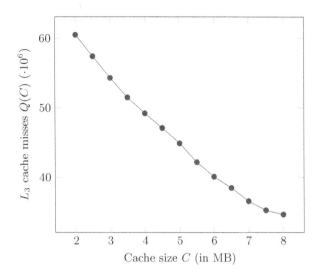

Figure 6: Number of shared cache misses of the sequential MT algorithm for varying cache sizes.

	L_3 cache misses	Time (ms)	Speedup
Sequential ($C = 2$MB)	$60.5 \cdot 10^6$	5015	0.66
Sequential ($C = 8$MB)	$34.7 \cdot 10^6$	3320	1.00
NoWindow	$55.3 \cdot 10^6$	1137	2.92
SlidingWindow	$38.4 \cdot 10^6$	964	3.44

Table 1: Performance of the two parallel MT algorithms NoWindow and SlidingWindow compared to the sequential algorithm.

We now consider the SlidingWindow algorithm where cores operate on elements at distance at most m in the cell sequence. Let $r(m)$ be the maximum number of distinct memory references when processing $m - 1$ consecutive elements of the cell sequence. In the worst case, when processing the last element of the window, all other elements have been processed accessing at most $r(m)$ additional distinct elements compared to the sequential algorithm. Thus the reuse distance is increased by at most $r(m)$. The number of cache misses of the SlidingWindow algorithm is

$$Q_w(C) \leq \sum_{d=C+1}^{\infty} H(d - r(m)) = Q(C) + \sum_{d=C+1-r(m)}^{C} H(d).$$

As we assumed the sequence has good temporal locality, $r(m)$ is small compared to m and $H(d)$ is small for large d. Therefore $\sum_{d=C+1-r(m)}^{C} H(d)$ is small and the SlidingWindow algorithm induces approximately the same number of shared cache misses as the sequential algorithm.

We experimentally verify this result by computing the number of shared cache misses for the sequential algorithm $Q(C)$ for cache sizes C varying from 2MB to 8MB on the Xeon E5530 (*cf.* Figure 6). We used a mesh composed of 150,000,000 cells. The number of cache misses for a cache of 2MB is much greater than when using an 8MB cache. Thus, we expect that using the SlidingWindow algorithm will result in a big gain in cache misses compared to the NoWindow algorithm on the 4 cores of the Xeon E5530. It is the case (*cf.* Table 1): the NoWindow exhibits almost the same number of misses as the sequential algorithm using four times less cache. Consequently its speedup is hindered

	L_3 cache misses	Time (ms)
Linux	$37.1 \cdot 10^6$	4124
Cache Control	$34.7 \cdot 10^6$	3320
Optimized Cache Control	$23.7 \cdot 10^6$	3090

Table 2: Performance of the sequential MT algorithm with 3 different allocation policies.

by its poor use of this application locality. On the contrary, as expected, the SlidingWindow version induces only a few more cache misses than the sequential algorithm and offers a better speedup.

6. DATA STRUCTURE(S) ISOLATION

Our objective, in this section, is to distribute as best as possible the cache available to the application. Our approach works in two steps: first we estimate from a derivative of the working sets analysis the cache requirements associated to each data structure of the application. Secondly, we use our cache controller to distribute the cache according to the first analysis. This method is especially effective in identifying the data structures (or memory regions) that would benefit the most from an increased cache size. We first use it to inhibit the negative effects of a streaming access pattern in the MT application. Then, we demonstrate better cache allocation strategies on a stencil algorithm similar to multigrid applications.

6.1 Avoiding Cache Pollution Due to Streaming Accesses in MT

When examining the access patterns of the MT algorithm, one can notice that only accesses to points exhibit data reuse. The other two access patterns, reading the cell sequence and writing the generated triangles, are pure streaming accesses and waste cache space. To avoid this negative effect, our implementation of the MT uses non temporal instructions to write the triangle sequence [7]. These instructions bypass the cache to avoid polluting it with useless data. We would like to do the same while reading the cell sequence. Unfortunately, non temporal read instructions do not exist. However, our cache controller can avoid the cache pollution by streaming-like access patterns by isolating them to a small portion of the cache. We have added this optimization on the cell array of the mesh in our MT implementation and compared the resulting 3 methods to allocate our data structures in Table 2.

In the first method, denoted Linux, we simply allocate them using `malloc`. In the second one, denoted Cache Control, we allocate them with our cache controller in a single region using all available colors thus realizing a perfect mapping of virtual to physical memory. In the last one, denoted Optimized Cache Control, we allocate the point array in a region composed of 100 colors and the cell and triangle arrays in the remaining 28 colors. As expected, due to a better color distribution in allocated pages, using a perfect mapping reduces the number of cache misses and improves the running time. Moreover, allocating more cache space to the array that exhibits reuse while confining the data structure accessed in streaming into a small cache region greatly reduces the number of cache misses (by 36%) and offers the best performance, a speedup of 1.33 over the unmodified application.

6.2 Multigrid Stencil

To demonstrate the full potential gains that can be obtained when using our cache partitioning scheme, we programmed a toy application derived from classical stencil filters. Our application makes a simultaneous use of three different matrices that reside in memory to compute the elements of a result matrix. The input matrices form the multigrid structure, it is made of a large matrix ($Y \times X$ 64 bytes elements), a medium-sized matrix (one fourth of the large matrix size) and a small matrix (one sixteenth of the large matrix size). The resulting matrix has the same size as the large matrix. Each of its elements is a linear combination of nine points stencils taken from each input matrix at the same coordinates (interpolated for smaller matrices).

This application is interesting for two reasons: it is extremely memory intensive and it makes a simultaneous use of several working sets of different sizes. Our nine points stencil forms a cross (a center element, the two elements above it, the two elements on the right, and so on) and it is included in five lines of a matrix. Thus, in the ideal case, if five lines of each input matrix can remain in the cache during the computation, the stencil will be computed with a maximal reuse. This translates into a cache space of $X \times 64 \times 5$ bytes for the large matrix, half of this size for the medium one and one fourth of this size for the small one. Of course if these working sets are not mapped to disjoints colors sets, they will mutually trash each other's cache when running the application.

Because the previous testing architecture (Intel Xeon) is known to prefetch memory too aggressively for the kind of access patterns our application contains, the following experiments were done on an Intel Core 2 Duo System. It contains 2 cores, with a L_1 Data cache size of 32 KB, a L_2 Unified cache, 16 ways associative of 4 MB. All caches have 64 B lines. From a coloring point of view, the L_2 cache contains 64 colors, each being 64 KB wide.

As we want to measure the cache requirements of each data structure independently, we modified our stencil so that it can use a different cache partition for each of the matrices. Then, for each application run, we isolated one of the matrices in a dedicated partition and the others in another one. The experiment consists in measuring the cache misses of the whole application while varying the size of the cache part associated to the isolated data structure. As the rest of the application is confined in a cache part of fixed size, the variation of cache misses can only be the result of the variation of the cache size given to the isolated data structure. As a result, we obtain the shape of the working sets of each data structure present in the application.

Figure 7 gives the resulting working sets for a partition size varying between 8 and 56 colors. The other data structures are contained in a fixed partition of 8 colors. This application was run with $X = 7168$ and $Y = 100$. Matrices are named from the smallest one M_1 ($X/4$ by $Y/4$) to the biggest M_3 (X by Y), the result matrix is named M_r.

Notice that, on such experiments, a difference in cache misses between structures for a given number of colors does not convey any significance: different structures are present in the small, static cache partition, inducing a different number of cache misses for the rest of the application. Thus, only the shape of the curve (the variation in cache misses for each structure) is of interest.

These working sets match the theoretical analysis of this

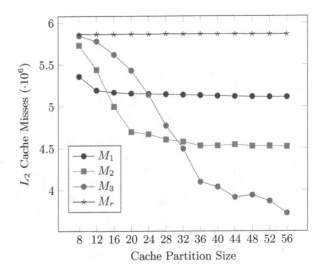

Figure 7: Multigrid Stencil: L_2 **cache misses per partition size for each data structure.**

	L_2 cache misses	Time (ms)
Linux	$3.6 \cdot 10^6$	139
Cache Control	$3.3 \cdot 10^6$	78
Optimized Cache Control	$2.2 \cdot 10^6$	57

Table 3: Performance of the stencil application with 3 different allocation policies.

application: each matrix needs to cache 5 rows at most to benefit optimally from cache, except for M_r which is only written to (needing no cache at all). As each matrix M_i is two times larger than M_{i+1} (in X), each matrix needs twice more cache than the previous. Given those working sets, we choose an optimized cache partitioning with 9 colors for M_1, 18 for M_2, 35 for M_3 and 2 for M_r. Table 3 presents the resulting performance of our application compared to the unmodified (Linux) and the single partition (Cache control) versions.

Using our cache controller, compared to the unmodified application, we achieve a tremendous performance improvement of 38% in L_2 cache misses and a speedup of 2.4 regarding the execution time. This very good speedup can be explained easily: a cache miss cost a lot more in execution time than a cache hit. Thus, reducing the number of cache misses significantly improves the running time of our application.

Of course, such results are only an indication of the kind of performance improvements our cache control scheme makes available. This stencil application is specially tailored so that an unmanaged cache is not able to use the locality of each data structure while a good partitioning can fit in the whole cache. Nevertheless, we can safely assume that any application containing streaming access patterns or very different reuse distances per data structure should benefit from our scheme.

7. RELATED WORKS

Soft-OLP [19], a tool making cache partitions at the object level inside an application using page coloring, is the closest work related to our proposal. However Soft-OLP relies, like most previous works, on binary instrumentation techniques: to determine a good partitioning among objects, they measure reuse distances for each object on instrumented runs (with Pin). As the authors acknowledge, instrumented runs are 50 to 80 times slower than real executions. To cope with longer execution times, they extrapolate the cache usage of each object in real word instances using measurements on small inputs (supposed representative). Our tool does not suffer from such limitations: measuring working sets is as fast as unmodified runs and thus can handle real sized instances. Instead of using Pin, we isolate each object in its own cache partition and measure misses with varying partition size.

A small part of the optimizations presented here were also discussed by Soares et al. in 2008 [25]. They proposed a OS scheme capable of detecting streaming access patterns using hardware performance counters. More precisely, they detected the virtual pages causing the most cache thrashing and isolated them to a small partition (using page coloring). Such techniques can also be related to cache-bypassing instructions found on most modern architectures [7]. We believe our scheme goes further, by balancing cache usage between data structures (even if overall they do not fit in cache). We demonstrated its use both to reduce streaming access patterns influence on performance and to better distribute the cache among data structures of an application.

Several studies have already resulted in the implementation of a Linux kernel module to provide a basic software cache partitioning mechanism using page coloring [5,17,18]. However, these papers were focused on a different context: cache sharing issues among multiple running processes on the same core. Such issues require tedious OS optimization and complicated heuristics whereas our proposal deals with only one thread per core, focusing on providing good colors to the right memory region used by the thread. Moreover, not a single paper has provided its implementation to the community, limiting the reuse of these works.

Most existing implementations of page coloring also make a trade-off between protecting processes from each other and avoiding cache trashing inside an address space. Several papers presented a cooperation between hardware mechanisms and compilers do cope with the latter [4,23]. Unfortunately such methods are limited to data reorganization techniques inside compilers and QoS strategies of the OS, whereas our cache control allows any application programmer to fine tune the cache usage of each of its data structures.

Finally, control of the virtual memory subsystem by user programs has also been suggested in the domain of micro and exokernels [11,12]. In those cases, an application could ask the OS to use other virtual memory managers than the default one, thus making it possible to rewrite a virtual memory manager fine tuned for a single memory access pattern. Several issues prevented those works to ever be made available in standard HPC configurations. First, all the virtual memory manager (not just the physical memory allocator) needed to be replaced. Such OS component is among the most complicated and it is considered too cumbersome to rewrite it for the improvement of a single application. Second, most of those specific operating systems are designed for single processor architectures and were never ported to HPC ones.

8. CONCLUSION

The International Exascale Software Project Roadmap [9] defines the support for explicit management of the memory hierarchy by runtime systems/user applications as one of the most critical aspect of future operating systems for HPC.

We believe our cache control tool to be a first step in the design of such mechanism. We presented a simple scheme, based on a well understood technique (page coloring) to expose to user applications control of the partitioning of the cache hierarchy. We validated this tool in Linux, one of the most popular OS in HPC. Our implementation is simple to use, efficient both in CPU and memory and does not necessarily require modifications of the target application. To the best of our knowledge, our tool is the first to allow measurements of the working sets of an application or of its data structures using only a small number of runs.

We also have presented a collection of experiments that highlight different usages of our proposal. We demonstrated how the analysis of application working sets can give hints about the proper parallelization scheme to use for them. We applied to two different applications our methodology for fine cache optimization. First, we used the analysis of the working sets of each data structure of a parallel scientific visualization application to remove cache thrashing due to small-reuse access patterns inside it. Then, this working sets analysis was used on a stencil application to design a dramatic optimization of its cache behavior. These experiments assessed that our methodology was sound, useful and might produce a reduction in caches misses of up to 38% in the most favorable cases and similar (or even better) improvements in execution time.

As future works, we plan to study the possible additional improvements that could be obtained when using a partitioning scheme sensitive to the cache hierarchy. To further improve the reach of our tool we will also study integrating it into parallel runtimes like OpenMP or MPI.

Our cache control tool as well as all the code used for our experiments are available on `http://ccontrol.ligforge.imag.fr`.

9. REFERENCES

[1] K. Beyls and E. D'Hollander. Reuse distance as a metric for cache behavior. In *Proceedings of the IASTED Conference on Parallel and Distributed Computing and systems*, volume 14, pages 350–360, 2001.

[2] C. Bienia, S. Kumar, J. P. Singh, and K. Li. The parsec benchmark suite: characterization and architectural implications. In *Proceedings of 17th International Conference on Parallel Architecture and Compilation Techniques*, pages 72–81, 2008.

[3] S. Browne, J. Dongarra, N. Garner, G. Ho, and P. Mucci. A portable programming interface for performance evaluation on modern processors. *The International Journal of High Performance Computing Applications*, 14(3):189–204, 2000.

[4] E. Bugnion, J. Anderson, T. Mowry, M. Rosenblum, and M. Lam. Compiler-directed page coloring for multiprocessors. *ACM SIGOPS Operating Systems Review*, 30(5):255, 1996.

[5] S. Cho and L. Jin. Managing distributed, shared l2 caches through os-level page allocation. In *Proceedings*

of the 39th Annual IEEE/ACM International Symposium on Microarchitecture, pages 455–468, 2006.

[6] J. Corbet, A. Rubini, and G. Kroah-Hartman. *Linux Device Drivers*. O'Reilly Media, 3rd edition, 2005.

[7] I. Corporation. *Intel Architecture Software Developer's Manual, Volume 2: Instruction Set Reference*.

[8] M. Dillon. Design elements of the FreeBSD VM system.

[9] J. Dongarra et al. The international exascale software project roadmap. *International Journal of High Performance Computer Applications*, 25(1), 2011.

[10] U. Drepper. What every programmer should know about memory, 2007.

[11] D. R. Engler, M. F. Kaashoek, and J. O'Toole. Exokernel: An operating system architecture for application-level resource management. In *Proceedings of the Fifteenth ACM Symposium on Operating System Principles*, pages 251–266, 1995.

[12] K. Harty and D. R. Cheriton. Application-controlled physical memory using external page-cache management. In *Proceedings of the Fifth International Conference on Architectural Support for Programming Languages and Operating Systems*, pages 187–197, 1992.

[13] J. L. Hennessy and D. A. Patterson. *Computer Architecture: a quantitative approach*. Morgan Kaufmann Publishers Inc., San Francisco, CA, USA, 2nd edition, 1996.

[14] R. R. Iyer. CQoS: a framework for enabling QoS in shared caches of cmp platforms. In *Proceedings of the 18th International Conference on Supercomputing*, pages 257–266, 2004.

[15] C. Johnson and C. Hansen. *Visualization Handbook*. Academic Press, Inc., 2004.

[16] R. E. Kessler and M. D. Hill. Page placement algorithms for large real-indexed caches. *ACM Transactions on Computer Systems*, 10:338–359, 1992.

[17] S. Kim, D. Chandra, and Y. Solihin. Fair cache sharing and partitioning in a chip multiprocessor architecture. In *Proceedings of the 13th International Conference on Parallel Architectures and Compilation Techniques*, pages 111–122, 2004.

[18] J. Lin, Q. Lu, X. Ding, Z. Zhang, X. Zhang, and P. Sadayappan. Gaining insights into multicore cache partitioning: Bridging the gap between simulation and real systems. In *Proceedings of the 14th International Conference on High-Performance Computer Architecture*, pages 367–378, 2008.

[19] Q. Lu, J. Lin, X. Ding, Z. Zhang, X. Zhang, and P. Sadayappan. Soft-olp: Improving hardware cache performance through software-controlled object-level partitioning. In *Proceedings of the 18th International Conference on Parallel Architectures and Compilation Techniques (PACT)*, pages 246–257, 2009.

[20] C. Luk, R. Cohn, R. Muth, H. Patil, A. Klauser, G. Lowney, S. Wallace, V. Reddi, and K. Hazelwood. Pin: building customized program analysis tools with dynamic instrumentation. In *Proceedings of the 2005 ACM SIGPLAN conference on Programming language design and implementation*, pages 190–200, 2005.

[21] H. Meuer, E. Strohmaier, H. Simon, and J. Dongarra. 35th release of the TOP500 list of fastest supercomputers, 2010.

[22] N. Nethercote and J. Seward. Valgrind: a framework for heavyweight dynamic binary instrumentation. In *Proceedings of the ACM SIGPLAN 2007 Conference on Programming Language Design and Implementation*, pages 89–100, 2007.

[23] T. Sherwood, B. Calder, and J. S. Emer. Reducing cache misses using hardware and software page placement. In *Proceedings of the 13th International Conference on Supercomputing*, pages 155–164, 1999.

[24] M. Snir and J. Yu. On the theory of spatial and temporal locality. Technical report, 2005.

[25] L. Soares, D. K. Tam, and M. Stumm. Reducing the harmful effects of last-level cache polluters with an os-level, software-only pollute buffer. In *41st Annual IEEE/ACM International Symposium on Microarchitecture (MICRO)*, pages 258–269, 2008.

[26] M. Tchiboukdjian, V. Danjean, T. Gautier, F. Le Mentec, and B. Raffin. A work stealing scheduler for parallel loops on shared cache multicores. In *Proceedings of the 4th Workshop on Highly Parallel Processing on a Chip (HPPC 2010)*, 2010.

[27] M. Tchiboukdjian, V. Danjean, and B. Raffin. Binary mesh partitioning for cache-efficient visualization. *Transactions on Visualization and Computer Graphics*, 16(5):815 –828, sep. 2010.

Cosmic Microwave Background Map-Making At The Petascale And Beyond

Rajesh Sudarsan   Julian Borrill   Christopher Cantalupo
Theodore Kisner   Kamesh Madduri   Leonid Oliker   Horst Simon   Yili Zheng
Computational Research Division, Lawrence Berkeley National Laboratory
Berkeley, CA 94720, USA
{rsudarsan, jdborrill, cmcantalupo, tkisner, kmadduri, loliker, hdsimon, yzheng}@lbl.gov

ABSTRACT

The analysis of Cosmic Microwave Background (CMB) observations is a long-standing computational challenge, driven by the exponential growth in the size of the data sets being gathered. Since this growth is projected to continue for at least the next decade, it will be critical to extend the analysis algorithms and their implementations to petascale high performance computing (HPC) systems and beyond. The most compute-intensive part of the analysis is generating and reducing Monte Carlo realizations of an experiment's data. In this work we take the current state-of-the-art simulation and mapping software and investigate its performance when pushed to tens of thousands of cores on a range of leading HPC systems, in particular focusing on the communication bottleneck that emerges at high concurrencies. We present a new communication strategy that removes this bottleneck, allowing for CMB analyses of unprecedented scale and hence fidelity. Experimental results show a communication speedup of up to $116\times$ using our alternative strategy.

Categories and Subject Descriptors

D.1.3 [**Programming Techniques**]: Parallel Programming

General Terms

Algorithms, Performance

Keywords

Sparse Allreduce, Hybrid Programming, Petascale Computing

1. INTRODUCTION

The CMB is the remnant radiation from the Big Bang itself. Last scattered when the Universe first cooled enough for neutral hydrogen to form, some 400,000 years after the Big Bang, it provides the earliest possible image of the Universe. Tiny fluctuations in the CMB across the sky encode not only the basic parameters of cosmology, but also, using the Big

Bang as the ultimate particle accelerator, insights into fundamental physics at energies some 12 orders of magnitude higher than those of the Large Hadron Collider beams [6]. However the faintness of these fluctuations requires us to gather and process enormous data sets to achieve sufficient signal-to-noise to decode them, and as a result, CMB data analysis is an extremely compute-intensive endeavor. Since CMB data sets have been growing exponentially in the last two decades, and are projected to continue to do so for at least the next decade, their analysis presents a long-standing challenge to scale the algorithms and implementations to the largest supercomputers available at any epoch.

The main focus of this work is to scale MADmap – a state-of-the-art massively parallel CMB analysis code – to the next generation of peta-scale supercomputers in order to be able to apply it to CMB experiments currently being fielded. Previous work by Cantalupo et.al [8] has shown that the inter-node communication phase in MADmap becomes a bottleneck when it is scaled to more than $O(10^4)$ MPI tasks. The highly irregular communication required in MADmap cannot be efficiently captured via nearest neighbor-based or tree-based all-to-all communication schemes. We present a novel approach that minimizes the data volume communicated, and is generally applicable to any sparse, irregular data distribution.

This paper presents two new optimizations towards alleviating the communication bottleneck and scaling up MADmap. The first one involves implementing the new communication algorithm that replaces MPI_Allreduce with an approach that uses MPI_Allgather operations (discussed in more detail in Section 3.3). We also employ "hybrid" programming to reduce the number of MPI tasks. We utilize one MPI task per socket, together with as many with OpenMP [18] threads as there are cores on the socket. We evaluate the costs and benefits of these optimizations by running a strong scaling experiment on up to 16K cores on four different systems, and show that these combined optimizations significantly reduce the communication bottleneck, achieving a speedup of up to $116\times$. The goal of this work is to provide an application-level portable optimization for a broad variety of supercomputers used for production CMB analysis. The proposed optimizations can also be applied to problems that require non-trivial global computation on large distributed and sparse data set. Examples include sparse matrix computations in scientific computing, in particular, applications that use conjugate gradient as a core component, graph traversal-based algorithms (social network analysis methods, modeling and analysis of dynamic networks), combinatorial graph-based problems in computational biology (e.g., distributed-memory genome assembly), and in general, data-parallel computations over sparse data sets with key-value pairs.

The remainder of the paper is laid out as follows: Section 2 gives an overview of CMB science in cosmology and a brief introduction to the analysis of current and future CMB experiments; Section 3 details the design and implementation of MADmap, its current communication bottleneck, and the optimizations implemented to alleviate it; Section 4 discusses the experimental setup used to evaluate the performance of these new approaches; Section 5 shows the benefits of these optimizations across a number of HPC systems; finally Section 6 presents our conclusions and directions for future research.

2. CMB SCIENCE

Observations of the CMB have already had a profound effect on our understanding of the Universe. Its very existence sounded the death-knell for the Steady State cosmology, while its extraordinary isotropy posed questions that were effectively addressed by the theory of Inflation, which posits a period of exponential expansion in the first moments after the Big Bang. However, it is the tiny fluctuations in the CMB temperature and polarization that carry the most detailed imprint of our cosmology. Already they have provided the strongest evidence for Inflation, as well as constraining the age, composition and overall geometry of the Universe [15].

At the turn of the millennium, CMB results coupled with the accelerating expansion of the Universe deduced from observations of type 1a supernovae, led to the surprising but now widely accepted "Concordance Cosmology", in which the Universe is believed to comprise around 70% dark energy, 25% dark matter and 5% ordinary matter [7]. Future observations of the CMB promise to yield even greater insight into the foundations of the Universe. The Planck satellite [19] – launched in May 2009, and following in the footsteps of the very successful COBE [5, 22] and WMAP [27] missions – will provide the definitive measurement of the temperature anisotropies, as well as the most detailed polarization observations to date. These results will be an essential complement to the numerous experiments currently being developed to improve our understanding of the dark energy (indeed the expected Planck results are routinely assumed as given in such experiments' performance projections). Beyond Planck, first a series of sub-orbital experiments and ultimately another satellite mission will search for the faintest CMB signal, its B-mode polarization, which is expected to carry, amongst other signals, the imprint of gravity waves emitted during Inflation. Precise measurement of this polarization signal on all angular scales constitutes the next great frontier for CMB research.

2.1 CMB Data Analysis

Most CMB experiments gather their data by scanning the sky with an array of detectors at multiple frequencies to produce a time-ordered data set comprising sky signal (both CMB and astrophysical foregrounds) and instrument noise. These data are reduced to pixelized maps of the intensity (I) and two polarization components (Q, U) of the microwave sky at each observing frequency. These maps are then combined to separate the CMB from the foreground contami-

nants, and the CMB IQU map-triplet is then used to determine the auto- and cross-angular power spectra of the CMB temperature (T) and E- and B- polarization modes, from which fundamental cosmological parameters can be determined.

This analysis is essentially data compression, progressively reducing the dimensionality of the data from time samples through multi- to single-frequency sky pixels to angular power spectral coefficients and ultimately cosmological parameters. Under minimal assumptions it is possible to write down maximum likelihood expressions for the maps given the time-ordered data and for the power spectra given the maps, and to show that these represent lossless compression [4]. However, a key feature of CMB data is that their three major components – the CMB itself, foregrounds, and detector noise – are individually correlated, and moreover, each is most simply described in a different domain. Detector noise is piecewise correlated in the time-domain; foregrounds signals are spatially correlated pixel-templates; and the azimuthally symmetric CMB signal can be represented by its angular correlations – indeed it is precisely the strength of these that we want to determine. These various correlations precludes the kind of divide-and-conquer embarrassingly parallel approaches used to analyze very large data sets in disciplines like accelerator physics. Instead, any CMB analysis has to be able to manipulate an entire data set simultaneously and coherently, ideally keeping track not just of the data in each basis, but also of their correlations as they are reduced.

In practice the computational tractability of any CMB analysis depends on two data parameters: the numbers of time-samples $(\mathcal{N}_t)$ and sky-pixels $(\mathcal{N}_p)$. The first is the product of the number of time streams, their sampling rate(s) and the duration of the observation, while the second comes from the ratio of the fraction of the sky observed to the size of the detector beams. Together these set the overall sensitivity of the experiment and the lower and upper limits of its angular power spectral range.

Using preconditioned conjugate gradient techniques [10] and exploiting the piecewise stationarity of the time-time noise correlations, the floating point operation count for maximum likelihood map-making scales as $\mathcal{O}(\mathcal{N}_t)$. However the maximum likelihood power spectrum estimation flopcount scales as $\mathcal{O}(\mathcal{N}_p^3)$, making it impractical for data sets with more than a few hundred thousand pixels; while it can still play a role for low-resolution (low multipole) analyses of current and future data sets, it has largely been replaced by Monte Carlo pseudo-spectral methods [11]. These methods scale with the simulation and map-making costs, both $\mathcal{O}(\mathcal{N}_t)$, and both with significant pre-factors.

Over the next 15 years we can expect CMB time-ordered data volumes to grow by three orders of magnitude; coincidentally this exactly matches the projected growth in computing power over the same period assuming a continuation of Moore's Law. Since today's CMB data analyses are already pushing the limits of current HPC systems, this implies that the algorithms and their implementations will have to continue scaling on the leading edge of HPC technology for the next 10 epochs of Moore's Law if we are to be able fully to support first the design and deployment of these missions and then the scientific exploitation of the data sets they gather.

3. MADMAP

3.1 The Current MADmap Package

The last decade has seen the development of a general purpose massively parallel CMB map-making code, MADmap, together with its application to real and simulated data from a number of experiments on many generations of HPC systems. As shown in Figure 1, MADmap has already successfully been scaled through a 100-fold increase in concurrency, 600-fold increase in peak system performance and 1000-fold increase in data volume; the next step is to enable MADmap to make effective use of the next generation of peta-scale HPC systems, with the particular scaling challenges they will present, in order to be able to analyze the next generation of CMB polarization experiments.

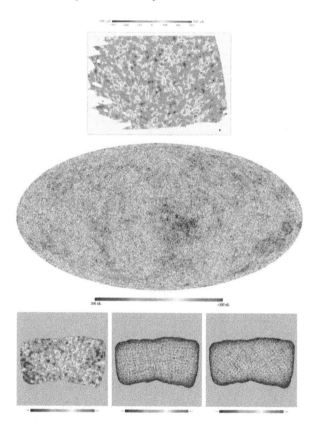

Figure 1: MADmap scaling to date: an O(10^8-sample, 10^5-pixel) BOOMERanG-98 temperature map calculated in 2000 on 128 Cray T3E processors, an O(10^{10}-sample,10^8-pixel) single-frequency simulated Planck temperature map calculated in 2005 on 6000 IBM SP3 processors, and an O(10^{11}-sample,10^5-pixel) simulated EBEX temperature and polarization map triplet calculated in 2008 on 15360 Cray XT4 cores.

MADmap is a massively parallel implementation of a pre-conditioned gradient (PCG) solver for maximum likelihood CMB map-making under the assumption that the noise is Gaussian and piecewise stationary. Each datum is the sum of instrument noise and a sky signal (CMB+foregrounds)

$$d_t = n_t + s_t = n_t + P_{tp}\, s_p$$

where P_{tp} is the pointing matrix, giving the weight of each

sky pixel p in sample t. Given the inverse time-time noise correlation matrix $N_{tt'}^{-1}$ the maximum-likelihood map m is then given by [23, 24]

$$m = \left(P^T\, N^{-1}\, P \right)^{-1} P^T\, N^{-1}\, d$$

Writing

$$
\begin{aligned}
M &= P^T\, N^{-1}\, P \\
b &= P^T\, N^{-1}\, d
\end{aligned}
$$

this can be cast in PCG form

$$Q^{-1}\, M\, m = Q^{-1}\, b$$

for some pre-conditioning matrix Q – typically chosen to be the trivially-invertible block-diagonal white noise approximation to M, with each 3×3 IQU-block constructed using just the diagonal of N^{-1}. Key to the MADmap implementation is to note that, by construction, N^{-1} is block band Toeplitz in the time domain (with each block corresponding to an interval over which the noise is stationary) and therefore diagonal in the Fourier domain. Multiplying a pixel-domain vector by M is therefore most efficiently performed by explicitly un-pointing the vector to the time-domain, Fourier transforming it, multiplying by the diagonal matrix, inverse Fourier transforming it, and re-pointing to the pixel-domain.

Until recently, the bottlenecks to scaling MADmap have been its IO requirements – specifically reading the time-ordered pointing and observation data. Like many massively parallel CMB codes, MADmap uses the M3 data abstraction layer [8,16] to isolate the generic analysis algorithm from the particular details of a specific experiment's data format and distribution, since these are invariably unique to each experiment. Instead of individually recasting data to each application's preferred format and distribution, as used to be the norm, the M3 data abstraction layer provides a simple API for each CMB data type and uses an XML description of the data files included in a particular analysis (in a run configuration file, or RunConfig) to enable an application's generic data requests to be converted into the appropriate specific file operations. By virtue of its support of arbitrary data formats and distributions, M3 also allows application codes transparently to access compressed, multi-component or virtual data by uncompressing, combining or simulating the requested data on demand.

Historically, CMB experiments would reconstruct the pointing for every sample from every stream and save these on disk to be accessed by subsequent analyses. However this detector-specific full pointing came from first reconstructing the pointing of a single fiducial line-of-sight (such as the telescope boresight) from instruments like star trackers and gyroscopes that are sampled much less frequently than the detectors. Reducing the IO load of the pointing data has been achieved by using the Generalized Compressed Pointing (GCP) library which takes the sparse-sampled fiducial pointing and calculates the detector-specific full pointing over some specific interval only when the application code requests that data through the M3 interface. This compresses the pointing data volume by factors of (i) the number of detectors (10^3-10^4) and (ii) the ratio of the sampling rate of the detectors to the sampling rate of the pointing instruments (10^2-10^3), for an overall reduction of 5-7 orders of magnitude so that even the largest projected experiment only requires a few GB of pointing data.

Unlike the pointing data, real detector data does not have the kind of redundancy that allows for compression and reconstruction on the fly. However, by far the majority of the detector data used in CMB analyses is simulated – either for mission design studies, or as Monte Carlo realizations for power spectrum estimation. In these cases simulation is immediately followed by analysis, which has traditionally meant first performing the simulation and writing the detector data out to disk, and then reading those data back in for analysis. To reduce the IO load of such detector data the On-The-Fly Simulation (OTFS) library simulates an interval of a particular detector's data data only when requested by the analysis application, again through the M3 data abstraction interface. Since these data now need never touch disk, this approach can completely solve the simulated detector data IO problem for any application using the M3 interface, albeit at the cost of re-calculation for each re-analysis.

3.2 Communication Bottleneck

With the IO bottleneck solved, the next scaling issue to emerge has been in MADmap's communication requirements. Since the dominant computational cost scales with the number of time samples, load-balancing requires these time ordered data to be equally distributed over the processes. Given this data distribution, each process then has some of the information about some subset of the pixels (i.e. those pixels observed by its time-ordered data). At each PCG iteration, these pixel data must be reduced over all of the processes to generate the complete updated map.

The mapping between time-ordered data and sky pixels depends on the experiment's scanning strategy. Resolving CMB maps in the presence of non-white detector noise means that a fraction of the pixels in the map must be re-observed after some significant time has passed, and preferably in an orthogonal direction to the first scan. This technique is known as cross-linking, and it is precisely these re-observed pixels that end up being shared across the processes.

The required communication can most simply be performed with MPI's global reduction collective MPI_Allreduce, although often there is insufficient memory available to each process to store the entire map and the reduction must be buffered. Having chosen a supportable buffer size (n_b), a pipelined reduction on the entire map is performed with one call to MPI_Allreduce for each buffer. The buffer is filled with the value stored locally, or the identity of the reduction operator if no data is stored locally. The reduction is then performed, and each process copies the pertinent values out of the buffer into a local pixel vector before the operation is repeated.

We can utilize a simple network performance model to describe the complexity of this communication step. Assume that the time taken to send a message between two processes is given by $\alpha + n\beta$, where α is a term that accounts for the latency per message, β is the transfer time per byte (inverse of bandwidth), and n is the message size. This model does not account for network congestion, message sizes, or the network topology. However, prior work [9,12,21] suggests that this is a reasonable first-order approximation for comparing alternative algorithmic approaches.

Most current MPI implementations employ Rabenseifner's approach [20,25] for MPI_Allreduce with large message sizes. This algorithm performs a reduce-scatter using the recursive-halving technique and then a gather operation using a binomial tree approach. For p processes, the complexity of this algorithm in terms of the α-β model is

$$2 \log p\, \alpha + 2n \frac{p-1}{p} \beta$$

The bandwidth component of this algorithm is a notable reduction over an older binomial tree-based algorithm for Allreduce, which has a $n \log p\ \beta$ term. Our buffered reduction approach based on Rabenseifner's Allreduce algorithm would thus have a complexity of

$$2 \frac{\mathcal{N}_p}{n_b} \log p\, \alpha + 2\mathcal{N}_p \frac{p-1}{p} \beta$$

Note that the volume of data exchanged in this approach may be much larger than necessary. If every process observes every pixel (i.e., we perform a reduction over a dense vector), then this approach would be optimal. On the other hand if the number of pixels shared between processors is comparatively small (as is often the case), then much of the data communicated in this technique will be the identity operator for the reduction, which is wasteful. Although Rabenseifner's algorithm may not be used in all MPI implementations, any binomial tree-based reduction algorithm only changes our analysis by a $\log p$ multiplicative factor to the bandwidth component.

3.3 Collective Communication Optimization

The collective problem in MADmap can be generalized and formally stated as follows: each process i locally stores n_i key-value pairs, with $\Sigma_1^p n_i = n_{all}$. The keys are non-negative integers that lie in the range $[0, C]$. A global reduction operation with a binary associative operator is performed, but a process only needs to store the updated values of its local keys. Our objective is to minimize the total execution time for this collective operation, which is a sum of the local computation time and time spent in communication (which we will express in terms of the α-β model). Also, let o_{ij} denote the key counts shared by processes i and j, and $n_{lmax} = \max{(n_i)}, 1 \leq i \leq p$.

This problem definition captures several common global communication patterns observed in parallel scientific computing. For instance, consider the Allreduce collective over a dense vector. In this case, $n_i = n_{lmax} = n_{all}/p = C$ for all $1 \leq i \leq p$ and $o_{ij} = C$ for all $1 \leq i, j \leq p$. Further, since keys are ordered in $[0, C]$ and sorted, they need not be explicitly represented. In this case, Rabenseifner's algorithm may be appropriate, as it achieves a good balance between the number of messages sent and the data volume exchanged over the network.

Nearest-neighbor communication would correspond to the case where o_{ij} is non-zero when $|i-j| = 1$, and 0 for all other $i \neq j$. Here, the optimal strategy would be to have neighbors exchanging the data they share and then performing reductions locally. The corresponding communication cost would be $2\alpha + 2n_{lmax}\beta$.

A third case that lies in between the dense vector reduction and nearest neighbor communication patterns is when each process shares data with a few other processes (say, more than one, but less than $\log p$). Hoefler et al. [13] study this problem and its variations, and design new, specialized

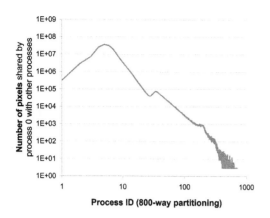

Figure 2: A depiction of the overlap pattern exhibited by a typical distributed sky-pixel data representation (Planck simulation data, $\mathcal{N}_p$ is 150 million).

collectives to address this problem. Hoefler and Träff [14] also make the case for better support of "sparse" communication patterns within MPI, where the sparsity refers to the number of communicating processes.

Clearly, the distribution of keys within $[0, C]$ for each process, the key overlap count between pairs of processes, the count of keys owned by each process, the values of C and n_{all}, all contribute to determining the optimal reduction strategy for a parallel platform.

To drive our design of a faster communication approach, we analyze the sparsity pattern exhibited by the sky pixel data partitioning . Figure 2 gives the count of sky pixels shared by one MPI process (process 0 in this case) with all other processes, for an experiment where $\mathcal{N}_p$ is 150 million. The data represents a distribution of pixels corresponding to a year of Planck simulated data using four 217 GHz channel detectors. Analysis shows that process 0 shares a significantly large fraction of its total number of local pixels (98.5%) with a few other processes (in this case, process IDs 1-20), and shares at least few pixels (say, < 1000) with almost all other processes. Conversely, few pixels appear in the local partitions of almost all processes, and a majority of pixels appear in the local partitions of less than 20 processes. Additionally, the actual pixel integer identifiers that are local to each process are not contiguously ordered, i.e., process 0 contains roughly $\mathcal{N}_p/p$ pixels, but the pixel identifiers IDs are spread out in the entire range of $[0, \mathcal{N}_p]$. Restating these observations in terms of the collective problem definition, C would be equal to N_p, n_{all} is typically 2-6$\times$ the value of C, and the overlap counts and patterns are neither nearest-neighbor nor amenable to a sparse collective implementation. Furthermore, the values of C can be very large, and thus accumulation of all pixel identifiers and values on a single process may not possible.

Our new algorithm is primarily motivated by the potential data volume reduction that can be achieved by avoiding the buffered Allreduce approach. Note that n_{all} is not more than 6 times the value of N_p at process concurrencies up to 8000, and that the pixel counts per process are roughly the same. Furthermore, analysis of Figure 2 shows that Σo_{ij} is bounded by $2n_{lmax}$ for all the processes. Thus, if each process were to exchange only the data it shares with other processes and then perform the reduction locally, the

bandwidth term in the α-β model would decrease from N_p to $2n_{lmax}$, which is almost a $\mathcal{O}(p)$ reduction.

This pairwise exchange scheme is implemented in a two-step approach. In the first "preprocessing" routine, each process determines the pixel identifiers (keys) that it shares with all other processes. Since the cumulative pixel overlap count per process is bounded, this information can be stored in memory for the duration of the simulation. Whenever a global reduction needs to be performed, each process only sends the values corresponding to the keys it shares with every other process. This is accomplished using a single call of the MPI_Alltoallv collective, which internally relies on pair-wise sends and receives to communicate the data.

Figure 3 presents the execution time of the various subroutines in the preprocessing step, on the Franklin system (described in Section 4). Our algorithm stores the local pixel identifiers in a sorted array on every process, and begins by determining n_{lmax}, which allows the estimate of n_{all} and the associated buffer sizes used for all the communication steps. Next, we allocate memory and initialize the data buffers to be exchanged (labeled as "Init buffer index" in Figure 3). At this stage, we calculate all pairwise overlap counts and shared pixel locations. Exploiting symmetry, the pairwise count can be reduced from p^2 to $p(p-1)/2$. Instead of pairwise exchanges of data, the MPI_Allgather routine is utilized in a buffered fashion ("MPI Allgather" in Figure 3). This reduces the number of pairwise message exchanges, as MPI Allgather implementations typically utilize a tree-based algorithm. Each process inspects the pixel identifiers received from all other processes and notes the shared pixels. The local pixels are then stored in a Judy array data representation [3] to permit very fast membership queries. The step labeled "Sifting" in the figure captures the time taken for these lookups. Finally, the overlap pixels identifiers are stored compactly in a sorted array. The communication complexity of the preprocessing step is

$$\log p \frac{n_{lmax}}{n_b} \alpha + p n_{lmax} \frac{p-1}{p} \beta$$

in the α-β model (dominated by the MPI_Allgather step), and the local computation is $O(p n_{lmax})$ due to the initialization and sift operations. Figure 3 indicates that these three steps – Allgather, sift, and initialization – are indeed the steps that dominate the overall execution time. Future work will investigate additional performance optimizations such as simultaneous, asynchronous execution of the gather and sift steps using non-blocking collectives, and further optimization of the initialization routines.

Subsequent calls to a global reduction involve pairwise data exchanges utilizing the shared pixel information collected in the preprocessing routine. This step would be dominated by the cost of the Alltoallv routine: $p\alpha + k n_{lmax}\beta$, where k is a small number that bounds the overlap count in terms of n_{lmax}. The quadratic scaling of the number of messages exchanged may be a potential drawback of our scheme. All-to-all communication is a known bottleneck for MPI implementations and high concurrency runs [2]. However, this message count is inevitable if we rely on pairwise exchanges of data and try to minimize the total data volume. In future work, we will investigate approaches that would reduce the number of messages from p to a smaller, manageable value. For instance, the subset of pixels identifiers that appear on a majority of processes can be identi-

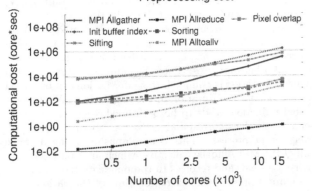

Figure 3: A breakdown of the local computation and communication components (on the Franklin system) in the preprocessing phase of the new collective algorithm.

fied in the preprocessing step and reduced separately. This may necessitate an increase in the preprocessing step's local computation. Note that our approach does not directly utilize hardware-accelerated collective primitives for communication, but instead, optimizes code for compliant MPI functions. Our communication algorithm will automatically benefit from vendor-optimized MPI, which we expect will leverage hardware acceleration internally where available.

3.4 Threading Optimization

Our approach can also alleviate the communication cost by reducing the total number of MPI tasks p. To do so, we adopt a hybrid implementation that uses a single MPI task per socket or node, and as many OpenMP threads per task as there are cores per socket/node. This hybrid approach required the implementation of new multithreaded routines for computationally demanding MADmap components, including FFTs (using the threaded ACML [1] or IMKL [17] libraries depending on their availability on a particular platform); the mapping of global to local pixel indices (using a threaded lookup with Judy arrays [3]); and the pointing matrix-vector multiplication, calculation and application of the pre-conditioner in the conjugate gradient calculation, calculation of the pixel overlap in the communication preprocessing step, and parts of the GCP and M3 libraries (all primary in their for-loops). OpenMP pragmas are used to parallelize the code, creating additional auxiliary data structures wherever required (such as thread-local copies for private buffers) in a space-efficient manner.

A few computational phases have not yet been threaded because of for-loops present in non-canonical form. These include inverse matrix multiplication, derivation of pixel data distribution, initializing data structures for convolution algorithm, calculation involved before writing output maps, and some parts of M3. Due to these unthreaded components, the cumulative computational time of threaded MADmap is currently 50% slower than the unthreaded case (i.e, with one MPI task per core). Implementing multithreaded versions of these remaining components as well as increasing the efficiency of threading in MADmap will be a key area of focus in our future work.

4. EXPERIMENTAL SETUP

To investigate the benefits of the new communication algorithm and hybrid programming in MADmap, we performed strong scaling experiments on a typical Planck-scale data set on four different implementations of MADmap on five HPC systems, described in Section 4.2 — Franklin and Hopper at NERSC, Jaguar at Oak Ridge National Lab, and Pleiades-H and Pleiades-W at NASA Ames Research Center.

4.1 Data Analyses

MADmap is evaluated at eight different concurrencies ranging from 256 to 16384 cores, at powers of two for Franklin and Pleiades-H (with four cores per socket) and at the closest multiple of six to these for Hopper, Jaguar, and Pleiades-W (with six cores per socket). At each concurrency, we measured the overhead for communication, computation, and disk I/O incurred by MADmap when analyzing simulated data corresponding to a year of Planck observations of the entire sky from all 12 detectors at one of its key observing frequencies, so that ($\mathcal{N}_t \sim 7.5 \times 10^{10}$ and $\mathcal{N}_p \sim 1.5 \times 10^8$). All the runs were executed for 50 iterations of the PCG solver, a typical number for mapping polarized data, and to compare performance of four different MADmap versions.

Unthreaded Allreduce: The existing (original) version of MADmap that uses MPI_Allreduce for communication. This application is not threaded and runs with one MPI process per core.

Unthreaded Allgather: This version of MADmap replaces MPI_Allreduce with the new collective communication algorithm discussed above, but without threading (one MPI task per core). Since the cost of our new algorithm is dominated by the MPI_Allgather in the preprocessing step, we refer to this as the Allgather-based approach. Evaluating this version at various concurrencies addresses the question of whether the new algorithm by itself is sufficient to eliminate the high concurrency communication bottleneck.

Threaded Allreduce: In this version, existing implementation of MADmap is threaded using OpenMP pragmas. Evaluating this version tells us whether reducing the number of communicating processes with threading alone can provide a solution to the communication bottleneck at high concurrencies.

Threaded Allgather: This version includes both the optimized communication algorithm as well as OpenMP threading, and quantifies the impact of including both the optimization strategies.

Note that both Threaded Allreduce and Threaded Allgather run with one MPI task per socket, combined with as many OpenMP threads as there are cores in that socket.

4.2 Architectural Platforms

To evaluate MADmap in a range of HPC environments we conduct our experiments on five large-scale HPC platforms, the Cray XT4, XT5 and XE6 and two generations of Intel/Infiniband clusters. The Cray XT is designed with tightly integrated node and interconnect fabric, opting for a custom network ASIC and messaging protocol coupled with a commodity AMD processor. In contrast, the Intel/IB cluster is assembled from off-the-shelf high-performance networking components and Intel server processors. These represent common design trade-offs in the high performance computing arena. Table 1 shows architectural highlights of the examined platforms.

Table 1: Highlights of CPU and node architectures for examined platforms, all evaluated processors are superscalar, out-of-order. MPI bandwidth is measured as the maximum MPI point-to-point bandwidth with message sizes from 4 Bytes to 256 Mbytes. MPI latency is measured with 4-Byte messages.

Core Architecture	AMD Budapest	AMD Istanbul	Intel Harpertown	Intel Westmere	AMD Magny-Cours
Clock (GHz)	2.30	2.6	3	2.93	2.1
DP Peak (GFlop/s)	9.20	10.4	12	11.72	8.4
Private L1 Data Cache	64 KB	64 KB	32 KB	32 KB	64 KB
Private L2 Data Cache	512 KB	512 KB	—	256 KB	512 KB
Socket/Node Architecture	**Opteron 1356 Budapest**	**Opteron 2435 Istanbul**	**Xeon E5472 Harpertown**	**Xeon X5670 Westmere**	**Opteron 6172 Magny-Cours**
Cores per Socket	4	6	4	6	12
Shared Cache per Socket	2 MB L3	6 MB L3	12 MB L2	12 MB L3	12 MB L3
Sockets per SMP	1	2	2	2	2
Node DP Peak (GFlop/s)	36.8	124.8	96	140.6	201.6
DRAM Pin Bandwidth (GB/s)	12.8	25.6	21.33	32.0	25.6
Node DP Flop:Byte Ratio	2.9	4.9	4.5	4.4	7.9
System Architecture	**Cray XT4 Franklin**	**Cray XT5 Jaguar**	**Intel Cluster Pleiades-H**	**Intel Cluster Pleiades-W**	**Cray XE6 Hopper**
Interconnect	Seastar2 3D Torus	Seastar2+ 3D Torus	Infiniband DDR	Infiniband QDR	Gemini 3D Torus
Total Nodes	9,660	18,688	5,888	2,048	6,392
Peak Bandwidth (GB/s per direction)	3.8	4.8	2.5	5	7
Measured MPI point-point bandwidth (GB/s)	1.65	1.6	1.66	3.13	5.95
Measured MPI latency (μs)	8.15	8.26	1.32	1.83	1.4
Compiler vendor, version	PGI 10.1	PGI 10.3	Intel 11.1	Intel 11.1	PGI 10.9
MPI Vendor, MPT version	Cray 4.0.3	Cray 4.0	SGI 1.25	SGI 1.25	Cray 5.1.2

Franklin: Cray XT4: Franklin, a 9,660 node Cray XT4 supercomputer, is located at Lawrence Berkeley National Laboratory (LBNL). Each XT4 node contains a quad-core 2.3 GHz AMD Opteron processor, which is tightly integrated to the XT4 interconnect via a Cray SeaStar2 ASIC through a HyperTransport (HT) 2 interface capable of 6.4 Gbyte/s. All the SeaStar routing chips are interconnected in a 3D torus topology with each link is capable of 7.6 Gbyte/s peak bidirectional bandwidth, where each node has a direct link to its six nearest neighbors. Typical MPI latencies will range from 4.5 - 8.5 μs, depending on the size of the system and the job placement. The Opteron Budapest processor is a superscalar out-of-order core that may complete both a single instruction-multiple data (SIMD) floating-point add and a SIMD floating-point multiply per cycle, the peak double-precision floating-point performance (assuming balance between adds and multiplies) is 36.8 GFlop/s. Each core has both a private 64 Kbyte L1 data cache and a 512 Kbyte L2 victim cache. The four cores on a socket share a 2 Mbyte L3 cache. Unlike Intel's older Xeon, the Opteron integrates the memory controllers on chip and provides an inter-socket network (via HT) to provide cache coherency as well as direct access to remote memory. This machine uses DDR2-800 DIMMs providing a DRAM pin bandwidth of 12.80 Gbyte/s per socket.

Jaguar: Cray XT5: The 18,688 node Jaguar XT5 platform is currently the number two system on the TOP500 [26]. This successor to the XT4 line contains nodes with two hexa-core 2.6 GHz AMD Opteron processors, and a Cray SeaStar2+ 3D torus interconnect capable of 9.6 Gbyte/s. Typical MPI latencies will range from 4.5 - 8.5 μs, depending on the size of the system and the job placement. The next-generation Opteron Istanbul processor has a larger 6MB semi-exclusive L3 cache and a peak theoretical node rate of 124.8 double-precision GFlop/s. To mitigate snoop effects and maximize the effective memory bandwidth, Istanbul uses 1MB of each 6MB cache for HT assist (a snoop filter). The snoop filter enables higher bandwidth on large multi-socket SMPs.

Pleiades-H: Intel Harpertown Cluster: The 9,216 node Pleiades cluster, located at NASA Ames Research Center consists of three Xeon-based clusters, two of which are examined in this study. The Pleiades-H cluster consists of 5,888 dual-socket nodes utilizing 3.0 GHz quad-core Intel Harpertown processors, connected via a DDR IB network in partial 11D hypercube. Providing an interesting comparison to the Opterons, the Xeon E5472 (Harpertown) uses a modern superscalar out-of-order core architecture coupled with an older frontside bus (FSB) architecture in which two multichip modules (MCM) are connected with an external memory controller hub (MCH) via two frontside buses. Unfortunately the limited FSB bandwidth (10.66 Gbyte/s) bottlenecks the substantial DRAM read bandwidth of 21.33 Gbyte/s (subsequently released Nehalem processors have abandoned the front-side bus in favor of on-chip memory controllers). Each core runs at 3 GHz, has a private 32 KB L1 data cache, and, like the Opteron, may complete one SIMD floating-point add and one SIMD floating-point multiply per cycle. Unlike the Opteron, the two cores on a chip share a 4 Mbyte L2 and may only communicate with the other two cores of this nominal quad-core MCM via the shared frontside bus.

Pleiades-W: Intel Westmere Cluster: Our study also examines performance on the Pleiades-W cluster that consists of 2,048 dual-socket nodes containing 2.93 GHz octal-core Intel Westmere processors connected via a QDR IB network. This recently released design the latest enhancement to the Intel "Core" architecture, and represents a dramatic departure from Intel's previous multiprocessor designs. It abandons the front-side bus (FSB) in favor of on-chip memory controllers. The resultant QuickPath Interconnect (QPI) inter-chip network is similar to AMD's HyperTransport (HT), and it provides access to remote memory controllers and I/O devices, while also maintaining cache coherency. Each core has a private 256 KB L1 and a 1 MB L2 cache, and each socket instantiates a shared 12 MB L3 cache. Additionally, each socket integrates three DDR3 memory controllers providing up to 32 GB/s of DRAM bandwidth to each socket.

Hopper: Cray XE6: The 6392 node Hopper cluster debuted this year as the fifth fastest system on Top 500 list. Each node contains two 12-core 2.1 GHz AMD 'Magny-Cours' processors and a Cray Gemini interconnect with an effective bandwidth of 168 GB/s. Each processor has 2 dies with 6 cores on each die. Each die has 2 memory channels and is a NUMA node. There are 4 HyperTransport 3 (HT3) links per processor providing a peak bandwidth of 25.6 GB/s per processor. Each core has private L1 and L2 caches with 64KB and 512KB respectively and a L3 cache of 12 MB shared between the two dies in a processor. The processors are interconnected in a 3D torus topology with each node providing an aggregate bandwidth of 168 GB/s.

5. RESULTS AND DISCUSSION

For each code configuration and concurrency, we time the calculation, communication and IO components, across all evaluated HPC systems — reporting our results in total core-seconds; a constant value therefore represents perfect scaling for this problem. Figure 4 shows the performance of Unthreaded Allreduce, Unthreaded Allgather, Threaded Allreduce and Threaded Allgather on Franklin, Jaguar, and Pleiades-H and -W[1]. Each column compares the performance of the various implementations on a single system and each row compares the performance of a particular implementation across the systems. The threaded implementations are run with one process per socket and as many threads as there are cores per socket; in addition, for all dual-socket systems use the Threaded Allgather approach alone via a single process per node with as many threads as cores on the node.

5.1 Comparison Across Implementations

Results show that on all systems, the communication bottleneck emerges in the Unthreaded Allreduce, with communication dominating above a few thousand cores. The Unthreaded Allgather approach increases the concurrency at which communication become a bottleneck. But once it does, its cost rapidly comes to exceed that of the Un-

threaded Allreduce. In both of the threaded cases, the communication cost is reduced, marginally for the Allreduce and significantly for the Allgather. Both of these observations are consistent with our complexity analyses, in which the Allreduce latency depends on $\log p$, the Allgather latency on $p \log p$, and the transfer time on p. At a concurrency of 16K processors, the improvement in communication overhead is maximum on Jaguar with a speedup of 14.2× using threaded Allgather. On Franklin, Hopper, Pleiades-W, and Pleiades-H the communication speedups are 1.95×, 2.35×, 3.44× and 4.65× respectively. At the same time, the calculation cost increases due to the incomplete threading — as expected from Amdahl's Law — and the IO cost decreases, since much of the data ingest is implemented by process 0 performing a serial read and broadcasting, now to a smaller number of processes.

To check whether our theoretical expressions for the communication costs are indicative of observed execution times in practice, we perform a least-squares fit of the observed data to linear model. Figure 5 depicts the MPI_Allreduce and MPI_Allgather execution times per iteration and the calculated trend line. For MPI_Allgather, we fit the data to the complexity cost of a ring-based (not tree-based) algorithm, since the MPI implementations employ a ring-based algorithm for the buffer sizes in our experiments. Observe from Figure 5 that the linear α-β model is a reasonable fit for MPI_Allreduce, and a very good fit for MPI_Allgather. The slope of the line corresponds to β in our model, which is the inverse of the sustained per-node network bandwidth for the collectives. Examining these values shows that the sustained bandwidth per process for the threaded case is greater by a factor of two for both MPI_Allreduce and MPI_Allgather. The measured point-to-point bandwidth and the small message latency (see Table 1) are upper and lower bounds respectively for the empirically-determined α and β values, thereby providing validation of our performance model. The impact of latency term is negligible in the MPI_Allreduce cost, due to the large message sizes and the tree-based algorithm employed. To summarize, we observe a sustained bandwidth of 0.86 GB/s for threaded Allreduce, 0.25 GB/s for unthreaded Allreduce, 1.15 GB/s for threaded Allgather and 0.58 GB/s for unthreaded Allgather. The communication costs on the remaining systems can be similarly analyzed, to estimate the potential for improvement in performance of the MPI collectives, and will be the focus of future investigations.

For the four evaluated systems with dual-socket nodes, threading per node performance can be compared against threading per socket. Since the former halves the number of MPI tasks, one might expect node-level threading to result in a similar reduction in the communication cost (see Figure 6. However, at higher concurrencies, the communication cost actually increases on Jaguar and Pleiades-H, and stays roughly constant on Pleiades-W. This is likely because a single process per node is insufficient to saturate the available network injection bandwidth on Jaguar and Pleiades-H. Results also show the calculation cost roughly doubling due to the partial threading of the application and NUMA effects of a single process running on two sockets. Therefore, in our current implementation, threading beyond the socket level does not gain any additional benefit.

---

[1]To date we have been unsuccessful in completing 16K-way unthreaded allgather run on Pleiades-H, and are working with NASA Ames staff to resolve this in time for publication

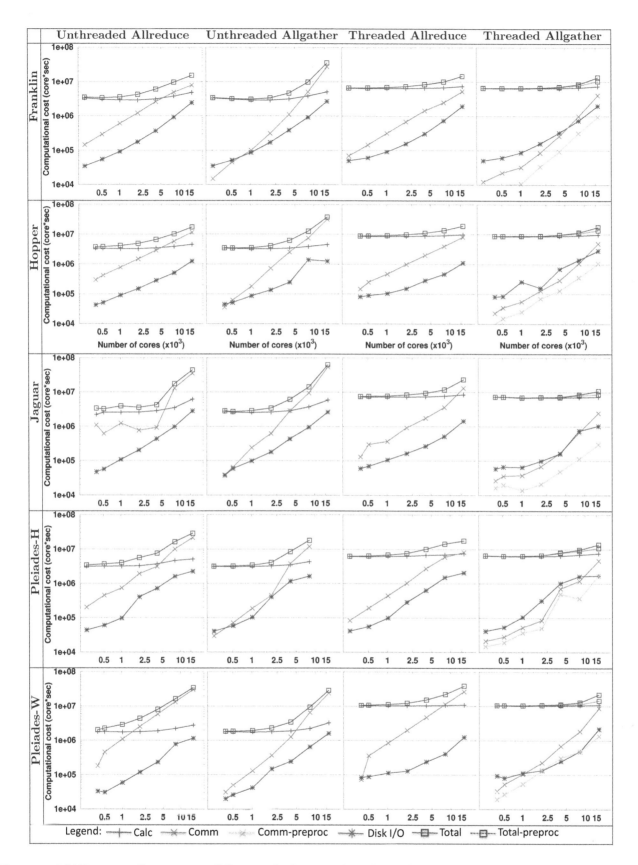

Figure 4: MADmap scaling runs on different platforms. Threaded Allgather and Threaded Allreduce execute with one process per socket with four or six threads. The dotted lines in Threaded Allgather represent the total and communication time without the preprocessing overhead.

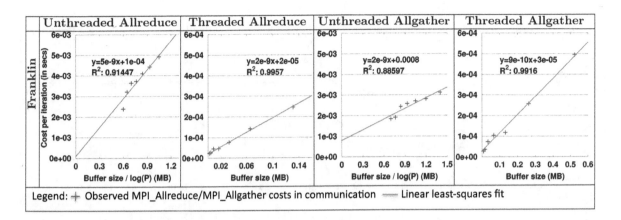

Figure 5: A least-squares fit of the observed Franklin communication costs (scatter data) for MPI_Allgather and MPI_Allreduce, to the linear α-β model expressions. The R^2 value indicates the deviation of the observed data from the fit, with a value close to 1 indicating a good fit.

5.2 Comparison Across Systems

The communication cost for Unthreaded Allreduce at 16K processors on Jaguar, Pleiades-W, Pleiades-H and Hopper are 4.45, 3.85, 2.71 and 1.5 times the cost on Franklin respectively. The reason for this slowdown is due to the increased number of communicating processes per node on these systems: 4, 12, 12, 8 and 12 for Franklin, Jaguar, Pleiades-W, Pleiades-H, and Hopper, respectively. As a result, the per-node bandwidth is shared by all the processes per node on these systems, although Hopper has roughly three time the bandwidth per node compared to the other systems and about 1.5 times the bandwidth per node compared to Pleiades-W. Also, since the messages from multiple processes is serialized at the network interface of the node, increasing the number of MPI tasks per node limits scalability. In addition, variability due to other factors such as the type of interconnect used (Seastar2 or Infiniband), its configuration (3D Torus or Hypercube), and MPI implementation details also influence the communication costs.

At a concurrency of 16K in threaded MADmap, Franklin and Pleiades-H use 4096 MPI processes whereas Jaguar, Pleiades-W and Hopper use only 2730 processes. Threaded Allreduce reduces the communication overhead by 1.51, 2.66, 2.64, 1.12 and 1.44 with respect to their unthreaded counterparts on Franklin, Jaguar, Pleiades-H, Pleiades-W, Hopper respectively at a concurrency of 16K processors. As seen in the unthreaded case, the cost of Threaded Allreduce on Jaguar, Pleiades-H, Pleiades-W and Hopper is 2.54, 1.55, 5.15 and 1.54 times slower than Franklin. Although the total number of processes compared to Franklin is lower in Jaguar, each node has two MPI processes that share the inter-node network bandwidth; whereas Franklin has just one process per node. Compared to Franklin, the data per process on Jaguar is more, which in turn increases the number of communicating MPI tasks (since the message size is maintained constant). Unlike Jaguar and Pleiades-W that have two MPI processes sharing the node bandwidth, Hopper has four MPI processes per node. Thus even with more processes per node, the communication cost on Hopper is lower than all the other dual-socket node systems due to the availability of high bandwidth per node. Threaded Allgather further reduces the communication as the expensive preprocessing cost is incurred only once. At a concurrency of

16K processors, the communication cost for Threaded Allgather on Jaguar is 3.44 times lower than Franklin. The main reasons for this improvement is that the overhead of per-iteration communication is relatively inexpensive. The communication cost on Pleiades-H is comparable to the cost on Franklin as they use same number of total MPI processes. The marginal increase in cost in Pleiades-H can be attributed to the overhead due to serialization of messages at the network interface from two processes in a single node. On Pleiades-W, due the undetermined variability in the MPI implementation, the MPI_Allgather cost in preprocessing increases steeply at higher concurrency, thereby increasing the overall cost of communication. Additionally, Figure 4 shows that the communication cost on Hopper is comparable to Franklin and Pleiades-H.

The calculation cost with 16K processors for unthreaded MADmap are comparable on Franklin, Jaguar, Hopper and Pleiades-H. On Pleiades-W the application runs almost twice as fast compared to Franklin, Jaguar, Hopper and Pleiades-H respectively, as seen in Figure 4. Although Pleiades-H has a faster processor clock frequency compared to Pleiades-W, the bus to core ratio in Pleiades-W is 22 compared to 7.5 in Pleiades-H — account for its faster calculation cost, as higher ratio indicates greater bandwidth to transfer data. In addition the Pleiades-W processors support a maximum turbo frequency of 3.3GHz along with a Quick Path Interconnect (QPI) rate of 6.4GT/s compared to a front side bus frequency of 1600MHz in Pleiades-H.

However, the calculation cost for threaded MADmap on Pleiades-W is highest relative to the other platforms, including Pleiades-H The reason for this slowdown is likely due to different instruction set used in the compilation of application binary. Threaded MADmap was compiled on Pleiades-H with SSE4.1 instruction set whereas unthreaded MADmap uses the application binary compiled on Pleiades-W with the SSE4.2 instruction set. We could not successfully execute the threaded binary compiled with SSE4.2 on Pleiades-W and are investigating the problem. Finally, note that in all cases, the calculation cost remains roughly constant across all concurrencies, indicating a near-linear speedup. Table 2 summarizes the performance speedups on individual systems with respect to Franklin.

Table 2: Calculation and communication speedups relative to Pleiades-W for threaded allgather at 16K concurrency. Performance values on Pleiades-W have been normalized to unity.

Component	Franklin	Hopper	Jaguar	Pleiades-H	Pleiades-W
Calculation	1.46	1.11	1.46	1.44	1.00
Communication	2.16	1.78	3.54	1.89	1.00
Communication w/o preprocessing	1.43	1.28	4.49	0.81	1.00

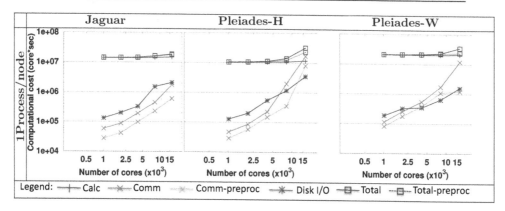

Figure 6: MADmap scaling runs on Jaguar, Pleiades-W and Pleiades-H with 1 process per dual-socket node.

5.3 Monte Carlo Analyses

While these results focus on a single analysis, actual CMB data computations are dominated by generating (simulating and mapping) sets of hundreds to tens of thousands of Monte Carlo data realizations. For these large-scale experiments, our methodology allows a single, off-line preprocessing step once — since the communication pattern will be common to all the realizations. Figure 7 shows the speedup achieved by the Threaded Allgather on all the platforms when the preprocessing is excluded, showing the overall speedup (written for each platform) as well as highlighting the dramatic reduction of communication overhead. Although the calculation costs have increased in the threaded code, this is more than offset by the communication improvements, and will be further optimized in subsequent studies. The overall speedups attained are 4.14×, 2.88×, 2.41×, 1.48×, 1.27× for Jaguar, Pleiades-H, Pleiades-W, Franklin and Hopper (respectively). The (preprocessing amortized) communication speedups now account for only 2% — 4% of the overall runtime, showing impressive speedups compared to the original version of up to 116× on Jaguar, with improvements of 8.3×, 22.3×, 12.7×, and 10.8× on Franklin, Pleiades-W, Pleiades-H and Hopper (respectively).

6. CONCLUSIONS

Observations of the CMB have the profound effect on our understanding of the Universe and hence of fundamental physics at the highest energies. However, the exponential growth in the size of CMB data sets over the next 15 years means that our analyses have to stay on the bleeding edge of high performance computing for the next 10 epochs of Moore's Law. At present, the state-of-the-art in simulating and mapping CMB data sets is the MADmap code, but it suffers from a serious communication bottleneck when using more than a few thousand MPI tasks.

In this work we presented a two step approach to al-

leviate the communication bottleneck. The first step involves using a new algorithm that minimizes the communication data volume by replacing global reductions with pairwise point-to-point communication, which only includes data that must be communicated. The second step leverages the OpenMP/MPI hybrid programming model, reducing the number of MPI tasks to only one per socket. Our work presents an extensive performance evaluation of these steps (both individually and in concert) across a wide range of large-scale HPC platforms and shows that at high concurrencies, our combined methodologies result in significant improvement of communication overhead — with reductions of one to two orders of magnitude compared to the original approach. As a result of these optimizations, the communication cost is no longer the bottleneck, thus causing the calculation phase to emerge as the dominant overhead component. This bottleneck shift is well suited for next generation supercomputers whose computational throughput is expected to grow faster than interconnect messaging speeds. Future work will focus on effectively threading the remaining unthreaded computations, as well as exploring the potential of using accelerator-based systems such as GPUs to reduce the computation time. We will also investigate generalizing communication optimization for applications to other data-intensive scientific computations.

Overall, this work enables CMB data analysts to take advantage of the largest peta-scale HPC systems, which will be essential to achieve the full scientific potential of the coming generation of B-mode CMB experiments.

7. ACKNOWLEDGEMENTS

This research used resources of the National Energy Research Scientific Computing Center, which is supported by the Office of Science of the U.S. Department of Energy under Contract No. DE-AC02-05CH11231, the Oak Ridge Leadership Facility at the Oak Ridge National Laboratory, which

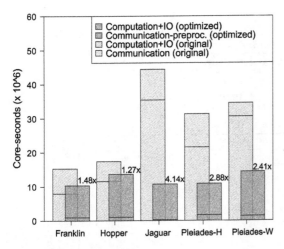

Figure 7: The speedup achieved using our new communication optimizations and inter-socket threading on the five different parallel platforms and 16K core concurrency. 'Original' and 'optimized' correspond to unthreaded Allreduce and threaded Allgather respectively. The overall speedup value is indicated above the optimized implementation bar. The new communication algorithm preprocessing time is not included in the cost of the optimized implementation, as it is amortized over 50 iterations.

is supported by the Office of Science of the U.S. Department of Energy under Contract No. DE-AC05-00OR22725, and the NASA Advanced Supercomputing facility at the Ames Research Center. This work was supported by the NSF PetaApps program under grant AST-0905099.

8. REFERENCES

[1] AMD Core Math Library, 2010. http://www.amd.com/acml.

[2] P. Balaji, D. Buntinas, D. Goodell, W. Gropp, S. Kumar, E. Lusk, R. Thakur, and J.L. Träff. Mpi on a million processors. In *Proc. 16th European PVM/MPI Users' Group Meeting on Recent Advances in Parallel Virtual Machine and Message Passing Interface*, pages 20–30. Springer-Verlag, 2009.

[3] D. Baskins. Judy arrays web page, 2004. http://judy.sourceforge.net/.

[4] J.R. Bond, A.H. Jaffe, and L. Knox. Estimating the power spectrum of the cosmic microwave background. *Phys. Rev. D*, 57(4):2117–2137, 1998.

[5] COBE, 2010. http://lambda.gsfc.nasa.gov/product/cobe.

[6] S. Dodelson. *Modern Cosmology*. Academic Press, 2003.

[7] J. Dunkley et al. Five-year Wilkinson microwave anisotropy probe observations: Likelihoods and parameters from the wmap data. *The Astrophysical Journal Supplement Series*, 180(2):306, 2009.

[8] C.M. Cantalupo et al. MADmap: A Massively Parallel Maximum Likelihood Cosmic Microwave Background Map-maker. *The Astrophysical Journal Supplement Series*, 187:212, 2010.

[9] J. Pješivac-Grbović et al. Performance analysis of MPI collective operations. *Cluster Computing*, 10(2):127–143, 2007.

[10] G.H. Golub and C.F. Van Loan. *Matrix computations*. Johns Hopkins University Press, 3rd edition, 1996.

[11] E. Hivon et al. MASTER of the cosmic microwave background anisotropy power spectrum: A fast method for statistical analysis of large and complex cosmic microwave background data sets. *The Astrophysical Journal*, 567(1):2, 2002.

[12] R.W. Hockney. The communication challenge for MPP: Intel Paragon and Meiko CS-2. *Parallel Computing*, 20(3):389–398, 1994.

[13] T. Hoefler, C. Siebert, and A. Lumsdaine. Scalable communication protocols for dynamic sparse data exchange. In *Proc. 15th ACM SIGPLAN symposium on Principles and practice of parallel programming (PPoPP '10)*, pages 159–168. ACM, 2010.

[14] T. Hoefler and J.L. Träff. Sparse collective operations for mpi. In *Proc. 14th Int'l. Workshop on High-Level Parallel Programming Models and Supportive Environments (HIPS09)*, 2009.

[15] E. Komatsu et al. Five-year Wilkinson microwave anisotropy probe observations: Cosmological interpretation. *The Astrophysical Journal Supplement Series*, 180(2):330, 2009.

[16] M3 data abstraction library, 2010. http://crd.lbl.gov/~cmc/M3/.

[17] Intel Math Kernel Library, 2010. http://software.intel.com/en-us/intel-mkl.

[18] The OpenMP API specifications, 2010. http://openmp.org/wp.

[19] Planck science team home, 2010. http://www.rssd.esa.int/index.php?project=PLANCK.

[20] R. Rabenseifner. New optimized MPI reduce algorithm, 2010. https://fs.hlrs.de/projects/par/mpi/myreduce.html.

[21] R. Rabenseifner and J.L. Träff. More efficient reduction algorithms for non-power-of-two number of processors in message-passing parallel systems. In *Proc. Recent Advances in Parallel Virtual Machine and Message Passing Interface*, pages 309–335, 2004.

[22] G.F. Smoot et al. Preliminary results from the COBE differential microwave radiometers - large angular scale isotropy of the cosmic microwave background. *Astrophysics Journal*, 371:L1–L5, 1991.

[23] R. Stompor et al. Making maps of the cosmic microwave background: The MAXIMA example. *Phys. Rev. D*, 65(2):022003, 2001.

[24] M. Tegmark. CMB mapping experiments: A designer's guide. *Phys. Rev. D*, 56(8):4514–4529, 1997.

[25] R. Thakur, R. Rabenseifner, and W. Gropp. Optimization of collective communication operations in MPICH. *Int'l. Journal of High Performance Computing Applications*, 19(1):49–66, 2005.

[26] Top500 supercomputer sites, 2010. http://top500.org.

[27] WMAP, 2010. http://map.gsfc.nasa.gov.

A QHD-Capable Parallel H.264 Decoder

Chi Ching Chi   Ben Juurlink
Embedded Systems Architectures
Technische Universität Berlin
10587 Berlin, Germany
{cchi, juurlink}@cs.tu-berlin.de

ABSTRACT

Video coding follows the trend of demanding higher performance every new generation, and therefore could utilize many-cores. A complete parallelization of H.264, which is the most advanced video coding standard, was found to be difficult due to the complexity of the standard. In this paper a parallel implementation of a complete H.264 decoder is presented. Our parallelization strategy exploits function-level as well as data-level parallelism. Function-level parallelism is used to pipeline the H.264 decoding stages. Data-level parallelism is exploited within the two most time consuming stages, the entropy decoding stage and the macroblock decoding stage. The parallelization strategy has been implemented and optimized on three platforms with very different memory architectures, namely an 8-core SMP, a 64-core cc-NUMA, and an 18-core Cell platform. Evaluations have been performed using $4k \times 2k$ QHD sequences. On the SMP platform a maximum speedup of $4.5\times$ is achieved. The SMP-implementation is reasonably performance portable as it achieves a speedup of $26.6\times$ on the cc-NUMA system. However, to obtain the highest performance (speedup of $33.4\times$ and throughput of 200 QHD frames per second), several cc-NUMA specific optimizations are necessary such as optimizing the page placement and statically assigning threads to cores. Finally, on the Cell platform a near ideal speedup of $16.5\times$ is achieved by completely hiding the communication latency.

Categories and Subject Descriptors

D.1.3 [**Software**]: Programming Techniques—*Concurrent Programming*; I.4 [**Image Processing and Computer Vision**]: Compression (Coding)

General Terms

Algorithms, Design, Performance

Keywords

H.264, $4k \times 2k$, decoding, Cell, NUMA, SMP, parallel

1. INTRODUCTION

A major concern for moving to many-core architectures is the usefulness from an application point-of-view. As a recent study shows [6], contemporary desktop applications rarely require more compute power to justify the parallelization effort. Video decoding, however, is one of the application domains that follow the trend of demanding more performance every new generation [15].

With the introduction of the H.264 video coding standard, compression rate, quality, but also the computational complexity have significantly increased over previous standards [12, 24]. For H.264 video decoding, contemporary multicores can be used to deliver a better experience. Next-generation features like $4k \times 2k$ Quad High Definition (QHD), stereoscopic 3D, and even higher compression rates, on the other hand, will demand full multicore support.

A full parallelization of the H.264 decoder, however, is not obvious. Higher compression is achieved by removing more redundancy, which in turn complicates the data dependencies in the decoding process. Most previous works, therefore, focused mainly on the Macroblock Decoding (MBD) stage, which exhibits fine-grained data-level parallelism. Attempts at parallelizing the Entropy Decoding (ED) stage are rare and have not resulted in a scalable approach. The ED stage is about as time consuming as the MBD stage and has, therefore, been found to be the main bottleneck [5, 8, 10, 13, 19]. Furthermore, previous works have not evaluated their parallelization strategies on several parallel platforms, and therefore have not evaluated the performance portability of their approaches.

In this paper a fully parallel, highly scalable, QHD-capable H.264 decoding strategy is presented. The parallel decoding strategy considers the entire application, including the ED stage. The parallelization strategy has been implemented and optimized on three multicore platforms with significantly different memory architectures. The main contributions of this work can be summarized as follows.

- We propose a fully parallel and highly scalable H.264 decoding strategy, which is compliant with all the H.264 coding features for higher compression rate and quality. Function-level parallelism is exploited at the highest level to pipeline the decoder stages. In addition, data-level parallelism is exploited in the ED stage and the MBD stage.

- We target QHD resolution, while all previous works targeted FHD or lower resolutions. QHD is more meaningful, because contemporary high performance processors, e.g., Intel Sandybridge or AMD Phenom II, can achieve the computational requirements of FHD using a single thread, while for QHD this is not the case.

- We implement and evaluate the parallel decoding strategy on three platforms with significantly different memory hierarchies, namely an 8-core SMP, an 64-core cc-NUMA, and an 18-core Cell platform. Optimization for the memory hierarchy are performed and compared for each platform.

This paper is organized as follows. Section 2 provides an overview of related work. Section 3 describes the parallel H.264 decoding strategy. Section 4 details the experimental setup. Sections 5 to 7 present the implementations, optimizations, and experimental results for each platform. Finally, in Section 8 conclusions are drawn.

2. RELATED WORK

Roitzsch [19] proposed a slice-balancing approach to improve the load balance of exploiting slice-level parallelism. Slice-level parallelism, however, is impaired by a reduced compression rate due to adding more slices in a frame. Finchelstein et al. [10] addressed this by line interleaving the slices. The coding inefficiency of regular slicing is in this approach reduced by allowing context selection over slice boundaries. This approach, however, would require a change of the H.264 standard.

Baik et al. [4] combined function-level parallelism (FLP) with data-level parallelism (DLP) to parallelize an H.264 decoder for the Cell Broadband Engine. The entropy decoding, motion compensation, and deblocking filter kernels are pipelined at the granularity of macroblocks (MBs), and the motion compensation of the MB partitions are performed in a data-parallel fashion using three SPEs. Nishihara et al. [18] and Sihn et al. [21] used similar approaches for embedded multicores. Nishihara et al. investigated prediction based preloading for the deblocking filter to reduce memory access contention. Sihn et al. observed memory contention in the parallel motion compensation phase and introduced a software memory throttling technique to reduce this. The parallelism in these approaches is limited, however.

Van der Tol et al. [23] considered FLP as well as DLP and argued that the most scalable approach is the use of DLP in the form of MB-level parallelism within a frame. Alvarez et al. [1] analyzed this using trace driven simulation with several dynamic scheduling approaches. Meenderinck et al. [16] showed that a 3D-wavefront strategy, which combines intra- and inter-frame MB-level parallelism, results in huge amounts of parallelism. Azevedo et al. [3] explored this further using a multicore simulator and showed a speedup of 45× on 64 cores. The employed simulator, however, does not model memory and network contention in detail but assumes that the average shared L2 access time is 40 cycles.

Seitner et al. [20] performed a simulation based comparison of several static MB-level parallelization approaches for resource-restricted environments. Baker et al. [5] used Seitner's "single row" approach in their Cell implementation. This approach is promising due to the abundant parallelism and low synchronization overhead. In our previous work [7] a variant of the "single row" approach with distributed control was implemented on the Cell processor. By exploiting the Cell memory hierarchy a scalability was achieved that

approached the theoretical limit. In most of these works (e.g., [1, 3, 5, 7, 16, 20, 23]), the entropy decoding was not considered or mapped on a single core, which causes a scalability bottleneck.

Cho et al. [8] recently presented a parallel H.264 decoder for the Cell architecture in which the entropy decoding is also parallelized. They found that the dependencies in the entropy decoding between MBs in different frames are only to the co-located MBs. They exploited this using a parallelization strategy similar to the Entropy Ring (ER) approach presented in this paper. Their approach can cause load imbalance, however, due to high differences in entropy decoding times of different types of frames, and we introduce the B-Ring (BR) approach to address this. Furthermore, their Cell implementation only uses the PPEs for the entropy decoding and the SPEs for the MB decoding, which causes a bottleneck. In our Cell implementation the entropy decoding can be performed on both the PPEs and any number of SPEs simultaneously, resolving the entropy decoding bottleneck.

3. PARALLEL H.264 DECODER

In this section the highly scalable parallel H.264 decoding strategy is introduced. In this strategy parallelism is exploited in two directions. Function-level parallelism (FLP) is exploited to pipeline the decoder stages and data-level parallelism (DLP) is exploited within the time-consuming ED and MBD pipeline stages. A MB is a 16×16 pixel block of the frame, e.g., a QHD frame has 240 MBs in the horizontal direction, forming a MB line, and 135 of such MB lines in the vertical direction. Previous work mostly exploited either the limited FLP or the DLP in the MBD stage. Without combining FLP and DLP, however, significant speedup over the entire application cannot be achieved. First, the pipelining approach is discussed, followed by the strategies for exploiting the DLP within the ED and MBD stages.

3.1 Pipelining H.264

Figure 1 depicts a simplified overview of the pipeline stages of our H.264 decoder. The stages are decoupled by placing FIFO queues between the stages, buffering the indicated data structures. The Picture Info Buffer (PIB) and Decoded Picture Buffer (DPB) are not needed to pipeline the stages, but for the H.264 decoding algorithm. The PIB is used in the Entropy Decoding (ED) which needs the Picture Info (PI) of previous frames. A PIB entry consists of the motion vectors, MB types, and reference indices of an entire frame. A DPB entry contains an output frame and is used both as the reference and display buffer. The PIB and DPB buffer entries are not released in a FIFO manner, but when they are no longer needed.

The *read* stage reads the H.264 stream from memory or disk and outputs raw H.264 frames. The *parse* stage parses the header of the H.264 frame and allocates a PIB entry. The parsed header and the remainder of the H.264 frame are sent to the ED stage.

The *ED* stage reads the H.264 frame and produces a work unit for each MB of a frame. This stage includes CABAC decoding, filling prediction caches, motion vector calculation, deblocking filter parameter calculation, as well as other calculations. Copies of the motion vector, MB type, and reference indices of each MB are stored in the allocated PIB entry. The produced work units for an entire frame are

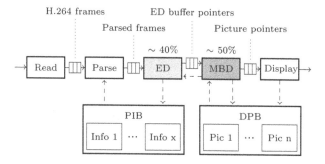

Figure 1: Each pipeline stage in the parallel H.264 decoder processes an entire frame. FIFO queues are placed between the stages to decouple them. Dashed arrows show the buffer release and allocation signals.

placed in an internal ED buffer entry. At the end of the ED stage, if the frames are no longer needed, one or more PIB entries are released and a pointer to the ED buffer entry is sent to the MBD stage. Pointers are passed as ED buffer entries are fairly large (43.5MB for QHD sequences). The internal ED buffer has multiple entries to be able to work ahead. This reduces the impact of dependency stalls when the ED stage temporarily takes more time than the MBD stage and vice versa. In this paper four entries are used as more did not improve performance.

The *MBD* stage processes the work units produced by the ED stage and performs the video decoding kernels that produce the final output frame. This includes intra prediction, motion compensation, deblocking filter, and other kernels. At the start of the MBD stage a DPB entry is allocated for the output frame. At the end of the stage the used ED buffer entry is released by sending a signal to the ED stage. Then one or more reference frames are marked as no longer referenced or released if they have already been displayed. Since the DBP functions both as the reference and as the display buffer, frames must be both displayed and no longer referenced before they can be released. Finally, a pointer to the produced frame is sent to the display stage.

The *display* stage reorders the output frames before displaying them because the decoding order and the display order are not the same in H.264. After a frame has been displayed, it is released if it is no longer referenced, otherwise it is marked as displayed.

Pipelining is effective as long as the pipelining overhead, caused by the buffering operations, does not dominate. The decoupling of the ED and the MBD stage requires an ED buffer of 43.5 MB. This is too large to stay in the cache which causes capacity misses. Further pipelining the ED or the MBD stages would cause even more capacity misses, and has, therefore, not been performed. Instead DLP is exploited in the ED and MBD stages, which is not impaired by the buffering penalty. As indicated in Figure 1, the ED and MBD stages of the H.264 decoder take approximately 40% and 50% of the total execution time, respectively. These percentages have been measured on the SMP platform with the QHD Park Joy sequence.

3.2 Entropy Decoding Stage

In the ED stage, the CABAC decoding is performed, which does not exhibit DLP within a frame. The ED stage, however, does exhibit DLP between frames, but frames are not fully independent. MBs in B-frames can have a *direct* en-

coding mode. In this mode the motion vectors of the MB are not encoded in the stream, but instead the motion vectors of the co-located MB in the closest reference frame are reused. A potential dependency pattern and the parallelism between frames are illustrated in Figure 2.

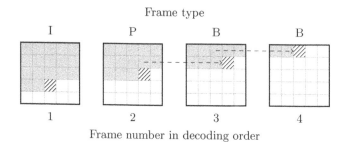

Figure 2: Parallel ED of consecutive frames. Colored MBs have been entropy decoded. Hashed MBs are currently being decoded in parallel

Figure 2 shows that frames can be decoded in parallel as long as the co-located MBs have been decoded before. This is ensured by Entropy Ring (ER) strategy illustrated in Figure 3, which is similar to the strategy used by Cho et al. [8]. In this strategy there are n Entropy Decoding Threads (EDTs) and EDT_i decodes frames i, $n+i$, $2n+i$,... etc. Each EDT performs the same function as the the single threaded ED stage and has four ED buffers entries to be able to work ahead. The Dist thread distributes the frames over the EDTs. The EDTs are organized in a ring structure to ensure that the co-located MB is decoded before the MB that depends on it. To ensure this, at any time EDT_{i+1} is not allowed to have processed more MBs than EDT_i.

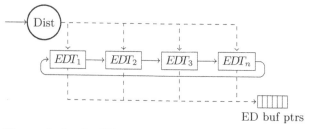

Figure 3: In the ER strategy the EDTs are organized in a ring to maintain dependencies.

The parallelism in the ER strategy scales with the frame size, since there can be as many EDTs as MBs in a frame. In addition, the synchronization overhead is low, since it consists of incrementing a counter containing the number of decoded MBs. Its efficiency is not optimal, however, due to load imbalance. Figure 4 depicts the time it takes to entropy decode each frame in the QHD stream Park Joy [26]. It shows that I- and P-frames take longer to entropy decode, which could cause the EDTs that decode B-frames to stall.

To address this load imbalance, we introduce a slightly more complex B-Ring (BR) strategy, which is illustrated in Figure 5. In this strategy the Split thread splits the I- and P-frames from the B-frames. As depicted in Figure 2, only B-frames have dependencies, since I- and P-frames do not have MBs with a direct encoding. Because B-frames have a relatively constant entropy decoding time, the number of

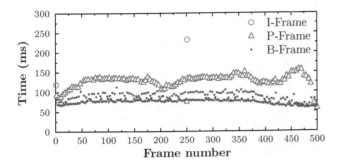

Figure 4: Entropy decoding times of the different frames in the QHD Park Joy sequence.

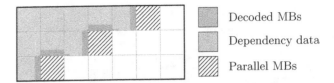

Figure 6: Illustration of spatial MB-level parallelism and dependencies. To decode a MB, data of adjacent MBs is required. The data is available after the upper right and left MB have been decoded.

dependency stalls is reduced, increasing the efficiency. Furthermore, this strategy also exploits that I- and P-frames can be decoded fully in parallel and out-of-order.

The DistB thread distributes the B-frames in a round-robin fashion over the B-frame EDTs. It stalls when a B-frame has a dependency to a not completed I- or P-frame, and then waits for the Reorder thread to signal its completion. The Reorder thread is responsible for reordering the produced ED buffers of the I-, P- and B-frames to their original decode order, before signaling them to the DistB thread and submitting them to the MBD stage. The reordering abstracts the parallel entropy decoding of frames from the MBD stage, thereby reducing the overall complexity and increasing modularity.

The maximum number of parallel B-frame EDTs is equal to the number of MBs in a frame. As this number is very large, we choose to signal the next B-frame EDT after completing an entire MB line, instead of each MB to reduce the synchronization overhead.

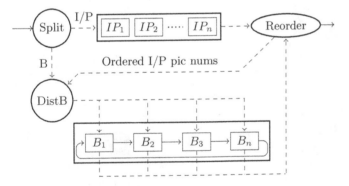

Figure 5: B-Ring strategy. IP denotes an EDT that processes I/P-frames and B denotes an EDT that processes B-frames

3.3 Macroblock Decoding Stage

The MBD stage exhibits DLP within frames as well as between frames, also referred to as spatial and temporal MB-level parallelism, respectively. In our previous work [7] we introduced the Ring-Line (RL) strategy, which exploits only spatial MB-level parallelism. The spatial MB dependencies and parallelism are illustrated in Figure 6. For every MB the data dependencies are satisfied if their upper right and left MB have been decoded. Due to these dependencies, at most one MB per MB line can be decoded in parallel.

In this paper, an improved version of the RL strategy is introduced, referred to as the Multi-frame Ring-Line (MRL) strategy. Figure 7 illustrates the MRL strategy. In the MRL strategy macroblock decoding threads (MBTs) are organized in a ring. Each MBT decodes a MB line of the frame. By decoding the lines from left to right the dependency to the left MB is implicitly resolved. The dependency to the upper right MB is satisfied if MBT_{i+1} "stays behind" MBT_i. More specifically, at any time MBT_i must have processed at least two more MBs than MBT_{i+1}. The MBT processing the last line of a frame informs the Release thread of the frame completion. The Release thread releases the ED buffer and one or more reference frames if they are no longer needed. Finally, it signals the decoded picture to the *display* stage. A separate Release thread is used to be able to quickly continue with the next frame.

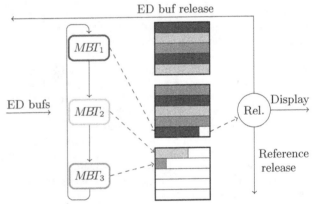

Figure 7: Illustration of the MRL strategy.

The previous RL strategy uses a barrier between consecutive frames. This results in recurring ramp-up and ramp-down inefficiency for each frame, because there are only a few parallel MBs at the beginning and the end of each frame. The new MRL strategy eliminates this inefficiency by overlapping the execution of consecutive frames. Previously this was not possible because the ED stage was not executed parallel to the MBD stage, which is solved in this paper.

Overlapping the MBD stage of consecutive frames, however, may introduce additional temporal dependencies when using too many MBTs, because the required reference picture data for the motion compensation might not be completely available. To ensure that all required reference data is available, the number of in-flight MB lines, thus the number of MBTs, needs to be restricted. The maximum number of MBTs, MBT_{max}, is given by the following equation:

$$MBT_{max} = \lceil (H - MMV)/16 \rceil, \qquad (1)$$

where H is the vertical resolution in pixels and MMV is the maximum motion vector length in pixels. For QHD, assuming that the MMV of QHD will be twice that of FHD, MBT_{max} is $(2160-1024)/16 = 71$. Additionally, the picture border needs to be extended directly after decoding a MB line, because areas outside the actual picture can be used as reference data in H.264.

4. EXPERIMENTAL SETUP

For the evaluation QHD sequences of Xiph.org Test Media [26] are used. These sequences have a framerate of 50 frames per second (fps) and use a YUV 4:2:0 color space. The sequences are 500 frames long, but for the evaluation they have been extended to 10000 frames by replicating them 20 times. The sequences have been encoded with x264 [25], using settings based on the High 5.1 profile. The encoding properties are listed in Table 1. The average bitrates of the encoded QHD sequences varied between 77.6 and 259.8 Mbps. In comparison, 16 Mbps FHD sequences with 25 fps are considered high quality. The parallel H.264 decoder has been evaluated using two QHD sequences, Park Joy and Ducks Take Off, which have a bitrate of 117.8 Mbps and 259.8 Mbps, respectively. For conciseness only the results for the Park Joy sequence, which represents the average case, are provided. In general higher bitrate sequences translate to lower framerates, but higher speedups compared to lower bitrate sequences.

Table 1: X264 encode setting for the Ducks and Park QHD sequences.

Option	Value	Brief description
–cfr	23	Quality-based variable bitrate
–partition	all	All MB partition allowed
–b-frames	16	Number of consecutive B-frames
–b-adapt	2	Adaptive number of B-frames
–b-pyramid	normal	Allow B-frames as reference
–direct	auto	Spatial and Temporal Direct MB encoding
–ref	16	Up to 16 reference frames
–slices	1	Single slice per frame

The parallel H.264 decoder is evaluated on three platforms with significantly different memory architectures. An overview of the platforms is provided in Table 2. To determine the performance the wall clock time of the entire H.264 decoder is measured. This includes all stages depicted in Figure 1, except the display stage. The display stage is disabled since the evaluation platforms do not provide this feature.

The baseline implementation is the widely-used and open-source FFmpeg transcoder [9]. FFmpeg offers a high performance H.264 decoder implementation with, among others, SSE and AltiVec optimizations for the MBD kernels and an optimized entropy decoder. It is one of the fastest single threaded implementations [2]. The FFmpeg framework, however, does not allow a clean implementation of our parallelization strategy. The provided codec interface enforces that only a single frame is in-flight at a time. To solve this, FFmpeg has been dismantled of everything not related to

Table 2: Platform specifications.

	SMP	cc-NUMA	Cell
Processor	Xeon X5365	Xeon 7560	PowerXCell 8i
Sockets	2	8	2
Frequency	3 GHz	2.26 GHz	3.2 GHz
Cores	8	64	18
SMT	-	off	2-way PPE
Local store	-	-	4 MB
Last level $	16 MB	192 MB	1MB
Interconnect	FSB	QPI	FlexIO
Memory BW	8.5 GB/s	204.8 GB/s	25.6 GB/s
Linux kernel	2.6.28	2.6.36	2.6.18
GCC	4.3.3	4.4.3	4.1.1
Opt. level	-O2	-O2	-O2

H.264 decoding and rebuilt in a lightweight parallel version using the POSIX thread library facilities for parallelization and synchronization. Based on the decoupled code also a new sequential version is developed which serves as the baseline performance.

5. BUS-BASED SMP

The first platform that we consider is a Symmetric MultiProcessor (SMP) platform. This platform has 8 homogeneous cores with symmetric memory access via a single memory controller through a shared Front Side Bus (FSB). While it is possible to extend this architecture with more cores and memory controllers, the shared FSB constitutes a scalability bottleneck. The programming effort for such a system, however, is relatively low as there are no or few specific optimizations required for the memory architecture. Some general optimizations have been performed to minimize false sharing, such as duplicating the motion compensation scratch pad and the upper border buffers, which improves performance on all cache coherent architectures.

The performance and speedup results are depicted in Figure 8 for the Park sequence. Each bar in the figure is labeled by n-m, where n denotes the number of EDTs and m the number of MBTs. For conciseness, n denotes the combined number of EDTs and, therefore, has a minimum of two, corresponding to one IP-frame and one B-frame decoding thread. The ratio of the number of IP-frame EDTs to B-frame EDTs does not differ very much and is about 1 to 2 for all platforms. The read, parse, display, split, distribute, reorder and release threads are not taken into account in this total thread number. There is one of each such threads.

The SMP platform exhibits reasonable performance and scalability. A maximum speedup of 4.5× is achieved, with a performance of 25.9fps. The sequential decoder, which is based on the decoupled code used for the SMP parallel version, is slightly slower than the original FFmpeg code in which the ED and MBD stages are merged. The difference is around 15% and is observed on all platforms. The performance degradation is caused by additional cache misses introduced by using the large ED buffers needed to decouple the ED and MBD stages, as mentioned in Section 3.1.

The figure shows that using more than 4 MBTs reduces performance considerably. The reason for this is as follows. Since there are more threads than cores, some MBTs will be temporarily descheduled. Because MBTs depend on each other, however, this will stall other MBTs. Here it needs

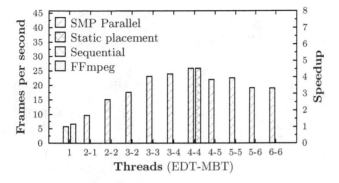

Figure 8: Performance and scalability on the 8-core SMP for the Park sequence.

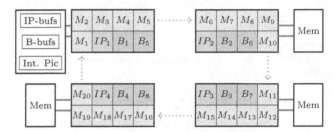

Figure 9: Static thread placement on the cc-NUMA platform.

to be remarked that thread synchronization has been implemented using busy waiting, because it incurs lower overhead than blocking. The EDTs are less likely to stall than MBTs since, as shown in Figure 6, the MBT that decodes a certain MB line has to stay at least two MBs behind the MBT that processes the previous MB line. Therefore, MBTs can tolerate running out of pace for only a few MBs compared to a few MB lines for EDTs.

The reduced scaling efficiency is mostly caused by the limited memory bandwidth of this platform. To show that the FSB is not the bottleneck, Figure 8 also depicts the results for the *Static placement* version. In the Static placement version, consecutive MBTs are placed on the same node to reduce cache coherence misses and, therefore, FSB traffic. No performance improvement is observed, however. Other possible causes for the saturated scalability are insufficient application parallelism and threading overhead. If either of these is the cause, it would also limit the scalability on the other platforms, which is shown to be not the case in the following sections.

6. CACHE COHERENT NUMA

Our second evaluation platform is an 8-socket cc-NUMA machine [11] based on the Nehalem-EX architecture. Each socket contains 8 homogeneous cores, for a total of 64 cores. Each socket is also a memory node as it accommodates an individual memory controller. Inter-node cache coherence and memory traffic use the QPI network with an aggregate bandwidth of 307.2 GB/s. Together with an aggregate memory bandwidth of 204.8 GB/s, this platform offers very high communication bandwidth, per-core 3 to 5 × higher than the SMP platform. To exploit this communication bandwidth, however, NUMA specific optimizations are required. First, the NUMA optimizations performed to the SMP implementation are described, followed by the experimental results.

6.1 cc-NUMA Optimizations

To optimally utilize the NUMA memory hierarchy, the parallel H.264 decoder requires specific optimizations. Page placement on the cc-NUMA platform uses the "first touch" policy. This policy maps a page to the node that accesses it the first time. A poor initial thread placement can cluster large parts of the working set in a single memory node. A way to ensure a balanced memory distribution is to statically assign threads to cores. For this only the EDTs and MBTs are considered, since they access most of the working set.

Figure 9 illustrates the static thread placement strategy for a 4-socket configuration. In the figure, IP_i and B_i denote the IP- and B-frame EDTs, respectively. M_i denotes the MBTs.

The EDTs are placed in a round-robin fashion over the sockets. This ensures that the ED buffers are distributed evenly over the memory nodes, as the EDTs are the first to access them. This static thread placement also improves data locality, since the EDTs always find the ED buffer data in their local memory node. The MBTs are placed in a block distributed fashion over the available sockets. This ensures that the picture data is distributed evenly in a block interleaved manner over the memory nodes. Furthermore, placing consecutive MBTs on a single node increases locality as they share an overlapping part of the picture data. In this way most coherence traffic stays on the same node. Some MBTs still need to access a remote memory node, but contention is minimized and the node distance is always only one hop. In addition, the static placement reduces thread migration as threads are bound to cores. Thread migrations are expensive on cc-NUMA platforms [14], which can cause a lot of dependency stalls.

The static thread placement yields a page distribution that is optimal for the ED stage and MBD stage *separately*, but which is not *globally* optimal. A single EDT produces an entire ED buffer entry for a frame, but several parallel running MBTs consume this ED buffer to process the frame further. Since complete ED buffers are allocated in a single node, all MBTs will have to access this node at the same time, resulting in a temporal memory access hotspot.

This hotspot is avoided by letting the MBTs first touch the ED buffers, instead of the EDTs. This ensures that both the input ED buffer entry pages and DPB entry output pages of each MBT are distributed evenly, as illustrated in Figure 10. The downside, however, is that now each EDT will have to write to remote memory nodes. But because the overall contention is reduced and because read latency is more important than write latency, this page placement improves the overall performance.

In addition to letting the MBTs first touch the ED buffer entries, the MBTs are assigned to process the MB lines corresponding to the pages they touched. Without this, depending on the number of MB lines per frame and the number of MBTs, the MBTs process different MB lines in each frame. For example, when there are 8 MB lines in a frame and 3 MBTs, MBT_1 decodes MB lines 1, 4, and 7 of the first frame, MB lines 2, 5, and 8 of the second frame, etc. MB line 2 of the second frame, however, resides in a different memory node as it is first touched by MBT_2, which results in a lot of inter-node memory accesses.

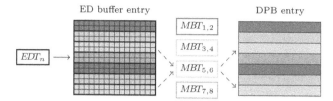

Figure 10: Illustration of the globally optimized page placement and the MBT to MB lines binding. The colors denote the thread and page placement to different nodes.

6.2 cc-NUMA Experimental Results

Four versions of the parallel H.264 decoder have been evaluated on the cc-NUMA platform. The first version, referred to as "SMP parallel", is the same as the one used on the SMP platform. The second version, referred to as "Interleaved" employs a round-robin page placement policy instead of first touch. The third version, referred to as "Static placement" uses the static thread placement presented in Section 6.1. The fourth version, referred to as "NUMA optimized", applies in addition to the static thread placement, the globally optimized page placement of the ED buffers and the MBT to line binding.

Figure 11 shows the performance and scalability of each version for 1, 2, 4, and 8 sockets. The figure shows the results obtained using the best performing thread configurations, which have been found through a design space exploration. An exception to this is the Interleaved version, which uses the same thread configuration as the SMP parallel version. The optimal thread configurations are depicted in Table 3. Figure 11 shows that the parallel H.264 decoder is able to scale to very high performance levels. The maximum achieved frame rate is 200 fps with a speedup of $33.4\times$.

While the performance is very high, the scaling efficiency decreases with more sockets. For example, the SMP parallel and Interleaved versions exhibit reasonable scaling up to 2 sockets, with a speedup of $11.6\times$ on 16 cores. However, they become less efficient when deploying 4 and 8 sockets for which a speedup of $26.6\times$ is observed on 64 cores. When using a static thread placement the performance and scalability increase considerably for 4 and 8 sockets. For example, for 8 sockets the performance of the Static placement version is 200 fps versus 157 fps for the SMP parallel version.

The NUMA optimized version performs slightly better for 4 sockets and slightly worse for 8 sockets compared to the Static placement version. The reason why the NUMA optimized version is slightly slower on 8 sockets is that only 56 threads (EDTs + MBTs) are used versus 64 threads for the Static placement version. Because the number of MBTs is less flexible due to the static binding of MB lines to MBTs the optimal performance is obtained with a smaller thread configuration. To increase the performance of the MBD stage the number of MBTs have to be increased from 27 to 34. This, however, leaves no cores to increase the number of EDTs. We expect that the performance difference between the NUMA optimized version and the Static placement version would increase with more sockets and/or cores.

The impact of the NUMA optimized version is, however, visible in the thread configurations. With more sockets the ratio between the number of EDTs and the number of MBTs changes in favor of the number of MBTs in the Static place-

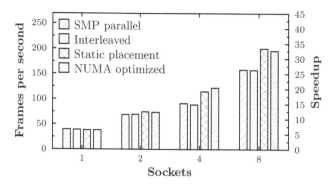

Figure 11: Performance and scalability on a 8-socket cc-NUMA machine for the Park sequence.

Table 3: Optimal thread configuration for the Park sequence. E denotes the combined number of EDTs, M denotes the number of MBTs.

	1		2		4		8	
	E	M	E	M	E	M	E	M
SMP parallel	5	4	8	8	12	19	23	40
Interleaved	5	4	8	8	12	19	23	40
Static placement	5	3	8	8	14	18	24	40
NUMA optimized	5	3	9	7	16	15	29	27

ment version. The efficiency of scaling the number of MBTs, therefore, decreases considerably with more sockets due to increased contention when reading from an ED buffer entry. For the NUMA optimized version this ratio remains fairly constant because in the globally optimized page placement the ED buffer entries are read from all memory nodes simultaneously, thereby avoiding contention.

Optimizing the thread mapping and page placement yields performance improvements of up to 27.3%. A static thread placement, however, is undesirable because other programs might map their threads to the same cores, while there are other cores available. Our results indicate, however, that techniques that give priority to locality over load balancing, such as resource partitioning, locality-aware scheduling [22], and runtime page migration [17], can provide significant performance benefits, when increasing the number of cores.

7. CELL BROADBAND ENGINE

Our final platform has a local store memory architecture, and consists of two Cell Broadband Engines processors with 2 PPE cores and 16 SPE cores. The Cell architecture is very different from the previous two platform, as it exposes the on-chip memory hierarchy to the programmer. On the one hand, the programmer is given control of regulating the data flow between the cores and the off-chip memory. On the other hand, the programmer is now responsible for fitting the data structures in the on-chip memory, which is performed transparently by the hardware in cache-based processors.

On the Cell architecture the same parallel H.264 decoding strategy is used. The differences are in the implementations of the ED and MBD stages. As most of the time is spent in these stages, it is necessary to port both of them to the SPEs to gain overall speedup. The other stages of the decoder and the control threads run on the PPEs using the Pthread base code. The implementations and optimizations of the ED

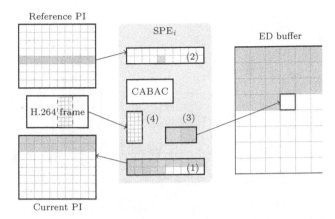

Figure 12: Overview of the SPE EDT implementation. Data structures in the orange background are located in the local store. The other data structures reside in the main memory.

and MBD stages on the Cell SPEs are discussed in the next two sections, followed by the experimental results.

7.1 Entropy Decoding on the SPE

From the threads in the ED stage depicted in Figure 5 only the I/P- and B-frame entropy decoding threads are executed on the SPEs. Although the I/P- and B-frame decoding threads process different types of frames, their SPE implementations are quite similar. Therefore, the base SPE EDT implementation is presented first and the differences between the two are described later. Figure 12 depicts a simplified overview of the EDT implementation. The color of the structures denote the "state" of the data. Blue denotes that it has been produced in this frame, gray denotes that is has been produced in a previous frame, red denotes that it is used for the ED of the current MB, and green denotes that it is produced by the ED of the current MB.

Each EDT requires access to several data structures that do not fit in the local store. The required input data structures are the CABAC tables and buffers, H.264 frame data, and the reference Picture Info (PI). The output data structures are the PI and the ED buffer of the current frame. The CABAC tables and buffers are able to fit in the local store. The other data structures are too large and, furthermore, their size increases with the resolution.

Close examination of the ED algorithm reveals that there is little reuse of data. Performing the ED of a MB only uses the PI data produced by the ED of the upper and left neighboring MBs. From the reference PI only the data corresponding to the co-located MB is used. This allows keeping only a small window (1) of the PI data in the local store. With a window of two MB lines in the local store, the PI data produced by decoding the current MB line can be written back during the decode of the next MB line. Furthermore, the data of the upper MB stays in the local store until it is used for decoding the lower MB. For the reference PI also a buffer of two MB lines (2) is allocated in the local store to be able to prefetch the next MB line. The motion vectors of the reference PI, however, cannot be prefetched for a complete MB line due to local store size constraints. Instead, the motion vectors of 4 MBs are prefetched at a time.

The ED buffer elements are not reused by the EDT. Therefore, only two buffer elements (3) are required in the local

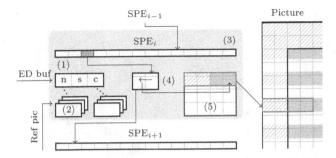

Figure 13: Overview of the SPE MBT implementation. Data structures in the orange background are located in the local store of SPE$_i$.

store to perform a double buffered write back. The only data that is not double buffered is the H.264 frame window (4), because the total amount of traffic for reading the H.264 frame is small. We have, therefore, decided to decrease the local store usage and code complexity, by keeping a single H.264 frame window with a size of 4KB in the local store.

The total local store footprint of the described EDT implementation for QHD resolutions is 238 kB, of which 63 kB is program code. The ED implementation for I/P-frames does not require a reference PI window. In the B-frame EDT implementation, after decoding each line a signal is sent to the next EDT in the B-ring to maintain the dependencies between co-located blocks.

7.2 Macroblock Decoding on the Cell

Similar to the ED stage, only the MBTs of the MBD stage are mapped to the SPEs. The problems of porting the code and performing the data partitioning have already been solved for a large part in our previous work [7]. Some improvements are necessary to support the QHD resolution and to overlap execution of consecutive frames. A simplified overview of the data allocation in the SPE MBT implementation is shown in Figure 13.

Each MBT uses an ED buffer entry and one or more reference pictures as input to produce the output picture data. As is the case for the EDTs, these data structures are too large to fit completely in the local store and several smaller data windows are allocated in the local store to hold only the active part of the data structures.

The MBD algorithm only requires one ED buffer element at a time to decode a MB. Three ED buffer elements (1) and two motion data buffers (2) are allocated in the local store to be able to prefetch both the ED buffer elements and the motion reference data. In Figure 13, element c denotes the element for the current MB, n denotes the element for the next MB, and s denotes the element for the second next. Element s and the motion data of element n can be prefetched, while element c is used to decode the current MB. After decoding each MB the roles of the elements rotate. Element n, of which the motion data has been prefetched, becomes the current element c, element s becomes the next element n, and element c can be reused to hold the new second next element.

To decode a MB, the picture data produced by decoding the upper-left to upper-right MBs is needed. Each SPE, therefore, has a buffer (3) to receive the filtered and unfiltered lower lines of these upper MBs from the previous MBT in the ring. In this way the data is kept on chip, reducing the number of off-chip memory transfers. The buffer has 240 entries, one for each MB in a MB line of a QHD frame.

For the picture data, a working buffer with a size of 32×20 pixels (4) is needed to fit the picture data of two MBs and their upper borders. Before decoding the MB, the upper borders are copied into the working buffer. After decoding the MB, the data of the previously decoded MB, residing in the left side of the working buffer, is copied to the DMA buffer (5), then the picture data produced by decoding the current MB is copied to the left part of the working buffer to act as the left border of the next MB. The produced picture data cannot be copied directly to the DMA buffer as the deblocking filter not only modifies the picture data of the current MB, but also the picture data of the left MB and the received upper border data. Therefore, the write back of the picture data has to be delayed by one MB and also includes the lower lines of the upper MB.

In our previous implementation [7], the upper border buffer and the picture data buffer were joined to avoid the additional copy steps performed in the working buffer. This approach, however, required an entire MB line to be allocated in the local store, which is not feasible for QHD resolution. Another difference with our previous implementation is the DMA buffer. This buffer is enlarged to be able to perform the picture border extension directly after decoding a MB line to support the overlapped execution of two consecutive frames, as mentioned in Section 3.3.

In total, the local store footprint of the SPE MBT implementation is 197 kB, of which 121 kB is program code. As everything fits in the local store, techniques such as code overlaying, which have been used in other implementations [5, 8], are not required in our implementation.

7.3 Cell Experimental Results

To show the efficacy of the optimizations described in the previous sections, two versions of the Cell implementation are evaluated. The *Non-blocking* version employs the DMA latency hiding, double buffering techniques described in the previous section. The *Blocking* version does not use these techniques, but blocks when fetching data. Furthermore, in order to evaluate the impact of the available memory bandwidth, both versions are evaluated with only one and both memory controllers (MCs) enabled.

Figure 14 presents the performance and scalability results for the Cell platform. The figure shows that the *Non-blocking* version achieves a near ideal speedup of $16.5\times$. The speedup is relative to the single-threaded version (without multi-threading code) running on one PPE. The results are shown for 4 to 16 SPEs in steps of 4 SPEs. The results for 18 threads are obtained by executing two additional I/P-frame EDTs on the PPEs. The near ideal speedup implies that the SPE EDT and MBT implementations are as fast as their PPE counterparts.

In the *Non-blocking* version almost all data transfers are completely overlapped with the computation, which results in an up to 34% higher performance than the *Blocking* version. Data transfer latencies only reduce the performance in the *Non-blocking* version when they actually take longer than the computation. In our implementation this does not not occur until the application starts to become bandwidth limited. The results show that the memory bandwidth of one MC is saturated at around 20 fps. The performance

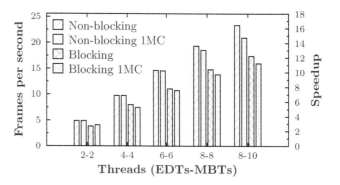

Figure 14: Performance and scalability on the Cell platform for the Park sequence.

of the *Blocking* version, however, is already reduced by disabling one MC at a lower frame rate, which indicates the effect of memory access contention.

For the Cell implementation additionally several FHD sequences are evaluated to be able to compare to the implementation of Cho et al. [8]. To be comparable, these FHD sequences are encoded using a 2-pass encoding to get an average bit rate of 16 Mbps instead of the constant quality mode used for the QHD sequences. Table 4 depicts the performance results of our Cell implementation and the results obtained by Cho et al. Compared to the work of Cho et al., the performance is between $2.5\times$ and $3.3\times$ higher. This difference is mostly caused by being able to use the SPEs for parallel entropy decoding, while the implementation of Cho et al. uses only the two PPEs for that stage.

Table 4: Performance comparison of the Cell implementation using 16 Mbps FHD sequences.

Sequence	EDT-MBT	Our decoder	Cho et al. [8]
Pedestrian	9-9	91 fps	37 fps
Tractor	10-8	81 fps	31 fps
Station 2	9-9	79 fps	24 fps
Rush Hour	8-10	88 fps	34 fps

8. CONCLUSIONS

In this paper a high-performance, fully parallel, QHD-capable H.264 decoder has been presented. The employed parallelization strategy exploits the available parallelism at two levels. First, function-level parallelism is exploited by pipelining the decoder stages. This allows several frames to be processed concurrently in different stages of the decoder. In addition, data-level parallelism is exploited within the entropy decoding (ED) and macroblock decoding (MBD) stages, as these two stages account for more than 90% of the total execution time. In the ED stage data-level parallelism between frames is exploited using a novel B-ring strategy. By separating the I- and P-frames from the B-frames, the I- and P-frames can be processed completely in parallel, while load balancing is improved for the B-frames. In the MBD stage mostly MB-level parallelism within a frame is exploited. Limited parallelism at the beginning and end of each frame is avoided by overlapping the execution of consecutive frames.

The parallel decoder has been implemented on three multicore platform with substantially different memory architectures. On the 8-core SMP platform the limited memory bandwidth restricts the scalability to about 4.5×. Furthermore, the SMP parallel version is reasonably performance portable to the 64-core cc-NUMA platform as it achieves a speedup of 26.6×. On the cc-NUMA platform, due the non-uniform memory hierarchy and the large number of cores, specific optimizations are necessary to obtain the highest achievable performance and scalability. To efficiently exploit the distributed memory, a locality-aware static thread placement and page placement scheme have been presented. These optimizations yield additional improvements of up to 27.3% over the SMP parallel version, with a maximum performance of 200 fps. Scalability on the Cell platform is close to ideal with 16.5× on 18 cores. Due to vigorous overlapping of communication with computation, the Cell implementation is tolerant to DMA transfer latencies, which allows more efficient use of the memory bandwidth. Lack of portability and the required programming effort are known disadvantages of the Cell architecture, however.

The evaluation on the three platforms shows that our parallel H.264 decoding strategy scales well on a wide range of multicore architectures. Furthermore, the performance obtained on the cc-NUMA shows that multicores provide computational headroom that can be used to further innovation in the video coding domain. Finally, the performance results also show that exploiting the memory hierarchy becomes increasingly critical when the number of cores increases.

9. ACKNOWLEDGEMENTS

The research leading to these results has received funding from the European Community's Seventh Framework Programme [FP7/2007-2013] under the ENCORE Project (www.encore-project.eu), grant agreement n° 248647. We would like to thank the Future SOC Lab of the Hasso Plattner Institut and the Mathematics department of TU Berlin for giving us access to their platforms. Finally, we would like to thank the anonymous reviewers for their constructive remarks.

10. REFERENCES

[1] M. Alvarez, A. Ramirez, A. Azevedo, C. Meenderinck, B. Juurlink, and M. Valero. Scalability of Macroblock-level Parallelism for H.264 Decoding. In *Proc. 15th Int. Conf. on Parallel and Distributed Systems*, 2009.

[2] M. Alvarez, E. Salami, A. Ramirez, and M. Valero. A Performance Characterization of High Definition Digital Video Decoding using H.264/AVC. In *Proceedings IEEE Int. Symp. on Workload Characterization*, 2005.

[3] A. Azevedo, C. Meenderinck, B. Juurlink, A. Terechko, J. Hoogerbrugge, M. Alvarez, and A. Ramirez. Parallel H.264 Decoding on an Embedded Multicore Processor. In *Proc. 4th Int. Conf. on High Performance Embedded Architectures and Compilers*, 2009.

[4] H. Baik, K.-H. Sihn, Y. il Kim, S. Bae, N. Han, and H. J. Song. Analysis and Parallelization of H.264 Decoder on Cell Broadband Engine Architecture. In *Proc. Int. Symp. on Signal Processing and Information Technology*, 2007.

[5] M. A. Baker, P. Dalale, K. S. Chatha, and S. B. Vrudhula. A Scalable Parallel H.264 Decoder on the Cell Broadband Engine Architecture. In *In Proc. 7th ACM/IEEE Int. Conf. on Hardware/Software Codesign and System Synthesis*, 2009.

[6] G. Blake, R. G. Dreslinski, T. Mudge, and K. Flautner. Evolution of thread-level parallelism in desktop applications. In *Proc. 37th Int. Symp. on Computer Architecture*, 2010.

[7] C. C. Chi, B. Juurlink, and C. Meenderinck. Evaluation of Parallel H.264 Decoding Strategies for the Cell Broadband Engine. In *Proc. 24th Int. Conf. on Supercomputing*, 2010.

[8] Y. Cho, S. Kim, J. Lee, and H. Shin. Parallelizing the H.264 Decoder on the Cell BE Architecture. In *Proc. 10th Int. Conf on Embedded software*, 2010.

[9] The FFmpeg Libavcodec. http://ffmpeg.org.

[10] D. Finchelstein, V. Sze, and A. Chandrakasan. Multicore Processing and Efficient On-Chip Caching for H.264 and Future Video Decoders. *IEEE Trans. on Circuits and Systems for Video Technology*, 2009.

[11] Hewlett-Packard. HP ProLiant DL980 G7 server with HP PREMA Architecture. Technical report, 2010.

[12] M. Horowitz, A. Joch, F. Kossentini, and A. Hallapuro. H.264/AVC Baseline Profile Decoder Complexity Analysis. *IEEE Trans. on Circuits and Systems for Video Technology*, 13(7), 2003.

[13] N. Iqbal and J. Henkel. Efficient Constant-Time Entropy Decoding for H.264. In *Proc. Conf. Design, Automation Test in Europe*, 2009.

[14] T. Li, D. Baumberger, D. A. Koufaty, and S. Hahn. Efficient Operating System Scheduling for Performance-Asymmetric Multi-core Architectures. In *Proc. ACM/IEEE Conf. on Supercomputing*, 2007.

[15] N. Ling. Expectations and Challenges for Next Generation Video Compression. In *Proc. 5th IEEE Conf. on Industrial Electronics and Applications*, 2010.

[16] C. Meenderinck, A. Azevedo, B. Juurlink, M. Alvarez Mesa, and A. Ramirez. Parallel Scalability of Video Decoders. *Journal of Signal Processing Systems*, 57, November 2009.

[17] D. S. Nikolopoulos, T. S. Papatheodorou, C. D. Polychronopoulos, J. Labarta, and E. Ayguadé. A Case for User-Level Dynamic Page Migration. In *Proc. 14th Int. Conf. on Supercomputing*, 2000.

[18] K. Nishihara, A. Hatabu, and T. Moriyoshi. Parallelization of H.264 video decoder for embedded multicore processor. In *Proc. IEEE Int. Conf. on Multimedia and Expo*, 2008.

[19] M. Roitzsch. Slice-balancing H.264 video encoding for improved scalability of multicore decoding. In *Proc. 7th Int. Conf. on Embedded software*, 2007.

[20] F. H. Seitner, R. M. Schreier, M. Bleyer, and M. Gelautz. Evaluation of Data-Parallel Splitting Approaches for H.264 Decoding. In *Proc. 6th Int. Conf. on Advances in Mobile Computing and Multimedia*, 2008.

[21] K.-H. Sihn, H. Baik, J.-T. Kim, S. Bae, and H. J. Song. Novel Approaches to Parallel H.264 Decoder on Symmetric Multicore Systems. In *Proc. Int. Conf. on Acoustics, Speech and Signal Processing*, 2009.

[22] D. Tam, R. Azimi, and M. Stumm. Thread Clustering: Sharing-Aware Scheduling on SMP-CMP-SMT Multiprocessors. In *Proc. 2nd ACM SIGOPS/EuroSys European Conference on Computer Systems*, 2007.

[23] E. van der Tol, E. Jaspers, and R. Gelderblom. Mapping of H.264 Decoding on a Multiprocessor Architecture. In *Proc. SPIE Conf. on Image and Video Communications and Processing*, 2003.

[24] T. Wiegand, G. Sullivan, G. Bjontegaard, and A. Luthra. Overview of the H.264/AVC Video Coding Standard. *IEEE Trans. on Circuits and Systems for Video Technology*, 13(7), 2003.

[25] X264. A Free H.264/AVC Encoder. http://www.videolan.org/developers/x264.html.

[26] Xiph.org. http://media.xiph.org/video/derf/.

MP-PIPE: A Massively Parallel Protein-Protein Interaction Prediction Engine [*]

A. Schoenrock
School of Computer Science
Carleton University
Ottawa, Canada
aschoenr@scs.carleton.ca

F. Dehne
School of Computer Science
Carleton University
Ottawa, Canada
frank@dehne.net

J.R. Green
Department of Systems and
Computer Engineering
Carleton University
Ottawa, Canada
jrgreen@sce.carleton.ca

A. Golshani
Institute for Biochemistry
Carleton University
Ottawa, Canada
agolshan@connect.carleton.ca

S. Pitre
School of Computer Science
Carleton University
Ottawa, Canada
sylverbullit@hotmail.com

ABSTRACT

Interactions among proteins are essential to many biological functions in living cells but experimentally detected interactions represent only a small fraction of the real interaction network. Computational protein interaction prediction methods have become important to augment the experimental methods; in particular sequence based prediction methods that do not require additional data such as homologous sequences or 3D structure information which are often not available. Our *Protein Interaction Prediction Engine* (PIPE) method falls into this category. Park has recently compared PIPE with the other competing methods and concluded that our method "significantly outperforms the others in terms of recall-precision across both the yeast and human data". Here, we present MP-PIPE, a *new* massively parallel PIPE implementation for large scale, high throughput protein interaction prediction. MP-PIPE enabled us to perform the first ever complete scan of the entire *human* protein interaction network; a *massively parallel* computational experiment which took three months of full time 24/7 computation on a dedicated SUN UltraSparc T2+ based cluster with 50 nodes, 800 processor cores and 6,400 hardware supported threads. The implications for the understanding of human cell function will be significant as biologists are starting to analyze the 130,470 *new* protein interactions and possible new pathways in *Human* cells predicted by MP-PIPE.

Categories and Subject Descriptors

J.3 [**Computer Applications**]: Life and Medical Sciences

[*]Research partially supported by the Natural Sciences and Engineering Research Council of Canada.

General Terms

Parallel Computing

Keywords

Massively Parallel Application, Computational Biology, Protein Interaction Prediction, High Throughput.

1. INTRODUCTION

1.1 Background

Interactions among proteins are essential to many biological functions in living cells but experimentally detected interactions represent only a small fraction of the real interaction networks (e.g. [5]). Computational protein interaction prediction methods have become important to augment the experimental methods (e.g. [8]). Protein-protein interaction (PPI) prediction tools aim to exploit the set of known PPIs, as determined through classical wet-lab techniques, in order to determine whether two proteins will physically interact. There are several approaches to this problem including *sequence-based* prediction techniques (i.e. only the amino acid sequence of the query proteins are required as inputs), examination of the *genetic encoding* of the input proteins, *phylogenetic analysis* of the query proteins, and comparing the query proteins with previously solved *3D structures* of protein complexes (see e.g. [9] for a survey). Sequence based prediction methods are of particular importance in practice because they do not require additional data such as homologous sequences or 3D structure information which are often not available (e.g. [8]). Our algorithm, termed Protein Interaction Prediction Engine (PIPE) [10, 12, 11], falls into this category. An outline of our PIPE algorithm is presented in Section 3. Park [8] has compared PIPE with other sequence based methods [7, 5, 13] and concluded that our method "significantly outperforms the others in terms of recall-precision across both the yeast and human data". Another important consideration is that protein interaction networks are very sparse. Typically less than 0.1% of all possible protein pairs do actually interact. As discussed by Yu et al [14], it is critical that any method that is to be used for protein network wide high-throughput analysis operates

precision = $\frac{TP}{TP+FP}$	specificity = $\frac{TN}{TN+FP}$
recall = $\frac{TP}{TP+FN}$	sensitivity = $\frac{TP}{TP+FN}$

Table 1: Precision/recall vs. sensitivity/specificity. (TP=number of true positives. FP=number of false positives. TN=number of true negatives. FN=number of false negatives).

at extremely high specificity lest the predicted interactions be completely dominated by false positive predictions. (Biologists often consider sensitivity/specificity instead of precision/recall; see Table 1.1.) At these high specificities (up to 99.95% i.e. less than 0.05 % false positives), our method is particularly effective and achieves significantly higher sensitivity than all other methods [8].

1.2 Summary of Results

Since our PIPE method is more effective and achieves significantly higher sensitivity than competing methods in particular for high specificities (up to 99.95% i.e. less than 0.05 % false positives) [8], PIPE is a prime candidate for scanning the entire protein interaction network (proteome) of organisms. However, this is a massive computational undertaking because, for most organisms, the numbers of proteins pairs is very large. Typical model organisms such as *S.Cerevisiae* and *C.Elegans* have 18,000,000 and 280,000,000 protein pairs, respectively. For the *Human* protein interaction network, 253,000,000 protein pairs need to be tested for possible interactions.

In this paper, we present **MP-PIPE**: a *new* massively parallel PIPE implementation for large scale protein interaction prediction. This is, to our knowledge, the first massively parallel high throughput protein interaction prediction engine which is capable of scanning the entire protein interaction network of organisms. MP-PIPE is able to compute the entire protein interaction network for *C.Elegans* in about one week (on a SUN UltraSparc T2+ based cluster with 50 nodes). This is the first ever complete scan of the *C.Elegans* protein interaction network. For the *Human* protein interaction network, the task was considerably more complicated. Not only does the *Human* protein interaction network have more interactions but the calculation/prediction of these interactions is considerably more time consuming. Whereas nearly all individual interactions for *C.Elegans* could be predicted within seconds, some of the human protein interactions took hours (even days) to predict because of very large numbers of interaction candidate strings. Even though the problem is "embarrassingly parallel", given 253,000,000 protein pairs to work on, the large variation in computation time for individual pairs (from seconds to hours to days) created a massive scale load balancing problem. A considerable portion of our new massively parallel *MP-PIPE* method presented in this paper is dedicated to solving this load balancing problem. In a *large scale* computational experiment, which took three months of full time 24/7 computation on a dedicated SUN UltraSparc T2+ based cluster with 50 nodes, 800 processor cores and 6,400 hardware supported threads, MP-PIPE has been the first system ever to scan the entire *Human* protein interaction network. In addition to the 41,678 previously known *Human* protein interactions, MP-PIPE discovered more than 130,000 *new* protein interactions

with high confidence (0.05% false positive rate), potentially more than quadrupling the number of known *Human* protein interactions. The implications for the understanding of human cell function will be significant as biologist are starting to analyze these *new* protein interactions and implied possible new pathways in *human* cells predicted by MP-PIPE.

The remainder of this paper is organized as follows. Section 3 gives a brief review of our sequential PIPE algorithm and Section 4 discusses sequential performance optimization. Section 5 presents MP-PIPE and Section 7 shows a performance evaluation of MP-PIPE on various size clusters. Section 8 outlines the scientific results produced so far by MP-PIPE: the first complete scans of the *C.Elegans* and *Human* protein interaction networks.

2. RELATED WORK

Due to the high computational complexity of many problems in Computational Biology, parallel systems have been designed for numerous bioinformatics tools (see e.g. Rocks Cluster Bio Roll, http://www.rocksclusters.org). The most well known parallel systems for bioinfomatics include parallel simulations such as parallel protein folding [1] and parallel similarity searches such as parallel BLAST (e.g. mpiBLAST [2] and pioBLAST [6]). For protein interaction prediction there is, to our knowledge, no prior work on large scale *parallel* protein interaction prediction systems such as MP-PIPE. As indicated in Section 1.1 there is however a large body of work on sequential protein interaction prediction methods including *sequence-based* prediction techniques, *genetic encoding* based methods, *phylogenetic analysis*, and *3D structure* based techniques. Our Protein Interaction Prediction Engine (PIPE) falls into the category of *sequence based* prediction methods which are of particular importance in practice because they do not require additional data such as homologous sequences or 3D structure information which are often not available. Among the sequence-based methods there are two principle categories: *domain* based methods and *sequence similarity* based methods. Domain based methods (see e.g. [9]) search the query proteins for sequence similarly to known protein domains. If the query proteins contain a pair of domains which have been previously annotated as mediating a PPI, then the query proteins are predicted to also interact. The obvious limitation of domain based methods is that they require previously characterized protein domains for the species in question and cannot identify novel interaction sites outside of the set of known interacting domains. Sequence similarity based methods try to overcome these problems by discovering PPI mediating sequences from known interactions. A number of machine learning approaches (see e.g [5, 7, 13, 14]) examine features derived from the physiochemical properties of the amino acid residues using support vector machines. A limitation of these methods is the complexity of feature extraction, classifier training, and PPI prediction which precludes them from being used for high-throughput protein network wide analysis. More importantly, since protein interactions are typically mediated by small protein segments (15-30 amino acids) and unaffected by the amino acids outside these segments, the prediction accuracy (precision-recall) of these support vector machine based methods is limited because the interaction location is unknown. Our PIPE method [10, 12, 11] overcomes these problems. Rather than using a general purpose learning method such as support vector machines, PIPE is a custom designed algorithm for detecting interaction sites among proteins. PIPE provides two advantages: improved processing speed and improved prediction accuracy. For protein network wide analysis, involving many many million protein pairs, executing a support vector machine based classification for each pair is not computationally feasible. Most importantly, even it was possible, scanning entire protein networks with machine learning approaches such as [5, 7, 13, 14] would provide results that are completely dominated by false positives. As outlined in Section 1.1, an independent study by Park [8] showed that PIPE significantly outperforms all other sequence based methods in terms of recall-precision. In fact, PIPE is the first method to achieve very high specificities (up to 99.95% i.e. less than 0.05 % false positives) that are sufficient to scan entire protein networks. Furthermore, PIPE requires only positive PPI data for training. Machine learning based methods will change PPI prediction behavior as the ratio of positive-to-negative interactions changes in their training set. Considering that the actual ratio of protein pairs expected to participate in true PPIs is unknown for most species, this is particularly problematic for such methods.

3. REVIEW OF THE BASIC (SEQUENTIAL) PIPE ALGORITHM

For a given organism (e.g. *S.Cerevisiae*, *C.Elegans*, or *Human*) the PIPE algorithm relies on a database of known and experimentally verified protein interactions. For example, for the 22,513 *Human* proteins, only 41,678 interactions are known (out of 253,406,328 possible protein pairs). Considering that experimental verification of a single protein interaction can take days, this is already a massive amount of lab work. Since experimental verification can have large numbers of false positives (up to 40%, see e.g. [10]), the PIPE database is carefully constructed to avoid false data and stores only protein interactions that have been independently verified by multiple experiments. The database represents an *interaction graph* G where every protein corresponds to a vertex in G and every interaction between two proteins X and Y is represented as an edge between X and Y in G. The remainder of this section outlines how, for a given pair (A, B) of query proteins, our PIPE method predicts whether or not A and B interact.

In the first step of the PIPE algorithm, protein A is split up into overlapping fragments of size w by using a sliding window of size w on A. For each fragment a_i of A, where $0 \leq i \leq (|A| - w + 1)$, we search for fragments "similar" to a_i in every protein in graph G. A sliding window of size w is again used on each protein in G, and each of the resulting protein fragments is compared to a_i. For each protein that contains a fragment similar to a_i, all of that protein's neighbors in G are added to an initially empty list, referred to as list R in the remainder.

Before proceeding to the next step, we need to discuss the meaning of the term "similar" used above. To determine whether two protein fragments are similar, a score is generated with the use of a substitution matrix that has a row and column for each amino acid and the value stored at matrix location (i, j) is the probability that the amino acid j is replaced (through evolutionary processes) by amino acid i after a given evolutionary period. The PAM1 matrix [3] represents probabilities of amino acids changing into other

amino acids where only a single mutation occurs per 100 amino acids. For PIPE, the PAM120 matrix (i.e. the PAM1 matrix multiplied by itself 120 times) [3] was used to account for longer evolutionary processes. Two sequences of amino acids are considered "similar" if the sum of the PAM120 matrix values of corresponding amino acids pairs is larger than a given threshold S_{PAM}.

In the next step of the PIPE algorithm, protein B is split up into overlapping fragments b_j of size w ($0 \leq j \leq (|B| - w + 1)$) and these fragment are compared to all (size w) fragments of all proteins in the list R produced in the previous step. We then create a *result matrix* of size $n \times m$, where $n = |A|$ and $m = |B|$ and initialize it to contain zeros at the beginning. For a given fragment a_i of A, every time a protein fragment b_j of B is similar to a fragment of a protein Y in R, the cell at position (i, j) in the result matrix is incremented by one. An illustration of the PIPE algorithm is shown in Figure 1.

Row i of the result matrix corresponds to fragment a_i of protein A and column j corresponds to fragment b_j of protein B. The result matrix indicates how many times a pair (a_i, b_j) of fragments co-occurs in protein pairs that are known to interact. A visualization of PIPE's result matrix for two pairs of *S.Cerevisiae* proteins is shown in Figure 2. The x and y axis represent the amino acid fragment locations for proteins A and B, respectively, and the z axis represents the value of the result matrix for each pair of fragment locations. The proteins in Figure 2a are predicted to not interact because the result matrix values are all small. The proteins in Figure 2b are predicted to interact because of the large value (peak) around $x \approx 780$ and $y \approx 150$ which indicates a predicted interaction location.

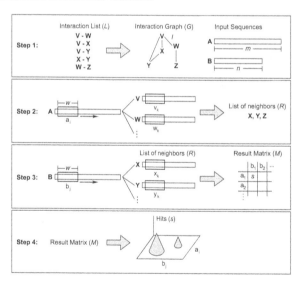

Figure 1: Illustration of the PIPE algorithm.

A possible cause of false positive PIPE predictions are "popular" protein fragments that simply occur very often but have no relationship to protein interactions. It turns out that such false positives typically correspond to very narrow peaks in the result matrix whereas true positives typically correspond to peaks with a wider base. Therefore, a median filter was applied to the output matrix in order to eliminate narrow peaks [12]. However, applying a median filter is com-

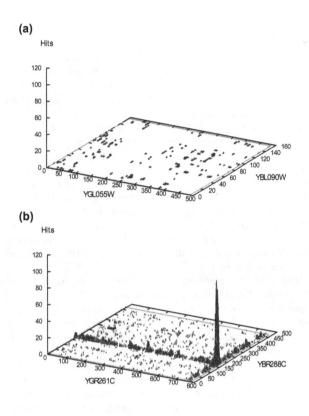

(a)

Hits

YGL055W

YBL090W

(b)

Hits

YGR261C

YBR288C

Figure 2: Visualization of PIPE's result matrix for two pairs of *S.Cerevisiae* proteins.

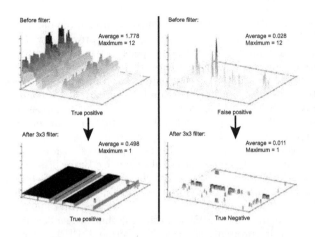

Before filter:

Average = 1.778
Maximum = 12

True positive

After 3x3 filter:

Average = 0.498
Maximum = 1

True positive

Before filter:

Average = 0.028
Maximum = 12

False positive

After 3x3 filter:

Average = 0.011
Maximum = 1

True Negative

Figure 3: Illustration of the simplified median filter. Impact of applying a 3x3 filter on a PIPE result matrix. Left: Example of two interacting proteins (true positive). Right: Example of two not interacting proteins (true negative).

putationally expensive. Thus, a simplified median filter was used: For a given cell c, if its neighbors consisted of more zeros than non-zeros then c would be set to zero, otherwise c would be set to 1. After this simplified median filter, the average value of all cells of the result matrix is calculated, and if the average is above a given threshold then the proteins are predicted to interact. An illustration is shown in Figure 3. The threshold parameters of PIPE were tuned using a true positive set and true negative set of 1,274 pairs each and applying leave-one-out cross-validation.

4. SEQUENTIAL PERFORMANCE OPTIMIZATION

It is important to note that before proceeding with a parallelization of PIPE, considerable efforts were made to *optimize* the sequential PIPE implementation. We would like to highlight three performance improvements that were particularly successful. (1) The character based amino acid representation of the proteins was converted into binary. This rather simple change removed the need for a character-to-index lookup when adding up the PAM120 scores. (2) The "sliding the window" process across proteins was improved, making use of incremental updates (moving both fragments one position in sync requires only one addition and deletion each). (3) We observed that many protein fragment comparisons are repeated multiple times, in particular when predicting interactions between many protein pairs. After all, query proteins and their fragments are from the given protein set of the organism under consideration. Therefore, we pre-computed all possible protein fragment comparisons

and stored all matches of similar fragments. For a set of query proteins, all relevant fragment comparisons are found via lookup instead of string comparison. In the remainder, we will refer to the graph G of previously known protein interactions as the *PIPE interaction graph* and the above precomputed fragment comparisons as the *PIPE database*.

5. MP-PIPE OVERVIEW

An important design goal for MP-PIPE was to obtain a *flexible* and *portable* parallel system that can be scaled to parallel architectures of different size depending on the complexity and size of the protein interaction network to be processed. We targeted in particular three popular parallel architectures: small scale local workstation networks, medium scale processor clusters, and large scale processor clusters. As discussed in Section 1, the main goal for MP-PIPE is to enable a *complete scan of all protein pairs for a given organism*, and the most important application is the first ever scan of the entire *Human* protein interaction network with its 253,000,000 protein pairs of which only a fraction has been evaluated so far. Another important requirement for MP-PIPE was therefore *fault tolerance* and *crash recovery*. The MP-PIPE run for the *Human* proteome took three months of full time 24/7 computation on a dedicated SUN UltraSparc T2+ based cluster with 50 nodes, 800 processor cores and 6,400 hardware supported threads. Needless to say, there were many hardware and system software crashes during such an extended time period where the cluster was run at maximum capacity.

In addition, preliminary experiments showed an interesting challenge that made the scan of the *Human* protein interaction network considerably harder than scanning the proteomes of other organisms such as *S.Cerevisiae* and *C.Elegans*. Note that the number of *Human* proteins and protein pairs is not exceptional. Simple organisms such a *C.Elegans* actually have more proteins and protein pairs than *Human*. However, the *Human* protein interaction network has more interactions and a more complex structure. In particular, the calculation/prediction of these interactions is consid-

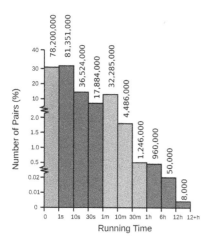

Figure 4: Distribution of running times for *Human* protein-protein interaction prediction. (Numbers above bars indicate approximate number of protein pairs with a running time within the given range.)

erably more time consuming. Previous PIPE experiments for *S.Cerevisiae* [10, 12, 11] and experiments for *C.Elegans* reported in Section 8 below showed that PIPE can process each individual protein pair within seconds. However, for *Human* proteins, the picture changes dramatically. As shown in Figure 4, the running time for one individual protein pair can fluctuate between less than a second and more than 12 hours. *Human* proteins have a much more complex structure which appears to lead, in some cases, to a very large number of fragment similarities found by PIPE. For two query proteins A and B, if a fragment a_i in A finds many nodes in G associated with proteins that contain fragments similar to a_i then every fragment b_j in B needs to be tested against all those proteins. If that happens for many a_i, as seems to be the case for certain *Human* proteins, then the running time can escalate from seconds to hours. Furthermore, a large number of fragment matches and excessive runtime does not increase the likelihood that those proteins are predicted to interact. One could imagine that many fragment matches imply high peaks in the result matrix and one could maybe simply stop the computation after a few minutes and predict an interaction but this is not the case. Many fragment matches do not necessarily lead to high counts in the result matrix. In fact, our experiments show that protein pairs with many fragment matches and requiring a large computation time have nearly the same probability of being predicted to interact than those protein pairs than can be processed within seconds. Therefore, even though processing 253,000,000 protein pairs is essentially an embarrassingly parallel problem, those 1,000,000 protein pairs that require more than one hour of processing time and in particular those 8,000 protein pairs that require more than 12 hours of processing time (see Figure 4) create an interesting load balancing problem.

The basic structure of MP-PIPE is a two-level master/slave model. A single *MP-PIPE scheduler* process is in charge of managing the main list of protein pairs to be processed as well as reporting the results. The MP-PIPE scheduler distributes work to several *MP-PIPE worker* processes in packets. Each packet contains a relatively small number of

protein pairs. Each MP-PIPE worker executes the PIPE algorithm on protein pairs received from the MP-PIPE Scheduler. By giving each worker only a relatively small amount of work at a time we ensure that if a worker does get stuck with an abnormally hard packet (one or more of those very time consuming protein pairs), the other workers will continue to work on their packets and, when they finish, they will request more work from the scheduler process and continue to work. It should be noted however that if the packet size is too small then the amount of communication between the scheduler and worker processes will negatively impact the running time of the system. It is therefore important to balance the packet size between being too small (too much communication overhead) and too large (too much work imbalance).

Algorithm 1: MP-PIPE Scheduler.

Split protein pairs into packets.
while *packets remain* **do**
    receive work request from worker x
    receive previous results from worker x
    send packet to worker x
    write results to output file
foreach *worker process* **do**
    receive work request from worker x
    receive previous results from worker x
    send KILL_SIGNAL to worker x
    write results to output file

Algorithm 2: MP-PIPE Worker.

Load PIPE interaction graph
$current\_packet \leftarrow \emptyset$
$current\_results \leftarrow \emptyset$
$work\_available \leftarrow$ TRUE
foreach *thread* **in parallel do**
    while *work_available* **do**
        if *current_packet* $= \emptyset$ **then**
            request work from scheduler
            send *current_results* to scheduler
            receive *message* from scheduler
            if *message = KILL_SIGNAL* **then**
                work_available $\leftarrow$ FALSE
                BREAK
            else
                current_packet $\leftarrow$ *message*
        retrieve pair from *current_packet*
        run PIPE algorithm on pair
        add results to *current_results*

To improve load balancing, MP-PIPE uses a two-level model where each MP-PIPE worker consists again of a number of parallel threads, called *worker threads*, among whom it distributes the protein pairs to be processed. The worker threads of an MP-PIPE worker are envisioned to be executed on a shared memory multi-core processor. A major concern is the efficient use of memory. The PIPE interaction graph

G and the large database of pre-computed protein fragment similarity matches requires considerable amounts of memory. For MP-PIPE, the PIPE interaction graph stored at an MP-PIPE worker was re-designed to become a parallel data structure on which all worker threads for that worker can operate concurrently. Much care was taken to implement the PIPE interaction graph and database as memory efficient as possible so that a single shared copy fits into the main memory of a processor node executing an MP-PIPE worker. In addition, the pre-computed database files were not all loaded at once at the start of the computation but were loaded only when needed. This allowed more threads to run simultaneously on a given processor node by reducing the overall memory usage.

The scheduler/worker part of MP-PIPE was implemented using MPI (on the SUN T2+ cluster: SunMPI within Sun Cluster Tool 6) and the worker threads within each MP-PIPE worker were implemented in OpenMP (on the SUN T2+ cluster: OpenMP within the SunOS SPARC 5.9C compiler). Pseudo code for the MP-PIPE scheduler and MP-PIPE workers are shown in Algorithm 1 and Algorithm 2, respectively.

Once the interaction graph G has been loaded by a MP-PIPE worker, it splits into a user defined number of worker threads. Each thread first checks if the packet they are working on still has pairs to process. If not, the thread requests more work from the scheduler process. When the scheduler process responds, the thread checks if the message is a signal to stop. If it is, it sets the *work_available* flag and exits. If not, it sets up the incoming packet to be processed by itself and the other threads, and continues. While there is work available in the current packet, each thread simply takes a pair from the packet, runs the PIPE algorithm on that pair (using the shared PIPE interaction graph) and then adds the result to the results array. It is important that the first thread to notice that the current packet is empty communicates directly with the scheduler and requests a new packet for the entire group of threads of the MP-PIPE worker without any interruption of the other threads. We refer to this mechanism as the *dynamic work request* design. The alternative *static work request* design is discussed below in Section 6.

6. DISCUSSION OF DESIGN ALTERNATIVES

Before arriving at the MP-PIPE algorithm outlined above, we considered various design alternatives, some of which we discuss here. One possible alternative solution would have been to parallelize the PIPE execution for each individual protein pair. As outlined in Section 3, each PIPE execution consists of a number of graph and string searches. Parallelizing graph and string searches is a non-trivial task and is known to lead in most cases to less than optimal speedup in practice (e.g. [4]). Furthermore, it would have interfered with some of the optimizations outlined in Section 4. For example, the sliding window optimization discussed in Section 4, Item (2), makes use of incremental updates to improve speed but introduces sequential dependencies between window queries. In contrast, MP-PIPE makes use of the massive parallelism available due to the millions of protein pairs that require separate PIPE executions. There are however various alternatives possible with respect to MP-PIPE's

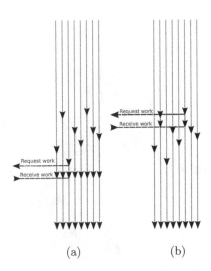

(a)   (b)

Figure 5: MP-PIPE worker thread implementation alternatives. The arrows represent worker threads where the red lines represent work on the first packet and the green lines represent work on a new packet after the first packet has been completed. (a) Static work requests. (b) Dynamic work requests implemented for MP-PIPE.

two level master slave structure using MPI and OpenMP. For example, we could have chosen an MPI only based implementation where each processor node as well as all threads within each node are MPI based. However, MPI threads do not support shared data structures and since each thread requires access to the PIPE interaction graph, we would have needed several copies of the interaction graph on each node. The memory available would have severely restricted the number of threads that can be executed on each node. For example, for the SUN UltraSparc T2+ based cluster with 50 nodes used in our experiments, it would not have been possible to utilize the available 6,400 hardware supported threads.

The MP-PIPE design outlined in Section 3 was aimed at providing high efficiency for a wide range of parallel architectures including small scale workstation clusters and very large scale clusters with large numbers of hardware supported threads. MP-PIPE's two level master slave structure also has the advantage to require only very little internode communication. In fact, after the PIPE interaction graph has been loaded onto each node, the only communication required are work packets and results sent between the scheduler and the workers. The amount of communication needed is in fact so low that we decided to have only one single scheduler process on one node responsible for all workers on all nodes. We also considered double buffering such as overlapping receiving results from workers and sending packets to workers in Algorithm 1. However, since the amount of communication between scheduler and workers as well as the computational load on the scheduler are so small, this had no measurable impact on MP-PIPE's performance.

Another important design choice is the *dynamic work request* scheme for assigning work to the worker threads of each node discussed in Section 5. While there is work available in the current packet, each thread takes a protein pair from the packet, runs the PIPE algorithm on that pair (using the shared PIPE interaction graph) and then adds the result to the results array. It is important that the first thread to notice that the current packet is empty communicates immediately with the scheduler and requests a new packet for the entire group of threads of the MP-PIPE worker without any interruption of the other threads. We refer to this as the *dynamic work request* design. Its implementation in OpenMP is not exactly in the spirit of OpenMP program design but the *dynamic work request* design is very important for efficiency because of those protein pairs with extremely long processing times. As illustrated in Figure 5, the alternative *static work request* design where all worker threads need to join/sync first before a new package of protein pairs is requested from the scheduler leads to wait times and is less efficient. In fact, because of those protein pairs with extremely long processing times, the difference in performance between the static and dynamic work request designs can be very large.

7. MP-PIPE PERFORMANCE

MP-PIPE's performance was tested on a small cluster (Cluster 1), a medium size cluster (Cluster 2) and a large cluster (Cluster 3). The precise cluster configurations are outlined below. The benchmark contains two tests for each cluster. The first test is designed to evaluate how MP-PIPE scales as more threads are used by a worker process. This test is done by using a single worker on a single cluster node, first starting with one thread and then increasing the number of threads until the point of maximum performance is found. For the second test, we evaluate how MP-PIPE scales as more workers are added, using the optimal number of threads per worker found in the first test. Tests are performed using a set of 5,000 random protein pairs except for some of the tests on the large cluster (Cluster 3) which required larger data sets (50,000 and 500,000 random protein pairs). All reported running times (and resulting speedups) are averages of 100 experiments and measured as wall clock times (between start of program until termination of the last cluster node).

7.1 Small Cluster

We tested MP-PIPE on a small cluster (Cluster 1) with six nodes connected by a gigabit Ethernet switch. Each node consisted of an Intel quad core processor (1.6GHz), 8 GB DDR2 RAM and a 320 GB hard drive, running Ubuntu Linux (10.04). The first test was performed to determine the optimal number of threads for each worker as described above. The results displayed in Figure 6 show the average running times and speedups with different numbers of threads for one worker running on one processor node. The data sets consisted of 5,000 random protein pairs. As shown in Figure 6, 5 threads per worker process provides the best speedup of 3.122. The second test examined how MP-PIPE scales when more processor nodes are added. Each processor node ran one MP-PIPE worker with 5 worker threads. The result are shown in Figure 7. Interestingly, we obtain a slightly above linear speedup with respect to the number of workers (processor nodes). The effect is due to the increase in total cache size and the fact that the MP-PIPE scheduler runs on one of the nodes together with one of the MP-PIPE workers. The scheduler process requires only a very small fraction of the computation required by an MP-PIPE worker but contributes to the artifact of a slightly

No. Threads per Worker	Average Running Time (s)	Speedup
1	2318.547131	1
2	1213.482118	1.911
3	835.571807	2.775
4	777.797144	2.981
5	742.669497	3.122
6	746.089079	3.108
7	745.651284	3.109
8	775.769684	2.989
9	790.394030	2.933
10	804.553819	2.882

Figure 6: MP-PIPE performance for different numbers of threads per worker on a small cluster (Cluster 1). Average running times for 5,000 random protein pairs, using one worker.

above linear speedup. The total speedup obtained by MP-PIPE on Cluster 1 is 21.485, the product of the speedup obtained by each worker/node (3.122) and the speedup for 6 workers (6.882).

7.2 Medium Size Cluster

We tested MP-PIPE on a medium size cluster (Cluster 2) with 32 nodes connected by a gigabit Ethernet switch. Each node consisted of four Opteron Cores (2.2 GHz), with 8 GB RAM running Linux (ROCKS). Again, the first test was performed to determine the optimal number of threads for each worker as described above. The results are displayed in Figure 8 and show the average running times and speedups with different numbers of threads for one worker running on one processor node. The data sets consisted of 5,000 random protein pairs. As shown in Figure 8, 5 threads per worker process provides the best speedup of 2.764. The second test examined again how MP-PIPE scales when more processor nodes are added. Each processor node ran one MP-PIPE worker with 5 worker threads. The results are shown in Figure 9. Interestingly, we obtain again a slightly above linear speedup with respect to the number of workers (processor nodes). As discussed in Section 7.1, the effect is due to the increase in total cache size and the fact that the MP-PIPE scheduler runs on one of the nodes together with one of the MP-PIPE workers. The total speedup obtained by MP-PIPE on Cluster 2 is 107.807, the product of the speedup obtained by each worker/node (2.764) and the speedup for 32 workers/nodes (39.004).

Number of Workers	Average Running Time (s)	Speedup
1	742.669497	1
2	331.018381	2.244
3	232.867967	3.189
4	168.935589	4.396
5	131.902550	5.630
6	107.919543	6.882

Small Cluster

Figure 7: MP-PIPE performance for different numbers of workers on a small cluster (Cluster 1). Average running times for 5,000 random protein pairs, using 5 threads per worker.

No. Threads per Worker	Average Running Time (s)	Speedup
1	3750.0589016	1
2	2027.0536836	1.850
3	1423.47368383	2.634
4	1359.32627749	2.759
5	1356.51471854	2.764
6	1372.91203179	2.731
7	1368.82533481	2.740
8	1406.15620157	2.667
9	1427.07301278	2.628
10	1441.51278317	2.601

Medium Cluster

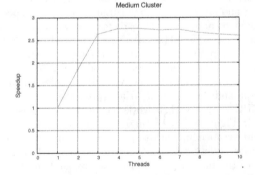

Figure 8: MP-PIPE performance for different numbers of threads per worker on a medium size cluster (Cluster 2). Average running times for 5,000 random protein pairs, using one worker.

Number of Workers	Average Running Time (s)	Speedup
1	1356.51471854	1
2	574.4489908	2.361
4	283.32493562	4.788
8	145.42208586	9.328
16	68.92684697	19.680
32	34.77818442	39.004

Medium Cluster

Figure 9: MP-PIPE performance for different numbers of workers on a medium size cluster (Cluster 2). Average running times for 5,000 random protein pairs, using 5 threads per worker.

7.3 Large Cluster

We tested MP-PIPE on a UltraSparc T2+ based "Victoria Falls" cluster (Cluster 3) with 50 nodes. Each node contains 2 UltraSparc T2+ chips (1.2 Ghz) with 8 compute cores per chip and 32 GB RAM. Each of these compute cores has 8 hardware supported threads, giving each node 128 hardware supported threads and providing 6,400 hardware supported threads in total.

The first test was again performed to determine the optimal number of threads for each worker process (running on one node). Due to the large number of hardware supported threads on a Victoria Falls node, the 5,000 random protein pairs were not sufficient to show the full scaling capabilities of a node. For this reason a second data set comprised of 50,000 random protein pairs was created. The 5,000 pair data set was used to examine the scaling of the code with a small number of threads (1 – 16 threads) and then the 50,000 pair data set was used for tests with 16 or more threads. The 50,000 pair data set was not used on the smaller number of threads because of the amount of time it would take to process. To calculate the speedup on the higher number of threads processing the 50,000 pair data set, the running time of a single thread to processes the 50,000 pair data set was approximated by taking the speedup from the trials on the 5,000 pair data set. The results are shown in Figure 10. The best result was achieved for 512 threads leading to a speedup of 8.701. The speedup curve shown in Figure 10 is essentially flat for more than 128 threads and we found that using more than 512 threads creates memory problems. In total, MP-PIPE's worker threads makes reasonably efficient use of the UltraSparc T2+ architecture. The slightly lower speedup compared to the small and medium size clusters can be explained by the increased number of threads spending more time waiting for new packets. On the small and medium size clusters, each node has only 5 concurrent threads and

No. Threads per Worker	Average Running Time (s)	Speedup
(5,000 protein pairs)		
1	9308.75325356	1
2	6622.24860655	1.406
4	4438.87609902	2.097
8	3259.65337563	2.856
16	2410.89934953	3.861
(50,000 protein pairs)		
1	80408.797712014086	1
16	20825.2934437	3.861
32	15325.5586534	5.247
64	11530.1009018	6.974
128	9259.13093131	8.684
256	9302.602417	8.644
512	9241.05782809	8.701

Large Cluster

[Speedup vs Threads plot]

Figure 10: MP-PIPE performance for different numbers of threads per worker on a large cluster (Cluster 3). Average running times for 50,000 random protein pairs, using one worker.

the chance of a thread waiting for another thread to finish communicating with the scheduler (for a new work packet) is very small. On the Victoria Falls cluster, each worker has 512 threads which increases the chance that threads have to wait. This also highlights the importance of the dynamic work request mechanism implemented for MP-PIPE (see Section 5).

The second test examined again how MP-PIPE scales when more workers/processors are added. Each cluster node ran one MP-PIPE worker with 512 worker threads. The result are shown in Figure 11. The performance of MP-PIPE scales almost linearly as the number of nodes used increases. This is an excellent result considering the vast number of threads involved.

8. SCIENTIFIC RESULTS

8.1 First Ever Complete Scan Of The C. Elegans Proteome

The first demonstration of MP-PIPE's performance was the first ever scan of the entire *C. Elegans* proteome.

- Total number of *C. Elegans* proteins: 23,684

- Total number of protein pairs to examine: 280,454,086

- Total number of known protein interactions: 6,607

Number of Workers	Average Running Time (s)	Speedup
1	18244.3975384	1
2	8992.99307318	2.029
4	4571.25758775	3.991
8	2294.45482244	7.952
16	1183.31196108	15.418
32	620.47111997	29.404

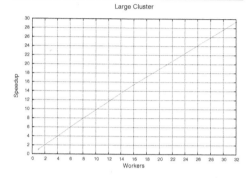

Large Cluster

Figure 11: MP-PIPE performance for different numbers of workers on a large cluster (Cluster 3). Average running times for 500,000 random protein pairs, using 512 threads per worker.

- Total number of proteins with at least one known interacting partner: 3,460

- Total number of proteins with no known interacting partners: 20,224

- Largest number of known interactions partners for a single protein: 512

- Smallest number of known interactions partners for a single protein: 0

- Average number of known interactions per protein: 0.55

- Average number of known interactions per protein with at least one interaction: 3.82

MP-PIPE evaluated all 280,454,086 possible protein pairs in the *C. Elegans* proteome. The work was split between the Victoria Falls cluster (Section 7.3) and Cluster 2 (Section 7.2). That is, MP-PIPE was run concurrently on both clusters. On the Victoria Falls cluster, 50 nodes were used. Each node executed one worker process running 512 worker threads. Hence, a total of 25,600 parallel computational threads were running on 6,400 hardware supported threads. On Cluster 2, 60 nodes were used each with its own worker process running 5 threads. This represents 300 parallel computational threads running on 240 cores. Both clusters executed sequences of "jobs" where each job contained approximately 10% of the total set of protein pairs to be processed. After a week of 24/7 computation, the first ever scan of the entire *C. Elegans* proteome was completed. At a specificity of 99.99%, MP-PIPE predicted 37,572 protein interactions. Of these high confidence predictions (0.001% false positive rate), 31,065 protein interactions are novel. Given that only

6,607 protein interactions are known for *C. Elegans*, this greatly increases our knowledge of the *C. Elegans* proteome.

Besides experimental verification and leave one out cross-validation, another standard method for evaluating a protein interaction prediction method is the "co-location test" which checks whether the proteins pairs predicted to interact are located in the same cellular component, have the same molecular function, or are involved in the same biological process (e.g. [8]). The results are shown in Figure 12. The percentage of pairs predicted by MP-PIPE that have similar function, occur in the same cellular component and participate in the same cellular process is 1.3%, which is consistent with the percentage for previously reported protein pairs (1.9% for 6,607 pairs). In contrast, for randomly selected protein pairs, the percentage of pairs that have similar function, occur in the same cellular component and participate in the same cellular process is only 0.2%. Similarly, for molecular function and biological processes, the MP-PIPE results are very similar to the previous experimentally confirmed protein interactions and very different from a control group of random protein pairs. It is important to note that the PIPE algorithm has no knowledge of the molecular function of proteins or which biological processes they are involved in. The probability that MP-PIPE could have found such co-occurrences by chance is extremely small.

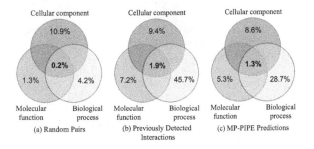

Figure 12: Co-Location Test: Percentages of *C. Elegans* protein pairs located in the same cellular component, with the same molecular function, or involved in the same biological process. (a) Random protein pairs [control group]. (b) Previous experimentally confirmed protein interactions. (c) Protein interactions predicted by MP-PIPE.

8.2 First Ever Complete Scan Of The Human Proteome

After the successful scan of the *C. Elegans* proteome, our group started a very large MP-PIPE run to perform the first ever complete scan of the *Human* proteome.

- Total number of *Human* proteins: 22,513

- Total number of protein pairs to examine: 253,406,328

- Total number of known protein interactions: 41,678

- Total number of proteins with at least one known interacting partner: 9,459

- Total number of proteins with no known interacting partners: 13,054

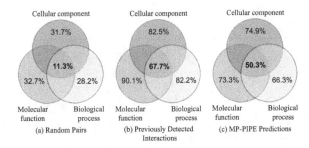

Figure 13: Co-Location Test: Percentages of *Human* protein pairs located in the same cellular component, with the same molecular function, or involved in the same biological process. (a) Random protein pairs [control group]. (b) Previous experimentally confirmed protein interactions. (c) Protein interactions predicted by MP-PIPE.

- Largest number of known interactions partners for a single protein: 265

- Smallest number of known interactions partners for a single protein: 0

- Average number of known interactions per protein: 3.70

- Average number of known interactions per protein with at least one interaction: 8.81

MP-PIPE evaluated all 253,406,328 possible protein pairs in the *Human* proteome. The work was again split between the Victoria Falls cluster (Section 7.3) and Cluster 2 (Section 7.2). The *Human* proteome has almost 7 times more known interactions than the *C. Elegans* proteome. The average *Human* protein has more than double the known interactions than a *C. Elegans* protein. Coupled with the fact that the *Human* proteins are, on average, longer than the *C. Elegans* proteins, this increases the complexity of scanning the entire *Human* significantly. Furthermore, as outlined at the beginning of Section 5 and illustrated in Figure 4, the running time for one individual protein pair can fluctuate between less than a second and more than 12 hours. This creates an additional load balancing problem that has been discussed in detail in Section 5. In fact, some individual protein pairs required 6 days of computation.

On the Victoria Falls cluster (Section 7.3), 50 nodes were used each with their own MP-PIPE worker process running 256 threads. This implies 12,800 parallel computational threads running on 6,400 hardware supported threads. The number of threads per node was scaled down from 512 threads used in the *C.Elegans* scan due to the fact that each individual thread needed significantly more memory. The Victoria Falls cluster was used to process the vast majority of protein pairs. If one of its worker threads got stuck with a protein pair that was running more than 12 hours, that protein pair was off-loaded to Cluster 2 (Section 7.2) since its individual cores are much more powerful than a single Victoria Falls thread.

After 3 months of 24/7 computation on the 50 fully dedicated nodes of the Victoria Falls cluster (plus the additional computation on Cluster 2), MP-PIPE finished the first ever complete scan of the *Human* proteome. At a specificity of 99.95%, MP-PIPE predicted 172,183 protein interactions. Of these high confidence predictions (0.05% false positive rate), 132,710 protein interactions are novel. Given that 41,678 *Human* protein interactions are known, MP-PIPE potentially more than quadrupled our knowledge of the *Human* proteome.

Besides experimental verification and leave one out cross-validation, another standard method for evaluating a protein interaction prediction method is the "co-location test" which checks whether the proteins pairs predicted to interact are located in the same cellular component, have the same molecular function, or are involved in the same biological process (e.g. [8]). The results are shown in Figure 13. The percentage of pairs predicted by MP-PIPE that have similar function, occur in the same cellular component and participate in the same cellular process is 50.3%, which is consistent with the percentage for previously reported protein pairs (67.7%). In contrast, for randomly selected protein pairs, the percentage of pairs that have similar function, occur in the same cellular component and participate in the same cellular process is only 11.3%. Similarly, for molecular function and biological processes, the MP-PIPE results are very similar to the previous experimentally confirmed protein interactions and very different from a control group of random protein pairs. As previously stated, the PIPE algorithm has no knowledge of the molecular function of proteins or which biological processes they are involved in and the probability that MP-PIPE could have found such co-occurrences by chance is extremely small.

9. CONCLUSION

In this paper, we presented **MP-PIPE**: a *new* massively parallel PIPE implementation for large scale protein interaction prediction. In a *large scale* computational experiment, which took three months of full time 24/7 computation on a dedicated SUN UltraSparc T2+ based cluster with 50 nodes, 800 processor cores and 6,400 hardware supported threads, MP-PIPE has been the first system ever to scan the entire *Human* protein interaction network (253,406,328 protein pairs). The biggest challenge here was that, while most protein pairs can be processed within seconds or minutes, some protein pairs require more than 12 hour or even several days of computation. This creates a non-trivial load balancing problem which MP-PIPE has been able to overcome. At a specificity of 99.95%, MP-PIPE predicted 172,183 protein interactions. Of these high confidence predictions (0.05% false positive rate), 132,710 protein interactions are novel. Given that currently only 41,678 *Human* protein interactions are known, MP-PIPE potentially more than quadrupled our knowledge of the *Human* proteome. We are currently building a publicly accessible database with the data generated by MP-PIPE. The implications for the understanding of human cell function will be significant as biologist are starting to analyze these *new* protein interactions and implied possible new pathways in *human* cells predicted by MP-PIPE.

10. REFERENCES

[1] A. Beberg and V. S. Pande. Folding@home: lessons from eight years of distributed computing. In *IEEE International Symposium on Parallel & Distributed Processing*, pages 1–8, 2009.

[2] A. E. Darling, L. Carey, and W. Feng. The design, implementation, and evaluation of mpiblast. In *ClusterWorld*, 2003.

[3] M. O. Dayhoff, R. M. Schwartz, and B. C. Orcutt. A model of evolutionary change in proteins. In M. O. Dayhoff, editor, *Atlas of Protein Sequence and Structure*, pages 345–352+. 1978.

[4] F.Dehne, A.Ferreira, E.Caceres, S.Song, and A.Roncato. Efficient parallel graph algorithms for coarse grained multicomputers and bsp. *Algorithmica*, 33:2:183–200, 2002.

[5] Y. Guo, L. Yu, Z. Wen, and M. Li. Using support vector machine combined with auto covariance to predict protein-protein interactions from protein sequences. *Nucleic Acids Res.*, 36(9):3025–30, 2008.

[6] H. Lin, X. Ma, P. Chandramohan, A. Geist, and N. Samatova. Efficient data access for parallel BLAST. In *IPDPS*, 2005.

[7] S. Martin, D. Roe, and J. L. Faulon. Predicting protein-protein interactions using signature products. *Bioinformatics*, 21(2):218–226, January 2005.

[8] Y. Park. Critical assessment of sequence-based protein-protein interaction prediction methods that do not require homologous protein sequences. *BMC Bioinformatics*, 10:419, 2009.

[9] S. Pitre, M. Alamgir, J. R. Green, M. Dumontier, F. Dehne, and A. Golshani. Computational methods for predicting protein-protein interactions. *Seitz, H (ed), Advances in Biochemical Engineering/Biotechnology (Springer-Verlag)*, 2008.

[10] S. Pitre, F. Dehne, A. Chan, J. Cheetham, A. Duong, A. Emili, M. Gebbia, J. Greenblatt, M. Jessulat, N. Krogan, X. Luo, and A. Golshani. PIPE: a protein-protein interaction prediction engine based on the re-occurring short polypeptide sequences between known interacting protein pairs. *BMC Bioinformatics*, 7:365, 2006.

[11] S. Pitre, M. Hooshyar, A. Schoenrock, J. Green, F. Dehne, and A. Golshani. Short co-occurring polypeptide regions can predict global protein interaction maps. *submitted*, 2011.

[12] S. Pitre, C. North, M. Alamgir, M. Jessulat, A. Chan, X. Luo, J. R. Green, M. Dumontier, F. Dehne, and A. Golshani. Global investigation of protein-protein interactions in yeast saccharomyces cerevisiae using re-occurring short polypeptide sequences. *Nucl. Acids Res.*, page gkn390, 2008.

[13] J. Shen, J. Zhang, X. Luo, W. Zhu, and K. Yu. Predicting protein-protein interactions based only on sequences information. *Proc. Natl. Acad. Sci. USA*, 104:4337–41, 2007.

[14] C. Yu, L. Chou, and D. Chang. Predicting protein-protein interactions in unbalanced data using the primary structure of proteins. *BMC Bioinformatics*, 11:167, 2010.

The Elephant and the Mice: The Role of Non-Strict Fine-Grain Synchronization for Modern Many-Core Architectures

Juergen Ributzka, Yuhei Hayashi, Joseph B. Manzano, and Guang R. Gao
University of Delaware
140 Evans Hall
Newark, DE 19716
{ributzka,hayashi,jmanzano,ggao}@capsl.udel.edu

ABSTRACT

The Cray XMT architecture has incited curiosity among computer architects and system software designers for its architecture support of fine-grain in-memory synchronization. Although such discussion go back thirty years, there is a lack of practical experimental platforms that can evaluate major technological trends, such as fine-grain in-memory synchronization. The need for these platforms becomes apparent when dealing with new massive many-core designs and applications.

This paper studies the feasibility, usefulness and trade-offs of fine-grain in-memory synchronization support in a real-world large-scale many-core chip (IBM Cyclops-64). We extended the original Cyclops-64 architecture design at gate level to support the fine-grain in-memory synchronization feature. We performed an in-depth study of a well-known kernel code: the wavefront computation. Several versions of the kernel were used to test the effects of different synchronization constructs using our chip emulation framework. Furthermore, we tested selected OpenMP kernel loops against existing software-based synchronization approaches.

In our wavefront benchmark study, the combination of fine-grain dataflow-like in-memory synchronization with non-strict scheduling methods yields a thirty percent improvement over the best optimized traditional synchronization method provided by the original Cyclops-64 design. For the OpenMP kernel loops, we achieved speeds of three to fourteen times the speed of software-based synchronization methods.

Categories and Subject Descriptors

C.4 [**Computer Systems Organization**]: Performance of Systems—*Design studies*

General Terms

Design

1. INTRODUCTION

During the 1970's and 1980's, a novel computational model was introduced by Dennis et al. [9] named Dataflow. Under this model, computation "flows" according to the availability of data, which means that several operations can run in parallel if the dependent data is available to them (and there are free resources to run them). Under the umbrella of Dataflow, several interesting structures and methods were proposed, like the actor's activity template structure for the Moonson Machine [16], static dataflow schemas [8] and the MIT tagged dataflow model [20]. Among these proposed methods, the I-Structure is a very interesting addition. The I-Structure was designed as a non-strict fine-grain memory centric (dataflow style) synchronization method in which the requesting operations will wait on the memory construct to be initialized. This behavior allows a consumer operation (i.e. read) to be issued before a producer operation (i.e. write) is issued or completed. The consumer operation will have to wait until the producer operation completes. However, the waiting happens on the I-Structure construct and frees the processor (i.e. producer and/or consumer) to do other useful work. This non-blocking issuing behavior is what we call the leniency property of the I-Structure. Another property of the I-Structure is that it allows a true data centric synchronization since it permits the synchronization on an element level (i.e. the I-Structure) instead of depending on certain control flow constructs such as barriers or signal-wait. Finally, it allows the synchronization to occur on finer granularity levels than its control-flow based counterparts. Nevertheless, it puts the restriction of "single assignment" on any given location. Due to the overwhelming trend of frequency scaling and uni-processor performance during the 1990's, Dataflow research was gently nudged out of mainstream computing. Due to the emergence of multi-core and many-core designs that have permeated the computer market in the last decade, research on Dataflow models and Dataflow style synchronization have seen a renaissance.

Although many synchronization methods exist today, most of them are defined under the control-flow style of computation (i.e. they are processor centric). Most of these methods are called coarse-grain since they allow synchronization of structures at a very high level. This incurs high overhead, which can be manageable on a small number of cores but quickly becomes a critical performance killer on a large number of cores. All these synchronization constructs are critical for applications that exhibit data races, a condition that occurs when two or more memory operations concurrently try to access a single memory element and at least one of them is a write. Data races, if not taken care of, can produce erroneous or unexpected results in a given application. Unfortunately, many of the real applications on High Performance Computing (HPC) exhibit this phenomenon due to the need to use previous computed values on its data space. Some of the most famous applications are stencil-like calculations such as the Finite Difference Time Domain (FDTD) and wavefront communication type algorithms like Sweep3D. Some of these problems can be parallelized by program re-structuring or by the insertion of coarse-grain synchronization.

One well known synchronization construct is signal-wait. Under this model, the producer sends a signal to the consumer after its write has been completed. Such behavior guarantees the producer operation to be completed before the consumer read arrives. However, this also implies that the consumer will have to block and wait for the signal to arrive. Although the way that the wait is implemented (busy-wait versus sleep-and-wakeup approaches) can have a huge impact on its performance, it still incurs an unnecessary substantial overhead for the consumer. Furthermore, this has a negative effect on the processor's and the toolchain's ability to schedule and reorder instructions. The reason for this is that although the signal and the memory operation are decoupled, they need to be scheduled in a very restricted manner, affecting other unrelated memory operations. Signal-wait methods can be implemented in several ways and may need hardware support depending on the architecture. For example, architectures which use out-of-order engines will require a memory *fence* instruction so that memory operations will not be incorrectly reordered across the wait and force the results of any memory operations to be "visible" to the whole system. These strict conditions apply to every memory operation in the processor, even the ones that do not need synchronization. Such overhead can be reduced by certain program transformations, such as loop unrolling, which allows having a synchronization operation every nth iterations if unrolled n times. Although this increases performance, it also increases the time delay until the next processor can continue program execution. Due to this behavior, it becomes difficult to scale, especially for small data sets.

Coarse-grain synchronization constructs like signal-wait cannot take full advantage of parallelism due to their strict behavior, overhead, the scheduling penalty, and the control-flow centric approach. Thus, many architectures have implemented fine-grain synchronization constructs in hardware. Some examples include the Denalcor HEP[19], Monsoon [16], the Tera MTA family of processors [2], MDP [5], Cedar [12], Multicube, KSR1, Alewife/Sparcle [1], the M-Machine [11], the J-Machine [15], ElDorado (aka Cray XMT) [10] and others. One popular way to implement the fine-grain constructs is to add an extra bit, called the full/empty bit, to each memory location. This enhancement, along with the addition of several extensions to the Instruction Set Architecture (ISA) to handle the full/empty bit, allows fast and efficient fine-grain dataflow-like synchronization. Since these bits are in each memory location, a synchronized operation will only complete if the memory word is in a pre-determined state (e.g. for loads the full/empty bit must be "full" and for stores the full/empty bit must be "empty"). Upon completion of the operation and according to the instruction type, the state

of the memory location might change to a different state or stay the same. The usage of fine-grain synchronization helps to achieve good performance and scalability as we will show in this paper.

Another factor that influences synchronization performance is the strictness of the operation. In general, strictness refers to the point of evaluation. If the value is evaluated when it is requested, it is called strict. If the value is evaluated when it is needed, it is called non-strict or lenient. In particular, strict operations stall or block execution until the operation is completed. Non-strict operations work in an asynchronous fashion and allow execution to continue even though the operation has not yet been completed.

Even though the addition of the extra bit to each memory location allows the implementation of fine-grain synchronization constructs, its cost might be very high. The Synchronization State Buffer (SSB) from Zhu et al. [22] mitigates this problem with a trade-off. This trade-off is based on the observation that the number of synchronizations at any given time is much smaller than the number of memory locations in the system. Therefore, the use of a small buffer to keep track of the full/empty bits was proposed. However, this approach lacked the non-strictness/leniency of the I-Structures and other dataflow-type synchronization constructs.

In this paper, we propose an Extended Synchronization State Buffer (E-SSB) that combines the advantages of a small synchronization buffer with the advantages of non-strict synchronization in a many-core architecture. By adding the non-strictness, this structure behaves more like an I-Structure and it can reap all the benefits of dataflow-like synchronization. We implemented the E-SSB at the gate-level using the hardware description language (HDL) code of the original Cyclops-64 architecture and extended it with our E-SSB implementation. A more detailed description of the Cyclops-64 architecture is given in Section 2.1. This enhanced architecture was then emulated on a gate-level accurate emulation platform, which was also used during the original chip verification. A more detailed description of the emulation platform is given in Section 3.1.

Problem Formulation

In the following sections we answer these questions:

How difficult is it to implement and support non-strict fine-grain synchronization?

New features in chips can be simulated and tested in a fast and reliable fashion using functional-accurate simulators, but the real complexity is often misunderstood or just not implementable. To determine the complexity of fine-grain synchronization, we performed an implementation at the hardware description level (HDL) of a real many-core architecture. Section 2.4 gives a more detailed description of the changes that were necessary to support fine-grain synchronization in the Cyclops-64 many-core architecture.

What are the implications on used chip estate?

The real hardware cost of a new architectural feature can, to a certain extent, be estimated by chip architects, but its final resource usage is unknown until an actual implementation has been performed. In Section 2.5 we discuss and describe both the additional hardware resources, which are required to support fine-grain synchronization, and how we obtained these results.

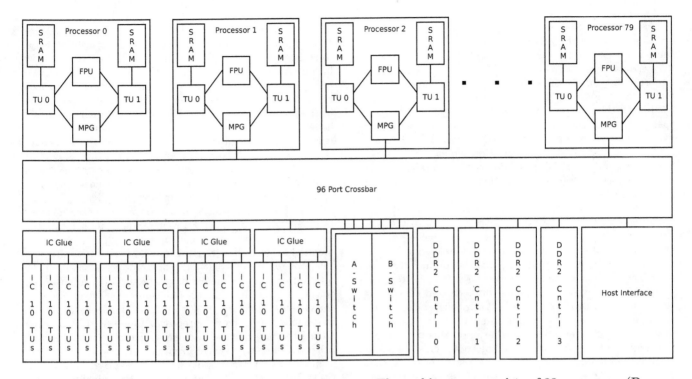

Figure 1: IBM Cyclops-64 (C64) Many-Core Architecture: The architecture consists of 80 processors (Processor 0 -79). Each processor has two Thread Units (TUs) called TU 0 and TU 1. Both share one Floating-Point Unit (FPU) and one crossbar port (MPG). Each TU is connected to a SRAM bank, which can be accessed by all other TUs via the crossbar. Ten TUs share one Instruction Cache (IC). The system has four on-chip DDR2 memory controllers to access off-chip memory. The A-Switch is used to connect to the six surrounding neighbors in a 3D-mesh network.

What are the performance gains of non-strict fine-grain synchronization?

The effort and cost of adding a new architectural feature has to be validated. In the case of our non-strict fine-grain synchronization construct, we expect a substantial performance increase. Otherwise, it may be more useful to use chip real estate for other features or even more cores. In Section 3, we compare and contrast fine-grain synchronization with other already existing synchronization constructs of the Cyclops-64 many-core architecture.

How do we ensure the correctness of our implementation and the given performance prediction with a very high degree of confidence?

The validation of new features and their true performance is difficult to measure with software simulators only. Software simulators may be cycle accurate, but they are slow and not useful to validate a full chip or even run a benchmark. Others might be fast, but sacrifice accuracy. In Section 3.1, we describe our emulation system and how we used it to obtain cycle-accurate performance results of the whole chip with a very high degree of confidence and the system's usefulness for whole chip and system software validation.

The remainder of the paper is structured as follows: Section 2 describes the design and implementation of non-strict fine-grain synchronization. Section 3 introduces the experimental testbed and shows our results. Section 4 gives a recap of the related work. Section 5 concludes the paper.

2. DESIGN AND IMPLEMENTATION OF FINE-GRAIN SYNCHRONIZATION

Before we go into the details of the design and implementation of fine-grain synchronization, we will first introduce the Cyclops-64 many-core architecture. We will then show our proposed design and its actual implementation for the given many-core architecture.

2.1 The IBM Cyclops-64 Architecture

The IBM Cyclops-64 (C64) architecture is logically partitioned into 80 homogeneous processors, which are connected to a 96-port crossbar. A processor contains two Thread Units (TUs), which share one Floating-Point Unit (FPU). Therefore, it is possible to have 160 independent and concurrent threads running at the same time. Every TU is attached to one SRAM bank and each TU can access all SRAM banks via the crossbar. The SRAM banks can be configured during chip boot-up into two distinct sections. One section contributes to the Global Interleaved Shared Memory; the other section can be used as Scratch Pad Memory (SPM). A TU has direct, low-latency access to its own SPM. The SPM of other TUs can still be accessed through the crossbar. Sequential Consistency is guaranteed for the Global Interleaved Shared Memory, but not for the SPM. TUs are in-order single-issue cores and use scoreboarding for out-of-order completion. They have a quad-ported register file (two read ports and two write ports) with 64×64 bit General Purpose Registers (GPRs). All TUs share a common signal bus, which provides fast barrier support in hardware. Ten TUs (five processors) share one Instruction Cache (IC) and four ICs share one crossbar port. There is no Data Cache. Off-chip DDR2 memory is connected through four on-chip DDR2 memory controllers and each memory controller is connected to its own crossbar port. Each chip can be connected to six neighboring chips in a 3-D mesh network. The network switch is also integrated into the chip and has seven connections to the crossbar. The host interface is connected to one crossbar port. In summary, the chip's crossbar interconnect possesses a total of 96 ports: eighty for the processors, four ports for the IC, four ports for on-chip DDR2 memory controllers, seven ports for inter-chip communication, and one port for the host interface. A logical overview of the chip is shown in Figure 1.

The architecture uses an explicit memory hierarchy similar to the one found in the NVIDIA CUDA or the Cell/B.E. architecture. Moreover, there is no paging or virtual memory support between all the memory hierarchy segments. More information about the C64 architecture and its system software can be found elsewhere [21, 6, 7].

2.2 SSB: A Recap

The Synchronization State Buffer (SSB) proposed by Zhu et al. is based on the observation that in any synchronized program only a small number of synchronized variables are needed at any point in time [22]. This means that a small buffer (added to each memory controller) is sufficient to keep the synchronization metadata of these variables. This reduces the overhead of keeping N bits for each memory word in the system as presented in other solutions [10]. Moreover, this buffer can store additional metadata for a specific variable for enabling such features as memory-based pointer forwarding and debugging/tracing capabilities.

In this paper we will only describe the usage of the metadata as full/empty bits in the context of Single-Writer-Single-Reader (SWSR) synchronization. The information saved in an SSB entry is implementation dependent, but it requires at least four parts in the original SSB: (1) a state field to indicate the current synchronization mode; (2) a counter field; (3) a thread identifier field; and (4) an address field to specify the memory address to which the entry applies.

The original SSB design had two different SWSR modes. Mode 1 employed a busy-wait approach for the reader until the data was ready. The second mode utilized the sleep-wakeup features of the architecture to reduce crossbar traffic and energy consumption. The operational semantics for the SSB synchronization constructs are described as follows:

SSB 1: Busy-Wait.

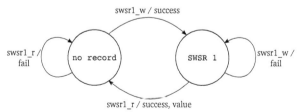

Figure 2: SSB 1: Busy-Wait

If the writer is first, then an entry is created in the SSB and the status "SUCCESS" is returned to the writer. When the load arrives, it is allowed to proceed and the entry is removed from the SSB. The value and the status "SUCCESS"

are returned to the reader. If the reader is first, then no entry is created and the status "FAIL" is returned to the reader. The reader has to retry until the status "SUCCESS" is returned. The corresponding state diagram is shown in Figure 2.

SSB 2: Sleep-Wakeup.

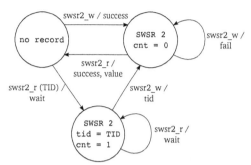

Figure 3: SSB 2: Sleep-Wakeup

If the writer is first, then an entry is created in the SSB and the status "SUCCESS" is returned to the writer. When the load arrives, it is allowed to proceed and the entry is removed from the SSB. The value and the status "SUCCESS" are returned to the reader. If the reader is first, then an entry is created and the status "WAIT" is returned to the reader. The reader goes to sleep and waits to be woken up by the writer. When the writer arrives, the Thread ID (TID) of the waiting reader is returned. The writer sends the wakeup signal to the waiting reader. The reader has now to retry the load again. This time it will succeed and the entry is removed from the SSB. The corresponding state diagram is shown in Figure 3.

If the buffer is full and a synchronization operation tries to add a new entry, an interrupt is generated and the software runtime will take control of the buffer. There is no automatic eviction of entries and flush to memory as a cache would do.

2.3 Design of the Extended Synchronization State Buffer (E-SSB)

In this section we will explain the design principles for non-strict fine-grain synchronization and its operational semantics. We implemented the original SSB and extended it with non-strict fine-grain synchronization. The major goal in designing our Extended Synchronization State Buffer (E-SSB) was to improve programmability and ease-of-scheduling for the compiler. Our major interest were the Single-Writer-Single-Reader (SWSR) synchronization operations. We added a third mode which eliminates the overhead of the synchronization operation with little additional hardware cost and added non-strict behavior. For the remainder of this paper we will refer to these three different modes as SSB 1, SSB 2 and SSB 3, respectively. Furthermore, we extended all modes to support any data size (byte, half word, word and double word) and signedness (signed and unsigned) of memory operations. To support these new features we extended the SSB entry with the following fields: (5) register identifier; (6) size; and (7) signdness.

The operational semantics of the non-strict synchronization is defined as follows:

SSB 3: Non-Strict.

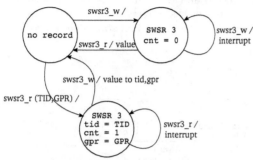

Figure 4: SSB 3: Non-Strict

If the writer arrives first, an entry is created in the E-SSB indicating this scenario. No status code is returned to the writer, as opposed to Modes 1 and 2. When the load operation arrives, its corresponding entry in the E-SSB is obtained (if available) and it is allowed to proceed. Finally, the entry is removed from the E-SSB and the value of the requested memory location is returned to the reader. If the reader arrives first, an entry is created in the E-SSB to store the Thread ID and register id of the requesting thread unit, and no data is returned. While waiting for the data to return, the reader uses scoreboarding to determine if it can continue issuing other instructions that do not depend on the return value. When the writer arrives, the value is stored in memory and also returned to the reader at the same time. Finally, the entry is removed from the E-SSB. Under this mode, the synchronization memory operations appear as normal load and store operations to the processor. The processor only stalls when a dependency is found between the synchronized operation and another operation. The corresponding state diagram is shown in Figure 4.

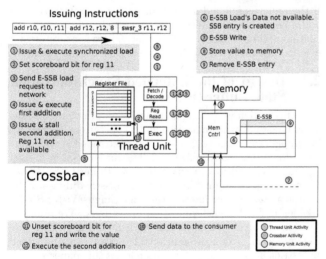

Figure 5: SSB 3 Read Example

Figure 5 illustrates the advantages of the non-strict behavior of an SSB 3 load operation. Even if the load operation is outstanding, other operations can be issued in order until a dependency is met. Register dependencies are enforced by the scoreboard. Another advantage of the non-strict version is that there are no additonal crossbar packages, meaning that zero overhead is incurred. An SSB 3 load or store oper-

ation produces the exact same number of crossbar packages as their normal memory load and store counterparts.

Using these operational semantics, we implemented the E-SSB in the Cyclops-64 architecture at the HDL level. The following section gives an overview of the required changes and implementation decisions.

2.4 Implementation of the Extended Synchronization State Buffer (E-SSB)

In this section, we will describe the architectural changes we performed to implement fine-grain synchronization in the Cyclops-64 many-core architecture. The Extended Synchronization State Buffer (E-SSB) required changes mostly in the Thread Unit (TU), because all the required logic related to the on-chip memory interface is located there. In particular, changes were required on the instruction decoder to support the new E-SSB instructions and the storage interface, which is responsible for routing memory requests from the network and the thread unit. Another module, the crossbar interface, which is shared by two thread units, had to be adapted to support new crossbar packages. Changes to the crossbar itself were not required.

The existing design allowed for an easy extension of the instruction decoder to support the new synchronization instructions. The Storage Interface (SI) of the TU required more extensive changes, because we added the E-SSB in this module. This was the actual buffer for the metadata and the associated control logic. The SI orchestrates the data routing between different requests coming from the network, TU, and E-SSB and the responses coming from the network and memory controller.

Some of the original SSB instructions require more than one result register. One register is required for the return code and one for the data. Due to restrictions in the instruction format, crossbar package format, and the register file, we use the result register and implicitly, the following register as bundled result registers. For example, the SSB 1 instruction `swsr1_rd rt,ra` reads a signed double word value from the address specified in register ra. The return code is written to register rt and the value is written to register rt+1. The write-back register is selected to be the next register after the return-code register in the register file. The SI in the TU was adapted to handle this special case and to generate crossbar packages for the new instructions if necessary. The actual implementation of the meta-data buffer is a 16-entry 8-way associative buffer and is 47 bits wide for each entry. The required fields for an E-SSB entry in this architecture are: state (4 bits), counter (8 bits), address (15 bits), processor id (7 bits), thread id (3 bits), register id (6 bits), size (2 bits), signdness (1 bit), and bits for implementation dependent features (in this case one bit).

The E-SSB creates special network return packages to accommodate support for E-SSB return codes, interrupts and performance counter events. The interrupt is always raised in the TU that produced it and not in the TU where the E-SSB is located. This is necessary because even if a TU is turned off, its SRAM can still be accessed by other TUs.

2.5 Logic Resource Usage of the Extended Synchronization State Buffer (E-SSB)

New architectural features may sometimes be implemented very easily, but the associated hardware cost can be overwhelming and may not be feasible to implement in hardware.

We did a comparison of the Cyclops-64 design with and without E-SSB. We converted the HDL code to VHDL and synthesized it with the design compiler, using the generic technology independent libraries (GTECH) to generate a VHDL netlist. We then used a tool to analyze the VHDL netlist and calculated the number of each design primitive. The design primitives reported for this study are NOT, AND, OR, XOR, Flip-Flops (FF), and SRAM. An exact gate number cannot be given, because this depends on the feature size of the process and the specific component libraries of the semiconductor foundry. The implementation of the first

Table 1: Logic Resource Usage of the Cyclops-64 Architecture.

Design Primitive	Original	with E-SSB	Increase
NOT	6,946,100	7,364,740	6.03%
AND	10,924,586	11,779,946	7.83%
OR	5,812,398	6,257,358	7.66%
XOR	1,171,951	1,200,671	2.45%
FF	2,140,299	2,350,619	9.83%
RAM(bit)	50,318,560	51,260,640	1.87%

two Single-Writer-Single-Reader Modes (SSB 1 and SSB 2) required additional buffers in the crossbar interface, which is solely responsible for an increase of 76,000 FF in the whole system. We only implemented the first two modes to have a fair comparison for benchmarking. In the final architecture it would not be necessary to implement all three modes and these additional FF will not be required. We still list them here for completeness to represent the current design.

3. EVALUATION

In this section we first introduce the experimental testbed, which was used to emulate the Cyclops-64 design. Then we present the results obtained from the experimental testbed, using the wavefront computation kernel and selected OpenMP kernel loops.

3.1 Experimental Testbed

For experimental performance evaluation, we implemented the proposed Extended Synchronization State Buffer (E-SSB) at the Hardware Description Language (HDL) level of the Cyclops-64 (C64) architecture. Moreover, we use the Delaware Enhanced Emulation Platform (DEEP) to emulate this many-core architecture. We selected this FPGA-based emulator due to several of its properties. This emulation platform is fast and cycle-accurate compared to software based methods. It is capable of emulating the whole many-core design with a relatively small number of FPGAs (32 Altera Stratix II) thanks to the Delaware Iterative Multiprocessor Emulation System (DIMES) mode. Since the whole Cyclops-64 design cannot fit into a single FPGA, neither the FPGAs in DEEP nor any other on the market today, the design is broken down into sub-modules. These sub-modules fit on a single FPGA, but many FPGA would be required to run the entire system and the communication overhead would be very high. On the other hand, DEEP, running in DIMES mode, takes an iterative emulation approach [18]. Combinatorial logic equivalent sub-modules are implemented on only one (or a few) FPGA(s); they are then iteratively utilized to emulate all instances of the sub-module. Moreover, stateful elements, like Flip-Flops (FF) and internal RAM

blocks, are isolated and kept independent of the sub-module instance. By using this approach, the required number of FPGAs to run the design is drastically reduced. All the steps described above are done automatically by the DEEP software stack. Finally, thanks to its debugging facilities and emulation modes, a design can be quickly debugged and run. For more information about the DEEP system and its various modes of operations (including DIMES), please refer to Ributzka et al. [17]. In the case of the C64 design (with E-SSB) the average emulation speed is around 20k cycles per second on DEEP (without using its tracing capabilities).

3.2 Experimental Results

Wavefront

We implemented the wavefront computation kernel in six different versions. The different versions are serial, barrier, signal-wait, and SSB Modes 1 to 3. All kernels were hand-coded in assembly. In all versions, the inner loop is unrolled four times to reduce the overhead of the synchronization and to allow for a better overlapping of memory operations and arithmetic computation. We run the benchmark on the emulation system for problem sizes starting at 16x16 elements at increments of 16 up to the maximum supported problem size of 512x512 elements. For each problem size, we run the wavefront benchmark with different numbers of threads, starting with one thread and going up by increments of one to 159 threads[1]. The runtime was calculated only for the kernel and the speedup was calculated based on the results of the serial version. Figure 6 shows the speedups of the different parallel versions.

Barrier: Even though the hardware-enabled barrier is very efficient, the speedup of the application is limited. The weakest link is the slowest thread. All other threads have to wait for it before they can continue doing useful work. Using barriers for these kinds of workloads is not necessarily a good choice, and dynamic scheduling approaches have achieved better results. We are aware of this, but we chose to demonstrate the barrier implementation for two important reasons. First, the barrier is supported in hardware and we wanted to compare different hardware supported synchronization constructs. Second, from a programming point of view the barriers seems to be an easy and efficient construct, because the work for each thread is the same. We wanted to show that this thinking cannot be applied anymore to many-core architectures and that congestion, bank conflicts, etc., can have unpredictable impacts on a thread's execution. The barrier version of the benchmark achieved a maximal speedup of 24x.

Signal-Wait: The signal-wait version can be implemented very efficiently on the Cyclops-64 architecture by taking advantage of the extensive atomic memory operation support and the local, low-latency scratch pad memory resulting in a speedup of 72x. Figure 7 illustrates the synchronization delay of the different benchmark versions. For all examples in this illustration, Thread 1 (consumer) always tries to read the shared data, whereas Thread 2 (producer) is producing this shared data. The first example shows the synchronization delay for signal-wait. The dashed arrows represent accesses to scratch pad memory via the back-door

---
[1] The architecture supports up to 160 hardware threads, but only 159 can be used, because the OS kernel is running on the first thread unit.

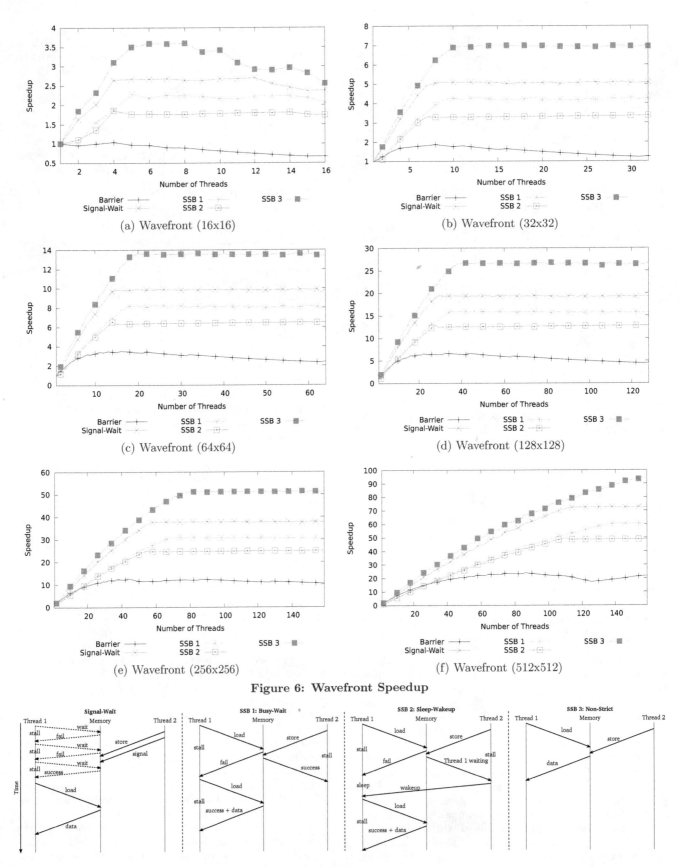

Figure 6: Wavefront Speedup

Figure 7: Synchronization Delay Illustration

each thread unit has to its own scratch pad memory. This access is much faster, because it does not have to go through the crossbar. Solid arrows represents memory operations that go through the crossbar and therefore take more time. Since the consumer spins on its own local synchronization variable, changes to this variable are observed with little delay. Once the signal from the producer arrives, the consumer can continue execution without any further synchronization related stalls. This allows the overlap of computation and memory operations after the wait. The producer does not need to stall at all. This makes signal-wait a very efficient synchronization construct on Cyclops-64.

Fine-grain In-Memory Synchronization: The different SSB versions of the benchmark achieved speedups of 60x, 50x and 94x respectively. We took a closer look at the benchmarks by using performance counters. In summary, we can say that the benchmark is not memory bound. The SSB 1 (busy-wait) version has a synchronization failure rate of 150%. That means every synchronizing load operation has to be repeated 1.5 times on average, because the data had not been written yet by the producer. The SSB 2 (sleep-wakeup) version on the other hand had a failure rate of only 1-2%. Nevertheless, the SSB 1 (busy-wait) approach still achieved better speedups. The second approach generates fewer memory operations and also saves power, but the price is a longer synchronization delay, which hinders parallelism and therefore performance. The SSB 3 (non-strict) version has a failure rate of 25%, but that only means that the load arrived before the store. No additional overhead or memory transactions were required to correct this, because the memory controller had already taken care of it. The second illustration in Figure 7 shows that SSB 1 employs a similar busy-waiting approach as signal-wait, but it has to go through the crossbar every time. Furthermore, the producer and the consumer have to stall and cannot overlap any other computation or memory operations until the memory operation on their side has successfully completed. The SSB 2 sleep-wakeup approach in the next example even further aggravates this problem, because now the producer has to wake up the consumer and the synchronization delay increases further. The last SSB mode solves all the problems of the previous versions by performing the synchronization completely in the memory controller. No further action is required from the producer or the consumer. In this mode synchronizing memory operations act like normal memory operations for the thread unit and the synchronization is transparent to them. This allows aggressive scheduling of synchronizing and non-synchronizing memory operations and arithmetic instructions.

OpenMP Kernel Loops

The kernel loops are extracted from SPEC OpenMP benchmarks, such as 314.mgrid and 318.galgel. As in the original SSB paper, we compare our SSB versions against the software-based approaches proposed by Kejariwal et al. [14]. All loops exhibit the same characteristics, namely, that dependencies between loop iterations are positive and constant. They also fulfill our requirement of Single-Writer-Single-Reader, so our SSB synchronization constructs can be applied. Figure 8 shows the speedup of the different parallel versions against the sequential version. SSB 3 clearly outperforms all other versions, both software and hardware based. Another interesting aspect is that we do not lose performance

when we increase the number of threads. K1's and K2's speedups are severely limited, but this is understandable and expected. K1 only performs a single arithmetic operation in the loop and therefore the speedup is clearly limited by it and the only form of parallelism can be obtained from the number of iterations that can be performed in parallel without dependence. K2's story is even worse, because the iteration dependence is 1. That means none of the iterations can be performed in parallel. Nevertheless, SSB 3 is still able to obtain instruction level parallelism between iterations through its fine-grain non-strict behavior and does not suffer any performance degradation as the other approaches. K3, K4 and K5 do not only provide sufficient iteration level parallelism due to a larger dependence distance of 8, but also a larger kernel that provides a great source of cross-iteration instruction level parallelism that can only be leveraged by SSB 3.

3.3 Analysis Breakdown

In this section we take an in-depth look at the different versions of the tested wavefront benchmarks. This in-depth look consists of breaking down the collected information into different important activities and overhead such as cycles spent on useful work, synchronization overhead, loop overhead, arithmetic stalls, and stalls due to synchronized and unrelated memory operations, among others. To obtain this instruction mix, we enabled the program tracing feature on the emulation engine and obtained the detailed trace of all 160 thread units. Figure 9 shows a break down of the in-

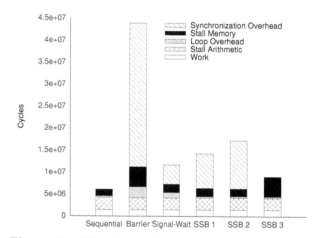

Figure 9: Wavefront Execution Runtime Breakdown: This histogram shows a breakdown of cycles spend on certain important aspects of the program. The Sequential version shows cycles spend by a single thread, whereas the other versions show the accumulated cycles spend by all 159 threads.

struction mix of the different benchmark versions. We used the maximum problem size (512x512) for the benchmark to fully utilize the whole system. The histogram shows the accumulated cycles spent by all thread units to complete the work. The serial version uses of course only one thread unit, whereas all the other versions use 159 thread units. To obtain the actual execution time, each version has to be divided by the number of threads used. "Work" contains all instructions necessary to perform the actual required computation. This includes the arithmetic instructions and the memory

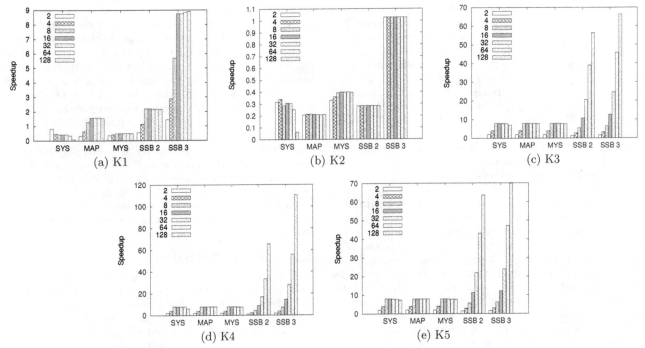

Figure 8: OpenMP Loops Speedup

operations to obtain the data. "Stall Arithmetic" contains all the stall cycles in the kernel due to dependence on an unfinished arithmetic instruction. "Stall Arithmetic" can bee seen as part of "Work", because it depends on the given schedule and the arithmetic instruction latency of the architecture. "Loop Overhead" contains pointer increments, loop exit checks, branches and branch delays. "Stall Memory" contains all the stall cycles inside the kernel due to instructions waiting on data to return from memory. "Synchronization Overhead" contains all the additional instructions, stalls and branch delays which were required to perform the actual synchronization. "Function Overhead" contains all the instructions, stall cycles, etc, which are not part of the kernel code, but the surrounding setup code of the function. "Stall Misc" contains stalls due to the fact that the crossbar port and the floating-point unit are shared between two thread units and other architecture related stall cycles. "Function Overhead" and "Stall Misc" are so small (less than 1%) that we omitted them in the figure.

The instruction mix break-down, overall, is predictable: "Work" and "Stall Arithmetic" are uniform across all benchmarks and indicate a compute-bound kernel. "Loop Overhead" should also be rather constant across all benchmarks, but signal-wait and barrier have a much higher loop overhead than the other versions. A detailed analysis showed that this increase is solely due to branch delays for the signal-wait version, because the loop does not fit completely in the instruction buffer. The barrier version suffers from the same problem, but it also has more complex loop exit checks on top of that. The barrier version also suffers a lot under a very large amount of memory related stall cycles. This is due to the pathologic nature of programs that use barriers, which have normally three distinct phases. During phase one, all threads try to obtain the data at the same time, followed by the computation phase with almost no memory operations. Finally, in the last phase the results are written

back to memory. This behavior makes the first phase a memory bound problem, which is responsible for the increase in memory related stall cycles.

Due to the factors described above, the main components that determine performance are the "Stall Memory" and the "Synchronization Overhead". The SSB 3 method shows no "Synchronization Overhead", because these cycles are hidden in the memory stall cycles. Thus, for a fair comparison, both of these components must be used together to evaluate our synchronization methods. Under these conditions, SSB 3 still clearly outperforms all other methods, even the highly optimized signal-wait version.

4. RELATED WORK

Our research was greatly influenced by previous work on fine-grain synchronization constructs by academia and industry. This includes research on dataflow constructs like the I-Structure [3], the Synchronization State Buffer (SSB) [22], and the Tera MTA/Cray XMT [2, 10]. The use of tagged memory, full/empty bits, and I-Structure has been explained in Section 1. E-SSB differs in the following aspect from previous work: It enables "virtual tagging" of the whole memory space like SSB; it also supports all data sizes of the architecture and it is not limited to double-word synchronization. Furthermore, it has been enhanced to support non-strict synchronization. It has the benefits of SSB, which means using fewer hardware resources, and the non-strict behavior of I-Structures. Another approach that gained momentum in recent years is Transactional Memory (TM) [13, 4], which also employs a non-blocking synchronization approach. The major difference with our approach is that in TM, if a transaction fails, all changes done inside a transaction must be rolled back and the transaction has to be restarted. This results in unnecessary computation every time a transaction has to be restarted. Our approach does not require this.

5. CONCLUSION AND FUTURE WORK

In this paper, we presented a new design for a dataflow-like fine-grain synchronization, based on the Synchronization State Buffer (SSB) presented in [22], and its implementation at the Hardware Description Level (HDL) of a "real" many-core architecture. Our experiments were performed on an emulation engine with gate-level accuracy. The results surpassed our expectations and show very good scalability for even small problem sizes. Even for larger problem sizes, our non-strict synchronization approach surpasses all other synchronization constructs, such as barriers with hardware support and signal-wait. The most noticeable result is that we achieve scalability beyond the 100 core barrier. E-SSB is the first step toward a new paradigm in code generation for many-core architectures and we intend to utilize this in future compiler research.

Acknowledgements

Our utmost respect goes to Monty Denneau for creating such a great architecture. We also would like to thank all the reviewers for their comments, suggestions, and help to improve this paper. This work would have not been possible without the support by NSF (CCF-0833122, CCF-0925863, CCF-0937907, CNS-0720531, and OCI-0904534), and other government sponsors.

6. REFERENCES

[1] A. Agarwal, J. Kubiatowicz, D. Kranz, B. Lim, D. Yeung, G. D'Souza, and M. Parkin. Sparcle: An Evolutionary Processor Design for Large-Scale Multiprocessors. *IEEE Micro*, 13(3):48–61, 1993.

[2] R. Alverson, D. Callahan, D. Cummings, B. Koblenz, A. Porterfield, and B. Smith. The Tera Computer System. In *Proceedings of the 4th International Conference on Supercomputing*, pages 1–6. ACM, 1990.

[3] R. Arvind, R. Nikhil, and K. Pingali. I-Structures: Data Structures for Parallel Computing. *TOPLAS*, 11(4):598–632, 1989.

[4] B. Carlstrom, A. McDonald, H. Chafi, J. Chung, C. Minh, C. Kozyrakis, and K. Olukotun. The Atomos Transactional Programming Language. *ACM SIGPLAN Notices*, 41(6):13, 2006.

[5] W. Dally, L. Chao, A. Chien, S. Hassoun, W. Horwat, J. Kaplan, P. Song, B. Totty, and S. Wills. Architecture of a Message-Driven Processor. In *Proceedings of the 14th Annual International Symposium on Computer Architecture*, pages 189–196. ACM, 1987.

[6] J. del Cuvillo, W. Zhu, Z. Hu, and G. Gao. TiNy Threads: A Thread Virtual Machine for the Cyclops64 Cellular Architecture. In *19th IEEE International Parallel and Distributed Processing Symposium, 2005. Proceedings*, page 8, 2005.

[7] J. Del Cuvillo, W. Zhu, Z. Hu, and G. Gao. Toward a Software Infrastructure for the Cyclops-64 Cellular Architecture. In *High-Performance Computing in an Advanced Collaborative Environment, 2006. HPCS 2006. 20th International Symposium on*, pages 9–9, 2006.

[8] J. Dennis. The Evolution of 'Static' Dataflow Architecture. *Advanced Topics in Data-Flow Computing*, pages 35–91.

[9] J. Dennis, J. Fosseen, and J. Linderman. Data Flow Schemas. In *International Symposium on Theoretical Programming*, pages 187–216. Springer, 1974.

[10] J. Feo, D. Harper, S. Kahan, and P. Konecny. Eldorado. In *Proceedings of the 2nd Conference on Computing Frontiers*, page 34. ACM, 2005.

[11] M. Fillo, S. Keckler, W. Dally, N. Carter, A. Chang, Y. Gurevich, and W. Lee. The M-Machine Multicomputer. In *Proceedings of the 28th Annual International Symposium on Microarchitecture*, pages 146–156. IEEE Computer Society Press, 1995.

[12] D. Gajski, D. Kuck, D. Lawrie, and A. Sameh. CEDAR: A Large Scale Multiprocessor. *ACM SIGARCH Computer Architecture News*, 11(1):7–11, 1983.

[13] M. Herlihy and J. Moss. Transactional Memory: Architectural Support for Lock-Free Data Structures. In *Proceedings of the 20th Annual International Symposium on Computer Architecture*, page 300. ACM, 1993.

[14] A. Kejariwal, H. Saito, X. Tian, M. Girkar, W. Li, U. Banerjee, A. Nicolau, and C. Polychronopoulos. Lightweight Lock-Free Synchronization Methods for Multithreading. In *Proceedings of the 20th Annual International Conference on Supercomputing*, pages 361–371. ACM, 2006.

[15] M. Noakes, D. Wallach, and W. Dally. The J-Machine Multicomputer: An Architectural Evaluation. In *ACM SIGARCH Computer Architecture News*, volume 21, pages 224–235. ACM, 1993.

[16] G. Papadopoulos and D. Culler. Monsoon: An Explicit Token-Store Architecture. *ACM SIGARCH Computer Architecture News*, 18(3a):82–91, 1990.

[17] J. Ributzka, Y. Hayashi, F. Chen, and G. Gao. DEEP: An Iterative FPGA-based Many-core Emulation System for Chip Verification and Architecture Research. In *Proceedings of the 19th ACM/SIGDA International Symposium on Field Programmable Gate Arrays*, pages 115–118. ACM, 2011.

[18] H. Sakane, L. Yakay, V. Karna, C. Leung, and G. Gao. DIMES: An Iterative Emulation Platform for Multiprocessor-System-On-Chip Designs. In *2003 IEEE International Conference on Field-Programmable Technology (FPT), 2003. Proceedings*, pages 244–251, 2003.

[19] B. J. Smith. Architecture and applications of the HEP multiprocessor computer system. *Real-Time Signal Processing IV*, pages 241–248, 1982.

[20] K. R. Traub. A Compiler for the MIT Tagged-token Dataflow Architecture. 1986.

[21] Y. Zhang, T. Jeong, F. Chen, H. Wu, R. Nitzsche, and G. Gao. A Study of the On-Chip Interconnection Network for the IBM Cyclops64 Multi-Core Architecture. In *20th International Parallel and Distributed Processing Symposium (IPDPS)*, page 10. IEEE, 2006.

[22] W. Zhu, V. Sreedhar, Z. Hu, and G. Gao. Synchronization State Buffer: Supporting Efficient Fine-Grain Synchronization on Many-Core Architectures. In *Proceedings of the 34th Annual International Symposium on Computer Architecture*, page 45. ACM, 2007.

F²BFLY: An On-Chip Free-Space Optical Network with Wavelength-Switching

Jin Ouyang†, Chuan Yang§, Dimin Niu†, Yuan Xie†, Zhiwen Liu§
†Dept. of Computer Science and Engineering*
§Dept. of Electrical Engineering
Pennsylvania State University, University Park, PA 16802
jouyang@cse.psu.edu, czy111@psu.edu

ABSTRACT

The increasing number of cores in contemporary and future many-core processors will continue to demand high throughput, scalable, and energy efficient on-chip interconnection networks. To overcome the intrinsic inefficiency of electrical interconnects, researchers have leveraged recent developments in chip photonics to design novel optical network-on-chip (NoC). However, existing optical NoCs are mostly based on passively switched, channel-guided optical interconnect in which large amount of power is wasted in heating the micro-rings and maintaining the optical signal integrity.

In this paper we present an optical NoC based on *free-space* optical interconnect in which optical signals emitted from the transmitter is propagated in the free space in the package. With lower attenuation and no coupling effects, free-space optical interconnects have less overheads to maintain the signal integrity, and no energy waste for heating micro-rings. In addition, we propose a novel cost-effective *wavelength-switching* method where a refractive grating layer directs optical signals in different wavelengths to different photodetectors without collision. Based on the above interconnect and switching technologies, we propose **free flattened butterfly** (F²BFLY) NoC which features both high-radix network and dense free-space optical interconnects to improve the performance while reducing the power. Our experiment results, comparing F²BFLY with state-of-the-art electrical and optical on-chip networks, show that it is a highly competitive interconnect substrate for many-core architectures.

Categories and Subject Descriptors

B.4.3 [**Hardware**]: Interconnections (Subsystems)

*J. Ouyang, D. Niu, and Y. Xie are supported in part by NSF CCF-0903432, CNS-0905365, SRC grant, and DoE's ASCR program under under award number DE-SC0005026.

General Terms

Design, Experimentation

Keywords

free-space optical interconnects, network-on-chip

1. INTRODUCTION

In an era when shrinking device size and exploiting instruction-level parallelism (ILP) gain diminishing returns in frequency and application throughput, many-core architectures which better leverage high device density and task-level parallelism (TLP) is proposed as a more efficient solution to continuous performance improvement. The increasing number of cores in a chip, however, places rapidly increasing communication burden on the on-chip interconnect substrate. Therefore, high throughput, scalable, and energy-efficient on-chip interconnection networks become the key enabler of future large scale many-core processors. Towards this objective, researchers have been focused on either designing novel router architectures and network topologies, or leveraging emerging on-chip interconnect technologies which are intrinsically more efficient than conventional electrical interconnects.

1.1 Electrical NoCs

A major branch of contemporary NoC researches inherit ideas from the long-established computer and multiprocessor networks [1]. However, the on-chip environment adds extra constraints and opportunities, which leads to various specially optimized architectures. Driven by the requirements of low latency and low complexity, researchers have been working on reducing the router pipeline stages and efficient switching mechanisms [2, 3, 4]. An interesting recent trend is to leverage the ample on-chip wiring resources to build high-radix, richly interconnected NoCs that features both high bi-section bandwidth and low network diameter [5, 6, 7, 8]. Grot *et al.* [7] generalize these high-radix NoCs as *express cube topologies* and perform a comprehensive study of the design space of express cubes. Their results show that by wisely utilizing the abundant wiring resources, express cubes can produce significantly higher performance and consume lower power than conventional topologies.

However, future performance elevation with electrical NoC is impeded by the slow improvement in the on-chip interconnect technology. The wiring density is not increasing as fast as device density, since to maintain acceptable signal integrity, the feature size of wires cannot scale at the

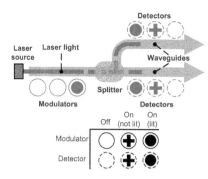

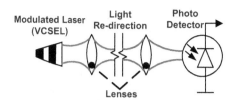

Figure 2: Free-space optical interconnects: the actively modulated VCSEL emits encoded optical signals, which are then collimated and redirected by a series of optical devices, and finally detected by the photodetector.

While channel-guided optical interconnects with DWDM are shown to be more energy-efficient than electrical interconnects, it has significant energy wastes that offset the energy-efficiency of optical interconnects. First, the external laser source needs to continuously produce lights used for modulation. To make things worse, existing optical NoCs typically have a large number of long waveguides due to the lack of optical buffering. This requires the external laser source to provide high laser power on the order of tens of watts. Second, to achieve high bandwidth thousands of micro-rings are used as modulators and detectors. Thermal trimming is needed to ensure all the micro-rings to work with the right resonance frequencies. Besides technical difficulties, the total power needed for trimming is so high to be comparable with the laser source power. Analysis shows that the laser source power and the trimming power accounts for 75% of total power in channel-guided optical networks [20]. Note that the above two power components are static powers and pure overheads.

1.2.2 Free-Space Optical Interconnects

Most recently, free-space optical interconnects (FSOI) gains interests as it overcomes the inefficiencies of channel-guided optical interconnects. Figure 2 shows a conceptual view of FSOI. Compared with channel-guided interconnects, the major differences include:

• **Laser source and modulation:** Light is emitted from on-chip integrated vertical-cavity surface-emitting lasers (VCSELs) [21, 22, 23, 24]. By switching on and off the VCSEL, active modulation is achieved with the laser source.

• **Light propagation:** Modulated lightwave propagates in the free-space in the package. In order to direct lightwave onto intended photodetectors, optical elements are inserted to achieve multiple functionalities of collimation, diffraction, and collection of light signal. We will discuss more about how to control the light's direction below and in the following section.

• **Detection:** Instead of using micro-rings to couple light out of waveguides for detection, photo diodes are employed. Light beams are projected onto corresponding photo diodes under the control of optical elements.

From the above discussion, we can see that free-space optical interconnects eliminate the needs of external laser source and micro-rings, which are the sources of significant energy wastes. In addition, optical signals propagating in the free space experience no coupling and lower attenuation, which further improves the efficiency of optical links.

However, new challenges are also introduced: directing the emitted laser beam to the intended photodetector. As exist-

Figure 1: Channel-guided optical interconnects: a continuous laser beam is provided by the external laser source, propagated in on-chip waveguides, and modulated and detected by micro-rings.

same pace as devices. In addition, the increase of metal levels has almost stopped, and it is projected that from now to the 11nm node by 2022, only 4 more metal levels will be added (from 11 to 15 levels) [9]. Furthermore, the power spent by on-chip interconnects starts to dominate the overall chip power [10, 11]. The express cube topologies will suffer even more from above issues as the wiring intensity of these topologies increases with the network size ($O(N)$ for flattened butterfly [5] and $O(\sqrt{N})$ for MECS [6, 7], where N is the number of nodes in the network). This sets researchers on the quest of more scalable and power-efficient alternatives for on-chip interconnects.

1.2 Optical NoCs

Recent developments in nanophotonics have motivated researchers to design NoCs based on optical interconnects, which is intrinsically faster and less power consuming than electrical interconnects. The proposed optical NoCs [12, 13, 14, 15, 16, 17, 18] are mostly based on *channel-guided optical interconnects*, where optical signals are confined and propagated in on-chip waveguides.

1.2.1 Channel-Guided Optical Interconnects

Figure 1 provides a conceptual view of channel-guided optical interconnects and illustrates the necessary components. On-chip waveguides (fabricated with poly-Si, crystalline Si [14, 15], or polymer [19]) serve as the physical channel carrying optical signals. A continuous laser beam is provided by an external laser source and modulated into on-off digital signals. The modulated light continues to travel downstream, possibly duplicated by a splitter, and finally detected and removed from the waveguides. Modulation and detection are both performed by micro-rings placed beside the waveguides, which can be electrically tuned into and out of resonance with a certain wavelength. In the resonant state, the coupling between the micro-rings and the waveguides becomes so strong that the light is dropped by the micro-rings. Therefore, electrically tuning the micro-rings achieves on-off modulation, and dropping the optical signals to a photodetector completes detection. To further increase the bandwidth, dense-wavelength-division-multiplexing (DWDM) is used to enable the waveguide to carry multiple wavelengths simultaneously. The micro-ring can selectively modulate or drop a given wavelength by adjusting its resonance frequency.

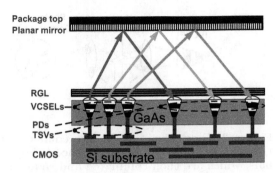

Figure 3: The optical system with 3D stacked RGL, optical substrate, and CMOS substrate.

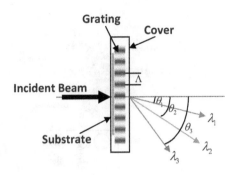

Figure 4: The volume phase holographic grating VPHG used as RGL.

ing VCSELs and photo diodes are all surface devices, they cannot be freely aimed at each other. Therefore, optical elements are placed in the optical path to control the direction of beam propagation. Xue *et al.* [25] propose to use angled micro-mirrors in the package to re-direct the beams. However, this method suffers from technological difficulties and complexities. Fabricating micro-mirrors requires unconventional processes that are incompatible with planar CMOS processes. To make things worse, aligning the micro-mirrors requires precise control of 5 free variables in the 3D space (x, y, z, inclination angle θ, and azimuth angle ϕ), whose feasibility remains a question. In addition, Xue *et al.* propose an all-to-all network where a laser beam will be reflected by multiple mirrors before reaching the destination. Planning the optical paths for all links in the complex all-to-all network is an intimidating task and adds more difficulties to alignment. Last but not the least, this also introduces problems to designing network architectures, which will be detailed in Section 3.

In contrast to previous approaches, we propose to achieve beam redirection with a single **Refractive Grating Layer** (RGL). A RGL is a planar thin-film diffractive optical element. One interesting feature of RGL is that the refractive angle (the extent to which the light direction is changed) depends on the wavelength of the incident light. That is, controlling the optical path is as simple as selecting the wavelength.

Figure 3 provides the high level view of our optical system. We leverage 3D integration to stack the optical substrate (GaAs) on CMOS substrate (Si). On the surface of the optical substrate, a planar RGL is in turn stacked. Laser beams generated by VCSELs are vertically incident onto the RGL, by which the laser beam get collimated and skewed. A planar mirror is deposited on the ceiling of the package, which bounces the beams back towards the corresponding photodetectors on the optical substrate. The advantages of this approach are: *(a)* the optical elements for beam redirection (planar mirror and RGL) can be fabricated with mature processes and *(b)* we only need to control 3 free variables (wavelength λ and 2D locations of VCSELs and detectors) to ensure that the laser beams are projected onto intended detectors. The relative positions of VCSELs and detectors can be precisely defined when fabricating the optical substrate; wavelengths λ is well controlled in contemporary multi-wavelength VCSELs [21, 22, 23, 24]. With the absence of alignment issues, the proposed optical system is more feasible to realize. Detailed analysis of the system is provided in Section 2.

Free Flattened Butterfly (F^{2}BFLY): We leverage the above proposed free-space optical interconnects to design an optical NoC called free flattened butterfly. Based on the special features of underlying interconnect technology, F^{2}BFLY features high-radix routers, rich connectivity, and low network diameter by fully exploiting the low latency and low power benefits of free-space optical interconnects. As we will show by experiment results, F^{2}BFLY outperforms electrical NoCs with both conventional mesh topology and high-radix express cube topologies. In addition, it is also more energy-efficient than state-of-the-art channel-guided optical NoCs. In designing the NoC architecture, we also propose optimizations to reduce the complexities of high-radix routers, resulting in a simple and low cost router suitable for on-chip implementation.

In the rest of the paper, we first provide in-depth description of the proposed free-space optical interconnects based on wavelength-switching (Section 2). We then present our architectural design in Section 3. To perform a comprehensive evaluation, we also investigate state-of-the-art electrical and optical NoCs together with our proposal, and introduce the simulation environment in Section 4. The simulation results are presented and discussed in Section 5. Finally, related work is reviewed and conclusion is drawn in Section 6 and 7.

2. DESIGNING FREE-SPACE OPTICAL INTERCONNECTS

In this section, we provide specific design considerations for the free-space optical interconnects illustrated in Figure 3, with a focus on enabling wavelength-switching with a high efficiency RGL:

• **RGL Design:** RGL is a thin-film component with periodic phase structure, which diffracts different wavelengths of light from a common input direction into different angular output directions (Figure 4). In this paper, we use the volume phase holographic grating (VPHG) as RGL due to its advantages in diffraction efficiency and system packaging [26, 27]. Figure 4 shows the structure of a VPHG. The core of a VPHG is a transmissive material whose refractive index is a periodic function of location, with a period of Λ. When a light beam passes through this structure, it is diffracted (or redirected) and the angle of the output beam θ depends on the wavelength λ and period Λ, as given by $\sin(\theta) = \lambda/\Lambda$. For example, in Figure 4 the incident light beam contains 3 different wavelengths which are redirected to different directions. In addition, the core of a VPHG is

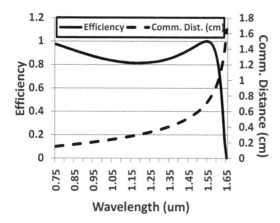

Figure 5: Diffraction efficiency (solid line) and communication distance (dash line) with respect to wavelength.

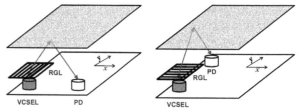

(a) Laser beam directed to the x-dimension

(b) Laser beam directed to the y-dimension

Figure 6: The two RGL patterns directing laser beams to two orthogonal directions.

Table 1: Optical System Design

Package Height	1.5mm
Communication Distances	
Max.	12mm
Min.	1.5mm
RGL	
Wavelength	.75–1.6um
Grating density	660 lines/mm
Grating efficiency	$\geq 75\%$
VCSEL [25]	
Frequency	40GHz
Power	6.3mW
Area	$20 \times 20\text{um}^2$
Photodetector [25]	
Frequency	40GHz
Power	4.2mW
Area	$20 \times 20\text{um}^2$

laminated by plates of glass or fused silica, which increase its durability for handling and system packaging.

The diffraction efficiency of the VPHG is high, reported to be better than 80% or even close to 100% [26, 27]. Based on the two-wave coupling theory, the diffraction efficiency depends on the grating thickness, the grating period, and the wavelength. Targeting at optical interconnect lengths in the range of 1.5mm to 12mm, we set the grating period to 1600nm (660 l/mm) and can achieve an efficiency greater than 75%. The diffraction efficiency and communication distance with respect to wavelength is plotted in Figure 5.

The index pattern of VPHG is generated by laser exposure, in a similar way to patterning silicon substrate. However, a single exposure run can only define one type of pattern, ruling out the possibility of defining arbitrary patterns on a single VPHG. Therefore in this work we only assume two types of patterns on the VPHG used: an x-pattern enabling x-dimension links and a y-pattern enabling y-dimension links (Figure 6). This restriction presents both challenges and opportunities for designing an free-space optical network, as we will discuss in detail in Section 3.

• **VCSELs and Photodetectors:** Contemporary integrated VCSELs feature small footprints on the order of tens of microns, high modulation speeds up to 40Gbps [28], and the ability to produce a single-wavelength laser beam from a wide range of wavelengths [21, 22, 23, 24]. The resonant cavity photodiodes incorporates the resonant cavity similar to VCSELs to amplify the received signal, and offers high sensitivity and bandwidth [29]. For the free-space optical links in this paper, we assume the high-speed VSCEL and photodetector design in [25]. The key parameters of the overall optical system is listed in Table 1.

3. FREE FLATTENED BUTTERFLY NOC

Leveraging the FSOI based on wavelength-switching in the previous section, we design F²BFLY with realistic hardware implementation in mind and its architecture is detailed in this section.

3.1 Topology

While an all-to-all network seems attractive to efficiently use optical interconnects, practical issues mentioned in the previous section prevent implementing FSOI links with arbitration directions. In addition, the hardware complexity per node of an all-to-all network grows in the order of $O(N)$, which will become difficult to accommodate on-chip when the network scale goes up.

Instead, we propose a topology that both exploits optical efficiency and has good scalability. First, the FSOI links in our system can have only two possible directions, chosen from the cardinal directions (x and y directions). This eliminates the complexities associated with building links with arbitrary directions. In addition, coupled with a dimensionally decomposed router architecture (see Section 3.2), RGL fabrication and alignment difficulties are further reduced.

Using only the two cardinal directions, a node in the network can reach any node in the same row or column with wavelength-switching as discussed in the previous section.

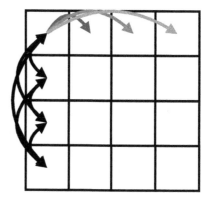

Figure 7: 1-d FSOI links and crossbar formed by wavelength-switching.

Figure 7 shows an example of a 16-node network, where 3 FSOI links using 3 different wavelengths from the node at the upper-left corner to all other nodes in the first row are shown. With FSOI links connecting any pair of nodes in the same dimension, a 1-dimensional crossbar is formed by the FSOI links for each row/column. For example, Figure 7 shows a 1-dimensional crossbar formed in the first column. Overall, the resulted network topology is equivalent to a 2-level flattened butterfly (FBFLY) [5], where the crossbars along the rows form the first level and those along the columns form the second level. With this topology, packets sent between nodes in the same row or column can reach the destination in one hop. For a packet sent to a node in both a different row and a different column, it is first routed in the first level (row dimension) and then in the second level (column dimension) to reach the destination. Therefore, any packet can reach the destination in at most 2 hops (the network diameter is 2 hops). Compared to all-to-all optical networks F^{2}BFLY introduces only one more hop and one more pair of O/E and E/O conversions, while both the implementation difficulty and hardware complexity per node (now $O(\sqrt{N})$) become significantly lower. In addition, it enables an efficient router architecture suitable for on-chip implementation, which will be detailed in the following subsection.

3.2 Router Architecture

Unlike 2D mesh whose routers have a constant number of output ports, F^{2}BFLY requires the output port counts of routers to increase in the order of $O(\sqrt{N})$. For example, a 16-node and a 64-node F^{2}BFLY requires routers with 7 and 15 output ports, respectively, including the ejection ports. Simply adopting the generic wormhole-switching router architecture [2] for such high-radix routers is inefficient, since the the hardware complexity of generic wormhole-switching routers grows quadratically with the radix. To design an efficient, high-radix router architecture for F^{2}BFLY, we propose to use *dimension-decomposition* to reduce the router complexity. In addition, we use only one virtual channel per input port and source routing to further simplify the router pipeline.

• **Dimension-Decomposition:** The idea of dimension-decomposition is to divide the router into a row module and a column module [30, 31], as shown in Figure 8a. As a result, the original 5×5 crossbar of the router is decomposed into 2 2×2 crossbars inside the row and column modules respectively. The incoming flits are guided to the row/column modules in order to traverse in the row/column dimension. Since the complexity of the crossbar grows quadratically with its port counts, the decomposed crossbars have lower hardware cost and power consumption than the original crossbar. Using the same approach, we can reduce the crossbar complexity of routers in F^{2}BFLY. For example, the 7×7 crossbar for a 16-node F^{2}BFLY can be decomposed into 2 4×4 crossbars whose overall complexity is lower.

There are further opportunities for optimization if we assume XY-routing is used. First, note that with XY-routing a flit can only turn from the row dimension to the column dimension but not reversely. Second, since in F^{2}BFLY a flit only takes at most 1 hop in each dimension, an incoming flit that is currently traversing in the row/column dimension will *not* continue to traverse in the same dimension. That is, an incoming flit using the row dimension will either turn

to the column dimension or go to the ejection port; an incoming flit using the column dimension will definitely go to the ejection port (it cannot turn to the row dimension with XY-routing). Based on these observations, the complexities of switching fabrics in each dimension module can be further reduced.

The resulted overall router architecture for 16-node F^{2}BFLY is shown in Figure 8b. For clarity, input buffers are omitted in the figure. The router is decomposed into a row and a column module. Each module has a transceiver block (Tx-Rx Block in the figure) and switching fabrics (crossbar or multiplexers). The transceiver block consists of VCSEL and photodetector arrays, which forms the input and output FSOI links for the corresponding dimension. For a 16-node F^{2}BFLY, each transceiver block has 3 input ports and 3 output ports. The switching fabric directs an incoming flit to one of the output ports of the transceiver block or to the ejection port. The switching fabric of the column module is a 4×4 crossbar, whose inputs are the injection port and the 3 input ports from the transceiver block in the row module, and whose outputs are the ejection port and the 3 output ports to the transceiver block in the column module. The switching fabric of the row module contains only one 3-to-1 multiplexer and one 1-to-3 de-multiplexer. The inputs to the multiplexer are the input ports from the transceiver block in the column module and the output is the the ejection port. The de-multiplexer, on the other hand, takes the injection port as the input and the outport ports to the transceiver block in the row module as the outputs. Since a flit can only turn from the row module to the column module and cannot continue traversing a same dimension, the optimized router architecture can maintain the connectivity of F^{2}BFLY while using low-complexity switching fabrics instead of a 7×7 crossbar.

• **Router Pipeline and Source Routing:** As network deadlock is already avoided with XY-routing, our F^{2}BFLY router uses only 1 virtual channel which removes virtual channel allocation (VA) stage from the pipeline. In addition, the fact that the network diameter is 2 hops motivates us to use source routing to eliminate the route computation (RC) stage. In source routing, the source of the packet computes the output port to use at each hop during the injection process and encodes this information in the packet header. In F^{2}BFLY, the packet header only needs to record 2 output ports along the path, which introduces very low overhead. For example, the first half of Figure 9 compares the routing information contained in the header for per hop routing and source routing respectively, in a 16-node F^{2}BFLY. For source routing, the first bit (the FD bit) of routing information indicates whether to traverse the row dimension or the column dimension first. The two pairs of bits of the following 4 bits (OP bits) record the output ports to use when traversing the row dimension and the column dimension respectively. If the FD bit indicates that the first dimension to traverse is column dimension, the output port information for the row dimension is ignored. As we can see, the source routing information is only 1 bit longer than the per hop routing information, adding negligible overheads to the header. Finally, the second half of Figure 9 shows the resulted router pipeline where only the switch arbitration (SA) and switch traversal (ST) stages are left.

• **Flow Control:** We use credit-based flow control with F^{2}BFLY to ensure no packet is dropped when being trans-

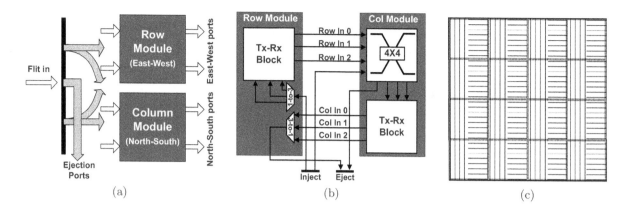

(a)   (b)   (c)

Figure 8: Free flattened butterfly: (a) concept of dimension-decomposition; (b) router architecture; (c) RGL pattern.

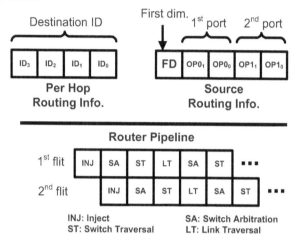

Figure 9: Up: routing information comparison for per hop routing and source routing. Down: router pipeline stages

ferred in the network. Each link employs one additional VCSEL-photodetector pair to transfer credits.

• **RGL Design:** With dimensionally-decomposed router architecture, designing the RGL pattern and align it with optical elements becomes even easier. Figure 8c illustrates one possible configuration. The RGL only needs to incorporate two types of patterns, each for one of the dimension module. Alignment is achieved as long as the patterns covers the corresponding dimension modules. Therefore, there is no need for complex RGL patterns and large alignment errors can be tolerated.

3.3 Comparison to Prior Approaches

All-to-all topologies gain favor in prior researches of optical networks, since these approaches seems to better leverage the efficiency of optical communication. In Corona NoC [15, 17], an optical crossbar is formed using multiple optical token rings to interconnect all nodes in the network. Collisions on the rings are avoided by using optical tokens to grant accesses to the rings. In Xue *et al.*'s work [25], every node in the network has FSOI links to all other nodes, and collectively these FSOI links form an optical crossbar. However, all-to-all networks scale poorly. Both Corona and Xue *et al.*'s work require a daunting number of optical devices.

In Corona the large number of waveguides and micro-rings also introduces great static power consumed by the external laser source and ring trimming. In Xue *et al.*'s work, accurately controlling all FSOI links becomes an intimidating design and implementation issue. Moreover, as the bandwidth density holds constant, the large number of FSOI links also reduces the bandwidth per link and increases serialization latency.

In addition to the difficulties with the optical technology, all-to-all topologies also complicates the router design at each node. For Corona, each router has at least a wide de-multiplexer to direct flits to queues on corresponding rings, and a complex arbiter to nominate a fix number of queues for optical arbitration and transmission [17]. For Xue *et al.*'s work [25], collision is handled by the exponential back-off algorithm with an initial window size of 3 and a fractional base of 1.1. It is not clear from their work how such a back-off algorithm can be implemented efficiently in the hardware. Adding to the difficulties, each of the $O(N^2)$ FSOI links needs to run a back-off algorithm independently. However, the costs of implementing the back-off algorithm is not considered in their paper.

In contrast, F^{2}BFLY trades some of the optical efficiency for better scalability, lower power consumption, and easy hardware implementation. Compared with Corona [15, 17], F^{2}BFLY has at most one more hop (3 network cycles) and one more pair of O/E and E/O conversion, but much lower static power consumption. Compared with Xue *et al.*'s work [25], it has fewer FSOI links and higher link bandwidth, and is more feasible to implement. In either case, the router of F^{2}BFLY has lower complexity and is more suitable for on-chip implementation.

4. EXPERIMENT SETUP

4.1 Methodology

We perform a comparative evaluation of F^{2}BFLY and other state-of-the-art electrical and optical networks using a cycle-accurate NoC simulator [32]. Besides synthetic traffic patterns, we also run trace-driven simulations of parallel benchmarks by interfacing the NoC simulator with an x86 CMP simulator [33]. We use ORION 2.0 [34] to estimate the power consumption of electrical routers. In addition, we use reported data in [14, 17, 18] to estimate the power for the external laser, ring modulation, and ring trimming. Finally, the power expended by VCSELs and photodetectors is estimated from the analysis presented in section 2. The network architectures evaluated are detailed in the following subsection.

4.2 Network Configuration

Table 2 lists configurations of the network architectures evaluated, including three electrical networks: mesh, flattened butterfly (FBFLY) [5], and multidrop express channels (MECS) [7]; and two optical networks: Corona and F^{2}BFLY. For each architecture, two network sizes (16-node and 64-node) are used in the evaluation.

Both FBFLY and MECS belong to the express cube family, which features high-radix routers and high wiring complexity. FBFLY is designed to leverage the rich on-chip wires and have a network diameter of 2 hops. From the topology perspective, FBFLY is exactly the same as our proposed F^{2}BFLY. However, FBFLY uses electrical links and suffers from the limited bandwidth density and power efficiency of electrical interconnects [7]. In contrast, F^{2}BFLY is built with FSOI links which provides much higher bandwidth with lower power consumption. In addition, in the original FBFLY work, the authors simply adapts a generic wormhole switching router as the high-radix router, which incurs high hardware and power overheads. In this paper, we adopt a dimension-decomposed router architecture which together with other optimizations significantly reduces hardware complexity and power consumption (see Section 3). The MECS architecture is proposed to overcome the high interconnect intensity of FBFLY. MECS has lower router radix but also more restricted connectivity, which makes it a compromise between complexity and connectivity. Corona is a channel-guided optical network. As we have discussed in Section 3.3, Corona is based on an optical crossbar formed by multiple optical token rings and has high implementation complexities and power consumption.

• **Concentration:** According to prior studies [35, 7], concentrated on-chip network provides better power-performance efficiency. In this work, we use 4-way concentration for all networks evaluated. The second and the third rows of Table 2 show the network sizes in terms of number of nodes and number of PEs. In addition, there are two kinds of concentration: *external* concentration first merges traffics of the 4 PEs and sends using a single port of the router; *internal* concentration adds more inject/eject ports to the router and directly connects the PEs to the additional ports. In general, internal concentration provides better performance but has higher hardware and power overheads. In our evaluation, we exam both internal concentration and external concentration for the electrical NoCs[1].

• **Link Bandwidth:** To perform a fair comparison, we use the iso-bandwidth analysis as that used by Grot *et al.* [7]: we keep the bi-section bandwidth constant (4,608-bit and 18,432-bit for the 16-node and the 64-node networks respectively), and calculate the link bandwidth for each of the three electrical networks. As we can see from the sixth row (link width) of Table 2, mesh has highest link bandwidth due to its lowest wiring complexity, while FBFLY has the lowest link bandwidth due to its highest wiring complexity.

---

[1]From our experiment results, power and performance of the two optical networks are both insensitive to concentration types.

Table 3: Configurations for the CMP

Frequency	5GHz
Processor Core	
Issue/Commit width	2
ROB size	128
L1 Cache	
Size	32KB per core
Associativity	4
Block size	64-byte
L2 Cache	
Size	1MB bank
Associativity	16
Block size	64-byte
Memory	
Size	4GB
Latency	260 cycles
Controllers	4 MCs on the corners

The results of MECS show a compromise between complexity and link bandwidth.

For Corona, we assume each waveguide carries 72 wavelengths and 4 waveguides forms a physical channel, leading to a 288-bit link. For F^{2}BFLY, by conservatively assuming that VCSELs and photodetectors have a pitch of 50um and the node area is 1.5mm×1.5mm, each FSOI link is 72-bit and 36-bit for the 16- and 64-node networks respectively. The frequencies of optical links are 10GHz and 40GHz for Corona and F^{2}BFLY respectively, conforming to the settings in [17] and [25].

• **Virtual Channels:** Only the mesh network employs multiple virtual channels, with each channel has a depth of 8-flit. For FBFLY and MECS, the depth of the input buffer is designed to account for the worst-case round-trip credit return latency. For Corona, the depth of the ejection queue is designed to cover the round-trip latency of optical tokens. Finally, since the FSOI link has a single cycle latency, the buffer size is fixed for both network sizes, also according to the credit return latency.

4.3 CMP Configuration

The CMP consists of 64 (256) PEs for networks with 16 (64) nodes. Each PE consists of an x86-like core, a private L1 cache and a shared L2 cache bank, and is connected to the corresponding router through a network interface. The whole CMP system including routers runs at 5GHz. Table 3 lists the detailed configuration for the CMP.

5. EXPERIMENT RESULTS

5.1 Results for Synthetic Traffics

We first study different networks with synthetic traffics. For each synthetic traffic, packets with a size of 576-bit (equivalent to a cache line transfer) are generated with the specified injection rates. The measurements are taken after the network reaches a steady state.

• **Performance:** Figure 10 shows the average packet latency against the injection rate for different networks. Let us first look at the results for the 16-node network. We notice that when the injection rate is low, FBFLY and MECS have comparable or slightly lower packet latencies than mesh. However, the packet latencies of both topologies rise rapidly when the inject rate increases, and the saturate throughputs are much lower than mesh. This is because, while the two high-radix networks have lower network diameter,

Table 2: Configurations of Different Network Architectures. The "-I" versions of networks refer to the cases with internal concentration.

		Mesh (-I)		FBFLY (-I)		MECS (-I)		Corona		F²BFLY	
Network	Number of nodes	16	64	16	64	16	64	16	64	16	64
	Number of PEs	64	256	64	256	64	256	64	256	64	256
	Concentration degree	4	4	4	4	4	4	4	4	4	4
	Network diameter	6	14	2	2	2	2	1	1	2	2
	Link width	576	576	144	72	288	288	288	288	72	36
Router	Input ports	5 (8)	5 (8)	7 (10)	15 (18)	7 (10)	15 (18)	1	1	7	15
	Output ports	5 (8)	5 (8)	7 (10)	15 (18)	3 (6)	3 (6)	15	63	7	15
	Switching fabrics	5×5 (8×8)	5×5 (8×8)	7×7 (10×10)	15×15 (18×18)	7×3 (10×6)	15×3 (18×6)	1-to-15	1-to-63	4×4 & 1-to-3 & 3-to-1	8×8 & 1-to-7 & 7-to-1
	VC per port	5	5	1	1	1	1	1	1	1	1
	VC depth	8	8	10	15	10	15	8	16	8	8

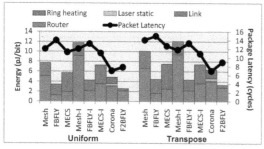

(a) 16-node network

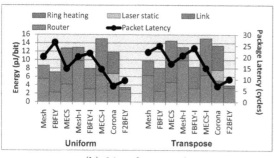

(b) 64-node network

Figure 11: Energy consumption for uniform and transpose traffics, when the injection rate is 0.05 packets/cycle/node.

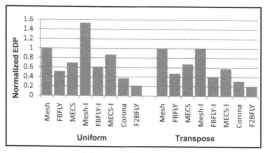

(a) 16-node network

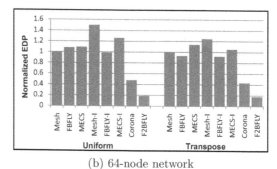

(b) 64-node network

Figure 12: Energy-delay products calculated from results in Figure 11.

the lower link bandwidth of them results in a longer serialization latency, which will cause the network to saturate early. On the other hand, both optical networks have consistently lower packet latencies than all the electrical networks, thanks to the significantly higher bandwidth of the optical links. It is worth noting that due to the higher hop counts, F²BFLY has slightly higher packet latencies than Corona. However, both networks have roughly the same saturation throughputs. Moreover, we also see that internal concentration improves the performances for the electrical networks for uniform and transpose traffics, due to the increased injection and ejection bandwidth. The performances for the hotspot traffic see almost no improvement, because in the hotspot traffic the performance is restricted by the single destination instead of the injection/ejection ports.

In the 64-node network, the packet latencies of MECS at low loads are even lower than mesh, due to the increased network scale. In contrast, the performance of FBFLY becomes worse, exhibiting largest packet latencies among all networks for all loads. The primary cause for this phenomenon is the

halved link bandwidth for FBFLY when the network size increases from 16-node to 64-node. This implies that FBFLY has inferior scalability than other networks. In the 64-node network, the two optical architectures continue to perform better than electrical networks. However, we notice that F²BFLY now has significantly lower saturation throughput than Corona. This is because we conservatively halved the link bandwidth of F2BFLY for the 64-node network, but optimistically keep the link bandwidth for Corona. Finally, internal concentration continue to improve the performances for electrical networks for uniform and transpose traffics. The results with internal concentration for the hotspot traffic are not shown, since internal concentration does not improve the performance in this case.

•**Power:** We set the injection rate to 0.05 packets/cycle/node and measure the energy consumption for the uniform and the transpose traffics. Figure 11 shows the results for all architectures for both 16- and 64-node networks. The black curve in each plot shows the average packet latencies. For the 16-node network, the F²BFLY has the lowest energy consumption. While Corona has slightly lower packet

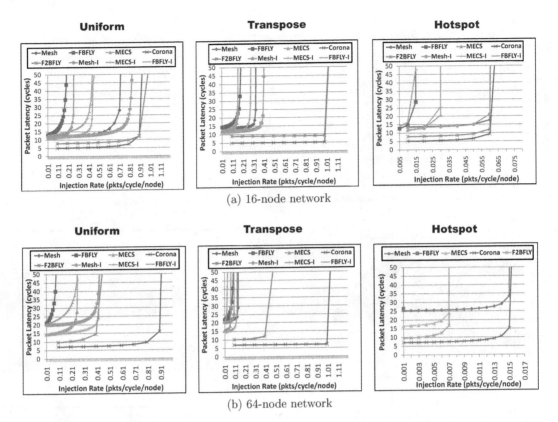

Figure 10: Performance results for synthetic traffics. The "-I" versions of networks refer to the cases with internal concentration. For the 64-node network, the results with internal concentration for the hotspot traffic are not shown, since we already show with the 64-node network it does not improve performance for the hotspot traffic.

latency than F²BFLY, it has significantly higher energy consumption due to the more complex router architecture and the static power consumed by the external laser source and ring trimming. For the 64-node network, we see a rapid increase of power spent by the laser source and ring trimming: the static energy accounts for more than 60% of total energy consumption of Corona, largely offsetting the power efficiency. This result implies that when the network size goes up, the static energy waste impedes the energy efficiency of Corona. Finally, we also notice that internal concentration results in slightly lower packet latency but also higher energy consumption.

For a more comprehensive comparison, we calculate the energy-delay products (EDP) from results in Figure 11 and plot them in Figure 12. As we can see, in the 16-node network, the two optical networks have the lowest EDP. In addition, the EDP of F²BFLY is 41% lower than that of Corona. In the 64-node network, while the optical networks continue to have the lowest EDP, Corona's EDP increases significantly due to the large static power consumption. In this case, F²BFLY's EDP is 80% lower than Corona's EDP. In addition, we see that the EDP results with and without internal concentration are roughly the same, because internal concentration slightly decreases the packet latency, but increases the power consumption.

5.2 Results for Applications

We further evaluate networks by simulating a CMP running different applications. To make the simulation time tractable, we only simulate a 16-node network with 64 pro-

cessing elements. Furthermore, for the electrical networks we only evaluate internal concentration since our studies above show that internal concentration results in slightly better performance and roughly the same EDP. The network and CMP configurations are detailed in Table 2 and 3. We collect traces from a diverse set of 33 benchmarks including SPEC CPU2006 benchmarks, applications from SPLASH-2 and SPEC OMP benchmark suites, and four commercial workloads (`sap`, `sjas`, `sjbb`, `tpcw`). In addition, we choose representative execution phases using [36] for all the workloads.

Figure 13 shows the results for network performance and power when running the applications. Due to space limit, we only show results for 10 representative applications out of the 33 benchmarks. The last set of bars in each figure show the average results for all 33 benchmarks. From the results, we first notice that the two optical networks have the lowest packet latencies and power consumptions across all benchmarks. Second, the high-radix electrical networks (FBFLY and MECS) have slightly lower latencies than mesh for some benchmarks (`gcc`, `astar`), but in general higher latencies than mesh for most benchmarks. A closer look at the benchmarks reveals that `gcc` and `astar` have quite low injection rates (less than 0.02 flits/cycle/node), however on average the injection rates of all benchmarks are high (around 0.1 flits/cycle/node) partly because of the 4-way concentration used.

Figure 13b shows the normalized energy-delay products. We notice that the EDPs for the high-radix electrical networks (FBFLY and MECS) are lower than mesh for some

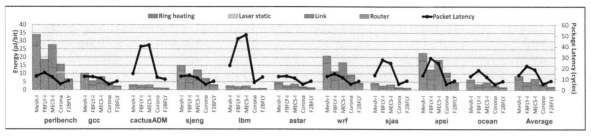

(a) Packet latency and energy consumption

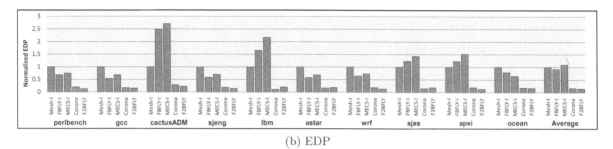

(b) EDP

Figure 13: Network performance and energy results for applications.

benchmarks, but higher for others. On average, the EDP for FBFLY is 10% lower and the EDP for MECS is 10% higher compared with mesh. Our proposed F^{2}BFLY is shown to have the lowest EDP, which is 15% better than Corona. While the saving in EDP is not as significant as with the synthetic traffics shown above, we believe the energy advantage of F^{2}BFLY will increase as the network size scales up as predicted by the synthetic traffic results.

6. RELATED WORK

Network-on-chip (NoC) has gained interests from researchers due to the high on-chip communication demands of contemporary and future many-core architectures. Conventional research efforts are focused on router architectures with lower router latencies [2, 3, 4] and efficient topologies [5, 6, 7, 8]. The seminal work by Peh et al. [2] establishes a low latency wormhole switching router architecture that is widely adopted by other researchers. Both Kim et al. [5] and Grot et al. [7] propose to use high-radix networks to better exploit the on-chip wiring resources. Dimension-decomposition is proposed by Kim et al. [30] to further simplify router architectures. Our proposed router architecture for F^{2}BFLY inherits the basic organization of the wormhole switching router proposed by Peh et al.'s. In addition, we apply dimension-decomposition to reduce the hardware complexity of the high-radix router, which results in lower hardware and power overhead than the high-radix routers used in prior work [5, 7]. While in terms of topology F^{2}BFLY is the same as FBFLY [5], we use both FSOI interconnects and an optimized router architecture to tackle the wiring and the hardware complexities.

To overcome the intrinsic inefficiency of electrical interconnects, researchers have explored optical NoCs based on emerging on-chip photonic technologies. Prior work [12, 13, 14, 15, 16, 17, 18] mostly uses channel-guided optical interconnects, which suffers from significant static power consumption and poor scalability. Most recently, Xue et al. [25] present an optical network based on FSOI links. However, in their approach micro-mirrors are used to guide laser beams

and an all-to-all architecture is proposed using large amount of optical elements. The resulted system is not amenable for on-chip implementation and has low scalability. In contrast, our proposed F^{2}BFLY is based on FSOI technologies with mature fabrication processes. In addition, in designing the network architecture, we trade slight performance reduction for lower hardware complexity and power consumption, resulting in an efficient optical network using FSOI links.

7. CONCLUSION

In this work, we present F^{2}BFLY network-on-chip which is based on novel FSOI technologies. Compared to state-of-the-art optical NoCs, it has lower hardware complexity and power consumption, and also better scalability. We evaluate F^{2}BFLY together with recently developed electrical and optical NoCs, and our results show that F^{2}BFLY has lowest power consumption and energy-delay products for both synthetic traffics and benchmarks. In addition, when the network scale grows up energy efficiency of F^{2}BFLY is even better than Corona, a representative channel-guided optical network. These results from comparative evaluation show that F^{2}BFLY is a potential solution for future efficient on-chip interconnection substrates.

8. REFERENCES

[1] J. Y. Duato, S. Yalamanchili, and L. Ni. *Interconnection Networks: An Engineering Approach.* Morgan Kaufman, 2003.

[2] L. Peh and W. J. Dally. A delay model and speculative architecture for pipelined routers. In *Proc. of the 7th Intl. Symp. on High Performance Computer Architecture*, page 255, 2001.

[3] L. Peh and W. J. Dally. Flit-reservation flow control. *IEEE Trans. on Parallel and Distributed Systems*, 3(3):194–205, 2000.

[4] M. Ahn and E.J. Kim. Pseudo-circuit: accelerating communication for on-chip interconnection networks. In *Proc. of the 43th Intl. Symp. on Microarchitecture*, pages 399–408, 2010.

[5] J. Kim, J. Balfour, and W. Dally. Flattened butterfly topology for on-chip networks. In *Proc. of the 40th Intl. Symp. on Microarchitecture*, pages 172–182, 2007.

[6] B. Grot and S.W. Keckler. Scalable on-chip interconnect topologies. In *Workshop on Chip Multiprocessors Memory Systems and Interconnects*, 2008.

[7] B. Grot et al. Express cube topologies for on-chip interconnects. In *Proc. of the 15th Intl. Symp. on High Performance Computer Architecture*, pages 163 –174, 2009.

[8] A. Kumar et al. Express virtual channels: towards the ideal interconnection fabric. In *Proc. of Intl. Symp. on Computer Architecture*, pages 150–161, 2007.

[9] 2007 International technology roadmap for semiconductors, at http://www.itrs.net

[10] L. Cheng et al. Interconnect-aware coherence protocols for chip multiprocessors. *Prof. of the 33rd Intl. Symp. on Computer Architecture*, 34(2):339–351, 2006.

[11] N. Magen et al. Interconnect-power dissipation in a microprocessor. In *Proc. of SLIP '04*, pages 7–13, 2004.

[12] N. Kirman et al. Leveraging optical technology in future bus-based chip multiprocessors. In *Proc. of the 39th Intl. Symp. on Microarchitecture*, pages 492–503, 2006.

[13] A. Shacham, K. Bergman, and L. P. Carloni. On the design of a photonic network-on-chip. In *Proc. of the First Intl. Symp. on Networks-on-Chip*, pages 53–64, 2007.

[14] C. Batten et al. Building manycore processor-to-dram networks with monolithic silicon photonics. In *Proc. of the 16th IEEE Symp. on High Performance Interconnects*, pages 21–30, 2008.

[15] D. Vantrease et al. Corona: System implications of emerging nanophotonic technology. In *Proc. of the 35th Intl. Symp. on Computer Architecture*, volume 36, pages 153–164. ACM, 2008.

[16] Y. Pan et al. Firefly: illuminating future network-on-chip with nanophotonics. 37(3):429–440, 2009.

[17] D. Vantrease et al. Light speed arbitration and flow control for nanophotonic interconnects. In *Proc. of the 42nd Intl. Symp. on Microarchitecture*, pages 304–315, 2009.

[18] X. Zhang and A. Louri. A multilayer nanophotonic interconnection network for on-chip many-core communications. In *Proc. of Design Automation Conference*, pages 657–660, 2010.

[19] M. Haurylau et al. On-chip optical interconnect roadmap: Challenges and critical directions. *IEEE Journal of Selected Topics in Quantum Electronics*, 12(6):1699 –1705, 2006.

[20] Y. Pan, J. Kim, and G. Memik. Flexishare: Channel sharing for an energy-efficient nanophotonic crossbar. In *Proc. of the 16th Intl. Symp. on High Performance Computer Architecture*, pages 1–12, 2010.

[21] A. Imamura, V. Karagodsky, B. Pesala, F. Koyama, and C.J. Chang-Hasnain. Multi-wavelength VCSEL array based on high contrast sub-wavelength grating.

[22] F. Koyama and M. Arai. Long-wavelength GaInAs/GaAs VCSELs and multiwavelength arrays. In *Photonics: Design, Technology, and Packaging*, volume 5277, pages 146–154, 2004.

[23] V. Karagodsky et al. Monolithically integrated multi-wavelength VCSEL arrays using high-contrast gratings. *Opt. Express*, 18(2):694–699, Jan 2010.

[24] B. E. Lemoff, D. Babic, and P. Schneider. Monolithic multiple wavelength VCSEL array, US Patent No. 6117699, 2000.

[25] J. Xue et al. An intra-chip free-space optical interconnect. In *Proc. of the 37th Intl. Symp. on Computer Architecture*, pages 94–105, 2010.

[26] J. A. Arns, W. S. Colburn, and S. C. Barden. Volume phase grating for spectroscopy, ultrafast laser compressors, and wavelength division multiplexing. In *Proc. SPIE*, volume 3799, 1999.

[27] P.-A. Blanche et al. Volume phase holographic gratings: large size and high diffraction efficiency. In *Opt. Eng.*, volume 43, 2004.

[28] P. Westbergh et al. 850nm VCSEL operating error-free at 40 Gbit/s. In *Proc. 22nd IEEE International Semiconductor Laser Conference*, pages 154 –155, 2010.

[29] A. Ramam, G. K. Chowdhury, and S. J. Chua. An approach to the design of highly selective resonant-cavity-enhanced photodetectors. *Applied Physics Letters*, 86(17):171104 –171104–3, 2005.

[30] J. Kim et al. A gracefully degrading and energy-efficient modular router architecture for on-chip networks. In *Proc. of the 33rd Intl Symp. on Computer Architecture*, pages 4–15, 2006.

[31] J. Kim et al. A novel dimensionally-decomposed router for on-chip communication in 3D architectures. In *Proc. of the 34th Intl Symp. on Computer Architecture*, pages 138–149, 2007.

[32] J. Kim et al. Design and analysis of an NoC architecture from performance, reliability and energy perspective. In *Proc. of the 2005 ACM Symp. on Architecture for Networking and Communications Systems*, pages 173–182, 2005.

[33] R. Das et al. Aérgia: exploiting packet latency slack in on-chip networks. In *Proc. of the 37th Intl. Symp. on Computer Architecture*, pages 106–116, 2010.

[34] A. B. Kahng et al. ORION 2.0: a fast and accurate NoC power and area model for early-stage design space exploration. In *Proc. of the Conference on Design, Automation and Test in Europe*, pages 423–428, 2009.

[35] J. Balfour and W. J. Dally. Design tradeoffs for tiled CMP on-chip networks. In *Proc. of the 20th Intl. Conf. on Supercomputing*, pages 187–198, 2006.

[36] H. Patil et al. Pinpointing representative portions of large Intel® Itanium® programs with dynamic instrumentation. In *Proc. of the 37th Intl. Symp. on Microarchitecture*, pages 81–92, 2004.

In *Proc. of LEOS Annual Meeting Conf.*, pages 811 –812, 2009.

Karma: Scalable Deterministic Record-Replay

Arkaprava Basu
Department of Computer Sciences
University of Wisconsin-Madison
basu@cs.wisc.edu

Jayaram Bobba*
Intel Corporation
jayaram.bobba@intel.com

Mark D. Hill
Department of Computer Sciences
University of Wisconsin-Madison
markhill@cs.wisc.edu

ABSTRACT

Recent research in *deterministic record-replay* seeks to ease debugging, security, and fault tolerance on otherwise nondeterministic multicore systems. The important challenge of handling shared memory races (that can occur on any memory reference) can be made more efficient with hardware support. Recent proposals record how long threads run in isolation on top of snooping coherence (IMRR), implicit transactions (DeLorean), or directory coherence (Rerun). As core counts scale, Rerun's directory-based parallel record gets more attractive, but its nearly sequential replay becomes unacceptably slow.

This paper proposes Karma for both scalable recording and replay. Karma builds an *episodic* memory race recorder using a *conventional* directory cache coherence protocol and records the order of the episodes as a directed acyclic graph. Karma also enables extension of episodes even after some conflicts. During replay, Karma uses *wakeup* messages to trigger a partially ordered parallel episode replay. Results with several commercial workloads on a 16-core system show that Karma can achieve replay speed (a) within 19%-28% of native execution speed without record-replay and (b) four times faster than even an *idealized* Rerun replay. Additional results explore tradeoffs between log size and replay speed.

Categories and Subject Descriptors

C.1 [**Processor Architectures**]: General

General Terms

Performance, Design

Keywords

Deterministic record-replay, multi-core processors.

1. INTRODUCTION

Today's shared-memory multiprocessors are not deterministic. The lack of repeatability makes it more difficult to do debugging (because bugs do not faithfully reappear on re-execution) [44], security analysis (attacks cannot be exactly replayed) [10], and fault tolerance (where a secondary set of threads attempts to mimic a primary set to detect faults) [24]. Moreover, dealing with multiprocessor nondeterminism -- heretofore limited to a few experts -- is now a concern of many programmers, as multicore chips become the norm in systems ranging from servers to clients to phones and the number of cores scales from a few to several to sometimes many.

To this end, researchers have explored software and hardware approaches for a *two-phase deterministic record-replay system* [10][17][22][27][30][34][41][42]. In the first phase, these systems record selective execution events into a *log* to enable the second phase to deterministically *replay* the recorded execution.

A great challenge for record-replay is handling *shared memory races* that can potentially occur on any memory reference, while other events, such as context switches and I/O can easily be handled by software [10][22][28]. Early hardware proposals for handling memory races [41][42] record when threads *do* interact, but require substantial hardware state to make log sizes smaller.

Three recent hardware race recorders reduce this state by instead recording when threads *don't* interact: Rerun [17], DeLorean [27] and Intel Memory Race Recorder (IMRR) [34]. Let *an episode (or chunk)* be a series of dynamic instructions from a single thread that executes without conflicting with any other thread. All three recorders use Bloom filters [5] to track coherence events to determine when to end episodes.

These recorders assume different coherence protocols that affect their scalability to many-core chips and complexity of implementation:

- IMRR assumes broadcast snooping cache coherence and proposes globally synchronized chunk termination among the cores for better replay speed. IMRR reliance on broadcast and globally synchronized operation limits its scalability.

- DeLorean relies on BulkSC/Bulk's [6][7] non-traditional broadcast of signatures to commit/abort implicit transactions and a centralized arbiter to record and replay chunk order. Thus DeLorean demands a *completely new* coherence protocol and support for implicit transactions to make its scheme for deterministic record-replay feasible.

- Rerun operates with relatively minor changes to more conventional point-to-point directory protocol that allows scalable recording while demanding minimal hardware extension.

Thus, going forward, Rerun's approach seems most promising as it is scalable to chips with many cores and to systems with multiple sockets, while requires moderate changes to conventional hardware. During replay, however, Rerun does *not* scale, because its replay is nearly sequential due to its use of Lamport scalar clocks [19]. Fast, parallel replay can expand the applicability of deterministic record/replay systems, which in turn, can further justify deploying them. Fast replay is valuable for scenarios that include:

- In *security analysis*, fast replay can help quick analysis of an attack and allow urgent fix to critical security flaws. A quick replay, even when the attack is underway, can help to trace the attacker [10].

- In *fault tolerance*, where one might wish to maintain availability of a critical primary server in presence of faults, a secondary server following the primary, needs to quickly

*Work done while at UW-Madison.

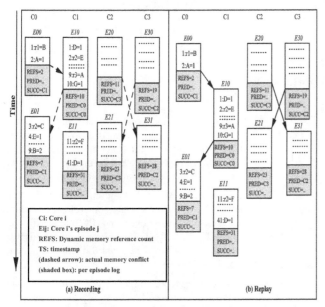

Figure 1. Rerun's Recording and "idealized" replay.

replay primary's execution to provide hot backup [24].

- For classic use of *debugging*, deterministic record/replay's utility will decline if scaling to 16, 32 or more cores, requires a sequential replay that is at least 16X, 32X or more slower. Replaying for small intervals of time may be acceptable, but the situation quickly worsens if replay for longer intervals and/or large number of cores are needed.

We believe that the need for scalable and fast Deterministic record-replay assumes further importance with respect to supercomputing where hundreds of cores/nodes interact during computation.

This paper proposes Karma for both scalable recording and replay, that minimally extends conventional directory coherence protocol. Karma's proposed novel episodic memory race recorder-replayer records the order of episodes as a *directed acyclic graph (DAG)*. Karma also extends lengths of episodes that conflict during recording by ensuring that they do not conflict during replay. During Karma's replay, special *wakeup* messages (like coherence acknowledgment messages) trigger parallel replay of independent episodes. We also show how to extend Karma from sequential consistency to Total Store Order (TSO), sufficient to implement the x86 memory model.

We evaluate Karma on a 16-core system and find that: (1) Karma can achieve replay speed within 19-28% of native execution with no-record-replay and about 4 times faster than even idealized Rerun's replay. (2) Karma's log size is similar to Rerun's, but (3) can be made smaller for uses that can tolerate slower replay.

2. Related Work and Rerun Review
2.1 Related Work

Classic all-software solutions to deterministic multiprocessor replay exist [11][22], but results show that they do not perform well on workloads that interact frequently. Three recent, promising approaches seek to reduce recording overhead, but consequently make replay more difficult. Park et al. [33] record partial information and retry replay until successful, while Altekar

and Stoica [2] seek only to replicate a bug, not an exact replay. Lee et al. [23] seeks to log minimal information but uses online replay on spare cores to validate whether logged information is sufficient to guarantee *output* deterministic replay.

Architecture researchers have focused on solutions that use hardware, at least for memory race detection. Bacon and Goldstein [3] recorded all snooping coherence transactions, which produced a serial and voluminous log. Xu et al.'s Flight Data Recorder (FDR) [41][42] created a distributed log of a subset of memory races, not implied by other races, but required substantial state with each core. Bugnet [31] shows how to enable record-replay by recording input values rather than memory race order. Strata [30] uses global strata to reduce this state, but does not scale well to many cores [17]. ReEnact [35] allowed deterministic reproduction of a recent buggy execution with Thread Level Speculation (TLS) support. As previously discussed, DeLorean, Rerun, and IMMR largely eliminate FDR's filtering state by focusing on when cores operate independently. More recently, Timetraveller [39] improved upon Rerun to reduce its log size further by delaying ending of episodes in Rerun. Herein we propose Karma to improve Rerun's replay speed, and we expect that Karma's improvements will apply to Timetraveller as well.

Importantly, Capo [28] discusses how to virtualize hardware deterministic replayers-including FDR, Rerun, and DeLorean-so that different parts of a machine can be in different modes: recorder, replay, or none. Fortunately, Karma, can also be virtualized with Capo.

Finally, there have been several recent efforts on obtaining deterministic execution, wherein a multithreaded program with a fixed input always executes the same way [4][9][32]. Somewhat related is Yu et al.'s work [44] to constrain production software runs to the set of interleaving observed during testing. While promising, these approaches are not (yet) generally adopted.

2.2 Rerun Review
We review Rerun here to better enable Section 3 to show how Karma supersedes it, even as both modestly extend conventional directory cache coherence protocols.

Record: Rerun dynamically breaks each core's execution into *episodes* during which a core does *not* interact with other cores. Rerun ends an episode when memory references of an episode conflict with a concurrent episode on another core. It can end episodes early, e.g., due to false conflicts, L1 cache evictions, or context switches. Rerun orders episodes with the timestamps based on a Lamport scalar clock [19]. Rerun's global log is a distributed collection of per-core logs. Each per-core log captures a core's sequence of episodes with each episode's size in dynamic memory references (REFS) and Lamport scalar clock based timestamp (TS). Figure 1(a) illustrates a Rerun recording, after threads at each core executed for some time initially. In Figure 1(a), when during episode E10, core C1 tries to read memory block A, a coherence intervention message is sent to core C0, which had written the same address as part of episode E00. This prompts C0 to end episode E00, as it detects a conflict and attaches its own timestamp in the coherence reply (dotted directed edge in Figure 1(a)). After receiving the coherence reply, core C1 adjusts the timestamp of episode E10 accordingly to capture the fact that E10 must be ordered after E00 during replay. The proposed Rerun implementation uses per-core read and write Bloom filters to detect when to end episodes and piggybacks timestamps on coherence response messages to capture the causal ordering among the episodes.

Replay: Rerun advocates software-based fully sequential replay of episodes in increasing order of their timestamps. In theory, however, scalar timestamps allow some parallelism, where episodes with the same timestamp can be replayed concurrently. We illustrate this *idealized* Rerun replay (non-sequential) in Figure 1(b). On one hand, it allows episodes E21 and E31 to be replayed concurrently. On the other hand, Lamport scalar clocks unnecessarily orders many independent episodes (e.g., E20 with episodes from cores C0 and C1).

3. Insights: Replaying Episodes in Parallel

As multi-threaded programs scale to more cores, replay must be parallelized otherwise it can become arbitrarily slow, limiting the utility of record-replay for online uses (e.g., fault tolerance, security analysis) and eventually debugging. To this end, this section introduces insights into Karma's parallel replay with both (a) ordering episodes with DAG and (b) extending episodes. While we present how Karma orders the execution in the cores, Karma-like FDR, Rerun, and DeLorean-can be virtualized by Capo [28].

3.1 Key Idea 1: Using Directed Acyclic Graph to Order Episodes During Replay

. The first key idea behind Karma is simple: *Use a directed acyclic graph (DAG) rather than scalar timestamps to partially order episodes during replay.* DAGs are well known to allow much greater parallelism than scalar timestamps and have been used in an offline analysis of replay speed potentials of deterministic recording schemes [34]. For ease of exposition, we first show the value of using a DAG by pretending that Karma's recording breaks the execution into exact same episodes as Rerun did in Figure 1, and then, in Section 3.2, present a second innovation that allows Karma to have longer episodes than Rerun permits.

To this end, Figure 2(a) illustrates how Karma can record memory dependencies among cores by triggering episode formation with DAG edges to successor episode(s). Karma's distributed log resembles Rerun's log with timestamps replaced by DAG edges (represented as PRED/SUCC sets explained below).

Figure 2(b) illustrates the parallelism of Karma's replay wherein successor episodes execute after their predecessors without other *artificial* ordering constraints. Importantly, this enables a parallel replay that is much faster than even Rerun's *idealized* replay. For example, while Rerun ordered episode E20 with independent episodes of cores C0 and C1 (Figure 1(b)), Karma's replay leaves episode E20 unordered with respect to the episodes of cores C0 and C1 (Figure 2(b)), facilitating more replay parallelism.

While the idea of using a DAG is simple, it is less simple to determine how to represent DAG edges to successor episode(s). For fastest replay, the DAG edge representation should facilitate an episode waking up the successor episode(s) quickly. Moreover, for low recording overhead, it should be fast to create during recording and compact to log. Using integer episode identifiers, as in a software representation of DAG edges, is a poor representation, as we see no way for replay to avoid indirecting through memory to determine the successor(s). Using these episode identifiers would also have severe negative impact on log size.

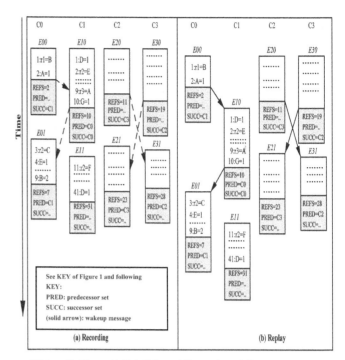

Figure 2. Karma's DAG-based Record and Replay with Rerun's Episode

As discussed in more details in Section 4.3, to efficiently record the DAG edges, Karma represents DAG edges with predecessor (PRED) and successor (SUCC) sets that name the cores of the predecessor and successor episodes respectively. During recording, these sets are populated from coherence traffic and then logged. During replay, a core awaits a wakeup message from each predecessor before beginning an episode and sends a wakeup message to each successor after completing an episode.

3.2 Key Idea 2: Extending Rerun's Episode

The second key idea behind Karma is subtle: *Concurrent episodes must not conflict during replay, but may conflict during recording.* In contrast, Rerun, DeLorean and IMRR always end episodes when they conflict during *recording*. For example in Figure 1(a) for Rerun, core C0 ends episode E00 when it gives block A to core C1 for episode E10. In Figure 2(a), we show Karma behaving similarly, but this is not necessary. More recently, Timetraveller [39] which improves upon Rerun's log size uses *post-dating* of scalar timestamps to also allow growing episodes even after some conflicts.

In contrast, as shown in Figure 3(a), Karma continues recording in episode E00 even as it conflicts with episode E10, as long as it orders E00 before E10 in the log. During replay, conflicting episodes E00 and E10 will not be concurrent, because the log entries will ensure that the end of E00 precedes the beginning of E10. In similar fashion, core C1 can cover its execution of 41 references with one episode E10 (Figure 3(a)), rather than two episodes E10 and E11 (Figure 2(a)). Beside the restriction discussed below, a core is not required to end a episode when either it (a) provides a block to another core or (b) obtains a block from another core. On one hand, this optimization seems too good to be true. Perhaps the authors of Rerun and DeLorean missed it, because they appear to be inspired by transactional memory systems [15][21] that usually abort when concurrent transactions conflict in an execution (as there is no distinction between recording and replay). Fortunately in *Dependence Aware* TM,

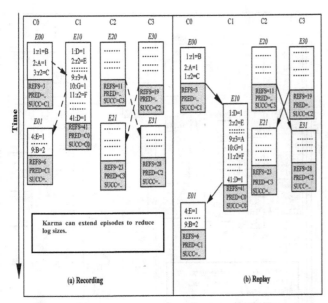

Figure 3. Karma's Record and Replay with Extended Episodes

Ramadan et al. [36] showed that conflicting concurrent transactions can all commit, provided that they are properly ordered. For example, they allow core C0's transaction T to pass a value to core C1's concurrent transaction U (and both commit) as long as T is ordered before U. Karma exploits a similar idea for episodes. Both are inspired by the greater freedom of conflict serializability over two-phase locking [12] and value forwarding among "episodes" in some thread-level-speculation systems (e.g., [13][37]).

On the other hand, full exploitation of the optimization is not possible. As depicted in Figure 3(a), a problem occurs when the core C0 later *attempts* to order E00 *after* core C1's episode E10 because of conflict in block E (memory reference 4 of core C0), but E00 was previously ordered *before* E10 due to block A (or conversely a core seeks to order an episode *before* another episode previously ordered *after*). Karma cannot do this without adding a cycle to the DAG, which is not allowed, as it would make ordering replay impossible. Instead, Karma always ends episode E00, begins episode E01 (with memory reference 4 as its first reference), and orders E01 after E10 of core C1.

Karma detects the possibility of cycle formation in the recorded DAG using Lamport scalar clock based timestamps [19] (but never logs them). Karma ends an episode when it receives a timestamp greater than the timestamp of the current episode. This ensures that the order of episodes is acyclic and can be replayed properly. Since Karma does *not* log timestamps, they *cannot* serialize replay and the sole purpose of this timestamp is to dynamically detect possibility of cycles while recording.

Finally, Karma enables a tradeoff between log size and replay parallelism, similar to one found in few other record-replay systems [27][42]. Growing longer episodes has two effects. First, larger episodes mean fewer episodes to cover an execution. This makes log size smaller. Second, longer episodes make replay less parallel and slower. This is because during replay the *end* of a predecessor episode happens *before* the beginning of a successor episode. For example, earlier we saw that Karma could cover core C1's execution of 41 memory references with one episode (Figure 3(a)) rather than two (E10 and E11 in Figure 2(a)). In Figure 3(b), we however observe that during replay, this means that episode

Table 1. Base system Configuration

Core	16 core, in-order, 3 GHz
L1 Caches	Split I&D, Private, 4-way set-associative, write-back, 64B lines, LRU, 3cycles hit
L2 Caches	Unified, Shared, Inclusive, 16M 8-way set associative, write-back, 16 banks, LRU replacement, 21 cycle hit
Directory	Full Bit vector at L2
Memory	4GB DRAM , 300 cycle access
Coherence	MESI Directory, Silent Replacement
Consistency Model	Sequential Consistency(SC) (with extension to TSO in Section 4.7)

E01 can only start execution after the merged bigger episode E10 completes its execution. For this reason, as we will find in Section 6, there is value in bounding the maximum episode size to balance log size and replay parallelism.

3.3 A Sketch of Karma Operation

This section sketches Karma's basic operation for recording and replay, but leaves details for Section 4.

Record Sketch: During recording, Karma grows episodes and passes timestamps on coherence response messages. Each core grows its episode until it receives a timestamp greater than its current timestamp (or a maximum size is reached, etc.). This indicates possibility of cycle in the DAG. At this point, it ends its episode, saves the corresponding predecessor/successor set for logging, and begins a new episode. When responding with a timestamp, a core sends its current timestamp for a block that matches in its read/write filter or its previous timestamp otherwise. For implementation reasons discussed later, a Karma core keeps the timestamp and predecessor/successor sets for both its immediately previous and current episodes. When an episode ends at a core, it logs the memory reference count, predecessor and successor set of the immediately previous episode, but *never* logs the timestamp.

Replay Sketch: During replay, a Karma core repeats four steps. (1) Read the predecessor/successor (PRED/SUCC) sets and reference count REFS for its next episode. (2) Wait for wake-up messages from each core in the episode's predecessor set. (3) Execute instructions for REFS memory references. (4) Send a wakeup message to each core in the successor set.

Online Replay? While we present the record and replay phases as separate, applications like fault tolerance may wish to "pipe" the log from recording to a concurrent replay. Karma's faster parallel replay makes this online replay more promising, but we leave detailed design issues to future work.

4. Implementing Karma

While the previous section presented the ideas behind Karma, this section presents a concrete hardware implementation and addresses additional issues.

4.1 Example Base System

We assume a base system as illustrated in Figure 4 with parameter values from Table 1. It is a multicore chip with private writeback L1 caches, shared multibanked L2 and a MESI directory protocol.

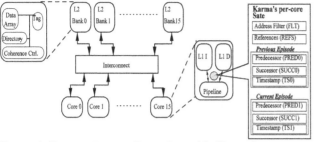

Figure 4. Base system configuration with Karma's state per core

4.2 Karma Hardware

As Figure 4 depicts, Karma adds eight registers (148 bytes) to each core: 128-byte address filter (FLT) (combining Rerun's read/write filters), 4-byte reference count (REFS), and for both the previous and current episodes, there are predecessor sets (PRED0 and PRED1), successor sets (SUCC0 and SUCC1) and 4-byte timestamps (TS0 and TS1). For 16 cores, all sets can be represented with 2-byte bit vectors, while more scalable representations are possible as many episodes have one or two predecessor or successor.

Karma assumes L2 cache blocks include a directory that tracks where a block is cached in the L1s, L1 cache shared replacements are silent, and L1 writebacks continue to remember the previous owner. Section 4.6 will discuss additional issues due to L1 and L2 caches being finite. Karma passes timestamps on coherence response messages. Karma also adds a single bit called *previouslyOrdered* in coherence response message, to be explained in next section. For supporting replay, Karma adds wakeup messages whose only payload is a source core identifier.

4.3 Predecessor and Successor Sets

This subsection discusses some subtle issues for how and why Karma represents DAG edges between episodes as predecessor and successor sets between cores. We implement each set with a 2-byte bit vector, but larger systems can use other encodings since most of these sets have just one or a few elements.

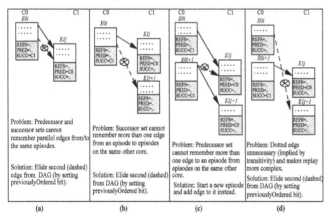

Figure 5. Subtle implementation issues regarding Predecessor and Successor Sets

Since predecessor and successor sets can only record a single edge from/to each other core, we take special care to avoid recording a second edge between the same two cores (Figure 5). When sending a message that would constitute a second outgoing edge from an episode to the same other core, we set the *previouslyOrdered* bit in the coherence reply message to indicate

that this message does not represent an edge, as depicted in Figure 5(a) and (b). This edge is redundant because of the previous edge to this core. On receiving a message that would be the second incoming edge from another core, we end the receiving core's episode, start a new episode, and add the edge to the otherwise empty new predecessor set (Figure 5(c)). This works, since cores can always end episodes early. On receiving a request message from a core already ordered after this core's current episode, this core responds with the *previouslyOrdered* bit set so that this message is also not a DAG edge, as depicted in Figure 5(d). This action is correct because the missing edge is implied by transitivity [41].

Karma's approach for representing DAG edges leads to a convenient invariant during replay (Section 4.5): when a core receives a wakeup message from core *req*, the message pertains to the receiving core's next episode whose predecessor set includes core *req*. This allows the wakeup message to physically name a core and yet have the edge be applied to a specific episode as in Figure 3(b).

4.4 Karma Recording

As depicted in Figure 6, the key to Karma recording is what actions Karma takes when a core/L1 sends a data response or acknowledgement (left side) and receives data or an acknowledgement in response to a coherence request it has made (right side). The top of Figure 6 repeats the Karma state from Figure 4.

During recording, each core sometimes sends a coherence reply (data and acknowledgement) in response to coherence request from another core *req* (Figure 6 (a)). The core first tests whether core *req* is already an element of SUCC1. If it is, the outgoing message's *previouslyOrdered* bit is set, so that the message does not create an edge in the DAG (Section 4.3) and no other actions are needed.

Otherwise, the core examines whether its address filter contains the message address (or a false positive). If so, then the core associates the outgoing edge with its current episode. It sets the message's timestamp to TS1 and *previouslyOrdered* bit to false. It then adds core *req* to SUCC1. If the filter does not match, the core associates the message with its previous episode and takes corresponding actions using TS0 and SUCC0. This is correct, because if a block is not touched by the current episode it was touched no later than the previous episode at that core.

During recording, a core executes instructions, which sometimes generate cache misses and coherence requests. Upon receiving a coherence response message (data or acknowledgement) from core *src*, a core may or may not take any actions for recording (Figure 6(b)). In particular, if the incoming message's *previouslyOrdered* bit is set, no action is needed, because the message comes from a core whose current or previous episode was already ordered with respect to this core's earlier or current episode.

If episode ordering is required, the incoming message may cause the current episode to end for two reasons. First, the episode ends if SUCC1 is not empty and the message's timestamp is greater than the current episode's timestamp. This is done to prevent cycles in the DAG. Second, the episode ends on incoming message from core *src* that is already in the current episode's PRED1.

363

State per core

REFS0: Memory Reference count
   for previous episode
REFS1: Memory Reference count
   for current episode
FILTER: Address filter

TS0: Timestamp of previous Episode
TS1: Timestamp of current Episode
PRED0: Predecessor set of previous Episode
SUCC0: Successor set of previous Episode
PRED1: Predecessor set of current Episode
SUCC1: Successor set of current Episode

Coherence Message Structure

src/req: Source or Requestor core id
previouslyOrdered: need an Edge in DAG?

dst: Destination   Addr: Address
TS: Timestamp   Payload: Data etc.

```
Action on sending data/Ack reply:

 receive_request_message(i_msg)
 if(SUCC1 contains i_msg.req) {
            /* No new edge in DAG neded */
     o_msg.previouslyOrdered = true
 } else {
       if(FLT contains i_msg.Addr){
             /* Current episode*/
           o_msg.TS = TS1
           o_msg.previouslyOrdered = false
           SUCC1.set(i_msg.req)
       } else {        /* Previous episode */
           if(SUCC0 contains i_msg.req) {
               /* No new edge required */
               o_msg.previouslyOrdered = true
           } else {
               o_msg.TS = TS0
               o_msg.previouslyOrdered = false
               SUCC0.set(i_msg.req)
           }
       }
 }
 /* Fill in other fields in o_msg according
    to coherence protocol */
 send_response_message(o_msg)
```

(a)

```
 Action on receiving data/Ack i_msg:
 if(i_msg.previouslyOrdered == true) {
        /* Do nothing */
 }else{
        if((SUCC1 not empty      && i_msg.TS>=TS1)
         || PRED1 contains i_msg.src){
           /* End episode */
           /* Log previous episode */
            write_to_log(REFS0,PRED0,SUCC0)
        /* Move current episode to previous*/
           TS0=TS1
           REFS0=REFS1
           PRED0=PRED1
           SUCC0=SUCC1
           /* Set up new episode */
           Clear PRED1,SUCC1 and FILTER
           PRED1.set(i_msg.src)
           REFS1=0
           TS1 = max(i_msg.TS+1,TS0+1)
        } else {
        /* Update the current episode */
           TS1 = max(i_msg.TS+1, TS1)
           PRED1.set(i_msg.src)
        }
 }
```

(b)

Figure 6. Karma's Recording Algorithm (at each core)

To end an episode, a core logs the previous episode's memory reference count and the predecessor/successor sets, copies the current episode's information to the previous one's, and then initializes the new current episode's values. In particular, the timestamp update follows Lamport scalar clock rules, the filter is cleared, the successor set made empty, and predecessor set made to contain only the message source (core *src*). The timestamp is not logged and thus has no role in replay.

4.5 Karma Replay

During replay, a Karma core repeats four steps, as depicted in Figure 7.

(1) When a core is ready to start a new episode, it reads the predecessor/successor (PRED1/SUCC1) sets and reference count REFS1 for the next episode from its per-core log. These values are stored in the same special registers as used in recording. Replay on this core is complete when its log is empty.

(2) The core waits for wakeup messages from each core in the episode's predecessor set PRED1. When the core has received a message for all cores originally in PRED1, it moves to the next step.

(3) The core executes instructions of the episode, decrementing REFS1 on each dynamic memory references, and stops execution when the episode REFS1 is zero and the episode is complete.

(4) The core sends a wakeup message to each core in its successor set SUCC1. When complete, the core goes back to step (1).

Karma's replay algorithm counts committed memory references, but never micro-architectural events, such as cache misses. Thus, Karma replay does not require the same caches or cache state as was present during Karma recording

The description above acts as if the wakeup messages arrive only during step (2), whereas they can actually arrive at any time. We implement a simple replayer that just buffers early messages. A more complex replayer could "pipeline" episodes by reading the next log entry early and gathering wakeup messages for the next episode while the current episode is still executing.

More subtly, wakeup messages for future episodes can arrive earlier than ones needed for the next episode(s), theoretically filling up any fixed sized message buffer. Fortunately, since the only information that must be remembered about a wakeup message is its source core identifier, a core can remember up to 8 wakeup messages per core (128 total) using a three-bit counter for each of 16 cores (6 bytes total). Moreover, these buffer counts can be made unbounded using known "limitless" techniques [8] that maintain rare overflow counts in software.

4.6 Effect of Finite Caches

Heretofore we assumed infinite L1 and L2 caches, but real systems have finite caches. Here we extend Karma to handle L1 and L2 cache replacements (from `Shared' and `Exclusive') and writebacks (from `Modified') [38]. Assume that a block is evicted by core C0 at episode E00 and next used by core C1 in episode E19. In all cases, episode E00 must be ordered before episode E19.

L1 Evictions: Karma handles L1 replacements and writebacks mostly like FDR [41]. There are three possible cases during L1 eviction that require attention. First, a shared replacement by C0 that is *silent* (i.e. coherence directory is not notified). A subsequent miss by C1 will send an invalidation to C0 whose acknowledgement message will order episode E19 after C0's current episode which is (long) after episode E00. Second, a writeback by C0 does not reset the block owner field at the L2, much like LogTM's sticky states [29] and FDR [41]. As in the first case, a subsequent miss by C1 will send an message to C0 whose acknowledgement message will order episode E19 after C0's current episode which is after episode E00.

Third, C0 could have written back the block and one or more other cores read it. Here Karma, extends the L2 directory by 4 bits (< 1% of a 64-byte cache block) to keep core identifier of the last writer to a block, so that reads can continue to get ordered after C0's current episode that is after E00. This is the same state that a MOESI coherence protocol needs to remember for an owner among sharers.

State per core:

```
PRED1: Predecessor set of current episode (executing/waiting)
SUCC1: Successor set of current episode (executing/waiting)
REFS1: Count of residual memory references of current episode
```

Wakeup message structure:

```
src: Source                                    dest: Destination
```

```
Before the start of a new episode:
    /* (1) Get next log entry */
    read_from_log(REFS1,PRED1,SUCC1)
    while(PRED1 not empty) {
      /* (2) Wait until all required wakeup messages arrive */
      when receive_wakeup_message(i_msg) {
          if(PRED1 contains i_msg.src) {
                PRED1.unSet(i_msg.src)
          }
      }
    }
     /* (3) Execute  the new episode */
     while(REFS1 != 0) {
         Execute instructions
         if(memory reference) {
                REFS1 = REFS1 - 1
         }
      } /* Finished episode execution*/

      /* (4) Send out wakeup messages */
      For each element P in SUCC1 {
           o_msg.src = own_core_id
           o_msg.dest = P
           send_wakeup_message(o_msg)
      }
```

Figure 7. Karma's replay algorithm (at each core)

L2 Evictions:

Karma seeks a different solution for L2 evictions, because (a) they are much less common and (b) we wish to add little or no state to main memory. The key idea is to compute a proxy core to order the eviction before any subsequent use. For example, the proxy core for victim block 100 with 16 cores might be 100 modulo 16 = C4. When the L2 seeks to evict block 100 last written by core C0, it will first order the current episode of C0 before the current episode of C4. (Much) later when C1 misses to memory for block 100, the L2 can re-compute the proxy C4 and order the current episode of core C4 before the current episode of core C1 which is E19. By transitivity, episode E00 is ordered before E19. Optionally, memory can use a single bit to remember whether a block was ever cached, as we assume in our simulations. Many other solutions are possible, including broadcasting on L2 misses in small systems or augmenting main memory to remember the previous writer if metabits are available.

4.7 Extending Karma to Support TSO (x86)

Hitherto, Karma implicitly assumed the sequential consistency (SC) memory consistency model [20], but now we show how to extend Karma to total store ordering (TSO) [14][40]. Unlike SC, TSO exposes (an abstraction of) write buffer for committed writes. Moreover, TSO provides a correct implementation of the x86 memory model [18] that exploits most of the flexibility that x86 allows. We extend Karma by adapting Xu et al.'s TSO solution from the dependence-based RTR[42].

TSO presents challenges as it allows a processor to *commit* a write (store) before a subsequent read (load) (in program order) and yet *order* the write (at logical shared memory) after the read. In practice, this relaxation of write-read ordering is leveraged using a *first-in-first-out* write buffer to hold writes that are committed but yet not ordered. Xu et al. [42] showed that such write buffers can cause their RTR system to record a cycle of dependences and deadlock the replay. To break these cycles, they propose a *order-value hybrid recorder* that detects a *problematic read* (or load) and reacts by recording the value read and not recording the write-after-read dependency that made the read problematic. Specifically, a problematic read is a read that gets its value V from the cache, while one or more earlier committed writes (in program order) are in the write buffer and cache block containing V is invalidated before all earlier writes are ordered. The execution is replayed following the now-acyclic dependencies and "bypassing" values to reads from the log whenever present. We found that Karma's replayer can also run into a similar situation for the same reasons, but fortunately, Xu et al.'s solution can be extended to episodic record/replay of Karma.

5. Evaluation Methods

We evaluate Karma using the multicore hardware presented in Section 4, except that we study scaling by varying core count: 4, 8, and 16 cores. When doing this, we keep the shared L2 cache size per core constant at 1MB, so the total L2 cache size is 4MB for 4 cores, 8MB for 8 cores, and 16MB for 16 cores.

For comparison purposes, we also evaluated Rerun [17] in the same setup, as it is the closest cousin to Karma, using the code obtained from Rerun's authors. More specifically, we compare against an *idealized* Rerun replayer (non-sequential) that (a) replays episodes with the same timestamp in parallel (as in Figure 1(b)) and (b) appears to wakeup episode(s) with the next timestamp after the last episode with the current timestamp completes. A practical implementation of Rerun replay would, of course, be slower than this idealized one.

We use the Wisconsin GEMS [26] full system simulation infrastructure, which models an enterprise-level SPARC server running on unmodified Solaris 9 operating system. This simulator uses the Simics [25] full system simulator as front end for the functional part of the simulation and uses the Ruby memory timing model to simulate different hardware platforms. In this work we concentrate on memory race recording and replaying and assume support for handling DMA, I/O, and external interrupts much like FDR [41] and software layer support much like Capo [28]. To approximate this, we dilate Simics's time to make sure interrupts arrive between the same dynamic instructions during both recording and replay.

We use the Wisconsin Commercial Workload suite [1] to drive evaluation. This workload suite consists of a task-parallel web server (Apache), a Java middleware application (Jbb), a TPC-C like online transaction processing (Oltp) workload on DB2, and a pipelined web server (Zeus). We stress-tested the Karma implementation with memory race ordering sensitive microbenchmark racey [16].

6. Experimental Results

This section will ask three basic questions and provide the answers summarized here:

Question #1: Does Karma speedup replay?

Yes, Karma replay can be 1.4X-7.1X faster than idealized Rerun replay. This translates to a modest 19%-28% slowdown for the replay over the base system without any record/replay in a 16 core system. With fewer cores the slowdown is even less.

Question #2: How can Karma trade off log size and replay speed?

By loosening the bound on maximum episode size, Karma can achieve smaller log sizes (e.g., 47%) for situations when slower replay is tolerable (e.g., 21% slower). This presents an effective control knob to trade off the log size versus replay speed, depending upon the requirement of a particular use of deterministic replay.

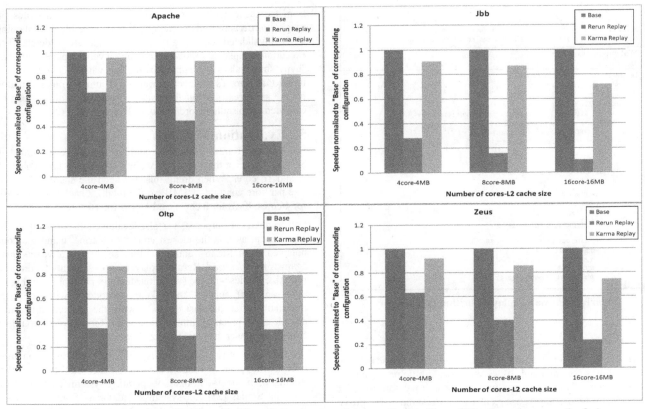

Figure 8. Comparison of Rerun's and Karma's Replay Speed (normalized to Base, 256-reference max. episodes)

Question #3: How does Karma's log size compare to Rerun's?

Karma and Rerun log sizes are comparable with a 256-memory-reference maximum episode size. As we increase episode size, Karma achieves substantial log size reduction (up to 43%) over Rerun and still replays much faster than Rerun.

6.1 Big Picture: Much Faster Replay While Retaining Fast Recording

Figure 8 displays the most important graphs in this paper. Each graph provides results for a different benchmark. Each cluster of bars within a histogram represents a different configuration of the CMP. The configuration here is characterized by the number of cores (4, 8, and 16) and total L2 cache size (4MB, 8MB, and 16MB). All histogram heights depict the speedup normalized to the native execution at corresponding CMP configuration with no recording or replay (Base). For example, bars clustered around x-axis point for 16core-16MB configuration are speedup normalized to execution for 16core-16MB L2 cache CMP configuration without any record/replay (Base).

Each cluster of bars in a histogram has three bars representing execution with no *record/replay (Base)*, *idealized Rerun replay* and *Karma replay*. Not shown are Rerun and Karma recording, as they are mostly very close to Base. All results in this section assume a maximum episode size of 256 memory references, which, as we will see later, produces a log size similar to Rerun's. By showing performance comparison of our system for different configuration points for CMP, we tried to demonstrate scalability and applicability of our proposed system under varying CMP configurations.

Question #1: Does Karma speedup replay?

Yes, Karma replay can be 1.4-7.1X faster than idealized Rerun replay depending upon the number of cores and the application. For Apache with 4, 8, and 16 cores, for example, Karma replay is 1.4X, 2X, and 3X faster than Rerun replay. This is not surprising, since even our idealized Rerun replay still does not expose enough parallelism due to scalar clock based ordering of episodes. Results for Oltp and Zeus are similar, while for Jbb, Karma replay speed is 7.1X of Rerun's. For the 16-core system, Karma replay is only 19%, 28%, 22% and 25% slower than the Base execute (without record/replay) for Apache, Jbb, Oltp and Zeus, respectively. For fewer cores, this slowdown is much less.

Recording: Karma's recording (not shown in the figure) is usually negligibly different from doing no recording/replay (i.e., Base), just like Rerun's recording. We observed for Apache, Jbb and Zeus, Karma recording runs nearly identically (<1% slowdown) with doing no recording (Base). Karma recording also works similarly well for OLTP with 4 and 8 cores, but adds a bit more overhead (~10%) to 16-core OLTP. More importantly, Karma recording scales well when applications scale well.

Bandwidth: Karma sends around 2% more traffic over the interconnect while recording than Rerun. This is because of extending few coherence messages (*previouslyOrdered bit*, etc.) and sometimes because of extra messages. This modest extra bandwidth could affect execution time substantially if the interconnect was near saturation (which it should not be). One would note that Rerun adds around 10% bandwidth overhead on the interconnect over a system with no record/replay.

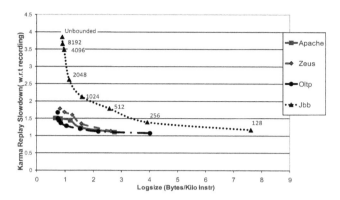

Figure 9. Tradeof between Logsize and Replay Slowdown
By varying maximum episode size across 128 (right end of each application's lines), 256, 512, ... 8K, and unbounded number of memory references, allow one tradeoff smaller log with some replay slowdown. Displayed results use 16 cores.

Sensitivity Analysis: The results above showed that Karma gains are robust with varying core count (4, 8 and 16) and shared L2 cache sizes (4, 8, 16 MB). Additional sensitivity analysis (not shown), confirms that results qualitatively hold during variations, e.g., doubling L1 size, doubling L2 size, and halving memory latency.

6.2 Obtaining Smaller Logs but Slower Replay

Above we showed that Karma replay performance is much better than Rerun's (1.4X-7.1X) for what will turn out to be a comparable log size. Some uses of record/replay, e.g., debugging, may wish to reduce rate of log size growth further, so that, for fixed log size, one can record a longer execution. Karma facilitates this for deterministic record/replay uses that can tolerate somewhat slower replay. This might be a good tradeoff when recording is much more common (e.g., always on) than replay (e.g., to investigate a crash).

Figure 9 illustrates Karma log size and replay speed for each of our four applications. The x-axis gives uncompressed log size growth in bytes per thousand instructions. The y-axis gives replay speed normalized to recording speed. For each application, each point on its lines, beginning from the right, provides the tradeoff with maximum episode sizes with memory reference counts: 128, 256 (the value used in Section 6.1), 512, ..., 8K, and unbounded.

Question #2: How can Karma trade off log size and replay speed? By loosening the bound on maximum episode size, Karma achieves smaller log sizes but slower replay. For example, increasing the maximum episode size from 256 to 2K references has the following effects: Apache generates 54% smaller log for 23% slower replay, Jbb generates 71% smaller log for 87% slower OLTP generates 60% smaller log for 21% slower replay, and Zeus generates 47% smaller log for 33% slower replay. Three of four benchmarks pay a modest replay slowdown, while Jbb is more sensitive.

Question #3: How does Karma log size compare to Rerun's? Karma and Rerun log sizes are comparable with a 256-memory-reference maximum episode size. Figure 10 displays Karma's uncompressed log size normalized to Rerun's uncompressed log size on a 16 core system. The x-axis varies both Karma and Rerun's maximum episode sizes (in memory

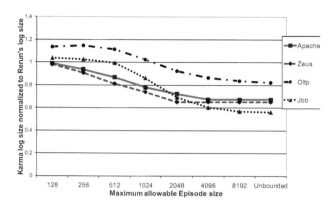

Figure 10. Logsize comparison between Karma and Rerun

references) for 128, 256, ..., 8K, and unbounded. For the default of 256 memory references, Karma's log sizes versus Rerun's varies from 10% smaller for Zeus to 17% larger for OLTP. As episodes grow larger, Karma's log size decreases faster than Rerun's. For maximum episode sizes of 1K references and greater, Karma's log is always smaller than Rerun's. With a maximum episode size of 8K references), Karma log size is smaller than Rerun's by 33%, 43%, 17% and 35% for Apache, Jbb, Oltp and Zeus, respectively.

If small logs are more important than faster replay, then it is reasonable to set the maximum episode size to 2K references. To this end we found out that with maximum episode size 2K references, Karma retains substantial replay speedups with respect to Rerun (e.g. 1.3X-4.8X) but they are smaller than with 256-reference episodes. Moreover, Figure 10 showed that Karma's log size is 8-35% smaller than Rerun's log size, when the maximum episode size is limited to 2K memory references in both systems.

7. Conclusions

This paper proposes Karma for both scalable recording and replay. Karma builds episode-based memory race recorder/replayer using a directory coherence protocol, without requiring any global communication. During recording, Karma records the order of episodes with a directed acyclic graph and extends episodes even after some conflicts. During replay, Karma uses wakeup messages to trigger parallel replay of independent episodes. Results with several commercial workloads on a 16-core multicore system show that Karma can achieve replay speed within 19%-28% of execution speed without record-replay and four times better than idealized Rerun replay.

8. ACKNOWLEDGEMENTS

We thank Derek Hower for providing the code for Rerun. We thank Brad Beckmann, Dan Gibson, Heidi Arbisi-Kelm, Rathijit Sen, Mike Swift, Haris Volos, Min Xu, the Wisconsin Multifacet group, the anonymous reviwers and the Wisconsin Computer Architecture Affiliates for their comments and/or proofreading. Finally we thank the Wisconsin Condor project, the UW CSL for their assistance.

This work is supported in part by the National Sicence Foundation (CNS-0551401, CNS-0720565 and CNS-0916725), Sandia/DOE (#MSN123960/DOE890426), and University of Wisconsin (Kellett award to Hill). The views expressed herein are not necessarily those of the NSF, Sandia or DOE. Bobba was PhD student at University of Wisconsin-Madison when this work was performed. Hill has a significant financial interest in AMD.

9. References

[1] A. R. Alameldeen, C. J. Mauer, M. Xu, P. J. Harper, M. M. K. Martin, D. J. Sorin, M. D. Hill, and D. A. Wood. Evaluating Non-deterministic Multi-threaded Commercial Workloads. In 5th Workshop on Computer Architecture Evaluation Using Commercial Workloads, 2002.

[2] G. Altekar and I. Stoica. ODR: output-deterministic replay for multicore debugging. In ACM Symposium on Operating systems principles (SOSP'09), 2009.

[3] D. F. Bacon and S. C. Goldstein. Hardware-Assisted Replay of Multiprocessor Programs. Proceedings of the ACM/ONR Workshop on Parallel and Distributed Debugging, published in ACM SIGPLAN Notices, 1991.

[4] T. Bergan, O. Anderson, J. Devietti, L. Ceze, and D. Grossman. CoreDet: a compiler and runtime system for deterministic multithreaded execution. In Proc. of the 15th Intl. Conf. on Architectural Support for Programming Languages and Operating Systems, March 2010.

[5] B. H. Bloom. Space/Time Trade-offs in Hash Coding with Allowable Errors. Communications of the ACM, 13(7):, July 1970.

[6] L. Ceze, J. Tuck, C. Cascaval, and J. Torrellas. Bulk Disambiguation of Speculative Threads in Multiprocessors. In Proc. of the 33nd Annual Intl. Symposium. on Computer Architecture, June 2006.

[7] L. Ceze, J. Tuck, P. Montesinos, and J. Torrellas. BulkSC: Bulk Enforcement of Sequential Consistency. In Proc. of the 34th Annual Intl. Symp. on Computer Architecture, June 2007.

[8] D. Chaiken, J. Kubiatowicz, and A. Agarwal. LimitLESS directories: A scalable cache coherence scheme. In ASPLOS-IV: Proceedings of the fourth international conference on Architectural support for programming languages and operating systems,, NY, USA, 1991.

[9] J. Devietti, B. Lucia, L. Ceze, and M. Oskin. DMP: Deterministic Shared Memory Multiprocessing. In Proc. of the 14th Inl. Conf. on Architectural Support for Programming Languages and Operating Systems (ASPLOS), March 2009.

[10] G. W. Dunlap, S.T. King, S. Cinar, M. Basrai, and P. M. Chen. ReVirt: Enabling Intrusion Analysis through Virtual-Machine Logging and Replay. In Proc. of the 2002 Symposium. on Operating Systems Design and Implementation, 2002.

[11] G. W. Dunlap, D. Lucchetti, P. M. Chen, and M. Fetterman. Execution Replay of Multiprocessor Virtual Machines. In Intl Conf. on Virtual Execution Environments (VEE), 2008.

[12] J. Gray and A. Reuter. Transaction Processing: Concepts and Techniques. Morgan Kaufmann, 1993.

[13] L. Hammond, B. Hubbert, M. Siu, M. Prabhu, M. Chen, and K. Olukotun. The Stanford Hydra CMP. IEEE Micro, 20(2), March-April 2000.

[14] S. Hangal, D. Vahia, C. Manoit J.-Yeu, J. Lu, and S. Narayanan. TSOtool: A Program for Verifying Memory Systems Using the Memory Consistency Model. In Proc. of the 31st Annual Intnl. Symp. on Computer Architecture, 2004.

[15] M. Herlihy and J. Eliot B. Moss. Transactional Memory: Architectural Support for Lock-Free Data Structures. Technical Report 92/07, Digital Cambridge Research Lab, 1992.

[16] M. D. Hill and M. Xu. Racey: A Stress Test for Deterministic Execution. http://www.cs.wisc.edu/ markhill/racey.html.

[17] D. R. Hower and M. D. Hill. Rerun: Exploiting Episodes for Lightweight Race Recording. In Proc. of the 35th Annual Intnl. Symp. on Computer Architecture, 2008.

[18] Intel, editor. Intel 64 and IA-32 Architectures Software Developer's Manual, volume 3A: System Programming Guide Part 1. Intel Corporation.

[19] L. Lamport. Time, Clocks and the Ordering of Events in a Distributed System. Communications of the ACM, 21(7): July 1978.

[20] L. Lamport. How to Make a Multiprocess Computer that Correctly Executes Multiprocess Programs. IEEE Transactions on Computers, 1979.

[21] J. R. Larus and R. Rajwar. Transactional Memory. Morgan & Claypool Publishers, 2007.

[22] T. J. Leblanc and J. M. Mellor-Crummey. Debugging Parallel Programs with Instant Replay. IEEE Transactions on Computers, C-36(4):, April 1987.

[23] D. Lee, B. Wester, K. Veeraraghavan, S. Narayanasamy, and P. Chen. Respec: efficient online multiprocessor replay via speculation and external determinism. In Proc. of ASPLOS, 2010.

[24] D. Lucchetti, S. K. Reinhardt, and P. M. Chen. ExtraVirt: Detecting and recovering from transient processor faults. In Symp. on Operating System Principles work-in-progress session, 2005.

[25] P. S. Magnusson et al. Simics: A Full System Simulation Platform. IEEE Computer, 35(2):,2002.

[26] M. M. K. Martin, D. J. Sorin, B. M. Beckmann, M. R. Marty, M. Xu, A. R. Alameldeen, K. E. Moore, M. D. Hill, and D. A. Wood. Multifacet's General Execution-driven Multiprocessor Simulator (GEMS) Toolset. CAN, 2005.

[27] P. Montesinos, L. Ceze, and J. Torrellas. DeLorean: Recording and Deterministically Replaying Shared-Memory Multiprocessor Execution Efficiently. In Proc. of ISCA, 2008.

[28] P. Montesinos, M. Hicks, S. T. King, and J. Torrellas. Capo: A Software-Hardware Interface for Practical Deterministic Multiprocessor Replay. In Proc.of ASPLOS 2009.

[29] K. E. Moore, J. Bobba, M. J. Moravan, M. D. Hill, and D. A. Wood. LogTM: Log-Based Transactional Memory. In Proc. of HPCA, 2006.

[30] S. Narayanasamy, C. Pereira, and B. Calder. Recording Shared Memory Dependencies Using Strata. In Proc. of ASPLOS, 2006.

[31] S. Narayanasamy, G. Pokam, and B. Calder. BugNet: Continuously Recording Program Execution for Deterministic Replay Debugging. In Proc. ISCA 2005.

[32] M. Olszewski, J. Ansel, and S. Amarasinghe. Kendo: Efficient Deterministic Multithreading in Software. In Proc. of ASPLOS, 2009.

[33] S. Park, Y. Zhou, W. Xiong, Z. Yin, R. Kaushik, K. H. Lee, and S. Lu. PRES: probabilistic replay with execution sketching on multiprocessors. In Proc. of SOSP 2009.

[34] G. Pokam, C. Pereira, K. Danne, R. Kassa, and A.R. Adl-Tabatabai. Architecting a chunk-based memory race recorder in modern CMPs. In Proc. of MICRO, 2009.

[35] M. Prvulovic and J. Torrellas. ReEnact: Using Thread-Level Speculation Mechanisms to Debug Data Races in Multithreaded Codes. In Proc. of ISCA, 2003.

[36] H. E. Ramadan, C. J. Rossbach, and E. Witchel. Dependence-Aware Transactional Memory for Increased Concurrency. In Proc. of MICRO, 2008.

[37] G.S. Sohi, S. Breach, and T.N. Vijaykumar. Multiscalar Processors. In Proc. of ISCA, 1995.

[38] P. Sweazey and A. Jay Smith. A Class of Compatible Cache Consistency Protocols and their Support by the IEEE Futurebus. In Proc. of ISCA 1986.

[39] G. Voskuilen, F. Ahmad, and T. N. Vijaykumar. Timetraveler: exploiting acyclic races for optimizing memory race recording. In 37th Annual Intnl. Symp. on Computer Architecture, 2010.

[40] D. L. Weaver and T. Germond, editors. SPARC Architecture Manual (Version 9). PTR Prentice Hall, 1994.

[41] M. Xu, R. Bodik, and M. D. Hill. A "Flight Data Recorder" for Enabling Full-system Multiprocessor Deterministic Replay. In the 30th Annual Intnl. Symp. on Computer Architecture, 2003.

[42] M. Xu, R. Bodik, and M. D. Hill. A Regulated Transitive Reduction (RTR) for Longer Memory Race Recording. In Proc. of ASPLOS, 2006.

[43] Min Xu, V. Malyugin, J. Sheldon, G. Venkitachalam, and B. Weissman. ReTrace: Collecting Execution Trace with Virtual Machine Deterministic Replay. In the 3rd Annual Workshop on Modeling, Benchmarking and Simulation, 2007.

[44] J. Yu and S. Narayansamy. A Case for an interleaving constrained shared-memory multi-processor. In Pro. Of ISCA 2009.

SRC: Information Retrieval as a Persistent Parallel Service on Supercomputer Infrastructure

Tobias Berka
University of Salzburg
Department of Computer Sciences
Jakob-Haringer-Strasse 2
Salzburg, Austria
tberka@cosy.sbg.ac.at

Marian Vajteršic
University of Salzburg
Department of Computer Sciences
Jakob-Haringer-Strasse 2
Salzburg, Austria
marian@cosy.sbg.ac.at

ABSTRACT

We seek to create a parallel search engine which outperforms conventional, loosely coupled distributed systems. We have (1) parallelized the vector space model with 120%–180% parallel efficiency, (2) introduced a highly parallel algorithm for text dimensionality reduction increasing the search accuracy measured with the mean average precision by 4.8 percentage points on the Reuters corpus and (3) developed a middleware for concurrent programming in parallel applications for index maintenance and multi-user operation. Using these building blocks, we present an overall system architecture that addresses the requirements of information retrieval as a persistently deployed parallel service.

Categories and Subject Descriptors

D.1.3 [**Software**]: Concurrent Programming—*Parallel programming*; G.1.0 [**Mathematics of Computing**]: Numerical Analysis—*Parallel algorithms*; H.3.3 [**Information Storage and Retrieval**]: Information Search and Retrieval—*Search process*

General Terms

Algorithms, Design, Performance

Keywords

Vector space model, Symmetric multiprocessing, Dense vector computations, Message Passing Interface

1. DESCRIPTION

The information explosion presents us with the challenge of organizing large amounts of unstructured data. A particular challenge is the search for documents, and the field of information retrieval (IR) provides us with a wide range of empirically proven algorithms; But the computational cost is considerate. As with many challenges of scalability, parallel processing comes as a natural fit. However, existing search engines are constructed as loosely coupled, distributed systems. In our research, we attempt to develop a truly parallel IR system for private memory systems using the message passing interface (MPI).

There are three key objectives for a parallel search engine: it must provide high quality search results within low response times at a very high query throughput for extremely large document collections, serve multiple users concurrently and allow concurrent index modification, and operate seamlessly for extended durations. The novelty of our work lies in the following issues: the parallelization of IR for dense vectors using MPI, a novel dimensionality reduction method for text and its parallelization with MPI, a middleware approach to concurrency support within parallel applications and a first attempt to develop a full-scale search engine as parallel, high-performance application for supercomputer infrastructure.

Regarding the first objective, we present our newly developed dimensionality reduction method for text [1] and a parallel algorithm for retrieval of dense vectors in the vector space model [2], along with our initial performance measurements and retrieval quality evaluation.

The second objective requires support for concurrent programming *within* a *parallel* application in order to add, remove and update documents while queries are being executed. We have to concurrently receive maintenance requests without interference on the communication channels. Thus, we have developed an additional layer of portable middleware on top of MPI to provide concurrency through threads in a safe, reliable and convenient manner.

The third objective calls for fault tolerance beyond the traditional requirements in parallel computing, but we illustrate that modern MPI implementations will provide sufficient features.

Together, these individual building blocks can be used to form an architecture for a parallel search engine for supercomputer infrastructure.

2. REFERENCES

[1] Tobias Berka and Marian Vajteršic. Dimensionality Reduction for Information Retrieval using Vector Replacement of Rare Terms. In *Proc. TM'11*, 2011.

[2] Tobias Berka and Marian Vajteršic. Parallel Retrieval of Dense Vectors in the Vector Space Model. *Computing and Informatics*, (2), 2011.

SRC: Damaris - Using Dedicated I/O Cores for Scalable Post-petascale HPC Simulations

Matthieu Dorier
ENS Cachan, Brittany - IRISA
Rennes, France
matthieu.dorier@eleves.bretagne.ens-cachan.fr
Advisor: Gabriel Antoniu, INRIA Rennes, France, gabriel.antoniu@inria.fr

As we enter the post-petascale era, scientific applications running on large-scale platforms generate increasingly larger amounts of data for checkpointing or offline visualization, which puts current storage systems under heavy pressure. Unfortunately, I/O scalability rapidly fades behind the increasing computation power available, and thereby reduced the overall application performance scalability. We consider the common case of large-scale simulations who alternate between computation phases and I/O phases. Two main approaches have been used to handle these I/O phases: 1) each process writes an individual file, leading to a very large number of files from which it is hard to retrieve scientific insights; 2) processes synchronize and use collective I/O to write to the same shared file. In both cases, because of mandatory communications betweens processes during the computation phase, all processes enter the I/O phase at the same time, which leads to huge access contention and extreme performance variability.

Previous research efforts have focused on improving each layer of the I/O stack separately: at the highest level scientific data formats like HDF5 [4] allow to keep a high degree of semantics within files, while leveraging MPI-IO optimizations. Parallel file systems like GPFS [5] or PVFS [2] are also subject to optimization efforts, as they usually represent the main bottleneck of this I/O stack.

As a step forward, we introduce Damaris (Dedicated Adaptable Middleware for Application Resources Inline Steering), an approach targeting large-scale multicore SMP supercomputers. The main idea is to dedicate one or a few cores on each node to I/O and data processing to provide an efficient, scalable-by-design, in-compute-node data processing service. Damaris takes into account user-provided information related to the application, the file system and the intended use of the datasets to better schedule data transfers and processing. It may also respond to visualization tools to allow in-situ visualization without impacting the simulation.

We tested our implementation of Damaris as an I/O backend for the CM1 atmospheric model[1], one of the application intended to run on next generation supercomputer BlueWa-

ters [1] at NCSA. CM1 is a typical MPI application, originally writing one file per process at each checkpoint using HDF5. Deployed on 1024 cores on BluePrint, the Blue-Water's interim system at NCSA with GPFS as underlying filesystem, this approach induces up to 10 seconds overhead in checkpointing phases every 2 minutes, with a high variability in the time spent by each process to write its data (from 1 to 10 seconds). Using one dedicated I/O core in each 16-cores SMP node, we completely remove this overhead. Moreover, the time spared by the I/O core enables a better compression level, thus reducing both the number of files produced (by a factor of 16) and the total data size. Experiments conducted on the French Grid5000 [3] testbed with PVFS as underlying filesystem and a 24 cores/node cluster emphasized the benefit of our approach, which allows communication and computation to overlap, in a context involving high network contention at multiple levels.

Categories and Subject Descriptors

D.1.3 [**Concurrent Programming**]: Parallel Programing; I.6.6 [**Simulations and Modeling**]: Simulation Output Analysis; E.5 [**Files**]: Optimization

General Terms

Design, Experimentation, Performance

Keywords

Exascale Computing, Multicore Architectures, I/O, Dedicated Cores

---

[1]This work was done in the framework of a collaboration between the KerData INRIA - ENS Cachan/Brittany team (Rennes, France) and the NCSA (Urbana-Champaign, USA) within the Joint INRIA-UIUC Laboratory for Petascale Computing.

1. REFERENCES

[1] The Blue Waters Project.
    http://www.ncsa.illinois.edu/BlueWaters/.
[2] P. H. Carns, W. B. Ligon, III, R. B. Ross, and R. Thakur. PVFS: A parallel file system for Linux clusters. In *Proceedings of the 4th annual Linux Showcase & Conference - Volume 4*, pages 28–28, Berkeley, CA, USA, 2000. USENIX Association.
[3] Grid5000. https://www.grid5000.fr.
[4] NCSA. Hierarchical Data Format HDF5,
    http://www.hdfgroup.org/HDF5/.
[5] F. Schmuck and R. Haskin. GPFS: A Shared-Disk File System for Large Computing Clusters. In *In Proceedings of the 2002 Conference on File and Storage Technologies (FAST)*, pages 231–244, 2002.

SRC: FenixOS - A Research Operating System Focused on High Scalability and Reliability

Stavros Passas
DTU Informatics
Technical University of Denmark
Richard Petersens Plads, Building 322
2800 Kgs. Lyngby, Denmark
stpa@imm.dtu.dk

Sven Karlsson
DTU Informatics
Technical University of Denmark
Richard Petersens Plads, Building 322
2800 Kgs. Lyngby, Denmark
ska@imm.dtu.dk

ABSTRACT

Computer systems keep increasing in size. Systems scale in the number of processing units, memories and peripheral devices. This creates many and diverse architectural trade-offs that the existing operating systems are not able to address. We are designing and implementing, FenixOS, a new operating system that aims to improve the state of the art in scalability and reliability.

We achieve scalability through limiting data sharing when possible, and through extensive use of lock-free data structures. Reliability is addressed with a careful re-design of the programming interface and structure of the operating system.

Categories and Subject Descriptors

D.4.7 [**Operating Systems**]: Organization and Design

General Terms

Design

Keywords

Operating systems, Performance, Reliability

1. INTRODUCTION

Computer systems increase in complexity rapidly. Systems scale in the number of cores, caches, interconnect networks, IO devices, accelerators and peripheral devices. This leads to scalability and reliability challenges for the operating system designers.

The existing operating systems are designed to scale for traditional server-based, high-performance workloads. However, we find multi-core systems in diverse environments and with varied purposes. Current workloads on systems are less predictable and more operating system intensive than the high performance benchmarks that we traditionally use as a base to measure and improve system's scalability. Often, we cannot simply tune an existing, general purpose operating system to meet the requirements of a particular system. For the above reasons, existing operating systems are not designed to efficiently handle state-of-the-art and complex systems.

2. APPROACH

We are designing and implementing *FenixOS*, an operating system that aims to improve the state-of-the art in scalability and reliability. To achieve scalability, we limit the data sharing between processing cores. When data sharing cannot be avoided, we seek to use lock-free data-structures.

To achieve reliability, we careful re-design the programming interface and structure of the operating system. We aim to minimize the amount of code that runs in kernel mode. We have designed a high performance, transactional based, server interface, that drivers use to run in user space. For the most common and performance critical devices, we support a limited number of in-kernel drivers.

We aim to improve system's performance, compared to state-of-the-art operating systems [1, 2, 3]. Barrelfish [1] forces cores to use explicit messages to communicate. We believe that use of lock-free data structures can reduce this communication overhead. Singularity [3] is a micro-kernel based system. That introduces overhead to the system. Our approach aims to decrease the overhead, without decreasing the operating system's reliability. Microdrivers [2], split drivers in kernel and user segments. We want most of our drivers to not reside in the kernel.

3. OUTLOOK

We have implemented a minimal kernel layer that supports the AMD 64 architecture and we are currently implementing support for the ARM architecture. We work on memory management, data locality and process scheduling. This will enable us to run our operating system on many different platforms. It will also allow us to perform experiments so as to expose interesting trade-offs.

4. REFERENCES

[1] A. Baumann, P. Barham, P.-E. Dagand, T. Harris, R. Isaacs, S. Peter, T. Roscoe, A. Schüpbach, and A. Singhania. The Multikernel: A new OS architecture for scalable multicore systems. In *Proceedings of the ACM SIGOPS 22nd Symposium on Operating systems principles (SOSP '09)*, pages 29–44, 2009.

[2] V. Ganapathy, M. J. Renzelmann, A. Balakrishnan, M. M. Swift, and S. Jha. The design and implementation of microdrivers. *SIGOPS Oper. Syst. Rev.*, 42:168–178, 2008.

[3] G. C. Hunt and J. R. Larus. Singularity: rethinking the software stack. *SIGOPS Oper. Syst. Rev.*, 41:37–49, 2007.

SRC: Soft Error Detection and Recovery for High Performance Linpack

Teresa Davies and Zizhong Chen (advisor)
Colorado School of Mines
Golden, CO, USA
{tdavies, zchen}@mines.edu

ABSTRACT

In high-performance systems, the probability of failure is higher for larger systems. Errors in calculations may occur that cannot be detected by any other means. To address this problem, we create a checksum-based approach that detects and recovers from calculation errors. We apply this approach to the LU factorization algorithm used by High Performance Linpack. Our approach has low overhead. In contrast to existing approaches that require repeated calculation, it repeats only a fraction of the calculation during recovery. The frequency of checking can be adjusted for the error rate, resulting in a flexible method of fault tolerance.

Categories and Subject Descriptors

C.4 [**Performance of Systems**]: Fault tolerance

General Terms

Reliability

Keywords

High Performance Linpack benchmark, LU factorization, fault tolerance, algorithm-based recovery

1. RELATED WORK

Algorithm-based fault tolerance [1, 2] is a technique that has been used to detect miscalculations in matrix operations. This technique consists of adding a checksum row or column to the matrices being operated on. For many matrix operations, some sort of checksum can be shown to be correct at the end of the calculation, and can be used to find errors after the calculation is done.

The original algorithm-based fault tolerance uses a checksum to determine at the end whether the calculation had been successful or not. If the sums are not consistent with the final result, the calculation is repeated. If the probability of a failure is p, the expected number of runs is $\frac{1}{1-p}$. If p is small, then the overhead of using this method on average is low, but the cost of repeating is larger the higher the probability of failure.

2. FAILURE MODEL

The type of failure that we handle with this technique is a fail-continue failure, where the failure is not evident except by the fact that the application has the wrong data. We use a set of checksums to both detect and correct errors. We assume that errors can only occur during calculation, so that stored values will not become wrong. Matrix elements can only potentially be wrong when they are changed.

3. CHECKSUMS

We use two types of checksums, global and local. High Performance Linpack (HPL) arranges the processes in a grid. Each process has a section of the matrix, referred to as its local matrix. The local checksum is a sum of elements in the local matrix on each process, and is stored in the same local matrix as an additional column. The global checksum is a sum of local matrices across the rows of the grid, and it is stored in an additional column of processes in the process grid. The local checksum is verified periodically; if the sum is not correct, then the global sum is used for recovery. No extra communication is needed unless an error occurs. Recovery requires a reduce across the affected row.

The most certainty of correctness comes from verifying the sums every step of the calculation, but the overhead can be reduced by less frequent checking. A small part of the matrix is most sensitive to errors in each step. Errors in certain areas can be propagated to the rest of the matrix in such a way that recovery from the global checksums is impossible. These areas of the matrix must be verified often to ensure correctness, but they are a small fraction of the total matrix. Better performance can be acheived by checking the rest of the matrix less often. The optimum rate of checking the entire matrix is related to the failure rate.

4. REFERENCES

[1] K.-H. Huang and J. A. Abraham. Algorithm-based fault tolerance for matrix operations. *IEEE Transactions on Computers*, C-33:518–528, 1984.
[2] F. T. Luk and H. Park. An analysis of algorithm-based fault tolerance techniques. *Journal of Parallel and Distributed Computing*, 5(2):172–184, 1988.

Poster: DVFS Management in Real-Processors

Vasileios Spiliopoulos
Uppsala University
Sweden
vasileios.spiliopoulos@it.uu.se

Georgios Keramidas
Industrial Systems Institute
Greece
keramidas@isi.gr

Stefanos Kaxiras
Uppsala University
Sweden
stefanos.kaxiras@it.uu.se

Konstantinos Efstathiou
University of Patras
Greece
efstathiou@ece.upatras.gr

ABSTRACT

We describe a framework for run-time adaptive dynamic voltage-frequency scaling in Linux systems. Our underlying methodology is based on a simple first-order processor performance model in which frequency scaling is expressed as a change (in cycles) of the main memory latency. Utilizing available performance monitoring hardware, we show that our model is powerful enough to i) predict with reasonable accuracy the effect of frequency scaling, and ii) predict the energy consumed by the core under different V/f combinations. To validate our approach we perform highly accurate, fine grained power measurements directly on the processor off-chip voltage regulator.

Categories and Subject Descriptors

C.0 **[General]**: Modeling of computer architecture; C.1.3 **[Processor Architectures]**: Other Architecture Styles - *Adaptable architectures*.

General Terms

Measurement, Performance, Design

Keywords

Dynamic Voltage and Frequency Scaling, Performance and Power Modeling, Performance Monitoring Hardware, Intel and AMD processors.

1. SUMMARY

The power-aware architecture landscape has been dominated by techniques based on supply voltage and clock frequency scaling. Dynamic Voltage and Frequency Scaling (DVFS) offers great opportunities to reduce energy/power consumption by adjusting both voltage and frequency levels of a system. While one can expect to lower power consumption by sacrificing performance, the promise of DVFS techniques lies in the exploitation of slack or "idleness." The objective is to take advantage of slack, so that performance is affected little by frequency scaling, while at the same time a cubic benefit in power consumption —with the help of voltage scaling— is achieved.

Our underlying methodology relies on the exploitation of the instruction slack due to the long latency, off-chip, memory operations [1]. The realization that inspired this work is that core frequency is nothing more than changing the memory latency measured in cycles. While our previous work was conducted in a controlled simulation environment —a cycle accurate simulator augmented with power models— our current view is to apply our methodology in real-life processors e.g., Intel or AMD processors.

As a first step towards this direction, we provide our experiences in building a strong framework (residing in linux kernel space) for power and performance run-time management for real life processors. Testing new ideas in real processors was motivated by the integration of a rich set of performance monitoring counters (PMCs) which resides in almost all modern processors. Live measurements allow a complete view of operating system and I/O effects and many other aspects of "real-world" behavior, often omitted in simulations. However, measuring live, running complex systems (e.g., multicore Intel or AMD processors) and relating gathered results to overall system hardware and software behavior is not as straightforward as in a simulator, because many details are omitted from the computer vendors.

As a result a systematic approach is required to reverse-engineer the hardware details of the target processors. Some of the points, we shed light on, are: i) How much power (static and dynamic) is consumed by the core and the uncore areas of the processors? ii) How real processors are affected by frequency scaling with respect to the behavior of the applications? iii) Is the performance monitoring hardware appropriate for power-oriented optimizations? iv) How much clock-gated are real processors?

Finally, we provide an experimental approach to justify the power and performance measurements and verify the correctness of the proposed framework. We use our methodology, presented in [1], as a basis and we apply it within the proposed framework. Our results indicate that our methodology [1] is proven powerful enough to i) describe and explain how real life processors are affected by frequency scaling with respect to workload's characteristics, ii) predict with reasonable accuracy the effect of frequency scaling (in terms of performance loss), and iii) predict the energy consumed by the core under different V/f combinations. The energy predictions are verified by directly measuring from the off-chip voltage regulator the power consumed by the core. Those power measurements are directly fed into our framework (in kernel space) using DLP-IO8, a USB analog–to–digital converter.

2. REFERENCE

[1] G. Keramidas, V. Spiliopoulos, and S. Kaxiras. Interval-based models for run-time DVFS orchestration in superscalar processors. Int. Conference on Computer Frontiers, 2010.

SRC: OpenSHMEM Library Development

Swaroop Pophale
University of Houston
4800 Calhoun Road, Houston, Texas.
1-832-818-5558

spophale@cs.uh.edu

ABSTRACT

OpenSHMEM is a PGAS programming library implementing an RMA-based point-to-point and collective communication paradigm which decouples data motion from synchronization. This results in a more scalable programming model than more common two-sided paradigms such as MPI. The OpenSHMEM project arose in an effort to standardize among several implementations of the decade-old SHMEM API, which exhibited subtle differences in the API and underlying semantics, inhibiting portability between implementations. In collaboration with Oak Ridge National Laboratory, the University of Houston is preparing an API specification and a portable, scalable, observable OpenSHMEM reference implementation.

Categories and Subject Descriptors

D.3.2 [**Language Classifications**]: *Concurrent, distributed, and parallel languages*; D.3.4 [**Processors**]: *Run-time environments*; D.2.4 [**Software/Program Verification**]: *Validation*

General Terms

Performance, Languages, Standardization, Verification

Keywords

ICS Poster, SHMEM, OpenSHMEM, PGAS

1. EXTENDED ABSTRACT

The Symmetric Hierarchical MEMory (SHMEM) API allows a programmer to write parallel applications using a Partitioned Global Address Space (PGAS) programming model. This model permits an explicit decoupling of data motion and synchronization to enhance application scalability. SHMEM is an SPMD programming model in which the parallel processes communicate through one-sided updates to the symmetric memory spaces of the participating processing elements (PEs) via the API's support for point-to-point (put/get) operations, remote atomic memory operations, broadcasts, and reductions with a simple set of ordering, locking, and synchronization primitives. The key concept in SHMEM is the use of data structures stored in symmetric memory, which is accessible to other PEs.

Such symmetric variables can be either statically allocated or dynamically allocated at run-time using a symmetric memory allocator. Thus data structures allocated from symmetric memory will have symmetric addresses on each PE. This makes it easy to address remote symmetric variables via locally generated addresses, and when enabled by the underlying hardware, allows SHMEM to do true "one-sided communication" with very low latency.

The SHMEM library has a long history as a parallel programming library. The SHMEM library was first introduced in 1993 by Cray Research Inc for their T3D systems. SHMEM was later adapted by SGI for its products based on the Numa-Link architecture and included in the Message Passing Toolkit (MPT). Other SHMEM implementations grew out of the SGI and Cray implementations. These implementations of the SHMEM API support C, C++, and Fortran programs; however, the differences between SHMEM implementations' semantics and APIs are subtle, resulting in portability and correctness issues.

Recently, the U.S. Department of Defense funded a collaboration between Oak Ridge National Laboratory and the University of Houston to develop a specification for a uniform SHMEM API. The OpenSHMEM specification was announced to address the divergence of the SHMEM APIs. In this poster we present our ongoing work on a reference implementation of OpenSHMEM and the challenges faced therein. We introduce the OpenSHMEM programming model and then touch on the key concepts of OpenSHMEM, our library development process, and our implementation based on the portable OpenSHMEM specification. Our goal is to make this library implementation observable and scalable by interfacing with profiling tools and making use of locality information. We will also use benchmarks to observe the speed-up obtained while using our library implementation and identify the strengths and weaknesses of our approach.

2. ACKNOWLEDGMENTS

I would like to thank Tony Curtis, Dr. B. Chapman, Jeffery Kuehn, and Stephen Poole for their guidance and support. Lastly, I would like to thank the Department of Defense for making this project possible.

SRC: Enabling Petascale Data Analysis for Scientific Applications Through Data Reorganization

Yuan Tian
Dept. Computer Science
Auburn University
Auburn, AL 36849
tianyua@auburn.edu

ABSTRACT

This work proposes a novel data reorganization strategy to enable petascale data analysis for large-scale scientific applications running on high-end leadership computers. This strategy achieves optimal data layout for scientific applications by: 1) using a Space Filling Curve to reorganize the data chunks of multidimensional datasets on large storage systems, thus achieving a consistent and balanced read performance for any access pattern; 2) harmonizing the optimal chunk size with underlying file system for more efficient data access. Experimental results demonstrate a maximum of 37 times speedup for S3D simulation on the Jaguar supercomputer.

Categories and Subject Descriptors

D 4.3 [**Operating System**]: File Systems Management—*Access Method, File organization*

General Terms

Design, Experimentation, Performance

Keywords

I/O, Space Filling Curve, Data Layout

1. INTRODUCTION

With storage system performance continuing to lag behind computational performance, many efforts have been focused on the output side of the I/O problem. However, few have systematically examined the read performance of scientific applications on large-scale supercomputers, despite the importance of read performance to the simulation and analysis workflows. In this work, we focus on reading orthogonal planes from a multidimensional array. This is very common in data analysis. However, much performance fluctuation is often observed because of the disparity between the access pattern and underlying storage. We propose two techniques: (1) use a Hilbert [2] Space Filling Curve (SFC) to reorganize the data chunks in the output file, and (2) tune the size of data chunks for more efficient data access. We experimentally show that a SFC-based layout is able to provide consistent and balanced read performance for planar reads, with negligible write overhead.

ICS'11, May 31–June 4, 2011, Tucson, Arizona, USA.
ACM 978-1-4503-0102-2/11/05.

2. DESIGN AND IMPLEMENTATION

We build our SFC-based data layout on top of ADIOS [3], an efficient I/O middleware which essentially employs data chunking within its log-based file format. However, we reorganize the data chunks along the order of the Hilbert curve to adjust the distribution of chunks on storage targets with improved concurrency. Thus all access patterns can enjoy good read performance. Furthermore, we tune the optimal decomposition of large data chunks to harmonize the SFC-based data chunks with the underlying file system, thus reducing the read overhead.

3. EXPERIMENTAL EVALUATION

We carry out a series of experimental evaluations with S3D [1] simulation on the Jaguar supercomputer at Oak Ridge National Laboratories. We demonstrate that by using SFC-based data reorganization, the performance of planar reads of multidimensional variables is improved in a balanced manner across all dimensions. Maximum speedups of 37 times and 7 times are achieved compared to Logically Contiguous and original ADIOS data layouts, respectively. Tuning the chunk size further improves the read performance of large datasets by up to a factor of 22. Moreover, the write overhead is negligible.

4. CONCLUSION

We introduce a SFC-based data reorganization strategy. It enables the petascale data analysis for large-scale scientific applications with balanced planar reads and negligible write overhead. A maximum of 37 times speedup is achieved for S3D.

5. ACKNOWLEDGMENTS

This research used resources of the NCCS at Oak Ridge National Laboratories, which is supported by the Office of Science of the U.S. Department of Energy under Contract No. DE-AC05-00OR22725. Special thanks to Dr. Weikuan Yu, Dr. Scott Klasky and the extended ADIOS team.

6. REFERENCES

[1] J. H. Chen et al. Terascale direct numerical simulations of turbulent combustion using S3D. *Comp. Sci. & Disc.*, 2(1):015001 (31pp), 2009.

[2] D. Hilbert. Ueber die stetige abbildung einer line auf ein flächenstück. *Math. Ann.*, 38:459–460, 1891.

[3] Oak Ridge National Laboratories. http://www.nccs.gov/user-support/center-projects/adios/.

SRC: Virtual I/O Caching: Dynamic Storage Cache Management for Concurrent Workloads

Michael R. Frasca
The Pennsylvania State University
University Park, Pennsylvania
mrf218@cse.psu.edu

Ramya Prabhakar
The Pennsylvania State University
University Park, Pennsylvania
rap244@cse.psu.edu

ABSTRACT

A leading cause of unpredictable application performance in distributed systems is contention at the storage layer, where resources are multiplexed among concurrent data intensive workloads. We target the shared storage cache, used to alleviate disk I/O bottlenecks, and propose a new caching paradigm to improve performance.

We present the virtual I/O cache, a dynamic scheme that manages a limited storage cache resource. Application behavior and the performance of a chosen replacement policy are observed at run time, and a mechanism is designed to avoid suboptimal caching.

Categories and Subject Descriptors

D.4.2 [**Software**]: Operating Systems—*Storage Management*

General Terms: Performance.

Keywords: Storage Cache, I/O Performance.

1. INTRODUCTION

Current system design trends employ resource consolidation, especially at the storage level, where disk resources are shared by numerous clients. Although this yields decreased costs, there are great performance challenges as independent applications compete for system resources. There is a clear need for intelligent and dynamic resource management.

We focus on the resource demands at the storage layer and develop a novel cache management strategy, the *virtual I/O cache*, to deliver increased hit rates and improved performance. Existing cache replacement policies monitor program application behavior to estimate which data blocks should be cached. We recognize that any cache policy makes a number of *a prior* assumptions, e.g., the LRU policy assumes that recency is correlated with access likelihood. The virtual I/O cache detects when these assumptions are violated and provides a unique compensation mechanism.

2. DESIGN

The virtual I/O cache has two main components, the Virtual Resource Monitor (VRM) and the Virtual-Physical Allocator (VPA), which are illustrated in Figure 1. A chosen replacement policy is abstracted as a priority queue, and the VRM monitors its run-time utilization. The priority queue

ICS'11, May 31–June 4, 2011, Tucson, Arizona, USA.
ACM 978-1-4503-0102-2/11/05.

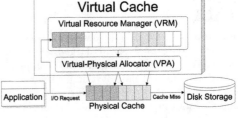

Figure 1: **Virtual I/O caching framework. The VRM tracks the baseline replacement policy in a ghost cache, and the VPA displaces underutilized blocks when the replacement policy is suboptimal.**

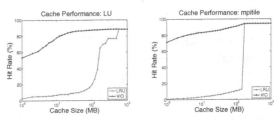

Figure 2: **Performance profile for several I/O Benchmarks. Significant gains are observed until the physical size approaches working set size.**

is modeled via a large ghost cache, and the baseline replacement policy uses measures of application data use to manage this queue. When the replacement policy preforms suboptimally, high block utilization is observed far from the head of the replacement priority queue.

The VPA uses the above measures to evaluate which queue positions are most valued and maps them to the physical cache. Accordingly, poor decisions by the baseline policy are avoided, and the precious physical cache space is better utilized. We replicate this design per application, which provides a powerful mechanism to minimize application interference and optimize system performance objectives.

3. RESULTS

Our experiments show large performance gains for numerous data-intensive workloads. We examine two benchmarks in Figure 2. If the baseline policy (e.g. LRU, LFU, ARC, etc) performs well, the VRM data confirms this fact and high performance is maintained. When this is not the case, we identify which positions in the priority queue are most valued and pack them into the small physical cache. These gains are magnified at increased resource pressure.

SRC: An Automatic Code Overlaying Technique for Multicores with Explicitly-Managed Memory Hierarchies*

Choonki Jang
School of Computer Science and Engineering
Seoul National University, Seoul 151-744, Korea
choonki@aces.snu.ac.kr
http://aces.snu.ac.kr

ABSTRACT

In this paper, we propose an efficient code overlay technique that automatically generates an overlay structure for a given memory size for multicores with explicitly-managed memory hierarchies. We observe that finding an efficient overlay structure with minimum memory copying overhead is similar to the problem that finds a code placement with minimum conflict misses in the instruction cache. Our algorithm exploits the temporal-ordering information between functions during program execution. Experimental results on the Cell BE processor indicate that our approach is effective and promising.

Categories and Subject Descriptors

D.3.4 [**PROGRAMMING LANGUAGES**]: Processors—
Code generation, Compilers, Optimization

General Terms

Algorithms, Design, Experimentation, Measurement, Performance

Keywords

Code overlays, Temporal ordering

1. INTRODUCTION

Explicitly managed memory hierarchies, where the programmer or software is responsible for managing code or data between different levels of the hierarchy, can also be found in recent high performance multicores because of the complicated design and implementation costs of coherent caches for manycores. In these processors, a *local store* is tightly coupled to each processor core or a group of processor cores instead of the coherent caches. The local store needs to be managed explicitly by the programmer or software. They are in charge of memory coherence and consistency. Moreover, the local store is used not only for data but also for code in the Cell BE processor and its size is limited to 256KB [2]. Thus, code memory space reduction in the local store is a very important issue to achieve high performance with the Cell BE processor. To reduce memory footprint due to instruction fetches, an overlay structure is required unless virtual memory is available.

In this paper, we propose an efficient automatic code overlaying technique for multicores with explicitly-managed memory hierarchies, especially for Cell BE architectures. We are dealing with a multicore context in which there is no virtual memory for the cores with the explicitly-managed memory hierarchy. In addition, a function is the granularity of the faulting mechanism in our overlaying technique. This incurs heavy run-time checking and memory copying overhead and requires overhead minimization. This paper addresses these two issues as efficiently as possible.

When two different code segments overlap each other in the memory, we say that they conflict with each other. A conflict miss occurs when a code segment is being referenced by the program and does not reside currently in the memory because it has been replaced with another code segment. To generate an efficient overlay structure, conflict misses due to the overlay structure must be minimized. We observe that conflict misses in an overlaid executable are similar to those in the conventional direct-mapped instruction cache. We apply the concept of temporal-ordering information to our overlay generation problem. Our approach exploits the temporal relationship graph (TRG) [1] that summarizes the temporal-ordering information between functions during program execution and is built upon the profiling information. The TRG estimates the degree of conflict misses between two different code segments when they are overlaid in the same memory region.

We propose a cost model that considers not only the degree of conflict misses, but also the degree of run-time checks by the glue code. The overhead due to the run-time checks is proportional to the number of invocations of overlaid functions. Consequently, to generate an efficient overlay structure for a given memory size, we need to minimize the overhead due to the runtime checks.

The experimental results on the Cell BE processor indicate that our approach is 3.51 times faster than the overlay technique used by the Cell compiler. Moreover, with more than 50% code memory savings, our approach achieves comparable performance to the overlay structure generated by the programmer who understands the application well.

2. REFERENCES

[1] N. Gloy, T. Blackwell, M. D. Smith, and B. Calder. Procedure placement using temporal ordering information. In *MICRO 30: Proceedings of the 30th annual ACM/IEEE international symposium on Microarchitecture*, pages 303–313, 1997.

[2] IBM, Sony, and Toshiba. *Cell Broadband Engine Architecture*. IBM, October 2007. http://www.ibm.com/developerworks/power/cell/.

---

*This work was supported by grant 2009-0081569 (Creative Research Initiatives: Center for Manycore Programming) and the BK21 project from the National Research Foundation of Korea funded by the Korean government (Ministry of Education, Science and Technology). ICT at Seoul National University provided research facilities for this study.

Poster: Programming Clusters of GPUs with OmpSs

Javier Bueno
Barcelona Supercomputing
Center
javier.bueno@bsc.es

Alejandro Duran
Barcelona Supercomputing
Center
alex.duran@bsc.es

Xavier Martorell
Barcelona Supercomputing
Center
Universitat Politècnica de
Catalunya
xavim@ac.upc.edu

Eduard Ayguadé
Barcelona Supercomputing
Center
Universitat Politècnica de
Catalunya
eduard.ayguade@bsc.es

Rosa M. Badia
Barcelona Supercomputing
Center
Consejo Superior de
Investigaciones Científicas
rosa.m.badia@bsc.es

Jesús Labarta
Barcelona Supercomputing
Center
Universitat Politècnica de
Catalunya
jesus@bsc.es

ABSTRACT

OmpSs is a programming model that provides an environment to develop parallel applications for cluster environments with heterogeneous architectures. Based on OpenMP and StarSs, it offers a set of compiler directives that can be used to annotate a sequential code. Additional features have been added to support the use of accelerators like GPUs. This schema offers a high productivity environment due to its simplicity compared to other models like MPI. Our current implementation has shown a good performance when running different benchmarks.

Categories and Subject Descriptors: D.1.3 [Concurrent Programming]: Distrubuted programming, Parallel programming

General Terms: Performance

Keywords: Heterogeneous architectures

1. INTRODUCTION

Cluster programming has always been a complex task. Because of this, many programming models and tools have been created in order to aid programmers to be more productive while developing parallel applications for clusters. However, new forms of hardware have kept adding new challenges to these tools. Nowadays, for instance, heterogeneous clusters of GPUs have become more popular due to their reduced cost compared to other homogeneous alternatives. Our proposal to address some of these new challenges that keep arising in the parallel programming field is OmpSs.

2. OMPSS AND NANOS++

OmpSs is a programming model based on OpenMP and StarSs, a programming model also developed at the Barcelona Supercomputing Center. We chose OpenMP due to its simple and smart usage based on compiler directives to annotate code. StarSs, while also being a programming model based on pragmas, had several features that were not present

on OpenMP, like data requirements and dependences specification between tasks. It offers a thread-pool execution model where the master thread creates additional tasks that are executed by the pool of threads. It assumes a non-homogeneous disjoint memory address space, therefore tasks must specify their data requirements in order to access it correctly. These data specifications are also used to compute the dependences between tasks, which are needed to schedule tasks in a data flow way. Tasks can target specific devices, in this work we have used CUDA based tasks in order to run them on GPUs.

The Nanos++ runtime library is the responible to run OmpSs applications generated by our Mercurium compiler. It executes task parallel applications making sure all constraints specified by the programmer are maintained. As the master thread starts creating new tasks, these will be scheduled locally or in remote nodes. Before a task is executed, it has to go through the dependence graph, which ensures that a task can be executed correctly. Next, the task scheduler decides in which resource (processor, node, GPU) is going to be run. The library moves the data required by tasks among the different address spaces (nodes or GPUs) present in the execution. In order to achieve good scalability the runtime implements techniques like data conscious scheduling, and communication and computation overlapping; all of this being completely transparent to the user.

3. CURRENT STATUS

Using clusters of SMPs, Nanos++ has been able to achieve a performance comparable or even higher than MPI, thanks to being able to express more irregular parallelism.

Currently we are starting to evaluate our system on a clusters of GPUs. Initial results show steady scalability up to 8 nodes using GPUs, but there is still room to improve since some optimization techniques are not yet fully implemented.

Acknowledgements

This work is supported by European Commission through the HiPEAC-2 Network of Excellence (FP7/ICT 217068), the Spanish Ministry of Education (TIN2007-60625, and CSD2007-00050), and the Generalitat de Catalunya (2009-SGR-980).

Poster: Revisiting Virtual Channel Memory for Performance and Fairness on Multi-core Architecture

Licheng Chen[1,2], Yongbing Huang[1,2], Yungang Bao[1], Onur Mutlu[3], Guangming Tan[1], Mingyu Chen[1]

[1]Key Laboratory of Computer System & Architecture, Institute of Computing Technology,
Chinese Academy of Sciences
[2]Graduate School of Chinese Academy of Sciences
[3] Carnegie Mellon University
{chenlicheng, baoyg, cmy}@ict.ac.cn {huangyongbing, tgm}@ncic.ac.cn onur@cmu.edu

Categories and Subject Descriptors: B.3.2, shared memory; B.3.1, dynamic memory (DRAM)

General Terms: Experimentation, Measurement, Performance

1. Introduction

In modern multi-core chip architecture, the DRAM system is shared by more and more cores and high bandwidth I/O devices. This trend raises the memory contention problem and the memory QoS problem. Meanwhile, we find that multicore architecture also brings a large amount of unexploited memory-level parallelism (MLP). In order to exploit the MLP, we revisit the obsolete Virtual Channel Memory (VCM) technology [3]. The experimental results show that VCM is a good alternative to traditional DRAM chip on multicore architecture because it can not only improve performance but also reduce unfairness. Thus, we suggest memory chip vendors reconsider the VCM technology for multicore architecture.

2. Implementing VCM on a multi-core architecture

Figure 1 illustrates VCM's conceptual organization. Two commands, *Prefetch* and *Restore*, are introduced to transfer data between row buffers and channel buffers, each row buffer is divided into 4~16 segments which is the basic transfer data size. Foreground operations and background operations can also be executed independently, so VCM can exploit more MLP than traditional DRAM chip. Figure 2 illustrates the VCM memory controller, the memory request buffers are distributed as a number of separated channel request buffers and the physical memory address is translated into VCM address in the form of <*bank, row, segment, column*>. Based on this, we further implement the state of the art scheduling algorithms on VCM, including FR-FCFS [4], PARBS [2], and ATLAS [1].

3. Experimental Results

Figure 3 shows the normalized IPC (NIPC) speedups of memory intensive applications running on a 16-core system with 8 memory banks. On average, VCM with 32 1KB-channel buffers achieves 2.08X performance speedup against the baseline FR-FCFS system, while eight 8KB-row buffers provide only 1.15X improvements.

Figure 4 shows the weighted speedup (system throughput) of heterogeneous memory intensive workloads on a 16-core system. For VCM with FR-FCFS, it improves system throughput by 1.66X. Since applying PAR-BS and ATLAS to VCM changes system throughput

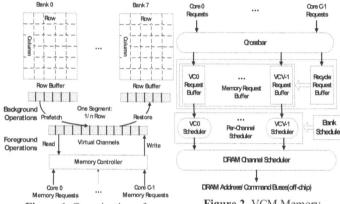

Figure 1. Organization of VCM

Figure 2. VCM Memory Controller

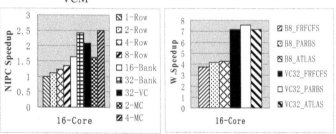

Figure 3. Performance improvements

Figure 4. Weighted Speedup

slightly, by only 5.9% and 0.03% respectively. This means that VCM is inherently able to eliminate unfairness and improve system throughput.

From our perspective, we suggest memory chip vendors reconsider the VCM technology for multicore architecture.

References

[1] Y. Kim, D. Han, O. Mutlu, and M. Harchol-Balter. ATLAS: A Scalable and High-Performance Scheduling Algorithm for Multiple Memory Controllers. in Proceedings of the 16th International Symposium on High-Performance Computer Architecture (HPCA). 2010.

[2] O. Mutlu and T. Moscibroda, Parallelism-Aware Batch Scheduling: Enhancing both Performance and Fairness of Shared DRAM Systems, in Proceedings of the 35th Annual International Symposium on Computer Architecture, 2008.

[3] Nec, 64M-bit Virtual Channel SDRAM data sheet, 1998.

[4] S. Rixner, W. J. Dally, U. J. Kapasi, P. Mattson, and J. D. Owens. Memory Access Scheduling. in Proceedings of the 27th annual international symposium on Computer architecture. 2000.

Poster: Implications of Merging Phases on Scalability of Multi-core Architectures

Madhavan Manivannan
Chalmers University of Technology
Gothenburg, Sweden
madhavan@chalmers.se

Ben Juurlink
Technische Universitat Berlin
Berlin, Germany
juurlink@ce.tu-berlin.de

Per Stenstrom
Chalmers University of Technology
Gothenburg, Sweden
per.stenstrom@chalmers.se

ABSTRACT

Amdahl's Law estimates parallel applications with negligible serial sections to potentially scale to many cores. However, due to merging phases in data mining applications, the serial sections do not remain constant. We extend Amdahl's model to accommodate this and establish that Amdahl's Law can overestimate the scalability offered by symmetric and asymmetric architectures for such applications.

Implications: 1) A better use of the chip area is for fewer and hence more capable cores rather than simply increasing the number of cores for symmetric and asymmetric architectures and 2) The performance potential of asymmetric over symmetric multi-core architectures is limited for such applications.

Categories and Subject Descriptors

C.1.2 [**Multiprocessors**]: Multiprocessors

General Terms

Performance, Design

Keywords

Amdahl's Law, Reduction Operations, Multi-core architecture

1. INTRODUCTION

This poster studies the scalability of a set of data mining workloads that have negligible serial sections. While the formulation of Amdahl's Law that optimistically assumes constant serial sections [1] estimates these workloads to scale to large number of cores, the overhead in carrying out merging (or reduction) operations makes scalability to peak at a much lower core count. We establish this by extending the Amdahl's speedup model to factor in the impact of reduction operations on the speedup of applications on symmetric as well as asymmetric chip multiprocessor (CMP) designs.

2. MODEL AND ITS IMPLICATIONS

The mathematical formulation of Amdahl's Law in [1] assumes that the serial section remains constant, independent of scaling. However our analysis of the clustering applications in the Minebench suite [2] reveals that serial sections do not remain constant with scaling. This behavior can be attributed to merging phases in the application where partial results computed by different threads are merged. Merging operations have an inherent serial component and its complexity grows as we scale. We extend the model in [1] to incorporate this observation and validate it by runs on simulators as well as real hardware [3].

Figure 1 shows the scalability prediction for kmeans using the model presented in [1] and the extended Amdahl's model that incorporates reduction. By factoring in reduction operations, speedup tapers off at a lesser core count (71.9 instead of 246.5). This shows that naively using Amdahl's Law can lead to speedup overestimation.

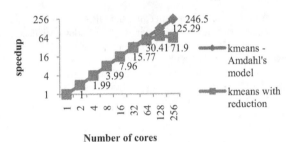

Figure 1. kmeans scalability using different models

We use the resource model presented in [1] to obtain the theoretical speedup limit for a hypothetical application that spends *1%* of the time on serial sections *(f=0.99)* with *256* simple cores (BCEs). Figure 2 compares the speedup obtained using the model presented in [1] (marked 'Amdahl') and the model with reduction (marked 'Reduction') for symmetric (sym) and asymmetric (asym) CMPs. We can observe that due to reduction overhead, the performance potential of asymmetric CMP over symmetric CMP is limited (43.3 against 36.2 as opposed to 162.3 against 79.7).

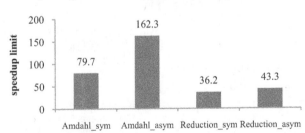

Figure 2. scalability on symmetric and asymmetric CMPs

3. REFERENCES

[1] Mark Hill and Mike Marty. Amdahl's Law in the multicore era. *IEEE Computer*, Vol. 41, no.7, pages 33-38, July 2008.

[2] Ramanathan Narayanan et al. MineBench: A Benchmark Suite for Data Mining Workloads. *In Proceedings of IISWC, 2006.*

[3] M. Manivannan, B. Juurlink, P. Stenstrom. Implications of Merging Phases on Scalability of Multi-core Architectures. *Technical Report.* Department of Computer Science and Engineering. Chalmers University.http://www.cse.chalmers.se/~madhavan/tr_madhavan_20 11_01.pdf

SRC: Facilitating Efficient Parallelization of Information Storage and Retrieval on Large Data Sets

Steven Feldman
University of Central Florida
Orlando, FL, USA
Feldman@knights.ucf.edu

Abstract

The purpose of this work is to develop a lock-free hash table that allows a large number of threads to concurrently insert, modify, or retrieve information. Lock-free or non-blocking designs alleviate the problems traditionally associated with lock-based designs, such as bottlenecks and thread safety. Using standard atomic operations provided by the hardware, the design is portable and therefore, applicable to embedded systems and supercomputers such as the Cray XMT. Real-world applications range from search-indexing to computer vision. Having written and tested the core functionality of the hash table, we plan to perform a formal validation using model checkers.

Categories & Subject Descriptors: E.2 [Data]: Data Storage Representations---Hash Table Representations

General Terms: Algorithms, Design, Languages.

Description of the insertion process

For a thread to insert an element, it rearranges the bits in its key, and then takes the first Y bits, where 2^Y is equal to the length of the memory array. The location to insert at is determined by those Y bits. If the main array points to another array, then that thread will set their local pointer, that was pointing to the main array and set it to the array it found, then take the next Y bits.

Once a regular node is found then if it is null, deleted, or a key match, then it CAS (Compare and Swap) the current node for its node. If the CAS fails, then the thread re-examines the node there. If it is a non-key match, then we will probe down until a valid spot is reached. If no valid spot is reached, then at the original location we tried to insert at, we create an array node and move elements over.

This is very simplified and some cases have been neglected, however, the information on our poster covers these effectively. The main advantage of arrays over linked lists is that they are able to take advantage of the fact that we use a perfect hashing and therefore, every node has a unique final position, giving all operations constant time, regardless of the number of collisions.

Bio

The speaker is a junior, undergraduate student at the University of Central Florida, majoring in Computer Science. He is researching under Dr. Dechev, studying lock-free, concurrent data structures. Steven's technical interests are in the efficient design of concurrent server applications, as well as data structures that can be operated on concurrently. The research he will be presenting was shown at UCF's "Showcase of Undergraduate Research Excellence" event, in April, 2011.

SRC: Automatic Extraction
of SST/macro Skeleton Models

Amruth Rudraiah Dakshinamurthy
University of Central Florida
Orlando, FL, USA
amruth.rd@knights.ucf.edu

Abstract

The utilization of large scale parallel event simulators such as SST/macro requires that skeleton models of underlying software systems and architectures be created. Implementing such models by abstracting the designs of large scale parallel applications requires a substantial manual effort and introduces the hazards of human errors. We outline an approach for the automatic extraction of SST/macro skeleton models from large scale parallel applications. Our methodology for deriving SST/macro skeleton models is based on the use of extensible and open-source ROSE compiler infrastructure. The SST/macro skeleton models are then combined with appropriate models of the network and hardware configurations.

Brief Description

Our motivation is to address the critical issue of interpolating application behavior for exascale machines when driving the SST/macro simulator by simplifying the process of creating skeleton applications. The key idea is to construct these reduced skeletons automatically from full applications by using program analysis modules provided by ROSE compiler. One aspect of compiler analysis to achieve this optimization is by abstracting away fragments of redundant computations and message data whose values do not affect the skeleton application's state. Another aspect is to identify the values that could affect program performance and to isolate the computations and communications that determine these values. These aspects of compiler analysis use a technique called program slicing which is done by extraction module of ROSE. The translation module of ROSE encodes the insertion and rewriting of actions from the input application code. The implementation of the translation module is achieved by matching expression patterns provided by SST/macro simulator against the sliced-out AST. This converts the ROSE AST annotated with input application instances into AST with SST/macro-specific nodes, thus creating the skeleton model.

Categories & Subject Descriptors:

D.2.4 [Software Engineering]: Software/Program Verification---Statistical methods; D.3.4 [Programming Languages]: Processors---Translator writing systems and compiler generators

General Terms:

Algorithms, Performance, Design, Experimentation, Human Factors, Verification.

Bio

The author is a graduate student of Computer Science at University of Central Florida. Amruth was previously a technology analyst at Infosys Technologies Limited. He is currently doing his research under Dr. Damian Dechev in Modern Programming Techniques Research lab. His research interests are in the area of static analysis, parallel computing, program analysis, and programming tools and techniques.

Author Index

NOTES

NOTES

NOTES

www.ingramcontent.com/pod-product-compliance
Lightning Source LLC
Chambersburg PA
CBHW080146060326
40689CB00018B/3870